Brief Contents

Contents

Contents

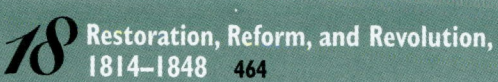

18 Restoration, Reform, and Revolution, 1814–1848   464

19 The Industrial Transformation of Europe, 1750–1850   492

20 New Powers and New Tensions, 1850–1880   517

Contents xv

Maps

Documents

Preface

In 1994 Thomas F. X. Noble, Barry S. Strauss, Duane J. Osheim, Kristen B. Neuschel, William B. Cohen, and David D. Roberts published *Western Civilization: The Continuing Experiment*. Our goal was to create a book that was balanced and coherent; that addressed the full range of subjects a Western civilization book needs to address; that provided the student reader with interesting, timely material; that was up-to-date in terms of scholarship and approach—in short, a book that helped the instructor to teach and the student to learn. In 1998 the Second Edition appeared, revised on the basis of what colleagues told us of their experience in using the book.

Some instructors said that they liked our book but there was just too much of it: To cover the course in a single term or to assign extensive supplementary readings, they had to have a shorter text. The Brief Edition, based on the Second Edition, is designed to meet their needs. With four hundred fewer pages, it is 40 percent shorter than the original book. Prepared by Jennifer Michael Hecht of Nassau Community College, the Brief Edition retains the conceptual and analytical strengths of the original text. It continues to develop large themes, providing carefully chosen illustrative details. Instructors and students will still find the important and long-captivating stories of Western history. In addition, Professor Hecht has drawn on her own research and teaching to provide new content and features for students of the survey course. For example, she has brought the book up to the present by adding a new discussion of postmodernism and by updating the coverage of NATO expansion and the European monetary union.

CENTRAL THEMES AND APPROACH

The Brief Edition retains a strong chronological narrative and the traditional division of Western civilization into ancient, medieval, early modern, and modern periods. By focusing on the most important people and developments, we highlight the most enduring aspects of the story.

To enhance the narrative line, we continue to examine power in all its senses: public and private; economic, social, political, and cultural; symbolic and real: Who had power and who did not? How was power gained, lost, and exercised in a given time and place? How did people talk about power? What kinds of rituals and ceremonies displayed power? In addition, the Brief Edition has further developed the treatment of gender and gender relations to reflect new scholarship, adding, for example, a new section on the women's movement in the nineteenth century.

The Brief Edition also shares its parent's distinctive vision of the West as extending far beyond Western Europe. The Celtic world, Scandinavia, and the Slavic world are integral parts of the story. We look often at the lands that border the West—Anatolia/Turkey, western Asia, North Africa, the Eurasian steppes—in order to show the to-and-fro of peoples, ideas, technologies, and products. And we consistently situate the West in its global context, in recognition of the fact that just as the West has influenced the rest of the world, the rest of the world has influenced the West.

DISTINCTIVE FEATURES

To make the book as accessible as possible to teachers and students, the Brief Edition includes several new features. As with the full edition, each chapter begins with a thematic introduction to engage the reader's interest and point to the major issues that will follow. But, new for the Brief Edition, the introduction is followed right away by a list of "Questions and Ideas to Consider," to focus student attention on the major themes to think about while reading. In addition, a new "Chapter Chronology" at the beginning of every chapter organizes and conveniently reviews major events and developments. At the end of each chapter a "Summary" draws together the major topics and themes, and an annotated list of "Suggested Reading" alerts students to scholarly classics and exciting new works.

To give students an opportunity to work with primary sources, each chapter contains two or three boxed documents, including one called "Encounters with the West." To advance the book's goal of situating the West in its global context, these boxes show Western people commenting on the non-Western world and non-Western people commenting on the West.

The Brief Edition provides a generous selection of maps illustrating key political and social developments. Each chapter is also enhanced by a number of illustrations, including several new photographs selected to accompany new discussions in the last two chapters.

To meet the varying needs of instructors, *Western Civilization: The Continuing Experiment*, Brief Edition, is available in the following formats: a complete version (Chapters 1–27); Volume I: To 1715 (Chapters 1–15); and Volume II: Since 1560 (Chapters 13–27).

THE CONTINUING EXPERIMENT

We ask, finally, that you note the subtitle of the book: *The Continuing Experiment.* It was carefully chosen to convey our resolve to avoid a deter-

ministic approach. We always try to give individual actors, moments, and movements the sense of drama, possibility, and contingency that they actually possessed. We, with faultless hindsight, always know how things turned out. Contemporaries often hadn't a clue. We respect them. Indeed, much of the fascination, and the reward, of studying Western civilization lies in its richness, diversity, changeability, and unpredictability. As you read and study our book, we hope that you will send us your own thoughts on how we might improve it. You can reach us at this e-mail address: college_history@hmco.com.

SUPPLEMENTS

We have thoroughly revised our array of text supplements provided to aid students in learning and instructors in teaching. These supplements include a *Study Guide,* an *Instructor's Resource Manual with Test Items,* a *Computerized Test Bank, Map Transparencies,* a *Videodisc Guide,* and a new multimedia supplement: a CD-ROM of interactive maps. Together, these items provide a tightly integrated program of teaching and learning.

The *Study Guide,* written by Miriam Shadi of Ohio University, includes an introductory essay on how to make the best use of your Western civilization course. Each chapter of the *Study Guide* contains learning objectives, an annotated outline of the chapter, multiple-choice questions keyed to the text, essay questions with guidelines, analytical questions, and map exercises.

The *Instructor's Resource Manual with Test Items,* prepared by Janice Liedl of Laurentian University, contains useful teaching strategies and tips for getting the most out of the text. Each chapter includes a summary and outline, learning objectives, lecture suggestions, discussion questions, recommended outside reading and writing assignments, and paper topics. For this edition, we have also expanded the *Instructor's Resource Manual* to include test questions and exercises that will help test the student's comprehension of the book.

An exciting addition to our map program is *GeoQuest™*, a CD-ROM of thirty interactive historical maps, available to both instructors and students. We also offer *The Western Civilization Videodisc/Videotape/Slide* program, a multimedia collection of visual images, as well as a set of *Map Transparencies* of all the maps in the text.

Finally, we are proud to announce the creation of our on-line primary-source collection, *BiblioBase™: Custom Coursepacks in Western Civilization*. This resource will allow instructors to elect from over six hundred primary-source documents to create their own customized reader.

doctorates and showmen: Amy, Carolyn, Darla, Gene, and Jamey. She would also like to express warm thanks to the six original authors of *Western Civilization: The Continuing Experiment* for welcoming yet another voice into their midst and allowing the brief version to take on a character and shape of its own.

Much thanks are due to our former editor, Elizabeth Welch, whose enthusiasm and insight influenced the book's trajectory even after she had moved off the project, and to Jennifer Sutherland for ably helping to carry the project to its conclusion. We are grateful to Christina Horn, our Senior Project Editor, for her cheerful assistance and good judgment, and to Jean Woy, Editor in Chief for History and Political Science, for her confidence in the project.

ACKNOWLEDGMENTS

Jennifer Michael Hecht would like to thank her colleagues at Nassau Community College, particularly Professors Paul Devendittis, Gil Schrank, and Glenn Whaley, for their helpful comments and advice. She also thanks Mary Keller and the whole Hecht clan of traveling

Thomas F. X. Noble
Barry S. Strauss
Duane J. Osheim
Kristen B. Neuschel
William B. Cohen
David D. Roberts
Jennifer Michael Hecht

About the Authors

Thomas F. X. Noble Since receiving his Ph.D. from Michigan State University, Thomas Noble has taught at Albion College, Michigan State University, Texas Tech University, and since 1980 at the University of Virginia. He is the author of *The Republic of St. Peter: The Birth of the Papal State, 680–825; Religion, Culture and Society in the Early Middle Ages;* and *Soldiers of Christ: Saints and Saints' Lives from Late Antiquity and the Early Middle Ages.* Noble's articles and reviews have appeared in many leading journals, and he has contributed chapters to several books and articles to three encyclopedias. Noble, who was a member of the Institute for Advanced Study in 1994, has been awarded fellowships by the National Endowment for the Humanities (twice) and the American Philosophical Society.

Barry S. Strauss Professor of history and classics at Cornell University, where he is also director of the Peace Studies Program, Barry S. Strauss holds a Ph.D. from Yale University. He has received several academic fellowships, including one from the National Endowment for the Humanities and a Rockefeller Visiting Fellowship. He is the recipient of the Clark Award for excellence in teaching from Cornell. His many publications include *Athens After the Peloponnesian War, Fathers and Sons in Athens, The Anatomy of Error: Ancient Military Disasters and Their Lessons for Modern Strategists* (with Josiah Ober), and *Hegemonic Rivalries from Thucydides to the Nuclear Age* (with R. N. Lebow).

Duane J. Osheim A Fellow of the American Academy in Rome with a Ph.D. in history from the University of California, Davis, Duane Osheim is professor of history and associate dean of the Graduate School of Arts and Sciences at the University of Virginia. He is the author of *A Tuscan Monastery and Its Social World* and *An Italian Lordship: The Bishopric of Lucca in the Late Middle Ages,* as well as numerous papers and articles on rural life, religious experience, and medieval plagues.

Kristen B. Neuschel Associate professor of history at Duke University, Kristen B. Neuschel received her Ph.D. from Brown University. She is the author of *Word of Honor: Interpreting Noble Culture in Sixteenth-Century France* and articles on French social history and European women's history. In 1988 she received the Alumni Distinguished Undergraduate Teaching Award for excellence in teaching at Duke.

William B. Cohen Since receiving his Ph.D. at Stanford University, William Cohen has taught at Northwestern University and Indiana University, where he is now professor of history. A previous president of the Society for French Historical Studies, Cohen has received several academic fellowships, among them a National Endowment for the Humanities and a Fulbright fellowship. Among his many publications are *Rulers of Empire, The French Encounter with Africans, European Empire Building, Robert Delavignette and the French Empire, The Transformation of Modern France,* and *Urban Government and the Rise of the French City.*

David D. Roberts After taking his Ph.D. in modern European history at the University of California, Berkeley, David Roberts taught at the Universities of Virginia and Rochester before becoming professor of history at the University of Georgia in 1988. A recipient of Woodrow Wilson and Rockefeller Foundation fellowships, he is the author of *The Syndicalist Tradition and Italian Fascism, Benedetto Croce and the Uses of Historicism,* and *Nothing but History: Reconstruction and Extremity after Metaphysics,* as well as numerous articles and reviews.

Jennifer Michael Hecht Since earning her Ph.D. from Columbia University in 1995, Jennifer Michael Hecht has taught European history and the history of science at Nassau Community College. Her studies of nineteenth-century French anthropology and philosophy have appeared in *French Historical Studies, The Journal of the History of the Behavioral Sciences,* and *Isis* (forthcoming). She has also written for *The Partisan Review, The Denver Quarterly, The Antioch Review,* and other journals.

CHAPTER 1

The Ancestors of the West

There is an ancient poem that asks how people learned to cultivate "the jewel and ornament of the plain, the holy furrows ... [where] grain grows." How did we learn to live in a "well-supplied" city, "awesome in its appearance," its temples "rich with abundance," its laws "perfected"?[1] These questions about the origins of civilization were written four thousand years ago in Sumer, and we are still trying to answer them.

We know that the first modern humans evolved from humanlike ancestors, but scholars debate whether the date was closer to 45,000 or 70,000 years ago. This chapter begins with those first humans, follows the great civilizations of Egypt and western Asia and Israel, and ends with a survey of the wider ancient world. This period witnessed the most momentous inventions in human history: representational art and religion, the shift from a food-collecting to a food-producing economy, and the first villages, from which grew the first cities and kingdoms.

We tend to have more information as we move forward in history, but we must begin by examining a period before the invention of writing— often called "prehistory"—and before the emergence of civilization. These innovations occurred at about the same time, around 3500–3000 B.C., because the complexity of civilization (sufficient agricultural advances to support centers of economic and cultural sophistication) created a need for the development of writing.

Civilization first emerged around 3100–1200 B.C. in two great river valleys: Mesopotamia, which lay between the Tigris and Euphrates Rivers in what is today Iraq, and Egypt, in the valley of the Nile. Soon after, two other civilizations emerged: one in what is today Pakistan and northwest India, the other in northern China.

~ *Questions and Ideas to Consider*

- Why didn't your professor assign a textbook from the nineteenth century? Since the ancient world has not changed, there must be new knowledge or new interpretations—or both. Try to identify some of these as you read.

- Scholars describe ancient Mesopotamia and ancient Egypt as having different world-views. What is the evidence of this, and how can we explain it? Think about the art and literature of these cultures and their attitudes toward death.

- What are some of the differences between the law codes of Hammurabi and the ancient Hebrews? How did the Hebrew conception of God influence these differences?

- The origins of modern languages, both written and spoken, can be traced back to the ancient world. Identify the major contributions of the Sumerians, Egyptians, Canaanites, and Hittites.

- If you could be sent back in time to any ancient civilization as a wealthy, unmarried woman, which one would you choose? How about as a man with neither money nor property? Why?

ORIGINS, TO CA. 3000 B.C.

There is still a lot of disagreement about the origins of human beings and human society. Physical anthropologists, archaeologists, and biochemists continue to make discoveries that call for the reassessment of previous theories. Still, there are some things about which we are relatively certain.

Over a period of several thousand years, beginning around 10,000 B.C., humans abandoned a mobile existence for a sedentary one. They learned to domesticate animals and cultivate plants. They replaced a food-collecting economy with a food-producing economy. They developed the first towns, from which, over several millennia, slowly evolved the first urban societies.

The First Human Beings

The earliest humanlike beings, ancestors of modern people, appeared in the tropics and subtropics of Africa at least 5 million years ago. By a little more than 2.5 million years ago, these hominids, or members of the human family, had evolved into humanlike creatures who invented simple stone tools—which is why we call this period the Stone Age. From about 2.0 to 1.6 million years ago, hominids migrated out of Africa to Asia and the eastern edge of Europe. Toward the end of this period, they developed into *Homo erectus* ("upright person"), a hominid with a large brain who used more complex stone tools and may have acquired language. The next important stage in human evolution was the gradual emergence, from separate *Homo erectus* populations in different places, of various archaic forms of *Homo sapiens*. Modern human beings, *Homo sapiens sapiens* (Latin for "wise, wise human being"), first appeared either more than 70,000 or more than 45,000 years ago, depending on which scholarly estimate we follow.

For many millennia, Europe represented a challenging environment for human habitation because the Ice Age, a period of fluctuating cycles of warm and cold, caused glaciers to ebb and flow over the land. The Ice Age began about 730,000 years ago and ended only about 10,000 years ago. Still, human beings managed to live through it. Recent finds in Spain show the presence of archaic humans in Europe about 800,000 years ago. Neandertals inhabited Europe from about 400,000 years ago to about 30,000 years ago. They were among the first people to bury their dead, often with grave offerings such as flint, animal bones, or flowers.

Neandertals, however, were not modern humans. Modern humans entered Europe from western Asia about 40,000 years ago, while the Neandertals were still around. Within 10,000 years of that time, Neandertals disappeared, perhaps through war or disease or perhaps through intermarriage with modern humans. The first modern humans tended to be taller and less muscular than Neandertals and other archaic people; they had

CHAPTER CHRONOLOGY

HUMAN ORIGINS

5 million years ago	Earliest hominids
1.6 million years ago	*Homo erectus*
800,000 years ago	First humans in Europe
70,000–45,000 years ago	*Homo sapiens sapiens*
40,000–10,000 B.C.	Upper Paleolithic era
10,000 B.C.	Last Ice Age ends
9000–2500 B.C.	Neolithic era

(All above dates are approximate.)

MESOPOTAMIA

3800–3200 B.C.	Uruk Period
3500–3100 B.C.	Writing invented
2800–2350 B.C.	Early Dynastic Period
2371–2316 B.C.	Reign of Sargon
2112–2004 B.C.	Third Dynasty of Ur
1900–1600 B.C.	Old Babylonian Period
1792–1750 B.C.	Reign of Hammurabi

EGYPT

3100 B.C.	Unification of Nile Valley
2695–2160 B.C.	Old Kingdom
2160–1963 B.C.	First Intermediate Period
1963–1786 B.C.	Middle Kingdom
1786–1550 B.C.	Second Intermediate Period; Hyksos
1550–1070 B.C.	New Kingdom

WESTERN ASIA AND THE LEVANT

1650–1450 B.C.	Hittite Old Kingdom
1450–1380 B.C.	Hittite Middle Kingdom
1380–1180 B.C.	Hittite New Kingdom (empire)
1250–1150 B.C.	Sea Peoples invade
ca. 1200–1000 B.C.	Israelites settle Palestinian hill country
ca. 1050–750 B.C.	Height of Phoenician city-states
965–928 B.C.	Reign of Solomon
ca. 750–664 B.C.	Height of Assyrian Empire
722 B.C.	Assyrians conquer kingdom of Israel
612 B.C.	Conquest of Nineveh
598 B.C.	Neo-Babylonians conquer kingdom of Judah
559–530 B.C.	Reign of Cyrus the Great
550–331 B.C.	Achaemenid Persian Empire
539 B.C.	Cyrus conquers Babylon; permits Jews to return to Palestine
ca. 425 B.C.	Judean assembly accepts the Torah

more precise use of the hand and walked more efficiently; and they lived longer. With its high forehead and tucked-in face, the modern human skull is distinctive, but differences between the modern and archaic human brain are a matter of scholarly debate. What no one debates, however, is that around 40,000 years ago modern humans put a revolution into effect: They invented culture.

From the Cave to the Town, ca. 40,000–5000 B.C.

Cave paintings and notations made on bone were the foundation of modern human culture, and they began in the Upper Paleolithic (Greek for "Old Stone") era, about 40,000 to about 10,000 B.C. At the beginning of this period, humans were living in hunter-gatherer societies; by the end of it they had domesticated animals and learned how to cultivate crops. This change precipitated the creation first of villages and then of walled towns.

Archaeology tells us something about early people's hunter-gatherer way of life, as do analogies from contemporary anthropology, for even today a tiny number of people still exist in such societies: for example, in the Kalahari Desert of Africa or in the Arctic. It seems that early humans lived in small groups, perhaps twenty-five to fifty persons related by kinship or marriage. They moved from place to place, following the seasonal food supply. They ate nuts and berries, largely provided by the women, who gathered foods as they walked, talked, and cared for the group's small children. This diet was supplemented by some meat. Hunting for game often required long excursions and much patience. As this was not an ideal setting for infants, men probably did most of the hunting. When the men were home, they too cared for the young.

During the Upper Paleolithic era, about 30,000 years ago, caves were sites of the earliest representational art. The most spectacular cave paintings yet discovered have been found in southern France (at Lascaux and at Chauvet Cave) and in Spain (at Altamira). European cave paintings of bison, horses, reindeer, and woolly mammoths (an extinct member of the elephant family with hairy skin and long tusks) are beautiful to the modern eye—realistic and skillfully rendered. The cave paintings may have been illustrations of past events, or attempts to control the future through magic.

Other early representational art includes stone engravings of animals, birds, and stylized human females, as well as female figurines carved from ivory or bone, usually represented with voluptuous figures. Moderns named these carvings "Venus sculptures," after Venus, the Greco-Roman goddess of love, and some have guessed that the statues were used in an attempt to control fertility through magic. It is also possible that the earliest artists were women and the Venus figurines were self-portraits by well-nourished, comfortable people.

It is unclear whether these early groups of people were matriarchal (literally, "rule by the mother") or patriarchal ("rule by the father"). Ancient Greek myths depicted women as the rulers of prehistoric society, and today some historians see evidence of matriarchy in the Venus figurines. Some tribes may have had no chief at all, but rather followed the decision of the community.

About fifteen thousand years ago, life in hunter-gatherer societies began to change dramatically. Humans began to specialize in the wild plants they collected and the animals they hunted. People seem to have begun by domesticating dogs, which were useful in hunting. Then they learned to keep sheep, goats, and cattle, which could replace hunting. Given the division of labor, men may have had a larger role in domestication of animals, while women discovered the secrets of agriculture. They learned first how to grow wheat and barley, then legumes (beans). The process began sometime after 10,000 B.C. in western Asia, in the warmer, damper climate that followed the Ice Age. Wild cereals became abundant in the "Fertile Crescent," an area stretching in a crescent shape from southern Jordan to southern Iran (Map 1.1). That may have led to a population explosion, which soon required that certain plants and animals be cultivated so that everyone could be fed. Scholars often describe the domestication of plants and animals as the "Neolithic" (literally, "New Stone") Revolution, but in truth the process was evolutionary, spread out over about five thousand years.

Small agricultural settlements were increasingly common after 7000 B.C. Thus was born the farming village. It is probably the place that most people have called home since the spread of agriculture around the world. Many villages were walled for defense. Jericho, in Palestine near the Dead Sea, is perhaps the oldest town on earth. It was surrounded by massive walls, 10 feet thick and 13 or more feet high, which enclosed an area of about 10 acres. Some Neolithic towns, such as Çatal Hüyük in south central Anatolia, were trading centers (see Map 1.1). Carbonization from fire has preserved a wealth of artifacts attesting to Çatal Hüyük's sophistication, including fabrics, obsidian mirrors,

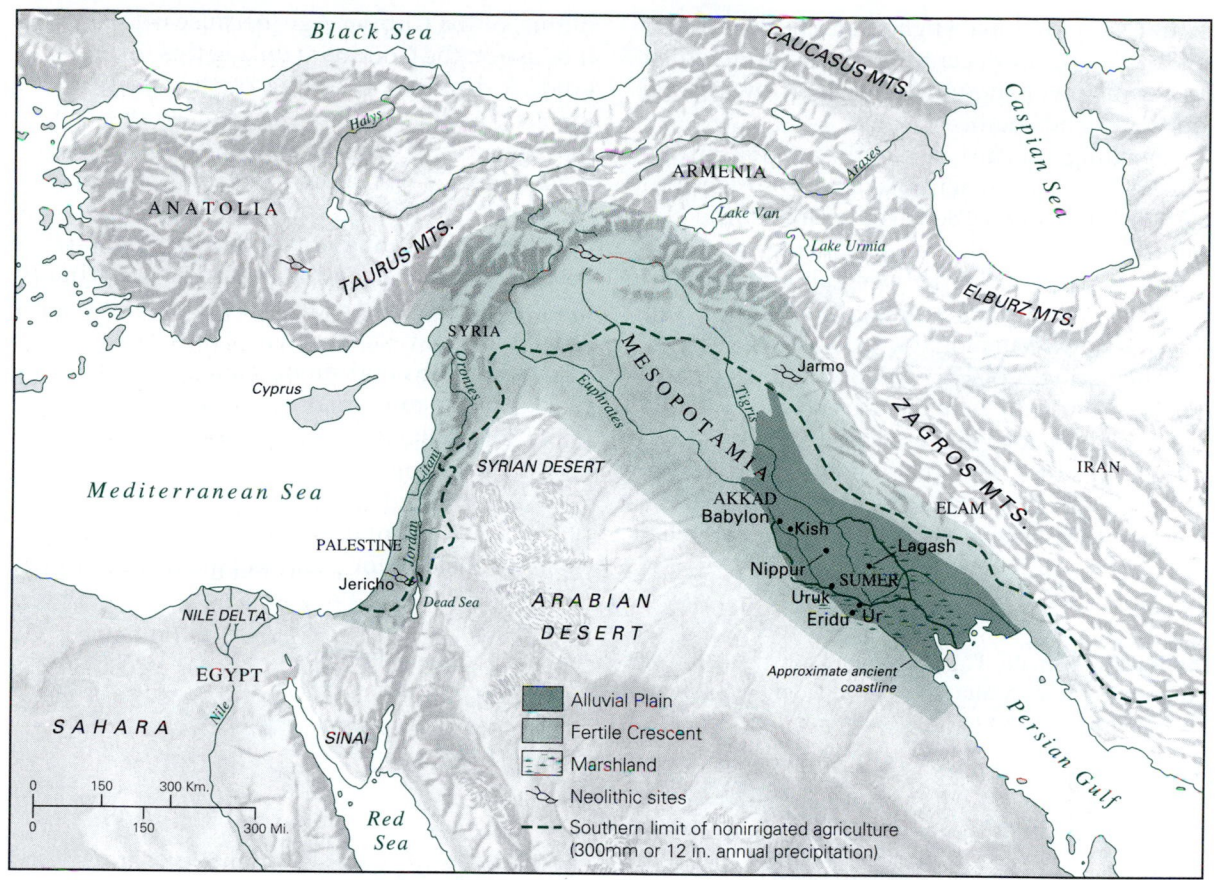

Map 1.1 Western Asia In the Fertile Crescent, an arc-shaped region of dependable annual rainfall, the Neolithic Revolution began after 10,000 B.C. In southern Mesopotamia, between the Tigris and Euphrates Rivers, the world's first urban civilization took root about 3500–3000 B.C.

wooden vessels, and sticks that were used to apply eye makeup. Along with these pleasant innovations came new problems: The concentrated population of settled life bred disease, and cultivation of a piece of land over time led to territoriality and war.

Neolithic and Copper Age Europe, 7000–2500 B.C.

Europe was one day to become the center of Western civilization, but the Continent lagged behind its neighbors at first. Innovations from the east reached Europe after 7000 B.C. and slowly transformed it, mixing with native traditions so that Europeans developed their own unique culture.

The continent of Europe comprises several very distinct regions. Southern Europe is made up of a rugged and hilly Mediterranean coastal strip, connected to northern Africa and western Asia by the sea and by similarities in climate and landscape. Northern Europe, by contrast, consists in large part of forested plain, indented here and there by great rivers. In the east, open and largely treeless plains stretch from Russia across central Asia to China. High mountains are found in the Alps of south central Europe, from which chains of lower mountains radiate toward the southwest and southeast.

Farming began in southeastern Europe around 7000 B.C., when migrants from western Asia brought the settled way of life of the Neolithic village. That food-producing economy spread across Europe between about 6000 and 4500 B.C., borne by colonization and native adaptation of new technologies.

The farmers of Early Neolithic Europe (ca. 7000–ca. 4500 B.C.) were pioneers. They tended to live in hamlets or villages surrounded by larger populations that remained hunter-gatherers. Between about 4500 and 2500 B.C., however, the majority of Europeans adopted a food-producing way of life. This era is known as the Late Ne-

olithic, or the Copper Age, because copper came into use on the Continent during this time, as did gold. A dramatic example of the use of these metals is a Bulgarian burial site of about 4000 B.C. in which a 45-year-old man was buried with 990 gold objects as well as copper and flint weapons.

Until about 3500 B.C., Copper Age Europeans developed in relative isolation from the more advanced east. For example, European metallurgy probably developed independently. On Europe's northern and western edges people began to set up stone tombs and monuments, often of huge blocks. These monuments, known as megaliths, may reflect the sense of time created by the spread of agriculture, with its seasonal rhythms.

Neolithic and Copper Age sculpture consists of many representations of females and few of males. Consider, for example, the huge sculpted

The Maltese Female This "Sleeping Lady," a terra-cotta statuette of the late fourth millennium B.C. from Malta, shows a reclining woman, perhaps a goddess or priestess. *(Erich Lessing/Art Resource, NY)*

female figures found in Malta's temples. Some scholars speculate that early Europeans worshiped goddesses of fertility, a religion replaced by that of the warlike invaders who brought male deities with them after 2000 B.C.

MESOPOTAMIA, 3000 B.C. TO CA. 100 B.C.

Civilization is derived from the Latin *civitas*, meaning "commonwealth" or "city." However, what differentiated the first civilizations from their Neolithic predecessors was not so much size (a city versus a town) as complexity. Once agriculture was improved so that fewer people were needed to feed the population, some people were free to devote their time to arts, crafts, and public service. With a sufficiently large and specialized labor force, and with a sufficiently strong government, it became possible to expand control over nature, to pursue advances in technology, to trade and compete over ever widening areas, to free an elite for ever more ambitious projects in art and thought, and to invent writing. In short, the advent of civilization in the fourth millennium B.C. marked a major turning point, when the human horizon expanded forever.

Civilization arose in southern Iraq, in the valley between the Tigris and Euphrates Rivers, a region that the Greeks called "Mesopotamia" (literally, "between the rivers"). At around the same time or shortly afterward, civilization began in the valley of the Nile River in Egypt. These two early civilizations developed independently but were also influenced by contacts with each other. Both Mesopotamia and Egypt are home to valleys containing alluvial land—that is, an essentially flat tract where fertile soil is deposited by a river. Otherwise, the two regions are quite different. Life in the Nile Valley was relatively easy. Every summer the Nile flooded in a relatively predictable manner, fertilizing the land with rich runoff water. The spring deluges of the Tigris and Euphrates were less predictable. The Nile's waters spread so broadly, moreover, that it

took little human effort to irrigate most of the available farmland in the Nile Valley. In southern Mesopotamia, by contrast, agriculture would not have been possible without irrigation and the use of channels, dikes, and dams to control floodwaters. One Mesopotamian text describes a farmer as "the man of dike, ditch, and plow."

With the development of a good irrigation system, southern Mesopotamia was transformed into rich farmland. But the lack of key raw materials, such as minerals and timber, meant that Mesopotamia had to depend on foreign trade. When human beings trade goods they also trade ideas, which can lead to turbulent change. Change also came through war: The Mesopotamians were frequently attacked by neighboring peoples who envied their rich cities.

Defense and management of the complex society created a need for cooperation and central direction. Mesopotamia consisted of numerous *city-states*—that is, independent political units each containing a rural countryside with villages controlled by a city. In the early Mesopotamian city, the temple was the most important authority, in politics and economics as well as religion. By 4000 B.C. the temple had become a monumental work of architecture built on a raised platform. Each city had at least one temple, the house of its patron god, and the common symbol of the community. Temples were wealthy and powerful and commanded deep loyalty.

Before the invention of writing, Mesopotamian people used tiny clay or stone tokens to represent objects being counted or traded. By 3500 B.C., with 250 different types of tokens, the system had grown unwieldy enough for people to start using signs to indicate tokens. Then they got rid of the tokens and simply made the signs on a clay tablet, using a reed stylus with a triangular point. The number of pictographs (pictures that stand for particular objects) grew, and these evolved into ideograms, symbols that are no longer recognizable as specific objects and thus can be used to denote ideas as well as things. In the centuries following its introduction, writing became standardized. Scholars call this writing *cuneiform* from the Latin for "wedge-shaped," a good description of what early writing looks like. Initially, cuneiform was used almost entirely to keep daily records, but by 2350 B.C. it had evolved enough to record the spoken language. As a system of about six hundred signs, cuneiform could now be used for poetry as easily as for bookkeeping. Cuneiform became the standard script of various languages of western Asia for several thousand years.

The formative era of Mesopotamian civilization, when writing was invented, is called the Uruk Period (ca. 3800–3200 B.C.) after one of its major archaeological sites. The Uruk Period encompassed a series of major technological breakthroughs, including the wheel and the plow, the first orchards—of dates, figs, or olives—and the first sophisticated metal casting processes. It witnessed the emergence of the first cities. Moreover, it marked a dramatic increase in the extent of territory and population, in warfare and political centralization, and in social complexity and institutional formality.

Professions and religious practices grew more complex. Women worked alongside men in most professions, but class differences were clear. For instance, priestesses were usually noblewomen from wealthy families. Most people had to rent land from temple or noble, and some peasants worked under foremen. There were also some slaves, originally captives from the mountains, but they were much outnumbered by free peasants.

The City-States of Sumer, ca. 3000–ca. 2350 B.C.

The city-states of Mesopotamia were the first civilization, and the dominant inhabitants of that civilization are called Sumerians. Present in southern Mesopotamia by 3200 B.C. and probably earlier, the Sumerians entered their great age in the third millennium B.C., when their city-states enjoyed a proud independence.

By the Early Dynastic Period (2800–2350 B.C.), a large Mesopotamian city might number fifty thousand people and cover 1000 acres surrounded by more than 5 miles of walls. Such a city was larger and more impressive than a Çatal Hüyük or Jericho, and it had mastered a more complex tech-

nology in order to reshape its agricultural hinterland. Most significant, it was part of a network of thirty such city-states with a common culture, commerce, and language. Despite their commonalities, however, Sumerian cities had a propensity to make war on each other. The scarcity of fresh water led to quarrels. Geography was an obstacle to unification because the cities were separated from each other by desert and swampland.

In each city, power flowed first from the temples to the wealthy landowning families and then finally to monarchs. Since the temple controlled large landed estates, the priests, scribes, and other temple officials were a major economic authority. Political power was largely in the hands of the Council of Elders, whose members were probably wealthy landowners. Some scholars argue that the council shared power with a popular assembly, creating, in effect, a primitive democracy—but we cannot be certain.

By about 2700 B.C., political power shifted from the council to the palace. It was a time of chronic intercity warfare, and the times demanded a strong hand. According to a plausible tradition, the earliest Sumerian monarchs were Enmebaragesi of the city of Kish; his son and successor, Agga; and Gilgamesh of Uruk, a hero of epic poetry whom many scholars consider a genuine historical personage. In the cities of Ur and Lagash the king's wife was often a power in her own right. Kish was ruled by Ku-baba (r. ca. 2450 B.C.), the first reigning queen of recorded history.

Conquest and Assimilation, ca. 2350–1900 B.C.

Mesopotamia's wealth drew a variety of hopeful conquerors from the surrounding peoples of the desert and mountains. Some attacked the city walls. Others, like Sargon (r. 2371–2316 B.C.), who spoke Akkadian (a Semitic language, related to Arabic and Hebrew) but lived in Sumer, rose to power from within, capitalizing on the discord among the Sumerian city-states. Either way, conquerors were sufficiently impressed by Sumerian culture to adopt many Sumerian customs. The conquering Akkadians, for example, adopted

Sumerian religion and wrote Akkadian in cuneiform.

As commander of one of history's first professional armies, Sargon conquered all Mesopotamia: His power extended westward along the Euphrates and eastward into the Iranian Plateau. Recent research suggests that Sargon's armies might have made use of the horse to draw war chariots, allowing them to cover much greater distances than earlier forces. Sargon's armies tore down the walls of conquered cities, leaving them defenseless and less likely to rebel. The old rulers were generally allowed to remain in office. The Akkadians were satisfied with loose control, as long as they could monopolize trade. Sargon and most of his successors presented themselves as mediators between human beings and the gods, but they usually stopped short of claiming to be gods themselves.

Although Sargon made Akkadian the official language of administration, he made politic concessions to Sumerian sensibilities. The cultures meshed. Sargon's daughter Enkheduanna, whom he appointed high priestess at Ur and Uruk, wrote poetry in Sumerian—poetry powerful enough to be often quoted in later Sumerian texts.

Around 2200 B.C. the Akkadian empire broke up into a series of smaller successor states. When the Sumerians returned to power under the Third Dynasty of Ur (2112–2004 B.C.), their rulers spoke of themselves as "kings of Sumer and Akkad." It was a title that would have a long and potent history; for the next fifteen hundred years many of the great kings of western Asia would label themselves, among other things, "king of Sumer and Akkad."

A new kingdom, under the rule of the Amorites, one of a group of raiding peoples who attacked Mesopotamia, emerged around 1900 B.C. in southern Mesopotamia. The kingdom of

The Uruk Vase This panel, from an alabaster vase of late-third-millennium-B.C. Uruk, is thought to depict either the goddess Inanna or one of her priestesses. She accepts a basket of gifts. Behind her are two bundles of reeds with streamers, symbols of the goddess. *(Frank Scherschel/Life Magazine © Time, Inc.)*

the Amorites, Semitic speakers, shared Mesopotamian culture and traditions. They made their capital at Babylon, in central Mesopotamia, which is why this era is often referred to as the Old Babylonian Period (1900–1600 B.C.). Its greatest era was under the reign of Hammurabi.

The Majesty of the Law

Hammurabi (r. 1792–1750 B.C.) ruled about six hundred years after Sargon. He created a Mesopotamian empire and ushered in an era of prosperity and cultural flowering. His famous text, Hammurabi's Code, became a legal and literary classic, often copied in later times. The code contains nearly three hundred rulings on topics ranging from family to commercial law, from wage rates to murder. However, there was no notion of abstract or universal principles in Mesopotamia (indeed, there was no word for "law"), and in that sense the document was less a code and more a collection of verdicts.

The earliest known law code had been promulgated by King Ur-Nammu of Ur around 2100 B.C., and other codes survive from the three centuries between Ur-Nammu and Hammurabi. Though we now tend to think of it as extraordinarily harsh, Hammurabi's Code was more lenient than some earlier documents. For example, family members sold or placed in servitude because of debt were automatically freed after three years. But Hammurabi's Code was the first to include such penalties as bodily mutilation, drowning, and impaling; earlier codes had stipulated payment in silver as punishment for crime. Hammurabi's Code also introduced the law of retaliation for wounds: "If a man has destroyed the eye of a member of the aristocracy: they shall destroy his eye. If he has broken his limb: they shall break the limb."

Inscribed in stone and put in a prominent public place, Hammurabi's Code and other Mesopotamian legal texts symbolized the notion that the law belonged to everyone. Yet Hammurabi's society was not egalitarian. There were three classes: slaves, free people who owned land, and *mushkenum* (a subordinate class whose members were legally free but landless and often dependent). Punishments were class-biased: Crimes against a free person received harsher punishment than crimes against a slave or a mushkenum. Debt frequently forced the poor to sell their children, especially daughters, into slavery. In general, crimes against women were punished just as crimes against men. Women could own and inherit property, work for wages, sue for divorce, and testify in court. The overall direction of the code, however, was patriarchal.

Divine Masters

The Old Babylonian Period was an era of great religious creativity. Many Sumerian gods arose out of the forces of nature—An, the sky-god; Enki, the earth-god and freshwater-god; and Enlil, the air-god. Others embodied human passions or notions about the afterlife—such as Inanna (Semitic, Ishtar), the goddess of love and war. The Sumerians were polytheists—that is, they had many gods—and their gods (like the later gods of Greece) were anthropomorphic, or human in form. Indeed, Sumerian gods were thought to be much like human beings, except that they were immortal and superpowerful. The Sumerians sometimes envisioned their gods holding an assembly, based perhaps on a boisterous Sumerian prototype.

Every Mesopotamian city had its main temple complex, the most striking feature of which was a *ziggurat*, a stepped tower. Unlike the pyramids of Egypt, ziggurats were not tombs but "stairways," providing a way for the gods to descend from heaven to earth. A typical ziggurat had two temples: a "high temple" at the top, to serve the god in the sky, and a "low temple" for the god to reach the earth. The "low temple" was the chief sanctuary of the city. To understand the divine will, the Mesopotamians engaged in various kinds of divination: the interpretation of dreams, the examination of the entrails of slaughtered animals, and the study of the stars (which stimulated great advances in astronomy).

Most people expected nothing glorious in the afterlife, merely a shadowy existence. It was thought that after death the person's spirit went on a journey to the Netherworld, under the earth. Mesopotamian texts describe the Netherworld as "the house wherein the dwellers are bereft of light,/Where dust is their fare and clay their food."[2] The dead stayed there permanently, though in some texts spirits returned to earth briefly, often with hostile intent toward the living.

Arts and Sciences

From Sumer to Babylon, the people of Mesopotamia were deeply inquisitive. They focused on the beginning and the end of things: "How did the world come into being?" "What happens to us when we die?" The Babylonian creation epic known from its first line as *Enuma Elish* ("When on high") is a poem about the triumph of the gods of order over the forces of chaos. This poem was recited annually during the New Year's festival by Babylonian priests. Another important Babylonian literary genre is known as wisdom literature, which gives general, sometimes sophisticated, advice. It eventually influenced the wisdom literature of the Hebrew Bible.

The best-known work of Mesopotamian literature is the *Epic of Gilgamesh.* Frequently translated and adapted by various west Asian peoples, *Gilgamesh* may be a Sumerian work perhaps dating back to about 2500 B.C. An epic poem is the story of heroic deeds, in this case those of Gilgamesh, king of Uruk. Gilgamesh was probably a real historical personage, but the poem primarily concerns his fictionalized personal life, in particular the painful wisdom he gains as he grows from arrogant youth to maturity. Much of the poem discusses Gilgamesh's close relationship with Enkidu, at first his rival, then his friend, and finally his educator. Enkidu's untimely death makes Gilgamesh aware of his own mortality and inspires his quest for immortality. The great power of the work is that Gilgamesh does not find immortality. Instead, he gains the wisdom to derive happiness from love, work, and friendship and accept the realities of mortal life. (See the box "Heroism and Death in Mesopotamia.") The *Epic of Gilgamesh* contains stories that presage the later biblical Eden and Flood narratives. There is little doubt that those narratives found their way from Mesopotamia to the Hebrew Bible.

Mesopotamian literature included some scientific works. Physicians made advances in the use of plant products for medicines and in rudimentary surgery. An Akkadian medical treatise speaks of general examples, like "a man who is feverish and has a burning abdomen" rather than the specific case of so-and-so. The Babylonians had a simple pregnancy test of moderate accuracy, and they were able to extract an aching tooth. When they became ill, however, most people in Mesopotamia set more store by magic and incantations than surgery or herbal medicine.

The Mesopotamians also made advances in mathematics, astronomy, and engineering. The Sumerians had two systems of numeration: a decimal system (powers of ten) for administration and business and a sexagesimal system (powers of sixty) for weights and mathematical or astronomical calculations. From this, the Babylonians came to divide hours by sixty, and it was also they who divided the day into two twelve-hour periods. Adept at arithmetic, the Babylonians could solve problems for which we would use algebra. A millennium before the Greek mathematician Pythagoras (who said that he had studied the Mesopotamian tradition) proved the theorem that bears his name, the Babylonians were familiar with the proposition that in a right triangle the square of the longest side is equal to the sum of the squares of the two other sides.

In many ways then, the Mesopotamians laid the groundwork for all future culture. Their difficult rivers seem to have demanded the cultivation of a cooperative work ethic. Harsh conditions also led them to a keen and often bitter awareness of human limitations and vanity. Knowledge of the erratic violence of nature, as well as the frailty of humanity, gave the Mesopotamians a world-view that encouraged both quiet cynicism and a deep appreciation for life.

Heroism and Death in Mesopotamia

The Epic of Gilgamesh sheds light on categories of gender and power in Mesopotamia. Men like King Gilgamesh and his friend Enkidu have heroic adventures and risk death. Women lead quieter lives but are wiser and more realistic, as the following excerpts show.

[Gilgamesh mourns the death of Enkidu.]

"Hear me, O elders and give ear unto me! It is for Enkidu, my friend, that I weep, Moaning bitterly like a wailing woman. The axe at my side, my hand's trust, The dirk in my belt, the shield in front of me, My festal robe, my richest trimming—An evil demon rose up and robbed me! O my younger friend, thou chasedst The wild ass of the hills, the panther of the steppe! Enkidu, my younger friend, thou who chasedst The wild ass of the hills, the panther of the steppe! We who have conquered all things, scaled the mountains, Who seized the Bull and slew him, Brought affliction on Hubaba, who dwelled in the Cedar Forest! What, now, is this sleep that has laid hold on thee? Thou art benighted and canst not hear me!" But he lifts not up his head; he touched his heart but it does not beat.

[Beginning lost. Gilgamesh is addressing Siduri, the ale-wife:]
"He who with me underwent all hardships—

Enkidu, whom I loved dearly, who with me underwent all hardships—has now gone to the fate of mankind! Day and night I have wept over him. I would not give him up for burial—in case my friend should rise at my plaint—seven days and seven nights, until a worm fell out of his nose. Since his passing I have not found life, I have roamed like a hunter in the midst of the steppe. O ale-wife, now that I have seen thy face, let me not see the death which I ever dread."

The ale-wife said to him, to Gilgamesh: "Gilgamesh, whither rovest thou? The life thou pursuest thou shalt not find. When the gods created mankind, death for mankind they set aside, Life in their own hands retaining. Thou, Gilgamesh, let full be thy belly, make thou merry by day and by night. Of each day make thou a feast of rejoicing, day and night dance thou and play! Let thy garments be sparkling fresh, thy head be washed; bathe thou in water. Pay heed to the little one that holds on to thy hand, let thy spouse delight in thy bosom! For this is the task of mankind!"

Source: James B. Pritchard, ed., *Ancient Near Eastern Texts Relating to the Old Testament*, 3d ed., with Supplement (Princeton: Princeton University Press, 1969), pp. 89–90. Copyright © 1969 by Princeton University Press. Reprinted by permission of Princeton University Press.

EGYPT, TO CA. 1100 B.C.

From Babylon to the Nile River Valley was about 750 miles by way of the caravan routes through Syria and Palestine: close enough to exchange customs, goods, and, sometimes, blows, but far enough for a distinct Egyptian civilization to emerge. Egypt developed writing around 3100 B.C.,

slightly after Mesopotamia (and possibly under Mesopotamian influence), but became a unified, peaceful kingdom much earlier than Mesopotamia.

Because of its pyramids, as well as its unique contributions in religion and politics, arts and sciences, Egypt has impressed scholars and lay people as few other ancient civilizations have. In the ancient world, Egyptian culture was distinct but influential, from the spread of such Egyptian notions as a Last Judgment in the afterlife to Egyptian techniques in architecture and sculpture.

Geography as Destiny

Because most of Egypt is desert, with only about 5 percent habitable by humans, its civilization was shaped by the Nile River (Map 1.2). For the most part, then, Egypt was narrow: The Nile Valley is nowhere more than about 14 miles wide. In the surrounding desert there were a few oases—and then there was the fertile Nile Delta. The delta is north on our maps, but is called Lower Egypt, since the Nile flows down on its way to the Mediterranean Sea.

The Nile's annual floods were regular and rarely damaging. As a result, Egyptian agriculture was one of the wealthiest in the ancient world. Bread and beer were the national staples. Unlike Mesopotamia, where scarcity provoked chronic warfare, Egyptian towns peacefully enjoyed plentiful water and fertile land. Nor was Egypt easily reached by outside invaders. The Nile was cut off by deserts to the east and west, by rapids to the south, and by the Mediterranean to the north. Egyptian art and literature betray little of the despair over the unpredictability of the universe or the idea of hard-won wisdom that developed in Mesopotamia.

Storm over Origins

Early Egypt developed a distinctive civilization, with no major invasion for over a thousand years after the beginning of the historical period around 3100 B.C. Historians argue over the extent of Egypt's isolation. Before World War II, most Egyptologists tended to see Egypt as part of the culture of western Asia rather than as part of Africa. Many imagined that ancient Egyptians looked much like modern white Europeans. After World War II, the liberation of Europe's former African colonies and the awakening of a growing interest in Africa by African Americans led some historians to consider the possibility that Egypt was primarily African in character and that the ancient Egyptians were black.

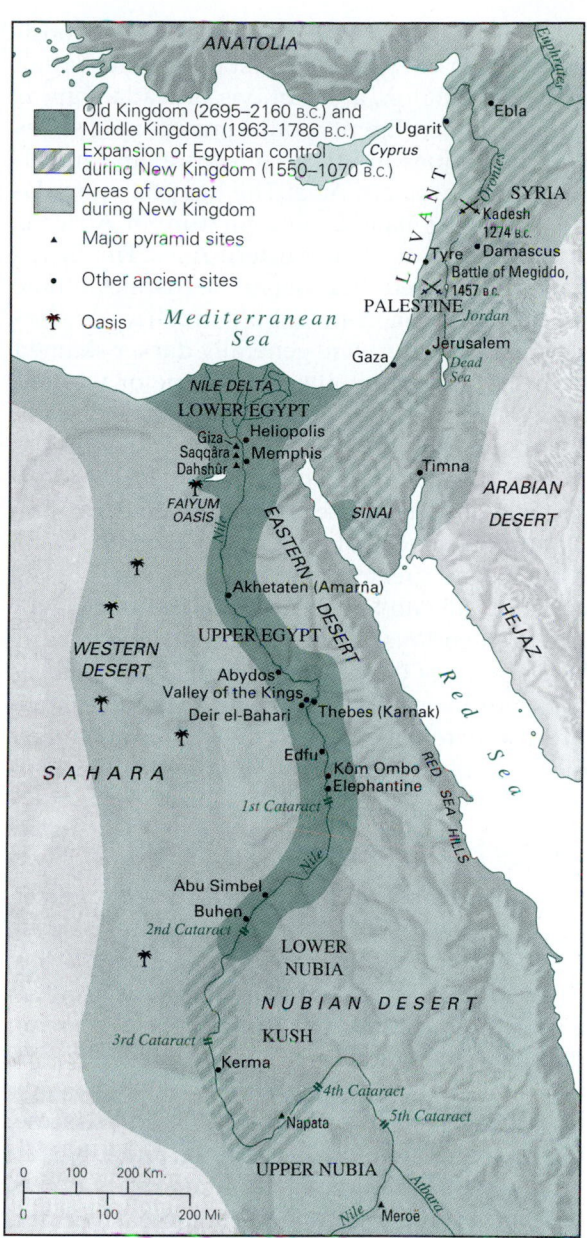

Map 1.2 Ancient Egypt and the Levant The unique geography of the Nile Valley left a stamp on ancient Egypt. Fertile soil made Egypt wealthy, and the surrounding desert led to periods of isolation from nearby African and Asian cultures.

The truth lies in between these two positions. Much of Egypt's earliest culture, including artwork, religion, and notions of leadership, is African. Later, Egypt would import new styles and techniques in art, architecture, and metallurgy from western Asia. The Egyptian population seems to have been a mixture of Africans and immigrants from western Asia. The Egyptians considered themselves a distinct ethnic group, unlike their neighbors in Africa or elsewhere. Egyptians were generally darker skinned than the ancient peoples of Europe or western Asia but lighter skinned than the peoples of sub-Saharan Africa; they included a considerable variety of skin colors and body types.

Scholars also argue over the relative originality and influence of Egyptian civilization. Some have taken great pains to show that Egypt copied from sub-Saharan Africa and that Egypt had tremendous influence on ancient Greece. While some of these specific claims have real validity, for the most part it seems that ancient cultures were relatively independent, though many of them influenced each other to some degree.

Divine Kingship

Agriculture and settled village life emerged in Egypt around 5000 B.C. For two millennia, Egyptian communities up and down the Nile Valley cleared marshes and expanded the amount of land under cultivation, to support a growing population. Around 3100 B.C., the Nile Valley became one unified kingdom of Egypt, with a capital city perhaps at Memphis. Around this time, monumental architecture, writing, and kingship arose—all a combination of indigenous invention and borrowing from Mesopotamia and perhaps Nubia.

The history of third- and second-millennium B.C. Egypt is usually divided into three distinct eras of great prosperity: the Old Kingdom (2695–2160 B.C.), the Middle Kingdom (1963–1786 B.C.), and the New Kingdom (1550–1070 B.C.). Central authority broke down in the Intermediate Periods between the kingdoms. Broadly speaking, the Old Kingdom was an era of spectacular creativity and originality, symbolized by the building of the Great Pyramids; the Middle Kingdom was an era of introspection, literary production, and increased political equality; and the New Kingdom was an era in which Egypt's traditional isolation gave way to international diplomacy, warfare, and expansion.

The early Egyptian government was the first to govern such a large territory. It managed this through a hierarchical power structure: A broad base of laborers and artisans supported a commanding elite and a single supreme leader. For centuries, Egyptians referred to the supreme office rather than to the person, calling it "the Great House": in Egyptian, *per-aa,* or "pharaoh." This eventually became the title of the ruler himself—or occasionally herself.

The pyramids give witness to the power of pharaoh. The ancients built thirty-five major and many smaller pyramids, of which the best known are the Great Pyramids of Giza—three gigantic, perfectly symmetrical limestone tombs. Nearly five thousand years later, the pyramid of King Khufu (r. 2589–2566 B.C.; better known by his Greek name, Cheops) is still the largest all-stone building in human history. Equally impressive is the Great Sphinx, a human-headed lion carved out of a huge rock outcropping.

When the Great Pyramids were constructed, the kingdom of Egypt was young and the king's power not yet secure. By ordering the construction of an astonishingly large project focused on his person, the king made a statement of his strength. The sheer size of the Great Pyramids demonstrated the king's ability to organize a vast labor force. Indeed, it has been suggested that the encampment of workers at Giza represented the largest gathering of human beings to that date.

In theory, the king owned all the land. In practice, Egypt's economy was a mixture of private enterprise and centralized control. Old Kingdom Egypt was one of the earliest great bureaucracies, run by provincial governors, military commanders, judges, treasurers, engineers, agricultural overseers, scribes, and others. The highest official was the vizier, a sort of prime minister, who had more day-to-day power than pharaoh himself.

Egyptian kingship was sacred monarchy: Pharaoh was deemed to be a god. According to Egyptian myth, the world was created when a god, sitting on a hill, made the waters recede. For farmers, especially in the desert, control of the earth's water was the most essential power. Pharaoh was thought to have such power, for it was he or she, they believed, who made the Nile rise and fall each year.

A wall of ceremony separated kings from ordinary human beings. Egyptians did not speak "to" the king but rather "in his presence." Pharaoh's exalted status was apparent on the occasion of a ceremonial "glorious appearance," especially at the Sed festival or jubilee, commemorating the anniversary of pharaoh's reign. The most traditional part of the ceremony was the appearance of the king and queen at the palace door on jubilee day wearing special jubilee clothes. Other features included an elaborate procession of boats on the Nile, the assembling of officials and foreign dignitaries standing according to rank, the distribution of gifts, a special breakfast (bread, beef, fowl, and beer), and the erection of festival buildings.

Life and Afterlife

Later peoples, beginning with the Greeks, have assumed that the ordinary Egyptian chafed under royal power. It is true that Egyptians were burdened with a variety of taxes (paid in agricultural produce) and that free people, both men and women, had an obligation of forced labor on public works, from irrigation projects to the pyramids. Sometimes this service caused resentment. We hear of worker discipline maintained by beatings, of fugitives, of the hope that there be no forced labor in the afterlife, and even, in one case, of a worker's strike. But the pyramid builders were not slaves laboring under a tyrant, as Greek writers assumed. In fact, they might have given their labor gladly, raising the man-god's tomb as an act of faith, just as people centuries later donated time and money to build

medieval cathedrals. There were material compensations too: ration supplements for ordinary laborers and steady employment for specialized craftsmen.

Egyptian religion tended toward syncretism—the combination of contradictory beliefs. For example, Egyptian mythology taught that the sky was a cow, or was held up by a god or a post, or was a goddess stretched over the earth. This was conceivable because the unity of the world seemed strong enough to support great variety in the way nature manifested itself. Egyptian religion was not usually monotheistic, which is the belief in one and only one god. Instead, it tended toward henotheism. Henotheists emphasize the worship of one god though they believe in many others, and they occasionally shift emphasis from one to another. The most important Egyptian god was Re, the sun, often called "universal lord," but he was sometimes syncretized with other gods to create a powerful new god. For example, Re-Atum was a combination of Re and a creator-god, while Amon-Re was a combination of Re and the invisible, omnipresent Amon. Egypt's religion had an abundance of greater and lesser deities, including human, animal, and composite gods.

The most striking feature of Egyptian religion was its focus on the afterlife. Unlike Mesopotamians, Egyptians believed that death could be an extremely pleasant continuation of life on earth. Egyptians distinguished between soul and body and believed that part of the soul, the *ka*, was immortal. Since a soul liked to return to its body from time to time after death, the Egyptians mastered the science of embalming, creating the Egyptian mummies.

In the Old Kingdom the afterlife was reserved for the king and his officials, but by the Middle Kingdom even ordinary Egyptians could live in the afterlife as gods—as long as they could pay for the relevant rituals and prayers for their graves. In the Middle Kingdom and its flanking Intermediate Periods, average people had more control over their own lives, arts and letters flourished, and there was a growing sense of community rather than hierarchy.

Miniature Coffin of Tutankhamon This miniature coffin (8⅞ inches long) is one of four containing the internal organs of the king (r. 1336–1327 B.C.) removed during the embalming process. Made of gold inlaid with colored glass and carnelian, the coffin is typical of the splendor and luxury of the objects discovered in the substantially intact royal tomb. Note the hiero-glyphic inscription offering divine protection to the remains. *(Egyptian Museum, Cairo)*

Access to the afterlife was dependent on in-cantations, magic spells, and prayers. Yet from time to time, especially during the Middle King-dom, there was an impressive insistence on ethi-cal behavior. Dead people were to appear before the court of a god, usually Osiris, for judgment. Before forty-two judges of the underworld, the dead would have a chance to declare their inno-cence of a variety of sins. The sinless were to be admitted into eternal life in the kingdom of the blessed; the guilty were wiped out. The system was identical for men and women.

In life, Egyptian women did not enjoy equal status with men, but they had a greater measure of equality than women in other ancient societies, particularly in legal matters. As in Mesopotamia, in Egypt a woman could buy or sell, bequeath or inherit, sue or testify in court; but an Egyptian woman, unlike her eastern sisters, could do so without a male guardian's approval. A married woman in Egypt retained her legal independ-ence; she could even own property without her husband's involvement, though there is little evi-dence that this often occurred. Although Egyp-tian women could work outside the home in a variety of enterprises, they were rarely managers and rarely received the same pay as men. Women worked in agriculture and trade, in the textile and perfume industries, in dining halls, in enter-tainment, and as priestesses. Still, women were expected to make the home the focus of their ac-tivities, so there was no real equality.

The humane attitudes of the Middle King-dom were swept away in the period from about 1700 to 1570 B.C., when Semitic-speaking immi-grants from Palestine, the Hyksos, settled in the delta region and conquered much of Egypt. In many ways gentle conquerors, the Hyksos wor-shiped Egyptian gods, built and restored Egyp-tian temples, and intermarried with their sub-jects. Eventually, however, the nobles of Upper Egypt waged a war to retake the kingdom. Egypt had had no standing army in its earlier period, but the Hyksos had brought advanced military technology to Egypt, including the horse-drawn war chariot, new kinds of daggers and swords, and bows. The native Egyptians learned to use these new military devices, and they drove the Hyksos out.

Ahmose I (r. 1550–1525 B.C.), the first restored Egyptian ruler of the New Kingdom, changed Egypt a great deal. Leaders who take power through military force rarely choose to dismantle a victorious, loyal army. Once the original battle was won, Egypt's new rulers turned their weaponry to aggressive campaigns abroad.

Expansion and Reform, 1540–1293 B.C.

Warlike, expansionist, and marked by a daring attempt at religious reform, the New Kingdom's Eighteenth Dynasty (1540–1293 B.C.) has long held a special fascination for historians. The great warrior-pharaoh Thutmose III (r. 1479–1425 B.C.) undertook the dynasty's expansion into Nubia and Syria. Before Thutmose reached adulthood, his stepmother, Queen Hatshepsut, had served as regent and then assumed the kingship herself (r. 1479–1457 B.C.). Hatshepsut's was the most successful female reign in Egypt before Cleopatra (r. 51–30 B.C.). Although she led Egyptian armies on campaign to Nubia, Hatshepsut is best known for her public works and temple rebuilding, and for leading a commercial expedition over the Red Sea to the "Land of Punt" (perhaps modern Somalia, in eastern Africa).

New Kingdom Egypt is also remembered for its dramatic religious revolution. Amon-Re was the chief deity of the New Kingdom. His temple priests supported the military and were rewarded with land and wealth until their power rivaled pharaoh's own. The pharaoh Amenhotep IV (r. 1352–1336 B.C.) resented this and outlawed the worship of Amon-Re. He announced a new god, Aton, the solar disk. Changing his own name to Akhenaton ("pleasing to Aton"), the king ordered the erasure of Amon-Re's name from monuments throughout Egypt. He even created a new capital city in central Egypt and called it Akhetaton (modern Amarna). Akhenaton's wife, Nefertiti, figures prominently in Amarna art, and she may have played an important role in the reform.

The reform shifted power from the priests to the king, but we need not doubt the reformers' sincerity. Contemporary literature suggests intense religious belief in Aton as a benevolent god. Although the Aton cult focused on one god, it was not monotheistic but henotheistic because Re and Akhenaton himself were recognized as gods as well. Indeed, only Akhenaton and his family were permitted to worship Aton directly; the rest of the Egyptian population worshiped the god through pharaoh.

Bold as the reform was, sustaining so dramatic a break with tradition proved impossible. After Akhenaton's death, his son-in-law and successor, Tutankhaton (r. 1336–1327 B.C.), reconciled with the priests of Amon-Re and changed his name to Tutankhamon. The Amon-Re cult was revived, the Aton cult abolished, and the city of Akhetaton abandoned.

Arts and Sciences

The Egyptians were superb builders, architects, and engineers. In addition to pyramids and irrigation works, they constructed royal tombs, palaces, forts, temples, and obelisks (pillars carved of a single piece of stone and inscribed with figures and hieroglyphs). At their best, Egyptian architects designed buildings in sublime harmony with the unique landscape.

The Egyptian court was one of the first and greatest patrons of the arts. Egyptian craftsmen were masters of gold jewelry-work, glassmaking, and woodworking. The major arts are well represented in temples and tombs, which were decorated with rich, multicolored wall paintings. There are scenes of the gods, court ceremony, ordinary life, war, and recreation amid the crocodiles and hippopotamuses of the Nile Valley. Egyptians also excelled in sculpture. Carved in stone, wood, or metal, Egyptian sculpture is a study in contrasts. The body is usually rigid and uniform while the face is full of character, representing the personality of an individual.

Ancient Egyptian literature was quite varied. Religious subjects, historical records, treatises in mathematics and medicine, and secular stories

⤳ ENCOUNTERS WITH THE WEST ⤳

Egyptian Attitudes Toward Foreigners

The story of Sinuhe is a well-known piece of Middle Kingdom prose literature. A court official, Sinuhe fled Egypt for Syria-Palestine after the assassination of the king. There he married the daughter of a tribal chief and became a successful chief himself. In his old age he received permission to return home. The tale demonstrates Egyptian curiosity about Palestine and Syria while it reveals Egyptian cultural snobbery toward what another Egyptian text calls "the miserable Asiatic."

This decree of the King: . . . Come back to Egypt! See the residence in which you lived! Kiss the ground at the great portals, mingle with the courtiers! For today you have begun to age. You have lost a man's strength. Think of the day of burial, the passing into reveredness.

A night is made for you with ointments and wrappings from the hand of Tait [goddess of weaving]. A funeral procession is made for you on the day of burial; the mummy case is of gold, its head of lapis lazuli. . . . You shall not die abroad! Nor shall Asiatics inter you. You shall not be wrapped in the skin of a ram to serve as your coffin. Too long a roaming of the earth! Think of your corpse, come back! . . .

Copy of the reply to this decree:

The servant of the Palace, Sinuhe, says: In very good peace! . . . May the fear of you resound in lowlands and highlands, for you have subdued all that the sun encircles! . . .

Re [the sun-god] has set the fear of you throughout the land, the dread of you in every foreign country. Whether I am at the residence, whether I am in this place, it is you who cover this horizon. The sun rises at your pleasure. The water in the river is drunk when you wish. The air of heaven is breathed at your bidding. . . . This servant has been sent for!

Your Majesty will do as he wishes! One lives by the breath which you give.

[Sinuhe returns to Egypt and is brought into the king's presence.]

Then the royal daughters were brought in, and his majesty said to the queen: "Here is Sinuhe, come as an Asiatic, a product of nomads!" She uttered a very great cry, and the royal daughters shrieked all together. They said to his majesty: "Is it really he, O king, our lord?" Said his majesty: "It is really he!" . . .

His majesty said: "He shall not fear, he shall not dread! He shall be a Companion among the nobles. He shall be among the courtiers. Proceed to the robing-room to wait on him!"

I left the audience-hall, the royal daughters giving me their hands. We went through the great portals, and I was put in the house of a prince. In it were luxuries: a bathroom and mirrors. . . . Every servant was at his task. Years were removed from my body. I was shaved; my hair was combed. Thus was my squalor returned to the foreign land, my dress to the Sand-farers. I was clothed in fine linen; I was anointed with fine oil. I slept on a bed. I had returned the sand to those who dwell in it, the tree-oil to those who grease themselves with it.

Source: Miriam Lichtheim, *Ancient Egyptian Literature,* Volume 1: *The Old and Middle Kingdoms* (Berkeley: University of California Press, 1973), pp. 229–233. Reprinted by permission of the Regents of the University of California and the University of California Press.

survive alongside business contracts and royal proclamations. A good example of Egyptian writing is *The Story of Sinuhe,* a prose tale that reveals both the charm of ancient Egyptian literature and its cultural chauvinism. (See the box "Encounters with the West: Egyptian Attitudes Toward Foreigners.") The existence of papyrus in Egypt, and the discovery that its fibers could be made into writing material (the word *paper* comes from *papyrus*) distinguishes Egyptian writing from the clay tablets of Mesopotamia. The best-known Egyptian writing is hieroglyphics, a system of pictures and abstract signs that represent sounds or ideas. Elaborate and formal, hieroglyphics were used only for monuments and ornamentation. Two simplified scripts served for everyday use.

Mathematical astronomy never reached the heights in Egypt that it did in Babylon, but the Egyptian calendar was an enduring achievement. Based on observation of the star Sirius, the 365-day Egyptian calendar approximated the solar calendar. Julius Caesar brought the Egyptian calendar to Rome, and, corrected to 365¼ days, it survives to this day (in adjusted form).

Egyptian medical doctors were admired in antiquity and were in demand abroad. They had a full battery of splints, sutures, adhesive plasters, and elementary disinfectants (from tree leaves). A brilliant treatise, the so-called Edwin Smith Papyrus, demonstrates their sophistication and rationalism. Dating from around 1750 B.C., the document claims to be a copy of an original from 2700 B.C. In this treatise physicians divide diseases into three categories: treatable, possibly treatable, and untreatable. There are signs of careful observation and tantalizing evidence of postmortem dissection.

Although Egyptian doctors distinguished between medicine and magic, they were happy to use magic when all else failed. In a letter of the thirteenth century B.C. to a Hittite king, Ramesses II declines the king's request for an Egyptian physician to treat his sister's infertility. A physician could do nothing, Ramesses explains, because the woman was past childbearing age. He goes on to say, however, that an Egyptian magician might be perfect for the job, and he has decided to send one.

ISRAEL, CA. 1500–400 B.C.

Sometime between 2000 and 1500 B.C., a semi-nomadic chieftain called Abraham apparently migrated from northern Mesopotamia and settled his people in Canaan, north and west of the Dead Sea. His language, Hebrew, was one of the many Semitic tongues spoken between the Mediterranean Sea and the Euphrates River. Archaeology does not confirm the biblical account of this long migration, but it does show it to be plausible. The civilization that arose following this journey was not extraordinary for its size, time, or technology—factors that justify study of ancient Mesopotamia and Egypt. The ancient Hebrews demand our attention because of the profound effect they had, and still have, on the culture of the Western world. Thousands of years ago, the ancient Hebrews put together a book of literature, history, poetry, law, ethics, general advice, politics, and worship. Its impact still resounds.

The Hebrew Bible

As literature and as religious teaching, the Bible is unquestionably the most important book in Western civilization. As a source of history, however, it presents difficulties. Much of the Hebrew Bible (called the "Old Testament" by Christians) is based on written sources that probably date back at least as far as the early Israelite monarchy of about 1000 B.C. Some scholars trace these written sources back several centuries earlier, to the religious leader Moses and the laws he is said to have promulgated. Other parts of the Hebrew Bible are probably the product of oral tradition, and the reliability of that tradition is also the subject of much scholarly debate.

The Hebrew Bible reached something close to its current form around 200 B.C. It consists of three main sections: (1) the Torah (literally, "teaching"), also known as the Pentateuch, or five books of Moses; (2) the Prophets, which are largely history and prediction; and (3) the Writings, books of poetry, proverbs, and wisdom literature. The books of the Hebrew Bible are canonical: One by one, each was accepted by established authority as sacred. Perhaps most important was the acceptance, in 425 B.C., of the assembled five books of the Torah. The introduction of the Torah made the Hebrews into what they have been ever since, "a people of the book," as the Muslims would put it many years later. Literacy and the written tradition became central to their culture.

The Hebrews are the first people we know of to have a single national history book, but it is not secular history. Indeed, one of the main actors of the narrative is God. All ancient peoples told stories of their semidivine foundation, but only the Hebrews believed their nation had been created by a treaty, the covenant, between them and their god. In the Hebrew Bible, there is an emphatic focus on the individual: Individual characters take actions that have moral consequences that unfold over time. History was understood as the story of the success or failure of the Hebrew people in carrying out God's commandments—and the ways in which God kept his part of the covenant.

Many of the themes, narrative details, and styles of writing in the Hebrew Bible derive from earlier cultures. The biblical Flood story, for example, seems to have been modeled on an episode in the *Epic of Gilgamesh*. Biblical poems in praise of God are often similar to Egyptian sacred poems, and biblical wisdom literature often recalls Egyptian or Babylonian parallels. All in all, however, the Hebrew Bible was a dramatically new kind of book, concentrating on one central theme: God's plan for humanity and his chosen people, the Hebrews. There is also passionate poetry here that seems to have been written for a human lover before it became a description of sacred worship. There are also passages that are stunning for their pragmatism, fatalism, and even secularism—especially in Ecclesiastes. Consider, for example, that book's injunction to "eat drink and be merry," and its advice that human beings "be not righteous overmuch." Ecclesiastes even tells us that the world, even under a just God, is not fair: "The race is not to the swift, nor the battle to the strong . . . but time and chance happeneth to them all" (Ecclesiastes 9:11).

The Emergence of Monotheism, ca. 1500–600 B.C.

According to the Bible, Abraham gave up Mesopotamian polytheism for belief in one god, and in return for Abraham's faith God said, "As a possession for all time I shall give you and your descendants after you the land in which you are now aliens, the whole of Canaan, and I shall be their God" (Genesis 17:8). Strictly speaking, Abraham was a henotheist rather than monotheist. Although he worshiped only one god, he did not deny the existence of other gods. Pure monotheism was the invention of the Hebrews, but it came later.

According to the biblical account, that turning point came several hundred years later. In a time of famine, many of Abraham's descendants had left Canaan for prosperous Egypt. At first they thrived, but in time they were enslaved and forced to build cities in the Nile Delta. Eventually, Moses, a divinely appointed leader, released the Hebrews from bondage in Egypt and led them back to Canaan and freedom.

The Exodus ("journey out," in Greek), as this movement has been called, was a rare example of a successful national liberation movement in antiquity, and it has served as a symbol of freedom ever since. Among those who accept its historicity, a date of about 1225 B.C. is frequently assigned to the Exodus. The Exodus is also one of the central events in the history of ancient Israel, because it marked another covenant, this time between the god of Abraham and the entire Israelite people. At Mount Sinai, traditionally located on the rugged Sinai Peninsula between Egypt and Palestine, the Israelites are said to have first accepted as their one god a deity whose name is represented in Hebrew by the letters corresponding to YHWH. YHWH is traditionally rendered in English as "Jehovah," though "Yahweh" is more accurate. The Israelites accepted Yahweh's laws, summarized in the Ten Commandments. In return for obedience, they would be God's chosen people, his "special possession; . . . a kingdom of priests, . . . [his] holy nation." The substance of the covenant is unique, but in form and style it bears a certain similarity to the treaties of international diplomacy of the period 1400–1200 B.C. The Bible places the Israelite covenant with God at around 1200 B.C., but modern scholars argue that the idea of monotheism may have come a bit earlier or even centuries later. In either case, it was centuries before ordinary Hebrews had committed themselves fully to monotheism.

The Ten Commandments are both more general and more personal than the laws of Hammurabi's Code. They are addressed to the individual, whom they commit to a universal standard. Punishments are not explicit, suggesting that the commandments were both an ethical code and a private arrangement between God and the individual. The text mentioned the existence of class difference but did not assign the various classes separate laws and punishments. Indeed, it insisted that the commandments were for everyone: On the Sabbath, servants, strangers, and even animals were to rest. It is also worth noticing that the commandments mention not only what one does, but what one thinks about. The injunction to "not covet" what belongs to others is more a piece of advice for personal contentment than it is a law for ensuring an orderly community.

Ethical gods were rare, but this was certainly not the first. What was new was that although other gods were part of nature, Israel's god transcended nature. He was its creator and master. This allowed him to give human beings dominion over nature—a gift that has had profound consequences for our relationship with the environment. In his immense power, Israel's god was further removed from human beings than other deities; but in his justice and mercy he was closer. He was both humane and unfathomably suprahuman.

During the twelfth and eleventh centuries B.C., the Hebrews completed the conquest of the Palestinian hill country from the Canaanites. The Hebrews were governed in this period by a series of judges. When the Philistines, one of the Sea Peoples (see page 26), captured the Palestinian coast, the Hebrew tribes appointed a centralized monarchy to resist the foe. The first Israelite king, Saul (r. ca. 1020–1004 B.C.), had some suc-

cess against the Philistines, but eventually fell in battle. The next king, David (r. 1004–965 B.C.), a former mercenary captain for the Philistines, defeated them decisively—symbolized in his biblical struggle with Goliath.

David conquered an empire that extended into modern Jordan, Lebanon, and Syria, as well as the Canaanite city of Jerusalem, which he made into Israel's capital. David's son and

City of David When David conquered Jerusalem around 1000 B.C. and made it his capital, it was a small, 15-acre town on a steep hill above the valley of Kidron (foreground), outside the walls of today's Old City. His successors expanded the city to include the Temple Mount, once the site of Solomon's Temple, today crowned with the Dome of the Rock, an Islamic mosque. (*Zev Radovan, Jerusalem*)

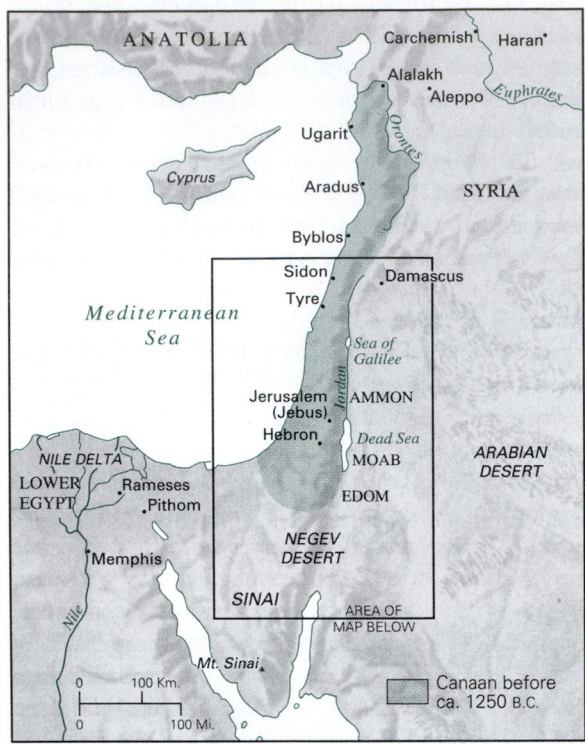

Map 1.3 Ancient Israel The Israelites settled in the Canaanite hill country west of the Jordan River and the Dead Sea after 1200 B.C. (left map). Control of Israelite territory after 928 B.C. was shared between two monarchies (right map): the kingdom of Israel (conquered by the Assyrians in 722 B.C.) and Judah (conquered in 598 B.C.).

successor, Solomon (r. 965–928 B.C.), was also a great king. His most famous act was to build the first Hebrew Temple. Before it was built, the Hebrews had worshiped at a humble, movable wooden chest called the Ark of the Covenant. Solomon's temple became a dramatic symbol of rootedness. Located in Jerusalem, it functioned as the center of religious life.

Solomon was the last monarch of the unified Hebrew people. Under his successors the monarchy was split into the large northern kingdom of Israel and a smaller southern kingdom of Judah centered on Jerusalem (Map 1.3). In 722 B.C. the

Assyrians conquered the kingdom of Israel. Judah survived, preserving its autonomy first as an Assyrian vassal and then as an independent power.

In the period of the two kingdoms (928–722 B.C.) and the Judean survivor-state (722–587 B.C.), the kings made the Temple at Jerusalem the unquestioned religious center of the whole Israelite people and began the process of canonizing the Hebrew Bible. The cohesion of the people and the doctrine was much aided by the prophets, who were prominent from approximately 900 to 500 B.C. Seers uttering divinely inspired predictions were universal figures in ancient religion. But no other culture of antiquity has anything like the Hebrew prophets: charismatic, uncompromising, terrible figures of God's wrath and ultimate forgiveness. The prophets were a reminder of the most radical spiritual teachings of Israel: absolute monotheism, insistence on righteousness, contempt for materialism and worldly power, and love of the powerless. They often supported the kings but did not shrink from confronting them and insisting on justice. Among them were Amos, a humble shepherd who preached the superiority of righteousness to ritual; Jeremiah, who prophesied the destruction of Jerusalem as punishment for the people's worship of gods other than Yahweh; and Isaiah, who predicted a new day of universal peace and justice to be inaugurated by a savior.

Exile and Return, 598–ca. 400 B.C.

Between 598 and 582 B.C., Judah was conquered by the Neo-Babylonians (see page 26), who destroyed Jerusalem and the Temple. The cultural, political, and economic elite was deported to Babylon. Those who could, fled for Egypt. The dispirited remnant in Palestine shared their land with migrant colonists from neighboring regions, with whom they intermarried and among whom their religion all but disappeared.

And that, given the usual fate of exiled and uprooted peoples in antiquity, should have been that. Yet not only did the Judeans in the Babylonian Captivity persevere in their religious loyalty, they actually returned to Palestine in large numbers. The Temple was rebuilt around 515 B.C., only seventy years after its destruction. This success was due in part to the Persians, who conquered Babylon in 539 B.C. and proclaimed the freedom of the Jews to rebuild the Temple in Jerusalem. Still, Persian benevolence would have availed little if not for the ability of the Judean elite to keep the faith burning among the exiles.

The Neo-Babylonian rulers allowed Jewish deportees to continue to practice their religion. Jews in Babylonia were not slaves; rather they rented land on royal estates, and some became quite prosperous. Although some Babylonian Jews assimilated to local ways, many continued a Jewish religious life. Communal worship was observed in open places, perhaps with associated buildings. Some scholars argue that synagogues ("gatherings" in Greek), modest centers of prayer and study that have been the focus of Jewish worship ever since, first emerged in Babylon.

As striking as the return to Palestine was the survival of large numbers of Judeans as an unassimilated people outside of Judah—in other words, as Jews. For the first time, membership in a community of worship was divorced from residence. Jewish communities flourished in Babylonia, Persia, and Egypt, but their members often chose not to become Babylonians, Persians, or Egyptians. From the sixth century B.C. on, a majority of Jews lived outside Palestine, and the Jewish Diaspora ("dispersion") became a permanent part of Western history.

Restoring the Jewish community in Judea (the Persian province corresponding to the former kingdom of Judah) did not prove easy. After many difficult years, that community was reestablished on a firm footing under the leadership of the Persian Jewish governor Nehemiah, who arrived in Judea in 445 B.C., and the Babylonian Jew Ezra, who probably arrived a generation later. Nehemiah overcame local and imperial opposition and built a new city wall for Jerusalem, which rendered the capital secure. A priest and scribe, Ezra oversaw the adoption of the Torah by the Judean community.

Society, Equality, and the People of Israel

A rough equality, limited government, and the rule of law under God were fundamental Israelite political notions. According to Israelite belief, humans were made in God's image. Thus all individuals were equal in a fundamental sense; all were bound by God's law. A king who disobeyed this law was illegitimate. Indeed, Israel was ambivalent at best about the institution of kingship, which was tolerated as an evil made necessary only by the country's armed enemies.

God's covenant with the Hebrews was a religious contract with political consequences: God was the only true king of Israel. Far from being gods themselves or even God's representatives, Israel's kings were merely his humble servants.

Israelite egalitarianism was restricted to men. Israelite women usually could not own or inherit property, as women could in Hammurabi's Babylon; or sue in court, as women could in pharaonic Egypt; or initiate a divorce, as women could in Athens. Monotheism meant that the powerful goddesses of other ancient cultures were absent in Israel. Women participated in the rituals of early Israelite religion and the original Temple (ca. 940–587 B.C.), but were segregated in a separate women's courtyard in the rebuilt Temple (ca. 515 B.C.–A.D. 79) and did not take part in temple ritual. Indeed, the perspective of the Hebrew Bible is predominantly male: Of the 1426 names in the Hebrew Bible, 1315 are male, and only men can bear the sign of the Lord's covenant with Israel—that is, circumcision.[3]

Nevertheless, Israelite women enjoyed honor as mothers and partners in running the household. Reproduction and hence motherhood assumed great importance in the Hebrew Bible; the Lord enjoins humans to "be fruitful and multiply" (Genesis 1:28). The Bible also commands that children honor both their father and their mother: The two parents are equal in parental authority (Exodus 20:12). The Hebrew Bible sometimes admires the strategies that women used to counter male power. Rebecca, for instance, is portrayed as clever when she tricks her husband into blessing Jacob, the son she prefers.

Only about a half-dozen women in the Hebrew Bible serve as leaders of Israel, but that is more than in the literature of most other ancient cultures. Deborah (ca. 1125 B.C.), a charismatic Israelite preacher, organizes an army that destroys the forces of a Canaanite commander. Centuries later Esther, a Hebrew woman, becomes the wife of a Persian king and defeats a conspiracy to wipe out her people. In the Book of Ruth, a selfless and loyal woman saves her mother-in-law, Naomi, from ruin and poverty. The Bible celebrates Ruth as Naomi's "devoted daughter-in-law, who has proved better to you [Naomi] than seven sons." Israelite culture prized women for their cunning, courage, and perseverance—qualities that allowed the people to survive. Although military prowess was highly valued in men, the Bible taught that "wisdom is better than weapons of war" (Ecclesiastes). Above all, the god of Israel prized righteousness.

WESTERN ASIA AND THE LEVANT, 1400–330 B.C.

So far we have concentrated our study of civilization on three distinct cultures. The ancient Mesopotamian, Egyptian, and Hebraic civilizations capture our attention because they were the earliest and most influential cultures of the third and second millennium B.C. Because of their political arrangements, literary and religious accomplishments, agricultural advancements, and scientific investigations, these civilizations take pride of place in our study. There was, however, a wider world.

Syria-Palestine, Hittites, and the First International System

In the third millennium B.C., while Mesopotamia and Egypt were flowering, city-states were flourishing elsewhere, particularly in the Levant—the geographical region known today as Syria, Lebanon, and Israel. The discovery in 1974 of a huge cuneiform archive in northern Syria has revolutionized our knowledge of one such city-state, Ebla (modern Tell Mardikh), in the mid-third millennium B.C. Another city-state, Ugarit (modern Ras Shamra), flourished in the second millennium B.C.

Ugarit was a thriving Mediterranean port of Syria around 1400–1200 B.C. (see Map 1.3). The indigenous inhabitants of Ugarit spoke a Semitic language and were part of the Canaanite culture of southern Syria and Palestine. The merchant community in Ugarit, however, was polyglot, including not only the Canaanite majority but

Babylonians, Egyptians, Moabites (a people from the region that is now Jordan), Hittites, and Hurrians, among others.

The most influential legacy of Ugaritic culture was the creation of the world's oldest alphabet. It may have been invented in order to set religious documents in writing, or perhaps commercial efficiency was the driving motive. Whatever the cause, Ugaritic scribes in the fourteenth century B.C. invented thirty cuneiform signs as an alphabet for their Semitic language. It was a true alphabet in that each sign stood for one and only one sound. Later adapted by the Phoenicians and, through them, the Greeks, the Ugaritic alphabet is the source of the English alphabet and most other alphabets in the world today.

Another people who had a profound influence on the future of language were the Hittites. Theirs was an Indo-European language, and nearly half of the world's people today speak an Indo-European language—such as English, Spanish, French, Italian, German, Greek, Russian, Iranian, and Hindi. Indo-European-speakers probably originated between 4500 and 2500 B.C. in southern Russia. A warlike, mobile, horse-riding people, they emigrated east and west, ruling Anatolia from their city of Hattusas (see Map 1.4).

Hittite history is divided into the Old Kingdom (ca. 1650–1450 B.C.), marked by the conquest and consolidation of Anatolia; the Middle Kingdom (ca. 1450–1380 B.C.), a period of retrenchment and loss of territory; the New Kingdom (ca. 1380–1180 B.C.), characterized by intervention in international politics and then collapse; and finally a Neo-Hittite era (ca. 1180–700 B.C.) of small successor states. The Hittite empire reached its zenith in the New Kingdom, when it extended into Syria and northern Mesopotamia.

Hittite politics of the Old Kingdom reflected the qualities of a warrior society: a weak king, a strong and boisterous nobility, and a measure of equality for forceful queens. The monarch was neither god nor god's representative but rather first among equals. He was supported by an armed, horse-riding nobility who, in return for land, supplied him with troops and mounts. The nobles met in assembly and rendered legal judgments.

Hittite queens and queen mothers had strong and independent positions. Puduhepa, wife of King Hattusilis III (r. 1278–1250 B.C.), played a memorable role in state affairs. Evidence suggests that Puduhepa was the prime mover in an important religious movement, whereby the Hurrian sun-goddess of Arinna (a shrine near the capital) became the chief deity of the Hittite state. The goddess was worshiped as "Queen of the Land of Hatti, Queen of Heaven and Earth, mistress of the kings and queens of the Land of Hatti, directing the government of the King and Queen of Hatti."[4]

The rise of the Hittite empire coincided with the first international system—and its collapse. An international system is a group of relatively stable interactions between competing international powers. This emerged in western Asia and northeast Africa between 1500 and 1150 B.C. Pharaohs in New Kingdom Egypt, for instance, pursued a forward defense policy, sending diplomats and, at times, large mobile armies into the Levant. Both for Egypt and for other large kingdoms such as that of the Hittites, Syria-Palestine became the battleground for power and influence.

The new international system was marked by war and diplomacy. War consisted of skirmishes marked by an occasional dramatic battle, such as at Kadesh in 1274 B.C., where twenty thousand Egyptian troops clashed with seventeen thousand Hittites. The two powers agreed to share control of Syria-Palestine, as a subsequent treaty attests. Quite a few treaties and letters between monarchs survive in cuneiform archives. The texts reveal a system of gift exchange and commerce, politeness and formality, alliance and dynastic marriage, subjects and governors, rebels and garrisons. Kings of other great powers address pharaoh as "brother," while Canaanite princes call him "my lord and my Sun-god" and assure him that they are "thy servant and the dirt on which thou dost tread."

The international system of the late second millennium B.C. came to a crashing end between about 1250 and 1150 B.C., as one state after another collapsed: Mesopotamia, Greece, Anatolia, and Egypt. Surviving evidence is fragmentary, but it suggests that both foreign and domestic problems led to the collapse. Raiders and invaders beset the eastern Mediterranean in this period. Called "Sea Peoples" by the Egyptians, they attacked both on land and at sea. There is evidence of famine and climatic change in some countries, leading to disruption and rebellion. Some states may have overextended themselves in war and thereby bred internal decay.

Whatever the cause, what followed would prove to be a different world. Yet the end of the state system did not result in the obliteration of ancient cultures. Considerable continuities reached into the first millennium B.C. and beyond. Eventually, each of these cultures would flower anew.

Assyrians, Neo-Babylonians, Phoenicians, ca. 1200–ca. 500 B.C.

Ruthless soldiers, brutal conquerors, and innovative administrators, the Assyrians established an empire in western Asia and Egypt during the eighth and seventh centuries B.C. (see Map 1.4). Their homeland was in what is today northern Iraq. They spoke a Semitic language. For most of the second millennium B.C. they had been a military and mercantile power, but around 1200 B.C. the Assyrian state collapsed. They held on to a small homeland of about 5000 square miles, roughly the size of the state of Connecticut. The toughened survivors emerged with an aggressive, expansionist ideology.

In the eighth and seventh centuries B.C., Assyria became the first state to rule the two great river valleys of the ancient Near East: the Tigris-Euphrates and the Nile. The key to Assyria's success was its army—from 100,000 to 200,000 men strong—which made an unforgettable impression on observers. The Israelite prophet Isaiah of Jerusalem said of Assyrian soldiers: "[Their] arrows are sharpened, and all their bows bent, their horses' hoofs are like flint, their chariot wheels like the whirlwind. Their growling is like that of a lion" (Isaiah 5:28–29). He might have added that Assyrian spearmen, archers, and cavalrymen were equipped with iron weapons and armor. Indeed, the first millennium B.C. is now

called the "Iron Age" because of the new techniques for combining carbon and iron ore—and the Assyrians were among the first to replace bronze with this stronger and cheaper alloy.

To control the restive subjects of their far-flung empire, the Assyrians met rebellion with ferocious reprisals. Disloyal cities were attacked and sometimes destroyed. Sculptured reliefs and inscriptions were set up to show, often in gruesome detail, the fate awaiting Assyria's enemies. We see and read of cities burned to the ground; men flayed alive, even though they had surrendered, and walls covered with their skin; and piles of human skulls.

The Assyrians engaged in mass deportation. They uprooted the people of a conquered country, resettled them far away—often in Assyria itself—and colonized their land with Assyrian loyalists. The so-called Ten Lost Tribes of Israel—the people of the northern Israelite kingdom—were conquered by Assyria in 722 B.C. and transported to Mesopotamia, where they disappeared from history. The political goal of forced deportation was to punish rebellion, the economic goal to create a varied labor force. Although it is estimated that the Assyrians deported several million people, they deported not whole populations but a carefully chosen cross section of professions. Also, they deported entire families together, to weaken deportees' emotional ties to their former homes. Such tactics increased their infamy as vicious conquerors. Eventually, in 612 B.C., a coalition army of Babylonians and of Medes (who had formed a powerful state in Iran) conquered the Assyrian capital, Nineveh. They defeated the remnants of the Assyrian army in battles in 609 and 605. Few subjects mourned the empire's passing.

The destruction of Assyria led to a brief political and longer-lived cultural revival for Babylon, whose rulers attempted to revive the glories of Hammurabi's day. For a short period, until the Persian conquest in 539 B.C., the Neo-Babylonian dynasty (founded in 626) was one of the dominant military forces in western Asia. King Nebuchadrezzar II (Nebuchadnezzar in the Hebrew Bible; r. 605–562 B.C.) conquered the kingdom of

Judah in 598 and destroyed Jerusalem, its capital, in 586. He deported thousands of Judeans to Babylon, an event remembered by Jews and Christians as the Babylonian Captivity. Most of the rest of western Asia also fell to Nebuchadrezzar's troops. His most enduring achievement was rebuilding Babylon on a grand scale. In addition to numerous temples, shrines, and altars, Nebuchadrezzar ordered the construction of the Hanging Gardens, a large terraced complex designed for the pleasure of his queen. Greek writers celebrated it as one of the seven wonders of the world.

The other major state in western Asia during this period was created by trade, not war. In the Hebrew Bible, the Phoenicians loom large as merchants and seamen, as "traders the world honored" (Isaiah 23:8). Phoenicians were Canaanites, speakers of a Semitic language, and heirs to the civilization that had prospered in Ugarit. After the invasions of the Sea Peoples and others around 1200 B.C., the Canaanites' once-large territory was reduced to a narrow strip along the Mediterranean. Between 1050 and 750 B.C. the inhabitants of the area flourished. Their purple-dyed textiles gave the Greeks their word for the color purple: "Phoenician."

The Phoenicians were great shipbuilders and sailors. Around 600 B.C. their ships accomplished the first known circumnavigation of Africa. Around 450 B.C. they made the first known commercial sailing trip to the British Isles. Some scholars think they even reached Brazil. The most lasting Phoenician achievement at sea was the planting of colonies in the Mediterranean, probably beginning in the ninth century B.C. (see Map 2.2 on page 40). Many of the colonies eventually became independent states. The greatest Phoenician colony was Carthage, founded around 750 B.C. It was the major port city of the western Mediterranean for much of the next thousand years.

Between 1000 and 800 B.C., when the small towns of Greece were slowly developing into city-states (see Chapter 2), the sophisticated Phoenicians represented an important outside stimulus. Phoenician traders introduced advanced material goods, slaves, and possibly law codes to the Greeks. It was probably from the Phoenicians, whose alphabet derived from Ugarit, that the Greeks adapted their alphabet.

Persia, ca. 1000–330 B.C.

The Persians were Indo-European-speaking peoples who arrived in western Iran around 900 B.C. and perhaps as early as 1500 B.C. In the twenty years following 550 B.C., the young Persian king Cyrus the Great (r. 559–530 B.C.) conquered most of western Asia and much of central Asia. His son Cambyses added Egypt and Libya; his successor, Darius (r. 521–486 B.C.), added northwestern India and Thrace (Map 1.4). This Achaemenid Persian Empire (named after a legendary founder, Achaemenes) survived for two hundred years, until it was destroyed by a Greco-Macedonian army under Alexander the Great, king of Macedon (r. 336–323 B.C.).

Persia was ruled by a warrior-aristocracy, but unlike the iron-fisted Assyrians, the Persians were relatively tolerant and respectful of their subjects' customs. The Greek historian Herodotus summarizes their traditional values as "riding, hunting, and telling the truth." The state was able to field a huge conscript army of about 300,000 men. Although the resultant hodgepodge of peoples from across the empire did not always fight as a unit, a crack infantry group, the 10,000 Immortals, provided a solid core. Persia was equally innovative at sea, where its subjects built the first great navy. Although Persians served as marines and sometimes as commanders, the rowers and seamen were usually Phoenicians or Greeks.

Unlike the Assyrians, the Persians considered generosity and tolerance to be more effective than terrorism and brutality. As Cyrus prepared to attack Babylon, for example, he portrayed himself as the champion of the traditional Babylonian deity Marduk, the power of whose priesthood had been challenged by the Neo-Babylonian kings. As a result, the Babylonians opened the city gates to the Persian army, allowing Cyrus victory without a battle. Cyrus overturned several cruel Assyrian and Neo-Babylonian imperial policies. Most famous today is his edict of 539 B.C. permitting the Jewish exiles in Babylon to return to Judea.

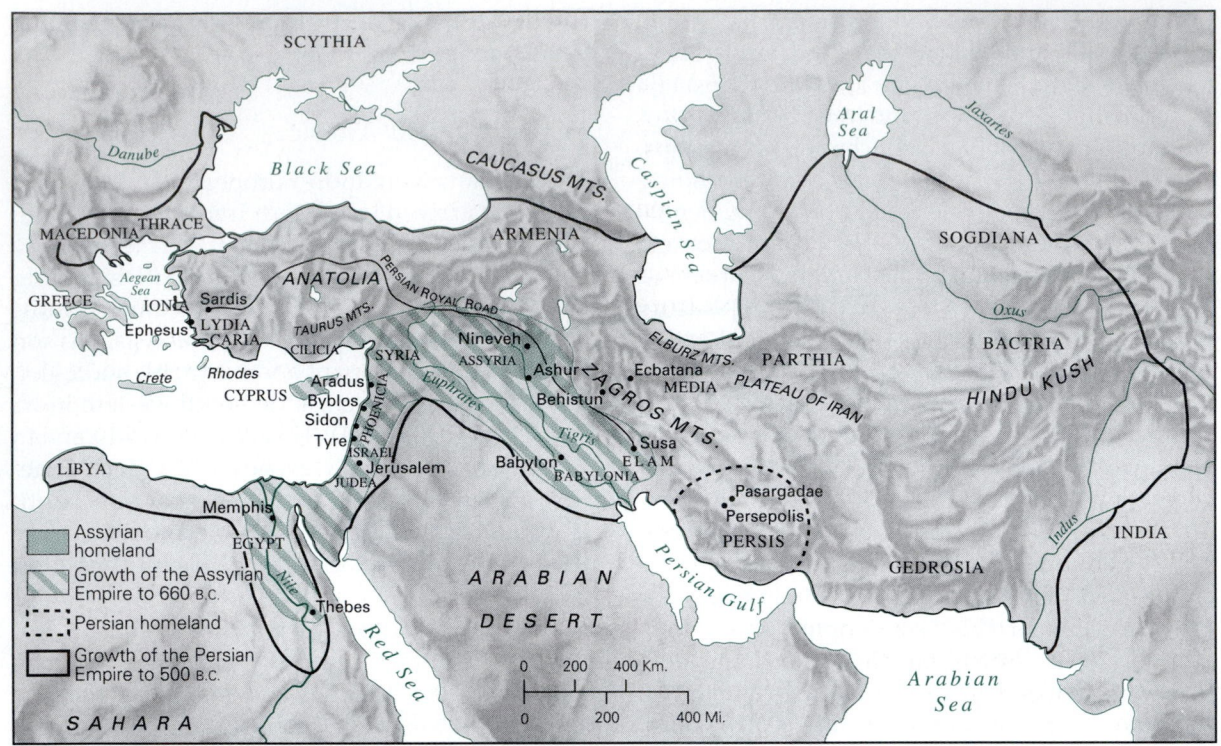

Map 1.4 The Assyrian and Persian Empires In the 660s B.C. the Assyrians ruled the largest empire the ancient world had seen yet, extending from the Tigris to the Nile. The Persian Empire was even greater. Around 500 B.C. it reached from its heartland in southwestern Iran westward to Macedonia and eastward to India.

The Persian domain was divided into units of administration and tax collection, called *satrapies.* For the first time, taxes could be paid with a stable, official coinage. (Coins had been invented in the kingdom of Lydia in western Asia Minor in the seventh century B.C. The expression "rich as Croesus" refers to Lydia's king, whom Cyrus conquered in 547 B.C.)

A network of good roads radiated from the main capital cities. The most famous road, the so-called Royal Road, stretched 1600 miles from western Iran to western Anatolia. Covering the whole distance took most travelers three months, but the king's relay messenger corps had a series of staging posts with fresh horses built along the

way and they could make the trip in a week. This helped to forge unity.

Language, too, built unity. Aramaic, a Semitic language related to Hebrew, was the empire's basic language of commerce and administration. It was composed of a simple and easily learned alphabet that facilitated the development of literacy and recordkeeping. Indeed, Aramaic would become the common language of western Asia for over a thousand years, until Arabic replaced it. Jesus was to be its most famous native speaker.

However mild Persian rule, however peaceful and prosperous, it was still rule by foreigners and it still involved taxation. Native resentment, particularly in Egypt, led to intermittent provincial revolts. The exaltation of the Persian king served as a counterweight to rebellious tendencies. The "King of Kings," as the monarch called himself, sat on a high gold and blue throne, dressed in purple, decked out in gold jewelry, wearing unguents and cosmetics, and attended by corps of slaves and eunuchs (castrated men employed in high positions). Although he was not considered a god, he had to be treated worshipfully. Anyone who came into his presence had to approach him with a bow to the ground, face down. Aspects of this ornate version of kingship were explicitly copied by future ambitious rulers, from Alexander the Great and the Caesars of Rome to the Byzantine emperors and Muslim caliphs.

One of Persia's most original contributions to civilization was religious. From obscure beginnings, Zoroastrianism became the religion of Persia until the Muslim conquest in the seventh century A.D. Although largely extinct in today's Iran, an overwhelmingly Islamic country, Zoroastrianism still survives in small communities elsewhere, primarily in India. Zoroastrianism is particularly interesting because of its *dualism*—the notion that life was a grand conflict between good and evil. We see this notion in Christianity, and many scholars argue that the Christian version was derived from Zoroastrianism; it certainly does not seem to have come from Judaism. Other compelling features of Zoroastrianism are its *eschatology* (interest in the end of the world) and *soteriology* (belief in a savior). These may have influenced similar beliefs in other religions, including Roman paganism and Indian Buddhism.

Zoroastrianism was founded by a great reformer named Zarathustra (Zoroaster in Greek). Zarathustra lived in eastern Iran. His teachings survive in the Gathas ("Songs"), a portion of the Zoroastrian holy book called the Avesta. Some scholars date Zarathustra as late as 550 B.C.; others prefer an earlier date, 750 or even 1000 B.C.

Zarathustra's society was dominated by warriors whose religion consisted of violent gods, animal sacrifice, and ecstatic rituals in which hallucinogens were eaten. Zarathustra rejected such practices in favor of an inward-looking,

intellectual, and ethical religion. Like the Jews, Zarathustra was a monotheist, believing in only one god, the supremely good and wise creator of the universe, whom he called Ahura Mazda ("Wise Lord"). Unlike the Jews, Zarathustra considered the problem of evil to be the central question of religion. If god was one, good, and omnipotent, how could evil exist?

Zarathustra's answer might be called *ethical dualism.* Ahura Mazda had twin children: the Beneficent Spirit and the Hostile Spirit. Each spirit had made a free choice: one for the "truth" and the other for the "lie"—that is, one for good and the other for evil. Each human being had to make the same choice. Zarathustra thus endowed humanity with great freedom and dignity. The more a person pursued spiritual purity, the greater was his or her ability to choose good.

Zarathustra believed that the world would end in a Last Judgment of everyone who had ever lived. Good would be rewarded, evil punished, and the dead restored to a glorious bodily existence. The notion of a savior who would initiate the Last Judgment was an early Zoroastrian belief, if perhaps not a doctrine of Zarathustra himself.

Zarathustra's followers compromised his rejection of Iranian paganism. Under the leadership of priests, known as *magi* in western Iran, the religion evolved and changed considerably. Lesser deities beneath Ahura Mazda were added to the Zoroastrian pantheon, in part to suit the religion to the needs of the huge, multicultural Persian Empire.

SUMMARY

About 2 million years ago, hominids wandered out of Africa, appearing in our modern form at least 40,000 years ago (possibly much earlier). Yet early humans did not start committing themselves to patches of land until as late as 10,000 B.C. Organized, complex city life, and the writing skills it necessitated, came into being about 3500 B.C. In comparison to our first, lost history as nomadic humans, we have not been living in civilization for very long at all.

First came the invention of human culture in the Upper Paleolithic era, based mostly on carvings and cave paintings. Next came the move, in the Neolithic era, from a food-collecting to a food-producing economy. From its origins in the Fertile Crescent region of western Asia (shortly after 10,000 B.C.), food production spread throughout Africa, Asia, and Europe by 5000 B.C.

The next important development was the emergence of civilization in Mesopotamia after 3500 B.C. By 3000, civilization was present in Egypt. These were the first and best remembered of the early civilizations. Their inventions are staggering; among them are the first cities, kingdoms, and multi-ethnic empires; the first monumental architecture; the first advances in agriculture sweeping enough to support a large urban population; the first writing, and with it the first recorded attempts to explore the meaning of life.

The religious, literary, and political innovations of the Hebrews were also extraordinary. The Israelites conquered Palestine and, even after losing it, held on to their identity by means of a tenacious belief in one god. They broke with tradition by insisting that the purpose of life was to serve God by acting righteously. The new religion eventually became Judaism. The Jews wrote down their religious and historical traditions in a book that proved to be the most influential single text in the history of the West: the Hebrew Bible.

The second millennium B.C. was a period of competition, exchange, and warfare among the various civilizations of the eastern Mediterranean region, but the great kingdoms of the second millennium collapsed, one after another, around 1250 to 1150 B.C. In the first half of the first millennium B.C., iron replaced bronze as the primary metal of work and war. The Assyrian Empire, marked by brutal and inhumane methods, stretched from western Iran to Palestine and briefly even to Egypt. Next came a period dominated by Neo-Babylonians and Medes, which also saw the expansion of the Phoenician city-states across the Mediterranean Sea. The Persians then established an empire that was larger, better organized, and more tolerant than the empire of the Assyrians. The Persians developed a new religion, Zoroastrianism, that emphasized ethics and redemption. As we will see in Chapter 2, the Greeks would soon address these profound issues with extraordinary new ideas.

NOTES

1. Samuel Noah Kramer, *History Begins at Sumer: Thirty-nine Firsts in Man's Recorded History*, 3d rev. ed. (Philadelphia: University of Pennsylvania Press, 1981), pp. 91, 94.
2. James B. Pritchard, ed., *Ancient Near Eastern Texts Relating to the Old Testament*, 3d ed. (Princeton: Princeton University Press, 1969), p. 107.
3. Carol L. Meyers, "Everyday Life: Women in the Period of the Hebrew Bible," in Carol A. Newsom and Sharon H. Ringe, eds., *The Women's Bible Commentary* (Louisville, Ky.: Westminster/John Knox Press, 1992), p. 245.
4. O. R. Gurney, *The Hittites*, 3d ed. Harmondsworth, England: Penguin, 1975), p. 139.

SUGGESTED READING

Bernal, Martin. *Black Athena: The Afro-Asiatic Roots of Classical Civilization. Vol. 1: The Fabrication of Ancient Greece 1785–1985. Vol. 2: The Archaeological Evidence.* 1987 and 1991. A stimulating but highly controversial argument. Some scholars agree with the author's arguments on nineteenth-century historians, but few accept his reconstruction of ancient history.

Bottéro, Jean. *Mesopotamia: Writing, Reasoning, and the Gods.* Translated by Zainab Bahrani and Marc Van De Mierrop. 1992. A provocative collection of essays arguing that Western civilization began in Mesopotamia; contains a useful glossary.

Cook, J. M. *The Persian Empire.* 1983. A clear and readable introduction, updating Olmstead's book (see below) in the light of recent archaeological discoveries, particularly inscriptions.

Crawford, H. *The Sumerians.* 1991. An excellent introduction to the way that recent archaeological excavation and survey have caused scholars to rethink many older ideas.

Cunliffe, Barry, ed. *The Oxford Illustrated Prehistory of Europe.* 1994. An introduction to European material culture from the Paleolithic era to the early medieval period, with chapters written by a dozen archaeologists. Especially valuable for its treatment of the early period and for its integration of Greco-Roman civilization and the wider continental context.

Drane, John. *Introducing the Old Testament.* 1987. An excellent introduction to the archaeology, history, and religion of biblical Israel.

Frankfort, H., et al. *Before Philosophy: The Intellectual Adventure of Ancient Man. An Essay on Speculative Thought in the Ancient Near East.* 1946. Brilliant essays on the religious and political outlook of people in Mesopotamia and Egypt, contrasting them with the Hebrews and Greeks.

Gabriel, Richard A. *The Culture of War. Invention and Early Development.* 1990. Although marred by factual errors, the book represents a very thoughtful essay on the origins and nature of war from the Stone Age to Rome.

Gowlett, John A. J. *Ascent to Civilization: The Archaeology of Early Man.* 1984. Beautifully illustrated introduction to prehistory.

Halpern, Baruch. *The First Historians: The Hebrew Bible and History.* 1988. Scholarly but readable introduction to the Hebrew Bible's contribution to the Western tradition of historiography.

Lefkowitz, Mary, and Guy MacLean Rogers, eds. *Black Athena Revisited.* 1996. A lively and scholarly collection of essays challenging Bernal's theses.

Lerner, Gerda. *The Creation of Patriarchy.* 1986. A theory of the origins of gender and class hierarchies in Mesopotamia, with developments in ancient Israel and classical Greece considered as well.

Lewin, Roger. *Human Evolution: An Illustrated Introduction.* 2d ed. 1989. A clear survey of a complex and rapidly changing field.

Lichtheim, Miriam. *Ancient Egyptian Literature.* 3 vols. 1975–1980. A large selection of translations of Egyptian literary and religious texts.

Macqueen, J. G. *The Hittites and Their Contemporaries in Asia Minor.* 2d rev. ed. 1986. A well-illustrated, thematic discussion.

Meyers, Carol. *Discovering Eve: Ancient Israelite Women in Context.* 1988. A sophisticated analysis combining archaeology, biblical scholarship, feminist theory, and comparative anthropology. The author argues for the existence of a tradition of powerful women in the Hebrew Bible, dating back to the gender equality of early Israelite peasant society.

Neugebauer, Otto. *The Exact Sciences in Antiquity.* 1962. An introduction to ancient astronomy and mathematics.

Oates, Joan. *Babylon.* Rev. ed. 1986. A well-illustrated introduction.

Oded, Bustenay. *Mass Deportations and Deportees in the Neo-Assyrian Empire.* 1979. A detailed study of an appalling practice.

Olmstead, A. T. *History of the Persian Empire.* 1948. Out of date in some of its findings but still an ambitious narrative history. The prose style is majestic.

Robins, Gay. *Women in Ancient Egypt.* 1993. Balanced and judicious introduction by an art historian, with many photographs.

Seltzer, Robert M., ed. *Religions of Antiquity: Religion, History, and Culture. Selections from The Encyclopedia of Religion, Mircea Eliade, Editor in Chief.* 1989. An excellent introduction to the religions discussed in this chapter.

Shanks, H., ed. *Ancient Israel. A Short History from Abraham to the Roman Destruction of the Temple.* 1988. Short, readable essay by scholars offering up-to-date introductions to the subject.

Strauss, Barry, and Josiah Ober. *The Anatomy of Error: Ancient Military Disasters and Their Lessons for Modern Strategists.* 1990. An analysis of eight case studies from the ancient world.

CHAPTER 2

Ancient Greece

The morning light reveals a hillside in the city of Athens: a natural auditorium. Its rocky slopes are covered with wooden benches facing a platform cut into the rock. The six thousand men gathered there constitute a heterogeneous group, ranging from farmers to philosophers, from dockyard workers to aristocrats. As they take their seats, these, the citizens of Athens, watch priests conducting prayers and a sacrifice. Then, a herald mounts the platform and asks the question that marks the start of business: "Who wishes to speak?" Someone rises to address the assembly. It is the first democracy in history—and this is the central laboratory in this great experiment in participation.

The history of ancient Greece encompasses several extraordinary periods. The first is the "Aegean Greece" of the Minoan and Mycenaean civilizations, and what we know of this period is based largely on archaeology. The epic poems the *Iliad* and *Odyssey* are set in this early period, though they were composed by Homer later. The next period is Archaic Greece, the era of the *polis* (plural, *poleis*), or "city-state." The two largest and most famous city-states, Sparta and Athens, got their start during this period. Sparta was a paragon of militarism, obedience, and austerity, scorning the life of the mind. Athens was the birthplace of democracy and prided itself on freedom and cultural attainments, including theater, history, and philosophy.

Athens rose to cultural dominance in the next period, the Classical age, but despite profound intellectual advancement and creative accomplishment, deep problems remained. Greek democracy, for example, failed to grant equal rights to women, immigrants, or slaves. Further, relations among poleis were less often a matter of cooperation than of combat. Indeed, this world of the polis was disrupted by frequent war, culminating in the Persian Wars and the Peloponnesian War. In the end, the city-states dissipated their strength fighting among each other, but the real blow came from Macedon, a northeastern Greek kingdom. Macedon rose meteorically under King Philip II, until it was the leader of Greece. Philip was a brilliant general, but his son, Alexander the Great, outstripped him, establishing the largest empire to that date. This was the beginning of the Hellenistic world.

Hellenistic Greeks were as likely to be subjects of a king as they were to be citizens of an independent city-state. Empire brought them in contact with new peoples, and the Greeks were introduced to new philosophies, religions, and modes of artistic expression. The prestige of royal women tended to promote improvements in the general status of Greek women. Overall, the Hellenistic period was one of momentous cross-fertilization among peoples of the ancient world.

∽ Questions and Ideas to Consider

■ How do archaeologists and historians tell the difference between Minoan and Mycenaean civilizations? Consider our knowledge of each culture's language, architecture, and lifestyle.

■ What was a polis? If such different places as Athens and Sparta can both be described as poleis, what are the defining characteristics? Consider geography, community attitude, and relations to other sovereign states.

■ Do you think that you would prefer life in Sparta to life in Athens? Why? In what ways is your answer dependent on gender and social class?

■ It is often said that the ancient Greeks invented philosophy, yet people had always wondered about the world and put forth theories about it. What was it about Greek thought that made it so special? Of the philosophies discussed here, which appeals to you most?

■ Alexander the Great created the Hellenistic world by conquering and uniting a tremendous amount of territory. How did the intermingling of different peoples and ideas change the nature of Greek culture?

EARLY GREECE, TO CA. 750 B.C.

To most people, "ancient Greece" means the city-states (ca. 700–300 B.C.) or the heroes portrayed in the *Iliad* and the *Odyssey*, the epic poems of Homer (ca. 750 B.C.). Both were products of the first millennium B.C. Civilization, however, flourished in Greece throughout the second millennium B.C., and Homer's works have roots in this earlier era. Scholars call this period "Aegean Greece" and, within it, archaeology illustrates the rise and fall of two monument-building, literate civilizations: the Minoans on the island of Crete and the Mycenaeans on the Greek mainland (Map 2.1).

The Minoans and Early Greece, 3000–1375 B.C.

The first agricultural villages appeared in Greece shortly after 7000 B.C.; bronze-making skills appeared after 3000. After 3500 B.C., Greece became a supplier of raw materials for western Asia and was influenced by its impressive cities. Both on the islands and the mainland there appeared small towns, sometimes fortified with stone walls. Between 3000 and 2400 B.C., people living on the Cycladic islands of the Aegean Sea produced exquisite marble sculptures and incised terra-cotta (baked clay) dishes.

Europe's first monumental, literate civilization originated on the Aegean island of Crete around 2000 B.C. When Crete's palaces were destroyed by earthquake, they were rebuilt on such a monumental scale that we recognize it as a new civilization—flourishing during the period from 1800 to 1550 B.C. We are not sure if the new palace builders were the original Cretans or invaders, but we call them and their civilization "Minoan," after King Minos (of later Greek myth), who was supposed to have ruled a great empire from his palace at Knossos.

There was indeed a palace at Knossos. It was the largest Cretan palace and the first to be excavated. The main building covers 3 acres and was built around a large central court that was

CHAPTER CHRONOLOGY

GREECE AND THE AEGEAN

2000 B.C.	First Minoan palaces on Crete
1800–1550 B.C.	Height of Minoan civilization
1626 B.C.	Eruption of Thera volcano
1375 B.C.	Palace at Knossos destroyed
1400–1200 B.C.	Height of Mycenaean civilization
1200 B.C.	Mycenaean palaces destroyed
750 B.C.	Homer

ARCHAIC GREECE

ca. 750 B.C.	Greek colonization of Magna Graecia begins
ca. 725 B.C.	Sparta conquers Messenia
594 B.C.	Solon is magistrate in Athens

ca. 560 B.C.	Peisistratus becomes tyrant of Athens
508 B.C.	Cleisthenes begins reforms in Athens

CLASSICAL GREECE

490 B.C.	Battle of Marathon
480–479 B.C.	Persian invasion of Greece
477 B.C.	Delian League founded
431–404 B.C.	Peloponnesian War
371 B.C.	Battle of Leuctra

THE HELLENISTIC WORLD

359–336 B.C.	Reign of Philip II of Macedon
336–323 B.C.	Reign of Alexander the Great
312 B.C.	Seleucus I conquers Babylon
304 B.C.	Ptolemy I king of Egypt
167–142 B.C.	Maccabean revolt in Judea

probably used for public ceremonies. A maze-like structure surrounded the court. Like the other Minoan palaces, it was a center of administration, religion, politics, and economics. Bureaucrats supervised a large sector of the economy, telling people how many products to make or grow and distributing the food and items so that everyone had what they needed.

The luxury of the palaces make clear that the Minoans exploited Crete's considerable natural wealth in agriculture and timber. The stunning artwork, often in precious metal; the sophisticated frescoes; and the vast and elaborate architecture all testify to prosperity. Archaeological and linguistic evidence indicates a widespread Minoan trading network from the Levant to Sicily. A Minoan settlement flourished on the Aegean island of Thera, 70 miles north of Crete. This settlement was destroyed in 1626 (or possibly 1628) B.C. by one of the most violent volcanic

eruptions in history. The huge eruption produced climate changes for several years. The changes are visible in the pattern of tree-rings in ancient wood, which is why scholars can offer so specific a date for Thera's destruction.

From the lack of fortifications around Cretan palaces and the small amount of arms and armor found in burial sites, it appears that the Minoans lived in relative peace. They worshiped a variety of gods and goddesses, whom they represented in their art. Minoan frescoes show that women played important roles in cult and ritual—perhaps even more than men. The women portrayed by Cretan artists are often beautiful, bejeweled, and elegant, the men often graceful and athletic. Landscapes and animals are frequently illustrated. In short, Minoan civilization gives an impression of peace, prosperity, and happiness. There is thus a lost-Eden quality about the violent destruction of Minoan civilization. All the palaces

Fresco at Thera This detail of the so-called Fresco of the Ladies shows one of a pair of murals from a shrine. We see a festively costumed woman carrying clothes and ornaments. She is bringing them to a seated woman (not shown), perhaps a goddess. (*The Ancient Art & Architecture Collection*)

except Knossos were destroyed around 1550 B.C. By whom? Archaeological evidence strongly supports the notion of an invasion from the Greek mainland. Knossos fell around 1375 B.C.

The Mycenaeans

Mainland Greece had enjoyed a period of Copper Age prosperity, but it crashed around 2300 B.C. Centuries of relative poverty followed. Then, rather suddenly, we see marks of real prosperity around 1700 B.C. at a series of burial sites in central Greece and the Peloponnesus. The most dramatic are at Mycenae. Scholars are not sure how these people got there or how they achieved their extraordinary wealth.

Unlike the earlier inhabitants of the Greek peninsula, the inhabitants of Mycenae were Greek-speakers. They and the wider civilization they represent are called Mycenaean. They were not an entirely original civilization. Archaeology shows that the Mycenaeans adopted and adapted technology, ideas, and art from their advanced neighbors in Crete, Egypt, Anatolia, and Syria-Palestine. The Mycenaeans traded with these neighbors. They also fought with them, for Mycenaean society was dominated by warrior-kings—raiders who exchanged booty with one another in competitive displays of wealth.

Around 1550 B.C., the mainland warriors achieved their greatest feat: the conquest of Crete. We know this in part because of a shift in the languages found on artifacts in Crete. Minoan Cretan writing had been a syllabary that we call "Linear A." Mycenaean-style artifacts dating from this period have been found in graves on Crete, and thousands of tablets inscribed mostly in the Mycenaeans' writing,

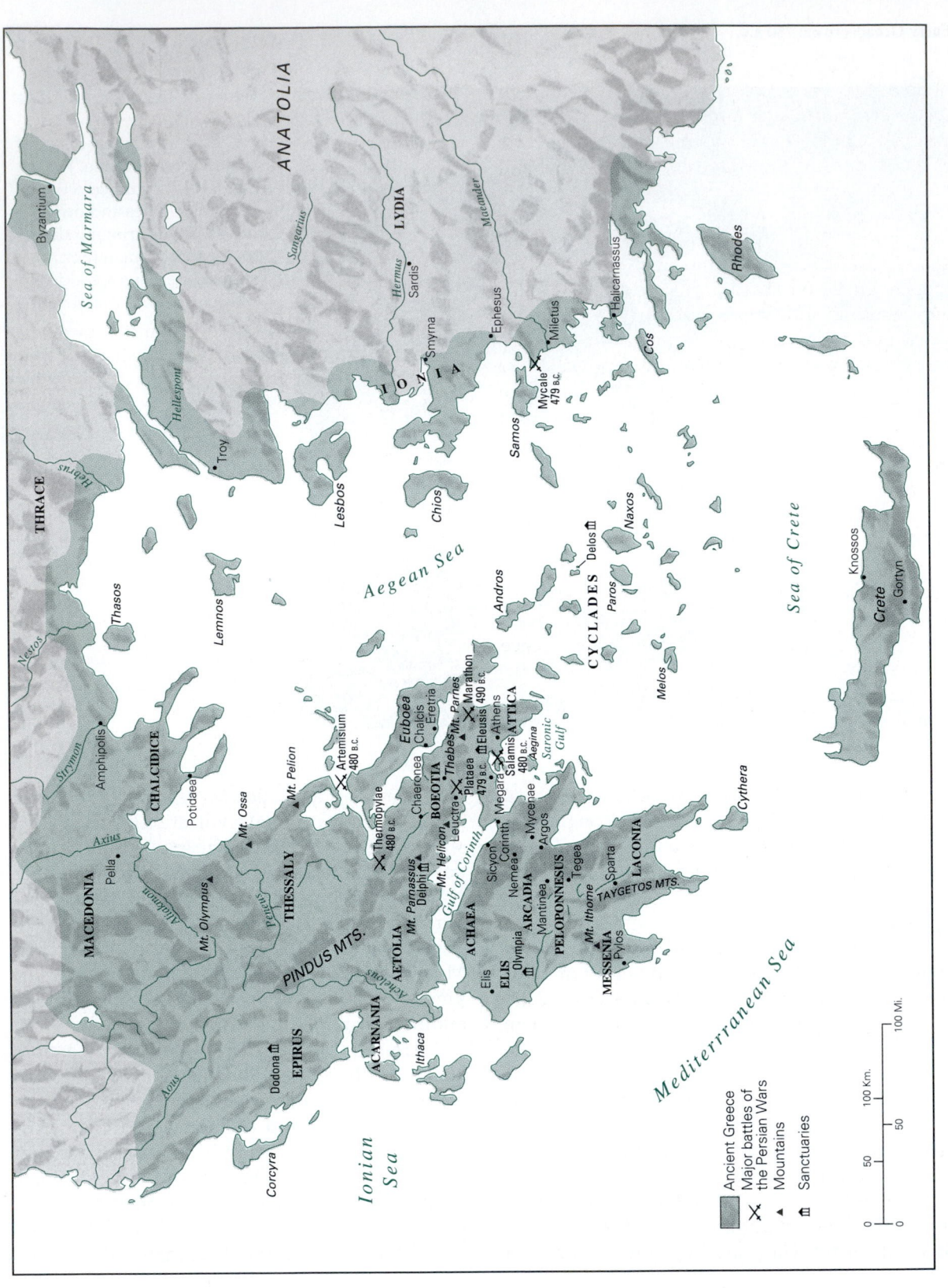

ANATOLIA

Sea of Marmara

Byzantium

Sangarius

LYDIA

Hermus

Sardis

Maeander

Smyrna

Ephesus

Miletus

Halicarnassus

Rhodes

Hellespont

Troy

I O N I A

Mycale
479 B.C.

Cos

THRACE

Hebrus

Samos

Lesbos

Chios

Strymon

Thasos

Nestus

Aegean Sea

Delos

Naxos

Knossos

CYCLADES

Paros

Andros

Sea of Crete

Gortyn

Crete

Amphipolis

CHALCIDICE

Potidaea

Lemnos

Melos

Pella

MACEDONIA

Axius

Mt. Olympus

Haliacmon

Mt. Ossa

Mt. Pelion

Artemisium
480 B.C.

Euboea

Chalcis

Eretria

Mt. Parnes

Marathon
490 B.C.

Peneus

THESSALY

Thermopylae
480 B.C.

Chaeronea

BOEOTIA

Thebes

Eleusis

Athens

ATTICA

Plataea
479 B.C.

Megara

Salamis
480 B.C.

Aegina

Saronic Gulf

PINDUS MTS.

AETOLIA

Mt. Parnassus

Delphi

Mt. Helicon

Leuctra

Corinth

Mycenae

Achelous

ACHAEA

Sicyon

Nemea

Argos

Gulf of Corinth

ACARNANIA

Ithaca

Elis

ELIS

ARCADIA

Mantinea

PELOPONNESUS

Tegea

Sparta

LACONIA

Aoüs

Dodona

EPIRUS

Olympia

Mt. Ithome

MESSENIA

Pylos

TAYGETOS MTS.

Cythera

Corcyra

Ionian Sea

Mediterranean Sea

Ancient Greece
Major battles of
the Persian Wars
Mountains
Sanctuaries

"Linear B" (an early form of Greek), have been discovered in the remains of the final stage of the palace at Knossos. When they took over, the Mycenaeans adopted a Minoan-style palace economy, with palace officials supervising the work of men, women, and children in agriculture, pasturage, and artisanry. Between about 1400 and 1200 B.C., Mycenaean civilization was at its height. Mycenaean artists excelled at pottery making and fresco painting, metal inlay work and ivory carving. Mycenaean builders constructed palaces, fortifications, bridges, huge vaulted tombs, and sophisticated drainage works. Abroad, Mycenaean merchants replaced Minoans. They exported wine and scented oils from Sicily to the Levant and brought back metals, ivory, and perhaps slaves.

In the thirteenth century B.C., at the height of Mycenaean power, trouble was brewing for the Mycenaean kings. Palaces at Mycenae and elsewhere were given strong fortification walls. By 1200 B.C., most of the fortified sites had been destroyed. It appears that Mycenaean Greece suffered from a combination of internal weakness and invasion from abroad similar to that of most of the eastern Mediterranean around 1250–1150 B.C., the era of the Sea Peoples (see page 26).

Mycenaean culture continued to flicker before finally fading in the early eleventh century B.C. From roughly 1100 to 800 B.C., Greece was largely a poor and illiterate society of small towns and low-level agriculture and trade. Nevertheless, it produced notable painted pottery and preserved an oral tradition of poetry handed down from the Mycenaean era. By the end of this period, the Greeks were poised to reach a milestone in narrative artistry: the epic poetry of Homer.

Map 2.1 Archaic and Classical Greece The region of the Aegean Sea was the heartland of Greek civilization around 750–350 B.C. The mountainous terrain, rugged coastline, and large number of islands encouraged political fragmentation.

Homer and History

The Greeks were polytheists and their gods were anthropomorphic, similar in many ways to the gods of Sumer. They share the foibles and foolishness of humanity but are immortal and far more powerful than humans. In comparison to Yahweh, the Greek gods are less powerful, less immediate, and less interested in the inner life of humans.

The Greek gods of the first millennium B.C. existed in Mycenaean times—offerings to them are recorded on Linear B tablets. Because they were thought to live on Mount Olympus, a 9500-foot-high peak in northern Greece, the gods were called the Olympians. The "household" of the Olympians—the early Greek pantheon was conceived of as a noble's household—included Zeus, a sky-god and the "father of gods and men," and his consort, Hera; Zeus's brother, Poseidon, god of the sea, earthquakes, and horses; Ares, god of war; and Aphrodite, goddess of love. Also in the "household" were Zeus's children: Athena, Hephaestus, Hermes, Apollo, and Artemis.

The Greek gods embodied the values of a warrior society that put a premium on *aretê*, excellence in battle. The heroes in Homer's poems, the *Iliad* and the *Odyssey*, seek glory through military exploits. They assume that the gods want precisely the same thing and will help those mortals whose achievements are most promising. Yet Zeus also wants justice and punishes those who break oaths or give false judgments or violate the laws of hospitality.

The *Iliad* and the *Odyssey* tell the story of the Trojan War—sparked by the abduction of Helen, the wife of the Greek king Menelaus, by the Trojan prince Paris—and its aftermath. The *Iliad* is set in the tenth year of the conflict. The strain of fighting leads to a quarrel between Agamemnon, king of Mycenae, and Achilles, the greatest Greek warrior. Troy is destroyed, but neither Greek nor Trojan nobles were generally motivated by hatred. Indeed, some were bound by hereditary ties of guest-friendship and declined to fight each other. (See the box "Encounters with the West: The Enemy as Honored Friend.")

≈ ENCOUNTERS WITH THE WEST ≈

The Enemy as Honored Friend

For Homer's aristocratic heroes, war was a struggle not of nations but of individual loyalties. Friendship and family ties mattered more than patriotism. This excerpt from Homer's Iliad *demonstrates that individual Greeks sometimes considered their enemies, the Trojans (and Trojan allies), to be respected rivals or even honored friends.*

Now Glaukos, sprung of Hippolochos, and [Diomedes,] the son of Tydeus came together in the space between the two armies, battle-bent. Now as these advancing came to one place and encountered, first to speak was Diomedes of the great war cry: "Who among mortal men are you, good friend? . . . unhappy are those whose sons match warcraft against me."

Then in turn the shining son of Hippolochos answered: ". . . Hippolochos begot me, and I claim that he is my father; he sent me to Troy, and urged upon me repeated injunctions, to be always among the bravest, and hold my head above others, not shaming the generation of my fathers, who were the greatest men in Ephyre and again in wide Lykia. Such is my generation and the blood I claim to be born from."

He spoke, and Diomedes of the great war cry was gladdened. He drove his spear deep into the prospering earth, and in winning words of friendliness he spoke to the shepherd of the people [Glaukos]: "See now, you are my guest friend from far in the time of our fathers. . . . Let us avoid each other's spears, even in the close fighting. There are plenty of Trojans and famed companions in battle for me to kill, whom the god sends me, or those I run down with my swift feet, many Achaians for you to slaughter, if you can do it. But let us exchange our armour, so that these others may know how we claim to be guests and friends from the days of our fathers."

So they spoke, and both springing down from behind their horses gripped each other's hands and exchanged the promise of friendship; but Zeus the son of Kronos stole away the wits of Glaukos who exchanged with Diomedes the son of Tydeus armour of gold for bronze, for nine oxen's worth the worth of a hundred.

Source: The Iliad of Homer, trans. Richmond Lattimore (Chicago: University of Chicago Press, 1951), pp. 63, 156–159.

The *Odyssey* tells the story of the struggle of the Greek hero Odysseus to return home to Ithaca and regain his kingship after ten years in the war at Troy and ten years wandering homeward. It also focuses on the loyalty and ingenuity of Odysseus's wife, Penelope, who saves the household in her husband's absence, and the maturation of their son, Telemachus, who helps his father regain his kingdom.

Homer was a bard, a professional singer of heroic poetry—of songs praising the deeds of the great. We do not know if any of his human char-

acters really existed. Homer did not live in the age he sings about or even on the Greek mainland. Most scholars today date Homer to about 750 B.C., a period of increasing change, growth, and ferment in Greece. Some scholars even doubt that there was just *one* Homer and argue that the *Iliad* and *Odyssey* are the works of two different poets.

All would agree that the poems sprang from a bardic tradition going back to the Mycenaean Age, from which the poet took stories, details, and language. Most scholars accept the theory that this tradition was oral, not written. This oral tradition gave Homer knowledge of a society that was long gone by his day. Although Homer studs his poems with details of Mycenaean palace life, the ideology of his characters generally reflects the beliefs of his own, post-Mycenaean society.

Homeric men and women hold aristocratic values and tend to look down on ordinary people. Scholarship shows, however, that society in Homer's day was more level and undifferentiated. Most people in the Greece of 750 B.C. were free farmers or shepherds. In each community the people were called the *demos*; the elite were called *basileis*, which means "kings," but it is more accurate to understand them as chiefs. No great difference of wealth existed between the basileis and ordinary free farmers. Homeric government is dominated by the basileis, but the demos is not entirely excluded.

Homer does not present women on an equal footing with men but he is less misogynistic than the classical culture of the city-states would turn out to be. He shows considerable interest in women, particularly in the *Odyssey*. Penelope, for example, personifies resourcefulness and honor. Believing her husband might still be alive, she refuses all marriage proposals. Finally, she tells her many suitors that she will accept a proposal when she has finished weaving a burial shroud for Odysseus's father. Every night she unravels what she has woven during the day. Penelope has thus become a symbol of cleverness and patience in the service of honor and love.

ARCHAIC SOCIETY AND THE RISE OF SPARTA, CA. 750–500 B.C.

Historians usually call the era in Greek history from roughly 750 to 500 B.C. the "Archaic period." Archaic Greece was a patchwork of hundreds of separate city-states, tribal leagues, and monarchies (see Map 2.1). In addition, the Archaic Greeks founded colonies throughout the Mediterranean and the Black Sea, establishing nearly as many cities as already existed in Greece

(Map 2.2). Southern Italy and Sicily were especially intense areas of Greek settlement, so much so that the Romans later called the region *Magna Graecia* ("Great Greece").

Trade and colonization inspired change at home, bringing the Greeks into contact with new ideas and institutions. One important consequence of foreign contact was the introduction to Greece of the Phoenician alphabet. The first datable examples of the Greek alphabet were inscribed on pots around 750 B.C. The alphabet spread rapidly and widely in the next century. Literacy underlay achievements in poetry, philosophy, and the law, but we must remember that ancient Greek culture remained primarily oral.

The City-State, the Hoplites, and the Rise of Tyranny

In the years around 700 B.C., the Greek city-state, or polis, began to emerge. A polis was not just a city—it was also the countryside that supported that city. Most poleis were small, many less than a hundred square miles in size; a typical polis contained between 5000 and 10,000 people. Athens was one of the largest (see Map 2.2). Its territory, known as Attica, covered a thousand square miles (approximately the size of the state of Rhode Island), and at its height (ca. 430 B.C.) the population of Athens was about 400,000. From the earliest times, the urban public space of a polis included both a defensible hill called a "high city" (*acropolis*) and a "gathering place" (*agora*) used as a marketplace and for meetings. There was usually at least one temple. After around 500 B.C. stone buildings, including council houses, theaters, covered porticoes, gymnasia, and baths, became increasingly common.

The polis was defended by a new type of army organization: the hoplite phalanx, a tightly ordered unit of heavily armed, pike-bearing infantrymen. The phalanx not only became the dominant military force in Archaic Greece but, with relatively few changes in equipment and tactics, remained supreme on land in Greece, western Asia, and other Mediterranean regions until its defeat by a Roman army in 197 B.C.

Map 2.2 Phoenician and Greek Colonization Both the Phoenicians (beginning perhaps after 900 B.C.) and the Greeks (beginning around 750 B.C.) established numerous colonies on the coasts of the Mediterranean and Black Seas.

Phalanx warfare developed in stages. Around 700 B.C. changes in society and technology meant that more men could afford to buy armaments. The heavily armed infantryman (hoplite) of the fighting unit (phalanx) wore bronze armor and carried a heavy shield, a pike with iron tip, and a short, iron stabbing-sword. Soldiers stood together in line, each man's shield overlapping his neighbor's. Hoplite battles were army against army, all-or-nothing affairs, rather than individual skirmishes or raids. The front line pounded the enemy with its pikes while the rear pushed forward. Finally one side would give way. Most of the defeated would escape by running away. For centuries, hoplite battle was virtually an annual occurrence in Greece.

Aretê, or "warrior prowess," was a central concept for the Greeks—indeed, the term would come to represent "virtue" in general. In Homer, a warrior fought mainly for personal and family honor. By around 650 B.C. aretê referred also to the community. According to the poet Tyrtaeus (ca. 650 B.C.), the ideal soldier not only fights bravely but "heartens his neighbor by his words." Should he die, his death brings glory not only to his father but also to his city and his countrymen.

Most hoplites were full-time farmers outside of the fighting season, which lasted only for the summer months. The notion of the farmer-soldier, important in later political theory, had an immediate, practical effect: Those who fought for society soon demanded a say in governing it. Before the introduction of the phalanx, most poleis were ruled by the elite basileis. The emergence of the hoplite encouraged potential leaders to overthrow this aristocracy, ushering in a period of rule by popular figures supported by fighter-farmers. These rulers were called *tyrants*. Clearly, the term originally referred to a champion of the people and not to an arbitrary and oppressive ruler. *Tyrant* did not become a pejorative word until the people soured on the second and third generation of tyrants.

Much of what the first-generation tyrants did was popular and progressive. They stimulated the economy by founding colonies, standardizing weights and measures, and encouraging the immigration of skilled craftsmen from other poleis. Tyrants built temples and instituted festivals, providing jobs and leisure-time activities. When tyrants passed power on to their sons, the second generation tended to rule oppressively. Few tyrannies lasted beyond the third generation, when they were overthrown and replaced by oligarchy ("rule by the few") or, less often, by democracy (literally, "power of the people"). By 500 B.C. tyranny had disappeared from most of Greece.

Sparta

The polis Sparta developed a uniquely austere and militaristic version of community. Located in Laconia, a fertile valley in Peloponnesus, the southern part of mainland Greece (see Map 2.1), Sparta was a closed society, suspicious of foreigners, secretive toward the outside world, and contemptuous of book learning. (Our word *laconic*, meaning "of few words," comes from Laconia.)

Spartans believed that their system had been created at one stroke by the legendary lawgiver Lycurgus. Nowadays, scholars are not certain that Lycurgus ever existed. They argue that Sparta developed slowly, beginning around 650 B.C., when a three-part class system emerged: helots, *perioikoi*, and Similars. The helots were unfree laborers who worked the land; they were not exactly slaves because they were owned not by individual masters but by the whole community. The *perioikoi* (roughly, "neighbors") were free but subordinate to the Similars. Similars were the only full citizens. Only men could be

Similars, for they were hoplites, the backbone of Sparta's army. The helots vastly outnumbered the other two classes.

When the system began around 650 B.C., there were about nine thousand Similars. Each Similar had the right, after reaching age 30, to attend a legislative assembly and hold public office. Each was given a land allotment that was worked by helots, freeing the Similar to fight. As the name implies, Similars were alike but not equal—some owned more land than the minimum allotment.

Sparta was so dependent on its army because there were so many helots. Most helots were not

Spartan Woman This bronze statuette (4¾ inches tall) from Laconia (ca. 530 B.C.) shows a woman running. Unlike other Greek women, elite Spartan women underwent physical education. Although personal freedom was limited in Sparta, women suffered fewer restrictions than their counterparts in democratic Athens did. *(National Archaeological Museum, Archaeological Receipts Fund, Athens)*

Spartans but Messenians. Their fertile territory had been conquered by Sparta in about 725 B.C., and they were forced to labor. Sparta profited, but it had to police the Messenian helots. A dramatic revolt sometime between 675 and 650 B.C. almost succeeded in expelling the Spartans. To keep Messenia, Sparta needed to train, nourish, and glorify its fighters, who had to be full-time soldiers. Hence, all Spartan hoplites became Similars.

Sparta was no democracy. The assembly of Similars constituted the popular element in the regime, but its powers were limited. Real power lay with the Council of Elders: Sparta's two kings—less monarchs than commanders of the army and chief priests—and twenty-eight men over 68 years old who generally belonged to a few wealthy families. The assembly approved laws, but only after prior approval by the Council of Elders. In reality, Sparta was an oligarchy, ruled by a few powerful figures.

The oligarchs did not lead lives of luxury, however, especially after around 550 B.C., when austerity became the order of the day. Society was re-ordered to ensure discipline, obedience, preparedness, and loyalty, the qualities needed to maintain control of the helots. For example, Spartans' diet was famous for its simplicity. The preferred meal was a black broth of pork cooked in its own blood and spiced with salt and vinegar.

At birth, all male Similar babies were examined by public inspectors. Those who were considered deformed or unfit were "exposed"—that is, abandoned without food or shelter. The victims might die, be sold into slavery, or even be secretly adopted. (Other Greeks also practiced exposure of infants but left the matter up to private families.) Surviving children were raised at home until the age of 7, at which point boys were taken from the family to be boarded in barracks with a "herd" of their age mates. Girls stayed home and, unlike most Greek girls, received a public education—though this was mostly limited to physical training. For boys, the years from age 7 to age 18 were a period of rigorous training called the *agoge* ("upbringing"). Boys learned only enough reading and writing for practical ends—for example, for messages to or from military headquarters.

Between the ages of 18 and 20, many boys served in the *krypteia* (secret service), an institution that combined the common Greek practice of initiatory service for young warriors with Sparta's security needs. Boys in the krypteia lived outdoors, in the hills of Messenia, where they survived by hunting, foraging, and stealing. They spied on the Messenian helots, whom they could kill with impunity. By age 20, all Similars became hoplites, and they continued to serve in the army until age 60. All those years, the Similars had to take all their meals at the barracks. Until they were 30, they slept there as well—even after marriage. Men had to sneak visits to their wives.

Marriage was designed to produce offspring, not to form a relationship that might undermine the Similar's loyalty to the state. This meant that Spartan women were more independent than women elsewhere in Greece. With the men off in training or warfare, women ran the day-to-day operations of life, controlling the helot farmworkers and servants, and raising the girls and the very small boys. Girls were schooled to assertiveness by youthful physical training outdoors. Unlike Athenian women, Spartan women were able to inherit property.

Young Spartan soldiers called their military trainers "father," thus strengthening the feeling that the military was the true family. Some demonstrated love for their fellow soldiers physically as well as emotionally. This valuing of state family over nuclear family minimized the significance of adultery. If the husband did not mind, it was perfectly acceptable for a woman to have a child with another man. The need for new soldiers gave childbearing an intense importance. While all other Spartans were buried anonymously, the tombstone of a woman who died in childbirth was marked with her name—a high honor for her sacrifice to the state. Bachelors, on the other hand, were humiliated and punished.

For more than three hundred years, Spartan soldiers dominated land warfare in Greece. Unlike most of the other poleis, Sparta had no walls; the inhabitants claimed that the Spartans themselves were sufficient defense. Beginning around 550 B.C., Sparta built up a network of alliances

Athens: Archaic Greece to the Classical Ideal, ca. 650–404 B.C.

43

(dubbed the "Peloponnesian League" by scholars) in the Peloponnesus and central Greece. After defeating Persia in 480, the league became the dominant land power in the entire eastern Mediterranean. It remained so until its breakup after the Peloponnesian War (431–404 B.C.).

ATHENS: ARCHAIC GREECE TO THE CLASSICAL IDEAL, CA. 650–404 B.C.

The Athenians invented democracy. The word *democracy* comes from the Greek, meaning "the power (*kratos*) of the people (*demos*)." A modern democracy is characterized by mass citizenship, elections, and representative government. Athenian *demokratia*, in contrast, was a democracy of direct participation in which citizenship was narrowly restricted, women were excluded from public life, resident aliens could almost never become citizens, and citizens owned slaves and ruled an empire. Modern democracies tend to emphasize individual rights. Athens, in contrast, often placed the community first. In spite of the differences, Athenian demokratia established principles that are enshrined in democracy today: freedom, equality, citizenship without property qualifications, the right of most citizens to hold public office, and the rule of law.

Athenian demokratia developed slowly. In the Archaic period, Athens's government was in the hands of the basileis, as in most poleis. The Athenian basileis, who proudly called themselves the Eupatrids ("well-fathered"), ruled through an aristocratic council. In 621 B.C. codification of the laws was issued in writing. This Code of Draco, named for its main drafter, was famous for its harsh provisions (hence the adjective *draconian*); it was written, as a later commentator observed, "not in ink but blood."

Solon and the Reformers

Draco's Code seems to have whetted an appetite for change. A non-Eupatrid elite of hoplites was emerging. Some were merchants grown rich exporting olive oil; most were prosperous farmers. They now wanted political power. As the wealthy grew restless, ordinary Athenians, typically working small family farms, were suffering. Over the years, bad harvests and soil exhaustion had sent many into debt. Those who had only themselves or their children as collateral ended up as slaves, sometimes sold abroad. Because both rich and poor Athenians had grievances against the Eupatrids, revolution was in the air. Enter Solon (ca. 630–ca. 560 B.C.), a Eupatrid merchant who was appointed to an emergency leadership position for one year, probably 594 B.C. He could have become tyrant, but he preferred to be a mediator; as such, he said, he "stood with a strong shield before both parties [the common people and the powerful] and allowed neither one to win an unfair victory."[1]

Solon enacted both economic and political reforms. He helped ordinary people by the "shaking off of burdens," canceling certain land dues and setting up a fund to redeem Athenians sold into slavery abroad. Solon disappointed many poor people by refusing to confiscate and redistribute land, but by canceling the land dues, he ensured Athens a large class of independent small farmers.

Solon also changed qualifications for office from birth to wealth, a boon to the non-Eupatrid elite. He established four census classes based on agricultural production. Most offices were reserved for men of property, but the poorest class, known as *thetes*, could participate in the assembly and courts. Solon probably established a Council of 400, which prepared the assembly's agenda.

Solon's moderation, respect for law, and liberation of the poor are milestones in Greek history. Yet Solon's middle way satisfied neither the Eupatrids nor the champions of the poor. After years of conflict, around 560 B.C. advocates of radical reform established a tyranny under Peisistratus (ca. 600–528 B.C.). Supported by the thetes, Peisistratus and his sons exiled many Eupatrids and redistributed their land. But the dynasty lasted only two generations. Athens's elites by birth and wealth wanted to establish an oligarchy, but something very different happened: the emergence of popular government.

The Rise of Democracy

A democratic revolution inaugurated Athens's Classical period. The revolution was led by the Eupatrid Cleisthenes (d. ca. 500 B.C.). Originally Cleisthenes aimed to head the oligarchy, but his rivals shut him out of power. He turned then to the better-off members of the demos, including owners of medium-size farms, artisans, and merchants but excluding the poorest Athenians, the thetes. He soon became their leader. Frightened by the assertive populace, the oligarchs called for Spartan military assistance, but to no avail: Cleisthenes rallied "the people" to victory.

Cleisthenes undermined Eupatrid power once and for all by attacking its local bases of support, especially that of the four traditional tribes. Cleisthenes abolished them and apportioned the people among ten new tribes. Immigrants or their descendants who had been excluded from the old tribes now joined natives in the new tribes. Each tribe annually chose fifty councilmen, and each tribe's councilmen served as a kind of executive committee for one of the ten months of the civic year. The army was divided into ten tribal units, so that every Athenian hoplite fought along with fellow tribesmen.

The centerpiece of the government was the assembly, some of whose members, emboldened by the new spirit of equality, now spoke up for the first time. The new Council—now with 500 members—prepared the assembly's agenda, as in the past, but now assemblymen felt free to amend it.

The last and most unusual part of the Cleisthenic system was ostracism, an annual opportunity to vote to expel someone from the community for ten years. Ostracism—the word came from the pieces of broken pottery (*ostraka*) on which the names were inscribed—was meant to protect the regime by defusing factionalism and discouraging tyrants. Judging by Athens's consequent political stability, it worked.

The Athenian government remained unchanged until the decade of the 450s, when payment for public service was introduced. Conservatives complained bitterly, because state pay made political activity by poor people possible.

State pay was, an Athenian said, "the glue of demokratia."

Demokratia became closely connected with Pericles (ca. 495–429 B.C.). An aristocrat who respected the common people, an excellent orator who benefited from an education in philosophy, an honest and tireless worker, a war leader and a builder in peacetime, Pericles was a political giant. Under his leadership, demokratia became firmly entrenched as the government and way of life in Athens. Large numbers of ordinary citizens attended the assembly on a regular basis and held public office or served on the Council of 500 for a year or two. In addition, military service was made universal for men from ages 18 to 59. (See the box "The Debate on Democracy.")

The central institution was the assembly. Open to all male citizens over age 20, assembly meetings were held in the open air on a hillside seating several thousand on benches. In the fourth century B.C. there was a minimum of forty meetings per year, one about every ten days. The assembly made decisions about war and peace, alliance and friendship; it granted honors and condemnations; it passed decrees relating to current issues and set up commissions to revise the laws. In the assembly great orators addressed the people, but everyone was theoretically entitled to speak. The judicial branch consisted of courts, which, with a few exceptions, were open to all citizens. Juries were large, commonly consisting of several hundred men chosen by lottery; small juries, it was felt, were easily bribed. Most public officials were chosen by lottery, which put rich and poor, talented and untalented, on an equal footing.

Metics, Women, Slaves

Some critics have charged that the Athenian people were uneducated, emotional, and easily swayed by oratorical tricks. Others say that demokratia degenerated into mob rule after the death of Pericles. Still others complain about the lack of a system of formal public education, which denied many citizens equality of opportunity. The harshest critique focuses on the people who could not become citizens at all.

The Debate on Democracy

Characters in Greek drama often discuss general principles. In this excerpt from Euripides'
tragedy **The Suppliant Women** *(ca. 420 B.C.), Theseus, legendary king of Athens, and a herald*
from Creon, tyrant of Thebes, debate the merits of democracy.

Herald
What man is tyrant in this land? To whom/
Must I give the word I bring from Creon,
ruler/In Cadmus' country [Thebes] . . . ?

Theseus
One moment, stranger./Your start was wrong,
seeking a tyrant here./This city is free, and
ruled by no one man./The people reign, in annual succession./They do not yield the power
to the rich;/The poor man has an equal share
in it.

Herald
That one point gives the better of the game/To
me. The town I come from is controlled/By one
man, not a mob. And there is no one/To puff it
up with words, for private gain,/Swaying it
this way, that way. . . . /The people is no right
judge of arguments./Then how can it give
right guidance to a city?/A poor man, working
hard, could not attend/To public matters, even

if ignorance/Were not his birthright. When a
wretch, a nothing,/Obtains respect and power
from the people/By talk, his betters sicken at
the sight.

Theseus
. . . Nothing/Is worse for a city than a
tyrant./In earliest days, before the laws are
common,/One man has power and makes the
law his own:/Equality is not yet. With written
laws,/People of small resources and the
rich/Both have the same recourse to justice.
Now/A man of means, if badly spoken of,/
Will have no better standing than the weak;/
And if the little man is right, he wins/Against
the great. This is the call of freedom:/"What
man has good advice to give the city,/And
wishes to make it known?" He who re-
sponds/Gains glory; the reluctant hold their
peace./For the city, what can be more fair than
that?

Source: Adapted from Euripides, *The Suppliant Women,* trans. Frank Jones, in *Euripides IV: The Complete Greek
Tragedies,* ed. David Grene and Richmond Lattimore (Chicago: University of Chicago Press, 1958), pp. 73–74. Copyright 1958 by the University of Chicago Press. Reprinted by permission.

There were never more than approximately
40,000 adult male citizens out of a total population—men, women and children, resident aliens,
and slaves—of about 400,000. To become a citizen, at age 18 a boy had to prove that he was the
legitimate descendant of a citizen father and maternal grandfather. Foreigners, women, and
slaves were left out.

Athenian ideology emphasized the homogeneity of Athenian citizens; they were, it was
claimed, "sprung from the soil itself." In reality,
many had ancestors who had immigrated to
Athens before 500 B.C. In the fifth and fourth centuries B.C. Athens had a large population of officially registered resident aliens, or *metics.* Some,
like Aristotle (a native of a Greek colony in Macedonia), were attracted by Athens's schools of philosophy, but most came because of its unparalleled economic opportunities. Although metics
could not own land in Athens and had to pay

extra taxes and serve in the Athenian military, they prospered in Athenian commerce and crafts.

Athenian women were excluded from politics and played only a small role in commerce as small retailers. Girls were never officially registered as citizens; Athenian women of citizen families were usually referred to as "city women." Women rarely received an education, even in physical activity. In legal and contractual matters they were almost always required to be represented by a male guardian. They had neither the legal rights of women in Egypt or Mesopotamia nor the honor as mothers and household partners of women in Israel.

The more power was distributed among the male citizenry, the more hostile to women's freedom Athens's citizen ideology became. Women were supposed to stay indoors almost all the time, though inner courtyards (possessed only by the rich) and trips to permitted funerals and festivals alleviated this to some degree. The extent of this ideology is clear in Aristotle's rhetorical question, "How is it possible to prevent the wives of the poor from going out?" "Poor" is a synonym for "ordinary" in ancient Greek. Ordinary women could not stay at home because they had to run errands and sometimes work for pay. The idealized goal of female seclusion represents the restrictions placed on Athenian women, but their real lives were perhaps less constrained than it might seem. Women did play a large role in Athenian religion. They were priestesses in more than forty major cults. They participated each year in many festivals, including several reserved for women only. One such festival, the Thesmophoria, a yearly celebration of fertility, featured a three-day encampment of women on a hillside in the city. Women attended funeral orations in honor of soldiers. Women probably attended the theater, and all women must have spent as much time as possible in one another's company.

Slavery was widespread in democratic Athens. Some slaves served in agriculture, some labored under miserable conditions in Athenian silver mines, and some were engaged in commerce or the military (where some rowers were slaves). Most, however, worked as domestics or in small workshops. The vast majority of slaves were non-Greek. Most were prisoners of war; some were debtors from states where, unlike Athens, citizens might still end up in debt-slavery.

The living conditions of slaves were usually poor and in the silver mines abysmal. Yet emancipation was more common in Athens than in the American South before 1865. A few ex-slaves rose to positions of wealth and power in Athens. A striking and unusual case was that of Pasion (d. 370 B.C.). Originally a slave employee of a banking firm, he bought his freedom and became the wealthiest Athenian banker of his day, as well as an Athenian citizen.

Athenian demokratia lacked many features of modern democracy: universal human rights, the possibility for immigrants to become citizens, gender equality, the abolition of slavery, and public education. To its small citizen body, however, Athenian demokratia offered extraordinary freedom, equality, and responsibility, and a degree of participation in public life seldom equaled.

STRUGGLES FOR HEGEMONY

The polis generated community spirit, but that spirit had to compete with a strong passion for personal glory. The citizen was often unwilling to make compromises for the public good; the polis recoiled at the thought of sacrificing its honor for the sake of other poleis. The result was a constant struggle in diplomacy and war among city-states, often arranged in leagues each under a *hegemon* (literally, "leader").

In 500 B.C. the most prominent power of the Greek mainland was Sparta, hegemon of the Peloponnesian League. Across the Aegean Sea in Anatolia, the Ionian Greek city-states had been under Persian rule for two generations, since their conquest in the 540s (see Map 2.1). In 499 B.C. a chain of events began that would throw the entire eastern Mediterranean into two hundred years of turmoil.

The Persian Wars, 499–479 B.C., and the Rise of the Athenian Empire

In 499 B.C., led by Miletus, the Ionian Greek city-states rose in revolt against Persia. Athens sent troops to help, but despite initial successes Athens lacked the will for a long war and its troops soon departed. The Ionian coalition broke down, and in 494 B.C. the Persian fleet crushed the Ionian navy. Miletus was besieged and destroyed, but otherwise Persia was relatively lenient.

Upstart Athens, however, could not go unpunished. In 492 B.C., Darius I sent a large naval expedition to Athens. It was destroyed by a storm, but in 490 he sent a second force of about 25,000 infantrymen and 1200 cavalrymen (with horses) to Marathon, some 26 miles from the city of Athens. Athens sent 10,000 men to defend Marathon. A great battle ensued.

Under the general Miltiades (550–489 B.C.), the Greeks attacked. Persian overconfidence and the superiority of the Greek phalanx over Persia's loosely organized infantrymen won Athens a smashing victory: Persia suffered 6400 casualties, Athens only 192. (There is an unconfirmed story that a messenger ran 26 miles to the city of Athens with the news, "Rejoice, we conquer!"—the basis for the modern marathon race.) After the battle, Athens experienced a burst of confidence that propelled it to power and glory.

Persia sought revenge. Darius's son and successor, Xerxes, decided on a joint land-sea expedition. He amassed a huge force of several hundred ships, vastly outnumbering the potential Greek opposition. Athens joined Sparta and twenty-nine other Peloponnesian poleis in a Hellenic League of defense, with Sparta in overall command. Most poleis either stayed neutral or collaborated with Persia.

Persia invaded Greece in 480 B.C. and won the opening moves. A small Spartan army under King Leonidas held the narrow pass of Thermopylae in central Greece (see Map 2.1). With local help, the Persians found a way to outflank Leonidas and take both ends of the pass. They crushed the Spartans, who died fighting to the last man (thereby adding to their reputation for courage). After a naval victory near Thermopylae, the Persians marched on Athens. Abandoned by its defenders, it was sacked.

Then the tide turned. The Greeks lured the Persian fleet into the narrow straits between Athens and Salamis. In this closed space, the Persians could not use their numerical superiority, and the Greeks had the home advantage. The result was a crushing Persian defeat under the eyes of Xerxes himself, who watched the battle from a throne on a hillside near the shore.

Xerxes and the remainder of his fleet sailed for home. Soon afterward the victorious Greeks liberated the Ionians. Not only had Persia failed to conquer the Greek mainland, but it had lost its eastern Aegean empire. Greeks did not remember the invader fondly. After 480 they thought of Persians not merely as enemies but as barbarians—that is, cultural inferiors. At the same time, Greeks became more conscious of their own common culture.

In 477 B.C., Athens became the hegemon of a new security organization, founded on the island of Delos in the Aegean Sea. The dual purpose of the so-called Delian League was to protect Greek lands and to attack and plunder Persian territory. Fearful as ever of entanglements outside the Peloponnesus, Sparta preferred to leave the Aegean to Athens. But many Spartans watched with unease and jealousy as Athenian power surged.

Athens, meanwhile, transformed its pride to arrogance. Within a generation, by the 450s, the Delian League was becoming an Athenian empire. In 454 B.C. the treasury was transferred from Delos to Athens on the pretext that it would be safer there. In the following decades, the allies were compelled to send delegations to Athenian festivals, to use Athenian weights, measures, and coinage, and to refer major court cases to Athenian juries.

One by one, beginning with Thasos in 465 B.C., the major allied states rebelled, but Athens crushed each rebellion. Sometimes, after surrender, rebels were executed and their wives and children sold into slavery. Allied complaints began to stir Sparta. A conflict between Greece's greatest land power, Sparta, and its greatest seapower, Athens, seemed all but inevitable.

The Peloponnesian War, 431–404 B.C.

When it came, the conflict between Athens and Sparta proved exceptionally bloody and bitter. Battles between huge fleets, economic warfare, protracted sieges, epidemic disease, and ideological struggle produced a devastating war.

In the era of the Peloponnesian War, both democratic Athens and oligarchic Sparta found themselves fighting to sustain their respective ideologies. In Athens a minority of oligarchs had never been reconciled to demokratia. When Athens began to falter in the war after 413 B.C., they seized the opportunity and twice installed oligarchy in Athens: first in 411 and again in 404. Each time, the democrats came back to power, the second time only after foreign intervention and civil war.

Given Spartan supremacy on land and Athenian mastery of the sea, it is not surprising that the war continued as long as it did. It was a decade and a half before the balance of power shifted, following an Athenian blunder. In 415 B.C. Athens launched a quick raid on Sicily, hoping to use its fabled wealth to reshape the Greek balance of power. Unfortunately for Athens, the raid became a quagmire and then a disaster, leading to total defeat and thousands of Athenian casualties.

By 412 B.C. most of the Athenian empire was in revolt and Persia had intervened on Sparta's side—in return for Sparta's restoration of Ionia to Persia, an ironic counterpoint to Sparta's role in driving Persia from Greece in 479. Athens, nevertheless, was sufficiently wealthy and plucky to hold out until 405 B.C., when the Spartans, led by the shrewd and aggressive Lysander (d. 395 B.C.), captured almost the entire Athenian fleet in the Hellespont. Athens surrendered the next year.

Peace, however, was elusive. The fourth century B.C. was marked by unproductive wars and infighting. Sparta had won the Peloponnesian War, but establishing a new Greek order proved beyond its grasp. Spartans made poor leaders: They were trained as soldiers, not diplomats; they lacked the oratorical skills valued by other Greeks; and worst of all, they were self-satisfied and contemptuous of others. Sparta took over Athens's former empire and quickly had a falling-out with its allies.

At this point Sparta began suffering from a vast decline in the number of citizens. The original nine thousand Similars of the seventh century B.C. had declined to about fifteen hundred in 371 B.C. The main problem seems to have been greed. Rich Spartans preferred to get richer by concentrating wealth in fewer hands rather than opening the elite to new blood. Thousands of men could no longer afford to live as elite soldiers. The result was military disaster. In 371 B.C. the army of the city-states of Boeotia, united under the hegemony of Thebes, crushed the Spartans at the Battle of Leuctra. In the next few years Boeotia invaded the Peloponnesus, freed the Messenian helots, and restored Messenia to independence after some 350 years of bondage. It was a fatal blow to Spartan power, but Boeotia, too, was exhausted. None of the Greek city-states had been able to maintain hegemony. The wars of the city-states in the fourth century B.C. accomplished nothing but leaving Greece prey to outsiders.

CULTURE: FROM ARCHAIC TO CLASSICAL GREECE

If one trend in Archaic culture was communal solidarity, as reflected in the hoplite phalanx, another was quite opposite: individualism. Increased prosperity and social mobility during the Archaic period encouraged the breakdown of old ties, and a new consciousness of the self became apparent in poetry and sculpture.

Archaic religion and thought, too, followed superficially opposite trends. While monumental stone temples were being erected, Greek thinkers were beginning to move away from divine and toward abstract and mechanistic explanations of the universe.

Public life was the central theme of Classical Greek art and literature. In Greek tragedy, for example, regardless of the particular hero or plot, the same character looms in the background: the polis. The Classical historians had little to say about private life. Classical philosophy ranged from biology to metaphysics, but it made politics its central focus.

Art and Religion

Between approximately 675 and 500 B.C. the dominant Greek literary form was lyric poetry. This form consisted of short poems written in a variety of styles but sharing a willingness to experiment, sometimes by revealing private feelings, sometimes by commenting on contemporary politics. In comparison to epic poetry, lyric was shorter and more personal.

Archilochus of Paros (ca. 700–ca. 650 B.C.) was the earliest known of the lyric poets. The son of a noble, he was a mercenary soldier who died in battle. The subjects of his poetry include love, travels, and war. He often sets a mood of privacy. Consider, for example, a lonely mercenary described by Archilochus as using his spear to knead bread and to lean on while drinking wine. Archilochus takes an ironic and detached view of hoplite ideals, freely admitting that he once tossed away his shield to escape the battlefield: "And that shield, to hell with it! Tomorrow I'll get me another one no worse."[2]

Sappho of Lesbos (ca. 625 B.C.) is also famous as a private poet, one who composed unsurpassed descriptions of intimate feelings, including love for other women. Sappho is one of the few women poets of antiquity whose work has survived. Unfortunately, most of her poetry was lost. Sappho was educated, worldly, and versed in politics. Like a modern experimental poet, she used language self-consciously. Sappho's sensuality comes through in a description of her feelings at seeing a woman whose company she wants: Her heart shakes, her tongue is stuck, her eyes cannot see, her skin is on fire. "I am greener than grass," Sappho writes, "I feel nearly as if I could die."[3]

Sappho discussed female sexuality, a subject Greek elite culture tended to ignore (along with the sexuality of nonelite males). Among the male elite, romantic love in both Archaic and Classical Greece was homosexual love or, to be precise, pederasty. The ideal relationship was supposed to involve a man in his twenties and a boy in his teens. The male elite was, strictly speaking, bisexual. By age 30 a man was expected to marry and raise a family. Perhaps bisexuality prevailed among elite females as well; Sappho, for example, eventually married and had a child.

Another sign of Archaic Greece's interest in the personal was the growing attention to the depiction of the human body in painted pottery and sculpture. Archaic artists displayed increasing skill and sensitivity in depicting the human form. The rich marble deposits in Greek soil gave sculptors promising material; baked clay (terra cotta) and bronze were other common sculptural media.

Early Archaic marble sculpture (seventh century B.C.) was strongly influenced by the way Egyptian sculpture represented the human body. As such, early Greek sculpture tended to be formal and frontal. Over the course of the seventh and sixth centuries B.C., Greek sculptors experimented with a variety of poses and with increasing realism in musculature and motion. Classical sculptors completed the process begun by their Archaic predecessors of mastering the accurate representation of the human body, though their aim was never absolute realism. Greek sculpture was intended to create idealized portraits of the human (and divine) form.

Despite momentous changes across the various eras of ancient Greece, the Olympian gods survived, adapted by successive ages to fit the Greeks' political and social structures. In the Archaic period, the Olympian gods were gods of the polis. The Olympians were worshiped throughout Greece, and each polis had its patron deity. It was considered important to build a "house"—that is, a temple—for the patron god or at least for his or her statue.

Temples were rectangular structures with a colonnade around all four sides and a pitched roof. The interior decoration of the temple was simple. Outside, however, brownish-red roof tiles, painted sculpture above the colonnade, and

The Parthenon   The temple of Athena Parthenos ("the Maiden") on the Athenian Acropolis, the Parthenon was dedicated in 438 B.C. One of the largest and most complex Greek temples, it was built of fine marble. The partially restored ruins symbolize the wealth, power, and greatness of Classical Greece. *(William Katz/Photo Researchers)*

terra-cotta roof ornaments created a festive and lively effect. The bare, white ruins seen today are misleading. The emphasis on exterior decoration in a Greek temple made sense because the main ceremonies took place outside.

As in other ancient cultures, divination was an important element of Greek religion. Divination was institutionalized in *oracles*, places where, it was believed, one could go to consult a god or hero for advice. The deity was thought to speak through the agency of his human servants, the priests and priestesses who tended the oracles. Of the various Greek oracles, that of Apollo at Delphi (in central Greece) became the most prestigious and respected. The priests of Delphi were regularly consulted by poleis as well as individuals. Tradition says that Sparta based its government on a pronouncement of the Delphic oracle.

A hallmark of Classical culture was the tension between the religious heritage of the Archaic period and the confident, worldly spirit of the Classical period. "Wonders are many on earth, and none more wondrous than man," said the Athenian tragedian Sophocles (ca. 495–406 B.C.). Yet Sophocles was also a deeply religious man who believed that people were doomed to disaster unless they obeyed the laws of the gods.

Classical religion was less sure of itself than its Archaic predecessor. A few people even questioned the existence of the gods, although most Greeks wanted religion to be adapted to the new age, not discarded altogether. Thus, Athenian religion was tailored to the needs of a democratic and imperial city. In the 440s B.C., under Pericles' leadership, Athens embarked on an ambitious and expensive temple-building project, which served as a large public employment program.

The Origins of Western Philosophy

Abstract, rationalistic, speculative thinking first emerged in Miletus, an Ionian city during the sixth century B.C. (see Map 2.2). The Ionians were not the first to ask questions about the nature of the universe; virtually every ancient people did so. Nor did the Ionians invent science. By 600 B.C., science had been thriving for over two thousand years in Egypt and Mesopotamia, a heritage with which the Ionians were familiar.

It was the Greeks, however, who invented philosophy: sustained inquiry into human life and the universe that did not rely on supernatural explanations. The Ionians did not always make a clear distinction between reason and revelation, but they tended toward abstract and mechanistic explanation of things. Greek philosophers were rarely (if ever) atheists, but they were increasingly secular in their reasoning.

The Ionians were particularly interested in natural phenomena. In their own day, they were called "wise men" (*sophoi*); to a later generation, they were "lovers of wisdom," *philosophoi* (from which *philosopher* comes). Thales, a Milesian thinker who successfully predicted a solar eclipse in 585 B.C., is credited with founding Greek geometry and astronomy. He also created the first general and systematic theory about the nature of the universe, asserting that all of nature was created from one primary substance: water.

A reply was not long in coming. Around 550 B.C., Anaximander of Miletus wrote the first known book of prose in Greek, attacking Thales for oversimplifying nature. He called the primary substance "the unlimited" rather than water. A third Milesian, Anaximenes, replied that the primary substance was air, whose properties symbolized the dynamic and changing nature of things.

Humble as these theories might seem today, they represent a dramatic development: an open debate among thinkers, each of whom was proposing an abstract and rational model of the universe. Early Greek philosophy in its second generation moved to other Ionian cities and then migrated westward across the Mediterranean. Heracleitus of Ephesus (ca. 500 B.C.) proposed fire as the primary substance. Although fire was ever changing, it had an underlying coherence. Heracleitus saw the universe as ruled by change, saying, "All things flow" and "You cannot step into the same river twice."

Heracleitus' contemporary, Pythagoras of Samos, was a kind of religious mathematician. He discovered a number of numerical relationships and saw in them a beauty and purity that seemed to harbor the secrets of the universe. His accomplishments were mathematical: He established the numerical ratios determining the major intervals of the musical scale and is known (questionably) as the discoverer of the Pythagorean theorem—that in a right triangle the hypotenuse squared is equal to the sum of the squares of the other two sides. Yet his math was intertwined with mysticism. Indeed, Pythagoras founded a religious community bound by a strict rule of secrecy.

The early Greek philosopher Parmenides of Elea (b. ca. 515 B.C.) was the first Western philosopher to propose a radical difference between the world of the senses and reality. He believed that reality was a world of pure being: eternal, unchanging, and indivisible. The change that Heracleitus had seen was, to Parmenides, a mere illusion. This fundamental strain of Western thought would be taken up by Plato and his followers and then passed to Christianity.

In the Classical period, concern shifted from the nature of the universe to how people should live. Success in democratic politics required oratorical skill. This demand was met in the late fifth century B.C. by the arrival in Athens of instructors of *rhetoric*, the art of speaking. Known as Sophists, they were the first professional teachers. For a large fee, Sophists taught young

Athenians how to be convincing. Their curriculum also touched on linguistics, ethics, psychology, and history to round out the education of an aspiring politician.

Protagoras (b. ca. 485 B.C.), perhaps the best-known Sophist, summed up the spirit of the age in his famous dictum "Man is the measure of all things." In other words, human beings create the appropriate truth for a given situation—there are no absolute truths. Because they taught respect for success over truth, the Sophists acquired a reputation as word-twisters. *Sophist* became a term of abuse in Athens and remains so today.

Nevertheless, the Sophists had a wide-ranging impact on many different branches of thought. For example, the Sophist-educated Democritus (b. ca. 460 B.C.) devised the idea that all things consist of tiny, indivisible particles, which he called *atoma*, "the uncuttable." Equally significant was the work of the physicians known as Hippocratics, from Hippocrates (b. ca. 460 B.C.), the first great thinker of their school. If they were not directly influenced by the Sophists, they shared many similar habits of thought. They considered disease to be strictly a natural phenomenon in which the gods played no part.

The relativism of the Sophists ultimately caused their downfall. If no absolute truths exist, what is the basis of virtue, religion, morality, and even the state? As the Sophists grew increasingly involved in teaching young people how to be clever politicians, a movement based on the reality of absolute truth arose against them. The leading figures of this movement were Socrates, Plato, and Aristotle.

Socrates (469–399 B.C.) differed from the Sophists in many ways. He charged no fees, had no formal students, and did not claim to teach any positive body of knowledge. In fact, his basic thesis was the radical ignorance of most people, including himself. His only superiority, he believed, was his awareness of his ignorance.

Socrates changed the emphasis of philosophy to human ethics. For Socrates, one became good by studying the truth, which is part of what he meant when he said, "Virtue (aretê) is knowledge." He also meant that no one who truly understood goodness would ever do evil. This outlook downgraded the importance of willpower and the emotions, but it made education a cornerstone of society. Socrates' favorite teaching technique was to lead people to realizations by asking meaningful questions. Pedagogy that relies on questioning is still called the "Socratic method."

Socrates was interested in political theory and what it meant to be a good citizen—and he lived by his ideas, serving as a hoplite during the Peloponnesian War. He had his doubts about Athenian democracy, which he criticized for inefficiency and for giving an equal voice to the uneducated. He preferred rule by a wise elite. He did not advocate revolution, but his critique of democracy and the Sophists got him into trouble. In 399 Socrates was tried, convicted, and executed by an Athenian court for alleged atheism and "corrupting the young." The trial of Socrates is usually considered one of history's great miscarriages of justice and one of Athenian democracy's greatest blunders.

Because Socrates never wrote anything down (he believed philosophy had to be spoken and discussed) we are dependent on others for our knowledge of him. Fortunately, Socrates' brilliant student Plato (427–348 B.C.) wrote down his teachings. Plato in turn was the teacher of Aristotle (384–322 B.C.). Together, these three men laid the foundations of the Western philosophical tradition.

Socrates grew up in confident Periclean days. Plato came of age during the Peloponnesian War, a period culminating in the execution of Socrates. Shocked and disillusioned, Plato turned his back on public life, although he was an Athenian citizen. Instead of discussing philosophy in public, he founded a private school in an Athenian suburb, the Academy. He held a low opinion of democracy and rarely intervened in politics.

In an attempt to recapture the stimulating give-and-take of a conversation with Socrates, Plato wrote dialogues rather than straightforward philosophical treatises. In most of them, the main speaker is named "Socrates": sometimes the historical Socrates, sometimes merely a mouthpiece for Plato's ideas.

The word that best characterizes Plato's legacy is *idealism*. Like Parmenides, Plato believed that the senses are misleading. Truth exists but is attainable only by training the mind to overcome common-sense evidence. The model for Plato's philosophical method is geometry. Just as geometry deals not with this or that triangle or rectangle but with ideal forms—with a pure triangle, a pure rectangle—the philosopher can learn to recognize purity. Plato believed in absolute good and evil.

In the *Republic,* a dialogue that is his best-known work, Plato envisioned a society in which the elite would study philosophy and attain enlightenment. In Plato's ideal state philosophers would rule as kings, benevolently and unselfishly. The ideal state would be like a small polis. Society would be sharply divided into three classes—philosophers, soldiers, and farmers—with admission based on merit rather than heredity. Poetry and drama would be strictly censored. Plato advocated public education and toyed with more radical notions: not only gender equality but the abolition of the family and private property, institutions that he felt led to disunity.

Plato's ideas have always been controversial, even in his own day. The writings of his great student Aristotle were more to contemporary tastes. Originally from Macedonia, Aristotle spent most of his life in Athens, first as a student at the Academy, then as the founder of his own school, the Lyceum. Aristotle's main extant works are treatises, largely compilations by students of his lecture notes. They reflect a wide-ranging intellect, discussing politics, ethics, poetry, botany, zoology, physics, metaphysics, astronomy, rhetoric, logic, and psychology.

Although he was influenced by Plato's idealism, Aristotle was more interested in worldly concerns. His father had been a doctor, which may account for Aristotle's interest in applied science and biology. Unlike Plato, Aristotle placed great emphasis on observation and classification. Aristotle agreed with Plato about the existence of absolute standards of good and evil, but unlike Plato, he considered the senses to be important guides. Change, he believed, was not an illusion but an important phenomenon. Aristotle's view of change was teleological—that is, he emphasized the goal (*telos* in Greek) of change. According to Aristotle, every organism grows toward a particular end. The entire cosmos is teleological, and every one of its parts has a purpose. Behind the cosmos was a principle that Aristotle called "the unmoved mover," the supreme cause of existence.

Aristotle defined *aretê* as the fulfillment of one's function in the cosmos. Aristotle agreed with Plato that only the philosopher achieved true aretê. Yet Aristotle did not imagine philosophers becoming kings. Neither did he advocate democracy, which he considered mob rule. Instead, Aristotle advocated a government of wealthy gentlemen trained by philosophers.

Aristotle may be the most influential thinker in Western history. His scientific writings not only were the most influential philosophical classics of Greek civilization, and of Roman civilization as well, but remained so during the Middle Ages in the Arabic and Latin worlds. For more than two thousand years there were no serious challenges to Aristotle's intellectual supremacy.

Drama and History

Perhaps the greatest art form that emerged in the polis was drama. Comedy and tragedy began in religious festivals honoring the god Dionysus but quickly became an independent forum for comment on public life. Ancient drama was poetry, not prose, and it highlighted the relation of the individual to the community, enacting the ideology of the polis.

According to ancient tradition, tragedy was first presented at the Dionysia festival in Athens by one Thespis in the 530s B.C. (hence the word *thespian* for "actor"). In the fifth century B.C. a play consisted of a chorus (a group of performers working in unison) and three actors who played all the individual speaking parts. Plays were performed in an open-air theater on a hillside of the Acropolis. Enormously popular, drama spread all over Greece, and eventually most poleis had a theater.

Classical Athenian tragedy was performed at the annual Dionysia. Each playwright would submit a trilogy of plays on a central theme, plus a raucous farce to break the tension afterward. Comedies, which were independent plays rather than trilogies, were performed both at the Dionysia and at a separate festival. Wealthy producers competed to outfit the most lavish productions, and judges awarded prizes for the best plays.

Tragedy is not easy to define, but, in general, it is when a good person comes to a bad fate—because he or she either took a virtue too far or had to choose between two contradictory truths. The point of watching tragedy was that, in the words of the playwright Aeschylus: *pathos mathei,* "suffering teaches." As Aristotle observed, tragedy derives its emotional power from the fear and pity it evokes and from the purification (*katharsis*) of the senses it produces.

The great period of Greek tragedy began and ended in the fifth century B.C. Aeschylus (525–456 B.C.), Sophocles (ca. 495–406 B.C.), and Euripides (ca. 485–406 B.C.) were and are considered the three giant playwrights. They were all concerned with justice and virtue—both human and divine. In Sophocles' *Antigone* (ca. 442 B.C.), for example, the heroine refuses to compromise with injustice. Her late brother had committed treason, for which his corpse is denied burial—the standard Greek punishment. Antigone wants to follow the rule of the state but also needs to follow Zeus's law, which demands that all bodies be buried. Loyalty to family and the gods wins out over loyalty to the state, but the result is turmoil and death.

Comedy, too, was invented in Athens in the Classical period. Like tragedy, comedy offered a moral commentary on contemporary Athenian life. The greatest writer of comedy in the fifth century B.C. was Aristophanes (ca. 455–385 B.C.). His plays are lively, ribald, and full of allusions to contemporary politics. Aristophanes loved to show the "little guy" getting the better of the powerful and women deflating the pretensions of men. In *Lysistrata* (411 B.C.), his best-known play, he imagined the women of Greece stopping the Peloponnesian War by going on a sex strike, which forces the men to make peace.

History also flourished in the exciting intellectual atmosphere of classical Athens. Its two greatest historians, Herodotus (ca. 485–ca. 425 B.C.) and Thucydides (ca. 455–ca. 399 B.C.), were among the founders of history-writing in the West. Herodotus and Thucydides were more rationalistic than earlier chroniclers, and their subject matter was war, politics, peoples, and customs—what we think of as the stuff of history-writing today. Indeed, the word *history* comes from a word used by Herodotus, *historiai,* meaning "inquiries" or "research."

Herodotus wrote about the Persian Wars, seeing them as one episode of a vast historical drama. Only a child at the time of the wars, Herodotus gathered information by interviewing older people in various countries and checking the surviving written records. Herodotus also wrote about earlier centuries and places he had not visited, but with uneven accuracy—alongside solid research were unconfirmed accounts and myths. Thucydides, by contrast, prided himself on accuracy. He confined himself mainly to writing about an event he had lived through and participated in: the Peloponnesian War. A failed Athenian general, Thucydides spent most of the Peloponnesian War in exile, carefully observing, taking notes, and writing.

ALEXANDER THE GREAT AND THE HELLENISTIC WORLD, 323–30 B.C.

The quarrelsome Greek poleis achieved neither internal stability nor durable peace with one another. In the last decades of the fourth century B.C., Greece was conquered by its northern neighbor, Macedon. Once the Macedonians had secured control of Greece they undertook a series of military campaigns that subjected the eastern Mediterranean and the Persian Empire to their control. Because they admired Greek culture, the Macedonians spread it wherever they went. This forced encounter between Hellenic, or Greek, culture and the diverse cultures of the worlds the Macedonians conquered ushered in a new period called "Hellenistic," or Greeklike.

Alexander the Great of Macedon

The Hellenistic world was founded by two conquerors: Philip II of Macedon (382–336 B.C.) and his son, Alexander III, known as Alexander the Great (356–323 B.C.). Philip conquered the Greek city-states in less than twenty years; in less time still, Alexander conquered Egypt and all of western Asia as far east as modern Pakistan.

As a leader of men, Alexander was popular, was inspiring, and shared risks with the troops. He knew the value of propaganda and took pains to depict his expedition to the Greek city-states as a war of revenge for Persia's invasion of Greece in 480 B.C. instead of what it actually was: an act of Macedonian imperialism. He loved the colorful gesture. He began his expedition to conquer Persia in 334 B.C. by sacrificing animals to the gods at Troy, a site evoking Homer's heroes. He was charismatic, handsome, intelligent, and well educated; as a teenager he had Aristotle himself as a private tutor. He founded twenty cities. Alexander was ruthless, though, as well as cultured. He

Dionysus on a Panther This rich mosaic of about 100 B.C. comes from the Aegean island of Delos, a thriving port in Hellenistic times. In this theatrical scene, the artist contrasts the ferocity of the panther with the calm and composure of the god. Dionysus holds a cymbal, recalling his patronage of music, dance, and drama. *(House of Masks, Delos/Archaeological Receipts Fund, Athens)*

began his reign with a massacre of his male relatives. First and foremost a warrior, Alexander was a battlefield commander of the Macedonian cavalry at age 18, and he devoted most of his adult life to war.

The last seven years of Alexander's life were marked by three things. First was an apparently open-ended military campaign. Having conquered Persia, he pushed his army not only into the eastern parts of the Persian Empire but beyond, into modern Pakistan, which had not been controlled by Persia since the early fifth century B.C. He stopped only because his exhausted and homesick men demanded it. The second characteristic of Alexander's later career was his increasing despotism. After conquering Persia in 330 B.C., Alexander turned on the Macedonian nobility, staging conspiracy trials and assassinations. The most spectacular example took place in 328 when, after a drunken quarrel, Alexander himself murdered Cleitus, one of his senior commanders. Another sign of Alexander's growing despotism was his demand for the trappings of Persian kingship. After conquering Persia he made independent-minded Greeks and Macedonians bow down before him and required the Greek city-states to deify him.

The third characteristic was his novel policy of fusion. After returning from the Indian subcontinent, Alexander began training an army of thirty thousand Iranians and dismissed a large number of Macedonian troops. He forced his main commanders to marry Iranian women, as he did himself. This was a sharp break with traditional Greek ethnocentrism. Aristotle, for example, had said that the peoples of western Asia were fit only to be slaves. Alexander's policy probably owed less to idealism than to a desire for a new power base independent of the Macedonian nobility.

Ptolemaic and Seleucid Monarchies

Alexander died in Babylon in June 323 B.C., probably of malarial fever, although some contemporaries suspected poison and some historians

have suggested drunkenness. He was 32. His most powerful successors were the Ptolemies in Egypt (descendants of one of Alexander's generals, Ptolemy) and the Seleucid kings in western Asia (who got their name from another of Alexander's generals, Seleucus).

The wealthiest and the longest lasting of the Hellenistic kingdoms was Ptolemaic Egypt (Map 2.3). Ptolemy became governor of Egypt in 323 B.C. and proclaimed himself king in 304. His dynasty lasted until Rome annexed Egypt in 30 B.C., after the suicide of the last of the line, Queen Cleopatra. Ptolemy I made arrangements to have himself proclaimed "Savior God" after his death; his successors took divine honors while still alive.

Ptolemaic rulers borrowed the pharaonic tradition of the command economy (see page 14), combining it with Greek practices of literacy and a monetary economy. The result was a highly complex and profitable economy. The Ptolemies sponsored irrigation and land reclamation, the introduction of new crops, and the greatly expanded cultivation of old ones. Most of the people of Egypt made their living in agriculture, either as independent farmers or as tenants on large estates. Government enriched itself through taxes, rents, demands for compulsory labor, state monopolies, and internal tolls. Under strong kings and queens in the third century B.C., Egypt became the most prosperous part of the Hellenistic world.

Although friction between immigrants and natives sparked from time to time, most Egyptians readily accepted the Ptolemies as pharaohs as long as they brought peace and prosperity. In 196 B.C., Ptolemy V Epiphanes celebrated his coronation in full pharaonic ceremonial in Memphis. The occasion was recorded in stone in a trilingual inscription (Greek, hieroglyphic, and demotic—ordinary Egyptian). Discovered by Frenchmen in 1798 and called the Rosetta Stone, it led to the decipherment of hieroglyphics.

The Greeks slowly assimilated Egyptian ways. In the countryside, intermarriage and bilingualism became common. Over the centuries, even wealthy, sophisticated, urban Greeks

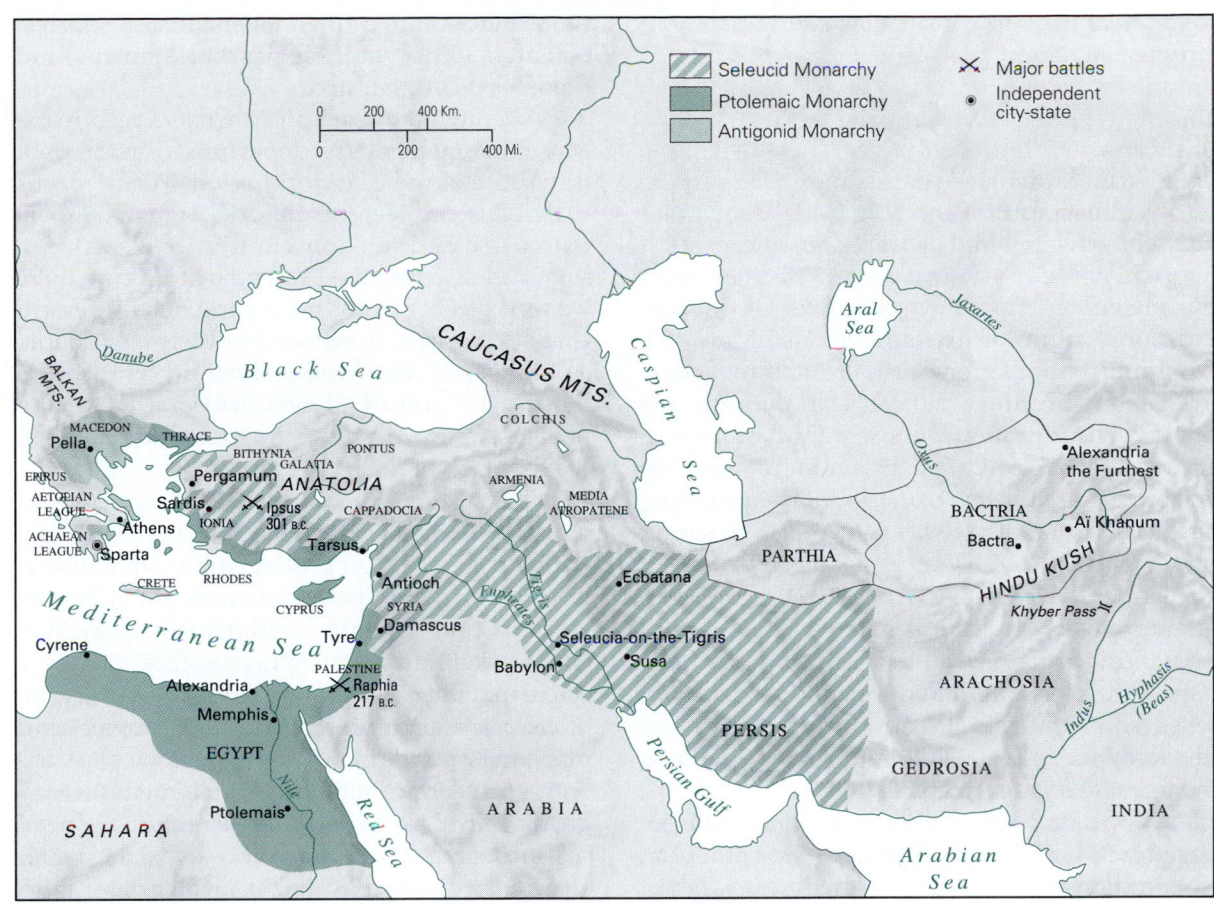

Map 2.3 Hellenistic Kingdoms, Leagues, and City-States, ca. 240 B.C. After Alexander's death, his empire lost its political unity. Great new cities and kingdoms arose in the lands he had conquered.

adopted a smattering of Egyptian customs. The Egyptian calendar, Egyptian names, and mummification were all in use.

The Seleucid kingdom began when Alexander's general Seleucus (ca. 358–281 B.C.) took Babylon in 312 B.C. and ended when Syria became a Roman province in 64 B.C. At its height, in the third century B.C., the Seleucid kingdom had three nerve centers: Ionia (in western Anatolia), Syria, and Babylonia (see Map 2.3).

Unlike the compact Nile Valley with its relatively homogeneous population, the far-flung and multi-ethnic Seleucid lands presented an enormous administrative challenge. To govern effectively, the kings adopted the Persian system of satraps (provincial governors), taxes, and royal roads and post, to which they added an army trained according to Macedonian traditions, a common coinage, and a Hellenistic ruler cult. Although Greek and Macedonian soldiers and administrators dominated the kingdom, the Seleucids also employed natives. The greatest Seleucid city was Antioch, which became one of the wealthiest cities in the eastern

Mediterranean; only Ptolemaic Alexandria outstripped it.

The Alexandrian Moment

In 331 B.C., at the site of a fishing village in the northwestern part of the Nile Delta, Alexander and his advisers had marked out the ground plan of a new city—a great eastern Mediterranean trading center. The new city, called Alexandria, did not disappoint its founders (see Map 2.3). Grown to a population of a half-million or more by the first century B.C., it was perhaps the largest, wealthiest, and most important city in the world. Greeks, Egyptians, and Jews were the largest groups in its cosmopolitan population, but no one would have been surprised to see an Indian or a Celt, an Italian or a Persian.

Under the Ptolemies, Alexandria became one of the great cultural centers of Hellenism. Alexandrians enjoyed an increase in leisure time, a growth in educational opportunities for both sexes, and royal patronage of culture. Even a limited knowledge of Greek literature could serve as the ticket to advancement.

In 294 B.C., King Ptolemy I invited the deposed tyrant of Athens, Demetrius of Phalerum, to found an institution of culture in Alexandria. The intention was to enjoy culture, to bring Ptolemy prestige, and to advance agricultural and military technology. The new institution was called the Museum ("House of the Muses," the female deities who inspired creativity). The Museum was a residence, study, and lecture hall for scholars, scientists, and poets. One of its key components was the Library, at the time the largest repository of Greek writing in the world. In the third century B.C. the Library contained 700,000 papyrus rolls, the equivalent of roughly 50,000 modern books.

The Library is one of several indicators of an increase in the size of the Hellenistic reading and writing public. As independence vanished, city-states changed their military training programs for young men into educational programs in literature and philosophy. The names of over a thousand writers of the Hellenistic era survive, and after 300 B.C. anthologies, abridgments, and school texts proliferated.

Although modeled on Athens's Lyceum, the Museum represented a departure from the public culture of the Classical period. The denizens of the Museum were an elite, dependent on royal patronage, and self-consciously Greek—as if to set up a barrier against Egyptians. Culture there was an object of study, not a part of civic life as in Classical Athens. Consider a witticism of Timon, a philosopher who lived in the third century B.C.: "In Egypt, land of diverse tribes, graze many pedants, fatted fowls that quarrel without end in the hen coop of the Muses."

Hellenistic mathematics and science were innovative. In his *Elements*, the Alexandrian Euclid (worked ca. 300 B.C.) produced a systematic exposition of geometry, hugely influential in both Western and Islamic civilizations. A Sicilian Greek, Archimedes of Syracuse (287–212 B.C.), calculated the approximate value of pi (the ratio of a circle's circumference to its diameter) and made important discoveries in geometry, astronomy, engineering, and optics. Archimedes was as great an inventor as he was a theoretician. One of his most important inventions was the water snail, a screwlike device for lifting water (also known as Archimedes' screw), which made it possible to irrigate previously barren land.

Advances in mathematics promoted advances in astronomy. Aristarchus of Samos (worked ca. 275 B.C.) is known for his heliocentric hypothesis, which confounded tradition by having the earth revolve around the sun. He was right, but Hellenistic astronomy lacked the data to prove his theory. Hellenistic medicine also thrived in Alexandria. The key to medical advance was the influence of both ancient Greek and ancient Egyptian medical science on the one hand and, on the other, the dissection of human cadavers in Alexandria—a first in the history of science. In Greece, religious tradition demanded that dead bodies not be mutilated, but in the frontier atmosphere of early Alexandria, tradition lost much of its force.

Men and Women in Art and Society

Hellenistic art attested to changing attitudes regarding gender. The portrait of Jason and Medea in Apollonius's *Argonautica* makes fun of masculine pretensions and celebrates the triumph of female intelligence. It also presents a sympathetic portrait of a woman's romantic desire for a man—in contrast to Classical focus on depictions of male homoerotic love. Also in contrast to the Classical period, Hellenistic sculpture affords many erotic examples of the female nude. Hellenistic vase-painting reflected a new emphasis on tenderness and domesticity, and Hellenistic men wrote with sensitivity about satisfying a woman's needs and desires. The vogue in Hellenistic art for representations of Hermaphrodite, the mythical creature who was half female and half male, suggests a belief that the feminine was as important a part of human nature as the masculine.

Hellenistic women enjoyed small improvements in political and legal rights and considerable improvements in economic and ideological status. Greek women, particularly in the elite, benefited from the spread of monarchy. For one thing, queens and princesses had power and prestige that had been denied to women in city-states. For another, under monarchy the ideal of the independent citizen-warrior was replaced with that of the loyal, cooperative subject. This required such virtues as legalism, compromise, and economic enterprise. Because Greek men associated these virtues with women, their respect for female qualities tended to increase. Also, in the new cities, as in many a frontier society, women were more often permitted to inherit and use property.

It was an era of powerful queens: Olympias, Alexander the Great's mother, played kingmaker after her son's death. Arsinoe II Philadelphus was co-ruler of Egypt with her husband (who was also her brother) for five years at the height of Ptolemaic prosperity around 275 B.C. The most famous Hellenistic woman, Cleopatra VII, was queen of Egypt from 51 to 30 B.C. A brilliant and ambitious strategist, she nearly succeeded in winning a world empire for her family. Among her lovers were two of the most powerful men in the world, the Romans Julius Caesar and Mark Antony.

Writers in the new Hellenistic cities often described freedom of movement for women. Although women generally continued to need a male guardian to represent them in public, in some situations, at least in Egypt (where the evidence is most plentiful), a woman could represent herself and petition the government on her own behalf. Widows and mothers of illegitimate children could give their daughters in marriage or apprentice their sons. A few cities granted women citizenship or even permitted them to hold public office. Some Hellenistic cities admitted women to the gymnasium, previously a male preserve. Heretofore only Sparta had promoted physical education for women, but by the first century A.D. women were even competing in the great Pan-Hellenic games.

The Hellenistic period also saw the re-emergence of women poets and the first appearance of women philosophers in the West. Before dying at age 19, Erinna, who lived on the Aegean island of Telos during the late fourth century B.C., wrote the *Distaff*, a 300-line poem in memory of girlhood that was famous in antiquity. Hipparchia of Maroneia (b. ca. 350 B.C.), like her husband, Crates of Thebes, studied Cynic philosophy. The Cynics, like another philosophical school, the Epicureans, supported a measure of equality between women and men. Hipparchia and Crates led an itinerant life as popular teachers and the Hellenistic equivalent of counselors.

Much of the explanation for the relative freedom of elite women lies in the new economic power of this group. There was probably a connection between one Phile's ability to hold a magistracy in Priene (in Anatolia) in the first century B.C. and her control of the financial resources to build the town a reservoir and an aqueduct. In many cities women could sell land, borrow money, and decide whether their husbands could make loans or contracts on the strength of their dowry. Free women could manumit slaves.

Philosophy and Religion

The intensely civic and individualistic philosophy of the Hellenic period evolved in new ways in the immense and impersonal realms of the Hellenistic world. Thinkers elaborated systems of ideas that focused on ethics, on a quest for peace of mind in confusing times, on ideas that were therapeutic.

Some thinkers taught that only by suspending judgment about great philosophical questions, accepting traditions, and avoiding politics could one find happiness. Such thinkers came to be called Skeptics. Others believed that happiness could be attained only by satisfying one's needs in the simplest possible ways. Such thinkers flouted conventions—luxury, comfort, fame—and came to be called Cynics. The name derives from the Greek word *kuon* meaning "dog," a creature the Greeks believed to be shameless.

Of more lasting importance were the Stoics and Epicureans. Stoicism, the philosophy taught by Zeno (335–263 B.C.), takes its name from the Stoa Poikile (the "painted porch"), where the master taught. Like Plato and Aristotle, Zeno sought an absolute standard of good. He found it in the divine reason (*logos*), which he considered the organizing principle of the universe. According to Zeno, a good life was to be spent pursuing wisdom, serving others, and freeing oneself from all passion—hence our word *stoical*, meaning indifferent to pain. For the stoic, self-denial led not to pain but to peace of mind. Stoics believed that all people had equal access to the divine reason and taught human brotherhood. Later Roman and Christian writers embraced many principles of stoicism.

Epicureanism descends from Epicurus (341–270 B.C.). Whereas Zeno taught in public, Epicurus held forth in a private garden. Zeno encouraged political participation but Epicurus counseled withdrawal from public life. "Calm" and "Live in hiding" are famous Epicurean maxims. For Epicureans the goal of life was the avoidance of pain and the cultivation of intellectual pleasure—*hedone* in Greek. Today *hedonism* and even *epicureanism* connote the pursuit of sensual excess, but in antiquity Epicureans were admired for the austerity of their lives.

Just as new social conditions provoked challenges to traditional philosophy, so too the Olympian deities came in for criticism. Among many new religious movements in the Hellenistic period, three stand out: the divinization of kings, the cult of Tyche, and the mystery religions. Under the Ptolemies and Seleucids, the ruler-worship that Alexander had demanded became standard practice. In some places Tyche, the goddess of fortune, was worshiped as the protector of a particular city. The mystery religions, so called because their adherents were initiated into secret rites and mysteries, offered ethical guidance, release from worries, and reassurance about suffering and death.

An important but unintended consequence of Alexander's conquests was the mixing of Greek and Jewish cultures. When the Macedonians conquered Judea, many upper-class Jews found Greek culture very attractive. They abandoned their ancestral customs for the Greek gymnasium, theater, and political institutions. Hellenizing Jews had Jerusalem proclaimed a Greek polis and rededicated the Temple to Zeus in 167 B.C. Traditionalists resisted and rallied the Jewish masses into opposition. A guerrilla revolt soon arose led by the Hasmonean family, also known as the Maccabees, whose successes are celebrated by Jews today at Hanukkah. The Seleucids were forced to tolerate an independent state under the Hasmonean dynasty.

In the meantime, millions of Jews had settled in Egypt, Syria, Anatolia, and Greece itself. It is estimated that Jews made up 40 percent of the population of Alexandria in the first century A.D. The growing visibility of such a large minority occasionally sparked anti-Semitic literature as well as violence and oppression.

SUMMARY

Ancient Greece witnessed the very first examples of philosophy, and the dramatic arts of comedy and tragedy, as well as vibrant innovations in science, politics, history-writing, sculpture, and painting. This surge of creativity occurred under various conditions, but, in general, the fo-

cus of Greek life and art was the city-state, or polis, wherein public duty was promoted as more
important than private advantage.

There were many tensions and contradictions. The Greeks invented democracy while at
the same time limiting the freedom of women
and immigrants, oppressing slaves, and engaging in imperialism. Although the Greeks originated the concept that natural phenomena have
natural causes, they nonetheless recognized the
power of the irrational—be it divine whims or
human emotions. With its democracy, freedom,
and high culture, Athens stands for one side of
the achievement of the polis while Sparta, with
its hierarchy, militarism, and austerity, stands for
another. The greatest of their art explored these
tensions.

Athens reached its peak under Pericles,
whose leadership in the mid-fifth century B.C.
ushered in a time of empire, prosperity, and cultural greatness. The major tragedians were all active, and the sophistic movement was at its most
optimistic and progressive. Periclean Athens was
unique, if not for the sheer concentration of talent, then for the sense that the state, the cultural
elite, and the people were united in a common
pursuit.

If later times witnessed a fall from that state
of grace, they did not suffer any decline in creative achievement. The Peloponnesian War
(431–404 B.C.) marked the beginning of a century
in which Greek warfare was more brutal than before. Yet this century also witnessed, among
other cultural achievements, the comedies of
Aristophanes, the history-writing of Herodotus
and Thucydides, and the philosophy of Socrates,
Plato, and Aristotle.

After Alexander the Great, culture continued
to thrive, though in very different ways. In the Hellenistic age, Greeks flourished alongside native
cultures in the multi-ethnic kingdoms of the
Ptolemies and Seleucids. Although Greeks and
Macedonians dominated these regimes, they never
imposed homogeneity, either in politics or culture.

The most important Greek cultural development of the age was a retreat from a complex of
values associated with the citizen-warrior ideal of
the Classical city-state. The polis came under the
shadow of federal leagues and kingdoms; philosophers questioned the very point of political activity. Women's role in public and private life grew
more active and valued. The female nude became
as important a subject for sculptors as the male
nude. Hellenistic women were freer than their predecessors in their movement and their ability to
hold property and have some say in public life.

NOTES

1. Excerpt from a poem by Solon, cited in Aristotle,
   Constitution of Athens, trans. Barry S. Strauss.
2. Charles Rowan Beye, *Ancient Greek Literature and
   Society*, 2d ed., rev. (Ithaca, N.Y.: Cornell University
   Press, 1987), p. 78.
3. Ibid., p. 79.

SUGGESTED READING

Beye, C. R. *Ancient Greek Literature and Society.* 2d ed.
   1987. A witty and readable analysis from Homer to
   the Hellenistic era.
Biers, W. *The Archaeology of Ancient Greece: An Introduction.* Rev. ed. 1987. A clear presentation of the
   achievements and variety of archaeological excavation of Greece.
Burkert, Walter. *Greek Religion.* 1985. A thorough and
   logical introduction.
Cohen, Shaye. *From the Maccabees to the Mishnah.* 1987.
   Excellent introduction by a distinguished scholar of
   Second Temple Judaism.
Crawford, Dorothy J. *Kerkeosiris: An Egyptian Village in
   the Ptolemaic Period.* 1971. A fascinating glimpse of
   local social history.
Dover, K. J. *Greek Homosexuality.* Updated edition.
   1989. A judicious introduction, with emphases on
   Athens, oratory, and vase painting.
Fantham, Elaine, Helene Peet Foley, et al. *Women in the
   Classical World: Text and Image.* 1995. Scholarly and
   readable introduction, up to date and well illus-
   trated.
Grant, Michael. *Cleopatra.* 1972. A very readable biography, well documented and nicely illustrated.
Green, P. *Alexander to Actium: An Essay in the Historical
   Evolution of the Hellenistic Age.* 1989. A collection of elegant essays synthesizing scholarship on a wide variety of topics in political, cultural, and social history.

Hall, Edith. *Inventing the Barbarian. Greek Self-Definition Through Tragedy.* 1989. Discusses the notion of the enemy as barbarian, as it emerges in fifth-century B.C. Athenian literature.

Hamilton, J. R. *Alexander the Great.* 1973. A reliable and remarkably concise introduction.

Humphreys, S. C. *The Family, Women and Death: Comparative Studies.* 2d ed. 1993. Provocative and stimulating essays, influenced by anthropology, on Classical Athenian society.

Hutchinson, G. O. *Hellenistic Poetry.* 1988. A good introduction, with an emphasis on the third century B.C.

Just, Roger. *Women in Athenian Law and Life.* 1989. A careful examination of the evidence to reconstruct the reality and ideology of women in Athens in the fifth and fourth centuries B.C.

Kuhrt, Amélie, and Susan Sherwin-White. *From Samarkhand to Sardis: A New Approach to the Seleucid Empire.* 1993. An important and controversial book. The authors argue that Seleucid rule was more multicultural than is usually thought.

Lloyd, G. E. R. *Early Greek Science: Thales to Aristotle.* 1971. A thoughtful and readable discussion of science in its social and cultural context.

Long, A. A. *Hellenistic Philosophy: Stoics, Epicureans, Sceptics.* 2d ed. 1986. A concise critical analysis of the ideas and methods of the major Hellenistic philosophers.

Morgan, Catherine. *Athletes and Oracles: The Transformation of Olympia and Delphi in the Eighth Century B.C.* 1990. An archaeological and historical study of the role of religious sanctuaries and athletic games in the rise of the Greek polis.

Pomeroy, Sarah B. *Goddesses, Whores, Wives, and Slaves: Women in Classical Antiquity.* 1975. An overview of women in politics and society in Greece, the Hellenistic world, and Rome.

——. *Women in Hellenistic Egypt from Alexander to Cleopatra.* 1984. A social history that documents women's growing autonomy.

Powell, Anton. *Athens and Sparta: Constructing Greek Political and Social History from 478 B.C.* 1988. A lively and scholarly introduction to the social and political history of the two most prominent Greek city-states of the fifth century B.C.

Strauss, Barry S. *Athens After the Peloponnesian War: Class, Faction, and Policy, 403–386 B.C.* 1987. A case study of the interaction of politics and society and of war and peace in Classical Athens.

Thomas, Rosalind. *Literacy and Orality in Ancient Greece.* 1992. A demonstration that ancient culture was primarily oral rather than written.

Vermeule, Emily. *Greece in the Bronze Age.* 1964, new preface 1972. Though written before some important excavations and discoveries of the past thirty years, this is still the best and most thorough overview of Greece from its beginnings to around 1100 B.C.

Von Staden, Heinrich. *Herophilus: The Art of Medicine in Early Alexandria.* 1989. A detailed, scholarly account.

CHAPTER 3

Rome: From Republic to Empire, ca. 509–44 B.C.

There are many monuments to the ancient Romans, ranging from amphitheaters and aqueducts to Spanish, French, and the other languages derived from Latin, the language of the Romans. The Romans were also innovators in legal science and masters of political mythmaking and propaganda. Yet they are probably best known as imperialists who turned an Italian city-state into one of the largest empires in history, comprising all the countries of the Mediterranean as well as substantial parts of western Asia and northern and central Europe. By holding this empire for centuries and by fostering prosperity, Rome planted in what would become Britain, France, Germany, and Spain (among other places) the seeds of the advanced civilizations of the Mediterranean.

Rome's innovation in civic behavior resonates in the modern vocabulary of politics—*president*, *inauguration*, and *forum* can all be traced back to Rome. After an early period of monarchy, Rome was for centuries a republic (Latin, *res publica*, literally "public business") before essentially becoming a monarchy again under the Caesars. The Roman Republic was far more hierarchical than Greek democracy. Greek democrats governed themselves; Romans elected their leaders, aristocrats with wide powers of office. To create an effective and stable regime, the elite divided power among separate government bodies, creating a system of checks and balances that tended toward consensus.

Fueled by fear, ambition, and greed, Roman expansion generated its own momentum. Masters of war and diplomacy, the Romans unknowingly weakened their society with every stone they added to the edifice of the empire. Romans borrowed from other societies, in particular from the

Greeks, with remarkable open-mindedness. Also fascinating is the shrewdness with which the Romans extended citizenship to conquered peoples, thereby strengthening Rome's grip.

Historians conventionally divide the Republic into three periods: Early (509–287 B.C.), Middle (287–133 B.C.), and Late (133–31 B.C.). This chapter begins with the origins of the city of Rome in the early first millennium B.C. and then traces the Republic from its foundation to its imperial conquests to its collapse under their weight.

≈ *Questions and Ideas to Consider*

- Describe the foundation of Rome and its development into a republic. List some of the factors that complicate our knowledge of these events.

- Discuss the Roman family. What was the relationship between family patterns and the structure of government?

- How were plebeians able to negotiate with patricians? What were their demands, and how successful were they in achieving these demands?

- Describe the origins of the Punic Wars. In what way were these wars representative of Roman expansion in general?

- There is a fascinating relationship between Roman success and Roman failure. Name at least two ways that the conquest of, or interaction with, a given area changed Roman society, economy, or culture.

BEFORE THE REPUBLIC

Romans believed that their city was founded by Romulus, the descendant of immigrants to Italy from far-off Troy. In the first century B.C., a Roman scholar even supplied a precise date for the founding: April 27, 753 B.C., by our reckoning. Although the name "Romulus" supplies a convenient etymology for "Rome," little stock can be placed in this story. No history of Rome was writ-

ten before the late third century B.C.—five hundred years after 753 B.C. Nevertheless, archaeology provides some confirmation of Roman tradition. Tombs from the tenth century B.C. have been found in Rome, and the first evidence of buildings comes from the eighth century B.C. A simple village of farmers and shepherds—a collection of huts—was established then on the Palatine Hill, one of the seven hills of what would be Rome and the place where tradition puts the settlement of 753. Other, similar settlements, followed on two or three of Rome's other hills (see inset, Map 3.2).

What, then, were Rome's origins? How did it grow? By examining the findings of archaeology and those elements in ancient historiography that seem to be based on accurate tradition, we can answer these questions, at least in outline.

Archaic Rome and Its Neighbors

Italy is a long peninsula, shaped roughly like a boot, extending about 750 miles from the Alps into the Mediterranean (Map 3.1). In the far north, the high Alps provide a barrier, though not an impenetrable one, to the rest of Europe. The Adriatic Sea to the east separates Italy from modern Slovenia and Croatia; to the west, the Tyrrhenian Sea faces the large islands of Sardinia and Corsica (and the smaller, but iron-rich island of Elba) and the coasts of France and Spain beyond. Across from the "toe" of the Italian boot, and separated from the mainland by a narrow, 3-mile strait of water, is the island of Sicily, large and in antiquity agriculturally rich. Sicily is only 90 miles from North Africa. Italy is thus centrally located in the Mediterranean and was both a tempting target for conquerors and a convenient springboard for conquest.

Italy's geographic regions comprise some of the ancient Mediterranean's most fertile and metal-rich land. There are many alluvial plains flanking sizable rivers. Traveling south along the west coast of Italy, one enters in turn the lowland alluvial plains of Etruria (modern Tuscany), Latium (the region of Rome), and Campania (the region of Naples). Although the Apennine mountains run southward along most of the Italian peninsula, they are low compared with the Alps and contain many passes, permitting the movement of armies.

In the first millennium B.C., Italy comprised a complex mix of peoples and languages. They included the Etruscans in the north, Greek colonists along the southern Italian coast and in Sicily, and such Apennine peoples as the Sabines, northeast of Rome, and the Samnites to the south. Latium was home to a number of small Latin-speaking towns, one of them Rome. In the fifth century B.C. another important people arrived on the Italian scene: Celts (called Gauls by the Romans), large numbers of whom crossed the Alps and settled in northern Italy. Most of these peoples spoke Indo-European languages, of which Latin, the language of the Romans (among other peoples of Latium), was one.

Rome's location in Latium gave it a central and strategic position in the Italian peninsula. Located 15 miles inland on the Tiber River, Rome was near the sea but far enough away to be safe from sea raiders. The seven hills of the city also offered defensive protection. A midstream island made Rome the first crossing place upstream from the Tiber's mouth, offering the Romans access north and south.

In the seventh century B.C., Archaic Rome (as the pre-Republican period is called) began to be transformed from a large village into a city. Signs of urbanization included Rome's first stone houses, first public building, and the first forum, or civic center. In the sixth century, streets, walls, drains, temples, and a racetrack followed. What caused the transformation? Probably the most important cause was contact with Magna Graecia, the Greek colonies to the south (see Map 3.1). Established in the eighth and seventh centuries B.C., the colonies transported westward the sophisticated urban civilization of the eastern Mediterranean.

More controversial was the impact of Rome on its neighbors to the north, the Etruscans. The twelve Etruscan city-states were organized in a loose confederation centered in Etruria. They grew wealthy from mining iron, copper, and silver, from piracy and trade, and from a network of influential Etruscan emigrants in central Italy, possibly including Rome's last three kings (traditionally dated 616–509 B.C.).

CHAPTER CHRONOLOGY

753–509 B.C.	Monarchy (traditional dates)
509–287 B.C.	Early Republic
494 B.C.	Latin League formed
449 B.C.	Law of the Twelve Tables
445 B.C.	Plebeian-patrician intermarriage permitted
367 B.C.	Consulship opened to plebeians
338 B.C.	Latin League dissolved; Roman citizenship extended
287 B.C.	Decisions of plebs legally binding
287–133 B.C.	Middle Republic
264–146 B.C.	Punic Wars
146 B.C.	Rome destroys Carthage and Corinth
133–31 B.C.	Late Republic
91–89 B.C.	Social War
66–62 B.C.	Pompey's eastern campaigns
58–50 B.C.	Caesar conquers Gaul
44 B.C.	Assassination of Julius Caesar

Scholars have long believed that the Etruscans conquered Rome and left a significant cultural and material legacy. Recent work, however, suggests a pattern of cross-fertilization and emigration rather than conquest; it argues that the Etruscan legacy in Rome was superficial. According to this view, to the extent that any outside culture influenced Archaic Rome, it was the Greeks—who also influenced the Etruscans and other central Italian peoples, for that matter. The Etruscan city-states were similar to Rome; they were its peer, not its elder sibling.

The new theory seems more plausible than the traditional one, given what we know of other ancient societies, but since so little evidence survives from Archaic Rome, we must be cautious. Our inability to decipher the Etruscan language also dictates caution. There is no need to be wary

Latium (inset map)

Roman territory, ca. 500 B.C.

Etruscans of Etruria
Expansion of Etruscans
Greeks
Carthaginians
OSCI Other peoples

Etruscan Tomb Painting
This wall painting from Tarquinia shows a married aristocratic couple at a banquet. The style of the figures is derived from Greek art, but the depiction of husband and wife dining on the same couch is characteristically Etruscan. (*National Museum, Tarquinia/Scala/Art Resource, NY*)

about noting the Etruscans' rich artistic legacy, however, or the high status of Etruscan elite women compared to their Greek and Roman counterparts. Etruscan women kept their own names, and Etruscan children bore the names of both parents. Etruscan elite women were welcome to attend athletic contests in spite of the presence of naked male athletes.

The Roman Monarchy, 753–509 B.C.

Tradition says that Rome was ruled by seven kings before the founding of the Republic. Although the number of kings may be a later in-

Map 3.1 Early Italy and Region of City of Rome.
Early Italy comprised a variety of terrain and peoples. Rome was located in the central Italian region of Latium. The Alps separate Italy from northern Europe. The Apennine mountain range runs almost the entire length of the Italian peninsula. Much of the rest of Italy is fertile plain.

vention, there is no doubt about the existence of the monarchy, which left its traces in Republican institutions. The king's power, called *imperium* (from *imperare*, "to command"), was very great, embracing religious, military, and judicial affairs. The king was advised by a council of elders, called the "fathers" (*patres* in Latin) or the "senate" (*senatus*, from *senex*, "old man").

In theory the senate was primarily an advisory body, but in practice it was quite powerful. Senators were often the heads of the most important families in Rome, so the king rejected their advice at his peril. Most senators were patricians, as early Rome's hereditary aristocracy was known. The rest of the people, the bulk of Roman society, were called plebeians. Plebeians were free; most were ordinary people, though some were wealthy. Patricians monopolized the senate and priesthoods, and they did not intermarry with plebeians. In the early years of the Republic, the patricians wore red shoes so that they would be easily differentiated from the rank and file.

Early Rome was a class-based society, but it was not closed to foreigners. Among others, Etruscans, Sabines, and Latins—as the inhabitants of other Latin-speaking towns were called—came to Rome. Unlike Athenians, who tried to hide the presence of immigrants in their country by a myth of indigenous origins, Romans openly discussed their mixed roots. At first, foreigners had a subordinate status, but they gained equality around 550 B.C. Military pressure made it necessary to expand the body of loyal infantrymen, so native Romans decided to incorporate the immigrants into their community. When Rome adopted the hoplite phalanx, any man with enough property to afford the necessary training and equipment could serve as a hoplite or cavalryman.

Like the early Greeks, the Romans moved toward a notion of citizenship based on military service. As in early Greece, military change bred political upheaval in Rome. Within several generations of the development of the Roman hoplite phalanx, Rome went from monarchy to republic.

SOCIETY AND CULTURE OF THE ROMAN REPUBLIC

The traditional date of the overthrow of the kings and the establishment of the Republic is 509 B.C. This event was probably part of a long process rather than a dramatic upheaval. Some scholars reject the date of 509 and put the transition years later. The Early Republic left us only a few documents as to its origins: inscriptions, temple dedications, and lists of public officeholders. For a coherent account, it is necessary to turn to the works of Roman historians. Written centuries after the events, these works tend to embroider the evidence—so, again, we must be cautious.

According to the historian Livy (59 B.C.–A.D. 17), the overthrow of the monarchy was an act of vengeance. The tyrant Tarquinius Superbus (r. ca. 534–509 B.C.) had imposed cruel and arbitrary rule on the Romans. After long humiliation, the Romans revolted when the king's son, Sextus, raped Lucretia, an aristocratic, married, Roman

woman. In Livy's version, Sextus forced himself on Lucretia by threatening to kill her and claim that he had found her in bed with a slave. Lucretia told her husband, Tarquinius Collatinus, and his kinsman, Lucius Junius Brutus, of Sextus's crime, then killed herself with her own dagger. To avenge her, Collatinus and Brutus drove out the Tarquin kings and established the Republic. This story is representative of Roman ideals: For Lucretia, honor—her own and that of her family—was more important than life.

The Roman Household

The Latin word *familia* is broader than the English word *family*: Better translated as "household," it included slaves, animals, and property, as well as the members of a nuclear family and their ancestors or descendants. The familia was the basic unit of Roman society. A center of production and consumption, it was also a model of political authority. In theory though not always in practice, the Roman household was an authoritarian institution governed by a man; thus, the familia was an example of patriarchy.

The legal head of the familia was the *paterfamilias*, the oldest living man—usually the father in a nuclear family, though occasionally the grandfather or, in cases of unusual longevity, the great-grandfather. According to Roman law, the paterfamilias had supreme power within the household. Although he was supposed to call a council of senior male relatives to consult on major decisions, he was not required to follow their advice. He had the right to sell family members into slavery and the rarely used power to kill an errant wife or child. A son, no matter how old, was always legally subject to the authority of a living paterfamilias. Only the paterfamilias could own property free and clear. Thus, a 30-year-old man might still be under the authority of his paterfamilias and dependent on him for an allowance.

Roman respect for the paterfamilias stemmed from Roman esteem for ancestors, who were far more important than in Greek culture. All patricians and some plebeians belonged to a *gens* (plural, *gentes*), a kinship group that traced its ancestry to a purported common ancestor. All Roman males had a personal and family name, and patricians and elite plebeians also had a third (middle) name, indicating their gens: for example, Gaius Julius Caesar (100–44 B.C.), whose personal name, Gaius, was followed by the gens name, Julius, and the familia name, Caesar.

In theory, the paterfamilias was the focus of power in the household, but practice was more complex. The sources are full of indications of fathers' affection, love, and even indulgence for their children. Moreover, given the low life expectancies, it was common for a man of 25 to have already buried his father. Many adult men were independent of a paterfamilias.

Roman women never became legally independent, even on the death of a paterfamilias. Instead of receiving a personal name, a daughter was called by the name of her father's gens. For example, Gaius Julius Caesar's daughter was called Julia; if Caesar had had a second daughter, she would have been Julia Secunda ("Julia the Second"). Although fathers were expected to support all their sons, they had to support only the first of their daughters. A father also arranged a daughter's marriage and provided her with a dowry. In theory, again, it was a severe relationship, but the evidence suggests considerable father-daughter affection, including married daughters who sought advice or aid from their fathers. Families controlled their size through the "exposure" of physically unfit or otherwise unwanted children. Infants were left in the open either to die or, as was more likely, to be adopted or raised as a slave.

Most women in early Rome married *cum manu* (literally, "with hand")—that is, they were "handed over" to their husbands, who became their new paterfamilias. Roman wives and mothers had more prestige and freedom than their counterparts in Classical Greece. Legends of early Rome mention some women who were peacemakers and negotiators. Roman women regularly shared meals and social activities with their parents and generally took an active interest in their husband's political life. Wealthy women led active lives, supervising the household slaves, guiding their children's education, giving and attending parties, and monitoring their own property.

The hierarchy of the household was applied to Roman society and politics. Romans conceived of the state as a collection of heads of household, each head competing for honor for his own familia and gens. The imperium (power) of the chief magistrates was analogous to the supreme power of the paterfamilias. An ordinary Roman was expected to obey the magistrates, just as he would obey his paterfamilias.

Patrons and Clients

Patron (from *pater,* "father") means "defender" or "protector." *Client* means "dependent." Roman society consisted of pyramidlike patron-client networks. Most patrons were themselves clients of someone more powerful; only a very few stood at the top of the pyramid. In the Roman view, justice required not equality between patron and client but mutual respect and obligation.

Various paths led to the status of client. A peasant in need of help on his farm might ask a wealthy neighbor to become his patron. A manumitted slave became the client of his former owner. A conquered foe became the client of the victorious general. The status of client or patron was hereditary.

Patron and client helped each other in many ways. A patron might provide a client with food or property for a dowry. He might settle disputes or provide legal assistance. In return, a client owed his patron respect and service. He escorted his patron in public on important occasions, because possession of a large clientele signified prestige and power. If his patron sought political office, the client voted for him. If his patron needed money, the client was obligated to contribute, perhaps to an election campaign or to pay fines or ransoms.

Cloaked in an elaborate language of goodwill, the patron-client relationship was considered a matter of *fides* ("good faith" or "trustworthiness"). Romans spoke not of a client submitting to a patron's power but rather of a client "commending himself" to the patron's fides. A patron spoke not of his clients but of his "friends," especially if they were men of standing. A patron was supposed to put clients before kin by marriage; only blood or adoptive relations took precedence. The Twelve Tables, a Roman law code of the mid-fifth century B.C., declared that a patron who defrauds his client is accursed and may be killed with impunity.

Patronage undergirded Roman domestic politics and foreign relations. Although Republican political institutions appeared to work through free elections and popular choice, the obligations of humble clients to wealthy patrons took precedence. If a man's clients grew discontented, another ambitious politician might offer himself as their new patron, leading in turn to political change. As for foreign affairs, experience as patrons schooled Roman leaders to treat the peoples they conquered as clients, often as personal clients. The Roman state sometimes took foreign countries into its collective fides, allowing Rome to extend its influence without the constraints of a formal alliance.

Religion and World-View

If we knew nothing about early Roman religion, we could deduce much about it from the familia and patronage. We would expect to find elements of patriarchy and contractualism, and both are indeed present. The task of a Roman priest, whether an official of the state or an individual paterfamilias, was to establish what the Romans called the "peace of the gods." Roman cults aimed at obtaining the gods' agreement to human requests, at "binding" the gods—the Latin term for which is *religio*.

The earliest Roman religion was animistic, centering on the belief that spirits haunted households, fields, and forests and determined the weather. The spirit of the hearth was Vesta; of the door, Janus; of the rain and sun, Jupiter (later identified with the Greek sky-god and the father-god Zeus); of crops and vegetation, Mars (later identified with the Greek war-god Ares). The Romans believed that these spirits needed to be appeased—hence the contractual nature of their prayers and offerings. Over the years, as a result

of Greek influence, anthropomorphism (that is, the worship of humanlike gods and goddesses) supplanted Roman animism.

Roman state religion grew out of house religion. Vesta, the hearth-goddess, became goddess of the civic hearth; Janus, the door-god, became god of the city's gates; Jupiter became the general overseer of the gods; and Mars became the god of war. When trade and conquest brought the Romans into contact with foreign religions, the Romans tended to absorb them. The senate screened and sometimes rejected new gods, but by and large Roman polytheism was tolerant.

The Republic sponsored numerous priestly committees, or colleges, to secure the peace of the gods. Originally restricted to patricians, most of the highest priesthoods were opened to plebeians by law in 300 B.C. Although some priesthoods were full-time jobs, most left the officeholder free to pursue a concurrent career as a magistrate or senator. The two most important priestly colleges were the augurs, who were in charge of divination, and the pontiffs, who exercised a general supervisory function over Rome's numerous rituals, sacrifices, offerings, prayers, temples, and festivals. The chief pontiff, the *pontifex maximus*, was the head of the state clergy. Until the fourth century B.C., the pontiffs alone controlled the interpretation of the law. The Romans allowed priests to interpret the law on the theory that an offense against humans was also an offense against the gods.

There were only two colleges of priestesses: those of Ceres, goddess of fertility and death, and those of the Vestal Virgins. The six Vestals were servants of the shrine of Vesta, the goddess of the hearth and the protector of families. Their job was to tend the eternal flame of Rome and make sure that it never went out, for Romans feared their city would be destroyed if the flame ever died. The Vestals were the only Roman women not under the authority of a paterfamilias. Chosen between the ages of 6 and 10 by the pontifex maximus, they remained virgins for thirty years. Their chastity symbolized the safety of the Roman family and that of the city itself.

By the Early Republic, class distinctions abounded in Rome. The elite papered over such differences by promoting an ideology of simple and austere farmers' virtues—discipline, hard work, frugality, temperance, and the avoidance of public displays of affection even between spouses. The supreme value of the household was *pietas*—devotion and loyalty to the familia, the gods, and the state. Household duties and gender obligations were clearly defined. Women were to be chaste, modest, and practical. Men were to display self-control and constancy and project *gravitas* (weight, seriousness), never lightness or levity. The masculine ideal was *virtus* (literally, "manliness"), which indicated excellence in war and government.

Roman men who attained virtus considered themselves entitled to the reward of *dignitas*, meaning not only public esteem but also a dignified position and official rank. The ultimate test of virtus, however, was war.

GOVERNMENT AND SOCIETY IN THE EARLY AND MIDDLE REPUBLIC, CA. 509–133 B.C.

The history of Republican politics is both as simple as the patriarchal framework of the Roman household and as complex as the crosscurrents of affection and manipulation that ran through it. Although Rome had no written constitution, a hierarchical arrangement of public officials and popular assemblies emerged by the third century B.C. Documentation is poor for the earlier period, and though there are later records that shed light on earlier practice, these present several problems of interpretation. Rome's constitutional forms often masked the realities of elite power and manipulation. Furthermore, perhaps the best source for the mid-Republican constitution, the historian Polybius (ca. 200–ca. 118 B.C.), a Greek and former hostage who lived in Rome, used Greek categories to analyze the Roman government, producing considerable distortion.

Political Institutions

Ancient theorists divided Roman political institutions into three branches: executive, deliberative, and legislative. Influenced by the Romans, the American founders adopted a similar division, but with the legislative and deliberative functions combined and a judicial branch added. In Rome, various magistrates of the executive branch administered justice in addition to their other responsibilities. The Roman senate, which made up the deliberative branch, was far more powerful than the American senate. The Roman legislative branch consisted of several popular assemblies.

The three parts of the Roman constitution, then, were the magistrates, the senate, and the people. Polybius described the Middle Republic as a "mixed constitution": the assemblies, a democratic element; the senate, an oligarchic element; and the magistrates, a royal element. Polybius's model of power-sharing was elegant but wrong. Hierarchy characterized Roman government, just as it did Roman society and the household. In the Early Republic the magistrates were very strong; in the Middle Republic the senate was the dominant power.

Executive power lay in the hands of the magistrates. They were more powerful and more elite figures than their counterparts in Greek democracies. Magistrates were elected by the Roman people rather than chosen by lottery, as in Greek democracy. Election required extensive campaigning, which in turn necessitated many clients. Magistracies were time-consuming jobs but offered no salary, unlike public office in Greek democracy. Only a wealthy, elite few could afford to be magistrates; almost all magistrates came from senatorial families. Competition for office among the elite was intense.

Eager for strong, effective magistrates but ever fearful that power might lead to corruption, Rome limited the tenure of office to only one year. The chief magistrates were eventually called consuls, of which there were two. Each consul had the power to veto the other's actions. Like the former king, each consul had imperium, the power to issue commands and order punishments, including execution.

From about 500 B.C. to about 300 B.C., other magistracies emerged to assist the consuls as administration grew more complex. Most important were the censors. Every four or five years, two ex-consuls were elected for an eighteen-month term as censor. At first their job was to supervise the census, the military register of citizens that recorded each man's property class. Later the censors began to punish those they considered bad citizens by consigning them to a lower census class. Censors could expel a man from the senate by simply placing a black spot next to his name. In this way, the censors became supervisors of public morals.

The Republic's government adapted flexibly to emergencies and changing borders. In times of emergency the Republic turned over power to a single magistrate. The dictator, as he was called, held imperium, and his decisions were beyond appeal, but he held office for only six months. Another sign of adaptability was the practice of promagistracy—that is, extending a magistrate's imperium past the normal term of office or temporarily investing a private citizen with imperium. First employed in the fourth century B.C., promagistracy met Rome's needs as a conquering power by greatly expanding the pool of leaders able to serve as administrators and commanders away from home.

The deliberative branch was the senate, which guided and advised the magistrates. During most of the Republic, it consisted of three hundred men. In the third century B.C. and later, one became a senator after holding a magistracy. Senators served for life. The senators' decisions were not legally binding, but their exalted social status—which they proclaimed in clothing as well as speech—made them difficult to ignore. Since magistrates hoped to become senators after their term was finished, they cultivated a congenial relationship. The senate sent and received ambassadors and supervised expenditures. Although the centuriate assembly, which we turn to next, formally declared war and ratified treaties, the senate was otherwise in charge of foreign policy.

The legislative branch of the constitution consisted of four popular assemblies: the curiate assembly, the centuriate assembly, the council of the plebs, and the tribal assembly. Roman assemblies were not democratic: Women were barred; assembly participants received no salary for attendance; and the ordinary Roman was unlikely to speak, if he participated at all. The patron-client system greatly constrained a client's voting freedom.

The curiate assembly was a survival from the period of monarchy, and it held a largely ceremonial role. The centuriate assembly better suited the military oligarchy of the Republic. Based on a military formation (the century was the smallest unit of the Roman army), this assembly offered the façade of popular participation but the reality of control by the wealthy. The assembly was divided according to wealth into census classes of fighting men. They voted in order of wealth. First came the equestrians, or cavalrymen, then five classes of infantrymen, and finally the *proletarii* ("breeders"), men who could not provide their own arms but could offer the state their fertility. Since the wealthiest men constituted an easy majority, they had all the power in this important body. The centuriate assembly elected consuls and lesser magistrates and, when needed, dictators. It voted on laws and treaties, accepted declarations of war and peace, and acted as a court in cases of treason and homicide.

The two other assemblies rose to prominence later: the council of the plebs and the tribal assembly. To understand this evolution, we turn now to the class conflicts in Rome during the fifth through third centuries B.C.

Conflict of the Orders

Social and political conflict, usually considered a struggle between the patrician and plebeian orders, tested the Roman state between 494 and 287 B.C. As in Archaic Greece, a relatively stable regime emerged: oligarchies and democracies in Greece, the Republic in Rome. As Rome reached a domestic political consensus, it presented an ever stronger military front to its external opponents. By 300 B.C., Rome was ready to grow from local power to dominance in Italy and then the Mediterranean.

Tradition gives Rome only 136 patrician families in 509 B.C., but they dominated the Early Republic. The plebs, in contrast, comprised masses of poor peasants and a tiny number of men who, though wealthy, were not patricians; there were plebeian artisans, traders, and shopkeepers, but they were only a small part of the population. All the plebeians wanted to break patrician power. Wealthy plebeians wanted unrestricted access to high office, from which they had been largely excluded. Ordinary plebeians demanded redistribution of land, codification and publication of the law, and relief from debt. For a century and a half, the two groups of plebeians made common cause, writing an important chapter in the history of political resistance.

Debt and hunger loomed large in the Early Republic. A form of debt-bondage called *nexum* forced a free man who defaulted on a loan to work off what he owed, often for the rest of his life. Plebeians wanted nexum abolished. The average peasant farm was too small to feed a family, rendering most peasants dependent on public land for farming and grazing. Time and again throughout Republican history, however, public land was occupied by the wealthy, who denied or restricted access to the poor.

In the fifth century B.C. the plebs organized themselves as a kind of state within the state, complete with their own assembly (the council of the plebs) and officials (the tribunes of the plebs). The decisions of the council of the plebs, called *plebiscita* (from which *plebiscite* comes), were binding only on the plebs; they did not achieve the full force of law for over two hundred years. Yet the plebs did not retreat. On several occasions during the Early Republic they resorted to secession: The plebs as a whole left the city for the Aventine Hill, where they stayed, refusing to serve in Rome's military, until their grievances were addressed (see inset, Map 3.2).

The ten tribunes, elected annually by the plebs, were the people's champions. A tribune's house always stood open to any plebeian who needed him, and he could not leave the city lim-its. Inside the city of Rome, a tribune also had the right to veto any act of the magistrates, assembly, or senate that harmed plebeians. In return, the plebs swore to treat the tribunes as sacrosanct and to lynch anyone who harmed them.

The patricians still had formidable resources. Patricians dominated important priesthoods. Thanks to patrician financial aid, patricians' many clients could afford to serve as heavy infantrymen and thereby render support for continued patrician rule. Furthermore, patricians exercised great power in the new tribal assembly, created around the same time as the council of the plebs, because the system of representation heavily favored landowners. The tribal assembly elected lower magistrates, voted on laws, and acted as a court of appeals.

Nevertheless, the plebeians pressed onward, wringing concession after concession from the patricians, until finally the patricians decided to divide the opposition by meeting the main demands of the plebeian elite. The outcome was a new, combined patrician-plebeian nobility. The compromise preserved most of the patricians' privileges. The personnel changed, but an elite continued to rule Rome.

Patricians made major concessions to wealthy plebeians and small concessions to poor ones. For example, a law code known as the "Twelve Tables" was published in 449 B.C. Though it was primitive and severe by modern standards, its very existence was a plebeian victory, because published law was accessible and dependable. Unfortunately, legal procedure remained a secret of the pontiffs for another 150 years, which ensured that no poor man could go to court without the help of a patron.

Around 445 B.C., the patricians accepted a law permitting patrician-plebeian intermarriage, a victory for wealthy plebeians. Rather than endure plebeians as consuls, however, patricians suspended the consulship altogether for about eighty years, sharing the consuls' powers among a group of military officers, most of them patricians. In 367 B.C., a compromise was reached: The consulship was re-established, and every year one of the two consuls had to be a plebeian. The same year a measure was passed for short-term debt relief. Nexum was finally abolished in 326 B.C.

After 367 B.C., the integration of patrician and plebeian elites proceeded despite conservative opposition. But the conventional starting date of the Middle Republic is not until 287 B.C., when the merging of the orders culminated in a law that made the decisions of the council of the plebs and the trial assembly binding. Although the patriciate survived and remained prestigious, its importance gradually declined. The new elite was based on wealth, not heredity. Its members were known as equestrians—men wealthy enough to serve as cavalrymen. The overwhelming majority of Romans remained excluded, as they had been from the patriciate.

Although ordinary plebeians had improved their lot, they still faced the twin problems of debt and land-hunger. No longer could they depend on wealthy plebeians as champions. Although their problems would come back with a vengeance in the Late Republic, plebeians found temporary relief in the new land that Rome acquired through conquest.

FROM ITALIAN CITY-STATE TO WORLD EMPIRE

At the beginning of the Republic (ca. 509 B.C.), Roman territory comprised about 500 square miles, about half the size of the state of Rhode Island. By 265 B.C., Rome controlled all of the Italian peninsula south of an imaginary line from Pisae (modern Pisa) to Ariminium (modern Rimini), an area of about 50,000 square miles (Map 3.2). In 146 B.C., Roman provinces included Sicily, Cisalpine Gaul (northernmost Italy), Sardinia, Corsica, and Spain. Once-great Carthage was the Roman province of Africa (roughly, modern Tunisia), and once-mighty Macedon was the province of Macedonia, whose governor was also effectively in charge of Greece. The Seleucid kingdom was free but fatally weakened. Rome was the supreme power between Gibraltar and the Levant. How and why did Rome reach this

height from its humble beginnings as a local power in Italy?

Republican Expansion: The Conquest of Italy, ca. 509–265 B.C.

There were several motives for Rome's expansion. Greed, particularly land-hunger, was a perennial theme, as was fear of outsiders. The personal ambitions of a warrior elite and the presence of conflict in early Italy were even more significant. Foreign adventure was a convenient way of deflecting plebeian energies. Also, Romans were frequently attacked by others, but often only after behavior by Rome had left its rivals little choice.

For the elite, victory in battle promised a reputation for virtus, the booty with which to reward clients, and success in a public career. Military achievement brought unique acclaim. Certain victorious generals were allowed to celebrate a triumph; there was no such triumph for peacemakers or distinguished judges or other public benefactors. The triumphant general rode a chariot through the city accompanied by his troops, by the spoils of victory including famous captives, and by magistrates and senators.

Rome could not have broken away from the Etruscans without warfare, but what began as a pragmatic response to immediate danger became a habit of meeting even remote threats with force. In the fourth century B.C., having gained control of Latium, Rome considered the Samnites of central and southern Italy to be a potential threat. In the third century B.C., once Rome controlled Italy, it felt threatened by Carthage. After Carthage, there was the threat of Macedon, Seleucid Syria, and so on. Sometimes Rome got embroiled in war when another power attacked a Roman client state and Rome was called upon to prove its trustworthiness as a patron.

Map 3.2 Roman Italy, ca. 265 B.C. Rome controlled a patchwork of conquered territory, colonies, and allied states in Italy, held together by a network of treaties and of roads. The city of Rome (inset) was built on seven hills beside the Tiber River.

ALPS

Extent of Roman Italy by 218 B.C.

Aquileia

Verona

Cremona

Po

Adige

Placentia

CISALPINE GAUL

Genua

Bononia

Ariminum (Rimini)

Ligurian Sea

Pisae (Pisa)

Arno

Florentia

Fanum Fortunae

Ancona

Arretium

UMBRIA

Castrum Truentinum

Populonia

ETRURIA

PICENUM

Elba

Saturnia

Castrum Novum

Corsica

Aleria

Tiber

Reate

Corfinium

Veii Rome

SAMNIUM

Appian Way

LATIUM

APULIA

Barium

Tarracina

CAMPANIA

Beneventum

Venusia

Brundisium

Capua

Appian Way

Sardinia

Misenum

Neapolis (Naples)

Paestum

LUCANIA

Tarentum

CALABRIA

Gulf of Tarentum

Neapolis

Thurii

Tyrrhenian Sea

Carales

Croton

BRUTTIUM

Messana

Locri

Rhegium

Mediterranean Sea

Lilybaeum

Sicily

Syracuse

Utica

Cape Bon

Hippo Regius

Carthage

Malta

NORTH AFRICA

Adriatic Sea

ILLYRIA

Rome inset

Rome

0   500   1000 M.

0   1500   3000 Ft.

Tiber

FIELD OF MARS

QUIRINAL HILL

VIMINAL HILL

CAPITOLINE MT.

Senate House

ESCULINE MT.

Forum

Regia

Temple of Jupiter

Tiber Island

PALATINE MT.

Circus Maximus

CAELIAN MT.

AVENTINE MT.

Servian Wall

Hills of Rome

Legend

- Roman territory (full citizens)
- Roman territory (citizens without suffrage)
- Roman allies
- Latin colonies
- Carthaginian possessions
- ■ Greek cities
- —— Major roads by 100 B.C.

0   50   100 Km.

0   50   100 Mi.

Plaque of a Soldier This ivory, one of a pair from Latium dated about 250–200 B.C., provides the best evidence for the dress of a Roman legionnaire of the Middle Republic. *(Alinari/Art Resource, NY)*

Rome cultivated qualities that served military needs. Roman ideology prized toughness, the Roman social system instilled obedience and organization, and the competitive ethos raised the stakes for Roman generals. Beginning in the fourth century B.C., Rome began to reward its soldiers with regular pay; this and the distribution of conquered land improved morale. Two other points are even more significant: the willingness to adopt foreign military technology and the combination of generosity and firmness with which Rome treated its allies.

Adopted by Rome in the sixth century B.C., the hoplite phalanx suited the relatively level ground of Latium but fared poorly in the rugged Apennines against the Samnites. Following a major defeat in 321 B.C., the Romans adopted the Samnites' equipment and tactics with great success. Unlike the hoplite, the legionnary, as the Roman soldier was now called, carried a throwing spear (javelin) instead of a pike, as well as a short sword. Unlike the phalanx, a Roman legion did not fight and maneuver as one thickly massed unit; rather, it contained a loose set of subunits. The tactical unit was the maniple ("handful"). Each maniple consisted of two centuries (literally "hundreds"), and each century was commanded by a centurion. Legions also contained light-armed troops and cavalry. Unlike hoplites, who engaged the enemy at short range, legionnaires first threw their javelins at long range. Then, having broken the enemy's order, they charged and fought with sword and shield. The semi-independence of the maniples created a more maneuverable army than that of the phalanx and one better suited for mountain fighting. When Rome's legions beat the Macedonian phalanx decisively in 197 B.C., military history entered a new era.

Rome became the leading power among the Latins, whom it led in an alliance known as the Latin League. Rome was first among equals, but the citizens of even the humblest Latin state had reciprocal rights of intermarriage and commerce with Romans. Under Roman leadership the Latin League successfully defended Latium's borders against a series of enemies during the fourth and fifth centuries B.C. But eventually

Rome had to confront a bitter two-year-long Latin revolt (340–338 B.C.).

The year 338 B.C. marked a turning point. Defeated peoples in the ancient world were often executed, deported, or enslaved, but the Romans pursued generosity against the vanquished Latins. The Latin League was dissolved. Some of its member states were annexed and their inhabitants became Roman citizens; others retained independence and alliance with Rome though no longer with one another. The non-Latin allies of the former rebels were annexed by Rome and received the unique halfway status of "citizenship without suffrage." As Rome conquered the rest of Italy, a number of privileged Italian cities (called *municipia*) received this status.

To keep an eye on potential rebels, Rome built a network of military roads and colonies crisscrossing Italy. Roman roads allowed the swift movement of troops and linked the growing network of colonies. Colonies were established in strategically vital areas and were constructed with military discipline. The inhabitants owed military service to Rome.

Manpower abundance won Rome's war (280–276 B.C.) against the Greek general Pyrrhus of Epirus (319–272 B.C.), an adventurer who had intervened in southern Italy. Although Pyrrhus won battle after battle, he was unable to match Rome's willingness to sustain thousands of casualties time and again. Pyrrhus's seeming victories thus turned out to be defeats, which sent him home to Greece disappointed and left us with the expression "Pyrrhic victory." By 265 B.C. Rome had emerged as the ruler of all of Italy south of the Pisae-Ariminium line. One might say that Rome unified Italy, although Italy was less a unified state than a patchwork of Roman territory and colonies each allied to Rome by separate treaty.

Rome Versus Carthage: The Punic Wars, 264–146 B.C.

The conquest of Italy made Rome one of two great powers in the central Mediterranean. Rome's rival was Carthage. Founded around

The Nurturing Goddess This terra-cotta statuette (late second or first century B.C.) may represent a Carthaginian goddess of fertility worshiped in both Punic and Roman Africa. The scene of mother and infant suggests later imagery of the Virgin Mary and Christ. (*Martha Cooper/Peter Arnold, Inc.*)

750 B.C. by Phoenicians from Tyre, Carthage controlled an empire in North Africa, Sicily, Corsica, Sardinia, Malta, the Balearic Islands, and southern Spain. (The adjective *Phoenician* is *Punicus* in Latin, hence the term *Punic* for Carthaginian.) Like Rome, Carthage was run by an oligarchy,

but its elite was mercantile rather than agrarian. Rome was a land power, Carthage a sea power. Rome had virtually no navy, but Carthage had a great war fleet, a mercantile monopoly of the western Mediterranean, and a major commercial presence in the east. Also, the Carthaginians were the first Mediterranean people to organize large-scale plantations of slaves for the production of single crops.

Carthage boasted brilliant generals, especially in the Barca family, whose most famous member was Hannibal (247–183 B.C.). Carthage might have seemed superior at the outbreak of its long wars with Rome in 264 B.C., yet the end result was disaster for Carthage. Unlike Rome, Carthage did not have a citizen army. The commanders were Carthaginian, but most of the soldiers were mercenaries and so of questionable loyalty. A second difference in the two states lay in the treatment of allies. Rome treated the Italians with considerable respect and tolerance. Carthage showed contempt for its allies, who repaid the favor by revolting whenever they had the chance. Third, although Carthage's military manpower resources were considerable, they were not as great as Rome's.

At the start of the Punic Wars, Rome had no navy or commanders to match the Barca family but it proved adaptable, tenacious, and ruthless. The First Punic War (264–241 B.C.) took place almost entirely in Sicily. After initial success, Rome realized that it could not win the war without building a fleet. Rome's solution was to capture a Carthaginian warship and use it as a prototype for the Roman navy.

The long and bloody war exhausted both sides. Rome won only because the Carthaginian government had had enough. Rome triumphed at sea, but the Carthaginian army in western Sicily under Hannibal's father, Hamilcar Barca (d. 229 B.C.), was undefeated. At first Rome granted a mild peace treaty, requiring only that Carthage evacuate Sicily and pay an indemnity. Several years later, however, when Carthage was immersed in a mercenaries' revolt, Rome seized Corsica and Sardinia and demanded an additional indemnity.

Forced to give in to these treacherous exactions, Carthage decided to build a new and bigger empire in Spain, beginning in 237 B.C., under Barca family leadership. With Spain's rich deposits of silver and copper at its disposal, Carthage once again posed a credible threat to Rome. In the mid-220s, an ever watchful Rome negotiated that the Ebro River in northeastern Spain be recognized as the boundary of Carthaginian territory. Rome felt free to intervene south of the Ebro, where, through a Roman client, it challenged Carthaginian power by proxy. When Carthage responded with force, Rome threatened war. The new Carthaginian commander, 27-year-old Hannibal Barca, was not to be cowed, and the Second Punic War ensued (218–201 B.C.).

Carthage was willing to risk war because Hannibal had promised a cheap and easy victory. Because Carthage no longer had a fleet, the Romans felt secure in Italy; Hannibal surprised them by marching overland to Italy, making a dangerous passage across the Alps. A tactical genius, Hannibal reckoned that he could defeat the Romans in battle and cause them enormous casualties. He was right: Hannibal's forces dominated the battlefield. But huge casualties alone could not bring the Roman elite to its knees. Nor did Rome's allies revolt en masse, as Hannibal had hoped. Most stood by Rome, partly out of loyalty and partly out of fear of Roman reprisals. Meanwhile, Rome's leaders pursued a cautious strategy of harassment, delay, refusal to fight, and attrition.

Eventually, a new Roman military star emerged: Publius Cornelius Scipio (236–183 B.C.). After conquering Carthage's Spanish dominions, Scipio forced Hannibal back to North Africa for a final battle in 202 B.C. near Zama (in modern Tunisia). As the conqueror of North Africa, Scipio was now surnamed Africanus.

The peace settlement of 201 B.C. stripped Carthage of its empire. But its economy soon rebounded, reviving Roman fears. In the Third Punic War (149–146 B.C.) Rome mounted a three-year siege, destroying the city of Carthage in 146 B.C. Approximately a century later, Carthage was refounded as a Roman colony and became one of the empire's greatest cities. In the meantime, it was left desolate, its people killed or enslaved.

Rome emerged from the Punic Wars as the greatest power in the Mediterranean. It had acquired new provinces in Sicily, Sardinia, Corsica, Spain, and North Africa. The road to further conquest seemed to lead in all directions.

Victories in the Hellenistic East, ca. 200–133 B.C.

Most countries would have savored peace after such an ordeal as the Punic Wars, but Rome leaped immediately into a long conflict in Greece and Anatolia. Rome expected a relatively quick and easy victory. It was not disappointed; in 197 B.C. the legions crushed the Macedonian phalanx at Cynoscephalae in central Greece (Map 3.3).

Rome had hoped to impose a patron-client relationship on Greece and Macedon, thereby avoiding a permanent military presence, but that hope failed. The independent-minded Greeks chafed at Roman domination. First, the Seleucids, under the ambitious king Antiochus III (r. 223–187 B.C.), challenged Rome for hegemony in the Greek peninsula. Driven out not only from Greece but Anatolia as well, the Seleucids in effect recognized Roman supremacy in the Mediterranean (188 B.C.).

Then came another war between Rome and Macedon (171–167 B.C.), settled by a complete Roman victory. Two decades later, after additional revolts, Macedon became a Roman province in 148 B.C. Greece, not formally a separate province until 27 B.C., was under the thumb of the Roman governor of Macedonia. Wherever democracy had survived in Greece, it was replaced with oligarchy. Greece suffered Roman neglect and taxation for nearly two hundred years.

By annexing Carthage, Macedon, and Greece in the mid-second century B.C., Rome created a dynamic for expansion around the entire Mediterranean. Before the century was over, southern Gaul was annexed, and Rome had gained a foothold in Asia. Two great Hellenistic states remained independent, the Seleucid kingdom and Ptolemaic Egypt. Roman ambassadors and generals frequently interfered in their affairs, however, and in the first century B.C. they too were annexed by Rome.

The Consequences of Expansion

Expansion led to enormous and unintended changes in Rome's society, economy, and culture. Already wealthy, the Roman elite now came into fabulous riches. Huge profits awaited the generals, diplomats, magistrates, tax collectors, and businessmen who followed Rome's armies. Conquest also enlivened the asceticism of Roman culture and, for many women, it loosened social constraints. For the poor, however, it created new hardships.

Rome learned much from its new encounters with foreign peoples—especially the Greeks. Romans adopted the workmanship and style of Greek coins, which facilitated commercial transactions. Previously, the Romans had made do with barter and uncoined bronze. Wealthy Romans displayed Greek jewelry, art objects, and other luxury goods in their homes. Conservatives bemoaned the decline of traditional Roman austerity, largely in vain.

Wealthy Romans cultivated an interest in Greek art and literature. Poor and rich alike enjoyed Greek drama after large numbers of Roman soldiers stationed in Magna Graecia were introduced to comedy, tragedy, and mimes. Before the mid-third century B.C., there had been virtually no Roman literature. An oral tradition of songs, ballads, and funeral oratory kept alive the deeds of the famous; writing was generally restricted to commercial and government records. The Romans conquered Italy without writing about it.

Contact with the Greek cities also brought changes in Roman education. Traditionally, parents had played the primary teaching role. In the second century B.C., wealthy Romans began acquiring Greek slaves to educate their children in Greek language and literature. Soon Greek freedmen began setting up schools, and similar Latin grammar schools also opened. Roman orators studied Greek models of rhetoric. Marcus Porcius Cato (234–149 B.C.), known as Cato the Censor, was the first Roman to publish his speeches;

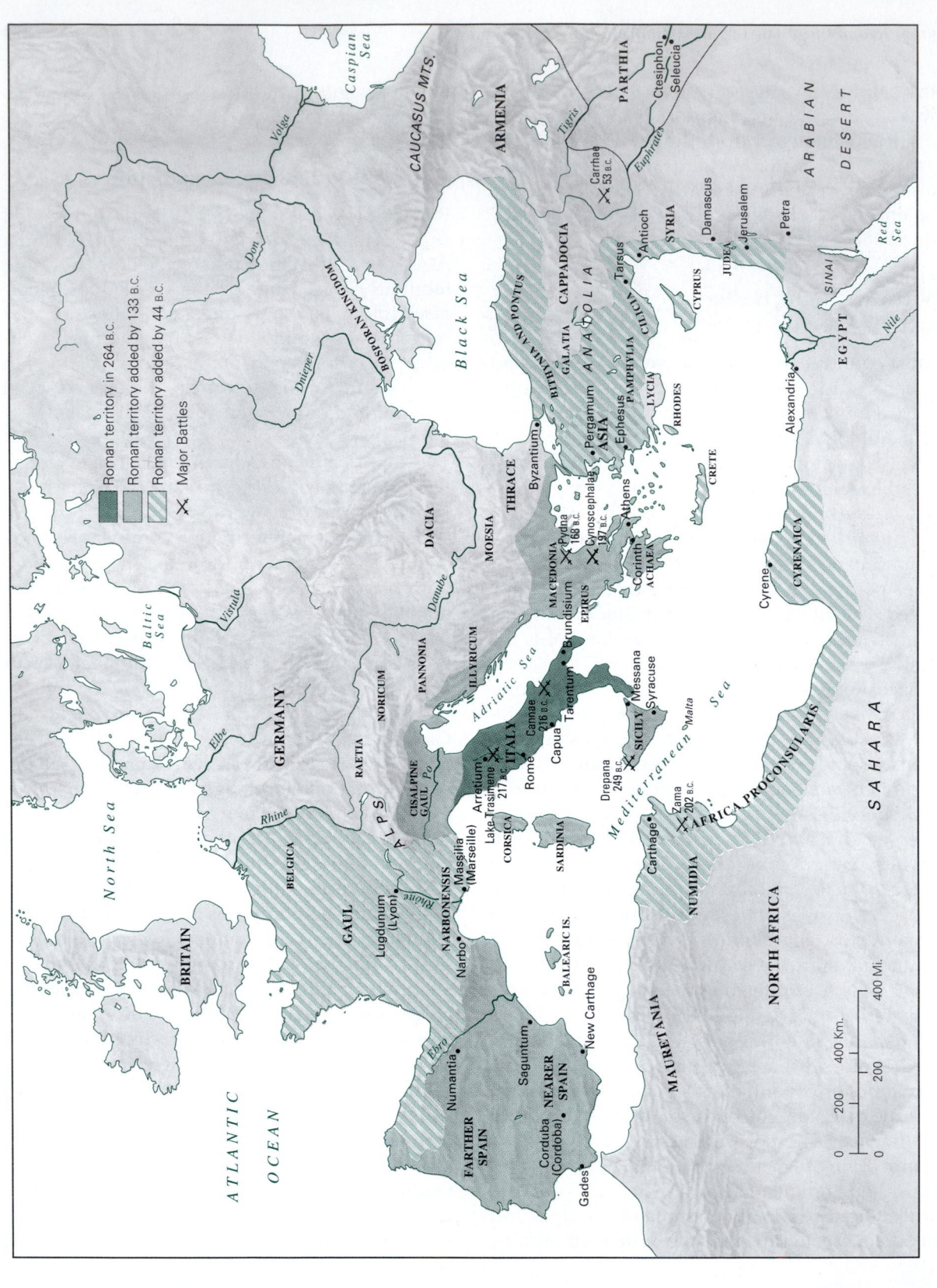

The Round Temple This elegant, circular, Corinthian-columned structure in the Forum Boarium in Rome, built around 150–100 B.C., is the oldest surviving marble temple in the city. Greek in style, it is an example of Roman borrowing from sophisticated Hellenistic culture. *(Scala/Art Resource, NY)*

he also wrote a book on rhetoric. Cato was the first historian of Rome to write in Latin. Despite his debt to Greek ideas, Cato was famously ambivalent about Greek culture. (See the box "Encounters with the West: Roman Attitudes Toward the Conquered.")

Changes in education, and the general loosening of cultural conservatism, affected women as well as men. In wealthy families girls were taught reading, literature, music, and conversational skills. In some cases, women were able to earn some cultural renown. An excellent example was the aristocrat Cornelia—an educated lover of Hellenism whose letters survived for several hundred years and were read as examples of elegant Latin prose. Like other women of her class,

Map 3.3 Roman Expansion, 264–44 B.C. Wars against Carthage, the major Greco-Macedonian powers, Gauls, Germans, North Africans, and other peoples brought Rome an empire on three continents.

she was greatly admired for her management of property and her accomplishments in raising virtuous citizens. Cornelia also earned great renown for bringing together distinguished guests in her villa. When her husband died, she chose to remain a widow, though the king of Egypt, among others, proposed marriage to her. Cornelia preferred to manage her own estate and supervise the education of her daughter and two sons, the future tribunes Tiberius and Gaius Gracchus.

It was Cornelia's wealth that allowed her so great a range of activity, but imperial expansion brought new opportunities to many Roman women. Few women were married *cum manu* anymore, that is, handed over to their husband by their father. A woman's father, not her husband, was most likely to be her *paterfamilias*, which meant that a husband's control over his wife's dowry was limited. Because most adult women had already lost their fathers, the result was more freedom.

∼ ENCOUNTERS WITH THE WEST ∼

Roman Attitudes Toward the Conquered

Roman attitudes toward the Greeks were complex, mixing admiration for Greek culture with fear of its corrosive effect on loyalty to the Roman state. In the following selection, the Greek writer Plutarch (ca. A.D. 50–ca. 120) discusses Greek philosophy in Rome.

Carneades the Academic and Diogenes the Stoic came as envoys from Athens to Rome [in 155 B.C.]. . . . The most studious of the youth at once went to wait upon these men, and frequently heard them speak with admiration. . . . The report spread far and wide that a Greek [Carneades] of amazing talent, who charmed and disarmed everybody, had infused a powerful passion into the young men, so that forsaking their other pleasures and pursuits, they were in ecstasies about philosophy. This pleased the other Romans, and they were glad to see the youth participating in Greek culture and consorting with such remarkable men. But Cato, when this passion for discussion came flowing into the city, from the beginning was distressed, fearing lest the youth, by diverting their ambitions in this direction, should prefer a reputation for speaking well before that of deeds and military campaigns. . . . Cato determined, under a specious pretext, to have all the philosophers cleared out of the city. And coming into the senate he blamed the magistrates for letting the envoys stay so long a time without settling the matter, though they were such persuasive persons that they could easily secure anything they wished; that therefore a decision should be made and a vote taken on the embassy as soon as possible, so that they might go home again to their own schools and lecture to the sons of the Greeks, while the Roman youth listened, as hitherto, to their own laws and magistrates.

Source: Plutarch, *Life of Cato the Elder,* in Naphtali Lewis and Meyer Reinhold, eds., *Roman Civilization: Selected Readings,* vol. 1, *The Republic and the Augustan Age,* 3d ed. (New York: Columbia University Press, 1990), pp. 528–529. © 1990 Columbia University Press. Reprinted by permission of the publisher.

Male or female, ordinary Romans did not share the elite's profit from Roman expansion. Indeed, a century of intensive warfare strained the Roman people to the breaking point. Hannibal's invasion left much of the farmland of southern Italy devastated and Italian manpower considerably reduced. Worse still, the average term of military service had lengthened to six years, with a maximum term of twenty years—and commanders were loath to release experienced legionnaires. The longer a man was in the army, the harder it was for his family to keep their farm running. The problem was compounded by the introduction to Italy of large-scale agricultural entrepreneurship. To set up Carthage-style plantations, the elite monopolized Italian farmland and imported huge numbers of slaves—destroying the free peasantry of Italy.

The last two centuries B.C. witnessed the transformation of Roman rural society from one of independent farmers to one in which slave labor played a major role. By the end of the first century B.C. there were an estimated 2 to 3 million slaves in Italy, about a third of the peninsula's total population. Prisoners of war and conquered civilians provided a ready supply of slaves. Their treatment was often abominable.

Conquests had gained Rome a plenitude of land in Italy, and individual Romans were legally entitled to take possession of about 320 acres of "public land." Many entrepreneurs flouted the law and took much more. They forced families of absent soldiers off private land, either by debt foreclosure or by outright violence. Sometimes families would move to the city, but usually they stayed on as tenants.

Poor Romans had sometimes been able to find land in colonies. By 170 B.C., Rome had established all the colonies in Italy that its security demanded, so this avenue of escape from poverty was closed. The situation of the Italian peasantry became increasingly miserable by the mid-second century B.C. as a direct result of the conquests of the Roman Empire.

THE REVOLUTION FROM THE GRACCHI TO CAESAR, 133–44 B.C.

After 350 years of expansion, a citizen of the Roman Republic in the mid-second century B.C. might have looked forward to a long and happy future for his country, unaware that the Republic was about to begin a century of domestic and foreign unrest that would bring down the whole system. In retrospect, the causes of this revolution are not hard to find. More than a century of warfare weighed heavily on the ordinary people of Italy. The Roman elite was bitterly divided over what to do about the problems of the peasants. One group wanted to redistribute land to the poor; another group had no sympathy for them. Both groups were willing to exploit the poor for their own ends.

By the Late Republic the city of Rome was crowded and populous: Scholars estimate the number of inhabitants at between 750,000 and 1 million. The government had to take charge of the grain supply to enable this vast community to survive. But the Late Republic was an age of individualism, and ambitious nobles were not willing to subordinate themselves to the community. It was not long before competing armies of land-hungry peasants were marching across Italy.

The Gracchi

In Rome, military service was a prestigious activity, and putting weapons in the hands of the poor was considered unwise. Therefore, a property qualification was imposed on conscripts. During the second century it became necessary to reduce the property qualification several times. By 150 B.C., a conscript had to own property worth 400 denarii—roughly a small house, a garden, and some personal belongings. If the peasantry continued to decline, Rome would have to either eliminate the property qualification altogether or stop fielding armies.

Into the breach stepped Tiberius Sempronius Gracchus (d. 133 B.C.). The son of Cornelia and a distinguished general and ambassador (whose name he shared), Tiberius was one of the ten tribunes for the year 133 B.C. He proposed a law restoring the roughly 320-acre limit on the amount of public land a person could own. A commission was to be set up to repossess excess land and redistribute it to the poor in small lots that were to be inalienable—that is, the wealthy could not buy them back. The former landowners would be reimbursed for improvements they had made, such as buildings or plantings.

The proposal was moderate, but wealthy landowners attempted to quash it. Part of the problem was that Tiberius's methods were disturbing. He had deposed one of his fellow tribunes, Octavius, for opposing reform. Also, Tiberius had somewhat illegally maneuvered to run for a second consecutive term as tribune. Many senators suspected that Tiberius wanted to set himself up as a kind of superpatron, buoyed by peasant supporters. While the tribal assembly prepared to vote on the new tribunes, some senators led a mob to the Forum and had Tiberius and three hundred of his followers clubbed to death.

This shocking event marked the first time in the Republic that a political debate had been settled by bloodshed in Rome itself. The ancient sources agree that it was the beginning of a century of revolution. Tiberius's killers had not merely committed murder; they had attacked the traditional inviolability of the tribunes. Over the next century, public violence became an increasingly common weapon of politics.

The land commission went ahead with its work, without Tiberius. His younger brother, Gaius (d. 121 B.C.), eager to continue Tiberius's work, became tribune in 123 B.C. Gaius expanded Tiberius's coalition, adding to it supporters from the equestrian order—rich men who were not in the senate. He also brought in the urban populace, mainly composed of slaves and freedmen. He gave the plebs cheap grain at subsidized prices and the power-hungry equestrians important positions in the courts.

Gaius's ultimate aims are uncertain, but the threat he posed to the senate's power was clear. He was denied a third term as tribune in 121 B.C. and shortly thereafter, one of the consuls had him and 250 of his followers killed. Another 3000 Gracchans were executed soon thereafter. Within a few years, the Gracchan land commission was abolished, after giving land to approximately 75,000 citizens. The law, however, was amended to permit the resale of redistributed land, and, with the wealthy poised to buy land, the settlers' future was uncertain. The senatorial oligarchy seemed to be back in control.

In the long run, the most important result of the Gracchi period was that the political community had been divided in two. On one side were the *optimates* ("the best people"), conservatives who asserted the rule of the senate against popular tribunes and the maintenance of the estates of the wealthy in spite of the agrarian crisis. On the other side were the *populares* ("men of the people"), who challenged the rule of the senate in the name of relief for the poor. The populares were not democrats. Like the optimates, they were Roman nobles who believed in hierarchy, but they advocated the redistribution of wealth and power as a way of restoring stability and strengthening the military.

Marius and Sulla

By 100 B.C., Rome's agrarian crisis had become a full-scale military crisis too. Roman armies under senatorial commanders fared poorly, both in Numidia (modern Algeria) and in southern Gaul

against Germanic invaders (see Map 3.3). The situation was saved by an outsider to established privilege, an equestrian named Gaius Marius (157–86 B.C.), the first member of his family to be elected consul, for 107 B.C. This "new man" proved to be a military reformer and a popularis. Marius streamlined the Roman army: Camp followers were reduced in number, individual soldiers were made to carry their own equipment, and the legions were reorganized. Most important, Marius abandoned the property qualification for the military. Roman soldiers were no longer peasants doing part-time military service but landless men making a profession of the military.

Marius won battles in North Africa and Gaul. He demanded and received six elections to the consulship, unconstitutional though that was. After restoring peace, Marius asked in 100 B.C. that land be distributed to his soldiers. Violent senatorial opposition made him back down, but this further revealed the senate's unpopularity. The land-hungry poor recognized that only military leaders like Marius offered to meet their needs. As a result, ordinary Romans, all of whom could join the army, transferred their loyalty from the senate to their commander.

The Republic was weak and became weaker still as a result of two new wars. First, its Italian allies rose against Rome in a bloody and bitter struggle from 91 to 89 B.C. known as the "Social War"—that is, war with the *socii* ("allies"). The allies fought hard, and Rome had to concede to them what they had demanded at the outset: full Roman citizenship. The war wrought devastation in the countryside, further destabilizing the Republic. The second conflict pitted Rome against Mithridates (120–63 B.C.), king of Pontus (northern Anatolia). Mithridates conquered the Roman province of Asia (western Anatolia) and slaughtered the numerous Italian businessmen and tax collectors there. Once again a military man rose to save the day for Rome: Marius's rival and former lieutenant, Lucius Cornelius Sulla Felix (ca. 138–78 B.C.), consul for the year 88 B.C., patrician and optimas.

The senate assigned Sulla the command against Mithridates, but Marius, though elderly, wanted it for himself. The troops decided the issue: first Sulla's, which marched on Rome and confirmed their leader's authority, then Marius's, which recaptured the city after Sulla's departure for the East. Victorious over Mithridates, Sulla returned to Italy in 83 B.C., eager to settle scores. Marius had died in 86 B.C., but his allies took up the challenge of civil war. Sulla won. His political opponents, as many as two thousand men, were executed. Their land was confiscated and their sons were disenfranchised. In Italy, Sulla expelled entire communities that had opposed him and settled his veterans, about eighty thousand men, on their land.

Having assumed the long-dormant office of dictatorship—now, unconstitutionally, for life—Sulla attempted to restore the senatorial oligarchy of pre-Gracchan days. To this end, he greatly weakened the tribunate and strengthened the senate. By adding several hundred equestrians, Sulla doubled the size of the senate, from about three hundred to about six hundred members. The move added both equestrians and Italians to the pool of potential leaders.

The most long-lasting of Sulla's measures was his reform of the courts. He abolished trials before popular assemblies and equestrian-staffed courts. Criminal cases were now heard before one of seven standing courts, whose juries were composed of senators. Although later Roman criminal law evolved considerably, it was founded on Sulla's actions. Generally only wealthy people had access to the standing courts; alleged crimes involving ordinary people were heard before lesser magistrates.

Sulla retired in 79 B.C. and died a year later. His hope of restoring law and order under the senate died with him. Discontent smoldered among the men whose land he had confiscated. Equally serious, many senators were more inspired by Sulla's achievement of personal power than they were by his actions to strengthen the collective interests of the senate.

Pompey and Caesar

The dominant leader of the seventies and sixties B.C. was the optimas Pompey the Great (106–48

B.C.), a brilliant general and a supporter of Sulla. Young Pompey went from command to command: He put down an agrarian rebellion in Italy and a revolt in Spain, cleared the Mediterranean of pirates, defeated Mithridates again, and added rich conquests to the empire in Anatolia, Syria, Phoenicia, and Palestine. In the fifties B.C. the tide began turning in favor of Gaius Julius Caesar (100–44 B.C.), an even more gifted general and politician, perhaps one of history's greatest. A popularis, Caesar's career depended on his dazzling oratory, his boldness, and his talent at war and politics. Caesar conquered Gaul, gained a foothold in Britain, and laid the foundations of Roman rule in Egypt (see Map 3.3).

While the elite of the Late Republic struggled to maintain order, ordinary people struggled for survival itself. Violence had become endemic in rural Italy. Many once-prosperous farmers, dispossessed peasants, and runaway slaves ended up as brigands or highwaymen. It was also an era of slave revolts, the most serious of which was led by the Thracian Spartacus from 73 to 71 B.C., at a time when Rome also faced major wars in Spain and Anatolia. An able commander, Spartacus beat nine separate Roman armies in two years before finally suffering defeat.

The political careers of Pompey and Caesar were linked closely with their romantic relationships. In 80 B.C., Pompey divorced his first wife to advance his career by marrying Aemilia, Sulla's stepdaughter. Aemilia was not only married at the time but pregnant by her first husband. Soon after her divorce and remarriage, she died in childbirth. One of Caesar's lovers was the queen of Egypt, Cleopatra, who may have encouraged his desire to become a monarch himself. Another of Caesar's lovers was Servilia, stepsister of Marcus Porcius Cato (Cato the Younger, 95–46 B.C.), great-grandson of the famous censor. She was also the mother of Brutus, the man who would eventually help murder Caesar.

Pompey was an optimas, Caesar a popularis, but the two of them agreed that they, not the senate or the assemblies, should rule Rome. In 60 B.C. they entered into a pact with a third ambitious noble, Marcus Licinius Crassus (d. 53 B.C.).

Known today as the "First Triumvirate," the coalition amounted to a conspiracy to run the state. Each man had an agenda that pooling resources in the triumvirate permitted him to fulfill: for Pompey, ratification of his acts in the East and land for his veterans; for Caesar, who became consul for 59 B.C., a long command with a free hand in Gaul; for Crassus, a rebate for the tax collectors of Roman Asia, and eventually a command in Syria to make war on Parthia (the revived Persian Empire).

Once it achieved its goals, the triumvirate did not long survive, but its very existence marked the demise of the Republic. Crassus died in inglorious defeat at Carrhae in Syria in 53 B.C. Pompey, frightened by Caesar's stunning victories in Gaul, returned to the senatorial fold, now led by Cato the Younger. In 49 B.C., Cato and his supporters ordered Caesar to give up his command in Gaul, but instead Caesar marched on Italy with his army. Italy's northern boundary was marked by a tiny stream called Rubicon; when Caesar crossed it, he declared, "The die is cast." Caesar swept to victory against the senate's army, led by Pompey in 48 B.C. Pompey fled but was assassinated. The complete destruction of the senate's forces took until 45 B.C. A talented writer, Caesar published two commentaries on his military campaigns: *On the Gallic War* and *On the Civil War,* the latter appearing after his death. These works served to glorify Caesar's conquests and justify his decision to wage a bloody civil war.

Named dictator by the senate, Caesar sponsored a vast number of reforms. His political goal was to elevate Italians and others at the expense of old Roman families. To achieve it, Caesar conferred Roman citizenship liberally, on all of Cisalpine Gaul (northernmost Italy) as well as on certain provincial towns. He enlarged the senate from six hundred to nine hundred, adding his supporters, including some Gauls, to the membership. Caesar also reduced debts and founded the first colonies outside Italy, where veterans and poor citizens were settled. He undertook a public building program in the city of Rome. Caesar's most long-lasting act was to introduce the calendar of 365¼ days, on January 1,

45 B.C. Derived from the calendar of Egypt, it is known as the Julian calendar.

Caesar often flaunted his contempt for Republican constitutional formalities. His acceptance of dictatorship for life offended the old guard, his flirtation with the notion of a monarchy even more so. With one eye toward avenging Crassus and another toward equaling the achievements of Alexander the Great, Caesar made preparations for a war against Parthia, but in vain. His ascendancy ended abruptly on March 15, 44 B.C. (the Ides of March by the Roman calendar), when sixty senators stabbed him to death. The assassination took place in the portico attached to the Theater of Pompey, where the senate was meeting that day. It had been eighty-nine years since the murder of Tiberius Gracchus.

The assassins called themselves Liberators, believing that they were freeing themselves from tyranny just as the founders of the Republic had done centuries before. One of the chief conspirators, Marcus Junius Brutus (ca. 85–42 B.C.), claimed descent from Lucius Junius Brutus, traditional leader of the revolt that had established the Republic. Like his co-conspirator Gaius Longinus Cassius (d. 42 B.C.), Brutus thought Caesar's murder was justified by the public interest, but the assassination led only to renewed civil war and the threat of tyranny far worse than Caesar's.

The World of Cicero

Marcus Tullius Cicero (106–43 B.C.) is one of the best-known figures of all antiquity. He was a wealthy equestrian from the central Italian town of Arpinum who, as consul (in 63 B.C.), became a "new man." Cicero was an optimas and defender of the senate, though he was ready for compromise with the equestrians, from whose ranks he himself had arisen. He made his name in the army by smashing a debtors' revolt in Etruria.

As a young man Cicero had studied philosophy and oratory in Greece, and this, along with his intelligence and ambition, enabled him to produce important writings. Never as original as Plato or Aristotle, Cicero nonetheless was crucial in making the Latin language a vessel for the heritage of Greek thought. He produced over a hundred orations, of which about sixty survive; several treatises on oratory; philosophical writings on politics, ethics, epistemology, and theology; poetry (of which little survives); and numerous letters. After his death in 43 B.C., his voluminous correspondence was published with little expurgation. The letters and speeches provide a vivid, detailed, and sometimes damning picture of politics in the Late Republic.

Few orators in history have matched Cicero's ability to lead and mislead an audience by playing on its feelings. His orations are masterpieces of technique, famous for their polish, wit, long, rolling sentences, and, above all, emotional power. (See the box "Cicero in Defense of Milo.") Although Cicero's talents were extraordinary, the elite in general prided itself on free speech and open debate. Oratory—sometimes great oratory—was common in the senate, assemblies, and court cases.

During the Late Republic it was possible for elite women as well as men to study oratory. Private tutors were common among the aristocracy, and girls often received lessons alongside their brothers. Girls sometimes profited from a father's expertise. A particularly dramatic case was that of Hortensia, daughter of Quintus Hortensius Hortalus (114–50 B.C.), a famous orator and rival of Cicero. An excellent speaker herself, Hortensia defied tradition by arguing successfully in the Roman Forum in 42 B.C. against a proposed war tax on wealthy women.

Cicero pilloried one elite woman who enjoyed considerable freedom: Clodia (b. ca. 95 B.C.). Sister of the notorious populist gang leader Clodius and wife of optimas politician Metellus Celer (d. 59 B.C.), Clodia moved in Rome's highest circles. Cicero accused her of poisoning her husband. (The charge was unprovable.) She is better remembered from the poems of Catullus (ca. 85–54 B.C.), where she is called Lesbia. In passionate and psychologically complex verse, Catullus described the ups and downs of their affair, which Clodia eventually ended.

The rise of poetry did not reflect social peace. Brawls and violence between the rival groups of Clodius, a supporter of Caesar, and Milo, a supporter of the senate, became increasingly common in the fifties B.C. As dictator, Caesar abolished the gangs. Meanwhile, among the elite, as Cicero's letters indicate, free speech gave way to gossip, plotting, factionalism, and flattery of Pompey and Caesar.

Cicero's works provide evidence of a crucial development in the practice of Roman law. Cicero's contemporaries invented the notion of the legal expert. Complex and intricate, Roman law needed interpretation. Much of the law was the work not of legislators but magistrates, who issued annual edicts setting forth how their courts would work. In the Early Republic only the pontiffs had the right to interpret the law, but in the third and second centuries B.C. a group of lay legal interpreters known as juriconsults emerged. In the first century they became true jurists; their interpretations began to be considered authoritative. No earlier Mediterranean society had a professional class of legal experts, but no earlier society had faced issues as complex and turbulent and none had 3 million citizens, as the Roman Republic did in the mid-first century B.C. The Western tradition of legal science has its roots in Rome.

Unlike its legal system, Rome's political system did not adapt flexibly to changing circumstances. The disenfranchised of the Late Republic had reasonable goals: land for those who had fought for their country and admission to the senate of a wider group. Yet the old elite resisted both. Cicero's proposed solution was to unite the senatorial and equestrian orders and widen the Roman ruling class to include the elite of all Italy. Cicero's vision for Rome was distinctly hierarchical.

In the turbulent times of the Late Republic, the Roman elite often turned to the Hellenistic philosophers. The poet Lucretius (ca. 94 B.C.–ca. 55 B.C.) described the Epicurean ideal of withdrawal into the contemplative life in a long didactic epic called *On the Nature of Things*. Most elite Romans, including Cicero, preferred the activist philosophy of Stoicism (see page 60). Cicero put forth a generous view of human brotherhood. He argued that all people are protected by natural law and share a spark of divinity. All

Cicero in Defense of Milo

On January 18, 53 B.C., a brawl between the rival gangs of Clodius and Milo on the Appian Way left Clodius dead. Cicero himself defended Milo, a fellow optimas, but Milo was convicted and exiled. As this excerpt shows, Cicero's speech to the jury reveals both the violence of Late Republican life and the elegance of his rhetoric.

As subsequent events demonstrated, his [Clodius's] plan was to take up a position in front of his own country manor, and set an ambush for Milo on the spot. . . .

Meanwhile, Milo . . . attended the Senate on that day, until the meeting was concluded. Then he proceeded to his home, changed his shoes and his clothes, waited for the usual period when his wife got ready, and then started off at just about the time when Clodius could have got back to Rome if it had been his intention to return at all on the day in question. But instead he encountered Clodius in the country. . . .

And so at about five in the afternoon, or thereabouts, he found himself confronted by Clodius before the gates of the latter's house. Milo was instantly set upon by a crowd of armed men who charged down from the higher ground; while, simultaneously, others rushed up from in front and killed the driver of the coach. Milo flung back his cloak, leapt out of the vehicle, and defended himself with energy. But meanwhile the people with Clodius were brandishing their drawn swords, and while some of them ran towards the coach in order to fall upon Milo from the rear, others believed he was already slain and began to attack his slaves who had been following behind him. A number of those slaves of Milo's lost their lives defending their master with loyal determination. Others, however, who could

see the fight round the coach but were unable to get to their master's help, heard from Clodius' own lips that Milo was slain, and believed the report. And so these slaves, without the orders or knowledge or presence of their master—and I am going to speak quite frankly, and not with any aim of denying the charge but just exactly as the situation developed— did what every man would have wished his own slaves to do in similar circumstances.

The incident, gentlemen, took place exactly as I have described it. The attacker was defeated. Force was frustrated by force; or, to put the matter more accurately, evil was overcome by good. Of the gain to our country and yourselves and all loyal citizens, I say nothing. It is not my intention to urge that the deed be counted in favor of Milo—the man whose self-preservation was destined to mean the preservation of the Republic and yourselves. No, my defense is that he was justified in acting to save his life. Civilized people are taught this by logic, barbarians by necessity, communities by tradition; and the lesson is inculcated even in wild beasts by nature itself. . . . That being so, if you come to the conclusion that this particular action was criminal, you are in the same breath deciding that every other man in the history of the world who has ever fought back against a robber deserves nothing better than death. . . .

Source: Cicero, "In Defense of Titus Annius Milo," in *Selected Political Speeches of Cicero*, trans. Michael Grant (Harmondsworth, England: Penguin, 1969), pp. 232–234. Copyright © 1969 by Michael Grant Publications Ltd. Reprinted by permission of Frederick Warne & Co. (Penguin Books UK).

therefore have value and importance. Such ideas would be influential in the new Roman Empire when, under the leadership of Augustus, fair treatment of provincials was a major theme (see Chapter 4). For Cicero, however, these ideas existed more as theory than as practice.

Cicero did not hide his lack of sympathy for his fellow citizens who were poor. In one speech he castigated "artisans and shopkeepers and all that kind of scum"; in a letter he complained about "the wretched half-starved populace, which attends mass meetings and sucks the blood of the treasury." Cicero also made his disdain for democracy clear: "The greatest number," he said, "should not have the greatest power."

Elitist as Cicero's views were, they were by no means extremist. Cassius, Brutus, and the other Liberators had little interest in even Cicero's limited compromises. Their stubbornness proved to be their downfall, for dispossessed peasants and ambitious equestrians would not submit. The Liberators were wiped out in renewed civil war, and a new generation of leaders emerged, weary for peace.

SUMMARY

From modest beginnings as a central Italian village urbanized after contact with its more sophisticated neighbors, Rome became a monarchy and then a republic. It practiced imperialism with extraordinary success, but ultimately the demands of empire brought down first the social system and then the political regime.

In the first centuries of its existence, the Republican oligarchy displayed a remarkable combination of flexibility and stability. It was able to accommodate not only the competitive instincts of the aristocracy and the newly rich but the land-hunger of the people. The old aristocracy of the patricians opened its ranks to the newly ambitious leaders of the plebeians and also made room in the government for popular representation. The ingrained hierarchy of the Roman social and cultural system helped keep politics stable.

Rome consolidated its control of central Italy by treating its allies with a mixture of firmness and generosity. By extending Roman citizenship, Rome gave its allies a stake in Roman hegemony. Having disposed of its nearest enemies, Rome mounted a quest for absolute security, a quest that led to conquest in Italy and the rest of the Mediterranean. Greed and ambition, as well as fear, were powerful motives of expansion.

Having defeated all opponents near and far, Rome seemed to have won absolute security by the mid-second century B.C. Yet its strength was deceptive. Contact with Greek culture liberated the Romans from ruder, peasant ways and loosened previous restraints. A huge influx of slaves made acquisition of large estates profitable. The Italian peasantry was already weakened by conscription and the devastation of farmland by chronic warfare, while the elite was arrogant from its military success. It became easy for the strong to confiscate the land of the weak. The result was a growing and dangerous social instability, with military and political ramifications. At the very moment of triumph, the Republic was in grave danger.

Since the Roman elite refused to share its wealth with the poor, the poor gave their support to new patrons, military leaders who raised private armies to win land for their followers and glory for themselves. By the first century B.C., the Republic had collapsed under the weight of political maneuvering, judicial murders, gang warfare, and civil war. The time was right for Augustus, first of the emperors.

SUGGESTED READING

Badian, E. *Foreign Clientelae (264–70 B.C.).* 1958. A classic study, vigorously written, of the ways in which the Roman elite transferred its domestic patron-client system to Rome's foreign conquests.

Beard, Mary, and Michael Crawford. *Rome in the Late Republic.* 1985. An unusual and innovative approach to the subject, emphasizing sociocultural and institutional analysis more than narrative.

Bonfante, Larissa, ed. *Etruscan Life and Afterlife: A Handbook of Etruscan Studies.* 1986. A well-illustrated collection of essays on history, economy, art, architecture, coinage, language, daily life, and religion.

Caven, B. *The Punic Wars.* 1980. A fluent and readable account, emphasizing military history.

Cornell, T. J. *The Beginnings of Rome: Italy and Rome from the Bronze Age to the Punic Wars (c. 1000–264 B.C.).* 1995. A readable and ambitious survey combining archaeological and literary evidence, often in support of iconoclastic conclusions.

Cornell, T. J., and J. Matthews. *Atlas of the Roman World.* 1982. A readable introduction to Roman history. The maps and photos are beautiful, among the best available.

Crawford, Michael. *The Roman Republic.* 1982. The best short introduction, sophisticated, lively, and concise.

Dixon, Suzanne. *The Roman Mother.* 1988. A thoughtful and sophisticated interpretation of the evidence.

Gelzer, M. *Caesar, Politician and Statesman.* 6th ed. Translated by P. Needham. 1968. An incisive, short treatment.

Gruen, E. *The Hellenistic World and the Coming of Rome.* 1984. Attuned to the ironies of international affairs, this groundbreaking book argues that the Romans were drawn into domination of the Greek world by the Greeks themselves, not by any Roman imperial design.

Gruen, E. S. *Culture and National Identity in Republican Rome.* 1992. A complex account of the ways in which Rome admired, distrusted, and finally absorbed Greek culture.

Heichelheim, F. M., C. A. Yeo, and A. M. Ward. *A History of the Roman People.* 2d ed. 1984. The best introductory textbook, readable and based on up-to-date scholarship.

Hopkins, Keith. *Death and Renewal: Sociological Studies in Roman History.* Vol. 2. 1983. An argument, against an older view, that the senatorial elite of the Late Republic and Early Empire was open to outsiders.

Discusses gladiatorial shows, funerals, mourning, and wills.

Keppie, L. *The Making of the Roman Army: From Republic to Empire.* 1984. A sensible and readable reconstruction of the evidence, with particular attention to tactics and organization.

Kunkel, Wolfgang. *An Introduction to Roman Legal and Constitutional History.* 2d ed. 1973. A survey of the evolution of Roman law in its social and political context from the earliest times to the early Byzantine era.

Ogilvie, R. M. *Roman Literature and Society.* 1980. A survey of literature in its social context from the Early Republic to the Early Empire. Good bibliographies.

Ramage, A., and N. Ramage. *Roman Art. Romulus to Constantine.* 1991. A thorough, readable, and well-illustrated introductory textbook.

Rawson, Elizabeth. *Cicero: A Portrait.* 1975. An intelligent, reliable, and readable introduction.

Saller, Richard P. *Patriarchy, Property, and Death in the Roman Family.* 1994. A sophisticated yet readable study of the interplay of authority, mutual obligation, and affection in the Roman family.

Scullard, H. H. *Roman Politics, 220–150 B.C.* 2d ed. 1973. A good example of the prosopographical approach to Roman politics, a methodology that emphasizes marriage and kinship ties.

Treggiari, Susan. *Roman Freedom During the Late Republic.* 1969. An introduction to a fascinating but often overlooked segment of Roman society, including discussions of legal status, careers, political activity, religion, and the family.

Wardham, A. *Rome's Debt to Greece.* 1976. An outline of opinions in Roman literature (from the first century B.C. to the second century A.D.) about Greeks and Greek thought.

CHAPTER 4

Imperial Rome, 27 B.C.– A.D. 284

T he first imperial family of Rome was generally represented as happy and virtuous—a symbol of the restoration of harmony in the state after generations of civil war. In practice, this was not always an easy matter, given the willful nature of its members, but carved in stone, the family radiated a stately grace. On a relief decorating a public monument, Augustus, first of the emperors, is joined by his wife, Livia; his daughter, Julia; Julia's husband, Agrippa; and various cousins and in-laws and their children. Dedicated on Livia's birthday in 9 B.C., the monument depicts the family on its way to a sacrifice, formally dressed in togas and gowns, heads wreathed. The men and women gaze seriously, while the boys and girls have impish looks, smiling mischievously as they hold their parents' hands. The senate, which had commissioned the monument, called it the Ara Pacis Augustae, or Altar of Augustan Peace.

Having made peace was no idle boast on Augustus's part. Not only did he end the Roman revolution, but he laid the foundation of a regime that would bring prosperity and stability to the Roman Empire for two hundred years. Augustus took advantage of Rome's war-weariness to create a new government out of the ruins of the Republic. Like the builders of the Early Republic's constitution, Augustus displayed the Roman genius for compromise. Although he retained the final say, he shared a degree of power with the senate. He made financial sacrifices to feed the urban poor and distribute farms to landless peasants. He ended Rome's seemingly limitless expansion and stabilized the borders of the empire. He began to raise the provinces to a status of equality with Italy.

The pax Romana ("Roman peace"), at its height between A.D. 96 and 180, was an era of enlightened emperors, thriving cities, intellectual vitality, and artistic and architectural achievement in an empire of 50 million or more people. The Roman peace was also an era of considerable spirituality. In the peaceful and diverse empire, ideas traveled from people to people, and Christianity began to spread around the Mediterranean and into northern Europe.

After 180, Rome slowly passed into a grim period marked in turn by bad emperors, civil war, inflation, plague, invasion, and defeat. After reaching a nadir around 235–253, Rome's fortunes began to improve under a series of reforming emperors. Their works culminated in the reigns of Diocletian (r. 284–305) and Constantine (r. 312–337), who would forge a stronger and vastly different empire.

∽ *Questions and Ideas to Consider*

- Augustus established the foundations for two centuries of Roman peace. How did he do this? Consider his military, social, and economic policies.

- Who were the "good emperors"? Consider the difference between the image and reality of the wives of the good emperors.

- What was the *curial order*? Why did people compete for positions as magistrates or on the local town council? Was everyone eligible for these positions? Consider the distinction between *honestiores* and *humiliores*.

- Discuss the term *Romanization*. In what ways were members of the vast empire integrated into Roman culture, society, and government? What were the limits of this?

- Why did Christianity spread so successfully? What were its rival religions at the time?

AUGUSTUS AND THE PRINCIPATE, 27 B.C.–A.D. 68

The assassination of Caesar in 44 B.C. threw Rome back into turmoil. Civil war raged for the next thirteen years, first between the Liberators and Caesar's partisans and then between the two leading Caesarians, Mark Antony (Marcus Anto-

nius, ca. 83–30 B.C.) and Octavian (Gaius Julius Caesar Octavianus, 63 B.C.–A.D. 14). Antony was Caesar's chief lieutenant and successor to the affections of the extraordinary queen of Egypt, Cleopatra. Octavian was Caesar's grandnephew and adopted son and heir. Antony's alliance with Cleopatra strengthened his hand, for she commanded a significant fleet. Octavian, though younger than Antony and not a general, was a man of unusual cunning. His forces defeated Antony and Cleopatra at the naval battle of Actium (northwestern Greece) in 31 B.C. Cleopatra fled with her fleet, and, to be certain that she would not be captured by Octavian, killed herself with a poisonous snakebite. Octavian conquered Egypt in 30 B.C. He spent the next forty-five years healing the wounds of a century of revolution, and in so doing, he laid the foundations for two centuries of peace (Map 4.1).

The Political Settlement

Octavian was both an astute politician and a lucky one. He was lucky in the length and violence of the civil wars. After Actium, most of his enemies were dead, so establishing one-man rule was relatively easy. He was also lucky to live to be nearly 80, so he had plenty of time to consolidate his rule. Octavian astutely learned the lesson of Caesar's mistake. He was a cagey man, a careful planner who loved to gamble with dice but never took chances in the game of power. He understood that the Roman elite, however weakened, was still strong enough to oppose a ruler who flaunted monarchical power. Octavian was infinitely diplomatic, aware that a cooperative senate could aid his rule greatly.

Rather than call himself Dictator, Octavian took the title of *Princeps* ("First Citizen"). From princeps comes *principate,* a term often used to describe the constitutional monarchy of the "Early Empire"—the period from 27 B.C. to A.D. 192. Four years after Actium, in 27 B.C., the senate granted Octavian the honorific title *augustus,* derived from the verb *augere,* "to grow." The name suggested prosperity and growth. Another name, *imperator* ("commander" and, later, "emperor"), recalled the military might that Augustus (as we shall henceforth call him) could call on if needed.

In 27 B.C. Augustus proclaimed "the transfer of the state to the free disposal of the senate and the people"—that is, the restoration of the Republic. Remembering similar claims by Sulla and Caesar, few Romans were likely to believe him, and few would have wanted the Republic restored in any case; they no doubt appreciated their ruler's tact, however. The new government that emerged, after trial and error, was a partnership between Augustus and the senate—an unequal partnership in which Augustus held the upper hand, but a partnership nonetheless.

Several things made it work. First, Augustus deftly claimed both consular imperium and tribunician authority without constant election as consul and tribune. He thereby separated his military and civil powers from Republican offices. Second, Augustus dispersed administrative authority to appease various groups and foster efficient government. One example was his division of the provinces into two categories. To check any new would-be Caesar, he kept for himself the frontier provinces, with the main concentration of armies, as well as grain-rich Egypt. The local commanders were loyal equestrians who owed their success to Augustus. Most of the other provinces continued to be ruled as before by the senate and its promagistrates.

A third and crucial point is that Augustus's senators hardly resembled their predecessors. After many senators were purged, the membership of the senate was reduced to about six hundred. The princeps reshaped the Roman ruling class by elevating to the senate large numbers of equestrians, particularly Italians. Where once optimates had monopolized power, now the wealthy classes of Italy eagerly administered the government of the man who had championed their cause. The senatorial order was still above the equestrians—a distinction made visible in the broad purple stripe that only senators could wear on their tunics. The equestrians' gold ring and narrow purple stripe marked them as the second highest order.

CHAPTER CHRONOLOGY

44 B.C.	Caesar assassinated
31 B.C.	Octavian defeats Antony at Actium
27 B.C.	Augustus establishes principate
ca. A.D. 27–30	Ministry of Jesus
ca. A.D. 67	Death of Paul of Tarsus
79	Eruption of Vesuvius
96–180	The "Five Good Emperors"
212	Almost all free inhabitants awarded Roman citizenship
235–283	Period of military anarchy

In order to use the senate as a sounding board, Augustus created a standing committee of magistrates and senators that evolved into an advisory group called the council of the princeps. In ordinary senate meetings, the presence of informers and secret agents ended the old freedom of speech. The popular assemblies fared even worse. Augustus clamped down on their already limited powers; even these were gradually assumed, in later times, by the senate.

Augustus also stationed his own personal guard in Rome. Called the praetorians, or Praetorian Guard, the name used for a Roman general's bodyguard, the guard would play a role in future imperial politics.

More important for the public good, Augustus established the first civil service for Rome, Italy, and the provinces, embodied in a series of prefectures—or departments—supervising the city watch, the grain supply, the water supply, the building of roads and bridges, tax collection, and the provisioning of the armies. Equestrians were prominent in these prefectures. Freedmen, too, rose rapidly in the imperial service. Since few public officials received a salary, bribes and corruption were common. Although one may speak loosely of "imperial bureaucracy," neither Augustus nor his

successors ever established a tight administrative grid on their far-flung empire. As in all ancient empires, Roman government tended to be decentralized and limited.

The Economic and Social Settlement

The old Roman ruling class made its peace with Augustus, but some never forgave him for ending their ancient privileges. Although Augustus was generally a mild ruler, several of his successors' rules were marked by treason trials, judicial murder, witch-hunts for alleged conspirators, and *damnatio memoriae*, the erasure from the public record of a condemned man's existence. The conservative historian Tacitus (A.D. 55–ca. 117) looked back wistfully to the Late Republic as a golden era of freedom, eloquence, and "the old sound morality." But Tacitus understood that the Principate was enormously popular with the vast majority of the inhabitants of the Roman world. The reason is simple: Augustus and his successors brought an age of peace and prosperity after a century of disasters under the Late Republic. The sternness of the emperor Tiberius (r. A.D. 14–37), the decadence of Caligula (r. 37–41), and the excesses of Nero (r. 54–68) affected only a tiny minority in the elite.

The Augustan period was one of affluence, especially in Italy; the other provinces caught up with Italy by the second century A.D. Agriculture flourished with the end of civil war. Italian industries became leading exporters of such luxury items as glass bowls and windowpanes, iron arms and tools, silver eating utensils and candlesticks, and bronze statues. Italian goods circulated from Britain and Norway to Sudan and eastward to south and central Asia. Augustus stimulated trade by creating the first stable imperial coinage. Brass and copper coins served everyday needs, and there were also gold and silver issues.

Map 4.1 The Roman World in the Early Empire
Many modern cities are built on the site of Roman foundations, evidence of the immense extent of the Roman Empire at its height.

The perennial problem of the Late Republic had been land-hunger, which drove peasants into the hands of ambitious generals. Augustus ensured his troops' contentment by compensating 300,000 loyal veterans with land, money, or both, often in new overseas colonies. At first he paid from his own private sources; after A.D. 6 he supported the army from new taxes on the rich. In other words, Augustus made the elite part of a property transfer that they had resisted since the time of the Gracchi. Still, rural poverty and slavery

Augustus of Prima Porta Named for the place where it was found, this statue (early first century A.D.) depicts an idealized and heroic Augustus. Scenes of victory, peace, and prosperity—symbols of the principate— decorate his breastplate. Riding a dolphin, the Cupid at Augustus's feet recalls the Julian family's claim of descent from the goddess Venus. (*Alinari/Art Resource, NY*)

continued in Italy. In the countryside, only the condition of soldiers and their families improved, but this was enough to ensure domestic peace.

To end the problem of renegade commanders that had so bedeviled the Late Republic, Augustus reduced the size of the army, gradually cutting the number of legions from over sixty to twenty-eight, around 140,000 men. About the same number of men served as light infantry or cavalry in the auxiliaries. This reduction freed the Roman economy of a considerable tax burden, but there was a cost in military strength. In A.D. 9 three Roman legions were wiped out in a native revolt in Germany. Augustus had to accept the Rhine River as Rome's new German frontier (see Map 4.1).

Imperial defense remained a major issue. The European frontier, with its hostile populations and lack of central authorities to negotiate with, required strong armies. When he could, Augustus and his immediate successors set up client kingdoms, such as Judea and Armenia, to protect Rome's provinces. With Parthia, Augustus negotiated a compromise settlement that failed to expand Roman territory but achieved the symbolic victory of a return of the legionary standards lost by Crassus at Carrhae in 53 B.C.

The urban poor, many of them freedmen, also benefited under Augustus. (See the box "Ordinary People.") He initiated a more efficient system of free grain distribution, and though many poor people lived on a sort of grain gruel and cheap wine, it was better than nothing. Augustus also increased the number of regularly held public spectacles. This policy of "bread and circuses" was designed to keep the masses content, often through extraordinarily violent spectacles. There were chariot races, fights between humans and wild animals, and criminal execution by savage beasts. Augustus also initiated vast public works programs to provide jobs for the poor. He prided himself on having found Rome "a city of brick" and having left it "a city of marble."

To promote his ideology of renewal, Augustus sponsored social legislation embodying the old Republican virtues. He passed a series of laws encouraging marriage and childbearing and discouraging promiscuity and adultery. Such legislation

was widely disobeyed. In 2 B.C. Augustus felt compelled to make an example of his own daughter, Julia (39 B.C.–A.D. 14), his only child, whose adulteries were the talk of Rome. As punishment she was banished to a barren islet. Despite the promotion of family, the slight increase in women's freedom that began in the Late Republic did continue into the empire. Wives could initiate and obtain a divorce without losing their personal property, for example. High infant mortality led women to have many children in order to ensure the survival of the family, though evidence suggests that some women did try to limit the number of their offspring through various methods of contraception.

The Culture of the Augustan Age

Like *Periclean*, the adjective *Augustan* has come to signify an era of literary and artistic flowering. In both periods there were strong elements of classicism in the arts—that is, an attempt to project heroic and idealized values, the values that the self-confident rulers of each epoch wished to promote. Both prose and poetry flourished in Augustus's empire. The emperor was a patron of a number of important poets, chief among them Virgil (70–19 B.C.) and Horace (65–8 B.C.). Also important was the historian Livy (59 B.C.–A.D. 17), who wrote his history of Rome from the founding of the city to 9 B.C. under Augustus. All three writers contributed to the Augustan renewal and rededication of Rome.

Virgil's masterpiece is an epic poem, the *Aeneid,* "the story of Aeneas," the legendary Trojan founder of Rome, or at least of the Latin town from which Rome's founders eventually came. Legend also made Aeneas the ancestor of Augustus. The *Aeneid* indirectly celebrates Augustus, often considered Rome's second founder. (If Virgil had written an epic directly about Augustus, he would have been constrained in what he could say.) The poem explores the pain and burden as well as the glory of empire.

If Virgil's work has the grandeur of marble, Horace's poems—*Odes, Epodes, Satires, Epistles,* and *Ars Poetica* (*Art of Poetry*)—are more like finely cut gems. They tend to be polished, highly complex, and less emotional than the *Aeneid.*

Ordinary People

These funerary inscriptions, chosen from different parts of the empire, are just a few of the tens of thousands of surviving epitaphs that shed light on the plain folk of the Roman world. They illustrate a variety of levels of success, ranging from a slave's poverty to a craftsman's prosperity to a boxing champion's money.

(a)
[Rome]   To the spirits of the departed. [Remains of] Marcus Canuleius Zosimus; he lived twenty-eight years; his patron erected this to a well-deserving freedman. In his lifetime he spoke ill of no one; he did nothing without his patron's consent; there was always a great weight of gold and silver in his possession, and he never coveted any of it; in his craft, Clodian [silver] engraving, he excelled everybody.

(b)
[Puteoli, Italy]   To Grania Clara, freedwoman of Aulus, a worthy freedwoman; she lived twenty-three years and never caused me any vexation, save by her death.

(c)
[Anatolia]   You see me a corpse, passers-by. My . . . name was Apollonis, my native town Apamea, but now in the soil of Nicomedia the thread of destiny spun by the Fates holds me fast to the ground. Eight times he won in athletic games, but in the ninth boxing match he met his fated end. Play, laugh, passer-by, knowing that you too must die. His wife

Alexandria erected this memorial out of his money as a remembrance. If anyone dares to disturb this monument, he shall pay a fine of 2,500 *denarii* to the fisc.

(d)
[Rome]   To the spirits of the departed. You wanted to precede me, most sainted wife, and you have left me behind in tears. If there is anything good in the regions below—as for me, I lead a worthless life without you—be happy there too, sweetest Thalassia, nurse of a *vir clarissimus* and married to me for forty years. Paprius Vitalis, of the painters' craft, her husband, built this for his incomparable wife, himself, and their family.

(e)
Sacred to the gods of the dead. To Hapate, a Greek stenographer [slave], who lived 25 years. Pittosus put this up for his sweetest wife.

(f)
To the gods of the dead. [The tomb] of Irene the wool-weigher. She lived 28 years. Olympus put this up [for] his well-deserving wife.

Sources: Inscriptions (a)–(d): Naphtali Lewis and Meyer Reinhold, *Roman Civilization. Sourcebook II: The Empire* (New York: Columbia University Press, 1966), pp. 261, 266, 284–285. Copyright 1966 by Columbia University. Reprinted by permission of the publisher. Inscriptions (e)–(f): Mary R. Lefkowitz and Maureen B. Fant, trans., in their *Women's Life in Greece & Rome: A Source Book in Translation*, 2d ed. (Baltimore: Johns Hopkins University Press, 1992), p. 223.

Horace explored the themes of war and peace and praised Augustus. "With Caesar [Augustus] holding the lands, I shall fear neither turmoil nor violent death," declares one of the *Odes.*

Another patron of writers in Augustus's circle was Messalla, himself an orator and states-man. Love poetry was his special interest. Among the poets he supported were Ovid, best known for works on love and mythology; Tibullus, an eligist; and Messalla's ward, Sulpicia. Although little survives of Sulpicia's work, she is the only Roman woman of whose poetry there exists more than fragments. She described her passion for one Cerinthus: "a worthy man . . . at last a love . . . of such a kind that my shame, Gossip, would be greater if I kept it covered than if I laid it bare."[1]

Only 35 of the original 142 books of Livy's ambitious history have survived. Livy was both a master storyteller and ironist. His anecdotes of Roman history are vivid and told in a grand rhetorical style, haunted by the theme of Late Republican decline. Livy is our major source of evidence for the Roman monarchy and Early Republic. By modern standards, he relied on too much hearsay and myth, but Livy was concerned with more than the facts of history. Known as an entertaining stylist, Livy was also a profound thinker on the meaning of history. He embroidered the facts and engaged in frank, subjective judgments intended to arouse patriotism and inspire reflection on the ironies of human action.

Augustus and his entourage were also great patrons of the arts and of architecture, which they considered propaganda tools. They sponsored many major building projects in Rome, from temples to a new Forum of Augustus, the Theater of Marcellus, the Baths of Agrippa, the Pantheon, and the Mausoleum of Augustus. Augustan sculpture also manifests the themes of peace and plenty. The most common subject was Augustus himself; his statues were ubiquitous throughout the empire. Gems, coins, and relief sculpture also celebrated Augustus and his family.

Augustus's rule marked the beginning of the classical period of Roman jurisprudence, during which the professionalism that had begun to mark Roman law in the Late Republic became a permanent fact. A few distinguished jurists were granted the exclusive right to issue legal opinions "on behalf of the princeps." This ensured that experts guided the administration of justice. The first law school was opened in Rome under Augustus. Although various provincial legal systems remained in use, the international system of Roman law was widely used in the provinces.

In religion, too, Augustus was a legislator and reformer. Many traditional Roman cults had been neglected during the Late Republic. Augus-tus restored their rituals and priesthoods; he claimed to have restored all of the eighty-two temples in Rome. The restoration of cults was intended to publicize Augustus as Rome's savior. The Romans deified Augustus after his death, just as Augustus and Antony had had Julius Caesar deified after his death. The provinces worshiped Augustus as a god even while he was still alive, and the civic calendar grew crowded with festival days celebrating him. The imperial cult of Augustus remained an important part of state propaganda until the empire became Christian in the fourth century A.D.

Augustus had established the Roman Empire on a completely new footing. Republican institutions had lost their old freedoms, but the emperor and his bureaucrats had brought stability. The peace of the Augustan Principate would last, with few interruptions, for two hundred years. Few people in history have created order so successfully.

The Julio-Claudians

Augustus and his successors presented the imperial household to the world as the model family, combining filial piety with marital fidelity and harmony: a paradigm of social order. The emperor's servants sowed the image throughout the empire on works of art and architecture, in inscriptions, and in rituals and ceremonies. Behind the walls of the palace, however, was a troubled and sordid reality.

Augustus had only one child, Julia, from his first marriage, which ended in divorce. In 38 B.C., Augustus took as his second wife Livia (58 B.C.–A.D. 29), who divorced her husband to marry Augustus even though she was pregnant with their second son. She did not bear Augustus children. Seeking a male successor, Augustus used Julia as a pawn in a game of dynastic marriage, divorce, and remarriage, but to no avail. Julia's first two husbands predeceased her, as did two sons, each of whom Augustus had adopted. In the end, Augustus was forced to choose as successor and adopted son a man he disliked, Tiberius (42 B.C.–A.D. 37), Livia's elder son.

Julio-Claudian Cameo Known as the Grand Camée de France, this superb gem depicts the imperial family in its glory. The central scene shows Tiberius, Livia, and, among others, the child Caligula (extreme left). The deified Augustus hovers above them while barbarian captives are below. *(Giraudon/Art Resource, NY)*

Livia was among the most powerful women of Roman history. One of Augustus's main advisers, she developed a reputation for intrigue aimed, so gossip had it, at securing the succession for Tiberius. Livia's enemies accused her of poisoning Julia's husbands and sons, her own grandson, Germanicus (a brilliant general whose popularity threatened Tiberius's), and even Augustus himself, who died after a short illness in A.D. 14. Yet when Tiberius finally became emperor, he resented Livia's influence; when she died, he refused to execute her will or permit her deification.

From A.D. 14 to 68, Rome was ruled by four emperors from Augustus's family. The dynasty, known as the Julio-Claudians, consisted of Augustus's stepson, Tiberius; great-grandson, Caligula; grandnephew, Claudius; and great-great-grandson, Nero. For many elite Romans, this was an era of decadence, scandal, and oppression of the old nobility. The main trends of the period were more prosaic. Equestrians and freedmen gained an increasing governmental role, while the senate's power declined. Treatment of the provinces improved, and imperial expansion was generally avoided.

The reign of Tiberius (r. 14–37) was marked by intrigue, treason trials, murders, and an increase of the power of the princeps at the expense of the senate. Though unpopular with the masses and the elite because he cut back on games and building projects, Tiberius was a skilled and prudent administrator. He wisely drew back from war in Germany and Parthia, preferring diplomatic solutions. He reduced taxes and expenditures and promoted honesty among provincial governors.

His successor was his nephew, Gaius (r. 37–41), nicknamed Caligula ("Baby Boots") after the boots he wore as a little boy in his father's army camp. Caligula made scandalous behavior into an art form, often in attempts to elevate himself to the status of a god and to humiliate the senate. He appointed his favorite horse not only high priest of a new cult in honor of Caligula the god but also a member of the senate. Caligula trumped up charges of treason in order to confiscate property. He wanted to have his statue erected in the Temple at Jerusalem. He would have had his way, but he was assassinated first, the victim of a high-level Roman conspiracy. After his death the senate debated restoring the Republic, but the imperial family made quite clear the realities of power.

Backed by the Praetorian Guard, Caligula's uncle, Claudius, forced the senate to name him princeps. Physically disabled and suffering from a speech impediment, Claudius (r. 41–54) was often not taken seriously by his contemporaries, but he was an extraordinary politician, historian, and priest and was fully versed in the cunning ways of his family. An activist emperor, he expanded the imperial offices with their powerful freedmen; oversaw the construction of an artificial harbor at Rome's silt-clogged port of Ostia; and conquered Britain, where Roman armies had not intervened since Julius Caesar's forays in 55–54 B.C.

Claudius's death may have been the result of poisoning by his wife and niece, Agrippina the Younger (A.D. 15–59); in any case, her son by a previous marriage, Nero, became emperor (r. 54–68). As princeps, Nero's scandalous behavior rivaled Caligula's, and his treason trials outdid Tiberius's. A great fire in 64 destroyed half of Rome. When Nero mounted an extravagant rebuilding program, he was accused of having started the fire so that he could become famous as a builder. Nero found a scapegoat for the fire in the members of a small and relatively new religious sect, the Christians, whom he persecuted.

In contrast to such behavior, Nero provided generally good government for the ordinary people of the empire, and they rewarded him with support. He was unpopular with the senatorial elite and, more serious, he failed to pay all his troops promptly. Confronted with a serious revolt in 68, Nero committed suicide. The next year, 69, witnessed Rome's first civil war in about a century. Three men each claimed the imperial purple after Nero. Finally, a fourth, Vespasian (Titus Flavius Vespasianus, r. 69–79), commander of the army quelling revolt in the province of Judea, was able to make his claim stick. Peace was restored, but not the rule of Augustus's family. Vespasian founded a new dynasty, the Flavians (r. 69–96), which was followed in turn by the Nervo-Trajanic (r. 96–138) and Antonine (r. 138–192) dynasties. The ultimate tribute to Augustus may be that his regime was stable enough to survive the extinction of his family.

THE ROMAN PEACE, A.D. 69–180

Much about Rome in the second century A.D. appears attractive today. Within the multi-ethnic empire, opportunities for inhabitants to become part of the elite were increasing. The central government was well on its way to granting Roman citizenship to every free person in the empire, a process completed in 212. The emperors emphasized sharing prosperity and spreading it through the provinces.

The Flavians and the "Good Emperors"

The Flavian dynasty of Vespasian (r. 69–79) and his sons Titus (r. 79–81) and Domitian (r. 81–96) offered good government, and their successors built on their achievements. Unlike the Julio-Claudians, Vespasian hailed not from the old Roman nobility but from an Italian propertied family. When Titus complained that a new latrine tax was beneath the dignity of the Roman government, Vespasian, a man of rough-and-ready character, is supposed to have replied, "Son, money has no smell." Unlike his father and brother, Domitian reverted to frequent treason trials and persecution of the aristocracy, which earned him assassination in 96, although the empire as a whole enjoyed peace and good administration during his reign.

The so-called Five Good Emperors who followed Domitian were Nerva (r. 96–98), Trajan (r. 98–117), Hadrian (r. 117–138), and the first two Antonines, Antoninus Pius (r. 138–161) and Marcus Aurelius (r. 161–180). They were in several ways examples of the principle of merit. Trajan, a Roman citizen born in Spain, was Rome's first emperor from outside Italy. Hadrian and Marcus Aurelius also came from Spain, Antoninus Pius from Gaul. Each of the Five Good Emperors except Marcus Aurelius adopted the most competent man, rather than the closest blood relative, as his son and successor, thus elevating duty over sentiment. Marcus Aurelius, a deeply committed Stoic, gave expression to his sense of duty in his *Meditations*, which he wrote in Greek while living in a tent on the Danube frontier, where he fought against German raids. Antoninus was surnamed "Pius" ("Dutiful") because of his devotion to his country, the gods, and his adoptive father, Hadrian.

The Five Good Emperors made humane generosity a theme of their reigns. Trajan founded a program of financial aid for the poor children of Italy. The emperors also went to great lengths to care for the provinces. Hadrian, a noted lover of Hellenism, lavished attention on Greece, particularly Athens. Both Hadrian and Antoninus Pius contributed generously to buildings in Roman Carthage. These emperors commonly received and answered petitions from cities, associations, and individuals in far-off provinces.

Like the Julio-Claudians, the Five Good Emperors spoke of their wives as exemplars of traditional modesty, self-effacement, and domesticity. In fact, these women were worldly, educated, and influential. Trajan's wife, Plotina (d. A.D. 121 or 123), acted as patron of the Epicurean school at Athens, whose philosophy she claimed as her own. She advised her husband on provincial administration as well as dynastic marriages.

Hadrian's wife, Sabina, traveled with her husband to Egypt (A.D. 130). There her aristocratic Greek friend Julia Balbilla commemorated the trip by writing Greek poetry, which she had inscribed on the leg of the colossal statue of Memnon.

A darker theme of the reigns of the second-century emperors was the constant problem of border defense. Augustus and the Julio-Claudians had established client kingdoms whenever possible to avoid the expense and political dangers of raising armies. Later emperors were inclined to be more aggressive. A new border policy begun by the Flavians was in full operation in the second century A.D.: stationary frontier defense. Expensive fortification systems of walls, watchtowers, and trenches were erected along the perimeter of the empire's border and manned with guards. A prominent example is Hadrian's Wall, which separated Roman Britain from the enemy tribes to the north. Stretching 80 miles, the wall required 15,000 defense troops.

The most ambitious policy was that of Trajan, who crossed the Danube to carve out the new province of Dacia (modern Romania) and seized on a pretext to invade Parthian Mesopotamia. Although Trajan swept all before him and reached the Persian Gulf, his Parthian campaign was ultimately a disaster. As soon as his army withdrew, Mesopotamia rose in a general revolt, and the Germans followed suit. Trajan's reign marked the empire's greatest geographical extent, but Trajan had overextended Rome's resources. When he died, his successor, Hadrian, had to abandon Trajan's province of Mesopotamia (see Map 4.1).

Prosperity and Romanization in the Provinces

Compared to a modern economy, the Roman economy was underdeveloped. Most people worked in agriculture, employed primitive technology, and lived at a subsistence level. Even so, the Roman Empire experienced modest economic growth during the first two centuries A.D. The chief beneficiaries were the wealthy few, but ordinary people shared in the economic expansion as well. In addition to stability and peace, several other factors encouraged economic development. The western provinces witnessed the opening of new lands to agriculture, where improved techniques were applied. The growth of cities increased agricultural demand. Changes in Roman law aided commerce by making it easier to employ middlemen in business transactions. Travel and communications were relatively easy and inexpensive.

The second century A.D. was a great age of city life. New cities were founded far from the Mediterranean. Many would be of permanent importance in European history: Cologne (Colonia Claudia Agrippensis), Paris (Lutetia Parisiorum), Lyon (Lugdunum), London (Londinium), Mérida (Emerita Augusta), Vienna (Vindobona), and Budapest (Aquincum). Some of the new cities were veterans' colonies. Some were army camps that grew into towns. Some were market towns that grew by slow accretion.

Whether old or new, cities attracted a large elite population. Urban people competed with each other for positions as magistrates or on the local town council, often called a *curia*; town councilors were called *decurions* and known collectively as the *curial order*. Decurions competed with each other in lavish expenditures on public buildings in the Roman style, one man endowing a new forum, another a triumphal arch, a third a library, a fourth public baths, and so on. From Anatolia to Britain, from Germany to Libya, a Roman could find familiar government institutions, architecture, and street plans.

Women did not usually hold magistracies, but wealthy women could and did lavish money on public benefactions, and rich women could become curials. Women endowed temples and synagogues, amphitheaters and monumental gateways, games and ceremonies. They were rewarded with wreaths, front-row seats, statues, priesthoods, and inscriptions honoring them as "most distinguished lady," "patron," and even "father of the city," to cite an extraordinary case from Roman Egypt.

The buildings were visible examples of Romanization, although the Romans did not use the term. Roman officials frequently established Roman buildings and monuments or Latin schools for the children of a conquered local elite, but the emperors did not attempt to impose uniformity on their subjects. Even if they had aspired to such a goal, it would have been impossible to achieve, given the size of the empire and the state of ancient technology. Scholarly estimates of the total population of the empire range between 50 and 100 million people, most of whom lived in the countryside. The small and largely urbanized Roman administration had little direct contact with most people. Only a minority of the inhabitants of the empire spoke Latin; in the East, Greek was the more common language of administration. Millions of people spoke neither Greek nor Latin. Celtic, Germanic, Punic, Berber, Coptic, Aramaic, and Syriac were other languages commonly spoken in Roman domains. In short, the empire lacked the unity of a modern nation-state.

What, then, might one mean by Romanization, besides buildings and language? One index has already been suggested: the participation of provincials in the central government, even as emperors. By around A.D. 200, about 15 percent of the known Roman equestrians and senators came from North Africa. By this time the senate was no longer dominated by Italians but was representative of the empire as a whole.

Participation in government implies another index of Romanization, the extension of Roman citizenship. Pompey and Caesar began the process of enfranchising individuals and communities outside the old borders of Roman Italy. The process continued under the Julio-Claudians and Flavians and flourished under the second-century emperors, who gave magistrates, decurions, or whole cities the privilege of citizenship. Citizens took the Roman names of the emperor or promagistrate who had enfranchised them. Thus the provinces were full of Julii, Claudii, and Flavii, among others. The provinces also provided many examples of the juxtaposition of Roman and local names. The existence of a Roman citizen named Gaius Julius Hannibal, for instance, says something about both the extent and limits of Romanization.

Double Portrait, Pompeii
This wall painting from a house joined to a bakery depicts a married couple, possibly the wealthy baker P. Paquius Proculus and his wife. The portraiture is realistic. The couple carry symbols of education: She holds wax tablets and a stylus (pen), while he grasps a sealed scroll. *(Scala/Art Resource, NY)*

Finally, by A.D. 212, in a law known as the *Constitutio Antoniana,* the emperor Caracalla (r. 211–217) declared nearly all of the free men and women of the empire to be Roman citizens. This law was probably less an expression of universal brotherhood than of a desire to collect increased taxes, for citizens had a heavier tax burden than noncitizens. Nor did near-universal citizenship mean an end to ingrained Roman social inequality. Privileges previously inherent in citizenship, such as exemption from flogging by officials, now tended to be based on a class distinction enshrined in private and criminal law: a distinction between *honestiores* (in general, the curial order) and *humiliores* (everyone else). Still, Caracalla's law was a landmark act. Near-universal Roman

citizenship was a kind of halfway point between ancient empire and modern mass democracy.

Two other institutions were crucial in Romanization: Roman law, with which local elites became familiar, and the Roman army. In antiquity as today, military service had an egalitarian and educational function. The legions were restricted to citizens; non-Romans served as auxiliaries. They received Roman citizenship after completing their regular term of service, twenty-five years. A Syrian or Gallic peasant who served in the Roman military would experience a way of life rooted in central Italy nearly a millennium before.

Non-Italians had the opportunity to rise high in the army or government. This was all to Rome's credit; yet as Italians became a minority in the Roman army, and as ever larger numbers of frontier peoples were recruited, it became conceivable that someday the army might give up its loyalty to Rome.

The Culture of the Roman Peace

In Latin poetry the century after the death of Augustus is often referred to as the "Silver Age," a term sometimes applied to prose as well. The implication is that this period fell short of the golden Augustan era. It might be fairer to say that the self-confidence of the Augustan writers did not last. As the permanence of monarchy became clear, many in the elite looked back to the Republic with nostalgia and bitterness. The Silver Age was an era of interest in antiquities and in compiling handbooks and encyclopedias, an era of self-consciousness and literary criticism. In the first two centuries A.D., Roman writers came from an ever greater diversity of provinces and backgrounds and wrote for an ever wider audience, as prosperity and educational opportunities increased.

Many writers of the era pursued public careers, which offered access to patronage. Tacitus, for instance, rose as high as proconsul of the province of Asia. Prominent literary families emerged, such as that of Pliny the Elder (A.D. 23–79), an encyclopedic author on natural science, geography, history, and art; and his nephew, Pliny the Younger (A.D. ca. 62–ca. 113), an orator and letter-writer. The most notable literary family was that of Seneca the Elder (ca. 55 B.C.–ca. A.D. 40), a historian and scholar of rhetoric; his son, Seneca the Younger; and Seneca the Younger's nephew, the epic poet Lucan (A.D. 39–65).

Seneca the Younger was the major literary figure of his age, a jack-of-all-trades: playwright, essayist, pamphleteer, student of science, and noted Stoic philosopher. Some have criticized his work as lively but insubstantial. Seneca's personal life, in contrast, was made of harsher stuff. He is known for his suicide, in which he opened his veins and bled to death while calmly discussing philosophy. Seneca's wife, Pompeia

Paulina, insisted on dying with him, in the tradition of the stern and courageous Roman woman. Nero had her arms bandaged and saved her life. He was thinking of his own reputation, which was already stained with enough cruelty, but gossip accused Paulina of betraying her husband.

A literary career was safer under the Five Good Emperors. Consider Tacitus and his contemporary, the poet Juvenal (ca. A.D. 55–130). Juvenal's *Satires* are bitter and brilliant poems offering social commentary. Juvenal lamented the past, when poverty and war had supposedly kept Romans chaste and virtuous. Amid "the woes of long peace," luxury and foreign ways had corrupted Rome, in his opinion. Critics often blamed society's woes on marginal groups. Juvenal, for example, launched harsh attacks on women and foreigners. Tacitus, too, was sometimes scornful of women. He noted, for example, the charge that Livia had "a woman's lack of self-control."

Tacitus, if biased on matters of gender, was far from ethnocentric. Few historians have expressed graver doubts about the value of their country's alleged success. Tacitus highlighted the simple virtues of the German tribes, so different from the sophisticated decadence of contemporary Rome. Nostalgia for the Republic pervades his two greatest works, *The Histories*, which covers the civil wars of A.D. 69, and *The Annals* (only parts of which survive), chronicling the emperors from Tiberius through Nero. A masterpiece of irony and pithiness, Tacitus's style makes an unforgettable impression on the reader.

Plutarch (ca. A.D. 50–ca. 120), whose *Parallel Lives of Noble Greeks and Romans* later captured the imagination of Shakespeare, was probably the best-known pagan Greek writer of the first two centuries A.D. Like Livy, Plutarch emphasized the moral and political lessons of history. A careful scholar, Plutarch found his true calling in rhetorical craftsmanship—polished speeches and carefully chosen anecdotes. As in Rome, rhetoric was the basis of much of Greek literary culture in this period.

THE CRISIS OF THE THIRD CENTURY, A.D. 180–284

The portrait sculpture of the Antonine era (A.D. 138–192) differs significantly from that of the third century A.D. Antonine sculpture recalls Augustan classicism: busts of the imperial family, for instance, show good-looking, hard-working women and men with regular, often idealized features and thoughtful expressions. In third-century imperial portrait busts, physical features are sharper, chisel work is coarser, and the uniformities of Greco-Roman classicism give way to diverse local styles. Third-century emperors are sometimes shown scowling or even looking anxiously into the distance.

The emperors had reason to be anxious. Leaving the relative calm of the second century A.D. behind, the third-century Roman Empire descended into an ever widening spiral of crisis. Barbarian invasions, domestic economic woes, plague, assassinations, brigandage, urban decline: The list of Rome's problems is dramatic. The empire went "from a kingdom of gold to one of iron and rust," as Dio Cassius put it, summing up Roman history after the death of Marcus Aurelius in A.D. 180.

Severan Ambitions

Stability first began to slip away during the reign of the last of the Antonines, Marcus Aurelius's birth-son, Commodus (r. 180–192), a man with Nero's taste for decadence and a penchant for terrorizing the senatorial elite. Dressed like Hercules, he appeared in the amphitheater, where he shot animals in the morning and fought as a gladiator in the afternoon. Ever suspicious of enemies, Commodus planned to kill both new consuls on New Year's Day 193, but they beat him to the punch on New Year's Eve by having him murdered: His training partner, a professional athlete named Narcissus, strangled Commodus in his bath. After several years of civil war, Septimius Severus, commander of the Danube armies, emerged as the unchallenged emperor (r. 193–211); he founded the Severan dynasty, which survived until 235.

Septimius and his family illustrated the decentralization of the Roman elite. Septimius was born in Roman Libya, into one of the leading families of the city of Lepcis Magna, an old Phoenician city. Of Phoenician descent, his family were Roman citizens; his grandfather had been educated in Italy. Septimius spoke Latin with a provincial accent; he knew Greek too, but not as well as Punic, which he needed to know when out in the family estates in the Libyan countryside. His wife, Julia Domna, was a Syrian from the city of Emesa, where Aramaic and Greek were the main languages. Her father, Julius Bassianus, was priest of the main local god, Elegabal, and descended from royalty. She was a powerful woman in a family of powerful women. Indeed, the reigns of the last two Severan emperors (218–235), Julia's two grandnephews, were dominated first by her sister and then by her niece.

The main theme of Septimius's reign was the transfer of power—from the senate to the army and from Italy to the provinces. Septimius believed that security demanded an extension of the Roman frontier in North Africa and western Asia. To achieve this goal, he expanded the army and improved pay and conditions of service. On his deathbed, he is said to have told his son: "Give the soldiers money and despise everyone else." Traditionalists decried the transformation of the principate into a military monarchy, whose great marshals elbowed aside civilian officials. Increasing border challenges seemed to necessitate this policy, however. Septimius's great mistake was indulging in war with Parthia (197–199)—unnecessary war, because the crumbling Parthian kingdom was too weak to threaten Rome. What the war *did* accomplish, however, was to inspire the enemy's rejuvenation under a new dynasty, the Sassanids.

Shock and Recovery

After the assassination of the last Severan emperor, Severus Alexander, in 235, the empire endured a half-century of one shock after another. The main problem was increased pressure on

≈ **ENCOUNTERS WITH THE WEST** ≈

Syria Between Rome and Persia

Rome and Persia fought three great battles in western Asia in A.D. 244, 252, and 260, all resulting in resounding victories for Persia under King Shapur I (r. ca. 241–272). This selection provides a Greek view of what Syria's inhabitants endured when Shapur "burned, ruined and pillaged" in A.D. 252. The selection comes from the **Thirteenth Sibylline Oracle,** *a verse commentary on contemporary events, purporting to be ancient prophecy.*

. . . the evil Persians . . .
. . . the Persians, arrogant men . . .
. . . the arrow-shooting Persians . . .
    Now for you, wretched Syria, I have lately been piteously lamenting; a blow will befall you from the arrow-shooting men, terrible, which you never thought would come to you. The fugitive of Rome will come, waving a great spear; crossing the Euphrates with many myriads, he will burn you, he will dispose all things

evilly. Alas, Antioch, they will never call you a city when you have fallen under the spear in your folly; he will leave you entirely ruined and naked, houseless, uninhabited; anyone seeing you will suddenly break out weeping. . . . Alas . . . they will leave ruin as far as the borders of Asia, stripping the cities, taking the statues of all and razing the temples down to the all-nourishing earth.

Source: D. S. Potter, trans., in his *Prophecy and History in the Crisis of the Roman Empire* (Oxford: Clarendon Press, 1990), p. 175.

Rome's frontiers. The Sassanid Persians overran Rome's eastern provinces and captured the emperor Valerian himself in 260. (See the box "Encounters with the West: Syria Between Rome and Persia.") The caravan city of Palmyra (in modern Jordan) took advantage of Rome's weakness to establish independence; its most famous leader was the warrior queen Zenobia. Meanwhile, two Germanic tribes, the Franks and the Goths, hammered the empire from the northwest and northeast.

Ever since the time of Augustus, financial restraint and political prudence had kept Rome's military manpower limited. The result of that limitation, plus fierce resistance by Germans, Britons, and Persians, was little overall expansion of Rome's borders during the Early Empire. The invasions of Roman territory in the third century stretched the system to the breaking point and beyond. To pay for defense, the emperors deval-

ued the currency. The result was massive inflation. As if this were not bad enough, a plague broke out in Egypt in midcentury and raged through the empire for fifteen years, compounding Rome's military manpower problems.

Assassinations and civil wars shook the government. Between 235 and 284 twenty men were emperor. Civilians suffered. Pretenders to the purple needed to raise armies, and therefore taxes. To keep one step ahead of the tax collector and military recruiter, some city-dwellers fled to the countryside, where some of them turned to brigandage. Those who remained in town faced greater financial burdens. Recognizing a shortage of potential benefactors and decurions, the emperors decreed that membership in the curial order would become hereditary and that decurions would be responsible for financing public services. Such decrees were easier to promulgate than enforce.

The ability of the empire to rebound from such problems was a tribute to Roman resilience and a sign of the disunity among the empire's enemies. Recovery began during the reign of Gallienus (r. 253–268), who ended the Frankish threat and nearly polished off the Goths. Gallienus excluded senators from high military commands and replaced them with professionals. Moreover, he adopted a more modest policy of border defense. The Romans now conceded much of the frontier to the enemy. They instead used fortified cities near the frontier as bases from which to prevent deeper enemy penetration into Roman territory.

Gallienus's reforms pointed the way to imperial reorganization, but they remained to be completed by the two great reforming emperors at the end of the third century and the beginning of the fourth: Diocletian (r. 284–305) and Constantine (r. 306–337), subjects of the next chapter.

EARLY CHRISTIANITY

Increasing contact between Rome and its western provinces served to plant Roman cities, Roman law, and the Latin language (or its derivatives) in western Europe. As Rome in turn owed much to other Mediterranean peoples, it may be said that the Roman Empire was a vessel that transported ancient Mediterranean civilization to northern and western Europe. No feature of that civilization was to have a greater historical impact than the religion born in Tiberius's reign: Christianity.

Christianity began as a Jewish movement in the provincial backwater of Palestine. Although the dominant language there, Aramaic, was understood by few in Rome, Christianity soon spread to speakers of the main languages of the empire, Greek and Latin. By the reign of Diocletian, Christians had grown from the twelve apostles, Jesus's original disciples, to millions. In the fourth century A.D., Christianity unexpectedly became the official religion of the entire Roman Empire, replacing paganism—one of the most momentous changes in Mediterranean history. We turn to that change in the next chapter; here we consider the career of Jesus and the early spread of the Christian Gospel (literally, "Good Tidings").

Jesus of Nazareth

Many Western scholars would distinguish the Jesus of theology, the object of faith, from the Jesus of history, the figure who lived in first-century Palestine. Recent work argues that the historical Jesus must be understood within the Judaism of his day. He was a product of the popular culture of the Palestinian countryside, a culture that was peasant and oral. Much of what the Gospels have to say about Jesus, some argue, must be rejected as later invention.

In the first century A.D., Judaism was in a state of creative and turbulent ferment. In this era there was not one normative Judaism but a variety of Judaisms. The Essenes, for example, lived apart from society in pursuit of a new covenant with God. The community at Qumran in the Judean desert, whose history was documented in the Dead Sea Scrolls, ancient texts discovered in 1947, was probably Essene. The tenets of Qumran included frugality, sharing, participating in a sacred communal meal, and avoiding oath-taking. Adherents anticipated the coming of the Messiah and an end of days, in which God would punish the wicked. Although Essene doctrine has much in common with early Christianity, early Christians did not withdraw from the world as the Essenes did.

The most popular group among Palestinian Jews was the Pharisees. They focused on the spiritual needs of ordinary folk. Pharisees believed that law was central to Judaism but argued that it could be interpreted flexibly, in light of the oral tradition that had grown up alongside the Hebrew Bible. The Pharisees believed in the superiority of spiritual to political matters. They emphasized charity toward the poor. They spoke in parables, vivid allegories that made their teaching accessible.

It is difficult to tell how much Jesus was influenced by these various doctrines, because, for all its historical importance, Jesus's life is poorly documented. The main sources of information about it are the New Testament books of Matthew, Mark, Luke, and John. Jesus left no writings of his own. Early Christians, however, wrote a great deal. Between the second and fourth centuries A.D., Christians settled on a holy book consisting of the Hebrew Bible, called the "Old Testament" by Christians, and a collection of writings about Jesus and his followers, called the "New Testament." The account of the Gospel According to Mark, probably the earliest Gospel, was most likely written about forty years after Jesus's crucifixion; several of the letters written by Paul of Tarsus date from the forties A.D.

Jesus was Jewish and spoke Aramaic. He may have also known at least some Greek, widely spoken by both Jews and non-Jews in the several Hellenized cities of Palestine. He began his teaching in the northern region of Galilee, where he lived in the town of Nazareth (see inset, Map 4.2). Jesus was probably born not long before the death in 4 B.C. of Herod, the Roman-installed client-king of Judea (the date of 1 A.D. for Jesus's birth, a mistaken calculation of Late Antiquity, does not accord with the data of the New Testament). At around age 30 Jesus was hailed by the preacher John the Baptist; soon afterward Herod Antipas, the Romans' client-king of Galilee, ordered the execution of John. John preached the imminence of God's kingdom, a time of universal perfection, and an end of misery. In preparation, sinful humankind needed to repent. Precisely how much influence John had on Jesus is a matter of debate, as is the question of John's relationship to the religious community of the Essenes.

Jesus was neither a Pharisee nor an Essene, but some of his positions were similar. Like the Pharisees, he strongly criticized the pillar of the Jewish establishment, the Sadducees, a small group of priests and wealthy men who saw the Jerusalem Temple and its rites as the heart of Judaism. Also like the Pharisees, Jesus rejected the growing movement of the Zealots, who advocated revolt against Roman rule, although there were Zealots among his followers. Jesus emphasized the notion of God as a loving and forgiving

father. He often spoke in parables and was said to be capable of working miracles, particularly faith healing. He welcomed marginalized groups, including such sinners as prostitutes and tax collectors. As a result, he won a wide following.

Jesus's teaching is typified in the Sermon on the Mount, addressed to his followers in Galilee. He praised the poor and humble and scorned the pursuit of wealth instead of righteousness. He called for generosity and forgiveness, recalling the traditional Jewish Golden Rule—to treat others as one would like to be treated. He said that prayer, fasting, and acts of charity should be conducted in private, not in public, in order to emphasize purity of motive.

Jesus spoke with conviction and persuasiveness—with "authority," as his followers said. To them, Jesus was Christ—"the anointed one" (from Greek *Christos*), the man anointed with oil and thus marked as the king of Israel. They considered him, that is, the Messiah foretold in the Hebrew Bible who would redeem the children of Israel and initiate the kingdom of heaven. In Galilee they greeted him as king. For some this was purely a spiritual designation; others planned an overthrow of Roman rule. In any case, his teachings provoked hostility from the Sadducees, stung by his criticisms. By going to Jerusalem, and by timing his visit to coincide with the feast of Passover, Jesus ensured the largest possible audience.

Jesus challenged central authority by going to Jerusalem and teaching and healing in the Temple under the eyes of the priests he had criticized. He drove merchants and moneychangers out of the Temple precincts by overturning their tables and perhaps even threatening them with a whip. Jesus attracted large crowds of followers, at least some of whom were armed. Sadducee authorities feared trouble, and so did the overlords of Judea, the Romans. The governor, Pilate (Pontius Pilatus), had already endured vehement Jewish objections to the display in Jerusalem of an imperial medallion and an inscription that seems to have asserted Augustus's divinity. Pilate had no need of further uproar. Temple police and Roman soldiers were called on to arrest Jesus quietly.

Map 4.2 The Expansion of Christianity to A.D. 200 After its origin in Palestine, early Christianity found its main centers in the Greek-speaking cities of the Roman East. Missionaries like Paul also brought the new faith to the Latin-speaking West, as well as to Ethiopia and Mesopotamia.

Jesus's subsequent trial and execution have always been controversial. The New Testament emphasizes the role of the Jewish leadership and the Jerusalem mob in Jesus's death. Written after the First Jewish Revolt (A.D. 66–77), however, the Gospels may have reflected anti-Jewish sentiment in the empire. Crucifixion, the method used to execute Jesus, was a Roman penalty (the traditional Jewish method was stoning) imposed and carried out by Romans. He suffered slow death on Golgotha (Calvary) Hill just outside the city. It was a spring Friday, on the eve of the Passover festival, around A.D. 30.

Paul of Tarsus

According to the Gospel-writers, Jesus died on a Friday and rose from the dead on Sunday, an event commemorated at Easter. He is said to have then spent forty days on earth, cheering his disciples in Galilee and working miracles, before finally ascending to heaven. Heartened, the disciples returned to Jerusalem and spread Jesus's teachings. Their movement spread in the thirties and forties A.D. throughout Palestine and into Syria. In Jerusalem Christians were known as Nazarenes—that is, followers of Jesus of Nazareth; it was at Antioch that they were first called "men of Christ" (*christianoi*).

Even as late as this, the followers of Jesus—those who considered him to be the Messiah—had no intention of starting a new religion. They saw themselves as good, faithful Jews and continued to follow the laws and rituals of the Sinai covenant. Although Sadducees and Jewish civil officials were hostile, early Jewish Christians found much support among Pharisees. The radical break came with the conversion of Paul of Tarsus (d. A.D. 67?), a pious Jew and Roman citizen.

Only Jesus himself played a greater role than Paul in the foundation of Christianity. A remarkable figure, Paul embodied three different and interlocking worlds. Born with the name of Saul, he was a Jew of the Diaspora (see page 23) from the southern Anatolian city of Tarsus. A learned Pharisee, Paul was a native speaker of Aramaic and knew Hebrew and Greek. His father had attained Roman citizenship, a rare privilege (for Jews) that Paul inherited. Paul's heritage speaks volumes about the variety of the Roman peace, and his religious odyssey speaks volumes more (see Map 4.2).

At first Paul joined in the persecution of the Christians, whom he considered blasphemous. Around A.D. 36, however, he claimed to have seen a blinding light on the road to Damascus, a vision of Jesus that convinced him to change from persecutor to believer. It was a complete turnaround, a *conversio* ("conversion"), to use the Latin word that would grow so important in years to come. Saul changed his name to Paul and became a Christian.

He also changed what being a Christian meant. Before Paul, part of being a Christian meant being a Jew and following the many rules of Jewish law. Because these included complex dietary and hygienic codes as well as the ritual of

circumcision, the idea of following Jesus was unattractive to people who were not already Jewish. Paul declared that adherence to Jewish law was no longer necessary. Whereas the Jerusalem church had baptized converts and considered them Jews, Paul considered them not Jews but converts in Christ. Also, before Paul, followers of Jesus tended to emphasize his teachings and his life. Paul emphasized Jesus's death and resurrection, and the suggestion that this event offered all humanity the hope of resurrection and salvation. From the late forties to the early sixties A.D., Paul undertook missionary journeys through the cities of the Roman east and to Rome itself. Roman authorities concluded that he was a criminal troublemaker and executed him sometime around A.D. 64.

Paul started Christianity on the road to complete separation from Judaism. Events over the next century widened the division. Jews and Christians competing for converts emphasized their differences. Also, although many Jews made their peace with Rome in A.D. 70, enough Jewish-Roman hostility remained to lead to uprisings in the Diaspora in 115 and to the Second Jewish Revolt in 132–135. Both were suppressed by Rome, and Judaism became ever more stigmatized among Gentiles, or non-Jews.

Bereft of the Temple at Jerusalem, Judaism nonetheless continued to prosper as a religion. The rabbis, the religious leaders of the Pharisees, emerged as the mentors of Judaism. Popular among Jews, the rabbis also appealed to the Romans, because most rabbis opposed revolt. Both after A.D. 70 and 135, the Romans made the rabbis responsible for Jewish self-government in Palestine. The rabbis left their mark on history, however, in an intellectual movement and not administration. Continuing in the tradition of the Pharisees, the rabbis amplified the oral law; that is, they wrote interpretations of the Hebrew Bible that clarified the practice of Judaism. They developed the notion of the "dual Torah," that is, the divine authority of the oral law as well as of written law of the Hebrew Bible. The notion legitimized the rabbis' enterprise, which made it possible for Judaism to evolve flexibly. The basic text of rabbinic Judaism is the Mishnah (ca. A.D. 200), a study of Jewish law. In rabbinic Judaism lay the basis of the medieval and modern forms of the Jewish religion.[2]

Expansion, Divergence, Persecution

Although Jesus's mission was mainly in the countryside, early Christianity quickly became primarily an urban movement. Initially concentrated in the Greek-speaking East, by the second century A.D. there were churches in North Africa and Gaul and, beyond Roman boundaries, in Parthian Iraq and in Ethiopia (see Map 4.2).

By around A.D. 200 an orthodox Christianity had emerged. Rooted in Judaism, it was a distinct and separate religion finding most of its supporters among Gentiles. A simple "rule of faith," emphasizing belief in one God and the mission of his son Jesus as savior, united Christians from one end of the empire to the other. Christianity attracted both rich and poor, male and female; its primary appeal was to ordinary, moderately prosperous city folk. Believers could take comfort from the prospect of salvation in the next world and in a caring community in the here-and-now. Christians emphasized charity and help for the needy, qualities all too often absent in Greco-Roman society. A Christian writer justly described a pagan's amazed comment on Christian behavior: "Look how they love each other." Most early Christians expected Christ's return to be imminent. This belief imparted urgency and excitement to their message.

Early churches were simple and relatively informal congregations that gathered for regular meetings. The liturgy, or service, consisted of readings from the Scriptures (the Old and New Testaments), teaching, praying, and singing hymns. Baptism was used to initiate converts. The Lord's Supper, a communal meal in memory of Jesus, was a major ritual. The most important parts of the meal were the breaking and distribution of bread at the beginning and the passing of a cup of wine at the end; these recalled the body and blood of Christ. As organizational structures emerged, churches in different cities were in frequent contact with each other, discussing common concerns and coordinating doctrine and practice.

Just as Jewish women were not rabbis, so early Christian women did not hold the priesthood. Jewish women, however, did hold office in the synagogue, and Christian women likewise served as deaconesses. Both endowed buildings and institutions. For example, the Italian Jewish woman Caelia Paterna was an officeholder honored by her congregation as "mother of the synagogue of the people of Brescia." Deaconesses played an active part in church charities and counseling and now and then gave sermons.

As Christianity spread it came to the attention of the authorities. The Romans expected all subjects to make sacrifices to the emperor as a sign of patriotism. The only exception was the Jews, who were permitted to forgo the imperial cult because their religion prohibited them from worshiping idols. When the Christians separated themselves from Judaism, they lost this privilege. As a result, the emperors considered Christianity at best a nuisance and at worst a threat. Christians were tested from time to time by being asked to sacrifice to the emperor; those who failed to do so might be executed. At times of stress when scapegoats were needed, Christians were sometimes brought to the arena to be fed to the animals. Until the fourth century Christians were occasionally persecuted. More often, Romans tacitly tolerated Christians as long as they kept their religion private. Christians could not proselytize in public places, put up inscriptions or monuments, or build churches. Christianity thus spread under restrictions, but spread it did, particularly in the cities of the East. The willingness of martyrs to die for the faith made a strong impression on potential converts. Although the number of Christians in the empire is not known, it is clear that by the late third century they were a significant and growing minority.

Mystery Religions

Roman policy toward Christianity by no means reflected an attempt to impose a single, unified religion on the empire. As polytheists, Romans were usually willing to admit new gods to their pantheon, as long as their worshipers took part in the patriotic emperor cult. Roman conservatism, moreover, fostered respect for other peoples' traditional faiths. Although from time to time during Roman history the authorities had tried to expel these faiths from the city of Rome itself, the spread of new religions during the first three centuries A.D. proved irresistible. Besides Christianity and Judaism, the most important were Greek mystery cults, including the cults of Dionysus and Demeter; the cults of Isis and Mithras; and

Mithraeum This sculpted relief comes from an underground sanctuary along the Rhine frontier. It shows the hero-god Mithras sacrificing a bull, the central symbol of Mithraism. Actual bull sacrifices were carried out in Mithraea. *(Hildesheim Museum/Richard Erdoes)*

Manichaeism. These religions displayed a tendency toward syncretism, often borrowing rites, doctrines, and symbols from one another.

The cult of Isis derived from the ancient Egyptian cult of Isis; her brother and husband, Osiris; and their son, Horus. Its central theme was eternal life through the promise of resurrection achieved by moral behavior in this life. Elements of Isis, who was often pictured with her young son, were later syncretized in the cult of the Virgin Mary, the mother of Jesus. Followers of Isis marched in colorful and at times terrifying processions through the streets of Roman cities, flagellating themselves as a sign of penitence.

Although men joined in the worship of Isis, the cult appealed particularly to women. The goddess's popularity crossed class lines; devotees ranged from slaves to one Julia Felix, whose estate at Pompeii included a garden shrine to Isis and Egyptian statuettes. The worship of Mithras, on the other hand, was generally limited to men and was especially popular with soldiers. Mithras, a heroic Persian god of light and truth, also promised eternal life. His worshipers believed that Mithras had captured and killed a sacred bull whose blood and body were the source of life. Accordingly, Mithraism focused on bull sacrifice carried out in a vaulted, cavelike temple called a *Mithraeum.* Initiates were baptized with bull blood and participated in various other rituals, including a sacramental meal. Their moral code advised a life led in imitation of their hero.

Manichaeism also originated in Persia, but later, in the third century A.D. Its founder, the Persian priest Mani, was martyred by conservative religious authorities. His cult recognized Jesus, Zoroaster, and Buddha as prophets. Manichaeism was characterized by philosophical dualism, emphasizing the universal struggle between good (Light) and evil (Darkness). According to believers, the world had been corrupted by Darkness, but eventually the Light would return. In the meantime, Manichaeans were to attempt to lead pure lives. Much attention was placed on proper diet. Manichaeism was a powerful religious force for two centuries; the great theologian Augustine flirted with it before becoming a Christian.

SUMMARY

Between the first century B.C. and the third century A.D., the Romans changed from a people who had come to destroy into a people who had come to fulfill. At the beginning of this period, the conquered provinces were oppressed by greedy bureaucrats and tax collectors, and Rome's imperial victories nearly ruined the Italian peasantry, who lost their farms while fighting in the Roman army. Members of the Roman elite raised private armies to win land for their followers and glory for themselves. The Republic collapsed under the weight of political maneuvering, judicial murders, gang warfare, and civil war.

A shrewd outsider, Octavian, confounded expectations by creating a new empire that would enjoy two centuries of stability; as Augustus, he served as its first emperor. Augustus reconciled the senatorial class by sharing a degree of power, but he guaranteed peace by keeping most of the armies in his own hand. He wisely accepted compromise with Parthia and defeat in Germany, reduced military spending, and stabilized the frontiers. He solved the problem of the landless peasantry by raising taxes to provide farms for all veterans. Perhaps most important, he began a new policy toward the provinces, which were slowly raised to equality with Italy. In short, Augustus initiated the prosperous Roman peace, an era lasting until the third century A.D. To survive the crises of that century, it was necessary for Rome to have a bigger army supported by higher taxes collected by a larger bureaucracy—requirements that would shake the social, political, and cultural foundations of the empire.

Literature and the arts flourished in the turbulent times of the Late Republic and the peaceful period of the Early Empire. In the provinces, the Roman peace made possible an era of architectural and literary flowering. Rome was a multi-ethnic empire whose inhabitants increasingly mixed with each other and exchanged ideas. None of these exchanges was more momentous than the emergence of several new religions, including Christianity.

NOTES

1. Translated by Mary R. Lefkowitz and Maureen B. Fant, *Women's Life in Greece & Rome. A Source Book in Translation*, 2d ed. (Baltimore: Johns Hopkins University Press, 1992), p. 9.
2. On these points see Lawrence H. Schiffman, *From Text to Tradition. A History of Second Temple and Rabbinic Judaism* (Hoboken, N.J.: Ktav Publishing House, 1991), pp. 1–16.

SUGGESTED READING

See also the suggested reading for Chapter 3; several of the works cited there cover the period of Chapter 4 as well.

Chadwick, Henry. *The Early Chuch*. 1967. A brief account of the first century B.C. through the sixth century A.D. Emphasizes theology.

Cohen, Shaye J. D. *From the Maccabees to the Mishnah*. 1987. Excellent synthesis of recent work that cites the origins of both Christianity and rabbinic Judaism in the turbulent history of Judaism in this era.

Crossan, John Dominic. *The Historical Jesus: The Life of a Mediterranean Jewish Peasant*. 1991. Innovative and controversial, the book presents Jesus as a Jew and an agrarian rebel, and questions the authenticity of much of what the Gospels report that Jesus said.

Earl, D. C. *The Age of Augustus*. 1968. A beautifully illustrated introduction to government, society, and religion.

Fantham, Elaine, Helene Peet Foley, Natalie Boymel Kampen, Sarah B. Pomeroy, and H. A. Shapiro. *Women in the Classical World: Image and Text*. 1994. Chapters 10–13 provide an excellent introduction to the social and cultural history of women in the Roman Empire.

Gardner, Jane F. *Women in Roman Law and Society*. 1986. A straightforward survey concentrating on the Late Republic and Early Empire.

Garnsey, Peter, and Richard Saller. *The Roman Empire: Economy, Society, and Culture*. 1987. A thematic rather than chronological introduction by two distinguished social historians.

Grant, Michael. *The Jews in the Roman World*. 1973. A good survey of Jews, Romans, and Christians, including a succinct account of the life and trial of Jesus.

Henig, M., ed. *Handbook of Roman Art.* 1983. A well-illustrated collection of essays by various authors, written for the beginner.

Johnson, Luke Timothy. *The Real Jesus: The Misguided Quest for the Historical Jesus and the Truth of the Traditional Gospels.* 1996. Well written, carefully argued, conservative and cautious, this book offers a good introduction to the question of the historicity of Jesus.

Kraemer, Ross. *Her Share of the Blessings: Women's Religions Among Pagans, Jews, and Christians in the Greco-Roman World.* 1992. Readable and thoughtful synthesis of important recent work emphasizing the prominence of women in ancient religion; uses a mixture of archaeological and literary sources.

Laistner, M. L. W. *The Greater Roman Historians.* 1963. A good, brief, general survey.

MacMullen, Ramsay. *Roman Government's Response to Crisis.* 1976. An analytical overview of the third century A.D. with special attention to institutions and society.

MacMullen, Ramsay. *Roman Social Relations, 50 B.C.–A.D. 284.* 1981. A wide-ranging essay in social history that moves between anecdote and general trend.

Millar, F. G. B. *The Roman Near East, 31 B.C.–A.D. 337.* 1993. A thoughtful, meticulous, and important study of ethnicity and empire, making special use of inscriptions.

Potter, D. S. *Prophecy and History in the Crisis of the Roman Empire.* 1990. A detailed historical study of the *Thirteenth Sybilline Oracle* as a contemporary comment on the troubles of the third-century empire.

Raaflaub, K., and M. Toher, eds. *Between Republic and Empire: Interpretations of Augustus and His Principate.* 1990. A good selection of the latest scholarly theories and controversies.

Russell, Donald. "The Arts of Prose: The Early Empire." In John Boardman, Jasper Griffin, and Oswyn Murray, eds., *The Roman World,* 243–266. 1988. A witty, perceptive, and concise treatment of Greek and Latin prose, excluding history writing, in the first two centuries A.D.

Saller, Richard. *Patriarchy, Property, and Death in the Roman Family.* 1994. A groundbreaking study of the demographic roots of familial sentiments.

Scullard, H. H. *From the Gracchi to Nero.* 5th ed. 1982. A concise and reliable introduction, with an emphasis on political history. Excellent bibliographies.

Thompson, Lloyd A. *Romans and Blacks.* 1989. A fascinating study of black Africans and the Roman Empire. Discusses Roman categories of race and ethnicity and contrasts stereotypes and the reality of social relations.

Treggiari, Susan. *Roman Marriage: Iusti Coniuges from the Time of Cicero to the Time of Ulpian.* 1991. An up-to-date and thorough discussion.

Zanker, Paul. *The Power of Images in the Age of Augustus.* 1988. Incisive study of Augustus's use of visual propaganda.

The World of Late Antiquity, ca. 300–600

Flavius Valerius Constantinus, known to history as Constantine the Great (r. 306–337), called himself "the restorer of the Roman Empire." It was a valid claim, but this restoration entailed a profound transformation. Constantine contracted treaties with various barbarian peoples that, in the long run, made it possible for those peoples to enter the empire and radically transform it. He instituted military reforms that paved the way to a massive militarization of public life in the Roman world. He also put an end to the persecution of Christianity, granted important privileges to the Christian church, and became a Christian himself—the first Roman emperor to do so. When Constantine died, the Roman Empire was stronger than it had been in generations. But it was also very different.

The reigns of Constantine and of his immediate predecessor, Diocletian (r. 284–305), inaugurate a period that scholars now label "Late Antiquity." For a long time educated people, often taking their lead from the elegant and influential *The Decline and Fall of the Roman Empire* by the British historian Edward Gibbon (1737–1794), believed that the Roman Empire "fell" in the fifth century, and the glories of classical civilization gave way to the gloom of the "Dark Ages." Today, on the contrary, specialists in the period from roughly A.D. 300 to 600 see vigor and achievement. Above all they see continuity, not tumult and collapse.

The most fundamental changes that occurred in this period involved the fragmentation of old structures and the creation of new ones. The imperial regime was militarized, the Germanic barbarians were incorporated into the Roman system, and the western provinces of the empire were transformed into a series of kingdoms allied with but basically independent of Rome. At the same time, Christianity developed an empire-wide organizational structure and a sophisticated intellectual tradition that made it first a competitor and then the successor to the classical culture that had dominated the Mediterranean world for over a millennium.

These were great changes, and yet, to a remarkable extent, the traditional Roman elite maintained itself. The Germanic warlords who replaced Roman administrators were tutored by the Romans themselves. The most prominent Christian clergy descended, in town after town, from the same powerful local families who had ruled for centuries. Christian culture borrowed not only the languages of the Roman Empire—Greek and Latin—but also the empire's philosophical traditions, legal customs, and art forms. The Roman Empire did not fall. It evolved. That evolution is the story of Late Antiquity.

∼ *Questions and Ideas to Consider*

- What was the tetrarchy, and why did the emperor Diocletian create it? How did the tetrarchy address the problem of succession?

- How did Christianity change the lives of women? What new choices, role models, and values did it offer them?

- In what ways did the institution of Christianity reflect the structures and practices of the empire in which it was created? Consider questions of administration, patterns of solving doctrinal disputes, and the concepts of honor, patronage, and deference.

- The "barbarian invasions" of the Roman Empire reflect compromise more than invasion. Discuss both the violent and the peaceful interactions between the Germanic peoples and Rome.

- Discuss the differences between the Eastern and Western churches around the time of Justinian. Consider doctrine, leadership, language, and architecture.

REBUILDING THE ROMAN EMPIRE

The third-century Roman Empire lurched from crisis to crisis. Three somewhat interrelated sets of problems demanded attention if Rome were to survive. First, the constant civil wars of the years between 235 and 284 had to be stopped and a stable form of transition from one reign to another found. Second, with the frontiers threatened in many sectors, the army needed to be expanded in size and deployed more effectively. Third, the economy had to be stabilized in order for the government to finance administrative and military reforms. Two rulers, with more than fifty years of rule between them, understood the empire's problems and legislated energetically to correct them.

The Reforms of Diocletian (r. 284–305)

By 293 the emperor Diocletian had put in place a regime that historians call the "tetrarchy," or rule by four (Map 5.1). Diocletian first selected an imperial colleague for himself, and then he and his colleague each selected a subordinate official. Diocletian and his colleague were called *augusti,* and the two subordinates were designated *caesares.* The names came from *Caesar,* which was both a family name and a general term for a ruler, and from the special title of *Augustus Caesar.* The system was intended to provide four men of imperial rank who could lead armies and make decisions in political and administrative matters. Each augustus was to adopt his caesar as his son and heir. In this way, the tetrarchy would provide for orderly succession to the imperial office and promote experienced, respected men. Diocletian retained the position of senior augustus and concentrated his efforts in the wealthy and populous eastern half of the empire.

Diocletian also addressed an ideological flaw in the Roman imperial system. Ever since the Principate (27 B.C.–A.D. 68), emperors kept Republican titles, though their real power was based on the military. Diocletian abandoned this pretense. He was addressed as *Dominus,* or

CHAPTER CHRONOLOGY

284–337	Reforms of Diocletian and Constantine	411–418	Settlement of Visigoths in Gaul
ca. 300	Emergence of Christian monasticism	430	Vandals seize North Africa
313	Edict of Milan grants toleration to Christianity	440–461	Pope Leo I elaborates doctrine of papal primacy
324–330	Founding of Constantinople	450–550	Angles and Saxons enter Britain
325	Council of Nicaea condemns Arian heresy	451	Council of Chalcedon condemns monophysite heresy
379–395	Reign of Theodosius the Great	476	Deposition of last Roman emperor in the West
382–392	Jerome prepares Vulgate Bible	481–511	Reign of Clovis: consolidation of Frankish kingdom
408–450	Theodosius II consolidates eastern Roman Empire	527–565	Reign of Justinian I
410	Visigoths sack Rome		

"Lord and Master." He adopted Eastern, especially Persian, habits, such as wearing ornate clothes and a jeweled diadem, sitting on an elevated throne, and rarely appearing in public.

When Diocletian ascended the throne, the Roman Empire was dramatically undergoverned given its size and problems. The empire had some fifty provinces, which differed greatly in size, population, wealth, strategic importance, and degree of Romanization. Rome had traditionally asked for relatively little from its empire, primarily taxes, military recruits, and loyalty. Local authorities generally did the tax collecting and military recruiting, with little interference by imperial agents. The imperial administration, made up largely of aristocratic amateurs, numbered only a few hundred men on Diocletian's accession.

Diocletian expanded the imperial administration by dividing old, large provinces into smaller ones and increasing the number of officials tending them. He then organized groups of provinces into thirteen dioceses and joined the dioceses into four prefectures. Each prefecture was equipped with an entourage of military, legal, financial, and secretarial officials headed by a praetorian prefect. By 350 the number of officers from the provincial

to the prefectorial level had risen from a few hundred to about forty thousand. Diocletian wished to fill the bureaucracy with trained administrators instead of with wealthy senators and equestrians who viewed government service as a tool to gain riches and prestige.

Diocletian also attended to Rome's military problems. His major initiative was an attempt to double the size of the army from about 300,000 to 600,000 men, although the final total ended up being only around 450,000. He also built new forts along the frontiers, improved the roads that supplied frontier defenders, and began the systematic incorporation of Germans into the army. Military careers had once been prized for providing Roman citizenship as well as a decent income. However, after citizenship became common—it was granted to almost everyone in the empire by 212—the dangers of military life far exceeded the attractions. But noncitizen Germans, whose only hope of citizenship was military service, found the army appealing.

These administrative and military reforms were expensive, so Diocletian attempted to regularize the tax system in the empire. A census was held to identify all taxpayers, and the productive

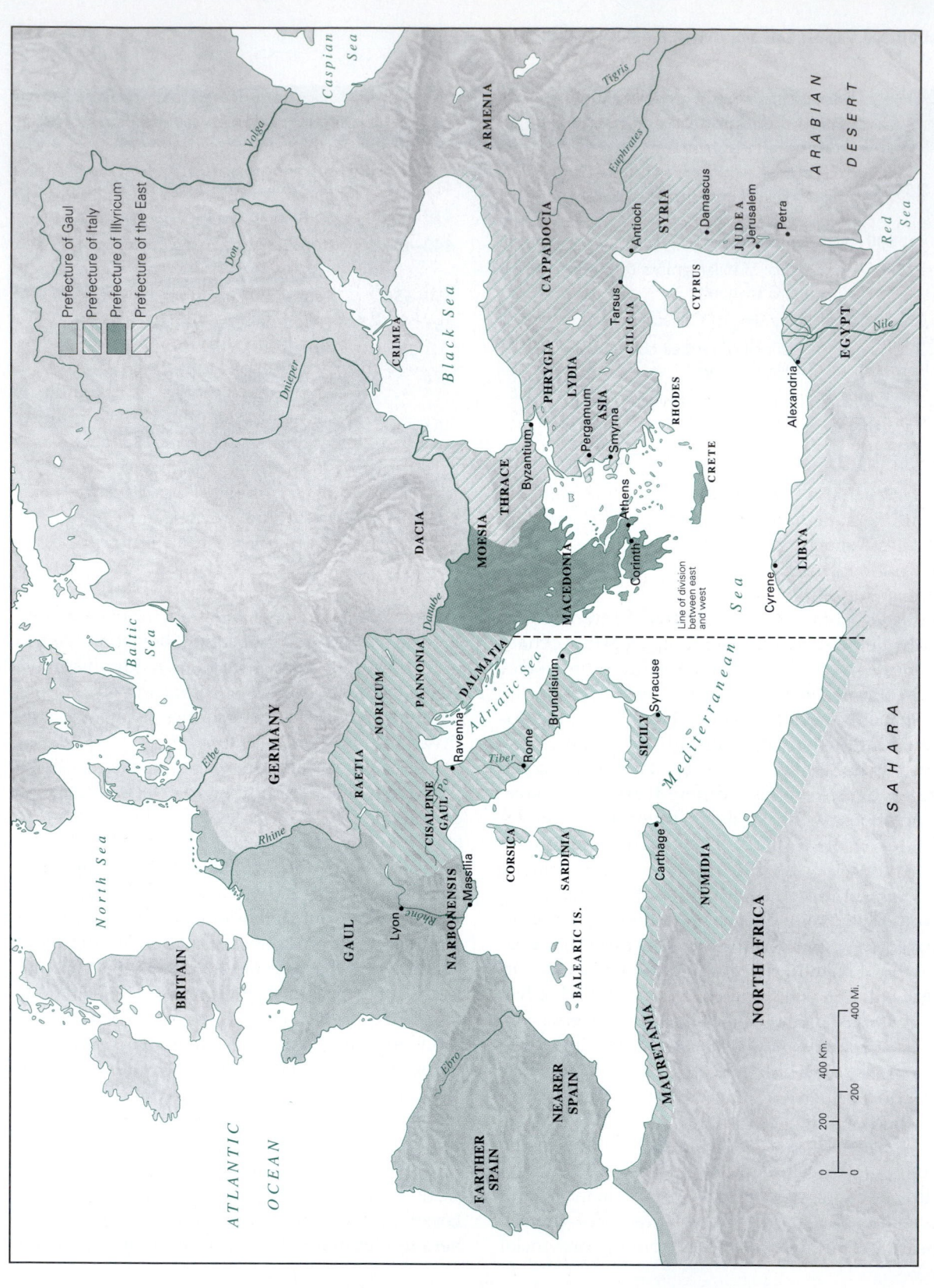

Prefecture of Gaul
Prefecture of Italy
Prefecture of Illyricum
Prefecture of the East

Caspian Sea
Volga
Don
Dnieper
Black Sea
CRIMEA
ARMENIA
Tigris
Euphrates
ARABIAN DESERT
SYRIA
Antioch
Damascus
JUDEA
Jerusalem
Petra
Red Sea
CAPPADOCIA
PHRYGIA
LYDIA
ASIA
Pergamum
Smyrna
Tarsus
CILICIA
CYPRUS
RHODES
EGYPT
Nile
Alexandria
THRACE
Byzantium
CRETE
Mediterranean Sea
LIBYA
Cyrene
DACIA
MOESIA
MACEDONIA
Athens
Corinth
Line of division between east and west
PANNONIA
DALMATIA
Adriatic Sea
Brundisium
Syracuse
SICILY
NORICUM
RAETIA
GERMANY
Elbe
Rhine
CISALPINE GAUL
Po
Ravenna
Tiber
Rome
CORSICA
SARDINIA
NUMIDIA
Carthage
NORTH AFRICA
SAHARA
Baltic Sea
North Sea
BRITAIN
GAUL
Lyon
Rhône
NARBONENSIS
Massilia
BALEARIC IS.
NEARER SPAIN
FARTHER SPAIN
MAURETANIA
Ebro
ATLANTIC OCEAN

400 Mi.
400 Km.
200
200
0
0

value of land was assessed. Tax reform was not enough, however. To address the escalating inflation of the third century and to halt skyrocketing prices, Diocletian issued in 302 the Edict of Maximum Prices, which froze prices and made many occupations hereditary to stop people from fleeing the countryside. The new taxes brought in revenue but caused widespread hardship by placing the burden on the most vulnerable: small farmers in particular. And with more officials handling vastly greater sums of money, corruption ran rampant.

Diocletian's reforms were sensible in principle but problematic in practice. In instituting his reforms, Diocletian stripped the senatorial order of military and civic responsibilities. He thus alienated a small but influential group numbering about two thousand. During the Principate, senators had gained enormous wealth, powerful offices, and prestige in return for their support of the imperial regime. That wealth, power, and prestige translated into immense personal influence that endured long after the senators' official power ceased. Moreover, the enlarged imperial administration necessarily reduced the autonomy of cities and their local leaders. Finally, the expanded administration cost a lot, especially for an empire already in serious economic distress. All of this caused resentment and weakened civic loyalty to Rome.

Tetrarchy Ideal and reality are both evident in this sculpture of the tetrarchy. The rulers, depicted equal in size, embrace one another but also bare their weapons—to one another and to the world. *(Scala/Art Resource, NY)*

The Reforms of Constantine (r. 306–337)

Diocletian's careful plans for the imperial succession collapsed almost immediately after his voluntary retirement in 305. When Constantius, Diocletian's western colleague as augustus, died in 306, his troops declared his son, Constantine, augustus. From 306 to 313, Constantine had several competitors; from 313 to 324, he shared rule with one man;

Map 5.1 Diocletian's Division of the Roman Empire Corresponding to the tetrarchy, the empire was divided into eastern and western halves, and each half was divided into prefectures. Four regions, rulers, and bureaucratic administrations replaced the ineffective rule of one man.

and from 324 to 337, he ruled alone, with his sons as caesars in various parts of the empire. This compromise between the hereditary and tetrarchal systems persisted for the next two centuries.

Constantine had entered the imperial court as a young man in 293, when his father was appointed augustus, and he later served with his father in Britain and Gaul. He knew the system and maintained the administrative structure that Diocletian introduced. Continuing the eastward shift of power begun under the tetrarchy, Constantine created a second imperial capital in the east. He selected an old Greek city, Byzantium, and renamed it after himself, "Constantine's polis" or Constantinople (modern Istanbul). The city was chosen because it straddled military roads between the eastern and western halves of the empire, overlooked crucial trade lanes to and from the Black Sea region, and was well sited to respond to threats along both the Balkan and the eastern frontiers (see Map 5.1).

In military affairs, Constantine expanded the use of mobile field armies to protect the empire's long frontiers. These armies, recruited largely (as under Diocletian) from Germans living along or beyond the frontiers, were stationed well behind the frontiers so that they could be mobilized and moved quickly. They were given their own command structures, under officers whom the Romans called "Masters of the Soldiers." The praetorian prefects became exclusively civilian officials. This separation of civilian and military command meant that no individual could combine the command of an army with one of the new and powerful government posts.

Scholars have long debated the wisdom of Constantine's arrangements. Moving experienced troops from the frontiers may have invited attacks. Recruiting Germans into the field armies may have created divided loyalties. Most Roman provincials had not lived near soldiers. Now the soldiers and the veterans of the field armies became daily companions. The reforms of Diocletian and Constantine essentially transformed the Roman Empire into a vast, armed camp. The financial resources of that empire were now largely devoted to maintaining a military establishment that was expensive, socially diverse, and potentially politically volatile.

The Legalization of Christianity

Since the first century, Christianity had been spreading throughout the Roman world, and by 300 there were Christians in every province. Christianity's strong appeal to women drew many adherents. Another factor in the expansion of Christianity was its growing hierarchical organization. The Roman Empire was rich in varieties of religious experience, but no pagan cult combined compelling teachings with a sophisticated institutional foundation.

The earliest communities of Christians had three kinds of officials, whose customary titles in English are *bishop, priest,* and *deacon.* Bishops and priests presided at celebrations, preached, and taught; deacons were responsible for charitable works and for arranging meetings. Deacons were clearly subordinate to the other two, but distinctions between bishops and priests developed over time. Within towns, the eldest priest was gradually accorded precedence and designated "overseer," the literal meaning of *bishop.* The bishops became influential local officials, and by the fourth century, even modest towns had bishops. By the late fourth century, the bishops in the major cities of the empire were called *metropolitan bishops,* or sometimes *archbishops,* and they had responsibility for territories often called *dioceses.* The Christian church was adopting the administrative geography of the Roman Empire under Diocletian.

And yet Diocletian will always be remembered for undertaking the last persecution of Christianity, between 303 and 305. We shall never know exactly why he did it. He was a man of conventional piety, and it may be, as even Christian writers later said, that he was truly convinced that the presence of Christians in his army offended his ancestral gods. Whatever its cause, the persecution was harsh and well planned. Churches were closed and copies of the Scriptures were collected. Decrees demanded the arrest of the clergy and required citizens to present themselves at a temple for some act of sacrifice. But gauging the effect of the persecution is difficult. It may have drawn favorable attention to Christianity by creating heroic victims—the martyrs' blood, according to a contemporary, was "the seed of the church."

All this changed under Constantine. While marching toward Rome to fight for the imperial office to which his father's troops had elected him, Constantine believed that he saw, emblazoned on the sun, a cross accompanied by the words "In this sign you shall conquer." Constantine had been raised at the court of Diocletian, where he received a traditional pagan upbringing, but his mother, Helena, was

Santa Costanza, Rome, ca. 350 The overall decoration and the modeling of figures in this mosaic are fundamentally classical, but the theme is Christian: Christ hands a scroll of the law, signifying both the Hebrew law and the church, to Saint Peter in the presence of Saint Paul. The mosaic illustrates well the blending of classical and Christian cultures. *(Scala/Art Resource, NY)*

Christian. She had surely exposed her son to the new faith, and she may have influenced him significantly.

Constantine put Christian monograms on his soldiers' uniforms, and when they proceeded to win a crucial battle in 312, he declared that they owed the victory to the God of the Christians. In 313, Constantine and the western augustus issued the Edict of Milan, which made Christianity a legal religion in the empire. In the years ahead, Constantine promoted the Christian church, granting it tax immunities and relieving the clergy of military service. He provided money to replace the books and buildings that had been lost in persecutions. During his reign, Helena worked to preserve sites associated with Jesus's life. She traveled to convert pagans, intervened in religious controversies, and, with her son's help, sponsored vast church-building projects in Rome, Constantinople, and Jerusalem.

Many differences among Christians had gone almost unnoticed when the faith could not be practiced publicly. The Edict of Milan changed all that. Christian heresies almost immediately came to the emperor's attention. *Heresy* comes from a Greek word meaning "to choose." Heretics are people who choose teachings or practices that do not have official sanction. In Egypt first, but eventually in much of the empire as well, a dispute arose that centered on the foremost mystery of Christianity: the belief that God exists as three distinct but equal persons. Christians had long been stung by the charge that their monotheism was a sham, that they really worshiped three gods. A priest of Alexandria, Arius (ca. 250–ca. 336), sought to preserve monotheism by placing

Jesus later in time and slightly subordinate to the Father. Arianism, as the faith of Arius and his followers is called, won many adherents.

Constantine dealt with religious controversies by assembling church councils to debate issues and promulgate solutions. In 325 at Nicaea, near Constantinople (see Map 5.2), the emperor convened a council of more than three hundred bishops, who condemned Arius and his teaching. They maintained that Christ was "one in being with the Father," as the words of the Nicene Creed still have it. Arianism did not die at Nicaea, however, and Late Antiquity was never free of doctrinal disputes. Constantine claimed to be the specially chosen agent of God, though he did not ask to be worshiped, as earlier emperors had done. Constantine's acts entangled the church with the government just as divisions among Christians were coming into view.

THE FOURTH-CENTURY EMPIRE: AN ILLUSORY STABILITY

By 337 stability and good government had replaced the turmoil of 284. But as it turned out, the reforms of Diocletian and Constantine did not stabilize the empire so much as they provided a framework for its gradual transformation.

Imperial Politics: Families and Armies

Constantine had employed a combination of the tetrarchal and dynastic systems. Under him were three caesars, but they were all his sons, and they succeeded him when he died. Constantine's sons had no heirs, however, and they did not appoint subordinate caesars. When the last of them died in 361, the army turned to Julian (331–363), a nephew of Constantine. Julian was known as a great military leader and as a man who looked out for his troops. Familial and military politics were combining to secure the empire.

Julian ruled for only two years before he was killed fighting in Mesopotamia. He had no heirs and, acting on a long-standing precedent, the army controlled the succession. The choice fell on Valentinian (r. 364–375) and his brother, Valens (r. 364–378). Valentinian ruled in the west, his brother in the east. In 378, when Valens was killed in battle, Valentinian's sons sent their brother-in-law, Theodosius I (r. 379–395), to the east to maintain order. As a result of this act, Valentinian's dynasty would rule the Roman world for ninety-one years (364–455).

Until his own death in 395, Theodosius was the most powerful man in the Roman world, and after his last brother-in-law died in 392, he was Rome's only ruler. He enjoyed the confidence of the people and the army—the former because he was exceptionally competent and honest and the latter because he was a superb general. He divided the empire between his two sons without dynastic or military challenge. Dynastic and tetrarchal systems were blended effectively. Yet the army's influence was a troubling reminder of the third century.

Administrative Successes and Failures

In the time of Constantine, the empire may have numbered some 50 or 60 million inhabitants. Of these, not more than 5 to 10 million lived in towns. After Constantine, the futility of the effort to achieve unity in the increasingly diverse and populous empire became ever more apparent. Because Roman government was based on towns, it had a great deal of trouble keeping track of, taxing, and Romanizing the population.

Religious unity was also elusive. The Council of Nicaea (325) had tried in vain to eliminate Arianism. But Constantine's own son and successor, Constantius II (r. 337–361), was an avowed Arian, as was Valens later. For more than forty years, some of Rome's rulers embraced a faith that had been declared heretical. During this time, a Visigothic priest entered the empire, embraced Arian Christianity, and returned to spread this faith among his people. When the Visigoths settled in the empire in 376, they were considered heretics, despite the fact that when they had converted, in the 340s, the senior Roman ruler was an Arian.

Constantine's nephew, Julian, was called "the Apostate" by his Christian opponents because during his short reign (361–363), he attempted to restore paganism. He forbade Christians to hold most government or military positions or to teach in any school. He did not resort to persecution, however, believing that Christianity could be eradicated by appeals to tradition and by reasoned argument. He was wrong, and his efforts died with him. Julian's abortive pagan restoration was echoed a few years later in the affair of the victory altar. Emperor Gratian (r. 375–383), a Christian, removed the altar of victory from the Roman senate. This was a statue of the goddess of victory before which senators usually burned a bit of incense as they passed. Tradition held that this homage to victory had for centuries assured the success of Rome's armies. The removal of the altar provoked a cry of anguish from a number of prominent Roman senators, most of whom were still pagan and deeply respectful of Rome's ancient customs. The senators' inability to persuade Gratian to change his mind, coupled with Julian's failure, shows that Christianity was winning over paganism. But in what form?

The Development of the Catholic Church

After the Edict of Milan legalized Christianity, the Catholic church attracted a clear majority of the empire's population (Map 5.2). The continuing appeal of Christianity's basic doctrines was key to its growth, but so too were imperial patronage and the increasing prominence of the hierarchically organized Christian clergy. The rising significance of the clergy, particularly the bishops of Rome, eventually led to significant changes in the social and intellectual life, and even in the topography, of late antique towns.

All Christian bishops were understood to be the successors of the apostles. Because Jesus had told the original apostles to "Go forth and teach," it was believed that bishops continued to possess this teaching authority. The bishops of Rome coupled this general idea with a particular emphasis on the primacy of Peter (d. A.D. 67?) —the first

bishop of Rome. This notion emerged in the fourth and fifth centuries and was the theological basis of a political and administrative institution: the papacy. The New Testament accords a certain precedence to Peter among the apostles but provides no clear evidence that he possessed formal leadership. Yet by 380 the bishop of Rome, by then regularly addressed as *papa*, or "pope" in English, had become so prominent that Emperor Theodosius required all Christians to believe as the pope did.

Just as a council had been called at Nicaea to address the problem of Arianism, there continued to be church councils. Two principal issues attracted the attention of Christian thinkers and authorities. One of these concerned Trinitarian theology, the branch of theology that tries to explain how God can be triune (three in one). Arianism was the major Trinitarian heresy of antiquity. The second struggle concerned Christology, the branch of theology that attempts to understand how Jesus Christ could have two distinct natures: God and man. The great Christological heresy of antiquity, monophysitism (literally "one nature-ism"), maintained that although Jesus appeared as a human, he had only one, divine nature. The Council of Chalcedon of 451 condemned monophysitism.

Popes attempted to impose doctrinal decisions on the councils. Pope Leo I (r. 440–461) was the first great theoretician of papal power. His ideas constitute the Petrine theory of papal primacy. According to this doctrine, Peter had not just a moral precedence but a legal primacy, explicitly given to him by Jesus. Leo claimed that apostolic succession designated the pope as the overseer of the whole church. Such theoretical claims to papal supremacy eventually translated into real power, but it took centuries.

The final, decisive factor in the triumph of Christianity was the capture of the elite. By the last years of the fourth century, members of the social elite were everywhere entering the clergy and rising to its highest offices. The clergy became an outlet for their talents and ambitions. For some time, senators had been excluded from military offices and reduced in civilian influence, and decurions—town councilors—were growing

Map 5.2 The Spread of Christianity to A.D. 600 From its beginnings in Palestine (see Map 4.2 on page 109), Christianity, while still illegal, spread mainly in heavily urbanized regions. After Constantine legalized Christianity, the faith spread into every corner of the Roman world.

dissatisfied with public service. The *episcopal* office (the office of bishop) was desirable for many reasons. It was prestigious. Bishops wore distinctive clothing when officiating and were addressed by special titles—traditional Roman marks of respect. They had opportunities to control patronage in the way that prominent Romans always had done. They could intervene on behalf of individuals at the imperial court. They came to control vast wealth, as the generosity of pious Christians put more resources at their disposal. By the middle of the fifth century, the dominant

person in most towns was the bishop, not a civilian official. The bishops, however, were from the same families as those who had once dominated local society through civic service.

The fourth century at first saw little building on private initiative, but then came the construction of Christian cathedrals (churches presided over by bishops), episcopal residences, and local parish churches. Such buildings generally were placed not in the old city centers—which had associations with the pagan past—but on the edges of populated districts. Ancient towns were reconfigured around these Christian centers. As the imperial government became less important locally, the existence of an episcopal *see* (place of a bishop's authority) usually dictated whether a city survived.

Shifting Social Hierarchies

Roman society was hierarchical. From Republican times, Rome had been governed by a hereditary class. Although the members of this class affected a style of life that set them apart, they were never a closed caste. First, they did not reproduce themselves very effectively. About two-thirds of the Roman aristocracy was replaced every century—a typical pattern in premodern societies. There were significant opportunities for social mobility. Second, Late Antiquity saw the incorporation of provincial elites and Germans into the framework of power. Social change was masked as social continuity because when new people reached the top, they embraced the culture of those whom they had replaced.

We can characterize the elite by means of three ideals: *otium, amicitia,* and *officium. Otium,* leisure, meant that the only life worth living was one of retreat and composure in which the finer things of life—literature, especially—could be cultivated. *Amicitia,* friendship, meant patronage. The doorstep of every patron's household was crowded every morning with clients who accompanied the patron on his trip through town, accepted small offerings (often a basket of food), and attended to the patron's requests. Amicitia also meant the kinds of literary friendships that the thousands of surviving letters from Late Antiquity reveal. *Officium,* duty, was the sense of civic obligation that the Romans managed to communicate to the provincial upper classes.

In the West, in the growing absence of an imperial administration, Roman public power did not so much "decline and fall" as it splintered, becoming privatized and localized. Decurions in towns controlled local market privileges, building trades, police forces, fire brigades, and charitable associations. Their public and private means of persuasion and intimidation were im-mense. The system of patronage and clientage could be ruthless, because without a patron's help, much of the urban population lacked the influence to protect themselves.

Late Antiquity saw a trend in the countryside that continued into the Middle Ages: Freedom and slavery declined simultaneously. Many small, independent farmers, probably people who had long been the clients of local grandees, were actually handing over their possessions—*commending* them is the technical term—and receiving back the use of their former possessions in return for annual rents in money or in kind. They were becoming *coloni,* tenants. Their patrons promised to protect them from lawsuits or from severe economic hardship. More and more, these coloni, formerly clients, were bound to their places of residence and were forced to perform labors or to pay fees that marked their status as less than fully free even though they had not been reduced to slavery. At the same time, many landlords were finding it economically unprofitable to house, feed, and equip slaves. As a result they were manumitting their slaves and elevating them to the status of coloni. Probably there was little change in the daily lives of the rural population.

Women's lives are not as well known to us as men's, but it is clear that they lived under great hardship and prejudice. Ancient philosophy held that women were intellectually weaker than men, science claimed they were physically inferior, and law maintained that they were naturally dependent. In the Roman world women could not enter professions, and they had limited rights in legal matters. Christianity offered women conflicting models. There was Eve, the temptress through whom sin had fallen upon humanity, and then there was Mary, the immaculate, virginal Mother of God. The Bible also presented readers with powerful, active women, such as Deborah and Ruth, and loyal, steadfast ones, such as Jesus's female disciples. Despite the social constraints placed on them, we can still detect some independent and influential activity on the part of women.

Girls usually did not choose their marriage partners. Most marriages took place around age 16. A daughter could rarely reject her father's choice, and divorce was possible only in restricted cases. A divorced woman was at a distinct disadvantage unless she had great wealth.

Christianity prized virginity and celibacy and, thus, gave women the viable option of declining marriage. The church at Antioch in Syria, for example, supported three thousand virgins and widows. Christianity also taught that both men and women were to be faithful, whereas Roman custom permitted men, but not women, recourse to lovers, prostitutes, and concubines. Further, Christianity's opposition to divorce altered life for both husbands and wives as both marriage partners now had more security but might be constrained to stay in a difficult or abusive relationship.

Traditionally, women were not permitted to teach in the ancient world, though we do hear of women teachers such as Hypatia of Alexandria (355–415), renowned for her knowledge of both philosophy and mathematics. Some Christian women were formidably learned. The Christian church had deaconesses until at least the sixth century. They had important responsibilities in the instruction of women and girls. Medical knowledge was often the preserve of women, particularly in areas such as sex, conception, and childbirth.

In Jewish society, a woman who demonstrated skill and hard work in her domestic labors was rewarded with praise and even prestige. Women's work however, was arduous, including grinding corn, laundering, preparing meals, nursing children, and working wool. Christian writers tried to attract women to the celibate life by emphasizing that housework was drudgery. Although the church won only some women away from the domestic realm, Christianity also affected daily life. Teachings on modesty demanded that clothing expose little skin, that hair be veiled, and that jewelry and cosmetics be used in moderation. Women were told to avoid the public baths and latrines.

Male or female, Christians thought and lived in distinctive new ways. All Christians were sinners, and so all were equal in God's eyes and equally in need of God's grace. Neither birth nor wealth nor status was supposed to matter, but Christianity did have hierarchies of its own:

popes, archbishops, bishops, priests, deacons. At councils, a hierarchy of seniority was observed. In these respects, the structure of the church was very much like that of the secular world.

The church also introduced some novel status distinctions. Holiness, rather than office or achievement, became a badge of honor. The holy dead were thought to be as present in Christian society as the holy or sinful living. Sanctuaries were dedicated to saints, and people visited the tombs of the saints to pray and to seek healing from physical and spiritual ailments. Christianity produced a society that the ancient world had never known, a society where the living and the dead jockeyed for place in a hierarchy that was at once earthly and celestial. Yet Christianity reconfirmed traditional Roman patron-client bonds, joining client sinners in this world to sanctified patrons in heaven.

FROM WESTERN ROMAN EMPIRE TO GERMANIC KINGDOMS

The years from the 370s to the 530s were decisive in the history of the Roman Empire in the west. When this period opened, the dynasty of Valentinian was firmly in control. By the 530s the western Roman Empire had vanished. Where it had been, there were now Franks in Gaul, Visigoths in Spain, and Anglo-Saxons in Britain. Each had created a stable political entity and thus set the stage for the eventual rise of Europe (Map 5.3).

This change of power happened for several reasons. The most important is that, beginning with Constantine, Rome's best rulers were concerned mainly about the East, leaving the West to its own devices. In addition, beginning with the Visigoths, certain Germanic peoples were settling in their own kingdoms on Roman soil. From Diocletian on, the army was increasingly Germanized, and Germanic military men gained high offices in the state. Those leaders were able to negotiate treaties favorable to their peoples. Provincial elites had long been accustomed to prominent Germans in their midst, so the new situation certainly did

Map 5.3 The Germanic Kingdoms in the Sixth Century By the late sixth century, the western provinces of the Roman Empire (compare Map 4.1 on page 94) had evolved into Germanic kingdoms. Just as provincial boundaries had changed numerous times, the existence and extent of kingdoms were also not permanent.

not feel revolutionary. The process that brought the Germanic barbarians into contact with the Romans was complicated. Roman policies played as great a role in it as barbarian plans. Many barbarians were peacefully accommodated into the Roman system on essentially Roman terms. The settlement of the Germans thus illustrates the paradox of continuity and change evident in so many aspects of late antique life.

Invasions and Migrations

Few images of the ancient world are more fixed in the popular imagination than the "barbarian invasions": hordes of savages overrunning the Roman Empire and ushering in a dark age. The Romans inherited the word *barbarian* (literally, "babblers") from the Greeks, who had divided the world between those who spoke Greek and those who spoke a foreign language. After the Romans granted citizenship to virtually everyone in the empire in 212, they adopted a Greek-style differentiation between Romans and barbarians, considering barbarians to be inferior. However, Romans and barbarians did not face each other as declared enemies. Individual groups of barbarians did invade the empire in various places at different times, but there was no single, coordinated barbarian invasion of the Roman world. Peaceful encounters were also common. The Romans had long traded with the Germanic peoples, carried out complicated diplomacy with them, and recruited them into their armies.

The idea of barbarian migrations is sometimes offered as an alternative to invasions. Archaeological evidence collected to date, however, makes it clear that the Germans were settled agriculturalists. If barbarians moved from one place to another, this movement cannot be attributed to migratory habits.

The Germans can be differentiated from the Celtic and Slavic peoples with whom they shared much of central and eastern Europe, but apart from some minor linguistic variations, it is difficult to distinguish Germans from one another. What are we to make of the profusion of names offered to us by our sources: Franks, Alemans, Saxons, Gepids, Heruls, Vandals, Alans, Visigoths, Ostrogoths, Lombards, Burgundians? These were not discrete ethnic communities. The Romans referred to the German peoples as tribes, but that does not mean they were actually groups of related people. Every Germanic tribe was a confederation, and these confederations formed, dissolved, and re-formed many times. The confederated tribes intermarried and adopted common languages, laws, and lifestyles.

Incorporating the Barbarians

The transformation of the western Roman Empire began as a result of an unexpected set of events involving the Huns, a people from the steppes of central Asia. Classical sources first mention these nomadic warriors in 172, but for the next two centuries they confined themselves to plundering the frontiers of Persia and China. Then, in the middle of the fourth century, they encountered formidable opposition and moved west. Until the 420s, the rulers in the east saw the Visigoths as the greater menace; but then the Huns began raiding in the Balkans, preying on trade routes that crossed the region, and demanding tribute from the eastern emperor. At

the same time, a Roman general in Gaul concluded an alliance with the Huns in an attempt to use them as a check on the Burgundians, a "federate" (from *foedus*, meaning "treaty") people who lived in the central Rhineland and were expanding their territories.

In 434 the Huns chose Attila as their king. In return for a huge imperial subsidy, he agreed to cease raiding in the Balkans, and he marched west, having accepted the alliance against the Burgundians. Attila and the Romans together dealt the Burgundians a severe defeat, but Attila saw the weakness of the Roman position and attacked Gaul in 451. The Roman leaders then defeated Attila with a vast network of alliances made up of Romans, Visigoths, Burgundians, and Franks. Attila turned to Italy in 452, even approaching Rome, where Pope Leo I, not the emperor, convinced him to withdraw. Attila died in 454. Before another year was out, the Hunnic kingdom, largely Attila's personal creation, had vanished. (See the box "Encounters with the West: A Roman View of the Huns.")

The history of the Visigoths presents another instructive example of Romano-Germanic relations. The Visigoths lived just across the Danube from imperial territory (see Map 5.3). Since the reign of Constantine they had been a federate people defending a section of the frontier as auxiliary troops. In 376 the Visigoths, alarmed about the movement into the Danube basin of the Huns, requested permission to enter the empire, to cross the Danube and settle in the Balkans. While the central government considered how to deal with them, local authorities sold them food at exorbitant prices and even traded dog meat for Gothic children, who were then enslaved. Barbarians had no monopoly on barbarity. It took until 382 for Theodosius to grant the Visigoths what they had been demanding: land to settle on and official status for their king. A spokesman for Theodosius captured the emperor's position: "Which is better: To fill Thrace with corpses or with farmers? To fill it with graves or with people? To travel through wilderness or cultivated land?" For

> ∼ **ENCOUNTERS WITH THE WEST** ∼
>
> ## A Roman View of the Huns
>
> *The dread and disgust inspired by the Huns is well captured in this passage from the Roman historian Ammianus Marcellinus.*
>
> From the moment of their birth they make deep gashes in their children's cheeks, so that when in due course hair appears its growth is checked by the wrinkled scars; as they grow older this gives them the unlovely appearance of beardless eunuchs. They have squat bodies, strong limbs, and thick necks, and are so prodigiously ugly and bent that they might be two-legged animals. Their shape, however disagreeable, is human. They have no use for seasoned food, but live on the roots of wild plants and the half-raw flesh of any animal, which they warm a little by placing it between their thighs and the backs of their horses. They have no buildings to shelter them. They wear garments of linen or of the skins of field-mice stitched together. Once they have put their necks into some dingy shirt they never take it off or change it until it rots and falls to pieces. They have round caps of fur on their heads, and protect their hairy legs with goatskins. They are ill-fitted to fight on foot, and remain glued to their horses, hardy but ugly beasts, on which they sometimes sit like women to perform their everyday business and they even bow forward over their beasts' narrow necks to enjoy a deep and dreamy sleep.
>
> *Source:* Ammianus Marcellinus, *The Later Roman Empire (A.D. 354–378),* ed. and trans. Walter Hamilton (Harmondsworth, England: Penguin, 1986), 31.2, pp. 411–412.

decades, barbarians had been settling inside the Roman frontiers, and they had served loyally in the army. Beginning in the fourth century, most high military officers in the Roman world were barbarians. The only peculiar thing about the Visigoths' situation was that never before had the Romans admitted a whole people, as a people.

For about thirty years the Visigoths struggled to improve the terms of their settlements in the Balkans. Alaric, the Visigothic king after 395, grew tired of unfulfilled promises and of being a pawn in other people's games. He forced matters by attacking Italy. The Visigothic sack of Rome in 410 was a psychological shock to contemporaries, and it has loomed large for centuries in popular ideas about the "fall" of the Roman Empire. Actually, it was a ploy by Alaric

to adjust the terms of his already official status. In 418 the Roman government gave in. A new treaty permitted the Visigoths to settle in southern Gaul, with Toulouse as their base of operations. They were assigned the task of protecting the area from bands of brigands. In return for their service, the Visigoths were given land on which to settle and a portion of Roman tax receipts as pay.

The Visigoths' treaty with Rome made theirs the first Germanic kingdom on Roman soil. Between 466 and 484, the Visigothic kingdom in Gaul reached its high point and Southern Gaul, one of Rome's oldest and richest provinces, passed from the hands of the Roman bureaucracy and the local nobility into the control of the Visigoths. Nevertheless, from Constantine's first treaty with the Visigoths through the continuing recognition by the Romans of Visigothic kings in the fifth and sixth centuries, the Romans generally remained in control.

More Kingdoms: The End of Direct Roman Rule in the West

In 476 Odoacer, a Germanic general, deposed the last of the western emperors and then sent the imperial regalia to Constantinople, declaring that the West no longer needed an emperor. This is all that happened in 476, the traditional date for the "fall" of the Roman Empire.

In Gaul a vast coalition of Romans, Visigoths, Burgundians, and Franks had defeated the Huns. But as soon as the Huns were beaten, a new problem arose: The Visigoths were expanding into central Gaul. To check this advance, the Roman commander in Paris forged an alliance with the Franks. The Franks, long Roman federates, had been expanding their settlements southward across modern Holland and Belgium since the third century. Occasionally the Romans had halted their advance, but usually they had left the Franks alone. They now enlisted the Franks to help stop the Visigoths.

The leader of the Frankish kingdom was Clovis. He became king of one group of Franks in 481 and spent the years until his death in 511 subjecting all the other bands of Franks to his rule. He gained the allegiance of the Frankish people by leading them to constant military victories that brought territorial gains, plunder, and tribute. The greatest of Clovis's successes came in 507, when he defeated the Visigoths and drove them over the Pyrenees into Spain (see Map 5.3).

Clovis was popular not only with the Franks but also with the Gallo-Roman population. There were three reasons for his popularity. First, Clovis and the Romans had common enemies: Germanic tribes still living beyond the Rhine and pirates who raided the coast of Gaul. Second, whereas most of the Germanic peoples were Arian Christians, the majority of the Franks passed directly from paganism to Catholicism. Clovis himself was a convert, having been convinced by his Christian wife, Clothilde. Her arguments

were religious, but conversion made good political sense, too, permitting Clovis to portray his war against the Visigoths as a crusade against heresy. Third, Clovis appeared publicly in the dress of a Roman official, eagerly sought formal recognition and titles, and practiced such imperial rituals as distributing gold coins while riding through crowds. The Frankish kingdom under Clovis's family—called "Merovingian" from one of his semilegendary ancestors—became the most successful of all the Germanic realms.

To meet threats elsewhere, the Romans had begun pulling troops out of Britain in the fourth century and abandoned the island to its own defense in 410. Thereafter, raiding parties from Scotland and Ireland as well as seaborne attackers, called "Saxons" by contemporaries because some of them came from Saxony in northern Germany, ravaged Britain. Down to the 450s the British continually appealed to the military authorities in Gaul for aid, but to no avail. Between 450 and 600, much of southern and eastern Britain was taken over by diverse peoples whom we call the "Anglo-Saxons." These newcomers jostled for position with the Celtic Britons, who were increasingly confined to the north and west of the island. Gradually several small, impermanent kingdoms emerged. Although Britain retained contacts with Gaul, the island had virtually no Roman inheritance.

There were several unsuccessful Germanic kingdoms. The Burgundian kingdom that had once prompted the Romans to ally with the Huns was swallowed up by the more powerful Franks in the 530s. The Vandals, who crossed the Rhine in 406 and headed for Spain, crossed to North Africa in 429 (see Map 5.3). They were ardent Arians who persecuted the Catholic population. They constantly plundered the islands of the western Mediterranean and the Italian coast, even sacking Rome in 455. The Romans eliminated the Vandals in 534.

The Ostrogoths had been living in Pannonia since the 370s, subjects of the Huns for much of that time. They were sent to Italy in 493 by the Romans to remove Odoacer, the man who had deposed the last western emperor in 476. Odoacer had earned the displeasure of the Roman administration by laying hands on the sentimentally significant land of Italy—and by doing so on his own initiative, instead of by Roman directive. The government at Constantinople was familiar with the Ostrogoths' king, Theodoric, because he had been a hostage there for several years. Also, the emperor wished to remove the Ostrogoths from the Danube basin. Sending Theodoric to Italy seemed like a way to solve two problems simultaneously.

Theodoric got rid of Odoacer quickly enough and set up his capital in Ravenna, the swamp-surrounded and virtually impregnable city that had sheltered the imperial administration after the Visigothic attack had exposed the weakness of Rome's defenses. Through the force of his personality, and by a series of marriage alliances, Theodoric became the dominant ruler in western Europe. In Italy he promoted peace, stability, and good government. Still, Theodoric had two strikes against him. One, he and his people were Arians. Two, although the population of Italy was accustomed to having an imperial court dominated by Germans, they had never been directly ruled by a German, and some of them resented it. By the 520s Theodoric grew increasingly suspicious and dictatorial. After he died in 526, the government in Constantinople began a twenty-year war that put an end to the Ostrogothic kingdom.

The New Old West

The Germanic kingdoms had a great deal in common with one another and with the late Roman Empire, which had been their common tutor. Each realm was led by a king who usually appeared in two distinct guises. To his people, the king was the military leader. The essential bond of unity among each Germanic people was loyalty to the leader, who repaid his followers in booty, land, judicial protection, and military security. To the Romans, the king appeared as an ally and magistrate. Almost all Germanic kings bore such Roman titles as *consul* or *patrician*, and in these officially conferred titles resided the authority to govern Roman populations. The kings also succeeded to a long line of German Masters

of the Soldiers, the title of the highest military officers in a prefecture. Each monarchy was led by a dynasty—for example, the Merovingians among the Franks—that was pre-eminent in wealth and possessed a sacral aura not unlike that of the Roman emperors. The dynasties provided strength through continuity but also tension as family members competed with one another and with envious outsiders.

The most common local official was the *count*, a combined civilian-military position that made its first appearance in the fifth century. Initially a direct representative of the central government, a count had financial, judicial, and military responsibilities. Kings were careful to promote important locals to the office of count. During this period, local administration continued to be based in cities and towns. Taxes continued to be paid to royal governments throughout the sixth century. Latin remained the language of administration. Germanic kingdoms issued law codes that were essentially local adaptations of Roman law. In short, people's daily lives do not seem to have changed much as a result of the replacement of Roman provinces by Germanic kingdoms.

The Germans generally shared the Christian faith with the provincial populations, although the Vandals, Visigoths, and Ostrogoths were Arians. Cooperation between the Franks and the Gallo-Romans derived from many sources, but one of the strongest was a shared faith.

THE ROMAN EMPIRE IN THE EAST

As the western empire was being parceled out into kingdoms, there emerged an eastern Roman Empire that became the sole heir of the imperial tradition. The creation of the tetrarchy had separated the two halves of the Roman Empire administratively (see Map 5.1). Although in theory there was only one empire, ruled by one senior augustus, the reality was different. The East was more populous, more heavily urbanized, and more prosperous. Greek in culture, it was also livelier intellectually than the West. Eastern rulers, who ushered the Germans through the Balkans and into the West, lost virtually no territory to them.

Constantinople and Its Rulers

Constantius II (r. 337–361), Constantine's son and successor, began making Constantinople, the capital of the eastern empire, a truly imperial city. He gave "New Rome" a senate and a set of urban magistrates of its own, placing the city on an equal constitutional footing with old Rome. Constantinople did not have an ancient aristocracy, so Constantius created a senatorial order. He did this by promoting cultivated persons from cities in the eastern half of the empire. Almost immediately rivalries arose between the senates of East and West.

With the exception of the founder, the ablest members of the dynasty of Valentinian ruled in the East. The greatest of these was Theodosius II (r. 408–450), who enjoyed the longest imperial reign in Roman history. Through skillful diplomacy and occasional force, he managed to keep the eastern empire free of serious Germanic incursions and the Persians at bay in Mesopotamia. To protect his capital city, he built on the landward side massive walls whose ruins are impressive even today. Along with his wife and his sister, he added and beautified important buildings and promoted learning in the city. Theodosius and his family made the new capital a genuine intellectual center.

Theodosius's greatest achievement, however, was the law code that he issued in 438. The most comprehensive collection of Roman law yet produced, this code brought together all Roman laws issued since Constantine and arranged them in systematic fashion. The principal Germanic kingdoms were established just after the Theodosian code was issued. From this text, and from the Roman institutional structures that employed it, the Germans were taught the rule of law and regulations for the conduct of daily affairs.

The Emperor Justinian (r. 527–565)

After Theodosius II died in 450, the eastern empire endured seventy-seven years of rule by military men who lacked the culture, vision, or administrative capacity of their predecessors. But they preserved the empire and kept its government functioning. It was from these rough soldiers that Justinian arose. Until his death in 565, he worked tirelessly in many fields, earning the nickname of "the emperor who never sleeps." He was the greatest ruler of Late Antiquity, one of the greatest of all Rome's emperors.

Justinian rose from the Illyrian (Croatian today) peasantry through the military to the imperial throne. Despite growing up in rural military camps, Justinian showed a wide range of interests and abilities. He surrounded himself with remarkable people and gave them considerable latitude. He flouted convention by marrying an actress—the daughter of a bear keeper. Her name was Theodora (d. 548), and she became widely known for her wit and courage. A contemporary member of the government, John Lydus, called her "superior in intelligence to any man." The statement demonstrates that at that time female intelligence was considered remarkable, but it is still a meaningful assessment. Theodora became one of Justinian's key advisers. For instance, during the Nika Revolts of 532 (see page 133), her speech in the Council of State convinced Justinian that they should not flee. He sought her opinion on matters domestic, military, and legal. Theodora fought for her own initiatives as well. She helped to bring about legal changes that gave women more property rights. In her effort to improve the lives of girls sold into prostitution, Theodora bought some women their freedom and gave them money. She encouraged laws against brothels and set up a convent for former prostitutes.

Justinian identified and promoted such previously obscure figures as the gifted general Belisarius, the administrative genius John the Cappadocian, and the greatest legal mind of the age, Tribonian. Justinian put John the Cappadocian to work reforming an administration that had been little altered in two centuries despite vast changes in the scope of the empire. John worked to secure tighter control of provincial administrators, to ensure a steady flow of tax revenue, and to eliminate corruption. Tribonian and a commission were as-

Theodora This magnificent sixth-century mosaic from Ravenna depicts Empress Theodora in all her power and majesty. *(Scala/Art Resource, NY)*

signed the task of producing the first comprehensive review of Roman law since that of Theodosius II in 438. Between 529 and 533, Justinian's code was issued in three parts: The *Code* was a systematically organized collection of all imperial legislation; the *Digest* was a collection of the writings of the classical Roman jurists; and the *Institutes* was a textbook for law students. Justinian's code constitutes the most influential legal collection in history. It summarized a thousand years of legal work, was used in the eastern empire for another thousand years, and has affected almost every state and legal system in the modern world.

Not long after undertaking his legal and administrative reforms, Justinian launched an attempt to reconquer the empire's lost western provinces. Belisarius retook Africa from the Vandals and Italy from the Ostrogoths. Justinian also attempted, in vain, to recapture Iberia from the Visigoths. Although he enjoyed some military successes in the west, Justinian faced constant threats in the Balkans from Bulgars and Slavs and in Mesopotamia from Persians. The emperor's campaigns were so expensive that his administrative reforms wound up looking like contrivances to make more money for the emperor to waste. In the Nika Revolts in 532 violent mobs coursed through Constantinople demanding the dismissal of John the Cappadocian and other imperial agents.

Justinian's religious policy also met with sharp opposition. A genuinely pious man, he legislated frequently on behalf of the church and practiced, along with Theodora, generous charitable benefactions. Still, by both personal conviction and a sense of official duty, Justinian desired religious unity. Although the Council of Chalcedon had condemned monophysitism in 451, Justinian was mildly monophysite, and Theodora was enthusiastically so. Justinian tried again and again to find a compromise that would bring all parties together. His church council of 553 assembled amid high hopes but in the end alienated the clergy in Syria, Egypt, and Rome.

In one of his most famous acts, Justinian arranged for two famous mathematicians, Anthemius of Tralles and Isidore of Miletus, to design a church in Constantinople that would represent the place where heaven and earth touched. It was to be the regular meeting place of the emperor, the patriarch (the archbishop of Constantinople), and the people. The result was the extraordinary church of Hagia Sophia, Holy Wisdom. It was the largest Christian church ever built, but its size is almost the least of its qualities. The outside is a complex structure of squares, circles, and arches, crowned by a dome. The inside is a riot of color achieved by marble fittings in almost every imaginable hue, by mosaics and frescoes of indescribable beauty, and by the mysterious play of light and shadow. The effect of the whole is disorienting. Space in most basilicas is ordered, controlled, elegant. Space in Hagia Sophia is horizontal and vertical, straight and curved, square and round. The inside is by turns dark and light, purple and green, red and blue. When Justinian first saw his church in its completed state, he said, "Solomon, I have outdone thee."

It is appropriate that in inspecting his great church Justinian should have looked backward to Solomon, the Hebrew king who built Jerusalem's Temple. In almost all respects Justinian was a backward-looking ruler. In everything from his legal code and administrative restructuring to his religious policies and attempt to restore direct rule in Rome's former western provinces, Justinian was concerned with shoring up old accomplishments and returning to the past.

CHRISTIAN CULTURE AND LIFE

Christian culture involved institutions that claimed people's allegiance, communities that nurtured them, ideas that inspired them, and a history that defined them. Christianity grew and spread in the Roman world. It spoke that world's languages, borrowed its philosophical and legal terminology, adapted its administrative structures, reinterpreted its celebrations, and recruited its ablest citizens.

The True Church: Competing Visions

Catholicism takes its name from a Greek word meaning "universal." It is no accident that a Catholic church grew up in a Roman world steeped in ideas of universality. The most deeply held tenet of Roman ideology maintained that Rome's mission was to civilize the whole world and bend it to Roman ways.

The Catholic church, in seeking to assume that mission, met opposition from the secular world. The popes had been working to gain leadership in the church and to make themselves final arbiters of doctrine. When Emperor Anastasius (r. 491–518) intervened in a quarrel between the Catholics and the monophysites, Pope Gelasius I (r. 492–496) sent him a harsh letter in which he protested the emperor's intervention. Gelasius told the emperor that the world was governed by the "power" of kings and by the "authority" of priests. Ordinarily, the pope said, the jurisdictions of kings and priests are distinct. In a controversy between them, however, priestly authority must have precedence because priests are concerned with the salvation of immortal souls but kings rule only mortal bodies. Gelasius was telling the emperor to stay out of theology, but he was also implying that the church was above the whole secular regime.

Gelasius could take this position because he was in Rome, where there was no longer an em-

Hagia Sophia This interior view of Hagia Sophia conveys some sense of the dazzling complexity of this greatest of all late antique buildings.
(Giraudon/Art Resource, NY)

peror. The emperor took sharp exception to Gelasius's arguments, but more pressing business faced him. He could not achieve unity among warring Christian factions, and he had to think about his frontiers more than about the writings of a troublesome priest in old Rome. Christians in the East agreed with Gelasius's views on priestly authority and kingly power only to the extent that they were already opposed to the emperor's theological pronouncements.

This controversy reveals several conflicting visions. Was the church a branch of the state and thus subject to imperial command? The emperor thought so, but the pope denied it. Was the pope the final arbiter of doctrine? Neither the emperor nor the pope's theological opponents were prepared to admit this. Would the pope actually have any real influence in the East? It seemed unlikely. But it also seemed unlikely that the emperor could impose his will in matters of religion, in the East or the West.

The other major challenge to the church was that several Christian communities were claiming to represent a universal—a catholic—tradition. The Latin Christian church in the West was staunchly Nicene and Chalcedonian and took its bearings from Latin church writers. The Orthodox church in the East centered primarily on the emperors and patriarchs, used Greek, and followed Greek Christian writers. The Coptic church in Egypt was monophysite, followed the teachings of the patriarchs of Alexandria, and used the Coptic language. The Jacobite church, a mildly monophysite, Syriac-speaking tradition, was originally strong in Syria, from where it spread to Mesopotamia and beyond. Each of these churches produced a literature, an art, and a way of life that marked its members as a distinct community, reflecting a Christian reinterpretation of very old cultures and ideals.

The Rise of Christian Monasticism

Christian monasticism emerged in Egypt in the last decades of the third century, but the forces that combined to produce monasticism are ancient and universal. Monks did not wish to work to change this world for the better. They wished to escape this world in order to avoid all that might come between them and God. Hidden away, they developed a theology and an institution that were among the most creative and long-lived of all the achievements of Late Antiquity.

The practice of rigorous self-denial (*askesis*) was common to several religious and philosophical sects in antiquity—for example, the Pythagoreans and the Stoics—and was well known among the Jews in the time of Christ, as the Essenes show (see page 107). Widespread opinion held that if one could conquer the desires of the body, one could reach a higher plane, unencumbered by lust for food, drink, sex, knowledge, and adventure. Sometimes ascetic practices were adopted by tightly knit groups, sometimes by solitaries.

These traditions met in Egypt in the person of Anthony (d. 356). At about age 20, Anthony gave away all his possessions and went to live in the Egyptian desert, seeking to imitate the life of Christ. His spiritual quest became famous, and many disciples flocked to him. Eventually, he decided to organize them into a very loose community. Anthony's form of monasticism is called *eremitic*, from the Greek *heremos* for "desert." The

name *eremitic*, signifying extreme asceticism, gives us the word *hermit*.

Pachomius (290–346) created a second form of monastic life. He was a Roman soldier who left the service in 313, was baptized a Christian, and retired to the Egyptian desert, where he studied with a hermit. Eventually Pachomius founded a community of ascetics, and before long his community, and dozens like it, had thousands of members. An anomalous situation had arisen: Literally thousands of people were living alone but together in veritable cities out in the desert. Pachomius wrote the first Rule, or code for daily living, for a monastic community. He designed a common life based on routines of private prayer, group worship, and work. Pachomius's pattern of monasticism is called *cenobitic*, from the Greek for "common life." People living this common life were called *monks*, and the place where they lived this life was called a *monastery*. The head of the community was designated *abbot*, a word meaning "father."

Monasticism spread from Egypt by means of texts such as the very popular *Life of Anthony*, collections of the wise sayings of famous desert abbots, and books written by persons who went to Egypt seeking a more perfect life—among whom were several prominent women. The appeal of monasticism grew greater after Christianity gained official status. Those who were attracted to monasticism saw it as a form of Christian life that was purer than the hierarchical church and its wealth, power, and controversy. The ascetic life was popular with women for individual reasons and because offices in the church hierarchy were denied to women, whereas positions in monasteries, including that of abbess, provided outlets for female talent. Monasticism gave women a chance to choose a kind of family life different from the one available in households dominated by fathers and husbands. Some women's monasteries began in ways quite independent of men's, as when the Councils of Nicaea and Chalcedon gave certain groups of pious Christian widows official recognition for their work with the sick and the poor. Later, women from respectable households could choose a monastic life, after examples set by women like Paula and her daughter, Eustochia. Abandoning the life of rich senatorial Romans, the two traveled with the monastic scholar Jerome (331–420), teaching, praying, and fasting. When they came to Bethlehem and saw the monastery established by another wealthy Roman, Melania the Elder, Paula set up four new communities: three female and one male. (See the box "Melania the Younger: The Appeal of Monasticism to Women.") Interestingly, when Pope Damasus commissioned Jerome to prepare a Latin version of the Bible (translated from the Hebrew Scriptures and Greek New Testament), Eustochia edited this important work for him. It came to be called the "Vulgate" because it was the Bible for the "people" (*vulgus*).

As monasticism spread from Egypt, it adopted these two basic patterns. In the East, the eremitic pattern was prominent. Eastern monasticism produced a great legislator in Basil (330–379), who wrote the most influential Rule in the Orthodox church. Generally these monks assembled only for weekly worship and otherwise ate, prayed, and worked alone. Eremitic monasticism arrived in the West in the person of Martin of Tours (336–397). Like Pachomius, Martin was a pagan Roman soldier who, after his military service ended, embraced both Christianity and asceticism. Even though he was elected bishop of Tours, Martin kept to his rigid life of denial. Still, in the West, the cenobitic pattern was dominant. The first great center from which cenobitic monasticism spread was Lérins in the south of Gaul, where a community was founded in 410.

The most famous monastic founder in the West was Benedict of Nursia (480–545), a middle-class Roman who abandoned legal studies to pursue a life of prayer. Benedict attracted a crowd of followers, and in about 520 he drew up a Rule. This Rule is marked by shrewd insights into the human personality. It emphasizes the bond of mutual love among the monks and obedience to the abbot. The abbot is assigned wide powers but is told to exercise them gently. Monks are permitted a reasonable diet and decent, though modest, clothing. Although punishment is provided for, loving correction is preferred. In Late Antiquity the monks of Lérins were the monastic elite of the West, giving way, in later centuries, to Benedict's Rule.

The Quest for a Catholic Tradition

The Christian clergy attracted not only talented administrators but also gifted intellectuals. As the church became first free and then triumphant, those intellectuals were able to reflect publicly on their faith and its place in the ancient world.

Christianity drew much from the pagan and Jewish environments within which it grew, but its fundamental inspiration was the collection of writings called in modern times the *Bible*. From the second century until the middle of the fifth century, Christian writers worked to define a canon, a definitive list of genuine Old and New Testament scriptures. There was also a need for a creedal statement that would settle debates about the priesthood, the church, and the problem of human free will. These challenging problems were addressed by the Church Fathers, a group of Greek and Latin writers impressive for their intellectual breadth, elegant style, and trenchant reasoning. Their era is called "patristic" (from *patres*, the Latin word for "fathers").

Many Christian writers addressed themselves to the difficulty of moral living in the world. Ambrose of Milan wrote *On Duties*, a treatise that attempted to Christianize the public ethos that Cicero had spelled out many years before in his book *On Duties*. Cicero had discussed citizens' obligations to one another and to the law, and he had stressed the need for those in power to be above reproach in their personal lives (see page 86). Ambrose reinterpreted these ideas as duties that Christians owed to one another because of their common worship of God. At about the same time, the patriarch of Constantinople, John Chrysostom (347–407), castigated the immorality of the imperial court and aristocracy. By setting a bad example, Chrysostom insisted, they endangered the souls of their subjects.

The most influential Christian thinker after Saint Paul was Augustine (354–430). He was born in North Africa to a family of modest

Melania the Younger: The Appeal of Monasticism to Women

The appeal of monasticism was great for men and women, rich and poor, as the career of Melania (383–438) shows. She came from a wealthy Roman family but renounced her possessions and traveled widely in Italy, North Africa, Egypt, and Palestine, visiting holy men and women. These selected passages from her biography provide glimpses of her life.

Melania was foremost among the Romans of senatorial rank. Wounded by divine love, she had from earliest youth yearned for Christ, and longed for bodily chastity. Her parents, because they were illustrious members of the Roman senate and expected that through her they would have a succession of the family line, forcibly united her in marriage . . . when she was fourteen and her husband, seventeen. [After having two children, Melania persuaded her husband to join her in renouncing the world.] She bridled nature and delivered herself to death daily, demonstrating to everyone that woman is not surpassed by man in anything

that pertains to virtue, if her decision is strong. She was by nature a gifted writer and wrote without mistakes in notebooks. She decided for herself how much she should write every day, and how much she should read in the canonical books and in the collections of homilies. Then she would go through the Lives of the fathers as if she were eating dessert. The blessed woman read the Old and New Testaments three or four times a year. The most holy fathers [Egyptian abbots] received her as if she were a man. In truth, she had been detached from the female nature, and had acquired a masculine disposition, or rather, a heavenly one.

Source: Elizabeth A. Clark, ed. and trans., *The Life of Melania the Younger,* cc. 1, 12, 23, 26, 39, *Studies in Women and Religion,* vol. 14 (New York: Edwin Mellen Press, 1984), pp. 27–28, 35, 46, 53–54. Reprinted by permission of Edwin Mellen Press.

means, and he received, at great sacrifice, the best education available. His career as a professor of rhetoric took him to Rome and then to Milan, which in the fourth century was the unofficial western capital. There, Augustine fell under the spell of Ambrose and embraced the Christianity that his mother had been urging on him throughout his life. He later chronicled his quest for spiritual fulfillment in his *Confessions,* a classic of Western literature. In 395, Augustine became a bishop and until his death served the North African community at Hippo.

Augustine never set out to provide a comprehensive exposition of the whole of Christian doctrine. Instead, he responded to problems as they arose. Living in a time of turmoil, he had

opportunities to speak on a wide array of issues, such as the relationship between God and humanity, the nature of the church, and the overall plan of God's creation. In the early fifth century some people believed that they could achieve salvation by the unaided operation of their own will. Augustine responded that although God did indeed endow human beings with free will, Adam and Eve had abused their will to rebel against God. Ever since that first act of rebellion, a taint, called by theologians "original sin," predisposed humans to continual sin. Only divine grace can overcome sin, and only by calling on God can people receive grace. Here was a decisive break with the classical idea of humanity as good in itself and capable of self-improvement, perhaps even perfection, in this world. According to Augustine, all people were flawed, all were sinners, all were in need of God's redemption.

Augustine also responded to the North African heresy that regarded sacraments celebrated by unworthy priests as invalid. Augustine believed that the efficacy of the sacraments—ritual celebrations that were considered to be channels for the communication of God's grace—did not depend on the personal merit of the minister. The church, in this reckoning, was a community of acknowledged sinners that was being led by its clergy in a quest for eternal salvation. To Augustine, only God was truly good, and God was a purely spiritual being.

Augustine wrote the most brilliant and difficult of all his works, *The City of God*, after the sack of Rome by the Visigoths in 410. Many people in the Roman world argued that Alaric's seizure of Rome was repayment for Rome's abandonment of its traditional gods. *The City of God* rejected this. It was a theological history, which was a rather new phenomenon. The traditional classical view of time was cyclical: Time moved, but it was not actually headed anywhere. Some ancient societies had valued the past above the present or future; the Classical period had valued the present. Some religions, including Judaism, had begun to value the imagined future, but the world was not going to reach that future by a linear path. Rather, one day an event of great importance would simply end this world. According to Augustine, however, God's plan has been in operation since the creation of the world, and this plan will govern all human activity until the end of time. Life is a struggle between those who call on divine grace, who are citizens of the City of God, and those who keep to the ways of the world.

Even though the Roman Empire was officially Christian, Augustine refused to identify his City of God with it. Nor would he say that the church and the City of God were identical. What he did say was that the sack of Rome was irrelevant because earthly kingdoms come and go; only the eternal kingdom of God is important. Romans

had cherished the belief that the world would last exactly as long as Rome's dominion. Augustine's dismissal of Rome's destiny sounded the death knell of the classical world-view.

Augustine also addressed the problem of education. Almost the entire educational establishment was pagan in design and content. Students learned rhetoric and grammar—Latin in the West, and Greek in the East. Confined mainly to the elite, education had generally been a steppingstone toward employment in the imperial or urban service. In Late Antiquity, however, public schools were fast disappearing as the imperial service (all but gone by the sixth century) faded in the West. The Church Fathers were generally dismissive of the Roman heritage, but the church still needed educated persons, so it provided schools in cathedrals and monasteries.

In a treatise entitled *On Christian Doctrine* Augustine expressed some ideas about education that proved influential for a millennium. He said that everything that one needs to know for salvation is contained in the Bible. But the Bible is full of difficult images and allusions. How is an ordinary person to learn what he or she needs to know in order to master this great book? Augustine used the expressive image of "spoiling the Egyptians," borrowed from the account of the Hebrews' Exodus from Egypt, when they took with them whatever they could use. Augustine's attitude toward classical learning was that it was useful to the extent that it taught the things one needed to know in order to understand the Bible.

Highly influential as well was the treatise *On Divine and Human Readings* by the Italian writer Cassiodorus (ca. 485–580). Cassiodorus agreed with Augustine's idea of "spoiling the Egyptians." Because there were no Christian grammars or rhetorical manuals, Cassiodorus's "human readings" were classical pagan texts. These were preparatory to "divine readings," which consisted of the Bible, the commentaries on it, and the writings of the Church Fathers. For centuries schools for the clergy were organized on the model established by Augustine and Cassiodorus.

SUMMARY

The paradox of Late Antiquity, the years from around 300 to around 600, is the nearly invisible boundary between change and continuity. When the period opened, Rome's vast and diverse empire was struggling. The classical culture that had evolved over more than a millennium in the Mediterranean world seemed to have lost much of its vigor and appeal. But the energetic rulers Diocletian and Constantine undertook a half-century of intense military, economic, and administrative reform that put the empire on firm footings while changing forever the basic nature of the Roman state.

To address pressing military threats, the empire's army was expanded and reorganized. This sensible reform had the unintended result of militarizing many aspects of public life. Traditional civilian government receded slowly into the background as the Roman economy was harnessed to the needs of the military. Tax burdens pressed on every level of society and called into question the cost of Roman leadership. To administer the empire more efficiently, the small amateur government of the early empire was transformed into a bureaucratic system that stripped local elites of much of their traditional autonomy. To put a halt to the endemic civil war of the third century, a tetrarchal system of imperial rule was installed, and enhanced imperial ceremony used to exalt the emperor. The paradox was that every reform made sense, but every reform contributed to altering the basic nature of the traditional Roman system. The Roman Empire itself survived only in the east. Over a long time, and facilitated by Roman policies, Germanic peoples took over key military and administrative positions in the west and built kingdoms that imitated the late Roman state.

The rise of a Mediterranean-wide Christian ecclesiastical structure parallels in some ways the elaboration of the late Roman government after Diocletian. In 303, Christianity, still a minority religion almost everywhere, endured severe persecution. A decade later, it was made legal. Within seventy-five years, it became the official religion of the state. Within two centuries, popes declared that the Christian priesthood was above the imperial office itself. This remarkable transformation was made possible by the conversion of the emperor Constantine and by the patronage of the church by his successors and by the social elites. Once it could function openly, the church developed a sophisticated system of governance. No pagan cult had ever built such a structure, which was crucial to the success of Christianity. Slowly a Catholic tradition emerged around the Bible, the creeds—especially the Nicene—and the patristic writings. That Catholic tradition interpreted fundamental Christian ideas in light of centuries-old pagan philosophical ideas and appropriated traditional literary and artistic forms.

By 600, new elites (or reorganized old elites) and the Catholic church were poised to refashion the world that would succeed Rome. Not surprisingly, the Roman world of Justinian in the East and the Germanic world of the West were going to look very different in the future. But Rome was to have a third heir, too, in the followers of the Prophet Muhammad. In the next chapter we will observe how ancient Mediterranean traditions, Jewish and Christian religious beliefs, Roman structures, and new ethnic communities formed three great civilizations—European, Byzantine, and Islamic—that for nearly a thousand years dominated the age we call "medieval."

SUGGESTED READING

Brown, Peter. *Augustine of Hippo: A Biography.* 1969. A penetrating account of the life and world of a man described by the author as possessing "a mind of terrifying acuteness."

———. *The Cult of the Saints: Its Rise and Function in Latin Christianity.* 1981. A lively, imaginative discussion of holy men and women and of their places in this world and the next.

———. *Power and Persuasion in Late Antiquity: Toward a Christian Empire.* 1992. A brilliant account of the emergence of the Christian bishops as a dominant force.

———. *The World of Late Antiquity.* 1971. A sprightly and beautifully illustrated interpretation of cultural cross-currents by the most gifted interpreter of Late Antiquity.

Browning, Robert. *Justinian and Theodora*. Rev. ed. 1987. A readable, reliable, and well-illustrated account of two fascinating people and a remarkable period.

Cameron, Averil. *The Mediterranean World in Late Antiquity, A.D. 395–600*. 1993. A superb and readable survey of all the major problems and interpretations.

Chitty, Derwas J. *The Desert a City*. 1966. A comprehensive, readable account of monastic origins in Egypt and dissemination to the east.

Clark, Gillian. *Women in Late Antiquity: Pagan and Christian Lifestyles*. 1993. A first-ever attempt to capture the lives of late antique women in all respects.

Elm, Susanna. *Virgins of God: The Making of Asceticism in Late Antiquity*. 1994. A fascinating and challenging discussion of the role of women in the making of late antique monastic culture.

Goffart, Walter. *Barbarians and Romans, A.D. 418–584: The Techniques of Accommodation*. 1980. An important, stimulating, and controversial book on how the barbarians were actually integrated into the Roman system on essentially Roman terms.

Harries, Jill. *Sidonius Apollinaris and the Fall of Rome*. 1994. A difficult but rewarding study of a major Gallic aristocrat who became a bishop and whose letters are a key source.

Holum, Kenneth G. *Theodosian Empresses: Women and Imperial Dominion in Late Antiquity*. 1982. A fascinating account of the behind-the-scenes roles played by female members of the imperial family in the fifth century.

Honoré, Tony. *Tribonian*. 1978. This difficult book repays close study by showing how legal thinkers in Justinian's world actually worked. One learns from it a great deal about law in general.

Jones, A. H. M. *The Later Roman Empire, 284–602*. 2 vols. 1964. Despite its age, this massive work remains the best history of the Roman Empire. Its great strength is its detailed treatment of the Roman government.

Markus, Robert. *The End of Ancient Christianity*. 1990. This stimulating and beautifully written book explores the meanings of sacred and secular in the period from 400 to 600.

Musset, Lucien. *The Germanic Invasions: The Making of Europe, A.D. 400–600*. Translated by Edward and Columba James. 1975. Since its first appearance in 1965, this book has become the standard treatment of the movement of the barbarians into the Roman world.

Pagels, Elaine. *Adam, Eve, and the Serpent*. 1988. A fascinating but controversial assessment of the evolution of attitudes toward women by the clergy.

Stancliffe, Claire. *St. Martin and His Hagiographer: History and Miracle in Sulpicius Severus*. 1983. Simultaneously an account of early Western eremitic monasticism and of how we know about it.

Thompson, E. A. *The Huns*. 1996. A revised and updated version of a classic study that presents a sympathetic portrait of this feared people.

Williams, Stephen, and Gerard Friell. *Theodosius: The Empire at Bay*. 1995. An exciting account of the reign of one of Rome's greatest emperors. Strong on currents in scholarly interpretation.

Wolfram, Herwig. *History of the Goths*. Translated by Thomas J. Dunlap. 1988. Not only a history of the Goths, this brilliant book explains current ethnographic thinking about the barbarians.

CHAPTER 6

Early Medieval Civilizations, ca. 600–900

time traveler transported to the Mediterranean world of 600 would almost certainly predict only two heirs to antiquity: the Roman East and the barbarian West. In fact, a new faith, Islam, was about to burst upon the scene and create a third extraordinary culture. Spreading across huge territories, Islam eventually gave rise to the rich and variegated Muslim world. In this chapter, then, three areas engage our attention. For each, the seventh century was an era of dramatic change, the eighth century an era of reform and consolidation, and the ninth century a time of upheaval. The similarities are not merely chronological. A new imperial tradition developed in each area, a tradition rooted in a particular territory whose people believed themselves to be specially chosen by God and whose rulers defined themselves as God's earthly agents. In all three realms the interaction of local traditions with the Roman past produced new forms of central government. Commercial ties began to transform the Mediterranean world into a community of peoples who needed to balance mutual interests with bitter rivalries.

The formative period from 600 to 900 is commonly called the "early Middle Ages" or "early medieval period." The terms originated in the seventeenth century when a Dutch scholar wrote of the *Medii Aevi*, the "Middle Times" that lay between antiquity and the dawning modern world. The name stuck. As a label for the post-Roman world, "Middle Ages" (whose adjectival form is "medieval") has become traditional. The fact that we no longer talk of an abrupt and catastrophic "fall" of the Roman Empire means that we no longer use the word *medieval* in exclusively pejorative ways.

Questions and Ideas to Consider

- Islam, like Christianity before it, attracted a wide range of people because it drew on several different religious and cultural traditions. What were some of these? What else accounts for the extraordinary spread of Islam?

- What were the issues at stake in the struggle between iconoclasts and their opponents? Discuss some of the political consequences of this religious schism.

- Compare the developments of early medieval Spain, Italy, and England. What did they have in common, and in what ways did they differ?

- What kind of roles did women play in Carolingian religion, culture, and politics? Contrast the roles that were truly public with those that were important because of private influence.

- Discuss the relationship between church and state in the Muslim, the Byzantine, and the Carolingian Empires. How and why was religious unity enforced? To what degree was it attainable?

THE ISLAMIC EAST

To ancient writers, the Arabs, who inhabited much of the area from the Arabian peninsula to the Euphrates River, played a small role in the history of antiquity, and they took little notice of them. Shortly after 600, however, a prophet appeared among them preaching a faith old in its basic elements but new in its formulation. Converts to that new faith burst forth with unprecedented spiritual and military fervor, and they conquered territories from Spain to the frontiers of China. Slowly, those lands were gathered into an imperial system with a coherent ideology and government apparatus.

Arabia Before Muhammad

The Arab world in the early seventh century was large and turbulent. Long dominated by the Ro-man and Persian Empires, the region had no stable, large-scale political entities. People belonged to close-knit clans that in varying associations formed tribes—the key element in Arab society. A tribe was in theory a group of people tracing descent from a known ancestor, but it was actually a diverse group of relatives, allies, and political or economic partners.

As complex as its political situation was the region's religious composition. The Roman world was overwhelmingly Christian, though there were many kinds of Christians. The Persian realm was officially Zoroastrian, but it had Jewish, Christian, Manichaean, and Buddhist minorities. The Arabs themselves were generally pagans, but Arabia had Jewish and Christian minorities.

The Arab East was also economically intricate. Bedouins (Arabs who were nomadic pastoralists) provided for their own needs from their herds of sheep and goats, from small-scale trading in towns, and from regular raids on one another and on caravans. There were some farmers, but in many areas soils were too poor and rain too infrequent to foster agriculture. Cities supported traders who moved luxury goods, such as spices, incense, and perfumes, from the Indian Ocean region and southern Arabia. These traders formed the elite of Arabia, and they led the tribes. Mecca, dominated by the powerful tribe of the Quraysh, was the foremost city of Arabia (see Map 6.1), but competition among cities and tribes was fierce.

A solution to the competition among tribes and towns for control of trade routes was the institution of *harams*, or sanctuaries—places where contending parties could settle disputes peacefully. Usually the founding of a haram was attributed to a holy man whose prestige added to the sanctity of the spot. Mecca was one of the chief harams in Arabia, and its founding was attributed to the Israelite patriarch Abraham and one of his sons, Ishmael. The focus of the sanctuary was the black stone shrine known as the Kaaba. For centuries people from all over Arabia had made pilgrimages to Mecca, to the Kaaba.

CHAPTER CHRONOLOGY

568	Lombards enter Italy	710	Spain invaded by Muslims
570–632	The life of Muhammad	717–741	Reign of Byzantine emperor Leo III
589	Visigoths convert to Catholicism	726–787	Iconoclastic controversy
590–604	Pontificate of Gregory I	750	Abbassid dynasty of caliphs founded
610–641	Reign of Byzantine emperor Heraclius	751	Carolingians become kings in Frankish world
632–634	Islamic conquest of Arabia	757–796	Offa of Mercia greatest early Anglo-Saxon ruler
634–640	Muslims conquer Byzantine provinces	800	Imperial coronation of Charlemagne
661–750	Umayyad dynasty of caliphs		
664	England chooses Roman over Celtic Christianity	840s–850s	Vikings attack France, British Isles
		843	Division of the Carolingian Empire
674–678,		867–886	Reign of Byzantine emperor Basil I
716–718	Arab sieges of Constantinople	889	Magyars attack western Europe

The Prophet and His Faith

Muhammad was born in 570 to a respectable though not wealthy or powerful clan of the Quraysh tribe. His father died before he was born, his mother shortly afterward, and Muhammad was raised by his grandparents and an uncle. Like many young Meccans he entered the caravan trade. By the time he was 20, Muhammad held such a reputation for competence and moral uprightness that he became financial adviser to a wealthy Quraysh widow, Khadija (555–619). Although older than Muhammad, she became his wife in 595. It seems that they had a happy life together until her death.

From his youth, Muhammad was a spiritual man. He went into the desert or to caves near Mecca to fast and contemplate. In 610 he experienced the first of many revelations that commanded him to teach all people a new faith that called for an unquestioned belief in one god, Allah, and an uncompromised commitment to social justice for believers. Muhammad began teaching in Mecca, but he converted few people outside his own circle. His wife was his first con-

vert. Because he preached against idolatry, some Meccans feared that Muhammad might question the legitimacy of the shrines in Mecca. That could jeopardize the traditional pilgrimages to the Kaaba and the trade that accompanied them. By 619, Muhammad's well-connected wife and uncle were dead, and his position was precarious.

At this juncture some of his followers in Medina, a smaller trading community, asked Muhammad to establish a haram there, in the hope that he would mediate the town's religious and political dissension. In the summer of 622, small groups of Muhammad's disciples made their way to Medina, and in September Muhammad joined them. His journey from Mecca to Medina, the *hijra,* marks the beginning of a new era, symbolized to this day in the Arab world by a calendar that dates "In the year of the Hijra."

When Muhammad was fully in control in Medina, he decided that he needed Mecca in order to convert the rest of Arabia. His followers began attacking Meccan caravans and battled with the Meccans several times in the 620s. In 630, Muhammad and many of his followers returned to Mecca in triumph. Muhammad left the Quraysh in con-

Map 6.1 The Expansion of Islam to 732 This map vividly illustrates the spectacular gains by Islam in the time of Muhammad, under the first caliphs, and under the Umayyads. Later there were slow, steady gains in Africa, central Asia, and India.

trol, and he retained the Kaaba as a focus of piety. He then set about winning over the Bedouins of the Arabian desert. When Muhammad died in 632, he had converted most of Arabia (Map 6.1).

To what had Arabia converted? People were asked to surrender completely to Allah, the one, true God—that is, they were asked to make *al-Islam*, "the surrender." Those who surrendered became *Muslims* and joined the *umma muslima*, a completely new kind of community in which membership depended on belief in Allah and acceptance of Muhammad as Allah's final prophet. Such figures as Moses and Jesus were seen as previous, lesser prophets of Allah. All members of the umma were understood to have responsibility for all other members. Because of the experience of the hijra, Islam was a religion of exile,

of total separation from the ordinary world, and of total dependence on God.

Islamic religious thought pertains to practice and allegiance more than ideas. The point is not to *know* Islam but to *live* it. The basic teachings of Islam are traditionally described as "Five Pillars": (1) the profession of faith; (2) individual prayer five times daily, plus group prayers at noon on Friday in a *mosque*, a Muslim house of prayer—at first men and women worshiped together; later they came to pray in separate areas; (3) the sunup-to-sundown fast for one month per year; (4) the giving of 10 percent of a person's income to the poor; (5) pilgrimage to Mecca at least once in a lifetime. These pillars built up a sense of community and sustained a faith that laid great stress on simple, uncompromising belief. There was no clergy. Men called *imams* led the Friday prayers in the mosque and usually offered sermons, but there was no ordained priesthood as in Judaism or Christianity and no hierarchy as in Christianity.

When Muhammad taught his followers, he claimed to be transmitting a direct, verbal revelation from God. That revelation came in the form of "recitations" that make up the *Quran*, the scriptures of Islam. After Muhammad's death his closest followers arranged the recitations into 114 *Suras*, or chapters. The Quran contains legal and wisdom literature, and moral teaching and rules for personal conduct. For example, the Quran forbids alcohol and gambling, censures luxury and ostentation, and imposes extreme sexual re-

straints on both men and women. Women are expected to shroud all but their eyes when they appear in public. (See the box "The Message of the Quran.")

After the prophet's death, people felt the need for an authoritative teaching, and their efforts resulted in two important collections. One of these was the *sunna,* which means the "good practice"— that is, the habits of Muhammad himself. The second was the *hadith,* the "sayings" of the prophet, presumably the comments he made about how God's revelation was to be understood. Extant compilations of the sunna and hadith date from the ninth century, and scholars are not sure what portion of them derives authentically from the age

Dome of the Rock This magnificent mosque in Jerusalem (built in 691–692) is the second holiest shrine of Islam—after the Kaaba in Mecca. Muslims believe that Muhammad ascended to heaven from this spot. *(Michael Holford)*

The Message of the Quran

*The Quran consists of 114 **Suras**, literally the "steps" by which one rises to knowledge of Allah; we might say chapters. The Quran in its earliest versions was also equipped with a running commentary. The first four extracts below illustrate the simplicity and elegance of Muslim prayer and the absolute transcendence of Allah. The last two extracts demonstrate the profound sense of religious continuity that marked Muhammad's teaching.*

Sura 1: In the name of Allah, Most Gracious, Most Merciful./Praise be to Allah, the Cherisher and Sustainer of worlds;/Most Gracious, Most Merciful./Master of the Day of Judgment./Thee do we worship and Thine aid we seek. Show us the straight way, the way of those on whom Thou hast bestowed Thy grace, Thou whose portion is not wrath, and who do not go astray.

Sura 4.171: O People of the Book! Commit no excesses in your religion, nor say of Allah anything but truth. Christ Jesus the son of Mary was a messenger of Allah . . . so believe in Allah and in his messengers. Say not "Trinity" . . . for Allah is One God. Glory be to Him for He is exalted above having a son. To him belong all things in the heavens and on earth.

Sura 3.84: Say ye: We believe in Allah, and the revelation given to us, and to Abraham, Ismail, Isaac, Jacob and the descendants (children of Jacob), and that given to Moses and to Jesus and that given to all prophets from their Lord, but we make no difference between one and another of them, and we bow to Allah.

Sura 2.87: We gave Moses the book and followed him up with a succession of messengers; We gave Jesus the son of Mary clear signs and strengthened him with the Holy Spirit.

C. 48: If the People of the Book rely upon Abraham, let them study his history. His posterity included both Israel and Ismail. Abraham was a righteous man of Allah, a Muslim, and so were his children. Abraham and Ismail built the Kaaba as the house of Allah and purified it, to be a centre of worship for all the world: For Allah is the God of all peoples.

C. 56: God's truth is continuous, and His prophets from Adam, through Noah and Abraham, down to the last of the prophets, Muhammad, form one brotherhood. Of Imran father of Moses and Aaron sprang a woman, who devoted her unborn offspring to Allah. That child was Mary the mother of Jesus. Her cousin was the wife of the priest Zakariya, who took charge of Mary. To Zachariya, in his old age, was born a son Yahya, amid prodigies: Yahya was the herald of Jesus the son of Mary and was known as John the Baptist.

Source: *The Meaning of the Holy Qur'an*, New Edition with Revised Translation, Commentary, and Newly Compiled Comprehensive Index by Abdullah Yusuf 'Ali (Beltsville, Maryland: Amana Publications, 1998), pp. 14, 40, 51, 55–56, 134–135. Reprinted with permission.

of the prophet. Quran, sunna, and hadith form the core of a dynamic spiritual message.

The Expansion of Islam

When Muhammad died in 632, the Meccan elite chose Abu Bakr as *caliph*, or "successor to the prophet." Abu Bakr and his three successors down to 661 (Umar, Uthman, and Ali) were all Meccans, relatives of the prophet by marriage, and early converts. Islamic tradition calls them the "Rightly Guided Caliphs."

Abu Bakr left his successor, Umar, a united Arabia (see Map 6.1). Umar began the Muslims' lightning conquests of much of the Roman and Persian Empires. He also began the policy of granting choice positions in the expanding caliphate, the Muslim empire, to old converts and of ranking them according to precedence in conversion. Muslim administrators collected personal taxes and land taxes from all conquered people. Converts to Islam paid only land taxes. Arab settlers paid no taxes and received salaries from the taxes paid by others. Numerous Arabs profited handsomely from the Muslim conquests.

Umar was murdered by a slave in 644, leaving his successor, Uthman, a huge empire to administer. Uthman succeeded in centralizing the regime, but his attempt to preserve the advantages of the old Meccan elite alienated many of the new elite, particularly in Egypt, Syria, and Iraq. Uthman was murdered in 656 and replaced by Ali, the husband of Muhammad's daughter Fatima. Ali's goal was to create a truly Islamic government by emphasizing the religious side of the caliph's office. Ali was killed by a disillusioned follower in 661, but years later some Muslims looked back to Ali as the true model for the caliph. These Muslims formed the *Shi'ites*, the "Party of Ali." In the late ninth and early tenth centuries a deep religious split emerged between the Shi'ites and the mainstream Sunna Muslims. Shi'ites believed that caliphs should be chosen from the line of Ali and Fatima, and only according to a strict standard of moral and spiritual worthiness. Sunnis, always the majority, accepted the legitimacy of the caliphs after Ali, as well as a broader interpretation of doctrine. Enmity based on these issues continues even today.

After Ali, the caliphate passed to the Umayyad family, who held it from 661 to 750. They built many of the centralizing institutions that characterized the caliphate until the tenth century. This involved the introduction of a unified coinage, the Arabization of the administration (granting all key positions to Arabs), and the tight control of provincial governors and taxes. The Umayyads moved the capital of the caliphate to Damascus in their own power base of Syria—more centrally located than the old towns of Mecca and Medina. The Umayyads also presided over the final territorial expansions of the caliphate (see Map 6.1). These extended, in the west, to North Africa and Spain, and even into Gaul, and in the east as far as the Indus River valley. Sieges against Constantinople were unsuccessful.

The pace was astonishing. Rome's empire expanded for 350 years, but the caliphate reached its zenith in scarcely 100. External factors go a long way toward explaining this phenomenal growth. Byzantium and Persia had weakened themselves in a series of wars that ended just as the caliphate of Umar commenced. Moreover, those two states were exceedingly diverse, and the Muslim armies dismantled them piecemeal. Both old empires had deep religious divisions. Coptic Egypt and Jacobite Syria, for example, willingly yielded to the Muslims, who demanded taxes and submission but, unlike the Byzantines, did not force conversions. The Byzantines and Persians tended to depend on large armies that could not be quickly mobilized. Aware of this, the Muslims rarely risked great pitched battles. They preferred a gradually expanding military frontier gained by numerous lightning strikes.

Internal factors were also significant. For centuries, raiding and plundering had been a way of life in Arabia, but because Islam forbade Muslims from raiding other Muslims, a new outlet for traditional violence was needed. The prophet had believed in the need to expand the faith, and his successors agreed. Muslim ideology divided the world into the "House of Islam" and the "House of War." In the House of Islam, Allah reigned supreme. In the House of War, *jihad*, holy war, was the rule. Christians and Jews, as fellow "Peoples of the Book"—sharers in a scriptural tradition reaching back to Abraham— were spared the choice of conversion or death. "Infidels" were expected to convert. Many converted by choice in order to join in the wealth of the new regime. The Muslim conquests were carefully planned to channel violence out of Arabia, to populate much of western Asia with loyal Muslims, and to permit members of the umma to enjoy vast rewards.

The Abbassid Revolution

The Umayyads were not popular, despite their military and administrative successes. Many people resented their bureaucratic centralization. Such resentment was acute in areas heavily populated by recent converts, who had always disliked the old Arabian elites, and in frontier provinces, where Arab immigrants and local converts both desired autonomy. Further, the secular nature of Umayyad rule offended some pious Muslims. The opposition came to a head in a series of rebellions that culminated in the naming of a rival caliph, Abu'l Abbas, in 749. In 750 he defeated his Umayyad rival, and the Abbassids reigned until the thirteenth century. In their earliest phases, especially in the caliphate of Harun al-Raschid (r. 786–809), they brought the Islamic world its first golden age. Harun's reign was marked by political stability, economic prosperity, and cultural achievements.

With their frontier origins, the Abbassids always understood the concerns of the caliphate's provincial populations. Thus, they created a more international regime, based on the idea of the fundamental equality of all believers. Key government posts were given to Iranians and other non-Arabs. Some provincial posts went to members of the Abbassid family, but local persons always got some choice positions. The capital of the caliphate was moved from Syria to Iraq, but to avoid favoring any existing city the Abbassids built a new one, Baghdad (see Map 6.1). By addressing regional and ethnic sensitivities in an effective way, they were able to extend the centralized state of the Umayyad period.

The death of Harun in 809 sparked a century of intense family rivalries, bureaucratic corruption, and palace intrigues. The army became more and more a professional body comprising non-Arabs, especially Turks, hired from the frontiers and beyond because Arabs, enjoying their salaries, declined to serve. The parallel with the Germanization of the late Roman army is striking. Religious divisions intensified. Many felt the Abbassids had not gone far enough in erecting a truly Islamic regime. Abbassid sensitivity to regional desires for autonomy resulted in the grad-ual loss of territory. Spain had been lost at the time of the Abbassid takeover in 750, when an Umayyad, Abd al-Rahman, erected an independent emirate at Cordoba. North Africa fell away in the mid-ninth century, and by the middle of the tenth century, Abbassid power in southern Iraq, Syria, Egypt, and Arabia was negligible. After the early tenth century the Abbassid caliphs had little effective power.

Culturally, however, this was a time of strength and renewal. In 832 an Abbassid caliph endowed the "House of Wisdom," an academy for scholars in Baghdad, and from this point on Muslim scholars had the leisure and wherewithal to begin tackling the corpus of Greek thought. Muslims showed little interest in the literary heritage of antiquity, seeking mainly to master the scientific learning of the past. The resultant culture was an amalgam of the ideas of the Quran and those of the Greek heritage. Over time, the Muslim empire mixed Iranian, Turkish, and even Hindu elements into a culture already rich with Arab, Christian, and Jewish ingredients.

THE BYZANTINE EMPIRE

The century after Justinian's death in 565 was difficult for the eastern Roman Empire. It suffered attacks by Persians, Bulgars, and Muslims, as well as internal rebellions, plagues, and famines. In 610 a process of reform and recovery began that had the long-term effect of transforming the eastern Roman regime into one that we call "Byzantine," from Byzantium, the ancient Greek name for the capital city, Constantinople. Before those reforms took hold, however, the eastern Roman state had to fight for its survival.

From the Eastern Roman Empire to the Byzantine Empire

In 610 Heraclius, a gifted, experienced ruler, ascended the throne. He ruled until 641 and set the basic pattern for the rest of the seventh century.

The eastern, Greek nature of the empire was emphasized over western ties. Military entanglements in the west were abandoned in favor of security in the east. Institutional reforms were initiated to meet new cultural, political, and diplomatic realities.

Heraclius and his successors faced military challenges on two fronts. In the east, Byzantium was the victim of a cruel irony. Between 612 and 619, the Persians conquered Syria, Palestine, Mesopotamia, and Egypt. Heraclius reorganized his military and finances and between 622 and 629 fought a series of campaigns that recovered almost everything. When the unexpected Muslim challenge appeared in 634, an exhausted Byzantium had no effective response. In the Balkans, the Byzantines enjoyed some successes against Slavs, who had been pushing south for years, and against Avars and Bulgars (peoples related to the Huns), who had settled in the Balkans. In the west, Spain and North Africa were abandoned to Muslims. In Italy and Sicily, effective imperial authority was minimal. The west was distant, divided, and distracting. It was clear that the east and the Balkans were critical. The change from the days of Justinian could not have been more apparent.

Several cultural indicators point to the emergence of a regime that laid increasing stress on its Greek and Christian roots. For example, the emperors used Greek to call themselves "Emperor of the Romans." As Justinian had looked to his Latin and Roman roots, so Heraclius and his successors were unashamedly Greek and Eastern in their outlook. The emperor saw himself as God's specially chosen and protected agent with full authority over the church and over the religious life of all Christian people. To emphasize the religious foundations of their imperial office, the emperors began putting images of Christ on their coins. In one of his official titles the emperor was "The Thirteenth Apostle." Heraclius sought religious unity, but his efforts to enforce conversion met opposition from popes as well as Coptic and Jacobite Christians. The differences between Orthodox and other Christians became ever more visible.

The Eighth-Century Recovery

In 717, Leo III became emperor in a moment of acute crisis. Muslim armies had seized most of Anatolia and had laid siege to Constantinople itself. The city would surely have fallen had it not been for "Greek fire," a mixture of petroleum, sulfur, saltpeter, and lime that ignited on contact with water, making it impossible for the Muslim navy to operate beneath the seaward walls. Leo ruled until 741 and was followed until 775 by his able son, Constantine V. Together they extended the seventh-century focus on the eastern frontiers and on the Greek and Orthodox empire. Although official ideology in the eighth century claimed that the Roman Empire of Augustus was still in existence, under Leo and Constantine a new regime, the Byzantine, was consolidated.

After a century of military reverses, Leo III and Constantine V were often victorious (Map 6.2). They defended Constantinople, recovered Anatolian territory from the Muslims, and checked the advance of the Bulgars. Their successes stemmed from military reforms. For centuries the Romans had used tax revenues to recruit, pay, and equip soldiers for both standing armies and frontier auxiliaries. Leo and Constantine brought to completion a new system that began emerging in the sixth century. Men from frontier regions were recruited and then settled on farms in military districts called *themes*. All themes, whether naval ones or army, stood under a commander who was simultaneously the civil and military chief of his theme. The farmer-soldiers did not pay tax on their lands but discharged their obligations to the state by personal service. Some standing troops were retained, but several thematic armies now constituted the backbone of the Byzantine military.

Leo and Constantine did more than just reform military structures. In 726, Leo issued the *Ecloga*, the first major revision of Roman law since Justinian's. But where Justinian's *Code* was beyond the capacity of all but the most sophisticated lawyers in Constantinople, the *Ecloga* was "a selection of laws," "an abridgment" whose purpose was to provide a simplified, unified body of law for provincial judges in the Byzantine Empire.

Leo and Constantine initiated far-reaching reforms in an imperial administration little changed since Late Antiquity. Roman administration had consisted of a few very large departments headed by officials with immense responsibilities and power. The new Byzantine system was characterized by a profusion of departments under officers who had more prestige than actual power. The emperors neutralized the bureaucrats by drawing them by merit from all social classes, paying them well, giving them fancy titles and public recognition, but dividing their responsibilities and curtailing their actual power.

Leo and Constantine also tried to achieve religious and cultural unity. The so-called iconoclastic controversy serves as an example of their policies. Icons of Christ, Mary, and saints began to play a prominent role in Orthodox devotions in the fifth century. Some *iconodules*—defenders of icons—said that icons served to bring to mind the person depicted and thus helped individuals in their spiritual life. Other iconodules felt that icons had theological significance by affirming the humanity of Christ: If Christ was truly human, then he could be depicted like any other human. By contrast the Jewish and Muslim traditions considered any attempt to depict God as idolatry, as sinful. Some influential Christian voices also said that any icon was really an idol.

In 726, Leo removed an icon of Christ from the gate of one of the imperial palaces, and for several years he and like-minded clergy agitated against icons. In 731, an imperial decree banned all images of Christ or the saints. Why did an emperor faced with so many threats devote so much energy to this issue? In the preface to the *Ecloga*, Leo portrays himself as an Old Testament king who has a duty to lead his people in the path of righteousness. He seems to have believed quite sincerely that icons were idols and that they provoked God so strongly that God had permitted Byzantium's enemies to prosper. Constantine V, who was much better educated than his father, was opposed to icons for theological reasons. To him, icons laid excessive emphasis

on the humanity of Christ—Christological quarrels had not disappeared.

Personal convictions played a role, but public issues were important, too. Many famous icons were housed in monasteries. Monasteries were often given generous gifts by pious laymen, and many extremely talented people embraced the monastic life rather than serving the state. The emperors had for a long time exercised control over the patriarchs, but they had never really gotten control of the monastic clergy. Attacking icons was in some ways an attempt to complete the emperor's control of the church.

Though extraordinarily destructive, iconoclasm had limited success. Many ordinary people cherished icons and ignored imperial policy. The emperors occasionally made an example of prominent iconodules by exiling or executing them, but most people were left alone. Monks were popular, in some areas as popular as the emperor himself. Thus, attacks on monasteries sometimes backfired. Christians in Egypt or Syria, to the extent they knew about iconoclastic policies, regarded the emperor as a heretic. In Rome, a succession of popes rejected iconoclasm itself and, like their predecessors, wrote to the emperor to tell him that he had no business interfering in church doctrines. Unity based on religion remained as elusive for emperors as it was for caliphs.

Ninth-Century Problems

The dynasty of Leo III might have continued indefinitely but for a rapid accumulation of misfortunes in the last decades of the eighth century. Constantine V's promising son, Leo IV, died suddenly in 780, leaving a 6-year-old son, Constantine VI, and a remarkable widow, Irene (753–803). Shortly after assuming the regency for her son, Irene began planning the restoration of icons. This was a matter of personal conviction with her, but it also owed a lot to an awareness that the controversy over icons had not brought religious or political unity to the empire but had isolated the Byzantine church from all other Christian communities. This isolation meant that the Byzantine Empire had no allies against Muslims

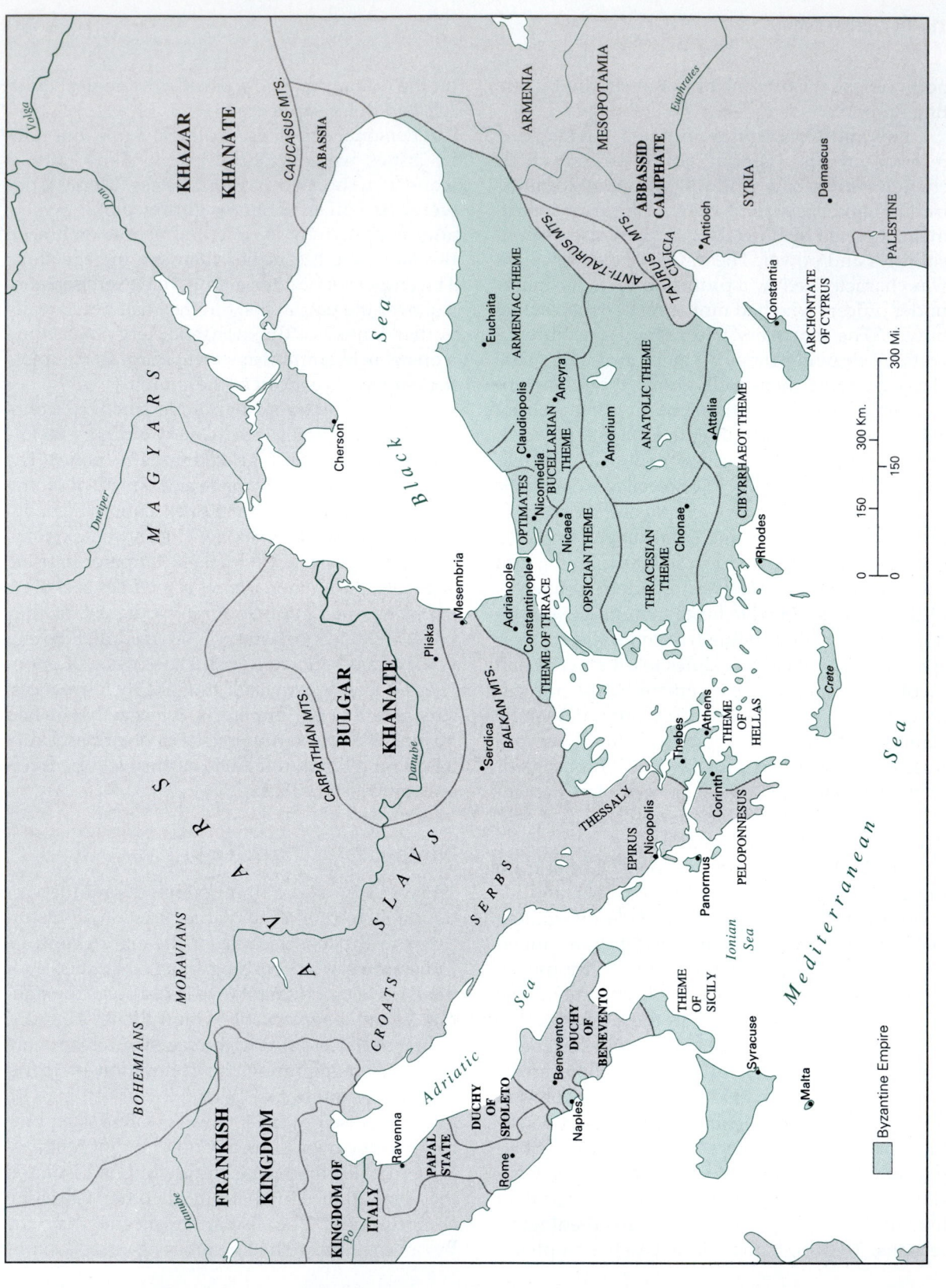

KHAZAR KHANATE

CAUCASUS MTS.

ABASSIA

ARMENIA

MESOPOTAMIA

Volga

Don

ABBASSID CALIPHATE

SYRIA

•Damascus

Euphrates

Antioch•

PALESTINE

Sea

ARMENIAC THEME

ANTI-TAURUS MTS.

TAURUS MTS.

CILICIA

ARCHONTATE OF CYPRUS

•Constantia

MAGYARS

Dnieper

Euchaita•

Claudiopolis•

Ancyra•

ANATOLIC THEME

•Attalia

CIBYRRHAEOT THEME

•Rhodes

Cherson•

Black

Sea

OPTIMATES

•Nicomedia

BUCELLARIAN THEME

Amorium•

Nicaea•

OPSICIAN THEME

THRACESIAN THEME

Chonae•

300 Mi.

300 Km.

150

150

0

0

Mesembria•

Adrianople•

Constantinople•

THEME OF THRACE

Pliska•

BULGAR KHANATE

Serdica•

BALKAN MTS.

Danube

CARPATHIAN MTS.

Crete

THESSALY

Athens•

Thebes•

THEME OF HELLAS

Corinth•

Mediterranean Sea

A

R

S

EPIRUS

Nicopolis•

PELOPONNESUS

S

L

A

V

S

SERBS

Panormus•

Ionian Sea

MORAVIANS

CROATS

THEME OF SICILY

BOHEMIANS

Adriatic Sea

Benevento•

DUCHY OF BENEVENTO

Syracuse•

Ravenna•

DUCHY OF SPOLETO

Naples•

•Malta

FRANKISH KINGDOM

Danube

KINGDOM OF ITALY

Po

PAPAL STATE

Rome•

Byzantine Empire

and Bulgars. In 787, Irene convened a church council at Nicaea that pronounced against the iconoclastic decrees.

What Irene could not do was control her frivolous son, who refused to attend to the business of state and trysted with girls who served in his mother's chamber. Exasperated, she blinded him in the very room in which he had been born. Because any physical deformity rendered a person unfit for rule, Irene intended merely to disqualify her son and then to succeed in her own right. Instead, he died from his wounds, and she incurred the name of murderess. From 797 to 802, Irene ruled the empire, but her authority was never really accepted. Many people were horrified at her treatment of her son; others were simply unprepared to accept a woman as ruler. (See the box "Encounters with the West: Muslim and Byzantine 'Diplomacy'?") Finally, however, she was the victim of a coup d'état because she could not retain the loyalty of the army or the bureaucracy. The irony in all this is that Irene was able, intelligent, resourceful, and, in truth, the real heir to Leo IV.

From the deposition of Irene in 802 until the accession of Basil I (r. 867–886), the history of the Byzantine Empire is a study in contradictions. There were assassinations and usurpations but also effective rulers. Military successes were recorded but also defeats. The state was often short of cash, and its attempts to raise money angered many people. Religious policy shifted several times, too. For example, icons were again outlawed from 815 to 842, with no more effect than in the first period of iconoclasm.

Basil, himself a usurper, was a great soldier, a gifted administrator, and a hard-headed ruler who brooked no opposition. His dynasty, the Macedonian, reigned for two centuries and eventually won great victories in the Balkans and in

Saint Peter A rare pre-iconoclastic icon from Mount Sinai: Peter is depicted as a late antique magistrate—wise and distinguished—not as a simple fisherman. The medallions depict Christ in the center, Mary on the right, and John the Evangelist on the left. In a late antique depiction of a consul, the images would have had the emperor in the center, the empress on the right, and the co-consul on the left. (*Alexandria-Michigan-Princeton Archeological Expedition to Mount Sinai/Roger Wood/Corbis-Bettmann*)

Map 6.2 The Byzantine Empire in the Eighth and Ninth Centuries After suffering tremendous territorial losses to barbarians and Muslims, the Byzantine Empire transformed its military, institutional, and cultural structures to create a regime that survived until it was conquered by Crusaders in 1204.

Anatolia. Macedonian rulers were sometimes scholars themselves and usually patrons of learning. They promoted but also controlled the church and went far to soothe the divisions of the iconoclastic era.

∼ ENCOUNTERS WITH THE WEST ∼

Muslim and Byzantine "Diplomacy"?

This excerpt from an Arabic chronicle reveals something of the attitudes of Muslims and Byzantines toward each other. Notice the mistakes and misunderstandings.

A woman [Irene] came to rule over the Romans because at the time she was the only one of their royal house who remained. She wrote to the Caliphs with respect and deference and showered them with gifts. When her son [Constantine VI] grew up and came to the throne in her place, he brought trouble and disorder and provoked [Harun] al-Raschid. The empress, who knew al-Raschid and feared his power, was afraid lest the kingdom of the Romans pass away and their country be ruined. She therefore overcame her son by cunning and put out his eyes so that the kingdom was taken from him and returned to her. But the people disapproved of this and hated her for it. Therefore Nicephorus [emperor, 802–811] rose against her. . . . He wrote to al-Raschid, "From Nicephorus, the king of the Romans, to al-Raschid, the king of the Arabs" as follows: "That woman [Irene] put you in the place of kings and put herself in the place of a commoner. I put you in a different place and am preparing to invade your lands and attack your cities unless you repay me what that woman paid you. Farewell." Al-Raschid replied, "In the name of God, the Merciful, the Compassionate, from the servant of God, Harun, Commander of the faithful, to Nicephorus, dog of the Romans" as follows: "I have understood your letter, and I have your answer. You will see it with your eye, not hear it." Then he sent an army against the land of the Romans.

Source: Abu'l-Faraj al-Isfahani, *Al-Aghani*, in Bernard Lewis, ed., *Islam from the Prophet Muhammad to the Conquest of Constantinople*, vol. 1 (New York: Harper & Row, 1974), pp. 27–28. Copyright © 1974 by Bernard Lewis. Reprinted by permission of HarperCollins Publishers, Inc.

CHRISTIAN KINGDOMS IN THE WEST

In the West, the seventh century was full of challenges, the eighth century was marked by innovation and accomplishment, and the ninth century was characterized by new challenges and in some areas near collapse. Parallels with the Islamic and Byzantine worlds are striking. Christian Europe developed slowly, through the evangelization of the countryside, the spread of an ecclesiastical hierarchy, the shift of papal interests away from the Mediterranean world toward western Europe, and the evolving relationship between royal governments and the Catholic church.

The Struggles of Christian Spain

After Clovis's victory over them in 507, the Visigoths were never able to re-establish dynastic continuity. As a result, Spain witnessed rebellions and usurpations more frequently than any other early medieval area in the West. The accomplishments of the Visigothic king Leovigild (r. 568–586) are remarkable given the state of Spain on his accession. He nearly unified the country, and he established a capital (Toledo) and a seat of government—which the Visigoths had been lacking since they lost Toulouse in 507. Leovigild's greatest problem was the Arianism of the Visigothic minority in the midst of the

Catholic Hispano-Roman population. An Arian himself, he tried hard to convert Catholics to Arianism but failed. In 589, under King Reccared (r. 586–601), the Visigoths officially embraced Roman Catholicism.

The conversion of the Visigoths permitted close cooperation between the church and the monarchy and placed the human and material resources of the church at the disposal of the king as he attempted to unite and govern the country. By the mid-seventh century, economic prosperity, assimilation between Goths and Hispano-Romans, and a brilliant culture marked the high point of Visigothic Spain. The succession problem, however, was never overcome, and a stable central government remained beyond reach.

In 710, Muslims from North Africa invaded Spain. Within five years Berbers (native North Africans and recent converts to Islam who were led by Arabs) completed the conquest of much of the Iberian Peninsula. Christians in the rugged mountains of the northwest—the region called Asturias—could not be dislodged, and the Muslims' part of Spain—known as al-Andalus—was plagued by the same ethnic and religious divisions as the Islamic East. Secure in mountainous Asturias (see Map 6.3), Christian kings built a capital at Oviedo and, in the ninth century, launched attacks against al-Andalus. For six hundred years this conflict between Christians and Muslims was the chief dynamic of Spanish history.

Italy and the Papal State

In 600 the Italian political scene was crowded. Several Germanic groups, four Byzantine outposts, and the popes were all contending for power. By the late eighth century, the Franks dominated northern Italy, the popes had created a state in the center, and the Byzantines clung to Naples and Sicily. That basic pattern then persisted for three hundred years.

After defeating the Ostrogoths, the Byzantines were in principle masters of Italy, but their attempts to restore order were thwarted by the Lombards, who invaded in 568. These people had long lived in the Pannonian plain. Their invasion caused the Byzantines to introduce a largely military regime under officers called *exarchs*. The exarchate was not strong because its population refused to pay heavy taxes to Constantinople when the receipts were spent in the Balkans instead of against the Lombards. Also, Catholic Italy rejected Byzantine Christology and iconoclasm. Gradually the popes organized the defense of central Italy against the Lombards, stood up for the oppressed locals against Byzantine tax collectors, and led the opposition to unpopular theologies. Even though the Lombard kings converted from Arianism to Catholicism by 680, formed a strong government, and then issued the most sophisticated Germanic law code, they were not sufficiently unified to achieve stability.

By attacking Rome, the strongest Lombard king of the eighth century, Aistulf (r. 749–757), caused the pope to turn to Pepin III, the king of the Franks, for protection. Pepin came to Italy in 755 and 756, defeated Aistulf, and forced him to give to the pope all the lands he had taken. A few years later Aistulf's successor reopened hostilities in central Italy. In 774, Charlemagne, Pepin's son and successor, defeated the Lombards, deposed their king, and took the Lombard crown for himself. The Franks guaranteed to the popes undisputed possession of a substantial territory in central Italy. This first papal state was the culmination of three processes. First, as Roman imperial power declined in Late Antiquity, bishops often became the effective leaders of their towns. The popes found themselves responsible for Rome's food and water supply and the upkeep of its public buildings and charitable services. To pay for these functions, the popes began to organize the efficient administration of the patrimonies, the lands of the Roman church. Second, the popes took the lead in protecting many people in central Italy from Byzantine taxes and heresy. This effort, too, forged bonds between the popes and the Italians. Third, eighth-century

A Mother Hen and Seven Chicks This delightfully frivolous object may have been a gift from Pope Gregory I to the Lombard queen Theudelinda. It helps us to appreciate the aesthetic tastes of the barbarians. *(Cathedral Treasure, Monza/Scala/ Art Resource, NY)*

Rome spawned a justification for papal temporal rule. According to the *Donation of Constantine*, a document written in Rome (probably in the 760s), when Constantine departed Rome for the East in the 320s, he gave to the pope the authority to rule the whole West. In reality, no pope ever made such grandiose claims, but the existence of the document signals a progression from landlordship to direct rule. As a consequence, while kingdoms were collapsing, a papal state was created that survives to this day as Vatican City.

The medieval popes who were simultaneously head of a church and of a state were the heirs of Pope Gregory I (r. 590–604). Scion of a Roman senatorial family, Gregory held important secular offices before deciding to become a monk. He had wanted a life of monastic retreat, but when the people and clergy of Rome elected him pope, he threw himself into his new responsibilities. Gregory negotiated with emperors and kings, disciplined churches and clerics throughout the West, and began creating and refining the bureaucratic apparatus of the papacy. He was also a brilliant theologian, the last of the Latin

Church Fathers. He wrote biblical commentaries, books on moral living, and the *Pastoral Rule*, which circulated for a thousand years as a guide for bishops. Gregory was the founder of the medieval papacy.

The Fate of the British Isles

Britain was less thoroughly Romanized, more quickly abandoned by the Romans, and more deeply influenced by Germanic peoples than any other locality in the West. Around 600, the small Anglo-Saxon kingdoms created in the sixth century took the first steps toward converting to Christianity, transforming Britain into England, and joining England inseparably to the European world.

But there was another history unfolding in the British Isles, that of the Celtic peoples in the north and west of Britain itself and in Ireland. The Celts were the people who inhabited Britain before the Romans invaded in the first century. They were related to peoples who lived in a broad band from Anatolia to Ireland and Spain. The Anglo-Saxons confined the British Celts to the western regions of Cornwall and Wales and to the northern area of Scotland. Ireland had almost no Roman or Anglo-Saxon imprint.

In the period between 600 and 900, the development of the Catholic church preceded political organization in the Celtic realms. Each Celtic region produced a mythology connected with missionaries who supposedly brought the Christian faith in Late Antiquity. The best-known stories swirl around Ireland's Saint Patrick (390?–461?). The son of a minor Roman official in the north of Britain, Patrick was captured by pirates, enslaved in Ireland, freed, made a priest, and then returned to Ireland as a missionary. Patrick and his successors spread Christianity, and a vigorous monasticism, throughout the island. Historical too is the Irish aristocrat Columba (521–597), who, after his family lost a great battle, emigrated in 563 to the isle of Iona off the coast of Scotland. From his monastery there, Columba and his successors began the evangelization of Scotland.

Among the most successful Anglo-Saxon kingdoms were Wessex, Northumbria, and Mercia (see Map 6.3). Each had a reasonably large population and territory and opportunities for expansion, and ambitious rulers whose wars provided booty, land, and glory for old followers and new recruits.

Foreign connections also played a role in their success. Kent and East Anglia had diplomatic connections with the Franks, and Aethelbert (561–616), the greatest Kentish king, married Bertha, the daughter of a Frankish king. East Anglia's far-flung connections are revealed by a ship burial unearthed near Sutton Hoo in 1939. The ship, either a grave for or a memorial to an unknown king, had been hauled up onto the land, filled with treasures, and buried. The array of goods found at Sutton Hoo is astonishing. They show influences ranging from the Mediterranean to the Rhineland, Scandinavia, and Ireland. The fine scepter found at Sutton Hoo indicates that English kings had adopted symbolic aspects of rule to legitimize their authority. Northumbrian kings were preceded by banners and a royal standard. Most kings issued coins in their own name.

In relations with the church, two issues proved crucial: the conversion to Christianity and the development of an ecclesiastical hierarchy. In 597, Pope Gregory I sent a small band of missionaries under a Roman monk named Augustine (d. 604) to King Aethelbert of Kent, whose Christian wife, Bertha, had prepared the ground for the newcomers. From their base of operations at Canterbury in southeastern England, Augustine and his successors had limited success spreading Christianity, but a new field of influence was opened to them when Aethelbert and Bertha's daughter married a king of Northumbria and took missionaries to her new home. Monks from Iona, as noted, were already spreading Christianity in Scotland. When later Northumbrian kings turned to Iona for missionaries, Roman and Celtic Christianity came face to face in Northumbria.

The Christianity brought from Ireland did not differ in fundamental ways from the Roman Christianity imported at Canterbury. Indeed, the Irish were Roman Catholics. But Ireland had been isolated from the centers of Christian life since Late Antiquity, and its church had developed a number of distinctive local customs. For example, the two traditions used different calendars and thus celebrated Christian holidays on different dates. In 664, the Northumbrian king Oswy called a synod, a church council, at the monastery of Whitby, whose abbess was the former royal princess Hilda (614–680), a champion of Celtic customs. At Whitby, Roman and Irish representatives debated their positions. Oswy, choosing the universal over the particular, decided for Rome.

In 668 the pope sent to England a new archbishop of Canterbury, Theodore (r. 668–690). He came from Rome but was a Syrian monk, so neither the "Romans" nor the "Irish" in England could easily view him as a partisan. Theodore reconciled the conflicting parties, built up a typical Roman ecclesiastical structure using Roman canon law, and promoted Christian education. Theodore laid the foundations for a unified English church that contributed to the eventual political unification of England.

Ecclesiastical peace led to the flourishing of monastic life. Monasteries played two important roles in this period. First, they led the way in bringing Christianity to ordinary people. Despite early gains among kings and nobles, Christianity had barely begun to penetrate the countryside. Second, monks maintained international connections that attached England to the major intellectual currents of the day and enabled the English to make their own contributions. In Canterbury and in Northumbria (another important center of learning), English, Irish, Frankish, and Roman currents came together, as revealed by the extraordinary illuminated manuscripts produced by the schools of Canterbury, Lindisfarne, and Jarrow. These books of texts and gorgeous paintings were the masterpieces of the early Middle Ages.

The greatest product of this intellectual tradition was Bede (673–735), a great teacher, an erudite scholar, and a superb Latin stylist. His *Ecclesiastical History of the English People* was the most important source for English history from the fifth century to the eighth. His biblical commentaries remained influential all over Europe for centuries, and his studies of temporal reckoning popularized the use of A.D. dating, which replaced a bewildering array of local systems.

The career of King Offa of Mercia (r. 757–796) illustrates the key trends in early Britain. His ancestors were pagans, but he was a patron of the church and recipient of papal envoys. He dominated all of Britain and was the first to call himself "King of the English." He issued a law code and signed England's first international trade agreement—with Charlemagne. After Offa's death, however, Viking raiders destroyed whatever unity had been achieved.

Beginning in 865, the Vikings conquered most of eastern and central England and began threatening the south. In 871 Alfred the Great (r. 871–899) ascended the throne, won a series of military victories, rallied the English, and began the slow reconquest of the rest of England from the Vikings. Alfred promoted intellectual recovery, church reform, and political stability. After two generations of chaos, Alfred revived the centralizing and unifying work of his eighth-century predecessors and laid the foundations for the English state of the tenth and eleventh centuries.

THE WORLD OF CHARLEMAGNE

Clovis and the Franks created the most effective of the early Germanic kingdoms (see page 130). During the seventh century that kingdom experienced difficulties but did not disappear. Then a Frankish family, called "Carolingian" from the name of its greatest member, Charlemagne, assembled the talent and resources of the Frankish realm in a new way. Charlemagne (Carolus Magnus, "Charles the Great," in Latin) reformed his government and church, patronized learning, and resurrected the western empire.

The Rise of the Carolingian Family

When Clovis died in 511, he divided his realm among his sons, and it soon became clear that several kingdoms would coexist. The Merovingian royal families feuded constantly. Trade and intellectual life declined, and some regions that had been conquered in the sixth century slipped away. Nevertheless, the *idea* of a single kingdom of the Franks persisted. Kings and aristocrats in the small kingdoms competed for leadership of the realm as a whole.

In the seventh century, the classicizing culture of late antique Gaul was largely gone, but a creative Christian monastic culture was growing up all over of the Frankish kingdom. Monks from the monasteries were converting the countryside to Christianity. The Carolingian family appeared in history just after 600 and thereafter monopolized the office of mayor of the palace (sort of a prime minister to the king) in Austrasia (the easternmost kingdom; see Map 6.3). The Carolingians were the wealthiest family in Austrasia, perhaps in the Frankish world. Within two generations they unified the Frankish realm and increased their own power.

The Carolingians used several methods to accomplish their ends. They formed alliances with powerful noble families in many regions, and they waged war against the enemies of the Franks. Charles Martel (d. 741), Charlemagne's grandfather, led the Frankish forces that put an end to Arab raiding in Gaul, defeating a large force near Poitiers in 733. With booty from their wars, tribute from conquered peoples, and even lands seized from the church, the Carolingians rewarded more and more followers until no one, not even the Merovingians, could challenge them.

For years the Carolingians were content with the office of mayor of the palace. Then in 749, Pepin III (son of Charles Martel) decided to ask the pope whether it was right that the person who had all the power in the land of the Franks was not the king. The pope responded that this situation contravened the divine plan. Accordingly, in 751, the last Merovingian king was deposed, and Pepin was elected in his place (r. 751–768). Pepin had prepared his usurpation very carefully with his Frankish supporters, but he appealed to the pope to lend his reign the air of divine approval. The pope, for his part, needed an ally against the Lombards in Italy. Three years later the pope visited the Frankish kingdom, where he crowned and anointed Pepin and his sons, including Charlemagne. The new royal dynasty would last for more than two centuries.

The Empire of Charlemagne

Charlemagne (r. 768–814) was a great and complex leader. He spoke and read Frankish, Latin, and some Greek but never learned to write. He promoted Christian morality but perpetrated unspeakable brutalities on his enemies. Many battles were fought in his name, but he rarely accompanied his armies and fought no campaigns that are remembered for strategic brilliance. Determination and organization were the hallmarks of his forty-six-year reign.

It took until the mid-780s for Charlemagne to assess his world (Map 6.3). His first major achievement was the articulation of a new ruling ideology in the Latin West. In *capitularies*—royal executive orders—of 789, Charlemagne required all males to swear an oath of allegiance to him,

and he compared himself to a biblical king in his responsibility to teach and to set an example for his people. No distinctions were to be made among Franks or Bavarians or Saxons. Everyone was to be equal in allegiance to the king and in membership in a sort of Augustinian City of God.

Einhard (ca. 770–840), Charlemagne's friend and biographer, said that Augustine's *City of God* was the king's favorite book. The king understood it to mean that there was a City of God consisting of all right-thinking Christians—the "New Israel"—and a City of Man consisting of pagans, heretics, and infidels. To Charlemagne, as to his Muslim and Byzantine contemporaries, no boundary existed between church and state. Religion and state were complementary attributes of a polity whose end was salvation, not victory in war, domestic security, or personal fulfillment.

The most disputed event in the reign of Charlemagne was his imperial coronation in Rome on Christmas in 800. In April 799, some disgruntled papal bureaucrats and their supporters attacked Pope Leo III (r. 795–816) in an attempt to depose him. Leo was saved by an ally of Charlemagne and then traveled all the way to Saxony, where the king was with his army. Charlemagne agreed to restore the pope to Rome and to investigate those who had attacked him. When Charlemagne went to Saint Peter's Basilica on Christmas Day, he prayed before the main altar. As he rose from prayer, Pope Leo placed a crown on his head, and the assembled Romans acclaimed him as emperor. Einhard later said that if Charlemagne had known what was going to happen he would not have gone to church, even though it was Christmas. What Einhard meant was that although Charlemagne saw himself as a Frankish and Christian emperor, leader of the Frankish "Israel," he did not want to be a *Roman* emperor, beholden to the pope and to the Romans.

Charlemagne's policies did not change after his coronation. He continued his program of legal and ecclesiastical reform and put the finishing touches on some military and diplomatic campaigns. In 806 he divided his empire among his three legitimate sons; but when two of them died he made Louis his sole heir and successor.

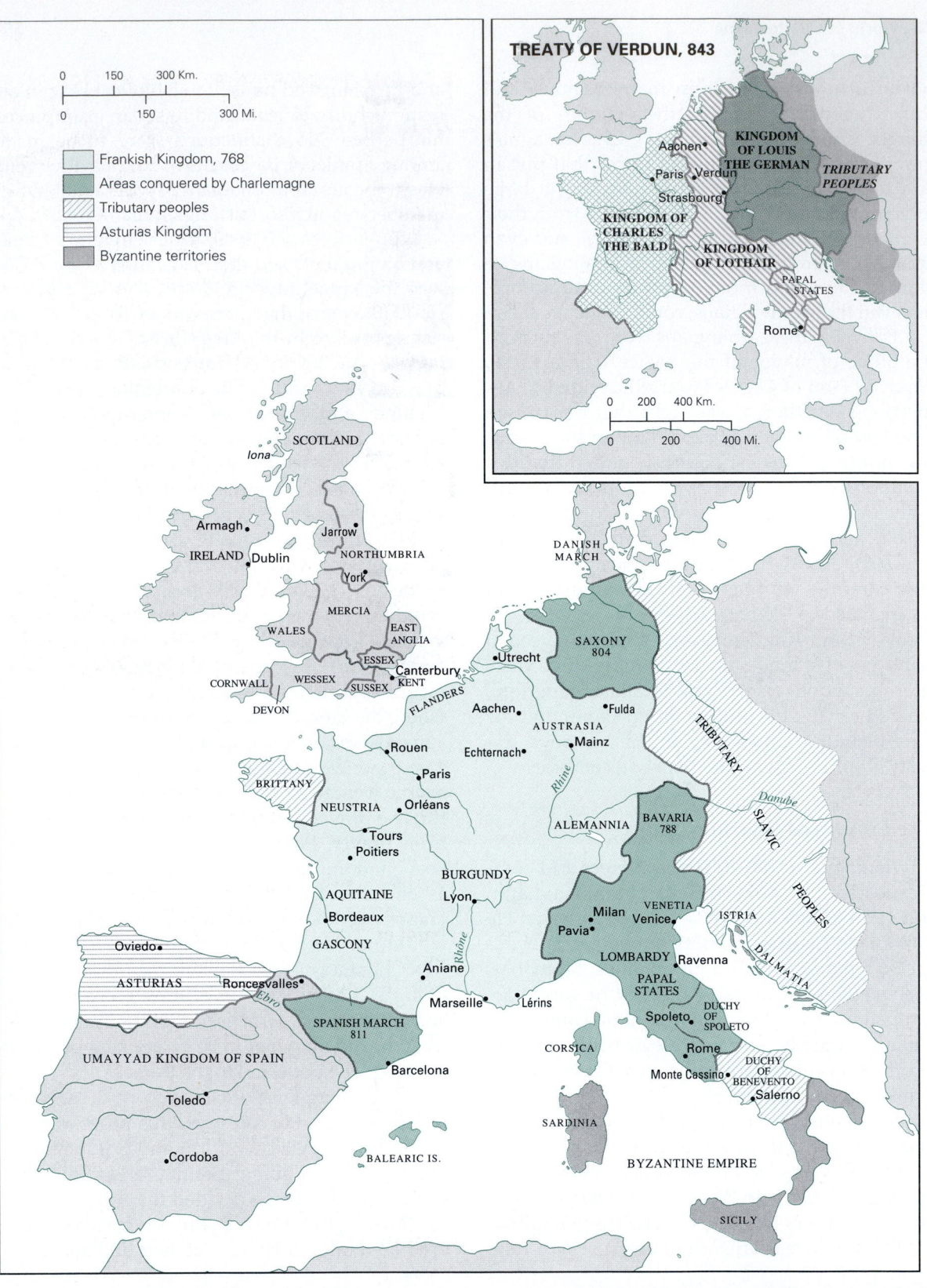

KINGDOM
OF LOUIS
THE GERMAN

*TRIBUTARY
PEOPLES*

Aachen

Paris • Verdun

Strasbourg

KINGDOM OF
CHARLES
THE BALD

KINGDOM
OF LOTHAIR

PAPAL
STATES

Rome

0   200   400 Km.

0   200   400 Mi.

Frankish Kingdom, 768

Areas conquered by Charlemagne

Tributary peoples

Asturias Kingdom

Byzantine territories

0   150   300 Km.

0   150   300 Mi.

SCOTLAND

Iona

Armagh

IRELAND Dublin

Jarrow

NORTHUMBRIA

York

MERCIA

WALES

EAST
ANGLIA

ESSEX

CORNWALL   WESSEX   SUSSEX

DEVON

KENT

Canterbury

DANISH
MARCH

Utrecht

FLANDERS

Aachen

AUSTRASIA

Echternach   Mainz

Rhine

Fulda

SAXONY
804

TRIBUTARY

BRITTANY

NEUSTRIA

Rouen

Paris

Orléans

Tours

Poitiers

BURGUNDY

AQUITAINE

Bordeaux

GASCONY

Lyon

Rhône

ALEMANNIA

BAVARIA
788

Danube

SLAVIC

Milan

Pavia

VENETIA

Venice

ISTRIA

PEOPLES

DALMATIA

LOMBARDY

Ravenna

Oviedo

ASTURIAS

Roncesvalles

Ebro

SPANISH MARCH
811

Aniane

Marseille

Lérins

PAPAL
STATES

Spoleto

DUCHY
OF
SPOLETO

CORSICA

Rome

Monte Cassino

DUCHY
OF
BENEVENTO

Salerno

UMAYYAD KINGDOM OF SPAIN

Barcelona

Toledo

Cordoba

BALEARIC IS.

SARDINIA

BYZANTINE EMPIRE

SICILY

Charlemagne outlived four wives, many of his children, and most of his friends. Old and alone, he died in early 814.

Charlemagne's legacy was great. He brought together the lands that would become France, Germany, and northern Italy and endowed them with a common government and culture. His vast supraregional and supra-ethnic entity, gradually called "Christendom," drew deeply on the universalizing ideals of its Roman, Christian, and Jewish antecedents but was, nevertheless, original. The Carolingian Empire was the final stage in the evolution of the Roman Empire, but it was also a new kind of regime that pointed to the future.

Carolingian Government

Charlemagne created institutional structures and governmental patterns that lasted in many parts of Europe until the twelfth century. The king (or emperor—the offices differed little in practical importance) was the heart of the system. In theory, the king ruled by God's grace and did not have to answer for his conduct to any person. In reality, the king necessarily sought consensus through a variety of means. By controlling vast lands, money, and appointments to key positions, the king required others to come to him for power, wealth, and prestige.

The eastern contemporaries of the Carolingians relied on large numbers of trained, paid civil servants. In contrast, the Carolingians employed a limited number of men who were tied to them by bonds of familial and personal allegiance. At the Carolingian court there were cere-

Charlemagne's Throne, Aachen Palace Chapel Modeled on the biblical description of King Solomon's throne, Charlemagne's throne symbolized the wisdom and justice of the Frankish king who led the new Frankish "Israel" *(Erich Lessing/Art Resource, NY)*

monial officers and a domestic staff. For example, the treasurer was the keeper of the king's bedchamber, where the royal treasure chest was kept. Several chaplains, whose primary duty was to see to the spiritual needs of the court, kept official records. The queen controlled the domestic staff and the stewards who managed the royal estates.

Local government was mainly entrusted to counts. There were about six hundred counts in the empire and several times that number of minor officials. The counts were at once administrative, judicial, and military officials. Most came from prominent families, and the office increased the wealth and importance of its holders. Counts enforced royal orders and presided in regular

Map 6.3 The Carolingian World The area over which Charlemagne exerted direct or indirect control was vast. The areas beyond the Rhine and Danube had never been part of the Roman Empire. The Franks made these regions part of European civilization. The Treaty of Verdun (see inset), signed by Charlemagne's grandsons in 843, was the first and most important of several divisions of the Carolingian Empire that resulted in the emergence of France and Germany. The kingdom of Italy and many small territories evolved from the kingdom of Lothair.

sessions of local courts. They received one-third of the fines, so the pursuit of justice was in their interest.

The royal court and the localities were linked in several ways. Under Charlemagne and his successors it became usual for all major officers, whether secular (counts and their subordinates) or ecclesiastical (bishops, abbots), to be *vassals* of the king. In return for their offices and grants of land called *benefices,* vassals pledged loyalty and service to the king. Vassalage drew on both Roman patron-client traditions and the Germanic allegiance of warriors to a chief. But by connecting personal loyalty with public office and material reward, Charlemagne created something new. Only a few thousand men, a tiny fraction of the total population, were vassals at any time. They constituted the political and social elite.

Another connection between the king and his local agents was the assembly that met in various places once or twice a year. Most of the great Carolingian reforms were formulated in these assemblies by cooperation between the king and his most important subjects. The king also brought his power to bear locally by traveling. The monarchy possessed estates all over the kingdom, and the royal entourage often moved from one place to another, checking on local conditions and monitoring local officials.

In 788, Charlemagne began to build a palace at Aachen, and in the last twenty years of his life he was usually in residence there (see Map 6.3). The later Carolingian rulers all tended to have fixed residences, as did the Byzantines and the Abbassids. Elegant courts and intricate rituals were seen as important ways to enhance people's respect for their rulers. After taking up residence in Aachen, Charlemagne began to send out pairs of roving inspectors, *missi dominici,* to see that royal orders were being observed, that counts were just, and that persons of power were not oppressing the powerless.

The Carolingian Renaissance

Charlemagne's reforms culminated in a revival of learning that scholars have named the "Car-

olingian Renaissance" (from *renaissance,* French for "rebirth"). The Carolingians were the driving force behind intellectual growth in their era, but it was not intellectualism for its own sake. In all areas the Carolingians subordinated learning to their ideological vision: the rebirth of Western society as a "New Israel."

Charlemagne required every cathedral and monastery to establish a school. To set up and run those schools he summoned to his court many of the most able intellectual figures of the day, among them Franks, such as his biographer Einhard, grammar teachers from Italy, and Visigothic theologians from the Spanish border. His most famous recruit was the Anglo-Saxon Alcuin (735–804), the heir of the dynamic culture of Northumbria. Charlemagne wanted people to be taught the basic truths of Christianity so that he could lead them to salvation. A massive effort was undertaken to copy manuscripts of the Bible and of the writings of the Church Fathers, so they could be disseminated as widely as possible.

With this plan, personnel, and system of schools in place, Charlemagne took many concrete steps. He got from Rome a copy of the then-authoritative canon law of the church. After some years of study by his court scholars, this law was issued for his whole kingdom. Charlemagne also received from the pope a *sacramentary,* a service book for worship in cathedral churches, and, again after a period of study, this was imposed throughout the kingdom. The *Rule of St. Benedict* was imposed on all monasteries in the kingdom. Not since Rome had governments possessed either the desire or the means to promote such centralization.

Art of the Carolingian Renaissance is best represented by the manuscripts decorated under Charlemagne's patronage and then, for three generations, under the patronage of his descendants. They show respect but not awe for the past, and innovation, combining the animal and geometric decorative motifs of Irish and Anglo-Saxon art, the elegance and formality of classical art, elements of style from Byzantine painting, actual scenes from papal Rome, and the mysteries of Christian theology. Every element was borrowed, but the finished product was new.

Architecture shows the same trends. Charlemagne's palace complex at Aachen has parallels in imperial Constantinople, papal Rome, and Ostrogothic Ravenna. Workers and building materials were fetched from all over the empire. From 768 to 855, 27 cathedrals were built along with 417 monasteries and 100 royal residences. For basic buildings the Carolingians adapted the basilica. The basilica was fundamentally a horizontal building, but, by altering the western end and façade, the Carolingians added the dimension of verticality. In Romanesque and Gothic architecture this innovation would have a brilliant career.

The Fragmentation of the Carolingian Empire

The Carolingian Empire itself did not outlive the ninth century. Both internal and external factors contributed to the breakup, and by 900 a profusion of small political entities replaced the empire.

The empire included many small regions—Saxony, Bavaria, Brittany, and Lombardy, for example—that had their own resident elites, linguistic traditions, and distinctive cultures, which had existed before the Carolingians came on the scene and persist to this day. The Merovingian and Carolingian periods were basically a unifying intrusion into a history characterized by regional diversity. The Carolingians made heroic efforts to build a common culture and to forge bonds of unity, but the obstacles were insuperable.

Another key issue in the breakup of the Carolingian Empire was dynastic. The Carolingians regularly tried to create subkingdoms for all their legitimate sons while preserving the imperial title for one of them. Unfortunately, younger sons rarely yielded to their older brothers, and cousins fought for a share. In the Treaty of Verdun in 843 (see the inset of Map 6.3) the three grandsons of Charlemagne—Charles the Bald, Louis the German, and Lothair—divided the empire into three realms. The lines drawn on the map at Verdun did not last even for a generation.

Slowly, large west Frankish and east Frankish kingdoms emerged and created a framework for the future France and Germany. But they competed with many smaller entities. Some of these, in Italy, the Rhineland, and southern France, were old and distinctive regions that recaptured their former independence. Other areas were essentially new creations, born in the absence of firm Carolingian control.

Scandinavian and Slavic principalities, newcomers on the scene, also began to consolidate as unified territories. Before the ninth century, Scandinavia knew only small-scale political units under local chieftains. Economic and political pressure from the Carolingians gradually began to push both Denmark and Norway in the direction of greater political consolidation. A single Danish monarchy has a continuous history from the late ninth century, and Norway's monarchy dates from the early tenth.

To the east of the Carolingian Empire lay a vast swath of Slavic lands. The Carolingians fought, allied, and traded with these peoples for decades. Charlemagne destroyed the Avar kingdom in the Danube basin in campaigns between 788 and 804, and by about 850 a cluster of Slavic states emerged in the region. The most durable consequence of this political restructuring was religious. In 863, on an invitation from the Slavic kingdom of Moravia and in hopes of countering the Franks, the Byzantine emperor sent the missionaries Cyril (826–869) and Methodius (805–884) into eastern Europe. Unfortunately for Byzantium, Cyril and Methodius agreed with the pope to introduce Roman Catholic Christianity in return for the pope's permission to use the Slavonic language in worship. Cyril and Methodius created a religious literature in "Church Slavonic" and initiated a new cultural realm in central Europe.

The external cause of the Carolingian Empire's fragmentation was a new wave of attacks. In the middle decades of the ninth century, Arabs, Vikings, and Magyars wreaked havoc on the Franks. Based in North Africa and the islands of the western Mediterranean, Arabs attacked Italy and southern France. In the 840s, Muslims raided the city of Rome. From the north came

Vikings, mainly Danes and Norwegians, seeking loot, glory, and political opportunity. Most Viking bands were formed by leaders who had lost out in the dawning institutional consolidation of the northern world. By the mid-ninth century, Vikings settled and began their own state-building activities in Ireland, England, France, and Russia. In eastern Europe, the lightning raids of the Magyars were equally destructive. Beginning in 889, these relatives of the Huns and Avars hit Italy, Germany, and even France.

All of these attacks isolated local regions. Commerce was disrupted everywhere, and schools suffered severe decline. These were raids, not wars, but their collective effect amounted to despair and disruption on a massive scale. The Carolingian Empire thus disintegrated, but the idea of Europe as "Christendom," as a single political-cultural entity, persisted. Carolingian governing structures were inherited and adapted by all of the successor states that emerged in the ninth and tenth centuries.

EARLY MEDIEVAL ECONOMIES AND SOCIETIES

The world of the early Middle Ages remained rural, society was hierarchical, and women were excluded from public power. But there was economic and social change. In rough terms, the Islamic world changed the most, the Byzantine the least, and the West fell somewhere between.

Trade and Commerce

Trade is a mechanism of exchange between producers and consumers that depends to some extent on markets. There are other exchange mechanisms. The Roman government, for example, moved large amounts of goods from the center of the empire to the frontiers to supply its armies. Tribute and plunder were also effective exchange mechanisms—the Franks collected tributes in cows from the Saxons. There were also diplomatic gifts: A caliph sent Charlemagne an elephant.

The commonest exchanges were intensely local, but several major trading networks operated during the early Middle Ages. Mesopotamia was linked by rivers to the Persian Gulf and to both east Africa and south Asia, by land and sea to Byzantium, and by land and rivers to the Black Sea region, Slavic Europe, and the Baltic. Byzantines traded mainly by sea. The whole Mediterranean was open to them, and from the Black Sea they received the products of the Danube basin. The Muslim world was fundamentally a land empire that had relatively poor roads and primitive wheeled vehicles, so transport considerations were crucial: A caravan of some five hundred camels could move only one-fourth to one-half of the cargo of a normal Byzantine ship.

The West had many trade routes. The North and Baltic Seas were the hubs of a network that linked the British Isles, the whole of the Frankish north—by means of its rivers—the Rhineland, Slavic Europe, Byzantium, and the Muslim world. The Danube was also a major highway. The main trade networks intersected at many points. Despite religious and ideological differences, Rome's three heirs regularly traded with one another.

Food and other bulk goods never traveled very far because the cost was prohibitive. Most towns were supplied with foodstuffs by their immediate hinterlands, so the goods that moved over long distances were portable and valuable. Cotton and raw silk were moved to the Mediterranean, where they were made into cloth in, respectively, Egypt and Byzantium. Paper and pottery were moved around the caliphate. Asian spices and perfumes were avidly sought everywhere. The Byzantines traded in silk cloth, fine ivories, delicate products of the gold- and silversmiths' art, slaves, and naval stores. Trade in the West was partly in high-value luxury goods but mainly in ordinary items such as plain pottery, raw wool, wool cloth, millstones, weapons, and slaves.

Town and Countryside

To think of the ancient world is to think of cities. Thinking of the medieval world brings to mind forests and fields. Actually, from 80 to 90 percent of people in antiquity lived in rural settings, and in the early Middle Ages the percentage was not much higher. What changed was the place occupied by towns in the totality of human life. Fewer government functions were based in towns, and cultural life was less bound to the urban environment.

Towns in the West lost Roman governmental significance but often survived as focal points of royal or, more often, ecclesiastical administration. A cathedral church required a large corps of administrators. Western towns were everywhere attracting *burgs,* new settlements of merchants, just outside their centers. Because Vikings frequently raided these burgs, their existence was precarious. Few Western towns were impressive in size or population. Rome may have numbered a million people in the time of Augustus, but it had only about 25,000—one-fortieth of that amount—in 800. Paris had perhaps 20,000 inhabitants before the Vikings arrived. These were the largest cities by far in Christian Europe.

In the Byzantine East, apart from Constantinople, the empire had a more rural aspect after the Muslims took control of the heavily urbanized regions of Syria, Egypt, and parts of Anatolia in the seventh century. Cities threatened by Muslims or Bulgars declined.

The Muslims were great city-builders. Baghdad—four times larger in area than Constantinople, with a million residents to the latter's 400,000—was created from scratch. The most magnificent city in the west was Cordoba, the capital of Muslim Spain. Its population may have reached 400,000, and its great mosque, begun in 785, held 5500 worshipers, more than any Latin church except St. Peter's. The city had 900 baths, 1600 mosques (Rome had about 200 churches), 60,000 mansions, and perhaps 100,000 shops. Its libraries held thousands of books when the largest Carolingian book collections numbered a few hundred.

Agriculture nevertheless remained the most important element in the economy and in the daily lives of most people in all three realms. Farming primarily meant the production of cereal grains, which provided diet staples such as bread, porridge, and beer. Olives and grapes were common in the Mediterranean area; cereals predominated around the Black Sea and in central Gaul. Animal husbandry was always a major part of the rural regime. English sheep provided wool and meat. In Frankish and Byzantine regions pigs, which were cheap to raise, supplied meat. Islam, however, adopted the Jewish prohibition against eating pork—pork was almost absent in the Muslim East.

A key development in the Frankish West was the appearance of a bipartite estate, sometimes called a "manor." On a bipartite estate, one part of the land was set aside as a reserve (or demesne), and the rest was divided into tenancies. The reserve, consuming from a quarter to half of the total territory of the estate, was exploited directly for the benefit of the landlord. The tenancies were generally worked by the peasants for their own support. The bipartite estate provided the aristocrats with a livelihood while freeing them for military and government service.

Estates were run in different ways. A landlord might hire laborers to farm his reserve, paying them with money exacted as fees from his tenants. Or he might require the tenants to work a certain number of days per week or weeks per year in his fields. The produce of the estate might be gathered into barns and consumed locally or hauled to local markets. The reserve might be a separate part of the estate, a proportion of common fields, or a percentage of the harvest. The tenants might have individual farms or work in common fields. Although the manor is one of the most familiar aspects of European life throughout the Middle Ages, large estates with dependent tenants were also evolving in the Byzantine and Islamic worlds.

Social Patterns

The elites in all three areas tended to be large landholders, to control dependent populations, and to have access to government offices. Scholars had more social rank in Byzantium than they had anywhere else; and churchmen, especially bishops, were powerful in Christian societies but had no counterparts in Muslim ones. Literature portrays the cultivated Muslim gentleman in the Abbassid period as marked by learning, good manners, and a taste for fine things. This social type does not appear in Byzantium or in the West until the twelfth century.

The middling classes show some disparities among the regions. Merchants, for example, often rose through the social ranks to become great aristocrats in Muslim societies. In Byzantium, traditional Roman prejudices against merchants and moneymaking activities persisted. Thus, there were rich merchants whose wealth gave them private power and influence but who lacked public power and recognition. In the West, merchants were neither numerous nor powerful in the Carolingian period. In some towns, Christian injunctions against moneymaking left the development of commerce to the Jews—outsiders in a militantly Christian society. In all three societies some farmers were personally free and owed no cash or labor services to anyone but the central government. In areas such as Abbassid Iraq, ordinary free farmers led a comfortable life. In the Frankish world, most peasants existed outside the dawning manorial system. They were free, and if they lived in areas of good land and political security, such as the Paris basin, their lives most likely were congenial. Byzantine peasants, though free, often lived in areas of military danger, and in some parts of the Balkans they eked a living from poor soils. They were highly taxed, and their freedom was small compensation for their economic and personal insecurity. All peasants were alike in their subjection to political forces over which they had no control.

At the bottom of the social scale everywhere were slaves. Christianity objected only to the enslavement of Christians, and Islam forbade Muslims to enslave other Muslims. Slaves therefore tended to be commonest in still-pagan societies—Scandinavia, for example—or in frontier regions where neighboring pagans could be captured and sold. There were more slaves in the Muslim world than in Byzantium, which had, in turn, more than the West.

Women were bound to the same social hierarchies as men, but they were admitted to few formal, public positions. Their influence, however great, tended to function in the private sphere, rarely revealed to us by sources that stem from the public realm. Aristocratic women had opportunities and power that were denied ordinary women. Irene ruled at Byzantium as empress. Frankish and Anglo-Saxon queens were formidable figures in the life of their realms. Carolingian queens managed the landed patrimony of the dynasty, dozens of huge estates with tens of thousands of dependents. A lack of evidence and the rigorous exclusion of women from public life in the Islamic world means that virtually no Muslim women emerge as distinct personalities in the early Middle Ages.

The conversion of England to Christianity was fostered by women. Most convents of nuns had aristocratic abbesses who presided over complex enterprises and, often, schools. In the Frankish world aristocratic women secured some learning, and one, Dhuoda, wrote in 841 a manual of advice for her son that conveys biblical and patristic teachings as well as practical wisdom. The Frankish convent at Chelles was a renowned center for the copying of manuscripts. Some Anglo-Saxon nuns owned ships and invested in commercial activities to support their convent. Almost all aspects of the cloth industry were in women's hands.

One example of the problems in the evidence concerning women is church roles. Women could not hold priestly office; and although there were deaconesses at Hagia Sophia in the sixth century, they disappeared soon after and had long ago vanished in the West. Religious power could come from personal sanctity as well as holding office, but one study of some 2200 saints from the early Middle Ages finds only about 300 females. It was hard for women to gain recognition as saints. If a woman did become a saint, her holiness was inevitably described either as "manly"—an extreme ascetic was praised for having the strength and courage of a man—or as beautiful, virginal, and domestic, in other words, with female stereotypes.

The domestic sphere is another difficult realm to enter. The Quran permitted a man up to four wives, if he could support them financially and treat them equitably. A Muslim woman, however, was given her dowry outright, and multiple marriages may have meant that relatively more Muslim women could gain a measure of security. In Byzantium and the West, families rarely arranged marriages for more than one or two daughters. Others remained single or entered convents. In antiquity a suitor usually paid a fee, a "bride price," to his prospective wife's father and then endowed his wife with "bridewealth," money or possessions of her own. Gradually this practice changed to a system whereby a bride's father paid a dowry to her future husband. Thus, a wife who was cast aside could be left impoverished, for in most places the law did not permit her to inherit land if she had brothers. A man could divorce, even kill, his wife for adultery, witchcraft, or grave robbing, and then marry again. A woman could usually gain a divorce only for adultery, and she could not remarry. For the vast majority of women, daily life was hedged about with legal limitations and personal indignities.

SUMMARY

We have traced three parallel trajectories in the history of the early Middle Ages. The first one is chronological. In the Islamic, Byzantine, and Latin worlds, the seventh century was an age of rapid, dynamic change, the eighth century a time of consolidation and reform, and the ninth century a period of renewed challenges.

The second trajectory is political, religious, and ideological. Three large imperial states were created out of diverse peoples and territories. Each state developed a central government around a leader who was seen as a specially chosen agent of God. Each state erected a system of rule that tied a government capital to its outlying regions. In the Muslim and Byzantine worlds, that system was highly bureaucratic; in the Frankish world, the system was more amateur and personal. Religion—Islam, Orthodox Catholicism, or Roman Catholicism—provided the social glue that held each society together and defined the mission of its government. The culture of each area strove to integrate powerful religious messages with older intellectual traditions.

The third trajectory concerns results. In the Islamic and Frankish worlds, large states broke down to leave many smaller heirs. In each instance, changes in the caliber of leadership, unpredictable foreign attacks, and the sheer diversity of the polity pulled the large state apart. The Byzantine Empire, much smaller than the Roman Empire had been, managed to defend its territory. A sense of common and present danger probably helped to preserve the Byzantine state even in the face of severe foreign threats and domestic disputes. Byzantium was not much less complex than the Islamic or Frankish realms, but it was centuries older, and from tradition come strength and confidence.

SUGGESTED READING

Andrae, Tor. *Mohammed: The Man and His Faith*. 1960. First published in 1936, this brief, engaging book remains the best introduction.

Brown, Peter. *The Rise of Western Christendom*. 1996. A verbal feast, this book presents a stimulating assessment of the place of Christianity in the rise of Western culture.

Collins, Roger. *Early Medieval Spain*. 2d ed. 1994. An intelligent, comprehensive history by a leading authority.

Crone, Patricia, and Martin Hinds. *God's Caliph: Religious Authority in the First Centuries of Islam*. 1986. A sensitive discussion of the emergence of the Islamic polity and the position of the caliphs.

Fell, Christine. *Women in Anglo-Saxon England*. 1984. Interesting and readable, this book concentrates on depictions of women in literature.

Geary, Patrick J. *Before France and Germany: The Creation and Transformation of the Merovingian World*. 1988. A readable narrative, this book makes accessible the best French and German scholarship.

Hussey, J. M. *The Orthodox Church in the Byzantine Empire*. 1986. By a great authority, this text provides not so much a thorough survey as a series of reflections by the author.

Kazhdan, A. P., and Giles Constable. *People and Power in Byzantium: An Introduction to Modern Byzantine Studies.* 1982. A series of penetrating essays on politics, ideology, religion, and culture across the whole Byzantine period.

Kennedy, Hugh. *The Prophet and the Age of the Caliphates: The Islamic Near East from the Sixth to the Eleventh Century.* 1986. Detailed but readable, this is the best modern introduction to the emergence and spread of Islam.

Mango, Cyril. *Byzantium: The Empire of New Rome.* 1980. By a brilliant art historian, this book is especially strong on cultural history.

McKitterick, Rosamond. *The New Cambridge Medieval History*, vol. II. 1995. Thirty well-written, comprehensive essays by experts covering the period 700 to 900.

Mütherich, Florentine, and Joachim Gaehde. *Carolingian Painting.* 1976. A fine introduction, with beautiful plates, for the student without a substantial background in art history.

Noble, Thomas F. X. *The Republic of St. Peter: The Birth of the Papal State, 680–825.* 1984. Detailed analysis of the emergence of papal temporal rule, the Franko-papal alliance, and the papal bureaucracy.

O Cróinín, Dáibhí. *Early Medieval Ireland, 400–1200.* 1995. Detailed and comprehensive yet readable and interesting, this is the best history of early Ireland ever written.

Ostrogorsky, George. *History of the Byzantine State.* Rev. ed. Translated by Joan Hussey. 1969. Massive and detailed, this remains the preferred general history.

Roesdahl, Else. *The Vikings.* 1991. A brief yet thorough discussion of all aspects of Viking culture and society in and after the age of invasions.

Stafford, Pauline. *Queens, Concubines, and Dowagers: The King's Wife in the Early Middle Ages.* 1983. Entertaining and informative, this book reveals much about the informal channels of power and influence open to women.

Sullivan, Richard, ed. *"The Gentle Voices of Teachers": Aspects of Learning in the Carolingian Age.* 1995. Eight intriguing essays that explore Carolingian culture from many vantage points. Massive bibliography.

Waddy, Charis. *Women in Muslim History.* 1980. A thoughtful account of the changing role of women in the Islamic world, from Muhammad's time to our own.

Webster, Leslie, and Janet Backhouse, eds. *The Making of England: Anglo-Saxon Art and Culture, A.D. 600–900.* 1991. A magnificently illustrated survey published to accompany a major British Museum exhibition in 1991–1992.

Wemple, Suzanne. *Women in Frankish Society: Marriage and the Cloister, 500–900.* 1981. A pioneering study, this book is not easy to read but contains much valuable information and many interesting interpretations.

Whittow, Mark. *The Making of Orthodox Byzantium, 600–1025.* 1996. Lively, readable, controversial, engaging, this book will become the standard against which others on Byzantium are judged.

CHAPTER 7

The Expansion of Europe, ca. 900–1150

In the late ninth century, western Europe was suffering from Magyar, Muslim, and Viking attacks and from political dislocation. It is difficult to imagine that Europe was on the verge of a vibrant renewal, but it was.

Between about 900 and 1150, Europe's population began one of its longest periods of sustained growth. People brought more land under cultivation, introduced new crops, and made agriculture more efficient. Villages, towns, and cities grew in number and size. The tenth century saw the emergence of myriad stable local communities. By the twelfth century, Europe witnessed the re-emergence of centralizing monarchies in France, England, and Spain, and a veritable explosion of new states along the frontiers of Carolingian Europe. Germany, Europe's most powerful state in 950, endured a tumultuous struggle with the papacy and found itself weakened and divided by 1150.

The church experienced several waves of reform activity. Monastic reformers attempted to improve the education, morals, and spiritual life of religious communities. Other reformers engaged in sometimes bitter ideological controversies with kings and emperors over the respective powers of secular and ecclesiastical rulers. Ecclesiastical schools and Latin letters remained important, but a superb vernacular literature began to appear all over Europe, complementing the Latin letters of the schools. "Romanesque" painting, sculpture, and architecture grew from Carolingian inspiration to triumphal realization.

Europeans spread aggressively in every direction. Normans conquered both England and southern Italy. Germans marched east into Slavic Europe. Spanish Christians pushed back the Muslims in the Iberian Peninsula. Armies of adventurers headed east in those remarkable expeditions, the Crusades. Expansion, in both the literal and the figurative sense, captures the spirit of the West in the tenth, eleventh, and early twelfth centuries.

∾ *Questions and Ideas to Consider*

- Consider the relationship between the surplus of food, due to agricultural advancements, and the rise of cities, specialized skills, and trade. How did advancements in transportation facilitate this process?

- The traditional medieval order of clergy, nobility, and peasantry may seem comprehensive and stable, but was medieval society so neatly divided? How were these three orders experienced differently by men and women? And where did townspeople and Jews fit into this tripartite scheme?

- What was the investiture controversy? Explain the specific factors that led to it as well as the underlying struggle between secular and religious power.

- How did monarchs create and strengthen unity in their kingdoms? Consider the establishment of patron saints and the elaborate itinerant courts, as well as the more administrative aspects of state-making. Why would a monarch desire this unity?

- How did the new Celtic, Scandinavian, and Slavic states contribute to the political expansion of this period?

- How is it that a religious controversy gave rise to the widespread study of logic? What did theologians believe about the relationship between faith and logic? Discuss the opinions of Anselm, Abelard, and Hildegard of Bingen.

- What factors led to the First Crusade?

SIGNS OF EXPANSION

Medieval people did not keep the kinds of records of births, deaths, population, or business activity that modern states routinely accumulate. Evidence for the economic expansion of Europe abounds but is more often qualitative than quantitative. We lack hard data, but much can be deduced from literary works and other contemporary descriptions.

The Growing Population

The population of Europe began rising slowly in the Carolingian period and may have doubled between 1000 and 1200. Scattered bits of evidence suggest that the total population of western Europe grew from around 30 million in 1000 to 55 or 60 million in 1200.

In a few regions where family size can be estimated, fertile marriages were producing on average 3.5 children in the tenth century and from 6 to 7 in the twelfth. Families of all social stations continued to experience the loss of children. The key change is that more babies were being born and people were living longer.

Everywhere in Europe, new land was brought into cultivation. Thousands of acres of forest were felled. Some 380,000 acres were drained along the western coast of France and probably twice that amount in both Flanders and England. This activity suggests a growing number of mouths to feed. Agriculture benefited from a warmer and drier climate through the whole of this period. Not a single vegetable blight was recorded. Animals were increasingly raised for their meat, and higher meat consumption meant more protein in the diet. Fine grains such as wheat replaced poorer cereals in many areas. People of every class and region were almost certainly eating better and living longer, healthier lives.

Technological Gains

The eleventh century was a decisive period in the spread of new technologies in Europe. Agricultural changes came first as a rising population created an increased demand for food that could be met only by new practices. Improvements in agriculture, coupled with others in transport, mining, and manufacturing, freed large numbers of persons not engaged in agriculture—urban dwellers, mainly—for other pursuits.

CHAPTER CHRONOLOGY

862	Foundation of Kiev	1066	Conquest of England by William of Normandy
ca. 900	*Beowulf*	1072–1085	Pontificate of Gregory VII
910	Foundation of Cluny	1077	Emperor Henry IV at Canossa
940–1003	Gerbert of Aurillac	1078	Papal decree against lay investiture
960–1028	Fulbert of Chartres		
962	Imperial coronation of Otto I	1079–1142	Peter Abelard
d. 970	Roswitha of Gandersheim	1085	Spanish reconquest of Toledo
972–1015	Reign of Vladimir in Russia	1086	Domesday Book
987	Accession of Hugh Capet in France	1090–1153	Bernard of Clairvaux
1000–1088	Berengar of Tours	1095	First Crusade proclaimed
1016	Conquest of England by Cnut	1098	Foundation of Cîteaux
ca. 1033–1109	Anselm of Canterbury	1098–1179	Hildegard of Bingen
ca. 1050–1150	Emergence of the Romanesque	ca. 1100	*The Song of Roland*
1059	Papal-Norman alliance in Italy	1122	Concordat of Worms

In the Carolingian period, the return on seed—the amount of seed realized for each seed sewn—is estimated at about 3 or 4 to 1. By the late twelfth century this ratio had risen in many areas to 8 or 10 to 1. Given that more land came under cultivation, the overall gains in the food supply were enormous. The increases can be accounted for in several ways. Horses were more frequently used as draft animals. They were more expensive to acquire than oxen but no more costly to feed, and they did, in a day, a third or half again as much work. Plows also improved. The light wooden scratch plow used by the Romans was satisfactory for the thin soils of the Mediterranean region but barely disturbed the heavy soils of northern Europe. The invention of a heavy wheeled plow with an iron coulter (or plowshare) was a real breakthrough. Wider adoption of nitrogen-fixing crops, such as peas and some kinds of beans, retarded soil exhaustion—and also put more protein in the diet. Leaving land fallow was another means of avoiding soil ex-

haustion. In the early Middle Ages this meant setting aside about half of the arable land every year (the two-field system) or working the land intensively for a few years and then moving on. By the twelfth century, three-field schemes of crop rotation were common. Under the three-field system, two-thirds of the arable land saw nearly constant use. The amount of an estate under cultivation rose from about 50 to 67 percent.

Surplus produce was intended mainly for the growing towns. To supply that market, improvements in transportation were necessary. Kings often passed laws to secure the safety of highways, and popes three times (in 1097, 1132, and 1179) threatened highwaymen with excommunication. Landlords required their dependents to maintain roads and bridges. Many stone bridges were constructed in France between 1130 and 1170 because wooden bridges were so vulnerable to fire.

Transport improved because of safer roads and better vehicles. Documents and works of art agree that the old two-wheeled cart, drawn

Twelfth-Century Timbered House, Rouen, France The house at the center of this picture was destroyed in World War II after holding its place for nearly eight hundred years. It shows one of the many uses of timber, and its narrow street gives an authentic feel of a medieval town. *(Roger-Viollet)*

keep the shafts and galleries free of water. Still, the exploitation of surface and near-surface veins of ore intensified, to supply the increased demand for plowshares, tools, weapons, construction fittings, and coins. Stone quarrying, the commonest form of mining in the Middle Ages, benefited directly from more efficient stone saws and indirectly from improvements in transport. This helps to explain the increase in the number of England's stone religious buildings from sixty to nearly five hundred in the century after 1050.

Forms of Enterprise

Agricultural specialization led to widespread growth in trade. Local trade continued to flourish. Italian wines and olive oil, for example, were not produced for far-off markets; they tended to move from countryside to town within a region. The same was true of French or English grains. French wines were much prized, however, especially in England; and certain products, such as English wool and Flemish cloth, were carried far and wide. Salt fish from the Baltic found its way all over Europe. Lumber was routinely traded across the Mediterranean to the wood-poor Muslim world.

The lumber industry reveals many facets of medieval economic activity. Before the twelfth century, wood was the main building material, and even after that time it yielded to stone mainly for the church and aristocracy. Also, the Venetian shipyards needed about twenty oaks, twenty good-size pines, and fifty or so beeches to make a ship. In the early twelfth century the Venetians were making about ten vessels a year, twice the number they had been building two centuries earlier. In England, to take another example, about 500 cords (a cord is a stack measuring 128 cubic feet) of wood, nearly 10 acres' worth, were needed to prepare 1 ton of silver. Under King Ethelred II (r. 978–1016) alone, moneyers coined 30 tons of silver, consuming in the process some 15,000 cords of wood. Better mining and increased trade both increased the demand for lumber.

by oxen or mules, began giving way to the sturdy four-wheeled, horse-drawn wagon. The fact that greater quantities of foodstuffs could be moved farther and faster meant that urban communities could be supplied from larger areas. This was a crucial factor in enabling cities to grow.

Evidence from various parts of Europe points to the years after 925 as the beginning of real growth in the mining industry. Mines were not deep because people lacked the means to

THE TRADITIONAL ORDER OF SOCIETY

Alfred the Great (r. 871–899) of England once said that a kingdom needed "men of prayer, men of war, and men of work." This imagined division provided neat places for the clergy, warrior-aristocrats, and the peasantry on whose labors the other two groups depended. The clergy and the nobility agreed that they were superior to the "workers," but fierce controversies raged over whether leadership in society belonged to the "fighters" or to the "prayers." This vision of society as nobles, clergy, and peasants excluded townspeople, who were becoming ever more important. It also excluded Europe's largest minority: the Jews. And where, we may ask, did women fit in Alfred's tripartite scheme?

Those Who Fight: The Nobility

Carolingian families had been large, amorphous groupings of people who traced their descent on both the male and the female sides. Such families tended to be fairly open to newcomers. From about the middle of the eleventh century, however, important changes appeared. Loose groupings of relatives began to think of themselves as lineages, the descendants of one male ancestor. They began to practice *primogeniture*—the transmittal of all family lands, offices, and titles to the eldest male heir. Lineages consolidated their landholdings into compact lordships, at the center of which was a castle.

The nobility was not yet closed or homogeneous. Fortunes and titles could be acquired quickly in turbulent frontier areas. In central France and Germany, conditions were more stable but movement was still possible. Mid-level nobles —usually vassals of the truly great—tried to improve their status and sometimes succeeded. There was a vast and growing class of ordinary knights and their families. Also, the consolidation of territorial lordships produced large numbers of men who had noble blood and upbringings but limited prospects. These men, called in contemporary sources "the young," wandered all over the medieval world in search of glory and a livelihood. These "young" men were often over 40.

Charlemagne had connected personal loyalty (vassalage) with public office and material reward (the benefice or fief). In the tenth and eleventh centuries, versions of this arrangement spread all over Europe. The result is sometimes, but misleadingly, called the "feudal system." *Feudalism* may be defined as a social and political system wherein public responsibilities and powers that had fallen into the hands of private individuals were fulfilled by men who had sworn personal fidelity to one another. By solemn acts of fealty, a vassal pledged never to do anything that would damage his lord's interests and also undertook to perform military service and appear at the lord's court. In return, the lord provided protection—physical, legal, or political— and gave the vassal a landed estate, called by modern scholars a *fief* and by medieval texts a *feudum* (whence *feudalism*). Today many historians prefer to speak of "lordship." The term *feudalism* masks an amazing array of local variations in a "system" that was never systematic, not even in northern France and southern England, feudalism's classical regions.

A specific ethos, chivalry, belonged to the warrior-aristocracy. Its name derives from *cheval*, French for horse, the conveyance of a knight. Military prowess was the most highly esteemed of early chivalric virtues, and literature of the time is full of accounts of combat between a single hero and impossible numbers of the enemy. Generosity was another key virtue. The truly noble person engaged in sumptuous display to manifest his power, to show concern for his dependents, and to attract more followers. Knights sought glory, the better to win a lord or a bride, but in a world based on promises of service and protection, honor and loyalty were the virtues that held society together.

In the early medieval period, women could be found in several public and semipublic roles. Convents of aristocratic nuns remained places where women could be highly educated and almost entirely in control of their own affairs. Matilda, daughter of the German empress

Château d'Angers, France Castles were private, residential, and military, and they dotted the landscape in the Middle Ages, bearing witness to the extremely decentralized power of the period. Remains of several hundred castles have been found in France alone. Their embankments, high walls, and other fortifications met the needs of a politically dominant warrior-aristocracy. *(Michael Holford)*

Adelaide, was abbess of Quedlinburg, mistress of vast estates in northern Germany, and a dominant figure in German politics. Gaita, wife of a Norman prince in Italy, fought in helmet and armor alongside her husband, as did Duchess Agnes of Burgundy. All over France, in the fluid political climate of the tenth and eleventh centuries, women were mistresses of castles and real powers in local politics.

By the late eleventh century, however, the elaboration of the chivalric ethos defined most key social and political roles as "manly" and thereby excluded women from them. Also, the consolidation of lineages by aristocratic families accompanied a moral campaign by the church to promote monogamous, unbreakable marriages. This situation subordinated women's freedom in the marriage market to the dynastic and patrimonial demands of great families.

Those Who Pray: The Clergy

Members of the clergy were overwhelmingly noble in origin. Whereas in the Carolingian world, the clergy served occasionally as an avenue of upward social mobility for talented outsiders, the later consolidation of families began to confine church offices to the younger sons of the nobility.

In the aftermath of the Carolingian collapse, a great spiritual reform swept Europe. It began in 910 when Duke William of Aquitaine founded the monastery of Cluny in Burgundy on lands that he freely donated. At a time when powerful families dominated almost all monasteries, Cluny was a rarity because it was placed under the direct authority of the pope. Cluny's abbots were European statesmen and became advisers to popes, French kings, German emperors, and aristocratic families.

In the tradition of the Carolingian monastic reforms, Cluny placed great emphasis on prayer. The monks spent hours in devotions and did little manual work. Because Cluniac prayer was thought to be especially efficacious, noblemen all over Europe donated land to Cluny and placed local monasteries under Cluniac control. By the twelfth century, hundreds of monasteries had joined in a Cluniac order. Individual houses were under the authority of the abbot of Cluny, and their priors had to attend an annual assembly. Although the majority of houses reformed by Cluny were male, beginning in the twelfth century, many convents of nuns also adopted Cluniac practices. Cluny promoted the idea that the role of the church was to pray for the world, not to be implicated deeply in it. Churches had to be free from lay control.

There were several other reforms, some of which built on Cluny, some of which criticized it. For example, customs of the monastery of Gorze resembled those at Cluny, but the Gorze reform was not so much to withdraw from the world as to improve it. Monks from both the Gorze and the Cluniac traditions preached against clerical marriage and *simony*, the buying and selling of church offices. The eleventh and early twelfth centuries also saw a proliferation of both male and female experiments in eremitic monasticism. These reformers, disenchanted with the opulence of Cluny and the worldliness of Gorze desired to recapture what they believed to be the way of life of the original apostolic community—a life of poverty, self-denial, and seclusion. Other Europeans believed that the apostolic life demanded active Christian ministry as well as personal renunciation. Cathedral clergy, called *canons*, adapted the Rule of Saint Augustine so that they could live a communal life and carry out priestly duties.

The greatest critics of the Cluniac tradition, and the real monastic elite of the early twelfth century, were the Cistercians. In 1098, Abbot Robert left his Burgundian monastery of Molesme because he believed it had abandoned the strict teachings of Saint Benedict. He founded a new monastery at Cîteaux in Burgundy. This house was to follow the Benedictine Rule literally and to refuse all secular entanglements: lands, rents, and servile dependents. A charismatic young Burgundian nobleman named Bernard (1090–1153) joined in 1112, and three years later he left to found a daughter house at Clairvaux. Bernard remained abbot there for the rest of his life. Through his writing, preaching, and personal example Bernard dominated the religious life of Europe in his lifetime. By the end of the twelfth century there were about 500 Cistercian (from the Latin for *Cîteaux*) monasteries in Europe.

With the monastic clergy gaining so much in prestige and visibility, the episcopal clergy countered with its own view of society. The bishops wanted to end the grossest examples of lay interference in the church. But because so many bishops came from great families and were so well connected, they were less inclined to be rigid about the line of demarcation between lay and clerical responsibilities. They advanced the king's interests in their areas of authority, but they were often men of spiritual depth, and they resented what they regarded as monastic carping about their worldliness. By the middle of the twelfth century, bishops had imposed on the church a view that monks belonged in their monasteries and that bishops should lead society.

In the turbulent world of gentlemen warriors, the church had its own ideas about what a perfect knight should do. Through the creation of military orders, the church attempted to make knights serve God and society. The Knights of St. John, or Hospitallers, and the Knights of the Temple, or Templars, are the major examples. Such orders generally pledged to follow monastic rule and either to defend pilgrims to the Holy Land or to protect the small states created by the Crusaders (see page 195).

Those Who Work: The Peasants

An extremely diverse segment of society, "peasants" ranged from slaves to free men and women of some means. Except in frontier zones, where victims were available and religious scruples diminished, slaves declined dramatically in numbers during the tenth and eleventh centuries. *Serfs*, persons bound to the soil, everywhere constituted the majority of the peasants, although their legal and social status differed considerably from place to place. Serfdom was a mixture of economic, legal, and personal statuses. The serf could be flogged in public, could be set upon by dogs, was excluded from many judicial proceedings, required approval to contract a marriage, and was denied the right to bear arms.

The tenth and eleventh centuries were a decisive period in the reshaping of rural society. As lordships of all kinds and sizes formed in the countryside, they drew communities of people. Castles were critical. Powerful men generally sited their castles in close proximity to wood, water, and iron. Sometimes a monastery, rural church, or graveyard also attracted a castle or else grew up near one. People from a fairly wide area settled in the vicinity of the castle. Many, originally free, commended themselves to the local lord by handing over their properties and receiving them back in return for rents or personal services. Other people fell into dependent status through military or economic misfortune. What eventually emerged was the *manor*, an institution wherein a powerful lord controlled the lives of an often large number of dependents. He required payments and services from them and regulated their ordinary disputes. His control was simultaneously public and private.

Certain trends were fairly consistent, however. As trade brought more and different products into Europe, and as a more consciously aristocratic lifestyle spread, the nobility began to want disposable cash. Thus, in many places *corvées* (labor services) were commuted into cash payments. But lords still needed provisions, so they sometimes split peasant payments into cash and kind. On many estates where the men had been largely freed from corvées, the women might continue to work in the lord's house cooking, sewing, slaughtering and skinning or plucking game, minding dogs, and tending to other household chores. The trend everywhere, however, was for labor services to diminish.

In the expanding economy of the eleventh and twelfth centuries, the peasants grew more prosperous, and their lords constantly sought new ways to extract the fruits of that prosperity. Peasants thus began to band together to demand that "customs" be observed. These customs were more-or-less formal agreements spelling out the terms under which work and fees would be arranged.

The European village was a key product of the tenth and eleventh centuries. People who originally gathered together around a castle began to form a durable human group. Their church and graveyard helped to form a community by tying together the living and the dead and by giving the village a sense of memory and continuity. Peasants generally worked only 250 to 270 days per year, so they had a good deal of time for festivals and celebrations. Births, baptisms, betrothals, and deaths provided opportunities for the community to come together and affirm its mutual ties. Market days and sessions of the lord's court also assembled the village. Villagers shared tools, plow teams, and wagons.

The status of women in peasant society tended to be, in legal theory and in daily reality, the same as that of men—at a time when the status of aristocratic women was declining. Marriage contracts from northern Italy show that brides often entered marriages with a comple-

ment of valuable tools. This suggests that peasant women retained some control over their own personal property and also reminds us that the huge gains in rural productivity are attributable in part to the work and ingenuity of women. (See the box "Furnishings of a Welsh Household.") Peasant women and men shared all but the heaviest jobs in the fields. When it was possible and useful for the family's well-being, women hired themselves out to perform an array of tasks for wages and trade.

Those Left Out: Townspeople and Jews

The tripartite model excluded two important groups of people. In the first group were the increasingly numerous citizens of Europe's growing towns. In the second group were Europe's principal religious minority, the Jews. Jews could be found almost everywhere, although they constituted only about 1 percent of the population as a whole and had, outside Rome and parts of Spain, no single community numbering more than 1500.

The central factor in the growth of towns was the rise in the productivity and profitability of medieval agriculture. For the first time there was a regular and substantial surplus to support an urban population that did not produce its own food. Increased local exchange, coupled with the relentless growth of a money economy, meant there were fortunes to be made and cash to be spent. A good part of the cash was spent by rural nobles, who earned it from rents, booty, and the profits of the private exercise of public power. When those nobles moved into towns, they created opportunities for merchants, craftsmen, day laborers, domestic servants, and professional people such as notaries and lawyers. This was particularly true in Europe's most heavily urbanized regions: Flanders, southern France, and northern Italy.

Town society was hierarchical, but its structures were new, ill defined, and flexible. Rich men built up bands of followers who supported them in urban politics, protected their neighborhoods, and occasionally raided the houses of their ene-

Furnishings of a Welsh Household

This passage from the laws of Howell the Good concerns the distribution of household property in case of divorce. The aim was to achieve a nearly even split. Notice the kinds of things a house might hold and who got what.

The husband shall have all the pigs, the wife the sheep. The husband shall have all the horses and mares, the oxen and cows, bullocks and heifers; the wife shall have the goats. . . . All the vessels for milk, except one pail, are the wife's; all the dishes, except one meat dish, are the husband's. One cart and yoke are the wife's. All the jars and drinking vessels are the husband's. Of the bedding, the husband shall have all the bedclothes which are beneath, the wife those which are above. The husband shall have the cauldron, the pillow, the winnowing sheet, the coulter, the wood axe, the gimlet [hole-borer], the fire dog, all the sickles except one, and the gridiron. The wife shall have the pan and the tripod, the broadaxe and the sieve, the ploughshare, the flax and the seed of the flax, and the precious things except gold and silver. If there are any of these (gold or silver) they are to be divided in two equal parts. The products of the loom shall be divided in two equal parts, both linens and woolens. The husband shall have the barn and the grain and whatever is above or in the ground, and the hens and the geese and one cat. The wife shall have the meat that is salted and the cheese that is fresh . . . and the vessel of butter . . . and the ham . . . and as much of the flour as she can carry. Each of them shall have his or her personal clothing, except the cloaks which shall be divided.

Source: Ian F. Fletcher, ed. and trans., *Latin Redaction A of the Law of Hywel* (Aberystwyth, Wales: Center for Advanced Welsh and Celtic Studies, 1986), pp. 58–59. Reprinted by permission.

mies in the next neighborhood. Relatives, friends, neighbors, people from a common rural district, or those engaged in similar trades tended to worship together in particular churches, observe certain festivals, and look after one another's families.

In the rapidly changing world of the tenth and eleventh centuries, towns provided numerous opportunities for women. In urban industries such as cloth making, tanning, laundering, and brewing there is evidence of women managing and owning enterprises. Apart, perhaps, from finance and the law, distinctions between male and female roles were not as sharp in towns as in rural areas.

If urban men and all women stood in an ambiguous relationship to the ideals of the male, rural, aristocratic elite, we can hardly imagine what it must have been like for Jews. Because the Byzantine and Islamic worlds vacillated between persecution and toleration, many Jews migrated to western Europe. Some laymen and many members of the clergy were bitterly hostile to the Jews, but from the time of Gregory I (r. 590–606) the papacy urged peaceful coexistence and prayers for Jewish conversion. The Carolingians protected the Jews, as did some kings in succeeding centuries. Although some Jews in Italy, Spain, and Germany owned farms and vineyards, most Jews settled in cities, where they could live and worship in community with other Jews. There was also strength in numbers for people who could at any moment fall victim to persecution and whose power was not based on landholding.

GERMANY AND THE EMPIRE

In 950 Germany was the most powerful state in western Europe (Map 7.1), but by 1150 it lay on the brink of collapse. That radical transformation is the most significant political fact in European history in the period from 900 to 1150. In the face of Viking and Magyar attacks, a series of resolute Saxon dukes built a kingdom, allied with the church, and revived the imperial title. German dynasties proved disastrously short-lived, however, and the monarchy's alliance with the church helped to precipitate the investiture controversy, a crisis in church-state relations. Promising beginnings for the German kingdom yielded meager results.

Unifying the Realm: The Saxon and Salian Rulers

After the Treaty of Verdun in 843 (see page 163), Louis the German and his successors managed to preserve the East Frankish Kingdom and created the possibility of an independent German kingdom. What lands that kingdom would possess was not yet clear. The Rhine has sometimes been Germany's river, sometimes its western boundary. Germany has no natural frontiers to the east, and incipient Slavic states resented German advances into their territories.

Germany consisted of several large duchies. Saxony, Franconia, Lorraine, Swabia, and Bavaria—the biggest—had a dual historical origin. They were formed of people with distinctive historical traditions, although their leaders, or dukes, were usually Frankish aristocrats appointed by the Carolingians. As the monarchy weakened, the dukes became the bearers of the German political destiny. In 911 the last legitimate Carolingian of the East Frankish line died, and in 919 the dukes elected Duke Henry of Saxony as his successor.

Henry I (r. 919–936) was chosen precisely because he offered the greatest hope of dealing decisively with the Viking threats in the north and the Magyar attacks in the east and south. Henry

was succeeded by his son, grandson, and great-grandson, all named Otto. These Saxon rulers created a solid German kingdom by consistently pursuing a few basic policies: warfare, control of Saxony and of the other duchies, domination of the church, and the acquisition of prestige.

Otto I (r. 936–973) continued Henry's policies but also raised a pan-German army. When Otto won a decisive victory over the Magyars in 955, he removed a serious threat to Germany and vastly enhanced his prestige. Otto II (r. 973–983) and Otto III (r. 983–1002) continued the German drive to the east into Slavic lands. The Ottonians' successful campaigns attracted more and more followers, who shared in the booty and received land.

In addition to building up a secure power base in Saxony, the Saxon dukes always tried to control one or more of the other German duchies. The German duchies had emerged together out of the late Carolingian world, and the Saxon dukes had not appointed and thus could not legally remove any of the other dukes. There was feudalism in Germany in the sense that all the dukes had vassals, but Germany was not a feudal monarchy because the dukes did not hold their duchies as fiefs granted by the king. The king's inability to control on a permanent basis any region but his own was a continuing weakness for the German state.

Control of the church partly compensated for the absence of central institutions or a hierarchy of vassalic bonds. Bishops and abbots remembered the Carolingian past when crown and church had worked harmoniously for the reform of the kingdom. They willingly supported the king and provided him with able, educated advisers. The royal chapel recruited capable, ambitious men from all over Germany, trained them, and then sent them back out as bishops or abbots. If the king could not appoint officials in Bavaria, for example, he could nevertheless name Bavaria's four bishops.

Finally, the Saxon rulers had a keen awareness of the value of prestige. Symbolic power substituted only partially for the lack of central institutions, taxes, and other aspects of Carolingian rule, but the Saxons used it for all it was

Map 7.1 Germany and Its Duchies Throughout the Middle Ages, the chief dynamic in German history was a contest for power between the kings and the dukes.

worth. The monarchy was itinerant; it moved about the country. One reason for this mobility was to consume on the spot the resources of various royal estates; another was to make a grand display of the king and his entourage, which numbered up to four hundred people.

The greatest enhancement of the prestige of the Saxon monarchy came with the restoration of the imperial title by Otto I in 962. From the middle of the ninth century, Carolingian aristocrats occasionally made themselves kings of Italy, but no one was able to protect or to rule Rome. When Muslims began attacking the city in 844, the popes themselves had to defend Rome. In the tenth century the papacy fell into its darkest period. It became the prize in the game of local Roman politics. One remarkable woman, Marozia (d. ca. 945), was at different times mother, wife, and mistress of various popes. During these difficult circumstances, Otto I went to Italy in 952. He made himself king of Italy and protector of the papacy. Ten years later he returned and prevailed on the pope to crown him emperor. Few concrete rights came to Otto as a result of his coronation, but he gained immensely in prestige, throughout Germany and the rest of Europe.

Otto III died without an heir. In 1002 and 1024 distant relatives of the Saxons were elected kings, and the Salian dynasty came to the throne. Based in Bavaria, the Salians rarely had any real power in the north, just as the Saxons had usually lacked power in the south (see Map 7.1). One of their first important rulers was Henry III (r. 1039–1056), a man of real ability and religious piety. He saw himself as the church's protector. Henry also felt that, as God's anointed ruler, he had a duty to control, even to purify, the church. In 1046 Henry was confronted with the scandal of three men claiming to be the legitimate pope. Deeply offended, he removed them all and replaced them with the first of several ardent German reformers. Henry's reign marked the high point of the so-called German imperial church.

The Investiture Controversy

When Henry died in 1056, his son, Henry IV, was a child; and until he came of age in 1066, anarchy reigned in Germany. Moreover, at Rome the reformers introduced by Henry III objected to *lay investiture* (the appointment of church officers by laymen) and to outside interference in the election of popes. Their concerns challenged the basis of the German imperial church and attacked a major source of Saxon-Salian prestige. They also signaled

that Rome was now taking the lead in church reform. Ironically, the reformers promoted by the Salians threatened to wreck the Salian system.

When Henry IV came of age, he controlled no duchies, faced a Saxony in open revolt, confronted bishops who had freed themselves of royal power, and had little idea of how the papacy would react to him. Henry had a high sense of his royal dignity and a burning desire to restore royal authority. He put down the revolt in Saxony, outmaneuvered most of the aristocrats who opposed him, and restored some control over the German church.

In 1072 the reformers in Rome elected as pope Cardinal Hildebrand, one of the reformers prominent since the 1050s. He took the name Gregory VII to cover himself with the mantle of spiritual authority possessed by Gregory the Great (see page 156). Gregory (r. 1072–1085) was a proud, brilliant, inflexible, self-righteous man who believed that laymen were in control of too many church offices, and rulers ought to defer to the pope. Gregory and Henry IV fell into the life-and-death struggle that is usually called the "investiture controversy."

By 1075, Henry decided to make a show of his restored power by intervening in the selection of a bishop at Milan. His decision came even though the papal court for some two decades had openly opposed such lay interference, and Gregory VII had made a series of strong claims about papal powers. Gregory's view was that God had assigned leadership of the whole Christian world to the pope and that kings existed only to do the pope's bidding.

The popes in the eleventh and twelfth centuries, unlike their eighth-century predecessors, did not concentrate on territorial rule. Instead, they turned to tightening the control exercised by the pope within the church. They used the weapon of *excommunication*—excluding a person from the sacraments and thus denying forever the hope of salvation—to coerce persons whom they believed to have violated canon law. They used papal legates, official envoys, to tie the pope to the Western church. The college of cardinals was slowly evolving into a kind of senate

Henry IV, Duchess Matilda of Tuscany, and Abbot Hugh of Cluny The embattled Henry IV here implores Matilda, a tremendously wealthy landowner and ally of Pope Gregory VII, to intercede with the pope. The powerful abbot of Cluny looks over the scene protectively. Written documents do not portray women's power as vividly as this image does. *(Vatican Library, Rome)*

for the church. The power of the papacy was expanding as never before.

Henry's view was that he was king by descent from his ancestors and by the election of God and thus had a perfect right—indeed, a profound duty—to supervise the church. But more than principle was at stake for Henry. The German kings had always ruled with the support and cooperation of the church. To ensure that support and cooperation, they had always played a key role in selecting bishops, and they had usually required those bishops to be their vassals. Given Henry's perilous position, he simply could not allow the church to slip from his control.

Gregory's response to Henry's action in Milan was to excommunicate him in 1076 and to release his subjects from their oaths of allegiance. Many churchmen and aristocrats abandoned Henry, not so much because they agreed with Pope Gregory but because they relished the opportunity to weaken the king. A meeting of German nobles and papal representatives was arranged to investigate Henry's fitness for the royal office. To forestall the meeting, Henry departed from Germany and met Gregory at Canossa in Tuscany in January 1077. The king stood in the snow before the castle where the pope was staying and begged his forgiveness. Gregory forgave Henry, which restored the king to the church's good graces and restored his subjects' duty of allegiance.

In Germany, the nobles felt betrayed by Gregory and proceeded to elect a new king. This action enraged Henry, whose ire increased when Gregory said that he would in due course decide between the claims of Henry and his rival. In addition, in 1078 Gregory issued a definitive decree against lay investiture. In response, Henry's propagandists unleashed a torrent of bitterly antipapal writing, the first such campaign in European history, to discredit Gregory. In 1080 the pope excommunicated the king once again, and Henry responded by marching to Rome, chasing Gregory out of the city, and installing a pope of his own, who promptly crowned him emperor (which Gregory had refused to do). Gregory died in exile five years later.

Henry never recovered his position in Germany. Both the material and the moral bases of the German crown were destroyed. The reign of Henry IV exposed the flaws in the German system. If the king tightly controlled one or more duchies and the church, and if there was a credible foreign threat, the king could be very powerful indeed. But if one or more of these props were kicked out from under the king, the monarchy threatened to fall. In 1106, Henry V actually deposed his pitiable father, who died within a few months.

Henry V (r. 1106–1125) struggled on for a generation trying to bring the investiture controversy to an end. In 1122 the Concordat of Worms between Henry V and Pope Calixtus II (r. 1119–1124) settled the matter. Henry agreed that episcopal elections would be free and canonical (carried out according to canon law), and he surrendered investiture with ring and staff, the symbols of the bishop's religious office. Elections were to take place in the royal presence, however, and after the election the king could invest the new bishop with purely secular offices. The concordat was a compromise; but, insofar as it spelled the end of the German imperial church system, it was a victory for the papacy.

Henry V died without heirs in 1125 and was followed by the dukes of Saxony and of Swabia in succession. The nobles elected these men precisely because they were not powerful. In the early tenth century, the nobles had affirmed the royal principle by electing the most powerful of

the dukes as kings. For nearly two centuries, when there were legitimate heirs of suitable age, the nobles had assented to their succession. Now, after three-quarters of a century of turmoil, the nobles elected weak men as kings. By 1150, Germany was weak and disunited.

SHAPING THE KINGDOM

Whereas the German Empire's trajectory in the period 900 to 1150 took it from strength to weakness, the course almost everywhere else was just the opposite. Both the variety of Europe's government patterns and the size of the individual governments expanded. Before about 1050, the majority of Europe's population was ruled, or misruled, by dukes and counts, by bishops and abbots, or by various petty magnates. After 1050 kingdoms began to have a measurable effect on the lives of most people.

The Rise of Capetian France

During the late ninth century and much of the tenth, France suffered from constant waves of Viking attacks and from repeated failures of the Carolingian family to produce adult heirs to the throne. Royal authority declined sharply because of the weakness of the later Carolingians, but what really damaged the royal office was the emergence of territorial principalities.

Whereas Germany produced five major duchies, France saw the appearance of more than a dozen principalities. Some were products of the years from 850 to 950, and some had existed before the Carolingians came on the scene. They re-emerged as districts with some sense of ethnic cohesion and of historical tradition. Confined largely to the Paris region, the king himself was a territorial prince.

Territorial princes built up their power by taking *bannal* (from the *ban*, the king's right to command) rights of the king into their own hands: the rights to raise armies, hold courts, collect taxes, and mint coins. The most successful of these territorial princes then reduced their less powerful neighbors to dependent status. Many formerly free men sought security in the entourage of powerful neighbors by handing over their possessions and then receiving them back in return for homage and service. France was becoming feudal.

Territorial princes ruled with little reference to the king, and the king had little power over them. But the Merovingian and Carolingian tradition was so strong that it never occurred to the French nobles to dispense with the monarchy. In 987 the nobles ignored the only legitimate Carolingian and turned to a family from Paris that had three times provided kings since 888. The man chosen was Hugh Capet (r. 987–996). The Capetian family would rule France in direct line until the fourteenth century.

The kings had a few real advantages. They possessed a landed patrimony—a *demesne*—that was situated strategically in the centrally located Paris basin. All the territorial princes were the king's vassals, and the king received oaths of fidelity from most important noblemen. The early Capetians usually could not force their nominal vassals to perform specific services for them, but no other nobleman could take up the oaths of his peers.

Powerful nobles, both secular and clerical, often had recourse to the royal court for arbitration of their disputes. Although the king could not demand that cases be brought to his court, he gained in prestige and political leverage whenever a case was heard there. In this way, kings created legal precedents for the later extension of their authority. The kings also controlled about two dozen bishoprics and around fifty monasteries in northern France. The kings got great material support from the church and, through their right to appoint bishops and abbots, inserted their influence into many of the territorial principalities. As in Carolingian times, churchmen were enthusiastic supporters of the monarchy.

The first four Capetian kings (987–1108) maintained the throne and enhanced royal power, even if only in small ways. Hugh Capet's son, Robert, called "the Pious" (r. 996–1030), ac-

quired a reputation for sanctity and got along especially well with the clergy. He also was the first French king to display the "royal touch," a ceremony in which the king was believed to cure people of scrofula (a common respiratory ailment) by touching them. This particular type of royal charisma sharply separated the king from any ordinary nobleman.

The early Capetians also began the practice of having their sons crowned and anointed during their own lifetime. The role of the nobility in electing kings, very great in the ninth and tenth centuries, had almost disappeared by the twelfth century. In this regard, France and Germany were quite different. In Germany, dynastic failure and papal excommunications afforded the nobility repeated opportunities to engage in kingmaking. Finally, the turmoil of the German investiture controversy was not visited on France. The king of France depended much less on his control of the church than the German ruler did, and the French king had less to lose by compromising with Rome.

In the twelfth century, France had two gifted kings in succession: Louis VI (r. 1108–1137) and Louis VII (r. 1137–1180). Louis VI suppressed the minor nobility in the royal demesne and turned his own principality into one of the best governed and most efficient in France. He made extensive use of the royal touch as a means of focusing loyalty on the king. He promoted Saint Denis (the legendary first bishop of Paris) as a patron saint for France, as a way of creating unity throughout the kingdom.

Louis VII began making ceremonial visitations around the kingdom, drawing attention away from the king's lack of real power by focusing attention on the monarchy's grandeur. He began to hold larger and more impressive assemblies than any since Carolingian times, and he was successful in getting some of the greatest lords of France to perform ceremonial duties in his court.

Before his accession, Louis VII had married Eleanor, the heiress of Aquitaine, and thereby multiplied by several times the amount of land under his direct control. Eleanor was a strong, independent leader and as queen of France she took a very active role, famously disputing church matters with Bernard of Clairvaux and leading her own troops to the First Crusade. But Eleanor of Aquitaine disliked her pious, abstemious husband, and he blamed her for their lack of sons. Compliant clerics annulled their marriage and Louis lost all the lands he had gained. Then Eleanor married Henry of Anjou, who was about to inherit Anjou, Maine, and Touraine from his father and who in two years would be crowned King Henry II of England. From his mother Henry would inherit Normandy. Through Eleanor, Henry got Poitou and Aquitaine and together they had three sons. Thus, Louis VII was faced with a vassal who controlled about three-fifths of France.

Anglo-Saxon England and the Norman Conquest

At the very time when continental kingdoms were collapsing in the late ninth century, Alfred the Great rallied the English. In the tenth century his successors constructed a peaceful, well-governed kingdom.

All of England was divided into administrative districts called *shires,* and each shire had a royally appointed representative, the shire-reeve, or *sheriff.* Taxes first levied on the kingdom in times of Viking danger began turning into routine sources of royal income. Alfred's burgs, originally defensive positions in the struggle against the Vikings, were purposefully transformed into towns with markets and merchants. English kings corresponded with popes, promoted learning, and shared in the spiritual reforms that were sweeping Europe. England's future could not have looked brighter.

Then in 978, Ethelred II, a boy of about 10, rose to the throne. He has become known as "Ethelred the Unready" (more accurately, Ethelred "of no counsel"), but this label is unfair. Shortly after his accession, England was drawn into the world of northern politics because King Swein of Denmark was conducting raids on the English coast. Many people in northern and eastern England were of Scandinavian extraction. Their loyalty to Ethelred may have been no stronger than their potential loyalty to Swein. Ethelred was not much of a soldier at a time when military gifts were needed, and his heavy taxes were unpopular. He fled to Normandy in 1013.

England fell to Swein in 1014, but his sudden death left the consolidation of the conquest to his son, Cnut. Cnut ruled England from 1016 to 1035, and his sons after him ruled to 1042. Cnut was one of the most powerful and capable men of his age. King of Denmark and England and briefly of Norway, too, he wed his daughter to Emperor Henry III, and later married Emma, Ethelred's widow. He was a Christian and had visited the pope in Rome. England had long enjoyed good government, and Cnut saw no reason to change things. He added a few Scandinavian aristocrats but did not purge the Anglo-Saxon nobility. Far from being disruptive, this first "Norman Conquest" actually benefited England.

Cnut's sons having died without heirs, the Anglo-Saxons invited the son of Ethelred and Emma, Edward, known as "the Confessor," to become their king. Edward was pious and well intentioned, but he had taken a vow of chastity and would leave no heir. The jostling for position among the Anglo-Saxon nobles began almost immediately, though Edward promised his throne to Duke William of Normandy.

When Edward died in 1066, Harold of Wessex, the most powerful of the Anglo-Saxon nobles, was voted king. William began to make preparations to fight for the English throne. Harold, meanwhile, had another challenger in the king of Norway and Denmark, Harald Hardrada, who claimed England in succession to Cnut. Harold of Wessex marched north to defeat Harald Hardrada, only to learn that William had landed in the south. Impulsively, he rushed south with a weary army and met William at Hastings. After one day's fighting, England was conquered for the second time in fifty years.

William "the Conqueror" ruled from 1066 to 1087. Although his power was based on conquest and on a brutal pacification campaign carried out between 1066 and 1071, William always claimed to be the legitimate heir of Edward. William maintained the traditional prerogatives of the Anglo-Saxon kings. He controlled his church with an iron hand, but his relations with Pope Gregory VII were generally cordial. Gregory probably did not wish to pick any more fights. In many ways, William's takeover, like Cnut's, was purely traditional.

In one critical area, William innovated. He turned most of the estates in England into fiefs and distributed them among the 180 or so of his greatest followers. Each of these vassals held his fief in return for a fixed quota of knights for the royal army. To raise the knights required by William, his vassals had to create vassals of their own. William exacted in 1087 the Salisbury Oath, thereby establishing the principle of *liege homage*, according to which the king was final lord of all vassals. By scattering his vassals' holdings around the kingdom, he kept the vassals from becoming too powerful in any one place.

William's keen sense of administrative order, along with his desire to know the value of his realm, led to the Domesday Book (named later by critics of the monarchy for the Day of Judgment, against which there was no appeal) of 1086. Inspectors were sent throughout the country to take the sworn testimony of people everywhere. William sought an enumeration of people, animals, buildings, mills, and anything else of significant value. No comparable undertaking was attempted again until the American census of 1790.

William was succeeded by two of his sons, William II (r. 1087–1100) and Henry I (r. 1100–1135), who kept most of their father's system intact while adding some features. The most important change came in 1107, when Henry effected a compromise with the church on the issue of lay investiture that anticipated the provisions of the Concordat of Worms.

Henry's only male heir drowned in the English Channel; so when the king died, the barons elected Stephen of Blois (r. 1135–1154), a grandson of William the Conqueror. Henry had tried in vain to convince the barons to accept his daughter Matilda as queen. Some barons rejected female rule, but many also feared Matilda's husband, the formidable Count Geoffrey of Anjou. Most English baronial families still had holdings in Normandy, and the Angevins were old enemies of the Normans. Stephen's reign was marked by constant plotting by Matilda and her supporters, and in 1153 Matilda's son, Henry of Anjou, prevailed on Stephen to recognize him as his heir. What would this turn of events mean for England? It is striking how the decade of the 1150s emerged as a turning point for Germany, France, and England.

Spain and Italy

Spain, too, faced a crisis in the 1150s. Historians perceive two driving forces in the rich and colorful history of medieval Spain. One is the constant interplay within the Iberian Peninsula of three vibrant cultures: Christian, Jewish, and Muslim. The other is the bloody experience of several centuries of war along an expanding frontier.

The caliphate of Cordoba (see page 149) began breaking up after 1002, and the emergence of tiny Muslim realms afforded an unprecedented opportunity to the Christians living in the north of the peninsula. King Sancho I (r. 1000–1035) of Navarre launched an offensive against the Muslims. This war, carried on intermittently until the fifteenth century, came to be called the *Reconquista*, the Reconquest.

Before he died, Sancho divided his realm among his sons; thus, the kingdoms of Aragon and Castile arose alongside Navarre. It was Alfonso I (r. 1065–1109) of Castile who really advanced the Reconquista. In 1085 his forces captured the Muslim stronghold and old Visigothic capital of Toledo, an important moral and strategic victory. Alfonso's military successes owed much to the dashing warrior Rodrigo Díaz de Vivar, known as "El Cid" ("the Lord" from the Arabic *sayyid*). Rodrigo, a gifted but slightly unprincipled mercenary, fought for both Muslims and Christians. His career shows just how turbulent Spain then was.

Throughout the twelfth century, the Christian states of Spain pressed slowly but relentlessly forward. The kings, especially the kings of Castile, managed to impose hereditary rule and to exact oaths of allegiance from all their free subjects. As the kingdoms grew and consolidated, the kings tried to force powerful nobles to become their vassals. They were more successful on the expanding frontier with Muslim Spain than at home. On the frontier, warriors could be given newly conquered fiefs in return for future military service. At home, in the old kingdoms, the local notables viewed their lands and rights as being independent of royal control.

To rally the Christians and give them a sense of belonging to a single country, the kings promoted the cult of Saint James of Compostella, Jesus's brother who allegedly preached Christianity in Spain. A royal council and judicial institutions also helped to unify the kingdom. In the end, however, it was the Reconquista that made the Spanish monarchy strong. In the 1150s the Muslims of Spain turned to North Africa for assistance. Help arrived, and the Reconquista was halted.

Unlike its European neighbors, Italy did not suffer a crisis in the mid-twelfth century. Italy in the period from 900 to 1150 was characterized by German and Norman involvement. As we have seen, the Germans involved themselves in the affairs of Italy, Rome, and the papacy. They were not alone. Even before the Norman conquests of England, bands of Norman adventurers began a conquest of southern Italy and Sicily. In 1026, Norman pilgrims bound for the Holy Land landed in southern Italy, where local people invited them to enlist in the fight against the Muslims. They ended up numerous enough to create their own state. From his capital at Palermo, Roger II "the Great" (r. 1130–1154) ruled at the juncture of the Latin, Greek, and Arab worlds. This Norman court was more advanced in finance and bureaucratic administration than any of its European contemporaries.

Another major factor in the history of northern and central Italy in the eleventh century was the creation of a new type of urban institution: the *commune*. Communes were sworn associations of the local nobility—the vassals of the bishops and counts—and their vassals. Commune members swore to uphold one another's rights

and called themselves the *popolo*, the "people," although the people as a whole had nothing to do with the early communes. The commune accorded a high degree of participation to its members in choosing leaders and in an assembly that voted on matters of common concern. The leaders of the early communes were usually called *consuls*. The number of consuls varied from four to twenty in different cities, and were usually elected for a single year. The consuls proposed suggestions to an assembly that then voted "yes" or "no." By the 1140s every significant city in northern and central Italy had a commune.

As communal governments became more established and confident, cities either refused to recognize papal or imperial overlordship or renegotiated the terms under which they would acknowledge the rule of their historic masters. The working out of this ongoing relationship was a major development in the history of the Italian cities in the twelfth century.

The Italian commune was a radical political experiment. Everywhere else in medieval Europe, power was thought to radiate downward—from God, the clergy, the emperor, the king. In a commune, power radiated upward from the popolo to its leaders. For several centuries, the Italian city was arguably the most creative institution in the Western world.

THE GROWTH OF NEW STATES

By 1150, a band of new states surrounded the old Carolingian core of Europe (Map 7.2). In the Celtic, Scandinavian, and Slavic worlds one new kingdom or principality after another emerged and attained a measure of stability. No previous period in European history had seen comparable political expansion.

The Celtic Realms

The most durable and distinctive Celtic regions evolved into Ireland, Wales, and Scotland. In the historical development of each of these regions,

Map 7.2 The States of an Expanding Europe The core states of Europe appeared inside the frontiers of the Roman Empire or just along them. After 900, new states, ranging from the Celtic realms in the west to Scandinavia in the north to Slavic regions in the east, surrounded and joined with the old core in a vastly larger, more diverse Europe.

England played a decisive role, though the Celtic lands also had complex relations with the wider European world.

In each of the Celtic realms the movement toward greater unity was opened by the efforts of powerful, ambitious leaders to subjugate numerous well-entrenched local potentates. In Ireland, Brian Boru (r. 976–1014) became the first ruler to exercise real authority over most of the island. In Wales, Rhodri the Great (d. 898) and Howell the Good (d. 950) were the first rulers to gain at least nominal authority over the whole of the land. Although disunity is a continuous theme of Scottish history, the centuries after the reign of Kenneth MacAlpin (r. 843–858) give evidence for the slow creation of a national tradition.

The course of development in the Celtic lands was disrupted by the English in the eleventh and especially in the twelfth century. The Norman Conquest of England brought adventurers to the frontiers of Wales and Scotland. Sometimes these continental knights advanced with the support of William the Conqueror and his sons, but more often they looked to wild frontier regions for opportunities to escape tight control.

Welsh Prince Grufydd ap Cynan (d. 1137) promised allegiance to King Henry I in 1114 if Henry would aid him in his quest to establish his authority all over Wales. From that time forward English kings usually claimed some authority over the region. Scottish kings managed to enlist a good many Norman knights into their service, but this process angered the English kings. Civil disturbances in Ireland induced King Rory O'Connor to turn to King Henry II of England for mercenaries to help him establish his power, but by 1171 Henry had invaded Ireland himself and inaugurated the complicated English involvement in the affairs of Ireland that persists to this day.

The Celtic realms participated vigorously in the European culture of the period. The coming of Christianity in the fifth century had introduced Mediterranean culture to the "end of the earth," as the Romans had dubbed Ireland. Irish schools had a high reputation, and both English and continental students went there. But Irish teachers and missionaries could also be found throughout Europe. Carolingian schools had prominent Irish teachers, as did twelfth-century schools. Celtic art forms, characterized by exuberantly intricate tracery, contributed to English, Carolingian, and Ottonian art. Cluniac and Cistercian monasticism struck deep roots in Ireland. In addition, the Irish Sea was a lively commercial basin linking the Celtic lands with England, Scandinavia, the Low Countries, and France.

Scandinavia and the Slavic World

Raiders, traders, and settlers, the Scandinavians fostered the expansion of Europe. They aided in the creation of trade routes that stretched from Byzantium and the Islamic world to the remotest reaches of the North Atlantic. Roman Christianity and Latin culture entered Scandinavia through both individual and state-sponsored missionary efforts. Germany, in particular, sought to expand its influence in the north through the church.

Because the sea made exit from Scandinavia so easy, and because the whole region had no tradition of unified government, kings had a hard time establishing their power. Essentially kings were war leaders with loyal bands of followers. Territorial states were thus built up as powerful leaders persuaded or forced more and more men to join them. Denmark's was the first of the northern monarchies to emerge in the early tenth century. Norway's monarchy arose a little later in the tenth century, but for much of the eleventh

century Norway was under Danish control. As the Danes fell increasingly under German influence in the eleventh century, Norway managed to break free. Sweden's monarchy was the last to emerge in the northern world; it was not fully stable until the twelfth century, but by 1300, it became the most powerful.

Much earlier, Swedes had laid the foundation for the Russian state when they built a permanent trading station at Kiev in 862. Kiev lay near the junction of several major trade routes based on the Volga and Dneiper Rivers. These river valleys were full of Slavic farmers. Russia emerged as Swedish warrior-merchants and Slavic farmers made common cause against the untamed peoples of the Russian steppes.

In 882, Prince Oleg of Novgorod, a northern Swedish station, extended his rule all the way to Kiev and became the first grand prince of Russia. A century later Vladimir (r. 978–1015) consolidated his power by neutralizing or exiling powerful nobles, converted to Orthodox Christianity, defended Kiev by means of fortifications, and went on the offensive against the steppe peoples. Despite Vladimir's efforts, Kiev did not remain in control of the young Russian state. Rule slowly passed to towns like Novgorod that enjoyed favorable commercial locations while also lying deep enough in the Russian forests to assure some protection from the steppe nomads who continually harassed Kiev.

For geographical and linguistic reasons, historians divide the Slavs into western, southern, and eastern categories. Russia was the greatest of the east Slavic states. The most important of the west Slavic states were Bohemia, Poland, and Hungary (see Map 7.2). Bohemia emerged in the late ninth century when a powerful local duke forged an alliance of the Czech people of Bohemia proper and the Slovak peoples to the east. Early in the tenth century a Polish duke laid the foundations for the kingdom of Poland. Poland might have become the most powerful of the west Slavic states had not a twelfth-century king divided his kingdom among his four sons. The origins of the Hungarian kingdom trace to the defeat of the Magyars by the Germans in 955. The Magyar leadership settled down in the Pannonian basin and ruled, as a minority, in conjunction with a large Slavic population. In the eleventh century the Hungarian kings profited from troubles in the German and Byzantine Empires to build an effective state.

The southern Slavs created a band of states reaching across the northern Balkans from the Adriatic to the Black Sea. In the extreme west the little states of Croatia, Slovenia, and Serbia appeared in the tenth and eleventh centuries. The greatest of the south Slavic states was Bulgaria. Like the Magyars, the Bulgars were a minority ruling over a numerically superior Slavic population. Bulgaria was the oldest of the Slavic states, reaching back to the seventh century. Under Khan Symeon (r. 893–927) the Bulgars made war on Byzantium and controlled trans-Balkan trade routes. The Byzantines so feared the Bulgars that they waged relentless war on them from 967 to 1018 and eventually destroyed the first Bulgar state.

CULTURAL LIFE IN AN AGE OF EXPANSION

As in the late antique and Carolingian periods, courts and churches were the great patrons of artists and authors. But in this age of expansion the number and geographic spread of such patrons rose dramatically. In addition to an increase in the sheer amount of cultural activity, the years between 900 and 1150 also witnessed innovations. Logic replaced grammar at the heart of the school curriculum. Latin letters remained ascendant, but literature in many vernacular (native) languages began to appear in quantity and quality. Romanesque art and architecture were fresh and original despite being lineal descendants of Carolingian ancestors. Europe's incipient urbanization produced the first stirrings of a distinctively urban culture.

Schools and Latin Letters

The breakup of the Carolingian Empire deprived schools and masters of the patronage that they had enjoyed for a century or more. Therefore, the tenth century was marked more by individual genius than by a program of learning.

Gerbert of Aurillac (940–1003) was the most distinguished intellect of his age. He left his home in Aquitaine to study in Spain and Italy before settling in Reims, in northern France, where he was a teacher and then briefly bishop. He attracted the attention of the emperor Otto III and spent some time at the German court, earning appointments as abbot, bishop, and, finally, pope. Gerbert followed Carolingian tradition in being a collector of manuscripts and critic of texts, but he departed from the norm in his interest in mathematics and in his study of logic, the formal rules of reasoning that, in the Western tradition, trace back over many thinkers to Aristotle.

Fulbert of Chartres (960–1028), Gerbert's finest pupil, elevated the cathedral school of Chartres to the paramount place in Europe. Fulbert wrote letters in elegant Latin and fine poems. He carried on his master's literary interests more than his scientific ones, and well into the twelfth century Chartres remained a major center of literary studies. Another figure of interest is the aristocratic German nun Roswitha of Gandersheim (d. 970). She wrote poems on saints and martyrs, as well as a story about a priest who sold his soul to the devil. In her mature years, Roswitha wrote Latin plays in rhymed verse based on the Roman writer Terence. In these plays she took tales from Roman and biblical history and used them to convey moral truths.

The eleventh century, more settled and prosperous than the tenth, was more diverse culturally. One of the chief accomplishments of the age came about almost by accident. Berengar (ca. 1000–ca. 1088), master of the school of Tours, wrote a treatise that denied Christ's presence in the Eucharist—the Holy Communion received by Catholics in the celebration of the mass. This position was heretical. Ordinarily, churchmen would have refuted it by simply quoting to Berengar various passages from the Scriptures or from the writings of the Church Fathers along with conciliar pronouncements. The evidence, however, was ambiguous. Berengar was finally refuted, at least to the satisfaction of his opponents, by the archbishop of Canterbury, Lanfranc. Lanfranc was an ardent reformer who had come from Normandy by the invitation of William the Conqueror. Against Berengar's heretical arguments, Lanfranc used precise logical argumentation.

Carolingian schools had focused on grammar, on the basic foundations of language. Now that logic had come to the aid of the faith in one critical case, people began using it widely to solve intellectual problems. Anselm (ca. 1033–1109), Lanfranc's successor as archbishop of Canterbury, developed an ingenious proof for the existence of God. The French theologian and philosopher Peter Abelard (1079–1142) used logic to reconcile apparent contradictions in the Scriptures and in the writings of the Church Fathers.

We must not suppose that Anselm and Abelard were skeptics. Anselm's motto was "Faith seeking understanding." Logic was for him the handmaiden of divine truth. He would have agreed completely with Abelard, who said that "Faith has no merit with God when it is not the testimony of divine truth that leads us to it, but the evidence of human reason." Anselm's distinguished works on logic and his theological treatise *Why God Became Man* (ca. 1100) served for three hundred years as a philosophical and theological explanation of the incarnation of Christ, the central mystery of the Christian faith.

Abelard rose to a keener understanding of Aristotle than anyone in centuries, and he developed a sharper sense of both the power and the limitations of language than anyone since the Greeks. He is remembered for his theological work, but also for his colorful life. He seduced and then secretly married Heloise, one of his pupils and the daughter of an influential Paris churchman. Heloise's relatives castrated Abelard for his refusal to live openly with his wife. Abelard then arranged for Heloise to enter a convent, and he joined a monastic community, where he continued writing and teaching. The two carried on a voluminous correspondence that reveals Heloise as a first-rate philosophical thinker. Some of Abelard's more imaginative

ideas earned him formal ecclesiastical condemnations in 1121 and 1140. He popularized the schools of Paris, however, attracting to them promising scholars from all over Europe.

In contrast to Abelard and Anselm's interest in logic, conservatives like Bernard of Clairvaux (1090–1153) and Hildegard of Bingen (1098–1179) believed faith and immediate divine inspiration were primary. To them, logical approaches to divine truth were the height of arrogance. Hildegard, well educated, gifted musically, and extremely observant, was the most profound psychological thinker of her age. She wrote a number of highly influential religious works, and her treatises on natural science and medicine were accepted by emperors and popes. More than anyone before her, Hildegard saw the Creator as feminine and nurturing. She, like Bernard, believed that God was to be found deep within the human spirit, not in books full of academic wrangling.

The Rise of Vernacular Culture

To know French or to write English did not make one a member of the community of scholars. Yet in the period 900 to 1150 many writers, most of them unknown to us by name, began to compose in their native tongues. The epic poem *Beowulf* is the first classic of English literature. We do not know who wrote it or when it was written. Scholars formerly assigned it to the eighth century, but they now usually place it later, in the ninth or possibly in the tenth century. The story focuses on three great battles against monsters and dragons and includes themes of adventure, heroism, and loyalty. It treats lordship, friendship, and kinship. The poem is barely Christian but nevertheless deeply moral. It speaks, in a mature, vigorous, and moving language, to and for the heart of a warrior society.

France produced a number of *chansons de gestes*, "songs of deeds" or celebrations of the great. The best is the *Song of Roland*, written around 1100. In 778 as Charlemagne's army was returning from Spain, Basques raided the baggage train and killed Count Roland. By 1100 this obscure event, long kept alive in oral traditions, had been transformed into a heroic struggle between Charlemagne and his retinue and an army of countless thousands of "paynim," who are crude caricatures of Muslims.

Like *Beowulf*, *Roland* is a story about loyalty and treachery, about bravery in the face of insuperable odds, about the kindness and generosity of leaders. They take us into a man's chivalric world. Women are all but absent. The two works do not show us personal hopes, fears, or motivations. What pours forth is the communal ethos and the dominant values of the elite, male social group. Although *Beowulf* is lightly clothed in Christianity, *Roland* is thickly vested in the faith. These texts are eloquent testimony to the literary attainments of the illiterate. Similar attainments could be chronicled for peoples and languages extending from Ireland to Russia.

The Romanesque Achievement

Romanesque, "in the Roman style," is a term coined in the nineteenth century to characterize the architecture and, to a lesser extent, the painting of the period from the end of Carolingian art to the full emergence of Gothic art in the late twelfth century. Today scholars define the Romanesque period as extending from roughly 1050 to 1150 and view the Romanesque style as transitional between Carolingian and Gothic.

At several places in Ottonian Germany a return of political stability led to the construction of churches. Ducal dynasties and women of the imperial family were among the most generous patrons. Pride in their Carolingian inheritance and their new imperial dignity led the Germans to a distinctive architectural style marked by very thick walls, alternating piers and columns in the nave, and galleries. As this architectural style spread all over Europe in the eleventh century, it produced true Romanesque, a style that differed from Roman and Carolingian styles mainly in the greater internal height and space made possible by vaulting (Figure 7.1).

Among the distinctive features of Romanesque churches were their wall paintings and frescoes, their sculpture, reliquaries, pulpits,

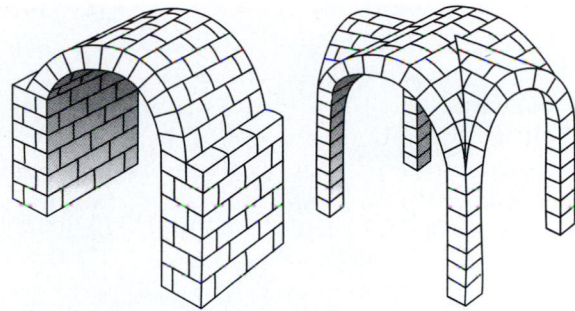

Figure 7.1 The Structure of Romanesque Architecture The basic structural element of Romanesque architecture was the barrel vault, which, when two were joined at right angles, formed a groin vault. These vaults produced great height and strength but gave buildings a massive, fortresslike appearance. (*Source:* Anne Shaver-Crandell, *The Middle Ages* [Cambridge, England: Cambridge University Press, 1982], p. 4. Used by permission.)

and baptisteries—in short, their exuberant decoration and ornament. Europe's growing wealth and sophistication, and the self-conscious feelings of the church's aristocratic patrons, are very much in evidence. Especially in the south of France, the façades of Romanesque churches provided space for sculpture. The tympanum above doors, a space seen by all who entered, was a favored location. Large-scale sculpture had made a comeback after its almost total absence in the early Middle Ages.

A CLASH OF CULTURES: THE FIRST CRUSADE

In 1096 an army of Christian knights who called themselves pilgrims left Europe to liberate the Holy Land from the Muslim "infidel." This was the first of many Crusades, so called because the warriors were *crucesignati*, "signed by the cross."

The First Crusade was made possible by Europe's expanding population, economic dynamism, political consolidation, and buoyant optimism. By the late eleventh century, Europe was

Saint Sernin, Toulouse This fortresslike church (ca. 1080–1120) was paid for by the offerings of pilgrims on their way to shrines in Spain. Its massive walls and numerous colonnades are typical of Romanesque architecture. The form of the building suggests the cross of Christ. *(Jean Dieuzaide, Toulouse)*

an impregnable fortress that had marshaled its resources for an attack on the world around it.

The Eastern Mediterranean Background

The Byzantine Empire experienced a period of vigorous, successful rule that began in 867 with the accession of Basil I—first of the Macedonian dynasty —and lasted until 1025. Although they fostered impressive cultural achievements, carried out significant administrative reforms, and achieved the kind of tight control of the church that had been so elusive in the iconoclastic era (see page 151), the Macedonians were primarily great soldiers. Along the Balkan frontier the Macedonian rulers managed to keep both the Bulgars and the incipient Russian state at bay while also neutralizing many smaller Slavic principalities.

By contrast, throughout the ninth and tenth centuries the ability of the caliphs in Baghdad to control their vast empire declined precipitously. Egypt and North Africa escaped Baghdad's control almost completely, and religious strife between Sunni and Shi'ite Muslims further destabilized the Islamic state. Although Byzantium at first profited from this situation by expanding its holdings in Anatolia, in the long run the inability of the caliphate to control its frontiers led to serious challenges for the Byzantines.

In the eleventh century, Byzantium suffered a long period of short reigns and abrupt changes in policy. In the capital, factional squabbling swirled around the imperial court, and in the person of Patriarch Michael Cerularius (r. 1043–1058) the church sought to break out from two centuries of domination. When in 1054 Cerularius and Pope Leo IX quarreled so bitterly over ecclesiastical customs that they excommunicated each other, the sometimes tense papal-Byzantine religious diplomacy gave way to a deep schism between the Roman and Orthodox churches. Religious tensions were complicated when the bitterly anti-Byzantine Normans began creating their kingdom in southern Italy.

It was in these divisive circumstances that the Seljuk Turks appeared on the eastern frontier of Anatolia. Bands of Turks, peoples from central Asia, had been serving the caliphs as mercenaries since the ninth century. With new leaders at their head, and with both the caliphate and the empire distracted, the Turks broke into Anatolia with a vengeance. In 1071 a skirmish between Byzantine and Turkish soldiers turned into a rout in which Byzantium lost an army, an emperor, and the Macedonian reputation for military prowess.

Ever since the emergence of the Turkish threat, the Byzantines had been seeking mercenary help; now they appealed to the West. Some troops were rounded up but not enough, so in 1095 Emperor Alexius Comnenus (r. 1081–1118) sent envoys to ask Pope Urban II to lend his support to an appeal for help against the Turks.

The Western Background

To most Westerners the Turkish threat to Byzantium was a matter of little consequence. What mattered to them were Turkish attacks on pilgrims to Jerusalem. The popes saw in the plight of the Byzantines and of Western pilgrims some opportunities to manifest their leadership of the church. The papacy also wanted very much to heal the Roman-Orthodox rift. The popes placed a high value on aiding the Byzantines.

Moreover, the crusade was perfectly consonant with the ethos of the knights of western Europe. Knights were born and trained to fight. The vernacular literature of the age glorified war and warriors. But churchmen had for some years been advancing an ideal of Christian knighthood that stressed fighting God's enemies and aiding God's people. In the late tenth century there arose, first in France and then in many other places, peace movements called the "Peace of God" or the "Truce of God." These movements sought to prevent war in certain seasons, such as around Christmas and Easter, and on certain days of the week, chiefly Sundays. The movement induced knights to fight non-Christians outside Europe.

As noted earlier, the simultaneous rise in population and consolidation of family lineages were producing, especially in France, large numbers of restless, landless "young." These young knights viewed the crusade as an opportunity to do what they did best: fight. In addition to adventure, the crusade provided an opportunity for military glory that might procure advancement back home or a chance to acquire lands and titles far from Europe's highly competitive aristocratic milieu.

The "Pilgrimage" to Jerusalem

Pope Urban II received Alexius's envoys in 1095 and then left Italy for France. He was actually a fugitive because Henry IV controlled Rome. In November, Urban delivered a rousing speech to a vast Christian assembly. He ignored the eastern emperor's appeal for aid and instead promised salvation to soldiers who would enlist in a great struggle to free the Holy Land. The crowd acclaimed his words with a shout of "God wills it."

By 1096 four large armies assembled, eventually swelling to perhaps 100,000 men—mostly French knights with a smattering of troops from other parts of Europe. The forces were to rendezvous at the Byzantine capital of Constantinople, where they seem to have expected a cordial imperial welcome and all necessary assistance. Alexius, however, took a rather different view. A ragtag band of ordinary people preceding the Crusaders had torn through the Balkans like a plague of locusts. Then, the crusading armies

~ **ENCOUNTERS WITH THE WEST** ~

An Arab Perspective on the First Crusade

The Muslim historian Ibn al-Athir (1160–1233) provides in his **Perfect History** *several interesting perspectives on the First Crusade. The Baldwin with whom his account opens is not historical; perhaps he is a composite of the many Baldwins then active in the West.*

Baldwin, their king, assembled a great army and sent word to Roger [of Sicily] saying: "I have assembled a great army and now I am on my way to you, to use your bases for my conquest of the African coast. Thus you and I shall become neighbors." Roger called together his companions and consulted them about these proposals. "This will be a fine thing for them and for us!" they declared, "for by this means these lands will be converted to the Faith." At this Roger raised one leg and farted loudly, and swore that it was of more use than their advice. "Why?" "Because if this army comes here it will need quantities of provisions and fleets of ships to transport it to Africa, as well as reinforcements from my own troops. Then, if the Franks succeed in conquering this territory they will take it over and will need provisioning from Sicily. This will cost me my annual profit from the harvest. If they fail they will return here and be an embarrassment to me here in my own domain. As well as this Tamim [the emir of Tunisia in North Africa] will say that I

have broken faith with him and violated our treaty, and friendly relations and communications between us will be disrupted. As far as we are concerned, Africa is always there. When we are strong enough we will take it."

He summoned Baldwin's messenger and said to him: "If you have decided to make war on the Muslims your best course will be to free Jerusalem from their rule and thereby win great honour. I am bound by certain treaties and promises of allegiance with the rulers of Africa." So the Franks made ready to attack Syria.

Another story is that the Fatimids [local rulers] of Egypt were afraid when they saw the Seljuqids extending their empire through Syria as far as Gaza, until they reached the Egyptian border and Atziz [a general] invaded Egypt itself. They therefore sent to invite the Franks to invade Syria and so to protect Egypt from the Muslims [the Fatimids, although militantly Muslim, were regarded as heretics by other Muslims]. But God knows best.

Source: Francesco Gabrieli, *Arab Historians of the Crusades* (Berkeley: University of California Press, 1969), pp. 3–4. Selected and translated from the Arabic sources by E. J. Costello. Copyright © 1969 by the University of California Press. Reprinted by permission of the Regents of the University of California and the University of California Press.

themselves sorely taxed the imperial authorities who spent a lot of time and money arranging their passage from the frontier of Hungary to the gates of Constantinople. Finally, Alexius wanted mercenaries to fight Turks in Anatolia, not armed pilgrims intent on liberating Palestine.

After receiving nominal promises of loyalty and the return or donation of any lands cap-

tured, Alexius moved the Crusaders into Anatolia. Almost immediately the Latin army defeated a Turkish force, thus earning a valuable, though short-lived, reputation for invincibility. (See the box "Encounters with the West: An Arab Perspective on the First Crusade.") The troops then entered Syria and laid siege to Antioch. At this point, rivalries among the Crusaders came into the open. One force went to the frontier of Armenia and carved out a principality. One of the ubiquitous Normans kept Antioch for himself. The main army, led by Godfrey of Bouillon, pressed on to Jerusalem and, after a short but fierce siege, conquered it in July 1099.

Judged on its own terms, the First Crusade was a success. The Holy Land was retaken from the infidel, and the pilgrim routes were passable once more. Entirely uncertain, however, were the prospects of the crusader states, the future course of Western relations with Byzantium, and the reaction of the Islamic world once it recovered from its initial shock.

SUMMARY

In 900 the survival of Europe's political, social, and intellectual order was in question. By 1150, Europe was prosperous, confident, and expansive. Population rose steadily. People everywhere brought new land under cultivation, adopted better agricultural techniques, and improved transportation. Agricultural gains promoted urban growth as some people were freed from farming to undertake commercial and artisanal pursuits. Never before had Europe's economy improved so rapidly.

Between 900 and 1150, European society assumed many of the distinctive features that it would bear until the modern period. A landed aristocracy competed with lesser nobles and with urban potentates for power and rank. In a militantly Christian society the clergy had great power and prestige, but it had to struggle continually with envious nobilities and governments in order to maintain its privileged status. Peasants gained ground economically and legally, but their position was always precarious.

Except in Germany, governments grew in power, scope, and sophistication. The Roman church expanded its governing structures. In particular, England, France, and Spain created effective centralized institutions. Cultural horizons expanded, too. There were more and better schools than at any time since the Carolingian Renaissance. The curriculum moved beyond an elementary focus on grammar to logic. Vernacular languages began taking their place alongside Latin as sophisticated tools for the expression of complex stories and ideas. Romanesque art represented richness, growth, and novelty.

But everything was fragile. No one in 1150 could have predicted whether the European economy would go on expanding. Cities and their residents might well have taken the lead in social and political life away from kings and landed nobles. Latin letters might have yielded their place to French or English. The death of Bernard of Clairvaux in 1153 might have signaled the end of traditional monasticism or an opening for new forms of religious expression. The years after 1150 would be creative, but in ways quite different from those between 900 and 1150.

SUGGESTED READING

Bisson, Thomas, ed. *Cultures of Power: Lordship, Status, and Process in Twelfth-Century Europe*. 1995. The thirteen sparkling essays in this book cover much of Europe and attempt to explain how power was wielded in an essentially "stateless" society.

Bloch, Marc. *Feudal Society*. Translated by L. A. Manyon. 2 vols. 1964. The best-known book by one of this century's greatest historians.

Blumenthal, Uta-Renate. *The Investiture Controversy: Church and Monarchy from the Ninth to the Twelfth Century*. 1988. Brief, readable, and remarkably comprehensive, this book is the best introduction in any language to the great upheaval.

Bynum, Caroline Walker. *Jesus as Mother: Studies in the Spirituality of the High Middle Ages*. 1982. A collection of extremely absorbing essays by a major historian makes the feminine in religious thought central to any discussion of medieval religion.

Chibnall, Marjorie. *Anglo-Norman England, 1066–1166*. 1986. Focusing on government, institutions, and society, this book is a remarkably effective introduction to a tumultuous century of English history.

Constable, Giles. *The Reformation of the Twelfth Century*. 1996. Long awaited, this book is the culmination of the life's work of America's most distinguished medievalist.

Demus, Otto. *Romanesque Wall Painting*. 1970. Although the commentary in this book is a little challenging, the pictures are numerous and superb.

Duby, Georges. *Medieval France.* 1991. The author of this original and entertaining book is France's leading medievalist.

Fichtenau, Heinrich. *Living in the Tenth Century: Mentalities and Social Orders.* Translated by Patrick Geary. 1991. Wide-ranging, readable, interesting, this is the best introduction to the post-Carolingian world.

Fletcher, Richard. *The Quest for El Cid.* 1990. As entertaining and engaging as a detective novel, Fletcher's book seeks both to recapture the historical Cid and to explain literary and historical accounts about him.

Fuhrmann, Horst. *Germany in the High Middle Ages, c. 1050–1200.* Translated by Timothy Reuter. 1986. Beautifully written and translated, this book presents the thought of Germany's leading medievalist.

Ganshof, François-Louis. *Feudalism.* 2d ed. Translated by Philip Grierson. 1964. The standard introduction to the personal and proprietary aspects of the feudal bond.

Gerber, Jane S. *The Jews of Spain: A History of the Sephardic Experience.* 1992. Fascinating, lively, and comprehensive.

Herlihy, David. *Opera Muliebria: Women and Work in Medieval Europe.* 1990. This brief and nontechnical book covers most of Europe in the thousand years after about 500.

Hyde, J. K. *Society and Politics in Medieval Italy: The Evolution of the Civil Life, 1000–1350.* 1973. A sophisticated introduction to the social complexity and institutional creativity of Italian towns.

Kubach, Hans Erich. *Romanesque Architecture.* 1988. Comprehensive and accessible, this is a standard introduction to a vast subject.

Leyser, Henrietta. *Hermits and the New Monasticism: A Study of Religious Communities in Western Europe, 1000–1150.* 1984. Brief, lively, and informative, this book explains the sources and history of the many religious movements that spread throughout medieval Europe, emphasizing the eremitic ideal.

Martin, Janet. *Medieval Russia, 980–1584.* 1995. Nicely written and very current, this is the place to start on Russian history.

Newman, Barbara. *Sister of Wisdom: St. Hildegard's Theology of the Feminine.* 1987. Interesting and readable, this path-breaking study not only introduces Hildegard but also opens up wholly new ways of thinking about twelfth-century spiritual culture.

Poly, Jean-Pierre, and Eric Bournazel. *The Feudal Transformation, 900–1200.* Translated by Caroline Higgett. 1991. This important book presents a synthesis of the best French thinking in the past generation on social and institutional development, mainly in France.

Reynolds, Susan. *Fiefs and Vassals.* 1994. Brilliant, controversial, and difficult, this massive book challenges many long-standing ideas about feudalism.

———. *Kingdoms and Communities in Western Europe, 900–1300.* 1984. After exploring the kinds of legal notions that guided community building, this lively book turns to actual communities, ranging from the parish to the kingdom.

Sedlar, Jean W. *East Central Europe in the Middle Ages.* 1994. Although difficult and confusingly organized, this book is as good an introduction as exists to central and eastern Europe.

Southern, Richard W. *Saint Anselm: A Portrait in a Landscape.* 1990. The distillation of a life's work by a master historian, this wonderful book introduces not only Anselm but also the intellectual and spiritual life of his world.

Stafford, Pauline. *Unification and Conquest: A Political and Social History of England in the Tenth and Eleventh Centuries.* 1989. The subtitle of this interesting and well-written book accurately describes its scope and contents.

Medieval Civilization at Its Height, ca. 1150–1300

Because he hated war and violence, Saint Francis of Assisi, the most charismatic religious figure of the High Middle Ages, set out in 1219 for Egypt, where a crusading army was encamped. He aimed to convert Malik al-Kamil, the sultan of Egypt, to Catholicism and thereby put an end to the Crusades. Captured by Muslim soldiers, Francis demanded to be taken before their leader. The audacity of Francis is remarkable. That a poor, humble man would think that he alone could, by power of persuasion, convert the mighty sultan of Egypt is astonishing. Yet audacious is in many ways a perfect description of many endeavors in late twelfth- and thirteenth-century Europe.

The papacy reached the high point of its institutional and ideological power, brought down kings and emperors, and yet was humiliated in a devastating conflict with France. The German Empire rebuilt its fortunes on the basis of an attempt to use Italy to control Germany, but ultimately the attempt failed. French and English kings refined their institutions as never before but emptied their treasuries in military adventures and infuriated their nobilities by constant attempts to neutralize them. Spanish rulers turned from wars of reconquest to struggles for political consolidation. Italian cities sought, with varying degrees of success, to attain a stability equal to their prosperity. Impressive political achievements in Europe's most easterly regions were cut short by the Mongols.

Agricultural innovation had fueled Europe's expansion before 1150, but urban and commercial development became decisive after that date. Particularly in the towns of high medieval Europe, social and religious movements arose, larger in scale than any seen previously.

In thinking about the period from 1150 to 1300, it is well to keep in mind the scene of Francis before the sultan. It reminds us of people's lofty aspirations in high medieval Europe.

∾ *Questions and Ideas to Consider*

- In the High Middle Ages, the papacy was extremely powerful and influential. Describe the ideology and institutional structure that supported it. What specific steps did the church take to increase its power and magnify the distinction between church and laity?

- Compare the development of central governments in France and England during this period. In both countries, monarchs succeeded in strengthening their control of the country. In what ways were the two countries following similar paths? How did their goals and methods differ?

- The great economic expansion of the early Middle Ages began to slow between 1150 and 1300, yet economic institutions in Europe were not in decline. Rather, they grew more complex and became more urban-based. How did this happen? Consider the rise of towns, the emergence of guilds, and the new ideologies surrounding usury and profit.

- Describe the similarities and differences between the new religious groups that were accepted by the church and those that were considered heretical. Discuss the role of women in the new religious groups of both types.

- Two important features of medieval culture were Scholasticism and the rise of vernacular literature. What were the major concerns of Scholastic thought? Describe three authors of vernacular literature and the styles that they represent.

THE EMPIRE AND THE PAPACY

The century between 1152, when Frederick I ascended the German throne, and 1250, when Frederick II died, was decisive for both Germany and the papacy. Under its new Staufen dynasty, Germany at first recovered from its early-twelfth-century malaise and then collapsed as its rulers became more interested in Italy than in Germany itself. The papacy battled the German kings on a wide range of issues and had the satisfaction of seeing an excommunicated Frederick II die without a successor. Meanwhile, unprecedented legal and institutional growth led to the elaboration of the papal monarchy.

Revival of the Empire, 1152–1190

After years of near anarchy, many parties in Germany desired a return to stability. In an act of genuine statesmanship, Conrad III in 1152 designated as his successor the powerful Duke Frederick of Swabia instead of his own young son. The dukes concurred. Frederick I (r. 1152–1190), known as Barbarossa ("red-bearded"), achieved a remarkable restoration of the fortunes of the German and imperial crowns. Frederick—athletic, handsome, chivalrous, and intelligent—was the grandest ruler of his generation.

Frederick controlled extensive territories in Swabia and, through his beloved wife, Beatrice, in Burgundy (Map 8.1). He was related to the family that dominated Bavaria and Saxony. Also, Frederick usually had the support of the most important members of the clergy. The German bishops had begun to regret the liberation they had achieved at Worms in 1122 (see page 182), because ducal domination more than fully replaced royal interference.

Inside Germany, Frederick pursued one basic policy. He supported the dukes in their attempts to achieve control in their own domains, as long as they agreed to swear fealty to him. Frederick attempted to create a network of vassalic bonds throughout Germany. Vassalic bonds were no substitute for solid institutional control, but they were a start. The best evidence for this came in 1180, when Frederick crushed Duke Henry "the Lion" of Saxony, his most formidable opponent in Germany. Henry had failed to answer a royal summons to serve in the army, and Frederick ordered him to court to answer for this

CHAPTER CHRONOLOGY

1135–1183	Chrétien de Troyes	1208	Albigensian Crusade
1154–1189	Reign of Henry II of England	1210–1280	Mechtild of Magdeburg
1155	Imperial coronation of Frederick Barbarossa	1212	Imperial coronation of Frederick II
1167	Formation of the Lombard League		Battle of Las Navas de Tolosa
1170	Murder of Thomas Becket	1215	Magna Carta
1170–1221	Dominic		Fourth Lateran Council
ca. 1177–1213	Mary of Oignies	1225–1274	Thomas Aquinas
1181–1226	Francis of Assisi	1226–1270	Reign of Saint Louis (Louis IX)
1183	Peace of Constance	1265–1321	Dante Alighieri
1194–1253	Clare of Assisi	1272–1307	Reign of Edward I of England
1198–1216	Pontificate of Innocent III	1285–1314	Reign of Philip IV (the Fair)
1204	Fourth Crusade	1295	First meeting of Parliament

refusal of a vassal's most basic duty. A century earlier, when Henry IV had tried to consolidate his authority, coalitions of dukes, bishops, peasants, townsmen, and popes opposed him. This time, such parties either stood aside or actively supported Frederick.

Frederick did face problems in Germany, however. He made little headway in getting control of his vassals' vassals. When Frederick brought down a rebellious subject, such as Henry the Lion, he could not routinely claim that subject's fiefs for himself, as often happened in France and England. He had to grant those fiefs to others as the price of their support. Having been elected himself, Frederick also faced difficulty in getting the nobles to accept his son as his successor.

It was in Italy that Frederick's regime nearly came to ruin. After three years spent gaining control of Germany, Frederick went to Italy in 1155 to help the pope crush a communal movement in Rome. As a reward for his trouble, the pope crowned Frederick emperor. In 1158, Frederick summoned representatives of the major northern and central Italian cities to demand full recognition of his *regalian*, or ruler's, rights. Even

a partial listing of these rights shows the difference between the powers of a feudal king and those of an emperor. Regalian rights included, in theory, military service; control of roads, ports, and waterways; tolls, minting, fines, vacant fiefs, and confiscated properties. Frederick's plans included an extension to Germany of this type of imperial control.

The Italians had no desire to be dominated anew by their northern neighbors, and the popes feared Frederick's growing power in Italy. For nearly twenty years Frederick and the papacy carried on a running battle. In 1157 a papal representative infuriated Frederick by telling him that the empire was a "benefice" held of the pope. Although the word could have a range of meanings, Frederick chose to interpret it as "fief." Recent popes had occasionally received vassals' oaths from kings of Norway, Poland, Bohemia, Bulgaria, England, parts of Spain, Sicily, and Jerusalem. Frederick rejected the idea that his imperial dignity came from Rome. He believed that his imperial authority came directly from God and that his actual office was an inheritance from the ancient Romans and from Charlemagne.

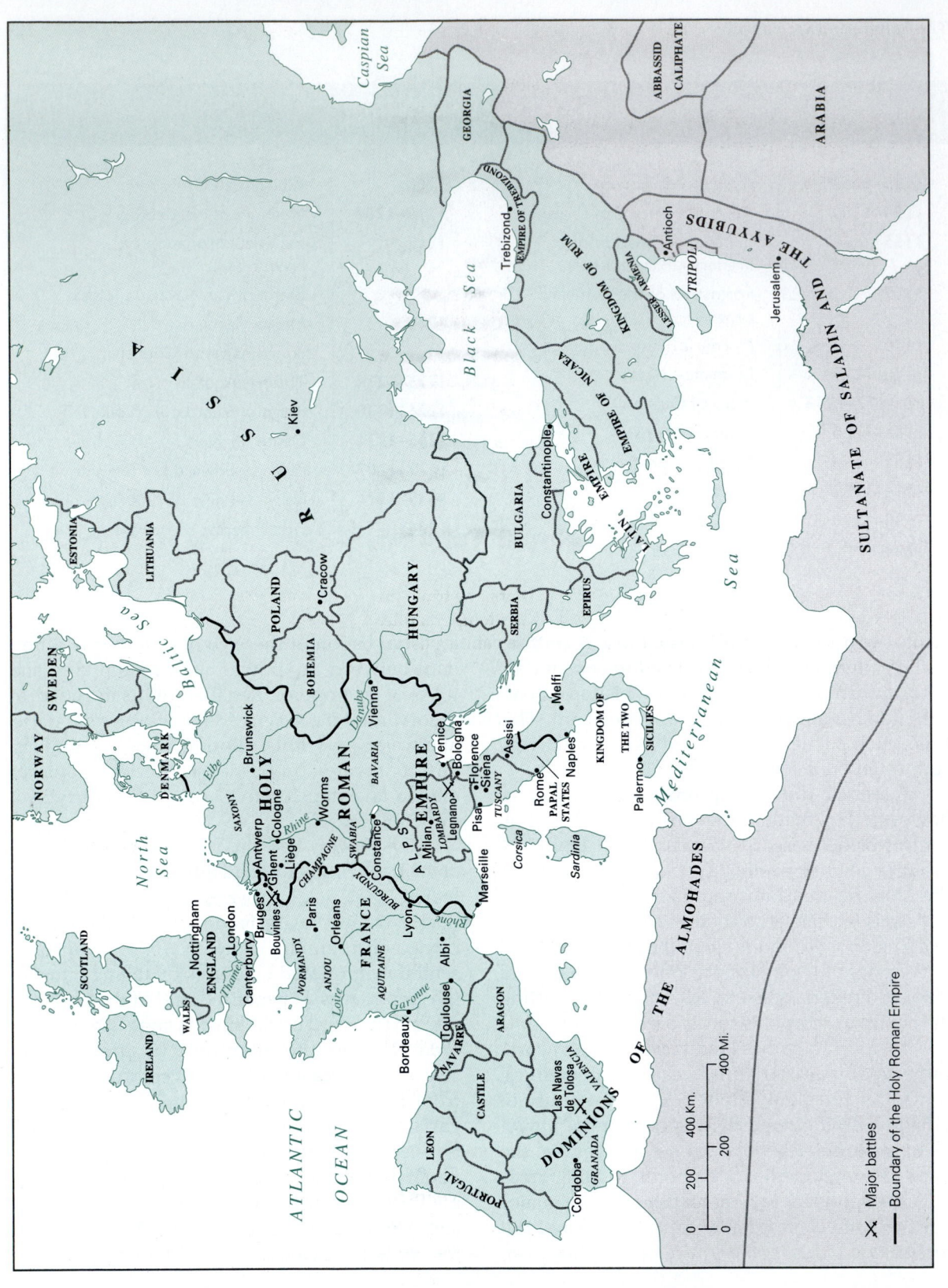

Innocent III In this wall painting, the pope wears a tiara, the triple crown that symbolizes his universal episcopate, supremacy of jurisdiction, and temporal rule. Though the greatest of popes, Innocent was also a friend of monks. This painting comes from the Holy Cave at Subiaco near Rome, where Benedict began his monastic life. *(Scala/Art Resource, NY)*

More serious for Frederick was the formation in 1167 of the Lombard League, an association of Italian towns under Milan's leadership that opposed the emperor at every turn. In 1176, Frederick led an army to Italy, but he suffered a devastating defeat at Legnano (see Map 8.1). In 1183 the Peace of Constance finally resolved the most serious outstanding issues. Frederick gave up his support for an *antipope*—a pope elected and acknowledged by Frederick and his supporters—and renounced direct control of Rome. The Lombard towns acknowledged a vague imperial suzerainty and paid some fees in recognition but were left largely independent.

Map 8.1 Europe, ca. 1220 By the early thirteenth century the European states that would exist into modern times were clearly visible, although each would continue to undergo changes. To gain a sense of the evolution of Europe, compare this map with Maps 4.1, 5.3, and 6.3.

Despite his troubles in Italy, Frederick was a ruler of real stature. His accidental drowning in Turkey on the Third Crusade was a blow to Germany, where legend has him sleeping under a mountain, to awaken when Germany needs him.

Imperial Authority and the Papal Challenge, 1190–1272

Henry VI (r. 1190–1197), Frederick's son, was accepted as king in Germany, so he headed for Sicily, whose Norman heiress, Constance, he had married some years before. Since the 950s, German rulers had concentrated on northern Italy. But because the Peace of Constance had made Lombardy and Rome difficult to dominate, it made sense for Henry VI to turn to Sicily as a base for his Italian policy. It took Henry several years to gain recognition of his authority in Sicily. Then, before the pope would crown him emperor, he had to give assurances that he would not try to control both northern and southern Italy. To buy time for his schemes in Italy, Henry gave the German princes virtual free rein. Suddenly, in 1197, Henry died without having consolidated imperial rule in Italy or royal rule in Germany.

The legitimate heir, Frederick II, was a 3-year-old whose mother, Constance of Sicily, had no standing in Germany and considerable opposition in Sicily from those who thought that she had sold out to the Germans. Shortly before her own death in 1198, Constance made her son the ward of Pope Innocent III (r. 1198–1216). In Germany, one party favored Staufen claims and wished to avoid anarchy, and another party preferred ducal rights over Staufen power.

Once again dynastic instability threatened Germany, affording Innocent an unprecedented opportunity to intervene. The pope wished both to arbitrate the imperial office and to limit German power in Italy. Meanwhile, Otto of Brunswick (son of Henry the Lion) emerged as leader of the anti-Staufen party and was crowned king in 1198. In return for papal recognition and imperial coronation, Otto promised to confine himself to Germany. Accordingly, in 1209, Otto was crowned emperor in Rome, but he immediately invaded Sicily, hoping to secure its riches for himself. Innocent responded to this betrayal by excommunicating Otto in 1211 and by crowning his ward, Frederick, as emperor in 1212. (See the box, "Innocent III on His Rights and Powers.")

Innocent got Frederick II (r. 1212–1250) to swear that he would not attempt to unite Italy and Germany. In 1220, Frederick issued the "Statute in Favor of the Princes," which almost totally abandoned regalian rights north of the Alps. Born in Sicily, Frederick loved the warm climate and cosmopolitan society of the south. All he wanted from the north was a vague recognition of his legitimacy. Frederick's actions stood the old Italian policy of the German rulers since the tenth century on its head. Now an essentially Italian ruler had a German policy.

Frederick was determined to unite almost all of Italy and run it with salaried officials appointed and removed at the emperor's will. Until his death in 1250, Frederick was constantly

hounded by opposition from popes, who excommunicated him several times, and from urban Italians, who resented his challenges to their local autonomy. Frederick has sometimes been seen as a very modern man: secular, rational, calculating. Actually, he was a man of his time. He was devoted to both astrology and the cult of saints. He wondered about the immortality of the soul but was no more skeptical than others. His bureaucratic reforms might seem very new, but they were based on Norman, papal, and Byzantine precedents.

In Germany, the period from 1250 to 1273 is called the "Great Interregnum" (the time "between the reigns"). For years the princes could not agree on the promotion of one of their own number until in 1273 they elected Rudolf of Habsburg king of Germany. He failed initially to establish a dynasty, although his family would be prominent in European politics until 1918. The powerful German state of the Saxons, and the revived state of the Staufen, had vanished.

Medieval Germany's failure was in some ways more apparent than real. It has never been easy to say just where or what Germany is. Through most of its history, Germany has been both an idea and a confederation of peoples and lands. Even today, German speakers and German lands are scattered all over the map of central Europe. Germany's medieval failure was really a failure of monarchy. Frederick Barbarossa built up his monarchy in ways very similar to those being used in France and England. What destroyed the medieval German monarchy were the Italian and papal entanglements and the inability of the German royal dynasties to produce heirs.

The Papal Monarchy

The papacy was strong. As we have seen, it was able to arbitrate the imperial succession and to break the Staufen. Between kings and popes, the struggle for power and prestige continued, but—with the legacy of the investiture controversy, of the Crusades, and of generations of spiritual reform—the church had taken the lead. The strength of the church rested not only on this ideological

Innocent III on His Rights and Powers

In this authoritative papal pronouncement from 1202, Innocent explains why he believes the pope has a right and duty to decide who is fit to be emperor.

Among other things certain princes urge this objection particularly, that our venerable brother the bishop of Palestrina, legate of the apostolic see, acted as either an elector [of the emperor] or as a judge of the election. If as an elector, he put his sickle in a stranger's harvest and, by intervening in the election, detracted from the dignity of the princes; if as a judge, he seems to have proceeded incorrectly since one of the parties was absent. . . . We indeed by virtue of our office of apostolic service owe justice to each man and, just as we do not want our justice to be usurped by others, so too we do not want to claim for ourselves the rights of princes. We do indeed acknowledge, as we should, that the princes have by ancient custom the right and power to elect a king who is afterwards to be promoted emperor; and especially so since this right and power came to them from the apostolic see which transferred the Roman empire from the Greeks to the Germans in the person of the great Charles. But the princes should acknowledge, and in-

deed they do acknowledge, that the right and authority to examine the person elected as king, who is to be promoted to the imperial dignity, belong to us who anoint, consecrate and crown him; for it is regularly and generally observed that the examination of a person belongs to the one to whom the laying-on of hands belongs. If the princes elected as king a sacrilegious man or an excommunicate, a tyrant, a fool or a heretic, and that not just by divided vote but unanimously, ought we to anoint, consecrate and crown such a man? Of course not. Therefore, . . . we maintain that our legate the bishop of Palestrina . . . did not act as either an elector . . . or as a judge when he approved King Otto and rejected Duke Philip. And so he in no way usurped the right of the princes or acted against it. . . . Rather he exercised the office of one who declared that the king was personally worthy and the duke personally unworthy to obtain the imperial dignity, not considering so much the zeal of the electors as the merits of those elected.

Source: Brian Tierney, *The Crisis of Church and State, 1050–1300* (Englewood Cliffs, N.J.: Prentice-Hall, 1964), pp. 133–134. Copyright © 1964 by Prentice-Hall, Inc., renewed 1992 by Brian Tierney. Reprinted by permission of Simon & Schuster.

victory, but also on its institutional organization. The twelfth-century popes refined their central government, which grew as never before. The ability of the Roman church to coerce secular rulers and to control local churches reached a high point. The canon law of the church surpassed all other contemporary legal systems in sophistication.

The papacy was an elective monarchy, but electoral procedures were a persistent problem. In 1059 an election decree had attempted to confine electoral participation to the cardinals but

had not specified how many votes were necessary for election. The twelfth and thirteenth centuries were thus filled with contested elections. In 1179 a council decreed that a two-thirds majority was required for election. One problem was solved, but another arose. Between 1241 and 1305, the papacy was vacant for almost ten years altogether, and once there was no pope for nearly three years. Groups of cardinals sometimes refused to show up for elections, or left Rome if events proceeded in a direction they disliked, or could not even get to Rome because of political struggles. In 1271 a *conclave* (shutting the cardinals in a room until they elected a pope) was used for the first time.

Who were the popes? Most of them were former cardinals with long experience in the government of the church. Many of the twelfth- and thirteenth-century popes were lawyers, which may explain, in part, their dedication to institutional and legal reforms. Not a single pope from this period has been canonized as a saint. One Englishman was elected; the rest were Roman, Italian, or French. Most were noblemen.

In Rome, the pope presided over the *curia,* the papal court. By the late twelfth century, the cardinals, who were increasingly drawn from all over Europe, were the key officers in that court. The cardinals headed the major branches of the papal administration and served as papal legates. In the thirteenth century these princes of the church began to wear their distinctive red hats. The curia presided over both financial and judicial institutions. Revenues came from the papal lands in Italy, from diverse fees from all over Europe, and from the pious offerings of pilgrims. The judicial institutions administered the rulings of the papal government, heard appeals for dispensations from the ordinary operations of canon law (such as requests for permission to marry from two persons who were closely related), and heard appeals against decisions made by local ecclesiastical courts.

The hearing of appeals from lower courts points to another growing area of activity by the papal government: control of the church throughout Europe. The pope and cardinals had numerous means to work their will. Beginning in 1123, the popes summoned a series of Lateran Councils, the largest since the councils of Late Antiquity. Now the great prelates of Europe met on a regular basis. "Papal provisions" enabled the pope to appoint bishops, and sometimes abbots, all over Europe. In the past, such officers had been elected locally and merely confirmed by Rome.

The Roman church also sharpened the tools that it used to make its will felt. Since the early days of Christianity, churchmen could excom-

municate a member of the faithful for some grievous offense. Separation from the sacraments of the church was always a serious punishment. In the Middle Ages, its severity increased because the excommunicated person was forbidden *all* social intercourse. Excommunication thus could be politically, socially, and economically disastrous. Another tool was the *interdict*—a decree that might be directed at a person but more often fell on a region. The interdict brought to a halt the celebration of most sacraments. Its aim was to generate a popular outcry for a particular outcome.

Gregory IX (r. 1227–1241) sought to bring a measure of order and legality to the process of identifying and punishing heretics. He began sending out teams of carefully trained inquisitors to take testimony according to precisely defined rules. The work of these inquisitors laid the foundation for the later courts of inquisition. In medieval society a person's religious faith was not a private matter of conscience but a public affair. The aim of the inquisitors was to reconcile the wayward, not to punish or execute them. The church could not administer corporal punishment or shed blood, so anyone found guilty in an inquisitorial proceeding was handed over to a secular court. Executions for heresy were comparatively rare.

This ever more bureaucratic and intrusive church related to the laity—to its members—in a variety of ways. The line between the clergy and the laity was drawn more sharply than ever before. Members of the clergy could not be notaries, secular lawyers, or doctors. Lay people were denied any right to preach, to expound on the Scriptures, or to stand in judgment of any offense that a cleric might commit. In the writings of thirteenth-century ecclesiastics, the word *church* usually referred to the institutional entity, to the clergy, and not, as before, to the body of all believers. Believers were expected to submit to the clergy in all respects, and effective institutions enforced their submission.

Ideology and institutions were important, but personalities mattered too. Innocent III (r. 1198–1216), for example, was the most powerful man ever to hold the papal office. He came from a minor Italian noble family, received early training in theology and law, and entered the papal administration while in his twenties. His entire life was dedicated to promoting the legal prerogatives of the papacy and the moral improvement of Christian society. As a young man Innocent wrote a book, *On the Contempt of the World,* in which he expressed his hope for a life of peace and private contemplation. As an older man he hurled legal thunderbolts at the greatest public figures of the day.

THE EVOLUTION OF CENTRAL GOVERNMENTS

The decade of the 1150s opened new opportunities all over Europe. In all of the major states of Europe the central governments increased in size, sophistication, and institutional effectiveness (see Map 8.1). This often meant that traditional nobilities lost power while obscure men rose to prominence in the service of kings. The growing competence of governments also brought up new problems in relations with the church. Governments found themselves needing more resources at a time when the great expansion of the eleventh and twelfth centuries began to slow.

France

The French king, Louis VII (r. 1137–1180), faced a single vassal, Henry II of England, who controlled more of France than he did (see page 184). Nevertheless, the French people increasingly dominated European culture. The First Crusade was widely seen as a French enterprise. The greatest twelfth-century monastic order, the Cistercian, was French. There were French quarters in almost all large towns outside France. The aristocracy of England conversed in French. French manners, style, and elegance were admired and emulated everywhere. The architecture that we know as Gothic was then called "the French style."

Louis VII and his son and successor, Philip II (r. 1180–1223)—usually called Philip Augustus—became masters at fomenting trouble in the vast continental holdings of Henry II of England, usually by setting the Angevin sons against their father and against one another. France's greatest gains came at the expense of King John of England. John (r. 1199–1216), son and successor to Henry II, was a vassal of the king of France for all of his father's vast continental holdings. He imprudently ran off with the fiancée of a French nobleman, who sued him in the court of Philip Augustus, feudal lord to them both. Philip summoned John to answer for his conduct. When John refused to answer the summons, Philip declared that his fiefs were "escheat"—that they were to revert to their lord. War ensued, and Philip won a resounding victory in 1204.

A decade later Philip confirmed his paramount position by defeating at Bouvines a joint attack on his kingdom by John and Otto IV of Germany, who were both trying to revive their sagging fortunes (see Map 8.1). French royal revenues at least doubled between 1180 and 1220. When Philip seized the Angevin lands, he did not give them to anyone as fiefs. To govern his new possessions, Philip extended, with some modifications, the old institutions of the royal demesne. Estates on the demesne had been governed by minor noblemen called *provosts,* but after 1204 non-noble officers called *bailiffs* became the overseers of the vastly expanded demesne. Bailiffs were often trained in law and were appointed for fixed terms.

Philip was succeeded briefly by his son, Louis VIII (r. 1223–1226). Louis VIII divided up some of the former Angevin lands into *apanages*—coherent blocks of land assigned to junior members of the royal family. In this way he kept land out of the hands of the nobility and provided resources and responsibility to persons who might otherwise be engaged in palace intrigue.

Louis IX (r. 1226–1270), known as "Saint Louis," ruled for more than four decades. It is worth remarking that the prestige of the Capetian dynasty was enough to produce a saint. Louis IX believed that the king's highest duty was the promotion of peace and justice. He revived the Carolingian practice of sending wandering officials around the kingdom to check on the work of the bailiffs. He also abolished serfdom and suppressed private warfare on royal lands. These reforms made people all over France look to the king rather than to local notables.

Before the reign of Louis VIII the French monarchy confined its activities to the regions north of the Loire River. Around the year 1200, however, the Cathar heresy in the south (see page 214) was attracting attention from outraged religious orders, and the papacy preached a crusade. The Crown refused to be distracted until it had defeated John and digested the Angevin lands, but Louis VIII and Louis IX, sensing political opportunities and religious duties, finally entered the fray. By the 1250s their forces had beaten the Albigensians—as the Cathars are usually called (the name derives from Albi, a Cathar stronghold; see Map 8.1). More important, the southeastern region of Langue d'Oc was taken over by the Crown. The Albigensian wars also served the kings of France by draining off some of the land-lust and violence of the nobility.

Saint Louis was succeeded by his son, Philip III (r. 1270–1285), and then by his famous grandson, Philip IV (r. 1285–1314), "the Fair." Philip IV began a series of dangerous military and diplomatic gambles to extend his power into Flanders and Gascony. His constant need for money to pay for his wars engendered resentment among various groups in France. He even resorted to seizing the property of the Jews of France and to repudiating his debts to Italian bankers. He died broke in 1314, but there was no reason to think that the impressive gains won by three centuries of Capetian policy would be lost. The kings of France were powerful and respected, and France was paramount in Europe.

England

When Henry II (r. 1154–1189) took the throne, he made it clear that he meant to rule England and also retain control of his vast continental inheritances. He sought to provide from the Angevin lands individual holdings for his four sons. The boys, however, abetted by their mother, Eleanor of Aquitaine, and by Louis VII and Philip II of France, plotted against their father and against one another. Henry never was able to unify law, institutions, economic practices, or culture in his far-flung "Angevin empire." Although he was first a French prince, and although he spent more time in France than in England, his greatest contributions were in his island kingdom.

By returning to the practices of the Norman kings and by innovating, Henry fashioned the institutions that turned England into the best-governed kingdom in Europe. Like his contemporaries, he used men of modest means but of great intelligence and careful training to staff government offices. He supported towns and the church in an effort to circumvent the nobility and to expand centers of royal influence. Henry increased both the size and the competence of the English government. He carried out two great inquests, one of knight's service and one of sheriffs. The latter resulted in the replacement of many of England's sheriffs, the key royal officers in the shires, with men who were more loyal to the king. It was from about this time that the Robin Hood stories arose, with their evocation of the evil, heartless sheriff of Nottingham. In fact, the sheriffs were neither more nor less evil than other men. They were just effective in doing the king's business.

Henry used judicial institutions to expand the central government. His objectives were to bring as much judicial activity as possible into royal courts and to diminish the role of the nobles. The justice dispensed in Henry's courts was swift and fair, and his courts were popular. Those who felt abused by powerful noble neighbors discovered that they could get real justice through recourse to royal courts. A common law began to grow up throughout the country. No other realm in Europe advanced so far so early on the road to legal unification.

Henry II also desired to bring "criminous clerks"—members of the clergy who had committed crimes—into the royal courts. This policy brought protest from Thomas Becket (ca.

1118–1170), the archbishop of Canterbury. Thomas had served loyally as Henry's chancellor (chief royal official) from 1155 to 1162, when the king instigated his election to Canterbury to attempt to gain tighter control over the church. As archbishop, however, Thomas held that only clergy could judge other clerics. When in 1164 Henry passed regulations on criminous clerks, the archbishop fled to France. Upon returning to England in 1170 after reconciliation with Henry, Thomas was murdered before the altar of his cathedral by four knights who thought they were doing the king's bidding. Becket was soon canonized as a saint, and Henry had to back down. The church was still powerful enough to defeat any attempt to diminish its prerogatives.

In 1189 Henry's charismatic, crusading son, Richard "the Lionhearted," became king and proved—in an ironic way—the strength of the foundations that his father had laid. Richard (r. 1189–1199) resided less than ten months in England during his ten-year reign. Mainly, he spent his time in France struggling with Philip II and going on the Third Crusade. Back in England the system put into place by Henry II functioned well in Richard's absence.

When John (r. 1199–1216) succeeded his brother Richard, he inherited some problems and created many of his own. Many English nobles were angry at having been circumvented by Henry II. The royal treasury was empty. A king's ransom, literally, had been raised to redeem Richard, who had been kidnapped on his way home from the Third Crusade.

The loss of Normandy in 1204 (see page 205) was a financial and moral disaster, but John managed to forge an alliance with Otto IV of Germany. The two rulers planned to attack and divide France. As we have seen, Philip Augustus defeated them, and John was humiliated yet again. What really got him in trouble, though, was his refusal to accept Pope Innocent's candidate for the archbishopric of Canterbury. The pope placed England under interdict and excommunicated John. John capitulated.

In June 1215 some English barons, supported by townspeople and members of the clergy,

forced John to sign the Magna Carta, the "Great Charter" (the "great" referring to its large size). Its sixty-three clauses spelled out in traditional ways royal prerogatives vis-à-vis vassals, towns, the church, and courts of law. The barons were trying to get the king to admit that he had to obey certain rules. Magna Carta's central premise was that everyone, even the king, was under the law.

Under John's son, Henry III (r. 1216–1272), and grandson, Edward I (r. 1272–1307), disputes over money and power in England repeatedly erupted between the king, the nobles, and the people. Until 1295, however, there was no mechanism for the arbitration of disputes. As early as 1236 a meeting of the English royal council was called a *Parliament,* from a French word that means "talking together." As yet this Parliament had no defined role, no procedures, no fixed membership, and no set times for meetings. The kings saw it as something of a rubber stamp. The barons viewed it as a means of controlling royal excess. The knights and townsmen thought they had gained a means of making permanent the loose alliance that they had enjoyed with the Crown since the twelfth century. The political quarrels of the thirteenth century had resulted in the creation of an institution that would eventually become dominant in the governance of England.

Spain

By around 1150 the Reconquista in Spain had stalled, not to resume until the early thirteenth century, when Pope Innocent III stirred up crusading zeal. The pope lent encouragement to clerics and nobles in Spain who wished to reopen hostilities against the Muslims. In 1212 a combined Castilian-Aragonese army won a decisive victory at Las Navas de Tolosa, south of Toledo (see Map 8.1). The victory of Las Navas de Tolosa was a turning point in Spanish history. The outcome of the Reconquista, which did not conclude until the fifteenth century, was never again in doubt.

In the thirteenth century Spain produced great kings, especially James I of Aragon (r.

Alfonso X "the Wise" The Spanish king, depicted here in a thirteenth-century manuscript from Spain, is judging his Muslim and Christian subjects. Alfonso's reputation for impartiality was important in his culturally diverse realm. *(El Escorial/Laurie Platt Winfrey, Inc.)*

1213–1276) and Ferdinand III (r. 1217–1252) and Alfonso X (r. 1252–1284) of Castile. These rulers were pious men, genuinely inspired by the ideal of the Crusades and zealous in the promotion of the church. They were also hard-headed rulers. James turned Aragon-Catalonia into the greatest naval power of the western Mediterranean and a formidable economic power, too. Ferdinand and Alfonso derived great prestige from their successful wars. Those wars also provided a flow of booty and a supply of lands to reward the Castilian nobles who spent their energy on the frontier, rather than using it to attack the king. Strong central institutions were created. Alfonso issued a major law book, the *Siete Partidas*, for the whole of Castile. These laws were based on Roman law and emphasized royal power. The *Cortes*, a representative assembly made up primarily of urban notables, began forging an alliance between the king and the towns. Spain was not united in

the thirteenth century, but it had evolved into four coherent blocks: a small Muslim region in Valencia and Granada and three vibrant kingdoms centered on Portugal, Castile, and Aragon.

Italy

Frederick Barbarossa's defeat at Legnano in 1176 and the Peace of Constance in 1183 left the Italian cities free to continue their distinctive political evolution. Although each Italian commune constituted an entity unto itself, a fairly coherent evolution is evident. By the late twelfth century, the consular communes were still governed by oligarchies of men whose wealth and power came from land, trade, and industry, but ordinary workers began to clamor for participation. The communes became increasingly volatile and violent.

One solution to this potential crisis was the introduction of the *podestà*, a sort of city manager chosen by the local oligarchy. The podestà often came from the outside, served for a set period (usually six months or one year), and underwent a careful scrutiny at the conclusion of his term. He was expected to be competent not only at ordinary administration but also at military leadership, so that he could police the city as well as defend it. He brought with him a group of seasoned officials as subordinates. Normally, he could not be a property owner in the town, marry into local society, or dine privately with any citizen. It is ironic that the Italian cities that had been feudal or episcopal principalities before the rise of the communes passed through a republican phase of wider and wider political participation, only to wind up under single rulers again.

Russia

In 1150, Russia's future was hard to predict. From their capital at Kiev, Russia's rulers had made some headway against both lawless nobles and the raids of frontier peoples. A flourishing church, deeply influenced by Byzantium, contributed to Russian unity. Commerce prospered.

In the early thirteenth century Russia faced a grave new threat from the Mongols. These were a loose coalition of pastoral nomads from Mongolia and Turkic soldiers. The charismatic leader Jenghiz Khan (1154–1227) turned the Mongols into an invincible fighting force, and he eventually built an empire reaching from China's frontier to Germany's. (See the box "Encounters with the West: William of Rubruck Reports on the Mongols.")

In 1221, the Mongols attacked Suzdal, and in 1240 they sacked Kiev (see Map 8.1). Jenghiz Khan died in 1227, and his successors divided his vast empire into several khanates. One of these, called the "Golden Horde" (from the splendid tent in which the khan presided), dominated Russia until the fifteenth century. The Mongols granted the Russians considerable local autonomy, but they demanded heavy taxes and occasionally carried out brutal raids to remind the Russians who was in control. Taxes fell most heavily on Russian peasants, who saw their status decline while that of Western peasants was rising. The Mongols also dominated trade and produced a weakening of both urbanization and the merchant classes.

A lasting consequence of the Mongol attack was the definitive shift of Russia's political center of gravity from Kiev and Suzdal to Moscow, a town far to the north and blanketed by deep forests, which afforded some protection from the Mongols. Centuries of Mongol domination initiated Russia's subsequently ambivalent relations with both Europe and Asia.

ECONOMIC LIFE

In 1150 the European economy was in full expansion. By 1300 that expansion had begun to moderate and, in some areas, to reverse. Decline, however, is not the central theme of economic life in this period. It is more accurate to speak of innovation and adaptation. Urban dynamism supplanted rural creativity. Economic institutions in Europe grew more complex, interdependent, and sophisticated.

The Roles of Cities and Towns

Although the vast majority of people still lived in the country, cities were growing as never before. Growth occurred in Bruges and Ghent, and in Paris, London, and other cities that were evolving into national capitals.

Cities were becoming centers for many activities. Governments, which required larger and larger staffs of trained personnel, settled in towns, even when kings continued to ride about the countryside or go off on crusade. Schools and eventually universities were urban institutions. Mercantile, industrial, and legal organizations were based in towns. Ecclesiastical organization was always urban based. Towns began to compete with royal and aristocratic courts as literary centers, and cathedrals, the great buildings of the age, were exclusively urban.

~ **ENCOUNTERS WITH THE WEST** ~

William of Rubruck Reports on the Mongols

The papacy tried to convert the Mongols to Catholicism in hopes of using them in a grand crusade against the Muslims. Here are extracts from the report of William of Rubruck, a Franciscan missionary, who visited the khan Baatu, the grandson of Jenghiz Khan and the founder of the Golden Horde, between 1253 and 1255. It is interesting to compare William's impressions with the boxes "A Roman View of the Huns" (page 129) and "Furnishings of a Welsh Household" (page 177).

The dwelling in which they sleep has as its base a circle of interlaced sticks, and is made of the same material; these sticks converge into a little circle at the top and from this a neck juts up like a chimney; they cover it with white felt . . . the felt around the top they decorate with lovely and varied paintings. Before the doorway they also hang felt worked in multicolored designs. . . . The married women make for themselves really beautiful carts. . . . A wealthy Mongol may well have a hundred such carts with chests. Baatu has twenty-six wives and each of these has a large house . . . belonging to each house a good two hundred carts. When they pitch their houses the wife places her dwelling at the extreme west end and after her the others according to their rank, so that the last wife will be at the far east end, and there will be the space of a stone's throw between the establishment of one wife and another. . . . The camp of a rich Mongol will look like a large town and yet there will be very few men in it. One woman will drive twenty or thirty carts, for the country is flat. They tie together the carts, which are drawn by oxen or camels, one after the other, and the woman will sit on the front one driving the ox. . . . When they have pitched their houses with the door facing south, they arrange the master's couch at the northern end. The women's place is always on the east side . . . and the men's place is on the west side. On entering the house the men would by no means hang up their quivers in the women's section. Over the head of the master there is always an idol like a doll or little image of felt which they call the master's brother, and a similar one over the head of the mistress, and this they call the mistress's brother. . . . In the winter they make an excellent drink from rice, millet, wheat, and honey . . . in the summer they do not bother about anything but *cosmos* [fermented mare's milk]. *Cosmos* is always to be found inside the house before the entrance door, and near it stands a musician with his instruments. Our lutes and viols I did not see but many other instruments that are not known among us. When the master begins to drink, then one of his attendants cries out in a loud voice "Ha!" and the musician strikes his instrument. When it is a big feast they are holding they all clap their hands and also dance to the sound of the instrument, the men before the master and the women before the mistress. . . . Then they drink all around, the men and the women, and sometimes they vie with each other in drinking in a really disgusting and gluttonous manner. . . .

Source: Christopher Dawson, ed., *The Mongol Mission* (New York: Sheed and Ward, 1953), pp. 93–98, 103–104, passim. Reprinted by permission of Sheed and Ward.

One distinctive urban phenomenon was the rise of guilds. In 1200, for example, Paris had one guild of merchants and four or five craft or trade associations. By 1292 the city had 130 craft or trade guilds. The guilds were meant to regulate standards of production, to fix prices, and to control membership in their respective trades. As towns grew larger and more impersonal, these associations of people engaged in similar occupations fostered a feeling of community. Members tended to live in the same areas and to worship together in a parish church. Growing wealth in general, coupled with fierce local pride, produced building competitions whose results are still visible in the huge neighborhood churches that survive in most European towns. The guilds indulged in elaborate festivals and celebrations, which sometimes turned into drunken debauches. The guilds were also mutual assurance societies. They saw to the funeral expenses of members and provided for widows and orphans.

The guilds played important roles in the political life of the towns. The older merchant guilds counted in their membership the urban elite. The newer craft guilds incorporated the workers in the industries that were growing up in cities. The former group had erected the first communes and reserved communal magistracies and council spots for itself. From the late twelfth century, masters in the craft guilds, or their elected representatives, began to demand positions on the city councils. Guilds thus contributed simultaneously to stability and to tension in cities.

The guilds had a damaging impact on women. As more economic activity came under the umbrella of the guild structures, women were more systematically excluded from guild membership. Usually women could become guild members only as wives or widows and could not open economic enterprises of their own.

Commercial Growth and Innovation

Towns were focal points in commercial networks. The basic trade routes and networks had existed since Carolingian times, but a novelty of the twelfth century was the emergence of the Champagne fairs as a meeting point for the commerce of north and south (see Map 8.1). Since the early Middle Ages there had been permanent fairs in a few locations and occasional fairs in many places. By 1150, however, the spices, silks, and dyes of the Mediterranean, the wool of England, the furs and linens of Germany, and the leather products of Spain began to be sold in a series of six fairs in the Champagne region of France that lasted seven weeks each from the spring to the autumn.

Because overland trade was so expensive, often multiplying the cost of goods tenfold, transport by water was preferred wherever possible. The stern rudder, better sails, the compass (in use by 1180), and better navigational charts facilitated sea travel, as did the growing use of larger ships. An Italian fleet sailed to Flanders in 1277, and within a few years the old overland trade routes, and with them the Champagne fairs, began a decline that was not reversed until the invention of the railroad in the nineteenth century.

Changing Economic Attitudes

As medieval society generated more wealth and populations concentrated in cities, people who were relatively well-off became more conscious of those who were less fortunate. Moralists began to argue that the poor were a special gift of God to the rich, who could redeem their own souls by generous charitable benefactions. Most towns established schemes of poor relief. But the numbers of poor people grew more rapidly than the support, particularly in large towns. Some hospitals began to refuse abandoned babies for fear that they would be deluged with them.

Efforts to alleviate the condition of the poor constituted one ethical concern of medieval thinkers, but two issues attracted even more attention. First, theologians and lawyers alike discussed the "just price," the price at which goods should be bought and sold. Christian teaching had long held that it was immoral to hoard food during a famine or knowingly to sell a damaged item. But what was the correct price in ordinary circumstances? A theological view, often dismissed as unrealistic, held that items could be sold for only the cost of the materials and the labor absolutely necessary to produce them. A commercial view, often dismissed as immoral, insisted that a fair price was whatever the market would bear, regardless of consequences. A working consensus held that a just price was one arrived at by bargaining between free and knowledgeable parties.

The other ethical issue concerned *usury*, the lending of money at interest. Christian writers were always hostile to commercial enterprise, and they had plenty of scriptural warrant for their view. Psalm 15 warned that no one can be blameless "who lends his money at usury." The Gospel According to Luke actually forbade the profit that makes most commercial enterprises possible. In the twelfth century, as churchmen began to be much more assiduous in their condemnations of usury, some remarkably inventive ways to get around the prohibitions emerged. One person might agree to sell another person an item at a certain price and then buy it back on a fixed date at a higher price. Exchange rates between currencies could be manipulated to mask usurious transactions. Some thinkers began to defend usury on the grounds that a person deserved to be compensated for the risks incurred by lending money. Theologians continued to treat all credit mechanisms as evidence of man's sinfulness. Still, fueled by the expansion of the European economy, individual profit began to be placed alongside community interest at the heart of social and economic thought.

SOCIAL AND RELIGIOUS MOVEMENTS

Twelfth- and thirteenth-century Europe witnessed several social movements unlike any that had occurred before. Spurred by increasingly intrusive governments, economic dislocation, and spiritual turmoil, they involved large numbers of people; cut across lines of gender, wealth, status, and occupation; and appeared in many places. Most of these movements had cohesive beliefs and well-determined goals. They are the first large-scale social movements in European history.

Reform from Within

Traditional monastic orders continued to win adherents, but new religious movements were being created by and for the laity. The novelty of these movements was especially meaningful for women, who suddenly had considerable opportunities to devote their lives to piety, study, and a cause. In the past such opportunities were severely limited. There was only one Cluniac house for women, and the Cistercians struggled to keep women out of their ranks. The wandering preachers of the twelfth century without exception acquired women as followers, but the usual results were either segregation of the women in cloisters or condemnation of the whole movement. In general, these reformers aimed to preach, to be poor, and to create formal but noncloistered religious orders. They submitted willingly to ecclesiastical authority.

The phenomenon began when Francis of Assisi (1181–1226), the son of a rich Italian merchant, decided to renounce the wealth and status that were his birthright. Francis had gradually grown tired of a life of ease and luxury, but he also experienced a blinding moment of spiritual insight when, by chance, his eyes fell on the passage in the Scriptures where Christ said, "Go, sell all you have, and follow me."

For a few years Francis wandered about Italy begging for his meager sustenance, repairing churches, caring for the sick, and preaching repentance to all who would listen. By 1210 he had attracted many followers, and together they set out to ask approval of Innocent III. After considering the matter for a while, Innocent decided to approve the new order of *friars* (that is, "brothers," from the Latin *fratres*) as long as they would accept monastic *tonsure* (a ritual haircut signifying submission), profess obedience to the pope, and swear obedience to Francis. The pope was genuinely won over by Francis himself, but he also sensed that by permitting the formation of the Franciscan order he could create a legitimate

Francis and Clare of Assisi
This beautiful, moving Gothic painting by Giotto (late thirteenth century) depicts Francis's funeral cortege passing by Clare's church of San Damiano. *(Scala/Art Resource, NY)*

and controllable repository for the explosive spiritual forces of the age. Along with another major new religious group, the Dominicans (see page 215), the Franciscan order provided zealous Christians with a pious, sanctioned alternative to joining the traditional church hierarchy.

In 1212, Francis attracted the aristocrat Clare of Assisi (1194–1253). She was eighteen and fleeing from an arranged marriage. She wanted to live the friars' life of poverty and preaching. Aware that the sight of women begging or preaching would be shocking, in 1215 Francis gave Clare and his other female followers their own rule. Clare became abbess of the first community of the "Poor Clares." Although cloistered and forbidden to preach, the Clares, or Sisters of

Saint Francis, lived lives of exemplary austerity and attracted many adherents.

Another important movement was that of the Beguines. Beguines were communities of women who lived together, devoted themselves to charitable works, but did not take vows as nuns. The Beguine movement grew from the work in Nivelles, near Liège (see Map 8.1), of Mary of Oignies (ca. 1177–1213). She renounced her marriage, gave away all her goods, worked for a while in a leper colony, and thought of preaching against the Cathars. Instead she formed a community.

Groups of Beguines appeared all over the Low Countries, western Germany, and northern France. This was the first exclusively women's movement in the history of Christianity. Beguines sometimes vowed poverty and sometimes did not. They sometimes cloistered themselves into communities and sometimes taught and served the poor and outcast. They neither challenged the officials and teachings of the church nor demanded a right to preach. As laywomen, they did not give rise to scandal as noncloistered nuns would have. They had no power in the outside world, but at least they had control over their own lives and communities.

Thirteenth-century Europe knew more female than male mystics, and female mysticism tended to focus on Jesus, especially on his presence in the Eucharist. Most of the mystics were either nuns or Beguines. Indeed, this is the first religious devotion that can be shown to have been more common to women than to men. As the clergy was defining its own prerogatives more tightly, and excluding women more completely from the exercise of formal public power, female communities provided a different locus for women's activity.

Women who spent their lives in community with other women reveal, in their writings and in writings about them, great moral and intellectual strength and self-confidence. Women understood to be in direct spiritual communion with God acquired, as teachers, mediators, and counselors in their communities, power that they simply could not have had outside those settings.

Heretics and Dissidents

Unity of belief was crucial in a Catholic ("universal") Christian Europe. In the twelfth century, the church reacted ever more strictly to challenges to its teachings or to its exclusive right to teach. The effort by the church to define its law, theology, and bureaucratic procedures with greater precision drew lines more sharply than ever before between what was and was not acceptable.

Heretics did not see themselves as secessionists from the true church. They saw themselves as its only representatives. Church teachings always encountered a degree of popular skepticism. Not everyone believed, for example, that Jesus was born of a virgin or that he was true God and true man. But such doubts had not previously led to mass defections. Before about 1150, challenges to the church came from people who saw themselves as inspired reformers. Some criticized the wealth and immorality of the clergy while others attacked the priesthood itself and the sacraments.

Coherent movements of much larger proportions emerged later in the century. In 1173, Waldo, a rich merchant of Lyon, decided to sell all his property, give the proceeds to the poor, and embrace a life of poverty and preaching. Waldo was motivated by the same quest for the apostolic life that had animated the eremitical movement of the eleventh century. But there was a difference: He was a layman. Waldo attracted many followers, men and women known as Waldensians, and in 1179 Pope Alexander III (r. 1159–1181) approved his vow of poverty. But the pope commanded Waldo to preach only when invited to do so by bishops. The bishops extended no such invitations.

Waldo and his "Poor Men of Lyon" went right on preaching and in 1184 were formally declared heretics. Until this point it was not their ideas so much as their appropriation of a clerical duty, preaching, that had gotten them into trouble. From this time on, however, the Waldensians became more radical in their attacks on the church. They spread all over southern France and Italy, into Germany, and as far away as Poland. Waldensian communities exist to this day.

The most serious of the popular heretical movements was Catharism (from the Greek *katharos,* meaning "pure"); as noted earlier, the movement is also sometimes called "Albigensian." There were Cathars all over Europe, although they clustered in northern Italy and southern France. Cathars were the religious descendants of Mani, a third-century Persian who explained life as a collection of polarities: good-evil, love-hate, flesh-spirit. Extreme Cathars abstained from flesh in all ways. They were vegetarians and renounced sexual intercourse so as not to produce offspring— that is, more flesh. Albigensians were staunchly opposed to the clergy of their day, seeing them as rich and corrupt. Probably radiating from Bulgaria, Cathar ideas had spread widely in the West by the 1140s. People of every station joined the new church, which, in its own view, was the only true church.

The Albigensians, like a number of other heretical sects, attracted many women. Unlike the Catholic church, which denied clerical, preaching, and teaching offices to women, the heretical sects tended to permit women to hold leading roles. With the Cathars, women had access to the highest positions in the group's hierarchy.

The Catholic church sent isolated preachers against the Cathars, but with little success. In 1198 and 1203, Pope Innocent III organized systematic preaching tours in southern France; but these too lacked solid results, and in 1208 the pope's legate was murdered by a supporter of the count of Toulouse, who was sympathetic to the Cathars. The killing led to the launching of the Albigensian Crusade, a loosely structured movement that lasted into the 1260s. Although the crusade itself was largely over by the 1220s, there was a massacre of Albigensians in 1244 and inquisitorial campaigns in 1246 and again in 1256–1257. Isolated resisters struggled on into the fourteenth century.

Less bloody approaches to the heretics spawned movements of their own. Dominic de Guzman (1170–1221), a priest and the son of a Spanish nobleman, went to Rome in 1206 to seek permission to preach against the heretics. Albigensian criticisms of the clergy could never be applied to Dominic and his fellow preachers because of their poverty and self-denial. In 1215, Dominic attempted to form a new order, but by that time Rome had forbidden the creation of new orders for fear of uncontrollable diversity. Thus, Dominic's "Order of Preachers" (the proper name for the Dominicans) adopted the Rule of Saint Augustine, which many communities had been using since the eleventh century. The Dominicans decided to disperse, some going to Paris, some (including Dominic) to Rome, some to other cities in Europe. Henceforth, the order saw its mission as serving the whole church. Dominican schools were set up all over Europe, and the order acquired a reputation for learning and scholarship.

The Franciscans, the "Poor Clares," the Beguines, and the Dominicans each reflected the widespread desire to emulate the apostolic life of the early church, and each submitted to legitimate authority. Albigensians and Waldensians, by contrast, did not seek to reform the Catholic church from within but departed from it or insisted that they alone represented it. These heretical movements marked the first serious challenge to the ideology of a uniformly Catholic Christendom.

The Later Crusades

The factors that produced the First Crusade— papal leadership, a more militant Christianity, religious zeal, surplus soldiers, a spirit of adventure—persisted throughout the thirteenth century. Crusading continued to be a popular social movement. Men from all over Europe and every social class participated in the Crusades. By 1300, however, the energies long channeled into crusading were being diverted elsewhere, though there was still talk of crusading in Europe even after 1500 (Map 8.2).

Crusading was intended to protect the Holy Land and keep open the pilgrim routes to Jerusalem. The creation of the small crusader states in the hostile environment of Syria and Palestine had made continued crusading almost inevitable. In 1144 the tiny crusader state at Edessa on the Armenian frontier fell to a Muslim army. Although the news saddened Europeans, it took the efforts of the pope and Bernard of Clairvaux to launch another crusade. They persuaded Conrad III of Germany and Louis VII of France to lead it, but neither would submit to the other's leadership, and the Second Crusade accomplished little. Its one achievement was an accident. In 1147 an army of English, French, and Flemish soldiers who were proceeding to the Holy Land by sea put in on the Iberian coast and captured Lisbon. This opened a new front in the Reconquista and laid the foundations for the later kingdom of Portugal.

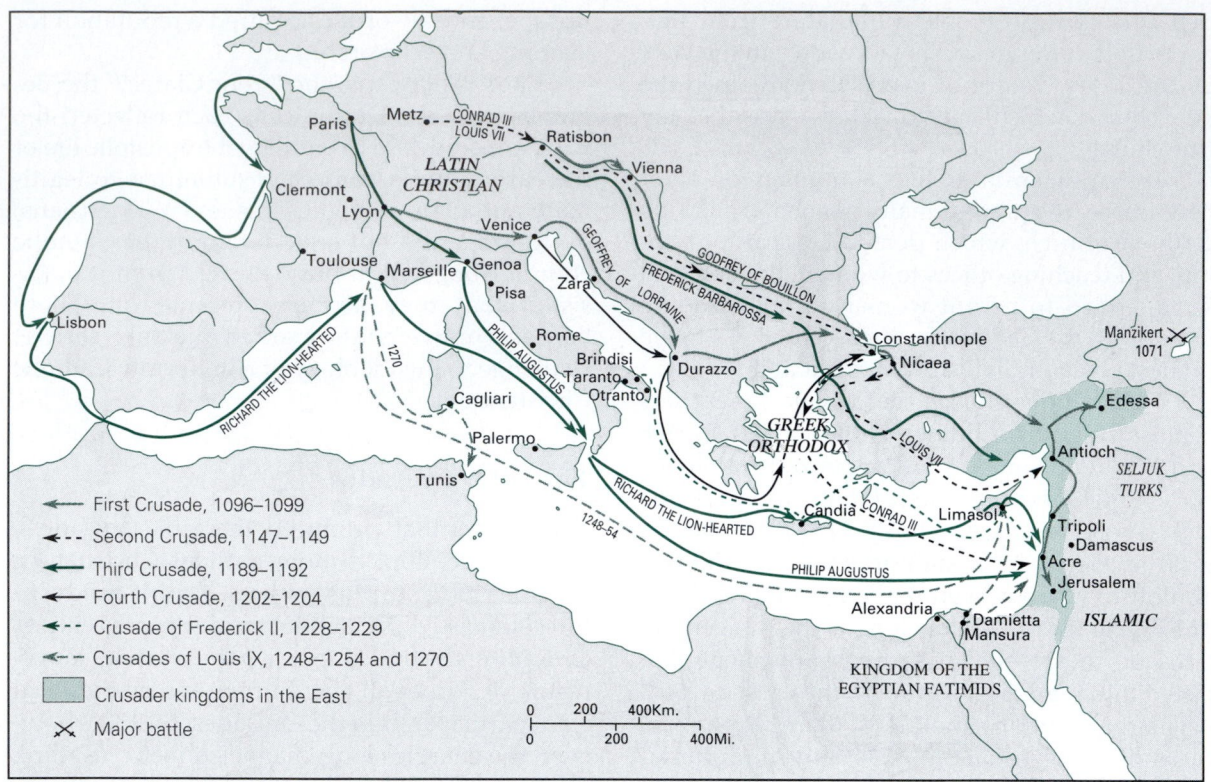

Map 8.2 The Crusades, 1095–1270 The long Western European interest in securing the Holy Land is illustrated by the repeated Crusades. Note the numerous routes taken, lands traversed, destinations attained, and points of cultural encounter.

The papacy called for the Third Crusade when Saladin (1138–1193), a powerful local leader typical of the disintegrating Abbassid caliphate, captured Jerusalem in 1187. The greatest crowned heads of the day—Frederick Barbarossa, Philip II, and Richard the Lionhearted—answered the call, but only Frederick did so enthusiastically. He died en route in 1190. Richard and Philip each went home soon after, and this crusade merely won access to Jerusalem for pilgrims.

Disappointed with the results of the Third Crusade, Innocent III began calling for another immediately on his election in 1198. Popular preachers summoned an army, once again largely French, and the pope and the Fourth Crusade's military leaders engaged the Venetians to construct a fleet of war and transport ships. In less than eighteen months they produced 50 galleys and 450 transports, a tribute to the awesome capabilities of the Venetian shipyards. Ships, however, were expensive. When too few Crusaders and too little money appeared, the Venetians suggested that the Crusaders could discharge some of their debt by recapturing from the Hungarians the formerly Venetian port of Zara (see Map 8.2). This idea outraged the pope, but he could do little about it. Then into the camp of the Crusaders came a pretender to the Byzantine throne, who promised that if the Crusaders would help him to claim his patrimony, he would contribute to the cost of the crusade. The Venetians urged the Crusaders to accept this offer, and, to the horror of Innocent III, the Fourth Crusade (1202–1204) turned to Constantinople.

Once in Constantinople, the Crusaders learned that their new ally had few friends in the Byzantine capital. The Venetians saw an opportunity to expand their commercial presence in the East, and the soldiers welcomed a chance to plunder the Mediterranean's greatest city and to avenge what they regarded as a century of Byzantine treachery. Thus, the Fourth Crusade captured not Jerusalem but Constantinople.

In later decades, popes began to take a more active role in planning Crusades. No pope wanted to lose control of a crusade as Innocent had done, and all popes saw that the liberation of Jerusalem required a solid base of operations in the eastern Mediterranean. Egypt was the objective of the Fifth Crusade (1218–1221)—when Saint Francis visited the sultan—and the Sixth Crusade (1248–1250). Despite a few victories, the Crusaders could not win a secure base. No further crusades to the East were organized in the thirteenth century. In 1291 Acre, the last Crusader stronghold, fell and the original crusading era ended.

A balance sheet for the crusading movement as a whole reveals more losses than gains. The Crusades exported many violent men from Europe, but it is not clear that Europe became a less violent place. Relations between Christian Europe and the Muslim world grew more bitter as a result of the Crusades. The Fourth Crusade mortally wounded Byzantium and worsened the already tense relations between the Catholic and Orthodox churches. Crusading zeal was directed deliberately against heretics and coincidentally against Jews. The Crusades did not create anti-Semitism, but they worsened it. Some women, particularly in France, from which the majority of all Crusaders came, may have enjoyed momentary benefits in terms of control of land, wealth, and people while their husbands were away. But the long-term trend in feudal society was disadvantageous to women, and the Crusades did not change that. Finally, the Crusades may have done as much to disrupt Mediterranean trade as to promote it. That a single new product, the apricot, entered Europe in the crusading era seems small recompense for such huge effort.

THE HEIGHT OF MEDIEVAL CULTURE

Between 1150 and 1300, theologians grappled with the totality of divine and human wisdom, architects in the new Gothic style created some of the world's most beautiful buildings, and Dante Alighieri wrote poetry of unmatched spiritual power and linguistic beauty. Universities, the new academic institutions that adorned some of Europe's major cities, brought unprecedented rigor and precision to intellectual life. Traditional Latin letters reached new heights of erudition, and the vernacular languages brought forth countless original and inspiring works.

The University

In the early decades of the twelfth century, students gathered wherever there were famous teachers. Such teachers—figures like Peter Abelard (see page 190)—clustered in a few centers, and the students congregated there as well. The last decades of the twelfth century saw a swarm of masters and students in Paris. Like members of secular guilds, the masters organized. They did so because they wanted to regulate the curriculum that students followed and to prescribe the requirements for entry into their own ranks. They also desired to set the fees to be charged for instruction. The University of Paris was the result of their efforts. By 1300 there were universities elsewhere in France, as well as in Italy, England, and western Germany.

In Bologna, the university developed a little differently. Here the students came primarily to study law, after acquiring a basic education elsewhere. These law students were usually older and more affluent than students elsewhere, and foreign to Bologna. Consequently, in Bologna the university arose from a guild of students who united to set standards in fees and studies and to protect themselves against unscrupulous masters.

Universities were known for certain specializations: Paris for arts and theology, Bologna for law, Salerno in Italy and Montpellier in France for medicine, Oxford for mathematical and scientific subjects. Still, the basic course of study was similar. The arts course, which was the prerequisite to all higher faculties, usually lasted from four to six years. The bachelor's degree was a license to teach, but to teach in a university one needed a master's degree. The master's degree required at least eight years of study (including the baccalaureate years), which culminated in a public, oral examination. A doctorate in theology, law, or medicine required ten to fifteen years of study.

In many ways, students were always foreigners. Although their presence in a town enhanced its prestige, townspeople charged them exorbitant prices for food and rent. For their part, students often earned the ire of the townspeople for fighting, drinking, and general carousing. England's Oxford and Cambridge were unique in always having residential colleges for students; Paris got one later. Typically, students were on their own.

Studies were difficult. The arts curriculum demanded a thorough acquaintance with all the famous texts of grammar, logic, and rhetoric. Higher studies added more of Aristotle, particularly his philosophical writings. In theology, the students had to master the Scriptures, the principal biblical commentaries from patristic times to the present, and the *Book of Sentences,* a theology textbook (ca. 1160) by the Italian Peter Lombard. In medicine, Arab texts supplemented the ancient writings of Galen and Hippocrates.

The basic method of teaching consisted of the recitation by the teacher of a short piece of a set text, followed by the presentation and discussion of many authoritative commentaries on that text, and concluded by the explanations of the teacher himself. This education focused on standard books and received opinions and required students to remember large amounts of material. The curriculum nevertheless produced thinkers of prodigious originality.

In principle, universities were open to all males, but in practice they were restricted to those who had the means to attend them. Women were not accepted at universities, either as students or as teachers. Women were furthermore denied entry into the learned professions of theology, law, and medicine, despite the fact that many rural and some urban medical practitioners were women. It was common for women to possess and transmit massive knowledge of remedies. For example, Trotula of Salerno, who probably lived in the twelfth century, wrote a learned treatise, *On the Diseases of Women*. Naples documents record the names of twenty-four women surgeons between 1273 and 1410. How these women were educated is not known.

Scholasticism

Scholasticism, the intellectual outlook of the medieval schools, was the product of several related forces. Most important was the Christian tradition. Other forces were the quickening pace of intellectual life occasioned by Latin Europe's encounter with the worlds of Arab and Jewish learning in the era of the Crusades; the need to reconcile natural philosophy, or the claims of reason, with revealed religion, or the realm of faith; and the style of intellectual life that resulted from the twelfth-century fascination with logic.

By 1150 the Christian tradition had a well-defined set of basic sources—the Scriptures and the authoritative commentators—and two different approaches to the sources. One approach was to rely on divine inspiration. This approach to the biblical text was often learned and tended toward the allegorical (a literary device in which abstract ideas are represented by characters or other concrete forms). The other approach was more concrete and rationalistic and got a potent impetus from the development of logical studies in the twelfth century. The old intellectual struggle within Christian circles between faith and reason was made more acute by the dawning awareness of just how much the ancient Greeks had actually written and by the simultaneous discovery that Arab and Jewish scholars were also struggling to come to grips with that intellectual heritage.

Aristotle had taught that the universe was eternal and mechanistic. In his thinking there was no room for creation or for a benevolent deity who intervened to alter the course of events.

Greek science, so obviously right about many things, seemed in this area to contradict fundamental Christian teachings. Also, Christians were aware that some Arab and Jewish thinkers looked at natural philosophy and suggested that the Quran and the Hebrew Scriptures contained only approximations to truth. Were the Scriptures true?

The answer of Thomas Aquinas (1225–1274) seemed most effectively to respond to the question. A Dominican friar, Thomas was educated at Naples, Cologne, and Paris. Apart from brief service at the papal court, he spent the years after 1252 teaching and writing in Paris. Of his many works, the two most famous are the *Summa Contra Gentiles* and the *Summa Theologiae*. No one before Thomas had so rigorously followed the dialectical method of reasoning through the whole of a field of knowledge, not just a particular problem. For thousands of pages, he poses a question, suggests answers, confronts the answers with objections, refutes the objections, and then draws a conclusion. Then he repeats the process. Thomas carefully distinguished between two kinds of truths. On the one hand were *natural truths*, truths (even theological ones) that anyone can know according to Thomas—for example, that God exists. On the other hand were *revealed truths*, truths that can be known only through faith in God's revelation—for example, the Trinity or the incarnation of Christ. Thomas maintained that natural and revealed truths simply could not contradict one another because God was ultimately the source of both. If natural truth—for example, Aristotle's contention that the world was eternal—appeared to contradict a revealed truth, then Aristotle was wrong. Thomas was accused by some contemporaries of applying reason too widely, and after his death some of his ideas were condemned by the church. But he actually steered a middle path between intellectual extremes.

The Gothic Image

Gothic art and architecture emerged just as the West was absorbing the recovery of Euclid's mathematical writings and everywhere applying the intensely ordered logic of Aristotle. One of the most familiar images of the Middle Ages is the inspiring beauty of the Gothic cathedral. It is thus ironic that the word *Gothic* first appeared in the sixteenth century as a term of derision for what was then regarded as an outmoded style so ugly that only the horrible conquerors of Rome, the Goths, could have been responsible for it. The name stuck, but today it simply identifies a period in European architecture, sculpture, and painting that lasted from the middle of the twelfth century to the early sixteenth century.

Gothic is a French invention. It was Abbot Suger (1085–1151) of St.-Denis, a monastery outside Paris, who, in rebuilding his basilica beginning in 1135, consciously sought a new style. He desired to achieve effects of lightness, almost weightlessness, in the stonework of his church and to admit large amounts of light to create a dazzling and mysterious aura on the inside. Suger combined a number of elements that had long existed and produced something original (Figure 8.1). A *pointed arch* permits the joining of two arches of identical height but different widths, which, in turn, permits complex shapes and sizes.

Figure 8.1 The Structure of Gothic Architecture The adoption of pointed arches, an import from the Islamic world, let Gothic builders join structures of identical heights but different widths (something that barrel and groin vaulting could not do; see Figure 7.1 on page 191). The resulting structures were high, light, airy, and visually interesting. (*Source:* Anne Shaver-Crandell, *The Middle Ages* [Cambridge, England: Cambridge University Press, 1982], p. 34. Used by permission.)

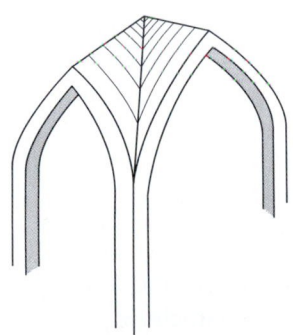

Interior of Notre-Dame, Paris The pointed vaults of the nave produce a verticality that is different in "feel" from the Romanesque. Note the triple elevation, the pointed arches, the ribbed vaulting, the ubiquitous glass that admits streams of multicolored light. The building can hold 10,000 people. *(Scala/Art Resource, NY)*

The *ribbed vault* exerts less stress than the groin vaults characteristic of Romanesque architecture and also facilitates experimentation with shapes. Finally, *point support*—basically, the support of structural elements at only certain points—permitted the replacement of heavy, stress-bearing walls with curtains of stained glass. The points of support might be massive internal piers or intricate skeletal frameworks, called *buttresses,* on the outside of the church. These elements produce a building that is characterized by verticality and

translucency. The effect is one of harmony, order, and mathematical precision.

The Gothic style soon spread in central and northern France. The thirteenth century was the most mature period for French Gothic architecture and also the time when Gothic spread most widely throughout Europe. This spread may be attributed to the superiority of French masons and stonecutters and also to the tremendous prestige of French culture. By 1300 there were distinctive Gothic traditions in almost all parts of Europe from Iceland to Poland.

Latin and Vernacular Culture

The prestige of French culture also points to the growing significance of vernacular literature. Most scholarly works, law books, and public documents were still written in Latin, but in a "vulgar" Latin that was reasonably close to the vernacular in areas where Romance languages (derived from Latin) were spoken. Technical manuals, on farming and animal husbandry, on warfare and armaments, or on law and government, were prepared in Latin, too, but in an extremely accessible style. What is most striking, however, is that Latin was rarely used, after about 1200, as the language for serious, original literary compositions. Here the change from the twelfth century—when theology and poetry, history and biography, and romance and adventure had been written in Latin— could not be more dramatic.

In the middle and last decades of the twelfth century, southern France added something new to Western literature: the love lyrics of the troubadours. This poetry, composed by both men and women, profoundly influenced an age and created the literary movement that has long been called "courtly love." Chivalry was initially a code for men interacting with other men. In the world of courtly love, chivalry became an elaborate set of rules governing relations between men and women.

Courtly love had several sources. The classical poet Ovid (43 B.C.–?A.D. 17), who wrote *The Art of Love,* a manual of seduction, was one. Another was the lyrical poetry of Muslim Spain. Ironically, feudal values such as loyalty and service played a critical role as men became, in effect, love vassals. The courtly poets sung of *fin'amours,* a pure love in contrast to the mere lust of the masses. A lover cherished an unattainable lady. He would do anything for the merest display of pleasure or gratitude on her part.

Male troubadours placed women on pedestals and worshiped them from afar. Women troubadours took a different line. Women's poems are more realistic, more human, more emotionally satisfying. Count William IX of Poitou (1071–1127) was among the first of the troubadours, and his daughter, Eleanor of Aquitaine, brought the conventions of this poetry and point of view to the French and Angevin courts. She and her daughters were the greatest literary patrons of the late twelfth century. The wives of kings and nobles who were frequently away from home maintained stunning courts and cultivated vernacular literature.

The romance and the lay were the chief new forms. Both drew on classical literature, the heroic Germanic past, and the Arthurian legends of the Celtic world to create stories of love and adventure. The romance usually develops a complex narrative involving several major characters. The lay is brief and focuses on a single incident. The most famous twelfth-century writer of romance was Chrétien de Troyes (1135–1183), the court writer of Marie of Champagne, a daughter of Eleanor of Aquitaine. The greatest writer of lays was Marie de France, who wrote at the Angevin court in the 1170s.

Although the romances and lays were by no means the preserve of the elite, very little is known about popular literature. Two exceptions are the mystery play and women's devotional writing. Mystery plays made their first appearance in the eleventh century. The liturgy of the church, which formally re-enacted the life of Christ, was confined to the clergy. But this limitation did not prevent troupes of actors from staging, on church porches or village greens, scenes from the life of Christ in simple, direct language. By the twelfth and thirteenth centuries, guilds in many towns sponsored the production of plays commemorating the Christian mysteries. Such plays served as both a form of popular entertainment and a device for teaching elementary Christian ideas. The female religious movements of the age gave rise to prose and verse works in various vernaculars. Mechtild of Magdeburg (1210–1280), a German Beguine, wrote *The Flowering Light of Divinity*, a mystical, allegorical account of the marriage between God and a spiritual woman. The vernaculars opened avenues of expression to women, who were normally denied Latin learning.

France led the way in the production of vernacular literature, but by the early thirteenth century centers of romantic poetry flourished in Germany and Italy. That French models did not inspire slavish imitation is proved by the master of all vernacular writers, Dante Alighieri (1265–1321). Dante began as a poet in *la dolce stil nuova,* "the sweet new style" that came from France and captivated Italians. But he moved beyond it in many ways. Dante was a man of extraordinarily wide learning and reading, best known for one of the masterpieces of world literature, the *Divine Comedy*. In exquisitely beautiful Italian, Dante took the most advanced theology and philosophy of his time, the richest poetic traditions, a huge hoard of stories, and many contemporary events, and wove them into an allegorical presentation of the journey of the whole human race toward God.

BONIFACE VIII AND PHILIP IV: CRISIS OF CHURCH AND STATE, 1294–1302

Even as Dante's poems transported their audience above the realm of daily affairs, the years around 1300 were disturbed by an all-too-earthly controversy between the king of France and the pope. This dispute encapsulates the major themes and particular issues that are discussed in this chapter.

The Issues

In 1294, Philip IV of France and Edward I of England both attempted to collect taxes from the clergy of their respective countries. They were at war in both Flanders and Gascony, their treasuries empty and their nobilities hostile. In 1296, Pope Boniface VIII (r. 1294–1303) issued the bull (letter) *Clericis laicos* forbidding the taxation of the clergy without explicit papal permission (repeating a decree of the Fourth Lateran Council of 1215). Edward I complied, but Philip responded with a propaganda campaign against the pope in France that was designed to rally popular support for the monarchy. He also issued an edict that forbade the export to Rome of bullion, coin, and valuables from France, an act meant to pressure Boniface by depriving him of vast ecclesiastical revenues.

The king felt he could not permit any power outside France to dictate when he could go to war by denying him valuable sources of income. In 1297, Boniface backed down. In the bull *Etsi de statu* he said that in a dire emergency "the conscience of the king" could decide whether or not to tax the clergy without papal permission. Philip's edict had affected Rome immediately because the greatest share of papal revenues came from France. Its impact was made all the greater by the precariousness of Boniface's position. An able, intelligent, experienced man, Pope Boniface carried out many important reforms. But the circumstances surrounding his election were questionable, because his predecessor, Celestine V (r. 1294), had resigned to return to a monastery. No other pope had ever resigned (and none has since), and it was not clear whether doing so was strictly legal. Moreover, although Boniface came from an old, rich, powerful Roman family, he was the mortal enemy of several equally well-placed families. Roman factions saw in the dispute with France a fine opportunity to attack the pope.

In 1297, Boniface canonized Philip's grandfather, Louis IX, as a saint—implying a reconciliation between Paris and Rome. Three years later, Boniface declared 1300 a jubilee year, a year of spiritual praise and thanksgiving, and Rome was filled with pilgrims, many of them French. The pope was working hard all the while to heal the rift between France and England so that the resources and energies of Europe could once again

be directed against the Muslims. Boniface still envisioned a militant and unified Christian Europe, with him at its head, going forth against the enemies of the faith.

In these circumstances, in 1301 Philip IV hauled a minor French bishop before the royal court on charges of heresy, blasphemy, and treason. Perhaps naively, he asked Boniface to concur. Instead, the pope sent the bull *Ausculta, fili carissime* to France. Its language was conciliatory but its message firm: No layman, not even the king of France, should dare to sit in judgment of a prelate of the church. Boniface also summoned the bishops of France to a council to investigate the whole matter. Boniface's actions challenged Philip's authority by implying that a power outside France could judge the actions of the French king and limit what he could do inside France. Philip's actions threatened the plenitude of papal power in the church and in Western society. Philip called a council of his own to decide if the pope was a heretic. Meanwhile, the pope's enemies in Rome, and also some clergy, were accusing the pope of heresy and questioning the legitimacy of his election.

The Outcome

Boniface pressed ahead and held his council in 1302. Few French bishops, and none from the north of France, attended. The council issued the bull *Unam sanctam*. Though fully rooted in the statements of popes going back to Gregory VII, *Unam sanctam* is the most blatant manifesto of papal triumphalism ever issued. Its argument is quite simple. Church and society are one, and the pope is the sole head. Philip responded by sending royal officials to Rome in 1303. They joined forces with Boniface's Roman foes and a gang of thugs and then seized and beat the pope—at Anagni, his summer residence. Boniface died three weeks later.

Comparisons are telling. Think of Germany's Henry IV, shivering in the snow beneath the walls of Canossa castle, begging forgiveness from Gregory VII. Then think of a Roman mob and of the minions of the king of France physically abusing an 80-year-old pope. All of our sources for the earlier events are in Latin and were written by clerics. Many sources for the events of 1302 are in French and Italian and were written by laymen. Henry II and Henry IV were advised by noble companions and relatives. Philip IV was counseled by trained lawyers. The times had changed.

SUMMARY

Comparisons between the Europe of 1150 and that of 1300 are instructive both as reminders of what had happened and as suggestions of what was to come. In 1150, Germany was promising but troubled. It reaped only the trouble. France and England showed great promise, too, and they realized much of it. France produced a strong government, a royal saint, and European cultural leadership. England developed a strong monarchy, a superb legal system, and a significant new institution, Parliament. But England and France were bitter rivals and had risked financial ruin to pursue their struggle. In Catalonia and Aragon, and to a degree in Portugal, the Iberian Peninsula witnessed the steady growth of monarchies with ideals and institutions much like those in France and England. The long Reconquista was not over, but its outcome seemed assured. Italian cities, as different from one another as they all were from the royal states of northern Europe, continued to be politically daring and socially volatile. Russia, despite promising beginnings and impressive resources, had been devastated by the Mongols. Recovery in this easternmost European region was anything but assured.

The papacy entered the thirteenth century with the powerful Innocent III and departed with the humiliated Boniface VIII. The church was still a formidable institution with the pope as its head, yet popes had lost the power to dictate to secular rulers as they had once done. Also, though the church was more unified than ever before as an institution, it was more diverse than at any time since Late Antiquity. Traditional monastic orders, the new communities, and dynamic women's or-

ders competed for places within the church, while growing numbers of heretics challenged the church from the outside. Along with the Crusades, these religious currents added up to Europe's first large-scale social movements.

Universities, fundamentally urban institutions, became dominant as centers of learning in England, France, Italy, and the Rhineland. The Gothic style, initially an urban architecture, barely existed in 1150, yet by 1300 it was about to develop a series of national forms. Scholasticism was just visible in the work of Anselm and Abelard but ascendant in Thomas Aquinas.

SUGGESTED READING

Barber, Malcolm. *The Two Cities: Medieval Europe, 1050–1320*. 1992. Readable, comprehensive, and reliable, this book is an excellent starting point for further explorations.

Brentano, Robert. *Rome Before Avignon: A Social History of Thirteenth-Century Rome*. 1974. Beautifully written, this book makes the reader feel as if he or she were walking the streets of Rome.

Bynum, Caroline Walker. *Holy Feast and Holy Fast: The Religious Significance of Food to Medieval Women*. 1987. An extraordinarily interesting and insightful discussion of late medieval female mystics.

Erler, Mary, and Maryanne Kowaleski. *Women and Power in the Middle Ages*. 1988. This fine collection of essays explores the various ways in which women exercised public and private power.

Grundmann, Herbert. *Religious Movements in the Middle Ages*. 1995. Translated into English sixty years after its appearance in German, this book has lost none of its interest or explanatory power.

Haverkamp, Alfred. *Medieval Germany, 1056–1273*. 2d ed. 1992. Covering every aspect of German life, this book is the best English introduction to the complex history of Germany.

Jantzen, Hans. *High Gothic: The Classic Cathedrals of Chartres, Reims and Amiens*. 1984. In the voluminous and technically daunting literature on Gothic style, this short book can be recommended for clarity and reliability.

Keen, Maurice. *Chivalry*. 1984. Out of the many books on this subject, Keen's can be recommended for its balance, readability, and reliability.

Klapische-Zuber, Christiane, ed. *A History of Women in the West*. Vol. 2, *Silences of the Middle Ages*. 1992. An excellent collection of essays concerning ideal images of women, medical descriptions of women, and religious doctrine intended for women.

Lambert, Malcolm. *Medieval Heresy: Popular Movements from the Gregorian Reform to the Reformation*. 2d ed. 1992. This book is the best history of medieval heresy ever written and one of the best books on medieval religion generally.

Le Goff, Jacques, ed. *Medieval Callings*. 1990. This interesting book has chapters on, among others, peasants, townfolk, merchants, monks, artists, and intellectuals.

Morris, Colin. *The Discovery of the Individual, 1050–1200*. 1972. Brief and readable, Morris's book has set off much controversy about the definition of individualism and the time of its first appearance in Europe.

Mundy, John H. *Europe in the High Middle Ages, 1150–1309*. 1973. A detailed and comprehensive introduction that is readable, witty, and sophisticated.

Munz, Peter. *Frederick Barbarossa: A Study in Medieval Politics*. 1969. An entertaining book that is sensitive more to political realities than to abstract theoretical problems.

Paterson, Linda M. *The World of the Troubadours: Medieval Occitan Society, c. 1100–1300*. 1993. A wonderfully evocative account of the history and culture of southern France.

Price, Betsy Barker. *Medieval Thought: An Introduction*. 1992. Comprehensive yet brief, readable, and non-technical, this book is an excellent introduction to Christian philosophy and theology that acknowledges and explains Jewish and Arab contributions.

Richard, Jean. *Saint Louis: Crusader King of France*. 1992. A detailed account of Louis's life and a compelling introduction to his age.

Riley-Smith, Jonathan. *The Crusades: A Short History*. 1987. The best introduction; its useful bibliography points to the detailed works.

Shahar, Shulamith. *The Fourth Estate: A History of Women in the Middle Ages*. 1983. Comprehensive and detailed, this book is best on the High Middle Ages and late periods.

Shaver-Crandell, Anne. *Cambridge Introduction to the History of Art: The Middle Ages*. 1982. Brief, carefully illustrated, and clearly written, this is an excellent starting point for the student of medieval art and architecture.

Van Caenegem, R. C. *The Birth of the English Common Law*. 2d ed. 1989. Written by a legal historian with a gift for clarity of presentation, this book provides immediate access to perhaps England's greatest legacy to the West.

Zink, Michel. *Medieval French Literature: An Introduction*. 1995. Clear and readable, this book does for the beginner what its title promises.

The Transformation of Medieval Civilization, 1300–1500

In the fourteenth century, God's judgment and the terrible fates awaiting sinners were constantly on the minds of Christians. The violence and plagues that ravaged late medieval Europe were thought to be premonitions of coming judgment. In this world, military, political, religious, economic, and social crises burdened Europe in the fourteenth and early fifteenth centuries.

Between 1337 and 1453, France and England fought what was in effect a world war. The Hundred Years' War, as it has come to be known, was primarily fought over English claims to traditionally French lands. Social and political disruptions and the economic burdens of the war allowed the nobles of England and France to limit royal power and made local administration more difficult. Both monarchies transformed themselves in the aftermath of political strife, however, in ways that preserved and even increased royal power. Similarly, in the towns of Germany and Italy, patrician classes moved to reduce the influence of artisans and laborers in government, instituting oligarchies or even aristocratic dictatorships in place of more democratic governments.

Questions of power and representation also affected the Christian church as ecclesiastical claims to authority came under attack. Disputed papal elections led to the Great Schism, a split between rival popes in Rome and Avignon (a city in what is now the south of France). In dealing with the schism and with other issues, the church hierarchy was challenged by those who argued that authority resided in the whole church and not just with its head, the pope. In the aftermath of the crisis, the papacy was forced to redefine its place in both the religious and the political life of Europe.

A series of economic and demographic shocks worsened these political and religious difficulties. Part of the problem was structural: The population of Europe grew too large to be supported by the resources available. Famine and the return of the bubonic plague in 1348 sent the economy into long-term decline. In almost every aspect of political, religious, and social life, then, the fourteenth and early fifteenth centuries marked a pause in the expansion that had characterized the previous century and a half.

Yet seeds of future growth were planted during this period. Two empires quite unlike the monarchical states of the twelfth and thirteenth centuries appeared in the fifteenth century. The marriage of the sovereigns of Aragon and Castile formed a new Spanish empire that would become the most powerful government in sixteenth-century Europe, while at the other end of the Mediterranean, a new Muslim Turkish empire replaced the weakened Byzantine Empire. Neither state had existed in 1300, and the future seemed to belong to them.

∼ *Questions and Ideas to Consider*

- How did the Great Schism change the relationship between the papacy and the governments of Europe? Discuss the results of this changed relationship. Consider the Pragmatic Sanction, the Spanish Inquisition, and the changing role of the Papal States.

- What were the immediate and the long-standing causes of the Hundred Years' War? What role did Joan of Arc play in the French military triumph?

- Governmental structures varied greatly in this period, and much depended on the relationship between a ruler and the nobility or parliamentary body. Compare the situation in France, England, Italy, Germany, and Scandinavia.

- To what can we attribute the strength of the Ottoman Empire under Mehmed II? Consider the situation of the Janissaries. Compare the attitudes toward religious diversity in the Ottoman Empire and in the Spain of Isabella and Ferdinand.

- What were the consequences of the Black Death? Consider economic, social, and religious factors. Describe the ways in which changes in the guilds altered the economic situations of men and women.

THE CRISIS OF THE WESTERN CHRISTIAN CHURCH

The French attack on Pope Boniface VIII in 1303 (see page 222) revealed the deep splits within the Christian community. After the death of Boniface, it was clear that the governments of Europe had no intention of recognizing papal authority as absolute.

The Babylonian Captivity, 1309–1377

It was largely in deference to Philip that the French archbishop of Bordeaux was elected Pope Clement V (r. 1305–1314). Clement chose to remain north of the Alps in order to seek an end to warfare between France and England and to prevent the king from carrying through his threatened posthumous heresy trial of Boniface. Clement's pontificate marked the beginning of the so-called Babylonian Captivity, a period during which the pope resided almost continuously in what is now the south of France. In 1309, Clement moved the papal court to Avignon, on the Rhône River in a region that was technically part of the Holy Roman Empire (the name that by the fourteenth century was given to the medieval empire whose origin reached back to Charlemagne). The papal court in Avignon became, perhaps, the largest in Europe. Although the thirteenth-century papal administration required only two hundred or so officials, the bureaucracy grew to about six hundred in Avignon. Artists, writers, lawyers, and merchants from across Europe were drawn to the new center of administration and patronage. Kings, princes, towns, and ecclesiastical institutions needed representatives at the papal court.

Not everyone approved of this situation. It was the Italian poet and philosopher Francesco

CHAPTER CHRONOLOGY

1309	Clement V moves the papal court to Avignon; beginning of the Babylonian Captivity	1417	Election of Martin V by the Council of Constance; end of the Great Schism
1311	English barons force Edward II to accept the Ordinances of 1311	1420	Treaty of Troyes
		1431	Joan of Arc is tried and executed
1327	Parliament deposes Edward II	1453	The last battle of the Hundred Years' War
1328	The last Capetian king dies; French nobles elect Philip of Valois king of France (Philip VI)	1469	Ferdinand of Aragon marries Isabella of Castile
1340	Edward III of England formally claims the French crown	1478	Spanish Inquisition is established
		1485	Death of Richard III
1356	Battle of Poitiers	1491	Charles VIII reclaims French control of Brittany by marrying Anne of Brittany
1377	End of the Babylonian Captivity		
1378	Elections of rival popes: Urban VI and Clement VII; start of the Great Schism	1492	Conquest of Granada; Columbus's first voyage; expulsion of Jews from Spain
1399	Abdication of Richard II; accession of Henry IV	1494	Charles VIII invades Italy
		1496	Joanna of Castile marries Philip of Habsburg
1415	Battle of Agincourt	1504	Expulsion of Muslims from Spain; death of Isabella; Ferdinand rules Castile as regent for his grandson, Charles I
	Council of Constance condemns and executes John Hus		

Petrarch (1304–1374) who first referred to a "Babylonian Captivity of the papacy." Recalling the exile of the Israelites and the image of Babylon as a center of sin and immorality, he complained of

[an] unholy Babylon, Hell on Earth, a sink of iniquity, the cesspool of the world. There is neither faith, nor charity, nor religion, nor fear of God, nor shame, nor truth, nor holiness.[1]

To Petrarch and to others, the exile of the papacy from Rome stood as an example of all that was wrong with the church. Those who came to the court were practical and worldly. Many people renowned for their piety, like Saint Catherine of Siena and Saint Bridget of Sweden, appealed to the pope to return to simpler ways and to Rome, his episcopal city.

Late in 1377, Pope Gregory XI (r. 1370–1378) did return to Rome. He found churches and palaces in ruin and the city violent and dangerous. He would have retreated to Avignon had he not died a few months later. In a tumultuous election, the cardinals finally elected a candidate acceptable both to the French cardinals and to the Roman mob. Urban VI (r. 1378–1389) was an Italian cleric from a French-controlled part of Italy. Within months the cardinals deposed the violent and intemperate Urban, electing in his place a French cardinal who took the name Clement VII (r. 1378–1394). Urban responded by denouncing the cardinals and refusing to step down. There were now two popes.

After some hesitation, Western Christians divided into two camps, initiating the Great Schism, which lasted almost forty years. Among the states of Europe, support for one pope or the other often had more to do with political rivalries than with religious conviction. The French supported Clement, who eventually resettled in

Avignon. The English, together with the Italians and most of the German Empire, supported Urban, the pope in Rome. Scotland, an enemy of the English, and Castile sided with the French.

The crisis gave impetus to new discussions about church government: Should the pope be considered the sole head of the church? Representative bodies in Europe—the English Parliament, the French Estates General, the Swedish Riksdag—already claimed the right to act for the realm, and in the city-states of Italy authority was thought to reside in the body of citizens. Canon lawyers and theologians called "conciliarists" similarly argued that the whole church had the right to come together in council to reform the church hierarchy.

The cardinals agreed to call a general council of the church. Meeting in Pisa in 1409, the council deposed both popes and elected a new pope. The council, however, lacked the power to force the rivals to accept deposition, and so the only result was that three men now claimed to be the rightful successor of Saint Peter. The Council of Pisa demonstrated that a solution would not come until secular rulers were willing to enforce it.

Heresy, Reunion, and Reform

The Holy Roman emperor, Sigismund (r. 1411–1437), with the support of other European powers, vigorously lobbied for a council. Resolution of the schism was only one of the items on the agenda of the council, which met from 1414 to 1417 in the German imperial city of Constance.

Sigismund faced a religious civil war in Bohemia, the most important part of his family's traditional lands (see Map 9.2 on page 239). Bohemia and its capital, Prague, were Czech-speaking. But Prague was also the seat of the Luxembourg dynasty of German emperors and the site of the first university in the German world. The issue centered on the Czech reformer John Hus (ca. 1370–1415). His criticisms of the church hierarchy, which in Prague was primarily German, fanned the flames of Czech national feeling. It was Sigismund's hope that a council might heal the rift within the church of Bohemia.

The council's response was based on the church's recent experience with heresy. In the 1370s, John Wyclif (1329–1384), an Oxford theologian and parish priest, began to criticize the state of the clergy. By 1387, Wyclif's ideas had been declared heretical. Wyclif gave special status to the Bible, criticizing the claims of authority of the church hierarchy. His followers, called Lollards, emphasized Bible-reading and popular piety and supported public preaching by women. According to one, "every true man and woman being in charity is a priest."[2]

Wyclif's most lasting impact was probably his influence on John Hus and the Hussite movement. Following the teachings of Wyclif, Hus attacked clerical power and privileges. By 1403 the German majority in the university had condemned Hus's teaching, initiating almost a decade of struggle between Czechs and Germans, Hussites and Catholics. In hopes of some sort of reconciliation, Sigismund offered Hus a safe-conduct pass to attend the Council of Constance. As matters progressed, however, it became clear that the councilors and Hus himself were in no mood to compromise. The council revoked the pledge of safe conduct and ordered Hus to recant his beliefs. He refused. The council condemned him as a heretic and burned him at the stake on July 6, 1415.

Far from ending Sigismund's problems with the Bohemians, the actions of the council provided the Czechs with a martyr and hero. Radical Hussites argued that the true church was the community of spiritual men and women. They had no use for ecclesiastical hierarchy of any kind. The German emperors were unable to defeat a united Hussite movement. So from 1430 to 1433 the emperor and moderate Hussites negotiated an agreement that allowed the Hussites to continue some of their practices while returning to the church. The Hussite war engulfed all of Bohemia and dragged on until 1436. Bohemia remained a center of religious dissent, and the memory of the execution of Hus at a church council would have a chilling effect on discussions of church reform during the Reformation in the sixteenth century.

The council was more successful in dealing with the schism. Gregory XII (r. 1406–1415), the Roman pope, submitted his letter of resignation, while the council deposed both of the other popes. The council justified its actions in what was perhaps its most important decree, *Haec sancta synodus* (This sacred synod): "sacred synod of Constance . . . declares . . . that it has its power immediately from Christ, and that all . . . including even the pope himself are bound to obey it in those matters that pertain to the faith."[3]

The Great Schism had ended. In the final sessions of the Council of Constance, Odo of Colonna, a member of an old Roman noble family, was elected pope of the newly reunified church. Taking the name of Martin V (r. 1417–1431), he presided over an institution that had changed dramatically. Ecclesiastical rights increasingly were matters for negotiation between popes and the governments of Europe.

The Reformed Papacy

The issue of papal reform was complex. Critics agreed that the pope no longer behaved like the "Servant of the Servants of Christ" but instead acted like the "Lord of Lords." Cardinals claimed to represent the church as counterweights to papal abuse, but as the nobility of the church, they and other members of the hierarchy required multiple benefices (paid public offices) to maintain their presence at the papal court. Both the cardinals and the popes viewed any reforms to the present system as potential threats to their ability to function. The council, however, recognized the need for further reforms, and in the decree *Frequens* (Frequently), it mandated that reform councils be called regularly. A reform council met at Basel from 1431 to 1449, but with little success. It tried again to reduce papal power but received no support from European governments.

Because of the continuing conciliarist threat, the papacy was forced to accept compromises on the issues of reform, ecclesiastical jurisdictions and immunities, and rights to papal revenues. Various lay rulers wanted church officials in their territories to be from local families. They wanted ecclesiastical institutions to be subject to local laws and administration. And by the 1470s, it was clear that they wanted to have local prelates named as cardinal-protectors, churchmen who could serve as mediators between local government and the papacy.

One of the most important compromises between the papacy and the monarchs was the Pragmatic Sanction of Bourges of 1438, by which the French crown established a claim to a church largely independent of papal influence. Among other reforms, the agreement reduced papal rights to appoint clergy within France without the approval of the local clergy or the Crown. The Pragmatic Sanction was the first of a number of claims for a unique "Gallican church," a national church free from outside interference. There were similar treaties throughout Europe. Perhaps the most momentous was a bull issued in 1478 by Pope Sixtus IV (r. 1471–1484) that allowed Ferdinand and Isabella of Aragon and Castile to institute a church court, the Spanish Inquisition, under their own authority.

The papal concessions signaled a changed relationship between the papacy and the governments of Europe. With reduced revenues from jurisdictions, annates, and appointments, the papacy of the fifteenth century was forced to derive more and more of its revenue and influence from its traditional Papal States in central Italy. By the late 1420s, the Papal States produced about half of the annual income of the papacy. Papal interests increasingly centered on protecting the papacy's influence among the Italian states. Thus, the papacy had to deal with many of the jurisdictional, diplomatic, and military challenges that faced medieval governments.

THE CHALLENGE TO MEDIEVAL GOVERNMENTS

A lawyer who served King Philip IV of France (r. 1285–1314) observed that "everything within the limits of his kingdom belongs to the lord king, especially protection, high justice and dominion."[4]

Royal officials in England and France generally believed that "liberties"—that is, individual rights to local jurisdictions—originated with the king. At almost the same time, however, an English earl challenged royal claims on his lands saying, "Here, my lords, is my warrant," and brandishing his longsword. "My ancestors came with William the Bastard [that is, with William the Conqueror in 1066] and conquered their lands with the sword, and by the sword I will defend them against anyone who tries to usurp them."[5] The old earl clearly believed that the rights and traditions of the aristocracy limited even royal attempts to centralize authority.

The issue throughout Europe in the late Middle Ages was whether central, regional, or even local authorities should dominate political and social life. In England and France traditional elites initially limited royal power, but by 1500 it was firmly re-established. From Italy through central Europe and into Scandinavia, however, late medieval monarchies found themselves hard-pressed to dominate political life. Yet as demonstrated by the development of the grand duchy of Tuscany, the independent feeling of the Swiss states, the free peasantry of Scandinavia, and the rise of Moscovy, political order and stability can characterize territorial states as well as centralized monarchies.

England, France, and the Hundred Years' War

In the twelfth and thirteenth centuries, as we have seen, centralization of royal power proceeded almost without interruption. In the fourteenth century, matters changed. Charles IV of France died in 1328 without heirs, and in England after the death of Edward I in 1307, monarchs found their power limited by forces largely beyond their control.

Fears arising from the growing power of the Crown and the weakness of an easily influenced king brought issues to a head during the reign of Edward II (r. 1307–1327). The barons, the titled lords of England, forced the king to accept the Ordinances of 1311. According to the ordinances,

the king could no longer wage war, leave the realm, grant lands or castles, or appoint chief justices without the approval of the barons in Parliament. Some of the ordinances were later voided, but the basic principle of parliamentary consent remained central to English constitutional history. As for Edward II, he suffered a humiliating defeat at the hands of the Scots at the Battle of Bannockburn (1314), and his position steadily deteriorated until he was deposed in 1327 by a coalition of barons led by Queen Isabella. After a short regency, his son, Edward III (r. 1327–1377), assumed the throne. He was a cautious king, ever aware of the volatility of the baronage.

Observing the civil strife and open rebellion that characterized England in the early fourteenth century, French thinkers prided themselves on the stability of the French monarchy. Nonetheless, a series of relatively weak kings during the fourteenth century made clear the limits of French kingship. Philip IV (r. 1285–1314) was succeeded by his three sons, each of whom died without a legitimate male heir. In 1328 the direct Capetian line, which had provided the kings of France since the election of Hugh Capet in 987, finally died out. Thus, the French nobility selected as king Philip of Valois (Philip VI; r. 1328–1350), a cousin of the late King Charles IV through the male line. He was chosen in preference to the daughters of the last Capetian kings and in preference to King Edward III of England, whose mother was the daughter of Philip IV. This question of inheritance was part of the reason for the Hundred Years' War, but the English claim to the crown was a reaction to older problems as well.

The mid-thirteenth-century Treaty of Paris stipulated English control of the duchy of Aquitaine, which the English king was to hold as a vassal of the French king (see Map 9.1). French kings claimed that as dukes of Aquitaine, the English kings owed *liege homage*—that is, while kneeling before the French king, they had to swear to provide military aid whenever the French king asked for it. Also, the treaty implied French sovereignty over Aquitaine, an area in which the French previously had enjoyed little

Ransoming Captives One English strategy during the first stages of the Hundred Years' War was seizing and ransoming French knights such as Charles of Blois, whose capture is illustrated here. (*Bibliothèque Nationale*)

influence. French kings claimed the right to incorporate Aquitaine into France. To the English kings, this was an unacceptable subversion of English jurisdiction. In frustration, Edward finally made his fateful claim to the French throne, thus igniting the war.

The Hundred Years' War was a series of short raids and expeditions punctuated by a few major battles and marked off by truces. The relative strengths of the two kingdoms dictated the sporadic nature of the struggle. France was far richer and more populous than England. On at least one occasion the French managed to field an army of over 50,000; at most the English mustered only 32,000. In almost every engagement the English were outnumbered. The most successful English strategy was to avoid pitched battles and engage in a series of quick, profitable raids during which they stole what they could and captured enemy knights to hold for ransom.

The war can be divided into four stages (Map 9.1). The first stage of the war, from 1337 to 1360, was characterized by English raids led by the crown prince Edward, later called "the Black Prince" because of the black armor he once wore. Though smaller in number, English armies did well in this period because they took excellent defensive positions and used the longbow to their best advantage. In the second phase of the war, from 1360 to 1396, careful French leaders managed to regain control of much of the land they had lost.

The situation soon changed again, ushering in the third stage of the war, from 1396 to 1422. King Charles VI (r. 1380–1422) of France suffered bouts of insanity throughout his long reign, which led to civil war. The English king Henry V (r. 1413–1422) renewed his family's claim to the French throne. At Agincourt in 1415, the English (led this time by Henry) enticed a larger French army into attacking a fortified English position. A hail of arrows from English longbows shattered the advance. With Burgundian aid, Henry gained control over Normandy, Paris, and much of northern France. By the terms of the Treaty of Troyes (1420), Henry married Catherine, the

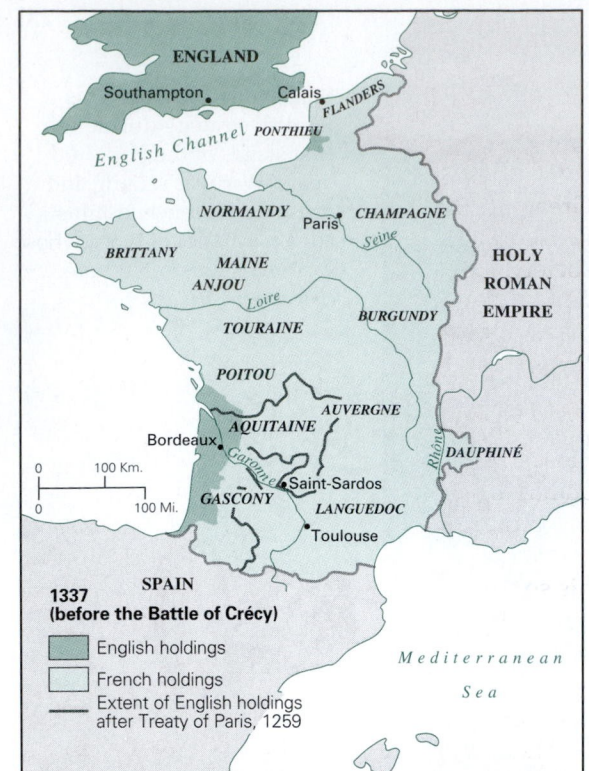

1337
(before the Battle of Crécy)

ENGLAND
Southampton
Calais
FLANDERS
PONTHIEU
English Channel
NORMANDY
Paris
CHAMPAGNE
Seine
HOLY
ROMAN
EMPIRE
BRITTANY
MAINE
ANJOU
Loire
TOURAINE
BURGUNDY
POITOU
AUVERGNE
AQUITAINE
Bordeaux
Garonne
Rhine
DAUPHINÉ
Saint-Sardos
GASCONY
LANGUEDOC
Toulouse
SPAIN
Mediterranean
Sea

0 100 Km.
0 100 Mi.

☐ English holdings
☐ French holdings
— Extent of English holdings
after Treaty of Paris, 1259

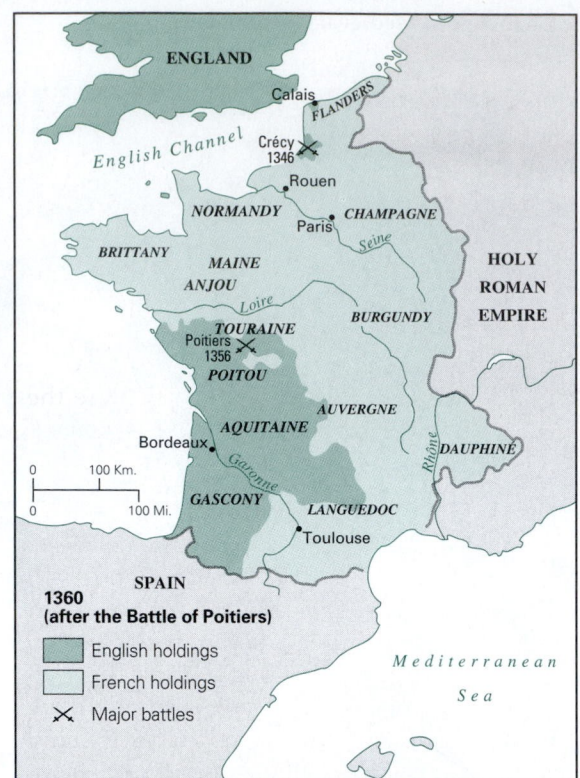

1360
(after the Battle of Poitiers)

ENGLAND
Calais
FLANDERS
Crécy
1346
English Channel
Rouen
NORMANDY
Paris
CHAMPAGNE
Seine
HOLY
ROMAN
EMPIRE
BRITTANY
MAINE
ANJOU
Loire
TOURAINE
Poitiers
1356
POITOU
BURGUNDY
AUVERGNE
AQUITAINE
Bordeaux
Garonne
Rhine
DAUPHINÉ
GASCONY
LANGUEDOC
Toulouse
SPAIN
Mediterranean
Sea

0 100 Km.
0 100 Mi.

☐ English holdings
☐ French holdings
✕ Major battles

ca. 1429
(after the siege of Orléans)

ENGLAND
Calais
FLANDERS
Agincourt
1415
English Channel
HOLY
ROMAN
EMPIRE
Rouen
Reims
NORMANDY
Paris
CHAMPAGNE
Seine
Domrémy
Orléans
BRITTANY
MAINE
ANJOU
Loire
Bourges
TOURAINE
DUCHY OF
BURGUNDY
COUNTY OF
BURGUNDY
POITOU
AUVERGNE
AQUITAINE
Bordeaux
Garonne
Rhine
DAUPHINÉ
GASCONY
LANGUEDOC
Toulouse
SPAIN
Mediterranean
Sea

0 100 Km.
0 100 Mi.

☐ English holdings
☐ French holdings
☐ Burgundian lands allied
with England to 1435
✕ Major battle

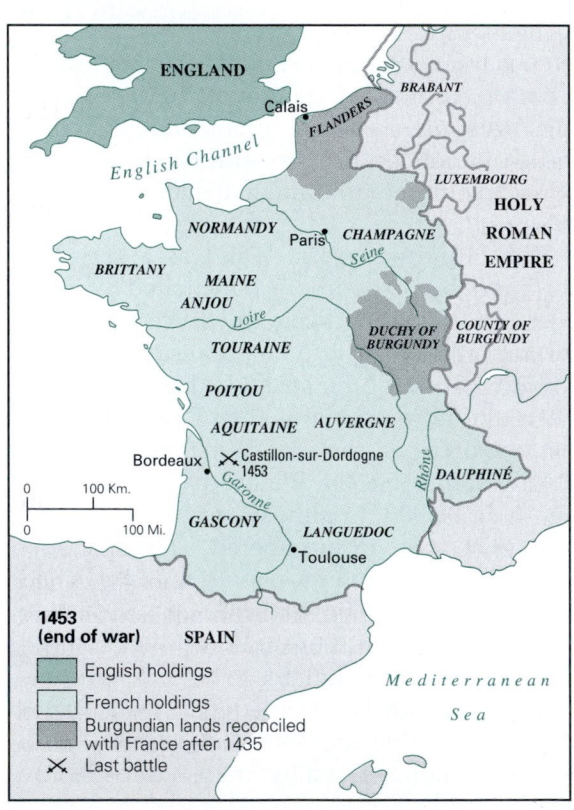

1453
(end of war)

ENGLAND
Calais
FLANDERS
BRABANT
English Channel
LUXEMBOURG
HOLY
ROMAN
EMPIRE
NORMANDY
Paris
CHAMPAGNE
Seine
BRITTANY
MAINE
ANJOU
Loire
DUCHY OF
BURGUNDY
COUNTY OF
BURGUNDY
TOURAINE
POITOU
AQUITAINE
AUVERGNE
Bordeaux
Castillon-sur-Dordogne
1453
Garonne
Rhine
DAUPHINÉ
GASCONY
LANGUEDOC
Toulouse
SPAIN
Mediterranean
Sea

0 100 Km.
0 100 Mi.

☐ English holdings
☐ French holdings
☐ Burgundian lands reconciled
with France after 1435
✕ Last battle

daughter of Charles VI, and became the heir to the French throne. A final English victory seemed assured, but both Charles VI and Henry V died in 1422, leaving the infant Henry VI with claims to both kingdoms. The kings' deaths ushered in the final stage of the war, the French reconquest, from 1422 to 1453. In a stunning series of events, the French were able to restore royal power.

In 1429, with the aid of Joan of Arc (d. 1431), Charles VII (r. 1422–1461) was able to raise the English siege of Orléans and begin the reconquest of the north of France. Joan was the daughter of prosperous peasants. Like other late medieval mystics she reported regular visions of divine revelation. Her "voices" told her to go to the king and aid him in driving out the English. Dressed as a man, she was Charles's most charismatic and feared military leader. Joan was captured during an audacious attack on Paris itself. Charles refused to ransom her, and eventually she fell into English hands. Because of her "unnatural dress" and her claim to divine illumination, she was condemned and burned as a heretic in 1431. Joan almost instantly became a symbol of French resistance. Pope Calixtus III reversed the condemnation in 1456, and in 1920 she was canonized. The heretic became Saint Joan, patron of France.

Despite Joan's capture, the French advance continued. By 1450 the English had lost all their major centers except Calais. In 1453, the French armies captured the fortress of Castillon-sur-Dordogne in what was to be the last battle of the war (see Map 9.1). There was no treaty, only a cessation of hostilities.

The Results of the War

The war touched almost every aspect of life in late medieval Europe: political, religious, economic, and social. It ranged beyond the borders

Map 9.1 England and France in the Hundred Years' War The succession of maps depicts both why hit-and-run tactics worked for the English early in the war and why the English were ultimately unable to defeat the French and take control of all of France.

of France as Scotland, Castile, Aragon, and German principalities were drawn at various times into the struggle. French and English support for rival popes prevented early settlement of the Great Schism in the papacy. Further, the war caused a general rise in the level of violence in society. During periods of truce, mercenary captains pillaged freely across Europe, kidnapping municipal officials and even laying siege to entire towns in order to extort money.

The war also helped consolidate the French monarchy's power. A key to French military successes had been the creation of a paid professional army, which, unlike the feudal host and mercenary companies of the fourteenth century, remained under the king's control. Along with his son, Louis XI (r. 1461–1483), Charles also expanded his judicial claims through the creation of new provincial parliaments.

French kings attacked the power of the great aristocratic families in two ways. In 1477, when Charles the Bold of Burgundy was killed, Louis quickly seized his duchy, ridding himself of the greatest independent power in the kingdom. The process of consolidation was completed in 1491 when Charles VIII (r. 1483–1498), Louis's son, married Anne of Brittany, the heiress of the last independent duke of Brittany.

The second key to maintaining royal influence was the rise of the French court as a political and financial center. Through careful appointments and judicious offers of annuities and honors, Charles VII and Louis XI drew the nobility to the royal court and made the nobles dependent on it. "The court," complained a frustrated noble, "is an assembly of people who, under the pretense of acting for the good of all, come together to diddle each other; for there's scarcely anyone who isn't engaged in buying and selling and exchanging."[6] By the end of the fifteenth century, France had recovered from the crisis of war. It was once again a strong and influential state.

In England during the fifteenth century, the Hundred Years' War became the backdrop for a series of struggles over royal power. Although the English generally agreed that the king could institute new taxes to pay for foreign wars, theorists and parliamentary leaders alike held that the king should live off the income of his traditional rights and properties and honor the influence of the aristocracy.

It was fear of the king's power that contributed to the downfall of King Richard II in 1399. Leaders of the peers captured Richard and forced him to abdicate. Parliament then elected as king Henry IV (r. 1399–1413), the first of the Lancastrian line.

In the beginning the Lancastrians were quite successful. Henry IV avoided war taxes and was careful not to alienate the magnates. Henry V, perhaps the most charismatic of the late medieval English kings, gave the Lancastrians their greatest moments: the victory at Agincourt in 1415 and the Treaty of Troyes in 1420, designed to unify the French and English crowns. Henry VI (r. 1422–1461), however, turned out to be weak-willed and immature.

The loss of virtually all French territories in 1453 led to the factional battles known as the "Wars of the Roses" because the red rose was the symbol of the Lancastrian dynasty and the white rose signified the Yorkist opposition. Edward of York eventually deposed Henry and claimed the crown for himself as Edward IV (r. 1461–1483). When he died, his brother, Richard, duke of Gloucester, claimed the protectorship over the 13-year-old king, Edward V (r. April–June 1483), and his younger brother. He seized the boys and placed them in the Tower of London. They were never seen again.

Richard proclaimed himself king and was crowned Richard III (r. 1483–1485). He withstood early challenges to his authority but in 1485 was killed in battle by Henry Tudor, a leader of the Lancastrian faction. Henry married Elizabeth, the surviving child of the late Edward IV. Symbolically at least, the struggle between the rival claimants to the crown appeared over.

Like his predecessor, Edward IV, Henry VII (r. 1485–1509) recognized the importance of avoiding war and taxation. Following Edward IV's example, Henry VII depended on a traditional system of royal patronage. Henry's skill in marriage politics gave England ties with Scot-

land and Spain. He arranged the marriage of his daughter, Margaret Tudor, to James IV of Scotland and the marriage of his sons, Arthur and (after Arthur's death) Henry, to Catherine of Aragon, daughter of the Spanish rulers Ferdinand and Isabella.

The success of Henry VII was based on several factors: the absence of powerful opponents; lowered taxation, the result of twenty-five years of peace under his rule; and the desire, shared by ruler and ruled alike, for an orderly realm built on the assured succession of a single dynasty.

Italy

Compared to France and England, fourteenth- and fifteenth-century Italy was a land of cities. In northern Europe a town of over 20,000 or 30,000 people was unusual. The 100,000 or more people who lived in London or Paris in the fourteenth century made these capitals unlike any other cities north of the Alps. Yet at one time or another in the late Middle Ages, Milan, Venice, Florence, and Naples all had populations near or exceeding 100,000, and countless other Italian towns boasted populations of over 20,000. In comparison to northern Europe, however, the Italian peninsula seemed a power vacuum. The northern and central provinces largely belonged to the kingdom of Italy and thus were part of the Holy Roman Empire. Most of central Italy was part of the Papal States. Neither emperor nor pope, however, wielded real political power.

By the late thirteenth century, political power in most Italian towns was divided among three major groups. The first was an old urban nobility that could trace its wealth back to grants of property and rights from kings and bishops in the tenth and eleventh centuries. They were joined by a second group, the merchant families who enriched themselves in the twelfth and thirteenth centuries as Italians led the European economic expansion into the Mediterranean. These old urban groups were challenged in the first decades of the thirteenth century by modest artisans and merchants who had organized trade, neighborhood, or militia groups and referred to themselves as the *popolo*, that is, "the people" (see page 186). In many towns they elected a virtual parallel government headed by their own small council of elders. As early as 1198, the popolo of Milan had elected their own Captain of the People. The rise of the popolo brought little peace, however. "War and hatred have so multiplied among the Italians," observed one Florentine, "that in every town there is a division and enmity between two parties of citizens." It was not simply a fight divided along class lines. Townsmen gathered themselves together in factions based on wealth, family, profession, neighborhood, and even systems of clientage that reached back into the villages from which many of the townsmen had come.

Riven with factions, townsmen would often turn control of their governments over to a *signor*, that is, a "lord," or "tyrant," often a local noble with a private army. In 1264, for example, Obizzo d'Este took control of the town of Ferrara. The rise of the Este lords of Ferrara seemed peaceful, but the force on which the transformation rested was clearer in Mantua. "[Pinamonte Bonacolsi (d. 1293)] usurped the lordship of his city and expelled his fellow-citizens and occupied their property," according to a chronicler. "And he was feared like the devil."[7]

The great republics of Venice and Florence escaped domination by signori, but only by undertaking significant constitutional change. In both republics political life was disrupted by large numbers of new citizens—immigrants drawn by the relatively greater economic opportunities in the towns and recently enriched merchants and speculators who demanded a voice in government. In 1297, reacting to increased competition for influence, the Venetian government enacted the so-called Closing of the Grand Council. The act guaranteed the political rights of the patriciate and froze out subsequent arrivals. The Venetian patriciate became a closed urban nobility.

In Florence, by contrast, political life was convulsed by the issue of citizenship. Violent noble families, immigrants, and artisans of modest backgrounds found themselves cut off from civic participation by the passage of a series of reforms that culminated in the Ordinances of Justice of 1293–1295. These reforms, largely promoted by wealthy guildsmen, restricted political participation in Florence to members in good standing of certain merchant and artisan guilds. After a political and diplomatic crisis in 1434 brought on by war and high taxes, virtual control of Florentine politics fell into the hands of Cosimo de' Medici, the wealthiest banker in the city. From 1434 to 1494, Cosimo, his son Piero, his grandson Lorenzo, and Lorenzo's son dominated the government in Florence. Always careful to appease Florentine republican traditions, Medici control was virtually as complete as that of the lords of towns like Ferrara or Milan.

In the fifteenth century, the great towns of Italy dominated their lesser neighbors. The aristocratic Visconti family had taken control of Milan by the early fourteenth century and secured the title of duke. The Viscontis and, later, their Sforza successors made marriage alliances with the French crown and created a splendid court culture in Milan.

Republican Florence and Venice followed similar policies in dealing with warfare and competition with other states. Relations among Milan, Venice, Florence, Rome, and Naples were stabilized by the Peace of Lodi and the creation of the Italian League in 1454. In response to endemic warfare in Italy and the looming threat of the Ottoman Turks in the eastern Mediterranean (see page 238), the five powers agreed to the creation of spheres of influence that would prevent any one of them from expanding at the expense of the others. The limits of these territorial states of Italy became clear when King Charles VIII of France invaded Italy in 1494 to assert his claims to the duchy of Milan and the kingdom of Naples.

The French invasion devastated Italy by touching off a series of wars called the Habsburg-Valois Wars. French control was immediately challenged by the Spanish, who themselves made claims on the south and much of Lombardy. The cost of warfare kept almost all governments in a state of crisis. Unrest brought on by the invasion allowed Pope Alexander VI (r. 1492–1503) to attempt to create a state for his son, Cesare Borgia (1475–1507), in central Italy.

In Florence, the wars destroyed the old Medici-dominated republic and brought in a new constitution. Republican, anti-Medici reformers were initially led by the popular Dominican preacher Girolamo Savonarola (1452–1498). Savonarola argued that true republican reform required a thoroughgoing religious reform of society. Gangs of youth flocked to his cause, attacking prostitutes and homosexuals. Many of his followers held "bonfires of vanities," burning wigs, silks, and other luxuries. In 1498, when his followers had lost influence in the government, Savonarola was arrested, tortured, and executed.

In spite of reforms, new fortresses, and a citizen militia, the Florentine government was unable to save itself from papal and imperial opposition. In 1512 the Medicis returned under papal and imperial protection. Eventually, the Medicis were named dukes and then grand dukes of Tuscany. The grand duchy of Tuscany remained an independent, integrated, and well-governed state until the French Revolution of 1789. Venice also managed to maintain its republican form of government and its territorial state until the French Revolution.

The Habsburg-Valois Wars continued for over a half-century, ending with the Treaty of Cateau-Cambrésis in 1559, which left the Spanish kings in control of Milan, Naples, Sardinia, and Sicily. Thus, war and the political integration of the fifteenth century destroyed the tiny city-republics and left the remaining territorial states in a position where they could no longer act independently of foreign powers.

Germany and Switzerland

The issue of central versus local control played a key role in German affairs as well. The Holy Roman Empire of the late Middle Ages was dramatically different from the empire of the early thirteenth century (see pages 198–202). Imperial power had previously rested on lands and castles in southwestern Germany. These strongholds melted away as emperors willingly pawned and sold the traditional crown lands in order to build up the holdings of their own families. Emperor

Henry VII (r. 1308–1313) and his grandson, Charles IV (r. 1347–1378), for example, pawned and sold imperial lands west of the Rhine in order to secure the house of Luxembourg's claims to the crown of Bohemia and other lands in the east. The Habsburgs in Austria, the Wittelsbachs in Bavaria, and a host of lesser families staked out claims to power and influence in separate parts of the empire. As a result, Germany was becoming a loose collection of territories.

The local power of regional authorities in the empire was further cemented by the so-called Golden Bull of 1356, the most important constitutional document of late medieval German history. In it, Emperor Charles IV declared that henceforth seven electors would be responsible for the choice of a new emperor: the archbishops of Cologne, Mainz, and Trier plus the secular rulers of the Rhenish Palatinate, Saxony, Brandenburg, and Bohemia. The result was a serious weaking of imperial power. Between the election of Rudolph of Habsburg in 1273 and 1519, there were fourteen emperors from six different dynasties, and only once, in 1378, did a son follow his father. The contrast between Germany and the monarchies of Iberia, France, and England is striking. By 1350, Germany had no hereditary monarchy, no common legal system, no common coinage, and no representative assembly. Political power rested in the hands of the territorial princes.

Territorial integration was least effective in what is now Switzerland, where a league of towns, provincial knights, and peasant villages successfully resisted a territorial prince. By 1410 the confederation had conquered most of the traditionally Habsburg lands in the Swiss areas. By the 1470s the Swiss had invented the myth of William Tell, the fearless woodsman who refused to bow his head to a Habsburg official, as a justification for their independent and anti-aristocratic traditions.

Scandinavia and Eastern Europe

In the fifteenth century, the Scandinavian kingdoms of Denmark, Sweden, and Norway—like the Swiss Confederation—lay open to economic and political influences from Germany. In

Denmark, rulers sought accommodations with the nobles and powerful cities of northern Germany. In Sweden and Norway, the situation was complicated by the fact that there was no nobility in the feudal sense of a class of vassals bound to a lord by an oath of homage. Aristocrats were merely leading landowners. Both they and the peasantry were traditionally represented in the Riksdag in Sweden and the Storting in Norway, popular assemblies that had the right to elect kings, authorize taxes, and make laws.

The elites of Scandinavia spoke similar Germanic languages and had close social and economic ties with one another. Thus, it is not surprising that the crowns of the three kingdoms were joined during short periods of crisis. In 1397, Queen Margaret of Denmark was able to unite the Scandinavian crowns by the Union of Kalmar, which would nominally endure until 1523. The Danes and Norwegians separately chose her as leader of their realms, calling her, for example, "the kingdom of Norway's mighty Lady and rightful Master." She then struggled with the rival claimant for the Swedish throne, and won, taking the title of queen of Sweden. Once established, her reign was a peaceful period for Scandinavia. She managed to create a strong centralized monarchy, eradicating the Swedish nobility's tax privileges, taking new lands for the Crown, and naming her own successor. The career of Margaret demonstrates as much about the precarious nature of elite women's lives in this period as it does about state building. If parliament elected a woman as queen, it was generally with the assumption that she would marry and give up her reign to her husband. An extraordinary woman could take advantage of such situations to prove her ability, take permanent control, refuse to marry, and provide strong leadership for a country—or, in this case, for three countries.

The political fluidity of Scandinavia was also typical of the Slavic East. German Teutonic knights controlled Prussia and, under the pretext of converting their pagan neighbors to Christianity, sought to expand eastward against the kingdom of Poland and the Lithuanian state. The conversion of the Lithuanian rulers to Christianity

slowed and finally halted the German advance to the east. More serious for the knights was their defeat in 1410 at Tannenberg Forest in Prussia by a Polish-Lithuanian army led by Prince Vytautus (r. 1392–1439) of Lithuania. The reign of Prince Vytautus represented the high point of Lithuanian dominion. He ruled much of modern Poland and western Russia as well as modern Lithuania.

During the fifteenth century, Lithuania faced a formidable new opponent, the grand duchy of Moscow. Since the Mongol invasions in the thirteenth century, various Russian towns and principalities had been part of a Mongolian sphere of influence. With the waning of Mongol control, however, the Muscovites annexed other Russian territories. By 1478, Ivan III (r. 1462–1505), called "the Great," had taken control of the famed trading center of Novgorod. Two years later he was powerful enough to renounce Mongol overlordship and refuse further payments of tribute. After marriage to an émigré Byzantine princess living in Rome, Ivan began to call himself "Tsar" (Russian for "Caesar"), implying that in the wake of the Muslim conquest of Constantinople, Moscow had become the new Rome. Landed aristocrats, called "boyars," came to control the provincial assemblies, or *dumas*. They used their political power to force formerly free peasants into a harsh serfdom from which the Russian peasantry would not emerge until the nineteenth century. It is too early to speak of a Russian national state, yet by 1500 the seeds of Russian dominion were sown.

With the exception of Italy and Germany, central monarchies emerged from the wars of the fourteenth and fifteenth centuries with their authority enhanced. By 1500 it did seem that the claim of the French king's lawyer—that all within the kingdom belonged to the king—was widely accepted. The Hundred Years' War and the resulting disorganization and unrest in France and England seemed to strike at the heart of the monarchies. But through the foundation of standing armies and the careful consolidation of power in the royal court, both countries grew stronger. And as the Italians learned in the wars following the French invasion of 1494, small regional states were no match for the monarchies.

FORMATION OF THE OTTOMAN AND SPANISH EMPIRES

In both Iberia and the eastern Mediterranean, political integration in the fifteenth century occurred because of political changes undreamed of in previous centuries. The rise of the Ottoman Empire and the unification of Spain created the two powers around which politics and diplomacy would revolve in sixteenth-century Europe.

The Ottoman Turks

In 1453 the Muslim Ottoman Turks breached the walls of Constantinople and killed Emperor Constantine XI (r. 1448–1453). They destroyed the last vestiges of the Byzantine Empire and ended the Roman imperial tradition. The sack of Constantinople sent shock waves through Christian Europe and brought forth calls for new crusades to liberate the East from the evils of Islam. It also stirred anti-Christian feelings among the Turks. The leader of the Turkish army, Sultan Mehmed II the Conqueror (r. 1451–1481), was acclaimed the greatest of all *ghazi*—that is, a crusading warrior who was, according to a Turkish poet, "the instrument of Allah, a servant of God, who purifies the earth from the filth of polytheism [i.e., the Christian Trinity]." The rise of the Ottoman Turks led to a profound clash between Christian and Muslim civilizations.

Turks had been invited into the Balkans as allies of the Byzantine emperors. Early in the fifteenth century, they were only one of the Balkan issues that concerned Christian Europe (Map 9.2). In the 1420s, for example, as the Turks and the Hungarians fought for control of Serbia, the Serbian king moved easily from alliance with one to alliance with the other. By changing religion, rulers often retained their political and economic influence. The Christian aristocracy of late-fifteenth-century Bosnia, for example, was welcomed into Islam and instantly created a cohesive elite fighting force for the Turks.

After the fall of Constantinople, the Turks worked to consolidate their new conquests. Anatolia was the heart of the vast Ottoman Empire, stretching from Syria and Palestine to Egypt, Croatia, and Greece. Turkish strength was based on a number of factors. The first was the loyalty and efficiency of the sultan's crack troops, the Janissaries. These troops were young boys forcibly taken from the subject Christian populations, trained in Turkish language and customs, and converted to Islam. Although they functioned as special protectors of the Christian community from which they were drawn, they were separated from it by their new faith. Seen as outsiders in both populations, they were particularly loyal to the sultan.

The situation of the Janissaries underlines a secondary explanation for Ottoman strength: the unusually tolerant attitudes of Mehmed II, who saw himself not only as the greatest of the ghazi but also as emperor, heir to Byzantine and ancient imperial traditions. Immediately after the conquest of Constantinople, he repopulated the city with Greeks, Armenians, Jews, and Muslims. Religious groups lived in separate districts centered on a church or synagogue, but each religious community retained the right to select its own leaders. Mehmed transferred the capital of the Turkish state to Constantinople. And by building mosques, hospitals, hostels, and bridges, he breathed new life into the city, which he referred to as Istanbul—that is, "the city." In the fifty years following the conquest, the population of the city grew an extraordinary 500 percent, from about 40,000 to over 200,000, making it the largest city in Europe, as it had been in antiquity. (See the box "Encounters with the West: A European View of the Ottoman Empire.") Christians and Jews were tolerated as long as they paid a special poll tax and accepted some Turkish supervision. Muslims and non-Muslims belonged to the same trade associations and traveled throughout the empire. At a time when Christian Europe seemed less and less willing to deal with non-Christian minorities, the Ottoman Empire was truly exceptional.

The Union of Crowns in Spain

While expanding across the Mediterranean, the Turks came in contact with the other new state

Map 9.2 Turkey and Eastern Europe With the conquest of Constantinople, Syria, and Palestine, the Ottoman Turks controlled the eastern Mediterranean and dominated Europe below the Danube River. The Holy Roman emperors, rulers of Italy, and kings of Spain had to be concerned about potential invasions by land or by sea.

of the fifteenth century, the newly unified kingdom of Spain. In 1469, Isabella, heir to the king of Castile, married Ferdinand, son of the king of Aragon and Catalonia. Five years later Isabella became queen of Castile, and then in 1479, Ferdinand took control of the kingdom of Aragon (see Map 10.1 on page 267). This union of crowns would lead to the creation of a united Spain.

The permanence of the union was surprising because the two kingdoms were so different. Isabella's Castile was much the larger and more populous state. It had taken the lead in the fight to reconquer Iberia and end Muslim rule. During the Reconquista, Castilians took control of large regions and turned them into ranges for grazing merino sheep, producers of the prized merino wool exported to the markets of Flanders and Italy. To maximize the profits from wool production, the kings authorized the creation of the Mesta, a brotherhood of sheep producers. By the early sixteenth century there were nearly 3.5 million sheep in Castile, and so great were the profits accruing to the Crown from the exporting of wool that all other aspects of the economy were sacrificed to the needs of the Mesta. Farmers

∾ ENCOUNTERS WITH THE WEST ∾

A European View of the Ottoman Empire

In the late fifteenth century, Italian governments began to send permanent ambassadors to foreign courts. They were the first governments to do so. The following report was written in 1585 by ambassador Gianfrancesco Morosini.

[The Turks] were organized as military squadrons or commando units until 1300 A.D., when one of their number, named Ottoman, a man of low birth, began to build a reputation as a strong and spirited leader. Shrewd and clever, he took advantage of rivalries among his people, attracted many of them to him, and led them in war and conquest, making himself master of various towns and provinces of both the Turks and their neighbors. . . .

They succeed to the throne without any kind of ceremony of election or coronation. According to Turkish law of succession, which resembles most countries' laws in this respect, the oldest son should succeed to the throne as soon as the father dies. But in fact, whichever of the sons can first enter the royal compound in Constantinople is called the sultan and is obeyed by the people and by the army. Since he has control of his father's treasure he can easily gain the favor of the janissaries and with their help the rest of the army and the civilians. . . .

The security of the empire depends more than anything else on the large numbers of land and sea forces which the Turks keep continually under arms. These are what make them feared throughout the world. The sultan always has about 280,000 well-paid men in his service. . . . These include roughly 16,000 janissaries who form the Grand Signor's advanced guard. . . .

The whole empire is inhabited by three groups of people: Turks, Moors [non-Turkish Muslims], and Christians. In Asia and Africa the Moors are more numerous than the Turks, while in Europe the largest number are Christians, almost all of whom practice the Greek rite. There are also many Jews since that is really their homeland, even though they live in it like strangers rather than natives.

In appearance they are very pious adherents of their false religion. . . . They are very regular in observing the hours of prayer and they always have the name of God on their lips, but never blaspheme. Every wealthy Turk builds a mosque, making it as splendid as he can, and provides a rich endowment for its upkeep. As a result, the mosques are kept so clean and orderly that they put us Christians to shame. . . . In addition to the mosques they also build asylums more pleasing than their own houses, and in many of these they will give food for three days to anyone who asks for it—not only Turks, but also Christians and Jews.

who lived along the routes by which the vast flocks moved often lost their crops to the hungry animals. The agricultural economy was virtually extinguished in some areas.

Economic power in Castile lay with the nobility, but political power rested with the monarch. Because the nobility was largely exempt from taxation, nobles ignored the *cortes*, the popular assembly, which could do little more than approve royal demands. No force was capable of opposing the will of the monarch. As John II of Castile (r. 1406–1454) asserted:

All my vassals, subjects, and people, whatever their estate, . . . are, according to all divine, human, . . . and even natural law, compelled and bound . . . to my word and deed. . . . The king holds this position not from men but from God, whose place he holds in temporal matters.[8]

The kingdom of Aragon was dramatically different. The center of the kingdom was Barcelona, an important trading center in the Mediterranean. In the fourteenth and fifteenth centuries the kings of Aragon concentrated their efforts on expanding their influence in the Mediterranean, south of France and Italy. By 1450 the Aragonese empire included the kingdom of Naples, Sicily, and Sardinia.

The power of the Aragonese king, in sharp contrast to the Castilian monarchy, was limited because the Crown was not unified. The ruler was king in Aragon and Navarre but was count in Catalonia. Aragon, Catalonia, and Valencia each maintained its own cortes. The power of the cortes is clear in the coronation oath taken by the Aragonese nobility: "We who are as good as you and together are more powerful than you, make you our king and lord, provided that you observe our laws and liberties, and if not, not."[9] The distinction with Castile could not be stronger.

The union of the crowns of Aragon and Castile did little to unify the two monarchies. Nobles fought over disputed boundaries, and trade duties continued to separate the two. The two realms even lacked a treaty to allow for the extradition of criminals from one kingdom to the other. Castilians never accepted Ferdinand as more than their queen's consort. After the death of Isabella in 1504, he ruled in Castile only as regent for his infant grandson, Charles I (r. 1516–1556). "Spain" would not emerge in an institutional sense until the late sixteenth century.

Nonetheless, the reign of Isabella and Ferdinand marked a profound change in politics and society in the Iberian kingdoms. The monarchs visited all parts of their realm, reorganized municipal governments, took control of the powerful military orders, strengthened the power of royal law courts, and extended the international influence of the monarchies. Ferdinand and Isabella married their daughter Joanna to Philip of Habsburg in 1496. Their intention was to get the Holy Roman Empire to help against the French invasion in Italy (see page 235). The marriage of their daughter Catherine of Aragon to Prince Arthur of England in 1501 was designed to obtain yet another ally against the French. Those two marriages would later have momentous consequences for European history.

The reign of Ferdinand and Isabella is especially memorable because of the events of 1492. In January of that year, a crusading army conquered Granada, the last Muslim stronghold in Iberia. In March, Ferdinand and Isabella ordered the Jews of Castile and Aragon to convert or leave the kingdom within four months. In April, Isabella issued her commission authorizing Christopher Columbus "to discover and acquire islands and mainland in the Ocean Sea" (see page 287).

The conquest of Granada and the expulsion of the Jews represented a radical shift in the Spanish mentality. Until the beginning of the fifteenth century, Spain maintained a level of religious tolerance unusual in Christendom. In the fourteenth century, perhaps 2 percent of the population of Iberia was Jewish, and the Muslim population may have been as high as 50 percent. One surprised northern visitor to Spain remarked that one noble's circle was filled with "Christians, Moors and Jews and he lets them live in peace in their faith."

This tolerant mingling of Christians, Muslims, and Jews came under attack by 1400, however. Many of the most important financiers and courtiers were Jews or *conversos* (converts), which increased tensions among the communities. The most conservative Christians desired a community free of non-Christian influences. Christians seemed concerned that many of the conversos were likely to reconvert, and this led many to advocate the institution of the Spanish Inquisition.

Inquisitions were well known in many parts of Europe, but the Spanish Inquisition was unique because in 1478, Pope Sixtus IV placed

Ferdinand and Isabella Interrogating a Jew Jews in Spain and many other parts of Europe were considered to be under the specific jurisdiction of local rulers. Jews and their converso relatives turned to the king and queen in 1492 when Jews faced the order to convert or leave the kingdom. *(Museo de Zaragoza)*

versos less than fully Christian. The "New Christians" tended to live near their Muslim or Jewish relatives, eat the foods enjoyed in their former communities, and observe holy days such as Yom Kippur, the Jewish day of atonement. Over four thousand converso families fled from Andalusia in southern Spain in the wake of the arrival of an inquisitor in 1490.

Because its administration, finances, and appointments were in Spanish hands, the Spanish Inquisition quickly became an important instrument for the expansion of state power. Many inquisitors used their offices to attack wealthy or politically important converso families both to drive them from public life and to fill the royal treasury, which was where the estates of those judged guilty wound up.

Ferdinand and Isabella seem to have concluded that the only way to protect the "New Christians" was to order all Jews who would not convert to leave the kingdom within four months. The order was signed on March 31, 1492, and published in late April after an unsuccessful attempt by converso and Jewish leaders to persuade the monarchs not to implement it. Many Jews could not dispose of their possessions in the four months allowed and so chose to convert and remain. But it is estimated that about ten thousand Jews left Aragon and that even more left Castile. Many moved to Portugal and then to North Africa. Some went east to Constantinople or north to the Low Countries. In 1504 the expulsion order was extended to include all Muslims.

The economic and social costs of the expulsion were profound. The exiles included many doctors, bankers, and merchants. Spanish culture, which had been open to influences from Muslim and Jewish sources, became less so in later centuries. As early as the first decades of the fifteenth century, some religious orders had refused to accept "New Christians." They required that their members demonstrate *limpieza de sangre,* a purity of blood. By 1500 the same tests of blood purity were extended to a majority of religious and public offices. Thus, by the end of the fifteenth century, the Iberian kingdoms had cre-

the grand inquisitor under the direct control of the monarchs. Like most Christian rulers, Ferdinand and Isabella believed that Christian orthodoxy was the only firm basis for a strong kingdom. Inquisitors attacked those aspects of converso tradition that seemed to make the con-

ated more powerful, unified governments, but at a terrible cost to the only area in Christendom that had ever practiced religious tolerance.

ECONOMY AND SOCIETY

People in many parts of Europe were living on the edge of disaster in 1300. Changes brought on by wars, plagues, and religious controversy affected the structure and dynamics of families, the organization of work, and the culture in many parts of Europe.

The Black Death and Economic Crisis

After nearly three centuries of dramatic growth, European society in 1300 was overpopulated and threatened by drastic economic and social problems. Estimates of Europe's population in 1300 have ranged from about 80 million to as high as 100 million. Given the low level of agricultural technology and the limited resources available, it became increasingly difficult for the towns and countryside to feed and support the growing population.

Farm size declined throughout Europe as parents divided their land among their children. Rents for farmland increased as landlords found they could play one land-hungry farmer off against another. Competition for jobs kept wages low, and when taxes were added to high rents and low wages, the peasant and artisan class began marrying later and having smaller families. Famines also cut the population. During the great famine of 1315–1322, wet and cold weather ruined crops in much of northern Europe. Food stocks were quickly exhausted, and mass starvation followed. So many people died, English chroniclers reported, that no one could keep up with the burials. At Ypres, in Flanders, 2800 people (about 10 percent of the population) died in just six months. And shortages continued. Seven other severe famines were reported in the south of France during the fourteenth century.

If Europe's problem had merely been one of famine brought on by overpopulation, recovery should have been possible. But, because of the return of a deadly epidemic disease, the economy did not recover. In 1348 bubonic plague returned to western Europe for the first time in six hundred years. Genoese traders contracted the plague in Caffa on the Black Sea coast, and infected sailors carried the disease south into Egypt and west to Sicily. From there it followed established trade routes and spread throughout Europe (Map 9.3).

The bacillus that caused "the great Mortality," as contemporaries called it, was *Yersinia pestis*. In its bubonic form, the plague attacks the lymphatic system, bringing painful, discolored swelling under the armpits and in the groin or lower abdomen. Some few who survived the first days of high fever and internal hemorrhaging recovered from the bubonic plague. No one, however, survived the rarer pneumonic or septicemic forms of the plague, which attacked the lungs and circulatory system. In the initial infestation of 1348–1351, from 25 to 35 percent of Europe's population may have died. In some of Europe's larger cities the figures may have risen to as high as 60 percent. (See the box "The Black Death.") After the initial outbreak, the plague returned again in 1363, and then for three centuries thereafter almost no generation would avoid it. Less is known about the plague in Muslim lands, but the situation seems to have resembled the European experience.

Lacking an understanding of contagion, fourteenth-century doctors depended on traditional theories inherited from the Greeks, especially the work of Galen. It was believed that good health could be upset by corrupt air, the movements of planets, and even violent shifts in emotions. In the fifteenth and sixteenth centuries, as the rhythms of the plague infestations became clearer, governments instituted quarantines to restrict the movement of goods and people from areas where the plague was raging.

Alongside medical theory, however, another class of explanations developed. A traditional religious response was to urge various moral reforms or penitential acts—charitable gifts, special prayers, processions. Charity and tolerance were not always the response, however. Women outside

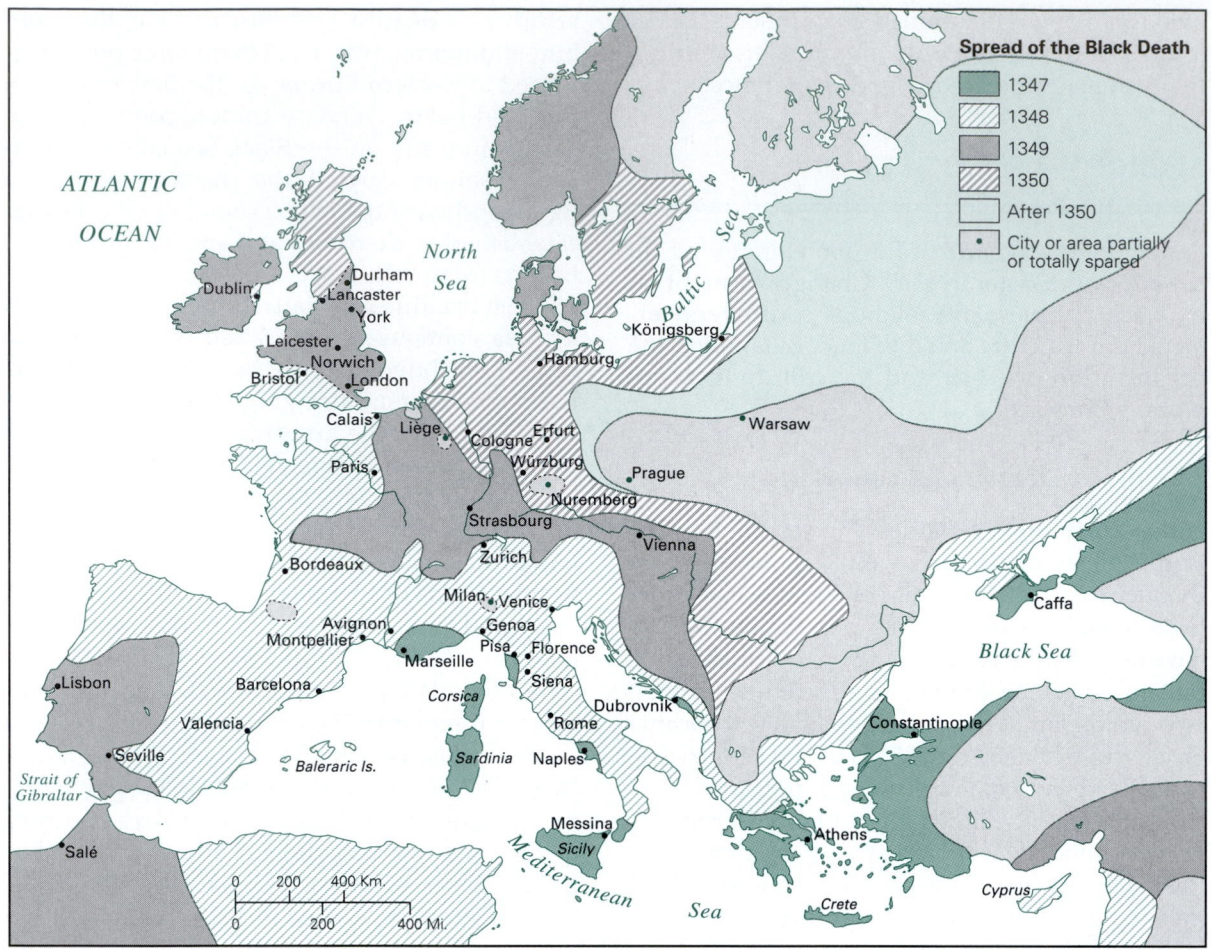

Map 9.3 The Progress of the Black Death The Black Death did not advance evenly across Europe; rather, as is clear from the dates at which it struck various regions, it followed the main lines of trade and communication.

the confines of family were often equated with moral dissolution and were sometimes persecuted during times of plague. In Muslim Egypt, women were ordered off the streets; in Christian Europe, prostitutes were driven out of towns.

In some parts of Europe there were murderous attacks on outsiders, especially Jews, who were suspected of spreading the contagion. Like many of the anti-Semitic myths, the stories of Jewish poisoners seemed to arise in the south of France and spread in their most virulent forms to

German towns along the Rhine. In many Rhineland towns, the entire Jewish population was slaughtered. In Strasbourg, attacks on Jews even preceded the arrival of plague.

A movement of penitents called "flagellants" arose in Hungary and spread quickly into Germany and across France and the Low Countries. These men and women moved from town to town urging repentance. In an imitation of Christ's sufferings, they ritually beat ("flagellated") themselves between the shoulders with

The Black Death

The plague of 1348 in Florence dominates the popular tales that form the bulk of the **Decameron** *by Giovanni Boccaccio (1313–1375). Boccaccio's description fits with everything scholars have since discovered about the first infestation of the plague in Italy and makes clear how the events affected the sensibilities of the people.*

This pestilence was so powerful that it was transmitted to the healthy by contact with the sick, the way a fire close to dry or oily things will set them aflame. And the evil of the plague went even further: not only did talking to or being around the sick bring infection and a common death, but also touching the clothes of the sick or anything touched or used by them seemed to communicate this very disease to the person involved. . . . There came about such fear and such fantastic notions among those who remained alive that almost all of them took a very cruel attitude in the matter; that is, they completely avoided the sick and their possessions; and in so doing, each one believed that he was protecting his good health.

There were some people who thought that living moderately and avoiding any excess might help a great deal in resisting this disease, so they gathered in small groups and lived entirely apart from everyone else. . . . Others thought the opposite: they believed that drinking excessively, enjoying life, going about singing and celebrating, and satisfying in every way the appetites as best one could, laughing, and making light of everything that happened was the best medicine for such a dis-

ease. . . . And in this great affliction and misery of our city the revered authority of the laws, both divine and human, had fallen and almost completely disappeared, for like other men, the ministers and executors of the laws were either dead or sick or so short of help that it was impossible for them to fulfill their duties. . . .

Others were of a crueler opinion (though it was, perhaps, a safer one): they maintained that there was no better medicine against the plague than to flee from it. . . . This disaster had struck such fear into the hearts of men and women that brother abandoned brother, uncle abandoned nephew, sister left brother, and very often wife abandoned husband and—even worse, almost unbelievable—fathers and mothers neglected to tend and care for their children as if they were not their own. . . . And since the sick were abandoned by their neighbors, their parents, and their friends and there was a scarcity of servants, a practice almost unheard of before spread through the city: when a woman fell sick, . . . she did not mind having a manservant (whoever he might be, no matter how young or old he was), and she had no shame whatsoever in revealing any part of her body to him. . . .

Source: Giovanni Boccaccio, *The Decameron*, trans. Mark Musa and Peter Bondanella (New York: New American Library, 1982), pp. 6–10. Translation copyright © 1982 by Mark Musa and Peter Bondanella. Reprinted by permission of Dutton Signet, a Division of Penguin Books USA Inc.

metal-tipped whips. The flagellants, in their quest for a purer, truly Christian society, brought suspicion on all those who were not Christian or were otherwise suspect.

It was a commonplace among contemporary chroniclers that "so many did die that everyone

thought it was the end of the world." Yet it was the young, the elderly, and the poor—those least likely to pay taxes, own shops, or produce new children—who were the most common victims. Even in towns with the highest mortality rates, recovery was rapid. Government offices were closed at

Lieferinxe: Saint Sebastian Interceding for the Plague-Stricken Lieferinxe depicts the major preoccupations of the plague years. In the foreground, a funeral proceeds, interrupted by a sudden death. A cart hauls more bodies out of the castle. In the sky, a demon and an angel quarrel over the souls of the dying. Above them, Christ listens to the prayers of Saint Sebastian. (*Walters Art Gallery, Baltimore*)

most for only a few weeks; markets reopened as soon as the death rate began to decline. Within two years tax receipts were back at preplague levels, but the shape of society had changed.

Patterns of Economic Change

In the aftermath of plague, the economy of Europe changed in a number of profound ways. Italy's domination of the European economy was challenged by the growth of trade and manufacturing in many parts of Europe. Other factors, such as the changing nature of the guilds, also contributed to the new economic situation.

Italy was the fulcrum of the international economy in 1300. Italian merchants sold woolens produced in Flanders and Italy to Arab traders in North Africa, who sold them along the African coast. The Italians used the gold that they collected in payment to buy spices and raw materials in the East, which they resold at the regional fairs of northern Europe. Because of their expertise in moving bullion and goods and their ready sources of capital, Italian merchants were ideal bankers and financial advisers to the papacy and European kings. Kings normally were expected to live off their own estates. They had few cash reserves. In time of war, when they needed money quickly, they tended to trade the rights to various revenues to Italian bankers, who had cash at hand. In the course of their operations, merchant-banking houses developed a network of couriers to move business mail, as well as bookkeeping procedures and techniques for the quick transfer of funds over long distances.

The most powerful bank in fifteenth-century Europe was the Medici bank of Florence. Founded in 1397 by Giovanni de' Medici (1360–1429), the bank grew quickly because of its role as papal banker. Cosimo de' Medici (1389–1464), son and successor of Giovanni, formed his bank as a series of partnerships with easily controlled junior partners in other parts of Europe.

International trade flourished in other areas besides Italy and Florence. By the end of the fifteenth century, Italians generally faced increased competition from local merchants and had never managed to penetrate beyond the Rhine in Germany. The Hanseatic League, an association of over a hundred trading cities centered on the German city of Lübeck, dominated northern commerce. By 1358 it was referred to as a "League of German Cities," and individual merchants could participate only if they were citizens of one of the member towns. The league's domination did not wane until the second half of the fifteenth century, when trade patterns diversified.

As wealthy as the great merchants were, in most parts of Europe prosperity was still tied to agriculture and the production of food grains. In northern and western Europe, foodstuffs were produced on the manorial estates of great churchmen and nobles. In the aftermath of plague and population decline, landlords and employers found themselves competing for the reduced number of farm laborers who had survived the plague. In 1351 the English crown issued the Statute of Laborers, which pegged wages and the prices of commodities at preplague levels. According to the statute, laborers "withdrew themselves from serving great men and others unless they have living [in food] and wages double or treble of what they were [before the plague]." Government attempts to stabilize prices and control wages had little effect, however. Many large landowners gave up direct farming of their estates and instead leased out lands to independent peasant farmers, who, for the most part, worked their lands with family labor. In southwest Germany some landowners reforested their lands, hoping to take advantage of rising prices for timber and charcoal. In both cases, landlords reduced their dependence on laborers.

Cloth manufacture, not agriculture, was the part of the European economy that changed most dramatically in the late Middle Ages. The production of light, cheap woolens moved out of the urban workshops of the cities and into the countryside. Rural cloth production was organized through the *putting-out system*. Merchants who owned the raw wool contracted with various artisans in the city, suburbs, or countryside—wherever the work could be done most cheaply—to process the wool into cloth. Rural manufacture was least expensive because it could be done as occasional or part-time labor by members of farming families during slack times of the day or season. Because production was likely to be finished in the countryside, guild masters had no control over price or quality.

All these patterns of economic change in the fifteenth century did not, however, bring new opportunities for women. Although men had controlled the guilds and most crafts in the thirteenth

and early fourteenth centuries, women in England and many other parts of northern Europe had been actively involved in the local economy. Unlike southern Europe, where women had few public roles, some northern towns apparently even had women's guilds to protect their members' activities as artisans and even peddlers. Because they often worked before marriage, townswomen in northern Europe tended to marry at a later age than did women in Italy. Since they had their own sources of income and often managed the shop of a dead husband, women could be quite independent. They were under less pressure to remarry at the death of a spouse. Although their economic circumstances varied considerably, up to a quarter of the households in northern towns like Bern or Zurich were headed by women—almost entirely independent widows.

The fifteenth century brought new restrictions into women's lives. In England, for example, brewing ale had been a highly profitable part-time activity that women often combined with the running of a household. The introduction of beer changed matters. Because hops were added to beer as a preservative, it was easier to produce, store, and transport in large batches. Beer brewing became a highly profitable full-time trade, reducing the demand for the alewife's product and providing work for men as beer-makers. At the same time the rights of women to work in urban crafts and industries were reduced. Guilds banned the use of female laborers in many trades and severely limited the right of a widow to supervise her spouse's shop. For reasons that are not entirely clear, journeymen objected to working alongside women—perhaps because they now saw their status as employees as permanent instead of temporary. By the early sixteenth century, journeymen in Germany considered it "dishonorable" for a woman to work in a shop, even the daughter or wife of the master.

Despite the narrowing of economic opportunities for women, the overall economic prospects of peasants and laborers improved. Lowered rents and increased wages in the wake of plague meant a higher standard of living for small farming

Women at Work   Although guild records tended to ignore the contributions of women, many women worked in their husband's shop. In this miniature, a woman is selling jewelry. Widows often managed the shops they inherited. *(Bibliothèque Nationale)*

families and laborers. Before the plague struck in 1348, when grain prices were high and wages relatively low, most poor Europeans had subsisted on bread or grain-based gruel, consuming meat, fish, and cheese a few times a week. A well-off peasant in England had lived on a daily ration of about two pounds of bread and a cup or two of oatmeal porridge washed down with three or four pints of ale; poorer peasants generally drank water. After the plague, laborers were more prosperous. Adults in parts of Germany may have consumed nearly a liter of wine and a third of a pound of meat along with a pound or more of bread each day. Hard times for landlords were good times for peasants and day laborers.

Landlords in England responded to their economic difficulties by converting their lands to grazing in order to produce for the growing woolen market and to reduce their need for labor. In eastern Europe, where landlords were able to take advantage of political and social unrest to force tenants into semifree servile status, there was increased emphasis on commercial grain farming. This "second serfdom" created an impoverished work force whose primary economic activity was in the lord's fields. Increasingly in the second half of the fourteenth century, grains raised in Poland and Prussia found their way to markets in England and the Low Countries. Europe east of the Elbe

River became a major producer of grain, but at a heavy social cost.

The loss of perhaps a third of the urban population due to the plague had serious consequences in the towns of Europe. Citizenship in most towns was restricted to masters in the most important guilds, and it was they who controlled government. In many towns, these citizens took advantage of this power in matters of taxation and worker's conditions. Peace and order in towns and in the countryside depended on a delicate balance of the interests of the well-to-do and the more humble—a balance easily destroyed by war, plague, and economic depression.

The Popular Revolts

The balance first broke in the 1330s, unleashing a wave of violence across Europe radically different from the violence of previous centuries. Some of the revolts seemed directed at the remnants of the old feudal and manorial elites. In that respect they were, as some historians have maintained, merely an extension of the struggle between landlords and tenants that had been going for at least two hundred years. Urban revolts, however, often seemed to be popular revolutions against exploitation by the patricians and guild masters who dominated local politics and controlled the local economy.

The first disturbance occurred in the industrial towns of Flanders during the 1330s. Flemish wealth was based on the manufacture of woolen cloth, which was dominated by the weavers of the towns of Ghent, Bruges, and Ypres. In 1338, just as the first battles of the Hundred Years' War were being waged, James van Artevelde was elected "captain," or emergency leader, of Ghent through the support of laborers and artisans who feared the weavers. Van Artevelde was assassinated in July 1345, in an act that was as much a personal vendetta as a political statement. Politics in Ghent quickly reverted to its traditional pattern: The well-to-do were again in control.

In the aftermath of war and plague, urban and rural risings also broke out in France. In the political upheaval that followed the disastrous French defeat at Poitiers (1356), Étienne Marcel, director of the merchants of Paris, mobilized a protest movement. He advocated ordinances that resembled a French Magna Carta, increasing the power of the Estates General. There was no real unity among the members of the Estates General, and Marcel's movement was not successful. It did, however, ignite a rural movement, the *jacquerie* (from *jacque*, French for the "jacket" typically worn by peasants), which began in response to long-standing economic and political grievances in the countryside that had been worsened by warfare. After extraordinary violence on both sides, the rebels were eventually defeated by aristocratic armies.

Two decades after the defeat of the French rebels, Europe again experienced insurrections. But the risings of the 1370s and 1380s differed from the previous revolts in several significant ways. Political unrest now was much more broadly based than it had been. There were political revolutions in many German towns as members of lowly artisan guilds claimed the right to sit alongside patricians in urban governments.

In 1378 a dramatic revolt occurred in central Italy. In reaction to a costly Florentine war with the papacy, the Ciompi, unskilled workers in the woolen industry, led a popular revolution hoping to expand participation in government and limit the authority of the guild masters over semiskilled artisans and day laborers. Barely six weeks after the Ciompi risings, however, wealthy conservatives quashed the new guilds and exiled or executed the leaders of the movement, leaving political and economic power even more firmly in the hands of the patricians.

Not long after the destruction of the Ciompi, England was rocked by the Rising of 1381, often called the Peasants' Revolt despite the fact that townsmen as well as peasants participated. England seethed with unrest as a result of plague, landlord claims for traditional dues, and finally a poll tax that placed a heavy burden on the common people. Popular armies led by Wat Tyler (d. 1381), who may have had some military experience, converged on London in June 1381. Tyler was murdered during a dramatic meeting with

Richard II outside London, and a reaction against the rebels quickly ensued.

SUMMARY

Europe in 1500 was profoundly different from the Europe of 1300. The economy had grown more complex in the wake of plague and demographic change. New patterns of trade and banking and new manufacturing techniques spread throughout Europe. Along with economic recovery came increased social and political consciousness, manifested in the urban and rural uprisings of the fourteenth century.

The kings of France and England, the princes and despots in Germany and Italy, and the papacy managed to overcome political and cultural crises. Military advances in the fifteenth century, such as the institution of standing armies, gave advantages to larger governments, but the Italian and German states demonstrated that regional powers, under certain circumstances, could remain virtually independent of royal control. Yet the strength of regional and local powers was largely overshadowed by the rise of the Turkish and Spanish empires. It was they who would dominate politics and diplomacy in the next century.

In the aftermath of schism and conciliar reform, the church also was transformed. Because of conciliar challenges to papal authority, popes had to deal much more carefully with the governments of Europe. The popes who returned to Rome from Avignon in the fifteenth century were adept at using art and literary culture to explain and magnify their court and their place in Christian history and society. Art and literature played an important role in the reform and explanation of public life.

NOTES

1. Quoted in Guillaume Mollat, *The Popes at Avignon, 1305–1378* (London: Thomas Nelson, 1963), p. 112.
2. Quoted in Margaret Aston, *Lollards and Reformers: Images and Literacy in Late Medieval Religion* (Ronceverte, W.Va.: Hambledon, 1984), p. 60.
3. Quoted in Francis Oakley, *The Western Church in the Later Middle Ages* (Ithaca, N.Y.: Cornell University Press, 1979), pp. 65–66.
4. Quoted in Charles T. Wood, *Joan of Arc and Richard III* (New York: Oxford University Press, 1988), pp. 56–57.
5. Quoted in Michael T. Clanchy, "Law, Government, and Society in Medieval England," *History* 59 (1974): 75.
6. Quoted in Peter Shervey Lewis, *Later Medieval France: The Polity* (New York: Macmillan, 1968), p. 15.
7. Salimbene de Adam, quoted in John Larner, *Italy in the Age of Dante and Petrarch, 1215–1380* (New York: Longman, 1980), p. 41.
8. Quoted in Angus MacKay, *Spain in the Middle Ages: From Frontier to Empire, 1000–1500* (London: Macmillan, 1977), p. 137.
9. Ibid.

SUGGESTED READING

Allmand, Christopher. *The Hundred Years' War: England and France at War, 1300–1450.* 1988. A summary of the war and its impact on late medieval politics, government, literature, and nationalism.

Brady, Thomas A., Jr., Heiko A. Oberman, and James D. Tracy. *Handbook of European History, 1400–1600.* 2 vols. 1994–1996. An excellent collection of studies by leading scholars in Europe and North America on all aspects of the period.

Carmichael, Ann G. *Plague and the Poor in Renaissance Florence.* 1985. A work directed at scholars that investigates the plague in a specific town, emphasizing the way in which the social and economic conditions that preceded the plague conditioned responses to the epidemic.

Cohen, J. *The Friars and the Jews: The Evolution of Medieval Anti-Judaism.* 1982. In a complex, closely argued study, Cohen describes the changed attitudes toward Jews in the thirteenth and fourteenth centuries.

Du Boulay, F. R. H. *Germany in the Later Middle Ages.* 1983. This survey of German history designed for students emphasizes the growth of territorial governments.

Duby, G. *France in the Middle Ages, 987–1460.* Translated by Juliet Vale. 1991. In this general survey, France's most distinguished medievalist concentrates on social and cultural life. Includes excellent pictures, maps, and diagrams.

Hanawalt, Barbara, ed. *Women and Work in Pre-Industrial Europe*. 1986. Sophisticated case studies of the changing status of women's work in the late Middle Ages in England, France, and Germany.

Hatcher, J. *Plague, Population, and the English Economy, 1348–1530*. 1977. Designed for students, this book provides a clear discussion of the effect of declining population on the economy of England.

Hay, Denys. *Europe in the Fourteenth and Fifteenth Centuries*. 1966. A well-written introductory survey of politics and society in Europe between 1300 and 1500; includes coverage of Scandinavia and the Slavic lands.

Herlihy, David. *Women, Family and Society in Medieval Europe: Historical Essays, 1978–1991*. 1995. A collection of essays on late medieval European society. Extremely thoughtful and well written.

Holt, P. M., Ann Katharine Swynford Lambton, and Bernard Lewis, eds. *The Cambridge History of Islam*. 1970. The essays in this volume provide a general introduction for nonspecialists.

Housley, N. *The Later Crusades: From Lyons to Alcazar, 1274–1580*. 1992. This comprehensive account of crusading history includes an especially good consideration of Christian and Muslim relations in Iberia and the Balkans.

Howell, Martha C. *Women, Production and Patriarchy in Late Medieval Cities*. 1986. After thoroughly reconstructing guild life in the Low Countries, the author argues that women were frozen out of the cloth industry. An interesting and important work.

Inalcik, H. *The Ottoman Empire: The Classical Age, 1300–1600*. 1973. A general discussion of the growth of the Ottoman state by Turkey's best medieval historian.

Kamen, H. A. F. *The Spanish Inquisition*. 1966. This is a passionate introduction to Spain's most controversial institution.

Klapisch-Zuber, Christiane. *Women, Family, and Ritual in Renaissance Italy*. 1987. A collection of essays that make clear the contradictory pressures placed on women in late medieval Italy. Very rewarding.

Larner, John. *Italy in the Age of Dante and Petrarch, 1215–1380*. 1980. A short introduction to the general developments in fourteenth-century Italy.

MacKay, A. *Spain in the Middle Ages: From Frontier to Empire, 1000–1500*. 1977. This short general introduction to Spain emphasizes the institutional changes that occurred in the late fourteenth and fifteenth centuries.

Miskimin, Harry A. *The Economy of Early Renaissance Europe, 1300–1460*. 1975. An excellent, readable survey of how the economies of various parts of Europe responded to economic decline and plague.

Mollat, Michel, and Philippe Wolff. *The Popular Revolutions of the Late Middle Ages*. 1973. The best survey of the major revolutions of the fourteenth century, emphasizing the local political conditions that brought on the revolutions.

Oakley, Francis. *The Western Church in the Later Middle Ages*. 1979. The best general history of the church in the Middle Ages. Oakley gives superior treatments of the Great Schism.

Swanson, Ronald N. *Religion and Devotion in Europe, c. 1215–c. 1515*. 1995. A general introduction to the place of the church in social life in the late Middle Ages.

Warner, Marina. *Joan of Arc: The Image of Female Heroism*. 1981. A studied and brilliant analysis of the changing political images of Joan of Arc in the centuries since her death. Very readable.

Ziegler, Philip. *The Black Death*. 1971. Although superseded on many specific points, this remains the best single volume on the plague in the fourteenth century.

CHAPTER 10

The Renaissance

Italians of the fourteenth and fifteenth centuries believed that the world needed to be dramatically reformed, and they were sure they knew why. "As the city of Rome had perished at the hands of perverse and tyrannical Emperors, so did Latin studies and literature undergo similar ruin and diminution. . . . And Italy was invaded by Goths and Lombards, barbarous, uncouth peoples, who practically extinguished all knowledge of literature."[1] This extinction of knowledge, according to Leonardo Bruni, a writer and chancellor in fifteenth-century Florence, was responsible for the moral and political decay he feared had weakened Italian public life. The only answer, he was sure, was to change the way Italians were educated and how they thought about their past.

Renaissance Italians wrote of themselves and their contemporaries as having "revived" arts, "rescued" painting, and "rediscovered" classical authors. In the sixteenth century the painter and art historian Giorgio Vasari described the revival as a *rinascità*, an Italian word meaning "rebirth." To this day we use the French translation of that word, *renaissance,* to describe the period between 1300 and 1600.

We also use *renaissance* to describe any time of intense creativity and change that differs dramatically from what has gone before. This definition of the word comes to us primarily from the work of the Swiss historian Jacob Burckhardt. In *The Civilization of the Renaissance in Italy* (1860), Burckhardt argued that the cultural brilliance of the period was the result of a new value system that placed personal merit over social status, loosening the medieval restraints of religion, guild, community, and family. Renaissance Italians, he believed, were the first individuals to recognize the state as an autonomous structure free from the strictures of religious or philosophical traditions. What Burckhardt thought he saw in Renaissance Italy were the first signs of the romantic individualism and the nationalism that characterized his own society.

Leonardo Bruni and Jacob Burckhardt both interpreted the period that separated classical antiquity from the culture of their own times as a "Dark Age" or a "Middle Age." It is true that the culture of Renaissance Europe was in many ways new and innovative, but today we see closer ties between the Renaissance and the ideas of the High Middle Ages. We no longer argue that the culture of Renaissance Europe was superior to the culture that preceded or followed it.

The Renaissance in Europe was an important cultural movement that aimed to reform and renew by making art, education, religion, and political life congruent with the reformers' conception of classical and early Christian traditions. Italians, and then other Europeans, came to believe that the social and moral values as well as the literature of classical Rome offered the best chance to change their own society for the better. This enthusiasm for a past culture became the measure for changes in literature, education, and art that would establish the standards of European cultural life for the next five hundred years.

~ *Questions and Ideas to Consider*

- What were the differences between Petrarch's humanism and the civic humanism that developed later? Consider the role of public service in each. How does the notion of public service versus private study intersect with traditional Christian descriptions of the pious life? How did divisions between public and private life affect women of the Renaissance?

- What was new about Renaissance art? Consider the close observations of nature, the study of classical models, and the discovery of the laws of perspective. How did the artist's role in society change?

- Who was Desiderius Erasmus? What were his contributions to European intellectual life? When humanism spread to northern Europe, it became known as Christian humanism. Why?

- What was life like at a noble court? Consider the life of Isabella d'Este and describe the situa-

tion of an elite, educated woman. What do you think of Castiglione's advice to the courtier?

- What was the relationship between the Renaissance artist and the Renaissance papacy? Did they support each other? How?

HUMANISM AND CULTURE IN ITALY, 1300–1500

Logic and Scholastic philosophy (see page 218) dominated university education in northern Europe in the fourteenth and fifteenth centuries. It had less influence in Italy, where education focused on the practical issues of town life rather than on theological speculation. Educated Italians of this period were interested in the *studia humanitatis*, which we now call humanism. By *humanism*, Italians meant rhetoric and literature—the arts of persuasion—not an ideological program based on philosophical arguments about human nature. Intellectual life centered on poetry, history, letter writing, and oratory based on aesthetic values consciously borrowed from ancient Greece and Rome.

As humanists discovered more about ancient culture, they were able to understand more clearly the historical context in which Roman and Greek writers and thinkers lived. And by the early sixteenth century their debates on learning, civic duty, and the classical legacy had led them to a new vision of the past and a new appreciation of the nature of politics.

The Emergence of Humanism

Humanism initially held greater appeal in Italy than elsewhere in Europe because the culture in central and northern Italy was significantly more secular and more urban than the culture of much of the rest of Europe. As we have seen, laymen, not members of the clergy, were likely to dominate government and education in Italy.

Differences between Italy and northern Europe are apparent in the structure of local education. In

CHAPTER CHRONOLOGY

1345	Petrarch discovers Cicero's letters to Atticus
1401	Lorenzo Ghiberti receives the commission for the doors of the Baptistery in Florence
1405	Christine de Pizan publishes *The Book of the City of the Ladies*
1416	Poggio Bracciolini discovers Quintilian's *Institutes of Oratory*
1419	Filippo Brunelleschi's Foundling Hospital in Florence is completed
1427	Masaccio completes his painting of the Trinity in Santa Maria Novella in Florence
1434	Jan van Eyck paints the Arnolfini wedding
1440	Lorenzo Valla publishes his *On the Donation of Constantine*
1444	Lorenzo Valla writes his *Annotations on the New Testament*

ca. 1452	Johann Gutenberg publishes his Bible
1469	Marsilio Ficino publishes his *Platonic Theology*
1478	Botticelli's *Primavera*
1494	Albrecht Dürer leaves on the first of two trips to Italy
1501	Michelangelo's *David*
1508	Michelangelo begins work on the Sistine Chapel ceiling
1511	Desiderius Erasmus writes *Praise of Folly*
1513	Niccolò Machiavelli writes *The Prince*
1516	Thomas More writes *Utopia*
1522	Francisco Jiménez de Cisneros's "Polyglot Bible" is completed
1528	Baldassare Castiglione publishes *The Book of the Courtier*

northern Europe, education was organized to provide clergy for local churches. In the towns of Italy, education was much more likely to be supervised by town governments to provide training in accounting, arithmetic, and the composition of business letters. In Italy it was common for town governments to hire lay grammar masters to teach in free public schools. They competed with numerous private masters and individual tutors who were prepared to teach all subjects. Giovanni Villani, a fourteenth-century merchant and historian, described Florence in 1338 as a city of about 100,000 people in which perhaps as many as 10,000 young girls and boys completed elementary education and 1000 boys continued their studies to prepare for careers in commerce.

In Italy there was much theorizing about towns as moral, religious, and political communities. Writers wanted to define the nature of the commune—the town government. They were practical thinkers trained in notarial arts—the everyday skills of oratory, letter writing, and the recording of legal documents.

Vernacular Literatures

The humanistic movement, however, was not simply a continuation of practical and literary movements. The extent of its innovation will be clearer if we look briefly at the vernacular literatures (that is, written in native languages, rather than Latin) of the fourteenth and fifteenth centuries. Vernacular literatures continued to treat traditional Christian moral and ethical concerns with reference to traditional values and ideas. Even the most famous and most innovative work of the fourteenth century, *The Decameron* by Giovanni Boccaccio (1313–1375), was in certain respects traditional (see page 245). Boccaccio hoped the lively and irreverent descriptions of contemporary Italians that make his *Decameron* a classic of European literature would also lead individuals to understand humanity and the folly of human desires. The tale describes a group of privileged young people who abandon friends and family during the plague of 1348 to go into the country, where on successive days they mix feasting, dancing, and song with one hundred tales of love, intrigue, and gaiety. With its mix of traditional and contemporary images, Boccaccio's book spawned numerous imitators in Italy and elsewhere.

Boccaccio's work influenced another vernacular writer, Geoffrey Chaucer (ca. 1343–1400), the son of a London burgher, who served as a diplomat, courtier, and member of Parliament. Chaucer's most well-known work, *The Canterbury Tales*, consists of stories told by a group of thirty pilgrims who left the London suburbs on a pilgrimage to the shrine of Saint Thomas Becket at Canterbury. The narrators and the stories themselves allow Chaucer to describe a variety of moral and social types, creating an acute, sometimes bitter, portrait of English life. The Wife of Bath is typical of Chaucer's pilgrims: "She was a worthy woman all her life, husbands at the churchdoor she had five." After describing her own five marriages, she makes the point that marriage is a proper way to achieve moral perfection, but it can be so only if the woman is master.

Despite the persistence of old forms of literature, new vernacular styles arose, although they still dealt with traditional values and ideas. Throughout Europe many writers directly addressed their cares and concerns. Some collected letters or wrote short works of piety, like *The Mirror for Simple Souls* of Marguerite of Porete (d. 1310). Though Marguerite was ultimately executed as a heretic, her work continued to circulate anonymously. Her frank description of love and God's love for humans inspired many other writers in the fourteenth and fifteenth centuries. Less erotic but equally riveting is the memoir of Margery Kempe, an alewife from England. She describes how she left her husband and family, dressed in white (symbolic of virginity), and joined with other pilgrims on trips to Spain, Italy, and Jerusalem.

One of the most unusual of the new vernacular writers was Christine de Pizan (1369–1430), the daughter of an Italian physician at the court of Charles V of France. Her father and later her husband had encouraged her to learn languages. When the deaths of both of these men left her with responsibility for her children and little money, she turned to writing. From 1389 until her death, she lived and wrote at the French court. She composed a short life of Joan of Arc and an instructional book for the education of the crown prince, but she is best known for *The Book of the City of the Ladies* (1405). In it she added her own voice to what is known as the *querelle des femmes*, the "argument over women." Christine de Pizan wrote to counter the many writings that characterized women as inferior to men and explained that any distinction between the abilities of men and women was due to unequal education: "If it were customary to send daughters to school like sons, and if they were then taught the natural sciences, they would learn as thoroughly and understand the subtleties of all the arts and sciences as well as sons." *The Book of the City of the Ladies* described an ideal city of women in which prudence, justice, and reason would reign.

All these vernacular writings built on popular tales and sayings as well as traditional moral and religious writings. Unlike the early humanists, the vernacular writers saw little need for new cultural and intellectual models. The humanists' need for new models seems to have developed out of particular Italian political and social needs.

Early Humanism

The first Italians who looked back consciously to the literary and historical examples of ancient Rome were a group of northern Italian lawyers and notaries who imitated Roman authors. Writers like Albertino Mussato of Padua (1262–1329) adopted classical styles in their poetry and histories celebrating their independent city-states and urging a renewal of republican values in the cities of the Po Valley. From its earliest, the classical

Women and Culture Christine de Pizan objected to male denigration of the moral and cultural value of women. This illumination from her *City of the Ladies* shows her ideal society, a place where women, like men, are allowed to study and create. *(Bibliothèque Nationale)*

revival in Italy was tied to issues of moral and political reform.

This fascination for the ancient world was transformed into a literary movement for reform by Francesco Petrarch (1304–1374), who popularized the idea of mixing classical moral and literary ideas with the concerns of the fourteenth century. Repelled by the urban violence and wars he had witnessed, Petrarch was highly critical of his contemporaries: "I never liked this age," he once confessed. He criticized what he named the "Babylonian Captivity" of the papacy in Avignon (see page 226); he supported an attempt to resurrect a repub-

lican government in Rome; and he believed that imitation of the values and culture of the ancient Romans was the only way to reform his world.

Petrarch believed that an age of darkness—he coined the expression "Dark Ages"—separated the Roman world from his own time and that the separation could be overcome only through a study and reconstruction of classical values: "Once the darkness has been broken, our descendants will perhaps be able to return to the pure, pristine radiance."[2] A brilliant poet and linguist and a tireless self-promoter, he lived his entire life as an example of the way in which classical values could serve as a vehicle for moral and intellectual reform.

Petrarch labored throughout his life to reconstruct the history and literature of Rome. He learned to read and write classical Latin. While still in his twenties, he discovered fragments of Livy's *Roman History*, an important source for the history of Republican Rome. He annotated and reorganized the fragments in an attempt to reconstruct the form Livy himself had intended. His work on Livy was merely the first step. In the 1330s he discovered a number of classical works, including orations by Cicero, the great philosopher, statesman, and opponent of Julius Caesar (see page 86).

Petrarch believed that study and memorization of the writings of classical authors could lead to the internalization of the ideas and values expressed in those works. He wrote *The Lives of Illustrious Men*, biographies of men from antiquity whose lives he thought were worthy of emulation. In some ways his admiration for the ancient moral philosophers put him at odds with Christian teachings, but Petrarch was a committed Christian. He recognized the tension between the Christian present and pagan antiquity. "My wishes fluctuate and my desires conflict, and in their struggle they tear me apart," he said.[3] Yet he prized the beauty and moral value of ancient learning.

Humanistic Studies

Petrarch's belief in humanism inspired a transformation of Italian intellectual life that affected discussions of politics, education, literature, and philosophy. Young scholars flocked to him. His style of historical and literary investigation of the past became the basis for a new appreciation of the present.

Petrarch's program of humanistic studies became especially popular with the wealthy oligarchy that dominated political life in Florence. The Florentine chancellor Coluccio Salutati (1331–1406) and a generation of young intellectuals who formed his circle evolved an ideology of civic humanism. Civic humanists wrote letters, orations, and histories praising their city's classical virtues and history. In the process they gave a practical and public meaning to the Petrarchan program. Civic humanists argued, like Cicero himself, that there was a moral and ethical value intrinsic to public life. In a letter to a friend, Coluccio Salutati wrote that public life is "something holy and holier than idleness in [religious] solitude." To another he added, "The active life you flee is to be followed both as an exercise in virtue and because of the necessity of brotherly love."[4]

More than Petrarch himself, civic humanists viewed their task as the creation of men of virtue who could take the lead in government. In the early years of the fifteenth century, civic humanists praised Florence for remaining a republic of free citizens rather than falling under the control of a lord. To civic humanists, the study of Rome and its virtues was the key to the continued prosperity of Florence and similar Italian republics.

One of Petrarch's most enthusiastic followers was Guarino of Verona (1374–1460), who became the leading advocate of educational reform in Renaissance Italy. His theories on educational reform were based on Greek models and were highly influential. One of his early students, Vittorino da Feltre (1378–1446), founded the Villa Giocosa, a school that became famous for employing games and physical exercise as well as formal study. In addition, Vittorino required that bright young boys from poor families be included among the seventy students normally resident in his school. Vittorino was so renowned that noblemen from across Italy sent their sons to be educated at the Villa Giocosa.

Humanistic education had its limits, however. Women participated in the cultural and artistic movements but not in the same way that men did. During the fifteenth century many women did learn to read and even to write. Religious women and wives of merchants read educational and spiritual literature. Some women needed to write in order to manage the economic and political interests of the family. Alessandra Macinghi-Strozzi of Florence (1407–1471), for example, wrote numerous letters to her sons in exile describing her efforts to find spouses for her children and to influence the government to end their exile. Yet many men were suspicious of literate women. Just how suspicious is evident in the career of Isotta Nogarola (b. 1418) of Verona. Isotta was well known as a gifted writer, but men's responses to her work were mixed. One anonymous critic suggested that it was unnatural for a woman to have such scholarly interests and accused her of equally unnatural sexual interests. Guarino of Verona himself wrote to her saying that if she was truly to be educated she must find "a man within the woman."[5]

When humanistically educated women tried to participate in creative pursuits, they were usually rebuffed and urged to hold to traditional Christian virtues of rejection of the world rather than to the values of civic humanism. A woman who had literary or cultural interests was expected to enter a convent. Throughout the fifteenth and early sixteenth centuries some women in Italy and the rest of Europe learned classical languages and philosophy, but they became rarer as time passed. The virtues of humanism were public virtues, and Renaissance Europe strained to keep women in the private sphere. (See the box "Cassandra Fedele Defends Liberal Arts for Women.") In this very restricted position, some elite women still managed to take an active part in the culture of the day. Isabella d'Este, wife of the duke of Mantua, was able to influence artistic trends and styles through the humanists and painters that she brought to her court, and she was widely recognized as having done so. Along with commissioning artwork, Isabella studied classical authors, made her own translations, and corresponded with noted scholars. Many other elite women found some creative satisfaction in directing culture through patronage.

Cassandra Fedele Defends Liberal Arts for Women

Cassandra Fedele (1465–1558) by the age of 12 had learned Latin and later learned Greek, rhetoric, and history. The Venetian senate praised her as an ornament of learning in the city, but there was no place for an educated woman. In this oration, she adds her own plea for education for women.

Aware of the weakness of my sex and the paucity of my talent, blushing, I decided to honor and obey [those who have urged me to consider how women could profit from assiduous study] . . . in order that the common crowd may be ashamed of itself and stop being offensive to me, devoted as I am to the liberal arts. . . . What woman, I ask, has such force and ability of mind and speech that she could adequately meet the standard of the greatness of letters or your learned ears? Thus daunted by the difficulty of the task and conscious of my weakness, I might easily have shirked this opportunity to speak, if your well-known kindness and clemency had not urged me to it. For I am not unaware that you are not in the habit of demanding or expecting from anyone more than the nature of the subject itself allows, or the person's own strength can promise of them.

Even an ignorant man—not only a philosopher—sees and admits that man is rightly distinguished from a beast above all by [the capacity of] reason. For what else so greatly delights, enriches and honors both of them than the teaching and understanding of letters and the liberal arts? . . . Moreover, simple men, ignorant of literature, even if they have by nature this potential seed of genius and reason, leave it alone and uncultivated throughout their whole lives, stifle it with neglect and sloth, and render themselves unfit for greatness. . . . But learned men, filled with a rich knowledge of divine and human things, turn all their thoughts and motions of the mind toward the goal of reason and thus free the mind, [otherwise] subject to so many anxieties, from all infirmity. . . . States and princes, moreover, who favor and cultivate these studies become much more humane, pleasing, and noble, and purely [through liberal studies] win for themselves a sweet reputation for humanity. . . . For this reason the ancients rightfully judged all leaders deficient in letters, however skillful in military affairs, to be crude and ignorant. As for the utility of letters, enough said. . . . Of these fruits I myself have tasted a little and [have esteemed myself in that enterprise] more than abject and hopeless; and armed with distaff and needle—woman's weapons—I march forth [to defend] the belief that even though the study of letters promises and offers no reward for women and no dignity, every woman ought to seek and embrace these studies for that pleasure and delight alone that [comes] from them.

Source: M. L. King and A. Rabil, *Her Immaculate Hand: Selected Works by and About the Women Humanists of Quattrocento Italy* (Binghamton, N.Y.: Center for Medieval and Early Renaissance Studies, State University of New York, 1983), pp. 74–77. Reprinted by permission.

The Transformation of Humanism

The fascination with education based on ancient authorities was heightened by the discovery in 1416 in the Monastery of Saint Gall in Switzerland of a complete manuscript of Quintilian's *Institutes of Oratory*, a first-century treatise on the proper education for a young Roman patrician. The discovery was hardly accidental. A Florentine antiquary, Niccolò Niccoli, coordinated and paid for this and other searchs for new manuscripts. A wealthy bachelor, Niccoli (1364–1437)

spent the fortune he had inherited from his father by collecting ancient statuary, reliefs, and,
most of all, books. When he died, his collection
of more than eight hundred volumes of Latin
and Greek texts was taken over by Cosimo de'
Medici. It became the foundation of the humanist library housed in the Monastery of San Marco
in Florence, and humanists from across Europe
came to Florence to study the collection. Similar
libraries were made elsewhere, and the Greek
and Latin sources collected there allowed humanists to study classical languages in a way not
possible before.

The career of Lorenzo Valla (1407–1457) illustrates the transformation that took place in the
fifteenth century. Convinced that the key to
philosophical and legal problems lay in histori-
cal-textual research, Valla came to realize that language changes—that it, too, has a life and a history. In 1440 he published a work called *On the
Donation of Constantine*. The *Donation of Constantine* purported to record the gift by the emperor
Constantine (r. 311–337) of jurisdiction over
Rome to the pope when the capital of the empire
was moved to Constantinople. In the High and
late Middle Ages, the papacy used the document
to defend its right to political dominion in central
Italy. The donation had long been criticized by legal theorists, who argued that Constantine had
no right to make it. Valla attacked the legitimacy
of the document itself. Because of its language
and form, he argued, it could not have been written at the time of Constantine:

Through his [the writer's] babbling, he reveals his
most impudent forgery himself. . . . Where he deals
with the gifts he says "a diadem . . . made of pure gold
and precious jewels." The ignoramus did not know
that the diadem was made of cloth, probably silk. . . .
He thinks it had to be made of gold, since nowadays
kings usually wear a circle of gold set with jewels.[6]

Valla was correct. The *Donation* was a forgery
written in the eighth century.

Valla later turned his attention to the New
Testament and made many important correc-
tions to the fourth-century Vulgate edition of the
Bible put together by Jerome (see page 137). His
annotations on the New Testament were highly
influential during the Protestant Reformation.

With the work of Valla and others, humanist
interest began to include philosophy along with
literary studies. In 1456, a young Florentine,
Marsilio Ficino (1433–1499), began studying
Greek in order to translate the works of Plato
into Latin and to interpret Plato in the light of
Christian tradition. Ficino wrote that everything
was connected along a hierarchy ranging from
the lowliest matter to the person of God. The human soul was located at the midpoint of this hierarchy and was a bridge between matter and
God. According to Ficino, logic and scientific observation did not lead to true wisdom, for humans know logically only that which they can
define in human language; they can, however,
love things, like God, that they cannot fully
comprehend.

Ficino's belief in the dignity of man was
shared by Giovanni Pico della Mirandola (1463–
1494), who extended Ficino's idea of the hierarchy
of being, arguing that humans surpassed even the
angels in dignity. Angels held a fixed position in
the hierarchy, just below God. In contrast, humans
could move up or down in the hierarchy. Pico was
one of the first humanists to learn Hebrew and to
argue that divine wisdom could be found in Jewish mystical literature. He studied the Jewish
Cabala, a collection of mystical and occult writings that humanists believed dated from the time
of Moses. Pico's adoption of the Hebrew mystical
writings was often controversial in the Jewish
community as well as among Christians. (See the
box "Encounters with the West: Rabbi Mordecai
Dato Criticizes the Humanists.")

Humanists of the fifteenth and sixteenth centuries also investigated astrology and alchemy.
By the late fifteenth century many humanists assumed that the stars profoundly affected personality as well as the ability to respond to certain
crises. For a century or more after 1500, astrol-
ogers were official or unofficial members of most
European courts. Interest in alchemy was
equally widespread though more controversial.
Alchemists believed that everything was made
of a primary material and that it was possible to

~ ENCOUNTERS WITH THE WEST ~

Rabbi Mordecai Dato Criticizes the Humanists

Beginning with Giovanni Pico della Mirandola, many Christian humanists became convinced that the Jewish Cabala shared an original wisdom with Egyptian magic, Greek mystical philosophy, and Christianity. And they enthusiastically studied Jewish literature in order to combine it with other traditions. In this selection, Rabbi Mordecai Dato (1525–ca. 1591), who lived in northern Italy, protests to a Jewish colleague that in trying to combine so many traditions, humanists misunderstand them.

Let me inform you of two things: first . . . that whatever is said by one of the sages of the *Safed* [the original Cabala mystics] . . . in the introduction to the works of Truth and Justice [i.e., Cabala] is based upon the words of the Book of Splendor [Zahor, a thirteenth-century book of mysticism]; their words are its words; they emerge from its radiance, and without them no man might raise his hands or feet . . . in learning or in criticism, to speak about this wisdom, for they fear the great fire which consumes that man who makes things up from his heart, who has not heard [them] from his teacher as required in the Book of Splendor. . . . They ought not to rely upon their understanding or their dialectics, [though] they are very great, save in the interpretation of some few sayings of the Book of Splendor which seem to contradict one another . . . and even this only under certain conditions stated in the book itself. Secondly, that the words of the Book of Splendor are based upon tradition, and that one may not question them.

Everything which is probable ought to be accepted graciously—and that which is without reason ought to be confirmed by reason. [However], one is not obligated to find a rational explanation of the kind which I have mentioned for all the words of the Book of Wisdom, for many have fallen [in the attempt]. Go and see how one of the sages of the [gentile] nations, Johannes Reuchlin, made himself wise in one work which he made, which I saw many years ago, bringing selection after selection, at random . . . to find words of favor and natural philosophic reason in the words of the Book of Wisdom. And in his many clever words, albeit he avoided corporealization, he compared the Creator to his form, and the servant to his master [that is, he made critical logical errors] . . . heaven forbid.

Source: Dato's letter is partially translated in Robert Bonfil, *Rabbis and Jewish Communities in Renaissance Italy* (Oxford and New York: Oxford University Press for The Littman Library, 1990), pp. 295–296. Reprinted by permission of Oxford University Press.

transmute one substance into another. The most popular version, and the most open to hucksters and frauds, was the belief that base metals could be turned into gold. The hopes of most alchemists, however, were more profound. They were convinced that they could unlock the explanation of the properties of the whole cosmos. On a religious level as well as on a material level, practitioners hoped to take the impure and make it pure. The interest in understanding and manipulating nature that lay at the heart of astrology and alchemy was an important stimulus to scientific investigations and, ultimately, to the rise of modern scientific thought.

Humanism and Political Thought

Petrarch and the civic humanists believed that rulers should exhibit all the classical and Christian virtues of faith, hope, love, prudence, temperance, fortitude, and justice. They viewed governments and laws as essentially unchanging and static. They believed that when change did occur, it most likely happened by chance—that is, because of fortune (the Roman goddess Fortuna). The only protection against chance was true virtue, for the virtuous would never be dominated by fortune. Thus, beginning with Petrarch, humanists advised rulers to love their subjects, to be magnanimous with their possessions, and to maintain the rule of law.

The French invasions of Italy in 1494 (see page 235) and the warfare that followed called into question many of the humanists' assumptions about the lessons and virtues of classical civilization. The best example of this can be found in the work of the Florentine Niccolò Machiavelli (1469–1527). After a humanistic education and service from 1494 to 1512 in the anti-Medicean republican government of Florence, Machiavelli was forced by the Medici to abandon public life and leave Florence. While living on his farm outside Florence, Machiavelli developed in a series of writings what he believed was a new science of politics. He wrote *Discourses on Livy*, a treatise on military organization, a history of Florence, and even a Renaissance play (*The Mandrake Root*). He is best remembered, however, for *The Prince* (1513), a small tract numbering less than a hundred pages.

Machiavelli felt that his contemporaries paid too little heed to the lessons of history. Thus, in his discourses on Livy he comments on Roman government, the role of religion, and the nature of political virtue, emphasizing the sophisticated Roman analysis of political and military situations. In *The Prince*, he explicitly rejects the assumption that human nature is essentially good and that individuals will naturally choose virtue over vice.

Machiavelli was vilified as amoral because he argued that in some situations "virtues" like prudence, magnanimity, and love could have violent, even evil, consequences. If, for example, a prince was so magnanimous in giving away his wealth that he was forced to raise taxes, his subjects might come to hate him. Conversely, a prince who, through cruelty to the enemies of his state, brought peace and stability to his subjects might be obeyed and perhaps even loved by them. A virtuous ruler must be mindful of the goals to be achieved—that is what Machiavelli meant by the phrase often translated as "the ends justify the means." Machiavelli rejected earlier humanistic assumptions that one needed merely to imitate the great leaders of the past. Because of the immoral behavior of others, including monarchs and popes, effective leaders must be more concerned with success than with personal morality.

With the writings of Machiavelli, humanistic ideas of intellectual, moral, and political reform came to maturation. Petrarch and the early humanists believed fully in the powers of classical wisdom to transform society. Machiavelli and his contemporaries admitted the importance of classical wisdom but also recognized the ambiguity of any application of classical learning to contemporary life.

THE ARTS IN ITALY, 1250–1550

Townsmen and artists in Renaissance Italy shared the humanists' perception of the importance of classical antiquity. In the middle of the fifteenth century the Florentine sculptor Lorenzo Ghiberti concluded that with the rise of Christianity "not only statues and paintings [were destroyed], but the books and commentaries and handbooks and rules on which men relied for their training." Italian writers and painters themselves recognized that the literary recovery of past practices was essential.

The Renaissance of the arts can be divided into three periods. In the early Renaissance artists first imitated nature. In the middle period artists rediscovered classical ideas of proportion.

In the High Renaissance, artists were "superior to nature but also to the artists of the ancient world," according to the artist and architect Giorgio Vasari (1511–1574), who wrote a famous history of the eminent artists of his day.

The Artistic Renaissance

The first stirrings of the new styles can be found in the late thirteenth century. The greatest innovator of the era was Giotto di Bondone of Florence (ca. 1266–1337). He traveled as far south as Rome and as far north as Padua painting churches and chapels. According to later artists and commentators, Giotto broke with the prevailing stiff, highly symbolic style and introduced lifelike portrayals of living persons. He produced paintings of dramatic situations, showing events located in a specific time and place. The frescoes of the Arena Chapel in Padua (1304–1314), for example, recount episodes in the life of Christ. In a series of scenes leading from Christ's birth to his crucifixion, Giotto manages to capture the drama of key events, like Judas's kiss of betrayal. Even

Giotto's Naturalism Later painters praised the naturalistic emotion of Giotto's painting. In this detail from the Arena Chapel, Giotto portrays the kiss of Judas, one of the most dramatic moments in Christian history. *(Scala/Art Resource, NY)*

Michelangelo, the master of the High Renaissance, studied Giotto's painting. Giotto was in such demand throughout Italy that his native Florence gave him a public appointment so that he would be required by law to remain in the city.

Early in the fifteenth century, Florentine artists devised new ways to represent nature that surpassed even the innovations of Giotto. The revolutionary quality of these artistic developments is evident from the careers of Lorenzo Ghiberti (1378–1455), Filippo Brunelleschi (1377–1446), and Masaccio (born Tomasso di ser Giovanni di Mone, 1401–ca. 1428). Their sculpture, architecture, and painting began an ongoing series of experiments with the representation of space through linear perspective. Perspective is a system for representing three-dimensional objects on a two-dimensional plane. It is based on two observations: (1) As parallel lines recede into the distance, they seem to converge; and (2) there is a geometrical relationship that regulates the relative size of objects at various distances from the viewer. Armed with these seemingly simple ideas, painters of the Renaissance were suddenly capable of an entirely new level of realism.

In 1401, Ghiberti won a commission to design door panels for the baptistery of San Giovanni in Florence. He was to spend the rest of his life working on two sets of bronze doors. The reliefs he created told the stories of the New Testament and the Old Testament. In the commissions for the Old Testament scenes, Ghiberti used the new techniques of linear perspective to create a sense of space into which he placed his classically inspired figures. His work made him famous throughout Italy. Later in the sixteenth century Michelangelo remarked that the Old Testament doors were worthy to be the "Doors of Paradise," and so they have since been known.

In the competition for the baptistery commission, Ghiberti had beaten the young Filippo Brunelleschi, who, as a result, gave up sculpture for architecture and later left Florence to study in Rome. While in Rome he is said to have visited and measured surviving examples of classical architecture—the artistic equivalent of humanistic literary research. According to Vasari, he was capable of "visualizing Rome as it was before the fall." Brunelleschi's debt to Rome is evident in his masterpiece, Florence's foundling hospital. Resembling a Greek stoa or an arcaded Roman basilica, the long, low structure is an example of how profoundly different Renaissance architecture was from the towering Gothic of the Middle Ages.

In the first decade of the fifteenth century, many commentators believed that painting would never be as innovative as either sculpture or architecture. They knew of no classical models that had survived for imitation. Yet the possibilities in painting became apparent in 1427 with the unveiling of Masaccio's *Trinity* in the Florentine church of Santa Maria Novella. Masaccio built on experiments in linear perspective to create a painting in which a flat wall seems to become a recessed chapel. The space created is filled with the images of Christ crucified, the Father, and the Holy Spirit.

In the second half of the fifteenth century, artists like the Florentine Sandro Botticelli (1445–1510) added a profound understanding of classical symbolism to the technical innovations of the early Renaissance. Botticelli's famous *Birth of Venus* and *Primavera* (1478), both painted for Medici houses, are filled with Neo-Platonic symbolism concerning truth, beauty, and the virtues of humanity.

The high point in the development of Renaissance art came at the beginning of the sixteenth century. Artists in Venice learned perspective from the Florentines and added their own tradition of subtle coloring in oils. Raphael Sanzio (1483–1520), who arrived in Rome from his native Urbino in 1508, demonstrated that artistic brilliance was not a Florentine monopoly. His decorations of the Vatican palaces in Rome included his *School of Athens*, a painting that portrays the great philosophers of the past gathered with contemporary artists. It is in effect the synthesis of the classical learning and artistic innovation for which the Renaissance is famous.

The work of two Florentines, Leonardo da Vinci (1452–1519) and Michelangelo Buonarroti (1475–1564), best exemplifies the sophisticated heights that art achieved early in the sixteenth century. Leonardo, the bastard son of a notary,

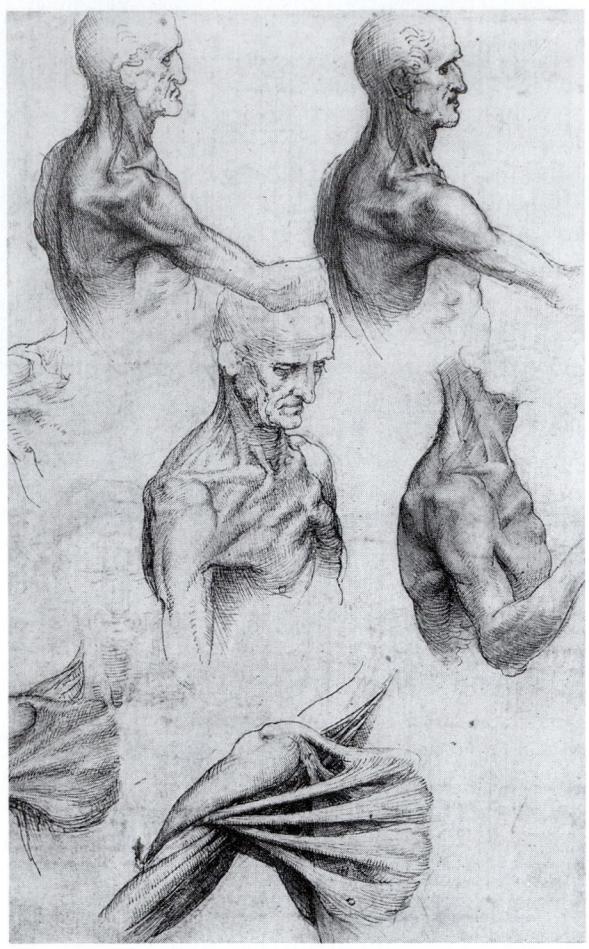

Leonardo da Vinci's Anatomical Drawings Leonardo studied carefully to record as accurately as possible the appearance of the human body. He was convinced that his keen observations made him the equal of any humanist. *(The Royal Collection © Her Majesty Queen Elizabeth II)*

was raised in the village of Vinci outside of Florence. Cut off from the humanistic milieu of the city, he defended his lack of classical education by arguing that all the best writing, like the best painting and invention, is based on the close observation of nature. Close observation and scientific analysis made him uniquely creative. Leonardo is famous for his plans for bridges, airships, submarines, and fortresses. There seemed to be no branch of learning in which he

was not interested. In painting he developed *chiaroscuro,* a technique using deep variations of light and shade to enhance a character and create dramatic realism. It was his analytical observation that made Leonardo so influential on his contemporaries.

The art of Michelangelo, by contrast, was more an expression of idealism than analytical observation—more concerned with philosophy than natural science. In his career we can follow the rise of Renaissance artists from the ranks of mere craftsmen to honored creators, courtiers who were the equals of the humanists. We can also discern the synthesis of the ideals of the Renaissance with a profound religious sensitivity.

Consider Michelangelo's statue *David* in Florence and his commissions in the Sistine Chapel of the Vatican in Rome. From his youth Michelangelo had studied and imitated antique sculpture. With the statue *David* (1501), Michelangelo combined this reverence for antiquity with new ideals, a vibrant depiction of human emotion, and the political concerns of the Renaissance. The statue represented David just after his defeat of Goliath saved Israel from conquest by the Philistines—a perfect symbol of the youthful Florentine republic struggling to maintain its freedom against great odds. Artists and citizens of Florence alike hailed the mammoth statue as a masterpiece, and the *David* was placed before the Palazzo Vecchio, Florence's city hall, where it could be seen by all.

Michelangelo was a committed republican and Florentine, but he spent much of his life working in Rome on a series of papal commissions. In 1508 he was called to Rome to work on the ceiling of the Sistine Chapel. Michelangelo spent four years decorating the ceiling with hundreds of figures and with nine scenes from the book of Genesis, including the famous *Creation of Adam.* In the late 1530s, he completed *The Last Judgment* on the wall above the altar. In that painting the techniques of perspective and the conscious recognition of debts to classical culture recede into the background as the artist passionately depicts his own spiritual struggle. He surrounds Christ in judgment with saints and sinners, including in the hollow, empty skin of Saint Bartholomew, a psychological self-portrait of the artist himself.

Art and Patronage

Artists in the modern world are accustomed to standing outside society as critics of commonly held ideas. In the late Middle Ages and Renaissance, artists were not alienated commentators. Their work provided symbols and images through which Italians could reason about the most important issues of their communities. Italians spent vast sums on art because of its ability to communicate social, political, and spiritual values.

Italy in the fourteenth and fifteenth centuries was unusually wealthy relative to the towns and principalities of northern Europe. Because of banking and international trade, Italians, and particularly Florentines, had money to spend on arts and luxuries. Whether as public or private patrons, they could afford to use consumption of art as a form of competition for social and political status.

Throughout Europe art fulfilled a devotional function. Painted crucifixes, altar paintings, and banners were often endowed as devotional or penitential objects. The Arena Chapel in Padua with its frescoes by Giotto was built and endowed by a merchant anxious to pay for his sins.

In the late Middle Ages and Renaissance, numerous paintings and statues throughout Italy (and much of the rest of Europe) were revered for their miraculous powers. During plague, drought, and times of war, people had recourse to the sacred power of the saints represented in these works of art. The construction of the great churches of the period was often a community project that lasted for decades, even centuries. These gigantic structures were mixtures of piety, civic pride, and religious patronage. The city council of Siena, for example, voted to rebuild its Gothic cathedral of Saint Mary, saying that the blessed Virgin "was, is and will be in the future the head of this city" and through veneration of her "Siena may be protected from harm." Thus, it is clear that although the subject of art was primarily religious, the message was bound up in civic concerns.

The first burst of artistic creativity in the fourteenth century was paid for by public institutions. Communal governments built and redecorated city halls to house government and to promote civic pride. In most towns there was a remarkable emphasis on the beauty of the work. Civic officials often named special commissions to consult with a variety of artists and architects before approving building projects.

In Florence public art was often organized and paid for by various guild organizations. Guild membership was a prerequisite for citizenship, so guildsmen set the tone in politics as well as in the commercial life of the city. Most major guilds commissioned sculpture for the Chapel of Or San Michele, a famous shrine in the grain market (its painting of the Virgin was popularly thought to have great powers) and seat of the city's most powerful political organization. Guilds took responsibility for the building and maintenance of other structures in the city as well. The guild of the cloth merchants paid for the frescoes in the baptistery of Saint John the Baptist (the city's patron saint) and commissioned the bronze doors by Lorenzo Ghiberti. The guild of the silk merchants oversaw the selection of Brunelleschi to design the foundling hospital. Guildsmen took pride in the creation of a beautiful environment, but the work reflected not only on the city but also on the power and influence of the guilds themselves.

The princes who ruled outside the republics of Italy often had similarly precise messages that they wished to communicate. Renaissance popes embarked on a quite specific ideological program in the late fifteenth century to assert their role as both spiritual leaders of Christendom and as temporal lords of a central Italian state. Rulers like the Sforza dukes of Milan constructed castles and decorated them with pictures that emphasized their noble virtues and their natural right to rule. In the Medici palace in Florence, the chapel holds a painting of the Magi (the three Wise Men who were said to have visited the infant Jesus) in which the artist, Benozzo Gozzoli (1420–1498), used faces of members of the Medici family for the portraits of the Wise Men and their entourage. The Magi, remembered as wise and virtuous rulers, were an apt symbol for the family that had come to dominate the city.

Artists at princely courts were expected to work for the glory of their lord. Often the genre of choice was the portrait. Perhaps the most successful portraitists of the sixteenth century were Sofonisba Anguissola (1532–1625) and her five sisters, all of whom were well-known painters. Anguissola won renown as a prodigy; one of her paintings was sent to Michelangelo, who forwarded it to the Medici in Florence. Later she was called to the Spanish court, where she produced portraits of the king, queen, and their daughter. She continued to paint after her marriage and return to Italy. Even in her nineties, painters from all parts of Europe visited her to talk about techniques of portraiture.

THE SPREAD OF THE RENAISSANCE, 1350–1536

By 1500, the Renaissance had spread from Italy to the rest of Europe. Even in the Slavic East, beyond the borders of the old Roman Empire, in Prague and Wroclaw one could find a renewed interest in classical ideas about art and literature. As ideas about the past and its relevance to contemporary life spread, however, the message was transformed in several important ways. Outside of Italy, Rome and its history did not play a dominant role. Humanists were interested more in religious than in political reform, and they responded to a number of important local interests. Yet the Renaissance idea of renewal based on a deep understanding and imitation of the past remained at the center of the movement. The key to the spread of humanistic culture was the rise of printing, which allowed for the distribution of texts that previously had been available only in Italy.

The Impact of Printing

In the fifteenth century the desire to have and to read classical works was widespread, but the number of copies was severely limited by the time and expense of hand-copying, collating, and checking manuscripts. Poggio Bracciolini's letters are punctuated with remarks about the time and expense of reproducing the various classical manuscripts he had discovered. One copy he had commissioned was so inaccurate and illegible as to be nearly unusable. Traveling to repositories and libraries was often easier than creating a personal library.

The invention of printing with movable lead type changed things dramatically. Although block printing had long been known in China and was a popular way to produce playing cards and small woodcuts in Europe, only with the creation of movable metal type in the 1450s did printing become a practical way to produce books. Johann Gutenberg (d. 1468) in the German city of Mainz produced between 180 and 200 copies of the so-called Gutenberg Bible in 1452–1453. It was followed shortly by editions of the Psalms.

German printers spread their techniques rapidly. As early as 1460, there were printing presses in Rome and Venice, and by 1470 the technique had spread to the Low Countries, France, and England. It has been estimated that by 1500 there were a thousand presses in 265 towns (Map 10.1). The output of the early presses in the first century of their existence was extremely varied. Gutenberg's first mass printing, for example, was of a thousand copies of a letter of indulgence, a remission of penance, for participation in a crusade. Early printers also produced highly popular and profitable small devotional books, abridged collections of saints' lives, and other popular literature, as well as editions of classical, humanistic, and theological texts.

There has been a long and complex debate over the impact of printing, but historians generally agree on a number of points. One unexpected aspect of print culture was the rise of the printshop as a center of culture and communication. The printers Aldus Manutius (1450–1515) in Venice and Johannes Froben (d. 1527) in Basel were humanists. Both invited humanists to work in their shops as they edited their texts and corrected the proofs before printing. Thus, printshops were natural sources of humanist ideas and later, in the six-

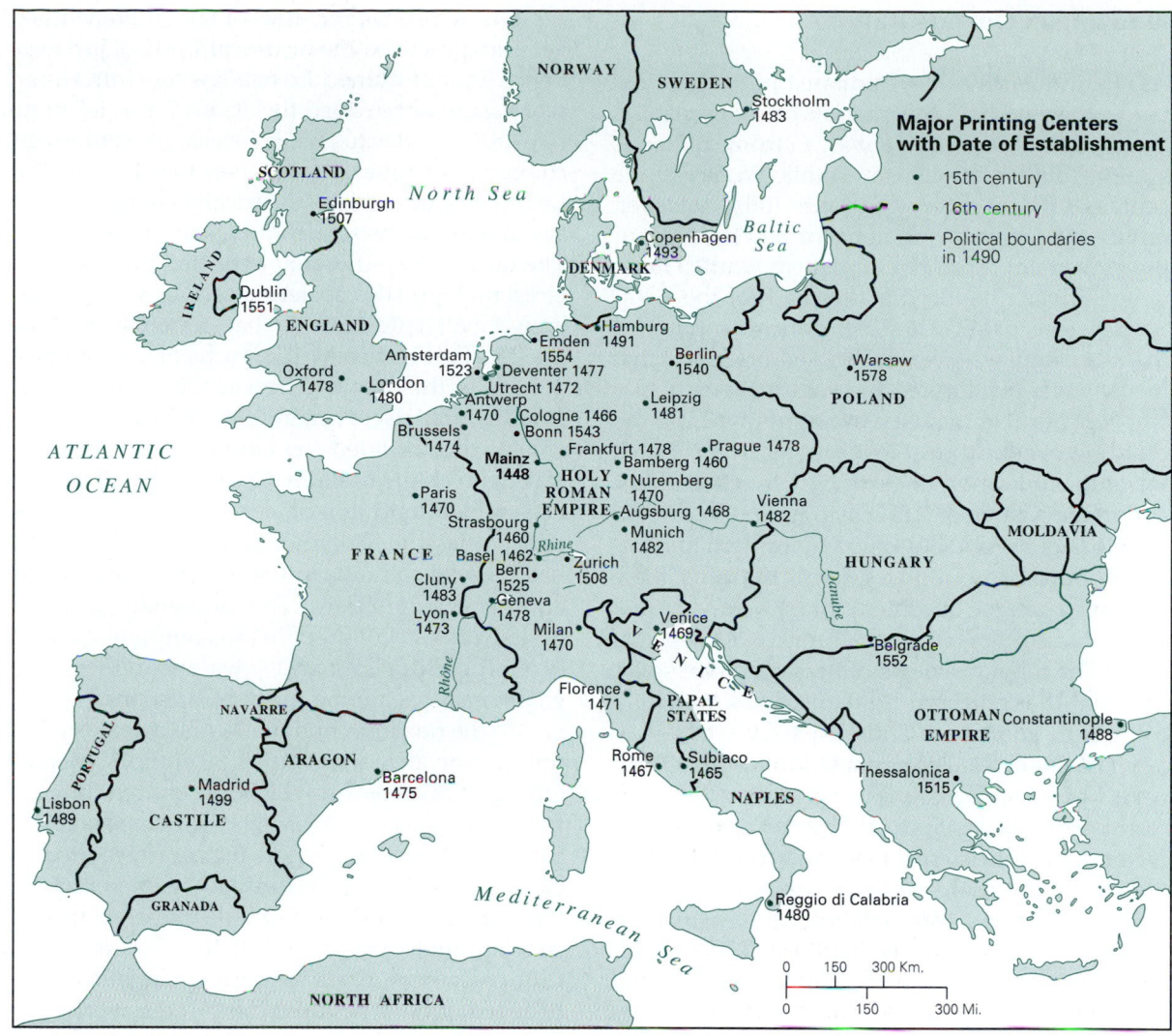

Map 10.1 The Spread of Printing Printing technology moved rapidly along major trade routes to the most populous and prosperous areas of Europe. The technology was rapidly adopted in highly literate centers such as the Low Countries, the Rhine Valley, and northern Italy.

teenth century, of Protestant religious programs. Printing allowed for the creation of agreed-upon standard editions of works in law, theology, philosophy, and science. Scholars in various parts of the world could feel fairly confident that they and their colleagues were analyzing identical texts.

Similarly, producing accurate medical and herbal diagrams, maps, and even reproductions of art and architecture was easier. Multiple copies of texts also made possible the study of rare and esoteric literary, philosophical, and scientific texts in all parts of the world.

Humanism Outside Italy

As the influence of the humanist movement extended beyond Italy, the interests of the humanists changed. Although there was a strong religious strain in Italian humanism, public life lay at the center of Italian reform. Outside Italy, however, moral and religious questions formed the heart of the movement. Northern humanists wanted to renew Christian life. In the aftermath of the Great Schism (see pages 226–228), critics complained that the clergy was wealthy and ignorant and that the laity was uneducated and superstitious.

Northern humanists were involved in the building of educational institutions, in the search for and publication of texts by Church Fathers, and in the writing of local customs and history. In the work of the two best-known northern humanists, Thomas More and Desiderius Erasmus, there is a sharp critique of contemporary behavior and, in the case of Erasmus, a call for a new sense of piety. The religious views of Erasmus were so influential that northern humanism has generally come to be known as "Christian humanism."

The intellectual environment of northern Europe had changed significantly since the thirteenth century. The universities of Paris and Oxford retained the status they had acquired earlier but found themselves competing with a host of new foundations. Most of these universities aspired, as the charter of Heidelburg (1386) noted, "to imitate Paris in all things." Like Paris, almost all had theological faculties dominated by scholastically trained theologians. Nevertheless, the new foundations often had chairs of rhetoric, or "eloquence," which left considerable scope for those who advocated humanistic learning. These new universities, from Bratislava in Slovakia (1465) to Uppsala in Sweden (1477), also reflected the increased national feeling in various regions of Europe. The earliest university in German-speaking lands, the Charles University in Prague (1348), was founded at the request of Emperor Charles IV of Luxembourg, whose court was in Prague. Numerous other universities owed their foundation to the pride and ambition of local rulers.

Humanists on faculties of law in French universities practiced the historical study of jurisprudence. Italian-trained French lawyers introduced what came to be called the "Gallican style" of jurisprudence. Because legal ideas, like language, change over time, they argued that Roman law had to be studied as a historically created system and not as an abstract and unchanging structure. The new universities also reflected humanist interest in linguistics, fostering serious study of Hebrew, Greek, and Latin so that students could understand more clearly the truths of Christianity. Typical of this movement was the archbishop of Toledo, Francisco Jiménez de Cisneros (1436–1517), who founded the University of Alcalá in 1508 with chairs of Latin, Greek, and Hebrew. He began the publication of a vast new edition of the Bible, called the "Polyglot Bible" (1522) because it had parallel columns in Latin, Greek, and, where appropriate, Hebrew. The university and the Bible were part of an effort to complete the conversion of Muslims and Jews and reform religious practices among the old Christians.

To the northern humanists, the discovery and publication of early Christian authors seemed critical to any reform within the church. Jacques Lefèvre d'Étaples (1455–1529) of France was one of the most famous of these humanistic editors of early Christian texts. He initially gained renown for his textual work on Aristotle. But after 1500 he concentrated on editions of texts by the early Church Fathers. The true spirit of Christianity, he believed, would be most clear in the works and lives of those who lived closest to the age of the apostles. Christian humanists inspired by Lefèvre became key players in the later Reformation movements in France.

Tensions between the humanists and the advocates of Scholastic methods broke out over humanist cultural and linguistic studies. Many humanists believed that there were universal moral and spiritual truths in other philosophies and religions. Debate over humanist Johannes Reuchlin's (1455–1522) study of the Jewish Cabala was particularly heated. In his own defense Reuchlin issued *The Letters of Illustrious Men*, a volume of letters that he had received in support of his position. This work gave rise to one of the great satires of the Renaissance, *The Letters of Obscure Men* (1516), written by anonymous authors and purporting to be letters from various narrow-minded Scholastics. Although the debate arose over the validity of Hebraic studies for Christian theology and not over humanistic ideas of reform or wisdom, it indicates the tension and divisions between the humanists and much of the Scholastic community. The early controversies of the Protestant Reformation were initially misunderstood by many as a continuation of the conflicts between humanists and Scholastic theologians.

Thomas More and Desiderius Erasmus

The careers of two humanists exemplified both the strength and the limits of the humanistic movement outside Italy: Sir Thomas More (1478–1535) of London and Desiderius Erasmus (1466–1536) of Rotterdam. After becoming close friends during one of Erasmus's visits to England, the two developed their careers along very different paths. More was a lawyer. He is most famous for his work *Utopia* (1516), the description of an ideal society located on the island of Utopia (literally "nowhere") in the newly explored oceans. This powerful and contradictory work is written in two books. Book I is a debate between Morus, a well-intentioned but practical politician, and Hythloday, a widely traveled idealist. Morus tries to make the bureaucrat's argument about working for change from within the system. Hythloday rejects the argument. As part of his critique of justice and politics in Europe, Hythloday describes in Book II the commonwealth of Utopia, in which there is no private property but strict equality of possessions, and, as a result, harmony, tolerance, and little or no violence. Since the publication of *Utopia*, debates have raged over the possibility and desirability of such a society. Some scholars have questioned how seriously More took this work—he seems to have written the initial sections merely to amuse friends. Yet whatever More's intentions, Utopia's society of equality and tolerance continues to inspire social commentators.

Not long after the completion of *Utopia*, More entered the service of King Henry VIII (r. 1509–1547), eventually serving as chancellor of England. As a staunch Catholic and royal official, More never acted on utopian principles of peace and toleration. He was, in fact, responsible for persecution of English Protestants in the years before Henry VIII's break with Rome (see pages 317–319). More was opposed to Henry's break with the papacy and divorce, and this led him to resign his offices. When he refused to acknowledge Henry as the head of the English church, he was imprisoned and executed.

Unlike More, who was drawn to the power of king and pope, Erasmus always avoided working for authorities. Often called the "Prince of Humanists," he was easily the best-known humanist of the early sixteenth century. He was born the illegitimate son of a priest in the Low Countries. Forced by relatives into a monastery, Erasmus disliked the conservative piety and authoritarian discipline of traditional monastic life. Once allowed out of the monastery to serve as an episcopal secretary, he never returned. Of all the humanists it was Erasmus who most benefited from the printing revolution. The printer Aldus Manutius invited him to live and work in Venice, and he spent the last productive years of his life at Johannes Froben's press in Basel. He left the city only when Protestant reformers took control of the city government.

Over a long career Erasmus sought to educate and amuse his readers. His *Adages*, first published in 1500, was a collection of proverbs from Greek and Roman sources, an immensely popular presentation of Greek and Roman wisdom. The *Colloquies* was a collection of popular stories, designed as primers for students, that taught moral lessons even as they served as examples of good language. His ironic *Praise of Folly* (1511) was dedicated to Thomas More. An oration by Folly in praise of folly, it was satire of a type unknown since antiquity. Folly's catalog of vices includes everyone from the ignoramus to the scholar. In effect, human existence is folly. Erasmus's Folly first made an observation that Shakespeare would refine and make famous: "Now the whole life of mortal men, what is it but a sort of play in which . . . [each person] plays his own part until the director gives him his cue to leave the stage."[7]

Erasmus's greatest contributions to European intellectual life were his edition of and commentaries on the New Testament. After finding and publishing in 1505 Lorenzo Valla's work on the New Testament, Erasmus embarked on creating a critical edition of the Greek text and a Latin translation independent of the fourth-century Latin Vulgate of Jerome. Like Valla, Erasmus corrected parts of the Vulgate. What was revolutionary in his edition was his commentary, which emphasized the literal and historical recounting of human experiences. This edition was the basis of later vernacular translations of the Bible during the Reformation.

Underlying Erasmus's scholarly output was what he called his "Philosophy of Christ." Erasmus was convinced that the true essence of Christianity was to be found in the life and actions of Christ. Reasonable, self-reliant, truly Christian people did not need superstitious rituals or magic. In his *Colloquies* he gives the example of a terrified priest who during a shipwreck promised everything to the Virgin Mary in order to be saved from drowning. Erasmus observed that it would have been more practical to start swimming. He hoped that classical and Christian wisdom would wipe away violence and superstition. Yet his philosophy, based on faith in the goodness and educability of the individual, was swamped in the 1520s and 1530s by the sectarian claims of both Protestants and Catholics.

Renaissance Art in the North

In the early fifteenth century, while Brunelleschi and Masaccio were revolutionizing the ways in which Italian artists viewed their world, artists north of the Alps, especially in Flanders, were making equally striking advances in the way they painted and sculpted. Artistic innovation in the North began with changes tied closely to the world of northern courts; only later did artists take up the styles of the Italian Renaissance.

Northern art of the late fourteenth and fifteenth centuries changed in two significant ways. In sculpture, the long, austere, vertical lines typical of Gothic sculpture gave way to a much more complex and emotional sculpture. In painting, Flemish artists moved from ornate, vividly colored paintings to experiments with ways to create a sense of depth. Artists strove to create works that more faithfully represented reality. Court painters like Jan van Eyck (ca. 1390–1441) also moved away from a highly formalized style to a careful representation of specific places. In Van Eyck's portrait of the Italian banker and courtier Giovanni Arnolfini and his bride, the image of the painter is reflected in a small mirror behind the couple, and above the mirror is written, "Jan van Eyck was here, 1434." Where Italians of the early fifteenth century tried to recreate space through linear perspective, the Flemish used aerial perspective, softening colors and tones to create the illusion of depth.

The influence of Renaissance styles in the north of Europe dates from the reign of the French king Francis I (r. 1515–1547), when Italian artists traveled north in significant numbers. Francis invited Italian artists to his court—most notably Leonardo da Vinci, who spent the last years of his life in France. The most influential of the Italian-style creations in France was doubtless Francis's château Fontainebleau, whose decorations contained mythologies, histories, and allegories of the kind found in the Italian courts. Throughout the sixteenth century, Italianate buildings and paintings sprang up throughout Europe.

Perhaps the most famous artist who traveled to Italy, learned Italian techniques, and then transformed them to fit the environment of northern Europe was Albrecht Dürer of Nuremberg (1471–1528). Son of a well-known goldsmith, Dürer became a painter and traveled to Italy and studied the work of Italian artists. Dürer was friends with some of Germany's leading humanists, and his work came to treat northern humanistic interests through Italian techniques of composition and linear perspective. Dürer worked in charcoal, watercolors, and

Portrait of a Black Man Albrecht Dürer sketched this portrait in the early sixteenth century, most likely in a commercial center such as Venice or Nuremberg. By that time it was common to show one of the Three Wise Men as black, but such depictions, unlike Dürer's drawing here, were rarely based on portrait studies. *(Graphische Sammlung Albertina)*

THE RENAISSANCE AND COURT SOCIETY

Art, literature, and politics merged in the brilliant life of the Renaissance Italian courts, both secular and papal. To understand fully the Renaissance and its importance in the history of Europe, we need to examine the uses of culture by governments, specifically investigating the transformation of European ideas about service at court during the fourteenth and fifteenth centuries. We will take as a model the politics and cultural life at one noble court: the court of the Gonzaga family of Mantua. We will also discuss the development of the idea of the Renaissance courtier made famous by Baldassare Castiglione, who was reared at the Gonzaga court. Finally, we will see how the Renaissance papacy melded the secular and religious aspects of art, culture, and politics in its glittering court in Rome.

The Elaboration of the Court

The courts of northern Italy interested themselves in the cultural and artistic innovations of the Renaissance humanists and artists inspired by classical civilization. They closely imitated many of the values and new styles that were developing in the courts of northern Europe, such as the court of Burgundy. Throughout Europe, attendance at court became increasingly important to members of the nobility as a source of revenue and influence. Kings and the great territorial lords were equally interested in drawing people to their courts as a way to influence and control the noble and the powerful.

Rulers in most parts of Europe instituted monarchical orders of knighthood to reward allies and followers. The most famous in the English-speaking world was the Order of the Garter, founded in 1349 by King Edward III. The orders were but one of the innovations in the organization of the court during the fourteenth and fifteenth centuries. The numbers of cooks, servants, huntsmen, musicians, and artists employed at court jumped dramatically in the late Middle Ages. The popes at Avignon in the fourteenth

paints, but his influence was most widely spread through the woodcuts that he produced on classical and contemporary themes.

Many other artists and engravers traveled south to see the great works of Italian artists. The engravings they produced and distributed back home made the innovations of the Italians available to those who were unable to travel to the south. In fact, some now lost creations are known only through the engravings produced by northern artists eager to learn Italian techniques.

century already had a household of nearly six hundred persons. Courts were becoming theaters built around a series of widely understood signs and images that the ruler could manipulate. On important political or personal occasions, rulers organized jousts or tournaments around themes drawn from mythology. The dukes of Milan indicated the relative status of courtiers by inviting them to participate in particular hunts or jousts.

The late fourteenth and fifteenth centuries were periods of growth in the political and bureaucratic power of European rulers. The increasingly elaborate and sumptuous courts were one of the tools that rulers used to create a unified culture and ideology. At the court of the Gonzagas in Mantua, one of the most widely known of the fifteenth-century courts, the manipulation of Renaissance culture for political purposes was most complete. Aristocratic values, humanism, and art all played a part in the creation of the Gonzaga reputation.

The Court of Mantua

The city of Mantua, with perhaps 25,000 inhabitants in 1500, was small in comparison with Milan or Venice—the two cities with which it was most commonly allied. Located in a rich farming region along the Po River, Mantua did not have a large merchant or manufacturing class. Most Mantuans were involved in agriculture and regional trade in foodstuffs. The town had been a typical medieval Italian city-state until its government was overthrown by the noble Bonacolsi family in the thirteenth century. Members of the family took control of most of the important communal offices, and friends of the Bonacolsis filled the representative assemblies. The Bonacolsis, in turn, were ousted from the city in 1328 by their former comrades, the Gonzagas, who ruled the city until 1627.

The Gonzagas faced a problem typical of many of the families who took control of towns in northern Italy. The state they were creating was relatively small, their right to rule was not very widely recognized, and their control over

the area was weak. The first step for the Gonzagas was the creation of fortresses and fortified towns that could withstand foreign enemies. The second step was to gain recognition of their right to rule. They had, after all, taken power in a palace revolution. In 1329 they were named imperial vicars, or representatives in the region. Later, in 1432, they bought the title "marquis" from Emperor Sigismund for the relatively low price of £12,000—equivalent to a year's pay for their courtiers. By 1500 they had exchanged that title for "duke."

Merely buying the title, however, did little to improve the status of the family. More was accomplished through the creation of a brilliant court. By 1500 there may have been eight hundred or more nobles, cooks, maids, and horsemen gathered in the court to amuse the ruling family. The Gonzagas were deeply involved in the cultural movement of humanism. It was under the tutelage of the Gonzagas that Vittorino da Feltre created his educational experiment in Villa Giocosa. It would be hard to overestimate the value for the Gonzagas of a school that attracted sons of great dukes and numerous lesser nobles.

The family also called numerous artists to Mantua. Antonio Pisano, called Pisanello (ca. 1415–ca. 1456), probably the most famous court artist of the fifteenth century, created a series of frescoes on Arthurian themes for the Gonzaga palace. Leon Battista Alberti redesigned the façade of the church of Sant'Andrea for the Gonzagas in the form of a Roman triumphal arch. The church, which long had been associated with the family, became a monument to the Gonzaga court.

The Gonzaga court, like most other courts, was both public and private. Finances for the city, appointments to public offices, and important political decisions were handled by the men who dominated the court. At the same time, as the prince's domestic setting, it was a place where women both were expected to be seen and had considerable influence. At court, the primary virtues were not military skill and political power, but rather wit, grace, good taste, and the ability to charm the rulers. Female courtiers of exceptional talent were held up as models for both women and men. From queens and duchesses to entertainers and artists, women were actively involved in creating the moral and political ideology of the court.

The arrival of Isabella d'Este (1494–1539) at court as the wife of Franceso Gonzaga marked the high point of the Renaissance in Mantua. Isabella's mother, Eleanora of Ferrara (1450–1493), was herself a well-educated woman who collected a religious and classical library at her court. Eleanora saw to it that her daughters as well as her sons were educated in Latin and Greek. Isabella had been taught by the son of Guarino of Verona. At her court in Mantua, she became an avid patron of art, architecture, and music. In her commissions she sometimes sketched a drawing of the characters and objects that she wanted portrayed and verbally specified the themes and the balance of the work—even telling the artist to "add nothing." Isabella was also an accomplished musician, playing a variety of string and keyboard instruments. She and others of the Gonzaga family recruited musicians from Flanders as well as Italians to their court. By the end of the sixteenth century, Mantua was the most important musical center of Europe. One festival brought 12,000 visitors to the city. It was in Mantua that Claudio Monteverdi (1567–1643) wrote works that established the genre of opera. The Gonzagas had secured for themselves a prominent place on the Italian, and the European, stage.

Castiglione and the Courtier

In 1528, Baldassare Castiglione (1478–1529) published *The Book of the Courtier*, a work in which he distilled what he had learned in his years at the various courts of Italy. Castiglione was born in Mantua, distantly related to the ruling Gonzaga family. He grew up at court and was sent to the Sforza court in Milan to finish his education. He returned home in 1499 to begin a career that would include service in Mantua, Urbino, and Rome. During his career Castiglione met the greatest lights of the Renaissance. While he was in Rome, he became friends with Michelangelo and Raphael as well as with numerous humanis-

tic writers. He died in Spain while on a mission for Pope Clement VII. When informed of his death, the emperor Charles V remarked, "One of the greatest knights in the world has died!" In his life and in his book Castiglione summed up the nature of late medieval chivalry.

The Book of the Courtier reports a series of fictional discussions at the court of Urbino held over the course of four nights in March 1507. Among the participants are the duchess of Urbino, Elizabeth Gonzaga; her lady-in-waiting; and a group of humanists, men of action, and courtiers. In their conversations, members of the circle debate the nature of nobility, humor, men, women, and love.

It was in many respects a typical gathering at court, and it reflects contemporary views of relations between men and women. The women organize the discussion, which is carried on by men. Women direct and influence the talk by jokes and short intervention but cannot afford to dominate discussion. "[A woman] must be more circumspect, and more careful not to give occasion for evil being said of them . . . for a woman has not so many ways of defending herself against false calumnies as a man has."[8]

Castiglione's popularity was based on his deliberate joining of humanistic ideas and traditional chivalric values. Although his topic was the court with all its trappings, Castiglione tells his readers that his models for the discussion are Greek and Latin dialogues, especially those of Cicero and Plato. He was a Platonist. He believed that there was an inborn quality of "grace" that all truly noble gentlemen had, but it had to be developed. Castiglione held that wisdom could be revealed only through careful imitation.

But what Castiglione's readers recalled most clearly was his advice about behavior. Francesco Guicciardini of Florence once remarked that "When I was young, I used to scoff at knowing how to play, dance, and sing, and other such frivolities. . . . I have nevertheless seen from experience that these ornaments and accomplishments lend dignity and reputation even to men of good rank."[9] Guicciardini's comment underlines the value that readers found in Castiglione's work.

Grace may be inbred, but it needed to be brought to the attention of those who controlled the court. Courtiers should study the military arts, but fight only in situations where their prowess would be noticed. Castiglione adds practical advice about how to dress, talk, and participate in music and dancing: Never leap about wildly when dancing as peasants might, but dance only with an air of dignity and decorum. Castiglione further urges the courtier to be careful in dress: The French are "overdressed"; the Italians too quickly adopt the most recent and colorful styles. Castiglione advises dark colors, which "reflect the sobriety of the Spaniards, since external appearances often bear witness to what is within."

Castiglione's book was an immediate success and widely followed even by those who claimed to have rejected it. By 1561 it was available in Spanish, French, and English translations. The reasons are not difficult to find. It was critical for the courtier "to win for himself the mind and favour of the prince." Castiglione's humanistic explanations and emphasis on form and fashion were essential to the cultured ladies and gentlemen of Renaissance and early modern Europe.

THE RENAISSANCE PAPACY

The issues of power and how it is displayed had religious as well as secular dimensions. After its fourteenth- and fifteenth-century struggles over jurisdiction, the Renaissance papacy found itself in need of a counterweight to the centrifugal forces of conciliarism, reform, and local feeling. Popes felt that they could reassert their primacy within the church by reviving the glory of Rome.

The first step in the creation of a new Rome was taken by Pope Nicholas V (r. 1446–1455), a cleric who had spent many years in the cultural environment of Renaissance Florence. Hoping to restore the church to its former grandeur, Nicholas and his successors patronized the arts, established a lively court culture, and sponsored numerous building projects. Nicholas was an

avid collector of ancient manuscripts that seemed to demonstrate the intellectual and religious primacy of Rome. He invited numerous artists and intellectuals to the papal court, including the Florentine architect and writer Leon Battista Alberti (1404–1472). On the basis of his research in topography and reading done in Rome, Alberti wrote his treatise *On Architecture* (1452), the most important work on architecture produced during the Renaissance. It was probably under Alberti's influence that Nicholas embarked on a series of ambitious urban renewal projects in Rome, which included plans for the rebuilding of Saint Peter's Basilica.

By reviving the style and organization of classical antiquity, the church sought to link papal Rome to an imperial tradition reaching back to Augustus and even to Alexander the Great. Papal restorers rebuilt the earliest Christian churches of the city, so that the continuity of the city itself became a demonstration of apostolic tradition and papal primacy.

The Sistine Chapel in the Vatican Palace vividly captures the cultural, religious, and ideological program of the papacy. Although best known for the decoration of the ceiling by Michelangelo, the chapel itself is of considerable significance. Begun by Pope Sixtus IV in 1475, it was to be an audience chamber in which an enthroned pope could meet the representatives of other states. In addition, it was thought that the college of cardinals would gather in the chapel for the election of new popes.

The decorations done before Michelangelo painted the ceiling reflect the intellectual and ideological values that Sixtus hoped to transmit to the churches and governments of Christendom. Along the lower sidewalls of the chapel are portraits of earlier popes, a feature typical of early Roman churches. More significant are two cycles of paintings of the lives of Moses and Christ, drawing parallels between them. To execute the scenes, Sixtus called to Rome some of the greatest artists of the period: Sandro Botticelli, Domenico Ghirlandaio, Luca Signorelli, and Pietro Perugino. The works illustrate the

Giving of the Keys to Saint Peter Pietro Perugino's painting of Saint Peter's receiving from Christ the keys to "bind and loose" on earth and in heaven illustrates the basis of papal claims to authority within the Christian church. This is the central message of the decorative plan of the Sistine Chapel. *(Scala/Art Resource, NY)*

continuity of the Old Testament and New Testament and emphasize the importance of obedience to authority. The meaning is most obvious in Perugino's painting of Saint Peter receiving the keys to the Kingdom of Heaven from Christ. The allusion is to Matthew 16:18: "Thou art Peter and upon this rock I shall build my church." The keys are the symbol of the claim of the pope, as successor of Saint Peter, to have the power to bind and loose sinners and their punishments.

The effects of Renaissance revival were profound. Rome grew from a modest population of about 17,000 in 1400 to 35,000 in 1450. By 1517 the city had a population of over 85,000, five times its population at the end of the Great Schism. The papal program was a success. Rome was transformed from a provincial town to a major European capital, perhaps the most important artistic and cultural center of the sixteenth century. Visitors to the Sistine Chapel, like visitors to the papal city itself, were expected to leave with a more

profound sense of the antiquity of the papal office and of the continuity of papal exercise of religious authority. Because the building and decorating were being completed as the Protestant Reformation was beginning in Germany, some historians have criticized the expense of the political and cultural program undertaken by the Renaissance popes. But to contemporaries on the scene, the work was a logical and necessary attempt to strengthen the church's standing in Christendom.

SUMMARY

Between 1300 and 1600, Europe experienced profound cultural innovation in literature, political and social thought, and art. This change can be overstated: Neither the world of Petrarch nor the world of courts described by Castiglione brought the beginning of modern individualism. And yet the attitudes toward the past and ideas about education formed in this period became the model of European cultural life for the next two hundred years.

The impulse for change arose from the belief, shared by thinkers from Petrarch to Machiavelli, that there was a great deal to be learned from study of the Roman past. This was the basis for humanistic innovations in language, history, and politics. Even revolutionary thinkers like Lorenzo Valla and Niccolò Machiavelli began with the study of classical literature and history. The same transformation is evident among the artists. Early in the fifteenth century, Florentines who experimented with perspective were intent on recovering lost Roman knowledge, and Michelangelo was praised not only for mastering but for going beyond Roman norms.

Issues of reform and renewal were less tied to public life in the monarchies of northern Europe. Moral and spiritual issues were more important. Yet the same movement from imitation to transformation is evident: Erasmus and Dürer assimilated the best of the new art and culture from Italy, but in the *Praise of Folly* and in Dürer's woodcuts, the use of past ideas and models was neither simple nor direct. The integration of art, literature, and public life was most evident in the ways that governments viewed and used art. The Gonzaga court and the papacy clearly recognized the value of artistic and literary works as a way to explain and justify power and influence.

As humanists came to know more fully the art and history of Greece and Rome, they recognized the extent to which classical culture represented only one source of legal, historical, or moral understanding. Europeans' recognition of other, often competing, traditions would be tested in the sixteenth century, when they came face to face with a previously unknown world. It is to the geographical discoveries and European expansion that we now turn.

NOTES

1. Quoted in Federico Chabod, *Machiavelli and the Renaissance* (New York: Harper & Row, 1958), p. 153.

2. Quoted in J. B. Trapp, ed., *Background to the English Renaissance* (London: Gray-Mills Publishing, 1974), p. 11.
3. Quoted in N. Mann, *Petrarch* (Oxford: Oxford University Press), p. 67.
4. Quoted in A. Rabil, Jr., *Renaissance Humanism: Foundations, Forms, and Legacy*, vol. 2 (Philadelphia: University of Pennsylvania Press, 1988), p. 236.
5. Quoted in R. M. San Juan, "The Court Lady's Dilemma: Isabella d'Este and Art Collecting in the Renaissance," *Oxford Art Journal* 14 (1991): 71.
6. K. R. Bartlett, *The Civilization of the Italian Renaissance* (Lexington, Mass.: D. C. Heath, 1992), p. 314.
7. Quoted in A. Rabil, Jr., *Renaissance Humanism: Foundations, Forms, and Legacy*, vol. 2 (Philadelphia: University of Pennsylvania Press, 1988), p. 236.
8. Quoted in R. M. San Juan, "The Court Lady's Dilemma: Isabella d'Este and Art Collecting in the Renaissance," *Oxford Art Journal* 14 (1991): 71.
9. Quoted in R. W. Hanning and D. Rosand, eds., *Castiglione: The Ideal and the Real in Renaissance Culture* (New Haven, Conn.: Yale University Press, 1983), p. 17.

SUGGESTED READING

Brown, Alison. *The Renaissance*. 1988. An excellent short introduction to Renaissance art and culture designed for those with little background in the field.
Burke, Peter. *The Fortunes of the Courtier: The European Reception of Castiglione's Cortegiano*. 1995. A fine survey of the influence of Castiglione's ideas.
Dempsey, Charles. *The Portrayal of Love: Botticelli's Primavera and Humanist Culture at the Time of Lorenzo the Magnificent*. 1992. A complex but rewarding demonstration of how artistic and literary culture are combined in a single work.
Eisenstein, E. L. *The Printing Press as an Agent of Change: Communications and Cultural Transformations in Early Modern Europe*. 1979. A discussion of the ways in which print culture changed social and intellectual life.
Elias, N. *The Civilizing Process*. 1978. A classic discussion of the transformation of manners and behavior at the courts of Renaissance Europe. Contains difficult analysis but lively descriptions.
Ettlinger, Leopold. *The Sistine Chapel before Michelangelo*. 1965. A scholarly discussion of the images and papal ideology discussed in this chapter.

Goodman, A., and A. Mackay, eds. *The Impact of Humanism*. 1990. A volume of basic surveys of the arrival of Italian humanistic ideas in the various lands of Europe.

Hale, John R. *The Civilization of Europe in the Renaissance*. 1994. A beautifully written survey of the culture of Europe from the fifteenth to the seventeenth centuries.

Hartt, F. *History of Italian Renaissance Art: Painting, Sculpture, Architecture*. 1987. A lavishly illustrated survey of Renaissance art that is sensitive to the social and political milieu in which artists worked.

Keen, Maurice. *Chivalry*. 1984. A well-written survey of chivalry and its transformation at the end of the Middle Ages.

Kelly, Joan. *Women, History & Theory*. 1984. Includes Kelly's famous "Did Women Have a Renaissance?" as well as an essay on the *querelle des femmes*.

King, M. L. *Women of the Renaissance*. 1991. A survey of the social, economic, and cultural experience of women during the Renaissance.

Klapisch-Zuber, Christine. *Women, Family, and Ritual in Renaissance Italy*. 1985. A collection of essays on private life and women's experience during the Renaissance.

Kohn, Benjamin, and Ronald Witt, eds. *Thgy of writings by fourteenth- and fifteenth-century civic humanists*. The general introduction is an especially clear discussion of civic humanism.

Letts, R. M. *The Renaissance*. 1992. An excellent introductory essay on the art of Renaissance Italy.

Mann, N. *Petrarch*. 1984. An excellent introduction to Petrarch's life and thought.

Marius, R. *Thomas More: A Biography*. 1984. A beautifully written biography that questions More's humanistic interests and looks at his divided feelings about religion and the state.

Murray, Linda. *The Late Renaissance and Mannerism*. 1967. An introductory survey that traces Renaissance themes as they move out of Italy, especially through France, Germany, and Flanders.

Nauert, Charles G., Jr. *Humanism and the Culture of Renaissance Europe*. 1995. An excellent short survey of European thought in the Renaissance.

Panofsky, E. *Renaissance and Renascences in Western Art*. 1969. A difficult but important essay on the concept of Renaissance and on the nature of the differences between the Renaissance and previous periods of creative innovation.

Pitkin, Hanna F. *Fortune Is a Woman: Gender and Politics in the Thought of Niccolo Machiavelli*. 1984. Brilliant, innovative discussion of the role of gender in political theory.

Stinger, Charles L. *The Renaissance in Rome*. 1985. An engaging survey of the cultural life at the papal court and in the city during the Renaissance.

Woodward, W. H., ed. *Vittorino da Feltre and Other Humanist Educators: Essays and Versions. An Introduction to the History of Classical Education*. 1987. A volume of essays and documents that are excellent introductions to the Renaissance educational program.

CHAPTER 11

Europe, the Old World and the New

In the spring of 1493, Christopher Columbus wrote to a friend and supporter at the court of Ferdinand and Isabella, reporting the glorious discoveries he had recently made during his successful trip to the Indies. "I found very many islands filled with people innumerable, and of them all I have taken possession for their Highnesses, by proclamation made and with the royal standard unfurled, and no opposition was offered to me."[1] His actions, as reported in the letter, seemed to establish Spanish claims to these lands. Columbus went on to enumerate the wealth, rivers, natural resources, and marvels to be found in this "new world." He concluded by promising he could send the monarchs "as much gold as they need" and "a thousand other things of value." This letter, rather than a more sober report sent to the monarchs themselves, was almost instantly printed and reprinted throughout Europe.

Columbus soon arrived at the Spanish court himself, accompanied by seven natives from the Caribbean and countless green parrots. His initial enthusiasm and awards were great, but neither lasted particularly long. Columbus's voyage was both a capstone of previous contacts with non-European societies and a prelude to dramatic, often tragic, encounters between Europe and the rest of the world. As we shall see, Europeans tended to respond to the challenges of this new world according to their view of themselves and the old world they had known.

Columbus's adventure was part of a series of voyages begun in the last decade of the fifteenth century that eventually carried Europeans to most parts of the world, unifying the "Old World" continents of Asia, Africa, and Europe with a "New World": the Americas and the islands of the Pacific. The story of the first navigators, their technological advances, and the colonies they established may seem straightforward, but scholars interested in the discoveries and expansion that occurred during the late fifteenth and sixteenth centuries have viewed these events in vastly different ways. Those who wanted to focus on the transfer of European religion and culture to new lands have viewed Christopher Columbus and the other early explorers as important symbols of the creation of a New World with new values. Others have seen Columbus's voyage across the Atlantic Ocean as proof that he was a "Renaissance man" who saw through the myths and superstitions of the Middle Ages. Some have focused on the fact that, in coming to the New World, the Europeans brought slavery, modern warfare, and epidemic diseases that virtually destroyed indigenous cultures. It is a simple story with complex ramifications.

Spain commissioned Columbus to sail west because the Portuguese already controlled eastern routes to Asia around the African coast and because certain technical innovations made long open-sea voyages possible. Thus, as those who celebrate Columbus's achievements have emphasized, the story includes national competition, the development of navigational techniques, and strategic choices. Another aspect of the story, however, is the cultural legacy of this meeting of two worlds. The Europeans overthrew the great empires of the Aztecs and Incas, but the transfer of European culture was never as complete as the Europeans expected. Blanketed by European language and law, elements of the language and customs of the conquered peoples survived.

~ Questions and Ideas to Consider

- Along with navigational technology, European exploration required both general interest in overseas voyages and prior geographical knowledge. These often went hand in hand as fantastic tales combined with accurate information. Discuss this phenomenon. Consider the works of Martianus Capella and Prester John, the *Travels of Sir John Mandeville*, and the *Catalan World Atlas* in your answer.

- Along the African coast and in trading centers in Asia, the Portuguese found that they could not always employ European economic traditions. How did they manage to create profitable situations for themselves? Consider the development of the slave trade, the cultivation of sugar cane, and the creation of naval and trading stations.

- Why did Columbus think he could sail to Japan? Was he right? Did his contemporaries agree with him?

- Why did Doña Marina help the Spanish invaders? How does her situation exemplify the cooperation between non-Aztec natives and the Spanish?

- Old World diseases had a major impact on the populations of the New World. How and why? Describe several encounters between the New and Old Worlds that were shaped or determined by disease.

THE EUROPEAN BACKGROUND, 1250–1492

Three critical factors for the exploratory voyages of the fifteenth and early sixteenth centuries were technology, curiosity, and geographical knowledge. A series of technical innovations made sailing far out into the ocean less risky and more predictable than it had been. The writings of classical geographers, myths and traditional tales, and merchants' accounts of their travels fueled popular interest in the East and made ocean routes to the East seem safe and reasonable alternatives to overland travel.

Navigational Innovations

The invention of several navigational aids in the fourteenth and fifteenth centuries made sailing in open waters easier and more predictable. Especially important was the fly compass, consisting of a magnetic needle attached to a paper disk

CHAPTER CHRONOLOGY

ca. 1350	The Madeira and Canary Islands are charted	**1507**	Waldseemüller issues the first map showing "America"
ca. 1400	The Azores are charted	**1519–1522**	Magellan's expedition sails around the world from east to west
1444	Cape Verde Islands are discovered by Prince Henry the Navigator	**1519–1523**	Cortés lands in Mexico, conquers the Aztecs, and destroys Tenochtitlán
1487	Dias is the first European to sail around the Cape of Good Hope	**1533**	Pizarro conquers Cuzco, the Incas' capital
1492	Columbus sails from Spain and discovers the New World	**1534**	Cartier discovers the St. Lawrence River
1494	Treaty of Tordesillas	**1542**	Charles V issues the New Laws
1497	Da Gama sails around the Cape of Good Hope and arrives in India; Cabot sights Newfoundland	**1545**	The Spanish discover the silver mines at Potosí
1501	Vespucci sails along the coast of Brazil and concludes that Columbus had discovered a new continent		

(or "fly"). The simple compass had been invented in China and was known in Europe by the late twelfth century, but it was not initially marked off in degrees so was only a rudimentary aid to navigation. By 1500 astrolabes and other devices enabling sailors to use the position of the sun and stars to assist in navigation were also available. An astrolabe allowed sailors to measure the altitude of the polestar in the sky and thereby calculate the latitude, or distance from the equator, at which their ship was sailing. Still, until the general adoption of charts marked with degrees of latitude, most navigators relied on the compass, experience, and instinct.

The most common Mediterranean ship of the late Middle Ages was a galley powered by a combination of sails and oars. Because of limited space and the need for a large crew of rowers, galleys were not ideal for long-distance travel or transport of bulky materials. Throughout the Mediterranean, shipbuilders experimented with new designs, and during the fifteenth century the Portuguese and Spanish perfected the caravel. Large, square sails caught the wind and propelled

the caravel forward, and smaller triangular sails (lateens) allowed the caravel to tack diagonally across a headwind, virtually sailing into the wind. The caravel was larger yet needed a smaller crew than the galley, and it was more maneuverable than ships with only square sails. Thus, by the 1490s the Portuguese and Spanish had developed the ships and techniques that would make long open-sea voyages possible. What remained was for Europeans to conclude that such voyages were both possible and profitable.

Lands Beyond Christendom

The Greeks and Romans had contacts with the civilizations of Asia and Africa, and in the Middle Ages interest in the lands beyond Christendom had never been lost. In the thirteenth and fourteenth centuries, European economic and cultural contacts with these lands greatly increased. The rising volume of trade between Europe and North Africa brought with it information about the wealthy African kingdoms of the Niger Delta. The Mongols in the thirteenth century allowed European merchants and missionaries to travel along trade routes extending all the way to China, opening regions formerly closed to them by hostile Muslim governments.

Trade in the Mediterranean also kept Christians and Muslims, Europeans and North Africans in close contact. Europeans sold textiles to Arab traders, who carried them across the Sahara to Timbuktu, where they were sold for gold bullion from the African kingdoms of Ghana and Mali located just above the Niger River. Italian merchants tried to trade directly with the African kingdoms, but Muslim merchants prevented any permanent contact.

Europeans enjoyed more successful trade connections farther east. The discovery in London of a brass shard inscribed with a Japanese character attests to the breadth of connections in the early fourteenth century. After the rise of the Mongols, Italian merchants regularly traveled east through Constantinople and on to India and China.

European intellectuals read the late classical and early medieval authors who described Africa, the Indies, and China. The work of the greatest of the classical geographers, Ptolemy of Alexandria (ca. A.D. 127–145), was known only

indirectly until the early fifteenth century, but medieval thinkers avidly read the works of authors from Late Antiquity. They discussed the works of Martianus Capella, who lived in the fifth century A.D. Martianus preserved fantastic myths along with geographical observations that he had gathered from the writings of Ptolemy and others. He reported that there were snakes in Calabria, in isolated southern Italy, that sucked milk from cows, and men who became wolves—the earliest mention of werewolves. Martianus assumed that a person who traveled to the south and east of Europe was more and more likely to find wonders. Further, it seemed to early geographers that the heat at the equator must be so intense that it would be impossible for life to exist there. By the twelfth century, fictitious reports circulated widely in the West of a wealthy Christian country in the East or possibly in Africa. The fictitious kingdom of Prester John was often associated with the Christian groups living near the shrine of Saint Thomas in India or the kingdom of Ethiopia. In the fifteenth century, European Christians looked to Prester John and eventually to the Christians of Ethiopia for aid against the Muslims.

The World Beyond Christendom
Medieval Christians believed that wondrous peoples lived beyond the borders of Christendom. Images of headless or one-legged men were usually included in travel accounts. This picture from Marco Polo's *Travels* shows what many Europeans expected to find when they traveled. (*Bibliothèque Nationale*)

Tales of geographical marvels are epitomized by the *Travels of Sir John Mandeville*, a book probably written in France but purporting to be the observations of a knight from St. Albans, just north of London. Mandeville says that he left England in 1322 or 1323 and traveled to Constantinople, Jerusalem, Egypt, India, China, Persia, and Turkey. In the first half of the book he describes what seems to be a typical pilgrimage to the Holy Land. As the author continues eastward, however, his descriptions turn to islands inhabited by dog-headed men, one-eyed giants, headless men, and hermaphrodites (people with both male and female reproductive organs). He not only describes his discovery of the lost tribes of Israel but records the location of Paradise. Less fantastically, Mandeville reports that the world could be—in fact has been—circumnavigated.

Mandeville's *Travels* and similar fabulous tales kept alive geographical speculation. They also raised expectations in travelers who actually did venture to the East. Thirteenth-century visitors to central Asia carefully asked their Mongol hosts about the exact locations of these wonders. Columbus, in his dispatches, included reports he had received of an island of Amazons in the Caribbean, and he believed that he had found the rivers flowing from Paradise along the coast of Venezuela.

More reliable information became available in the thirteenth century largely because of the arrival of the Mongols. Jenghiz Khan and his descendants created an empire that reached from eastern Hungary to China (see page 209). This *pax Mongolica*, or area of Mongol-enforced peace, was a region tolerant of ethnic and cultural differences. In the 1240s and 1250s a series of papal representatives traveled to the Mongol capital in Siberia. The letters of these papal ambassadors, who worked extensively to gain converts and allies for a crusade against the Turks, were widely read and greatly increased accurate knowledge about Asia. Other missionaries and diplomats journeyed to the Mongol court, and some continued farther east to India and China. By the early fourteenth century, the church had established a bishop in Beijing.

Italian merchants followed closely on the heels of the churchmen and diplomats. The pax Mongolica offered the chance to trade directly in Asia and the adventure of visiting lands known only from travel literature. In 1262, Niccolò and Maffeo Polo left on their first trip to China. On a later journey the two Venetians took Niccolò's son, Marco (1255–1324), who remained in China for sixteen or seventeen years. Marco dictated an account of his travels to a Pisan as they both sat as prisoners of war in a Genoese jail in 1298. It is difficult to know how much of the text really represents Marco's own observations and how much is invention by the Pisan. In any case, the book was widely known. Columbus himself owned and extensively annotated a copy of Marco Polo's *Travels*.

In his account Marco claims that he was an influential official in China, and he may, in fact, be the "Po-Lo" mentioned in Chinese sources as a low-level imperial bureaucrat of the emperor Kublai Khan. Marco describes the long, difficult trip to China, his equally arduous return, and the cities and industries he found. He was most impressed by the trade of Ch'nan (modern Hangzhou on the central coast of China)—one hundred times greater, he thought, than the trade of Alexandria in Egypt, a renowned port on the Mediterranean. Marco also visited modern Sri Lanka, Java, and Sumatra. His tales mix a merchant's observations of ports, markets, and trade with myths and marvels, including the kingdom of Prester John.

By 1300, Italian traders were traveling directly to the East, and there seems to have been a modest community of Italians in China. These merchants found that they had cheap access to spices, silks, and even porcelains, which they shipped back to the West. Fragmentary reports of Europeans in the Spice Islands, Japan, and India indicate that many Europeans traveled simply for the adventure of visiting new lands.

The Revolution in Geography

The situation changed significantly over the course of the fourteenth century. With the conversion of the Mongols to Islam, the breakdown of Mongol unity, and the subsequent rise of the Ottoman Turks in the fourteenth century, the highly integrated and unusually open trade network fell apart. The caravan routes across southern Russia, Persia, and Afghanistan were closed to Europeans. Western merchants once again became dependent on Muslim middlemen. The reports of travelers, however, continued to circulate long after the closing of the trade routes. This new information was avidly followed by Western geographers. Marco Polo's *Travels* and the classical geographical theories of Ptolemy contributed to a veritable revolution in geography in the decades before the Portuguese and Spanish voyages.

In 1375, Abraham Cresques, a Jewish mathematician from the Mediterranean island of Majorca, produced what has come to be known as the *Catalan World Atlas*. He combined the traditional medieval *mappamundi* (or world map) with a Mediterranean portolan. The mappamundi attempted to show both spatial and theological relationships. It often followed the O-T form—that is, a circle divided into three parts representing Europe, Africa, and Asia, the lands of the descendants of Noah. Jerusalem is always at the center of the map. The portolan, in contrast, was entirely practical. From the late thirteenth century, mariners had been developing atlases that included sailing instructions and accurate portrayals of ports, islands, and shallows along with general compass readings. The *Catalan World Atlas* largely holds to the portolan tradition but has more accurate representations of the lands surrounding the Mediterranean.

In the fifteenth century, following Ptolemy's suggestions, mapmakers began to divide their maps into squares marking lines of longitude and latitude. This format made it possible to show accurately the contours of various lands and the relationship of one landmass to another. Numerous maps of the world were produced in this period. The culmination of this cartography was a globe constructed for the city of Nuremberg in 1492, the very year Columbus set sail.

The Florentine mathematician Paolo Toscanelli, in a 1474 letter to the king of Portugal, included a map demonstrating, he believed, the short distance to be covered if one were to sail straight west first to Japan and then on to China. Columbus knew the letter, and some think he may have corresponded with the Florentine. After his voyages, Columbus observed that maps had been of no use to him, but without the accumulation of knowledge by travelers and the mingling of that knowledge with classical geography, it is doubtful whether he would have undertaken his voyages.

PORTUGUESE VOYAGES OF DISCOVERY, 1350–1515

Portugal led the European expansion. Portuguese sailors were the first Europeans to perfect the complex techniques of using the winds and currents of the south Atlantic, especially along the western coast of Africa (Map 11.1). As the Portuguese moved down the African coast and later as they tried to compete commercially in Asia, they found that they could not automatically transfer European economic traditions into new environments. In some areas the Portuguese created a network of relatively isolated naval and trading stations. In others they attempted to create large, dominant Portuguese colonies. In still other areas they used plantation slavery to create commercial products for the international market. Other European states would repeat these strategies in Asia and in the New World.

The Early Voyages

Portugal, like many late medieval European states, hoped that exploration and expansion would lead to "gold and Christians." The search for Christians was accelerated in the fifteenth century by the growing power of the Ottoman Turks. After the conquest of Constantinople in 1453 (see page 238), Turkish expansion into Syria and Palestine, and Turkish raids reaching into Austria and northeastern Italy, Europeans

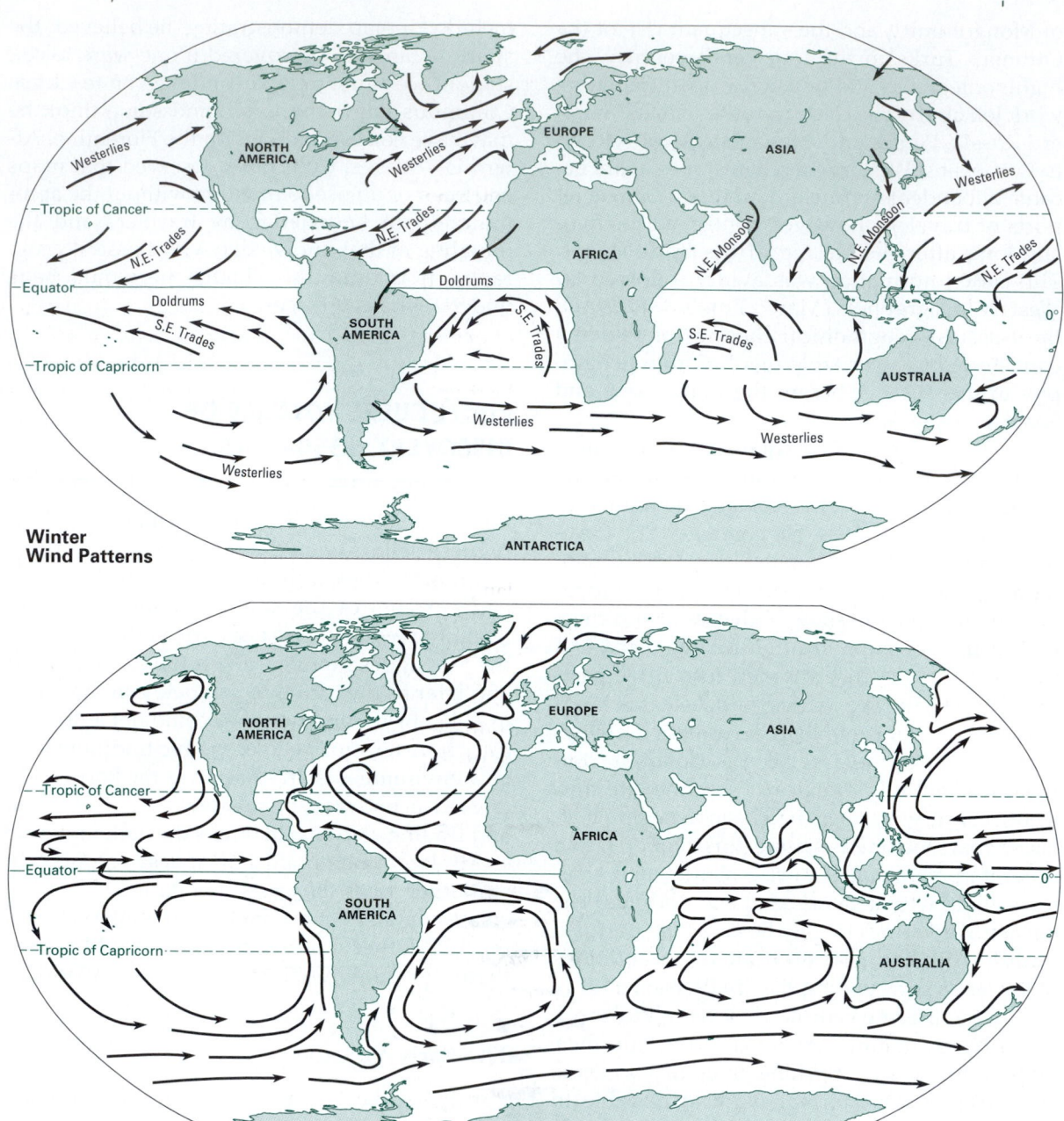

Map 11.1 Winds and Currents Winds and ocean currents move in giant clockwise and counterclockwise circles that limit the directions in which ships can sail efficiently. It was impossible, for example, for the explorers to sail directly south along the entire western coast of Africa.

increasingly hoped for an alliance with the mythical Christian kingdoms of the East to open a second front against the advancing Turks.

For Portugal, facing the Atlantic and insulated from the direct Turkish threat, the promise of gold was no doubt more alluring than the search for Christians. The nearest source of gold was well known to late medieval Christians: the African kingdoms of the Niger Delta. The problem for European traders was that commercial contacts with this wealthy region remained controlled by the Muslim Berbers of North Africa. The Portuguese and Spanish hoped to break the monopoly by taking control of the North African coast.

Actual exploration of the Atlantic had begun long before Europeans recognized the extent of the Turkish threat. By 1350 the Madeiras and the Canaries, groups of islands off the western coast of Africa, were regularly included on European maps. By 1400 the Azores, one-third of the way across the Atlantic, were known and from early in the fifteenth century were regular ports of call for Portuguese ships. These voyages were no mean feat, calling for sophisticated ocean sailing out of sight of land for weeks at a time.

In the 1410s the Portuguese expansion began in earnest with the capture of the Muslim port of Ceuta on the coast of Morocco (see Map 11.2). From then on, the Portuguese, led by Prince Henry "the Navigator" (1394–1460), younger son of King John I, moved steadily down the western coast of Africa. Contemporaries reported that Prince Henry was intent on reaching the "River of Gold"—that is, the Gold Coast of Africa and the Niger Delta. To accomplish this, he directed efforts to colonize the Canaries, the Azores, and Madeira, the largest of the Madeira Islands. He also sponsored a series of expeditions down the African coast, reaching Senegal and the Cape Verde Islands by 1444. The Portuguese quickly established trading stations in the region and soon were exporting gold and slaves to Lisbon.

Prince Henry is often credited with creating a virtual school of seamanship in his court at Sagres on the coast of Portugal, but his efforts at colonization may have had more importance. The islands off the coast of Africa were uninhabited, except for the Canaries. Thus, the Portuguese could not merely establish trading communities within a larger population, for there was no native population. As a result, by the early 1440s the Portuguese were bringing sheep, seed, and peasants to the hitherto uninhabited Azores and Madeiras,

Portuguese in India This watercolor by a Portuguese traveler shows the varied people and customs and the great wealth to be found in India. Europeans were fascinated by all that seemed different from their own world. *(Biblioteca Casanatense)*

and the Crown was forced to grant extensive lordships to nobles to encourage immigration to the Azores. The islanders survived largely by exporting sheep and grain to Iberia.

A significant transformation occurred on Madeira in the 1440s, when the Portuguese introduced sugar cane to the island. Within a decade sugar dominated the island's economy. By 1452, there was a water mill for processing the cane, and in the 1470s sugar revenues from Madeira constituted nearly 2 percent of the Crown's total income. Sugar production was capital- and labor-intensive. A great many workers were needed to cut the cane, and expensive mills were needed to extract and to produce sugar. On Madeira most of the work was done by Portuguese peasants. But when the Portuguese extended sugar cultivation to the newly discovered and colonized Cape Verde Islands in the 1460s, they found that Portuguese peasants would not work voluntarily in the sultry equatorial climate. Soon the Portuguese introduced a slave-based plantation system to produce sugar.

Slaves imported from the Black Sea areas had been used in agriculture since the introduction of sugar cultivation into the Mediterranean in the thirteenth century. The Portuguese themselves had been trading in slaves along the western coast of Africa since the late 1440s—the date from which black slaves appear in Lisbon. African slaves along with slaves from the East could be found in Italy and throughout the Mediterranean in the fifteenth century, most often as domestics or laborers in small enterprises. Since Roman times, however, there had been no slave-based industries on the scale of the Portuguese sugar plantations. Sugar production in the New World would be modeled on the slave-based system used by the Portuguese in their island colonies in the Atlantic.

The Search for a Sea Route to Asia

Until the middle of the fifteenth century, the Niger Delta remained the focus of Portuguese interest. Only after securing control of the western coast of Africa through the extension of sugar cultivation to Madeira and the Cape Verdes, developing the gold and slave trade in Senegal, and gaining access to most gold-producing areas of West Africa did the Portuguese look seriously at sailing around Africa and discovering a sea route to Asia.

The fifteenth-century sailors who first tried to sail down the coast of Africa faced enormous difficulties. Water and wind currents tend to move in clockwise and counterclockwise circles against which it is difficult for a sail-powered ship to make progress (see Map 11.1). In some zones and at certain times there are pockets of stillness with few breezes to propel ships. Sailing directly to and from a port was virtually impossible. By the second half of the fifteenth century, Portuguese sailors had learned to tack along a course, searching for favorable winds and currents.

Knowledge of winds and currents allowed Bartholomeu Dias (1450?–1500) in 1487 to explore the coast of southern Africa (Map 11.2). He followed the traditional Portuguese routes until southeasterly winds forced him to sail south and west, almost to the Brazilian coast. Then he rode the westerlies well past the southern tip of Africa, where he turned north. On his return he sighted what he called "the Cape of Storms," later renamed "the Cape of Good Hope" by the Portuguese king. Dias had perfected the techniques for searching out currents in the Southern Hemisphere and opened the way to India.

A decade after Dias's return from the Cape of Good Hope, Vasco da Gama (1460?–1524) embarked on a voyage that would take him to Calicut on the western coast of India. Da Gama set sail in 1497 with four square-rigged, armed caravels and over 170 men. He had been provided with maps and reports that indicated what he might expect to find along the eastern coast of Africa. He also carried textiles and metal utensils, merchandise of the type usually traded along the western coast of Africa. This was a trade mission and not really a voyage exploring the unknown.

Da Gama followed established routes beyond the Cape of Good Hope and into the Indian Ocean. He traveled up the coast until he reached Malindi in Mozambique, where he hired an Arab pilot who taught him the route to Calicut. Although the goods the Portuguese traders presented were not appropriate for the sophisticated Asian market, da Gama did manage to collect a cargo of Indian spices, which he brought back to Portugal, arriving in 1499. From 1500 until the Portuguese lost their last colonies in the twentieth century (Goa, 1961; Mozambique, 1975), Portugal remained a presence in the Indian Ocean.

The Portuguese in Asia

Trade in the Indian Ocean was nominally controlled by Muslims, but in fact a variety of ethnic and religious groups—including Muslims, Hindus, and Nestorian Christians—participated in the movement of cottons, silks, and spices throughout the region. The mixture of trade reflected the political situation. Vasco da Gama's arrival coincided with the rise of the Moguls, Muslim descendants of Jenghiz Khan. By 1530 they had gained control of most of northern India, and during the sixteenth century Mogul influence increased in the south. Throughout the sixteenth century the Moguls remained tolerant of India's religious, cultural, and economic diversity.

The Portuguese probably encountered some hostility, but there is no reason to believe that they could not have joined this complex mixture of traders. Local rulers collected taxes and ensured political control but otherwise left the various ethnic and religious communities to manage their own trade and manufacture. But the products the Portuguese brought from Europe had little value in sophisticated, highly developed Asian markets. In response to this, they created a "Trading-Post Empire," an empire based on control of trade.

Portugal's commercial empire in the East was based on fortified, strategically placed naval bases. As early as Vasco da Gama's second expedition in 1502, Portuguese bombarded Calicut and defeated an Arab fleet off the coast of India. This encounter set the stage for Portugal's most important strategist of empire, Alfonso d'Albuquerque (1453–1515), governor-general of Portuguese colonies in India. He convinced the monarchy that the key to dominance in the region was the creation of fortified naval bases designed to control access to the spices in the Spice Islands. Albuquerque was successful. By 1600 the Portuguese had created a network of naval bases that reached from the eastern coast of Africa to the western coast of India and to the island of Macao off the southeastern coast of China (see Map 11.2).

The Portuguese established a royal trading firm, the Casa da India, to control the trade in cinnamon, ginger, cloves, mace, and a variety of peppers. Although their control was far from total, the Portuguese did become significant exporters of spices to Europe. More significant was the creation of the Portuguese Estado da India, or India office, to control Portuguese naval forces, administer ports, and regulate maritime trade. Under the Portuguese system all merchants were expected to acquire export licenses and to ship products through Portuguese ports. Local boats were no match for the well-built Portuguese ships armed with cannon. Although the Portuguese navy was too small to enforce a complete blockade of clandestine trade, the Portuguese did manage to change the patterns of commerce in the area.

SPANISH VOYAGES OF DISCOVERY, 1492–1522

As early as 1479 the Spanish kingdoms had agreed to leave the exploration and colonization of the African coast to the Portuguese, yet they watched nervously as the Portuguese expanded their African contacts. The Castilians concentrated their efforts on what came to be called the "Enterprise of the Indies."

The Role of Columbus

The story of the enterprise begins with Christopher Columbus (1451–1506), a brilliant seaman, courtier, and self-promoter who has become a symbol of European expansion. During the

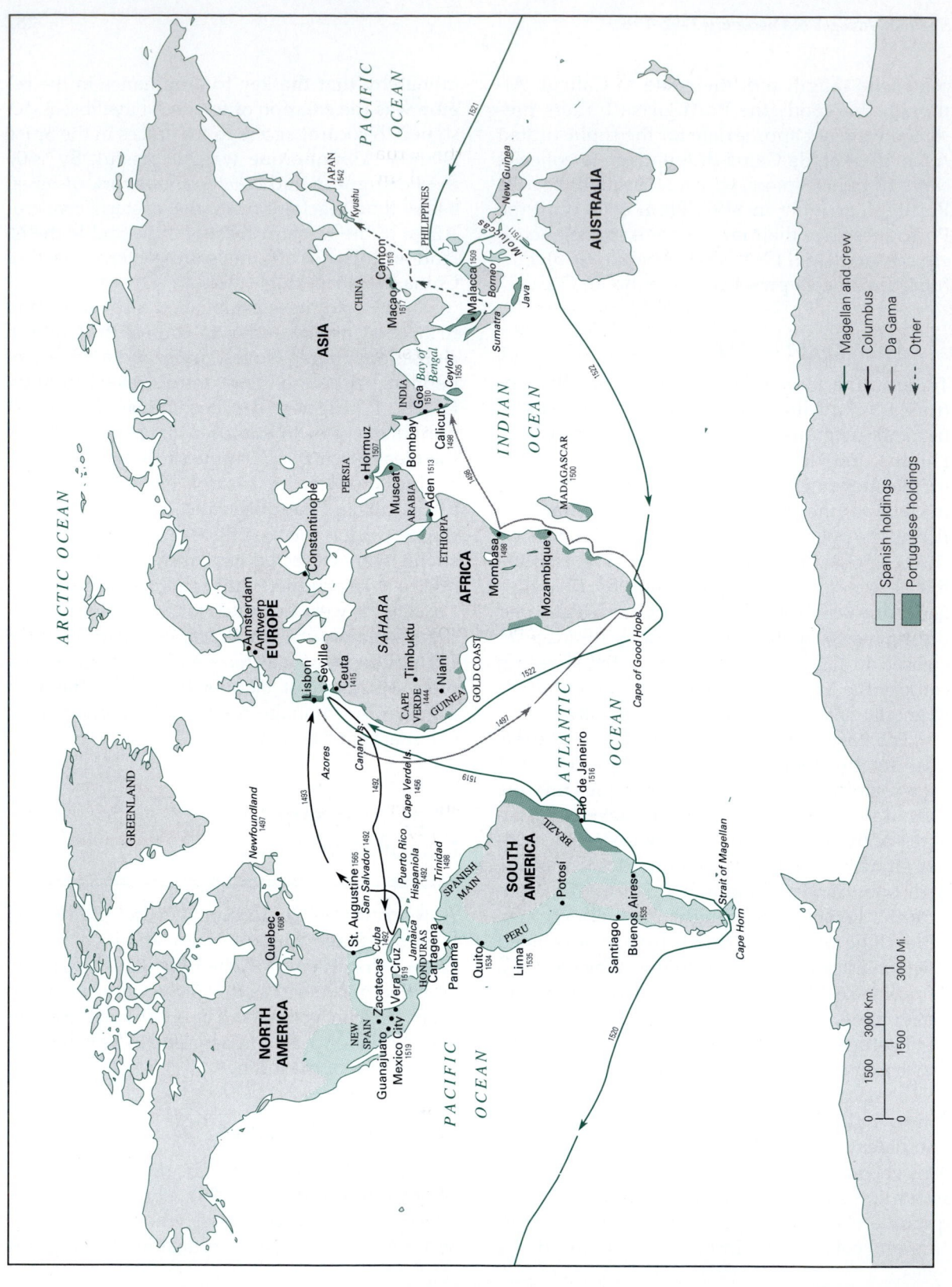

nineteenth century, patriots of the newly created United States of America celebrated Columbus as proof that the discovery and development of North America was not dependent on the British. By the early twentieth century, Italian immigrants to North America regarded him as a symbol of Italy's important role in the history of the Americas. And finally, modern historians have celebrated Columbus as one of the great men of the Renaissance who managed to break with medieval myth and superstition. Columbus, however, was not a "Renaissance man" of vision, the harbinger of a new, more rational world. And he certainly was not a bold pioneer who fearlessly did what no others could conceive of doing.

Columbus was born into a modest family in Genoa and spent his early years in travel and in the service of the Castilian and Portuguese crowns. He apparently first put his plans to sail west to Asia before King John II (r. 1481–1495) of Portugal. Only after Portuguese rejection did he approach the Spanish monarchs, Ferdinand and Isabella. His vision seems to have been thoroughly traditional and medieval. Studying information in *Imago Mundi* (*Image of the World,* 1410), by the French philosopher Pierre d'Ailly (1350–1420), he convinced himself that the distance between the coasts of Europe and Asia was much less than it actually is. Pierre d'Ailly had estimated that water covered only about one quarter of the globe. This estimate put the east coast of Asia within easy reach of the western edge of Europe. "This sea is navigable in a few days if the wind is favorable," was d'Ailly's conclusion.

D'Ailly's theories seemed to be confirmed by the work of the Florentine mathematician Paolo Toscanelli (see page 283). Columbus knew of Toscanelli's calculations and even revised them downward. From his own reading of an apocryphal book of the Bible (Esdras 6:42) that reported that only one-seventh of the world was

Map 11.2 World Exploration The voyages of Columbus, da Gama, and Magellan charted the major sealanes that became essential for communication, trade, and warfare for the next three hundred years.

covered with water, Columbus concluded that the distance from the west coast of Europe to the east coast of Asia was about 5000 miles instead of the actual 12,000. Columbus's reading of traditional sources put Japan in the approximate location of the Virgin Islands.

Like Marco Polo before him, Columbus expected to find the marvels reported in the classical sources. When Amerindians told him of Cuba, he concluded that it "must be Japan according to the indications that these people give of its size and wealth."[2] And on the basis of first-century descriptions, he assured Spanish authorities that King Solomon's mines were only a short distance west of his newly discovered islands. In addition to finding the gold of Solomon, Columbus also expected that by sailing west he could fulfill a series of medieval prophecies that would lead to the conversion of the whole world to Christianity. This conversion, he believed, would shortly precede the second coming of Christ. In Columbus's own view, then, his voyages were epochal not because they were ushering in a newer, more empirical world but because they signaled the completion of the long history of the creation and redemption.

Columbus's enthusiasm for the venture was only partially shared by Isabella and Ferdinand. Vasco da Gama was well supplied with large ships and a crew of over 170 men, but Columbus sailed in 1492 with three small ships and a crew of 90. Da Gama carried extra supplies and materials for trade and letters for the rulers he knew he would meet. Columbus had nothing similar. His commission did authorize him as "Admiral of Spain" to take possession of all he should find, but royal expectations do not seem to have been great.

After a stop in the Canary Islands, the small fleet sailed west. Columbus assumed that he would find the islands of Japan after sailing about 3000 miles. On October 12, about ten days later than he had calculated, he reached landfall on what he believed were small islands in the Japanese chain. He had actually landed in the Bahamas (see Map 11.2). Because Columbus announced to the world he had arrived in the Indies, the indigenous populations have since been

Christopher Columbus Describes His Discoveries

Columbus's hopes for wealth and titles for himself depended on getting and maintaining the goodwill of Ferdinand and Isabella. After each of his voyages he emphasized his accomplishments and their potential to enrich the Spanish monarchs. Columbus wrote this letter toward the conclusion of the first voyage, which he believed might secure his rights to lordship over all the new territories he found. He took pains to make clear that what he had found was what one would expect to find on the edge of Asia.

In conclusion, to speak only of what has been accomplished on this voyage, which was so hasty, their highnesses can see that I give them as much gold as they may need, if their highnesses will render me very slight assistance; moreover, spice and cotton, as much as their highnesses shall command; and mastic [yellow resin necessary for various adhesives], as much as they shall order to be shipped and which, up to now, has been found only in Greece, in the island of Chios, and the Seignory [of Venice] sells it for what it pleases; and also wood, as much as they shall order to be shipped, and slaves, as many as they shall order to be shipped and who will be from the idolaters. And I believe that I have found rhubarb and cinnamon [both were considered essential for medicine], and I shall find a thousand other things of value, which people I have left here will have discovered, for I have not delayed at any point . . . and in truth I shall have done more, if the ships had served me as reason demanded.

Source: C. Columbus, A. Bernáldez, et al., eds., *The Voyages of Christopher Columbus*, part 1 (London: Argonaut Press, 1930), p. 16.

called "Indians" and the islands are called the "West Indies." (See the box "Christopher Columbus Describes His Discoveries.")

Columbus returned to the New World three more times—in 1493, 1498, and 1502—exploring extensively in the Bahamas and along the coast of Panama and Venezuela. The enthusiasm his discoveries raised was evident on his second voyage. He oversaw a fleet of seventeen ships with 1500 sailors, churchmen, and adventurers. And Columbus's initial rewards were great. He was granted a hereditary title, a governorship of the new lands, and one-tenth of all the wealth he had discovered.

Columbus reported to the Spanish monarchs that the "Indians" on the islands were friendly and open to the new arrivals. He described simple, naked people, eager, he believed, to learn of Christianity and European ways. The Taínos, or Arawaks, whom he had misidentified, did live uncomplicated lives. The islands easily produced sweet potatoes, maize, beans, and squash, which along with fish provided an abundant diet. Initially these peoples shared their food and knowledge with the newcomers.

The Spanish, for their part, praised this smiling and happy people. Visitors commonly believed they had discovered a simple, virtuous people who, if converted, would be exemplars of Christian virtues to the Europeans. Columbus observed that "they are very gentle and do not know what evil is; nor do they kill others, nor steal; and they are without weapons. . . . They say very quickly any prayer that we tell them to say, and they make the sign of the cross, †. So your Highnesses ought to resolve to make them Christians."[3] Peace did not last. The settlers Columbus left at his fortress seized foodstocks, kidnapped women, and embarked on a frenzied search for gold. Those who did not kill one another were killed by the Taínos.

During succeeding voyages, Columbus struggled to make his discoveries the financial windfall he had promised the monarchs. He was unable to administer this vast new land. He quickly lost control of the colonists and was forced to allow the vicious exploitation of the island population. He and other Spanish settlers claimed larger and larger portions of the land and required the Indians to work it. Islands that easily supported a population of perhaps a million natives could not support those indigenous peoples and the Spanish newcomers and still provide exports to Spain. Largely because of diseases (see page 299), the native population of the islands fell precipitously—possibly to little more than thirty thousand by 1520. By 1550 the Arawaks had virtually disappeared.

Even in the face of mounting evidence to the contrary, Columbus maintained that Asia must be just beyond the lands he was exploring. With the islands in revolt and his explorations seemingly going nowhere, the Spanish monarchs stripped Columbus of his titles and commands. At one point he was returned to Spain in chains. After his final trip he still maintained that he had finally found either the Ganges River or one of the rivers that flow out of the earthly paradise.

In 1501, after sailing along the coast of Brazil, the Florentine geographer Amerigo Vespucci (1451–1512) drew the obvious conclusion from the information collected by Columbus's explorations. He argued that Columbus had discovered a new continent unknown to the classical world. These claims were accepted by the German mapmaker Martin Waldseemüller, who in 1507 honored Amerigo's claim by publishing the first map showing "America."

Columbus's Successors

Columbus's discoveries set off a decade-long debate over which nations had the right to be involved in trade and exploration. Finally, in the Treaty of Tordesillas (1494), Spain and Portugal agreed that the line of demarcation between them should be drawn 1480 miles west of the Azores. The treaty was signed just six years before Petro Alvares Cabral (1467–1520) discovered the coast of Brazil. Thus the Spanish unwittingly granted the Portuguese rights to Brazil.

The most important of the explorations that Columbus inspired was the voyage undertaken by Ferdinand Magellan in 1519 (see Map 11.2). Although his motives are unclear, Magellan (1480?–1521) may have planned to realize Columbus's dream of sailing to the Indies. By the 1510s mariners and others understood that the Americas were a new and hitherto unknown land, but they did not know what lay beyond them or what the distance was from the Americas to the Spice Islands of Asia. After sailing along the well-known coastal regions of South America, Magellan continued south, charting currents and looking for a passage into the Pacific. Early in 1520 he made the passage through the dangerous straits (now the Strait of Magellan) separating Tierra del Fuego from the mainland and marking the boundary of the Atlantic and the Pacific Oceans. Once into the Pacific, Magellan sailed north and west to escape the cold and to find winds and currents that would allow him to continue to Asia. It took almost four months to travel from the straits to the Philippines. During that time, a crew member reported, "We ate biscuit, which was no longer biscuit, but powder of biscuit swarming with worms, for they had eaten the good."[4] The crew suffered greatly from scurvy and a shortage of water and at times had to eat the rats aboard ship to survive. Nevertheless, Magellan managed to reach the Philippines by March 1521. A month later, he was killed by natives.

Spanish survivors in two remaining ships continued west, reaching the Moluccas (also known as the "Spice Islands"), where they traded merchandise that they had carried along for a small cargo of cloves. The Portuguese captured one of the ships as it tried to return to the Americas. The other proceeded on through the Indian Ocean, avoiding Portuguese patrols. It continued around Africa and back to Spain, landing with a crew of 15 at Cádiz in September 1522 after a voyage of three years and the loss of four ships and 245 men. No cargo of spices could have been worth the sacrifices, but the significance of the voyage was not the spice but the route established from South America to the Spice Islands. Further, Magellan completed and confirmed the knowledge of wind and ocean currents that European sailors had been accumulating.

Spanish adventurers were not the only ones to follow in Columbus's wake. The French and the English, however, concentrated their explorations farther to the north. Building on a tradition of fishing off the coast of New Foundland, English sailors under the command of John Cabot (1450?–1499?) sighted Newfoundland in 1497, and later voyages explored the coast as far south as New England. Cabot initiated an intense period of English exploration that would lead eventually to permanent settlement at Jamestown in 1607. French explorers followed Cabot to the north. In 1534, Jacques Cartier (1491–1557) received a royal commission to look for a passage to the East. He discovered the St. Lawrence River and began the process of exploration and trading that would lead to permanent settlements in Canada beginning in the early seventeenth century. But British and French settlements in the New World came later. The sixteenth century belonged to the Spanish.

Spanish penetration of the New World was not simply built on the model of the Portuguese in Asia. The Spaniards established no complex network of trade and commerce, and no strong states opposed their interests. A "Trading-Post Empire" could not have worked in the New World. To profit, the Spaniards needed to colonize and reorganize the lands they had discovered.

SPAIN'S COLONIAL EMPIRE, 1492–1600

Between 1492 and 1600, almost 200,000 Spaniards immigrated to the New World. New Spain, as they called these newly claimed lands, was neither the old society transported across the ocean nor Amerindian society with a thin patina of Spanish and European culture. To understand the history of New Spain, we will discuss the two major civilizations the Spaniards overthrew, the conquests themselves, and the institutions the Spaniards created in the wake of conquest. We will also discuss the attempts by some of the Spanish to secure fair treatment of the indigenous peoples who had been made part of the Spanish Empire.

The Americas Before the European Invasion

North and South America, along with Africa and the Eurasian landmass, were once part of a single supercontinent. The breakup of this supercontinent left the Americas, Africa, and Eurasia free to evolve in dramatically different ways. From one continent to another, the differences in plants and animals were so dramatic that one eighteenth-century naturalist confessed, "I was seized with terror at the thought of ranging to many new and unknown parts of natural history."[5] The continental breakup occurred millions of years ago, long before the appearance of human beings and many other forms of mammalian life.

In the period between 30,000 and 10,000 B.C., the Americas were temporarily rejoined to the Eurasian landmass by land and ice bridges. This allowed Asians to cross over the Bering Strait to the Americas. These hunter-gatherers seem to have played a significant role in the extinction of several large mammals—mastodons, mammoths, giant buffalo, and even early camels and horses. No easily domesticable large animals remained on the Continent. These peoples also came to the Americas long before the beginnings of the Neolithic agricultural revolution, so patterns of plant and animal domestication developed differently. The agricultural revolution in the Americas occurred around 3000 B.C., perhaps six thousand years after similar developments in the Old World (see page 4). The peoples of the Americas created complex societies, but those societies lacked large domesticated meat or pack animals (the llama was the largest), iron and other hard metals, and the wheel.

Population estimates for North and South America in the time around Columbus's arrival range from 30 million to 100 million—the lower figure is probably more correct. There were complex mound-builder societies in eastern North America and along the Mississippi River and pueblo societies in the deserts of the American Southwest, but the greatest centers of Amerindian civilization were in central and coastal Mexico and in the mountains of Peru.

In the late fifteenth century the two most powerful centers were the empires of the Aztecs and the Incas. When the collection of tribes now known as the "Aztec" (or Mexican) peoples appeared in central Mexico in the early fourteenth century, they found a flourishing civilization centered on the cities and towns dotting the Valley of Mexico. Through conquest, the Aztecs united the many Nahuatl-speaking groups living in the valley into a confederation centered on the Aztec capital of Tenochtitlán, a city of perhaps 200,000 people built on an island in Lake Texcoco (Map 11.3). In early-sixteenth-century Europe, only London, Constantinople, and Naples would have been as large as the Aztec capital. The Spanish conqueror Hernán Cortés described Aztec cities that literally rose out of the water of Lake Texcoco and "seemed like an enchanted vision." Only Venice could have equaled the sight. The whole valley supported an unusually high population of about a million, fed by farmers who raised a wide variety of crops on farms carefully formed beside canals and in the marshes on the edge of Lake Texcoco. Using canals along the edge of the lake and other canals in Tenochtitlán itself, merchants easily moved food, textiles, gold and silver ornaments, jewels, and ceremonial feathered capes into the city markets. Spaniards later estimated that fifty thousand or more people shopped in the city on market days.

Religion was integral to the Aztecs' understanding of their empire. They believed that the world was finite and that they lived in the last of five empires. It was only continued human sacrifice to Huitzilopochtli that allowed the world to continue. The Aztecs believed that the hearts of

sacrificial victims were necessary to sustain their god, to ensure that the sun would rise again each morning.

Tenochtitlán was the center of an imperial culture based on tribute. Towns and villages under Aztec control paid tribute in food and precious metals. To emphasize that their power and dominance were complete, the Aztecs not only collected vast quantities of maize, beans, squash, and textiles but demanded tribute in everything down to centipedes and snakes. The most chilling tribute, however, was in humans for sacrifice. When there were no longer wars of expansion to provide prisoners, the Aztecs and their neighbors fought "flower wars"—highly ritualized battles to provide prisoners to be sacrificed. Five thousand victims were sacrificed at the coronation of Moctezuma II (r. 1502–1520) in 1502. Even more, reportedly twenty thousand, were sacrificed at the dedication of the great temple of Huitzilopochtli in Tenochtitlán.

Aztec society maintained a perpetual state of war with the peoples beyond the mountains that ringed the Valley of Mexico—especially the people along the Caribbean coast. Given this state of war, plus the heavy burdens in tribute placed on the nearby subject cities, it is no small wonder that the Aztecs were obsessed by the contingencies of life. At the end of each calendar cycle of fifty-two years, all fires in the empire were extinguished until fire-priests ascertained that the world would continue.

The other great Amerindian empire of the fifteenth century, the empire of the Incas, was also of recent origin. During the fifteenth century the Incas formed efficient armies and expanded their control beyond the central highlands of Peru. Fifteen thousand miles of road and a sophisticated administrative system allowed the Incas to create a state that extended from Ecuador to Chile. As they expanded, they demanded political control and tribute but seem to have been tolerant of local traditions and language. The Incas perfected systems of irrigation and bridge-building initiated by earlier inhabitants of the region. The empire, centered on the city of Cuzco high in the mountains of Peru, was able to sustain a population

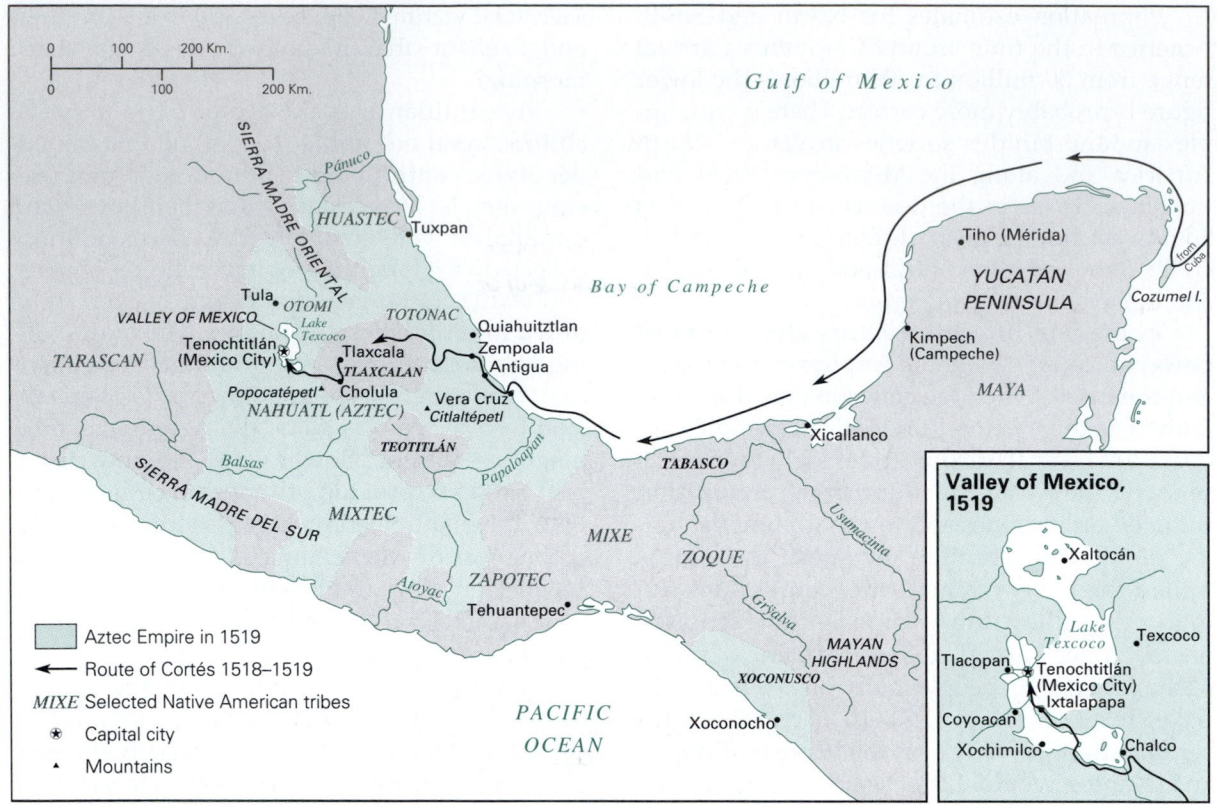

Map 11.3 Mexico and Central America The Valley of Mexico was a populous region of scattered towns, most of which were part of the Aztec Empire. As Cortés marched inland from Vera Cruz toward the valley, he passed through lands that had been in an almost constant state of war with the Aztecs.

that may have reached 10 million by the end of the fifteenth century. (See the box "Encounters with the West: An Inca Nobleman Defends His Civilization.")

Under the Inca system, the title Paca Inca, or "Great Inca," was inherited by the eldest son of the ruler's principal wife. The ruler's wealth, however, was retained by the rest of his family, who maintained the court as if the ruler still lived. Thus, each new ruler needed money to finance the creation of an entirely new court, and taxes were not only high but continuously increasing. Both great Amerindian empires, despite their brilliance, rested on uneasy conquests. Subject groups would be willing allies for any invader.

The Spanish Conquests

Hernán Cortés (1485–1546) was ambitious to make something of himself in the New World. Of a poor but aristocratic Spanish background, he had gone to the West Indies in 1504 to seek his fortune in the service of the governor of Cuba. The governor gave him a commission to lead an expeditionary force to investigate reports of a prosperous Indian civilization. From the very beginning, Spanish authorities seem to have distrusted his aims. He was forced to depart hastily from Cuba to evade formal notification that the governor of Cuba had revoked his commission because of insubordination.

∿ ENCOUNTERS WITH THE WEST ∿

An Inca Nobleman Defends His Civilization

Huamán Poma was born into a noble Inca family with a long history of service first to the Inca kings and later to the Spanish administrators. Although Huamán Poma became a Christian and adapted to Spanish rule, he wrote this letter to the king of Spain in 1613 explaining the great merits of the Inca civilization that he feared would be lost. In the excerpt included here, he describes the Inca understanding of the origins of the world. His "traditional world" is, however, one heavily influenced by his new Christian faith.

The first white people in the world were brought by God to this country. They were descended from those who survived the flood in Noah's Ark. It is said that they were born in pairs, male and female, and therefore they multiplied rapidly.

These people were incapable of useful work. They could not make proper clothes so they wore garments of leaves and straw. Not knowing how to build houses, they lived in caves and under rocks. They worshipped God with a constant outpouring of sound like the twitter of birds, saying: "Lord how long shall I cry and not be heard?" . . .

In their turn these first people were succeeded by the two castes: the great lords, who were the ancestors of our Incas, and the common people, who were descended from bastards and multiplied rapidly in number.

However barbarous they may have been, our ancestors had some glimmer of under-

standing of God. Even the mere saying of [God's name] is a sign of faith and an important step forward. Christians have much to learn from our people's good way of life. . . .

Their usual diet consisted of maize, potatoes and other tubers; cress, sorrel, and lupin; pond-weed, laver and a grass with yellow flowers; leaves for chewing; mushrooms, edible grubs, shells, shrimps, crab and various sorts of fish. . . . The burial of the dead was conducted with dignity, but without undue ceremony in vaults constructed for the purpose. There were separate vaults, which were whitewashed and painted, for people of high rank. The Indians believed that after death they would have to endure hard labor, torture, hunger, thirst and fire. Thus they had their own conception of Hell, which they called the place under the earth or the abode of demons.

Source: Huamán Poma, *Letter to a King: A Picture History of the Inca Civilization* (New York: E. P. Dutton, 1978), pp. 24–25, 30.

Cortés landed in Mexico at the site of the city he would name Vera Cruz ("True Cross") early in 1519 with a tiny command of 500 men, 16 horses, 11 ships, and some artillery. Aided by a devastating outbreak of smallpox and Amerindian peoples happy to overthrow Aztec control, Cortés and his troops managed to destroy the network of city-states dominated by the Aztecs of Tenochtitlán in two years.

Cortés, like Machiavelli, believed in the power of truly able leaders (men of virtú) to overcome chance through bold acts. Even so, an attempt to capture a city of 200,000 with an army of 500 appears more foolhardy than bold. Cortés seems to have attempted it simply because he found himself with very little choice. With his commission revoked by the governor of Cuba, Cortés arrived on the mainland as a rebel against both the governor of Cuba and the king of Spain. Much of what he did concerning the great Aztec Empire was an attempt to justify his initial act of insubordination and win back royal support. Cortés burned his ships so that his troops were forced to go with him. Then he founded the city of Vera Cruz, whose town government, which was his own creation, offered him a new commission to proceed inland to Tenochtitlán. He quickly found allies among native groups that for their own reasons wished to see the Aztec Empire destroyed.

Cortés was greatly aided by fortune in the form of Malintzin, a Mexican woman, who after her conversion to Christianity called herself Doña Marina (ca. 1501–1550). Malintzin was Cortés's interpreter and, later, they became lovers. Without her, one of Cortés's followers recalled, "We could not have understood the language of New Spain and Mexico." Her story illustrates many of the complex interactions at play in sixteenth-century Mexico. Born an Aztec, she was given away, ending up in the hands of Mayans, who gave her, along with twenty other women, to Cortés. Like many of the natives who felt no affection for the Aztecs of Tenochtitlán, it was not difficult for her to aid the Spaniard. Knowing the languages of the Mayans and Mexicans, and quickly learning Spanish, Malintzin was the one person who could mediate between Spaniard and native. She became Christian and after having a son with Cortés, married a Spanish gentleman and lived the rest of her life in Spain.

Despite the help of Malintzin and Spaniards who had previously lived with the natives, the meeting of Aztecs and Spaniards was marked by profound inability to communicate across cultures. This inability to communicate may explain why the Aztec king Moctezuma seemed to react so indecisively to the Spaniards. Neither in words nor in gestures did the two groups speak the same language. At first he appeared unconcerned about their presence. Then, hearing that the Spaniards were marching toward Tenochtitlán, Moctezuma sent ambassadors bearing gold, silver, and other costly gifts, which they presented in a most humble fashion to the Spaniards. To a modern ear the gifts sound like attempts to buy off the invaders. To Cortés, or any European or Asian resident of the Old World, such gifts were a sign of submission. But to Moctezuma and most Amerindians, the giving of gifts by powerful people could be a sign of wealth and status. Seen in that light, Moctezuma's lavish gifts and apparent humility probably demonstrated to the Aztecs' own satisfaction the superiority of their civilization, and Cortés's acceptance of the gifts seemed to indicate his recognition of his own inferior status.

Cortés took Moctezuma captive in 1521 and began what would be a two-year battle to take control of the city and its empire. Although weakened by the arrival of virulent Old World diseases, the Aztecs continued to fight even as more and more of the subject peoples joined the Spanish forces. The Spaniards cut off food and water to the capital, but still the Aztecs fought.

Different understandings of the rules of war, different traditions of diplomacy, and different cultures prevented the Aztecs and Cortés from reaching any understanding. The peoples of the Valley of Mexico tried to take captives to be sacrificed in temples. The Spaniards, to Aztec eyes, killed indiscriminately and needlessly on the battlefield. Cortés later complained of the Aztecs' refusal to negotiate: "We showed them more signs of peace than have ever been shown to a vanquished people." Thus, to end a war that neither side could resolve in any other way, in August 1523 Cortés and his allies completely destroyed Tenochtitlán.

Cortés's insubordination was a model for other adventurers. His own lieutenants later rebelled against his control and attempted to create their own governments as they searched for riches and Eldorado, a mythical city of gold. Later adventurers marched throughout the North American Southwest and Central and South America following rumors of hidden riches. Using private armies and torturing native peoples, veterans of Cortés's army and newly arrived speculators hoped to find wealth that would allow them to live like nobles on their return to Spain. Like Cortés, they claimed that they were acting for the monarchy and for Christianity, but in fact they expected that success would justify their most vicious acts.

Francisco Pizarro (1470–1541) was the most successful of the private adventurers. Poor, illegitimate at birth, he arrived in the Americas ambitious for riches and power. After participating in several slaving expeditions and helping to found Panama City, Pizarro was prosperous but still not wealthy. Rumors of Inca wealth filtered through to Central America. Pizarro and a partner resolved in 1530 to lead an expedition down the west coast of South America in search of the Inca capital. Benefiting from disorganization caused by a smallpox epidemic and ensuing civil war, Pizarro was able to find local allies. Aided by Amerindians eager to throw off Inca domination, he captured and executed the Paca Inca and conquered the capital of Cuzco by 1533. He later built a new capital on the coast at Lima, from where he worked to extend his control over all of the old Inca Empire. Pizarro and his Spanish partners seized vast amounts of gold and silver from the Incas. The Spanish eventually discovered silver mines at Potosí, which would be a critical source of revenue for the Spanish monarchy. Resistance to Spanish rule continued into the 1570s, when the last of the independent Inca strongholds was finally destroyed.

Colonial Organization

The Spanish crown needed to create a colonial government that could control the actions of the numerous adventurers and create an orderly economy. Although the Spaniards proclaimed that they would "give to those strange lands the form of our own [land]," the resulting political and economic organization of the new Spanish possessions was a curious mixture of the Old World and the New.

The head of the administration was the monarchy. As early as the reigns of Isabella and Ferdinand, Spanish monarchs had tried to curb the excesses of the explorers and conquerors who traveled in their name. Isabella initially opposed the enslavement of Amerindians and any

slave trade in the new lands. Further, they promoted a broad-based debate about the rights of Amerindians and the nature of religious conversion. Royal influence, however, was limited by the sheer distance between the court and the new provinces. It could take two years for a royal response to a question to arrive at its destination. Things moved so slowly that as one viceroy ruefully noted, "If death came from Madrid, we should all live to a very old age." Given these difficulties, the powers of local administrators had to be very broad.

By 1535, Spanish colonial administration was firmly established in the form it would retain for the next two hundred years. The king created a Council of the Indies located at court, eventually in Madrid, which saw to the new possessions. The new territories themselves were eventually divided into the viceroyalty of Mexico (primarily Central America and part of Venezuela) and the viceroyalty of Peru.

In Spain, Castilian conquerors completely dominated newly won lands, but in New Spain, royal administrators created Indian municipalities, or districts, in which Spaniards had no formal right to live or work. Government in these municipalities remained largely in the hands of pre-conquest native elites. Throughout the sixteenth century, official documents in these communities continued to be written in Nahuatl, the Aztec language. As long as taxes or tribute was paid and missionaries were allowed to circulate, the Spanish government tolerated considerable autonomy in the Indian municipalities.

The problem that most plagued the government was the conquerors' desire for laborers to work on the lands and in the mines that they had seized. From Columbus's first visit, the Spanish adopted a system of forced labor developed in Spain. A colonist called an *encomendero* was offered a grant, or *encomienda*, of a certain number of people or tribes who were required to work under his direction. In theory, the encomendero was to be a protector of the conquered peoples, someone who would Christianize and civilize them. In theory, Indians who voluntarily agreed to listen to missionaries or to convert to Christianity could not be put under the control of an encomendero. If they refused, however, the Spaniards believed they had the right of conquest. In fact, the conquerors assumed that they were entitled to encomiendas. Cortés himself claimed 115,000 people in Mexico, and Pizarro claimed 20,000 in Peru. In many areas encomenderos simply collected the traditional payments that the pre-conquest elites had claimed. In cases where the subject peoples were forced into mining districts, however, the conditions were brutal.

The pressures exerted by the encomenderos were worsened by the precipitous fall in the indigenous population. Old World diseases such as smallpox and measles swept through populations with no previous exposure to them. In central Mexico the pre-conquest population was at least 10 or 12 million and may have been twice that. By the mid-sixteenth century, the native population may have fallen to just over 6 million, and it probably declined to less than 1 million early in the seventeenth century before beginning to grow again. At first, sugar plantations and mines were worked by Amerindians, but when their numbers declined, the Spanish and Portuguese imported large numbers of slaves from Africa.

Africans had participated in the initial stages of the conquest. Some had lived in Spain and become Christian; indeed, Amerindians termed them "black whitemen." Most Africans, however, were enslaved laborers. African slaves were in Cuba by 1518; they labored in the mines of Honduras by the 1540s. After the 1560s the Portuguese began importing large numbers of African slaves into Brazil to work on the sugar plantations. It has been estimated that 62,500 slaves were imported into Spanish America and 50,000 into Brazil during the sixteenth century. By 1810, when the movement to abolish the slave trade began to grow, almost 10 million Africans had been involuntarily transported to the New World.

The conquerors had hoped to find vast quantities of wealth that they could take back to the Old World. In the viceroyalty of Mexico the search for Eldorado remained unsuccessful. The discovery in 1545 of the silver mines at Potosí in Peru, however, fulfilled the Spaniards' wildest dreams. Between 1550 and 1650, the Spanish probably sent back to Spain 181 tons of gold and 16,000 tons of silver, one fifth of which was paid directly into the royal treasury. In the 1560s, these precious metals made King Philip II of Spain the richest monarch in Europe.

The Debate over Indian Rights

To most conquerors the opportunities for wealth and power need little justification, but the more thoughtful among the Spaniards were uneasy. "Tell me," demanded Friar Antonio Montesinos in 1511, "by what right or justice do you hold these Indians in such cruel and horrible slavery? By what right do you wage such detestable wars on these people who lived idly and peacefully in their own lands?"[6]

Initially the conquerors claimed the right to wage a just war of conquest if Amerindians refused to allow missionaries to live and work among them. Later, based on reports of human sacrifice and cannibalism written by Columbus and other early explorers, Europeans concluded that the inhabitants of the New World rejected basic natural laws. Writers argued that nakedness and cannibalism were both signs that the Amerindians were "natural slaves," and some even implied that Indians were merely "humanlike," not necessarily human.

Franciscan and Dominican missionaries were especially vocal opponents of such views. To these missionaries, the Indians initially seemed innocent and ideal subjects for conversion to the simple piety of Christ and his first apostles. These mendicants saw themselves as advocates for Indians; they desired to protect the natives from the depredations of the Spanish conquerors and the corruptions of European civilization. The most eloquent defender of Indian rights was Bartolomé de las Casas (1474–1566), a former encomendero who became a Dominican missionary and eventually bishop of Chiapas in southern Mexico. Las Casas rejected the

Crusade for Justice The criticisms of Bartolomé de Las Casas were published widely and accompanied by woodcuts like this one showing the cruelty of the conquerors toward the Amerindians. In response to Las Casas, Charles V passed laws protecting the rights of the indigenous peoples. *(The John Carter Brown Library at Brown University, Providence)*

"humanlike" argument and passionately condemned the violence and brutality of the Spanish conquests. "All races of the world are men," he declared. All are evolving along a historical continuum. Like all other peoples, he added, Indians had reason. That being the case, even the most brutal could be civilized and Christianized. There was, in the view of Las Casas, no argument for natural slavery.

Charles V (who was king of Spain as well as Holy Roman emperor) accepted Las Casas's criticisms of the colonial administration. In 1542 he issued "New Laws" aimed at ending the virtual independence of the encomenderos. Further, he abolished Indian slavery and greatly restricted the transfer of encomiendas. From the 1540s Indians were protected from the most extreme exploitation. We should have no illusion, however, that these measures reflected an acceptance of cultural pluralism. The very people who protected Indians assumed that Westernization and Christianization would quickly follow.

THE COLUMBIAN EXCHANGE

The conquerors, adventurers, and traders who followed in the wake of Christopher Columbus and Vasco da Gama profoundly altered the Old World and the New. Before 1492 there had been a system of world trade, but now, as the Spanish proclaimed, Europe and especially Spain were at the center of economic and political life. As the Spanish and other Europeans moved throughout the world, they carried with them religions, ideas, diseases, people, plants, and animals—forever uniting the Old World and the New. This amalgamation of culture is known as the "Columbian Exchange."

Disease

Columbus and those who followed him brought not only people to the New World but also numerous Old World diseases. "Virgin-soil" epidemics—that is, epidemics of previously unknown diseases—are invariably fierce. Although the New World may have passed syphilis to Spain, from which it quickly spread throughout the Old World, diseases transferred from the Old World to the New were much more virulent than syphilis. Smallpox spread from Cuba to Mexico as early as 1519. It was soon followed by diphtheria, measles, trachoma, whooping cough, chickenpox, bubonic plague, malaria, typhoid fever, cholera, yellow fever, scarlet fever, amoebic dysentery, influenza, and some varieties of tuberculosis. At many critical points, disease served as the silent ally of the conquerors.

Lacking sources, historians cannot trace accurately the movement of epidemic disease or its effect on the New World populations, yet many archaeologists and historians remain convinced that Old World diseases moved north from Mexico and ravaged and disrupted Amerindian populations in eastern North America long before the arrival of European immigrants. In most of the New World, 90 percent or more of the native population was destroyed by wave after wave of previously unknown diseases. Explorers and colonists did not so much enter an empty land as an "emptied" one.

It was at least partially because of disease that both the Spanish and the Portuguese needed to import large numbers of African slaves to work their plantations and mines (see page 298). With the settlement of southeastern North America, plantation agriculture was extended to include the production of tobacco and later cotton. In the Caribbean and along the coasts of Central and South America the Africans created an African-Caribbean or African-American culture that amalgamated African, European, and American civilizations.

Plants and Animals

It became increasingly clear to the Spaniards that the New World had been completely isolated from the Old World. The impact of Old World peoples on native populations was immediately evident to all. But scholars have recently argued that the importation of plants and animals had an even more profound effect than the arrival of Europeans. The changes that began in 1492 created "Neo-Europes" in what are now Canada, the United States, Mexico, Argentina, Australia, and New Zealand. The flora and fauna of the Old World, accustomed to a relatively harsh, competitive environment, found ideal conditions in the new lands.

The most important meat and dairy animals in the New World—cattle, sheep, goats, and pigs—are imports from the Old World. Sailors initially brought pigs or goats aboard ship because they were easily transportable sources of protein. When let loose on the Caribbean islands, they quickly took over. The spread of horses through what is now Mexico, Brazil, Argentina, the United States, and Canada was equally dramatic. To the list of domesticated animals can be added donkeys, dogs, cats, and chickens. The changes these animals brought were profound. Cattle, pigs, and chickens quickly became staples of the New World diet. Horses enabled Amerindians and Europeans to travel across and settle on the vast plains of both North and South America.

The flora of the New World was equally changed. Even contemporaries noted how Old World plants flourished in the New. By 1555, European clover was widely distributed in Mexico—Aztecs called it "Castilian grass." Other Old World grasses, as well as weeds like dandelion, quickly followed. Domesticated plants like apples, peaches, and artichokes spread rapidly and naturally in the new environment. Early in the twentieth century it was estimated that only one-quarter of the grasses found on the broad prairies of the Argentine pampas were native before the arrival of Columbus. Studies of plant life in California, Australia, and New Zealand offer much the same results. The Old World also provided new and widely grown small grains like oats, barley, and wheat.

Crops from the New World also had an effect on the Old World. By the seventeenth century maize (or American corn), potatoes, and sweet potatoes had significantly altered the diets of Europe and Asia. It was the addition of maize and potatoes that supported the dramatic population growth in areas like Italy, Ireland, and

Scandinavia. With the addition of the tomato in the nineteenth century, much of the modern European diet became dependent on New World foods. The new plants and new animals, as well as the social and political changes initiated by the Europeans, pulled the Old World and the New more closely together.

Culture

During the sixteenth century, colonists set about remaking the world they had found. The acculturation of indigenous peoples was facilitated by the Spanish tendency to place churches and shrines at the sites of former Aztec temples. The shrine of the Virgin of Guadalupe (north of modern Mexico City), for example, was located on the site of the temple of the goddess Tonantzin, an Aztec fertility-goddess of childbirth and midwives. Early missionaries reported that Indians quickly took to Christianity, although investigations later in the sixteenth century raised questions about the depth of their belief. Nonetheless, Christianity quickly became the dominant religion of the peoples of the New World.

There were many other changes. In 1573, King Philip II (r. 1556–1598) established ordinances requiring all new cities to be based on a uniform grid with a main plaza, market, and religious center. The new cities became hubs of social and political life in the colonies. In these cities, religious orders founded colleges for basic education much like the universities they had organized in the Old World. The Crown had authorized the foundation of universities in Mexico City and Lima modeled after the great Spanish university of Salamanca. Colonists attempted to recreate in all essentials the society of Spain.

The experience of the Spanish and the Portuguese in the sixteenth century seemed confirmed by the later experiences of the French and English in the seventeenth century. In seventeenth-century New England, the English Puritan John Winthrop concluded, "For the natives, they are nearly all dead of smallpox, so as the Lord hath cleared our title to what we possess."[7] A seventeenth-century Frenchman came to a similar conclusion: "Touch-

The Virgin of Guadalupe The shrine of the Virgin of Guadalupe in Mexico City is likely the holiest shrine in the Americas, visited by perhaps 15,000 pilgrims and tourists daily. The image the pilgrims venerate is a painting of a dark-skinned woman—standing in the shimmering light of the moon, seeming to combine Aztec and Spanish elements. The shrine is located on the site of the pre-conquest shrine of Tonantzin, an Aztec fertility-goddess. (*Enrique Franco-Torrijos*)

ing these savages, there is a thing that I cannot omit to remark to you, it is that it appears visibly that God wishes that they yield their place to new peoples."[8] Political philosophers believed that if there was no evidence that a land was being cultivated by the indigenous people, the rights to that land passed to those who would use and improve it. Thus, colonists believed that they had divine and legal sanction to take and to remake these new lands in a European image.

SUMMARY

Modern historians considering decolonization, economic revolutions in many parts of Asia, and multiculturalism have been changing their ways of thinking about European expansion in the fifteenth century. The expansion of Europe was not the movement of highly developed commercial economies into underdeveloped areas. In Asia, the Portuguese and later the Dutch and English were a military presence long before they were an economic one. In the New World, even as the Spanish conquered people and changed their language, government, and religion, many aspects of Amerindian culture survived in the local Indian municipalities.

The economic, political, and cultural changes brought about by the conquest created a hybrid culture. The mix of peoples and ideas produced great things over the course of time, translating the voices, images, and behaviors of the New World and the Old into an original, vital culture. In its origins, however, this culture was marked by extraordinary misunderstanding, intolerance, arrogance, and violence. The inability to understand and tolerate others was to be a key to the strife created by the other great event of the sixteenth century, the movement to reform church and society.

NOTES

1. Quoted in John H. Parry and Robert G. Keith, eds., *The New Iberian World: A Documentary History of the Discovery and Settlement of Latin America to the Early Seventeenth Century*, vol. 2 (New York: Times Books, 1984), p. 59.
2. Quoted in William D. Phillips, Jr., and Carla Rahn Phillips, *The Worlds of Christopher Columbus* (Cambridge, England: Cambridge University Press, 1992), p. 163.
3. Quoted ibid., p. 166.
4. Quoted in J. H. Parry, ed., *The European Reconnaissance: Selected Documents* (New York: Harper & Row, 1968), p. 242.

5. Quoted in Alfred W. Crosby, *Ecological Imperialism: The Biological Expansion of Europe, 900–1900* (Cambridge, England: Cambridge University Press, 1986), p. 11.
6. Quoted in Mark A. Burkholder and Lyman L. Johnson, *Colonial Latin America* (Oxford: Oxford University Press, 1990), p. 29.
7. Quoted in Crosby, p. 208.
8. Quoted in ibid., p. 215.

SUGGESTED READING

Bethell, Leslie, ed. *The Cambridge History of Latin America*. Vol. 1. 1984. A standard work with excellent discussions of America before the conquest and after.

Boxer, C. R. *The Portuguese Seaborne Empire, 1415–1825*. 1977. A classic political and institutional narrative of the Portuguese empire.

Burkholder, Mark A., and Lyman L. Johnson. *Colonial Latin America*. 1990. A thorough introduction to the conquest and colonization of Central and South America by the Spanish and Portuguese.

Campbell, Mary B. *The Witness and the Other World: Exotic European Travel Writing, 400–1600*. 1988. A literary study of the narratives written by or about travelers, emphasizing especially the interest Columbus had in the reports of previous travelers.

Clendinnen, Inga. *Ambivalent Conquests: Maya and Spaniard in Yucatan, 1517–1570*. 1987. A skillful, ironic study of the attempts of Maya and Spaniard to understand each other. It concentrates on the way in which Mayans transformed European Christianity, including many of their pre-conquest beliefs and practices.

———. *Aztecs: An Interpretation*. 1991. A dramatic, beautifully written essay on the Aztecs that shows how daily life, religion, and imperialism were linked.

Crosby, Alfred W. *The Columbian Voyages, the Columbian Exchange, and Their Historians*. 1988. A short pamphlet about historical writing on Columbus and the expansion of Europeans; an excellent place for a beginning student to start.

———. *Ecological Imperialism: The Biological Expansion of Europe, 900–1900*. 1986. A discussion of how migrating peoples carried with them plants, animals, and diseases; has an excellent collection of maps and illustrations.

Curtin, P. *The Tropical Atlantic in the Age of the Slave Trade*. 1991. An introductory pamphlet that is an excellent first work for students interested in the history of slavery and the movement of peoples from Africa to the New World.

Elliott, John H. *The Old World and the New, 1492–1650*. 1970. Besides supplying the title for this chapter, these essays are excellent considerations of the reciprocal relations between the colonies and the kingdoms of Spain.

———. *Spain and Its World, 1500–1700: Selected Essays*. 1989. Essays by the greatest living historian of Spain and the New World. The essay on the mental world of Cortés is especially important.

Fernandez-Armesto, Felipe. *Before Columbus: Exploration and Colonization from the Mediterranean to the Atlantic, 1229–1492*. 1987. A well-written and accessible political and institutional narrative, especially valuable on the early Portuguese voyages.

Fuentes, Carlos. *The Buried Mirror: Reflections on Spain and the New World*. 1992. An essay with numerous illustrations, many in color, on the melding of the cultures of Spain and the New World, by one of Mexico's greatest writers. The author's reflections on the merging of Christianity and indigenous religions are particularly valuable.

Hanke, L. *Aristotle and the American Indians: A Study in Race Prejudice in the Modern World*. 1959. The most general of Hanke's books about race and prejudice in the Old World and New. Hanke states clearly the philosophical basis of debates over equality from classical Greece to the nineteenth century.

Levenson, J. A., ed. *Circa 1492: Art in the Age of Exploration*. 1991. A museum catalog showing art from Asia, Africa, America, and Europe at the time of Columbus; it includes essays on politics and culture aimed at a general audience.

Moseley, M. E. *The Incas and Their Ancestors: The Archaeology of Peru*. 1992. This general introduction to the Incas includes excellent maps and illustrations.

Pagden, Anthony. *The Fall of Natural Man: The American Indian and the Origin of Comparative Ethnology*. 1982. A brilliant, difficult, and rewarding book on the debate over Indians' rights in the sixteenth century.

Parry, J. H. *The Age of Reconnaissance*. 1981. A classic introductory survey of Portuguese, Spanish, English, and French exploration and conquest to the end of the seventeenth century.

Phillips, J. R. S. *The Medieval Expansion of Europe*. 1988. The best survey of European interest in and knowledge of the world beyond Christendom; especially good on European travelers to the East in the thirteenth century.

Phillips, W. D., Jr., and C. R. Phillips. *The Worlds of Christopher Columbus*. 1992. Though written for a popular audience, this is an excellent survey of Columbus and his voyages with an up-to-date summary of recent work on Columbus.

Scammell, Geoffrey. *The First Imperial Age: European Overseas Expansion, 1400–1715*. 1989. As the title implies, this is an introductory survey of European colonial interests through the early eighteenth century. The author puts the Spanish and Portuguese explorations in the context of later French and English experiences.

Smithsonian Institution. *Seeds of Change*. 1991. This museum catalog has excellent illustrations and introductory essays on the transfer of diseases and plants between the Old World and the New.

CHAPTER 12

The Age of the Reformation

O n November 5, 1529, Charles V, king of Spain and emperor-elect of the Holy Roman Empire, entered Bologna, the site of his coronation. Charles and his advisers believed that God had selected him to re-establish the power of the empire and cement the special relationship between emperor and pope. But by the end of Charles's reign in 1556, the empire had become little more than a German state. And the coronation of Charles by Pope Leo X in Bologna was, in fact, the last papal coronation of an emperor.

This dramatic reversal resulted from a series of political, diplomatic, and religious crises that changed forever the face of Europe. The key issue was the sixteenth-century movement known as the Reformation, an ever widening controversy over the nature of Christianity and the role of government in society. The struggle began as an apparently minor theological controversy in Germany—a "quarrel between monks," as the papacy saw it. Debates about salvation, however, quickly widened into arguments about the sacraments—that is, the means by which individuals receive God's grace. By the middle of the century, disagreements had expanded to the point that both the Christian religion and politics were changed forever. In the heat of this religious crisis the modern Christian churches, both Protestant and Catholic, were formed.

The Roman Catholic, Lutheran, Calvinist, and Anglican churches all came into being in the sixteenth century, but to speak of "Lutheran" or "Roman Catholic" during the first decades of the Reformation is to ignore the fluidity of the situation in which Europeans found themselves. At first, no one foresaw that the result of the controversies would be separate churches.

The reformers of the first half of the sixteenth century shared many characteristics. Most had been influenced by humanist study of Latin,

Greek, and Hebrew. Almost all emphasized the Bible as the unique source of religious authority. Initially, they all rejected any claim of special status or authority for the priesthood.

The debates over religion that raged during this period did not occur in a political vacuum. In Germany, the emperor and papal supporters faced hostile towns and princes as well as French and Turkish military threats—all of which made action against religious dissidents impossible. In England and Scandinavia, by contrast, reformers soon found themselves with royal patrons.

By the second half of the sixteenth century it was clear that there would never again be a single Christian church in western Europe. Protestant and Catholic churches concentrated their energies on a process of theological definition and institutionalization that historians call the "Second Reformation," or "Confessionalization." The increased moral control by all churches accompanied and even fostered the growth in state power that would characterize the late sixteenth and seventeenth centuries.

～ Questions and Ideas to Consider

- Religion in the late medieval period was varied and strong. New movements and new expressions of religious belief erupted from all levels of society, initiated by both men and women. Describe some of them. What did they have in common?

- In what ways did the reform movements differ from the various religious movements of the late medieval period? Why was Protestantism such a serious break with the past?

- What is the doctrine of "predestination"? Whose idea was it? Does it offer any incentive to do good works?

- Compare the religious settlement in Germany with that of England. In what ways can we describe English Protestantism as more political than religious? How was Queen Elizabeth able to resolve the English religious question?

- How did the Catholic church respond to the reform movements? Discuss the results of the Council of Trent. What were the goals and techniques of the Jesuits?

THE REFORMATION MOVEMENTS, CA. 1517–1545

In 1517 a little-known professor of theology at the University of Wittenberg in Saxony began a protest against practices in the late medieval church. Martin Luther had no carefully formulated idea about the nature of the church and salvation, but his theology struck a responsive chord with many of his contemporaries. All the reformation movements, even the most radical, shared a sense that the sacramental and priestly powers claimed by the medieval church were illegitimate.

"Protestant" is the label we now use to describe the churches that arose in opposition to the medieval Christian church. Interestingly, the word *Protestant* was originally a political term used to describe German princes who opposed imperial interference with the religious reformers in the 1530s. Only later was *Protestant* applied to the resulting churches. Until then, reformers tended to call themselves "evangelical reformed Christians." They were evangelical in that they believed that authority derived from the Word of God, the Bible. They were reformed Christians because their aim was merely to restore Christianity to its original form.

The Late Medieval Context

Questions of an individual's relationship to God and to the Christian community remained at the heart of theological speculation in the sixteenth as in previous centuries. Nominalist theologians were the leading thinkers of the late Middle Ages. They rejected the key assumption of previous Scholastics—that there were universal ideas and generally applicable rules of order for moral

CHAPTER CHRONOLOGY

1513–1517	Fifth Lateran Council meets to consider reform of the Catholic church
1517	Luther makes public his "Ninety-five Theses"
1518	Zwingli is appointed people's priest of Zurich
1521	Luther appears at the Diet of Worms
1524–1525	Peasant revolts in Germany
1527	Imperial troops sack Rome
1530	Melanchthon composes the Augsburg Confession summarizing Lutheran belief
1534	Calvin flees from Paris; Loyola founds the Society of Jesus
1535	The Anabaptist community of Münster is destroyed
1536	Calvin arrives in Geneva and publishes the first edition of *Institutes of the Christian Religion*
1545–1563	Council of Trent meets to reform the Catholic church
1555	Emperor Charles V accepts the Peace of Augsburg

life. In the words of William of Ockham (ca. 1285–1347), "No universal really exists outside the mind." Truth was to be found in daily experience or in revealed scripture, not in complex logical systems. At the heart is Ockham's method—known as "Ockham's razor"—that what can be explained with only a few logical speculations "is vainly explained by assuming more."

Nominalist theologians rejected vast logical systems, but they held on to the traditional rituals and beliefs that tied together the Christian community. They believed in a holy covenant in which God would save those Christians who, by means of the church's sacraments and through penitential acts, were partners in their own salvation. Foremost among the penitential acts was the feeding of "Christ's Poor," especially on feast days. The most common religious practice of the late Middle Ages was participation in religious brotherhoods. Members vowed to attend monthly meetings, to participate in processions on feast days, and to maintain peaceful and charitable relations with fellow members.

Kingdoms, provinces, and towns all had patron saints who, believers thought, offered protection from natural as well as political disasters. Festivals in honor of the saints were a major event in the town or kingdom. The most revered saint in the late Middle Ages was the Virgin Mary, the mother of Jesus. The most popular new pilgrimage shrines in the north of Europe were dedicated to the Virgin. It was she, the Sienese maintained, who protected them from their Florentine rivals. As the veneration of the Virgin Mary shows, in the late Middle Ages it was not possible to distinguish between religion and society, church and state.

Women played a prominent role in late medieval religious life. Holy women were usually thought of as such because they reported having visions or prophetic gifts like knowledge of the status of souls in purgatory. Reputations for sanctity provided a profound moral authority. The Italian Blessed Angela of Foligno (ca. 1248–1309) had several visions and became the object of a large circle of devoted followers. She was typical of a number of late medieval female religious figures who on the death of a spouse turned to religion. Like Angela, these women tended to gather "families" around them, people whom they described as their spiritual "fathers" or "children." They offered moral counsel and warned businessmen and politicians of the dangers of lying and sharp dealings.

In the late Middle Ages religious houses for women probably outnumbered those for men. For unmarried daughters, convents were an economical, safe, and controlled environment. The general public believed that well-run communities of women promoted the spiritual and physical health of the community. The experience was surely difficult for some women who felt rejected by the larger world, but for many, convent life had much to recommend it. In a society in which women were not allowed to control their own property and in which women outside the nobility lacked a visible role in political and intellectual life, a religious vocation appealed to women because it allowed them to define their own religious and social relationships.

Some women declined to join convents, which required vows of chastity and obedience to a rule and close male supervision. Margery Kempe (ca. 1373–1439) of Lynn, England, traveled throughout Christendom on a variety of pilgrimages. She left her husband and family, dressed in white (symbolic of virginity), and joined with other pilgrims on trips to Spain, Italy, and Jerusalem. Many other women chose to live as anchoresses, or recluses, in closed cells beside churches and hospitals or in rooms in private houses. Men and women traveled from all parts of England seeking the counsel of the Blessed Julian of Norwich (d. after 1413), who lived in a tiny cell built into the wall of a parish church.

The Beguines were women who lived in communities without taking formal vows and often with minimal connections to the local church hierarchy (see page 213). By the early fifteenth century, clerics began to resent Beguines because these independent women rejected traditional religious cloistering and the moral leadership of male clergy. Critics maintained that unsupervised Beguines held to what was called the "Heresy of the Free Spirit," a belief that one who had achieved spiritual perfection was no longer capable of sin. Although some Beguines may have held such a belief in spiritual perfection, the majority certainly did not. These pious women were slandered by an ecclesiastical hierarchy that resented female independence.

A more conservative movement for renewal in the church was the Brothers and Sisters of the Common Life founded by the Dutchman Geert Groote (1340–1384). Brothers and Sisters of the Common Life lived in quasi-monastic communities and supported themselves as book-copyists and teachers in small religious schools in the Low Countries. Members of these communities followed a strict, conservative spirituality that, paradoxically, has come to be known as the *devotio moderna,* or "modern devotion." Their ideas are encapsulated in *The Imitation of Christ,* written by Thomas à Kempis (ca. 1380–1471).

Religious life in the late medieval period was broadly based and vigorous. Theologians, lay women and men, and popular preachers could take heart they were furthering their own salvation and that of their neighbors. Thus, if reform was to be radically new, it would have to involve more than simple moral change.

Martin Luther and the New Theology

Throughout his life, Martin Luther (1483–1546) seems to have been troubled by a sense of his own sinfulness. Luther's father, a miner, had hoped that his son would become a lawyer, but the young man chose to enter a monastery. There he was tortured by worries over his own salvation. According to late medieval theology, the life of a Christian was a continuing cycle of sin, contrition, confession, and penance, and the only way to achieve salvation was to have confessed all one's sins and at least begun a cycle of penance at the time of one's death. Christians lived in fear of dying suddenly without having any chance to confess. The purchase of *indulgences* (the remission of penalties owed for sins), membership in penitential brotherhoods, ritualized charity, and veneration of popular saints were seen as ways to acquire merit and salvation in the eyes of God.

Luther came to believe that the church's system of penance was wrong. Instead, citing the New Testament, he argued that salvation (or *justification*) was God's gift to the faithful. Luther's belief is known as "justification by faith." Acts of charity were important products of God's love, but in Luther's opinion, they were not necessary for salvation. Late in his life, Luther explained how he came by these ideas:

Though I lived as a monk without reproach, I felt that I was a sinner before God with an extremely disturbed conscience. I could not believe that he was placated by

Cranach: The True Church and the False This woodcut was designed to make clear the distinction between the evangelical church and the papacy. On one side Christ and his sacrifice are clearly at the center; on the other the pope and innumerable church officials are caught in the flames of Hell. *(Staatliche Kunstsammlungen Dresden)*

my [acts of penance]. I did not love, yes, I hated the righteous God who punishes sinners. . . . At last, by the mercy of God, . . . I gave context to the words, namely, "In it the righteousness of God is revealed, as it is written, 'He who through faith is righteous shall live.'" There I began to understand that . . . the righteous lives by a gift of God, namely by faith. . . . Here I felt that I was altogether born again and had entered paradise itself through open gates.[1]

Other critics had complained of impious priests, an unresponsive bureaucracy, and a church too much involved in matters of government, but the theology that Luther developed struck at the very structure of the church itself. Luther separated justification from acts of sanctification—from the good works or charity expected of all Christians. In Luther's theology acts of piety were quite unnecessary for salva-

tion. Justification came entirely from God and was independent of human acts. Luther argued that the Christian was at the same time sinner and saved, so the penitential cycle and careful preparation for a "good death" were, in his opinion, unnecessary.

Luther also attacked the role of the priesthood. The church taught that, through the actions of ordained priests, Christ was really present in the bread and wine of the sacrament of Holy Communion. Luther agreed that the sacrament transformed the bread and wine into the body and blood of Christ, but he denied that priests had a role in the transformation. Priests distributed only the bread to the laity, reserving the consecrated wine for themselves—further emphasizing their own special status. Priests, in Luther's view, were not mediators between God and individual Christians. Luther argued for a "priesthood of all believers."

In the years before 1517, Luther's views on salvation and his reservations about the traditional ways of teaching theology attracted little interest outside his own university. Matters changed, however, when he challenged the sale of indulgences. The papacy frequently authorized the sale of indulgences to pay various expenses. Unscrupulous priests often left the impression that purchase of an indulgence freed a soul from purgatory. After getting no response to his initial complaints, Luther made public his "Ninety-five Theses"—probably by posting them on the door of the Wittenberg church, the usual way to announce topics for theological discussion. Luther's text was quickly translated and printed throughout German-speaking lands. His complaints encapsulated German feelings about unworthy priests and economic abuses by the clergy.

In a debate with a papal representative in Leipzig in 1519, Luther was forced to admit that in some of his positions he agreed with the Czech heretic John Hus (see page 228). In the Leipzig debate and in the following year Luther responded to his critics and tried to explain more fully the nature of the changes he advocated. Three tracts were especially important. In *Address to the Christian Nobility of the German Nation,* Luther urged the princes to reject papal claims of temporal and spiritual authority. In *On the Babylonian Captivity of the Church,* he argued for the principle of *sola scriptura*—that is, authority in the church had to be based on teachings found in the Bible. In *On Christian Freedom,* he explained his understanding of salvation: "A Christian has all he needs in faith and needs no works to justify him." Luther was speaking of spiritual freedom from unnecessary ritual, not political freedom. This distinction would later be crucial to his opposition to political and economic protests by peasants and artisans.

In 1520, Pope Leo X (r. 1513–1521) condemned Luther's teachings and gave him sixty days to recant. Luther refused to do so and publicly burned the papal letter. In 1521, Emperor Charles V called an imperial *diet,* or parliament, at Worms to deal with the religious crisis. Charles demanded that Luther submit to papal authority. Luther, however, would not retract anything. The emperor placed Luther under an imperial ban—that is, declared him an outlaw. Luther spent the next year in hiding, during which time he translated the New Testament into German, using Erasmus's edition of the Greek New Testament as the source. This New Testament became an influential literary as well as religious work.

The Reformation of the Communities

Luther challenged the authority of the clerical hierarchy and called on lay people to take responsibility for their own salvation. His ideas spread rapidly in the towns and countryside of Germany because he and his followers took advantage of the new technology of printing. Perhaps 300,000 copies of his early tracts were published in the first years of the protest.

The impact of Luther's ideas quickly became evident. If the active intercession of the clergy was not necessary for the salvation of individuals, then, according to Luther's followers, there was no reason for the clergy to remain unmarried and celibate, and there was no reason for monasteries or convents. Also, maintained Luther's partisans, there was no need to restrict the laity's participation in the sacrament of the Eucharist. Thus, the priest must distribute wine to the laity along with the bread. Because Luther's followers believed that penitential acts were not prerequisites for salvation, they set aside the veneration of saints and stopped making pilgrimages to the shrines and holy places all over Europe.

The reform message seems to have spread especially quickly among artisan and mercantile groups, which put pressure on town governments to press for reform. Agitation was often riotous. One resident of Augsburg exposed himself during a church service to protest what he believed to be evil and idolatrous. To quell disturbances and to arrive at a consensus within the community, town councils often set up debates between reformers and church representatives. Because the church hierarchy rarely approved of such debates, traditional views were often poorly represented, giving a great advantage to the reformers. The two sides argued over the authority of the church hierarchy, the nature of salvation, and whether papal authority and the seven sacraments could be demonstrated in the Bible. At the conclusion of such a debate, many town governments ordered that preaching and practice in the town should be according to the "Word of God"—a code for reformed practice. The city council would then become a council of elders for the church. Thus, civil government came to play an important role in the local organization of the church.

The case of Zurich is instructive. In 1519 the people's priest of Zurich was Huldrych Zwingli (1484–1531), son of a rural official from a nearby village. After a university education, he became a typical late medieval country priest, right down to his numerous lovers. Yet after experiences as a military chaplain and an acquaintance with the humanist writings of Erasmus, Zwingli began to preach strongly biblical sermons. In 1522 he requested episcopal permission to marry. Early in 1523, he led a group of reformers in a public debate over the nature of the church. The city council declared in favor of the reformers, and Zurich became, in effect, a Protestant city.

Unlike Luther, Zwingli believed that town governments should take the lead in bringing reform to the community. Zwingli explained that moral regeneration of individuals was an essential precondition for God's gift of grace. In the years following 1523, the reformers restructured church services, abolishing the mass; they also removed religious images from churches. Zwingli further disagreed with Luther about the nature of the sacrament of Holy Communion. Whereas Luther, like Catholic theologians, accepted that Christ was truly present in the bread and wine, Zwingli argued that the bread and wine merely signified Christ. Such disagreements made a common response to papal or imperial pressure difficult (Map 12.1).

The reform message spread from towns into the countryside, but often with effects that the reformers did not expect or desire. Many peasants and modest artisans believed Luther's message of biblical freedom carried material as well as theological meaning. Luther disagreed.

Throughout Germany villagers and peasants found themselves under increasing pressure from landlords and territorial princes. Taking advantage of changed economic and political conditions, these lords were intent on regaining claims to ancient manorial rights, on suppressing peasant claims to use common lands, and on imposing new taxes and tithes. Peasants argued that new tithes and taxes did not just go against tradition but violated the Word of God. Peasants from the district of Zurich, for example, petitioned the town council in 1523–1524, claiming that they should not be required to pay tithes on their produce because there was no biblical justification for doing so. Townsmen rejected the peasants' demand, noting that the Bible did not forbid such payments and saying that the peasants should make them out of love.

Demands that landlords give up human ordinances and follow "Godly Law" soon turned to violence. Peasants, miners, and villagers in 1524 and 1525 participated in a series of uprisings that began on the borderlands between Switzerland and Germany and spread throughout southwest Germany, upper Austria, and even into northern Italy. Bands of peasants and villagers, perhaps a total of 300,000 in the empire, revolted against their seigneurial lords or even their territorial overlords.

Luther initially counseled landlords and princes to redress the just grievances. As reports of riots and increased violence continued to reach Wittenberg, however, Luther condemned the rebels as "mad dogs" and urged that they be destroyed. Territorial princes and large cities quickly raised armies to meet the threat. The peasants were defeated and decimated in a series of battles in April 1525. When it became clear that the reformers were unwilling to follow the implications of their own theology, villagers and peasants lost interest in the progress of the re-

Map 12.1 Reform in Germany The pattern of religious reform in Germany was complex. Although some territorial princes, such as the dukes of Bavaria, rejected the reform, most free towns, particularly those in the southwest, adopted it.

form. As a townsman of Zurich commented, "Many came to a great hatred of the preachers, where before they would have bitten off their feet for the Gospel."[2]

John Calvin and the Reformed Tradition

In the 1530s, the theological arguments of the reformers began to take on a greater clarity, mostly because of the Franco-Swiss reformer John Calvin (1509–1564). Calvin had a humanistic education in Paris and entered the law before coming under the influence of reform-minded thinkers in France. In 1534 he fled Paris as royal pressures against reformers increased. He arrived in Geneva in 1536, where he would remain, except for a short exile, until the end of his life.

Calvin's ideas about salvation and the godly community rapidly spread to France, the Low Countries, Scotland, and England. The heart of Calvin's appeal lay in his formal theological writings. In 1536 he published the first of many editions of *Institutes of the Christian Religion,* which was to become the summa of reform theology. In it Calvin laid out a doctrine of the absolute power of God and the complete depravity and powerlessness of humanity. Calvin believed that from the beginning of time God had elected those to be saved and those to be damned and that human actions play no part in the divine plan. This idea of *predestination* means that "the word of God takes root and grows only in those whom the Lord, by his eternal election, has predestined to be his children." The elect—that is, the people to whom God graciously grants salvation—freely do good works in response to "God's benevolence."

Calvin suggested that the elect would benefit from "signs of divine benevolence," an idea that would have a profound impact on the Calvinist understanding of the relationship of wealth to spiritual life. By the seventeenth century, followers of Calvin widely believed that the elect had a duty to work in the secular world and that wealth accumulated in business was a sign of God's favor. It was an idea nicely suited to the increasingly wealthy world of early modern Europe.

That connection between salvation and material life, however, lay in the future. The aspect of election that most interested Calvin was the creation of a truly Christian community by the elect. To accomplish this, Calvinist Christians, later to be known as members of the Reformed church, purged their churches of any manifestation of "superstition." Like Zwingli they rejected the idea that Christ was really present in the sacrament of Holy Communion. They rejected the role of saints. They removed from their churches and destroyed paintings and statuary that they believed were signs of idolatry.

Public officials were to be "vicars of God." They had the power to lead and correct both the faithful and the unregenerate sinners who lived in Christian communities. In his years in Geneva, Calvin tried to create a "Christian Commonwealth," but Geneva was far from a theocracy. Calvin's Reformed church hierarchy was made up of four offices: preachers, teachers, deacons, and elders. Preachers and teachers saw to the care and education of the faithful. Deacons, as in the early church, attended to the material needs of the congregation. The elders—the true leaders of the Genevan church—were selected from the patriciate that dominated the civil government of the city. Thus, it makes as much sense to speak of a church governed by the town as a town dominated by the church. *Consistories,* or church courts, made up of community elders who enforced community moral and religious values, became one of the most important characteristics of Reformed (Calvinist) communities.

Radical Reform

Anabaptists (or "rebaptizers" because of their rejection of infant baptism) tended to take biblical commands more literally than the mainline reformers. They rejected infant baptism as unbiblical, and they refused to take civil oaths or hold public office, for to do so would be to compromise with unreformed civil society.

The earliest of the radicals allied themselves with the rebels of 1525. Thomas Müntzer (1490–1525) was an influential preacher who believed in divine revelation through visions and dreams. His own visions told him that the poor were the true elect and that the end of the world was at hand. An active participant in the revolts of 1525, Müntzer called on the elect to drive out the ungodly. After the defeat of the rebels, he was captured and executed by the German princes.

Other Anabaptist radicals, such as the revolutionaries who took control of the north German city of Münster, rejected infant baptism, adopted polygamy, and proclaimed a new "Kingdom of Righteousness." The reformers of Münster instituted the new kingdom in the city by rebaptizing those who joined their cause and driving out those who opposed them. They abolished private property rights in Münster and instituted new laws concerning morality and behavior. Leadership in the city eventually passed to a tailor, Jan of Leiden (d. 1535), who proclaimed himself the new messiah and lord of the world. The Anabaptists were opposed by the prince-bishop of Münster, the political and religious lord of the city. After a sixteen-month siege, the bishop and his allies recaptured the city from the Anabaptists in 1535. Besieging forces massacred men, women, and children. Jan of Leiden was captured and executed by mutilation with red-hot tongs.

With the destruction of the Münster revolutionaries in 1535, the Anabaptist movement turned inward. Under leaders like Menno Simons (1495–1561), who founded the Mennonites, and Jakob Hutter (d. 1536), who founded the Moravian Societies, the radicals rejected the violent establishment of truly holy cities. They tended to close themselves off from outsiders and enforce a strict discipline over their members. The elders of these communities were empowered to excommunicate or "shun" those who violated the community's precepts. Anabaptist communities have proved surprisingly durable. Moravian and Mennonite communities continue to exist in western Europe, North America, and even in parts of what used to be the Soviet Union.

Like Luther, all of the early reformers appealed to the authority of the Bible in their attacks on church tradition. Yet in the villages and towns of Germany and Switzerland, many radicals were prepared to move far beyond the positions Luther had advocated. When they did so, Luther found himself in the odd position of appealing for vigorous action to the very imperial authorities whose inaction had allowed his own protest to survive.

THE EMPIRE OF CHARLES V

Luther believed that secular authorities should be benevolently neutral in religious matters. In his eyes, the success of the early Reformation was God's will:

I simply taught, preached and wrote God's Word; otherwise I did nothing. And while I slept or drank Wittenberg beer with my friends . . . , the Word so greatly weakened the Papacy that no prince or emperor ever inflicted such losses on it. I did nothing; the Word did everything.[3]

As great as the word of God was, Luther must have known that even as he drank his beer, the Holy Roman emperor could have crushed the reform movement if he had chosen to enforce imperial decrees. But attempts to resolve religious conflict became entangled with attempts to hold together the family lands of the Habsburg emperor and with political rivalries among the various German princes. The eventual religious settlement required a constitutional compromise that preserved the virtual autonomy of the great princes of Germany.

Imperial Challenges

Emperor Charles V (r. 1519–1556) was the beneficiary of a series of marriages that, in the words of his courtiers, seemed to re-create the empire of Charlemagne. From his father, Philip of Habsburg, he inherited the imperial crown, claims to Austria, and Burgundian lands that included the Low Countries and the county of Burgundy. Through his mother, Joanna, the daughter of Ferdinand and Isabella of Spain, Charles became heir to the kingdoms of Castile, Aragon, Sicily, Naples, and Spanish America. During the Italian wars of the early sixteenth century, Charles's holdings in Italy expanded to include the duchy of Milan and most of the rest of Lombardy. By 1506 he was duke in the Burgundian lands; in 1516 he became king of Aragon and Castile; and in 1519 he was elected Holy Roman emperor. His chancellor enthused, "[God] has set you on the way towards a world monarchy, towards the gathering of all Christendom under a single shepherd."

Charles seems to have sincerely desired to create a united Christian monarchy, but each of the areas under his control challenged his authority. In Castile, for example, grandees, townsmen, and peasants complained that too many of his officials were foreigners whom he had brought with him from his home in Flanders. Protests festered and finally broke out into a revolt called the Comunero (townsmen's or citizens') movement. Between 1517 and 1522, when religious reform was making dramatic advances in Germany, many of the most important towns of Spain were in open rebellion against the Crown. Charles's forces eventually took control of the situation, and by 1522 he had crushed the Comuneros. Between 1522 and 1530, he was careful to spend much of his time in his Spanish kingdoms.

Charles's claims in Italy, as well as his claims to lands in the Pyrenees and in the Low Countries, brought him into direct conflict with the Valois kings of France. In the critical 1520s, the Habsburgs and the Valois fought a series of wars (see page 258). In the course of the struggle, the Catholic Francis I of France, whose title was "the Most Christian king," found it to his advantage to ally himself with Charles's most serious opponents, the Protestants and the Turks. The Habsburg-Valois Wars finally ended with the Treaty of Cateau-Cambrésis in 1559.

Charles was not the only ruler to claim the title "emperor" and a succession reaching back to the Roman Empire. After the conquest of Constantinople in 1453, the sultan of the Ottoman Turks began to refer to himself as "the Emperor." After consolidating control of Constantinople and the Balkans, Turkish armies under the command of Emperor Suleiman (r. 1520–1566), known as "the Magnificent," resumed their expansion to the north and west. Charles appealed for unity within Christendom against the threat. Even Martin Luther agreed that Christians should unite during invasion.

Suleiman's army besieged Vienna in 1529 before being forced to retreat. Turks also created a navy in the Mediterranean and, with French encouragement, began a series of raids along the coasts of Italy and Spain. The Turkish fleet remained a threat throughout the sixteenth century. Turkish pressure was yet another reason why Charles was unable to deal with German

Protestants in a direct and uncompromising way. (See the box "Encounters with the West: Duels Among Europeans and Turks.")

German Politics

The political configuration of Germany had an ongoing influence on the course of the religious reform. In 1500 Germany was much less centralized than France or England. Since 1495 seven electoral princes and a larger circle of imperial princes had claimed the right to representation in the imperial council, and nearly three hundred other towns or principalities demanded various exemptions from imperial control. The power of the emperor depended on his relations with the towns and princes of Germany.

In the first years after Luther issued his "Ninety-five Theses," he was defended by the elector Frederick of Saxony, who held a key vote in Charles's quest for election as Holy Roman emperor. As long as Frederick protected Luther, imperial officials had to proceed against him with caution. In 1522 and 1526 the emperor again tried to enforce the ban, but imperial officials were bluntly informed that the towns refused to conform. At the Diet of Speyer in 1526, delegates passed a resolution empowering princes and towns to settle religious matters in their territories as they saw fit.

Especially in the self-ruling towns, many decisions about religion often depended on the choices made by competitors. Rival sections of the province of Saxony, for example, split on the issue of reform: Electoral Saxony, Luther's homeland, was Lutheran, and ducal Saxony was Catholic. The Grand Master of the religious order of the Teutonic Knights, Albrecht von Hohenzollern (1490–1568), who controlled the duchy of Prussia, renounced his monastic vows and, at the urging of Luther, transferred his order's estates from church to private ownership. These lands became East Prussia, hereditary lands of the Hohenzollern family. In other territories, rulers managed to claim the proper-

ENCOUNTERS WITH THE WEST

Duels Among Europeans and Turks

A Flemish diplomat in the service of Ferdinand I of Austria, Augier Ghislain De Busbecq (1522–1592) was twice sent to Constantinople as ambassador. The following selection is part of a letter written from Constantinople in 1560. In it, Busbecq discusses violence among the Turks and contrasts it with Europeans' behavior.

The mention I made a while ago of matters in the confines of Hungary, gives me occasion to tell you, what the Turks think of duels, which among Christians are accounted a singular badge of personal valor. There was one Arstambey, a sanjack [district official], who lived on the frontier of Hungary, who was very much famed as a robust person [Arsta signifies a lion in Turkey]. He was an expert with the bow; no man brandished his sword with more strength; none was more terrible to his enemy. Not far from his district there also dwelt one Ulybey, also a sanjack, who was jealous of the same praise. And this jealousy (initiated perhaps by other occasions) at length occasioned hatred and many bloody combats between them. It happened thus, Ulybey was sent for to Constantinople, upon what occasion I know not. When he arrived there, the Pashas [governors] had asked many questions of him in the Divan [court] concerning other matters. At last they demanded how it was that he and Arstambey came to fall out? . . . To put his own cause in the best light, he said that once Arstambey had laid an ambush and wounded him treacherously.

Which he said, Arstambey need not have done, if he would have shown himself worthy of the name he bears because Ulybey often challenged him to fight hand to hand and never refused to meet him on the field. The Pashas, taking great offense, replied, "How dare you challenge a fellow soldier to a duel? What? Was there no Christian to fight with? Do both of you eat your emperor's bread? And yet, you attempt to take one another's life? What precedent did you have for this? Don't you know that whichever of you had died, the emperor would have lost a subject?" Whereupon, by their command, he was carried off to prison where he lay pining for many months. And at last, with difficulty, he was released, but with the loss of his reputation.

It is quite different among us Christians. Our people will draw their swords many times against each other before they ever come in sight of a public enemy, and unfortunately, they count it a brave and honorable thing to do. What should one do in such a case? Vice has usurped the seat of virtue and that which is worthy of punishment is counted noble and glorious.

Source: The Four Epistles of A. G. Busbequius Concerning His Embassy to Turkey (London: J. Taylor & J. Wyat, 1694), pp. 196–198.

ties of suppressed religious orders. Even when, as in the case of Count Philip of Hesse (1504–1567), much of the revenue from secularization was used to create an organized system of charity, the reforming prince was still enriched. Not all rulers welcomed the reformers.

Some found their personal reservations about Luther reinforced by their fears of popular unrest. Luther's call for decisions based on personal conscience seemed to the dukes of Bavaria, for example, to be a call for attacks on princely authority.

The Religious Settlement

With the fading of the Turkish threat on Vienna in 1529, Charles V renewed his pressure on the German principalities at a meeting of the imperial diet at Augsburg in 1530. It was for this diet that Philip Melanchthon (1497–1560), Luther's closest adviser, prepared the Augsburg Confession, which would become the basic statement of the Lutheran faith. Melanchthon hoped that the document would form the basis of compromise with Catholic powers, but the possibility was rejected out of hand by the imperial party. Charles aimed to affirm his strength in Germany by forcing the princes to end the reform movement and enforce the papal and imperial bans on Luther's teachings.

The Protestant princes responded by forming the League of Schmalkalden. At first, the founders of the league claimed that they were interested in protecting Reformed preaching, but the league quickly developed as a center of opposition to imperial influence in general. Eventually Charles and a group of allied princes managed to defeat the league at the Battle of Mühlberg in 1547. The emperor was unable to continue pressure on the Protestants, however, because he had depended on the support of some Protestant princes in his battles with the league. As a result, even after military defeat the Protestant princes were able to maintain religious autonomy. In the Religious Peace of Augsburg of 1555 the emperor formally acknowledged the principle that sovereign princes could choose the religion to be practiced in their territories, *cuius regio, eius religio* ("whose territory, his religion"). There were limits, however, for leaders could only remain under papal authority or adopt the Augsburg Confession outlined by Melanchthon. Reformed churches associated with Zwingli or Calvin were not legally recognized (Map 12.2).

Shortly after the settlement, Charles abdicated his Spanish and imperial titles. Exhausted by years of political and religious struggle, he ceded the imperial crown to his brother, Ferdinand (r. 1556–1564). His possessions in the Low Countries, Spain, Italy, and the New World he ceded to his son, Philip II (r. 1556–1598). Charles had believed that his duty as emperor was to unite Christendom under one law and one church. But in no part of his empire did he ever command the authority that would have allowed him to unite his lands politically, let alone re-establish religious unity. Following his abdication, Charles retired to a monastery in Spain, where he died in 1558.

THE ENGLISH REFORMATION, 1520–1603

England was closely tied to Germany. Since the twelfth century, large numbers of German merchants had lived and traded in England, and there was a major English community in Cologne. Anglo-German connections became especially significant during the Reformation. Reformers from Wittenberg and other Protestant towns had contact with English merchants from London who traded and traveled on the Continent. One reformer, William Tyndale (ca. 1494–1536), served as a bridge between the Continent and England. Forced by the church hierarchy to flee London, he visited Luther in Wittenberg before settling in Antwerp, where he completed his translation of the New Testament. By 1526 copies of his translation and his religious tracts flooded into England. By the 1520s Lutheran influence was noticeable in London and Cambridge. To some extent the ground may have been prepared for the reformers by the few surviving Lollards, the followers of Wyclif, who had argued for church reform in the late fourteenth and fifteenth centuries (see page 228). Lollards, who tended to be literate, were an ideal market for Tyndale's English Bible and his numerous tracts.

As in Germany, institutional change in the church followed from both secular issues and reform ideas. In England, a Catholic monarch began to tolerate reform ideas when he perceived the papacy as an unbiblical, tyrannical force blocking essential state policy.

Henry VIII and the Monarchical Reformation

Henry VIII (r. 1509–1547) began his reign as a popular and powerful king. At first, he was quite hostile to Luther's reform ideas and wrote *Defense of the Seven Sacraments*, which earned him the title "Defender of the Faith" from a grateful Pope Leo X. Throughout his life Henry remained suspicious of many Protestant ideas, but he led the initial phase of the break between the English church and the papacy because of his political problems with the highly orthodox Holy Roman emperor Charles V. The first phase of the English Reformation was thus a monarchical reformation.

Henry VII had initiated closer relations with Spain when he married his eldest son, Arthur, prince of Wales, to Ferdinand of Aragon's daughter, Catherine. After Arthur's death the future Henry VIII was married to Catherine in 1509. Henry VIII later tried to further the Anglo-imperial alliance when he arranged for the emperor Charles V, who was Catherine of Aragon's nephew, to marry Catherine and Henry's daughter, Mary Tudor. But by the late 1520s the Anglo-imperial alliance fell apart when Charles, responding to Spanish pressures, renounced the proposed marriage and instead married a Portuguese princess.

Henry's relations with Charles were further weakened by what the English called "The King's Great Matter," that is, his determination to divorce Catherine of Aragon. Henry believed that he needed a son to ensure Tudor control of the English crown. By 1527 Henry and Catherine had a daughter, Mary, but no living sons. Henry became convinced that he remained without a male heir because, by biblical standards, he had committed incest by marrying his brother's widow. As Leviticus 20:21 says, "If a man takes his brother's wife, it is impurity; . . . they shall remain childless." Henry desired an annulment. Unfortunately for him, Leo X's successor, Pope Clement VII (r. 1523–1534), was a virtual prisoner of imperial troops who had recently taken control of most of Italy. As long as Charles sup-

ported Catherine of Aragon and his forces occupied Rome, there would be no possibility of a papally sanctioned annulment of the marriage.

The king's advisers quickly divided into two camps. Sir Thomas More, the royal chancellor and a staunch Catholic, urged the king to negotiate with the papacy and destroy the growing Protestant party. Until his resignation in 1532, More led royal authorities in a vigorous campaign against the dissemination of the newly translated Tyndale Bible and against the spread of Protestant ideas. More was opposed and eventually ousted by a radical party of Protestants led by Thomas Cranmer (1489–1556) and Thomas Cromwell (1485?–1540), who saw in the king's desire for a divorce an effective wedge to pry Henry out of the papal camp. Cromwell, who eventually replaced More as chancellor, advised the king that the marriage problem could be solved by the English clergy without papal interference.

Between 1532 and 1535, Henry and Parliament took a number of steps that effectively left the king in control of the English church. Early in 1533, Cranmer was named archbishop of Canterbury. Later in the year Parliament ruled that appeals of cases concerning wills, marriages, and ecclesiastical grants had to be heard in England. In May an English court annulled the king's marriage to Catherine. Four months later, Henry's new queen, Anne Boleyn, gave birth to a daughter, Elizabeth.

Even before Cromwell became chancellor, Henry had attacked absentee clergy, restricted church courts, and prohibited the payment of certain papal taxes. After the split began, the king started to seize church properties. Parliamentary action culminated in the passage of the Act of Supremacy in 1534, which declared the king to be "the Protector and only Supreme Head of the Church and the Clergy of England." Henry meant to enforce his control by requiring a public oath supporting the act. Sir Thomas More refused to take the oath and was arrested, tried, and executed for treason. In some respects, Parliament had acted as an instrument of reform, much like the councils of the German and Swiss towns. In England, however, Parliament and

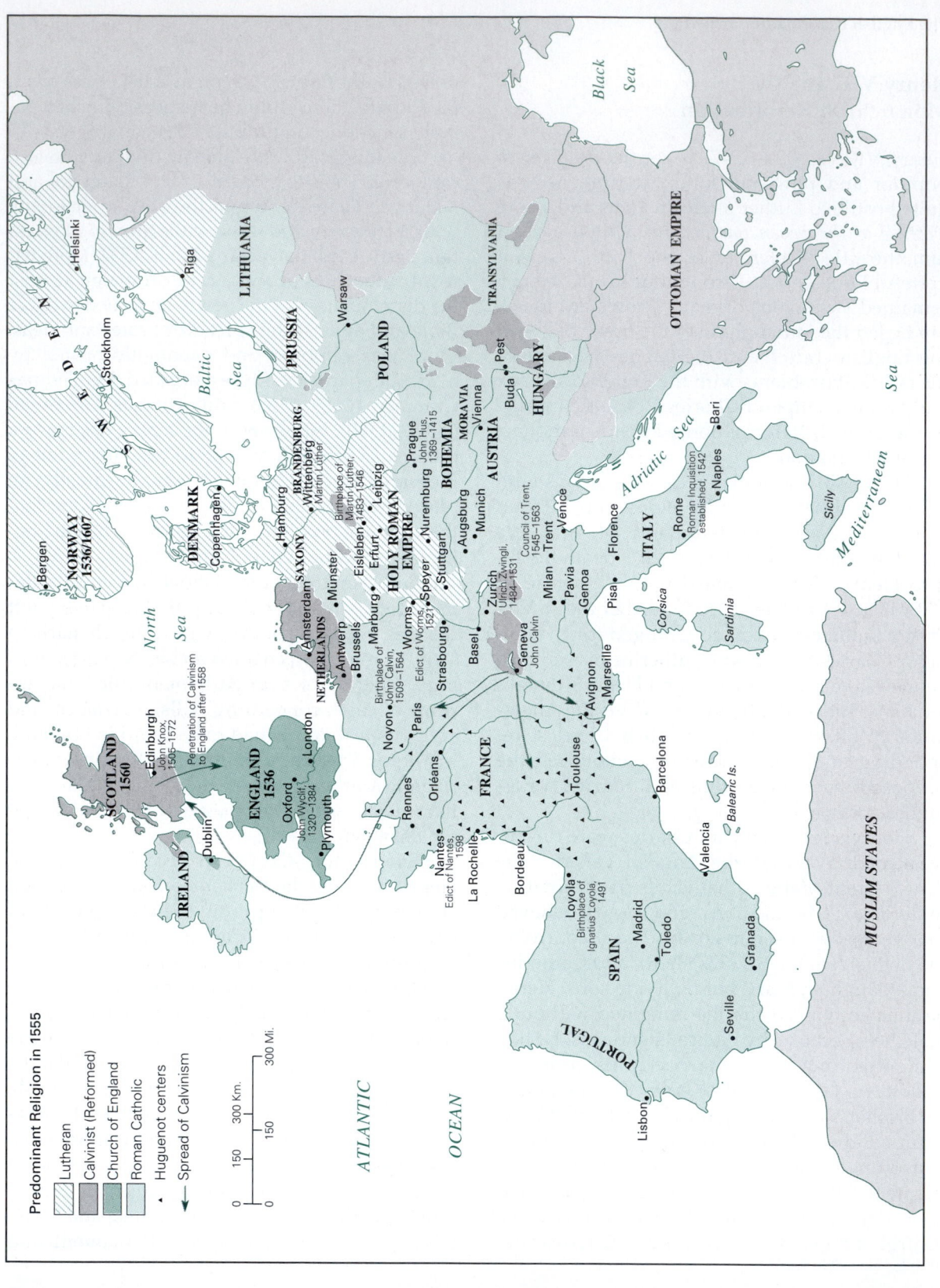

Predominant Religion in 1555

	Lutheran
	Calvinist (Reformed)
	Church of England
	Roman Catholic
◄	Huguenot centers
→	Spread of Calvinism

Scale: 0 – 150 – 300 Mi.

0 – 150 – 300 Km.

NORWAY 1536/1607

SWEDEN

Helsinki
Riga
Stockholm
Bergen

LITHUANIA

PRUSSIA

Warsaw

POLAND

Baltic Sea

DENMARK

Copenhagen
Hamburg

BRANDENBURG

Wittenberg
Birthplace of Martin Luther
Leipzig

Eisleben, 1483–1546
Erfurt

SAXONY

Münster

HOLY ROMAN EMPIRE

Prague
John Hus, 1369–1415

BOHEMIA

MORAVIA

TRANSYLVANIA

Pest

HUNGARY

Buda
Vienna

AUSTRIA

OTTOMAN EMPIRE

Nuremberg
Augsburg
Munich
Speyer
Stuttgart

Birthplace of Marburg

Worms
Edict of Worms, 1521

NETHERLANDS

Amsterdam
Antwerp
Brussels

Strasbourg

Noyon
Birthplace of John Calvin, 1509–1564

Paris

Basel

Zurich
Ulrich Zwingli, 1484–1531

Geneva
John Calvin

Milan
Pavia
Genoa

Venice

Adriatic Sea

Bari
Naples

Rome
Roman Inquisition established, 1542

Council of Trent, 1545–1563
Trent

ITALY

Florence
Pisa

Corsica

Sardinia

Sicily

Mediterranean Sea

Black Sea

Avignon
Marseille

Toulouse

FRANCE

Rennes
Orléans

Nantes
Edict of Nantes, 1598

La Rochelle

Bordeaux

Barcelona

Valencia

Balearic Is.

SCOTLAND 1560

Edinburgh
John Knox, 1505–1572

Penetration of Calvinism to England after 1558

ENGLAND 1536

Oxford
John Wyclif, 1320–1384

London

Plymouth

IRELAND

Dublin

Loyola
Birthplace of Ignatius Loyola, 1491

SPAIN

Madrid
Toledo

Seville
Granada

PORTUGAL

Lisbon

MUSLIM STATES

North Sea

ATLANTIC OCEAN

perhaps a majority of the laity perceived this reformation primarily as a political issue.

Cromwell and Cranmer had hoped to use the "King's Great Matter" as a way to begin a Lutheran-style reform of the church. But Henry remained suspicious of religious changes. He objected to the parts of the older tradition that he called "idolatry and other evil and naughty ceremonies," but he rejected the Protestant understanding of justification and what anti-Protestant critics called "bibliolatry." He complained of radicals who used Scripture "to subvert and overturn as well the sacraments of Holy Church as the power and authority of princes and magistrates." Between 1534 and Henry's death in 1547, neither the Protestant nor the Catholic party was able to gain the upper hand at court or in the English church. Substantive changes in the English church would be made by Henry's children.

Reform and Counter-Reform Under Edward and Mary

Prince Edward, Henry's only surviving son in 1547, was born to Henry's third wife, Jane Seymour. He was only 10 years old at his father's death. By chance, at the time of Henry's death, Edward Seymour, who was Prince Edward's uncle, and the Protestant faction were in favor. Seymour was named duke of Somerset and Lord Protector of the young king Edward VI (r. 1547–1553). Under Somerset, the Protestants were able to make significant changes in religious life in England. The Protestant party quickly reformed the Eucharist, allowing the laity to take both bread and wine. In an act of great symbolic meaning, priests were legally allowed to marry; many had already done so. Fi-

Map 12.2 Protestants and Catholics in 1555
Christendom in western Europe was divided into three major groups. Lutheran influence was largely confined to parts of Germany and Scandinavia, while Calvinist influence spread from Switzerland into Scotland, the Low Countries, and parts of France. Most of the West, however, remained within the Roman church.

nally, Archbishop Cranmer introduced the first edition of the English *Book of Common Prayer* in 1549. The book updated some late medieval English prayers and combined them with ideas taken from Luther, Zwingli, and Calvin. In its beautifully expressive English, it provided the laity with a primer on how to combine English religious traditions with reform theology. If Edward had not died of tuberculosis in 1553, England's reform would have looked very much like the changes that occurred in Switzerland and southern Germany.

Protestant reformers attempted to prevent Mary Tudor (r. 1553–1558), Henry's Catholic daughter, from claiming the throne, but they failed. Mary immediately declared previous reform decrees to be void. Cardinal Reginald Pole (1500–1558), who had advocated reform within the Catholic church, became the center of the Catholic restoration party in Mary's England. Pole rooted out Protestants within the church. More than eight hundred noblemen, clerics, and students fled England for the Protestant parts of the Continent. Three hundred mostly humble artisans and laborers were tried and executed by church courts, earning the queen her nickname, "Bloody Mary."

The policies of the queen brought about an abrupt return of the English church to papal authority. Most of the English quickly and easily returned to traditional religious practices. Statues were removed from hiding and restored to places of honor in churches and chapels. Although there is no conclusive evidence, the queen's initial successes may indicate that the Reformation was not broadly supported by the people. In fact, the restoration of Catholicism by Mary might have worked if the queen had not died after little more than six years on the throne.

The Elizabethan Settlement

Queen Elizabeth (r. 1558–1603), daughter of Anne Boleyn, succeeded to the throne at the death of her half-sister. The reign of Elizabeth was one of the most successful of English history. She managed to gain control of the various

The Queen in Parliament This image was meant to show the willingness of the Commons to support the queen, a key element of the Elizabethan Settlement. *(Bibliothèque Nationale)*

political and religious factions in the country and play off a variety of international powers against one another. She understood well the necessity of striking a balance between opposing forces.

Her first great problem was a religious settlement. Early in her reign she twice left church services at the elevation of the bread by the priest. Since in Catholic thought it was the action of the priest that made Christ present in the bread, she was indicating symbolically her opposition to a purely Catholic understanding of the sacraments. In the next few years she continued to work for

the restoration of many features of her father's and her half-brother's reforms. In 1559 the new Act of Supremacy and an Act of Uniformity reinstituted royal control of the English church and re-established uniform liturgical and doctrinal standards. The *Book of Common Prayer* composed by Cranmer was brought back, and final changes were made in the liturgy of the church.

Protestants had hoped for a complete victory, but the "Elizabethan Settlement" was considerably less than that. Although figures are lacking, it is likely that a large portion of the English population did not support a return to Henry's and Edward's reforms. After making clear her significant differences with Rome, Elizabeth confounded her most fervent Protestant supporters by offering a number of concessions to Anglo-Catholics. She herself remained celibate, and she ordered the Anglican clergy to do the same—although there was little she could do to prevent clerical marriage. As for her own refusal to marry: At this point in history, marriage almost necessarily placed women in a subordinate and submissive role. Elizabeth wanted to retain her freedom and dominance as well as her sanctity. The "Virgin Queen" commanded an image of political and military power over a forty-five-year reign.

She and her closest advisers allowed a great variety of customs and practices favored by Anglo-Catholics. These matters, the queen's supporters argued, were not essential to salvation, and thus individuals could be allowed to choose. Many of the prayers in the *Book of Common Prayer,* for example, seemed "papist" to the most radical Protestants. Similarly, many of the traditional clerical vestments and altar furnishings remained unchanged. Elizabeth probably knew that the Protestants had no alternative to supporting her and thus felt free to win back the support of the Anglo-Catholics.

REFORM IN OTHER STATES, 1523–1560

Considering England and the empire of Charles V, it would be hard to conclude, as Luther claimed, that "the Word did everything." Yet the religious reform movement cannot be reduced to the politics of kings and princes. The issues will be clearer if we survey politics and reform in the rest of Europe, noting to what extent the new ideas took root. In France, for example, widespread popular support of the old religion limited the options of the country's political leaders. Similarly, in northern Europe religious reform was an issue both of popular feeling and of royal politics.

France

Luther's work, and later the ideas of the urban reformers of southwestern Germany and Switzerland, passed quickly and easily into France. Geneva lies in a French-speaking area close to the French border, so it was easy for French Protestants to reach. French Protestants, known as Huguenots, were tied more closely to the Calvinists of Geneva than to the Lutherans of Germany.

At the height of the Reformation's popularity, Protestants probably represented no more than 10 percent of the total population of France. It has been estimated that there were about 2100 Protestant congregations in the 1560s—in a country that had perhaps 32,000 traditional parish congregations. Protestants seem to have been a diverse mix that included two of the three most important noble families at court: the Bourbon and the Montmorency families. Clerics interested in moral reform and artisans who worked at new trades, like the printing industry, also made up a significant portion of the converts. As a group Protestants tended to be of higher-than-average literacy. Protestants were well represented in towns; they were probably a numerical majority in the southern and western towns of La Rochelle, Montpellier, and Nîmes. Paris was the one part of the realm in which they had little influence, and their absence in the capital may have been their undoing.

The conservative theologians of the Sorbonne in Paris were some of Luther's earliest opponents. They complained that many masters at the University of Paris were "Lutheran." As early as 1523, Parisian authorities seized and burned books said to be by Luther. But as in Germany, there was no clear understanding of who or what a Lutheran was. They often complained about clerics who desired religious reform only within the traditional structures. King Francis's own sister, Margaret of Angoulême (1492–1549), gathered a group of religious persons at her court, even including several reformers. (See the box "The Conversion of Jeanne d'Albret.") But Margaret herself urged that theology be left to scholars; she believed that the laity should stick to simple pieties. Like Margaret, most French Christians did not believe that Protestant teachings required a complete break with medieval Christian traditions.

Like previous French kings, Francis I (r. 1515–1547) hoped to extend royal jurisdictions in France and make France an international power. Engaged in the seemingly intractable wars with the Habsburgs, Francis generally ignored religious questions. In 1525 he was taken captive in the wake of a military disaster at Pavia in Lombardy. He was held prisoner for nearly a year, during which time conservatives at the Sorbonne and in Paris moved actively against suspected Protestants. Francis was not initially opposed to what seemed to be moral reform within the church. His own view was that the king's duty was to preserve order and prevent scandal, and, at first, carrying out that duty meant protecting reformers whom the conservative militants persecuted.

On October 18, 1534, however, Francis's attitude changed when he and all Paris awoke to find the city covered with anti-Catholic placards containing, in the words of the writers, "true articles on the horrible, great and insufferable abuses of the Papal Mass." The response of the Parisians was immediate and hostile. They attacked foreigners, especially those who by dress or speech seemed "Lutheran"—that is, German or Flemish. Several months later Francis himself led a religious procession through Paris in honor of the Blessed Sacrament. The "Affair of the

The Conversion of Jeanne d'Albret

Jeanne d'Albret was the niece of King Francis I and mother of Henry of Navarre, the future Henry IV. In this letter, written in 1555 to a Huguenot supporter, she explains why she chose to become Protestant. After her conversion, her court became a center of the Huguenot movement.

I am writing to tell you that up to now I have followed in the footsteps of the deceased Queen, my most honored mother—whom God forgive—in the matter of hesitation between the two religions. The said Queen [was] warned by her late brother the King, François I of good and glorious memory, my much honored uncle, not to get new doctrines in her head so that from then on she confined herself to amusing stories. . . . Besides, I well remember how long ago, the late King, my most honored father . . . surprised the said Queen when she was praying in her rooms with the ministers Roussel and Farel, and how with great annoyance he slapped her right cheek and forbade her sharply to meddle in matters of doctrine. He shook a stick at me which cost me many bitter tears and has kept me fearful and compliant until after they had both died. Now that I am freed by the death of my said father two months ago . . . a reform seems so right and so necessary that, for my part, I consider that it would be disloyalty and cowardice to God, to my conscience and to my people to remain any longer in a state of suspense and indecision. . . . It is necessary for sincere persons to take counsel together to decide how to proceed, both now and in the future. Knowing that you are noble and courageous and that you have learned persons about you, I beg you to meet me.

Source: Nancy L. Roelker, trans., *Queen of Navarre: Jeanne d'Albret, 1528–1572* (Cambridge, Mass.: Harvard University Press, 1968), p. 127 (slightly adapted). Reprinted by permission of Harvard University Press.

Placards" changed Francis's ideas about the sources of disorder, and life became difficult for the reformers. John Calvin himself was forced to leave Paris and eventually France because he feared persecution. Between 1534 and 1560, some ten thousand Protestants fled France, many joining Calvin in Geneva.

By the middle of the sixteenth century it was clear that neither Protestant nor Catholic factions would be able to control religious and political life in France. Francis I died in 1547, and the stage was set for a series of destructive factional struggles over religion and political power that would continue for the rest of the century (see Chapter 13).

Eastern Europe

In some respects, a political vacuum in eastern Europe allowed for the expansion of Protestantism. The church hierarchy was not in a position to enforce orthodoxy. Some rulers were indifferent to religious debates, as were the Muslim Ottoman Turks, who controlled much of eastern Hungary and what is now Romania. Other rulers offered toleration because they could ill afford to alienate any portion of their subject populations.

Protestant ideas initially passed through the German communities of Poland and the trading towns along the Baltic coast. But in the 1540s

Calvinist ideas spread quickly among the Polish nobles, especially those at the royal court. Given the power and influence of some of the noble families, Catholics were unable to suppress the various secret Calvinist congregations. During the first half of the sixteenth century, Protestantism became so well established in Poland that it could not be rooted out. Throughout the sixteenth century, Protestantism remained one of the rallying points for those opposed to the expansion of royal power.

The situation was much the same in Hungary and Romania. Among German colonists, Magyars, and ethnic Romanians there were numerous individuals who were interested first in Luther's message and later in Calvinist revisions of the reformed theology. Some cities adopted a moderate Lutheran theology, and others followed a Calvinist confession. By the 1560s the Estates (representative assemblies) of Transylvania had decreed that both religions were to be tolerated. Further, when various radical groups migrated from the west in search of toleration, they too were able to create their own communities in Slavic and Magyar areas.

The Reformation was to have virtually no influence farther to the east, in Russia. The Russian church followed the traditions of the Greek church, and Western arguments over justification made little sense in Orthodox churches. Given the historic suspicion of the Orthodox for Rome, the Russians were more tolerant of contacts with the Protestants of northern Europe. But there would be no theological innovation or reform in Russia.

Scandinavia

By contrast, all of Scandinavia became Lutheran. Early influences drifted north from Germany, carried by Hanseatic merchants and students who had studied at the universities of northern Germany. Yet the reform in Sweden and Denmark, even more than in England, was a monarchical reformation. In both Scandina-

vian kingdoms the kings began with an attack on the temporal rights and properties of the church. Changes in liturgy and practice came later as reformers gained the protection of the kings.

Since 1397 all of Scandinavia had been united in theory in the Union of Kalmar (see page 237). But early in the sixteenth century the last pretenses of unity were shattered. Christian I of Denmark (r. 1513–1523) invaded Sweden and captured Stockholm, the capital. So great was his brutality that within a few years Gustav Vasa, a leading noble, was able to secure the loyalty of most of the Swedes and in 1523 was elected king of Sweden. Gustav's motto was "All power is of God." Like Henry VIII of England, Gustav (r. 1523–1560) moved carefully in an attempt to retain the loyalty of as many groups as possible. Although he never formally adopted a national confession of faith, the church and Swedish state gradually took on a more Lutheran character. In an effort to secure royal finances, the Riksdag, or parliament, passed the Västerås Ordinances, which secularized ecclesiastical lands and authorized the preaching of the "Pure Word of God." Olaus Petri (1493–1552), Sweden's principal reform preacher, was installed by royal order in the cathedral of Stockholm.

In Denmark the reformers also moved cautiously. Frederick I (r. 1523–1533) and his son, Christian III (r. 1534–1559), continued the policy of secularization and control that Christian I had started. Danish kings seemed interested in reform as a diplomatic means of attack on the Roman church and the political power of the bishops. It seems that in Denmark the old religion simply suffered from a sort of royal indifference. In 1538 the Danes finally accepted the Augsburg Confession, which was becoming the most widely accepted explanation of Lutheran belief. The transformation of practice proceeded slowly over the next decades. In the frontier regions of Scandinavia—Finland, Iceland, and Norway—the reform was undertaken as a matter of royal policy.

THE LATE REFORMATION,
CA. 1545–1600

In the first half of the sixteenth century, the term *Lutheran* applied to anyone who was anticlerical. Francesco Guicciardini (1483–1540), a papal governor in central Italy, remarked that had he not been a papal official:

I should have loved Martin Luther as much as myself— not so that I might be free of the laws based on Christian religion as it is generally interpreted and understood; but to see this bunch of rascals get their just deserts, that is, to be without vices or without authority.[4]

Guicciardini's remarks catch both the frustration many Christians felt with the traditional church and the very real confusion over just what it was that Luther had said. In parts of Germany by the late 1520s and across Europe by the 1550s, political and religious leaders attempted to make clearer to the peoples of Europe just what *Lutheran*, *Calvinist*, and *Catholic* had come to mean. Historians term the process of defining and explaining what each group believed, or confessed, the "Second Reformation," or "Confessionalization."

The profound changes that began in the sixteenth century continued into the seventeenth. People began to sort out what it meant to belong to one church instead of to another. Central governments supported religious authorities who desired religious uniformity and control over individual Christians. In all parts of Europe, both Protestants and Catholics became more concerned with the personal rather than the communal aspects of Christianity. After the sixteenth century, the nature of Christianity and its place in public life, whether in Protestant or in Catholic countries, differed profoundly from what it had been in the Middle Ages.

Catholic Reform

Historians commonly speak of both a movement for traditional reform and renewal within the

Catholic church and a "Counter-Reformation," which was a direct response to and rejection of the theological positions championed by the Protestants. It is useful, however, to consider the actions of the Roman church on their own terms, as both affirming traditional teachings and creating new institutions better fitted to the early modern world.

The idea of returning to purer, earlier church practices had been a commonplace for centuries. The great ecumenical Council of Constance early in the fifteenth century had called for "reform in head and members" (see page 229). In 1512, five years before Luther made his public protests, Pope Julius II (r. 1503–1513) convened another ecumenical council, the Fifth Lateran Council (1513–1517), which was expected to look into the problems of nonresident clergy, multiple benefices, and a host of other issues. This tradition of moral reform was especially strong in Spain, Portugal, and Italy, lands where political rulers were either indifferent or opposed to Protestant reforms.

The desire for reform along traditional lines was deeply felt within the church. In the wake of the sack of Rome by imperial troops in 1527, one Roman cardinal, Bishop Gian Matteo Giberti of Verona (1495–1543), returned to his diocese and began a thoroughgoing reform. He conducted visitations of the churches and other religious institutions in Verona, preached tirelessly, worked hard to raise the educational level of his clergy, and required that priests live within their parishes. Giberti believed that morally rigorous traditional reform and renewal could counter the malaise he perceived. Other reforming bishops could be found throughout Catholic Europe.

New religious foundations sprang up to renew the church. In Italy, France, and especially in Spain, a profusion of reformers chose to reform the church through austere prayer and contemplation. Teresa of Avila, who belonged to a wealthy *converso* (recently converted) family in Avila, led a movement to reform the lax practices within the religious houses of Spain. Famed for her rigorous religious life, her trances, and her raptures, Teresa animated a movement to reform the order of Carmelite nuns in Spain. Because of her writings about her mystical experiences she was named a "Doctor of the Church," a title reserved for the greatest of the church's theologians.

The most important of the new religious orders was the Society of Jesus, or Jesuits, founded in 1534 by Ignatius Loyola (1491–1556). A conservative Spanish nobleman, Loyola was wounded and nearly killed in battle. During a long and painful rehabilitation, he continuously read accounts of lives of the saints. After recovering, he went on a pilgrimage and experienced a profound conversion.

The structure of Loyola's order reflected his military experience. It had a well-defined chain of command leading to the general of the order and then to the pope. To educate and discipline the members, Loyola composed *Spiritual Exercises*, emphasizing the importance of obedience. He prohibited Jesuits from holding any ecclesiastical office that might compromise their autonomy. After papal approval of the order in 1540, the Jesuits directed their activities primarily to education in Catholic areas and reconversion of Protestants.

Throughout Europe, Jesuits gained fame for their work as educators of the laity and as spiritual advisers to the political leaders of Catholic Europe. In the late sixteenth and early seventeenth centuries they were responsible for a number of famous conversions, including that of Christina (1626–1689), the Lutheran queen of Sweden, who abdicated her throne in 1654 and spent the rest of her life in Rome. Raised to be queen, her rigorous education included hunting, riding, and statecraft. Once the crown was hers, however, the parliament insisted that she marry and take a more traditional role. Christina's Catholicism was surely part of her reason for choosing Italy as her new home, but it also reminds us that Catholicism offered an honored place for women who chose to live outside the traditional family. This option was generally

A Counter-Reformation Saint Saint Teresa of Avila came from a converso family. She believed that renewal within the Christian church would come through mysticism, prayer, and a return to traditional religious practices. She founded a reformed Carmelite order of nuns to further religious renewal in Spain. *(Institut Amatdler d'Art Hispanic, Barcelona)*

available only to wealthy women, but the existence of convents and sisterhoods had a symbolic significance in the culture at large.

Jesuits were especially successful in bringing many parts of the Holy Roman Empire back into communion with the papacy. They have rightly been called the vanguard of the Catholic reform movement. Catholic reformers were convinced that one of the reasons for the success of the Protestants was that faithful Christians had no clear guide about what were and what were not orthodox teachings. The first Catholic response to the reformers was to try to separate ideas they held to be correct from those they held to be incorrect. Successive popes made lists of books that they considered to be in error. The lists were combined into the *Index of Prohibited Books* in 1559. The climate of suspicion was such that the works of humanists like Erasmus were prohibited alongside the works of Martin Luther. The *Index* continued to be revised into the twentieth century. It was finally suppressed in 1966.

During the first half of the sixteenth century, Catholics joined Protestants in calls for an ecumenical council that all believed would solve the problems dogging the Christian church. It was finally called by Pope Paul III (r. 1534–1549) in 1545, when the hostilities between the Valois and Habsburgs had cooled. It is difficult to overemphasize the importance of the Council of Trent. It marked and defined the Roman Catholic church for the next four hundred years. Reformers within the Catholic church hoped that the council would define theological positions acceptable to the Protestants, making reunion possible. Unfortunately for the reformers, conservatives quickly took over the Italian-controlled council.

The Council of Trent sat in three sessions between 1545 and 1563. The initial debates were clearly meant to define Protestant heresy versus orthodox church doctrine. In response to the Protestant emphasis on the Scriptures, the council said that the church always recognized the validity of traditional teaching and understanding. Delegates rejected the humanists' work on the text of the Bible, declaring that the Latin Vulgate edition compiled by Jerome was the authorized text. In response to the widely held Protestant belief that salvation came through faith alone, the council declared that good works were not merely the outcome of faith but prerequisites to salvation. The council rejected Protestant positions on the sacraments, the giving of wine to the laity during Holy Communion, the marriage of clergy, and the granting of indulgences.

Protestant critics often list these positions and conclude that the work of the council was merely negative. To do so, however, is to ignore the many ways in which the decrees of the council were an essential part of the creation of the Roman Catholic church that would function for the next four centuries. The delegates at Trent generally felt that the real cause of the Protestant movement was the lack of leadership and supervision within the church. Many of the acts of the council dealt with that issue—either by confirming traditional authorities, such as the papacy, or by demanding that various church figures take on more responsive leadership roles. The council thus ordered that local bishops should reside in their dioceses, that they should establish seminaries to see to the education of parish clergy, and that, through regular visitation and supervision, they should make certain that the laity participated in the sacramental life of the church. At the final sessions of the council the basic position of the Roman Catholic church was summarized in the Creed of Pius IV.

Confessionalization

The labors of the Jesuits and the deliberations of the Council of Trent at midcentury made clear that reconciliation between the Protestant reformers and the Catholic church was not possible. The theological separation was marked in a number of ways. Churches in which both bread and wine were distributed to the laity during the sacrament of Holy Communion passed from Catholic to Protestant. Churches in which the altar was moved forward to face the congregation but the statuary was retained were likely to be Lutheran. Churches in which statues were destroyed and all other forms of art were removed were likely to be Reformed (Calvinist). Such matters as singing also differentiated the churches. Although the Calvinist tradition tended to believe that music, like art, drew the Christian away from consideration of the word, Luther believed that "next to the Word of God, music deserves the highest praise." Countless pastors in the sixteenth and seventeenth centuries followed Luther in composing hymns and even theoretical tracts on music. This tradition would reach its zenith in the church music of Johann Sebastian Bach (1685–1750), most of whose choral works were composed to be part of the normal worship service.

Music played an important role in Catholic services, too, so it was really architecture that

The Jesù in Rome This church is the center of the Jesuit order and the burial place of Saint Ignatius Loyola. Its baroque architecture set the tone for many later buildings in Rome and for many new Catholic churches elsewhere. *(Scala/Art Resource, NY)*

distinguished Catholic churches from Protestant churches in the late sixteenth and seventeenth centuries. In Rome, the great religious orders built new churches in the baroque style (see page 355). Baroque artists and architects absorbed all the classical lessons of the Renaissance and then went beyond them. Baroque art celebrates the supernatural, the ways in which God is not bound by the laws of nature. Where Renaissance art was meant to depict nature, baroque paintings and sculpture seemed to defy gravity. Its drama and power are clear in the construction of the Jesuit Church of the Jesù in Rome and especially in Gianlorenzo Bernini's (1598–1680) throne of Saint Peter made for the church of St. Peter in the Vatican. The construction of baroque churches, first in Spain and Italy but especially in the Catholic parts of Germany, created yet another boundary between an aus-

tere Protestantism and a visual and mystical Catholicism.

The Regulation of Religious Life

Medieval Christians had worried greatly about public sins that complicated life in a community. In the age of confessionalization, theologians—both Protestant and Catholic—worried about the moral status and interior life of individuals. Sexual sins and gluttony now seemed more dangerous than economic sins like avarice or usury. Even penance was understood as less a "restitution" that would reintegrate one into the Christian community than a process of coming to feel a true sense of contrition for sins. The changed attitude toward penance made the sense of Christian community less important and left individuals isolated and more subject to the influence of church authorities.

All of the major religious groups in the late sixteenth century emphasized education, right doctrine, and social control. In Catholic areas there was renewed emphasis on private confession by the laity to ensure a proper understanding of doctrine. During this period Charles Borromeo, archbishop of Milan (1538–1584), introduced the private confessional box, which isolated priest and penitent from the prying ears of the community. This allowed confessors time and opportunity to carefully instruct individual consciences. As early as the 1520s some Lutheran princes had begun visitations to ensure that the laity understood basic doctrine. Churchmen in both Protestant and Catholic areas used *catechisms*, handbooks containing instruction for the laity. The first and most famous was by Luther himself. Luther's *Small Catechism* includes the Lord's Prayer, Ten Commandments, and Apostles' Creed, along with simple, clear explanations of what they mean. More than Catholic rulers, Protestant rulers used church courts to enforce discipline within the community. Churchmen began to criticize semireligious popular celebrations such as May Day, harvest feasts, and the Feast of Fools, whose origins lay in popular myths and practices that preceded Christianity, because they seemed to encourage superstition and because they mocked the social and political order with, for example, parodies of fat or ignorant clergy and foolish magistrates.

Religious authorities also were concerned by what seemed to be out-of-control mysticism and dangerous religious practices, especially among women. The impact of the Reformation on the status of women has often been debated. The Protestant position is that the Reformation freed women from the cloistered control of traditional convents. Further, the Protestant attack on state-controlled prostitution reduced one of the basest forms of exploitation. To those who argued that unmarried men would always need sexual outlets, Luther replied that one cannot merely substitute one evil practice for another. Critics of the Reformation counter that a convent was one of

very few organizations that a woman could administer and direct. Women who took religious vows, Catholics point out, could engage in intellectual and religious pursuits similar to those enjoyed by men. The destruction of religious houses for women, Catholics argued, destroyed one of the few alternatives that women had to life in an authoritarian, patriarchal society.

In fact, in the late sixteenth and early seventeenth centuries, both Protestant and Catholic authorities viewed with suspicion any signs of religious independence by women. In the first years of the Reformation, some women did leave convents, eager to participate in the reform of the church. Early in the 1520s some women wrote tracts concerning the morality of the clergy. And there was for a time a tradition of women deacons in some Calvinist churches. Yet these religious women frightened Lutheran and Calvinist theologians, who argued that a woman's religious vocation should be in the care and education of her family. Similarly, even the most famous of the sixteenth- and seventeenth-century female Catholic mystics were greeted with suspicion and some hostility. Religious women in Catholic convents were required to subordinate their mysticism to the guidance they received from male spiritual advisers. For the laity in general and for women in particular, the late Reformation brought increased control by religious authorities.

SUMMARY

During the Age of the Reformation, Europe experienced a number of profound shocks. The medieval assumption that there was a unified Christendom in the West was shattered. No longer could Europeans assume that at heart they held similar views of the world and the place of individuals in it. Charles V had begun his reign with the hope that there would be one law and one empire. He ended it by dividing his empire and retiring to a monastery.

The Protestant challenge did not simply attack the institutional structure or the moral lapses as previous heretical movements had done. The early Protestant reformers rejected the very nature of the medieval church. Peasants and artisans argued that Luther's message of Christian freedom liberated them from both economic and spiritual oppression.

Monarchies and republics throughout Europe came to view religious institutions and religious choices as matters of state. In England and Sweden, calls for reform resulted in the secularization of church property, which put vast new sources of wealth in the hands of the kings. In the towns of Germany and Switzerland, governments redoubled their efforts to regulate religion and moral life. Thus, both Reformation and Counter-Reformation brought about a significant strengthening of religious and secular authorities.

Ironically, the reforms that Luther and other Protestants advocated on the basis of clear, incontrovertible religious truths eventually led to the suspicion that no truths could be known with certainty. Religious strife led some to conclude that in matters of religion toleration was the only appropriate option. Others concluded that if the truth could not be known, the state must be allowed to make the big decisions. And as we will see from the next chapter, the states of the seventeenth century were quite willing to do so.

NOTES

1. Martin Luther, *Works*, vol. 34 (Philadelphia: Fortress Press, 1955; St. Louis: Concordia Publishing House, 1986), pp. 336–337.
2. Quoted in Robert W. Scribner, *The German Reformation* (London: Macmillan, 1986), p. 32.
3. Quoted in Euan Cameron, *The European Reformation* (Oxford, England: Clarendon Press, 1991), pp. 106–107.
4. Francesco Guicciardini, *Maxims and Reflections (Ricordi)*, trans. Mario Domandi (Philadelphia: University of Pennsylvania Press, 1965), p. 48.

SUGGESTED READING

Bossy, John. *Christianity in the West, 1400–1700.* 1985. A subtle, important essay arguing that the Reformation ended communal Christianity and created in its place a more personal religion emphasizing individual self-control.

Brady, Thomas A. *Turning Swiss: Cities and Empire, 1450–1550.* 1985. A masterful history of the political and ideological concerns of the townsmen of southwestern Germany.

Cameron, Euan. *The European Reformation.* 1991. The best recent history of the Reformation, emphasizing the common principles of the major reformers.

Chatellier, Louis. *The Europe of the Devout: The Catholic Reformation and the Formation of a New Society.* 1989. An important study of the reconstruction of Catholic Christianity in the late sixteenth century.

Davidson, Nicholas S. *The Counter Reformation.* 1987. A short introduction emphasizing how the accomplishments of the Council of Trent laid the basis for a Catholic revival.

Dickens, Arthur G. *The English Reformation.* 1964. A classic, clear discussion of English religion, emphasizing the popular enthusiasm for reform, which Dickens believes is connected to the earlier Lollard movements.

Dickens, Arthur G., and John Tonkin. *The Reformation in Historical Thought.* 1985. A comprehensive survey of debates over the meanings of the Reformation, beginning with the earliest historians and continuing into the twentieth century.

Dillenberger, John, ed. *Martin Luther: Selections from His Writings.* 1961. A fine collection of writings that allows readers to follow the evolution of Luther's thought.

Eisenstein, Elizabeth. *The Printing Revolution in Early Modern Europe.* 1983. A general study of the printing revolution that includes a chapter on the importance of printing in the spread of reform.

Englander, David, Diana Norman, Rosemary O'Day, and W. R. Owens, eds. *Culture and Belief in Europe, 1450–1600: An Anthology of Sources.* 1990. A collection of documents illustrating religious and social values and giving an excellent overview of popular reform.

Fenlon, Dermot. *Heresy and Obedience in Tridentine Italy: Cardinal Pole and the Counter Reformation.* 1972. A complex book that argues that there was a strong interest in church reform in papal circles until the middle of the sixteenth century.

Greengrass, Mark. *The French Reformation.* 1987. A short pamphlet to introduce students to the political and religious development of the Reformation in France.

Haigh, Christopher, ed. *The English Reformation Revised.* 1987. A collection of essays criticizing Dickens's thesis on the popular basis of reform in England.

Hsia, R. Po-Chi, ed. *German People and the Reformation.* 1988. A collection of essays that introduce and comment on the various currents of research on the German Reformation.

McGrath, Alister E. *A Life of John Calvin: A Study in the Shaping of Western Culture.* 1990. An excellent biography emphasizing the definitive role of Calvin's religious thought.

Moeller, Bernt. *Imperial Cities and the Reformation.* 1972. Three classic essays on why townsmen responded so enthusiastically to the reform message.

Monter, E. William. *Calvin's Geneva.* 1967. A fascinating introduction to life in Geneva during the Reformation, emphasizing that the city was not a theocracy controlled by Calvin.

Moxey, Keith. *Peasants, Warriors, and Wives: Popular Imagery in the Reformation.* 1989. A study that shows how social and religious ideas spread throughout Germany by means of woodcuts; it contains numerous illustrations.

Oberman, Heiko. *Luther: Man Between God and the Devil.* 1989. A brilliant, beautifully written essay connecting Luther to prevailing late medieval ideas about sin, death, and the devil.

Ozment, Steven. *The Age of Reform, 1250–1550.* 1980. A well-written introduction to the ways in which reformers transformed medieval theological debates.

Potter, George R., and Mark Greengrass, eds. *John Calvin.* 1983. Selections from Calvin's most important works, along with short introductions.

Roper, Lyndal. *The Holy Household: Women and Morals in Reformation Augsburg.* 1990. A study of domestic values in a Protestant city, demonstrating the ways in which reform ideas limited women's religious role to instruction within the family.

CHAPTER 13

Europe in the Age of Religious War, 1555–1648

I n the early hours of August 24, 1572, armed noblemen accompanied by the personal guard of the king of France hunted out about one hundred other nobles, asleep in their lodgings in and around the royal palace in Paris, and murdered them in cold blood. The attackers were Catholic, their victims were Protestant—but all were French nobles, many of them related to one another. The king and his counselors had planned the murders as a preemptive strike because they feared that other Protestant noblemen were gathering an army outside of Paris. But when ordinary Parisians joined in, the calculated strike became a general massacre. About three thousand Protestants were murdered in Paris over the next three days.

This massacre came to be called the Saint Bartholomew's Day Massacre for the Catholic saint on whose feast day it began. Though particularly horrible in its scope (indeed, thousands more people were murdered in the French provinces as word of events in Paris spread), the massacres were not unusual in the deadly combination of religious and political antagonisms they reflected. Throughout Europe ordinary people took religious conflict into their own hands as rulers, for their part, tried to enforce religious uniformity, or at least religious peace.

Existing political tensions contributed to instability and violence, especially when reinforced by religious difference. Royal governments continued to consolidate authority, but resistance to royal power by provinces, nobles, or towns accustomed to independence now might have religious sanction. In several conflicts between Spain and the Netherlands, for example, religious issues were inseparable from political struggles. Tensions everywhere were also worsened by the rise of prices and unemployment as the sixteenth century wore on. These economic problems affected the rich as well as the poor and created particular hardship for working women. Economic stress was heightened because changes in military technology and tactics made warfare itself more destructive than ever before.

The late sixteenth and early seventeenth centuries were a period of extraordinary violence, but they were also distinguished by great innovation in statecraft. Queen Elizabeth transformed England through inspired diplomacy, aggressive development of the country's talent and resources, and strong leadership in military and religious conflicts. This was also a period of innovation in the arts. The plays of Shakespeare, for example, mirrored the passions but also reflected on the tensions of the day and helped to analyze Europeans' circumstances with a new degree of sophistication.

∾ *Questions and Ideas to Consider*

- In what ways did economic distress affect men and women differently?

- What was "iconoclastic fury"? What did it suggest about the relations between Spain and the Netherlands? What did Margaret of Parma do about the situation?

- Queen Elizabeth of England was widely recognized as an extraordinarily intelligent and able ruler. What were the chief accomplishments of her reign? How did she negotiate the difficulties of being a female ruler in a patriarchal society?

- What was the Defenestration of Prague? Why was it significant?

- When printing and literacy were first becoming widespread, cultures of drama and oral expression were still vibrant. Using specific examples from Montaigne, Shakespeare, and Cervantes, discuss this phenomenon.

SOCIETY AND THE STATE

Religious strife, warfare, and economic change disrupted the lives of whole communities in the late sixteenth and early seventeenth centuries.

The sixteenth century, especially, saw profound economic transformation that, by the end of the century, altered power relations in cities, in the countryside, and in the relationship of both to central governments.

The most obvious economic change was a steady rise in prices, which resulted in the concentration of wealth in fewer hands. Economic change did not spawn all of this era's social and political change: States made war for religious and dynastic reasons more than for calculated economic advantage. Nevertheless, the movements of the economy and the effects of war together created notable shifts in centers of wealth and power.

Economic Transformation and the New Elites

Sixteenth-century observers attributed rising prices to the inflationary effects of the influx of precious metals from Spanish territories in the New World. Historians now believe that there were also European causes for this "price revolution." Steady population growth caused a relative shortage of goods, particularly food, and the result was a rise in prices. Both the amount and the effect of price changes were highly localized, depending on factors such as the structure of local economies and the success of harvests. Between 1550 and 1600, however, the price of grain may have risen between 50 and 100 percent, and sometimes more, in cities throughout Europe— including eastern Europe, the breadbasket for growing urban areas to the west. Where we have data about wages, we can estimate that wages lost between one-tenth and one-fourth of their value by the end of the century. The political and religious struggles of the era thus took place against a background of increasing want.

These economic changes affected the wealthy as well as the poor. During this period, monarchs were making new accommodations with the hereditary aristocracy—with the Crown usually emerging stronger, if only by making concessions to aristocrats' economic interests. Underlying this new symbiosis of monarchy and traditional warrior-nobles were the effects of economic

CHAPTER CHRONOLOGY

1559	Peace of Cateau-Cambrésis; Act of Supremacy (England)
1565	Netherlands city councils and nobility ignore Philip's law against heresy
1566	Calvinist "iconoclastic fury" begins
1567	Duke of Alba arrives in the Netherlands; Margaret of Parma resigns her duties as governor-general
1571	Defeat of Turkish navy at Lepanto
1576	Sack of Antwerp
1579	Union of Utrecht
1588	Defeat of Spanish Armada
1598	Edict of Nantes
1603	Death of Elizabeth I
1609	Truce is declared between Spain and the Netherlands
1618	Bohemian revolt against Habsburg rule Defenestration of Prague
1619	Ferdinand II is elected Holy Roman emperor
1619	Frederick, elector of the Palatinate, is elected king of Bohemia
1620	Catholic victory at Battle of White Mountain
1621	Truce between Spain and the Netherlands expires; war between Spain and the Netherlands begins
1626	Imperial forces defeat armies of Christian IV of Denmark
1629	Peace of Alais
1631	Swedes under Gustav Adolf defeat imperial forces
1632	Death of Gustav Adolf
1635	Peace of Prague
1640–1653	The "Long Parliament" is in session
1648	Peace of Westphalia

changes that would eventually blur the lines between these noble families and new elites and simplify power relationships within the state.

Conditions in the countryside, where there were fewer resources to feed more mouths, grew less favorable. But at the same time expanded production and trade delivered more capital to wealthy families to invest in the countryside. As a result, a stratum of wealthy, educated, and socially ambitious "new gentry," as these families were called in England, began to appear. Many of the men of these families were royal officeholders. Many bought titles or were granted nobility as a benefit of their offices. They often lent money to royal governments, as the monumental expense of wars made becoming a lender to the government an attractive way to live off one's capital. Monarchs deliberately favored these new gentry as counterweights to independent aristocrats.

City governments also changed character as wealth accumulated in the hands of formerly commercial families. By 1600 traditional guild control of government had been subverted in many places. Town councils came to be dominated by successive generations of privileged families, and towns became more closely tied to royal interests by means of the mutual interests of the Crown and town elites. The long medieval tradition of towns serving as independent corporate bodies had come to an end.

Economic Change and the Common People

The growth of markets in Europe and Spanish possessions overseas had a profound effect on urban producers in western Europe. Production of cloth on a large scale for export, for example, now required huge amounts of capital—much more than a typical guild craftsman could amass. In many regions, guild members lost political power, and the guild structure itself began to break down. Master artisans began to treat apprentices virtually as wage laborers, at times letting them go when there was not enough work.

The effect on women workers was particularly dramatic. One of the first reflections of the dire circumstances faced by artisans was an attempt to lessen competition at the expense of the artisans' own mothers, sisters, daughters, and sons. Increasingly, widows were forbidden to continue practicing their husbands' trades, though they headed from 10 to 15 percent of households in many trades. Women had traditionally learned and practiced many trades but rarely followed the formal progress from apprenticeship to master status. A woman usually combined work of this kind with household production, with selling her products and those of her husband, and with bearing and nursing children. Exclusion of women from guild organization appears as early as the thirteenth century but now began regularly to appear in guild statutes. In addition, town governments tried to restrict women's participation in work such as selling in markets, which they had long dominated. Even midwives had to defend their practices, even though as part of housewifery women were expected to know about herbal remedies and practical medicine. (See the box "A Woman Defends Her Right to Practice Healing.") Single women and widows experienced increasing difficulty supporting themselves and their children.

Many women found work in cloth production, for spinning was a life skill that women learned as a matter of course. Cloth production was changing, too; it became increasingly controlled by new investor-producers with significant capital and access to distant markets. These entrepreneurs bought up large amounts of wool and hired it out to be cleaned, spun into thread, and woven into cloth by wage laborers in urban workshops or by pieceworkers in their homes. In the countryside, thousands of women and men helped to support themselves and families in this way.

In western Europe, countless peasants lost their lands to wealthy elites, "rentiers," who lent them money and claimed the land when the money was not repaid. Other peasants were unable to rent land as rents rose. To survive, some sought work as day laborers. Many found their way to cities, where they swelled the ranks of the poor. Others became part of the expanding network of cloth production, combining spinning and weaving with subsistence farming. One bad harvest might send them out on the roads begging or odd-jobbing; many did not long survive such a life.

In eastern Europe, peasants faced other dilemmas. The more densely urbanized and wealthy western Europe sought grain, from eastern Germany, Poland, and Lithuania. Thus, there was an economic incentive for landowners in eastern Europe to bind peasants to the land just as the desire of their rulers for greater cooperation had granted the landlords more power. Serfdom now spread in eastern Europe at the same time that it was gradually disappearing in the West.

Coping with Poverty and Violence

The common people of Europe did not submit passively either to economic difficulties or to the religious and political crises of their day. Whether Catholic or Protestant, common people took the initiative in attacking members of the other faith. At the community level, heretics were considered to be spiritual pollution that might provoke God's wrath. Thus, ordinary citizens believed that they had to eliminate heretics if the state failed to do so.

Townspeople and country people participated in riots and rebellions to protest their circumstances when the situation was particularly dire. The devastation of civil war in France, for example, led to a number of peasant rebellions and urban uprisings. Former soldiers, prosperous farmers, or even noble landlords whose economic fortunes were tied to peasant profits might lead rural revolts. If they succeeded, it would be only to relieve a local problem, such as a local tax burden. Urban protests often

A Woman Defends Her Right to Practice Healing

In this document, Katharine Carberiner testifies to the city council of Munich that she does not deliberately compete with male doctors but has skills that might lead other women to choose her rather than male medical practitioners.

I use my feminine skills, given by the grace of God, only when someone entreats me earnestly, and never advertise myself, but only when someone has been left for lost. . . . I do whatever I can possibly do . . . using only simple and allowable means that should not be forbidden or proscribed in the least. Not one person who has come under my care has a complaint or grievance against me. If the doctors, apothecaries or barber-surgeons have claimed this, it is solely out of spite.

At all times, as is natural, women have more trust in other women to discover their secrets, problems and illnesses, than they have in men—but perhaps this jealousy came from that. Undoubtedly as well, husbands who love and cherish their wives will seek any help and assistance they can, even that from women, if the wives have been given up (by the doctors) or otherwise come into great danger.

Because I know that I can help in my own small way, I will do all I can, even, as according to the Gospel, we should help pull an ox out of a well it has fallen into on Sunday.

Source: Merry Wiesner, "Women's Defense of Their Public Role," in Mary Beth Rose, ed., *Women in the Middle Ages and the Renaissance* (Syracuse: Syracuse University Press, 1986), p. 9.

began spontaneously when new grievances worsened existing problems. In Naples, in 1585, food riots were provoked not simply by a shortage of grain but by a government decision to raise the price of bread during the shortage. The property of the privileged was sometimes seized and city leaders were sometimes killed, but these protests rarely generated lasting political change.

Governments tried to cope with the increasing problem of poverty by changing the administration and scale of poor relief. In both Catholic and Protestant Europe, caring for the poor became more institutionalized and removed from religious impulses. In the second half of the sixteenth century, public almshouses to distribute food or to care for orphans sprang up in towns throughout Europe. These institutions reflected an optimistic vision, drawn from humanism, of an ideal Christian community. But by the end of the century, the distribution of food was accompanied by attempts to distinguish "deserving" from "undeserving" poor, by an insistence that the poor be forced to work to receive their ration of food, and even by an effort to compel the poor to live in almshouses and poorhouses. European elites were beginning to view the poor as a social problem, in need of collective control and institutional discipline.

The Hunt for Witches and the Illusion of Order

Between approximately 1550 and 1650, Europe saw a dramatic increase in the persecution of women and men for alleged witchcraft. Approximately a hundred thousand people were tried and about sixty thousand executed. The surge in witch-hunting was closely linked to the aftermath of the Protestant Reformation.

Food and Clothing Distributed by Government Officials In this rendering, a poor woman receives bread, and a destitute man clothing. Wealthy citizens' wills began to reflect the new definition of charity: Bequests to institutions increased and personal donations to the poor dwindled. *(The British Library)*

Certain kinds of witchcraft had long existed in Europe. So-called black magic of various kinds—one peasant casting a spell on another peasant's cow—had been common since the Middle Ages. What began to make black magic seem menacing to authorities were theories linking black magic to Devil worship. Religious leaders and legal scholars first began to advance such theories in the fifteenth century. By the late sixteenth century, both Catholic and Protestant elites viewed a witch not only as someone who might cast harmful spells but also as a heretic. Persecution for witchcraft rose dramatically after the initial phases of the Reformation ended, reflecting a continuation of reforming zeal directed at the traditional forms of folk religion and magic.

As far as we can tell, no proof that an accused person ever attended a Devil-worshiping "black" Sabbath was ever produced in any witch trial. Nevertheless, authorities were certain that Devil worship occurred, so convinced were they that Satan was in their midst and that the folkways of common people were somehow threatening.

Contemporary legal procedures allowed the use of torture to extract confessions. Torture or the threat of torture led most of those accused of witchcraft to "confess." Probably willing to say what they thought their captors wanted to hear, many named accomplices. In this way, a single initial accusation could lead to dozens of prosecutions. In regions where procedures for appealing convictions and sentences were fragile or nonexistent, prosecutions were pursued with zeal. They were widespread, for example, in the small principalities and imperial cities of the Holy Roman Empire, which were virtually independent of all higher authority.

Prosecutions numbered in the thousands in Switzerland, Poland, France, and Scotland. The majority—perhaps 80 percent—of those convicted and executed in all areas of Europe were women, many of them poor. The marked increase in poverty during the late sixteenth and early seventeenth centuries made poor women particularly vulnerable to accusations of witchcraft. It was easier to find such a person menacing—and to accuse her of something—than to feel guilty because of her evident need. The modern stereotype of the witch as an ugly old crone dates from this period.

Christian dogma and classically inspired humanistic writing portrayed women as morally weaker than men and thus as more susceptible to the Devil's enticements. Devil worship was described in sexual terms, and the prosecution of witches had a voyeuristic, sexual dimension. The bodies of accused witches were searched for the "Devil's mark"—a blemish thought to be the imprint of the Devil. Both Protestantism and Catholicism taught that sexual lust was evil. One theory has found the roots of witch-hunting in the guilt elite men suffered over their own sexual longings.

The witch-hunts virtually ended by the late seventeenth century, as intellectual energies shifted from religious to scientific thought. Reflecting religious fear and guilt and class divisions, the witch-hunts are central to an understanding of European life in this period.

IMPERIAL SPAIN AND THE LIMITS OF POWER

To contemporary observers, no political fact of the late sixteenth century was more obvious than the ascendancy of Spain. Philip II (r. 1556–1598) presided over the greatest empire since the time of Rome. Yet imperial Spain did not escape the turmoil of the era. An explosive combination of religious dissent and political disaffection led to revolt against Spain in the Netherlands. This conflict reflected the tensions of sixteenth-century political life: towns, provinces, and nobles trying to safeguard medieval liberties against efforts at greater centralization, with the added complications of economic strain and religious division. The revolt also demonstrated the material limits of royal power, since even with

gold and silver from the American colonies pouring in, Philip could at times barely afford to keep armies in the field.

The Revolt of the Netherlands

Philip II's power stemmed in part from the far-flung territories he inherited from his father, the Habsburg Holy Roman emperor Charles V: Spain, the Low Countries (the Netherlands), the duchy of Milan, the kingdom of Naples, and the conquered lands in the Americas (see Map 13.2). Treasure fleets bearing precious metals from the New World began to reach Spain regularly during Philip's reign. In addition, Spain now belonged to an expanding trading economy unlike any that had existed in Europe before. To supply its colonies, Spain needed timber and other shipbuilding materials from the hinterlands of the Baltic Sea. Grain from the Baltic region fed the urban population of Spain (where wool was the principal cash crop) and the Netherlands, while the Netherlands, in turn, was a source of finished goods, such as cloth. The major exchange point for all these goods was the city of Antwerp in the Netherlands, the leading trading center of all of Europe.

Thus, Spain's expanding trading network necessitated tight links with the Netherlands, the real jewel among Philip's European possessions. These seventeen provinces (corresponding roughly to the modern nations of Belgium and the Netherlands; Map 13.1) had been centers of trade and manufacture since the twelfth century. Each province had a representative assembly (Estates) that controlled taxation, but each also acknowledged a governing council sitting in Brussels as the central administrative authority. Heading the principal council of state was a governor-general, typically, like Philip, a member of the Habsburg family. Yet political power, here and elsewhere, was still highly decentralized, and Philip, like other rulers, could rule effectively only with the cooperation of local elites. Philip's clumsy efforts to adjust this distribution of power in his favor pushed his subjects in the Netherlands into revolt.

Map 13.1 The Netherlands, 1559–1609 The seven-teen provinces of the Netherlands were strikingly di-verse politically, economically, and culturally. Like his father, Philip was, technically, the ruler of each prov-ince separately: He was count of Flanders, duke of Brabant, and so forth.

Tensions arose partly over taxation and partly over Spanish insistence on maintaining tight control. When the Peace of Cateau-Cambrésis of 1559 brought an end to the fighting between the Habsburgs and the Valois kings of France, the people of the Netherlands hoped for lower taxes and reduced levels of Spanish control.

Philip, born and raised in Spain, had little real familiarity with the densely populated, lin-guistically diverse Netherlands and never vis-ited there after 1559. He appointed as governor-general his half-sister, Margaret of Parma, who presided over a council made up exclusively of Spaniards and men with close ties to the Spanish court. These arrangements affronted local nobles who were accustomed to positions of influence in the council of state.

To economic and political tensions were added severe religious problems created by Philip's ag-gressive pursuit of Protestant "heretics." Unlike his father, Philip directed the hunt for heretics not just at lower-class dissenters but also at well-to-do Calvinists, who now existed in increasing num-bers. Punishment for heresy now included confis-cation of family property as well as execution of the individual. By 1565, municipal councils in the Netherlands were routinely refusing to enforce Philip's religious decrees, believing that urban prosperity—as well as their personal security—de-pended on relative restraint in the prosecution of heresy.

During the spring and summer of 1566, reli-gious dissension in the Netherlands grew dra-matically. Encouraged by greater tolerance, Protestants began to hold open-air meetings, and in many towns ordinary people began to embrace Protestantism for the first time. In a series of actions called the "iconoclastic fury," townsfolk stripped Catholic churches of the relics and statues deemed idolatrous by Calvin-ist doctrine. Food riots also occurred. Both Span-ish authorities and local elites feared the out-break of general unrest.

By early 1567, Calvinist insurgents had seized two towns in the southern Netherlands, hoping to spark a general revolt that would secure freedom of worship. Although some nobles also supported a widening rebellion, Margaret of Parma success-fully quelled the uprisings by rallying city gov-ernments and loyal nobles, now alarmed for their own power and property. But she then learned that far away in Spain a decision had been made to send the Spanish duke of Alba with an army of ten thousand men.

Alba arrived in August 1567 and acted more like a conqueror than a peacemaker. He billeted troops in friendly cities, established new courts to try rebels, arrested thousands of people, executed about a thousand rebels (including Catholics as well as prominent Protestants), and imposed new taxes to support his army. Thus, Alba repeated every mistake of Spanish policy that had triggered rebellion in the first place.

Margaret of Parma resigned in disgust and left the Netherlands. Protestants escaped into exile and were joined by nobles who had been declared treasonous for minor lapses of loyalty. The most important of these was William of Nassau, prince of Orange (1533–1584), whose lands outside of the Netherlands, in France and the empire, lay out of Spanish reach and so could be used to finance continued warfare against Spain. Thus, a significant community with military capability began to grow in exile.

In 1572 ships of exiled Calvinist privateers known as the "Sea Beggars" captured some fifty towns in the northern provinces. The towns' impoverished inhabitants—eager to strike a blow at expensive Spanish rule—welcomed the exiles. For the rest of the century, the northern provinces became increasingly Calvinist strongholds and were the center of opposition to the Spanish, who concentrated their efforts against rebellion in the wealthier southern provinces. Occasionally the French and English lent aid to the rebels. The Spanish never had the resources to crush the rebellion.

Some northern cities improved their fortifications by constructing new defensive works known as "bastions"; such cities could not be taken by storm but had to be besieged for long periods. Military campaigns in the Netherlands now consisted of grueling sieges, skirmishes in a city's surrounding area for control of villages' supplies, and occasional pitched battles between besiegers and forces attempting to break the siege. Inevitably, the army put a great strain on the countryside, and both soldiers and civilians suffered great privations. On occasion, Spanish troops reacted violently to difficult conditions and to delayed pay (American treasure dwindled badly between 1572 and 1578). In 1576, Spanish troops sacked the hitherto loyal southern city of Antwerp and massacred about eight thousand people, an event long remembered as the "Spanish Fury."

In 1579 the northern provinces concluded a defensive alliance, the Union of Utrecht, against

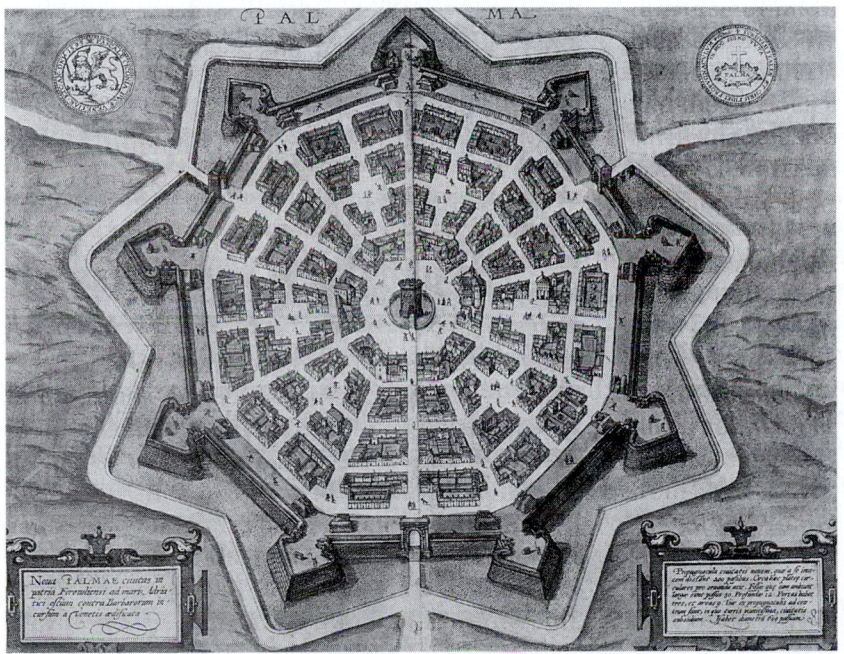

The Bastion Seen here in an example from an Italian fortress, the bastion was the triangular projection from the fortress wall. It enabled defenders to fire on the flanks of besieging forces; lower than medieval fortress walls and reinforced with earth, walls built in this manner were also less vulnerable to artillery blasts. (*Universitäts und Stadtbibliothek Cologne*)

the Spanish-controlled south, now governed by Margaret's son, Alexander, duke of Parma. Parma met with losses and faced declining resources as Spain diverted money to conflicts with England and with France. In 1609 a twelve-year truce was finally concluded between Spain and the northern provinces. This truce did not formally recognize the "United Provinces" as an independent entity, though in fact they were.

The independent United Provinces (usually called the Netherlands) was a fragile state, an accident of warfare. But commercial prosperity had begun to emerge as its greatest strength. Much of the economic activity of Antwerp had shifted north to Amsterdam in the province of Holland because of fighting in the south. Philip's policies had created a new enemy nation and had enriched it at his expense.

The Failure of the Invincible Armada

The political and economic importance of the Netherlands lured Spain into wider strategic involvement, most notably against England. England and Spain had long maintained cordial relations. They had a common foe in France and common economic interests. Philip's marriage to Mary Tudor, the Catholic queen of England (r. 1553–1558), had been a logical step in that relationship. Even after the accession of the Protestant queen Elizabeth (r. 1558–1603), Spanish-English relations initially remained cordial.

Relations started to sour, however, when Elizabeth began tolerating the use of English ports by the rebel Sea Beggars and authorizing English attacks on Spanish treasure fleets. In response, Spain supported Catholic resistance to Elizabeth within England, including a series of plots to replace Elizabeth on the throne with Mary, Queen of Scots. Greater Spanish success in the Netherlands, raids by the Spanish and English on each other's shipping, and Elizabeth's execution of Mary in 1587 prompted Philip to order an invasion of England. A fleet (armada) of Spanish warships sailed in 1588.

"The enterprise of England," as the plan was called in Spain, represented an astounding logis-

tical effort. The Spanish Armada was supposed to clear the English Channel of English ships in order to permit an invading force—troops under Parma in the Netherlands—to cross the Channel on barges. The fleet of about 130 ships also carried troops from Spain, as well as large quantities of supplies. The sheer number of ships required meant that some, inevitably, were slower supply ships, or naval vessels designed for the more protected waters of the Mediterranean. The fleet as a whole was slower and less maneuverable than the English force it faced. The English also had the advantage in arms, since they had better long-range artillery and better-trained gunners.

When the Armada entered the Channel on July 29, the English fleet fell in behind them. They could harass the Spanish with artillery from a distance without sustaining much damage themselves. On the night of August 7, the English launched eight fireships into the anchored Spanish fleet; at dawn on August 8, they attacked the disorganized enemy off Gravelines, and their advantage in arms was decisive (see Map 13.2).

The Battle at Gravelines was the first major gun battle by sailing ships and helped set the future course of naval warfare. For the Spanish, it was a disaster. Many ships were sunk or forced into hostile harbors as the Spanish rounded the northern tip of the British Isles and sailed for home. Fifteen thousand sailors and soldiers died in battle or on the return journey. Less than half of Philip's great fleet made it back to Spain.

Successes at Home and Around the Mediterranean

Many of Philip's interests still centered on the Mediterranean, despite the new overseas empire and his preoccupation with the Netherlands. Spain and the kingdom of Naples had exchanged trade for centuries. Newer ties had been forged with the duchy of Milan and the city-state of Genoa, whose bankers were financiers to the Spanish monarchy. Charles V had tried to secure the western Mediterranean against the Turks and their client states along the African coast, but it was under Philip that the Turkish threat in the western Mediterranean receded.

The years of the greatest Turkish threat coincided with the beginning of the Netherlands' revolt. To Philip and his advisers, the Turks represented a potential internal threat to Spain as well. Philip thus inaugurated a new wave of persecution of his Muslim subjects, eventually provoking a major rebellion in Granada between 1568 and 1571. After this revolt was crushed, the Muslim inhabitants of Granada were forcibly exiled farther north in Spain. The Spanish allied temporarily with the papacy and Venice—both were concerned with the Turkish advances in the Mediterranean—and their combined navies inflicted a massive defeat on the Turkish navy at Lepanto, off the coast of Greece, in October 1571. The Turks remained a power in the eastern Mediterranean, but their ability to threaten Spain was over.

Philip's powers in each of his Spanish kingdoms were circumscribed by the traditional privileges of towns, nobility, and clergy. In Aragon, for example, he could raise revenues only by appealing to local assemblies, the Cortes. In Castile, the king was able to levy taxes with greater ease. Philip established his permanent capital, Madrid, and his principal residence, the Escorial, there. The Spanish Empire became more and more Castilian as the reign progressed.

Philip made significant inroads into Aragonese independence by the end of his reign. Noble feuds and peasant rebellions had combined to create virtual anarchy in some areas of Aragon by the 1580s, and in 1591 Philip sent in veteran troops from the Netherlands campaigns to establish firmer royal control. Philip was successful in Aragon because he used adequate force, followed by constitutional changes that were cleverly moderate. Finally, he cemented the peace by doing what he had failed to do in the Netherlands. He appeared in Aragon in person, in the words of a contemporary, "like a rainbow at the end of a storm."[1]

Philip also invaded and annexed Portugal in 1580, completing the unification of the Iberian Peninsula. The annexation was assured by armed force but had been preceded by careful negotiation to guarantee that Philip's claim to

Philip II in 1583 Dressed in the austere black in fashion at the Spanish court, Philip holds a rosary and wears the Order of the Golden Fleece, an order of knighthood, around his neck. At age 56 Philip had outlived four wives and most of his children. *(Museo del Prado, Madrid)*

the throne—through his mother—would find some support within the country. This was old-fashioned dynastic politics at its best. When Philip died in 1598, he was old and ill, a man for whom daily life had become a painful burden. His Armada had been crushed; he had never quelled the Netherlands' revolt. Yet he had been more successful, by his own standards, in other regions that he ruled.

Spain in Decline

Spain steadily lost ground economically and strategically after the turn of the century. Imports of silver declined. The American mines were depleted, and the natives forced to work in them were decimated by European diseases and brutal treatment. Spain's economic health was further threatened by the very success of its colonies: Local industries in the Americas began to produce goods formerly obtained from Spain. The increasing presence of English, French, and Dutch shipping in the Americas provided colonists with rival sources for the goods they needed. Often, these competitors could offer their goods more cheaply than Spaniards could.

Spain renewed hostilities with the United Provinces in 1621, after the truce of 1609 had expired. Philip IV (r. 1621–1645) also aided his Habsburg cousins in the Thirty Years' War in the Holy Roman Empire (see page 348). Squeezed for troops and revenue for these commitments, other Spanish territories revolted. The uprisings reflected both economic distress and unresolved issues of regional autonomy.

In Portugal, a war of independence began in 1640, also with a popular revolt. The Spanish government tried to restore order with troops under the command of a leading Portuguese prince, John, duke of Braganza. The duke, however, was the nearest living relative to the last king of Portugal, and he seized this opportunity to claim the crown of Portugal for himself. Although war dragged on until 1668, the Portuguese under John IV (r. 1640–1656) succeeded in winning independence from Spain. In 1647 there would also be upheaval in Spain's Italian possessions of Sicily and Naples. By midcentury, Spain had lost its position as the pre-eminent state in Europe.

RELIGIOUS AND POLITICAL CRISIS IN FRANCE AND ENGLAND

Civil war wracked France from 1562 until 1598. As in the Netherlands, the conflicts in France had religious and political origins as well as international implications. Though a temporary resolution was achieved by 1598, religious division persisted.

England, however, was spared dramatic political and religious upheaval in the second half of the sixteenth century, in part because of the talents—and long life—of its ruler. In the seventeenth century, constitutional and religious dissent began to reinforce each other in new and dramatic ways and threaten the stability of the realm.

The French Religious Wars

The king of France, Henry II (r. 1547–1559), had concluded the Peace of Cateau-Cambrésis with Philip II in 1559, ending the Habsburg-Valois Wars, but Henry died in July of that year from wounds suffered at a tournament held to celebrate the new treaty. His death was a political disaster. Nobles from the Guise and Bourbon families vied for influence over his 15-year-old son, Francis II (r. 1559–1560). The queen mother, Catherine de' Medici (1519–1589), worked carefully and intelligently to balance their interests. She gained greater authority when, in late 1560, the sickly Francis died and was succeeded by his brother, Charles IX—a 10-year-old for whom Catherine was officially the regent. But keeping the conflicts among the great courtiers from boiling over into civil war proved impossible.

Noble conflict invariably had a violent component. Noble men went about armed and accompanied by armed entourages. Although they relied on army commands from the Crown, the Crown depended on their services. Provincial nobles had the resources for private warfare and assumed a right to wage it.

Religious tension was rising throughout France. Public preaching and secret meetings of Protestants (known as "Huguenots" in France) were causing unrest in towns. At court, members of the Bourbon family and other leading nobles had converted to Protestantism and worshiped openly in their rooms in the palace. In 1561, Catherine convened a national religious council to reconcile the two faiths. When it failed, she decided that the only practical course was at least provisional religious toleration, so she issued a limited edict of toleration in the name of the king in January 1562. Protestants, however, ignored the edict's restrictions and armed themselves. Townspeople of both faiths attacked one another at worship sites and religious festivals. Then in March, the duke of Guise's men killed a few dozen Protestants gathered in worship near the duke's estate at Vassy.

The killing at Vassy began the first of eight civil wars because it brought together the military power of the nobility with the broader problem of religious division. In some ways the initial conflict was decisive. The Protestant army lost the principal pitched battle of the war, near Dreux, west of Paris, in December. This defeat ultimately checked the growth of the Protestant movement, but the turning point most obvious to contemporaries came a decade later. In 1572, the Protestant nobleman Gaspard de Coligny was pressing for a war against Spain to aid Protestant rebels in the Netherlands. Alarmed by this pressure and by rumors of Protestant armies outside of Paris, Charles IX (r. 1560–1574) and his mother authorized royal guards to murder Coligny and other Protestant leaders on August 24, 1572— Saint Bartholomew's Day. Coligny's murder touched off a massacre of Protestants throughout the kingdom.

The Saint Bartholomew's Day Massacre revealed the degree to which religious differences had strained the fabric of community life. Neighbor murdered neighbor, and bodies of the dead, including Coligny's, were torn apart. When a truce was finally called, members of both Huguenot and Catholic forces refused to stop fighting—against the wishes of the Crown.

Another impetus to the breakdown of royal authority by the 1580s was the accession to the throne of Charles's brother, Henry III (r. 1574–1589), another king of limited abilities. Middle-aged, Henry had no children. The heir to his throne was the Protestant Henry of Navarre, and the assumption of the throne by a Protestant was unimaginable to the Catholics. By the end of Henry III's reign, the king had almost no royal authority left to wield. In December 1588, he resorted to murdering two members of the Guise family who led the ultra-Catholic faction, and, in turn, he was murdered by a priest in early 1589.

Henry of Navarre, who became Henry IV (r. 1589–1610), was able to force acceptance of his rule only after agreeing to return to Catholicism. After his conversion in 1593, the wars continued for a time, but after thirty years of civil war many of his subjects realized that only rallying to the monarchy could save France from chaos. The civil wars had demonstrated the power of the warrior-nobility to disrupt the state. But now nobles grew increasingly disposed, for both psychological and practical reasons, to cooperate with the Crown. The civil war period thus proved to be an important phase in the accommodation of the nobility to the power of the state.

In April 1598, Henry granted toleration for the Huguenot minority in a royal edict proclaimed in the city of Nantes. Nobles were allowed to practice the Protestant faith on their estates; townspeople were granted more limited rights to worship in selected towns in each region. Protestants were guaranteed access to schools, hospitals, royal appointments, and separate judicial institutions to ensure fair treatment. They were also guaranteed rights of self-defense—specifically, the right to maintain garrisons in about two hundred towns. About half of these garrisons would be paid for by the Crown.

The problem was that the Edict of Nantes, like any royal edict, could be revoked by the king at any time. Moreover, the provision allowing Protestants to keep garrisoned towns meant that living peacefully with religious diversity was not yet thought to be possible. Henry IV successfully ended the French religious wars, but the problem of religious and political division within France had not been solved.

The Consolidation of Royal Authority in France, 1610–1643

During Henry IV's reign, France recovered from the long years of civil war. Population and productivity began to grow; the Crown encouraged internal improvements to facilitate commerce. Yet Henry's regime was stable only in comparison with the preceding years of civil war.

The power of the great nobility had not been definitively broken. Several leading nobles plotted with foreign powers, including Spain, to influence French policy and gain materially themselves. Moreover, to raise revenue after decades of civil war, the king had agreed to a provision, known as the *paulette* (named for the functionary who first administered it), that allowed royal officeholders not merely to own their offices but also to bequeath those offices to their heirs in return for the payment of an annual fee. Although the paulette helped cement the loyalty of royal bureaucrats, their privileged position made them largely immune from royal control. A position in the royal bureaucracy now became property, like the landed property of the traditional nobility.

Henry IV was assassinated by a fanatical Catholic in 1610, when his son, Louis XIII (r. 1610–1643), was only 9 years old. Louis's mother, Marie de' Medici, acted ably as regent but soon after Louis took control of government from her, he faced a major Huguenot rebellion in southwestern France. Huguenots felt threatened by the recent marriage of the king to a Spanish princess and by Louis's reintroduction of Catholic institutions in nearby Navarre, an independent border territory he had inherited from his father (see Map 13.2). Huguenot nobles initiated fighting in 1621 as a show of force against the king. These religious wars persisted, on and off, until 1629. They reflected the continuing military might of great nobles and the importance of fortifications in warfare: The Crown had difficulty successfully besieging even small fortress towns. In the end, the Peace of Alais (1629) was a political triumph for the Crown because it broke the connection between religious dissent and political upheaval. The treaty reaffirmed the policy of religious toleration but rescinded the Protestants' military and political privileges. Most of the remaining great noble leaders began to convert to Catholicism.

The Peace of Alais was also a personal triumph for the king's leading minister, who crafted the treaty: Armand-Jean du Plessis (1585–1642), Cardinal Richelieu. From a provincial noble family, Richelieu had risen in the service of the queen mother. At court he was admired and feared for his skill in the political game of seeking and bestowing patronage. His control of many lucrative church offices gave him the resources to build up a large network of clients.

Richelieu favored an aggressive foreign policy to counter what he believed to be the greatest threat to the French crown: the Spanish Habsburgs. War had resumed between the Netherlands and Spain when the truce expired in 1621; since then, Richelieu had used his power to direct limited military campaigns against Spanish power in Italy. After 1630, with the king's full confidence, he superintended large-scale fighting against Spain in the Netherlands itself, as well as in Italy, and subsidized armies fighting the Spanish and Austrian Habsburgs in Germany as part of the Thirty Years' War (see page 348).

By 1640, Richelieu's expensive policies had caused taxes to triple. Courtiers and provincial elites' own power was also directly threatened by Richelieu's monopoly of patronage and by his creation of new mechanisms of government that bypassed their offices. The French had won territory along their northern and eastern borders by their successes against Habsburg forces. But when Richelieu and Louis XIII died within five months of each other, in December 1642 and May 1643, Richelieu's legacy was tested. Louis XIII was succeeded by his 5-year-old son, and the warrior-nobility as well as royal bureaucrats would dramatically challenge the Crown's authority.

England: Precarious Stability, 1558–1603

England experienced no civil wars during the second half of the sixteenth century, but religious dissent challenged the power of the monarchy. In Elizabeth I (r. 1558–1603), England—in stark contrast to France—possessed an able and long-lived ruler. Elizabeth was well educated in the humanistic tradition and was already an astute politician when she acceded to the throne at the age of 25. Religious, political, and constitutional disputes existed in England as elsewhere, but they did not provoke violence on anything like the continental scale.

Elizabeth came to the throne at the death of her Catholic half-sister, Mary Tudor (r. 1553–1558), wife of Philip II. Elizabeth faced the urgent problem of crafting a consensus in religious matters—a consensus that could embrace the two extremes of the Catholic-like doctrine and practice of Anglicanism and Calvinist-inspired Protestantism.

Elizabeth quickly issued a new Act of Supremacy (1559), intended to restore the monarch as head of the Church of England. She was willing to accept some difference of belief, but church liturgy, clerical vestments, and, above all, the hierarchical structure of the clergy closely resembled Catholicism. Elizabeth handled resistance to the Act of Supremacy with resolute firmness: She arrested the bishops and lords whose votes would have blocked its passage by Parliament.

The problem of religious dissent, however, was not definitively solved. Catholicism continued to be practiced. Loyal nobility and gentry in the north of England practiced it with discretion. But priests returning from exile, beginning in the 1570s, practiced it more visibly. In the last twenty years of Elizabeth's reign, approximately 180 Catholics were executed for treason; two-thirds of them were priests.

In the long run, the greater threat to the English crown came from growing tensions with the most radical Protestants in the realm, known (by their enemies initially) as Puritans. Puritanism was a movement for reform of church practice along familiar Protestant lines: Puritans emphasized Bible reading, preaching, and private scrutiny of conscience and wanted to simplify church ritual and reduce clerical authority. A significant Presbyterian underground movement began to form among them. Presbyterians wanted to dismantle the episcopacy, the hierarchy of bishops and archbishops, and govern the church with councils, called "presbyterys," that included lay members of the congregation. Laws were passed late in the reign to enable the Crown more easily to prosecute, and even force into exile, anyone who attended "nonconformist" (non-Anglican) services.

The greatest challenge Elizabeth faced from Puritans came in Parliament, where they were well represented by many literate gentry. Parliament met only when called by the monarch and in theory could merely voice opinions; it could not initiate legislation or demand changes in royal policy. However, only Parliament could vote taxes. During Elizabeth's reign, Puritans used meetings of Parliament to press their cause of further religious reform. In 1586 they went so far as to introduce bills calling for an end to the episcopacy and the Anglican prayer book. Elizabeth had to resort to imprisoning one Puritan leader to end Parliament's right to address the issue.

Elizabeth's reign saw the beginnings of English expansion overseas, but great interest in overseas possessions lay in the future; Elizabeth, like all her forebears, felt her interests tightly linked to affairs on the European continent. Her prime concern lay in safeguarding the independence of the Netherlands. Philip II's policy in the Netherlands increasingly alarmed her. She began to send small sums of money to the rebels and allowed their ships access to southern English ports, from which they could raid Spanish-held towns on the Netherlands coast. In 1585 she committed troops to help the rebels.

Her decision represented a reaction not only to the threat of a single continental power dominating the Netherlands but also to the threat of Catholicism. Spain had threatened her interests, and even her throne, in other ways. From 1579 to 1583, the Spanish had helped the Irish to resist English domination and were involved in several plots to replace Elizabeth with her Catholic cousin, Mary, Queen of Scots. Eventually, in 1588, the English faced the Spanish Armada and the threat of invasion that it brought. The English victory ended any Catholic threat to Elizabeth's rule. In the wake of victory, a mythology quickly began that portrayed Spain as an aggressive Goliath confronting the tiny David of England.

The defeat of the Armada has tended to overshadow other aspects of Elizabeth's foreign policy, such as the struggle over Ireland. Since the twelfth century, an Anglo-Irish state had been loosely supervised from England, but most of Ireland remained under the control of Gaelic chieftains.

Elizabeth I: The Armada Portrait Both serene and resolute, Elizabeth is flanked by "before" and "after" glimpses of the Spanish fleet; her hand rests on the globe in a gesture of dominion that also memorializes the circumnavigation of the globe by her famous captain, Sir Francis Drake, some years before. See the discussion of Elizabeth's image on page 355. *(By kind permission of Marquess of Tavistock and Trustees of Bedford Estate)*

Henry VIII's minister, Thomas Cromwell, had proposed that the whole of Ireland be brought under English control by making the Irish chieftains vassals of the king of England.

Under Elizabeth, this legalistic approach gave way to virtual conquest. Elizabeth's governor, Sir Henry Sidney, inaugurated a policy whereby Gaelic lords could be entirely dispossessed of their land. Any Englishman capable of raising a private force could help enforce these dispossessions and settle his conquered lands. Eventually, the Irish, with Spanish assistance, mounted a major rebellion, consciously Catholic and aimed against the "heretic" queen. The rebellion gave the English an excuse for brutal suppression and massive transfers of land to English control. To Elizabeth and her English subjects the conquests in Ireland seemed as successful as the victory over the Spanish Armada. Overall, the English enjoyed remarkable peace at home during Elizabeth's reign.

Rising Tensions in England, 1603–1642

In 1603, Queen Elizabeth died. Her successor to the throne, James I (r. 1603–1625), was the son of Mary, Queen of Scots, and his ascension began a period of severe financial problems for the monarchy. James's leanings toward extravagance were partly to blame for his financial problems, but so were pressures for patronage from elites. There were considerable debts left from the Irish conflicts and wars with Spain.

To raise revenue without Parliament's consent, James relied on sources of revenue that the Crown had enjoyed since medieval times: customs duties granted to the monarch for life, wardship (the right to manage and borrow liberally from the estates of minor nobles), and the sale of monopolies, which conveyed the right to be sole agent for a particular kind of goods. James increased the number of monopolies sold and added other measures, such as the sale of noble titles. These financial expedients were resented: Merchants opposed monopolies' arbitrary restriction of production and trade; common people found that the prices of certain ordinary commodities, like soap, rose prohibitively.

Under James's son, Charles I (r. 1625–1649), tensions between Crown and Parliament increased. Charles declared war on Spain and supplied costly support to the Huguenots in France. Wealthy merchants opposed this foreign policy because it disrupted trade. In 1626, Parliament was dissolved without granting any monies in order to stifle its objections to royal policies. The Crown's reliance on unpopular financial expedients continued. Above all, Charles's religious policies were a source of controversy. Charles was personally inclined toward "high church" practices: an emphasis on ceremony and sacrament reminiscent of Catholic ritual. In time he clashed with gentry who leaned toward Puritanism.

Charles was an intensely private man whose cold style of rule worsened religious, political, and economic tensions. When Charles again summoned Parliament in 1628 to get funds for his foreign policy, the members presented him with a document called the Petition of Right, which protested his financial policies as well as arbitrary imprisonment. (Seventeen members of Parliament had been imprisoned for refusing loans to the Crown.) Charles dissolved the Parliament in March 1629, having decided that the money he might extract was not worth the risk. For eleven years, he ruled without Parliament. In 1639, Charles started a war against his rebellious Scottish subjects but, lacking men and money, he was forced to agree to a peace treaty. Intent on renewing the war, he summoned Parliament in 1640 to obtain funds. By now royal finances were in desperate straits and religious tension had risen markedly.

Instead of voting Charles the funds he wanted, Parliament questioned the war with the Scots and other royal policies. Frustrated, Charles dissolved what is now known as the "Short Parliament" after just three weeks. But another humiliating defeat at the hands of the Scots later in 1640 made summoning another Parliament imperative. Members of Parliament could now exploit the king's predicament. This Parliament is known as the "Long Parliament" because it sat from 1640 to 1653. Charles was forced to agree not to dissolve Parliament without the members' consent and to summon Parliament at least every three years. Parliament abolished many of his unorthodox and traditional sources of revenue and removed his leading ministers from office. The royal commander deemed responsible for the Scottish fiasco, Thomas Wentworth, earl of Strafford, was executed without trial in May 1641.

Meanwhile, Parliament began debating the religious question. A bare majority of members favored abolition of Anglican bishops as a first step in thoroughgoing religious reform. Working people in London, kept apprised of the issues by the regular publication of parliamentary debates, demonstrated in support of that majority. Moderate members of Parliament, in contrast, favored checking the king's power but not upsetting the Elizabethan religious compromise.

Another revolt in Ireland in October 1641 brought matters to a head. Few trusted the king with the troops necessary to quash the rebellion, and Parliament demanded control of the army to put down the rebellion. In November the Puritan majority introduced a document known as the "Grand Remonstrance," a long catalog of grievances against the king. By a narrow margin, it was passed, further setting public opinion against Charles. The king's remaining support in Parliament eroded in January 1642, when he attempted to arrest five leading members on charges of treason. When the attempt failed, the king withdrew from London and began to raise an army. In mid-1642 the kingdom stood at the brink of civil war.

THE HOLY ROMAN EMPIRE AND THE THIRTY YEARS' WAR

The Holy Roman Empire enjoyed a period of comparative quiet after the Peace of Augsburg halted religious and political wars in 1555. By the early seventeenth century, however, fresh causes of instability brought about renewed fighting. Especially destabilizing was the drive by the Habsburgs, as emperors and territorial princes, to reverse the successes of Protestantism both in their own lands and in the empire at large and to consolidate their rule.

In the Thirty Years' War (1618–1648), as it is now called, we can see the continuation of conflicts from the sixteenth century—religious tensions, regionalism versus centralizing forces, rivalries between rulers. The war was particularly destructive because of the size of the armies and the degree to which army commanders evaded control by the states for which they fought. Some areas of the empire suffered catastrophic losses in population and productive capacity. As a result of the war, the empire was eclipsed as a political unit by the regional powers within it.

Peace Through Diversity, 1555–ca. 1618

The Habsburgs ruled over a diverse group of territories. Most lay within the boundaries of the empire, but many were not German. Though largely contiguous, the territories comprised independent duchies and kingdoms, each with its own institutional structure. Habsburg lands included speakers of Italian, German, and Czech, as well as other languages. The non-German lands of Bohemia and Hungary had been distinct kingdoms since the High Middle Ages. Most of Hungary was now under Ottoman domination, but Bohemia, with its rich capital, Prague, was a wealthy center of population and culture in central Europe.

Unlike the Netherlands, these linguistically and culturally diverse lands were still governed by highly decentralized institutions. The Habsburg family often divided rule of the various territories among themselves. For example, during the lifetime of Holy Roman Emperor Charles V, his brother Ferdinand (d. 1564) was more active than he in governing these family lands. At Ferdinand's death, rule of the various provinces and kingdoms was split among his three sons. One member of the family was routinely elected Holy Roman emperor. Unlike most of their contemporaries, the Habsburgs made no attempt to impose

religious uniformity in this period. Ferdinand was firmly Catholic but tolerant of diverse reform efforts within the church, including clerical marriage. His son, Emperor Maximilian II (r. 1564–1576), granted limited rights of worship to Protestant subjects within his lands and kept his distance from policies pursued by Catholic rulers elsewhere—most notably, those of his cousin, Philip II, in the Netherlands. During Maximilian's reign a variety of faiths flourished side by side. In this tolerant atmosphere, education, printing, and humanistic intellectual life flourished.

Given the course of events elsewhere in Europe, this late Renaissance was unlikely to last. Members of the Jesuit order had begun to appear in Habsburg lands in the reign of Maximilian. During the reign of Maximilian's son, Rudolf II (r. 1576–1612), they established Catholic schools and became confessors and preachers to the upper classes. Self-confident Catholicism emerged as one form of cultural identity among the German-speaking ruling classes and thus as a religious impetus to further political consolidation of all these Habsburg territories.

The Thirty Years' War, 1618–1648

In the seventeenth century, tensions between Catholic and Protestant states (and among Protestants, for Calvinists and Lutherans were not necessarily allies) were heightened by a succession crisis: The childless emperor Rudolf II was aging.

Bohemia (the core of the modern Czech Republic) had a large Protestant population. Rudolf II had set up his court in Prague, its bustling capital. Although Catholicism was reclaiming lost ground, Protestants had been confirmed in their rights to worship in the early seventeenth century both by Rudolf and by his younger brother, Matthias, who hoped to succeed Rudolf as king of Bohemia and as Holy Roman emperor. Since the crown of Bohemia was bestowed by election, rival claimants to this wealthy throne needed the acquiescence of the ruling elites, both Protestant and Catholic.

When Matthias did become king of Bohemia and Holy Roman emperor (r. 1612–1619), he reneged on his promise to the Protestants. The Habsburg succession to the Bohemian throne seemed secure, and concessions to Protestant elites seemed less necessary. As in the Netherlands, there was in Bohemia a delicate balance between regional integrity and Bohemia's expectation of sharing its ruler with other regions. As Philip II had done, Matthias appointed a council of regents that enforced unpopular policies. The right to build new Protestant churches was denied, and Bohemian crown lands were given to the Catholic church.

On May 23, 1618, delegates to a Protestant assembly that had unsuccessfully petitioned Matthias to end these policies marched to the palace in Prague where the hated royal officials met. After a confrontation over their demands, the delegates "tried" the officials on the spot for treason and, literally, threw them out the window. The incident became known as the Defenestration of Prague (from the Latin, *fenestra*, "window"). The officials' lives were saved only because they fell into a pile of manure. The rebels proceeded to set up their own government.

The new Bohemian government deposed Matthias's successor as king, his Catholic cousin, the Holy Roman emperor Ferdinand II. Instead they elected Frederick, a Calvinist prince whose territories in west central Germany carried with them the right to be one of the seven electors who chose the emperor.

This new success seemed to threaten the religious balance of power in the empire. Other Protestant princes saw their chance to make political gains. Rival claimants to Habsburg rule in Hungary took up arms. The Protestant king of Denmark, Christian IV (r. 1588–1648), who was also duke of Holstein in northern Germany, sought to take advantage of the situation and conquer more German territory. Powers outside the empire were also interested in these events. England practiced a pro-Protestant foreign policy, and the English king, James I, was Frederick's father-in-law. Spain's supply routes north from Italy to the Netherlands passed next to Frederick's lands in western Germany. France's first interest was its rivalry with Spain. In addi-

tion, it was in France's interest, much to the disgust of the devout Catholic faction at the French court, to keep Protestant as well as Catholic rulers in the empire strong enough to thwart Austrian Habsburg ambitions.

The revolt in Bohemia thus triggered a widespread war not only because it challenged Habsburg control but because other princes felt their interests to be involved. From the outset, the war was over the balance of power in the empire and in Europe (Map 13.2).

After the Protestant king Frederick was defeated by Ferdinand's forces at the Battle of White Mountain in Prague in the fall of 1620, fighting became widespread. The truce between Spain and the Netherlands, established in 1609, expired in 1621. At this point, Christian IV, the Danish king, decided to seize more territory. Christian received little help from Protestant allies, however; the Dutch were busy with Spain, the English were still wary of continental entanglements, and Denmark's regional rivals, the Swedish, were uninterested in furthering Danish ambitions. Imperial forces defeated Christian's armies in 1626. Yet, alarmed at the possibility of greater imperial control in northern Germany, Catholic princes arranged a truce that led to Denmark's withdrawal from the fighting on relatively generous terms.

Christian's rival, Gustav Adolf, king of Sweden (r. 1611–1632), then assumed the role of Protestant champion. Gustav Adolf was a brilliant and innovative military leader. When he was killed at the Battle of Lützen in late 1632, the tide turned in the favor of imperial forces. A decisive imperial victory over a combined Swedish and German Protestant army led to a peace treaty favorable to the Catholics: the Peace of Prague (1635).

The Peace of Prague brought only a temporary peace, however, because French involvement increased now that other anti-Habsburg forces had been eclipsed. France tried to seize imperial territory along its eastern border and generously subsidized Protestant mercenaries fighting within the empire. Fighting dragged on. The Swedes re-entered the war, hoping to obtain

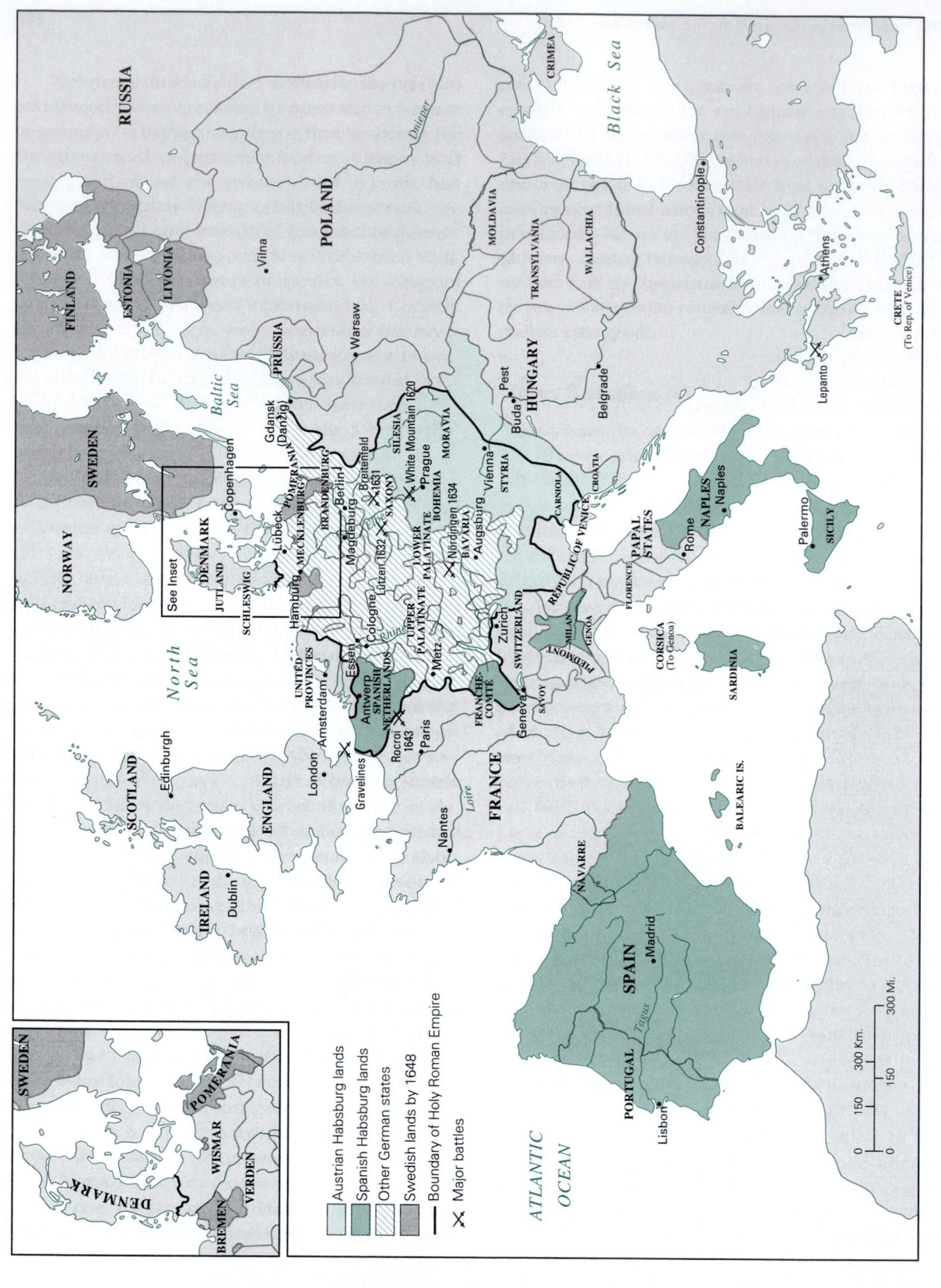

RUSSIA

POLAND

Vilna

Warsaw

CRIMEA

Black Sea

FINLAND

ESTONIA

LIVONIA

MOLDAVIA

TRANSYLVANIA

WALLACHIA

Constantinople

Athens

CRETE
(To Rep. of Venice)

SWEDEN

Dnieper

PRUSSIA

Baltic Sea

HUNGARY

Pest

Buda

Belgrade

Lepanto

Gdansk (Danzig)

POMERANIA

BRANDENBURG

SILESIA

MORAVIA

White Mountain 1620

Prague

BOHEMIA

STYRIA

CARNIOLA

CROATIA

REPUBLIC OF VENICE

NAPLES

Naples

Palermo

SICILY

NORWAY

Copenhagen

Lübeck

MECKLENBURG

Berlin

Magdeburg

Breitenfeld 1631

SAXONY

Lützen 1632

LOWER PALATINATE

Nördlingen 1634

BAVARIA

Augsburg

Vienna

PAPAL STATES

FLORENCE

Rome

CORSICA
(To Genoa)

SARDINIA

DENMARK

JUTLAND

SCHLESWIG

Hamburg

Cologne

UPPER PALATINATE

Metz

Rhine

SWITZERLAND

Zurich

Geneva

SAVOY

PIEDMONT

Milan

GENOA

See Inset

North Sea

UNITED PROVINCES

Amsterdam

Essen

Antwerp

SPANISH NETHERLANDS

Rocroi 1643

Paris

FRANCHE-COMTÉ

SCOTLAND

Edinburgh

ENGLAND

London

Gravelines

Loire

Nantes

FRANCE

NAVARRE

BALEARIC IS.

IRELAND

Dublin

SPAIN

Madrid

Tagus

PORTUGAL

Lisbon

ATLANTIC OCEAN

300 Mi.
300 Km.
150
150
150
0
0

Austrian Habsburg lands

Spanish Habsburg lands

Other German states

Swedish lands by 1648

Boundary of Holy Roman Empire

Major battles

Inset:

SWEDEN

POMERANIA

WISMAR

VERDEN

BREMEN

DENMARK

territory on the northern coast. In the south, rivals to the Habsburgs in Hungary tried to seize territory. By the end of the war, order had disintegrated so completely in the wake of the marauding armies that both Catholic and Protestant rulers made alliances with religious enemies to safeguard their states.

A comprehensive peace treaty did not become possible until France withdrew its sponsorship of continued fighting. There were domestic reasons for France's withdrawal. Louis XIII (r. 1610–1643), the king of France, had died, leaving a child to rule and face the burden of war debt. France wanted only a workable balance of power in the empire, but territorial rivalry continued with the Spanish Habsburgs. Fighting between them continued until 1659.

The Effects of the War

The Thirty Years' War caused economic devastation and population decline in many parts of the empire and had long-term political consequences for the empire as a whole. One reason for the war's devastation was the heightened application of firepower. The new development was volley fire: Foot soldiers were arranged in parallel lines so that one line of men could fire while another reloaded. Gustav Adolf refined this new tactic, amassing large numbers of troops and increasing the rate of fire to create a virtually continuous barrage. This increased both the size of armies and their deadly force in battle.

Although armies of all the major states adopted these new offensive tactics, defensive tactics—such as holding fortresses—remained important, and pitched battles still tended to be part of sieges. The costs in resources and human life of this kind of warfare reached unheard-of dimensions. Popular printed literature and court drama both condemned the irrationality of the war.

Map 13.2 Europe in the Thirty Years' War The Thirty Years' War was fought largely within the borders of the Holy Roman Empire. It was the result of conflicts within the empire as well as the meddling of neighbors for their own strategic advantage.

Where fighting had been concentrated, such as in parts of Saxony, between a third and half of the inhabitants of villages and major towns may have disappeared. Many starved, were caught in the fighting, or were killed by marauding soldiers. The most notorious atrocity occurred in the aftermath of the siege of Magdeburg in 1631. After the city surrendered to besieging Catholic forces, soldiers ate and drank themselves into a frenzy, raped and killed indiscriminately, and set fires that destroyed the town (killing some of their own ranks in the process).

Compounding the misery of war were the actions of armies hired by enterprising mercenary generals. The generals contracted to provide, supply, and lead troops and thus were more willing than the princes would have been to allow troops to live on plunder.

A series of treaties known as the Peace of Westphalia (1648) finally ended fighting in the empire. The treaties recognized Calvinism as a tolerated religion within the empire. The requirement that all subjects must follow their rulers' faith was retained, but some leeway was allowed for those who found themselves under new rulers. The property of those who decided to move elsewhere for religious reasons was protected. In its recognition of religious plurality, the Peace of Westphalia effectively put an end to religious war in the empire. The rights of states, however, were still enforced over the desires of individuals.

The treaties reflected some of the recent successes of the Swedish by granting them Baltic coast territory. France gained important towns on its eastern border. The United Provinces (the Netherlands) and Switzerland were recognized as independent states. Most of the major Catholic and Protestant rulers in the empire extended their territories at the expense of smaller principalities. From this point forward, each major state of the empire would conduct its own foreign policy; the Holy Roman Empire was no longer a meaningful political entity. Though weakened as emperors, the Habsburgs were strengthened as rulers of their own hereditary lands on the eastern fringes of the empire. They moved their capital from Prague to Vienna, and the government of Habsburg lands gained in importance as administration of the empire waned.

SOCIETY AND CULTURE

In the late sixteenth and early seventeenth centuries, both literature and political speculation often addressed questions of the legitimacy of rulers and divine authority—an urgent problem in an age of religious division. The form as well as the content of thought reflected its context. Authors and rulers alike often relied on still-prevalent oral modes of communication. Indeed, some of the greatest literature of the period and some of the most effective political statements were presented as drama and not conveyed in print. Nevertheless, literacy continued to spread and led to greater opportunities for knowledge and reflection. In the visual arts, the dramatic impulse was wedded to religious purposes to create works of great power and emotion.

Literacy and Literature

Traditional oral culture changed slowly under the impact of the spread of printing, education, and literacy. Works of literature from the late sixteenth and early seventeenth centuries incorporate material from traditional folktales, consciously reflecting the coexistence of oral and literature culture. In *Don Quixote*, by Spain's Miguel de Cervantes (1547–1616), the title character and his companion, Sancho Panza, have a long discussion about this subject. The squire Panza speaks in the style that was customary in oral culture—a rather roundabout and repetitive style, by our standards, that enabled the speaker and listener to remember what was said. Much of the richness of *Don Quixote* is due to the interweaving of prose styles and topical concerns from throughout Cervantes' culture—from the oral world of peasants to the world of court life.

The spread of education and literacy in the late sixteenth century had a dramatic impact on attitudes toward literature and on literature itself.

The value of education—particularly of the continuing humanist recovery of ancient wisdom—was reflected in much of the literature of the period. Writers found in humanistic education a vision of what it meant to be cultivated and disciplined. This vision provided the beginnings of a new self-image for members of the warrior class.

Certain elite women who were able to secure a humanistic education were moved to reflect on their own situation in society. The French poet Louise Labé (1526–1566), writing in 1555, described the benefits of education for women but exaggerated its availability:

> Since the time has come . . . when the severe laws of men no longer prevent women from applying themselves to the sciences and other disciplines, it seems to me that those of us who can should use this long-craved freedom to study and let men see how greatly they wronged us when depriving us of its honor and advantages.[2]

As for men, it is customary to regard the French author Michel de Montaigne (1533–1592) as the epitome of the reflective and—most important—self-reflective gentleman. Montaigne had been a judge in the parlement of Bordeaux; in 1570 he resigned and retired to his small château, where he wrote his *Essais* (from which we derive the word *essays*), a collection of short reflections that were revolutionary in form and content. Montaigne invented writing in the form of a sketch, a "try" (the literal meaning of *essai*), which enabled him to combine self-reflection with formal analysis.

Montaigne's reflections ranged from the destructiveness of the French civil wars to the consequences of European exploration of the New World. Toward all of these events, Montaigne was able to achieve an analytic detachment remarkable for his day. For example, he noted the irony in Europeans labeling New World peoples "savage," given Europeans' seemingly endless violence against those "savages" and against each other. (See the box "Encounters with the West: Montaigne Discusses Barbarity in the New World and the Old.")

Montaigne's greatest achievement was the deep exploration of his own private moral and

~ **ENCOUNTERS WITH THE WEST** ~

Montaigne Discusses Barbarity in the New World and the Old

In one of his most famous essays, Michel de Montaigne ironically compares the customs of Native Americans, about whom he has heard, with the customs of his own society.

They have their wars with [other] nations, to which they go quite naked, with no other arms than bows or wooden spears. . . . It is astonishing that firmness they show in their combats, which never end but in slaughter and bloodshed; for, as to routs and terror, they know nothing of either.

Each man brings back as his trophy the head of the enemy he has killed. . . . After they have treated their prisoners well for a long time with all the hospitality they can think of . . . they kill him with their swords. This done, they roast him and eat him in common and send some pieces to their absent friends.

I am not sorry that we notice the barbarous horror of such acts, but am heartily sorry that . . . we should be so blind to our own. I think there is more barbarity . . . in tearing by tortures and the rack a body still full of feeling, in roasting a man bit by bit, having him bitten and mangled by dogs (as we have not only read but seen within fresh memory . . . among neighbors and fellow citizens, and what is worse, on the pretext of piety and religion).

Three of these men (were brought to France) . . . and [someone] wanted to know what they had found most amazing. . . . They said that in the first place they thought it very strange that so many grown men, bearded, strong and armed who were around the king . . . should submit to obey a child. . . . Second (they have a way in their language of speaking of men as halves of one another), they had noticed that there were among us men full and gorged with all sorts of good things, and that their other halves were beggars at their doors, emaciated with hunger and poverty; and they thought it strange that these needy halves could endure such injustice.

Source: Donald M. Frame, trans., *The Complete Essays of Montaigne* (Stanford, Calif.: Stanford University Press, 1948), pp. 153, 155–159. Reprinted by permission of the publisher.

intellectual life, detached from any vocation or social role. Thanks to the spread of printing and literacy, Montaigne had a virtually unparalleled opportunity to juxtapose different events, values, and cultures. His writings thus reflect a distancing from his own society and a tolerance of others. His essays also reveal a distancing from himself, and this distancing is another result of literacy—the ability to enjoy long periods of solitude and reflection in the company of other solitary voices contained in books. Montaigne's works mark the beginning of what we know as the "invention" of private life, in which an individual is known more by internal character and personality traits than by social role and past behavior.

Dramatists, poets, and prose writers like Montaigne ask profound and in some ways timeless questions about the meaning of human experience; however, the kinds of questions thought important change as society changes. The works of the great English poet and playwright William Shakespeare (1564–1616) are still compelling to us because of the profundity of the questions he asked about love, honor, and political legitimacy, though he posed these questions in terms appropriate to his own day. One of his favorite themes—evident in *Hamlet* and *Macbeth*—is the legitimacy of rulers. He also explored the contradictions in values between the growing commercial world he saw around him and the older, seemingly more stable world of feudal society. Subtle political commentary distinguishes Shakespeare's later plays, written near and shortly after the death of Queen Elizabeth in 1603, when political problems were becoming increasingly visible. Shakespeare explored not only the duties of rulers but also the rights of their subjects.

Shakespeare, Cervantes, and other writers of their day were also representatives of what were starting to be self-consciously distinct national literatures. The spread of humanism added a historical dimension to their awareness of their own languages and to their subject matter: their own society and its past. This kind of self-consciousness is evident in Shakespeare's play *Richard II*:

This royal throne of kings, this sceptred isle,
This earth of majesty, this seat of Mars,
This other Eden, demi-paradise,
This fortress built by Nature for herself
Against infection and the hand of war,
This happy breed of men, this little world,
This precious stone set in the silver sea,
Which serves it in the office of a wall,
Or as [a] moat defensive to a house,
Against the envy of less happier lands;
This blessed plot, this earth, this realm, this England . . .
(*Richard II*, act 2, sc. 1, lines 40–50)[3]

The Great Age of Theater

Shakespeare's career was possible because his life coincided with the rise of professional theater. In the capitals of England and Spain, professional theaters first opened in the 1570s. Some drama was produced at court or in aristocratic households, but most public theaters drew large and very mixed audiences, including the poorest city dwellers. Playwrights, including Shakespeare, often wrote in teams under great pressure to keep acting companies supplied with material. The best-known dramatist in Spain in this period, Lope de Vega (1562–1635), wrote more than fifteen hundred works on a wide range of topics.

Over time, theater became increasingly restricted to aristocratic circles. In England, Puritan criticism of the "immorality" of public performance drove actors and playwrights to seek royal patronage. The first professional theater to open in Paris, in 1629, was dependent on Cardinal Richelieu's patronage. As court patronage grew in importance, the subject matter treated in plays began to narrow to topics of aristocratic concern, such as family honor and martial glory. These themes were depicted in the work of the Frenchman Pierre Corneille (1606–1684), whose great tragedy of aristocratic life, *Le Cid*, was one of the early successes of the seventeenth-century French theater.

That drama was one of the most important art forms of the late sixteenth and early seventeenth centuries is reflected in its impact on the development of music: The opera, which weds drama to music, was invented in Italy in the early seventeenth century. The first great work in this genre is generally acknowledged to be *Orfeo* (*Orpheus*, 1607) by Claudio Monteverdi (1567–1643). The practice of music itself changed. Monteverdi was the first master of a new style known as monody. Monodic music was inherently dramatic, creating a sense of expectation and resolution through the progression of chords.

Sovereignty in Ceremony, Image, and Word

Whether produced formally on stage or in some less-structured setting, drama was a favored method of communication in this era because people responded to and made extensive use of oral communication. Dramatic gesture and storytelling to get a message across were commonplace and were even important components of politics.

When great noble governors entered major towns, such as when Margaret of Parma entered Brussels, a solemn yet ostentatious formal "entry" was often staged. The dignitary would ride into the town through its main gate, usually beneath a canopy made of luxurious cloth. The event might include costumed townspeople acting in brief symbolic dramas and end with an elaborate banquet. A remnant of these proceedings survives today in the ceremony by which distinguished visitors are given "the keys to the city," which, in the sixteenth century, really were useful.

Royalty began to make deliberate and careful use of dramatic ceremony for royal entries into towns, at royal funerals, and on other occasions. In France, for example, the ritual entry of the king into Paris had originally stressed the participation of elites such as the leading guild members, judges, and administrators. But in the last half of the sixteenth century, the procession began to glorify the king alone.

Queen Elizabeth had the particular burden of assuming the throne in a period of instability. Hence, she paid a great deal of attention to the image of herself that she fashioned in words and authorized to be fashioned in painting. Elizabeth styled herself variously as mother to her people and as a warrior-queen. Having refused to marry (despite the wishes of Parliament and the resultant absence of an heir), Elizabeth made artful use of the image of her virginity. Avoiding the status of wife, with all its connotations of dependence and submission, she adopted an image of self-contained purity, sanctity, and inviolability. In this way, she presented herself as the wholly devoted, chaste mother (which, of course, had religious tradition behind it) and as an androgynous, aggressive ruler. (See the box "Elizabeth I Addresses Her Troops.")

More formal speculation about constitutional matters also resulted from the tumult of the sixteenth and seventeenth centuries. In France, the Huguenot party advanced an argument for the limitation of royal power, particularly after the Saint Bartholomew's Day Massacre. The best-known Huguenot tract (probably authored by the well-educated nobleman Philippe Duplessis-Mornay), *Defense of Liberty Against Tyrants* (1579), advanced the notion of a contract between the king and the people. Under the terms of this contract,

obedience to the king was conditional, dependent on his acting for the common good—above all, maintaining and protecting God's true church.

Alternative theories enhancing royal authority were offered, principally in support of the Catholic position though also simply to buttress the beleaguered monarchy itself. The most famous of these appeared in *The Six Books of the Republic* (1576), by the French legal scholar Jean Bodin (1530–1596). Bodin was a Catholic but offered a fundamentally secular perspective on the source of power within a state—namely, that there is a final sovereign authority, which, for Bodin, was the king. Bodin's theory of sovereignty was immediately echoed in other theoretical works, most notably that of Hugo Grotius (1583–1645). A Dutch jurist and diplomat, Grotius developed the first principles of modern international law. His major work, *De Jure Belli ac Pacis* (*On the Law of War and Peace*) (1625), was written in response to the turmoil of the Thirty Years' War. Grotius argued that relations between sovereign states could be based on respect for treaties and that war must be justified. He developed criteria to distinguish just wars.

Baroque Art and Architecture

Speculation about and celebration of power, as well as of dramatic emotion, also occurred in the visual arts—most notably in painting and architecture, in the style now known as "baroque." The word *baroque* comes from the Portuguese *barroco*, used to describe irregularly shaped pearls; the term as applied to the arts was initially derogatory, describing illogic and irregularity. Baroque architecture modified the precision, symmetry, and orderliness of Renaissance architecture to produce a sense of greater dynamism in space. Façades and interiors were both massive and, through clever use of architectural and decorative components, suggestive of movement. Baroque churches were impressively grand and emotionally engaging at the same time. Baroque techniques were pioneered in Italy in the late sixteenth century and spread slowly,

Elizabeth I Addresses Her Troops

The day after English ships dispersed the Spanish Armada in 1588, Elizabeth addressed a contingent of her troops. She used the opportunity to fashion an image of herself as a warrior above all but also as the beloved familiar of her people, unafraid of potential plots against her.

My loving people, we have been persuaded by some that are careful of our safety, to take heed how we commit ourselves to armed multitudes, for fear of treachery. But I assure you, I do not desire to live to distrust my faithful and loving people. Let tyrants fear. I have always so behaved myself that, under God, I have placed my chiefest strength in the loyal hearts and good will of my subjects; and therefore I am come amongst you, as you see, at this time, not for my reaction or disport, but being resolved, in the midst and heat of the battle, to live or die amongst you all, to lay down for my God, and for my kingdom, and for my people, my honor and my blood, even in the dust. I know I have the body of a weak and feeble woman, but I have the heart and the stomach of a king, and of a king of England too, and think foul scorn that Parma or Spain, or any prince of Europe should dare to invade the borders of my realm; to which, rather than any dishonor shall grow by me, I myself will take up arms, I myself will be your general, judge, and rewarder of every one of your virtues in the field.

Source: J. E. Neale, *Queen Elizabeth I* (New York: Anchor, 1957), pp. 308–309.

with many regional variations, throughout Catholic Europe especially, during the seventeenth century.

The most influential baroque painter in northern Europe was Peter Paul Rubens (1577–1640), a native of Flanders in the southern Netherlands. His early career in Italy, from 1600 to 1608, was profoundly important both in shaping him as an artist and in establishing his secondary career as a diplomat, trusted by his princely patrons. Throughout his life, he undertook diplomatic missions on behalf of the viceroys in the Spanish Netherlands, to Spain, France, and England, where he also gained artistic commissions. He simultaneously maintained a large studio in Antwerp where he could train students. Rubens's subject matter varied widely. It included church design and decoration as well as portraiture and landscapes. His technique was distinguished by the brilliant use of color and by the dynamic energy of his figures, often executed on a very large scale.

SUMMARY

The late sixteenth and early seventeenth centuries were an era of intense struggle over political and religious authority. Rulers everywhere tried to buttress and expand royal power. They were resisted by traditional centers of power, such as independent-minded nobles. But they were also resisted by the novel challenge of religious dissent, which empowered subjects to claim a greater right to question authority and risk more in their attempts to oppose it. In some areas of Europe, such as the Holy Roman Empire, the struggles reached some resolution. In other countries, such as England, decades of bloody conflict still lay ahead.

On the whole, these conflicts did not result in victories for ordinary people, since for the most part it was victorious elites who decided matters of religion and governance in their own interests. In addition, the difficult economic circumstances of these decades meant that working people, desperate for a secure livelihood, rioted or took up arms out of economic as well as religious concern.

Yet however grim the circumstances people faced, the technology of print and the spread of literacy helped spur speculative and creative works by providing the means for reflection and the audiences to receive it. Ironically, the increased importance of court life, although a cause of political strain, was also a source of patronage for art, literature, and drama. Some of the works, such as Rubens's paintings, portray the splendor and power of court life. Other works, such as Shakespeare's plays, reflect the tensions and contradictions in the society of the day: for example, the importance of the stability provided by royal authority and the dignity and wisdom of ordinary people, who had no claim to power at all.

NOTES

1. Quoted in A. W. Lovett, *Early Habsburg Spain, 1517–1598* (Oxford, England: Oxford University Press, 1986), p. 212.
2. Quoted in Ann Rosalind Jones, "City Women and Their Audiences: Louise Labé and Veronica Franco," in Margaret W. Ferguson et al., *Rewriting the Renaissance: The Discourses of Sexual Difference in Early Modern Europe* (Chicago: University of Chicago Press, 1986), p. 307.
3. From *The Riverside Shakespeare*, 2d ed. (Boston: Houghton Mifflin, 1997), p. 855.

SUGGESTED READING

Bonney, Richard. *The European Dynastic States, 1494–1660*. 1991. A recent, rich survey of the period. Good on eastern as well as western Europe but does not consider England as part of Europe.

Braudel, Fernand. *The Perspective of the World*. Vol. 3, *Civilization and Capitalism, 15th to 18th Century*. Translated by S. Reynolds. 1984. A particularly useful volume by this celebrated author of economic history concerning overall patterns in the European and international economies.

Davis, Natalie Zemon. *Society and Culture in Early Modern France*. 1975. Essays on social and cultural changes of the period, including important studies of women's participation in Protestantism.

Diefendorf, Barbara. *Beneath the Cross: Catholics and Huguenots in Sixteenth-Century Paris*. 1991. Traces the intersection of political and religious conflict in the French capital during the religious wars. Excellent bibliography.

Eagleton, Terry. *William Shakespeare*. 1986. A brief and highly readable interpretation of Shakespeare that emphasizes the tensions in the plays caused by language and by ideas from the new world of bourgeois, commercial life.

Elliott, J. H. *Europe Divided, 1559–1598*. 1968. An older but still reliable and readable survey by a leading scholar of Spanish history.

Evans, R. J. W. *The Making of the Hapsburg Monarchy*. 1979. A thorough survey of the rise of the Austrian Habsburg state from the breakup of Charles V's empire, emphasizing the importance of the ideology and institutions of Catholicism in shaping the identity and guaranteeing the coherence of the Habsburg state.

Greenblatt, Stephen. *Renaissance Self-Fashioning*. 1979. An interpretation of sixteenth-century literature and culture that emphasizes the "invention" of interior self-reflection and self-awareness.

Holt, Mack P. *The French Wars of Religion, 1562–1629*. 1995. An up-to-date synthesis that evaluates social and political context while not slighting the importance of religion.

Huppert, George. *After the Black Death: A Social History of Early Modern Europe*. 1986. A survey of developments in social and economic history throughout Europe from the fifteenth through the seventeenth centuries. A brief but very usable bibliography will guide further reading.

Jütte, Robert. *Poverty and Deviance in Early Modern Europe*. 1994. Discusses poverty, poor relief, and peasant rebellion.

Kelley, Donald R. *The Beginnings of Ideology: Consciousness and Society in the French Reformation*. 1981. A study of political thought, including but not limited to formal theory, as inspired by the experience of the wars of religion.

Klaits, Joseph. *Servants of Satan*. 1985; and Levack, Brian P. *The Witch-Hunt in Early Modern Europe*. 1987. Two surveys of witch-hunting in the sixteenth and seventeenth centuries. Levack synthesizes the work of various historians with particular care; Klaits's work is more interpretive.

Lynch, John. *Spain, 1516–1598: From Nation-State to World Empire*. 1991. An excellent survey.

Mattingly, Garret. *The Armada*. 1959. A well-crafted and gripping narrative of the sailing of the Armada and all the interrelated events in France, the Netherlands, England, and Spain, told from an English perspective.

Ong, Walter J. *Orality and Literacy: The Technologizing of the Word*. 1982. A synthesis of scholarship that concentrates on the psychological and cultural impact of literacy.

Parker, Geoffrey. *The Dutch Revolt*. 2d ed. 1985. The best survey of the revolt available in English.

———. *The Military Revolution*. 1988; and Black, Jeremy. *A Military Revolution?* 1991. Two works that disagree about the nature and extent of the changes in military practices and their significance for military, political, and social history.

———. *The Thirty Years' War*. 2d ed. 1987. A readable general history by one of the best-known military historians.

Patterson, Annabel. *Shakespeare and the Popular Voice*. 1989. An interpretation of Shakespeare's work that emphasizes his connection to the complex political and social milieu of his day.

Regosin, J. *The Matter of My Book: Montaigne's "Essais" as the Book of the Self*. 1977. One of the leading scholarly treatments of Montaigne's work.

Smith, A. G. R. *The Emergence of a Nation-State: The Commonwealth of England, 1529–1660*. 1984. A good place to start through the immense bibliography on the Elizabethan period.

Wiesner, Merry. *Women and Gender in Early Modern Europe*. 1993. Discusses all aspects of women's experience, including their working lives.

CHAPTER 14

Europe in the Age of Louis XIV, ca. 1610–1715

Toward the end of his reign, the subjects of Louis XIV of France began to grumble that he had lived too long. Indeed, he outlived his own son and grandson and was followed on the throne by a great-grandson when he died in 1715. In his prime, Louis symbolized the success of royal power in surmounting the challenges of warrior-nobles, in suppressing religious dissent, in tapping the wealth of the nation's population, and in waging war. A period of cultural brilliance early in his reign and the spectacle of an elaborate court life crowned his achievements. By the end of his reign, however, France was struggling under economic distress brought on by the many wars fought for his glory. Although Louis outlived his welcome, he was then, and is for us now, a central symbol of the age that ended with his death.

In England, by contrast, the Crown was not as successful in overcoming political and religious challenges to its authority. Resistance to the king, led by Parliament, resulted in a revolutionary overturning of royal authority that was temporary but had long-term consequences. In central and eastern Europe, a period of state building in the aftermath of the Thirty Years' War led to the dominance in the region of Austria, Brandenburg-Prussia, and Russia. The power of these rulers derived, in part, from the economic relationship of their lands to the wider European economy.

The seventeenth century also witnessed a dynamic phase of European overseas expansion, following on the successes of the Portuguese and the Spanish in the fifteenth and sixteenth centuries. Eager migrants settled in the Americas in ever increasing numbers, while forced migrants—enslaved Africans—were transported by the thousands to work on the profitable plantations of European colonizers. Aristocrats, merchants, and peasants back in Europe jockeyed to take advantage of—or to mitigate the effects of—the local political and economic impact of Europe's expansion.

∼ *Questions and Ideas to Consider*

- The seventeenth-century courtier relied on ceremony, etiquette, and conversational skills to exert influence and secure favor. Why? How did this experience differ for men and women?

- If Louis XIV was so effective at streamlining government and bringing revenues into the treasury, why did he experience desperate financial difficulties toward the end of his reign? What effect did this have on government?

- What was the Glorious Revolution?

- After the Thirty Years' War, what three powers came to dominate central and eastern Europe? How did Peter the Great pull his country into interaction with the rest of Europe?

- Why was slavery set up in the New World?

FRANCE IN THE AGE OF ABSOLUTISM

Absolutism describes the power achieved by monarchs, most notably Louis XIV (r. 1643–1715), in the seventeenth century. Louis continued the expansion of state power begun by his father's minister, Cardinal Richelieu. The extension of royal power, under Louis as well as his predecessor, was driven by the desire to sustain an expensive foreign policy. The policy itself was a traditional one: fighting the Habsburg enemy and generally seeking military glory. Louis XIV's successes in these undertakings made him both envied and emulated by other rulers; the French court became a model of culture and refinement. But increased royal authority was not accepted without protest.

The Last Challenge to Absolutism

Louis came to the throne as a 5-year-old child in 1643. As regent, his mother, Anne of Austria

(1601–1666), had to defuse a serious challenge to royal authority during her son's minority. Together with her chief minister and personal friend, Cardinal Jules Mazarin (1602–1666), she faced opposition from royal bureaucrats and the traditional nobility as well as the common people.

Revolts against the concentration of power in royal hands and against the high taxation that had prevailed under Louis's father began immediately. Several provincial parlements tried to abolish the special ranks of officials created by Richelieu. In 1648, after a few more years of foreign war and the financial expedients to sustain it, the most serious revolt began, led by the Parlement and the other sovereign law courts in Paris.

The source of the Parlement's leverage over the monarchy was its traditional right to register laws and edicts, which amounted to a right of judicial review. Now, the Parlement attempted to extend this power by debating and even initiating government policy. The courts sitting together drew up a reform program abolishing most of the machinery of government established under Richelieu and calling for consent to future taxation. The citizens of Paris rose to defend the courts when royal troops were sent against them. In the countryside, the machinery of government, particularly tax collection, virtually ceased to function.

Mazarin was forced to accept the proposed reform of government, at least in theory. He also had to avert challenges by great nobles for control of the young king's council. Civil war waxed and waned around France from 1648 until 1653. These revolts, derisively termed the "Fronde" after a children's game of the time, posed a serious challenge to the legacy of royal government as it had developed under Richelieu. It ended without a noteworthy impact on the growth of royal power for several reasons. First, Mazarin methodically regained control of the kingdom through armed force and by making concessions to win the loyalty of individual aristocrats eager for the fruits of royal service. In addition, when civil war threatened starvation as well as political unrest, the Parlement of Paris and many citizens of the capital welcomed a return to royal authority.

Unlike in England, there was in France no single institutional focus for resistance to royal power. A strong-willed and able ruler, such as Louis XIV proved to be, could face down challenges to royal power, particularly when he satisfied the ambitions of aristocrats and those bureaucrats who profited from the expansion of royal authority.

France Under Louis XIV, 1661–1715

Louis XIV assumed full control of government at Mazarin's death in 1661. It was a propitious moment. The Peace of the Pyrenees in 1659 had ended—in France's favor—the wars with Spain that had dragged on since the end of the Thirty Years' War. As part of the peace agreement, Louis married a Spanish princess, Maria Theresa. Louis was physically attractive and extremely vigorous. He had been lovingly coached in his duties by Mazarin and his mother, Queen Anne, and he proved a diligent king. He worked consistently at the affairs of state while sustaining the ceremonial life of the court with its elaborate hunts, balls, and public events.

In the first ten years of his active reign, Louis achieved a degree of control over the mechanisms of government unparalleled in the history of France or anywhere else in Europe. He did not invent any new bureaucratic devices but rather used existing ranks of officials in new ways that increased government efficiency and the centralization of control. He radically reduced the number of men in his High Council, the advisory body closest to the king, to only three or four great ministers of state affairs. This intimate group, with Louis's active participation, handled all policy-making. The ministers of state, war, and finance were chosen exclusively from men of modest backgrounds whose training and experience fitted them for such positions. Jean-Baptiste Colbert (1619–1683), perhaps the greatest of them, served as minister of finance and of most domestic policy from 1665 until his death; he was from a merchant family and had served for years under Mazarin.

Several dozen other officials, picked from the ranks of up-and-coming lawyers and administra-

CHAPTER CHRONOLOGY

1643	Louis XIV comes to the French throne
1648	Peace of Westphalia
1648–1653	"Fronde" revolts in France
1649	Execution of King Charles I
1659	Peace of the Pyrenees
1660	Monarchy restored in England
1661	Louis XIV assumes full control of government
1664	East India Company and the West India Company established
1682	Peter the Great takes the Russian throne
1683	Death of Colbert
1685	Revocation of the Edict of Nantes
1688	The Glorious Revolution
1713	The Peace of Utrecht
1715	Death of Louis XIV

tors, drew up laws and regulations for execution at the provincial level. These officials at the center were often sent to the provinces on special supervisory missions. The effect of this system was largely to bypass many entrenched provincial officials, particularly many responsible for tax collecting. The money saved by the more efficient collection of taxes enabled the government to streamline the bureaucracy: Dozens of the offices created to bring cash to the Crown were bought back by the Crown from their owners.

The system still relied on the bonds of patronage and personal service, however. Officials rose through the ranks by means of service to the great, and family connection and personal loyalty were still essential. Of the seventeen men who were part of Louis XIV's High Council in the course of his reign, five were members of the Colbert family, for example.

Some of the benefits of centralized administration can be seen in certain achievements of the early years of Louis's regime. Colbert encouraged France's economic development by reducing internal tolls and customs barriers and promoting industry with state subsidies and protective tariffs. He also set up state-sponsored trading companies, including the East India Company and the West India Company, both established in 1664.

Mercantilism, the philosophy behind Colbert's efforts, stressed self-sufficiency in manufactured goods, tight control of trade to foster the domestic economy, and the absolute value of bullion. Capital for development—bullion—was presumed to be limited in quantity. Protectionist policies were believed necessary to guarantee a favorable balance of payments. Although this static model did not wholly fit the reality of growing international trade in the seventeenth century, mercantilist philosophy was helpful to France. France became self-sufficient in the all-important production of woolen cloth, and French industry expanded notably in other sectors. Colbert's greatest success was the expansion of the navy and merchant marine. By 1677 the size of the navy had increased almost six times, to 144 ships. By the end of Louis XIV's reign, the French navy was virtually the equal of the English navy.

A general determination to manage national resources distinguished Louis's regime. Colbert and other ministers began to develop the kind of planned government policymaking we now take for granted. They tried to formulate policy based on carefully collected information. How many men of military age were available? How abundant was the harvest? Answers to such questions enabled them to formulate economic policy and manage production and services effectively—especially the recruitment and supply of the king's vast armies.

Beginning in 1673, Louis also tried to bring the religious life of the realm more fully under royal control by claiming for himself some of the church revenues and powers of appointment in France that still remained to the pope. Partly to bolster his position with the pope, he also began to attack the Huguenot community in France. He offered financial inducements for conversions to Catholicism, then quartered troops in Huguenot households to force them to convert. In 1685 he declared that there was no longer any Protestant community and revoked the Edict of Nantes (see page 343). A hundred thousand Protestant subjects who refused even nominal conversion to Catholicism chose to emigrate.

Despite Louis's achievement of unprecedented centralized control, "absolutism" overstates the situation. By modern standards, the power of the Crown was still greatly limited. Louis was not above the law. Louis's foremost apologist, Bishop Jacques Bossuet (1627–1704), asserted that although the king was guided only by fear of God and his own reason in his application and interpretation of law, he was obligated to act within the law. The "divine right" of kingship did not mean unlimited power to rule; rather it meant that hereditary monarchy was the divinely ordained form of government.

Absolutism meant not iron-fisted control but rather the successful focusing of energy and loyalties on the Crown, in the absence of alternative institutions. Much of the glue holding the absolutist state together lay in informal mechanisms such as patronage and court life, as well as in the traditional hunt for military glory—all of which Louis amply supplied.

The Life of the Court

An observer comparing the lives of prominent noble families in the mid-sixteenth and mid-seventeenth centuries would have noticed striking differences. By the second half of the seventeenth century, most sovereigns had the power to crush revolts. The nobility had relinquished its former independence but retained economic and social supremacy and, as a consequence, considerable political clout. Nobles also developed new ways to safeguard their privilege by means of cultural distinctions. This process was particularly dramatic in France as a strong Crown won out over a powerful nobility.

Louis maintained a brilliant court life. No longer able to wield independent political power, aristocrats lived at court whenever they could, in order to participate in the endless jostling for patronage and prestige—for commands in the royal army and for offices and honorific positions at court. Instead of safeguarding one's status with a code of honor backed up by force of arms, the seventeenth-century courtier relied on elegant ceremony, precise etiquette, and clever conversation.

As literacy became more widespread and the power of educated bureaucrats of humble origin became more obvious, more and more nobles from the traditional aristocracy began to use reading and writing as a means to think critically about their behavior—in the case of men, to reimagine themselves as gentlemen rather than warriors. Noble women and men alike began to reflect on their new roles—in letters, memoirs, and the first novels. The most influential early French novel was

Louis at Versailles Louis XIV (center, on horseback) is pictured among a throng of courtiers at a grotto in the gardens of Versailles. The symbol of the sun appeared throughout the palace; the image of Louis as the "Sun King" further enhanced his authority. *(Château de Versailles/Art Resource, NY)*

The Princess of Cleves by Marie-Madeleine Pioche de la Vergne (1634–1693), known by her title, Madame de Lafayette. Mme. de Lafayette's novel treats the particular difficulties faced by aristocratic women who, without military careers to buttress their honor, were more vulnerable than men to gossip and slander at court.

Louis XIV's court is usually associated with the palace he built at Versailles, southwest of Paris. Some of the greatest talent of the day worked on the design and construction of Versailles from 1670 through the 1680s. The palace was a masterpiece of luxury, and yet it symbolized order in its restrained, geometrical, baroque styling. Life there was sumptuous and grand. And yet, the great conglomeration of people in a building without much technology for the removal of waste or the maintenance of heat suggests that amid all the gaiety, comfort was unlikely. Still, nobles wore gorgeous clothes; meals and entertainments were extravagant. Ritual and ceremony surrounded the king, and his attention was sought constantly. Both women and men struggled to secure royal favor for themselves, their relations, and their clients. (See the box "Politics and Ritual at the Court of Louis XIV.")

The early years of Louis's personal reign were the heyday of French drama. The comedian Jean-Baptiste Poquelin, known as Molière (1622–1673), impressed the young Louis with his productions in the late 1650s and was rewarded with the use of a theater in the main royal palace in Paris. Like Shakespeare earlier in the century, Molière explored the social and political tensions of his day. He satirized the pretensions of the aristocracy, the social climbing of the bourgeoisie, the self-righteous piety of clerics. Some of his plays were banned, but most were not only tolerated but extremely popular with the elite audiences they mocked—their popularity is testimony to the confidence of Louis's regime in its early days.

Also popular at court were the tragedies of Jean Racine (1639–1699), a master of the poetic use of language. His plays, which treated familiar classical stories, focused on the emotional and psychological life of the characters and tended to stress the limits that fate places even on royal persons. The pessimism in Racine foreshadowed the less successful second half of Louis's reign.

Louis XIV and a Half-Century of War

Wars initiated by Louis XIV dominated the attention of most European states in the second half of the seventeenth century. Louis's wars sprang from traditional causes: the importance of the glory and dynastic aggrandizement of the king and the preoccupation of the aristocracy with military life. But they were more demanding on state resources than any previous wars.

In France and elsewhere, the size of armies grew markedly. The new offensive tactics developed during the Thirty Years' War changed the character of armies and increased the burden on governments to provide for them (see page 348). A higher proportion of soldiers became gunners, whose effectiveness lay in how well they operated as a unit. Since drill and discipline were vital to success, armies began to train seriously off the field of battle. The number of men on the battlefield increased somewhat, while the total numbers of men in arms supported by the state at any one time increased dramatically.

Louis's first war reflected the continuing French preoccupation with Spanish power. The goal was territory along France's eastern border to add to the land recently gained by the Peace of Westphalia (1648) and the Peace of the Pyrenees (1659). Louis invoked rather dubious dynastic claims to demand, from Spain, lands in the Spanish Netherlands and the large independent county on France's eastern border called the Franche-Comté.

War began in 1667. French troops first seized a wedge of territory in the Spanish Netherlands without difficulty and then, in early 1668, occupied the Franche-Comté. When the brief conflict ended later that year, the French retained only some towns in the Spanish Netherlands. Louis had already begun to negotiate with the Austrian Habsburgs over the eventual division of Spanish Habsburg lands, for it seemed likely that the Spanish king, Charles II (r. 1665–1700), would die without heirs. For the moment, Louis was content

Politics and Ritual at the Court of Louis XIV

This document is from the memoirs of Louis de Rouvroy, duke of Saint-Simon (1675–1755), a fa-vored courtier but one critical of Louis's power over the nobility. Notice his descriptions of court ceremony focusing on the most private moments of the king—an example of Louis's deliberate and exaggerated use of tradition, in this case of personal familiarity among warriors.

The frequent fetes, the . . . promenades at Ver-sailles, the journeys, were means on which the king seized in order to distinguish or mortify courtiers, and thus render them more assidu-ous in pleasing him. He felt that of real favors he had not enough to bestow. . . . He therefore unceasingly invented all sorts of ideal ones, lit-tle preferences and petty distinctions, which answered his purpose as well.

He was exceedingly jealous of the attention paid him. . . . He looked to the right and to the left, not only upon rising but upon going to bed, at his meals, in passing through his apart-ments, or his gardens of Versailles . . . ; not one escaped him, not even those who hoped to re-main unnoticed. He marked well all absences from court. . . .

At eight o'clock [every morning] the chief valet . . . woke the king. At the quarter [hour] the grand chamberlain was called, and those who had what was called the *grandes entrées.* The chamberlain or chief gentleman drew back the [bed] curtains and presented holy water from the vase. . . . The same officer gave [the king] his dressing gown; immediately after, other privileged courtiers entered, and then everybody, in time to find the king putting on his shoes and stockings. . . . Every other day we saw him shave himself; . . . he often spoke of [hunting] and sometimes said a word to some-body.

Source: Bayle St. John, trans., *The Memoirs of the Duke of Saint-Simon on the Reign of Louis XIV and the Regency,* 8th ed. (London: George Allen, 1913); quoted in Merry Wiesner et al., eds., *Discovering the Western Past,* 3d ed., vol. 2 (Boston: Houghton Mifflin, 1997), pp. 37–38.

to return the Franche-Comté, confident that he would get it back, and much more, in the future.

Louis's focus then shifted from Spain to a new enemy: the Dutch. The Dutch had been al-lied with France since the beginning of their exis-tence as provinces in rebellion against Spain. The French now turned against the Dutch for reasons that reflected the growth of the international trad-ing economy—specifically, the Dutch dominance of seaborne trade. "It is impossible that his Majesty should tolerate any longer the insolence and arrogance of that nation," asserted the prag-matic Colbert in 1670.[1] The Dutch War began in 1672, with Louis personally leading one of the largest armies ever fielded in Europe—perhaps

120,000 men. At the same time, the Dutch were challenged at sea by England. The English had fought the Dutch over trading issues since the 1650s; now Louis secretly sent the English king a pension to ensure his alliance with the French.

At first, the French were spectacularly suc-cessful against the tiny Dutch army. Louis, how-ever, presumptuously overrode a plan to move decisively on Amsterdam so that he could preside at the solemn reinstatement of Catholic worship in one of the Dutch provincial cathedrals. The Dutch opened dikes and flooded the countryside to protect their capital, and what had begun as a French rout became a stalemate. Moreover, the Dutch were beating the combined English and

French forces at sea and gathering allies who felt threatened by Louis's aggression. The French soon faced German and Austrian forces, and in 1674 the English made a separate peace with the Dutch and withdrew from the fighting. Nonetheless, the French managed to hold their own, and the Peace of Nijmegen, in 1678, gave the illusion of a French victory. From Spain France received further border areas in the Spanish Netherlands as well as the Franche-Comté.

Ensconced at Versailles since 1682, Louis seemed to be at the height of his power. Yet the Dutch War had cost him more than he had gained. Internal reforms ended under the pressure of paying for war, as the old financial expedients of borrowing money and selling privileges were revived. Colbert's death in 1683 dramatically symbolized the end of an era of innovation in French government.

Louis's unforgiving Dutch opponent, William of Orange, king of England from 1689 to 1702 (see page 370), renewed former alliances against him. The war, known as the Nine Years' War, or King William's War, was touched off late in 1688 by French aggression—an invasion of Germany to claim an inheritance. In his ongoing dispute with the pope, Louis seized the papal territory of Avignon in southern France. Boldest of all, he helped the exiled Catholic claimant to the English crown mount an invasion to reclaim his throne.

A widespread war began with all the major powers—Spain, the Netherlands, England, Austria, the major German states—ranged against France. This time there was no illusion of victory for Louis. In the Treaty of Ryswick (1697), Louis had to give up most of the territories in Germany, the Spanish Netherlands, and northern Spain that he had managed to occupy by war's end. Avignon went back to the pope. The terrible burden of taxes to pay for the wars combined with crop failures in 1693 and 1694 caused widespread starvation in the countryside. French courtiers began to criticize Louis openly.

The final major war of Louis's reign, now called the War of Spanish Succession, broke out in 1701. Both Louis and Holy Roman Emperor Leopold I (r. 1657–1705) hoped to claim for their heirs the throne of Spain, left open at the death in 1700 of the Spanish king, Charles II. The Dutch and the English responded to the prospect of a Frenchman on the throne of Spain by joining the emperor in a Grand Alliance in 1701.

Again the French fought a major war on several fronts on land and at sea. Again the people of France felt the cost in crushing taxes worsened by harvest failures. Major revolts inside France forced Louis to divert troops from the war. For a time it seemed that the French would be soundly defeated, but they were saved by a dynastic accident: Unexpected deaths in the Habsburg family meant that the Austrian claimant to the Spanish throne suddenly was poised to inherit rule of Austria and the empire as well. The English were more afraid of a revival of unified Habsburg control of Spain and Austria than of French domination of Spain, so they opened peace negotiations with France. The Peace of Utrecht in 1713 helped to set the agenda of European politics for the eighteenth century. Louis XIV's grandson, Philip of Anjou, became Philip V of Spain, on condition that the Spanish and French crowns would never be worn by the same monarch. To maintain the balance of power against French interests, the Spanish Netherlands and Spanish territories in Italy were ceded to Austria, which for many decades would be France's major continental rival. The Peace of Utrecht also marked the beginning of England's dominance of overseas trade and colonization. The French gave to England lands in Canada and the Caribbean and renounced any privileged relationship with Spanish colonies. England was allowed to control the highly profitable slave trade with Spanish colonies.

Louis XIV had added small amounts of strategically valuable territory along France's eastern border, and a Bourbon ruled in Spain. But the costs in human life and resources were great for the slim results achieved. Moreover, the army and navy had swallowed up capital for investment and trade, and strategic opportunities overseas were lost, never to be regained. Louis's government had been innovative in its early years but remained constrained by traditional ways of imagining the interests of the state.

THE ENGLISH REVOLUTION

In England, unlike in France, a representative institution—Parliament—became an effective, permanent brake on royal authority. The process by which Parliament gained a secure role in governing the kingdom was neither easy nor peaceful, however. As we saw in Chapter 13, conflicts between the English crown and its subjects centered on control of taxation and the direction of religious reform. Beginning in 1642, England was beset by civil war between royal and parliamentary forces. The king was eventually defeated and executed, and there followed a period when the monarchy was abolished altogether. The monarchy was restored in 1660, but Parliament retained a crucial role in governing the kingdom, a role that was confirmed when, in 1688, it again deposed a monarch whose fiscal and religious policies became unacceptable to its members.

Civil War and Revolution, 1642–1649

Fighting broke out between Charles I and parliamentary armies in the late summer of 1642. The Long Parliament (see page 347) continued to represent a broad coalition of critics and opponents of the monarchy, ranging from aristocrats concerned primarily with the abuses of royal prerogative to radical Puritans eager for thorough religious reform and determined to defeat the king. Fighting was halfhearted initially, and the tide of war at first favored Charles.

In 1643, however, the scope of the war broadened. Charles made peace with the Irish rebels and brought Irish troops to England to help his cause. Parliament, in turn, sought military aid from the Scots in exchange for a promise that Presbyterianism would become the religion of England. Meanwhile, Oliver Cromwell (1599–1658), a Puritan member of the Long Parliament and a cavalry officer, helped reorganize parliamentary forces in order to defeat the king's forces. The eleven-hundred-man cavalry trained by Cromwell, known as the "Ironsides," helped parliamentary and Scottish infantry defeat the king's troops in July 1644. The victory made Cromwell famous.

Shortly afterward, Parliament reorganized its forces to create the New Model Army, rigorously trained like Cromwell's Ironsides. Upper-class control of the army was reduced by barring sitting members of Parliament from commanding troops. The New Model Army won a convincing victory in 1645, and in the spring of 1646, Charles surrendered to a Scottish army in the north. In January 1647, Parliament paid the Scots for their services in the war and took the king into custody. In the negotiations that followed, Charles tried to play his opponents off each other, and, as he hoped, divisions among them widened.

Most members of Parliament were Presbyterians, Puritans who favored a strongly unified and controlled state church along Calvinist lines. They wanted peace with the king in return for acceptance of the new church structure and parliamentary control of standing militias for a specified period. They did not favor expanding the right to vote or other dramatic constitutional or legal changes. These men were increasingly alarmed by the rise of sectarian differences and the actual religious freedom that many ordinary people were claiming for themselves. With civil war and the weakening of royal authority, censorship was relaxed and public preaching by ordinary women and men who felt a religious inspiration was becoming commonplace.

Above all, Presbyterian gentry in Parliament feared more radical groups in the army and in London. Most officers of the New Model Army were Independents, Puritans who favored a decentralized church, a degree of religious toleration, and a wider sharing of political power among men of property, not just among the very wealthy gentry. In London, a well-organized artisans' movement known as the Levellers favored universal manhood suffrage, reform of law, and better access to education in addition to decentralized churches—in short, the separation of political power from wealth and virtual freedom of religion. Many of the rank and file of the army were deeply influenced by Leveller ideas.

In May 1647 the majority in Parliament voted to offer terms to the king and to disband the New Model Army without first paying most of the soldiers' back wages. This move provoked the first direct intervention by the army in politics. Representatives of the soldiers were chosen to present grievances to Parliament but, when this failed, the army seized the king and, in August, occupied the palace of Westminster, where Parliament met.

However, in November, Charles escaped from his captors and raised a new army among his erstwhile enemies, the Scots, who were also alarmed by the growing radicalism in England. Civil war began again in early 1648. Although it ended quickly with a victory by Cromwell and the New Model Army in August, the renewed war hardened political divisions and enhanced the power of the army. The king was widely blamed for the renewed bloodshed, and the army did not trust him to keep any agreement he might now sign. When Parliament, still dominated by Presbyterians, once again voted to negotiate with the king, army troops under a Colonel Thomas Pride prevented members who favored Presbyterianism or the king from attending sessions. The "Rump" Parliament that remained after "Pride's Purge" voted to try the king. Charles I was executed for "treason, tyranny and bloodshed" against his people on January 30, 1649.

The Interregnum, 1649–1660

A Commonwealth—a republic—was declared. Executive power resided in a council of state. Legislative power resided in a one-chamber Parliament, the Rump Parliament (the House of Lords was abolished). Declaring a republic proved far easier than running one. The execution of the king shocked most English and Scots people and alienated many elites from the new regime. The legitimacy of the Commonwealth government would always be in question.

The tasks of making and implementing policy were made difficult by the narrow political base on which the government now rested. The majority of the reformist gentry had been purged from Parliament. Also excluded were the more radical Levellers. Within a few years, many disillusioned Levellers would join a new religious movement called the Society of Friends, or Quakers, which espoused complete religious autonomy. Quakers refused all oaths or service to the state and refused to acknowledge social rank. New religious sects tended to promote gender equality as well, and many Quaker women became popular preachers.

Above all, the new government was vulnerable to the power of the army, which had created it. In 1649 and 1650, Cromwell led expeditions to Ireland and Scotland, partly for revenge and partly to put down resistance to the new English government. In Ireland, Cromwell's forces acted with great ruthlessness. English control there was furthered by more dispossession of Irish landholders, which also helped pay off the army's wages. Meanwhile, Parliament could not agree on systematic reforms, particularly the one reform Independents in the army insisted on: more broadly based elections for a new Parliament. Fresh from his victories in the north, Cromwell led his armies to London and dissolved Parliament in the spring of 1652.

In 1653 some army officers drew up the "Instrument of Government," England's first and only written constitution. It provided for an executive, the Lord Protector, and a Parliament to be based on somewhat wider male suffrage. Cromwell was the natural choice for Lord Protector, and whatever success the government of the Protectorate had was largely due to him.

Cromwell was an extremely able leader who was not averse to compromise. Although he had used the army against Parliament in 1648, he had worked hard to reconcile the Rump Parliament and the army before marching on London in 1652. He believed in a state church, but one that allowed for local control by congregations. He also believed in toleration for other Protestant sects, as well as for Catholics and Jews, as long as no one disturbed the peace.

As Lord Protector, Cromwell oversaw impressive reforms in law that testify to his belief in the limits of governing authority. For example, contrary to the practice of his day, he opposed

Popular Preaching in England Many women took advantage of the collapse of royal authority to preach in public—a radical activity for women at the time. This print satirizes the Quakers, a religious movement that attracted many women. *(Mary Evans Picture Library)*

capital punishment for petty crimes. The government of the Protectorate, however, accomplished little because Parliament remained internally divided and opposed to Cromwell's initiatives. For example, Cromwell was challenged by radical republicans in Parliament who thought the Protectorate represented a step backward, away from republican government. Yet in the population at large, there were still royalist sympathizers, and a royalist uprising in 1655 forced the temporary division of England into military districts administered by generals.

Cromwell died of a sudden illness in September 1658, and the Protectorate did not long survive him. In February 1660, the decisive action of one army general seeking a solution to the chaos enabled all the surviving members of the Long Parliament to rejoin the Rump. The Parliament summarily dissolved itself and called for new elections. The newly elected Parliament recalled Charles II, son of Charles I, from exile abroad and restored the monarchy. The chaos and radicalism of the late civil war and *interregnum*—the period between reigns, as the years from 1649 to 1660 came to be called—had provoked a conservative reaction.

The Restoration, 1660–1685

Charles II (r. 1660–1685) claimed his throne at the age of 30. He had learned from his years of uncertain exile and the fate of his father. He did not seek retribution but rather offered a general pardon to all but a few rebels (mostly those who had signed his father's death warrant), and he suggested to Parliament a relatively tolerant religious settlement that would include Anglicans as well as Presbyterians. He was far more politically adept than his father and much more willing to compromise.

That the re-established royal government was not more tolerant than it turned out to be was not Charles's doing but Parliament's. Anglican orthodoxy was reimposed, including the re-establishment of bishops and the Anglican *Book of Common Prayer*. All officeholders and clergy were required to swear oaths of obedience to the king and the established church. As a result, hundreds of them were forced out of office. Holding nonconformist religious services became illegal, and Parliament passed a "five-mile" act preventing dissenting ministers from visiting or even traveling near their former congregations. Property laws were strengthened and the criminal codes made more severe.

The king's attitudes began to mimic prerevolutionary royalist positions. Charles II began to flirt with Catholicism, and his brother and heir, James, openly converted. Charles promulgated a declaration of tolerance that would have included Catholics as well as nonconformist Protestants, but Parliament would not accept it. When Parliament moved to exclude James from succession to the throne, Charles dissolved it. A subsequent Parliament, cowed by fears of a new civil war, backed down. By the end of his reign, Charles was financially independent of Parliament due to more revenue from overseas trade and to secret subsidies from France, his recent ally against Dutch trading rivals (see page 365).

But it was impossible to silence dissent. After two decades of religious pluralism and broadly based political activity, there were well-established communities of various sects and a self-confidence that bred vigorous resistance. Also, anti-Catholic feeling still united all Protestants. Parliament focused its attention on anti-Catholicism, passing an act barring all but Anglicans from Parliament itself.

The clearest reflection of the regime's revolutionary background was Parliament's ability to assert its policies against the desires of the king. And yet Charles retained a great deal of power. If he had been followed by an able successor,

Parliament might have lost a good measure of its independence.

The Glorious Revolution, 1688

When James II (r. 1685–1689) succeeded Charles, Parliament initially cooperated, granting him customs duties for life and funds to suppress a rebellion by one of Charles's illegitimate sons. James did not try to impose Catholicism on England, but he did try to achieve toleration for Catholics in two declarations of indulgence in 1687 and 1688. His efforts were undermined by his heavy-handed tactics. When several Anglican bishops refused to read the declarations from their pulpits, he had them imprisoned and tried for seditious libel. The jury acquitted them.

James also failed because of the coincidence of other events. In 1685, at the outset of James's reign, Louis XIV of France had revoked the Edict of Nantes. The possibility that subjects and their monarch could be of different faiths seemed increasingly unlikely. Popular fears of James's Catholicism were thus heightened early in his reign, and his later declarations of tolerance, though also benefiting Protestant dissenters, were viewed with suspicion. In 1688 the king's second wife, who was Catholic, gave birth to a son, raising the specter of a Catholic succession.

In June 1688, seven leading members of Parliament invited William of Orange, the husband of James's Protestant daughter Mary, to come to England. William mounted an invasion that became a rout when James refused to defend his throne and fled to France. William called Parliament, which declared James to have abdicated and offered the throne to him and to Mary. James eventually invaded Ireland in 1690 with French support but was defeated by William at the Battle of the Boyne that year.

The substitution of William (r. 1689–1702) and Mary (r. 1689–1694) for James, known as the "Glorious Revolution," was engineered by Parliament and confirmed its power. Parliament presented the new sovereigns with a Bill of Rights that defended freedom of speech, called for frequent Parliaments, and stipulated that no

Catholic could ever succeed to the throne. The effectiveness of these documents was reinforced by Parliament's power of the purse.

The issues that had faced the English since the beginning of the century were common to all European states: religious division and elite power, fiscal strains and resistance to taxation. Yet events in England were unusual in that the assumption of authority by a well-established institution, Parliament, made challenge of the monarchy more legitimate and more effective. Political participation also developed more broadly in England than in other states. In the long run, the strength of Parliament would make easier the task of broadening participation in government.

NEW POWERS IN CENTRAL AND EASTERN EUROPE

By the end of the seventeenth century, central and eastern Europe were dominated by three states: Austria, Brandenburg-Prussia, and Russia. After the Thirty Years' War, the Habsburgs' power as emperors waned, and their interest in the coherence of their own territories, centered on Austria, grew. Brandenburg-Prussia, in northeastern Germany, grew to a position of power rivaling that of the Habsburg state. The rulers of Brandenburg-Prussia had gained lands in the Peace of Westphalia, and astute management transformed their relatively small and scattered holdings into one of the most powerful states in Europe. Russia's new stature in eastern Europe resulted in part from the weakness of its greatest rival, Poland, and the determination of one leader, Peter the Great, to assume a major role in European affairs. Sweden controlled valuable Baltic territory through much of the century but by the end of the century it, too, was eclipsed by Russia as a power in the region.

The development of states in central and eastern Europe was closely linked to developments in western Europe. This was true politically and strategically as well as economically. One of the most important factors influencing the internal political development of these states was their relationship to the wider European economy: They were sources of grain and raw materials for the more densely urbanized west.

The Consolidation of Austria

In 1648 the main Habsburg lands were a collection of principalities comprising modern Austria, the kingdom of Hungary (largely in Turkish hands), and the kingdom of Bohemia (Map 14.1). In 1713 the Peace of Utrecht ceded to Austria the Spanish Netherlands, renamed the "Austrian Netherlands," and substantial territories in Italy. Although language and ethnic differences prevented the establishment of an absolutist state along French lines, Leopold I (r. 1657–1705) instituted political and institutional changes that enabled the Habsburg state to become one of the most powerful in Europe in the eighteenth century.

Much of the coherence that already existed in Leopold's lands had been achieved by his predecessors in the wake of the Thirty Years' War. The lands of rebels in Bohemia had been confiscated and redistributed among loyal, mostly Austrian, families. In return for political and military support for the emperor, these families were given the right to exploit their newly acquired land and the peasants who worked it. The desire to recover population and productivity after the destruction of the Thirty Years' War gave landlords an incentive to curtail peasants' autonomy sharply, particularly in devastated Bohemia. Austrian landlords throughout the Habsburg domains provided grain and timber for the export market, and elite families provided the army with officers. This political-economic arrangement provoked numerous serious peasant revolts, but the peasants were not able to force changes in a system that suited both the elites and the central authority.

The institutions of the imperial government still functioned in Leopold's capital, Vienna, but Leopold worked to extricate the government of his own lands from the imperial offices, which were staffed largely by Germans more loyal to imperial than to Habsburg interests. In addition,

Map 14.1 New Powers in Central and Eastern Europe The balance of power in central and eastern Europe shifted with the strengthening of Austria, the rise of Brandenburg-Prussia, and the expansion of Russia at the expense of Poland and Sweden.

Leopold used the Catholic church as an institutional and ideological support for the Habsburg monarchy.

Leopold's personal preoccupation was the re-establishment of zealous Catholicism throughout his territories. Acceptance of Catholicism became the litmus test of loyalty to the Habsburg regime, and Protestantism vanished among elites. Leopold encouraged the work of Jesuit teachers and members of other Catholic orders. These men and women helped staff his government and administered religious life down to the most local levels.

Leopold's most dramatic success, as a Habsburg and an ardent Catholic, was his reconquest of Hungary from the Ottoman Empire. Since the mid-sixteenth century, the Habsburgs had controlled only a narrow strip of the kingdom. Preoccupied with countering Louis XIV's aggression, Leopold did not himself choose to begin a reconquest. His centralizing policies, however, alienated nobles and townspeople in the portion of Hungary he did control, as did his repression of Protestantism, which had flourished in Hungary. Hungarian nobles began a revolt, aided by the Turks, aiming for a fully united Hungary under Ottoman protection.

The Habsburgs emerged victorious in part because they received help from the talented Polish king Jan Sobieski, whose own lands in Ukraine were also threatened by the Turks. The Turks overreached their supply lines to besiege Vienna in 1683. After the siege failed, Habsburg armies slowly pressed east and south, recovering Buda, the ancient capital of Hungary, in 1686 and Belgrade in 1688. The Danube basin was once again in Christian hands.

Leopold gave land in the reclaimed kingdom to Austrian officers whom he believed were loyal to him. The traditions of Hungarian separatism, however, were strong, and the great magnates retained their independence. The peasantry, as elsewhere, suffered a decline in status as a result of the Crown's efforts to ensure the loyalty of elites. In the long run, Hungarian independence weakened the Habsburg state, but in the short run Leopold's victory over the Turks and the recovery of Hungary were momentous events, confirming the Habsburgs as the pre-eminent power in central Europe.

The Rise of Brandenburg-Prussia

In addition to Austria, three German states gained territory and stature after the Thirty Years' War: Bavaria, Saxony, and Brandenburg-Prussia. By the end of the seventeenth century, the strongest was Brandenburg-Prussia, a conglomeration of small territories held, by dynastic accident, by the Hohenzollern family. The two principal territories were electoral Brandenburg, in northeastern Germany, with its capital, Berlin, and the duchy of Prussia, a fief of the Polish crown along the Baltic coast east of Poland proper (see Map 14.1). In addition there was a handful of small principalities near the Netherlands. The manipulation of resources and power that enabled these unpromising lands to become a powerful state was primarily the work of Frederick William, known as "the Great Elector" (r. 1640–1688).

Frederick William took advantage of a war between Poland and its rivals, Sweden and Russia, to win independence for the duchy of Prussia from Polish overlordship. When his involvement in the war ended in 1657, he kept the general war commissariat intact and bypassed traditional civilian councils and representative bodies. He also used the standing army to force the payment of high taxes. Most significantly, he established a relationship with the *Junkers*, hereditary landholders, which assured him both revenue and loyalty. He agreed to allow the Junkers virtually total control of their own lands in return for their agreement to support his government—in short, to surrender their accustomed political independence.

Peasants and townspeople were taxed, but nobles were not. The freedom to control their estates led many nobles to invest in profitable agriculture for the export market. The peasants were serfs who received no benefits from the increased productivity of the land. Frederick William further enhanced his state's power by sponsoring state industries. These industries did not have to fear competition from urban producers because the towns had been frozen out of the political process and saddled with heavy taxes. Although an oppressive place for many Germans, Brandenburg-Prussia attracted many skilled refugees, such as Huguenot artisans fleeing Louis XIV.

In contrast to Brandenburg-Prussia, Bavaria and Saxony had vibrant towns, largely free peasantries, and weak aristocracies, but they were less powerful in international affairs. Power on the European stage depended on military force. Such power, whether in a large state like France or in a small one like Brandenburg-Prussia, usually came at the expense of the state's inhabitants.

Competition Around the Baltic: The Demise of the Polish State and the Zenith of Swedish Power

The rivers and port cities of the Baltic coast were conduits for the growing trade between the Baltic hinterland as well as its coastline and the rest of Europe; transit tolls on timber, grain, and naval stores were an important source of local income, and the commodities themselves brought profits to their producers. This trading system had profound consequences for all of the states bordering the Baltic Sea in the seventeenth century.

First, it was a spur to war. Through the sixteenth and seventeenth centuries, Sweden, Denmark, and Russia fought over access to and control of the Baltic trade, and in the seventeenth century, Poland and Russia fought over grain- and timber-producing lands. Second, profits from grain exports reinforced the power of large landholders, particularly in Poland, where most of the grain was produced.

In 1600 a large portion of the Baltic hinterland, as well as its coastline, lay under the control of Poland-Lithuania, a dual kingdom at the height of its power. A marriage in 1386 had brought the duchy of Lithuania under a joint ruler with Poland; earlier in the fourteenth century, Lithuania had conquered Belarus and Ukraine. Like the neighboring Habsburg lands, Poland-Lithuania was a multi-ethnic state, particularly in the huge duchy of Lithuania, where Russian-speakers predominated. Poland was Catholic but had a large minority of Protestants

and Jews. Lithuanians were mostly Catholic, while Russian-speakers were Orthodox.

Internal strains and external challenges began to mount in Poland-Lithuania in the late sixteenth century. The economic power of Polish landlords gave them political clout; the king was forced to grant concessions that bound peasants to the nobles' estates. The spread of the Counter-Reformation, encouraged by the Crown, created problems for both Protestant and Orthodox subjects. In Ukraine, communities of Cossacks, nomadic farmer-warriors, grew as Polish and Lithuanian peasants fled harsh conditions to join them. The Cossacks had long been tolerated because they were a military buffer against the Ottoman Turks, but now Polish landlords wanted to reincorporate the Cossacks into the profitable political-economic system that they controlled.

In 1648 the Cossacks staged a major revolt, defeated Polish armies, and established an independent state. In 1654 they transferred their allegiance to Moscow and became part of a Russian invasion of Poland that, by the next year, had engulfed much of the eastern half of the kingdom. At the same time, the Swedes seized central Poland and competed with the Russians for control elsewhere; the Swedes were helped by Polish and Lithuanian aristocrats acting like independent warlords.

Often called the First Great Northern War, this war is remembered in Poland as "the Deluge." The population of Poland may have declined by as much as 40 percent, and vital urban economies were in ruins. The religious tolerance that had distinguished the Polish kingdom and had been mandated in its constitution was thereafter abandoned. Polish royal armies managed to recover much territory, but much of this was only nominal. In parts of Lithuania inhabited by Russian-speaking peoples, the Russian presence during the wars had achieved local transfers of power from Lithuanian to Russian landlords loyal to Moscow.

The elective Polish crown passed in 1674 to the brilliant military commander Jan Sobieski (r. 1674–1696), who would become known as "Vanquisher of the Turks" for his victory in raising the siege of Vienna. Given Poland's internal weakness, Sobieski's victories helped the Austrian and Russian rivals of the Turks more than the Poles. His successor, Augustus II of Saxony (r. 1697–1704, 1709–1733), dragged Poland back into war, from which Russia would emerge the obvious winner in eastern Europe.

On the Baltic coast, however, Sweden remained the dominant power through most of the seventeenth century. Swedish efforts to control Baltic territory began in the sixteenth century, first to counter the power of its perennial rival, Denmark, in the western Baltic. It then competed with Poland to control Livonia (modern Latvia), whose principal city, Riga, was an important trading center for goods from Lithuania and Russia. Swedish intervention in the Thirty Years' War came when imperial successes against Denmark both threatened the Baltic coast and created an opportunity to strike at Sweden's old enemy. The treaty of Westphalia (1648) confirmed Sweden's earlier gains and added control of further coastal territory, mostly at Denmark's expense.

The port cities held by Sweden were profitable though their revenue mostly went to pay for the wars necessary to seize and defend them. All of these efforts to hold Baltic territory were driven by dynastic and strategic needs as much as economic rationales. For example, Sigismund Vasa, son of the king of Sweden, had been elected king of Poland in 1587 but also inherited the Swedish throne in 1592. The one permanent gain Sweden realized from its aggression in the First Great Northern War was the renunciation of the Polish Vasa line to any claim to the Swedish crown. Owing to its earlier gains, Sweden remained the dominant power on the Baltic coast until the end of the seventeenth century, when it was supplanted by Russia.

The Expansion of Russia: From Ivan "the Terrible" Through Peter "the Great"

The Russian state expanded dramatically in the sixteenth century. Ivan IV (r. 1533–1584) was proclaimed "Tsar [Russian for "Caesar"] of All the Russias" in 1547. This act was the culmination of the accumulation of land and authority by the princes of Moscow through the late Middle Ages, when Moscow had vied for pre-eminence with other Russian principalities. Ivan IV's grandfather, Ivan III (r. 1462–1505), the first to use the title *tsar*, had absorbed neighboring Russian principalities and ended Moscow's subservience to Mongol overlords.

Ivan IV is also known as Ivan "the Terrible" ("awe-inspiring" is a better translation of the Russian). He was the first actually to be crowned tsar and routinely to use the title. His use of the title aptly reflected his imperial intentions, as he continued Moscow's push westward and, especially, eastward against the Mongol states of central Asia. The Russians pushed eastward over the Ural Mountains to Siberia for the first time. Within this expanding empire, Ivan IV used ruthless methods, including the torture and murder of thousands of subjects, to enforce his will. The practice of gathering tribute for Mongol overlords had put many resources in the hands of Muscovite princes, but Ivan IV was able to bypass noble participation and intensify the centralization of government by creating ranks of officials, known as the service gentry, loyal only to him.

A period of disputed succession known as the Time of Troubles followed Ivan's death in 1584. Aristocratic factions fought among themselves as well as against armies of Cossacks and other common people who wanted a less oppressive government. Nonetheless, the foundations laid by Ivan enabled Michael Romanov to rebuild autocratic government after being chosen tsar in 1613. The Romanovs were an aristocratic family related to Ivan's. Michael (r. 1613–1645) was chosen by an assembly of aristocrats, gentry, and commoners more alarmed by civil wars than by the prospect of a return to strong tsarist rule. Michael was succeeded by his son, Alexis (r. 1645–1676), who presided over the extension of Russian control to Ukraine in 1654 and developed interest in further relationships with the West. Shifting the balance of power in eastern Europe and the Baltic in Russia's favor was also the work of Alexis's son, Peter I, "the Great" (r. 1682–1725). Peter accomplished this by military successes against his enemies and by forcibly reorienting Russian government and society.

Peter was almost literally larger than life. Nearly 7 feet tall, he towered over most of his contemporaries and had physical and mental energy to match his size. He set himself to learning trades and studied soldiering by rising in the ranks of the military like any common soldier. He traveled abroad to learn as much as he could about other states' economies and government. He wanted the revenue, manufacturing, technology and trade, and, above all, the up-to-date army and navy that other rulers enjoyed.

Peter initiated a bold and even brutal series of changes in Russian society upon his accession to power. Peasants already bore the brunt of taxation, but their tax burdens increased. Peter noticed that European monarchs coexisted with a privileged but educated aristocracy and that a brilliant court life symbolized and reinforced the rulers' authority. So he set out to refashion Russian society in what amounted to an enforced cultural revolution. (See the box "Peter the Great Changes Russia.") He provoked confrontations with Russia's traditional aristocracy over everything from education to matters of dress. He elevated new families to the ranks of gentry and created an official ranking system for the nobility, to encourage service to the government.

Peter's effort to reorient his nation toward Europe was most apparent in the construction of the city of St. Petersburg on the Gulf of Finland, which provided access to the Baltic Sea. In stark contrast to Moscow, dominated by the medieval fortress of the Kremlin and churches in the traditional Russian style, St. Petersburg was a modern European city with wide avenues and palaces designed for a sophisticated court life. But although Peter was intelligent, practical, and determined to create a more productive society, he was also cruel and authoritarian. The building of St. Petersburg cost staggering sums in money and in workers' lives. Peter's entire reform system was carried out autocratically; resistance

was brutally suppressed. Victims of Peter's oppression included his son, Alexis, who died after torture while awaiting execution for questioning his father's policies.

The primary reason for the high cost of Peter's government to the Russian people was his ambition for territorial gain and for an improved army and navy. Working side by side with workers and technicians, many of whom he had recruited while abroad, Peter created the Russian navy from scratch. Peter also modernized the Russian army by employing tactics and training he had observed in the West. By 1709, Russia was able to manufacture most of the up-to-date firearms it needed. He also introduced military conscription.

Russia waged war virtually throughout Peter's reign. Initially, he struck at the Ottomans and their client state in the Crimea, with some success. But later phases of these conflicts brought reverses. Peter had his greatest success against Sweden in contests for control of the weakened Polish state and the Baltic Sea. The conflicts between Sweden and Russia, known as the Second Great Northern War, raged from 1700 to 1709 and, in a less intense phase, lasted until 1721. The acquisitions of this war made Russia the pre-eminent Baltic power at Sweden's and Poland's expense (see Map 14.1).

THE RISE OF OVERSEAS TRADE

During the seventeenth century, European trade and colonization expanded and changed dramatically. The Dutch not only became masters of the spice trade but led the expansion of trade to include many other commodities. In the Americas, the expansion of sugar and tobacco production created a new trading system linking Europe, Africa, and the New World. French and English colonists began settling in North America in increasing numbers. Overseas trade had a dramatic impact on life within Europe: on patterns of production and consumption, social stratification, and the distribution of wealth.

Peter the Great Changes Russia

Peter the Great's reforms included not only monumental building and a new relationship with elites but also practical changes in education, technology, and administration. Writing about a hundred years after the end of Peter's reign, the Russian historian Mikhail Pogodin (1800–1875) reflected on all the changes Peter had introduced, perhaps exaggerating only the respect Peter earned in foreign eyes in his lifetime.

Yes, Peter the Great did much for Russia. . . . One keeps adding and one cannot reach the sum. We cannot open our eyes, cannot make a move, cannot turn in any direction without encountering him everywhere, at home, in the streets, in church, in school, in court, in the regiment. . . .

We wake up. What day is it today? . . . Peter ordered us to count the years from the birth of Christ; Peter ordered us to count the months from January.

It is time to dress—our clothing is made according to the fashion established by Peter the First, our uniform according to his model. The cloth is woven in a factory which he created. . . .

Newspapers are brought in—Peter the Great introduced them.

You must buy different things—they all, from the silk neckerchief to the sole of your shoe, will remind you of Peter. . . . Some were ordered by him . . . or improved by him, carried on his ships, into his harbors, on his canals, on his roads.

Let us go to the university—the first secular school was founded by Peter the Great.

You decide to travel abroad—following [his] example; you will be received well—Peter the Great placed Russia among the European states and began to instill respect for her; and so on and so on.

Source: Nicholas V. Riasanovsky, *A History of Russia,* 2d ed. (London: Oxford University Press, 1969), pp. 266–267.

The Growth of Trading Empires: The Success of the Dutch

By the end of the sixteenth century, the Dutch and the English were trying to make incursions into the Portuguese-controlled spice trade with areas of India, Ceylon, and the East Indies. Spain had annexed Portugal in 1580, but the drain on Spain's resources from its wars with the Dutch and the French prevented Spain from adequately defending its enlarged trading empire in Asia. The Dutch and, to a lesser degree, the English rapidly supplanted the Portuguese in this lucrative trade.

The Dutch were particularly well placed to be successful competitors in overseas trade. They already dominated seaborne trade within Europe, including the most important long-distance trade, which linked Spain and Portugal—with their wine and salt, as well as spices, hides, and gold from abroad—with the Baltic coast, where these products were sold for grain and timber produced in Germany, Poland-Lithuania, and Scandinavia. The geographic position of the Netherlands and the fact that the Dutch consumed more Baltic grain than any other area because of their densely urbanized economy help to explain their dominance of this trade. In addition, the Dutch had improved the design of their merchant ships to enhance their profits.

The Dutch were successful in Asia because of institutional as well as technical innovations. In 1602 the Dutch East India Company was formed. The company combined the government management of trade, typical of the period, with both public and private investment. In the past, groups of investors had funded single voyages or small numbers of ships on a one-time basis. The formation of the Dutch East India Company created a permanent pool of capital to sustain trade. The risks and delays of longer voyages could be spread among larger numbers of investors. The English East India Company, founded in 1607, also supported trade, but it had one-tenth the capital of the Dutch company. The Bank of Amsterdam, founded in 1609, became the depository for the bullion that flowed into the Netherlands with trade. The bank established currency-exchange rates and issued paper money and instruments of credit to facilitate commerce.

A dramatic expansion of trade with Asia resulted from the Dutch innovations, so much so that by 1650 the European market for spices was glutted and traders' profits had begun to fall. To control the supply of spices, the Dutch seized some of the areas where they were produced. Control of supply helped prop up prices, but these gains were somewhat offset by greater military and administrative costs.

The Dutch and English further responded to the oversupply of spices by diversifying their trade. The proportion of spices in cargoes from the East fell from about 70 percent at midcentury to just over 20 percent by the century's end. New consumer goods such as tea, coffee, silks, and cotton fabrics took their place. Eventually, the Dutch and the English even entered the local carrying trade among Asian states. Doing so enabled them to make profits without purchasing goods, and it slowed the drain of hard currency from Europe—currency in increasingly short supply as the silver mines in the Americas were worked out. (See the box "Encounters with the West: Agents of the Dutch East India Company Confront Asian Powers.")

The "Golden Age" of the Netherlands

The prosperity occasioned by the Netherlands' "mother trade" within Europe and its burgeoning overseas commerce helped foster social and political conditions unique within Europe. The

concentration of trade and shipping sustained a large merchant oligarchy as well as an extensive and prosperous artisanal sector. Disparities of wealth were smaller than anywhere else in Europe. The shipbuilding and fishing trades, among others, supported large numbers of workers with a high standard of living for the age.

Political decentralization in the Netherlands persisted: Each of the seven provinces retained considerable autonomy. However, merchant oligarchs in the Estates of the province of Holland in fact constituted the government for the whole for long periods because of Holland's economic dominance. The head of government was the *pensionary* (executive secretary) of Holland's Estates. An Estates-General existed but had no independent powers of taxation.

The only competition in the running of affairs came from the House of Orange, aristocratic leaders of the revolt against Spain. They exercised what control they had by means of the office of *stadholder*—a kind of military governorship. They continued to lead the defense of the Netherlands against Spanish attempts at reconquest until the Peace of Westphalia confirmed Dutch independence in 1648. Their power also came from the fact that they represented the only counterweight within the Netherlands to the dominance of Amsterdam merchant interests. Small towns dependent on land-based trade or rural areas dominated by farmers and gentry looked to the stadholders of the Orange family to defend their interests.

As elsewhere, religion was a source of political conflict. The stadholders favored rigid Calvinism. The pensionaries and regents of Holland (as the leading families were known) were more relaxed, reflecting the needs of the diverse mercantile communities of Holland, where thousands of Jews as well as Catholics and various kinds of Protestants lived. Foreign policy also turned on Holland's desire for peace in order to foster commerce versus the stadholder's greater willingness to engage in warfare for territory and dynastic advantage.

These differences notwithstanding, Dutch commercial dominance drew them into costly

~ **ENCOUNTERS WITH THE WEST** ~

Agents of the Dutch East India Company Confront Asian Powers

This 1655 letter from a local agent of the Dutch East India Company to its board of directors (the "Seventeen") shows that the Dutch had to maintain good working relationships with local powers in Asia—in this case, with the king of Siam (modern Thailand). The letter discusses the Dutch blockade of Tennasserim, a major port under Siamese control, and the promises of help the Dutch, via their local agents, had made the king for some of his military ventures.

It appears that the merchant Hendrich Craijer Zalr had promised, so they [the Siamese] say, 20 ships, which was a very rash proceeding on his part, and thereupon they made the above-mentioned expedition, which they said, if our support did not appear, would be obliged to return unsuccessful and with shame and dishonor to the crown, as was actually the case. Moreover, it happened that a writing had come unexpectedly from the governor of Tennasserim that two Dutch ships had held the harbor there for 2 months, and had prevented the entrance and departure of foreign traders, which caused great annoyance in Siam, especially at Court, and embittered everyone against us. This gave the [English] Companies very favorable opportunity to blacken us and to make us odious to everyone, and to change the King's feeble opposition into open enmity, the more so since the news has from time to time been confirmed and assured, and no one there doubts it any longer.

Wherefore the resident Westerwolt, who was convinced of the contrary, since he would certainly have been informed before any such action was taken, finally found himself obliged to ask that certain persons, on the King's behalf and on his own, should be deputed and sent overland to Tennasserim, in order to discover on the spot the truth of the case, which request was granted by the King, and on our behalf the junior merchant, Hugo van Crujlenburgh was sent.

Meanwhile the aforementioned resident Westerwolt had on various occasions made complaint of the bad and unreasonable treatment received, . . . so that the resident was in very great embarrassment and did not know whether even his life was any longer safe. These questions were for the most part on the subject of the help asked for against Singgora, the Siamese professing to have gone to war with the Spanish on our account, and to have suffered much damage in the same, and that we now refused to assist his Majesty against the rebels with ships and men; whereas the beforementioned merchant, Hendrich Craijer, had definitely made him such promises.

Source: Records of the Relations Between Siam and Foreign Countries in the Seventeenth Century (Bangkok: Council of the Vajiranana National Library, 1916), vol. 2. Quoted in Alfred J. Andrea and James H. Overfield, The Human Record: Sources of Global History, 2d ed., vol. 2: Since 1500 (Boston: Houghton Mifflin, 1994), pp. 134–135.

wars throughout the second half of the century. Between 1657 and 1660 the Dutch defended Denmark against Swedish ambitions in order to safeguard the sea-lanes and port cities of the Baltic. Other, more costly conflicts arose from rivalries with other states, notably England and France. Owing largely to the land war with France, the Estates in Holland lost control of policy to William of Nassau (d. 1702), who was prince of Orange after 1672. William drew the Netherlands

Rembrandt: The Syndics of the Cloth Drapers' Guild (1662) In this painting, the last group portrait of his career, Rembrandt depicts the guild members with artful, stylized simplicity. It was Rembrandt's genius also to be able to convey a sense of personality and drama in such commissioned portraits. *(Rijksmuseum-Stichting, Amsterdam)*

into his family's long-standing close relationship with England. Like other members of his family before him, William had married into the English royal family: His wife was Mary, daughter of James II.

Ironically, after he and Mary assumed the English throne in 1689, Dutch commerce suffered more in alliance with England than in its previous rivalry. William used Dutch resources for the land war against Louis XIV and used the English navy for the fight at sea. Dutch maritime strength was being eclipsed by English seapower by the end of the century.

To contemporaries, the Netherlands appeared to be an astonishing exception to the normal structures of politics. In France and most other states in Europe, political life was dominated by a court where aristocrats and ministers mingled and conspired and an elaborate ritual of honor

and deference glorified the king. The princes of Orange surrounded themselves with splendid trappings, but their court was not the sole focus of political life in the Netherlands. The portraits of the Dutch painter Rembrandt van Rijn (1606–1667) portray the austerity of the merchant oligarchs; theirs was a novel kind of power that could be symbolized with ostentatious simplicity.

The Growth of Atlantic Colonies and Commerce

In the seventeenth century, the Dutch, English, and French joined the Spanish as colonial and commercial powers in the Americas. The Spanish colonial empire, in theory a trading system closed to outsiders, was in fact vulnerable to incursion by other European traders. In 1628, for example, a Dutch captain seized the entire Spanish treasure fleet. But by then Spain's goals and those of its competitors had begun to shift, due largely to the declining output of the Spanish silver mines during the 1620s. The Spanish and their Dutch, French, and English competitors expanded the production of the cash crops of sugar and tobacco.

The European demand for sugar and tobacco grew steadily in the seventeenth century. European entrepreneurs had developed the *plantation system*—the use of forced labor to work large tracts of land—on Mediterranean islands during the Middle Ages. They imported slaves from the Black Sea region to supplement the local labor force. Sugar production by this system was established on Atlantic islands, using African labor, and then in the Americas by the Spanish and Portuguese. The French, English, and Dutch followed their lead and established sugar plantations on the Caribbean islands they held. Sugar production in the New World grew from about 20,000 tons in 1600 to about 200,000 tons by 1770. The Dutch became the official supplier of slaves to Spanish plantations in the New World and the chief supplier to most other regions. They made handsome profits until the end of the seventeenth century, when they were supplanted by the British.

Aware of the great Spanish territorial advantage in the New World and hoping for treasures such as the Spanish had found, the English, French, and Dutch were also ambitious to explore and settle North America. From the early sixteenth century, French, Dutch, English, and Portuguese seamen had fished and traded off Newfoundland. By 1630, small French and Scots settlements in Acadia (in modern Nova Scotia) and on the St. Lawrence River and English settlements in Newfoundland had been established to exploit the timber, fish, and fur of the north Atlantic coasts.

In England population growth and consequent unemployment, as well as religious discontent, created a large pool of potential colonists. The first English settlement to endure in what was to become the United States was established at Jamestown, named for James I, in Virginia in 1607. ("Virginia," named for Elizabeth I, the "vir-

gin" queen, was an extremely vague designation for the Atlantic coast of North America and its hinterland.)

The Crown encouraged colonization, but a private company similar to the companies that financed long-distance trade was established to organize the enterprise. The directors of the Virginia Company were London businessmen. Investors and would-be colonists purchased shares. Shareholders among the colonists could participate in a colonial assembly, though the governor appointed by the company was the final authority.

The colonists arrived in Virginia with ambitious and optimistic instructions. They were to open mines, establish profitable cultivation, and search for sea routes to Asia. At first they struggled merely to survive. The indigenous peoples in Virginia, unlike those in Spanish-held territory, were not organized in urbanized, rigidly hierarchical societies that, after conquest, could provide the invaders with a labor force. Indeed, the native Americans in this region were quickly wiped out by European diseases. The introduction of tobacco as a cash crop a few years later saved the colonists economically—though the Virginia Company had already gone bankrupt and the Crown had assumed control of the colony. With the cultivation of tobacco, the Virginia colony became dependent on forced, eventually slave, labor.

Among the Virginia colonists were impoverished men and women who came as servants indentured to those who had paid their passage. Colonies established to the north, in what was called "New England," also drew people from the margins of English society: Early settlers there were religious dissidents. The first to arrive were the Pilgrims, who arrived at New Plymouth (modern Massachusetts) in 1620. They were religious separatists who had originally emigrated to the Netherlands from England. Following the Pilgrims came Puritans escaping escalating persecution under Charles I. The first, in 1629, settled under the auspices of another royally chartered company, the Massachusetts Bay Company. Among their number were many prosperous Puritan merchants and landholders. Independence

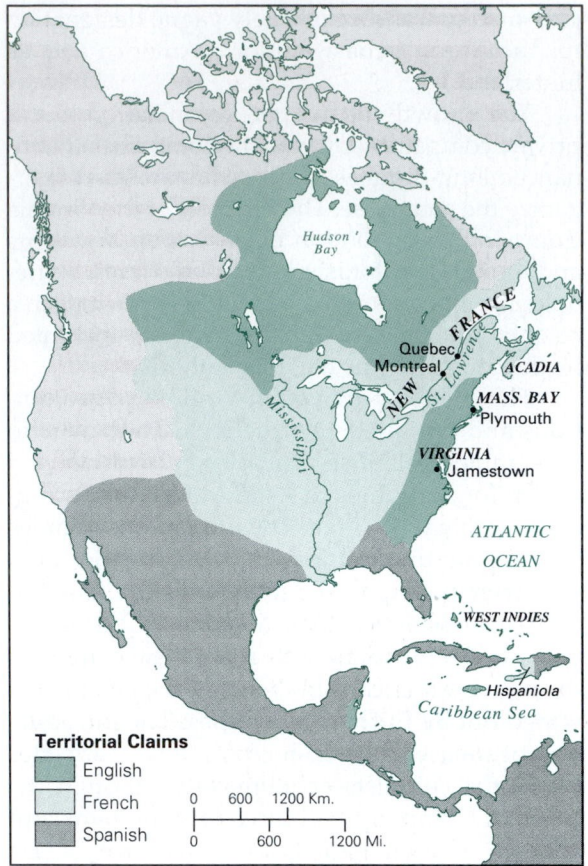

Territorial Claims

- English
- French
- Spanish

0   600   1200 Km.
0   600   1200 Mi.

Map 14.2 British and French in North America, ca. 1700 By 1700 a veritable ring of French-claimed territory encircled the coastal colonies of England. English-claimed areas, however, were more densely settled and more economically viable.

The colonies' greatest strength, from the English viewpoint, was that the settlements continued to attract migrants. By 1640, Massachusetts had some fourteen thousand European inhabitants. Through most of the next century, the growth of colonial populations in North America would result in an English advantage over the French in control of territory. In the long run, however, the size of the colonial communities would help lead them to seek independence.

The French began their settlement of North America at the same time as the English, in the same push to compensate for their mutual weakness vis-à-vis the Spanish (Map 14.2). The French efforts, however, had very different results, because of the scant number of colonists from France. There seems to have been less economic impetus for colonization from France than from England. And, after the French crown took over the colonies, there was no religious impetus, for only Catholics were allowed to settle in New France. Control by the Crown forced a traditional hierarchical political organization on the French colonies, and large tracts of land were set aside for privileged investors. There was little in North America to tempt people of modest means.

The first successful French colony was established in Acadia in 1605. A few years later, the intrepid explorer Samuel de Champlain (1567?–1635) navigated the St. Lawrence River and founded Quebec City. French explorers went on to establish Montreal, farther inland on the St. Lawrence (1642), and to explore the Great Lakes and the Mississippi River basin (see Map 14.2).

Such investment as the French crown was able to attract went into profitable trade, mainly in furs, not the difficult business of colonization. Although French men and women of Catholic religious orders sought new converts among the Indians, French trappers and traders ventured into wilderness areas without establishing European-style communities. Quebec remained more of a fur-trading outpost, dependent on supplies from France, than a thriving urban community. By the middle of the seventeenth century, all of New France had only about three thousand European inhabitants.

from investors in London allowed them an unprecedented degree of self-government once the Massachusetts Bay colony was established.

Nevertheless, the colonies in North America were disappointments to England because they generated much less wealth than expected. Shipping timber back to Europe proved too expensive, fur traders found indigenous competition, and although certain colonists profited enormously from the tobacco economy, the mother country did so only moderately. The demand in Europe for tobacco never grew as quickly as the demand for sugar.

For both England and France the major profits and strategic interests in the New World lay to the south, in the Caribbean. The Dutch experience in North America reveals the degree to which North America was of secondary importance, for all colonial powers, to the plantation profits farther south. In 1624 the Dutch founded a trading center, New Amsterdam, at the site of modern New York City. In 1664 they relinquished it to the English in return for recognition of the Dutch claims to sugar-producing Guiana (modern Suriname) in South America. Consequently, by far the largest group of migrants to European-held territories in the Americas were forced migrants: African men and women sold into slavery and transported across the Atlantic. A conservative estimate is that approximately 1,350,000 Africans were transported as slave labor to the New World during the seventeenth century.

The Beginning of the End of Traditional Society

Within Europe, the economic impact of overseas trade was profound. Merchants and investors in a few of Europe's largest cities reaped great profits. Mediterranean trading centers such as Venice and Genoa, once the heart of European trade, fell into decline while Atlantic ports flourished. The population of Amsterdam increased from about 30,000 to 200,000 in the course of the seventeenth century.

All capital cities, however, not just seaports, grew substantially in the seventeenth century. Increasing numbers of government functionaries, courtiers and their hangers-on, and people involved in trade lived and worked in capital cities. These cities also grew from the demand such people generated for services and products. For the first time, cities employed vast numbers of country people. Perhaps as much as one-fifth of the population of England passed through London at one time or another, creating the mobile, volatile community so active in the English civil war and its aftermath.

The economy became more productive and flexible as it expanded, but social stratification

ÆTAT. SUÆ XXXX.

LA MERE MARIE DE L'INCARNATION Premiere Superieure des Ursulines de la nouvelle france decedeé a Quebec en odeur de Saintete le dernier jour d'avril 1672. ageé de 72 ans 6 mois 13 j.ᵉ

Marie de l'Incarnation, Colonial Settler Marie Guyart (1599–1672), as she was known in lay life, was an Ursuline nun who abandoned her own family in France to help found a convent and school for girls in Quebec, Canada. She welcomed both settlers' daughters and girls from native tribes to the school; she also learned several Amerindian languages during her life. *(Thomas Fisher Rare Book Library, University of Toronto)*

increased. Patterns of consumption in cities reflected the economic gulfs between residents. Most people could not afford to buy imported pepper or sugar. Poverty increased in cities, even in vibrant Amsterdam, because they attracted people fleeing rural unemployment. As growing central governments increased their tax burdens on peasants, many rural people were caught in a cycle of debt; they abandoned farming and made their way to cities.

People on the margins of economic life were increasingly vulnerable to both economic forces and state power. Thousands of rural people, particularly those close to thriving urban centers, supplemented their farm income by means of the *putting-out system*, or cottage industry. An entrepreneur loaned, or "put out," raw materials to rural workers, who processed them at home and returned the finished products to the entrepreneur. In the long run, the putting-out system left workers open to exploitation of a new, more modern, sort. A local harvest failure might still endanger them, and so might a foreign war that affected the long-distance trade for their product.

Peasant rebellions recurred throughout the century. In western Europe, they were directed against escalating taxation. Countryfolk were accustomed to defending themselves as communities—against brigands and marauding soldiers, for example. Local gentry and even prosperous peasants sometimes led such revolts, convinced that they represented the legitimate interests of the community. The scale of peasant violence meant that at times thousands of troops had to be diverted from a state's foreign wars; as a matter of routine, soldiers accompanied tax officials to enforce collection all over Europe. Thus, as the ambitions of rulers grew, so did the resistance of ordinary people to the exactions of the state.

SUMMARY

The beginning of the seventeenth century was marked by religious turmoil and by social and political upheaval. By the end of the century, the former had faded as a source of collective anxiety, and the latter was largely resolved. Nascent political configurations in the Low Countries, in the Holy Roman Empire, and on the frontiers of eastern Europe had evolved into new centers of power: the Netherlands, Brandenburg-Prussia, and the Russia of Peter the Great. Most European states had moved from internal division—with independent provinces and aristocrats going their own way—to relative stability. This internal

stability was both cause and consequence of rulers' desire to make war on an ever larger scale. By the end of the century, only those states able to field large armies were competitive on the European stage.

At the beginning of the century, overseas trade and colonization had been the near monopoly of Spain and Portugal; at the century's end, the English, French, and Dutch controlled much of the trade with Asia and were reaping many profits in the Americas. Beneath all these developments lay subtle but significant economic, social, and cultural shifts. One effect of the increased wealth generated by overseas trade and the increased power of governments to tax their subjects was a widening of the gulf between poor and rich. New styles of behavior and patterns of consumption highlighted differences between social classes. Overseas voyages had long-term effects on European attitudes. Along with the intellectual changes that culminated in the development of modern science, these shifts in attitude would have revolutionary consequences for European culture.

NOTES

1. Quoted in D. H. Pennington, *Europe in the Seventeenth Century*, 2d ed. (London: Longman, 1989), p. 508.

SUGGESTED READING

Alpers, Svetlana. *The Art of Describing: Dutch Art in the Seventeenth Century*. 1983. An innovative approach to Dutch art, considering it in its social and broader cultural context.

Aylmer, G. E. *Rebellion or Revolution? England from Civil War to Restoration*. 1987. A useful work that summarizes the important studies on each facet of the revolution; has an extensive bibliography.

Beik, William. *Absolutism and Society in Seventeenth-Century France*. 1984. A case study focusing on a province in southern France but nevertheless an important interpretation of the nature and functioning of the absolutist state; has an extensive bibliography.

Bercé, Yves-Marie. *Revolt and Revolution in Early Modern Europe*. 1987; and *History of Peasant Revolts*. 1990. The first work is a general, comparative survey of revolts and revolutionary movements of all sorts across Europe between 1500 and 1800; the second is a more intensive study of French peasant movements.

Bérenger, Jean. *A History of the Hapsburg Empire, 1273–1700*. 1990. A detailed and nuanced history of all the Habsburg domains and of the Habsburgs' relationship to Europe as a whole.

Boxer, C. R. *The Dutch Seaborne Empire*. 1965. The standard work detailing the development of the Dutch empire.

Collins, James B. *The State in Early Modern France*. 1995. An up-to-date synthesis by one of the leading scholars of French absolutism.

Curtin, Philip D. *The Rise and Fall of the Plantation Complex*. 1990. A good starting place for understanding the Europeans' establishment of plantation agriculture in the New World.

De Vries, Jan. *The Economy of Europe in an Age of Crisis, 1600–1750*. 1976. The single most important work on the development of the European economy in this period, integrating developments within and around Europe with the growth of overseas empires.

Gibson, Wendy. *Women in Seventeenth-Century France*. 1989. A comprehensive study of women's lives.

Goubert, Pierre. *The French Peasantry in the Seventeenth Century*. 1986; and *Louis XIV and Twenty Million Frenchmen*. 1970. Two works that consider political and social history from a broad analytic framework that includes long-term economic, demographic, and cultural data.

Hill, Christopher. *The World Turned Upside Down*. 1972. An exploration of Levellers and other groups of lower-class participants in the English revolution.

Howard, Michael. *War in European History*. 1976. A general study of warfare emphasizing the relationship between war making and state development.

Kirby, David. *Northern Europe in the Early Modern Period, 1492–1772*. 1990; and Oakley, Stewart P. *War and Peace in the Baltic, 1560–1790*. 1992. Two excellent surveys of the Baltic region in the early modern period.

Mack, Phyllis. *Visionary Women: Ecstatic Prophecy in Seventeenth-Century England*. 1992. An inquiry into the beliefs and practices of female prophets, including a discussion of the religious experience of ordinary people.

Pennington, D. H. *Europe in the Seventeenth Century*. 2d ed. 1989; and Bonney, Richard. *The European Dynastic States, 1494–1660*. 1991. Two general histories covering various portions of the century.

Riasanovsky, Nicolas V. *A History of Russia*. 2d ed. 1969. A reliable survey of Russian history from medieval times; has an extensive bibliography of major works available in English.

Ritchie, Robert C. *Captain Kidd and the War Against the Pirates*. 1986. An interesting work on the communities of castoffs and adventurers that grew up in the Caribbean during European expansion and their place in the Atlantic economic and political worlds.

Stone, Lawrence. *The Causes of the English Revolution, 1529–1642*. 1972. A brief and clear introduction.

Vierhaus, Rudolf. *Germany in the Age of Absolutism*. 1988. A concise survey of the development of German states from the end of the Thirty Years' War through the eighteenth century.

Wandycz, Piotr. *The Price of Freedom: A History of East Central Europe from the Middle Ages to the Present*. 1992. A lively survey of the histories of Poland, Hungary, and Bohemia.

Wolf, Eric R. *Europe and the People Without History*. 1982. A survey of European contact with and conquest of peoples after 1400; includes extensive treatments of non-European societies and detailed explanation of the economic and political interests of the Europeans.

CHAPTER 15

A Revolution in World-View

As famous as the confrontation between the religious rebel Martin Luther and Holy Roman Emperor Charles V in 1521 is the confrontation between the astronomer Galileo and the judges of the papal inquisition that ended on June 22, 1633. On that day, Galileo knelt before the seven cardinals who represented the inquisition to renounce his errors and receive his punishment. His "errors" included publishing scientific propositions that disagreed with views accepted by the church—particularly the view that the earth is stationary and does not spin on its axis and orbit the sun. As Galileo left the cardinals' presence, he is supposed to have muttered, "Eppur si muove" ("But it *does* move").

This seems a wonderful moment of historical drama, but we should be suspicious of it because it oversimplifies historical circumstances. The changes that we know as "the Reformation" and "the Scientific Revolution" were far more complex than the actions of a few individuals. And Galileo never made the defiant statement he is credited with.

Moreover, we cannot treat the new scientific views simply as truth overcoming ignorance and error. The history of scientific thought is not merely a history of discovery about the world; it is also a history of explanations of the world. From its beginnings the Scientific Revolution was a broad cultural movement. Copernicus, Galileo, and others contributed important new data to the pool of knowledge, but even more important was their collective contribution to a fundamentally new view of the universe and the place of the earth and human beings in it.

By the end of the seventeenth century, the idea of an infinite but orderly cosmos accessible to human reason had largely replaced the medieval vision of a closed universe centered on earth and suffused with Christian purpose. Religion became an increasingly subordinate ally of science as confidence in an open-ended, experimental approach to knowledge came to be as strongly held as religious conviction. It is because of this larger shift in world-view, not because of particular scientific discoveries, that the seventeenth century may be labeled the era of the scientific *revolution*.

～ *Questions and Ideas to Consider*

- What was the major contribution of Copernicus? Why was it so significant?

- How did most of the scientists support themselves? How did systems of patronage and appointment favor certain groups of people? Consider the experience of Copernicus or Tycho Brahe on the one hand, and that of Maria Sibylla Merian or Maria Winkelman on the other.

- Descartes fashioned a systematic explanation for the operations of nature that replaced the medieval view. What was it? Discuss some of the ways that his contemporaries responded to it. Consider, for example, Pascal, Cavendish, and Locke.

- How did the new science undermine traditional social and political hierarchies, and, in light of this, why did governments tend to support scientific research?

- Why did Hobbes and Locke disagree? How were their theories dependent on the rise of the new science, and how did they come to such different conclusions? Consider the political context of their work.

THE REVOLUTION IN ASTRONOMY

Because the Scientific Revolution was a revolution within science itself as well as a revolution in intellectual life more generally, we must seek its causes within the history of science as well as in the broader historical context. Many of the causes are familiar. They include the intellectual achievements of the Renaissance, the challenges that were posed by the discovery of the New World, the expansion of trade and production, the spread of literacy and access to books, and the increasing power of princes and monarchs.

The scientific origins of the seventeenth-century revolution in thought lie, for the most part, in developments in astronomy. Advances in astronomy spurred dramatic intellectual transformation because of astronomy's role in the explanations of the world and of human life that had been devised by ancient and medieval scientists and philosophers. In the early seventeenth century, fundamental astronomical tenets were successfully challenged. The consequence was the undermining of both the material explanation of the world (physics) and the philosophical explanation of the world (metaphysics) that had stood for centuries.

The Inherited World-View and the Sixteenth-Century Context

Ancient and medieval astronomy accepted the perspective on the universe that unaided human senses support—namely, that the earth is at the center of the universe and the celestial bodies rotate around the earth. The intellectual and psychological journey from the notion of a closed world centered on the earth to an infinitely large universe of undifferentiated matter was an immense process with complex causes.

The regular movements of heavenly bodies and the obvious importance of the sun for life on earth made astronomy a vital undertaking for both scientific and religious purposes in many ancient societies. Astronomers in ancient Greece carefully observed the heavens and learned to calculate and predict the seemingly circular motion of the stars and the sun about the earth. The orbits of a few of the lights in the sky were more difficult to explain, for they seemed to travel both east and west across the sky at various times and with no regularity that could be mathematically understood. These were called *planets*, from a Greek word meaning "wanderer."

We now know that all the planets orbit the sun at different speeds and at different distances from the sun. The relative positions of the planets thus constantly change; sometimes other planets

CHAPTER CHRONOLOGY

1543	Copernicus, *On the Revolution of Heavenly Bodies*
	Vesalius, *On the Fabric of the Human Body*
1576	Construction of Brahe's observatory begins
1591	Galileo's law of falling bodies
1609	Kepler's third law of motion
1610	Galileo, *The Starry Messenger*
1620	Bacon, *Novum Organum*
1628	Harvey, *On the Motion of the Heart*
1632	Galileo, *Dialogue on the Two Chief Systems of the World*
1637	Descartes, *Discourse on Method*
1660	Boyle, *New Experiments Physico-Mechanical*
1668	Cavendish, *Grounds of Natural Philosophy*
1687	Newton, *Principia*

are "ahead" of the earth and sometimes "behind." In the second century A.D. the Greek astronomer Ptolemy attempted to explain the planets' occasional "backward" motion by attributing it to "epicycles"—small circular orbits within the larger orbit. Although Ptolemy's mathematical explanations of the imagined epicycles were extremely complex, neither Ptolemy nor medieval mathematicians and astronomers were ever able fully to account for planetary motion.

Ancient physics, most notably the work of Aristotle (384–322 B.C.), explained the fact that some objects (such as cannonballs) fall to earth but others (stars and planets) seem weightless relative to the earth by presuming that objects are made up of different sorts of matter. Aristotle thought that different kinds of matter had different inherent tendencies and properties. In this view, all earthbound matter falls because it is naturally attracted to the earth.

The universe was thought to be literally a closed world with the stationary earth at the center. Revolving around the earth in circular orbits were the sun, the moon, the stars, and the planets. The motion of all lesser bodies was caused by the rotation of all the stars together in the crystal-like sphere in which they were embedded. In the Christian era, the Aristotelian explanation of the universe was infused with Christian meaning and purpose. The heavens were thought to be made of different, pure matter because they were the abode of the angels. Both earth and the humans who inhabited it were changeable and corruptible, but God had given it, and its human inhabitants, a unique and special place in the universe.

A few ancient astronomers theorized that the earth moved about the sun. Some medieval philosophers also adopted this heliocentric thesis (*helios* is the Greek word for "sun"), but it remained a minority view because it seemed to contradict both common sense and observed data. The sun and stars *appeared* to move around the earth with great regularity. Moreover, how could objects fall to earth if the earth was moving beneath them? Also, astronomers detected no difference in the angles from which observers on earth viewed the stars at different times. Such differences would exist, they thought, if the earth changed position by moving around the sun. It was inconceivable that the stars could be so distant that the earth's movement would produce no measurable change in its position with respect to the stars.

Several conditions of intellectual life in the sixteenth century encouraged new work in astronomy and led to a revision of the earth-centered world-view. The most important was the humanists' recovery of and commentary on ancient texts. Now able to work with new Greek versions of Ptolemy, mathematicians and astronomers discovered that his explanations for the motions of the planets were imperfect and not simply inadequately transmitted, as they had long believed. The discovery of the New World also undermined Ptolemy's authority by disproving many of his geographic assertions.

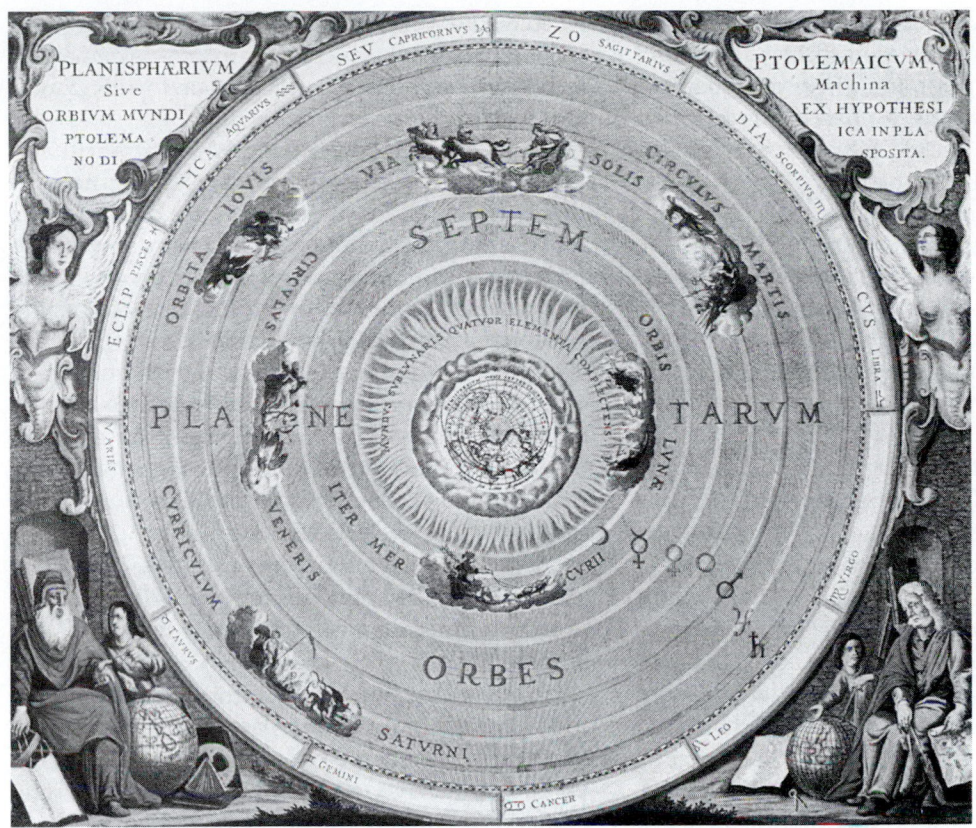

The Traditional Universe In this print from around 1600, heavenly bodies are depicted orbiting the earth in perfectly circular paths. In fact, the ancient astronomer Ptolemy believed that the planets followed complex orbits-within-orbits, known as *epicycles,* moving around the stationary earth. *(Hulton-Getty/Liaison)*

The desire to explain heavenly motions better was still loaded with religious significance in the sixteenth century and was heightened by the immediate need for reform of the Julian calendar (named for Julius Caesar). Ancient observations of the movement of the sun, though remarkably accurate, could not measure the precise length of the solar year. By the sixteenth century, the cumulative error of this calendar had resulted in a change of ten days: The spring equinox fell on March 11 instead of March 21. An accurate and uniform system of dating was necessary for all rulers and their tax collectors and recordkeepers but was the particular project of the church, because the calculation of the date of Easter was at stake.

Impetus for new and better astronomical observations and calculations arose from other features of the intellectual and political landscape as well. Increasingly as the century went on, princely courts became important sources of patronage for and sites of scientific activity. Rulers eager to buttress their own power by linking it symbolically to dominion over nature sponsored investigations of the world, as Ferdinand and Isabella had so successfully done, and displayed the marvels of nature at their courts. Sponsoring scientific inquiry also yielded practical benefits: better mapping of the ruler's domains and better technology for mining, gunnery, and navigation.

Finally, schools of thought fashionable at the time, encouraged by the humanists' critique of Scholastic tradition, hinted at the possibilities of alternative physical and metaphysical systems. One was Paracelsianism, named for the Swiss physician Philippus von Hohenheim (1493–1541), known as Paracelsus. Paracelsus offered an alternative to the theory, put forth by the ancient master, Galen (ca. 131–ca. 201), that the imbalance of bodily "humors" causes illness. He substituted a theory of chemical imbalance.

Neo-Platonism, another school of thought, had a more systematic and far-reaching impact. A revival primarily in Italian humanist circles of certain aspects of Plato's thought, Neo-Platonism emphasized the abstract nature of true knowledge: Things might not be as they seemed. Neo-Platonists prized mathematical investigation because they associated it with abstract truth. This provided a spur to astronomical studies, which, since ancient times, had been primarily concerned with mathematical analysis of heavenly movements (more than with physical explanations for them). Also, like Paracelsianism, Neo-Platonism had a mystical dimension. Neo-Platonists were particularly fascinated by the sun as a symbol of the one divine mind or soul at the heart of all creation.

The Copernican Challenge

Nicolaus Copernicus (1473–1543), the son of a prosperous Polish merchant, pursued wide-ranging university studies in philosophy, law, astronomy, and mathematics—first in Cracow in Poland and then in Bologna and Padua in Italy. In Italy he was exposed to Neo-Platonic ideas. He took a degree in canon law in 1503 and became a cathedral canon in the city of Frauenburg in East Prussia (modern Poland), where he pursued his interests in astronomy while carrying out administrative duties for the cathedral. When the pope asked Copernicus to assist with the reform of the Julian calendar, he replied that reform of the calendar required reform in astronomy. His major work, *On the Revolution of Heavenly Bodies* (1543), was dedi-

cated to the pope in the hopes that it would help with the task of calendar reform—as indeed it did. The Gregorian calendar, issued in 1582, was based on Copernicus's calculations.

Copernicus did not assert that the earth and the other planets orbit the sun. Rather, he suggested that if we pretend this is the case we get a mathematical construct that is very useful for predicting the movements of planets, stars, and the sun. But though he did not claim that his heliocentric system corresponded to reality, we cannot be certain what he believed. He had searched in ancient sources for thinkers who believed the earth did move. Also, if he had not sensed that his work was a revolutionary description of the real world, why would he have waited until 1542, twelve years after finishing it, to send it to be published? For years, other astronomers familiar with his work had urged him to publish. Instead, he was on his deathbed when he first held the book in his hand.

Copernicus's work was immediately useful. The schema made possible a simpler prediction of planetary motion and accounted for most backward motion. But since Copernicus still assumed that the planets traveled in circular orbits, he retained some epicycles to account for the difference between his model and his observations. The Copernican account of planetary motion appealed to other astronomers of the age for both its usefulness and its beauty; as they worked with his calculations, they sought new evidence to support his theory.

But Copernican theory led to a conceptual revolution only gradually, because Copernicus had failed to resolve the physical problems his theory raised. If Copernicus were right, the earth would have to be made of the same stuff as other planets. But if the earth is not made of some special earth-stuff, why do objects "on" earth fall toward it? Also, Copernicus's system explained the motion of the stars as *apparent* movement due to the motion of the earth. This obviated the need for rotating crystalline spheres for the stars, but what about the planets? What made them move?

Copernicus was not as troubled by these questions as we might expect him to have been. Since ancient times, mathematical astronomy—the science of measuring and predicting the movement of heavenly bodies—had been far more important than and had proceeded independently of physical explanations for observed motion. Still, his theories directly contradicted many of the supposed laws of motion. The usefulness of his theories to other astronomers meant that the contradictions between mathematical and physical models for the universe would have to be resolved. Copernicus might be best understood as the last Ptolemaic astronomer, working within inherited questions and with known tools. His work did not constitute a revolution, but it certainly initiated one.

The First Copernican Astronomers

We can see the effects of Copernicus's work on the first generation of astronomers that followed him. His impressive computations rapidly won converts among fellow astronomers. Several particularly gifted astronomers continued to develop the Copernican system. By the second quarter of the seventeenth century, they and many others accepted the heliocentric theory as reality and not just as a useful mathematical fiction. The most important astronomers to build on Copernican assumptions were the Dane Tycho Brahe (1546–1601), the German Johannes Kepler (1571–1630), and the Italian Galileo Galilei (1564–1642).

Like generations of observers before him, Tycho Brahe had been stirred by the majesty of the regular movements of heavenly bodies. After witnessing a partial eclipse of the sun, he abandoned a career in government and became an astronomer. Brahe was the first truly post-Ptolemaic astronomer because he was the first to improve on the data that the ancients and all subsequent astronomers had used. Ironically, *no* theory of planetary motion could have reconciled the data that Copernicus had used: They were simply too inaccurate, based as they were on naked-eye observations and marred by errors of translation and copying, accumulated over centuries.

In 1576 the king of Denmark showered Brahe with properties and pensions enabling him to build an observatory, Uraniborg, on an island near Copenhagen. At Uraniborg, Brahe improved on ancient observations with large and very finely calibrated instruments that permitted precise measurements of celestial movements by the naked eye. His attention to precision and the frequency of his observations produced results that were twice as accurate as any previous data had been.

As a result of his observations, Brahe agreed with Copernicus that the planets rotate around the sun, not the earth. He still could not be persuaded that the earth itself moved, for none of his data supported such a notion. Brahe's lasting and crucial contribution was his astronomical data. They would become obsolete as soon as data from use of the telescope were accumulated about a century later. But in the meantime, they were used by Johannes Kepler to further develop Copernicus's model and arrive at a more accurate heliocentric theory.

Kepler was young enough to be exposed to Copernican ideas from the outset of his training, and he quickly recognized in Brahe's data the means of resolving the problems in Copernican analysis. Though trained in his native Germany, Kepler went to Prague, where Brahe spent the last years of his life after a quarrel with the Danish king, and became something of an apprentice to Brahe. After Brahe's death in 1601, Kepler kept his mentor's records of astronomical observation and continued to work at the imperial court as Rudolf II's court mathematician.

Kepler's contribution to the new astronomy, like that of Copernicus, was fundamentally mathematical. In it, we can see the stamp of the Neo-Platonic conviction about the purity of mathematical explanation. Kepler spent ten years working to apply Brahe's data to the most intricate of celestial motions—the movement of the planet Mars—as a key to explaining all planetary motion. Mars is close to the earth but is farther from the sun than the earth is. This combination produces very puzzling and dramatic variations in the movement of Mars apparent to an earthly observer.

The result of Kepler's work was laws of planetary motion that, in the main, are still in use. He eliminated the need for epicycles (see the caption on page 389) by correctly asserting that planets follow elliptical and not circular orbits and that the speed of a planet in its orbit slows proportionally as the planet's distance from the sun increases. He also showed that the distance of each planet from the sun and the time it takes each planet to orbit the sun are in a constant ratio.

Kepler's work was a breakthrough because it confirmed the Copernican heliocentric hypothesis mathematically. Kepler's laws invited speculation about the properties and motion of heavenly and terrestrial bodies alike; a new physics would be required to explain the novel motions Kepler had posited. Kepler himself, in Neo-Platonic fashion, attributed planetary motion to the sun:

[The sun] is a fountain of light, rich in fruitful heat, most fair, limpid and pure . . . called king of the planets for his motion, heart of the world for his power. . . . Who would hesitate to confer the votes of the celestial motions on him who has been administering all other movements and changes by the benefit of the light which is entirely his possession?[1]

Galileo and the Triumph of Copernicanism

Galileo Galilei holds a pre-eminent position in the development of astronomy for several reasons. He provided compelling new evidence to support Copernican theory, and he contributed to the development of a new physics—or, more precisely, mechanics—that could account for the movement of bodies in new terms. Just as important, his efforts to publicize his findings and his condemnation by the church spurred debate about Copernican ideas in literate society.

Born to a minor Florentine noble family, Galileo studied medicine and mathematics at the University of Pisa and became professor of mathematics there in 1589 at the age of 25. He had already completed important work on mechanics and within three years was given a chair at the University of Padua, where Copernicus had once studied. He continued to work in mechanics during the 1590s but did not publish the results of his experiments until much later. In-

stead, he became famous for the results of his astronomical observations, which he published in 1610. *Sidereus Nuncius* (*The Starry Messenger*) described in lay language the results of his scrutiny of the heavens with a telescope that he had built.

Galileo was the first person that we know who used a telescope to look at the sky. In *The Starry Messenger*, he documented sighting new (previously invisible) stars, another blow to the ancient descriptions of the universe. He noted craters and other "imperfections" on the surface of the moon and the existence of moons orbiting the planet Jupiter. Three years later he published his observations of sunspots in *Letters on Sunspots*. Sunspots are regions of relatively cool gaseous material that appear as dark spots on the sun's surface. For Galileo the sunspots and the craters of the moon constituted proof that the heavens were not perfect and changeless but rather were like the supposedly "corrupt" and changeable earth.

Galileo's principal contribution to mechanics lay in his working out of an early theory of inertia. As a result of a number of experiments with falling bodies (balls rolling on carefully constructed inclines—not free-falling objects that, according to myth, he dropped from the Leaning Tower of Pisa), Galileo ventured a new view of what is "natural" to bodies. Galileo's view was that uniform motion is as natural as a state of rest. According to ancient and medieval theories, all motion needed a cause, and all motion could be explained in terms of purpose. "I hold," Galileo countered, "that there exists nothing in external bodies . . . but size, shape, quantity and motion."[2] In fact, Galileo retained the old assumption that motion was somehow naturally circular. Nevertheless, his theory was a crucial step in explaining motion according to new principles and in fashioning a world-view that accepted a mechanical universe devoid of metaphysical purpose. These theories were published only toward the end of his life, however. His astronomical theories were more influential at the time.

Galileo's books were widely read, and his work became common currency in the scientific societies already flourishing in his lifetime and in courtly circles where science was encouraged. In 1610, Galileo became court mathematician to Cosimo de' Medici, the grand duke of Tuscany (r. 1609–1620), as a result of the fame brought by *The Starry Messenger.* Soon after his arrival, however, rumors that "Galileists" were openly promulgating heliocentrism led to an investigation and, in 1616, the official condemnation of Copernicus's works by the inquisition in Rome. The condemnation allowed room for maneuver. After meeting personally with the pope, Galileo was assured that he could continue to use Copernican theory, but only as a theory.

In 1632, Galileo issued a bold response to that limitation. *Dialogue on the Two Chief Systems of the World* was perhaps the most important single source for the popularization of Copernican theory. The work consists of a debate among three characters on the merits of Copernican theory. Simplicio, the character representing the old world-view, was, as his name suggests, an example of ignorance, not wisdom. In this work, Galileo expressed his supreme confidence—bordering on arrogance—in his own powers and in human power generally to use reason to understand the physical world.

By publishing the *Dialogue,* Galileo defied the papal ban on advocating Copernicanism. In an earlier work, *Letter to the Grand Duchess Christina* (1615), Galileo had also been impolitic, trespassing on the church's authority to interpret the Scriptures. He was tried for heresy and forced to condemn his "errors" in 1633, though Pope Urban VIII (r. 1623–1644) intervened to give him the light sentence of house arrest at his villa in Tuscany. There, Galileo continued his investigations of mechanics until his death in 1642.

THE SCIENTIFIC REVOLUTION GENERALIZED

Galileo's work found such a willing audience because, like Kepler and Brahe, he was not working alone. Dozens of other scientists were attacking old problems from the fresh perspective offered by the breakthroughs in astronomy. Many of these thinkers addressed the metaphysical issues that their investigations inevitably raised.

The Promise of the New Science

Francis Bacon (1561–1626), lord chancellor of England during the reign of James I, wrote a utopian essay extolling the benefits of science for a peaceful society and for human happiness. In *New Atlantis,* published one year after his death, and in *Novum Organum* (1620), Bacon revealed his faith in science by advocating patient, systematic observation and experimentation to accumulate knowledge about the world. He argued that the proper method of investigation "derives axioms from . . . particulars, rising by gradual and unbroken ascent, so that it arrives at the most general axioms of all. This is the true way but untried."[3]

Bacon himself did not undertake experiments, though his widely read works were influential in encouraging both the *empirical method* (relying on observation and experimentation) and *inductive reasoning* (deriving general principles from particular facts). Bacon's writing reflected the fact that an interest in exploring nature's secrets and exercising "dominion over nature" had become an indispensable part of princely rule. Princely courts were the main source of financial support for science and a primary site of scientific work during Bacon's lifetime. Part of the impetus for this development came from the civic humanism of the Italian Renaissance, which had celebrated the state and service to it.

Rulers' newfound enthusiasm for science reflected the growing scope of their resources and ambitions: They wanted technical expertise in armaments, fortification, building projects in general, navigation, and mapmaking. The promise of the New World and the drive for overseas trade and exploration especially encouraged support of science. This took the form of geographical investigation, from mapmaking to navigation, as well as a variety of other empirical studies. For example, information was compiled about the new territory of Virginia, including the first dictionary of any Native American language.

Science could be an ideological as well as a practical tool. Most courts housed collections of marvels, specimens of exotic plants and animals, and mechanical contrivances. These demonstrated the ruler's interest in investigation of the world—his or her status, in other words, as an educated person. These collections and the work of court experts also enhanced the ruler's reputation as a patron and enlivened the image of the ruler's power. Galileo was playing off such expectations when he named some of his newly discovered bodies "Medician Stars."

Exploring the secrets of nature became an honorable activity for scholars and courtiers. By the beginning of the seventeenth century, private salons and academies were another major site of scientific investigation. These, too, had their roots in the humanist culture of Italy, where circles of scholars without university affiliations had formed.

The earliest scientific academy was the Accadèmia Segreta (Secret Academy), founded in Naples in the 1540s. The members pursued experiments together, in order, in the words of one member, "to make a true anatomy of the things and operations of nature itself."[4] For the rest of the sixteenth century and into the seventeenth, academies sprang up in many cities. The most celebrated was the Accadèmia dei Lincei, founded in Rome by an aristocrat in 1603. Its most famous member, Galileo, joined in 1611. The name "Lincei," *lynx*, was chosen because of the legendary keen sight of that animal, an appropriate mascot for "searchers of secrets."

Galileo's notoriety and the importance of his discoveries forced acceptance or rejection of Copernicanism on all communities. Throughout the seventeenth century, the investigation of natural phenomena continued in increasingly sophisticated institutional settings. The flowering of scientific thought in the seventeenth century occurred because of the specific innovations in astronomy and the general spread of scientific investigation that had been achieved by the end of Bacon's life.

New Cosmologies and New Procedures

Philosophers, mathematicians, and educated elites engaged in lively debate and practical investigation throughout Europe in the first half of the seventeenth century, but in France questions about cosmic order were posed at a time of political disorder. The years following the religious wars saw the murder of Henry IV, another regency, and further civil war in the 1620s (see page 344). In this environment, questions about order in the universe and the possibilities of human knowledge took on particular urgency. It is not surprising that it was a Frenchman, René Descartes (1596–1650), who created the first fully articulated alternative world-view.

Descartes's work emerged in dialogue with a circle of other French thinkers. His ideas became more influential among philosophers and lay people than those of some of his equally talented contemporaries because of his thoroughness and rigor, his mathematical expertise, and his graceful, readable French. His system was fully presented in his *Discourse on Method* (1637).

Descartes accepted Galileo's conclusion that the heavens and the earth are made of the same elements. In theorizing about the composition of matter, Descartes drew on ancient atomic models that previously had not been generally accepted. His theory that all matter is made up of identical bits, which he named "corpuscles," is a forerunner of modern atomic and quantum theories. Descartes believed that all the different appearances and behaviors of matter can be explained solely by the size, shape, and motion of these "corpuscles." Descartes's was an extremely mechanistic explanation of the universe. It permitted new, more specific observations and hypotheses and greater understanding of inertia. For example, because he reimagined the universe as being filled with "corpuscles" free to move in any direction, "natural" motion no longer seemed either circular (Galileo's idea) or toward the center of the earth (Aristotle's idea). The new understanding of motion would be crucial to Isaac Newton's formulations later in the century.

A Collection of Naturalia Displays of exotica, such as these specimens in Naples, symbolized the ruler's authority by suggesting his or her power over nature. *(From Ferrante Imperato,* Dell' Historia Naturale *[Naples, 1599]. By permission of the Houghton Library, Harvard University)*

The collapse of the old explanations about the world made Descartes and other investigators doubt not only what they knew but also their capacity to know anything at all. Their physical senses—which denied that the earth moved, for example—had been proved untrustworthy. Descartes's solution was to re-envision the human rational capacity, the mind, as completely distinct from the world—that is, as distinct from the human body—and the betraying sense data it offers. In a leap of faith, Descartes presumed that he could count on the fact that God would not have given humans a mind if that mind were to betray them. For Descartes, God became the guarantor of human reasoning capacity, and humans, in Descartes's view, were distinguished by that capacity. This is the significance of his famous claim "I think, therefore I am."

Descartes thus achieved a resolution of the terrifying doubt about the world by exalting the role of the human knower. The Cartesian universe was one of mechanical motion, not purpose or mystical meaning, and the Cartesian human being was pre-eminently a mind that could apprehend that universe. The term *Cartesian dualism* came to signify Descartes's notion that the material world of bodies and things is quite distinct from the mind of the human observer.

Descartes's ambitious view of human reason had important implications. One was the emphasis on *deductive reasoning* (a process of reasoning in which the conclusion follows necessarily from the stated premises), which naturally followed from his rejection of sense data. In actuality, Descartes did rely on sense data; he did experiments. But philosophically he emphasized logical sense above observed information. In the short run, Descartes's embrace of absolute certainty proved very useful to the advancement of knowledge because it gave natural philosophers the confidence to speculate despite their enormous uncertainty about specific problems.

Descartes's vision of the enhanced position of the individual knower, and of the power of the knower's reason, was also attractive to educated lay people. Elites used science to affirm their status in the world, which could now be expressed in terms of intellectual power and power over nature, rather than only as political power. Descartes was careful not to advocate the "madness" of applying reason to changing the state. The state alone had made humans civilized, he maintained; and although he and other thinkers had to rebuild knowledge of the universe from its foundations, he believed it was "unreasonable for an individual to conceive the plan of reforming a state by changing everything from the foundations."[5]

The notion of detached rationality appeared in other people's work around this time. Renaissance painters, for example, utilized the principles of linear perspective to present views of the world as detached still life. Michel de Montaigne (1533–1592) was also exploring a similar detachment (see page 352). Descartes's was the most radical detachment of all, for he claimed objectivity. Though much of Cartesian physics would be surpassed by Newton at the end of the century, Descartes's assumption about the objectivity of the observer would become an enduring part of scientific practice. The sense of detachment from the world also fostered a belief in humans' ability to control nature. In our own time, we have become aware of the limits of our ability to control nature, as well as the arbitrariness of Descartes's distinction between mind and body. In Descartes's day, the most radical aspect of his thought was the reduction of God from being an active presence in the world to serving as the guarantor of knowledge. Later generations of scientists would be fearful of Descartes's system because it seemed to encourage "atheism." In fact, a profound faith in God was necessary for Descartes's creativity in imagining his new world system—but the system did work without God. Although Descartes would have been surprised and offended by charges of atheism, he knew his work would antagonize the Catholic church. He moved to the Netherlands to study in 1628, and his *Discourse* was first published there.

A contemporary of Descartes, Blaise Pascal (1623–1662), challenged Descartes's confident rationalism by drawing attention to the limits of scientific knowledge. Son of a royal official, Pascal was one of the most brilliant minds of his generation. A mathematician like Descartes, he stressed the importance of mathematical representations of phenomena, built one of the first calculating machines, and invented probability theory. He also carried out experiments to investigate air pressure, the behavior of liquids, and the existence of vacuums.

Pascal's career alternated between periods of intense scientific work and religious retreat. Today he is best known for his writings on the human soul and psyche. His *Pensées* (*Thoughts*, 1669) consists of the published fragments of his defense of Christian faith, which remained unfinished at the time of his early death. Pascal's appeal for generations after him may lie in his assumption that matters of faith and feeling must also be open to investigation. His most famous statement, "The heart has its reasons which the reason knows not," can be read as a statement of the limits of the Cartesian world-view.

The new science had adherents and practitioners throughout Europe by 1650. Dutch scientists in the commercial milieu of the Netherlands, for example, had the freedom to pursue practical and experimental interests. The Dutch investigator Christiaan Huygens (1629–1695) worked on a great variety of problems, including air pressure and optics. He invented and patented the pendulum clock in 1657, the first device accurately to measure small units of time, essential for a variety of measurements.

In England, on the other hand, science was deeply informed by religion and politics because of the English civil war. In the 1640s natural philosophers with Puritan leanings were encouraged in their investigations by dreams that science, of the practical Baconian sort, could be used to bring about the perfection of life on earth and accelerate the end of history: the reign of the saints preceding the Second Coming of Christ. The best-known member of this group was Robert Boyle (1627–1691).

Boyle and his colleagues initially attacked the university system, still under the sway of Aristotelianism, and proposed widespread reform of education. But as the English revolution proceeded, they were forced to moderate many of their positions. Radical groups such as the Levellers believed that each person was capable of divine knowledge without the coercive hierarchy of officials of church and state. In response, Boyle and his colleagues worked to articulate a theoretical position that combined the orderliness of mechanism, a continued divine presence in the world, and a Baconian emphasis on scientific progress. This was attractive to the educated elite of the day because it offered the certainties of science without invalidating all of the authoritarian aspects of the old Christian world-view.

Boyle and his colleagues' most creative contribution was their refinement of experimental philosophy and practice. In 1660, Boyle published *New Experiments Physico-Mechanical*, describing the results of his experiments with an air pump he had designed and laying out general rules for experimental procedure. The work was significant for its nominal results (demonstrating that a vacuum could exist). The experiment is also interesting because Boyle's defense of the results did not meet modern standards of scientific rigor. When a Cambridge scholar criticized one of Boyle's interpretations of his experiments, Boyle replied that he could not understand his

critic's objections, "the experiment having been tried both before our whole society [the Royal Society of London], and very critically, by its royal founder, his majesty himself."[6] Rather than debate differing interpretations, Boyle chose to fall back on the authority and prestige of the participants themselves. In English science in the mid-seventeenth century, the various aspects of the modern scientific profession—the agreement on principles, the acceptance of experimental procedures, and the authority of practitioners—were all being worked out simultaneously.

The Newtonian Synthesis: The Copernican Revolution Completed

It was the Englishman Isaac Newton (1642–1724) who completed the explanation of motion in the heavens and on earth that Copernicus's work had initiated and that Kepler, Galileo, and others had sought. In Newton's career, we can see how different the climate for science was by the second half of the seventeenth century. When Newton entered Cambridge University as a student in 1661, Copernicanism was studied, the benefits of scientific investigation were debated, and much attention was focused on the problems of Descartes's explanations of matter.

Like all the natural philosophers before him, Newton was as concerned by questions of metaphysics as by physics. In the 1680s, he devoted himself primarily to the study of church history, theology, and alchemy. As a student at Cambridge he was strongly influenced by the work of a group of Neo-Platonists who were critical of Cartesian dualism, which posited God as a cause of all matter and motion but removed God as an explanation for the behavior of matter. As Newton says in some of his early writing while a student, "However we cast about we find almost no other reason for atheism than this [Cartesian] notion of bodies having . . . a complete, absolute and independent reality."[7] Like all earlier natural philosophers, Newton had concerns that were both religious and scientific; he, too, sought to harmonize science with a securely Christian world-view following the "excesses" of the English revolution.

Newton combined his scientific skepticism and his religious certainty to posit the existence of gravity—a mysterious force that accounts for the movement of heavenly bodies. Others had speculated about the existence of gravity, but Newton's extraordinary contribution was the mathematical computation of the laws of gravity and planetary motion, which he combined with a fully developed concept of inertia. The concept of inertia, as it had been elaborated by Galileo, Descartes, and others were suggested the need for the concept of gravity. Otherwise, if a planet was "pushed" (say, in Kepler's view, by the "motive force" of the sun), it would continue along that course forever unless "pulled back" by something else.

In 1687, Newton published *Philosophiae Naturalis Principia Mathematica* (*Mathematical Principles of Natural Philosophy*). In this mathematical treatise—so intricate that it was inaccessible to lay people, even those able to read Latin—Newton laid out his laws of motion and expressed them as mathematical theorems that could be used to test future observations. Then he demonstrated that these laws also apply to the solar system, confirming the data already gathered about the planets. His supreme achievement was his law of gravitation, with which he predicted the discovery of an as-yet-unseen planet. This law states that every body, indeed every bit of matter in the universe, exerts over every other body an attractive force proportional to the product of their masses and inversely proportional to the square of the distance between them. Newton not only accounted for motion but united heaven and earth with a single explanatory scheme and created a convincing picture of an orderly nature.

Newton did not claim that his theorems resolved all the questions about motion and matter. He did not know what gravity actually is, and we still do not know today. Yet Newton's laws of motion still adequately account for most problems of motion. The fact that so fundamental a principle as gravity remains unexplained in no way diminishes Newton's achievement but is clear evidence about the nature of scientific understanding: Science provides explanatory schemas that account for many—but not all—observed phenomena. When a scientific explanation ceases to account satisfactorily for enough data, it collapses. No schema explains everything, and each schema contains open doorways that lead to further discovery and blind alleys that lead to mistaken impressions. Newton, for example, also studied alchemy during his most productive years. He assumed that the spiritual forces that somehow accounted for gravity could be harnessed to change metals into gold.

Other Branches of Science

Innovations in astronomy that led to the new mechanistic view of the behavior of matter did not automatically spill over to other branches of science. Developments in astronomy were very specific to that field. Other branches of science followed their own paths, though all were strongly influenced by the mechanistic world-view.

In chemistry, the mechanistic assumption that all matter was composed of small, equivalent parts was crucial to understanding the properties and behavior of compounds (combinations of elements). But knowledge of these small units of matter was not yet detailed enough to be of much use in advancing chemistry conceptually. Nevertheless, the flawed conceptual schema did not hold back all discovery and development. Lack of understanding of gases and the specific elements that compose them did not prevent the development and improvement of gunpowder, for example. Indeed, unlike the innovations in astronomy, conceptual innovation in chemistry and biology owed a great deal to the results of experiment and the slow accumulation of data.

A conceptual leap forward was made in biology in the sixteenth and seventeenth centuries, however. Because biological knowledge was mostly a byproduct of the practice of medicine, biological studies had been and remained very practical and experimental. But the discovery of *On Anatomical Procedures,* a treatise by the ancient master Galen, encouraged dissection and other practical research. Andreas Vesalius (1514–1564), in particular, made important advances by heed-ing Galen's exhortation to conduct anatomical research. Born in Brussels, Vesalius studied at the nearby University of Louvain in Belgium and then at Padua, where he was appointed professor of surgery. He ended his career as physician to Emperor Charles V and his son, Philip II of Spain. In his teaching at Padua he embodied newly discovered Galenic precepts by doing dissections himself rather than leaving the work to technicians. In 1543 he published versions of his lectures as an illustrated compendium of anatomy, *On the Fabric of the Human Body*. His dissections of human corpses, revealed in this work, demonstrated a number of errors in Galen's knowledge of human anatomy, much of which had been derived from dissection of animals. Neither Vesalius nor his immediate successors, however, questioned overall Galenic theory about the functioning of the human body, any more than Copernicus had utterly rejected Aristotelian physics.

The slow movement from new observation to changed explanation is clearly illustrated in the career of the Englishman William Harvey (1578–1657). Like Vesalius, Harvey was educated first in his own land and then at Padua, where he benefited from the tradition of anatomical research. Returning to England, Harvey became a practicing physician in London and at the courts of James I and Charles I.

Harvey postulated the circulation of the blood—postulated rather than discovered because, owing to the technology of the day, he could not observe the tiny capillaries where arterial blood flows into the veins. His vivisectional experiments on animals revealed the actual functioning of heart and lungs; from there he reasoned that circulation must occur. He carefully described his experiments and his conclusions in *On the Motion of the Heart* (1628).

Harvey's work challenged Galenic anatomy and, like Copernicus's discoveries, created new burdens of explanation. According to Galenic theory, the heart and the lungs helped each other to function. The heart sent nourishment to the lungs through the pulmonary artery, and the lungs provided raw material for the "vital spirit," which the heart gave to blood to produce and sustain life. One chamber of the heart was supposedly reserved for the cleansing of waste products from venous blood—thought to be entirely separate from the "nourishing" blood pumped out by the heart.

From his observations, Harvey came to think of the heart in terms consonant with the new mechanistic notions about nature: as a pump to circulate the blood. But Harvey did not leap to a new conceptualization of the body's function. Rather, he adjusted but did not abandon Galenic theories, for example, concerning how "vital spirit" was made. The lungs had been thought to "ventilate" the heart. In light of his discovery of the pulmonary transit (that all of the blood is pumped through the lungs and back through the heart), Harvey suggested that the lungs help the blood to concoct the "vital spirit." Only in this context could the heart be thought of as a machine, circulating this life-giving material.

Harvey's explanation of bodily functions thus did not constitute a rupture with Galenic tradition. But by the end of his life, Harvey's adjustments of Galenic theory were suggesting new conceptual possibilities. His work inspired additional research in physiology, chemistry, and physics. Robert Boyle's efforts to understand vacuums can be traced in part to questions Harvey raised about the function of the lungs and the properties of air.

SCIENCE AND SOCIETY

Scientists wrestled with questions about God, human ability, and the possibilities of understanding the world every bit as intensely as they attempted to find new explanations for the behavior of matter and the motion of the heavens. Eventually, the implications of the new scientific posture would affect thought and behavior throughout society. Once people no longer thought of the universe in hierarchical terms, it became easier to question the hierarchical organization of society. Once people questioned the authority of traditional knowledge about the universe, the way was clear for them to begin questioning traditional views of the state and social order.

Such profound changes of perspective happened gradually. In the short term, Louis XIV and other rulers welcomed the new science for its practical value, and the practice of science remained wedded to religion. The advances in science would eventually lead to revolutionary cultural change, but until the end of the seventeenth century traditional institutions and ideologies circumscribed this change.

The Rise of Scientific Professionalism

Institutions both old and new supported the new science developing in the sixteenth and seventeenth centuries. Universities were the setting for many scientific breakthroughs, but courts continued to serve as patrons of scientific activity. The development of the Accadèmia dei Lincei, to which Galileo belonged, and other academies was a step toward modern professional societies of scholars, although these new organizations also depended on patronage.

Royally sponsored scientific societies were founded in both England and France in the third quarter of the seventeenth century. The Royal Society of London, inaugurated in 1660, received royal recognition but no money and remained an informal institution sponsoring amateur scientific interests as well as specialized independent research. The Académie Royale des Sciences in France, established in 1666 by Jean-Baptiste Colbert, Louis XIV's minister of finance, sponsored research and supported chosen scientists with pensions. These associations were extensions to science of traditional kinds of royal recognition and patronage. Thus, the French Académie was well funded but tightly controlled by the government of Louis XIV, while the Royal Society of London received little of Charles II's precious resources or his scarce political capital.

An important role of academies and patrons was to support the publication of scientific work. The Accadèmia dei Lincei published two of Galileo's best-known works. The Royal Society of London published its fellows' work in *Philo-*

sophical Transactions of the Royal Society, beginning in 1665.

The practice of seventeenth-century science took place in so many diverse institutions—academies, universities, royal courts—that neither *science* nor *scientist* was rigorously defined. Science as a discipline was not yet detached from broad metaphysical questions. Boyle, Newton, Pascal, and Descartes all concerned themselves with questions of religion, and all thought of themselves not as scientists but, like their medieval forebears, as natural philosophers. Natural philosophers belonged to the elite who met in aristocratic salons to discuss literature, politics, and science with equal ease and interest. Still, the narrowing of the practice of science to a tightly defined, truly professional community was becoming evident. Robert Boyle and his fellow advocates of experimentalism, for example, claimed that their procedures alone constituted true science.

The importance of court life and patronage to the new science had at first enabled women to be actively involved. Women ran important salons in France, aristocratic women everywhere were important sources of patronage for scientists, and women themselves were scientists, combining, as did men, science with other pursuits.

Noblewomen and daughters of gentry families had access to education in their homes, and a number of such women were active scientists—astronomers, mathematicians, and botanists. The astronomer Maria Cunitz (1610–1664), from Silesia (a Habsburg-controlled province, now in modern Poland), learned six languages with the support and encouragement of her father, a medical doctor. Later, she published a useful simplification of some of Kepler's mathematical calculations. Women from artisanal families might also receive useful training at home. Such was the case of the German entomologist Maria Sibylla Merian (1647–1717). Merian learned the techniques of illustration in the workshop of her father, an artist in Frankfurt. Later, she used her artistic training and her refined powers of observation to study and record the lives of insects and plants. Merian's career typifies many women's scientific careers in this period because it began within the artisanal tradition. She emerges as an extraordinary figure because her work was celebrated during her life and because of her ability to exit the tight confines of women's roles and follow an adventurous pursuit of science. In the 1670s she was an artist of some renown, but she was also working, raising children, and keeping house in a pattern usual to women of the artisan class. In 1692, however, she left her husband, taking refuge with a radical Protestant group that defended her right to divorce on the grounds that her husband was a nonbeliever. In 1699 she and her daughter, Dorothea, set off for the tropical Dutch colony of Suriname to collect and study the insects there. They traveled unaccompanied by a man and were not sponsored by any government or religious institution. After they returned, Merian's great work, *Metamorphosis of the Insects of Suriname*, established her as an important member of the scientific community of Amsterdam. Merian's life serves as an example of an extraordinary human being who managed to work despite tremendous cultural barriers; it also serves as a reminder of the many women who helped to advance the process of science by working at family-based, commercially motivated, artisanal crafts.

Margaret Cavendish (1623–1673) was a woman scientist from a very different tradition. Cavendish was the duchess of Newcastle. She worked at science in much the same way that many male English scientists did: from the comfort of an independent financial situation, and for the purpose of fulfilling her own intellectual desires. Cavendish wrote several major philosophical works, including *Grounds of Natural Philosophy* (1668). She was a Cartesian but was influenced by Neo-Platonism. She disagreed with Cartesian dualism in its strict separation of matter and mind, but she criticized English philosophers with whom she agreed on some matters because, like Descartes, she distrusted sense knowledge as a guide to philosophy. In many ways, she was disputing the contemporary belief that human knowledge of nature would lead to human control of nature—even control over natural causes and effects. Her arguments had con-

Astronomers Elisabetha and Johannes Hevelius were one of many collaborating couples among the scientists of the seventeenth century. Women were usually denied pensions and support for their research when they worked alone, however. *(From Hevelius,* Machinae coelestis. *By permission of the Houghton Library, Harvard University)*

siderable influence, but despite her accomplishments, she was barred from membership in the Royal Society of London.

Women were regularly accepted in Italian academies but they were excluded from formal membership in the academies in London and Paris. They could use the academies' facilities, however, and received prizes from the societies for their work. One reason for the exclusion of women was the limited amount of patronage available: Coveted positions automatically went to men.

Moreover, the hierarchical distinction signified by gender made the exclusion of women a ready way to define the academies as special and privileged.

Cavendish was aware of the degree to which her participation in scientific life depended on informal networks and her personal wealth and status. (See the box "Margaret Cavendish Challenges Male Scientists.") Women scientists from more modest backgrounds, without Cavendish's resources, had to fight for the right to employment as public institutions gained importance as settings for the pursuit of science. The German astronomer Maria Winkelman (1670–1720), for example, tried to succeed her late husband in an official position at the Berlin Academy of Sciences in 1710. She had received advanced training and worked as an astronomer as a young woman. Her marriage to a leading astronomer was beneficial to them both, and she was her husband's unofficial partner during his tenure as astronomer to the academy. She attained a wide reputation for her abilities and discoveries (she found a new comet, for example, in 1702), and when he died she sought to continue her work to support her four children. The academy refused to extend an official position to Winkelman, despite her experience and accomplishments. The secretary of the academy stated:

That she be kept on in an official capacity to work on the calendar or to continue with observations simply will not do. Already during her husband's lifetime the society was burdened with ridicule because its calendar was prepared by a woman. If she were now to be kept on in such a capacity, mouths would gape even wider.[8]

Winkelman worked in private observatories, and was able to return to the Berlin Academy only as the unofficial assistant to her son, whose training she herself had supervised.

The New Science and the Needs of the State

The new natural philosophy had implications for traditional notions about the state. The new world-view that all matter was alike and followed discernible natural laws gradually undermined political systems resting on a belief in the inherent inequality of persons and royal prerogative. By the middle of the eighteenth century, a fully formed alternative political philosophy would argue for more "rational" government in keeping with the rational, natural order of things. But change came slowly, and while it was coming, the state of Louis XIV and other rulers found much to admire and make use of in the new science.

Many new inventions were very attractive to governments and members of ruling elites. Experiments with vacuum pumps had important applications in the mining industry. The astronomy professor at Gresham College in London was required to teach navigation, and other professors at Gresham worked to improve the design of ships.

Governments also sponsored purely scientific research. Members of the elite, such as Colbert in France, recognized the opportunity not only for practical advances but also for prestige and, most important, confirmation of the orderliness of nature. It is hard to overestimate the psychological impact and intellectual power of this fundamental tenet of the new science—namely, that nature is an inanimate machine that reflects God's design not through its purposes but simply by its orderliness. Human beings could now hope to dominate nature in ways not possible before. Dominion, order, control—these were the goals of ambitious and powerful rulers in the seventeenth century.

Thus, in the short run, the new science supported a vision of order that was very pleasing to a monarch of absolutist pretensions. Louis XIV, among others, energetically sponsored scientific investigation by the Académie des Sciences and reaped the benefits in improved ships, increasingly skillful military engineers, and new industrial products.

Religion and the New Science

Because of Galileo's condemnation, the Catholic church is often seen as an opponent of scientific thought, and science and religion are often seen

Margaret Cavendish Challenges Male Scientists

In her preface to her earliest scientific work, **The Philosophical and Physical Opinions** *(1655), Cavendish addresses scholars at Oxford and Cambridge Universities with deceptive humility. She implies that the seeming limitations of women's abilities are in fact the consequence of their exclusion from education and from participation in affairs.*

Most Famously Learned,

I here present to you this philosophical work, not that I can hope wise school-men and industrious laborious students should value it for any worth, but to receive it without scorn, for the good encouragement of our sex, lest in time we should grow irrational as idiots, by the dejectedness of our spirits, through the careless neglects and despisements of the masculine sex to the female, thinking it impossible we should have either learning or understanding, wit or judgment, as if we had not rational souls as well as men, and we out of a custom of dejectedness think so too, which makes us quit all industry towards profitable knowledge, being imployed only in low and petty imployments which take away not only our abilities towards arts but higher capacities in speculations, so that we are become like worms, that only live in the dull earth of ignorance, winding ourselves sometimes out by the help of some refreshing rain of good education, which seldom is given us, for we are kept like birds in cages, to hop up and down in our houses . . . ; thus by an opinion, which I hope is but an erroneous one in men, we are shut out of all power and authority by reason we are never employed either in civil or martial affairs, our counsels are despised and laughed at and the best of our actions are trodden down with scorn, by the over-weening conceit men have of themselves and through a despisement of us.

Source: Moira Ferguson, ed., *First Feminists: British Women Writers, 1578–1799* (Bloomington and New York: Indiana University Press and The Feminist Press, 1985), pp. 85–86.

as antagonists. But this view is an oversimplification. Indeed, scientific thought remained closely tied to religion during the seventeenth century. Both religion and the Catholic church as an institution were involved in scientific advancement from the time of Copernicus. Copernicus himself was a cleric, as were many philosophers and scientists active in the early seventeenth century. This is not surprising, for most research in the sciences to this point had occurred within universities sponsored and staffed by members of religious orders.

Moreover, religious and metaphysical concerns were central to the work of virtually every scientist. The entire Cartesian edifice of reasoning about the world, for example, was founded on Descartes's certainty about God. God's gift of the capacity to reason was the only certainty that Descartes claimed. Copernicus, Kepler, and other investigators perceived God's purpose in the mathematical regularity of nature. In addition, traditional Christian views of the operations and purpose of the universe were evident in the work of all scientists from Copernicus to Newton—from Galileo's acceptance of perfect circular motion to Newton's theological writings.

Yet adjusting to a new view of nature in which God was less immanently and obviously represented was not particularly easy for the Catholic church. First of all, the church itself mirrored the hierarchy of the old view of the universe in its own hierarchy of believers, priests, bishops, popes, and saints. Moreover, in its sponsorship of institutions of higher learning, the church was the repository of the old view. In scientific disagreements spawned by the new theories, the church was both theoretically and literally invested in the old view.

Nevertheless, the church's condemnation of Galileo shocked many clerics, including a number of whom were scientists themselves, as well as three of Galileo's judges, who voted for leniency at his trial. Over the centuries, several apparent conflicts between scientific arguments and sacred teachings had been resolved with great intelligence and flexibility. Many scientists who were also clerics continued to study and teach the new science when they could; for example, Copernicanism was taught by Catholic missionaries abroad. (See the box "Encounters with the West: Jesuits and Astronomy in China.")

The rigid response of the church hierarchy to Galileo's challenge must be seen in the context of the Protestant Reformation, which, in the minds of the pope and others, had demonstrated the need for a firm response to any challenge. The condemnation of Galileo had a chilling effect on scientific investigators in most Catholic regions of Europe. They could and did continue their research, but many could publish results only by smuggling manuscripts to Protestant lands. Descartes, as we have seen, left France for the more tolerant Netherlands; he also sojourned at the Swedish court at the invitation of Queen Christina. After the middle of the seventeenth century, many of the most important empirical and theoretical innovations in science occurred in Protestant regions.

At first, Protestant leaders were not receptive to Copernican ideas because they defied scriptural authority. Protestant thinkers were also as troubled as Catholics by the metaphysical problems the new theories seemed to raise. In 1611, one year after the publication of Galileo's *Starry Messenger*, the English poet John Donne (1573–1631) reflected in "An Anatomie of the World" on the confusion about human capacities and social relationships that Copernican astronomy had caused:

[The] new Philosophy calls all in doubt,
The Element of fire is quite put out;
The Sun is lost, and th'earth, and no man's wit
Can well direct him where to look for it.[9]

The dilemma of accounting in religious terms for the ideas of Copernicus and Descartes became more urgent for Protestants as the ideas acquired an anti-Catholic status after the trial of Galileo in 1633. Religious, political, and scientific viewpoints became inextricably mixed. Religion did not merely remain in the scientists' panoply of explanations; it remained a fundamental building block of scientific thought, just as it remained central to most scientists' lives.

The Mechanistic World Order at the End of the Seventeenth Century

By the middle of the seventeenth century, political theory was beginning to show the impact of the mechanistic world-view. Political philosophers no longer viewed the world and human society as an organic whole in which each part was distinguished in nature and function from the rest. Thomas Hobbes, John Locke, and others reimagined the bonds that link citizens to each other and to their rulers.

Because of the political turmoil in England, Thomas Hobbes (1588–1679) spent much of his productive life on the Continent. After the beginnings of the parliamentary rebellion, he joined a group of royalist émigrés in France. He met Galileo and lived for extended periods in Paris, in contact with the circle of French thinkers that included Descartes.

Hobbes is best known today for *Leviathan* (1651), his treatise on political philosophy. Hobbes held a mostly Cartesian view of nature as composed of "self-motivated," atomlike structures. He understood people as no less mechanistic than the rest of nature. For him, people were made up of appetites of various sorts. The ideal state, concluded Hobbes, is one in which a strong sovereign controls the disorder that inevitably arises from the clash of desires. Unlike the medieval philosophers, Hobbes did not draw analogies between

~ ENCOUNTERS WITH THE WEST ~

Jesuits and Astronomy in China

The Italian Matteo Ricci (1552–1610) was one of the first of a series of Jesuit missionaries to establish himself at the imperial court in China. He was appreciative as well as critical of Chinese science, but his remarks are more interesting to us because they reveal that Ricci himself regarded expertise in mathematics and astronomy as worthy of esteem. Ricci's own scientific knowledge was crucial to his acceptance at court; Jesuit missionaries who followed Ricci in the seventeenth century found their scientific expertise equally valued, and several openly taught Copernican theory there.

The Chinese have not only made considerable progress in moral philosophy but in astronomy and in many branches of mathematics as well. At one time they were quite proficient in arithmetic and geometry, but in the study and teaching of these branches of learning they labored with more or less confusion. They divide the heavens into constellations in a manner somewhat different from that which we employ. Their count of the stars outnumbers the calculations of our astronomers by fully four hundred, because they include in it many of the fainter stars which are not always visible. And yet with all this, the Chinese astronomers take no pains whatever to reduce the phenomena of celestial bodies to the discipline of mathematics. Much of their time is spent in determining the moment of eclipses and the mass of the planets and the stars, but here, too, their deductions are spoiled by innumerable errors. Finally they center their whole attention on that phase of astronomy which our scientists term astrology, which may be accounted for the fact that they believe that everything happening on this terrestrial globe of ours depends upon the stars.

Some knowledge of the science of mathematics was given to the Chinese by the Saracens [Mongols], who penetrated into their country from the West, but very little of this knowledge was based upon definite mathematical proofs. What the Saracens left them, for the most part, consisted of certain tables of rules by which the Chinese regulated their calendar and to which they reduced their calculations of planets and the movements of the heavenly bodies in general. The founder of the family which at present regulates the study of astrology prohibited anyone from indulging in the study of this science unless he were chosen for it by hereditary right. The prohibition was founded upon fear, lest he who should acquire a knowledge of the stars might become capable of disrupting the order of the empire and seek an opportunity to do so.

Source: Louis J. Gallagher, trans., *China in the Sixteenth Century: The Journals of Matthew Ricci: 1583–1610* (New York: Random House, 1953), pp. 30–31. Copyright 1953 by Louis J. Gallagher. Reprinted by permission of Random House, Inc.

---

the state and the human body (the king as head, judges and magistrates as arms, and so forth). Instead, Hobbes compared the state to a machine that "ran" by means of laws and was kept in good working order by a skilled technician—the ruler.

Hobbes's pessimism about human behavior and his insistence on the need for order imposed

from above reflected his concern for order in the wake of political turmoil. This concern was one reason he was welcomed into the community of French philosophers, who were naturally comfortable with royalty as a guarantor of order. But Hobbes's work, like theirs, was a radical departure because it envisioned citizens as potentially

Science Gains an Audience The greatest scientific popularizer of the period was Bernard de Fontenelle. This illustration comes from his *Conversation on the Plurality of Worlds* (1686), and it reveals the audience for which the work was intended. A gentleman, sitting with a lady in a formal garden, gestures to a depiction of the solar system as it was then understood; the lady is presumed to understand and to be interested in the information. *(By permission of Houghton Library, Harvard University)*

equal and constrained neither by morality nor by natural obedience to authority.

Another Englishman, John Locke (1632–1704), offered an entirely different vision of social order. Locke's major works, *Essay on Human Understanding* (1690) and *Two Treatises on Government* (1690), combined the experimentalism of Robert Boyle, the systematizing rationality of Descartes, and other strands of the new scientific thought. Locke's treatises on government reflected his empiricism as well as his particular experiences as a member of elite circles in the aftermath of the English revolution. A trained physician, he served as personal physician and general political assistant to Anthony Ashley Cooper (1621–1683), Lord Shaftsbury, one of the members of Parliament most opposed to Charles II's pretensions to absolutist government. When James II acceded to the throne in 1685, Locke remained in the Netherlands, where he had fled to avoid prosecution for treason. He became an adviser to William of Orange and returned to England with William and Mary in 1688. Not surprisingly, Locke's view of the principles of good government reflected the pro-parliamentary stance of his political milieu.

Unlike Hobbes, Locke argued that people are capable of restraint and mutual respect in their pursuit of self-interest. The state arises from a contract that individuals freely enter into to protect themselves, their property, and their happiness from possible aggression by others. They can invest the executive and legislative authority to carry out this protection in monarchy or any other governing institution, though Locke believed the English Parliament was the best available model. Because sovereignty resides with the people who enter into the contract, rebellion against abuse of power is justified. Thus, Locke freed people from the arbitrary bonds of authority to the state.

Locke's status as a member of the elite of his society is apparent in his emphasis on private property, which he considered a fundamental human right. (See the box "Locke's View of the Purpose of Government.") Indeed, there was no place in his political vision for serious disagreement about the nature of property. Locke even found a justification for slavery. He also did not consider women to be political beings in the same way as men. The family, he felt, was a separate domain from the state, not bound by the same contractual obligations.

Locke's dismissal of women from the realm of politics and of questions of power and justice from the family was not an accident. The ability of Locke and many other seventeenth-century thinkers to imagine a new physical or political order was constrained by the prevailing view of gender as a "natural" principle of order and hierarchy. Gender distinctions are in the main socially ascribed roles that are easily misinterpreted as "natural" differences between women and men. Although Margaret Cavendish (see the box on page 403) and other women disputed the validity of such distinctions, men frequently used them. Locke's use of gender as an arbitrary organizing principle gave his political vision a

claim to being "natural." The use of gender-specific vocabulary to describe nature itself had the effect of making the new objective attitude toward the world seem "natural." Works by seventeenth-century scientists are filled with references to nature as a woman who must be "conquered," "subdued," or "unveiled."

Traditional gender distinctions limited and buttressed most facets of political thought, but in other areas the fact of uncertainty and the need for tolerance were embraced. Another of Locke's influential works was the impassioned *Letter on Toleration* (1689). In it he argued that religious belief is fundamentally private and that only the most basic Christian principles need be accepted by everyone. Others went further than Locke by removing traditional religion as a fundamental guarantor of morality and order. Fostering such religious skepticism were religious pluralism in England and the irrationality of religious intolerance—demonstrated by Louis XIV's persecution of Protestants.

Pierre Bayle (1647–1706), a Frenchman of Protestant origins, argued that morality can be wholly detached from traditional religion. Bayle cited the philosopher Baruch Spinoza (1632–1677) as an example of morality. Spinoza believed the state to have a moral purpose and human happiness to have spiritual roots. Yet he was not a Christian at all but a Dutch Jew who had been ejected from his local synagogue for supposed atheism. One need hardly be a Christian to be a moral being, Bayle concluded.

Bayle's skepticism toward traditional knowledge was more wide-ranging than his views on religion. His best-known work, *Dictionnaire historique et critique* (*Historical and Critical Dictionary*, 1702), was a compendium of observations about virtually every thinker whose works were known at the time, including recent figures such as Descartes and Newton. Bayle was the first systematic skeptic, and he relentlessly exposed errors and shortcomings in all received knowledge. Informative, critical, and lively, his works were very popular with elite lay readers avid to take part in the revolutionary new worldview.

Locke's View of the Purpose of Government

In this passage from the second of his treatises on government, Locke describes men as naturally free and willing to enter into communities only for the protection of property. Notice how Locke justifies private property as "natural" by linking it to an individual's labor.

Men being . . . by nature all free, equal, and independent, no one can be put out of this estate and subjected to the political power of another without his own consent. The only way whereby any one divests himself of his natural liberty and puts on the bonds of civil society is by agreeing with other men to join and unite into a community for their comfortable, safe, and peaceable living amongst one another, in a secure enjoyment of their properties and a greater security against any that are not of it. This any number of men may do, because it injures not the freedom of the rest; they are left as they were in the liberty of the state of nature. When any number of men have so consented to make one community or government, they are thereby presently incorporated and make one body politic wherein the majority have a right to act and conclude the rest. . . . And thus that which begins and acutally constitutes any political society is nothing but the consent of any number of freemen capable of a majority to unite and incorporate into such a society. And this is that, and that only, which did or could give beginning to any lawful government in the world.

   If man in the state of nature be so free . . . , and if he be absolute lord of his own person and possessions, equal to the greatest, and subject to nobody, why will he part with his freedom, why will he give up his empire and subject himself to the dominion and control of any other power?

   The great and chief end, therefore, of men's uniting into commonwealths and putting themselves under government is the preservation of their property. . . . Though the earth and all inferior creatures be common to all men, yet every man has a property in his own person; this nobody has any right to but himself. The labor of his body and the work of his hands, we may say, are properly his. Whatsoever then he removes out of the state that nature has provided and left it in, he has mixed his labor with, and joined to it something that is his own, and thereby makes it his property. It being by him removed from the common state nature has placed it in, it has by this labor something annexed to it that excludes the common right of other men. For this labor being the unquestionable property of the laborer, no man but he can have a right to what that is once joined to, at least where there is enough and as good left in common for others. . . . As much land as a man tills, plants, improves, cultivates, and can use the product of, so much is his property. He by his labor does, as it were, enclose it from the common.

Source: Second Treatise, in John Locke, *Two Treatises of Civil Government* (London: G. Routledge & Sons, 1884).

SUMMARY

The Scientific Revolution began, as innovation in scientific thinking often does, with a specific problem whose answer led in unexpected directions. Copernicus's response to traditional astronomical problems led to scientific and philosophical innovation because of his solution and because of the context into which it was received.

   Other scientists built on the theories of Copernicus, culminating in the work of Galileo, who supported Copernican theory with additional data and widely published his findings. The Frenchman Descartes was the first to fashion a systematic explanation for the operations of nature to replace the medieval view. The political climate in England, meanwhile, encouraged the development of experimental science and inductive reasoning. Isaac Newton provided new theories to explain the behavior of matter and expressed them in mathematical terms that applied to both the earth and the cosmos; with his work, traditional astronomy and physics were overturned.

Rulers made use of the new science for the practical results it offered despite the ideological challenge it presented to their power. By the end of the seventeenth century, the hierarchical Christian world-view grounded in the old science was being challenged on many fronts.

NOTES

1. Quoted in Thomas S. Kuhn, *The Copernican Revolution* (Cambridge, Mass.: Harvard University Press, 1985), p. 131.
2. Quoted in Margaret C. Jacob, *The Cultural Meaning of the Scientific Revolution* (Philadelphia: Temple, 1988), p. 18.
3. Quoted in Alan G. R. Smith, *Science and Society in the Sixteenth and Seventeenth Centuries* (New York: Science History Publications, 1972), p. 72.
4. Quoted in Bruce T. Moran, ed., *Patronage and Institutions: Science, Technology and Medicine at the European Court* (Rochester: The Boyden Press, 1991), p. 43.
5. Quoted in Jacob, *Cultural Meaning*, p. 59.
6. Quoted in Steven Shapin, *A Social History of Truth* (Chicago: University of Chicago Press, 1994), p. 298.
7. Quoted in Jacob, *Cultural Meaning*, p. 89.
8. Quoted in Londa Schiebinger, *The Mind Has No Sex?* (Cambridge, Mass.: Harvard University Press, 1989), p. 92.
9. *Complete Poetry and Selected Prose of John Donne*, ed. John Hayward (Bloomsbury, England: Nonesuch Press, 1929), p. 365; quoted in Kuhn, *The Copernican Revolution*, p. 194.

SUGGESTED READING

Biagioli, Mario. *Galileo Courtier.* 1993. A recent study that stresses the power of patronage relations to shape scientific process.

Bordo, Susan R. *The Flight to Objectivity: Essays on Cartesianism and Culture.* 1987. A collection that studies Descartes's work as a metaphysical and psychological crisis and discusses implications of Cartesian mind-body dualism.

Cohen, I. Bernard. *The Newtonian Revolution.* 1987. A brief introduction to Newton and the meaning of his discoveries; a good place to start on Newton.

Davis, Natalie Zemon. *Women on the Margins: Three Seventeenth-Century Lives.* 1995. The third section of this excellent study concentrates on Maria Sibylla Merian; rich in historical detail and cultural context.

Frank, Robert G., Jr. *Harvey and the Oxford Physiologists.* 1980. An explanation of Harvey's work in the context of traditional Galenic medicine and a discussion of the community of scholars who accepted and built on his innovations.

Geneva, Ann. *Astrology and the Seventeenth-Century Mind: William Lilly and the Language of the Stars.* 1995. Provides an excellent guide to the basics of seventeenth-century astrology.

Hall, A. Rupert. *The Revolution in Science, 1500–1800.* 1983. A thorough introduction to all scientific disciplines that de-emphasizes the larger context of scientific development but explains many of the innovations in detail.

Hunter, Michael. *Science and Society in Restoration England.* 1981. A study that sets English science in its political and cultural contexts; critical of Webster's classic study (see the next page).

Jacob, Margaret C. *The Cultural Meaning of the Scientific Revolution.* 1988. An account that moves from the Scientific Revolution through the industrial transformation of the nineteenth century.

———. *The Newtonians and the English Revolution.* 1976. A work that links the development of Newtonian science to its political and social context and examines the simultaneous evolution of religion that could accept the new science yet maintain traditional perspectives.

Kearney, Hugh. *Science and Change.* 1971. A readable general introduction to the Scientific Revolution.

Kuhn, Thomas. *The Copernican Revolution.* 1985. A readable treatment of the revolution in astronomy that also lucidly explains the Aristotelian world-view; the first thing to read to understand the Copernican revolution.

———. *The Structure of Scientific Revolutions.* 1970. A path-breaking work that argues that all scientific schemas are systems of explanation and that science progresses by shifting from one general paradigm to another, not from error to "truth."

Lindberg, D. C., and R. S. Westman. *Reappraisals of the Scientific Revolution.* 1990. Essays re-evaluating classic interpretations of the Scientific Revolution. Includes a rich bibliography.

Mandrou, Robert. *From Humanism to Science.* 1978. A general intellectual history of the period 1450–1650 that sets the Scientific Revolution in the context of broader intellectual, social, and economic currents.

Merchant, Carolyn. *The Death of Nature: Women, Ecology and the Scientific Revolution.* 1980. An important corrective interpretation that focuses on the changing definition of nature—particularly how nature became something to be dominated and consumed—and the way in which this definition reinforced negative cultural views of women.

Moran, Bruce T., ed. *Patronage and Institutions: Science, Technology and Medicine at the European Court.* 1991. A work that looks at royal courts as shaping and sustaining institutions for science from the early sixteenth century onward.

Redondi, Pietro. *Galileo Heretic.* 1987. A careful account of Galileo's confrontation with the church.

Schiebinger, Londa. *The Mind Has No Sex?* 1989. An examination of the participation of women in science and an explanation of how science began to reflect the exclusion of women in its values and objects of study.

Shapin, Steven, and Simon Schaffer. *Leviathan and the Air-Pump.* 1985. One of the most important studies of seventeenth-century science; it traces the conflict between Cartesian science, as represented by Hobbes, and experimental science, in the work of Boyle.

Thomas, Keith. *Religion and the Decline of Magic.* 1971. An exploration of the changing character of religious belief and "superstitious" practice; finds roots outside of science for changing, increasingly secular world-views.

Thoren, Victor E. *The Lord of Uraniborg: A Biography of Tycho Brahe.* 1990. An up-to-date study of the life and work of the Danish astronomer.

Webster, Charles. *The Great Instauration.* 1975. A classic study that links the development of the modern scientific attitude to the Puritan revolution in England.

Westfall, Richard S. *The Construction of Modern Science: Mechanisms and Mechanics.* 1977. A general treatment of the Scientific Revolution that emphasizes and explains the mechanistic world-view.

CHAPTER 16

Europe on the Threshold of Modernity, ca. 1715–1789

A customer in one of the growing number of cafés in Paris on February 10, 1778, might have wondered if the king himself was entering the city, such was the commotion as Parisians turned out to welcome a former resident. Now 84, this old man had journeyed to the city to preside at the opening of his latest play, but everyone realized that this most likely would be his last visit, and he was given a hero's welcome. Literary and political elites clamored to meet him; Benjamin Franklin brought his grandson to receive the old man's blessing. Though he was treated like royalty, the man was not a ruler, but a political thinker and writer: the philosopher Voltaire.

Voltaire was the best known of dozens of thinkers who made up the philosophical movement we know as the Enlightenment. The Enlightenment constituted a revolution in political philosophy, but it was much more. The era witnessed the emergence of an informed body of public opinion, critical of the prevailing political system, that existed outside the corridors of power. The relationship between governments and the governed had begun to change: Subjects of monarchs were becoming citizens of nations.

Frederick the Great of Prussia, Catherine the Great of Russia, and other rulers self-consciously tried to use Enlightenment precepts to guide their efforts at governing. They had mixed success. Powerful interests opposed their efforts at reform, and their own hereditary and autocratic power was incompatible with Enlightenment perspectives. Elites still sure of their power, as well as the traditional interests of states, dominated eighteenth-century politics.

Nevertheless, profound changes in economic, social, and political life began in this period. Economic growth spurred population growth, which in turn stimulated industry and trade. The increasing economic and strategic importance of overseas colonies made them focal points of international conflict. The dramatic political and social changes that began as the century closed had their roots in the intellectual, economic, and social ferment of eighteenth-century life.

~ *Questions and Ideas to Consider*

■ What were the guiding principles of Enlightenment thought? What ideas did the various Enlightenment thinkers share? In what ways did they disagree? Consider, for example, the ideas of Voltaire, Smith, Rousseau, and Wollstonecraft.

■ What were Enlightenment salons? Who generally ran them, and why were they so important?

■ What was "enlightened monarchy"? To what degree did Catherine the Great of Russia succeed in implementing Enlightenment ideas?

■ The eighteenth century was a period of warfare. What were the major issues of these conflicts?

■ In the changing economy of the eighteenth century, states attempted to gain further control over their populations, and in many instances, people began to resist that control. Discuss the changing relationship between the state and those who made a living on the seas. Consider new attitudes toward piracy, privateering, navies, and traders.

THE ENLIGHTENMENT

One of Isaac Newton's countrymen wrote the following epitaph for the English scientist:

Nature and Nature's Laws lay hid in Night.
God said, "Let Newton be," and all was Light.

The most important works of Enlightenment philosophy reflected the intellectual confidence that Newton's work generated. The poet's assertion that "all was Light" evokes the confidence of an intellectual elite that felt it held a new key to truth. In this sense, the Enlightenment was nothing less than the transfer into general philosophy, particularly political and social thought, of the intellectual revolution that had already taken place in the physical sciences.

Enlightenment philosophy occurred in the context of increasingly widespread publications and new opportunities in literary societies, clubs, and salons for the exchange of views. This context shaped the outline of Enlightenment thought, which was for the most part an elite set of preoccupations. It also determined the radicalism of the Enlightenment, by helping to ensure that an entire level of society shared attitudes that were fundamentally critical of that society.

Voltaire and the Enlightenment

The Enlightenment was not so much a body of thought as an intellectual and social movement. Originating in France, it consisted, first, of the application to political and social thought of the confidence in the intelligibility of natural law that theoretical science had recently achieved. Enlightenment thinkers combined an optimistic belief in the intelligibility of the world and its laws with confidence in the human capacity to discern and work in concert with those laws. The most dramatic effect was the desacralizing of social and political bonds—a new belief that society could be grounded on rational foundations to be determined by humans, not arbitrary foundations determined by God.

A wide range of thinkers participated in the Enlightenment. In France they were known as *philosophes,* a term meaning not a formal philosopher but rather a thinker and critic. To most philosophes, the main agenda was clear. For too long, humans had been mired in ignorance, oppressed by arbitrary laws and institutions. Lack of proper education and the tyranny of the church had condemned them to ignorance. French thinkers singled out the Catholic church as the archenemy because of its opposition to their positive views of human nature and because it controlled much education and was still a force in political life.

The following passage from Voltaire's *Dictionnaire philosophique* (*Philosophical Dictionary*, 1764) is typical of his work in its casual format and biting wit and is also typical of the venomous Enlightenment view of the church:

A hundred times [you clerics] have been spoken to of the insolent absurdity with which you condemned Galileo, and I shall speak to you for the hundred and first. . . . I desire that there be engraved on the door of your holy office: Here seven cardinals assisted by minor brethren had the master of thought of Italy thrown into prison at the age of seventy, made him fast on bread and water, because he instructed the human race.

The life of Voltaire (1694–1778) almost spanned the century. Born François-Marie Arouet to a middle-class family, he took the pen name Voltaire in 1718, after one of his early plays was a critical success. He produced a vast array of written work: plays, epic poems, novelettes—some of which have explicit philosophical or political content—as well as philosophical tracts. Voltaire moved in courtly circles. Mockery of the regent, the duke of Orléans, led to a year's imprisonment in 1717, and an exchange of insults with a leading courtier some years later led to enforced exile in Great Britain for two years.

After returning from Britain, Voltaire published his first major philosophical work. *Lettres philosophiques* (*Philosophical Letters*, 1734) revealed the influence of his British sojourn and helped to popularize Newton's achievement. Voltaire portrayed Great Britain as a more rational society than France. He was particularly impressed with the religious and intellectual toleration evident there. The British government had a more workable set of institutions, its economy was less crippled by the remnants of feudal privilege, and education was not strictly controlled by the church.

After the publication of his audacious *Lettres*, Voltaire was forced to leave Paris, and he resided for some years in the country home of a woman with whom he shared a remarkable intellectual

CHAPTER CHRONOLOGY

1721	Montesquieu, *Persian Letters*
1721–1742	Robert Walpole first British "prime minister"
1734	Voltaire, *Philosophical Letters*
1740–1748	War of the Austrian Succession
1748	Montesquieu, *The Spirit of the Laws*; Hume, *Essay Concerning Human Understanding*
1756–1763	Seven Years' War
1758	Voltaire, *Candide*
1751–1765	Diderot, *The Encyclopedia*
1762	Rousseau, *The Social Contract*
1764	Voltaire, *Philosophical Dictionary*
1772	First Partition of Poland
1776	Smith, *The Wealth of Nations*
1784	Kant, *What Is Enlightenment?*
1792	Wollstonecraft, *A Vindication of the Rights of Woman*
1795	Condorcet, *The Progress of the Human Mind*

and emotional relationship: Emilie, marquise du Châtelet (1706–1749). Châtelet was a mathematician and a scientist. She prepared a French translation of Newton's *Principia* while Voltaire worked at his accustomed variety of writing, which also included a commentary on Newton's work. Because of Châtelet's tutelage, Voltaire became more knowledgeable about the sciences and more serious in his efforts to apply scientific rationality to human affairs. He was devastated by her sudden death in 1749.

Shortly afterward, he accepted the invitation of the king of Prussia, Frederick II, to visit Berlin. His stay was stormy and brief because of disagreements with other court philosophers. He resided for a time in Geneva, until his criticisms of the city's moral codes forced yet another exile on him. He spent most of the last twenty years of his life at his estates on the Franco-Swiss border,

Etablissement de la nouvelle Philosophie.
Notre Berceau fut un Caffé.

Café Society The caption under this contemporary illustration reads: "Establishment of the new philosophy; our cradle was the café." Cafés were one of the new settings where literate elites could discuss the new philosophy and explore its implications for social and political life. *(Musée Carnavalet, Paris/Edimedia)*

where he could be relatively free from interference by any government. There he produced his best-known satirical novella, *Candide*, in 1758. It criticized aristocratic privilege and the power of clerics as well as the naiveté of philosophers who took "natural law" to mean that the world was already operating as it should.

Voltaire's belief that one must struggle to overturn the accumulated habits of centuries was reflected in his political activity. He became involved in several celebrated legal cases in which individuals were pitted against the authority of the church, which was still backed by the authority of the state. In the most famous case, Jean Calas (1698–1762), a Protestant from southern France, was accused of murdering his son, allegedly to prevent him from converting to Catholicism. Calas maintained his innocence until his execution in 1762. Voltaire saw in this case the worst aspects of religious prejudice and injustice and worked tirelessly to establish Calas's innocence as a matter of principle and so that his family could inherit his property. In pursuit of justice in these cases, and in criticism of the church, Voltaire added a stream of political pamphlets to his literary output.

Voltaire died in Paris in May 1778, shortly after his triumphal return there. By then he was no longer the leader of the Enlightenment in strictly intellectual terms. Thinkers and writers more radical than he had come to prominence during his long life and had dismissed some of his beliefs, such as the notion that reform could be introduced by a monarch. But Voltaire had provided a crucial stimulus to French thought with his *Lettres philosophiques*. His importance lies also in his embodiment of the critical spirit of eighteenth-century rationalism: its confidence, its increasingly practical bent, its wit and sophistication.

The Variety of Enlightenment Thought

Differences among philosophes grew as the century progressed. In the matter of religion, for example, there was virtual unanimity of opposition to the Catholic church among French thinkers, but no unanimity about God. Voltaire was a *theist*—believing firmly in God as creator of the universe, but not a specifically Christian God. To some later thinkers, God was irrelevant—the creator of the world, but a world that ran continuously according to established laws. Some philosophes were atheists, arguing that a universe that ran according to discoverable laws needed no divine presence to explain, run, or justify it. In Protestant areas of Europe, in contrast to France, Enlightenment thought was often less hostile to Christianity.

Philosophes also pondered questions about the social and political order, as well as about human rationality itself. Charles de Secondat (1689–1755), baron of Montesquieu, a French judge and legal philosopher, combined the belief that human institutions must be rational with Locke's assumption of human educability. Montesquieu's treatise *De l'esprit des lois* (*The Spirit of the Laws,* 1748) went through twenty-two printings in just two years. In it Montesquieu maintained that laws were not meant to be arbitrary rules but derived naturally from human society: The more evolved a society was, the more liberal its laws. This notion provided a sense of the progress possible within society and government and deflated Europeans' pretensions in regard to other societies, for a variety of laws could be equally "rational" given differing conditions. Montesquieu is perhaps best known to Americans as the advocate of the separation of legislative, executive, and judicial powers that later became enshrined in the U.S. Constitution. To Montesquieu, this scheme paralleled the balance of forces observable in nature and seemed the best guarantee of liberty.

The "laws" of economic life were also investigated, most notably by the Scotsman Adam Smith in his treatise *An Inquiry into the Nature and Causes of the Wealth of Nations* (1776). A professor at the University of Glasgow, Smith (1723–1790) is best known today as the originator of "laissez-faire" economics: the assumption that an economy will regulate itself without government interference and, of more concern to Smith, without the monopolies and other restrictions on trade that were common in his day. Smith shared Locke's optimistic view of human nature and human rationality. Humans, Smith believed, can direct their drives and passions through their reason and inherent sympathy for one another. Thus, Smith said, in seeking their own achievement and well-being, they are often "led by an invisible hand" to benefit society as a whole.

Other philosophers disagreed about the nature and limits of human reason. David Hume (1711–1776) was radical in his critique of the human capacity for knowing, doubting even the reliability of sense data. These views, which he expounded in his *Essay Concerning Human Understanding* (1748), ran counter to the prevailing spirit of confidence in empirical knowledge.

Mainstream confidence in empirical knowledge and in the intelligibility of the world was quite evident in the *Encyclopédie* (*Encyclopedia*), a seventeen-volume compendium of knowledge, criticism, and philosophy assembled by leading philosophes in France and published between 1751 and 1765. The volumes were designed to contain state-of-the-art knowledge about arts, sciences, technology, and philosophy. The guiding philosophy of the project, set forth by its chief editor, Denis Diderot (1713–1784), was a belief that human happiness could be achieved through the advance of knowledge. The *Encyclopédie* intrigued and inspired intellectuals and was used by thousands of government officials and professionals. Catherine the Great, empress of Russia, remarked in a letter that she consulted its pages to find guidance concerning one of her reform schemes.

Reaction to the encyclopedia project illustrated the political context of Enlightenment thought as well as its philosophic premises. The Catholic church placed the work on the Index of prohibited books, and the French government might well have barred its publication but for the fact that the official who would have made the decision was drawn to Enlightenment thinking. Many other officials, however, worked to suppress it. By the late 1750s, losses in wars overseas had made French officials highly sensitive to political challenges of any kind. Thus, like Voltaire, the major contributors to the *Encyclopédie* were lionized by certain segments of the elite and persecuted by others.

The *Encyclopédie* reflected the complexities and limitations of Enlightenment thought on another score—the position of women. One might expect that the Enlightenment penchant for challenging received knowledge and traditional hierarchies would have led to revised views of women's abilities and rights. Indeed, some contributors did blame women's social and political inequality on the customs and laws that had kept women from education and valued public roles. However, others simply substituted scientific-sounding assertions of women's inferiority in place of traditional religious assertions of gender inequality.

Both positions were represented in Enlightenment thought as a whole. The assumption of the natural equality of all people provided a powerful reason for arguing the equality of women with men. Some thinkers, such as Mary Astell (1666–1731), challenged Locke's separation of family life from the public world of free, contractual relationships. (See the box "An English Feminist Criticizes Unenlightened Views of Women.") Most advocated increased education for women, if only to make them more fit to raise enlightened children. By the end of the century, the most radical thinkers were also advocating full citizenship rights for women and equal rights to property.

The best-known proponent of those views was an Englishwoman, Mary Wollstonecraft (1759–1797), the author of *A Vindication of the Rights of Woman* (1792). She argued that women had been weakened by excessive refinement. Like both sexes in the aristocracy, women of the middle class were taught to prize superficial, decorative attributes above more substantial virtues. Wollstonecraft wanted women to stop enjoying their frivolous privileges and the superficial praise that, she argued, masked insulting assumptions about their nature. She strenuously asserted that the responsibilities of citizenship, the leavening of education, and economic independence would make women happier, fuller human beings and that from this new position, women could help to work for the betterment of society. In any case, she noted, working women needed these rights simply to survive.

Wollstonecraft specifically criticized the misogynistic attitudes of Jean-Jacques Rousseau (1712–1778). Like Locke, Rousseau could conceive of the free individual only as male, and he grounded his critique of the old order and his novel political ideas in an arbitrary division of gender roles. Rousseau's view of women was part of a critique of the cosmopolitan elite society of his day, in which aristocratic women were fully involved. He believed that this society was corrupting and that the true citizen had to cultivate virtue and sensibility, not manners, taste, or refinement. Rousseau designated women as guarantors of the "natural" virtues of children and as nurturers of the emotional life and character of men—not as fully formed beings in their own right.

Rousseau's emphasis on the education and virtue of citizens was the underpinning of his larger political vision, set forth in *Du Contrat social* (*The Social Contract*, 1762). He imagined an egalitarian republic in which men would consent to be governed because the government would determine and act in accordance with the "general will" of the citizens. The "general will" was not majority opinion but rather what each citizen *would* want if he were fully informed and acting in accordance with his highest nature. The "general will" became apparent whenever the citizens met as a body and made collective decisions, and it could be imposed on all inhabitants. This was a breathtaking vision of direct democracy—but one with ominous possibilities, for Rousseau rejected the institutional brakes on state authority proposed by Locke and Montesquieu. Also Rousseau believed that the demands of citizenship in a direct democracy necessitated that half the population serve in an obedient, supportive role, that is, that women's lives be subordinated to those of male citizens.

Rousseau's emphasis on private emotional life anticipated the romanticism of the early nineteenth century (see page 467). It also reflected his own experience as the son of a humble family, always sensing himself an outcast in the brilliant world of Parisian salons. He had a love-hate relationship with this life, remaining attached to several aristocratic women patrons even as he decried their influence. His own personal life did not match his prescriptions for others. He completely neglected to give his four children the nurturing and education that he argued were vital; indeed,

An English Feminist Criticizes Unenlightened Views of Women

Both male and female writers criticized the failure of some Enlightenment thinkers to view ideas about women with the same rationalism that they brought to other subjects. One of the earliest was the Englishwoman Mary Astell (1666–1731). In this excerpt from Some Reflections on Marriage *(1700), Astell criticizes, in an ironic tone, negative assessments of women's capacities, Locke's separation of the public and private spheres, and the denial to women of the rights that men enjoy in public life.*

'Tis true, through want of learning, and that of superior genius which men, as men, lay claim to, she [the author] was ignorant of the natural inferiority of our sex, which our masters lay down as self-evident and fundamental truth. She saw nothing in the reason of things to make this either a principle or a conclusion, but much to the contrary.

If they mean that some men are superior to some women, this is no great discovery; had they turned the tables, they might have seen that some women are superior to some men. . . .

Again, if absolute sovereignty be not necessary in a state, how comes it to be so in a family? Or if in a family why not in a state, since no reason can be alleged for the one that will not hold more strongly for the other? If the authority of the husband, so far as it extends, is sacred and inalienable, why not that of the prince? The domestic sovereign is without dispute elected and the stipulations and contract are mutual; is it not then partial in men to the last degree to contend for and practice that arbitrary dominion in their families which they abhor and exclaim against in the state? For if arbitrary power is evil in itself, and an improper method of governing rational and free agents, it ought not to be practiced anywhere.

Source: Moira Ferguson, ed., *First Feminists* (Bloomington: Indiana University Press, 1985), pp. 191–193.

he abandoned them all to a foundling home. Rousseau's work reflected to an extreme degree a central tension in Enlightenment thought generally: It was part of elite culture as well as its principal critic.

The Growth of Public Opinion

It is impossible to understand the significance of the Enlightenment without an analysis of how it was a part of public life. Indeed, the clearest distinguishing feature of the Enlightenment may be the creation of an informed body of public opinion that stood apart from court society.

Increased literacy and access to books and other print media were an important part of the story. Perhaps more important, the kinds of reading that people favored began to change. We know from inventories made of people's belongings at the time of their death (required by inheritance laws) that ordinary people now read secular and contemporary philosophical works. As the availability of such works increased, reading itself evolved from a reverential encounter with traditional material to a critical encounter with new ideas. Solitary reading for reflection and pleasure became more widespread.

In the eighteenth century, forerunners of modern lending libraries made their debut. In Paris, for a fee, one could join a *salle de lecture* (literally, a "reading room"), where the latest works were available to members. Booksellers, whose num-

The Growth of the Book Trade Book ownership dramatically increased in the eighteenth century, and a wide range of secular works—from racy novelettes to philosophical tracts—was available in print. In this rendering of a bookshop, shipments of books have arrived from around Europe. Notice the artist's optimism in the great variety of persons, from the peasant with a scythe to a white-robed cleric, who are drawn to the shop by "Minerva" (the Roman goddess of wisdom). *(Musée des Beaux-Arts de Dijon)*

bers increased dramatically, found ways to meet readers' demands for inexpensive reading matter. One might, for example, pay for the right to read a book in the bookshop itself. In short, new venues encouraged people to see themselves not just as readers but as members of a reading public.

Among the most famous and most important of these venues were the Parisian salons, where Voltaire and others read aloud their works in progress and discussed them. The great majority of salons were run by women. Most were wealthy but of modest social status. They invited courtiers, bureaucrats, and intellectuals to meet in their homes at regular times each week. The *salonnières* (salon leaders) read widely in order to facilitate the exchange of ideas among their guests. This mediating function, along with the choice of guests, was crucial to the success of the salons. Manners and polite conversation had been a defining feature of aristocratic life since the seventeenth century, but they had largely been a means of displaying status and safeguarding honor. The leadership of the salonnières and the protected environment they provided away from court life enabled a further evolution of "polite society" to occur: Anyone with appropriate manners could participate as an equal.

The influence of salons was extended by the wide networks of correspondence that salonnières maintained. Perhaps the most famous salonnière in her day, Marie-Thérèse Geoffrin (1699–1777), corresponded with Catherine the Great, the reform-minded empress of Russia, as well as with philosophes outside of Paris and would-be participants in her salon. The ambassador of Naples regularly attended her salon before returning to his native city, from which he exchanged weekly letters with her. He reflected on the importance of salon leaders when he wrote from Naples, lamenting,

[our gatherings here] are getting farther away from the character and tone of those of France, despite all [our] efforts. . . . There is no way to make Naples resemble Paris unless we find a woman to guide us, organize us, *Geoffrinise* us.[1]

Various clubs, local academies, and learned and secret societies copied some features of the salons of Paris. Hardly any municipality was without a private society that functioned both as a forum for political and philosophical discussion and as an elite social club. Ideas circulated beyond the membership of even the many far-flung clubs by means of print. Newsletters reporting the goings-on at salons in Paris were produced by some participants. Regularly published periodicals in Great Britain, France, and Italy also disseminated enlightened opinion in the form of reviews, essays, and published correspondence. Some of these journals had been established in the second half of the seventeenth century as a means to circulate the new scientific work. Subscribers now included Americans eager to keep up with intellectual life in Europe.

In all these arenas, Enlightenment ideas encouraged and legitimized a type of far-reaching political debate that had never before existed, except possibly in England during the seventeenth century. The first and greatest impact of the Enlightenment, particularly in France, was not the creation of a program for political change but the creation of a culture of politics that could generate change.

Art in the Age of Reason

Just as the market for books and the reading public expanded, so did the audience for works of art. The modern cultured public—a public of concertgoers and art-gallery enthusiasts—began to make its first appearance. Some performances of concerts and operas began to take place in theaters and halls outside the royal courts and were more accessible to the public.

Beginning in 1737, one section of the Louvre palace in Paris was devoted annually to public exhibitions of painting and sculpture (though by royally sponsored and approved artists). In both France and Britain, public discussion of art began to appear in published reviews: The role of art critic was born. Some works of art were now sold by public auctions, and as works became more available by such means, demand grew and production increased. Late baroque painters contributed to an exploration of private life and emotion sometimes called the "cult of sensibility." Frequently, they depicted private scenes of upper-class life, especially moments of intimate conversation or flirtation.

The cult of sensibility was fostered by literature as well. In England, the novels of Samuel Richardson (1689–1761)—*Pamela* (1740) and *Clarissa* (1747–1748)—explored personal psychology and passion. In the wake of these important works, the novel became an increasingly important genre for exploring human problems and relationships. Rousseau followed Richardson's lead in structuring his own novels, *La Nouvelle Héloïse* (1761) and *Emile* (1762). The cult of sensibility carried the message that honest emotion was a "natural" virtue and that courtly manners, by contrast, were irrational and degrading. The enormous popularity of Rousseau's novels came from the fact that their intense emotional appeal was considered to be uplifting.

There was a great revival of classical subjects and styles after the middle of the century. Classical revival architecture illustrated a belief in order, symmetry, and proportion. Americans are familiar with its evocations because it has been the architecture of their republic, but even churches were built in this style in eighteenth-century Europe. The classical movement in music reflected both the cult of sensibility and the classicizing styles in the visual arts. Embodied in the works of Austrians Franz Josef Haydn (1732–1809) and Wolfgang Amadeus Mozart (1756–1791), this movement saw the clarification of musical structures, such as the modern sonata and symphony, and enabled melody to take center stage.

Another trend in art was a fascination with nature and with the seemingly "natural" in human culture—less "developed" or more historically distant societies. Folk life, other cultures, and untamed nature itself began to be celebrated just when they were being more definitively conquered. Their disappearance made them exotic, and images of this exotic, natural world reinforced Europeans' sense of their own sophistication and dominance.

EUROPEAN RULERS AND EUROPEAN SOCIETY

Mindful of the lessons of the revolution in England and the achievements of Louis XIV, European rulers in the eighteenth century redoubled their efforts to govern with greater effectiveness. Some, like the rulers of Prussia and Russia, were encouraged in their efforts by Enlightenment ideas. In the main they, like Voltaire, believed that monarchs could be agents for change. In Austria, significant reforms were made, including the abolition of serfdom. The changes were uneven, however, and at times owed as much to traditional efforts at better government as to enlightened persuasion.

In all cases, rulers' efforts to govern more effectively meant continual readjustments in relationships with traditional elites. Whether or not elites played a formal role in the governing process, such as in the British Parliament, royal governments everywhere were still dependent on their participation. Enlightened monarchs were changing their view of themselves and their image from the diligent but self-glorifying image

of Louis XIV to that of servant of the state. By redefining their role on a utilitarian basis, monarchs undermined the dynastic claim to rule. The state was increasingly seen as separate from the ruler.

France During the Enlightenment

It is one of the seeming paradoxes of the Enlightenment era that critical thought about politics flourished in France, an autocratic state. Yet in France there was a well-educated elite, a tradition of scientific inquiry, and a legacy of cultured court life that, since the early days of Louis XIV, had become the model for all Europe. French was the international intellectual language, and France was the most fertile center of elite cultural life. Both Adam Smith and David Hume spent portions of their careers in Paris and were welcomed into the salons. In fact, the French capital encouraged debate and dissent precisely because of the juxtaposition of the new intellectual climate with the institutional rigidities of the French political system—a system that excluded many talented and productive members of the elite from its privileged circles.

In the last decades of the reign of Louis XIV (d. 1715), many French people began to criticize the seemingly endless foreign wars. The intoxicating blend of stability, effective government, national interest, and the personal glory of the monarch was beginning to loose its hold on the French people.

Louis XIV was followed on the throne by his 5-year-old great-grandson, Louis XV (r. 1715–1774). During the regency, nobles clamored for the establishment of councils so that they could become more active partners in government. Likewise, the supreme law courts, the parlements, reclaimed the right of remonstrance—the right to object to royal edicts and thus to exercise some control over the enactment of laws. Throughout the years of Louis XV's reign, his administration locked horns with the parlements, particularly as royal ministers tried to cope with France's financial crises. Louis XIV had left the nation financially exhausted—in need of both money and new and more reliable ways to get money. During Louis XV's reign the pressures of further wars intensified the need for wholesale reform.

By the late 1760s, the weight of government debt finally forced the king into action. He threw his support behind the reforming schemes of his chancellor, Nicolas de Maupeou. Maupeou dissolved the parlements early in 1771 and created new law courts whose judges would not enjoy independent power.

Public opinion was split over this conflict between the monarch and the parlements. A number of Louis XV's ministers shared Enlightenment hopes of doing away with privileges such as the exemption of the nobility from taxation—and the Enlightenment views of the efficiency of creating economic change from the top. However, the role of consultative bodies and the separation of powers beloved of Montesquieu, himself a parlementaire, were much prized, and the parlements were the only institutions that could legitimately check monarchical powers.

From about the middle of the century, enlightened public opinion, nurtured in salons and other new settings, had begun proposing ways to enhance representation and consultation and implement reform. There were calls to revive the moribund Estates General, the cumbersome representative assembly last called in 1614, as well as for the establishment of new councils or local, decentralized representative assemblies. The workability of these proposals is less important than the fact that they were being made.

The Crown lost control of reform in 1774, when Louis XV died. His grandson, Louis XVI (r. 1774–1792), who was well-meaning but insecure, allowed the complete restoration of the parlements. Further reform efforts, sponsored by the king and several talented ministers, came to naught because of parlementary opposition. By the time an Estates General was finally called in the wake of further financial problems in 1788, the enlightened elites' habit of carrying on political analysis and criticism of government outside the corridors of power had given rise to a volatile situation.

Monarchy and Constitutional Government in Great Britain

After the deaths of William (d. 1702) and Mary (d. 1694), the British crown passed to Mary's sister, Anne (r. 1702–1714), and then to a collateral line descended from Elizabeth (d. 1662), sister of the beheaded Charles I. Elizabeth had married Frederick, elector of the Palatinate (and had reigned with him briefly in Bohemia at the outset of the Thirty Years' War), and her descendants were Germans, now electors of Hanover. The new British sovereign in 1714, who reigned as George I (r. 1714–1727), was both a foreigner and a man of mediocre abilities. Moreover, his claim to the throne was immediately contested by Catholic descendants of James II, who attempted to depose him in 1715 and his son, George II (r. 1727–1760), in 1745.

The second attempt was more nearly successful. In 1745, the son of the Stuart claimant to the throne, Charles (known in legend as Bonnie Prince Charlie), landed on the west coast of Scotland and marched south into England with surprising ease. Most of the British army (and George II himself) was on the Continent, fighting in the War of the Austrian Succession (see page 428). Scotland had been formally united with England in 1707 (hence the term "Great Britain" after that time), and Charles found some support among dissatisfied Scots.

But the vast majority of Britons did not want the civil war that Charles's challenge inevitably meant, especially on behalf of a Catholic pretender who relied on support from Britain's great rival, France. Landholders and merchants in lowland Scotland and northern England gathered militia to oppose Charles until regular army units returned from abroad. Charles's army, made up mostly of poor Highland clansmen, was destroyed at the Battle of Culloden in April 1746. Charles fled back to France, and the British government used the failed uprising as justification for the brutal and forceful integration of the still-remote Highlands into the British state.

Traditional Highland practices, from wearing tartans to playing bagpipes, were forbidden.

Land was redistributed to break the bonds of clan society. Thousands of Highlanders died at the battle itself, in prisons or deportation ships, or by deliberate extermination by British troops after the battle. Despite this serious challenge to the dynasty and the brutal response it occasioned, the British state enjoyed a period of relative stability as well as innovation in the eighteenth century. The events of the seventeenth century had reaffirmed both the need for a strong monarchy and the role of Parliament in defending elite interests. The power of Parliament was reinforced by the Act of Settlement, by which the Protestant heir to Queen Anne had been chosen in 1701.

It was in the eighteenth century that political parties—that is, distinct groups within the elite favoring certain foreign and domestic policies—came into existence. Two groups, the Whigs and the Tories, had begun to form during the reign of Charles II (d. 1685). The Whigs (named derisively by their opponents with a Scottish term for horse thieves) had opposed Charles's toleration of Catholicism and had wholly opposed his Catholic brother and successor, James II. Initially, the Whigs favored an aggressive foreign policy against continental opponents, particularly France. The Tories (also derisively named—for Irish cattle rustlers) tended to be staunch Anglicans uninterested in anti-Catholic agitation. They favored isolationism in foreign affairs and deference toward monarchical authority. Whigs generally represented the interests of the great aristocrats or wealthy merchants or gentry. Tories tended to represent the interests of provincial gentry and the traditional concerns of landholding and local administration. The Whigs were the dominant influence in government through most of the century to 1770. William and Mary as well as Queen Anne favored Whig religious and foreign policy interests.

The long Whig dominance of government was assisted by the talents of Robert Walpole (1676–1745). Walpole, from a minor gentry family, was brought into government in 1714 with other Whig ministers in George I's new regime. An extremely talented politician, he took advan-

tage of the mistakes of other ministers and, in 1721, became both the first lord of the treasury and chancellor of the exchequer. There was not yet any official post or title of "prime minister," but the great contribution of Walpole's long tenure—1721–1742—was to create that office in fact, if not officially. He chose to maintain peace abroad where he could and thus presided over a period of recovery and relative prosperity that enhanced the stability of government.

Initially, Walpole was helped in his role as go-between for king and Parliament by George I's own limitations. The king rarely attended meetings of his council of ministers and, in any case, was hampered by his limited command of English. Gradually, the Privy Council of the king became something resembling a modern cabinet dominated by a prime minister. The notion of "loyal opposition" to the Crown within Parliament was also taking root. In some respects, the maturation of political life in Parliament resembled the lively political debates in the salons of Paris; political life was being legitimated on a new basis in both realms. In England, however, that legitimation was enshrined in a legislative institution, which made it especially effective and resilient.

Parliament was not yet representative of the British population. Because of strict property qualifications, only about 200,000 adult men could vote. In addition, representation was very uneven, heavily favoring traditional landed wealth. Agitation for reform began in the late 1760s as professionals, such as doctors and lawyers without landed property, and merchants in booming but underrepresented cities began to demand the vote. As the burden of taxation grew—the result of the recently concluded Seven Years' War—these groups felt increasingly deprived of representation. Indeed, many felt kinship and sympathy with the American colonists who opposed increased taxation by the British government on these same grounds and began a revolt in 1775.

The reform movement faltered over the issue of religion. In 1780, a tentative effort by Parliament to extend some civil rights to British Catholics provoked rioting in London (known as the Gordon Riots, after one of the leaders). The riots lasted for eight days and claimed three hundred lives. Pressure for parliamentary reform had been building as Britain met with reversals in its war against the American rebels, but this specter of a popular movement out of control temporarily ended the drive for reform.

"Enlightened" Monarchy

Arbitrary monarchical power might seem antithetical to Enlightenment thought, which stressed the reasonableness of human beings and their capacity to act in accord with natural law. Yet many contemporaries believed that the work of curtailing the influence of the church, reforming legal codes, and eliminating barriers to economic activity might be done most efficiently by a powerful monarch. Historians have labeled a number of rulers of this era "enlightened despots" because of the arbitrary nature of their power and the enlightened or reformist uses to which they put it.

"Enlightened despotism" aptly describes certain developments in the Scandinavian kingdoms in the late eighteenth century. In Denmark, the Crown had governed without significant challenge from the landholding nobility since the mid-seventeenth century. The nobility, however, had guaranteed its supremacy by means of ironclad domination of the peasantry. In 1784, a reform-minded group of nobles, led by the young Crown Prince Frederick (governing on behalf of his mentally ill father), began to apply Enlightenment remedies to the kingdom's economic problems. They encouraged freer trade and sought, above all, to boost agriculture by improving the status of the peasantry. With increased legal status and with land reform, which enabled some peasants to own the land they worked for the first time, agricultural productivity in Denmark rose dramatically. These reforms constitute some of the clearest achievements of any of the "enlightened" rulers.

In Sweden, in 1772, Gustav III (r. 1771–1796) staged a coup with army support that overturned the dominance of the Swedish parliament, the Riksdag. Bureaucrats more loyal to parliamentary patrons than to the Crown were replaced, restrictions on trade in grain and other economic controls were liberalized, the legal system was rationalized, the death penalty was strictly limited, and legal torture was abolished. Despite his abilities (and his charm), Gustav III was criticized for advancing reform by autocratic means in a kingdom with a strong tradition of representative government. In 1796 he was mortally wounded by an assassin hired by disgruntled nobles.

Another claimant to the title of "enlightened" monarch was Frederick II of Prussia (r. 1740–1786), "the Great." Although Frederick continued to reside in his imperial electorate of Brandenburg, the state he ruled was now referred to as "Prussia," the duchy his father had seized from Poland and ruled as king. In many ways, the Prussian state *was* its military victories, for Frederick's father and grandfather committed the resources of the state to a military machine of dramatic proportions. Prussia was a power on the European stage only because of the degree of that commitment.

The institutions that constituted the state and linked the various provinces under one administration were dominated by the needs of the military. There was no tradition of political participation—even by elites—and little chance of cultivating any. Nor was there any political or social room for maneuver at the lower part of the social scale. The rulers of Prussia had long ago acceded to the aristocracy's demand for tighter control over peasant labor. Thus, there was a stark limit to the kinds of social, judicial, or political reforms that Frederick could hope to carry out.

Frederick tried to introduce more efficient agricultural practices and improve the condition of peasants, but he met stiff resistance from noble landholders. He did succeed in abolishing serfdom in some regions. He tried to stimulate the economy by sponsoring state industries and trading monopolies but met opposition from the tightly controlled merchant communities. Simplifying and codifying the inherited jumble of local laws was a goal of every ruler. A law code published in 1794, after Frederick's death, was partly the product of his efforts.

Frederick's most distinctive "enlightened" characteristic was the seriousness with which he took his task as ruler. In his book *Anti-Machiavel* (1741) he argued that a ruler has a moral obligation to work for the betterment of the state. He styled himself as the "first servant" or steward of the state. However superficial this claim may appear, in his energy and diligence he compares favorably to Louis XV of France, who, having a much more wealthy and flexible society to work with, did much less.

Describing Frederick as "enlightened," however, masks the degree to which his activities reflected the traditional goals of security and prosperity as much as the impetus of "enlightened" thinking. Indeed, some of the most thoroughgoing administrative, legal, and economic reforms were accomplished in rival Austria entirely within such a traditional framework, during the reign of Maria Theresa (r. 1740–1780), the daughter of Emperor Charles VI (r. 1711–1740).

Maria Theresa was a remarkable ruler. Diligent and determined, she overcame the difficulties that surrounded her accession, survived the near dismemberment of Austrian territories in the war that opened her reign, and embarked on an energetic reform program to address the weaknesses in the state that the conflict had revealed (see page 428). The Austrian monarchy was still a highly decentralized state. Maria Theresa worked to streamline and centralize administration, finances, and defense. She created new centralized governing councils and, above all, reformed the tax system so that the Crown could better tap the wealth of its subjects. She established new courts of justice and limited the exploitation of serfs by landlords. In general, she presided over an effort to bypass many of the provincial and privatized controls on government still in the hands of the great nobility. She accomplished all of this without being in any way "enlightened" herself. For example, she had a traditional suspicion of freedom of the press and insisted on religious orthodoxy.

Her son, Joseph, was an interesting contrast. Self-consciously "enlightened," Joseph II (r. 1780–1790) carried out a variety of reforms that his mother had not attempted, including freedom of the press and limited freedom of religion. Some of his reforms were particularly dramatic, such as drastic curtailment of the death penalty and encouragement of widespread literacy. Many of Joseph's reforms, however, were simply extensions of his mother's. For example, he extended further legal protection to peasants and abolished hereditary serfdom in all Habsburg lands. And in some ways he was less successful than Maria Theresa had been. Though persuaded of the benefits of enlightened government, he was by temperament an inflexible autocrat, whose methods antagonized many of his most powerful subjects. Joseph's policies provoked simmering opposition and open revolt in a number of his lands, and some of his reforms were repealed even before his death.

Catherine the Great and the Empire of Russia

Another ruler who consciously staked a claim to the title "enlightened despot" was Catherine, empress of Russia (r. 1762–1796). Catherine was one of the ablest rulers in the eighteenth century and perhaps the single most able of all the rulers of imperial Russia. She combined intelligence with vision, diligence, and skill in handling people and choosing advisers. Her determination and political acumen were obvious early in her life in Russia simply from the fact that she survived at court. In 1745 she had been brought to Russia from her native Germany to marry the heir to the Russian throne. Treated badly by her husband, Tsar Peter III, Catherine engineered a coup against him in the summer of 1762. Peter was overthrown and killed, and Catherine ruled alone as empress for most of the rest of the century.

Catherine the Great, as she came to be called, was the true heir of Peter the Great in her abilities, policies, and ambitions. Under Catherine, Russia committed itself to general European affairs in addition to its traditional territorial ambitions. In situations involving the major European powers, Russia tended to ally with Britain (with which it had important trading connections, including the provision of timber for British shipbuilding) and with Austria (against their common foe, Turkey), and against France, Poland, and Prussia. In 1768, Catherine initiated a war against the Turks from which Russia gained much of the Crimean coast. She also continued Peter's efforts to dominate the weakened Poland. Here she was aided by Frederick the Great, who proposed the deliberate partitioning of Poland. In 1772, portions of Poland were gobbled up in the first of three successive "grabs" of territory (Map 16.1). Warsaw itself eventually landed in Prussian hands, but Catherine gained all of Belarus, Ukraine, and modern Lithuania—which had constituted the former duchy of Lithuania. Like any successful ruler of her age, Catherine counted territorial aggrandizement among her chief achievements.

Nevertheless, Catherine also counted herself a sincere follower of the Enlightenment. While young, she had received an education that bore the strong stamp of the Enlightenment. She took an active role in the intellectual community, corresponding with Voltaire over the course of many years and acting as patron to Diderot. One of Catherine's boldest political moves was the secularization of church lands. Although Peter the Great had extended government control of the church, he had never touched church lands. Catherine licensed private publishing houses and permitted a burgeoning periodical press. The number of books published in Russia tripled during her reign. This enriched cultural life helped bring forth a great flowering of Russian literature in the early nineteenth century.

The stamp of the Enlightenment on Catherine's policies was also visible in her attempts at legal reform. In 1767 she convened a legislative commission and provided it with a guiding document, the *Instruction*, which she had written. The commission was remarkable because it comprised representatives of all classes, including peasants, and provided a place for the airing of grievances. Catherine hoped for a general codification of law as well as reforms such as the abolition of torture and capital punishment—reforms that made the *Instruction* radical enough to

Catherine the Great Catherine was a German princess who had been brought to Russia to marry another German, Peter of Holstein-Gottorp, who was being groomed as heir to the Russian throne. There had been several Russian monarchs of mixed Russian and German parentage since the time of Peter the Great's deliberate interest in and ties with other European states. *(Wernher Collection, Somerset House, London)*

be banned in other countries. She did not propose changing the legal status of serfs, however, and class differences made the commission unworkable in the end. Most legal reforms were accomplished piecemeal and favored the interests of landed gentry. Property rights were clarified and strengthened; judicial procedures were streamlined but constructed to include legal privileges for the gentry.

Like the Austrian rulers, Catherine undertook far-reaching administrative reform to create more

Map 16.1 The Partitions of Poland and the Expansion of Russia, 1772–1795 Catherine the Great acquired modern Lithuania, Belarus, and Ukraine, which had once constituted the duchy of Lithuania, part of the multi-ethnic Polish kingdom.

effective local units of government. Here again, political imperatives were fundamental, and reforms in local government strengthened the hand of the gentry. The legal subjection of peasants in serfdom was also extended as a matter of state policy to help win the allegiance of landholders in newly acquired areas. Gentry, on whom the stability of her government depended, were rewarded with estates and serfs to work them.

Catherine's reign was marked by one of the most massive and best-organized peasant rebellions of the century. Occurring in 1773, the rebellion expressed the grievances of the thousands of peasants who joined its ranks and called for the abolition of serfdom. The revolt took its name from its Cossack leader, Emelian Pugachev (d. 1775), and also reflected the dissatisfaction with the Russian government of this semiautonomous people.

The dramatic dilemmas Catherine faced illustrated both the promise and the costs of state formation throughout Europe. State consolidation permitted the imposition of internal peace, a coordinated economic policy, and the reform of justice, but at the price of coercion of the population. Thus, we can see from the alternative perspective of Russia the importance of the political sphere that was opening up in France and being consolidated in England.

STATES IN CONFLICT

In the eighteenth century a new constellation of states emerged to dominate politics on the Continent. Along with the traditional powers of England, France, and Austria were Prussia in central Europe and Russia to the east (see Map 16.1). Certain characteristics common to all these states account for their dominance, and none was more crucial than their ability to field effective armies. Traditional territorial ambitions accounted for many wars in the eighteenth century, but the increasing importance of overseas trade and colonization was the most significant source of conflict between England and France.

A Century of Warfare: Circumstances and Rationales

The large and small states of Europe continued to make war on each other for both strategic and dynastic reasons. The expense of war, the number of powerful states involved, and the complexities of their interests meant that wars were preceded by the careful construction of complex systems of alliances and followed by the changing control of many bits of territory.

States fought over territory that had obvious economic and strategic value. Although rational and defensible "national" borders were important, collecting isolated bits of territory was still the norm. The wars between European powers became extremely complex strategically; for example, France might strike a blow against Austria by invading an Italian territory in order to use it as a bargaining chip in the eventual peace negotiations.

The state of military technology, tactics, and organization shaped the outcome of most conflicts. In the eighteenth century, weapons and tactics became increasingly refined. More reliable muskets were used. A bayonet that could slip over a musket barrel without blocking the muzzle was invented. Coordinated use of bayonets required even more rigorous drilling of troops. Artillery and cavalry forces were also subjected to greater standardization of training. One sure result of the new equipment and tactics was that war became more expensive than ever before. It became increasingly difficult for small states such as Sweden to compete. Prussia, a small and relatively poor state, supported large forces by means of an extraordinary bending of civil society to the needs of the army. In Prussia, twice as many people were in the armed forces, proportionally, as in other states, and a staggering 80 percent of meager state revenue went to support the army.

Most states introduced some form of conscription in the eighteenth century. The very poor often volunteered for army service to improve their lives, but the conscription of peasants imposed a significant burden on peasant communities and a sacrifice of productive members to the state. Governments everywhere supplemented volunteers and conscripts with mercenaries and even criminals, as necessary, to fill the ranks without tapping the wealthier elements of the community. Common soldiers were increasingly seen not as members of society but as its rejects. A French war minister commented that armies had to consist of the "scum of people and of all those for whom society has no use."[2] Brutality became an accepted tool for governments to use to manage such groups of men. From the eighteenth century, the army increasingly became an instrument of social control used to manage and make use of individuals who otherwise would have had no role in society.

The Power of Austria and Prussia

Major continental wars had a marked impact on the balance of power among states in western and central Europe. The first of these, now known as the War of the Austrian Succession, began in 1740. Emperor Charles VI died that year without a male heir, and his daughter, Maria Theresa, succeeded him. Charles VI had negotiated tirelessly to persuade the various provinces of the Habsburg monarchy and the states of Europe to accept the Pragmatic Sanction, an act recognizing his daughter as his heir. In 1740, however, Frederick II of Prussia took advantage of Habsburg vulnerability by invading the wealthy Habsburg province of Silesia (see Map 16.1), to which he had a hereditary claim of sorts.

Maria Theresa proved a much more tenacious opponent than Frederick had anticipated. In the end, he was lucky to be able to hold onto Silesia, which was on the northern edge of Maria Theresa's territories. Although Austrian forces were never able to dislodge Frederick, they did best most of the forces ranged against them by their perpetual opponent, France, and other German states allied with Frederick.

The War of the Austrian Succession dragged on until 1748, when a final treaty was signed. Austria's succession was not disrupted and its lands were not dismembered. Prussia, because of the annexation of Silesia and the psychological impact of victory, emerged as a power of virtually equal rank to the Habsburgs in Germany.

The unprecedented threat that Austria now felt from Prussia caused a veritable revolution in alliances across Europe. So great in Austrian minds was the change in the balance of power that Austria was willing to ally with France, its traditional enemy, in order to isolate Prussia. In the years before what would later be known as the Seven Years' War (1756–1763), Austrian officials approached France to propose a mutual defensive alliance—a move that became known as the "Diplomatic Revolution." Sweden and Russia, with territory to gain at Prussia's expense, joined the alliance system.

Frederick initiated hostilities in 1756, hoping, among other outcomes, to prevent consolidation of the new alliances. Instead, he found that he had started a war against overwhelming odds. Limited English aid kept him in the field. The English, engaged with France in the overseas conflict known as the French and Indian War, wanted France to be heavily committed on the Continent. What saved Frederick was Russia's withdrawal from the alliance against him when a new ruler took the throne there in 1762. Prussia managed to emerge intact—though strained economically and demographically.

The results of the war confirmed Prussia and Austria as the two states of European rank in German-speaking Europe. Their rivalry would dominate German history until the late nineteenth century.

The Atlantic World: Trade, Colonization, Competition

The importance of international trade and colonial possessions to the states of western Europe grew dramatically in the eighteenth century. Between 1715 and 1785, Britain's trade with North America rose from 19 to 34 percent of its total trade, and its trade with Asia and Africa rose from 7 to 19 percent of the total. By the end of the century, more than half of all British trade was carried on outside of Europe; for France, the figure was more than a third.

European commercial and colonial energies were concentrated in the Atlantic world, where the profits were the greatest. The population of British North America grew from about 250,000 in 1700 to about 1.7 million by 1760. The densely settled New England colonies provided a market for manufactured goods from the mother country, though they produced little by way of raw materials or bulk goods on which traders could make a profit. Maryland and Virginia produced tobacco, the Carolinas rice and indigo. England re-exported all three throughout Europe, at considerable profit.

The French in New France, numbering only 56,000 in 1740, were vastly outnumbered by the British colonists. Nevertheless, the French successfully expanded their control of territory in Canada. Despite native resistance, the French extended the fur trade—the source of most of the profits that New France generated—west and north along the Great Lakes, consolidating their hold as they went by building forts. They cut into the British trade run out of Hudson Bay to the north and contested the mouth of the St. Lawrence River and the Gulf of St. Lawrence. The British held Nova Scotia and Newfoundland, the French held Cape Breton Island, and both states fished the surrounding waters.

The commercial importance of all of these holdings, as well as those in Asia, paled beside the profits generated by the Caribbean colonies. The British held Jamaica and Barbados; the French, Guadeloupe and Martinique; the Spanish, Cuba and San Domingo; and the Dutch, a few small islands. Sugar produced by slave labor was the major source of profits, along with other cash crops such as coffee, indigo, and cochineal (another dyestuff). The tiny Dutch possession of Guiana on the South American coast required twice as many visits by Dutch ships as the Dutch East India Company sent into Asia.

The economic dependence of the colonies on slave labor meant that the colonies were tied to their home countries not with a two-way commercial exchange but with a three-way "triangle" trade (Map 16.2). European manufactures were shipped to western ports in Africa, where they were traded for slaves. The enslaved Africans were then transported to South America, the Caribbean, or North America, where planters bought and paid for them with profits from their sugar and tobacco plantations. (See the box "Encounters with the West: An African Recalls the Horrors of the Slave Ship.") Sugar and tobacco were then shipped back to the mother country to be re-exported at great profit throughout Europe. Merchants in cities such as Bordeaux in France and Liverpool in England invested heavily in the slave trade and the re-export business.

The proximity and growth of French and British settlements in North America ensured conflict (see Map 16.3). The Caribbean and the coasts of Central and South America were strategic flashpoints as well. The British were making incursions along the coastline claimed by Spain and were trying to break into the monopoly of trade between Spain and its vast possessions in the region. Public opinion in both Britain and France became increasingly sensitive to colonial issues. For the first time, tensions abroad would fuel a major conflict between two European states.

Great Britain and France: Wars Overseas

In the eighteenth century, England became the dominant naval power in Europe. Its navy protected its far-flung trading networks, its merchant fleet, and the coast of England itself. England had strategic interests on the Continent as well and consistently promoted a variety of powers there, so that no one of them could pose too great a threat to England, its coastline, or its widespread trading system. The French, who had dispatched a fleet to aid the Stuart claimant to the British throne (see page 421), seemed a particular threat.

A second, dynastic consideration in continental affairs was the electorate of Hanover, the large principality in western Germany that was the native territory of the Hanoverian kings of England. Early in the century especially, the interests of this German territory were a significant factor in British foreign policy. Unable to field a large army, given their maritime interests, the British sought protection for Hanover in alliances and subsidies for allies' armies on the Continent. The money for these ventures came from the profits on overseas trade.

After the death of Louis XIV in 1715, England's energies centered on colonial rivalries with France, its greatest competitor overseas. There were three major wars between England and France in colonial regions. The first two were concurrent with the major land wars in Europe: the War of the Austrian Succession (1740–1748) and the Seven Years' War (1756–1763). The third war

	Great Britain
	France
	Portugal
	Spain
	Netherlands

Hudson Bay

LOUISIANA

MEXICO

NEW FRANCE
QUEBEC

NEWFOUNDLAND
(To Gr. Br., 1713)

NOVA SCOTIA
(ACADIA)
(To Gr. Br., 1713)

Tobacco

Furs

Colonial products

GREAT
BRITAIN

NETH.

FLORIDA

Silver

FRANCE

CUBA

Sugar

Manufactured goods

JAMAICA

PORTUGAL SPAIN

Porto
Bello

HISPANIOLA

ATLANTIC OCEAN

GUADELOUPE
(Fr.)

CANARY IS.
(Spain)

MARTINIQUE
(Fr.)

NEW GRANADA

BARBADOS
(Gr. Br.)

DUTCH
GUIANA

FRENCH
GUIANA

AFRICA

Amazon

Sugar

CAPE VERDE IS.
(Port.)

Cape
Verde

PERU

European forts and trading stations

BRAZIL

Slaves

ANGOLA

∾ ENCOUNTERS WITH THE WEST ∾

An African Recalls the Horrors of the Slave Ship

Olaudah Equiano (ca. 1750–1797) was one of the few Africans sold into slavery in the Americas to leave a written record of his experiences. An Ibo from the Niger region, he first experienced slavery as a boy when kidnapped from his village by other Africans. But nothing prepared him for the brutality of the Europeans who bought and shipped him to Barbados, in the British West Indies. He eventually regained his freedom and received an education.

The first object which saluted my eyes when I arrived on the [African] coast was the sea and a slaveship . . . waiting for its cargo. . . . When I was carried on board I was immediately handled, and tossed up, to see if I were sound, by some of the crew. . . . I was soon put down under the decks, and there I received such a salutation in the nostrils as I had never experienced in my life; so that, with the loathsomeness of the stench . . . I became so sick and low that I was not able to eat. . . . I now wished for the last friend, death, to relieve me; but soon, to my grief, two of the white men offered me eatables; and, on my refusing to eat, one of them held me fast by the hands and laid me across, I think, the windlass, and tied my feet while the other flogged me severely.

One day, when we had a smooth sea and a moderate wind, two of my wearied countrymen, who were chained together, preferring death to such a life of misery, somehow made through the nettings and jumped into the sea; immediately another dejected fellow who [was ill and so not in irons] followed their example. . . . Two of the wretches were drowned, but they got the other and afterwards flogged him unmercifully for thus attempting to prefer death to slavery. In this manner we continued to undergo more hardships than I can now relate. Many a time we were near suffocation for want of fresh air. . . . This, and the stench of the necessary tubs, carried off many.

Source: Philip D. Curtin, *Africa Remembered* (Madison: University of Wisconsin Press, 1967), pp. 92–96.

coincided with the rebellion of British colonies in North America—the American Revolution—beginning in the 1770s. Inevitably more committed to affairs on the Continent than were the British, the French were able to hold their own successfully in both arenas during the 1740s, but by 1763,

Map 16.2 The Atlantic Economy, ca. 1750 The "triangle trade" linked Europe, Africa, and European colonies in the Americas. The most important component of this trade for Europe was the profitable plantation agriculture that depended on enslaved Africans for labor.

though pre-eminent on the Continent, they had lost many of their colonial possessions to the English.

In the 1740s, France and England tested each other's strength in scattered colonial fighting, which began in 1744 and produced a few well-balanced gains and losses. Peace was made in 1748 but tension was renewed almost immediately at many of the strategic points in North America. The French reinforced their encirclement of British colonies with more forts along the Great Lakes and the Ohio River. The French and Indian War was sparked when British troops (at one point led by the colonial commander George Washington) attempted to strike at these forts in 1754.

In India, meanwhile, the French and the British attempted to strengthen their commercial footholds by making military and political alliances with local Indian rulers. A British attack on a French convoy provoked a declaration of war by France in May 1756, three months before fighting in the Seven Years' War broke out in Europe. For the first time, a major war between European nations had started and would be fought in their overseas possessions, signifying a profound change in the relation between Europe and the rest of the world.

The French had already committed themselves to an alliance with Austria and were increasingly involved on the Continent after Frederick II initiated war there in August 1756. Slowly, the drain of sustaining war both on the Continent and abroad began to tell, and Britain scored major victories against French forces after an initial period of balanced successes and failures. The French lost a number of fortresses on the Mississippi and Ohio Rivers and on the Great Lakes and, finally, also lost the interior of Canada with the fall of Quebec and Montreal in 1759 and 1760, respectively (Map 16.3).

In the Caribbean, the British seized Guadeloupe, the main French sugar-producing island. Superior resources in India enabled the British to take several French outposts there. The cost of involvement on so many fronts meant that French troops were short of money and supplies. They were particularly vulnerable in North America because the territory they had occupied remained sparsely settled and dependent on the mother country for food.

By the terms of the Peace of Paris in 1763, France regained Guadeloupe. In India, France retained many of its trading stations but lost its political and military clout. British power in India was also enhanced by victories over the Indian rulers who had sided with the French. British political rule in India, as opposed to merely a mercantile presence, began at this time. The British now also held Canada. They emerged as the preeminent world power among European states.

ECONOMIC EXPANSION AND SOCIAL CHANGE

The intellectual and cultural ferment of the Enlightenment laid the groundwork for domestic political changes to come, just as British victories in the Seven Years' War shifted the balance of power abroad. More subtle and more profound changes were occurring in the European countryside, however: Population, production, and consumption were beginning to grow beyond the bounds that all preceding generations had known.

More Food and More People

Throughout European history, there had been a delicate balance between available food and numbers of people to feed. Population growth had accompanied increases in the amount of land under cultivation. From time to time, population growth surpassed the ability of the land to produce food, and people became malnourished and prey to disease.

There were few ways to increase the productivity of land. Peasants safeguarded its fertility by alternately cultivating some portions while letting others lie fallow or using them as pasture. Manure provided fertilizer, but during the winter months livestock could not be kept alive in large numbers. Limited food for livestock meant limited fertilizer, which in turn meant limited production of food for both humans and animals.

After the devastating decline in the fourteenth century due to the Black Death, the European population experienced a prolonged recovery, and in the eighteenth century the balance that had previously been reached began to be exceeded for the first time. Population growth occurred because of a decline in the death rate for adults and a simultaneous increase in the birthrate in some areas owing to earlier marriages.

The primary reason adults were living longer, despite the presence of various epidemic diseases, was that they were better nourished and thus better able to resist disease. Food production increased because of the introduction of new crops

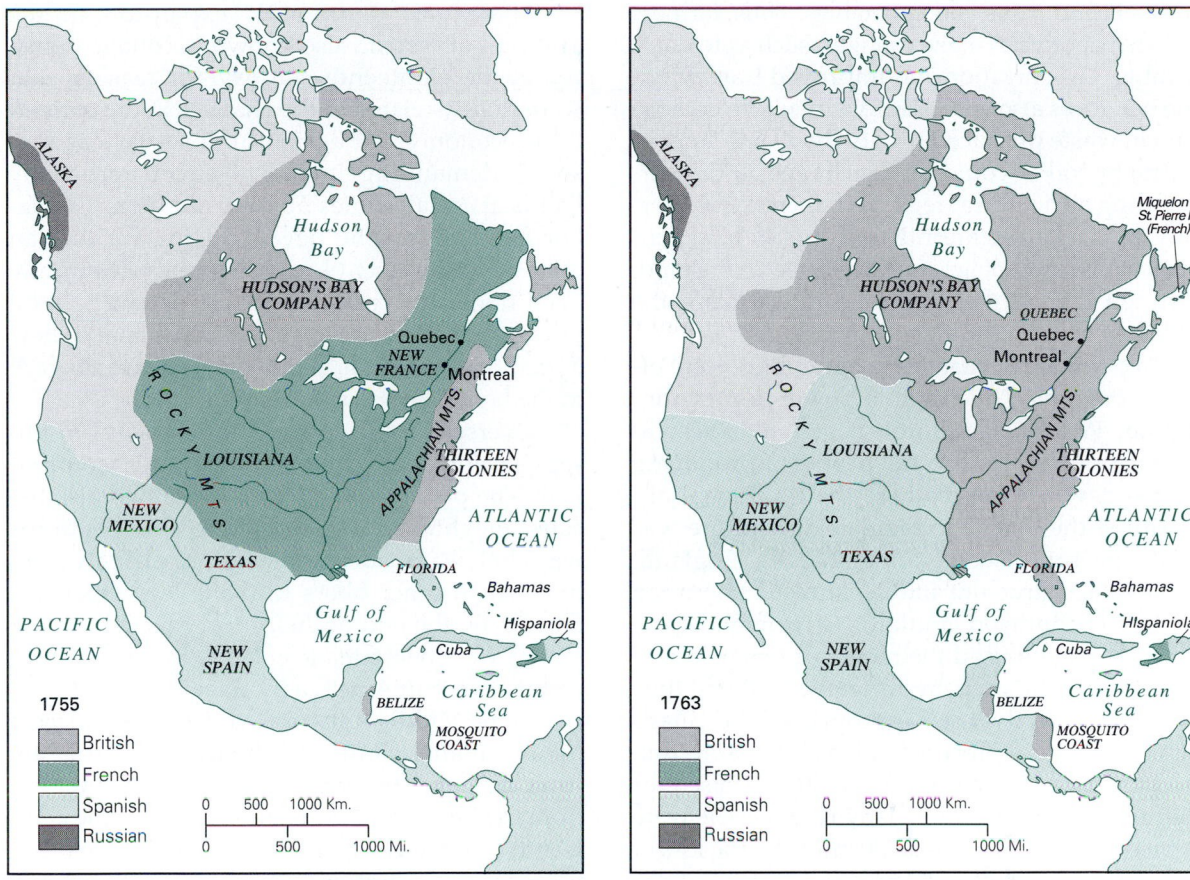

Map 16.3 British Gains in North America The British colonies on the Atlantic coast were effective staging posts for the armies that ousted the French from North America by 1763. However, taxes imposed on the colonies to pay the costs of the Seven Years' War helped spark revolt—the American Revolution—a decade later.

and other changes in agricultural practices. The cumulative effect of these changes was so dramatic that historians have called them an "agricultural revolution." The new crops included fodder, such as clover, legumes, and turnips, which did not deplete the soil and could be fed to livestock over the winter. The greater availability of animal manure, in turn, boosted grain production. The potato, introduced from the Americas in the sixteenth century, is nutrient-dense and can feed more people per acre than can grain.

More food being produced meant more food available for purchase. A family that could pur-

chase food might decide to convert its farm into a dairy farm. In such a case, many families could be supported from a piece of land that had formerly supported a single family engaged in traditional agriculture. Over a generation or two, several children might share the inheritance of what had previously been a single farm, yet each could make a living from his or her share, and population could grow as it had not done before.

Capitals like London and Amsterdam and trading centers such as Glasgow and Bordeaux were booming. Such cities demanded not only grain but also specialized produce such as dairy products and fruits and vegetables. Thus, farmers had an incentive to make changes, such as to dairy farming. Urbanization and improved transportation networks also encouraged agriculture because human waste produced by city dwellers—known as "night soil"—could be distributed in the surrounding agricultural regions to increase soil fertility. By the late eighteenth century, pockets of intensive, diversified agriculture existed in England, northern France, the Rhineland in Germany, the Po Valley in Italy, and Catalonia in Spain.

In other areas, changes in agriculture were often accompanied by a shift in power in the countryside. Wealthy landlords began to invest in change in order to reap the profits of producing for the new markets. Where the traditional authority of the village to regulate agriculture was weak, peasants were vulnerable. In England, weak village structure and the attraction of urban markets encouraged landlords to treat land speculatively. They raised the rents farmers paid and changed cultivation patterns on the land that they controlled directly. They appropriated the village common lands, a process known as *enclosure*, and used them for cash crops such as sheep (raised for their wool) or beef cattle. Many rural people were driven off the land or made destitute by the loss of the resources of common lands.

Thus, the agricultural revolution that allowed the population to grow because of an increased production of food per individual inhabitant did not mean increased prosperity for most people.

The Growth of Industry

Agricultural changes fostered change in other areas of economic and social life. As more food was grown with less labor, peasants were freed to do other work. Since there was work to be had making other products that people needed, the nonagricultural population continued to grow. More people meant more consumers, and the demand for goods helped continue the cycle of population growth, changes in production, and economic expansion. A combination of forces increased the number of people who worked at producing a few essential materials and products.

There was a dramatic expansion in the putting-out system, also known as cottage industry, in the eighteenth century, for reasons that were closely related to the changes in the agricultural economy. All agricultural work was seasonal, demanding intensive effort and many hands at certain times but few at others. The labor demands of the new crops meant that an even larger number of people might periodically need nonfarm work to make ends meet. Rural poverty, whether as a result of traditional or new agricultural methods, made manufacturing work in the home attractive to more people.

Overseas trade spurred the demand in Europe's colonies for cloth and other finished products. The production of cloth expanded also because heightened demand led to changes in the way cloth was made. Wool was increasingly combined with other fibers to make less expensive fabrics. By the end of the century wholly cotton fabrics were being made cheaply in Europe from cotton grown in America by slave labor.

In the Middle Ages, weavers had produced a luxury-quality cloth, and their profits came not from demand, which was relatively low, but from the high prices consumers paid. In the eighteenth century, cheaper kinds of cloth were made for mass consumption. Producing more became important.

The invention of machines to spin thread in the late eighteenth century brought a marked increase in the rate of production and profound changes to the lives of rural workers who had been juggling agricultural and textile work according to season and need. The areas of England, France, and the Low Countries where the new technologies were introduced stood, by the end of the century, on the verge of a massive industrial transformation that would have dramatic political and social consequences.

Control and Resistance

The economic changes of the century produced both resistance and adaptation by ordinary people and, at times, direct action by state authorities. Sometimes ordinary people coped in ways that revealed their desperation. In many cities, the number of abandoned children rose greatly because urban families, particularly recent immigrants from the countryside, could not support their offspring. The major cities of Europe put increasing resources into police forces and city lighting schemes. Charitable institutions run by cities, churches, and central governments expanded. By 1789, for example, there were more than two thousand *hôpitaux*—poorhouses for the destitute and ill—in France. The poor received food and shelter but were forced to work for the city or to live in poorhouses against their will. Men were sometimes taken out of poorhouses and forced to become soldiers.

Resistance and adaptation were particularly visible wherever the needs of common people conflicted with the states' desire for order and

for revenue. Consider, for example, the suppression of piracy. Piracy had been a way of life for hundreds of Europeans and colonial settlers since the sixteenth century. From the earliest days of exploration, European rulers had authorized men known as privateers to commit acts of war against specific targets; the Crown took little risk and was spared the cost of arming the ships but shared in the plunder. True piracy—outright robbery on the high seas—was illegal, but the difference between piracy and privateering was often small. As governments' and merchants' desire for regular trade began to outweigh that for the irregular profits of plunder, and as national navies developed in the late seventeenth century, a concerted effort to eliminate piracy began.

Life on the seas became an increasingly vital part of western European economic life in the eighteenth century, and it began to resemble life

An Idle Apprentice Is Sent to Sea, 1747 In one of a series of moralizing engravings by William Hogarth, the lazy apprentice, Tom, is sent away to a life at sea. The experienced seamen in the boat introduce him to some of its terrors: On the left dangles a cat-o'-nine-tails, and on the distant promontory is a gallows, where pirates and rebels meet their fate. *(Reproduced with permission)*

on land in the amount of compulsion it included. English-speaking seamen alone numbered about thirty thousand around the middle of the eighteenth century. Sailors in port were always vulnerable to forcible enlistment in the navy by impressment gangs, particularly during wartime. A drowsy merchant sailor sleeping off a night of celebrating with newgotten wages could wake up to find himself aboard a navy ship. Press gangs operated throughout England and not just in major ports, for authorities were as interested in controlling "vagrancy" as in staffing the navy. Merchant captains occasionally filled their crews by such means, particularly when sailing unpopular routes.

Like soldiers in the growing eighteenth-century armies, sailors in the merchant marine as well as the navy could be subjected to brutal discipline and appalling conditions. Merchant seamen attempted to improve their lot by trying to regulate their relationship with ships' captains. Contracts for pay on merchant ships became more regularized, and seamen often negotiated their terms very carefully, including, for example, details about how rations were to be allotted. Sailors might even take bold collective action aboard ship. The English-language term for a collective job action, *strike*, comes from the sailing expression "to strike sail," meaning to lower the sails so that they cannot fill with wind. Its use dates from the eighteenth century, from "strikes" of sailors protesting unfair conditions.

Seafaring men were an unusual group because they were a large and somewhat self-conscious community of workers for wages. Not until industrialization came into full swing a century later would a similar group of workers exist within Europe itself.

SUMMARY

It is important not to exaggerate the degree to which circumstances of life changed in the eighteenth century. The economy was expanding and the population growing beyond previous limits, and the system of production was being restructured. But these changes happened incrementally over many decades and were not recognized for the fundamental changes they were.

Most of the long-familiar material constraints were still in place. Roads, on which much commerce depended, were generally impassable in bad weather. Shipping was relatively dependable and economical—but only relatively. Military life likewise reflected traditional constraints. Despite technological changes and developments of the state to equip, train, and enforce discipline, the conduct of war was still hampered by problems of transport and supply that would have been familiar to warriors two centuries before.

Similarly, though some rulers were inspired by precepts of the Enlightenment, all were guided by traditional concerns of dynastic aggrandizement and strategic advantage. Among the reading public, the women who held Enlightenment salons, and even the leading Enlightenment authors, there was no consensus as to the level of equality desirable in a society. There was certainly a great deal of fear associated with democracy—and there would be for a long time to come.

The most visible and dramatic change would happen first in politics, where goals and expectations nurtured by Enlightenment philosophy clashed with the rigid structure of the French state. Whether they were referring to the rights of women, or religious toleration, or the ideal form of government, Enlightenment philosophes argued that thinking based on empirically established facts or demonstrable logic could discover truths more conducive to human happiness than the pronouncements of tradition, church, and monarch. Even if only a limited number of people understood the specifics of the ideas being advanced, the Enlightenment generally fostered reading and education as routes to freedom and power, advocated change, and suggested that traditional social hierarchies might be questioned. Yet the Enlightenment was not simply an intellectual movement. It also encompassed the public and private settings where "enlightened" opinion flourished. The revolutionary potential of Enlightenment thought came from belief in its rationality and from the fact that it was both critical of its society and fashionable to practice.

NOTES

1. Quoted in M. S. Anderson, *Europe in the Eighteenth Century*, 3d ed. (London: Longman, 1987), pp. 218–219.
2. Dena Goodman, *The Republic of Letters: A Cultural History of the French Enlightenment* (Ithaca: Cornell University Press, 1994), p. 89.

SUGGESTED READING

Carsten, F. L. *The Origins of Prussia.* 1982. An introduction to the growth of the Prussian state in the seventeenth and eighteenth centuries.

Chartier, Roger. *The Cultural Uses of Print in Early Modern France.* 1987. A discussion of changes in reading habits and in the uses of printed materials throughout the eighteenth century in France.

Cipolla, Carlo. *Before the Industrial Revolution.* 1976. A comprehensive treatment of the development of the European economy and technology through this period.

Colley, Linda. *Britons: Forging the Nation, 1707–1837.* 1992. A history of the British that emphasizes the interrelationships of political, social, and cultural history.

Darnton, Robert. *The Literary Underground of the Old Regime.* 1982. One of several important works by Darnton on the social history of print culture.

Devine, T. M. *Clanship to Crofters' War: The Social Transformation of the Scottish Highlands.* 1994. A brief and readable study that follows the destruction and transformation of Highland culture from the Late Middle Ages to the nineteenth century.

De Vries, Jan. *The Economy of Europe in an Age of Crisis, 1600–1750.* 1976. Essential reading for understanding the changes in Europe's economy and in its trade and colonial relationships throughout the world.

Doyle, William. *The Old European Order, 1660–1800.* 1978. A general history.

Gagliardo, John. *Enlightened Despotism.* 1968. A general introduction to the concept and to the rulers of the era.

Gay, Peter. *The Enlightenment: An Interpretation.* 2 vols. 1966–1969. A detailed study of Enlightenment thought by one of its foremost modern interpreters.

———. *Voltaire's Politics.* 1959. A lively introduction to Voltaire's career as a political and social reformer.

Goldgar, Anne. *Impolite Learning: Conduct and Community in the Republic of Letters, 1680–1750.* 1995. Erudite study of international literary and scientific communities.

Goodman, Dena. *The Republic of Letters: A Cultural History of the French Enlightenment.* 1994. Indispensable for understanding the social context of the Enlightenment and the role of women.

Gullickson, Gay. *Spinners and Weavers of Auffay.* 1986. Focuses on a specific community in western Europe, providing a detailed analysis of the changes in the European economy in the seventeenth and eighteenth centuries.

Hubatsch, Walter. *Frederick the Great.* 1981. A biography that illuminates Frederick's system of government.

Hufton, Olwen. *The Poor of Eighteenth-Century Paris.* 1974. An analysis of the lives of the poor and the responses of the state.

Kennedy, Paul. *The Rise and Fall of British Naval Mastery.* 1976. The authoritative work on the rise of British seapower from the sixteenth century to modern times.

Laslett, Peter. *The World We Have Lost.* 1965. An innovative study of premodern society and culture, emphasizing the differences in habits and values that separate our society from preindustrial times.

Madariaga, Isobel de. *Russia in the Age of Catherine the Great.* 1981. The best recent biography of Catherine.

Parry, J. H. *Trade and Dominion: The European Overseas Empires in the Eighteenth Century.* 1971. A reliable survey of developments.

Treasure, Geoffrey. *The Making of Modern Europe, 1648–1780.* 1985. A broad study covering political, social, economic, and cultural developments.

CHAPTER 17

Revolutionary Europe, 1789–1815

One day in early July 1792, a troop of national guardsmen from the city of Marseille in southern France marched into Paris, singing as they came:

Allons enfants de la patrie,	(Come, children of the nation)
Le jour de gloire est arrivé	(The day of glory is at hand)
Contre nous de la tyrannie	(Against us is raised)
L'étendard sanglant est levé!	(The bloody standard of tyranny!)

Their song, soon known as the "Marseillaise," became famous as the rally cry of the French Revolution and three years later was officially declared the French national anthem. This choice is appropriate, for the Revolution, which was unfolding that July, profoundly shaped the growth and character of modern France.

Part of the Revolution's significance lay in the power of symbols, such as the "Marseillaise," to challenge an old political order and legitimate a new one. Challenges to the power of the king were not new, but the Revolution overthrew his right to rule at all. Indeed, in the course of this Revolution, Louis XVI was transformed from the divinely appointed father of his people to an enemy of the people, worthy of execution. A new political world was emerging.

The Revolution began because of a governmental financial crisis, and at several important junctures it was further ignited by bread shortages, but these material causes led only to remarkable innovation (both horrible and hopeful) because of the intellectual and political climate in which they occurred. Enlightenment philosophy influenced the decisions of French public figures and inspired the imaginations of the people. The example of the American Revolution moved the French reformers to believe that change was both desirable and possible. Expectations ran high.

In its initial phase, the French Revolution established the principle of constitutional government and ended many traditional political privileges. These moderate gains were swept aside as the Revolution became increasingly radical. The reasons for this were various, including the king's intransigence, foreign war, counterrevolution, and food riots. Most dangerous, perhaps, was inexperience with the compromises and delays necessary in the normal processes of democratic institutions. The Revolution's most radical phase, the Terror, produced its most effective legislation but also its worst violence.

Today the Revolution is considered the initiation of modern European as well as modern French history. Events in France reverberated throughout Europe because the overthrow of Louis XVI threatened other monarchs. By the late 1790s the armies of France would be led in outright conquest of other European states by one of the most talented generals in European history, Napoleon Bonaparte. What he brought to the continental European nations was an amalgam of imperial aggression and revolutionary fervor.

~ Questions and Ideas to Consider

- In what ways did the American Revolution influence the French? Consider the ideological influences as well as the economic demands of the American Revolution and the experiences of Lafayette and other French officers.

- Over the course of the French Revolution, many people took an active role in politics for the first time. Consider the experience of Parisian women. In what ways, old and new, were they able to express their views and effect political change?

- What were the goals of the Terror? Did it achieve these goals? Scholars have long debated the moral significance of the Terror. What do you think? If great and arbitrary violence is necessary to create a regime of greater democracy and freedom, is such violence acceptable?

- Did Napoleon preserve the democratic and social accomplishments of the Revolution or dismantle them? Give evidence for both possible conclusions. Which do you think is more persuasive?

- Discuss the notion of political legitimacy. How do symbolic images and gestures help to give permanence and authority to a regime? Name several important symbols and symbolic acts of the revolutionary period.

BACKGROUND TO REVOLUTION

When the American colonists declared their independence from Britain in 1776, there were many consequences: British trading interests were challenged, French appetites for gains at British expense were whetted, and notions of "liberty" seemed more plausible and desirable. The victory of the American colonies in 1783, followed by the writing of the United States Constitution in 1787, heightened the appeal of liberal ideas elsewhere. There were attempts at liberal reform in several states, including Ireland, the Netherlands, and Poland. However, the American Revolution had the most direct impact on later events in France because the French had been directly involved in the American struggle.

Revolutionary Movements Around Europe

The war against the American colonies was not firmly supported by the British people. Many Britons had divided loyalties, and many others were convinced that the war was being mismanaged and called for reform of the ministerial government. In addition, a reform movement in Ireland began to spring up in 1779. The reformers demanded greater autonomy from Britain. Like the Americans, Irish elites felt like disadvantaged junior partners in the British Empire. Following the example of the American rebels, middle- and upper-class Anglo-Irish set up a system of locally sponsored voluntary militia to

CHAPTER CHRONOLOGY

May 5, 1789	Meeting of Estates General	**September 21, 1792**	National Convention declares France a republic
June 17, 1789	Third Estate declares itself the National Assembly	**January 21, 1793**	Louis XVI is guillotined
		February 1793	France declares war on Britain, Spain, and the Netherlands
June 20, 1789	Tennis Court Oath		
July–August 1789	Storming of the Bastille (July 14); abolition of feudalism (August 4); Declaration of the Rights of Man and of the Citizen (August 27)	**June 1793**	Radical Jacobins purge Girondins
		July 1793	Robespierre assumes leadership of Committee of Public Safety
October 5–6, 1789	Women's march on Versailles; Louis XVI's return to Paris	**July 1793–July 1794**	Reign of Terror
		July 1794	Robespierre is guillotined
July 1790	Civil Constitution of the Clergy	**August 1794**	Thermidorian reaction begins
June 1791	Louis XVI attempts to flee Paris; is captured and returned	**October 1795**	Directory is established
		November 1799	Napoleon seizes power
September 1791	New constitution is implemented; Girondins dominate newly formed Legislative Assembly	**1804**	Napoleon proclaimed emperor; Napoleonic Code
		1805	Battle of Trafalgar; Battle of Austerlitz
April 1792	France declares war on Austria	**1812**	Invasion of Russia
		1814	Napoleon abdicates
August 10, 1792	Storming of the Tuileries; Louis XVI arrested	**1815**	Battle of Waterloo

resist British troops if necessary. The Volunteer Movement was undercut when greater parliamentary autonomy for Ireland was granted in 1782, following the repeal of many restrictions on Irish commerce. Unlike the Americans, the Irish elites faced an internal challenge to their own authority—the Catholic population whom they had dominated for centuries—so they were willing to reach an accommodation with the British government.

Meanwhile, a political crisis with constitutional overtones was also brewing in the Netherlands. Tensions between the stadholder of the House of Orange and the merchant oligarchies of the major cities deepened during the American Revolution, because the Dutch were engaged in a commercial war against the British, to whom the stadholder was believed to be sympathetic. The conflict ceased to be wholly traditional because the representatives of the various cities, calling themselves the Dutch "Patriot" party, made wide claims to "liberty," like those of the American revolutionaries. Also, middling urban dwellers, long disenfranchised by these oligarchies, demanded "liberty," too—that is, political enfranchisement within the cities—and briefly took over the Patriot movement. An invasion in 1787 restored the power of the stadholder, the prince of Orange.

Both the Irish "volunteers" and the Dutch "Patriots," though members of very limited movements, echoed the American rebels in practical and ideological ways. Both were influenced by the economic and political consequences of Britain's relationship with its colonies. Both were inspired by the success of the American rebels and their claims for political self-determination.

Desire for political reform flared in Poland as well during this period. Reform along lines suggested by Enlightenment precepts was accepted as a necessity by Polish leaders after the first partition of Poland in 1772 had stripped the state of some of its wealthiest territories (see Map 16.1 on page 426). In 1788, however, reforming gentry in the *sejm* (representative assembly) went further, establishing a commission to write a constitution following the American example. The resulting document, known as the May 3 (1791) Constitution, was the first codified constitution in Europe; it was read and admired by George Washington.

The Constitution established a constitutional monarchy. However, Catherine the Great, empress of Russia, would not tolerate a constitutional government so close to her own autocratic regime; she ordered an invasion of Poland in 1792. The second, more extensive partition of Poland ensued, to be followed in turn in 1794 by a widespread insurrection against Russian rule. The uprising was mercilessly suppressed by Russian and Prussian troops. Unlike the Americans from whom they drew inspiration, the Poles' constitutional experiment was doomed by the power of its neighbor. A third partition in 1795 wiped Poland off the map—a situation that persisted for over 120 years.

The American Revolution and the Kingdom of France

As one of Britain's greatest commercial and political rivals, France naturally was drawn into Britain's struggle with its North American colonies. The consequences for France were momentous. First, the huge expense of aid for the American rebels helped accelerate a financial crisis in the French monarchy. Second, French involvement exposed many French aristocrats and common soldiers to the "enlightened" international community.

Rivalry with Great Britain gave France a special relationship with the American colonies and their fight for independence. In the Seven Years' War (1756–1763), France had lost many of its colonies, and some of the king's ministers pressed for an aggressive colonial policy to make up for these losses. The American Revolution seemed to offer the perfect opportunity. The French extended covert aid to the Americans from the very beginning of the conflict in 1775. After the first major American victory—at the Battle of Saratoga in 1777—France recognized the United States, established an alliance with them, and committed French troops. This support was decisive. In 1781 the French fleet kept reinforcements from reaching the British force besieged at Yorktown by George Washington. The American victory at Yorktown effectively ended the war; the colonies' independence was formally recognized by the Treaty of Paris in 1783.

The effect on France was complicated. Aid for the Americans saddled France with a debt equal to one-quarter of the government's total debt. A less tangible effect was also important. About nine thousand French soldiers, sailors, and aristocrats participated in the war. The best known was the Marquis de Lafayette, who became an aide to George Washington and helped command American troops. For many humble men, the war was simply employment. For others, it was a quest of sorts. For them, the Enlightenment belief in the rationality of men, natural rights, and natural laws by which society should be organized was brought to life in America.

Exposure to the American conflict occurred at the French court, too. Beginning in 1775, a permanent American mission to Versailles lobbied hard for aid and later managed the flow of that assistance. The chief American emissary was Benjamin Franklin (1706–1790), whose writings and scientific experiments were already known to French elites. His talents—among them a skillful exploitation of a simple, Quakerlike demeanor—succeeded in promoting the idealization of America at the French court.

The United States Constitution and the various state constitutions and debates surrounding them were all published in Paris and much discussed in salons and at court. America became the prototype of what Enlightenment philosophy said was possible. It was hailed as the place where the irrationalities of inherited privilege did not prevail. A British observer, Arthur Young (1741–1820), believed that "the American revolution has laid the foundation of another in France, if [the French] government does not take care of itself."[1]

By the mid-1780s there was no longer a question of whether the French regime would experience reform but rather what form the reform would take. The royal government was almost bankrupt. A significant minority of the politically active elite was convinced of the fundamental irrationality of France's system of government.

The Crisis of the Old Regime

The *Old Regime*—a term for the political structure that existed before the Revolution—was brought to the point of crisis in the late 1780s. Three main factors can be discerned: (1) an antiquated system for collecting revenue; (2) institutional constraints on the monarchy that defended privileged interests; and (3) an elite public opinion that envisioned thoroughgoing reform and pushed the monarchy in that direction. Another factor was the ineptitude of the king, Louis XVI (r. 1774–1793).

Louis was a kind, well-meaning man better suited to carry out the responsibilities of a petty bureaucrat than to be king. The queen, the Austrian Marie Antoinette (1755–1793), was unpop-

ular. She was regarded with suspicion by those for whom the alliance with Austria had never felt natural. She, too, was politically inept and widely rumored to be selfishly wasteful of royal resources.

The fiscal crisis of the monarchy was an outgrowth of the system in which the greatest wealth was protected by traditional privileges. At the top of the social and political pyramid were the nobles, a legal grouping that included warriors and royal officials. Since nobility conferred exemption from much taxation, the royal government could not directly tax its wealthiest subjects.

This situation existed throughout much of Europe, a legacy of the individual contractual relationships that had formed the political and economic framework of medieval Europe. Unique to France was the strength of the institutions that defended this system. Of particular importance were the royal law courts, the parlements, which claimed a right of judicial review over royal edicts. All the Parlementaires were noble. Louis XV (d. 1774) had successfully undermined the power of the parlements, but Louis XVI buckled under pressure and restored them to full power.

Deficit financing had been a way of life for centuries. After early efforts at reform, Louis XIV (d. 1715) had reverted to such old expedients as selling offices, which only added to the weight of privileged investment in the old order. England had established a national bank to free its government from the problem, but the comparable French effort early in the century had been undercapitalized and had failed.

Short-term economic crises added to the problem. During Louis XVI's reign there were several years of disastrously poor harvests, and there was a persistent downturn in the economy. The weakness of the economy proved to be a crucial reason for the failure of overall reform.

The king employed able finance ministers, who tried to replace the tangle of taxes with a simpler system in which all would pay and to eliminate local tariffs, which were stifling commerce. The parlements and many courtiers and aristocrats, as well as ordinary people, resisted.

Ordinary people did not trust the "free market" (free from traditional trade controls) for grain; most feared that speculators would buy up the grain supply and people would starve. Trying to implement such reforms in a time of grain shortage almost guaranteed their failure. Moreover, many supported the parlements out of self-interest and because they were the only institution capable of standing up to the monarchy. Yet not all members of the elite opposed reform. The imprint of "enlightened" public opinion shaped in salons and literary societies was apparent in the thinking of some aristocrats.

In 1787 the king called an "Assembly of Notables"—an ad hoc group of elites—to support him in facing down the parlements and implementing reform. He found little support even among men known to be sympathetic to reform. Some did not support particular reforms. Others, reflecting the influence of the American Revolution, maintained that a "constitutional" body such as the Estates General, which had not been called since 1614, needed to make these decisions.

Ironically, nobles and clergy who opposed reform supported the call for the Estates General, for they assumed that they could control its deliberations. Since the three Estates met and voted separately by "order"—clergy (First Estate), nobles (Second Estate), and commoners (Third Estate)—the clergy and nobles could nullify whatever the Third Estate might propose.

In 1788 deputies to the Estates General were elected by intermediate assemblies chosen by wide male suffrage. Louis assumed there was widespread loyalty to the monarchy in the provinces, and he wished to tap into it by means of this voting. Louis also agreed that the Third Estate should have twice as many deputies as the other two Estates, but he did not authorize voting by head rather than by order.

Louis faced a critical situation when the Estates General convened in May 1789. Political pamphlets abounded arguing that the Third Estate deserved enhanced power because it had the mandate of the people. The most important pamphlet was *What Is the Third Estate?* (1789) by Joseph Emmanuel Sieyès (1748–1836), a church official from the diocese of Chartres. The sympathies of Abbé Sieyès, as he was known, were with the Third Estate: His career had suffered because he was not noble. Sieyès argued that the Third Estate represented the nation because it did not reflect special privilege.

Among the deputies of the first two Estates were some men, like the Marquis de Lafayette (1757–1834), who were sympathetic to reform. More important, the elections had returned to the Third Estate a large majority of deputies who reflected the most radical political thought possible for men of their standing. Most were lawyers or government functionaries but, like Sieyès, of low social rank. They frequented provincial academies, salons, and political societies. They were determined on reform and had little stake in the system as it was.

1789: The Revolution Begins

The three Estates met at Versailles, and the ineptness of the Crown quickly became clear. On the first day of the meetings, Louis and his ministers failed to introduce a program of reforms for the deputies to consider. This failure raised doubt about the monarchy's commitment to reform. More important, it allowed the political initiative to pass to the Third Estate. The deputies challenged the Crown's insistence that the three Estates meet and vote separately. Deputies of the Third Estate refused to be certified (that is, to have their credentials officially recognized) as members of only the Third Estate rather than as members of the Estates General as a whole.

For six weeks the Estates General was unable to meet officially, and the king did nothing to break the impasse. During this interlude, more and more deputies were won over to the notion that the three Estates should meet together and that the reform process must begin in the most systematic way: France must have a written constitution.

By the middle of June, more than thirty reformist members of the clergy were sitting jointly with the Third Estate, which had invited the deputies of all three Estates to meet and be certified together. On June 17 the Third Estate declared itself the National Assembly of France. At first the king did nothing, but when the deputies arrived on the morning of June 20, they discovered they had been locked out of the hall. Undaunted, they assembled instead in a nearby indoor tennis court and produced the document that has come to be known as the "Tennis Court Oath." It was a collective pledge to meet until a written constitution had been achieved.

The king continued to handle the situation with both ill-timed self-assertion and attempts at compromise. As more and more deputies from the First and Second Estates joined the National Assembly, Louis "ordered" the remaining deputies to join it, too. Simultaneously, however, he ordered troops to come to Paris, which stirred unrest in the capital. Paris, with a population of about 600,000 in 1789, was one of the largest cities in Europe. Some assumed the king intended to starve Paris and destroy the National Assembly. Already they considered the Assembly to be a guarantor of acceptable government.

It took little—the announcement of the dismissal of a reformist finance minister—for Paris to erupt in demonstrations and looting. Crowds besieged City Hall and the royal armory, where they seized thousands of weapons. A popular militia formed as citizens armed themselves. Armed crowds assailed other sites of royal authority, including the huge fortified prison, the Bastille, on the morning of July 14. The Bastille now held only

The Tennis Court Oath   It was raining on June 20 when the deputies found themselves barred from their meeting hall and sought shelter in the royal tennis court. Their defiance created one of the turning points of the Revolution; the significance was recognized several years later by this painting's artist. *(Photographie Bulloz)*

a handful of petty criminals, but it was a symbol of royal power and, it was assumed, held large supplies of arms. The siege was successful because the garrison had not been given firm orders to fire on the crowds if necessary.

The citizens' victory was a great embarrassment to royal authority. The king had to embrace the popular movement. He came to Paris and in front of a crowd at City Hall donned the red and blue cockade worn by the militia and ordinary folk as a badge of resolve and defiance. This symbolic action signaled the legitimation of politics based on new principles.

Encouraged by events in Paris, inhabitants of cities and towns around France staged similar uprisings. In many, the machinery of royal government broke down completely. City councils, officials, and even Parlementaires were thrown out of office. Popular militias took control of the streets. There was a simultaneous wave of uprisings in rural areas. Most of them were the result of food shortages, but their timing added momentum to the political protests in urban areas. These events forced the members of the National Assembly to pass legislation to satisfy popular protests against economic and political privileges.

On August 4 the Assembly issued a set of decrees abolishing the remnants of powers that landlords had enjoyed since the Middle Ages, including the right to compel peasants to labor for them and the bondage of serfdom itself. Although largely symbolic, because serfdom and forced labor had been eliminated in much of France, these changes were hailed as the "end of feudalism." A blow was also struck at established religion by abolishing the *tithe*, an important church tax. At the end of August, the Assembly issued a Declaration of the Rights of Man and the Citizen, a bold assertion of principles condemning the old order.

In September, the deputies debated the king's role in a new constitutional government. Deputies known as "monarchists" fought with more radical deputies over the role of elites in government and whether the king should hold legislative veto power. After deliberation, the Assembly reached a compromise. The king was

Women's March on Versailles On October 5, 1789, Parisian marketwomen marched the 12 miles to Versailles, some provisioning themselves with tools, stolen firearms, and horses as they left the capital. *(Jean-Loup Charmet)*

given a three-year suspensive veto—the power to suspend legislation. This was still a formidable amount of power but a drastic limitation of his formerly absolute sovereignty.

Again, Louis resorted to troops. This time, he called them directly to Versailles, where the Assembly sat. News of the troops' arrival provoked outrage, which increased with the threat of another grain shortage. Early on the morning of October 5, women in street markets in Paris responded to the food shortages with immediate collective action, shouting for bread at the steps of City Hall. Women often led protests over bread shortages, because they procured food for their families. But this bread riot became political. A crowd of thousands gathered and decided to go all the way to Versailles, accompanied by the popular militia (now called the "National Guard"), to petition the king directly. At Versailles, they presented a delegation to the National Assembly, and a joint delegation of the women and deputies was dispatched to see the king. Louis ordered stored grain supplies distributed in Paris, and he agreed to accept the constitutional role that the Assembly had voted for him. The entire royal family was escorted back to Paris by militia and city women. The king was now in the hands of his people. He was still king, but his powers were limited, and his authority was badly shaken. The Assembly had begun to govern in the name of the "nation."

THE FRENCH REVOLUTION

The French Revolution was a complicated affair; consensus and stability were extremely elusive. Even among elites convinced of the need for reform there was a wide range of opinion. The people of Paris continued to be an important force for change. Country people also became active, primarily in resisting changes forced on them by the central government. The continuing problems that had precipitated the Revolution in the first place—the indebtedness of the government, economic difficulties, and recurrent short-ages of grain—remained unresolved. All of the wrangling within France was further complicated by foreign reaction. Managing foreign war soon became a routine burden for the fragile revolutionary governments.

The First Phase Completed, 1789–1791

At the end of 1789, Paris was in ferment, but there was no disastrous division between king and Assembly. The capital continued to be the center of lively political debate. Salons continued to meet; academies and private societies proliferated. Deputies to the Assembly swelled the ranks of these societies or helped to found new ones. Several would be important throughout the Revolution—particularly the Jacobin Club, named for the monastic order whose buildings the members used as a meeting hall.

The clubs represented a wide range of revolutionary opinion. Some, in which ordinary Parisians were well represented, focused on economic policies that would directly benefit common people. Women were active in a few of the more radical groups. Monarchists dominated other clubs. At first similar to the salons and debating societies of the Enlightenment era, the clubs increasingly became both sites of political action and sources of political pressure on the government. A bevy of popular newspapers also contributed to the vigorous political life in the capital.

The broad front of revolutionary consensus began to break apart as the Assembly forged ahead with decisions about the constitution and with policies necessary to remedy France's still-desperate financial situation. The largest portion of the untapped wealth of the nation lay with the Catholic church, an obvious target for anti-clerical reformers. The Assembly seized most of the vast properties of the church and declared them national property to be sold for revenue. The clergy became salaried officials of the state. Monasteries were abolished; monks and nuns were granted pensions to permit them to continue working as nurses and teachers where possible.

Since revenue was needed faster than church property could be inventoried and sold, government bonds (*assignats*) were issued against the eventual sale of the properties. Unfortunately, in the cash-strapped economy, the bonds were treated like money, their value became inflated, and the government never realized the hoped-for profits. The Civil Constitution of the Clergy, which required clergy to swear an oath of loyalty to the state, was passed by the Assembly in July 1790 because the clerical deputies opposing it were outvoted. More than half of the clergy did take the oath of loyalty. Those who refused, concentrated among the higher clergy, were in theory thrown out of their offices. Antirevolutionary sentiment grew among people to whom the church was still important.

Meanwhile, the Assembly proceeded with administrative and judicial reform. The deputies abolished the medieval provinces as administrative districts and replaced them with uniform *départements* (departments). They declared that local officials would be elected—a revolutionary dispersal of power that had previously belonged to the king.

As work on the constitution drew to a close in the spring of 1791, the king decided that he had had enough. Louis was now a virtual prisoner in the Tuileries Palace in the heart of Paris. Afraid for himself and his family, he and a few loyal aides worked out a plan to flee France. The king and the members of his immediate family set out incognito on June 20, 1791. However, the royal party missed a rendezvous with a troop escort and was stopped along the way—and recognized.

Louis and his family were returned to Paris and now lived under lightly disguised house arrest. The circumstances of his flight were quickly discovered. He had intended to invade France with Austrian troops if necessary. Thus, in July 1791, just as the Assembly was completing its proposal for a constitutional monarchy, the constitution it had created began to seem unworkable because the king was not trustworthy. Editorials and popular demonstrations against the monarchy echoed these sentiments. On September 14 the king swore to uphold the constitution. He had no choice. The event became an occasion for celebration, but tensions remained. Though a liberal document for its day, the constitution reflected the views of the elite deputies who had created it. The right to vote, based on a minimal property qualification, was given to about half of all adult men. But these men only chose electors, for whom the property qualifications were higher. The electors in turn chose the deputies to national bodies and also local officials.

Further, no political rights were accorded to women. Educated women had joined Parisian clubs such as the *Cercle sociale* (Social Circle), where opinion favored extending rights to women. Through such clubs, these women had tried to influence the National Assembly. But the Assembly granted neither political rights nor legal equality to women, nor did it pass other laws beneficial to women such as legalizing divorce or mandating female education. The prevailing view of women among deputies seemed to reflect those of the Enlightenment philosophe Rousseau, who imagined women's competence to be entirely circumscribed within the family. *A Declaration of the Rights of Woman* was drafted by a woman named Olympe de Gouges to draw attention to the treatment of women in the constitution.

The fragility of the new system became clear soon after the constitution was implemented. Since the National Assembly had declared that its members could not serve in the first assembly elected under the constitution, the members of the newly elected Legislative Assembly, which began to meet in October 1791, lacked any of the cohesiveness that would have come from collective experience. Also, unlike the previous National Assembly, they did not represent a broad range of opinion but were mostly republicans.

In fact, the Legislative Assembly was dominated by republican members of the Jacobin Club known as Girondins, after the region in France from which many of the club's leaders came. The policies of these new deputies and continued pressure from the ordinary citizens of Paris would cause the constitutional monarchy to collapse in less than a year.

The Second Revolution and Foreign War, 1791–1793

An additional pressure on the new regime soon arose from outside France. Antirevolutionary aristocratic émigrés had taken refuge in German states and were planning to invade France. Although the German rulers did little to aid the émigrés, Austria and Prussia declared in the Declaration of Pilnitz of August 1791 that they would intervene if necessary to support the monarchy in France.

The threat of invasion seemed more real to the revolutionaries in Paris than it actually was. Many deputies wanted war. They assumed that the outcome would be a French defeat, which would lead to a popular uprising that would rid them, at last, of the monarchy. In April 1792, under pressure from the Assembly, Louis XVI declared war against Austria. From this point, foreign war would be an ongoing factor in the revolution.

At first, the war was a disaster for France. The army had not been reorganized into an effective fighting force after the loss of many aristocratic officers and the addition of newly self-aware citizens. On one occasion, troops insisted on putting an officer's command to a vote. The defeats heightened criticism of the monarchy.

By July 1792, tensions had become acute. There was a severe grain shortage due to a poor harvest and the needs of the armies; Austrian and Prussian troops were threatening to invade; and the populace was better organized and more determined than ever before. In each of the forty-eight "sections"—administrative wards—of Paris a miniature popular assembly thrashed out the issues of the day just as deputies in the nationwide Legislative Assembly did. Derisively called *sans-culottes*, "without knee pants" (worn by the elite), the Parisians in the section assemblies included shopkeepers, artisans, and laborers. Their political organization enhanced their influence with the Assembly, the clubs, and the newspapers in the capital. By late July most sections of the city had approved a petition calling for the exile of the king, the election of new city officials, the exemption of the poor from taxation, and other radical measures.

In August they took matters into their own hands. On the night of August 9, after careful preparations, the section assemblies sent representatives who constituted themselves as a new city government with the aim of "saving the state." They then proceeded with an organized assault on the Tuileries Palace, where the royal family was living. In the bloody confrontation, hundreds of royal guards and citizens died. The king and his family were imprisoned in one of the fortified towers in the city, under guard of the popularly controlled city government.

The storming of the Tuileries inaugurated the second major phase of the Revolution: the establishment of republican government in place of the monarchy. Since some deputies had fled, the people of Paris now physically dominated the Legislative Assembly. The Assembly was dissolved to make way for another body to be elected by universal manhood suffrage. On September 20, that assembly—known as the National Convention—began to meet. The next day, the Convention declared the end of the monarchy and began to work on a constitution for the new republic.

Coincidentally, on the same day, French forces won their first real victory over the allied Austrian and Prussian forces. It was a profound psychological victory. A citizen army had defeated professional, royal forces. The new republican regime let it be known that its armies were not merely for self-defense but for the liberation of all peoples in the "name of the French Nation."

The Convention faced the divisive issue of what to do with the king. Louis had not done anything truly treasonous, but some of the king's correspondence, discovered after the storming of the Tuileries, provided a pretext for charges of treason. The Convention held a trial for him, lasting from December 11, 1792, to January 15, 1793. He was found guilty by an overwhelming vote (683 to 39). Less certain was the sentence: Louis was condemned to death by a narrow majority, 387 to 334. On January 21, 1793, Louis mounted the scaffold in a public square near the Tuileries and was beheaded.

The Faltering Republic and the Terror, 1793–1794

In February 1793, the French republic was at war with virtually every state in Europe, except the Scandinavian kingdoms and Russia. Moreover, the regime faced massive and widespread counterrevolutionary uprisings within France. Nevertheless, for a time, the republican government functioned adequately. In May 1793, it passed the first Law of the Maximum, which tried to fix the price of grain so that urban people could afford their staple food.

The Convention established an executive body, the Committee of Public Safety. As the months passed, it acted with greater and greater autonomy to institute various policies and eradicate internal and external enemies. The broadly based republican government represented by the Convention began to disintegrate. In June 1793, a group of extreme Jacobins, pushed by the Parisian sections, purged the Girondin deputies from the Convention and arrested many of them. The Girondins were republicans who favored an activist government in the people's behalf, but they were less radical than the Jacobins and less willing to share power with the citizens of Paris. After the purge, the Convention still met, but most authority was held by the Committee of Public Safety.

New uprisings against the regime began. Added to counterrevolutionary revolts by peasants and aristocrats were new revolts by Girondin sympathizers. As resistance to the government mounted and the foreign threat continued, a dramatic event in Paris led the Committee of Public Safety officially to adopt a policy of political repression. A well-known figure of the Revolution, Jean Paul Marat (1743–1793), publisher of a radical republican newspaper very popular with ordinary Parisians, was murdered on July 13 by Charlotte Corday (1768–1793), a fervent supporter of the Girondins and their moderate republicanism. Shortly afterward, a long-time member of the Jacobin Club, Maximilien Robespierre (1758–1794), joined the Committee and called for "Terror"—the systematic repression of internal enemies.

Robespierre embodied all the contradictions of the policy of Terror. He was an austere, almost prim, man who lived very modestly—a model, of sorts, of the virtuous, disinterested citizen. The policies followed by the government during the year of his greatest influence, from July 1793 to July 1794, included generous, rational, and humane actions to benefit ordinary citizens as well as the policy of official Terror. (See the box "Robespierre Justifies the Terror.")

The guillotine had been at work against identified enemies of the regime since the previous autumn, but now a more energetic apparatus of terror was instituted. The Law of Suspects allowed citizens to be arrested simply on vague suspicion of counterrevolutionary sympathies. Revolutionary tribunals made arbitrary arrests and rendered summary judgments. In October a steady stream of executions began, beginning with the queen, imprisoned since the storming of the Tuileries the year before. The imprisoned Girondin deputies followed, and then the process continued relentlessly. In Paris there were about 2600 executions from 1793 to 1794.

Around France, verdicts from revolutionary tribunals resulted in approximately 14,000 executions. Another 10,000 to 12,000 people died in prison. Ten thousand or more were killed, usually by summary execution, after the defeat of counterrevolutionary uprisings. For example, 2000 people were summarily executed in Lyon when a Girondin revolt collapsed there in October. The repression in Paris, however, was unique because of the city's role in the nation's political life. The aim of the repression was not merely to quash resistance; it was also to stifle dissent. The victims in Paris included sans-culottes as well as aristocrats and former deputies.

The Terror notwithstanding, the government of the Committee of Public Safety was effective in providing direction for the nation at a critical time. It instituted the first mass conscription of citizens into the army (*levée en masse*), which created an effective popular army for the first time in the modern world. In the autumn of 1793, this army won impressive victories. Accomplishments in domestic policy included an extended

Robespierre Justifies the Terror

In this excerpt from a speech before the Convention in December 1793, Robespierre justifies the revolutionary government's need to act in an extraconstitutional manner. He echoes Rousseau's notion of a highly abstract sense of the public good.

The defenders of the Republic must adopt Caesar's maxim, for they believe that "nothing has been done so long as anything remains to be done." Enough dangers still face us to engage all our efforts. It has not fully extended the valor of our Republican soldiers to conquer a few Englishmen and a few traitors. A task no less important, and one more difficult, now awaits us: to sustain an energy sufficient to defeat the constant intrigues of all the enemies of our freedom and to bring to a triumphant realization the principles that must be the cornerstone of public welfare. . . . Revolution is the war waged by liberty against its enemies; a constitution . . . crowns the edifice of freedom once victory has been won and the nation is at peace. . . . The principal concern of a constitutional government is civil liberty; that of a revolutionary government, public liberty. [A] revolutionary government is obliged to defend the state itself against the factions that assail it from every quarter. To good citizens revolutionary government owes the full protection of the state; to the enemies of the people it owes only death.

Is a revolutionary government the less just and the less legitimate because it must be more vigorous in its actions and freer in its movement than ordinary government? . . . It also has its rules, all based on justice and public order. . . . It has nothing in common with arbitrary rule; it is public interest which governs it and not the whims of private individuals.

Thanks to five years of treason and tyranny, thanks to our credulity and lack of foresight . . . Austria and England, Russia, Prussia, and Italy had time to set up in our country a secret government to challenge the authority of our own. . . . We shall strike terror, not in the hearts of patriots, but in the haunts of foreign brigands.

Source: George Rudé, ed., *Robespierre* (Englewood Cliffs, N.J.: Prentice-Hall, 1967), pp. 58–63. Copyright © 1967 by Prentice-Hall, Inc. Renewed 1995 by George Rudé. Reprinted by permission of Simon & Schuster.

Law of the Maximum (September 1793) that applied to necessary commodities other than bread. Extensive plans were made for a system of free and universal primary education. Slavery in the French colonies was abolished in February 1794. Divorce, first legalized in 1792, was made easier for women to obtain.

In the name of "reason" and progress, traditional rituals and rhythms of life were changed. One reform of long-term significance was the introduction of the metric system of weights and measures. Equally "rational" but not ultimately successful was the elimination of the traditional

calendar. The traditional days, weeks, and months were replaced by forty-day months and *decadi* (ten-day weeks with one day of rest). All saints' days and Christian holidays were eliminated. The years had already been changed—Year I had been declared with the founding of the republic in 1792.

Churches were rededicated as "temples of reason." Believing that atheism left people with no basis for personal or national morality, Robespierre sought to promote a cult of the Supreme Being. Public festivals organized around this principle were solemn civic ceremonies intended

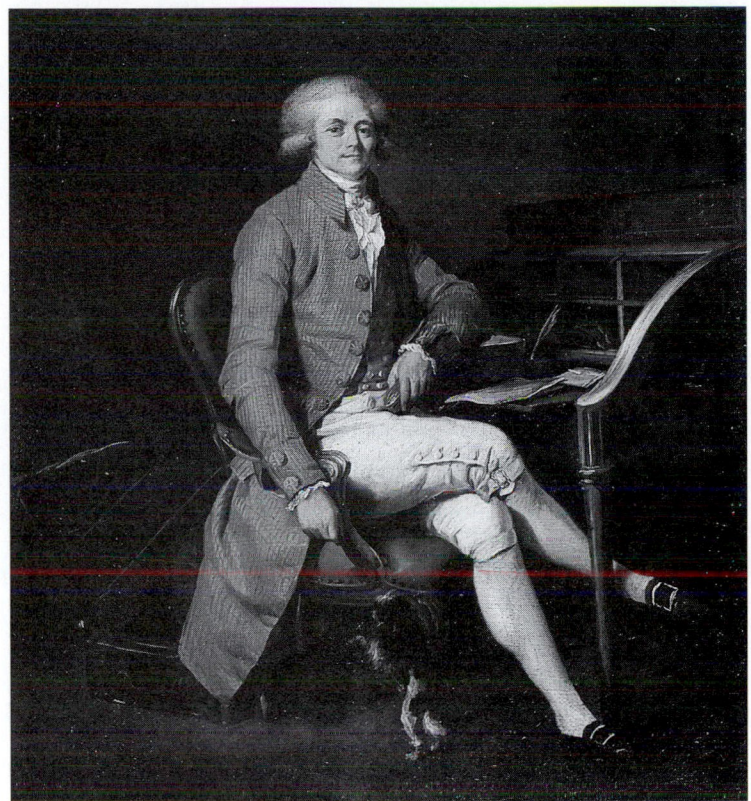

Robespierre the Incorruptible A lawyer who had often championed the poor, Robespierre was elected to the Estates General in 1789 and was a consistent advocate of republican government from the beginning of the Revolution. His unswerving loyalty to his political principles earned him the nickname "the Incorruptible." *(Musée des Beaux-Arts, Lille)*

to ritualize and legitimize the new political order. The various innovations were not necessarily welcomed. The French people generally resented the elimination of the traditional calendar. In the countryside, there were massive peasant uprisings over the loss of poor relief, community life, and familiar ritual.

Divorce law and economic regulation were a boon, especially to urban women, but women's participation in sectional assemblies and in all organized political activity—which had been energetic and widespread—was banned in October 1793. The particular target of the regime was the Society of Revolutionary Republican Women, a powerful club representing the interests of female sans-culottes. By banning women from political life, the regime hoped to ground its legitimacy, since the seemingly "natural" exclusion of women might make the new system of government appear part of the "natural" order. Elimination of women's clubs and women's participation in section assemblies also excluded a source of popular power from which the regime was now trying to distance itself.

Several critics of Robespierre and his allies were guillotined because they differed with them on policy and on the continuing need for the Terror itself. Their deaths helped precipitate the end of the Terror by further shrinking Robespierre's power. Deputies to the Convention finally dared to move against Robespierre in July 1794. French armies had scored a major victory over Austrian troops on June 26, so there no longer seemed to be any need for the Terror. In late July (the month of Thermidor, according to the revolutionary calendar), the Convention voted to arrest Robespierre. On July 28 and 29, Robespierre and his associates—about a hundred in all—were guillotined, and the Terror ended.

Thermidorian Reaction and the Directory, 1794–1799

After the death of Robespierre, the Convention reclaimed many of the executive powers that the Committee of Public Safety had seized. The Convention dismantled the apparatus of the Terror and forced the revolutionary tribunals to adopt ordinary legal procedures. The Convention also passed into law some initiatives, such as expanded public education, that had been proposed in the preceding year but not enacted. This phase of the Revolution that followed the Terror is called the "Thermidorian Reaction" because it began in the month of Thermidor (July 19–August 17).

The stability of the government, however, was threatened from the outset. There were counterrevolutionary uprisings in western France and popular uprisings against the Terror throughout France. Officials of the previous regime were lynched, and prorevolutionary groups were massacred by their fellow citizens.

With the apparatus of Terror dismantled, the Convention was unable to enforce controls on the supply and price of bread. Thus, economic difficulties and a hard winter produced famine by the spring of 1795. In May crowds marched on the Convention, chanting "Bread and the Constitution of '93," referring to the republican constitution drafted by the Convention but never implemented. The demonstrations were forcefully dispersed.

Fearful of a renewed, popularly supported Terror, or even of desperate popular support for a royalist uprising, the Convention drafted a new constitution. The new plan allowed fairly widespread (but not universal) male suffrage, but only for electors, who would choose the deputies. Property qualifications for being an elector were very high, so all but elite citizens were effectively disenfranchised.

In the fall of 1795, as the Convention was preparing for new elections, a final popular uprising shook Paris. When a crowd of twenty thousand or more converged on the Tuileries Palace, the officer in charge ordered his troops to fire. Parisian crowds never again seriously threatened the government, even though living conditions worsened as food prices soared. The army officer who issued the command to fire was Napoleon Bonaparte.

A new government took office under the provisions of the new constitution. It was called the Directory for the executive council of five men chosen by the upper house of the new legislature. To avoid the concentration of authority that had produced the Terror, the members of the Convention had tried to enshrine separation of powers in the new system. However, because of unsettled conditions throughout France, the governments under the Directory were never stable and never free from attempted coups. The most spectacular challenge, the Conspiracy of Equals, was led by extreme Jacobins who wanted to restore popular government and promote greater equality of property. The conspiracy ended with arrests and executions in 1797.

In 1799, conditions reached a critical juncture. France was again at war with a coalition of states and was faring badly. The demands of the war effort, together with other economic woes, brought the government again to the brink of bankruptcy. The government seemed to be losing control of the countryside; there were continued royalist uprisings and local political vendettas.

Two members of the Directory now invited General Napoleon Bonaparte to help them form a government that they could more strictly control. They plotted with Napoleon and his brother Louis Bonaparte to seize power on November 9, 1799.

THE NAPOLEONIC ERA

Talented, daring, and ruthless, Napoleon Bonaparte (1769–1821) was able to assess the situation in France and profit from the general state of political confusion. His audacity and personal magnetism were matched by his determination: He was a charismatic man of action who seemed capable of delivering both high ideals and social order. Once in power, he stabilized the political scene by enshrining in law the more conservative gains of the Revolution. He also used his abilities as a general to continue France's wars of conquest.

Napoleon's troops, in effect, exported the Revolution when they conquered most of Europe. Law codes were reformed, governing elites were opened to talent, and public works were undertaken in most states under French control. Yet French conquest also meant domination, pure and simple, and involvement in France's rivalry with Britain.

Napoleon: From Soldier to Emperor, 1799–1804

Napoleon was from Corsica, a Mediterranean island that had passed from Genoese to French control in the eighteenth century. The second son of a large gentry family, he was educated at military academies in France, and he married the politically well-connected widow Joséphine de Beauharnais (1763–1814), whose aristocratic husband had been a victim of the Terror.

By 1799, Napoleon was well known and popular because of his military victories. He had demonstrated his reliability and ruthlessness in 1795 when he ordered troops guarding the Convention to fire on the Parisian crowd. In 1796 and 1797 he conquered all of northern Italy, forcing Austria to relinquish that territory as well as the Austrian Netherlands, which revolutionary armies had seized in 1795. He then commanded an invasion of Egypt in an attempt to strike at British influence and trade connections in the eastern Mediterranean. The Egyptian campaign failed in its goals, but individual spectacular victories during the campaign ensured Napoleon's military reputation.

Napoleon's partners in the new government after the November coup in 1799 soon learned of his great political ambition and skill. In theory, the new system was to be a streamlined version of the Directory: Napoleon was to be first among equals in a three-man executive—First Consul, according to borrowed Roman terminology. But Napoleon soon asserted his primacy among them and began not only to dominate executive functions but also to bypass the various legislative bodies in the new regime.

Napoleon was careful to avoid heavy-handed displays of power. He cleverly sought ratification of each stage of his assumption of power through national plebiscites—a national referendum in which all eligible voters could vote for or against Napoleon's proposal. One plebiscite was for a new constitution in 1800; another, in 1802, confirmed support for his claim to consulship for life. Critical to the success of his increasingly authoritarian regime was his effort to include, among his ministers, advisers, and bureaucrats, men of many political stripes—Jacobins, reforming liberals, even former Old Regime bureaucrats. He welcomed many exiles back to France, including all but the most ardent royalists.

Napoleon combined toleration with ruthlessness. Between 1800 and 1804 he imprisoned, executed, or exiled dozens of individuals for alleged Jacobin agitation or royalist sympathies. His final gesture to intimidate royalist opposition came in 1804 when he kidnapped and coldly murdered a Bourbon prince who had been in exile in Germany.

By the terms of the Treaty of Amiens in 1802, Napoleon made peace with Britain, France's one remaining enemy. The short-lived peace only papered over the two countries' commercial and strategic rivalries, but it gave Napoleon room to establish his rule more securely in France. One of the most important steps had already been accomplished by the Concordat of 1801. The aim of this treaty with the pope was to solve the problem of church-state relations that for years had caused antirevolutionary rebellions. The agreement allowed for the resumption of Catholic worship and the continued support of the clergy by the state but also accepted the more dramatic changes accomplished by the Revolution. Church lands that had been sold were guaranteed to their new owners. Protestant churches were allowed and their clergy was paid, although Catholicism was recognized as the "religion of the majority of Frenchmen." Later, Napoleon granted new rights to Jews.

Napoleon Crossing the Great St. Bernard This stirring portrait by the great neoclassical painter Jacques-Louis David memorializes Napoleon's 1796 crossing of the Alps before his victorious Italian campaign, as a general under the Directory. The painting depicts the moment heroically rather than realistically (Napoleon wisely crossed the Alps on a sure-footed mule, not a stallion), in part because it was executed in 1801–1802. Napoleon, as First Consul, wanted images of himself that would justify his increasingly ambitious claims to power. *(Louvre © R.M.N.)*

The law code that Napoleon established in 1804 was much like his accommodation with the church in its limited acceptance of revolutionary gains. His Civil Code reflected the revolutionary legacy in its guarantee of equality before the law and its requirement for the taxation of all social classes; it also enshrined modern forms of property ownership and civil contracts. But neither the code nor Napoleon's political regime fostered individual rights, especially for women. Women lost all the rights they had gained during the Revolution. Fathers' control over their families was enhanced. Divorce was no longer permitted except in rare instances. Women lost all property rights when they married, and they generally faced legal domination by fathers and husbands.

More in keeping with the goals of the Revolution, Napoleon put France on a better financial footing by establishing a national bank. He also streamlined and centralized the administrative system, set up in 1789, by establishing the office of prefect to govern the départements. All prefects were appointed by Napoleon.

Some of these legal and administrative changes occurred after Napoleon's final coup— declaring himself emperor. This was a bold move, but Napoleon approached it dexterously. Years before, Napoleon had begun to sponsor an active court life appropriate to imperial pretensions.

The empire was proclaimed in May 1804 with the approval of the Senate; it was approved by another plebiscite. Members of Napoleon's family were given princely status, and a number of his favorites received titles. These brought no legal privileges but signaled social and political distinctions of great importance. Old nobles were allowed to use their titles again on this basis.

Conquering Europe, 1805–1810

Napoleon maintained relatively peaceful relations with other nations while he consolidated power at home, but the truces did not last. Tensions with the British quickly re-escalated when Britain resumed aggression against French shipping in 1803, and Napoleon countered by seizing Hanover, the ancestral German home of the English king. Then Napoleon seized several Italian territories and extended his influence in other German states. By 1805, all the states of Europe were threatened. Napoleon began to gather a large French force on the northern coast of France, with which he could invade England.

The British fleet, commanded by Horatio Nelson (1758–1805), intercepted the combined French and Spanish fleets that were to have been the invasion flotilla and inflicted a devastating defeat off Cape Trafalgar in southern Spain (see Map 17.1) on October 21, 1805. The victory ensured British mastery of the seas and contributed to Napoleon's eventual defeat.

In December 1805, after some preliminary small-scale victories, Napoleon's army confronted a Russian force near Austerlitz, north of Vienna (see Map 17.1). Tsar Alexander I (r. 1801–1825) led his own troops into a battle that he ought to have avoided. Austrian reinforcements could not reach him in time, and French armies shattered the Russian forces. The Battle of Austerlitz was Napoleon's most spectacular victory. Austria sued for peace. In further battles in 1806, French forces defeated Prussia as well as Russian armies once again. Prussia was virtually dismembered by the subsequent Treaty of Tilsit (1807), but Napoleon tried to work out terms to make Russia into a contented ally. His hold on

central Europe would not be secure with a hostile Russia.

Napoleon defeated Austria in the Battle of Wagram in July 1809 and, like Russia, Austria accepted French political and economic hegemony in a sort of alliance. By 1810, Napoleon had transformed most of Europe into allied or dependent states (Map 17.1). The only exceptions were Britain and the parts of Spain and Portugal that continued to resist France with British help.

The states least affected by French hegemony were its reluctant allies: Austria, Russia, and the Scandinavian countries. Most affected were the territories incorporated into France. These included the Austrian Netherlands, territory along the Rhine, and territories in Italy that bordered France. These regions were occupied by French troops and were treated as though they were départements of France itself.

In most other regions, some form of French-controlled government was in place, usually headed by a member of Napoleon's family. In northern Italy and, initially, in the Netherlands, where "sister" republics had been established after French conquests under the Directory, Napoleon imposed monarchies. Napoleon's brother Joseph was made king of Spain. Western German states of the Holy Roman Empire that had allied with Napoleon against Austria were organized into the Confederation of the Rhine, with Napoleon as its "Protector." In 1806, after a thousand years, the Holy Roman Empire ceased to exist.

Napoleon's domination of these various regions had complex, at times contradictory, consequences. French rule brought political and economic reform akin to that of the early phases of the Revolution, now enshrined in the Napoleonic Civil Code. Equality before the law was decreed, ending noble exemption from taxation where it still existed. In general, the complex snarl of medieval taxes and tolls was replaced with straightforward property taxes from which no one was exempt. As a consequence, tax revenues rose dramatically—by 50 percent in the kingdom of Italy, for example. Serfdom and forced labor were also abolished, as they had been in France in August 1789.

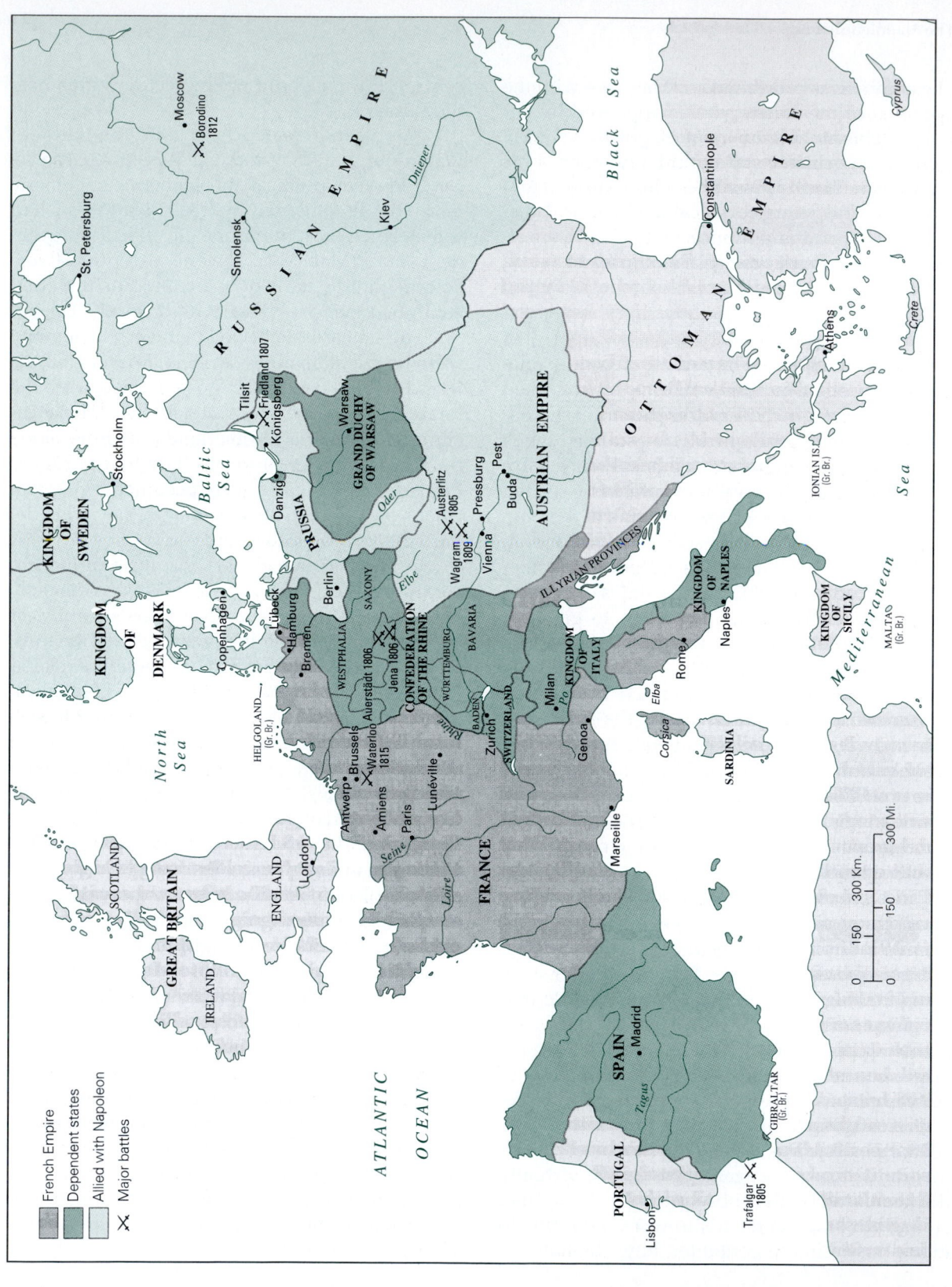

St. Petersburg
Stockholm
Moscow
Borodino 1812
Smolensk
Kiev
Dnieper
Black Sea
Constantinople
Cyprus
Crete
Athens
Tilsit
Friedland 1807
Königsberg
Danzig
Warsaw
GRAND DUCHY OF WARSAW
Austerlitz 1805
Pressburg
Pest
Buda
AUSTRIAN EMPIRE
OTTOMAN EMPIRE
IONIAN IS. (Gr. Br.)
Sea
Mediterranean Sea
KINGDOM OF SWEDEN
Baltic Sea
PRUSSIA
Oder
Wagram 1809
Vienna
Elbe
ILLYRIAN PROVINCES
KINGDOM OF NAPLES
Naples
MALTA (Gr. Br.)
KINGDOM OF SICILY
Berlin
SAXONY
BAVARIA
KINGDOM OF ITALY
Rome
Copenhagen
Lübeck
Hamburg
Bremen
HELGOLAND (Gr. Br.)
WESTPHALIA
Auerstädt 1806
Jena 1806
CONFEDERATION OF THE RHINE
WÜRTTEMBURG
BADEN
SWITZERLAND
Zurich
Milan
Po
Genoa
Elba
Corsica
SARDINIA
KINGDOM OF DENMARK
North Sea
Brussels
Waterloo 1815
Antwerp
Amiens
Paris
Lunéville
Seine
Rhine
Loire
FRANCE
Marseille
SCOTLAND
GREAT BRITAIN
IRELAND
ENGLAND
London
ATLANTIC OCEAN
SPAIN
Madrid
Tagus
GIBRALTAR (Gr. Br.)
PORTUGAL
Lisbon
Trafalgar 1805

300 Mi.
300 Km.
150
150
0
0

French Empire
Dependent states
Allied with Napoleon
Major battles

In most Catholic regions, the church was subjected to the terms of the Concordat of 1801. The tithe was abolished, church property seized and sold, and religious orders dissolved. Though Catholicism remained the state-supported religion in these areas, Protestantism was tolerated and Jews were granted rights of citizenship. Secular education, at least for boys, was encouraged.

And yet Napoleon would countenance only those aspects of France's revolutionary legacy that he tolerated in France itself. Meaningful participatory government was everywhere suppressed. This came as a blow to the Netherlands, which had experienced its own democratizing "Patriot" movement and had enjoyed republican self-government after invasion by French armies during the Revolution. Throughout the Napoleonic Empire, many of the benefits of streamlined administration and taxation were offset by the drain of continual warfare; deficits rose three- and fourfold, despite increased revenues.

Although true self-government was not allowed, a broad segment of the elites in all regions was won over to cooperation with Napoleon by being welcomed into his bureaucracy or into the large multinational army, the Grande Armée. Their loyalty was cemented when they bought confiscated church lands.

The impact of Napoleon's Continental System was equally mixed. Under this system, the Continent was closed to all British shipping and British goods. The effects were widespread but uneven, and smuggling became a major enterprise. Regions heavily involved in trade with Britain or its colonies or dependent on British shipping suffered in the new system, as did overseas trade in general when Britain gained dominance of the seas after Trafalgar. However, the closing of the Continent to British trade, combined with increases in demand resulting from the need to supply Napoleon's armies, spurred

the development of continental industries, at least in the short run. This industrial growth, enhanced by the improvement of roads, canals, and the like, formed the basis for further industrial development.

Defeat and Abdication, 1812–1815

Whatever its achievements, Napoleon's empire was ultimately precarious because of the hostility of Austria and Russia and the belligerence of Britain. Austria resented losing the Austrian Netherlands and lands in northern Italy. Russian landowners and merchants were angered when their vital trade in timber for the British navy was interrupted and when supplies of luxury goods, brought in British ships, began to dwindle. A century of close alliances with German ruling houses made alliance with a French ruler extremely difficult politically for Tsar Alexander I.

It was Napoleon, however, who ended the alliance by provoking a breach with Russia. He had reluctantly divorced Joséphine in 1809 because their marriage had not produced an heir, and he agreed to marry one of Alexander's younger sisters. Then he backed out and accepted the Austrian princess Marie Louise instead. In addition, he seized lands along the German Baltic seacoast belonging to a member of Alexander's family. When Alexander threatened a rupture of the alliance if the lands were not returned, Napoleon mounted an invasion. Advisers warned him about the magnitude of the task—particularly about the preparations needed for winter fighting in Russia, but their warnings went unheard.

Napoleon's previous military successes had stemmed from a combination of strategic innovations and audacity. Napoleon divided his forces into independent corps. Each corps included infantry, cavalry, and artillery. Organized in these workable units, his armies could travel quickly by several separate routes and converge in massive force to face the enemy. Leadership on the battlefield came from a loyal and talented officer corps that Napoleon had fashioned by welcoming returning aristocrats and favoring rising new talent. The final ingredient in the successful formula was

Map 17.1 Napoleonic Europe, ca. 1810 France dominated continental Europe after Napoleon's victories. Though French control would collapse quickly after defeats in Russia and Spain in 1812, the effects of French domination were more long-lasting.

the high morale of French troops under Napoleon. Napoleon's English nemesis, Arthur Wellesley (1769–1852), duke of Wellington, once remarked that Napoleon's presence on a battlefield was worth forty thousand men.

The campaign against Russia began in June 1812. It was a spectacular failure. Napoleon had gathered a force of about 700,000 men—about half from France and half from allied states—a force twice as large as Russia's. The strategy of quickly moving independent corps and assembling massive forces could not be implemented because of these large numbers. The supply system—always Napoleon's weakness—was simply not up to the task. Bold victories had often enabled Napoleon's troops to live off the countryside while they waited for supplies to catch up with them. But when the enemy attacked supply lines, when the distances traveled were very great, when the countryside was impoverished, or when battles were not decisive, Napoleon's strategies proved unworkable. In varying degrees, these conditions prevailed in Russia.

By the time the French faced the Russians at Borodino, the principal battle of the Russian campaign, the Grande Armée had been on the march for two and a half months and stood at less than half its original strength. After the indecisive but bloody battle, the French occupied and pillaged Moscow but found scarcely enough food and supplies to sustain them. When Napoleon finally led his troops out of Moscow late in October, the fate of the French forces was all but sealed. The army marched south to reach the warmer and better-provisioned Ukraine but was turned back by Russian troops. The French then retreated out of Russia. French soldiers who had not died in battle died of exposure or starvation or were killed by Russian peasants when they wandered away from their units. Of the original 700,000 French and allied troops, fewer than 100,000 made it out of Russia.

In the meantime, Napoleon had left his army. A coup attempt in Paris prompted him to return home before the French people realized the extent of the disaster in Russia. The collapse of his reign had begun, spurred by a coincidental

defeat in Spain. By the time Napoleon got back to Paris, his brother Joseph had been expelled from Spain, and an Anglo-Spanish force led by the duke of Wellington was poised to invade France.

Napoleon's most able generals rallied what remained of his troops and held off Prussian and Russian forces in the east until he arrived in April 1813 with a new army of raw recruits. With Britain willing to subsidize the allied armies, Tsar Alexander determined to destroy Napoleon, and the Austrians now anxious to share the spoils, Napoleon's empire began to crumble. Napoleon's forces were crushed in a massive "Battle of Nations" near Leipzig in October, during which some of his troops from German satellite states deserted him on the battlefield. The allies invaded France and forced Napoleon to abdicate on April 6, 1814. Napoleon was exiled to the island of Elba, off France's Mediterranean coast, but was installed as the island's ruler and treated somewhat royally.

The restored French king faced significant challenges. Louis XVIII (r. 1814–1824) was the brother of the executed Louis XVI; he took the number eighteen out of respect for Louis XVI's son, who had died in prison. In addition to the task of establishing his own legitimacy, he faced enormous practical problems, including pensioning off thousands of unemployed soldiers still loyal to Napoleon.

Napoleon saw his chance and returned surreptitiously to France on February 26, 1815. He had only a small band of attendants with him, but when the king sent soldiers to prevent Napoleon from advancing to Paris, they joined him instead. Louis XVIII abandoned Paris to the returned emperor.

Napoleon's triumphant return lasted one hundred days. Though many soldiers welcomed his return, ordinary French citizens had become disenchanted with him since the defeat in Russia, and with the high costs, in conscription and taxation, of raising new armies. Napoleon's reappearance galvanized the divided allies, who had been haggling over a peace settlement, into unity. Napoleon tried to strike first, but he was defeated by British and Prussian troops at Waterloo (in modern Belgium) on June 18, 1815. This time he was exiled to the tiny, remote island of St. Helena in the South Atlantic, from which escape would be impossible. He died there in 1821.

THE IMPACT OF REVOLUTION ON FRANCE AND THE WORLD

There had been extraordinary upheaval in France between 1789 and 1815, and yet this period began with Louis XVI on the throne and ended with Louis XVIII on the throne. That continuity had significance, but it could not mask the profound changes that had occurred in matters of political legitimacy, national sovereignty, and popular consciousness. The Revolution had changed the fundamental premises of political life in Europe.

The Significance of Revolution in France

Although the French monarchy was restored in 1815, the new king governed with a small group of representatives of the elite, whose participation slowly widened. The Revolution had established new principles on which to base a government: the right of "the people," however narrowly defined, to participate in government and enjoy due process of law.

Another legacy of the revolutionary era was a centralized political system. The nation was divided into départements rather than provinces. For the first time, a single code of law applied to all French people. Most officials—from département administrators to city mayors—continued to be appointed by the central government until the late twentieth century. The government sponsored national scientific societies, a national library and archives, and a system of teachers' colleges and universities. Particularly under Napoleon, there was a spate of canal- and road-building.

Napoleon's legacy, like that of the Revolution itself, was mixed. His self-serving reconciliation of aristocratic pretensions with the opening of careers to men of talent helped to ensure the long-term success of revolutionary principles from which the elite as a whole profited. His reconciliation of the state with the Catholic church helped stabilize his regime and preserve some revolutionary gains, since the restored monarchy could not renege on these arrangements. But Napoleon could hardly eliminate the antirevolutionary bent of the church, and it continued to be a reactionary force in France. The Napoleonic Code was a uniform system of law for the nation. But although it guaranteed equality under the law for men, it enshrined political and legal inferiority for women.

Napoleon's return to power in 1815 reflected the degree to which his power was always rooted in military adventurism and the loyalty of soldiers and officers. His bravado suggests the importance of personal qualities to the success of an authoritarian regime. But the swiftness of his collapse suggests that the legitimacy and security of his empire were as uncertain as the legitimacy and security of the revolutionary governments.

Although Louis XVIII acknowledged the principle of constitutionalism, it rested on fragile footing. Indeed, the fragility of new political systems was one of the most profound lessons of the Revolution. Politics, the Revolution revealed, takes place in part on a symbolic level. Symbols are effective because they link a specific political system to a broader, fundamental system of values. The religious symbolism used by the monarchy linked royal government to divine order. Similarly, the cults of reason and the Supreme Being promoted by Robespierre were attempts to link patriotism and support of the government to universal principles. Other, more limited, symbols were constantly in use: the red and blue cockades that supporters of the National Assembly put in their caps; the "liberty cap" that Louis XVI donned on one occasion; various representations of the abstract notion of "Liberty" in popular newspapers and journals.

Before the Revolution started, there was a significant shift in notions about political legitimacy. The deputies who declared themselves to be the National Assembly in June 1789 already believed that they had a right to do so. In their view, they represented "the nation," and their voice had legitimacy for that reason. The deputies brought to Versailles not only their individual convictions but also their experience in social settings where those ideas were well received. In their salons, clubs, and literary societies, they had experienced the familiarity, trust, and sense of community that are essential to effective political action.

The deputies' attempt to transplant their sense of community into national politics was not wholly successful. The National Assembly had scarcely inaugurated a secure system when its deputies undermined its workability by making themselves ineligible to hold office under the new constitution. Factions, competing interests, and clashes of personality were fatal to the government because it was so new—it did not have the authority and legitimacy that accrue over time, and its members were inexperienced. The British parliamentary system, by comparison, though every bit as elitist as the narrowest of the representative systems during the French Revolution, had a long history as a workable institution for lords, commoners, and rulers. This shared experience was an important counterweight to differences over issues, so that Parliament as an institution both survived political crises and helped solve them.

The Impact of the Revolution Overseas

Although French conquests in Europe were quickly overturned, the brief French domination had lasting effects. Elites were exposed to modern bureaucratic management, and equality under the law transformed social and political relationships. Although national self-determination had an enemy in Napoleon, the breaking down of ancient political divisions provided important practical grounding for later cooperation among elites in nationalist movements across Europe.

Europe's overseas colonies felt the impact of the Revolution in several ways. The British tried to take advantage of Napoleon's preoccupation with continental affairs by seizing French colonies and the colonies of the French-domi-

nated Dutch. In 1806 they seized the Dutch colony of Capetown—crucial for support of trade around Africa—as well as French bases along the African coast. In 1811 they grabbed the island of Java. In the Americas, French sugar colonies in the Caribbean were particularly vulnerable to English seapower. The sugar island of Haiti was an exception because British aggression there occurred in the context of a local revolution.

In Haiti the French Revolution had a direct impact. The National Assembly in Paris delayed abolishing slavery in French colonies, despite the moral appeal of such a move, because of pressure from the white planters on Haiti and out of fear that the French government would lose some of its profitable sugar trade. But the example of revolutionary daring in Paris and confusion about ruling authority invited challenges to authority in the colonies.

Many white planters hoped to seize the opportunity the Revolution provided to gain political and economic independence from France. White planter rule in Haiti was challenged, in turn, by wealthy people of mixed European and African descent and then by a full-fledged slave rebellion, beginning in 1791. (See the box "Encounters with the West: A Planter's Wife on the Haitian Slave Revolt.") Britain sent aid to the rebels when it went to war against the French revolutionary government in 1793. Only when the republic was declared in Paris and the Convention abolished slavery did the Haitian rebels abandon alliances with France's enemies and attempt to govern in concert with the mother country.

France never regained control of Haiti. Led by a former slave, François Dominique Toussaint-Louverture (1743–1803), the new government of Haiti tried to run its own affairs, though without formally declaring independence from France. Napoleon, early in his rule, decided to tighten control of the profitable colonies by reinstituting slavery and ousting the independent government of Haiti. In 1802, French forces fought their way onto the island. They captured Toussaint-Louverture, who died shortly thereafter in prison. But in 1803 they were forced to leave by another rebellion prompted by the threat of renewed slavery.

∾ ENCOUNTERS WITH THE WEST ∾

A Planter's Wife on the Haitian Slave Revolt

The following are excerpts from two letters of Madame de Rouvray, a wealthy planter's wife living in the French colony of Saint-Domingue (the western half of the island of Hispaniola), to her married daughter in France. The decree of May 15, 1791, that Madame de Rouvray mentions in her first letter granted civil rights to free persons of mixed race. Tensions between white planters, on the one hand, and mulattos and modest white settlers who favored revolutionary changes, on the other, enabled the well-organized slave rebellion to be dramatically successful. It began in late August 1791 and is the backdrop to Madame de Rouvray's second letter. Madame de Rouvray and her husband fled the island—renamed Haiti, the Native American term for Hispaniola, after the revolt—for the United States in 1793.

July 30, 1791   I am writing to you from Cap [a city on the island] where I came to find out what the general mood is here. . . . All the deputies who make up the general assembly [of the colony] left here the day before yesterday to gather at Léogane [another city]. If they conduct themselves wisely their first action should be to send emissaries to all the powers who have colonies with slaves in order to tell them of the decree [of May 15] and of the consequences that will follow from it, and ask for help from them in case it happens that the National Assembly actually abolishes slavery too, which they will surely do. After their decree of May 15, one cannot doubt that that is their plan. And you understand that all the powers who have slave colonies have a common interest in opposing such a crazy plan because the contagion of liberty will soon infect their colonies too, especially in nearby Jamaica. It is said that [the English] will send a ship and troops [which] would be wonderful for us. Your father thinks it won't be long before the English take control here.

September 4, 1791   If news of the horrors that have happened here since the 23rd of last month have reached you, you must have been very worried. Luckily, we are all safe. We can't say whether our fortunes are also safe because we are still at war with the slaves who revolted [and] who have slaughtered and torched much of the countryside hereabouts. . . . All of this will gravely damage our revenues for this year and for the future, because how can we stay in a country where slaves have raised their hands against their masters? . . . You have no idea, my dear, of the state of this colony; it would make you tremble. Don't breathe a word of this to anyone but your father is determined, once the rebels have been defeated, to take refuge in Havanna.

Source: M. E. McIntosh and B. C. Weber, *Une Correspondance familiale au temps des troubles de Saint-Domingue* (Paris: Société de l'Histoire des Colonies Françaises et Librairie Larose, 1959), pp. 22–23, 26–28. Trans. by Kristen B. Neuschel.

The View from Britain

Today the city of Paris is dotted with public monuments that celebrate Napoleon's victories. One of the main train stations is the Gare (Station) d'Austerlitz. A column in a city square, crowned with a statue of Napoleon, was made from the metal of enemy cannon captured at Austerlitz.

In London, another set of events and another hero is celebrated. In Trafalgar Square stands a statue of Lord Nelson, the British naval commander whose fleet destroyed a combined French and

Spanish fleet in 1805. Horatio Nelson was a brilliant tactician, whose innovations in maneuvering ships in the battle line resulted in stunning victories at Trafalgar and, in 1798, at the Nile Delta, which limited French ambitions in Egypt and the eastern Mediterranean. Trafalgar looms large in British history because it ensured British mastery of the seas, which enabled the British to seize colonies formerly ruled by France and its allies.

Since the late eighteenth century, the British had steadily made other gains abroad. In 1783, Britain had lost control of thirteen of its North American colonies; however, it had more successfully resolved the Irish rebellions. Similarly, in the Caribbean, British planter families, like Irish elites, were willing to accept tighter rule from the mother country in return for greater security against their subject population. In India, the East India Company was increasing its political domination and economic stranglehold on Indian manufacture and trade.

The British economy would expand dramatically in the nineteenth century as industrial production grew. The roots for that expansion can be found in this period in the countryside of Britain, where changes in agriculture and in production were occurring. These roots also lay in Britain's overseas possessions by the profits made there and also, increasingly, by the control of sources of raw materials, notably raw cotton raised in India. The export of Indian cotton grew significantly during the revolutionary period as part of an expanding trading system that included China, the source of tea.

Not every conquest had direct economic payoffs, but British elites were sure that strategic domination was a desirable step, wherever it could be managed. One Scottish landholder, writing in the opening years of the nineteenth century, spoke for many when he said that Britain needed an empire to ensure its greatness and that an empire of the sea was an effective counterweight to Napoleon's empire on land. Much as the French were at that moment exporting features of their own political system, the British, he said, could export their constitution wherever they conquered territory.

Thus, England and France were engaged in similar phases of expansion in this period. In both, the desire for power and profit drove policy. In each, myths about heroes and about the supposed benefits of domination masked the state's self-interest. In both, the effects of conquest would become a fundamental shaping force in the nineteenth century.

SUMMARY

The French Revolution was a watershed in European history because it successfully challenged the principles of hereditary rule and political privilege on which European states had hitherto been governed. The Revolution began when a financial crisis forced the monarchy to confront the desire for political reform by a segment of the French elite. Political philosophy emerging from the Enlightenment and the example of the American Revolution moved the French reformers to action. In its initial phase, the French Revolution established the principle of constitutional government and ended many of the traditional political privileges of the Old Regime.

The Revolution moved in more radical directions because of the intransigence of the king, the threat of foreign invasion, and the actions of republican legislators and Parisian citizens. Its most radical phase, the Terror, produced the most effective legislation for ordinary citizens but also the worst violence of the Revolution. A period of unstable conservative rule that followed the Terror ended when Napoleon seized power.

Though Napoleonic rule enshrined some of the gains of the Revolution, it also subjected France and most of Europe to the great costs of wars of conquest. After Napoleon, the French monarchy was restored but forced to accept many limitations on its power as a result of the Revolution. Indeed, hereditary rule and traditional social hierarchies remained in place in much of Europe, but they would not be secure in the future. The legacy of revolutionary change would prove impossible to contain in France or anywhere else.

NOTES

1. Quoted in Owen Connelly, *The French Revolution and Napoleonic Era* (New York: Holt, Rinehart and Winston, 1979), p. 32.

SUGGESTED READING

Baker, Keith Michael, ed. *The French Revolution and the Creation of Modern Political Culture*. 1987. A collection of essays by diverse scholars emphasizing the Revolution as a period of change in political culture.

Chartier, Roger. *The Cultural Origins of the French Revolution*. 1991. An interpretation of intellectual and cultural life in the eighteenth century with a view to explaining its revolutionary results; has a good bibliography.

Connelly, Owen. *Blundering to Glory: The Campaigns of Napoleon*. 1992. A new assessment of Napoleon's military achievements by an expert on Napoleonic warfare.

Furet, François. *Interpreting the French Revolution*. 1981. The major work by the outstanding French scholar of the Revolution of the current generation, written in reaction to liberal and Marxist interpretations.

Hufton, Olwen. *Women and the Limits of Citizenship in the French Revolution*. 1992. A series of essays by the leading scholar on the history of women in the Revolution.

Hunt, Lynn. *The Family Romance of the French Revolution*. 1992. A study of political ideology and symbolic politics emphasizing the vast cultural consequences of killing the king and queen.

———. *Politics, Culture and Class in the French Revolution*. 1984. A survey and assessment of other interpretations of the Revolution, emphasizing the role of symbols and symbolic politics.

James, C. L. R. *The Black Jacobins*. 1938. The classic study of the Haitian revolution in the context of events in Europe.

Jordan, D. P. *The King's Trial*. 1979. A readable study of Louis XVI's trial and its importance.

Landes, Joan. *Women and the Public Sphere in the Age of the French Revolution*. 1988. An analysis of the uses of gender ideology to fashion the new political world of the revolutionaries.

Lefebvre, Georges. *The Coming of the French Revolution*. Translated by R. R. Palmer. 1947. A beautifully written Marxist interpretation. The greatest work of this important French historian.

Lyons, Martyn. *Napoleon Bonaparte and the Legacy of the French Revolution*. 1994. A clear, readable, and up-to-date synthesis of scholarship on Napoleon.

Markham, Felix. *Napoleon*. 1963. The best biography in English of Napoleon.

Palmer, R. R. *The Age of Democratic Revolution*. 2 vols. 1959. A study of the American and European revolutions and their reciprocal influences; erudite and immensely readable.

Rudé, George. *The Crowd in the French Revolution*. 1959. A classic Marxist assessment of the importance of common people to the progress of the Revolution.

———. *Twelve Who Ruled*. 1941. A study of the principal figures of the Terror by one of the greatest American historians of the French Revolution.

Soboul, Albert. *The Sans-Culottes*. 1972. A study of the workers of Paris who were active in the Revolution, by Lefebvre's successor as the foremost Marxist historian of the Revolution.

Sutherland, D. M. G. *France, 1789–1815*. 1986. A dense and detailed treatment, with extensive bibliography, that emphasizes the revolutionary over the Napoleonic period.

Sydenham, M. *The First French Republic, 1792–1804*. 1974. A useful survey of the relatively neglected phases of the Revolution.

Tackett, Timothy. *Priest and Parish in Eighteenth-Century France*. 1977. A study of rural Catholic life before the Revolution and after the impact of the Civil Constitution of the Clergy.

Restoration, Reform, and Revolution, 1814–1848

I n 1791, in the midst of revolution, the comte de Provence had fled his homeland, disguised as a foreign merchant. Shunted from country to country he lived in exile, depending on subsidies from foreign courts. Since the revolutionaries had beheaded his brother, Louis XVI, and a nephew had died in captivity, when he returned to France after twenty-three years abroad, he did so as king of France, Louis XVIII (r. 1814–1824).

With Louis's return to French soil in April 1814, the Bourbons were restored. In many other states, too, with the fall of Napoleon, monarchy and aristocracy attempted to reassert, to "restore," their authority. Historians often call the period from 1814 to 1832 in Europe the "restoration." Yet the old world could not be re-created—from the beginning, efforts to restore it were challenged by forces that had appeared during the revolutionary years.

The Great Powers tried to re-establish as much of the old European state system as possible, but the international arrangements of the victorious powers—Austria, Great Britain, Prussia, and Russia—were soon shaken by outbreaks of nationalist fervor. Nationalists aimed either to create larger political units, as in Italy and Germany, or to win independence from foreign rule, as in Greece.

Domestically, the attempt to set the clock back also had limited success. The conservatism of European rulers and their opposition to change were at odds with the new dynamism of European society. Between 1800 and 1850, Europe's population increased by nearly 50 percent, from around 190 million to 280 million. Population growth and the development of industry created large cities where there had been small towns or rural areas. Manufacturing in factories was on the rise, reshaping class structures and the lives of workers. Romanticism, liberalism, and other systems of thought were redefining the relationship of the individual to society.

In 1814, European statesmen had consciously tried to forestall revolution, but in less than a generation they were challenged by waves of protest and violence, most notably in the revolutions of 1848. Revolutionaries did not win all their goals, and in many cases the forces of order crushed them. Yet major intellectual, social, and political changes had occurred by midcentury.

∼ Questions and Ideas to Consider

- Was the "restoration" worked out at the Congress of Vienna a true restoration of prerevolutionary Europe?

- What were the major ideas of romanticism? Why did romantic artists and intellectuals reject the classicism of the Enlightenment?

- Women found that both romanticism and socialism could be used to support gender equality. How? Consider the ideas of George Sand, Harriet Taylor Mill, Zoé Gatti de Gamond, and Flora Tristan.

- In western Europe, the political systems established in 1815 underwent important transformations by the 1830s. Reforms were instituted in many aspects of government. Discuss the mixture of conservatism and liberalism that shaped these transformations.

- What were the common factors of the revolutions of 1848? What were the results of these revolts? How is it that England avoided these upheavals?

THE SEARCH FOR STABILITY: THE CONGRESS OF VIENNA

The defeat of Napoleon put an end to French dominance in Europe. In September 1814 the victorious powers of the Quadruple Alliance—Austria, Great Britain, Prussia, and Russia—con-

vened a conference in Vienna to negotiate the terms of peace. The victors sought to draw territorial boundaries advantageous to themselves and to provide long-term stability on the European continent.

Although many small powers attended the Congress of Vienna, their role was limited to ratifying the large states' decisions. Having faced a powerful France that had mobilized popular forces with revolutionary principles, the victors decided to erect an international system to remove such threats. They restored the European order that had existed before the French Revolution. Thus, following principles of "legitimacy and compensation," they redrew the map of Europe (Map 18.1). Rulers who had been overthrown were restored to their thrones. As we have seen, the eldest surviving brother of Louis XVI of France became King Louis XVIII. In Spain, Ferdinand VII was restored to the throne from which Napoleon had toppled him and his father. The restoration, however, was not complete. Certain new realities had to be recognized. For example, Napoleon had consolidated the German states; the process was acknowledged with the creation of a loose German Confederation.

Negotiators at the Congress of Vienna strengthened the territories bordering France, enlarged Prussia, created the kingdom of Piedmont-Sardinia, joined Belgium to Holland, and provided the victors with spoils and compensation for territories bartered away. Russia's reward for its contribution to the war effort was most of Poland and all of Finland, which had belonged to Sweden. Sweden's king was compensated for the loss of Finland by being permitted to rule in a joint union over Norway, formerly under the Danish crown. Denmark was punished for adhering to the Napoleonic alliance longer than the victorious allies thought was appropriate. Britain acquired a number of colonies and naval outposts. Thus, even as they proclaimed their loyalty to the prerevolutionary past, conservative statesmen changed the map of Europe.

The leading personality at the Congress of Vienna was the Austrian foreign minister, Prince

CHAPTER CHRONOLOGY

EUROPEAN REVOLUTIONS, 1820–1831	
January 1820	Spain
July 1820	Naples
August 1820	Portugal
March 1821	Piedmont; Greece
December 1825	Russia
July 1830	France
August 1830	Belgium
September 1830	Brunswick; Saxony; Hesse-Cassel
November 1830	Poland
February 1831	Revolt in Piedmont, Modena, and Parma; revolt in Papal States

EUROPEAN REVOLUTIONS, 1848	
January	Sicily
February	France
March	Austria, Hungary, Croatia, Lombardy, Prussia
April	Bohemia
May	German National Assembly convenes in Frankfurt
January 1849	Roman Republic declared

Clemens von Metternich (1773–1859), who presided over the meetings. An aristocrat in exile from the Rhineland, which had been annexed by revolutionary France, he had gone into the service of the Habsburg empire and risen to become its highest official. Personal charm, tact, and representation of a state that for the time being was satisfied with its territories made Metternich seem a disinterested statesman. His influence at the Congress was great.

Made wary by their long war against France, the four powers of the Quadruple Alliance had pledged before the Congress of Vienna to cooperate to prevent any future French aggression. They planned to meet periodically to resolve all European issues, creating what was known as the "Concert of Europe." At Vienna the wily French foreign minister, Count Charles Talleyrand (1754–1838), was able to insinuate himself into the councils of the four Great Powers. The desire of Russia and Prussia for sizable territorial gains alarmed Austria and Great Britain, and France joined them in limiting Russian and Prussian ambitions. At Talleyrand's insistence, France was counted as one of five Great Powers.

The Concert of Europe, including France, met several times to try to resolve subsequent crises. Underlying the states' cooperation was the principle of a common European destiny.

IDEOLOGICAL CONFRONTATIONS

The international and domestic political systems established in 1815 were modified by a series of challenges and even revolts, culminating in revolutions throughout Europe in 1848. The order established in 1815 was inspired by conservatism. Its challengers advocated competing ideologies: romanticism, nationalism, liberalism, and socialism.

Conservatism

The architects of the restoration justified their policies with doctrines based on the ideology of conservatism, emphasizing the need to preserve the existing order. Conservatism emerged as a coherent movement during and after the French Revolution in reaction to the forces of change.

Edmund Burke (1729–1797), a British statesman and political theorist, launched one of the first intellectual assaults on the French Revolution. The revolutionary National Assembly had asserted that ancient prerogatives were superseded by the rights of man and principles of human equality based on natural law. In *Reflections on the Revolution in France* (1790), Burke said that such claims were abstract and dangerous and that the belief in human equality undermined the social order. Government should be anchored in tradition, he argued. No matter how poorly the French monarchy and its institutions had served the nation, they should be preserved; their very longevity proved their usefulness. Burke's writings were widely read and influential on the Continent.

In the English-speaking world, one of the most popular writers, Hannah More (1745–1833), who with her four sisters ran a prosperous school, saw piety as a rampart against rebellion. In a series of moral tracts, *Cheap Repository Tracts,* she advocated the acceptance of the existing order and the solace of religious faith. Costing but a penny, the tracts were often handed out by the rich together with alms or food to the poor. More was the first writer in history to sell over a million copies; within three years the sales doubled. Conservative values thus spread to a very large audience in both Britain and the United States, where one of her works appeared in thirty editions.

A more extreme form of conservatism was ultraroyalist or counterrevolutionary ideology. Its proponents wanted to restore society to its prerevolutionary condition. They had often had personal experience of the upheavals of the Revolution. Count Joseph de Maistre (1753–1821), a Savoyard (from the Franco-Italian border region) nobleman whose estates were occupied by the invading French, described monarchy as a God-given form of government in his *Considerations on France* in 1796. De Maistre advocated stern government control, including the generous use of the death penalty, to keep people loyal to throne and altar.

In Germany the influential thought of Georg Wilhelm Friedrich Hegel (1770–1831), philosophy professor at the University of Berlin, was interpreted by many of his disciples as a defense of the conservative order re-established by the restoration. In Hegel's view, history was propelled from one stage to another by the "world spirit" incarnate in the dominant power. Just as Rome had fulfilled divine plans by dominating the ancient world, so Napoleon was hailed by Hegel as a "world soul." The emperor's fall convinced Hegel that the true world soul was incarnate in the victorious allies, particularly Prussia. The state, Hegel said, showed "the march of God in the world"; the existing power, reactionary and authoritarian, was divinely ordained.

Conservatism was also influenced by romanticism, with its glorification of the past, taste for pageantry, and belief in the organic unity of society. But not all conservatives were romantics. Metternich, for instance, saw his work as the attempt of an enlightened mind to restore the world put in turmoil by the French Revolution. (See the box "Metternich's Cure for Europe.")

Romanticism

The romantic movement emerged in the 1760s as a rebellion against rationalism and persisted until the 1840s. It was primarily a movement in the arts. Writers, painters, and composers consciously rebelled against the Enlightenment and its values. In contrast to the philosophes with their emphasis on reason, romantics praised emotion and feeling. Jean-Jacques Rousseau's strong appeal to sentiment was taken up by the German writer Johann Wolfgang von Goethe (1749–1832), who declared that "Feeling is everything." Goethe's *Sorrows of Young Werther* (1774), the most widely read book of the era—Napoleon had a copy by his bedside—depicted the passions of the hero, who, depressed by unrequited love, kills himself. Many readers dressed in "Werther clothes" (tight black pants, blue vest, and an open yellow shirt) and in some cases emulated the tragic hero by committing suicide.

The Enlightenment studied nature for the principles that it could impart; romantics worshiped nature for its inherent beauty. The German composer Ludwig van Beethoven (1770–

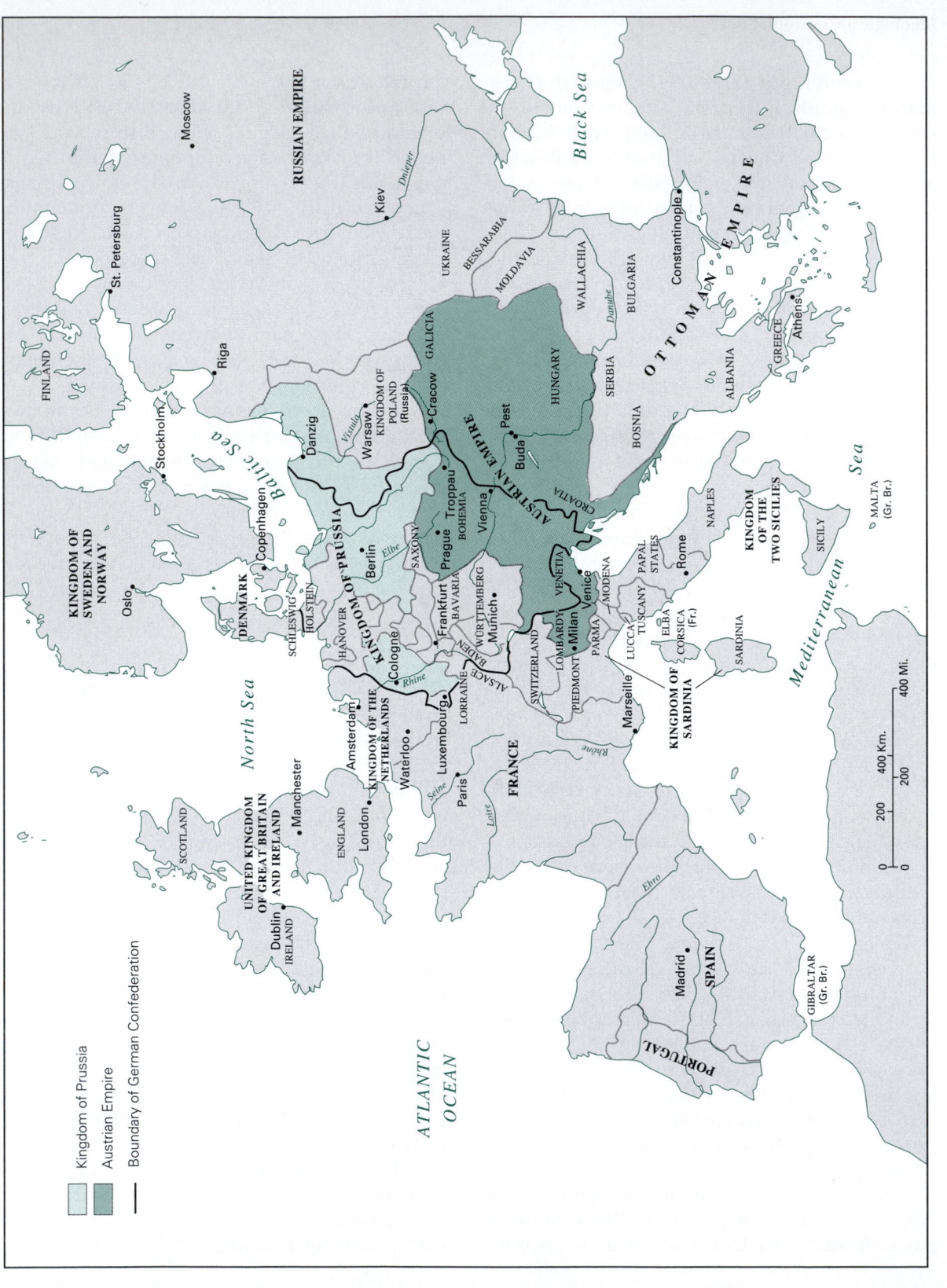

Moscow •

RUSSIAN EMPIRE

St. Petersburg •

Black Sea

FINLAND

Riga •

Kiev •
Dnieper

UKRAINE

BESSARABIA

MOLDAVIA

WALLACHIA

Danube

Constantinople •

OTTOMAN EMPIRE

Stockholm •

Baltic Sea

Danzig

GALICIA

KINGDOM OF POLAND (Russia)

Vistula

Warsaw •

Cracow •

BULGARIA

SERBIA

GREECE

Athens •

ALBANIA

Copenhagen •

KINGDOM OF SWEDEN AND NORWAY

Oslo •

DENMARK

SCHLESWIG

HOLSTEIN

Troppau

Vienna •

BOHEMIA

Prague •

AUSTRIAN EMPIRE

Pest •

Buda •

HUNGARY

CROATIA

BOSNIA

North Sea

KINGDOM OF PRUSSIA

Berlin •

Elbe

SAXONY

Frankfurt •

BAVARIA

Munich •

WÜRTTEMBERG

VENETIA

Venice •

MODENA

PARMA

LOMBARDY

Milan •

PIEDMONT

PAPAL STATES

Rome •

NAPLES

KINGDOM OF THE TWO SICILIES

SICILY

MALTA (Gr. Br.)

Mediterranean Sea

HANOVER

Cologne •

Rhine

BADEN

ALSACE

LORRAINE

SWITZERLAND

LUCCA

TUSCANY

ELBA

CORSICA (Fr.)

SARDINIA

KINGDOM OF SARDINIA

Marseille •

Amsterdam •

KINGDOM OF THE NETHERLANDS

Waterloo •

Luxembourg •

Seine

Paris •

FRANCE

Rhone

Manchester •

London •

ENGLAND

SCOTLAND

UNITED KINGDOM OF GREAT BRITAIN AND IRELAND

Dublin •

IRELAND

Loire

ATLANTIC OCEAN

Ebro

Madrid •

SPAIN

GIBRALTAR (Gr. Br.)

PORTUGAL

Kingdom of Prussia

Austrian Empire

Boundary of German Confederation

400 Mi.

400 Km.

200

200

0

0

Metternich's Cure for Europe

Metternich, Austria's foreign minister from 1809 to 1848, had an impact beyond his empire's borders, providing much of the leadership of the reactionary regimes of Europe between 1815 and 1848. In this secret letter to Russia's Tsar Alexander I, Metternich analyzed the current ailments of Europe and saw their cure in firm support for king and church.

Kings have to calculate the chances of their very existence in the immediate future; passions are let loose, and league together to overthrow everything which society respects as the basis of its existence; religion, public morality, laws, customs, rights, and duties all are attacked, confounded, overthrown, or called in question. . . .

Having now thrown a rapid glance over the first causes of the present state of society, it is necessary to point out in a more particular manner the evil which threatens to deprive it, at one blow, of the real blessings, the fruits of genuine civilisation, and to disturb it in the midst of its enjoyments. This evil may be described in one word—presumption; the natural effect of the rapid progression of the human mind towards the perfecting of so many things. This it is which at the present day leads so many individuals astray, for it has become an almost universal sentiment. . . .

The Governments, having lost their balance, are frightened, intimidated, and thrown into confusion, by the cries of the intermediary class of society, which, placed between the Kings and their subjects, breaks the sceptre of the monarch, and usurps the cry of the people. . . .

We are convinced that society can no longer be saved without strong and vigorous resolutions on the part of the Governments. . . . By this course the monarchs will fulfill the duties imposed upon them by Him who, by entrusting them with power, has charged them to watch over the maintenance of justice, and the rights of all, to avoid the paths of error and tread firmly in the way of truth. . . .

. . . [L]et the Governments govern. . . . Let them not encourage by their attitude or actions the suspicion of being favourable or indifferent to error: let them not allow it to be believed that experience has lost its rights to make way for experiments which at the least are dangerous.

Source: Metternich to Emperor Alexander, Troppau, December 15, 1820, in Prince Richard Metternich, ed., *Memoirs of Prince Metternich, 1815–1829*, vol. 3, trans. Mrs. Alexander Napier (New York: Scribner & Sons, 1881), pp. 455, 458–459, 468–470, 474.

1827) wrote his *Pastoral* Symphony in praise of nature. The English poets William Wordsworth (1770–1850) and Samuel Taylor Coleridge (1772–1834) treated untamed wilderness as a particular subject of wonder. Fellow Englishman Joseph Turner (1775–1851) displayed the raw passions of the sea in his paintings *Fire at Sea* (1834) and *Snowstorm, Steamboat Off a Harbour's*

Mouth (1842). To paint the latter, Turner is said to have tied himself to a ship's mast and braved a snowstorm for four hours. The Frenchman Théodore Géricault (1791–1824) also portrayed the impotence of human beings in the face of the natural world. His *Raft of the "Medusa,"* widely considered the most important painting of French romanticism, depicted an actual shipwreck off the coast of Africa. Passionate and dark, the painting includes all of romanticism's key themes: an exotic setting, powerful natural forces, and grand displays of human emotion.

Map 18.1 Europe in 1815 The map of Europe was redrawn at the Congress of Vienna.

Géricault: Raft of the "Medusa" This painting depicts a scandalous tragedy that occurred in 1816. A French government ship had been wrecked due to the incompetence of the captain, who had been appointed on the basis of his nobility and not his seamanship. Lacking sufficient lifeboats, 150 passengers were left on a makeshift raft. Before their chance rescue thirteen days later, most had died, and some of those who survived had engaged in cannibalism and murder. Partially because the government tried to hide these facts, Géricault's painting became an important symbol of antigovernment sentiment. *(Erich Lessing/Art Resource, NY)*

In their pursuit of feeling, many romantics rediscovered religion. In some areas of Europe, popular religion had anticipated the artists' romantic sensibilities. France experienced a revival of Catholicism. In the German states, pietism, which emerged in the seventeenth and eighteenth centuries, stressed the personal relationship of the individual to God. The influence of pietism, with its emphasis on feeling and emotion, spread throughout central Europe in schools and churches.

In England piety and emotionalism in religion expressed itself in the popularity of Methodism. Founded in the 1730s by the English preacher John Wesley (1703–1791), this movement emphasized salvation by faith. Appealing especially to the poor and desperate, Methodism had gained 70,000 members when it split off from the Church of England in the 1790s; within a generation it quadrupled its flock.

The philosophes had derided the Middle Ages, but romantics celebrated them. Sir Walter

Scott (1771–1832) in Scotland and Victor Hugo (1802–1885) in France celebrated chivalry and the age of faith in such popular works as *Ivanhoe* (1819) and *The Hunchback of Notre Dame* (1831). Painters frequently took as their theme Gothic buildings or ruins. Architects imitated the Gothic style in both private and public buildings.

After the French Revolution, monarchs and nobles ceased sponsoring art on a grand scale and were expected to conduct their lives soberly. Cut off from royal patronage, artists had to depend on members of the new middle class to buy paintings and books and attend plays and musical performances. Earning a livelihood had been difficult for artists in the past, but now it became even more so. Forced to live marginally, they cultivated the image of the artist as a bohemian, deliberately rejecting the conventions of society. The romantic period gave rise to the notion of the starving genius, alienated from society, loyal only to art.

Romantics often celebrated individualism. For this reason, they accepted unusual behavior— even when it challenged existing power relations and proprieties. The French writer Amandine-Aurore Dupin (1804–1876), better known by her pen name, George Sand, spoke for the emancipation of women from the close supervision of their husbands, fathers, and brothers. Sand practiced the freedom she preached, dressing like a man, smoking cigars, and openly pursuing affairs with the writer Prosper Mérimée (1803–1870), the poet Alfred de Musset (1810–1857), and the composer Frédéric Chopin (1810–1849). The English writer Mary Ann Evans (1819–1892), like George Sand, adopted a male pseudonym, George Eliot. She conducted her life in a nonconformist manner, living with a married man. The adoption of male pen names by both writers attests to the hostility that intellectual women still faced.

Determined to overthrow the smug present and create a new world, romantics consciously turned their backs on the classical tradition. Victor Hugo called for "no more rules, no more models" to constrain the human imagination. Such figures as the English romantic poet Percy Bysshe Shelley (1792–1822), the writer Mary Wollstonecraft (1759–1797), the painter Eugène Delacroix (1798–1863), and the poet George Gordon, Lord Byron (1788–1824), each expressed some aspect of romantic individualism, dedication to grand, passionate causes, and respect for the power of nature.

Nationalism

The ideology of nationalism emerged in this era. *Nationalism* is the belief that people derive their identity from their nation and owe their nation their primary loyalty. The idea of a "nation" grew out of the idea of a "country." While a country can be defined by its land and its government, a nation *is* its people. Nations tend to define themselves as a group of people with a common language and religion, as well as common traditions, daily habits, and shared historical experiences. No nation can claim all of these, and many areas that actually can claim many of these are not in fact nations. Nineteenth-century nationalists argued fiercely over what qualifications constituted a nation.

In an era that saw the undermining of traditional religious values, nationalism offered a new locus of faith. To people distressed by the erosion of the old order, nationalism held out the promise of a new community. Nationalism became an ideal espoused as strongly as religion. The Italian nationalist Giuseppe Mazzini (1805–1872) declared that nationalism was "a faith and mission" ordained by God. The religious intensity of nationalism helps explain its widespread appeal.

Many forces shaped nationalism. Its earliest manifestation, cultural nationalism, had its origins in Rousseau's ideas of the organic nature of a people. Johann Gottfried Herder (1744–1833), Rousseau's German disciple, declared that every people has a "national spirit." To explore the unique nature of this spirit, intellectuals all over Europe began collecting folk poems, songs, and tales. In an effort to document the spirit of the German people, the Grimm brothers, Jacob (1785–1863) and Wilhelm (1786–1859), collected fairy tales by traveling around German territories and asking women to recite the stories handed down from their own mothers. Fairy tales such as "Little Red Riding Hood" and "Snow White" had long been created and recounted by women, as many of their themes indicate. In making them public, the nationalist movement legitimated these stories but masked their true authors.

Political nationalism was born in the era of the French Revolution. When revolutionary France was attacked by neighboring countries ruled by kings and dukes, the Legislative Assembly called on the French people to rise and save the nation. The realm of the king of France had become the French nation.

Intellectuals in Germany and Italy embraced the spirit of nationalism, challenging France's claim to the right to lead the peoples of Europe. They argued variously that Germans were endowed with a special genius that had to be safeguarded for the well-being of all humankind or that Italians ought to be pre-eminent in Europe because they were the descendants and heirs of ancient Rome. Culture could also be invoked for the purpose of throwing off a foreign yoke. In the 1810s, as part of a campaign to free Greece from the Turks, Greek intellectuals re-issued the classics of ancient Greek literature in "purified" language, closer to classical Greek. Their purpose was to remind the population that they were the sons and daughters of Hellas.

For the most part, early nineteenth-century nationalism was generous and cosmopolitan in its outlook—excepting the French Revolution and the Napoleonic era. Herder and Mazzini believed that each of Europe's peoples was destined to achieve nationhood and that the nations of Europe would then live peacefully side by side. The members of dedicated nationalist groups like Young Germany and Young Italy were also members of Young Europe.

It is important to remember, though, that in the first half of the nineteenth century most people were likely to feel local and regional affinities more than national loyalties. Only after decades of propaganda would the ideology win wide support, and only then did it become natural for Europeans to think of dying for their nation.

Liberalism

Liberalism was a direct descendant of the Enlightenment's critique of eighteenth-century absolutism. Nineteenth-century liberals believed that individual freedom was best safeguarded by the reduction of government powers. They wanted to impose constitutional limits on government, to establish the rule of law, to sweep away all state regulation of the economy, and to ensure a voice in government for men of property and education. Liberalism was influenced by romanticism, with its emphasis on individual freedom and the imperative of the human personality to develop to its full potential.

Liberalism was both an economic and a political theory. In 1776, Adam Smith (1723–1790), the influential Scottish economist, published *An Inquiry into the Nature and Causes of the Wealth of Nations*, a systematic study of the economic knowledge of his era. Smith advocated freeing national economies from the fetters of the state. Under the mercantilist system, prevalent throughout Europe until about 1800, the state had regulated the prices and conditions of manufacture (see page 362). Smith argued for letting the forces of the marketplace shape economic decisions. He was the founder of the classical school of economics; this school rested on the belief that economics is subject to basic unalterable laws, which can be discerned and applied in the same fashion as natural laws. The economy is driven as if by an "invisible hand." In France, advocates of nonintervention by government in the economy were called supporters of *laissez faire* (to leave alone).

Wages and employment were also seen as subject to the law of supply and demand. Thomas Malthus (1766–1834), an Anglican minister, published *An Essay on the Principle of Population* in 1798. Malthus posited that if employers paid their workers higher salaries, workers would be able to afford to marry earlier and have more children, thus glutting the labor market and driving wages down. He wanted wages to be kept at subsistence level. Workers, Malthus suggested, are "themselves the cause of their own poverty."

The third giant among classical economists was the retired English stockbroker David Ricardo (1772–1823), who set forth his ideas in *Principles of Political Economy* (1817). Ricardo saw the capitalist system as typified by what he called the "iron law of wages." Since capitalists' major expenses were wages, to be competitive they had to keep depressing wages. According to the school of classical economics, the economy is driven by laws, and intervention of any sort will only make things worse.

In the political realm, liberals argued that power must be limited to prevent despotism. The French Revolution had proclaimed that the purpose of government is to ensure the happiness of humankind. As Thomas Jefferson (1743–1826), another child of the Enlightenment, asserted in the Declaration of Independence (1776), among the "unalienable rights" of individuals are "life, liberty, and the pursuit of happiness." The purpose of government is to safeguard and promote those rights.

The Enlightenment had posited natural law as the basis of government. French liberals in the nineteenth century continued to see human liberty as founded on natural law, but their English counterparts were less theoretical in outlook. The Englishman Jeremy Bentham (1748–1832) argued that the purpose of government is to provide "the greatest happiness of the greatest number." Bentham and his disciples believed that the test of government is its usefulness; they were known as "utilitarians."

John Stuart Mill (1803–1873), a disciple of Bentham, was the foremost proponent of liberalism, seeing it as ensuring the development of a free society. Individuals could best develop their talents if they were not hampered by the interference of the state. In his essay *On Liberty*, one of the fundamental documents of nineteenth-century liberalism, Mill argued for the free circulation of ideas—even false ones. In the free marketplace of ideas, false ideas will be defeated and truth will be vindicated. Mill also asserted that a free society should be free for all its members. In 1830, Mill met Harriet Taylor (1807–1856), an English feminist who became his wife years later (after her first husband's death). Harriet Taylor Mill's influential essay, "Enfranchisement of Women" (1851), had a tremendous impact on John Stuart Mill. After her death, he wrote his famous *On the Subjection of Women* (1861), crediting her with "all that is striking and most profound" in this work. Both Taylor and Mill asserted that women should vote and have access to equal educational opportunities as well as to the professions. Such equality would not only be just but would also have the advantage of "doubling the mass of mental faculties available for the higher service of humanity." Some people advocated women's right to vote on the principle that women would bring a special morality to the ballot box. Harriet Taylor and John Stuart Mill, however, were among those who argued that women deserved equal rights on the same liberal principles that gave men their rights.

Clearly, liberalism came in many forms. In the second half of the century, many people came to believe that the laws of the marketplace could not be allowed to operate without intervention. Even Mill grew to believe that some controls on market forces were needed to protect workers and consumers. Also, many liberals came to fear the masses and therefore vigorously opposed democracy. When less fortunate Frenchmen denounced the property requirements that prevented them from voting, the liberal statesman François Guizot (1787–1874) smugly replied, "Get rich."

In politics, however, the basic tenets of the liberal credo—the sanctity of human rights, freedom of speech and freedom to organize, the rule of law and equality before the law, and the abolition of torture—eventually became so widely accepted that even conservative and socialist opponents of liberalism accepted them as fundamental rights.

Socialism

The notion that human happiness can best be assured by the common ownership of property had been suggested by individuals as different as the Greek philosopher Plato (427?–347 B.C.) and Sir Thomas More (1478–1535), the English author of

Utopia. Troubled by the condition of the working classes, thinkers in Britain and France developed theories that, beginning in the 1820s, were called "socialist." Socialists believed that the "social" ownership of property, unlike private ownership, would benefit society as a whole.

In 1796, during the French Revolution, Gracchus Babeuf (1760–1797), a minor civil servant, participated in the Conspiracy of Equals (see page 452). The Revolution, however haltingly, had proclaimed political equality for its citizens, but it had failed to bring economic equality. Babeuf decided to resort to revolution to bring about a "communist" society—a society in which private property would be abolished and all property would be owned in common. Work would be provided for everyone; medical services and education would be free to all. Babeuf's plan was discovered and he was guillotined, but his theories and his example of conspiratorial revolutionary action would influence later socialists.

Several other important French thinkers made contributions to European socialism. Curiously, a French aristocrat, Henri de Saint-Simon (1760–1825), emphasized the need "to ameliorate as promptly and as quickly as possible the moral and physical existence of the most numerous class." The proper role for the state, Saint-Simon declared, was to ensure the welfare of the masses. Europe should be governed by a council of artists and scientists who would oversee the economy and ensure that everyone enjoyed a minimum level of well-being. Young intellectuals who gravitated to Saint-Simonism took on the master's faith in the capacity of technology to transform society. They became the dynamic entrepreneurs and engineers who in the 1850s would build up the French banking, investment, and rail systems.

Another vital contribution to socialist thought came from thinkers who tried to imagine an ideal world on an even wider scale. They were later derisively dismissed as dreamers, as builders of utopias, fantasy worlds (the Greek word *utopia* means "no place"). One of the earliest and most notable utopians was the Welsh mill-owner Robert Owen (1771–1858). In New Lanark, Scotland, beginning in 1800 he ran a successful cotton mill. He provided generously for his workers, guaranteeing them a job and a decent education for their children. In his writings Owen suggested the establishment of self-governing communes that would own the means of production. Essentials would be distributed to all members according to their needs. Owen's ideas for the new society included equal rights for women.

Owen received little support from fellow manufacturers and political leaders. In 1824 he established in New Harmony, Indiana, an ideal new society that was to be a model for others. Within four years of its founding, New Harmony ran into economic difficulty and was torn by internal dissension. Disheartened, Owen abandoned the community and returned to Britain.

Another influential contributor to early socialist theory was the Frenchman Charles Fourier (1772–1837). A clerk and salesman, Fourier wrote out his vision of the ideal future society in great detail. It would consist of cooperative organizations called "phalanxes," each with 1600 inhabitants who would live in harmony with nature and one another. Everyone would be assured of gainful employment. Work would be made enjoyable by rotating jobs and by sharing pleasurable and unpleasurable tasks. Cooperative communes often faced the issue of who would carry out the unpleasant tasks. Fourier thought that because children enjoy playing with dirt, they should be put in charge of picking up garbage.

Fourier's belief in equality of the sexes gave him an important female following. In Belgium, the activist Zoé Gatti de Gamond (1806–1854) cofounded a phalanx for women. She believed that if women could be assured of economic well-being, other rights would follow. Also inspired by Fourier, Flora Tristan (1801–1844) was an effective advocate for workers' rights. In her book *Union Ouvrière (Workers' Union)*, she suggested that workers should contribute to establish a "Worker's Palace" in every town, where the sick and disabled would have shelter and the workers' children could be given a free education. Like Fourier, she saw a profound link between the concerns of socialism and feminism and championed women's rights as prerequisite for a just society. Arguing that worker solidarity was damaged when underpaid women were employed in place of men, Tristan concluded that women's rights and worker's rights were profoundly interdependent. Crossing France on foot, she spread the word of workers' solidarity and self-help.

There were other approaches. The French socialist journalist Louis Blanc (1811–1882) saw in democracy the means of bringing into existence a socialist state. By securing the vote, the common people could win control of the state and direct it to serve their needs. The state could be induced to buy up banks, insurance companies, and railway systems and set up a commercial and retail chain that would provide jobs for workers and set reasonable prices. Once the workers controlled the state by the ballot, the state would establish worker-run workshops. The idea was to "Let each produce according to his aptitudes and strength; let each consume according to his need."

Blanc's contemporary, Louis Blanqui (1805–1882), suggested a more violent mode of action. He advocated seizure of the state by a small, dedicated band of men devoted to the welfare of the working class who would install communism for the equality of all. Blanqui was a perpetual conspirator, confined to state prisons for much of his long life. The thought of Blanqui and the other socialists would play a major role in shaping the thinking of the most important socialist of the nineteenth century, Karl Marx.

RESTORATION AND REFORM

Despite the new ideologies that emerged to challenge the existing order, efforts at restoration appeared successful until at least 1830. Indeed in central and eastern Europe, from the German states to Russia and the Ottoman Empire, the political systems established in 1815 would persist virtually unchanged until midcentury. In western Europe, however, important transformations would occur by the 1830s as reaction gave way to reform. Then in 1848, widespread revolution would break out on much of the Continent. The language of liberalism and nationalism and even the newer idiom of socialism would be heard on the barricades, in popular assemblies, and in parliamentary halls.

France

The restoration of the Bourbons in France turned the clock back not to 1789 but closer to 1791, when the country had briefly enjoyed a constitutional monarchy, and it went beyond that in maintaining the Napoleonic Code with its provisions of legal equality.

Louis XVIII granted France a charter confirming political and religious liberties and legal equality. The new constitution provided for a parliament with an elected lower house, the Chamber of Deputies, and an appointed upper house, the Chamber of Peers. Although suffrage to the Chamber of Deputies was limited to a small elite of men with landed property—100,000 voters, about 0.2 percent—it was a concession to representative government that had not existed in the Old Regime. Louis XVIII was unusual among European rulers because he accepted some aspects of the principle of popular sovereignty proclaimed by the French Revolution.

Louis was succeeded by his ultrareactionary brother, Charles X (r. 1824–1830). The new king encouraged passage of an indemnity bill to pay the aristocratic émigrés for property lost during the Revolution and Napoleon's regime. Bourgeois and lower-class taxpayers were outraged. Many resented the increased power granted the clergy and were shocked by the introduction of the death penalty for acts deemed sacrilegious. Charles X's dissolution of the National Guard, one of the bastions of the middle class, further alienated the bourgeoisie. Frustration mounted with an economic downturn in 1827, marked by poor harvests and increased unemployment in the cities. On July 26, 1830, after the humiliating defeat of his party at the polls, the king issued a set of decrees suspending freedom of the press, dissolving the Chamber of Deputies, and stiffening property qualifications for voters in subsequent elections. The king appeared to be engineering a coup against the existing political system.

The first to protest were the Parisian journalists and typesetters, directly threatened by the censorship laws. On July 28, others joined the protest and began erecting barricades across many streets and calling for a republic. After killing several hundred protesters, the king's forces lost control of the city. The uprising, known as "the three glorious days," drove the king into exile. However, the idea of a republic frightened the middle classes. A liberal constitutional monarchy seemed safer. Better organized than the republicans, they prevailed on the Chamber of Deputies to offer the throne to the king's cousin, the liberal-minded duke of Orléans, Louis Philippe (1773–1850).

Louis Philippe proclaimed himself "King of the French," acknowledging that he reigned at the behest of the people. Freedom of the press was reinstated; suffrage was extended to twice as many voters as before. The July Monarchy, named after the month in which it had been established by revolution, legitimated itself by celebrating the revolution of 1789. Louis Philippe commissioned huge canvasses celebrating great moments of the Revolution. On the site where the Bastille had been razed in 1789, the government erected a large column with the names of the victims of the July 1830 revolution, suggesting a continuity between those who had fought tyranny in 1789 and 1830.

But the regime allowed celebration only of the period until 1791, when France had a constitutional monarchy. Now that the revolution of 1830 had established a constitutional monarchy, the regime was suggesting, any further uprisings were illegitimate.

The July Monarchy was challenged from many quarters. Many people were nostalgic for the republic that had existed under the Revolution. Others longed for the glories of the Napoleonic era. Shortly after the revolution of 1830, another downturn in the economy led to further unemployment, followed by an epidemic of cholera that affected most of Europe. Also contributing to the unsettled atmosphere was labor agitation—including some bloody uprisings in Lyon in 1831 and 1834. In the countryside there were rumors of mass arson. In the face of unrest, the monarchy often resorted to censorship and other forms of repression. Foreign visitors from more authoritarian societies were impressed by France's apparently liberal institutions (see the box "Encounters with the West: A Moroccan Description of the French Freedom of the Press"), but many French liberals saw the regime as a travesty of the promises it had represented in 1830. Inaugurated by revolution, in a few years it would face revolution.

Great Britain

In comparison to the rest of Europe, Great Britain enjoyed considerable constitutional guarantees and a parliamentary regime. Yet liberals and radicals found their government retrograde and repressive. Traumatized by the French Revolution, the ruling class clung to the past, certain that advocates for change were Jacobins in disguise.

Social unrest beset Britain as it faced serious economic dislocation. The arrival of peace in 1815 led to a sudden drop in government expenditures and the return to the workplace of several hundred thousand men who had been away at war. The poor and the middle classes were incensed by the economic advantages that the landed classes, dominating Parliament, had secured for themselves in 1815 in passing the Corn Law. This legislation imposed high tariffs on imported "corn"— that is, various forms of grain. It thus shielded the domestic market from international competition and allowed landowners to reap huge profits at the expense of consumers. In response, there were demonstrations, petitions, protest marches, and other challenges to the authorities.

In August 1819, sixty thousand people gathered in St. Peter's Fields in Manchester to demand universal suffrage for men *and* women, an annual Parliament, and other democratic reforms. The crowd was peaceful and unarmed, but when a speaker whom the government con-

∾ ENCOUNTERS WITH THE WEST ∾

A Moroccan Description of the French Freedom of the Press

In 1845–1846 a Moroccan diplomatic mission visited Paris; the ambassador's secretary, Muhammad as-Saffar (d. 1881), wrote an account of this visit. He was struck by many aspects of French society, and in the following passage he described France's press.

The people of Paris, like all the French—indeed, like all of [Europe]—are eager to know the latest news and events that are taking place in other parts [of the world]. For this purpose they have the gazette. [In] these papers . . . they write all the news that has reached them that day about events in their own country and in other lands both near and far.

This is the way it is done. The owner of a newspaper dispatches his people to collect everything they see or hear in the way of important events or unusual happenings. Among the places where they collect the news are the two Chambers, the Great and the Small, where they come together to make their laws. When the members of the Chamber meet to deliberate, the men of the gazette sit nearby and write down everything that is said, for all debating and ratifying of laws is matter for the gazette and is known to everyone. No one can prevent them from doing this. . . .

. . . [I]f someone has an idea about a subject but he is not a member of the press, he may write about it in the gazette and make it known to others, so that the leaders of opinion learn about it. If the idea is worthy they may follow it, and if its author was out of favor it may bring him recognition.

No person in France is prohibited from expressing his opinion or from writing it and printing it, on condition that he does not violate the law. . . .

In the newspapers they write rejoinders to the men of the two Chambers about the laws they are making. If their Sultan demands gifts from the notables or goes against the law in any way, they write about that too, saying that he is a tyrant and in the wrong. He cannot confront them or cause them harm. Also, if someone behaves out of the ordinary, they write about that too, making it common knowledge among people of every rank. If his deeds were admirable, they praise and delight in him, lauding his example; but if he behaved badly, they revile him to discourage the like.

Moreover, if someone is being oppressed by another, they write about that too, so that everyone will know the story from both sides just as it happened, until it is decided in court. One can also read in it what their courts have decided.

Source: Susan Gilson Miller, ed. and trans., *Disorienting Encounters—Travels of a Moroccan Scholar in France in 1845–1846. The Voyage of Muhammad as-Saffar* (Berkeley: University of California Press, 1992), pp. 150–153. Reprinted by permission of the Regents of California and the University of California Press.

sidered a rabble-rouser took to the podium, mounted soldiers charged, attempting to arrest him. In the ensuing melee, eleven people were killed and four hundred wounded. The British public was shocked by this use of violence against peaceful demonstrators. Parliament responded in autumn 1819 by passing the Six Acts, which outlawed freedom of assembly and effectively imposed censorship.

The government began to embrace change in the 1820s. The provisions that prevented Catholics from holding any government position

"Peterloo" Massacre In August 1819 at St. Peter's Fields in Manchester, a crowd demanding parliamentary reform was charged by government troops, leading to bloodshed. Many English people derided the event and called it "Peterloo." *(Public Record Office)*

were removed in 1829. The number of crimes punishable by death was reduced to just one, homicide. Prison reforms were made. Sir Robert Peel (1788–1850), heir to a manufacturing fortune and an enthusiastic reader of Bentham's works, was the driving force behind many of these reforms. He became home secretary in 1828, and the following year he organized an efficient London police force, known ever after as "bobbies" in his honor, to control crime and contain popular protests.

The major political issue facing Britain in the early nineteenth century was the composition of Parliament. It did not reflect the dramatic population shifts that had occurred since the seventeenth century. Industrialization had trans-

formed mere villages into major cities, but those cities had no representation in Parliament, while localities that had lost population were still represented.

News of the July 1830 revolution in Paris encouraged liberals to push for reform and frightened some conservatives into softening their opposition. In 1831 the liberal Whig government of Earl Grey (1764–1845), a hereditary peer who was well attuned to the demands of the middle class, introduced a reform bill abolishing or reducing representation for sparsely populated areas and granting representation for the populous and unrepresented cities. The bill, which came to be known as the "Great Reform Bill of 1832," also widened the franchise by lowering property qualifications.

The reform was not particularly radical. Only the upper layers of the middle class were enfranchised, or one of seven adult males. The old franchise had not excluded women from the vote, but the new law did so. Still, Parliament better reflected the shift of economic power from agricultural landowners to the industrial and commercial classes. The bill's passage revealed the ability of the political system to bring about reform peacefully.

More reforms followed. The Poor Law of 1834 had a mixed impact. It denied aid to the able-bodied, no matter how destitute, offering them only the option of entering workhouses, where prisonlike conditions deterred all but the most desperate. But the law also abolished the long-standing policy of providing government supplements to very low salaries, which had made it unnecessary for employers to pay workers a living wage. The law of 1834 may thus have played some role in raising wages. Though harsh toward the poor, the Poor Law was an acknowledgment of a national responsibility for the underprivileged.

There were colonial reforms as well. In Britain opposition to slavery had been voiced since the 1780s. Slavery was an affront to liberal principles, and its persistence threatened the empire—in 1831, sixty thousand slaves rebelled in Jamaica. Parliament took heed of the call for change and in

1833 abolished slavery in the British Empire. The antislavery campaign led to the extension of British power into Africa. Having abolished the slave trade in 1807, the British worked to compel other nations to end it. The British navy patrolled the coast of West Africa, trying to suppress the traffic in humans. The minor settlements it established as bases for these patrols made Britain the predominant European power along the coast, foreshadowing the increasing European intrusion into African affairs.

Parliament's reforming zeal stimulated support for *Chartism*, a movement intended to transform Britain into a democracy. In 1838 political radicals with working-class support drew up a "people's charter" calling for universal male suffrage, equal electoral districts, salaries and the abolition of property qualifications for members of Parliament, the secret ballot, and annual general elections. Chartists hoped to end the dominance of narrow upper classes in Parliament. Chartism won wide support among men and women in the working class, sparking demonstrations and petition drives of unprecedented size. Women participated to a larger extent than in any other political movement of the day, founding over a hundred female Chartist organizations. Some Chartists, especially female members, asked for women's suffrage, but this demand was not supported by the overall membership.

Chartism lost some of its followers during a temporary economic upswing. The movement then fell under the sway of advocates of violence, who scared off many artisans and potential middle-class supporters. Lacking popular support, Chartism failed as a political movement. Still, it drew public attention to an integrated democratic program whose main provisions (except for yearly elections) would be adopted piecemeal over the next half-century.

In 1839 urban businessmen founded the Anti–Corn Law League for the purpose of abolishing the Corn Law of 1815, which was increasing the price of grain. Manufacturers knew that low food prices would allow them to pay low wages. The Corn Law was also unpopular with workers, who wanted bread at a price they could afford. The anti–Corn Law movement proved more effective than Chartism because it had the support of the middle classes. Parliament, alarmed by the threat of famine after the poor harvest of 1845, repealed the Corn Law in 1846.

Although repeal did not affect the price of grain, it was a milestone in British history because it showed how organized groups could bring about economic and social reform by putting pressure on Parliament. It also underscored what the Great Reform Act of 1832 had already revealed: Political and economic power was shifting away from the landed gentry to the urban industrial classes. The British political system responded more flexibly to this change than did the political systems of the Continent. When revolution broke out on the Continent, it did not cross the English Channel.

Spain

The term *liberal* was first coined in Spain, where the fate of liberals prefigured what would happen elsewhere in continental Europe. In 1812 the national parliament, the Cortes, elected during the Napoleonic occupation, issued a democratic constitution that provided for universal manhood suffrage and a unicameral legislature with control over government policy. Supporters and admirers of the constitution in Spain became known as "liberals," or friends of liberty.

The Bourbon king Ferdinand VII (r. 1808, 1814–1833) had been overthrown by Napoleon and replaced by his brother, Joseph Bonaparte (r. 1808–1813). In 1814, Ferdinand returned to power, promising to respect the 1812 constitution. But Ferdinand was a believer in the divine right of kings. He had no real intention of abiding by a document drawn up by the educated middle classes that reflected their anticlericalism and desire for power. Ferdinand drew his support from the aristocracy and from segments of the general population still loyal to the call of throne and altar. Liberals were arrested or driven into exile.

Ferdinand's plan to restore Spain to its earlier prominence included a reassertion of control over its American colonies. The Spanish dominions had grown restless in the eighteenth century, for they had witnessed the advent of an independent United States and French occupation of Spain itself. The dominions refused to recognize the Napoleonic regime in Madrid and became increasingly self-reliant. Their attitude did not change when French control of Spain ended. Ferdinand refused to compromise with the overseas territories. Instead, he gathered an army to subdue them. Some liberal junior officers, declaring the army's loyalty to the constitution of 1812, won support from the rank and file, who balked at going overseas. The military mutiny coincided with a sympathetic provincial uprising to produce the "revolution of 1820," the first major assault on the European order established in 1815 at the Congress of Vienna. Ferdinand appealed to the European powers for help. France intervened and crushed the uprising.

Ferdinand's reactionary regime was restored in Spain but could not regain its American colonies. The British, sympathetic to the cause of Latin American independence and eager for commercial access to the region, opposed reconquest. Naval dominance of the seas rendered Britain's opposition effective. The United States, meanwhile, had recognized the independence of the Latin American republics and wished to see their independence maintained. In 1823, President James Monroe issued the statement known as the Monroe Doctrine, proclaiming U.S. opposition to any European colonization or intervention in the affairs of independent republics in the Americas. The United States lacked the military power to back this proclamation, but the British navy effectively enforced it. By 1825 all Spain's colonies on the mainland in Central and South America had won their freedom.

The newly independent states patterned their regimes on the model of Spanish liberalism; all of them had constitutions, separation of powers, and guaranteed human rights. Brazil, the Portuguese empire in the Americas, was a monarchy for most of the rest of the nineteenth century, as was Mexico for a short time, but the other states all became republics, opting for what was then an unusual form of government. Although most of

the Latin regimes eventually became despotic, lip service continued to be paid to liberal values.

When Ferdinand died in 1833, Spain was torn by competing claims to the succession. A civil war between liberal and conservative factions led to extreme cruelty on both sides. The moderates and liberals won, but the military gained the upper hand in governing. A constitutional government was established, but the real power lay in the hands of the army. Several officers served as dictators of the country, replacing each other in a series of coups. One of them, General Ramón Narváez (1799–1868), brutally ran the country from 1844 to 1851. When he was on his deathbed, he was asked whether he forgave his enemies. He answered, "I have no enemies. I have shot them all."

Austria and the German States

The Austrian Empire's far-flung territories seemed to its Habsburg rulers to require a firm hand (see Map 18.1). Liberalism, which challenged imperial power, could not be countenanced. Nor, in this multinational empire, could nationalism be tolerated. The emperor, Francis I (r. 1792–1835), was opposed to any change; his motto was "Rule and change nothing." Prince Metternich, Francis's chief minister, viewed the French Revolution of 1789 and its aftermath as a disaster. Metternich established a network of secret police and informers to spy on the imperial subjects and keep them in check.

In most of the German states, the political order was authoritarian and inflexible. The states of Baden and Württemberg in the west and Bavaria in the south had been granted constitutions by their rulers, although effective power remained in the hands of the ruling houses. The king of Prussia had repeatedly promised a constitution, but none had materialized. A central, representative Diet would not meet until 1847. Prussia was ruled by an alliance of the king and the *Junkers,* the landowning aristocrats who staffed the officer corps and the bureaucracy. Both the officer corps and the bureaucracy were efficient enough to serve as models for the rest of Europe. Where Prussia lagged by liberal standards was in its political institutions.

Throughout the German states, the urban middle classes, intellectuals, journalists, university professors, and students were frustrated with the existing system. They were disappointed by the lack of free institutions and the failure of the patriotic wars against Napoleon to create a united Germany. University students formed *Burschenschaften,* or brotherhoods, whose slogan was "Honor, Liberty, Fatherland." Metternich imposed a policy of reaction on the Germanic Confederation and had it adopt the Carlsbad Decrees in July 1819, establishing close supervision over the universities, censorship of the press, and dissolution of the youth groups. Wholesale persecution of liberals and nationalists followed.

The outbreak of revolution in Paris in 1830 inspired further political agitation. Mounting demands for national unity led to the prosecution of outspoken liberals. Many associated with the nationalist Young Germany movement fled abroad. Nationalist fervor swept the German states again in the 1840s. The patriotic song "Deutschland, Deutschland über alles" ("Germany, Germany above all"), which became Germany's national anthem half a century later, was written at this time. Some German rulers who had been reluctant to support the national idea in the past now attempted to coopt it. In Bavaria, King Ludwig II built the Walhalla, named after the hall where fallen heroes gather in Germanic lore; Ludwig's Walhalla was to be a "sacred monument" to German unity, adorned with statues of famous Germans. The Cologne Cathedral, unfinished in its construction, became a symbol of German enthusiasm; from all over Germany donations came in to complete it. Prussia's King William Frederick IV (r. 1840–1861) declared it "the spirit of German unity and strength." These events suggested a broadening base for nationhood.

Italy

Austria continued to wield considerable power over the Italian states. In addition to Lombardy and Venetia, which it acquired in 1815 (see Map 18.1), Austria had dynastic ties to several ruling houses in the central part of the peninsula and political alliances with others, including the papacy. The only ruling house free of Austrian ties—and hence looked to by nationalists as a possible rallying point for the independence of the peninsula—was the Savoy dynasty of Piedmont-Sardinia.

Italy consisted of eight political states, and it was in Austria's interest to maintain disunity. Many Italian rulers imposed repressive policies, knowing that they could count on Austrian assistance in case of a popular uprising. Metternich's interventions to crush liberal rebellions generated hatred of Austria among Italian nationalists. Political reaction in the Italian states cannot be wholly blamed on Austria, however. Piedmont, which was free of Austrian influence, nevertheless embraced restoration. When the royal house of Savoy returned to power in 1815, it nullified all the laws passed during Napoleon's reign and banned from government service all officials who had served the French.

Throughout Italy, there was resistance to the restoration. The Carbonari (literally, "charcoal burners," suggesting men of simple occupations), a nationalist conspiratorial group that had been formed to fight the French occupation, after 1815 targeted the restoration regimes. In March 1821, liberal-minded young army officers in Piedmont, inspired by recent events in Spain, proclaimed their support of a constitution and their desire to evict Austria from Italy. The movement, essentially military, did not win much popular support. With the help of Austria, Piedmontese loyal to the monarch crushed the uprising.

A decade later, catalyzed by the July revolution in Paris, the same forces came to the fore. An uprising broke out in Piedmont, then spread to the Papal States and Modena. The revolt was aimed at the authoritarian rulers of the various Italian states, but it was also in support of a united Italy. Led by intellectuals and some members of the middle classes, the uprisings were fragmented by the participants' primary loyalties to their individual states and cities. The Austrians promptly crushed hopes for the liberty and unity of Italy.

Russia

By far the most autocratic of the European states was tsarist Russia. Since 1801 it had been ruled by Alexander I (r. 1801–1825), an enigmatic character whose domestic policy wavered between liberalism and reaction and whose foreign policy vacillated between brutal power politics and apparently selfless idealism. When the Congress of Vienna awarded additional Polish lands to Russia, he demonstrated his liberalism to the world by granting Poland a liberal constitution. But he offered no such constitution to his own people. He and his council discussed terms for the abolition of serfdom in 1803 and again in 1812, but like so many of his plans this one was not implemented. Although he earnestly desired freedom for the serfs, he was unwilling to impose any policy detrimental to the interests and privileges of the landed gentry.

Toward the end of his rule, Alexander became increasingly authoritarian and repressive, probably in response to growing opposition. Western liberal ideas, including constitutionalism, were adopted by Russian military officers who had served in western Europe, by Russian Freemasons who corresponded with Masonic lodges in western Europe, and by Russian intellectuals who read Western liberal political tracts. These groups formed secret societies with varying programs. Some envisioned Russia as a republic, others as a constitutional monarchy, but all shared a commitment to the abolition of serfdom and the establishment of a freer society.

Alexander died in December 1825, leaving it unclear which of his brothers was to succeed him. The younger brother, Nicholas, claimed to be the legal heir. Military conspirators declared in favor of the older brother, Constantine, in the belief that he favored a constitutional government. The "Decembrist uprising," as the ensuing struggle is known, quickly failed. The revolt in the Russian capital was badly coordinated with uprisings planned in the countryside, and Nicholas moved quickly to crush the rebellion. He had the leaders executed, sent to Siberia, or

sent into exile. Despite its tragic end, the Decembrist uprising served as an inspiration to Russians resisting tsarist oppression throughout the nineteenth century.

Coming to the throne after crushing a revolt, Nicholas I (r. 1825–1855) was obsessed with the danger of revolution and determined to suppress all challenges to his authority. The declared goal of his rule was to uphold "orthodoxy, autocracy, and nationality." Nicholas created a stern, centralized bureaucracy to control all facets of Russian life. He established the modern Russian secret police, called the "Third Section"; it was above the law—a state within the state. The tsar supported the primacy of the Russian Orthodox church within Russian society; the church in turn upheld the powers of the state. Nicholas also used nationalism to strengthen the state, glorifying the country's past and trying to Russify non-Russian peoples, especially the Poles, by imposing the Russian language on them.

Russia's single most overwhelming problem was serfdom. Economically, serfdom had little to recommend it; free labor was far more efficient. Moreover, public safety was threatened by the serfs' dissatisfaction with their lot. During Nicholas's thirty-year reign there were over six hundred peasant uprisings. Nicholas understood that serfdom had to be abolished for Russia's own good, but he could envision no alternative. Emancipation, he believed, would only sow further disorder. Except for a few minor reforms, he did nothing. Nicholas's death, followed by Russia's defeat in the Crimean War, eventually ended the institution that had held nearly half of the Russian people in bondage.

The Ottoman Empire

In its sheer mass, the Ottoman Empire continued to be a world empire. It extended over three continents. In Africa it ran across the whole North African coast. In Europe it stretched from Dalmatia (on the Adriatic coast) to Constantinople. In Asia it extended from Mesopotamia (present-day Iraq) to Anatolia (present-day Turkey). But it was an empire in decline, seriously challenged from within by nationalist movements and from outside by foreign threats.

The Ottoman bureaucracy, once the mainstay of the government, had fallen into decay. In the past, officials had been recruited and advanced by merit; now lacking funds, Constantinople sold government offices. Tax collectors ruthlessly squeezed the peasantry. By the eighteenth century the Janissaries, formerly an elite military force, had become an undisciplined band that menaced the peoples of the Ottoman Empire—especially those located at great distances from the capital. The reform-minded Sultan Selim III (r. 1789–1807) sought to curb the army, but he was killed by rebellious Janissaries, who forced the new ruler, Mahmud II (r. 1808–1839), to retract most of the previous improvements. The worst features of the declining empire were restored.

The Serbs and the Greeks successfully revolted against Ottoman rule at about the same time. The Serbs did so under the leadership of Milosh Obrenovich (r. 1815–1839). He was a formidable figure but success was determined from outside: Russia took an interest in fellow Slavs and members of the Orthodox faith, and in 1830 they pressured Constantinople to recognize Milosh as hereditary ruler over an autonomous Serbia. The Greek struggle was also determined by larger powers. Greeks encountered the ideas of the French Revolution and dedicated themselves to restoring Greek independence. The rest of Europe, excited by the idea of an independent Greece restored to its past greatness, widely supported the Greek movement for freedom. The Great Powers intervened in 1827, sending their navies and sinking Turkish ships. In 1830 an international agreement spelled out Greek independence.

When Egypt challenged the Ottoman Empire the Great Powers again intervened, this time on the empire's behalf. Mehemet Ali, the Egyptian ruler, modernized his army and used it to wrest Syria away in 1831. Britain and Russia helped Constantinople win it back because they were concerned that the Ottoman Empire might collapse and thus threaten the region's balance of power. The survival of the Ottoman Empire was beginning to depend on the goodwill of the Great Powers.

THE REVOLUTIONS OF 1848

From France in the west to Poland in the east, at least fifty separate revolts and uprisings shook the Continent in 1848, the most extensive outbreak of violence in nineteenth-century Europe. The revolts had an impact far beyond Europe's borders. Brazilians, inspired by the example of the European revolutions, rose up against their government. In Bogotá, Colombia, church bells rang to celebrate the announcement of a republic in France. And as a result of the Parisian revolution, slaves in French colonies were emancipated.

Roots of Rebellion

There were many reasons for the outbreak of discontent. In the countryside, changes in access to land (such as land enclosure) frustrated peasants. Although in the past many had enjoyed free access to village commons, increasingly these were coming under private control. Also, the poor were once allowed to forage in the forests for firewood, but the limitation of this right now led to frequent conflicts.

Points of friction were made worse by growing populations that put pressure on available resources. In the cities, artisans were being undercut by the putting-out system, or cottage industry, in which capitalists had goods produced in the countryside by cottagers—part-time artisans who supported themselves partly through agriculture and were thus willing to work for lower wages. Crises in the crafts hurt the journeymen; they had to serve far longer apprenticeships and in many cases could never expect to be masters. Where the guild system still existed, it was in decline.

These developing concerns came to a crisis as a result of the economic depression of 1845–1846. In 1845 a crop disaster, including the spread of the potato blight, destroyed the basic food of the poor in northern Europe. Food prices doubled from what they had been in the early 1840s. An industrial downturn accompanied these agricultural disasters, creating massive unemployment. Municipal and national governments seemed unable to deal with the crowding, disease, and unsanitary conditions. Tensions ran high in the cities, the sites of national governments. Revolts were triggered by discontent, but also by the hope for change.

France

Once again the spark for revolution was ignited in Paris. Economic crisis had a severe impact in the French capital. In some occupations as many as half the people were out of work. The price of bread had shot up to over one franc a pound, which meant that the entire salary of the average male worker—a franc a day—would not buy enough bread to sustain him. Thousands of workers were ready to pour into the streets to protest the government's seeming indifference to their desperation.

Meanwhile, liberals were agitating for the expansion of suffrage. When political meetings were forbidden in 1847, they resorted to banquets featuring long-winded toasts indistinguishable from political speeches. Such a banquet was scheduled for Paris on February 22, 1848, to celebrate the birthday of George Washington—an icon to French liberals. When the government banned the meeting, mass demonstrations broke out. Unlike the British with their professional urban police, the French had no forces trained in crowd control. The government called in the military, whose tactics were more appropriate to engaging an enemy army than to containing civilians. On February 23, soldiers guarding the Ministry of Foreign Affairs panicked and shot into a crowd; fifty-two people died.

Word spread that the government was shooting at the people. To protect themselves, residents of the traditionally revolutionary neighborhoods near the Bastille square erected barricades. On February 24, protesters attacked police and army posts and surrounded the royal palace. The National Guard, a civilian force recruited from the artisan and middle class and charged with restoring order, had become sympathetic to the protesters. Louis Philippe resigned as king and fled for London under the pseudonym "Mr. Smith."

The abruptness of the king's departure left the opposition in disarray. The protesters shared one goal, the extension of suffrage, but otherwise diverged sharply. The new regime, hastily organized under the pressure of a mob invasion of the Chamber of Deputies, lacked consensus. The provisional government consisted of well-known liberal opponents of the July Monarchy such as the poet Alphonse de Lamartine (1790–1869) and the journalist Alexandre Ledru-Rollin (1807–1874). Under pressure from the radicals, socialist journalist Louis Blanc and a worker known only as Albert also joined the government. At first, there was cooperation between liberal supporters of constitutional democracy and radical republicans committed to economic justice. Under the strain of events, however, the coalition fell apart by late spring.

Bowing to pressure from the poor and unemployed of Paris, the government established national workshops and a commission headed by Louis Blanc to study the problems of the poor. The national workshops were not a substitute for the capitalist order, as Louis Blanc had intended, but a stopgap measure to enable the unemployed to earn a livelihood. They nevertheless represented the most ambitious plan that any French government had yet undertaken to combat the misery of the poor.

The new republic was quick to institute other reforms. It abolished slavery in the colonies and the death penalty for political crimes. Imprisonment for debt ceased, and the workday was limited to ten hours in Paris, eleven hours in the départements. The most radical move was the adoption of universal male suffrage. In 1789 men had identified citizenship as a distinctly male prerogative, and they continued to do so.

In the general euphoria over human liberties, women asserted their rights. A new woman's newspaper, *La Voix des Femmes* (*The Voice of*

Women), argued for equal pay, political rights, and educational opportunities. Many of the militants took their cue from the women who had fought for their rights in 1789. Women's political clubs flourished in the capital as well as in Lyon and lesser provincial towns. (See the box "A Revolutionary of 1848 Calls for Women's Political Rights.") When women's political clubs petitioned for the vote, the revolutionary government abolished them. In light of women's active role at the barricades that had toppled the monarchy, this was a bitter disappointment.

The first universal-manhood elections took place in April. The results were surprising. Nearly everyone expected enfranchisement of the poor and uneducated to bring about the election of radicals. Most of France's population, however, consisted of rural peasants, and most peasants distrusted the radicalism of the capital and resented

the tax increases needed to support social programs. Peasants tended to vote for their social superiors: the local landowner, notary, or lawyer. Even Paris elected mostly moderate deputies. The new National Assembly elected by popular vote did not look much different from that of the July Monarchy. Among the new deputies, there were only seventeen workers and no peasants.

The government was soon at loggerheads with the radical workers in Paris. Under conservative pressure, in May the Assembly disbanded the national workshops, which were extremely expensive. At the news of the closings, people who depended on the workshops rose up in despair. After days of fighting in which 1500 were killed and 12,000 arrested, government forces regained control of the city. Passionate feelings on both sides led to savagery: Corpses were mutilated, and severed heads were paraded through

Revolutionary Women In this cartoon, entitled "The Divorced Women," Daumier ridicules women who fought for their rights in the revolution of 1848. They are seen as divorced, deprived of male companionship, and probably therefore crazed. This kind of depiction was one of many ways in which women were discouraged from participating in politics. *(Jean-Loup Charmet)*

A Revolutionary of 1848 Calls for Women's Political Rights

Jeanne Deroin was a French advocate of women's suffrage who served as editor of the newspaper representing women, L'opinion des femmes, *during the revolution of 1848. Frustrated that women were denied a role in the political process, she tried to run for parliament in 1849. In an election poster and in correspondence with a socialist paper, which although socially radical was opposed to female suffrage, Deroin proclaimed the rights of women.*

I present myself for your votes, out of devotion to the consecration of a great principle: the civil and political equality of the sexes.

It is in the name of justice that I appeal to the sovereign people against negating the great principles that are the foundation for the future of our society.

If using your right, you call upon women to take part in the work of the Legislative Assembly, you will consecrate our republican dogmas in all their integrity: Liberty, Equality, Fraternity for all women as well as for all men.

A Legislative Assembly composed entirely of men is incompetent to make the laws that rule a society of men and women, as an assembly composed entirely of privileged people to debate the interests of workers, or an assembly of capitalists to sustain the honor of the country. . . .

It is precisely because woman is equal to man, and yet not identical to him, that she should take part in the work of social reform and incorporate in it those necessary elements that are lacking in man, so that the work can be complete.

Liberty for woman, as well as for man, is the right to utilize and to develop one's faculties freely.

Life's unity can be considered to be in three parts: individual life, family life, and social life; this is a complete life. To refuse woman the right to live the social life is to commit a crime against humanity.

. . . this is a holy and legitimate protest against the errors of the old society and against a clear violation of our sacred principles of liberty, equality, and fraternity.

Source: Election poster to the Electors of the Department of Seine, *L'opinion des femmes,* April 10, 1849; *La Démocratie pacifique,* April 13, 1849. Trans. K. Offen. Reprinted in Susan Groag Bell and Karen M. Offen, eds., *Women, the Family, and Freedom: The Debate in Documents,* vol. I (Stanford: Stanford University Press, 1983), pp. 280–281.

the streets. Both the liberal Alexis de Tocqueville and the socialist Karl Marx called the June uprisings class warfare between the poor and the rich.

After the June uprisings, the propertied classes looked to the authorities for security. Of the several candidates for president in 1848, Louis Napoleon (1808–1873), a nephew of Napoleon Bonaparte, appealed to the largest cross section of the population. The bourgeoisie was attracted by the promise of authority and order, while peasants remained

loyal to the memory of Napoleonic glory. Workers were impressed by Louis Napoleon's vaguely socialistic program.

Louis Napoleon received nearly three times as many votes as all his opponents combined. His government was conservative, composed of men of the old order. Three years later, Louis Napoleon dissolved the National Assembly by force and established a personal dictatorship. In 1852 he declared himself Emperor Napoleon III.

Austria

In Austria, news of the overthrow of Louis Philippe and agitation in the German states prompted demonstrations and petitions calling for a constitution and the dismissal of Metternich, the symbol of the reactionary order. In the face of growing opposition, Metternich resigned, and the army withdrew from Vienna, which appeared to have fallen under the control of students and workers. On March 15, 1848, the imperial court, surrounded by crowds of students and workers, announced its willingness to issue a constitution. Even more important was the decision to abolish serfdom. There had been fear of a serf uprising, but the relatively generous terms of the emancipation mollified the peasantry.

The promised constitution was issued, but it was drafted by the emperor rather than by representatives of the people. It was probably acceptable to the male middle classes because it enfranchised them, but students and workers who favored popular sovereignty opposed it. Mass demonstrations and an invasion of the prime minister's office prompted the court to leave Vienna for Innsbruck on May 17.

The government also faced revolts in the non-German parts of the empire: in Italy, Hungary, the

Celebrating the Revolution of 1848 in Vienna What social issues are idealized in this painting of a barricade on May 26, in the early stage of the Austrian Revolution? Consider some of the individual groups of people and their interactions. Compare the women here with the portrayal of political women in Daumier's "The Divorced Women" on page 485. *(Historische Museen der Stadt Wien)*

Czech lands, and Croatia. In March, Vienna acquiesced to Hungary's demands; thereafter, Hungary was joined to the Austrian Empire by personal union to the emperor. Constitutional government was established in Hungary, but participation in the political process was limited to Magyars, who were the largest ethnic group but who made up only 40 percent of the population. The other peoples of Hungary—Romanians, Slovaks, Croats, and Slovenes—preferred the more distant rule of German Vienna to Magyar authority.

Many nationalities rallied to the Austrian Empire in 1848 for their own reasons—fear of falling under German rule in Bohemia, fear of Magyar rule in Hungary, fear of Polish rule in Galicia (the Austrian part of Poland)—and the empire survived. There was no solidarity among the various nationalities that rose up against Vienna's rule, yet the danger nationalism posed to its survival was clearly revealed.

The revolutions in Austria and its possessions were suppressed as soon as the court was able to gather an army and send it against the rebels. Prague was bombarded into submission in June and Vienna in November 1848. Absolutist rule was re-established by Prince Felix von Schwarzenberg (1800–1852), chief minister to the new emperor, Francis Joseph (r. 1848–1916).

Italy

In the years before 1848, the Italian peninsula was in the grip of economic hardship and social unrest; nationalists and liberals hoped somehow to see their program of a united and free Italy implemented. The election in 1846 of Pius IX (r. 1846–1878) was seen as a harbinger of change. The pope was not only a religious leader but also the secular ruler of the Papal States. Pius appeared to be a liberal and a supporter of Italian unification. In January 1848, a revolution forced the king of Sicily to grant a constitution to his subjects. The Sicilian revolution was the first to erupt in Europe, but it was news of the Paris uprising in February that stimulated revolutions elsewhere in Italy.

Italians under Austrian rule revolted, forcing the Austrians to evacuate their Italian possessions. The middle classes, though eager to be free of Austrian rule, saw working-class radicals as a threat. They believed that annexation to nearby Piedmont would provide security from both Austria and the lower classes. The king of Piedmont, Charles Albert (r. 1831–1849), reluctantly decided to unite Italy under his throne if doing so would prevent the spread of radicalism to his kingdom. On March 24, 1848, he declared war on Austria but was defeated in July and had to sue for an armistice.

The pope had expressed sympathy for Italian unification but provided no support for the cause. Republicans, disappointed by the pope's abandonment of the national cause, forced him to flee. In January 1849 they declared the Roman Republic. Hope ran high that it would become the capital of a united republican Italy. Giuseppe Mazzini was to be a member of the governing triumvirate. In Piedmont, Charles Albert declared war on Austria once again, in March 1849. Within six days his army was defeated, and he resigned his throne to his son, Victor Emmanuel II (r. 1849–1878).

The Austrians quickly reconquered their lost provinces and helped restore their puppets to power. Louis Napoleon, the newly elected president of France, eager to curry favor with Catholic voters, sent French troops to Rome, restoring the pope to power in July 1849. Nevertheless, profound liberal ideas—constitutional government, universal suffrage, abolition of the remnants of the Old Regime—had been expressed and in some cases implemented, though briefly. Most reforms were rescinded, but Piedmont's liberal constitution, the *Statuto*, implemented in 1848, was retained and later became the constitution of a united Italy.

The German States

News of the February uprising in Paris also acted as a catalyst for change in the German states. In response to large public demonstrations in the grand duchy of Baden in southwestern Germany, the duke—reluctant to suffer the same fate as Louis Philippe—dismissed his conservative prime minister and installed in March 1848 a government sympathetic to the aspirations of middle-class liberals. As the king of Württemberg observed, "I cannot mount on horseback against ideas." The wisest course appeared to be compromise. He and many of his fellow dukes and princes changed their governments, dismissing their cabinets and instituting constitutions.

Up to this point Prussia was untouched by the revolutionary wave. But when news of Metternich's fall reached Berlin on March 16, middle-class liberals and artisans demonstrated for reforms. To appease his subjects, King Frederick William IV appointed a liberal businessman to head a new government. Representative government was introduced, and suffrage was extended, though it was still restricted to men of property.

The revolutionary outbreaks in the German states in 1848 were triggered by dissatisfaction with local economic and political conditions, not by agitation for German unification. But once the revolutions had taken hold, preoccupying the two largest states, Prussia and Austria—which both opposed unification lest it undermine their power—the question of a single Germany quickly came to the fore. In March 1848, a self-appointed national committee invited five hundred prominent German liberals to convene in Frankfurt to begin the process of national unification.

The vast majority of those elected to the first all-German National Assembly came from the liberal professions; only four were artisans, and one a peasant. The liberals rejoiced that they controlled the new parliament, but it was unrepresentative and lacked broad popular support.

The first all-German elected legislature met in May 1848 to create a unified Germany. The most ambitious plan envisioned a *Grossdeutschland,* or large Germany, consisting of all the members of the Germanic Confederation. Such a country would have included many non-Germans, including Poles, Czechs, and Danes. The proponents of *Kleindeutschland,* or small Germany, which would exclude Austria and its possessions, saw their solution as a more likely scenario for national unity, although it would exclude many Germans. They succeeded in the end, largely because the reassertion of Austrian imperial power in the fall of 1848 made the areas under Vienna's control ineligible for inclusion.

The Frankfurt assembly formed a provisional government in June 1848. But since the individual states, including Prussia and Austria, did not recognize the assembly's authority, it was utterly powerless. The minister of war could not raise any soldiers, and the minister of finance could not impose taxes. The United States, enthusiastic about a new republic consciously modeled on its own, was one of the few nations to accept an ambassador from the all-German government.

The parliament might have succeeded if it had called for a national uprising against the princes, but the liberals in Frankfurt were loath to do so. They distrusted the populace. Force remained in the hands of the traditional authorities. In the fall of 1848, the king of Prussia brought soldiers into Berlin and dissolved the Prussian assembly. The Prussian reassertion of royal power, though partial, was a signal for other German rulers in late 1848 to dismiss their liberal ministers.

The moment for liberalism and national unification had passed by the time the Frankfurt assembly drew up a constitution in the spring of 1849. The parliament offered the throne to Frederick William IV, king of Prussia, because he ruled the largest state within the designated state boundaries and had the power of the Prussian army. But Frederick William feared that accepting the throne would lead to war with Austria. Also, he also did not want an office offered by representatives of the people. Disappointed, most members of the Frankfurt assembly went home. A series of uprisings in favor of German unity were crushed by the Prussian army.

So German unification failed. Liberalism was unable to bring about German unity; other means would be required to do so.

SUMMARY

The revolutions of 1848 released many of the forces for change that had been gathering strength since 1815. In spite of the Congress of Vienna's effort to restore the old order after Napoleon's fall, the generation after 1815 established a new order. The ideas of change that had powered the French Revolution of 1789 continued to shape an era that claimed to be rolling history back to prerevolutionary times. Liberalism contested authoritarianism.

Reform-minded regimes in Europe improved the lives of people in colonies overseas, abolishing slavery in British and then French colonies. Some states even turned away from monarchy and experimented with republicanism, a form of government that until then many had thought fit only for small states. All of the Latin American colonies except Mexico became republics on gaining independence from Spain. In Europe during 1848–1849 the French, German, Hungarian, and Roman republics were proclaimed. These experiments suggested new modes of political organization that were to become common in the following century.

The generation after 1815 experienced revolutions frequently and broadly. These uprisings usually failed, and the forces of order were able to recapture power. Yet the status quo was altered. In many cases absolutist rulers had to grant constitutions and accept ministers who were not their choice. Even though most of these arrangements were temporary, they established an important precedent. Unusual in the first half of the century, constitutions now became the norm. Nationalism arose in these years. The desire for national independence and unity was voiced in Italy, Germany, Hungary, Poland, and the land of the Czechs.

The middle classes found their position strengthened after 1848. They did not dominate the political system, but their influence was increasing with the growth of entrepreneurship. Middle-class professionals were recruited into the civil services of states determined to streamline their operation in order to withstand revolution more effectively. Revolutionary fervor waned after 1848, but the current of economic and social change continued to transform Europe. It is to these economic and social changes that we turn next.

SUGGESTED READING

Agulhon, Maurice. *The Republican Experiment*. 1983. A work that stresses how the splits between different French political groups made it difficult for revolutionaries to achieve their goals.

Anderson, Benedict. *Imagined Communities*. 1983. A noted anthropologist underscores the extent to which a nation is an "imagined community."

Brock, Michael. *The Great Reform Act*. 1973. An account that emphasizes the sense of crisis on the eve of the Great Reform Act.

Bushnell, David, and Neill Macaulay. *The Emergence of Latin America in the Nineteenth Century*. 1988. A brief but suggestive synthesis.

Carlisle, Robert B. *The Proffered Crown: Saint-Simonianism and the Doctrine of Hope*. 1987. A work that shows the originality of Saint-Simonian thought and its continuity after the founder's death.

Harrison, J. F. C. *Quest for the New Moral World: Robert Owen and the Owenites in Britain and America*. 1969. A good biography that views the movement as affected by contemporary religious notions of a coming millennium.

Hobsbawm, E. J. *The Age of Revolution, 1789–1848*. 1962. A compellingly argued book that describes the era as being dominated by two simultaneous revolutions, the French Revolution and the industrial transformation.

Jardin, André, and André-Jean Tudesq. *Restoration and Reaction, 1815–1848*. 1988. A general survey of France.

Johnson, Paul. *The Birth of the Modern World Society, 1815–1830*. 1991. A weighty but readable book providing a panoramic view of the era. Particularly strong in providing biographical sketches of some of the major figures.

Jones, Gareth Stedman. *The Languages of Class: Studies in English Working-Class History, 1832–1982*. 1983. A work that considers Chartism as a movement of the politically disenfranchised seeking a voice within the political system.

Kedourie, Elie. *Nationalism*. 1960. An account that describes the German romantics as developers of modern nationalism and creators of an essentially pernicious force.

Kissinger, Henry. *A World Restored*. 1957. A study by a future U.S. secretary of state that emphasizes the efforts of diplomats to build an international order resistant to revolution.

Lincoln, W. Bruce. *Nicholas I: Emperor and Autocrat of All the Russias*. 1978. A biography of the tsar, revealing the ruler's dedication to preserve the autocratic regime and its values.

Pinkney, David H. *The French Revolution of 1830*. 1972. The standard work on the subject.

Porter, Roy, and Mikulas Teich, eds. *Romanticism in National Context*. 1988. An up-to-date series of essays on romanticism in different national settings.

Price, Roger. *The Revolutions of 1848*. 1989. A general history of the European revolutions describing them as the result of discontent with an economic and political system.

Sheehan, James J. *German History, 1770–1866*. 1989. A survey of the variety and contrast of the German experience.

———. *German Liberalism in the Nineteenth Century*. 1978. The standard work revealing the difficulties that German liberals faced as early as the first half of the nineteenth century.

Sked, Alan. *The Decline and Fall of the Habsburg Empire, 1815–1918*. 1989. A brief, clear study stressing the threat the revolutions of 1848 posed to imperial survival.

Sperber, Jonathan. *The European Revolutions, 1848–1851*. 1994. The best up-to-date synthesis.

Taylor, Barbara. *Eve and the New Jerusalem*. 1983. A study of socialism and feminism in the nineteenth century that pays particular attention to the Owenite movement.

Woolf, Stuart Joseph. *A History of Italy, 1700–1860*. 1979. A consideration of the problems of political divisions in Italian life.

CHAPTER 19

The Industrial Transformation of Europe, 1750–1850

In the 1830s, the French socialist Louis Blanqui suggested that just as France had experienced a political revolution, so Britain was undergoing an "industrial revolution." Eventually, that expression entered the general vocabulary to describe the advances in production that occurred first in England and then in most of western Europe. Many economic historians now emphasize how gradual the changes were and question the appropriateness of the term. In the expanse of history, however, these vast transformations—in production, transportation, information, and construction—all occurred at an extraordinary pace.

Industrial development left its mark on just about every sphere of human activity. Economic activity became increasingly specialized. The unit of production changed from the family to a larger and less personal group. Significant numbers of workers left farming to enter mining and manufacturing, and major portions of the population moved from the countryside to the city. Machines replaced or supplemented manual labor.

The economic changes physically transformed Europe. Greater levels of production were achieved, and more wealth was created than ever before. Factory chimneys belched soot into the air. Miners in search of coal, iron ore, and other minerals cut deep gashes into the earth. Cities grew quickly, and Europe became increasingly urban.

Industrialization created unprecedented advancement and opportunity as well as unprecedented hardships and social problems. Different groups tried various strategies to strike a balance between the positive and negative effects. Many entrepreneurs and their sympathizers supported liberal principles based on classical economics. Workers, with a growing sense of solidarity, struggled for their common interests. Out of the socialist ideologies of the early nineteenth century, Karl Marx forged a militant ideology to address the needs of the industrial working class.

~ *Questions and Ideas to Consider*

- Why did industrialization begin where and when it did? Consider social, cultural, and economic factors.

- Describe the circumstances of the working class in industrialized, urban Europe. How did the situation differ for women, men, and children? How did the family function as an economic unit?

- Industrialization had harsh consequences on the environment. Describe both the immediate and the long-term effects.

- What were "friendly societies"? How were they different from unions?

- How does Marxism differ from the ideas of the utopian socialists? Compare the ideas of Flora Tristan, Charles Fourier, and Robert Owen (see pages 474–475) to those of Karl Marx.

SETTING THE STAGE FOR INDUSTRIALIZATION

No one can say with certainty which conditions were necessary for the industrialization of Europe. Nevertheless, we do know why industrialization did not spread widely to the rest of the world in the nineteenth century. A certain combination of conditions—geographic, cultural, economic, demographic—helped make industrialization possible in Europe.

Why Europe?

A fortunate set of circumstances seems to explain why Europe was the stage for industrial development. Since the Middle Ages, political transformations in western Europe had reduced risk and uncertainty while encouraging productive investment. With the development of legal due process, rich merchants did not run the risk of having their wealth confiscated—as they did, for instance, in the Ottoman Empire. The unfolding of state power in Europe reduced the frequency of brigandage—still common in many parts of the world—and thus encouraged trade. Discrepancies in risk are apparent in the differences in interest rates on borrowing money in the eighteenth century: 3 percent in England, 36 percent in China.

In Europe, disparities of wealth, though serious, were less extreme than in other parts of the world; thus, there was a better market for goods. At the time western Europe industrialized, the average yearly income per person was equivalent to $500—more than in many non-Western societies even today. And nearly half of the population was literate, again a very high proportion compared to non-Western societies.

Although population grew in Europe during the eighteenth century, late marriages and limited family sizes kept its rise in check; hence European society was rarely overwhelmed by the pressures of population. In India and China, by contrast, population growth was so dramatic that society had to be fully engaged in feeding the people and could not be readily mobilized for other production.

Europe enjoyed a measure of cultural, political, and social diversity unknown elsewhere. Challenges to the dominant religious and political powers had brought some religious diversity—a rarity outside the West. Diversity encouraged a culture that tolerated and eventually promoted innovation. Competitiveness drove states to try to catch up with each other. Governments actively encouraged industries and commerce to enrich a country and make it more powerful than its neighbors. None of these factors alone explains why industrialization occurred, but their combination seems to have facilitated the process when it did occur.

The industrialization of Europe radically transformed power relationships between the industrial West and nonindustrial Africa, Asia, and

CHAPTER CHRONOLOGY

1712	Steam-operated water pump invented by Thomas Newcomen	1793	Cotton gin invented by Eli Whitney
1733	Flying shuttle introduced by John Kay	1811–1812	Luddites smash textile machinery in Britain
1764	Spinning jenny invented by James Hargreaves	1848	General Workers' Brotherhood founded in Germany
1769	Water frame invented by Richard Arkwright		*Communist Manifesto* published by Karl Marx and Friedrich Engels
	Steam engine improved by James Watt	1859	Samuel Smiles publishes *Self-Help*
1779	The "mule" invented by Samuel Crompton	1868	Trades Union Congress founded in Britain
1784	Chlorine gas as a textile bleach discovered by C. L. Berthollet		

South America. By 1900 the latter were overwhelmed by the economic and military power of the former. Within Europe, power shifted to the nations that were most industrialized. Britain was the first to industrialize, and as France had been the dominant power in the eighteenth century, so Britain dominated the nineteenth. Britain was widely admired and seen not only as an economic model but also as a political and cultural one.

Transformations Accompanying Industrialization

A number of transformations preceded or accompanied and helped define the industrializing era. Changes in commerce, agriculture, population behavior, and transportation were the major stimuli of industrial development.

Changes in agriculture during the eighteenth century had dramatically increased the productivity of the land. In addition, new, more efficient plows enabled farmers to cultivate more land than ever before. The wealth created by agriculture allowed for investment in industry and for expenditures on infrastructure, such as roads and canal systems, useful to industry. The new

crops and the more efficient cultivation meant fewer farmworkers were necessary to feed the growing population, and surplus labor expanded the new urban industries.

In the seventeenth and eighteenth centuries, European trade had increased significantly, enriching businessmen and making them aware of the fortunes to be made in local and distant markets. A new dynamic ethos took hold of businessmen eager to venture into untried fields of economic endeavor.

The population continued to grow during the years of industrial transformation. It was significant enough to promote industrialization, yet not so large as to put a brake on economic expansion. From 1750 to 1850 the population of Europe doubled. This growing group of people supplied the labor force for the new industries and provided a large surge in consumers of industrial goods.

In the countryside industrialization was foreshadowed by a form of production that had developed in the seventeenth century—the putting-out system, or cottage industry (see page 434). During the winter and at other slack times, peasants took in handwork such as spinning, weaving, or dyeing. Entrepreneurs discovered that some individuals were better than others at specific tasks. Rather than have one household process the wool through all the steps of production until it was a finished piece, the entrepreneur would buy wool from one family, then take it to another to spin, a third to dye, a fourth to weave, and so on.

Some historians believe that this form of production, called *protoindustrialization,* laid the basis for industrial manufacture. Like the latter, it depended on specialization and supplied goods to a market beyond the producers' needs. In some areas, for instance, Flanders and northern Italy, protoindustry was followed by industrial manufacture; in other regions, such as western France, it became a substitute for industry. In still other areas, like Catalonia and the Ruhr region of western Germany, industry flourished without the previous development of cottage industries. Although cottage industry was an important contributor to industrialization in some regions, it did not play a role in every case.

A less ambiguous prerequisite for industry was a good transportation network. Transportation had improved significantly in the eighteenth century. Better roads were built; coaches and carriages were constructed to travel faster and carry larger loads. Government and private companies built canals linking rivers to each other or to lakes. All this made possible the movement of raw materials to manufacture and from there to market without too great an increase in the price of the finished good. In Great Britain these transformations occurred simultaneously with industrialization; on the Continent they preceded economic change.

In Britain, industrialization had begun before rail-building; yet once railroad expansion occurred, beginning in the 1830s, orders for iron rails, steam engines, and wagons sustained and advanced industrial growth. (See the box "Encounters with the West: A Persian Discovers the British Rail System.") On the Continent rail-building promoted industrialization, notably in Germany and later in Italy.

INDUSTRIALIZATION AND EUROPEAN PRODUCTION

Several important technological advances powered European industry, and breakthroughs in one field often led to breakthroughs in others. The first two industries to be affected were textiles and iron. New forms of energy drove the machinery, and novel forms of directing labor enhanced production. At first limited to the British Isles, industry spread to the Continent, a development that occurred unevenly in various regions.

Advances in the Cotton Industry

A series of inventions in the eighteenth century led the way to the mass manufacture of textiles. The flying shuttle, introduced in Britain in 1733 by John Kay (1704–1764), accelerated the weaving process to such an extent that it increased the demand for thread. This need was met in the 1760s by James Hargreaves (d. 1778), who invented the spinning jenny, a device that spun thread from wool or cotton. Improved spinning machines, such as the "mule" of Samuel Crompton (1753–1827), increased the efficiency of the spinning jenny so that by 1812 one spinner could produce as much yarn as two hundred had made before. In 1769, Richard Arkwright (1732–1792), a barber and wigmaker, invented the water frame. This huge spinning machine drove two pairs of rollers, moving at different speeds. It was installed in a single establishment with three hundred employees, forming the first modern factory. The frame was originally powered by horses or by a waterfall, but in 1777 Arkwright had James Watt construct a steam engine to operate it. With these innovations, cotton manufacturing increased 130-fold between 1770 and 1841.

In the past, finished cloth had been soaked in buttermilk and spread out in the meadows to be bleached by the sun. That method was hardly practical for the unprecedented quantities of cloth rolling out of the factories. The introduction

~ ENCOUNTERS WITH THE WEST ~

A Persian Discovers the British Rail System

In 1836 a delegation of three Persian princes visited England. Traveling widely, they had the opportunity to meet important Englishmen and to inspect and experience some of the new technological advances, including the railroad. One of the princes, Najaf-Kuli Mirza, wrote down his observations. In this entry on the new British rail system, he attempts to describe its workings to fellow Persians.

All the wonderful arts which require strong power are carried on by means of steam, which has rendered immense profits and advantages. The English then began to think of steam coaches, which are especially applicable to their country, because it is small, but contains an enormous population. Therefore, in order to do away with the necessity for horses, and that the land which is sown with horse-corn [rye] should be cultivated with wheat, so as to cause it to become much more plentiful (as it is the most important article of food), and that England might thereby support a much greater population, they have with their ingenious skill invented this miraculous wonder, so as to have railroads from the capital to all parts of the kingdom.

Thus, by geometrical wisdom, they have made roads of iron, and where it was necessary these roads are elevated on arches. The roads on which the coaches are placed and fixed are made of iron bars. The coach is so fixed that no air or wind can do it any harm and twenty or thirty coaches may be fixed to the first in the train, and these one after the other.

All that seems to draw these coaches is a box of iron, in which they put water to boil, as in a fire-place; underneath this iron box is like an urn, and from it rises the steam which gives the wonderful force: when the steam rises up, the wheels take their motion, the coach spreads its wings, and the travellers become like birds. In this way these coaches go the incredible distance of forty miles an hour.

We actually travelled in this coach, and we found it very agreeable, and it does not give more but even less motion than horses; whenever we came to the sight of a distant place, in a second we passed it. The little steam engine possesses the power of eighteen horses.

Source: Najaf-Kuli Mirza, *Journal of a Residence in England and of a Journey to and from Syria* II (London, 1839, Reprinted, Farnborough, England: Gregg International Publishers, 1971), pp. 11–12.

---

of sulfuric acid solved the problem. It was a far more economical bleach than buttermilk and sunlight and could be produced in commercial quantities. It in turn was replaced in the 1790s when the Frenchman C. L. Berthollet (1748–1822) discovered the bleaching powers of chlorine gas. Entrepreneurs or artisans made many of the other industrial inventions, but the breakthroughs in bleaching demonstrated that more and more, industry would be fueled by advances in scientific knowledge.

The cotton-manufacturing industry in Great Britain was based on cotton grown mainly in the U.S. South. Manufactured cotton was comfortable to wear, easy to wash, and cheap enough to compete with all handmade textiles. The popularity of cotton may have improved public health as well, for people could now own several changes of clothing and keep them clean. The higher demand for raw material put pressure on cotton growers in the United States, who opened up new land.

British Cotton Manufacture Machines simultaneously performed various functions. The carding machine (front left) separated cotton fibers, readying them for spinning. The roving machine (front right) wound the cotton onto spools. The drawing machine (rear left) wove patterns into the cloth. Rich in machines, this factory needed relatively few employees; most were women and children. *(The Granger Collection, New York)*

In 1793, the American Eli Whitney (1765–1825) invented the cotton gin, a device that mechanically removed the seeds from cotton. The cotton gin meant that more cotton could be processed and thus more could be grown. It increased the profitability of the U.S. southern plantation economy and the attractiveness of slave labor.

The cotton industry in Britain showed how local manufacturing could produce a ripple effect across the oceans. Among those benefiting overseas were American farmers, cotton traders, and merchants, as well as consumers of English cotton cloth around the world. Else-where, people were adversely affected— in Africa, where slaving raids increased, and in India, where local spinners were driven out of business.

No longer, as in preindustrial trade, were all goods locally made; nor did the consumer meet producers and buy from them. Increasingly, specialization became the norm. The results were high production and a low price for the finished product. For human beings, this often meant a sense of separation from the finished product and a loss of the pride and individuality of craftwork.

Iron, Steam, and Factories

Charcoal had traditionally fueled the smelting of iron. Britain, however, ran out of wood before other European countries did and needed an alternative source of fuel. There was plenty of coal, but it contained contaminating impurities, particularly sulfur. The discovery that coal in a blast furnace could smelt iron without contamination triggered the iron industry's use of coal. In 1777, the introduction of a steam engine to operate the blast furnace considerably increased efficiency. The output of the English iron industry doubled between 1788 and 1796 and again in the following eight years. Relatively cheap and durable iron machines replaced wooden machines, which had worn out rapidly. The new machines fueled further advances. The industrial change that had started with cotton was continued by breakthroughs in the use of iron and coal.

Before the age of industry, the basic sources of power were humans, animals, wind, and water. Humans and animals were limited in their capacity to drive the large mills needed to grind corn or operate a sawmill. Wind power was unreliable, and water-driven mills depended on the seasons—streams dried up in the summer and froze in the winter. And water mills could be placed only where there was a waterfall. The steam engine changed everything because it was a constant power source that could be located just about anywhere. The steam engine was first used to pump out coal mines. As mining shafts were dug ever deeper, water in the mines became an increasing hindrance. In 1712, Thomas Newcomen (1663–1729) invented a steam-operated water pump. James Watt (1736–1819) improved on the Newcomen engine considerably, making it twice as efficient in energy output. Eventually he made it capable of converting the reciprocating motion of the piston to rotary motion. This breakthrough enabled the steam engine to power a variety of machines. Its use spread rapidly. Cotton production in Britain grew more than 400-fold between 1840 and 1860. Assisted by machines, workers were enormously more productive than when they depended on hand-operated tools. In 1700 spinning 100 pounds of cotton took 50,000 worker-hours; by 1825, it took only 135.

The steam engine centralized the workplace. With the machine as a central power source, it became practical to organize work in factories. Large, austere edifices sometimes inspired by military architecture, factories imposed rigorous work discipline. The tall factory chimney became a common sight on the industrial landscape.

Factories ranged in size from small food-manufacturing operations to large textile mills. In the first half of the nineteenth century, the average number of employees in English and French textile mills was between two and three hundred. Some plants were big, but in 1850 the small workshop, worked by the owner and his relatives or a handful of employees, was still the most common site of manufacturing in Britain.

British production became truly industrial only after 1850. For decades industry coexisted with the artisan trades and other nonindustrial occupations, and indeed in a number of cases it aided their growth. Cheap industrially manufactured thread allowed handweaving to survive. Skilled craftsmen made by hand many of the machines and boilers used in factories. Income from the new industries created a wealthy middle class, which consumed more handmade goods and employed a great number of domestic servants; except for agriculture, domestic service was the single largest field of employment for women. In 1850 factory labor did not dominate the economy of western Europe, but it had become clear that it would be increasingly difficult for handmade products to compete.

Inventions and Entrepreneurs

The industrial age was triggered by inventions, and it was sustained by the steady flow of new ones. In the decade 1700–1709, 22 patents had been issued in Britain; between 1840 and 1849, 4581 were granted. Something revolutionary was occurring. People were seeing in their lifetime sizable growth in productivity, both in the factory and on the farm. Rather than cling to traditional methods, many entrepreneurs challenged tradition. In this age of invention, innovation was prized as never before.

Most of the early British industrialists belonged to merchant families; very few were landed noblemen, industrial workers, or artisans. However, in the iron industry, it was not uncommon for metalworkers to build a modest iron mill and then enlarge it. That was also the case with potters. Josiah Wedgwood (1730–1795), who pioneered the industrial manufacturing of china, came from a long line of artisan potters and is a good example of a self-made man. The thirteenth child of a potter who died when Josiah was 9 years old, he went to work for his brother as an apprentice and gradually established himself on his own. Richard Arkwright was a barber before his invention of the water frame brought him a knighthood and a fortune of half a million pounds. Many entrepreneurs began as farmers, became involved in the putting-out system, and graduated to industrial manufacture. Yet a disproportionate number of the early manufacturers were university educated. In fact, the self-made man was more the exception than the rule. Most entrepreneurs came from relatively privileged backgrounds.

Entrepreneurs took considerable financial risk when they invested in new enterprises. Most entrepreneurs ran a single plant by themselves or with a partner, but even in the early stages, some ran several plants. In 1788, Richard Arkwright and his partners had eight mills. Some enterprises were vertically integrated, controlling all stages of production. The entrepreneurs' dynamism and boldness fostered the growth of the British industrial system, making the small nation the "workshop of the world."

Britain's Lead in Industrial Innovation

Britain led the way industrially for many reasons. It was the first European country to have a standard currency, tax, and tariff system. It enjoyed the most emancipated labor. Although Britain was by no means an egalitarian society, it accommodated some movement between the classes. Ideas and experiments were readily communicated among entrepreneurs, workers, and scientists. Although other countries had scientific societies, several societies in Britain brought together theoreticians and businessmen—for example, the Lunar Society in Birmingham and the Literary and Philosophical Society in Manchester.

Britain was far more open to dissent than were other European countries at the time. The lack of conformity was reflected in religious diversity, as well as a willingness to try new methods of production. In fact, the two often went together. A large proportion of British entrepreneurs were Quakers or belonged to one of the dissenting (non-Anglican) churches. Perhaps they were accustomed to questioning authority and treading new paths. They were also well educated and, as a result of common religious bonds, inclined to provide mutual aid, including financial support.

England had gained an increasing share of international trade since the seventeenth century. This trade provided capital for investment in industrial plants. The world trade network also ensured that Britain had a market beyond its borders, as well as access to the raw materials it needed for its industry, the most important of which was cotton.

Earlier than its competitors, Britain had a national banking system to provide capital for expanding industries. In addition to numerous London banks, there were six hundred provincial banks by 1810. Banking could flourish because Britons had wide experience in trade, had accumulated considerable wealth, and had found a constant demand for credit.

Geographically, Britain was also fortunate. Coal and iron were located close to each other (Map 19.1). A relatively narrow island, Britain has easy access to the sea. This was a strategic advantage, for water was by far the cheapest means of transportation. Compared to the Continent, Britain had few tolls, and goods could move around easily.

On the whole, British workers were better off than their continental counterparts. They were more skilled, earned higher wages, and had discretionary income to spend on the manufactured

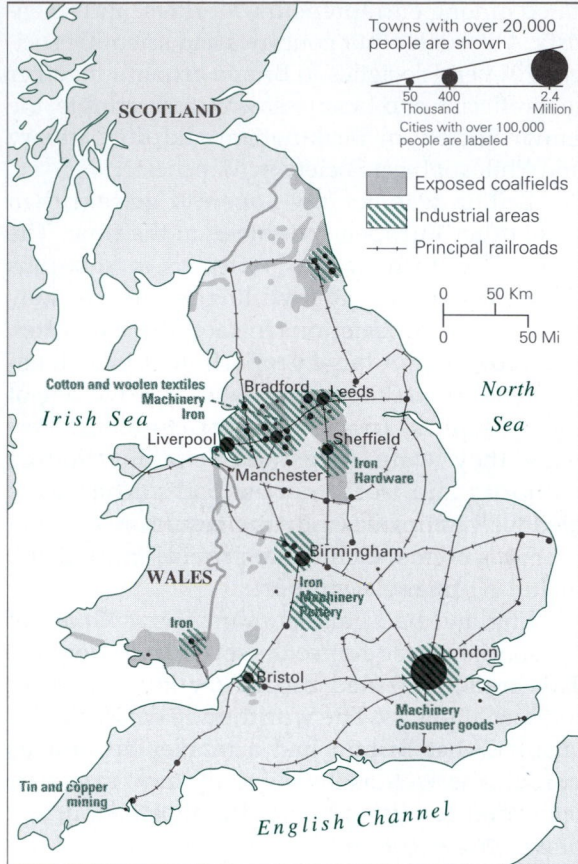

Map 19.1 The Industrial Transformation in England, ca. 1850 Industry developed in the areas rich in coal and iron fields. Important cities sprang up nearby and were linked to each other by a growing rail network.

goods now for sale. But because their wages were higher than wages on the Continent, there was an incentive for British business owners to find labor-saving devices and reduce the number of workers needed for production.

Population in Great Britain increased by 8 percent in each decade from 1750 to 1800. This swelling population expanded the market for goods. The most rapid growth occurred in the countryside, causing a steady movement of people from rural to urban areas. The presence of this work force was another contributing factor in Britain's readiness for change.

The timing of the industrial transformation in Britain was influenced by plentiful harvests in the years 1715–1750, creating low food prices and thus making possible low industrial wages. The demand for industrial goods was reasonably high. Farmers with good earnings could afford the new iron manufactured plows. It is likely that the income from farming helped bring about population growth, improvements to the transportation system, and the growing availability of capital for investment. Each change triggered more change, and the cumulative effect was staggering (see Map 19.1).

The Spread of Industry to the Continent

The ideas and methods that were changing industry in Britain spread to the Continent by direct contact and emulation. Visitors came to Britain, studied local methods of production, and returned home to set up blast furnaces and spinning works inspired by British design. Some visitors even resorted to industrial espionage, smuggling blueprints of machines out of Britain. Although a British law forbade local artisans from emigrating, some did leave, including entrepreneurs who helped set up industrial plants in France and Belgium. By the 1820s, British technicians were all over Europe.

The first country on the Continent to industrialize was Belgium, which had won its independence from the Netherlands in 1830. Like Britain, Belgium had iron and coal in proximity (Map 19.2). Belgium also had a long tradition of working cloth and iron and could readily adapt new methods to increase production of both. Belgium's location between Britain and Germany fostered the development of railroads. And rail-building facilitated industrialization by providing fast and cheap transportation and stimulating the iron industry. The Belgian government encouraged industrial modernization by building railroads and investing in the shipping industry. In the early years it kept tariffs high to protect nascent industries; later it negotiated free-trade agreements to provide expanded markets for its manufacturers.

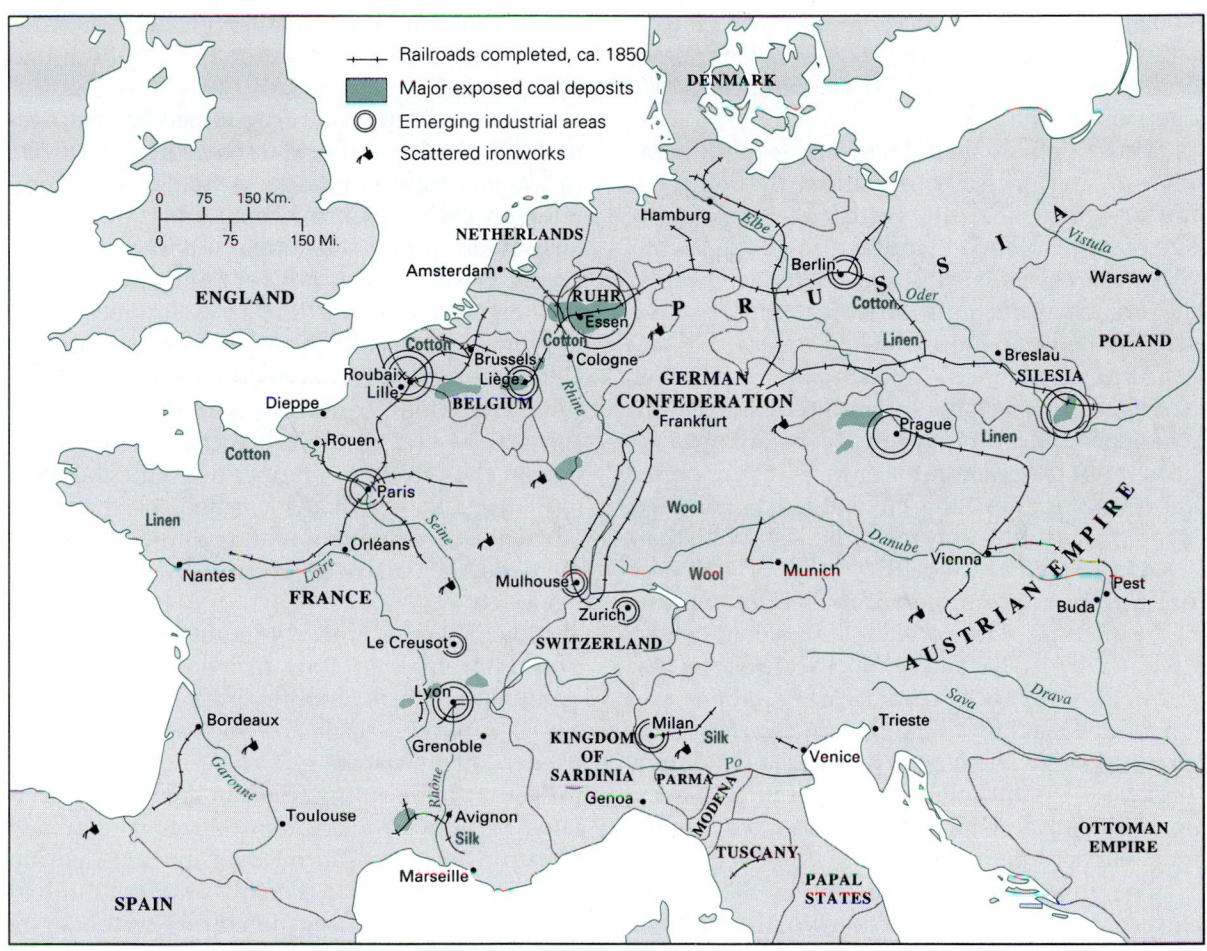

Map 19.2 Continental Industrialization, ca. 1850 Despite the fact that industry had begun on the Continent by the mid-nineteenth century, it was still sparse there, as was the rail network.

In the eighteenth century France seemed a more likely candidate for economic growth than Britain. France's overseas trade was growing faster than Britain's. In 1780, France's industrial output was greater than Britain's, though production per person was less. In the nineteenth century, however, while Britain's industry boomed, France's lagged behind. Why?

Historians have suggested several reasons. The war and revolution of the late eighteenth century were certainly contributing factors. They slowed economic growth and cut France off from the flow of information and new techniques from Britain. Moreover, in the 1790s, when the French peasants pressured for legislation to ease their situation, the revolutionaries responded positively. Thus, the misery of the peasantry was somewhat relieved, and peasants felt no urgency to leave the land and provide a cheap and ready labor supply, as in Britain. Further, since the Napoleonic Code of 1804 abolished primogeniture, younger sons were not forced off the land when their father died. Population figures provide another reason. Between

1800 and 1914, the population of France grew at half the average rate of the rest of the Continent. Finally, iron and coal in France were not close together (see Map 19.2).

Thus, French manufacturers found themselves facing British competition. By being the first to industrialize, the British had the advantage of being able to manufacture goods and to corner markets efficiently and relatively cheaply. The French were the first to feel the negative effects of being an industrial latecomer.

Although France's growth rate was lower than that of its neighbors, the French economy experienced slow but nearly constant growth throughout the nineteenth century. Taking population into account, the French did better than Great Britain and only slightly less well than Germany. From 1810 to 1850, the production of coal and the consumption of raw cotton quintupled. In 1830, France had 130 steam-driven machines; by 1852, it had 16,000. In ceramics, glass, porcelain, and paper manufacturing, France was a pioneer. Most French manufacturing, however, remained small; the typical firm had a handful of employees. Production by artisans, rather than by mass industrial production, continued longer there than in Britain or Germany.

The invasions of Germany by Napoleon caused considerable destruction but also brought some positive economic benefits. The example of the French Revolution led to important socioeconomic changes. Restrictive guilds declined. The French occupiers suppressed the small German states with their many tariffs and taxes, established a single unified legal system—which survived even after 1815—and introduced a single standard of measurement based on the metric system.

Governments in the German Confederation played an important role in the adoption of improved methods of manufacturing. The Prussian government invested in a transportation network to carry raw materials for processing and finished goods to their markets. To spur both trade and industrial growth, Prussia took the lead in creating a customs union, the *Zollverein*, which abolished tariffs among its members. By 1834 a German market embracing eighteen German states with a population of 23 million had been created.

German industrial growth accelerated dramatically in the 1850s. Massive expenditures on railways created a large demand for metal, which pressured German manufacturers to enlarge their plant capacities and increase efficiency. Germany was not yet politically unified, but the German middle classes saw economic growth as the route to prominence in Europe. Germany's growth was phenomenal. It successfully emulated Britain, overtook France, and toward the end of the nineteenth century pioneered the electrical engineering and chemical industries. The Germans avoided costly and inefficient experimentation and adapted the latest methods; they also entered fields the British had neglected.

Even by the end of the century, however, progress remained slow in many areas of Europe. As long as Russia retained serfdom (until 1861), it would lack the mobile labor force needed for industrial growth. And until late in the century, the ruling Russian aristocracy hesitated to adopt an economic system in which wealth was not based on land. In the Austrian Empire, Bohemia was the only important industrial center; otherwise, the empire was heavily agrarian (see Map 19.2).

The impoverished southern Mediterranean countries experienced little economic growth. With mostly poor soil, their agriculture yielded only a meager surplus. Spain, lacking coal or access to other energy sources, could not easily diversify its economic base. There was some industry in Catalonia, especially around Barcelona, but it did not have much impact on the rest of the country. The Italian peninsula was still industrially underdeveloped in the middle of the nineteenth century.

Although by midcentury only a few European nations had experienced industrialization to any great extent, many more would do so by the end of the century, pressured by severe competition from their more advanced neighbors. The potential threat was political and military as well as economic, for the industrialized nations represented military might and superiority. As compared to the rest of the world, Europe in the nineteenth century had a distinct material culture increasingly based on machine manufacture. Although only some regions of Europe were industrialized, many Europeans came to view their continent as obviously "superior" and the other continents as "inferior."

THE TRANSFORMATION OF EUROPE AND ITS ENVIRONMENT

Industry changed the traditional methods of agriculture, commerce, trade, and manufacture. It also transformed people's lives, individually and collectively. It altered how they made a livelihood, where and how they lived, and how they thought of themselves. Because industry required specialization, the range of occupations expanded dramatically.

The advent of industry transformed the way society functioned. Until the eighteenth century, the basis of influence and power was hereditary privilege, which meant aristocratic birth and land. The aristocracy did not disappear, but in the late eighteenth century it was challenged by a class of people whose wealth was self-made and whose influence was based on economic contributions to society. Cities grew dramatically as a result of industrialization, and Europeans faced urban problems and the pollution of their air and water.

Urbanization and Its Discontents

A sociologist at the end of the nineteenth century observed, "The most remarkable social phenomenon of the present century is the concentration of population in cities."[1] The number and size of cities had grown as never before. The major impetus for urban growth was the concentration of industry in cities and the resulting need of large numbers of urban workers for goods and services.

Industrialization was not the only stimulus. France provides many examples of urban growth with little industry. Increased commercial, trading, and administrative functions also led to the growth of cities. Neither Holland, Italy, nor Switzerland experienced much industrial development in the first half of the nineteenth century, yet their cities grew. In general, however, industry transformed people from rural to urban inhabitants.

Urban growth in some places was dramatic. In the entire eighteenth century, London grew by only 200,000; in the first half of the nineteenth century, it grew by 1.4 million, more than doubling its size. Liverpool and Manchester experienced similar growth. Census figures show that by 1851 Britain was a predominantly urban society, the first country to have as many people living in cities as in the countryside. For Germany that date was 1891, for France 1931. Although the proportion of people who were urban varied from place to place, the trend was clear.

In some cases factories were built in the countryside far from any town; as they prospered, cities grew up around them. In other cases industry gave rise to dramatic growth in once-modest towns. As industry stimulated urban growth, it was fueled in turn by urbanization. Large cities provided a labor pool and convenient markets for goods. The concentration of people encouraged the exchange of ideas. A large city was likely to have scientific societies and laboratories where engineers and scientists could discuss new ideas. After midcentury, industrialization was driven more and more by scientific and technical breakthroughs made in urban environments.

Cities pulled in people from near and far. Usually, the larger the city, the stronger its ability to attract migrants from great distances. While the medium-sized French town of Saint-Etienne drew migrants from the nearby mountains, Paris drew from the entire country. Industrial centers attracted people from beyond the nation's borders. The Irish arrived in large numbers to work in the factories in Lancashire, Belgians came for mining work in northern France, and Poles sought employment in the Ruhr in western Germany. Industrial activity stimulated world trade and shipping, taking merchant sailors far from home. Africans and Asians settled in port cities such as Amsterdam, Marseille, and Liverpool. Many large cities had heterogeneous populations, which included people of different languages, religions, and national origins, as well as, in some cases, of different races.

With the growth of cities came a multitude of urban ills. In the first half of the nineteenth century, mortality rates were higher in the cities than the countryside. There was a dramatic social inequality in the face of death. Factoring in the high child mortality rate, the average age at death for members of gentry families in Liverpool in 1842 was 35; for members of laborers' families it was 15. In 1800 boys living in urban slums were 8 inches shorter than their more fortunate contemporaries.

The rapid growth of the cities caught local authorities unprepared, and in the early stages of industrialization city life was particularly severe for the poor. Urban slums developed. The most notorious London slum was St. Giles, which became a tourist attraction because of its squalor. In many cities, large numbers of people were crammed into small areas. The houses were built back to back on small lots and had insufficient lighting and ventilation. Overcrowding was the norm. One study of a working-class parish in central London in midcentury showed three-quarters of the families living in single rooms. On one particular street, between twelve and twenty people were sleeping in each room. In Preston in 1842, 2400 persons slept three to a bed.

Sanitation was rudimentary or nonexistent. A single privy in a courtyard was likely to serve dozens of tenants—in some notorious cases in Britain and France, a few hundred. Waste from the privy might drain through open sewers to a nearby river, which was likely to be the local source of drinking water. Or the privy might be connected to a cesspool from which wastewater would seep and contaminate nearby wells. Some tenants lacked toilets and relieved themselves in the street. In the 1830s people living in the poorest sections of Glasgow stored human waste in heaps alongside their houses and sold it as manure.

In manufacturing towns factory chimneys spewed soot, and everything was covered with dirt and grime. Smoke created the famous London fog, which not only reduced visibility but posed serious health risks. City streets were littered with refuse; rotting corpses of dogs and horses were common. In 1858 the stench was so severe that the British House of Commons had to suspend its sessions.

It is not surprising that cholera, a highly infectious disease transmitted through contaminated water, swept the European urban centers. In the 1830s one of the first epidemics of modern times struck Europe, killing 100,000 in France, 50,000 in Britain, and 238,000 in Russia. Typhoid fever, also an acute infectious disease, hit mostly the poor but did not spare the privileged. Queen Victoria of Great Britain nearly died of it, and her husband, Prince Albert, did.

The Working Classes and Their Lot

In 1842 a middle-class observer traveling in industrial Lancashire noted that around the mills and factories there had developed a "population [that] like the system to which it belongs is NEW . . . hourly increasing in breadth and strength."[2] A French countess, using the pen name Daniel Stern, wrote in her memoirs of France in the 1830s and 1840s of the emergence of "a class apart, as if it were a nation within the nation," working in factories and mines, called "by a new name: the industrial proletariat."[3]

As industry advanced, more and more people depended on it for a livelihood. In the putting-out system, when there was an agricultural downturn, a cottager could spend more time on hand labor, and when there was a slack in demand for hand labor, the cottager could devote more time to the land. But people living in industrial cities were totally dependent on manufacturing. Neither skilled nor unskilled workers were assured of regular employment: Any downturn in the economy led to layoffs or loss of

St. Giles The most notorious London slum was St. Giles, whose human squalor made it a tourist attraction. *(Harvard College Library)*

jobs. In addition, the introduction of new industries often devastated laborers in older forms of production.

Most factory work was dirty and laborious, in grim plants with heavy machinery. Sixteen-hour days were common, and child labor was widespread. Because there were no safety provisions, the workers were prone to accidents—especially new workers unaccustomed to work routines or experienced workers untrained on new machines. Few factory owners protected their workers against dangerous substances or circumstances. Mercury used in hat manufacturing gradually poisoned the hatmakers and often led to dementia—the origin of the term *mad hatter*. Lead used in paints and pottery also had a devastating impact on workers' health. Metal grinding caused serious health problems. In Sheffield

in 1842, three-quarters of the cutlery workers had lung disease by the age of 40. In the 1840s the British military rejected four of ten rural volunteers because of some health deficiency; in the industrializing cities the rate of rejection was 90 percent.

Usually physically lighter than boys and often underfed, girls were faced with heavy labor that undermined their health. In 1842, 18-year-old Ann Eggley, a mineworker since the age of 7, hauled carriages loaded with ore weighing 800 pounds for twelve hours a day. She testified to a parliamentary commission that she was so tired from her work that when she came home she often fell asleep before even going to bed. Isabel Wilson, another mineworker, testified that she had given birth to ten children and had suffered five miscarriages. These women—overworked, exhausted, vulnerable to disease, and especially endangered by complications from giving birth—faced premature death. The mortality rate for adult women during the era of industrial transformation was slightly higher than that for men. The situation changed only toward the end of the nineteenth century.

Wages were so low that workers normally spent between two-thirds and three-fourths of their income on food. Family survival depended as much on intelligent purchasing and economizing as it did on money earned. Skill in negotiating the consumer economy could mean the difference between life and death. Women made the family's clothes, raised chickens or pigs, tended a potato patch, took in other families' laundry, collected rags to sell, and stretched food in whatever ways possible. Bread was the largest single item consumed; in Britain and Germany people also ate a lot of potatoes. A little bacon or other meat gave flavor to the meal, but meat was rarely consumed as a main course. Men generally took the choice piece of meat and the largest amount of food. Women and children ate what was left.

Despite such hardship, industrialization did increase wealth from the beginning. "Optimist" historians argue that some of the new wealth trickled down to the lower levels of society. "Pessimist" historians say that a downward flow did not necessarily occur. Statistics suggest that by the 1840s workers' lives in Britain did improve. Their real incomes rose by 40 percent between 1800 and 1850. In part this advance was due to an increase in the numbers of skilled workers, who were paid more than their unskilled counterparts. Although factory workers' wages took time to improve, they were usually higher than wages in the handicrafts. In Lille, in northern France, in the 1830s women in spinning mills were paid one-quarter to one-half more than lacemakers, whose work was done by hand.

Factory workers benefited not only from increased earnings but from the relatively low prices of many basic goods. In London, the price of 4 pounds of household bread fell from 15 pennies at the beginning of the nineteenth century to 8½ pennies in the 1830s. As the cost of cloth declined, there was a marked improvement in the dress of working-class people. In Germany workers' wages did not increase appreciably between 1800 and 1829, but by 1850 they had increased by 25 percent and by 1870 by another 50 percent.

Industrialization and the Family

Industrialization dramatically changed the character of the working-class family and household. Table 19.1 reveals the existence of a variegated, hierarchical work force with clear, separate functions and specified salaries. Job segregation reserved the best-paying jobs, such as carpenter and the running of certain machinery, for men. Especially in the textile industries, factory owners employed children and women in the lowest positions and paid them considerably less. Women generally received from 30 to 50 percent of men's wages, children from 5 to 25 percent. In 1839, Thomas Heath, a weaver in Spitalfields, a London neighborhood, earned 15 shillings a week, his wife but 3 shillings.

Factory work often undermined the ability of families to take care of their children. As farmers or cottagers, parents had been able to work and supervise their children at the same time. The factory, however, often separated the parents from their children. Many children were given heavy burdens at an early age, and it was not uncommon for an older child, sometimes only 5 or 6 years old, to be entrusted with the care of his or her sibling. Suzanne Monnier, the daughter of a French worker, described in her memoirs how her mother on giving birth had the 9-year-old Suzanne kiss her new sister and told her, "This is not a sister I am giving you, but a daughter."

Other workers resorted to more dangerous methods of child care. They might send a newborn to a "babyfarm," to individuals in the countryside who were paid to take care of the child. Very often these babies were neglected, and their mortality rate was extremely high. In many cases, babyfarming was no more than a camouflaged form of infanticide. Mothers who kept their children at home but were obliged to leave them unwatched during factory hours sometimes

Table 19.1		Wage Differentials in Verviers, Belgium, 1836–1869				
		Wages (francs per day)				
		1836	1846	1856	1863	1869
Male Occupations	Carpenter*	1.90	2.25	2.65	2.87	3.50
	Dyer	1.40	1.46	1.60	2.60	3.37
	Spinner	1.80	1.90	2.90	3.12	3.40
	Tanner*	1.83	2.00	2.25	3.00	3.25
	Hand weaver*	1.97	1.70	2.85	3.00	3.00
	Joiner*	1.98	2.00	2.25	2.75	3.00
	Presser	1.47	1.78	1.78	2.15	3.00
	Comber	0.84	1.27	1.50	1.75	2.65
	Laborer	—	1.25	1.50	1.87	2.50
Female Occupations	Mender	0.73	0.80	1.10	1.40	2.25
	Wool sorter	0.98	1.08	1.70	1.85	2.00
	Seamstress*	0.73	0.80	1.10	1.40	—
	Scourer	0.70	0.75	0.85	1.35	1.62
Children's Occupation	Piecener	—	0.70	0.90	1.10	1.60

*Artisans. (Those not starred were industrial workers.)

Source: Adapted from Chamber of Commerce of Verviers, *Rapport général sur la situation du commerce et de l'industrie en 1868* (Verviers, 1869), p. 69; repr. in George Alter, *Family and the Female Life Course—The Women of Verviers, Belgium, 1849–1880* (Madison: University of Wisconsin Press, 1988), p. 103. Used by permission of the University of Wisconsin Press.

pacified them with opium, readily available from the local druggist.

Working-class women carried a heavy burden in the family. In addition to sometimes working outside the home, they were responsible for running the household, managing the family income, and taking care of the children—providing most of the nurture and supervision they required. Because of the many demands on married women, their employment pattern followed the life cycle. Young women might work before marriage or before giving birth, then stay home until the children were older, and then return to work. Factory work had a harsh impact on women's lives, but most women did not work in factories; far more were in agriculture, crafts industries (which still flourished despite poor working conditions), and domestic service.

Some sectors of industry had a large proportion of women in them. In France, for example, where textiles were still the predominant product after the turn of the nineteenth century, women made up two-thirds of the textile work force as late as 1906. In iron and, later, steel plants, men were dominant. But in Belgium, women represented a full 15 percent of miners.

The textile industry found employment for children once they were over the age of 5 or 6. Their size made them useful for certain jobs, such as reaching under machines to pick up loose cotton. Because of their small hands they were also hired as "doffers," taking bobbins off frames and replacing them. Elizabeth Bentley began work as a doffer in 1815 at the age of 6. At the age of 23, when she testified before a parliamentary commission, she was "considerably deformed . . . in consequence of this labor." (See the box "The Young Girl in the Factory.")

Families changed their behaviors, but continued to function as cooperative economic units. Grandparents often moved from the country to live with the family and take care of children.

The Young Girl in the Factory

Reformers in Parliament, among them Michael Sadler, denounced the appalling conditions in the factories. Sadler was appointed to head a commission to hold hearings; workers appeared before it giving vivid descriptions of their lot. Public and parliamentary outrage at the conditions revealed by these hearings led to the Factory Act of 1833. Among the witnesses was Elizabeth Bentley, a 23-year-old weaving machine operator, who gave the following testimony.

What age are you?—23 . . .

What time did you begin to work in a factory?—When I was 6 years old. . . .

What were your hours of labor? . . . —From 5 in the morning till 9 at night, when they were thronged.

For how long have you worked that excessive length of time?—For about half a year.

What were your usual hours of labor when they were not so thronged?—From 6 in the morning till 7 at night.

What time was allowed for your meals?—40 minutes at noon. . . .

Your labor is very excessive?—Yes, you have not time for anything.

Suppose you flagged a little, or were too late, what would they do?—Strap us. . . .

Girls as well as boys?—Yes.

Severely?—Yes.

Could you eat your food well in that factory? —No, indeed, I had not much to eat, and the little I had I could not eat it, my appetite was so poor, and being covered with dust; and it was no use taking it home, I could not eat it . . . .

Did you live far from the mill?—Yes, two miles.

Had you a clock?—No, we had not. . . .

Were you generally there in time?—Yes; my mother has been up at four o'clock in the morning and at two o'clock; the colliers used to go to their work at about three or four o'clock, and when she heard them stirring she has got up out of her warm bed, and gone out and asked them the time; and I have sometimes been at Hunslet Car at 2 o'clock when it was steaming down with rain, and we have had to stay till the mill was opened [at 5 A.M.].

Source: Great Britain, *Sessional Papers, House of Commons,* Hearing of June 4, 1832, vol. XV (1831–1832), pp. 195–197.

A study of Verviers, an industrial city in eastern Belgium, showed that at mid-nineteenth century a sizable number of children over the age of 20 continued to live with their parents and contribute to the financial well-being of the family unit. When industrial workers married, they often settled with their spouses on the same street or in the same neighborhood where their parents lived. Although industry had the potential to undermine traditional family structures— sometimes giving women unprecedented opportunities to survive outside the family—the historical evidence shows that the family economic unit was the most effective way for men and women to survive in the industrial world.

The Land, the Water, and the Air

Industrialization seriously challenged the environment, transforming the surface of the earth, the water, and the air. To run the new machinery, coal was mined in increasing amounts. Iron and

Manchester, England, 1851 A small, unimportant town of 20,000 in the 1750s, Manchester—as a result of industrialization—had 400,000 inhabitants in 1850. In this 1851 painting, the polluted industrial city is contrasted with its idealized rural suburb. *(The Royal Collection © 1993 Her Majesty Queen Elizabeth II)*

other minerals were also in great demand. The exploitation of coal ushered in the modern age of energy use, in which massive amounts of nonrenewable resources are consumed.

To extract coal and other minerals, miners dug deep tunnels. Millions of tons of earth, rock, and other debris were removed from underground. This material, plus slag and other waste from the factories, was heaped up in mounds that at times covered acres of land, creating new geological formations. In one district in England in 1870, a million cubic yards of soda waste occupied 50 acres.

People cut down millions of trees to supply the wood to build shafts for coal, iron, and tin mines, or to make charcoal for glassmaking.

Between 1750 and 1900, industrial and agricultural needs led to the clearing of 50 percent of all the forests ever cleared. Many of Europe's major forests disappeared or were seriously diminished. Deforestation in turn sped up soil erosion.

Factories dumped waste ash into rivers, changing their channels and making them considerably shallower. Because of pollution from industrial and human waste, by 1850 no fish could survive in the lower Thames River in England. Smoke and soot darkened the skies. Foul odors from factories could be detected at several miles' distance. Not merely unpleasant, various air pollutants caused cancer and lung disease.

RESPONSES TO INDUSTRIALIZATION

The misery of people in the new industrial classes was disquieting evidence of the impact of industrialization. What should be done about the working classes—or for them? These new classes developed their own sense of a common interest and fate. The result was a resounding cry for political and social democracy that began in the first half of the nineteenth century and became increasingly insistent. Many solutions were proffered. The proposals became powerful ideologies shaping the nineteenth and twentieth centuries, not only in Europe but also in most of the world.

Middle-Class Ideology

The classical economists of the late eighteenth and early nineteenth centuries (see page 472) had argued in favor of laissez faire, the policy of non-intervention by the government in the economy. The laws of supply and demand, they contended, if allowed to operate unhindered, would provide for the well-being of both the individual and society. Their arguments formed the basis of middle-class ideology in the nineteenth century.

The classical economists' argument that government should do nothing to regulate industry and trade was now extended to mean that government should do nothing to regulate the distribution of wealth. The gospel of free enterprise spawned elaborate justifications of the tremendous differences in living conditions between rich and poor. *Self-Help* by Samuel Smiles (1812–1904), published in 1859, was such a justification—and one of the most influential books of the nineteenth century. *Self-Help* argued that the rich were rich because they deserved it—if the poor lived thrifty, industrious lives, the good life would come to them too. Although some people made extraordinary fortunes during the industrial transformation, others were barely surviving, unable to resort to the old sources of aid, for industrialization had broken down the charity and mutual-aid systems of the church and village. Yet Smiles argued that nothing need be done to help, for improvement depended on the character of the individual, not on society. Considering the ability of Smiles's books to assuage feelings of guilt in the middle class, their extraordinary popularity is not surprising.

Building on earlier liberals' advocacy of laissez-faire policies, others also argued against any government action to improve the condition of the working classes. The British social theorist Herbert Spencer (1820–1903) took the lessons of classical economics to extremes. Although he lived on inherited money, he asserted that wealth reflected innate virtue and poverty indicated innate vice. According to Spencer, the state should guarantee the right of everyone to pursue freedom as long as the pursuit did not infringe on others. In *Social Statics* (1851), Spencer opposed relief for the poor on the grounds that it unfairly deprived some—the rich—of their property. He also argued that schooling was outside the authority of the state.

Applying to human society Charles Darwin's principle of "survival of the fittest" (see page 559), Spencer was a Social Darwinist. Society, he believed, should be established in such a way that the strongest and most resourceful would survive. The weak, poor, and improvident were not worthy of survival. If the state helped them survive—such as by providing education—it would only perpetuate the unfit. Spencer's harsh doctrines were widely acclaimed.

Many of those who favored laissez-faire policies criticized some aspects of the market economy, however. In France in the first half of the nineteenth century, commentators on the factory system, including industrialists, expressed fear that factory work would undermine the stability of family life and hence of society itself. At midcentury, in the face of unsanitary urban conditions, child labor, and other alarming results of industrialization, some governments began to intervene in areas of concern that would have been unthinkable a half-century earlier.

The Growth of Working-Class Solidarity

At some point workers stopped thinking of themselves as members of a given craft and began to think of themselves as members of the working class. The decline of the guilds, which had included apprentices and masters, rich and poor, was one factor in this shift. Unlike the skilled handicrafts that required years of apprenticeship, much of industrial production did not require lengthy periods of training. The system of dependence between apprentice and master became irrelevant. Although guilds faded in importance, the solidarity and language born of the guild system continued to shape workers' attitudes throughout much of the nineteenth century. New experiences also reinforced the sense of belonging to a group and sharing common aspirations.

Cultural forces fostered workers' sense of solidarity. The common language of religion and shared religious practice united workers, and many religious groups were born as a result. Emphasis on equality before God fueled the sense of injustice in a world where some lived in luxury while others worked for a pittance. Joanna, a self-proclaimed prophet active in the 1810s in England, announced both salvation and the coming of a new world of material well-being. In France, workers believed the new society would come about by their martyrdom; like Jesus, the workers would suffer, and from their suffering would emerge a new, better society. Ideas of social justice were linked in the country-side with religious broadsides speaking of "Jesus the worker."

Social institutions also encouraged class unity. In the eighteenth century both husband and wife were usually in the same craft. By 1900 it became more common for workers to marry across their crafts, thereby strengthening the sense of solidarity that encompassed the working class as a whole.

Other cultural and social factors created bonds among workers. Housing was increasingly segregated. Workers lived in low-rent areas—in slums in the center of cities or in outlying areas near the factories. Thus, urban workers lived close together, in similar conditions of squalor and hardship. Entrepreneurs who built factories or established mineworks in the countryside had to provide housing in order to attract and retain workers. Although this housing was sometimes better than the quarters of urban workers, it nevertheless reinforced the workers' solidarity and sense of commonality.

Workers increasingly spent their leisure time together, drinking in pubs and taverns, attending theaters and new forms of popular entertainment such as the circus, or watching traditional blood sports like boxing or cockfights. Popular sports emerged in the 1880s. In sports such as soccer, which developed in England at this time, both players and fans were drawn overwhelmingly from the working class.

Faced with the uncertainties of unemployment and job-related accidents, in addition to disease and other natural catastrophes, workers formed so-called friendly societies in which they pooled their resources to provide mutual aid. These societies, descendants of the benefit organizations of the Middle Ages and Renaissance, combined business activity with feasts, drinking bouts, and other social functions.

Friendly societies had existed as early as the seventeenth century, but they became increasingly popular after industrialization. Their strength in a region often reflected the degree to which the area was industrialized. First started to provide aid for workers in a particular trade, they soon included members in several crafts. They federated into national organizations, so that a worker who moved to a new town could continue membership in the new locale. Connected by common membership in friendly societies, workers expressed group solidarity beyond their individual occupations. Though far from accomplished, a working class was in the making.

Collective Action

Militant and in some cases violent action also strengthened workers' solidarity. In 1811–1812, British hand weavers, faced with competition from mechanized looms, organized in groups claiming to be led by a mythical General Ned Ludd. In the name of economic justice and to protect their livelihood, the "Luddites," as the general's followers were called, smashed machines or threatened to do so. To bring the Luddite riots under control, twelve thousand troops were dispatched, and in January 1813, British authorities executed ten people for Luddism. Similarly, in Saxony in eastern Germany in the 1830s and 1840s, weavers went on machine-crushing campaigns.

In Lyon, France, in 1831 and 1834, workers led uprisings demanding fair wages for piecework. Angered when silk merchants lowered the amount they would pay, the workers marched in the streets bearing banners proclaiming "Live Working or Die Fighting." Troops were brought in to restore order to the riot-torn city. Although conditions of the silk trade had been the immediate impetus for the uprising, the workers appealed for help to workers in other trades.

Labor agitation increased in the 1840s in much of Europe; a wave of strikes involving twenty thousand workers broke out in Paris in 1840. In the summer of 1842, an industrial downturn in England led to massive unemployment and rioting. During the summer of 1844 in Silesia, in eastern Prussia, linen handloom weavers desperate because of worsening conditions brought on by competition from machine-made cotton fabrics attacked the homes of the wealthy.

Labor unions were illegal in Britain until 1825, in Prussia until 1859, and in France until the 1860s. The advantages offered by unions were well understood. As a French workers' paper declared in 1847, "If workers came together and organized . . . nothing would be able to stop them." An organized group could threaten to withhold labor if the employer did not grant decent wages and acceptable conditions. Unions made workers a countervailing force to the factory owners.

Discipline in the factory was often severe. Workers had to conform to rigid rules not only in the workplace but also away from it. Workers in some factories were forbidden to read certain newspapers, had to attend religious services, and could marry only with the owners' permission. Workers resisted these attempts at control. They wanted freedom from outside regulation, and unions were a way to ensure that freedom.

The process of unionization was difficult. By 1850 many countries had passed laws supporting employers against the workers. Censorship and the use of force against organized strikes were not uncommon. Population growth made it difficult for workers to withhold labor lest they be replaced by others only too willing to take their place. Foreign workers—for example, the Irish who streamed into England and the Belgians and Italians who streamed into France—were often desperate for work and not well informed about local conditions.

In many countries, workers formed unions before they were legalized. Most were centered around a single craft or a single industry. In Britain, however, there were early attempts to organize unions on a national basis. In 1834, Welsh socialist Robert Owen (1771–1858) helped launch the Grand National Consolidated Trades Union. The organization's goal was to use the principles of cooperation to unite all of labor against the capitalist system. Internal strife and government repression kept this organization from succeeding. Not until 1868 was a federal structure created for the British unions—the Trades Union Congress.

In Germany the General Workers' Brotherhood was founded in 1848. Its first members came from many walks of life, but eventually its membership included workers only. Most were craftsmen and artisans: skilled workers such as cigar makers, book printers, typesetters. The year after its founding, the General Workers' Brotherhood had 15,000 members and 170 locals. After 1859, when labor unions were legalized, they grew significantly.

The composition of union membership evolved over time. Because labor unions originated in the crafts tradition, the earliest members were skilled craftsmen who organized to protect their livelihood from the challenges of industrialization. Literate and long-time residents of their communities, they provided the labor movement with much of its leadership and organization. Skilled craft workers played a strong role in developing a sense of class consciousness. The language and institutions they had developed over decades and sometimes over centuries became the common heritage of workers in general.

Workers looked to political action as the means to improve their situation. In the 1830s and 1840s, English workers agitated for the right to vote; they saw voting as a way to put themselves on equal footing with the privileged and win better conditions. When the Great Reform Bill of 1832 failed to grant them the vote, many workers backed the Chartist movement of the 1840s (see page 479).

In France urban laborers had played an important part in the various stages of the Revolution of 1789, and they continued to shape political events. In July 1830 workers helped topple the Bourbon monarchy and bring Louis Philippe (r. 1830–1848) to the throne. They insisted that their labor had created the wealth of the nation and that their self-sacrifice had brought in a freer government. Workers were disappointed by their failure to win political representation under the July Monarchy, and their sense of betrayal strengthened their class solidarity.

However vague their ideas, European workers showed that their organizations were legitimate representatives of the people and that the lot of the worker should be the concern of government. In general, workers upheld the ideal of a moral economy—one in which all who labored got a just wage and a minimum level of well-being was assured to all.

The working class was never a monolithic group. It consisted of people with varying skills, responsibilities, and incomes. Many skilled workers looked with contempt on the unskilled. If both sexes worked side by side, there was little solidarity between them. Men worried that the presence of women devalued their work because women were regularly paid. Men often excluded women from their unions and even went on strike to force employers to discharge women. An exception to this practice was Belgium, where labor organizations were remarkably receptive to female members. Nor was there solidarity across nationalities. Foreign workers were heartily despised. British workers were hostile to their Irish colleagues, the French to the Belgians and Italians

in their midst. Thus, many forces fostered dissension in the working class in the nineteenth century. Nevertheless, various experiences broadened and deepened workers' sense of a common fate and goal.

The middle classes came to believe that all workers formed a single class. By the mid-nineteenth century, they had developed a clear fear of workers, not only as individuals but as a group, as a class. It was not unusual for members of the elite to refer to workers as "the swinish multitude" or, as the title of a popular English book put it, *The Great Unwashed* (1868). In France reference was alternately made to "the dangerous classes" and "the laboring classes." Not just workers but even the privileged seemed to see relations between the groups as a form of class war.

Marx and Marxism

Socialism provided a powerful language for the expression of working-class interests. Many of the workers enfranchised in the latter part of the century joined political parties espousing this doctrine. As we have seen, socialism existed before Karl Marx came on the scene. Henri de Saint-Simon and Charles Fourier in France and Robert Owen in Great Britain were its foremost prophets (see page 474). Marx drew on their theories and gave them a very special twist; in the end his became the dominant form of socialist thought.

Karl Marx (1818–1883), the son of a lawyer, grew up in the Rhineland, in western Germany, an industrializing area that was particularly open to political ideas and agitation. The Rhineland had been influenced by the ideas of the French Revolution and was primed for political radicalism. As a young man Marx studied philosophy at the University of Berlin and joined a group known as the "Young Hegelians," self-declared disciples of the idealist philosopher G. W. F. Hegel (1770–1831). Marx showed an early interest in political liberty and socialism. In 1842–1843 he edited a newspaper that spoke out for freedom and democracy in Germany. The following year in Paris, he met several of the French socialist writers. Even as a young man, he was perceived by his contemporaries as brilliant and extraordinarily determined.

Because of his radical journalism, he was exiled from the Rhineland and lived briefly in Paris, then Brussels. In 1849 he settled in London, where he lived for the rest of his life, dedicated to establishing his ideas on what he viewed as scientific bases. Deriving a modest income from writing for the *New York Daily Tribune* and from funds provided by his friend and collaborator Friedrich Engels (1820–1895), Marx was never able to provide well for his family, which constantly lived on the edge of poverty. Of the six children born to the Marx household, three died in infancy.

In 1848, Marx and Engels published the *Communist Manifesto*. A pamphlet written for the Communist League, a group of Germans living

Karl Marx Through his writings and agitation, Marx transformed the socialism of his day and created an ideology that helped shape the nineteenth and twentieth centuries. *(Corbis-Bettmann)*

in exile, the manifesto was an appeal to the workers of the world. The league deliberately called itself "Communist" rather than "Socialist." Communism was a radical program, bent on changing property relations by violence; socialism was associated with peaceful transformation. The pamphlet was too late and too obscure to influence the revolutions of 1848. However, it laid out Marx's basic ideas, calling on the working class to rise—"You have nothing to lose but your chains"—and create a society that would end the exploitation of man by man. The exploitation of women was not especially interesting to Marx. Marxists noted that even in the poorest household, husbands were tremendously privileged over their wives, but most merely insisted that after "the revolution" such injustices would end.

A number of political and polemical works flowed from Marx's pen, but most of them remained unpublished during his lifetime. The first volume of his major work, *Capital,* was published in 1867; subsequent volumes appeared posthumously. Marx agreed with Hegel that human history has a goal. Hegel believed that the goal was the realization of the world spirit (see page 467); Marx believed it was the abolition of capitalism, the victory of the proletariat, the disappearance of the state, and the liberation of all humankind.

Whereas Hegel thought that ideas govern the world, Marx insisted that material conditions determine it. Hegel said that truth evolves by a "dialectic method": A person states a proposition and then states its opposite; from the clash of the two emerges a synthesis that leads to a higher truth. Marx called his philosophy "dialectic materialism." Following Hegel, he posited a world of change but said that it was embedded in material conditions, not in a clash of ideas. Ideas, to Marx, were but a reflection of the material world.

Marx grouped human beings into classes based on their relationship to factories and machines—the means of production. Capitalists were one class, because they owned the means of production. Workers were a separate class—the proletariat—because they did not own any of the means of production and their income came from their own hands. Because these two classes had different relationships to the means of production, they had different—in fact, antagonistic—interests and were destined to engage in a class struggle.

Marx saw the conflict as necessary to advance human history, and he sought to validate his thesis by the study of the past. In the Middle Ages, he pointed out, the feudal class dominated society but eventually lost the struggle to the commercial classes. Now, in turn, the capitalists were destined to be overwhelmed by the rising proletariat.

Marx found not only justification for but irrefutable proof of the "scientific" basis of his ideas in history and economics. Capitalism was creating the forces that would supplant it. The large industrial plants necessitated an ever greater work force with a growing sense of class interest. The inherently competitive nature of capitalism would inevitably drive an increasing number of enterprises out of business, and there would emerge a form of monopoly capitalism, abusive of both consumers and workers. As a result of ever more savage competition, more businesses would fail, and more workers would become unemployed. Angry and frustrated, workers would overthrow the system that had abused them for so long: "The knell of private property has sounded. The expropriators will be expropriated." The proletariat would take power and to solidify its rule would temporarily exercise the "dictatorship of the proletariat." Once that had taken place, the state would wither away, class war would end, and the ideal society would prevail. History would be over.

Marx's study of economics and history proved to him that socialism was not only desirable—as the utopians had thought—but inevitable. The laws of history dictated that capitalism would collapse, having created within itself the means of its own destruction—namely, the rising proletariat. For millions of people, Marxism was a doctrine of hope founded on scientific principles.

SUMMARY

Industrial transformation altered the face of Europe. The process, which started around 1750 in parts of England, spread by 1850 to other states of Europe. The proximity of coal and iron, the relative ease of domestic transportation, a culture open to innovation and entrepreneurship, and the existence of an already relatively dynamic economy help explain why Britain was the first nation to industrialize.

Economies based on industry changed power relations within Europe and altered the relationship of Europe to the rest of the world. As a result of the transformation in its economy Britain became in the nineteenth century the most powerful nation in Europe and achieved worldwide influence. Although Europe was industrialized only in certain areas, many Europeans came to think of their continent as economically and technologically superior to the rest of the world.

Industry changed the nature of work for large numbers of Europeans. Machines replaced human energy in the workplace. By the application of science and technology, manufacturing productivity increased significantly. A decreasing number of people worked in agriculture, and more entered manufacturing. Population patterns changed; cities grew dramatically, and for the first time European cities had over a million inhabitants.

The massing of workers in factories and urban areas called attention to their misery and also to their potential power. Eager to improve their lives and working conditions, workers began to express their solidarity. They organized into groups that were more broadly based and therefore more powerful than workers' groups of the past. As workers began to think of themselves as a group, the dominant groups within society began to perceive them as such.

Confronted by the realities of industrialization, many people changed their intellectual convictions. It was obvious that the laissez-faire system could not meet many workers' needs. Classical liberal economists revised their orthodoxy; the state became more interventionist, trying to remove some of the worst abuses.

Drawing on earlier strands of socialism, Karl Marx articulated this ideology in a new and compelling way. Marxism gave a powerful voice to the new proletarian class that industrialization had created, and it was to cast a shadow far into the next century.

NOTES

1. Adna Ferrin Weber, *The Growth of Cities in the Nineteenth Century: A Study in Statistics* (New York: Macmillan, 1899; Ithaca, N.Y.: Cornell University Press, 1963), p. 1.
2. W. Cooke Taylor, *Notes of a Tour in the Manufacturing Districts of Lancashire, in a Series of Letters to His Grace the Archbishop of Dublin* (London, 1842), pp. 4–6. Quoted in E. P. Thompson, *The Making of the English Working Class* (New York: Vintage, 1963), p. 191.
3. Marie de Flavigny d'Agoult [Daniel Stern], *Histoire de la Révolution de 1848*, 2d ed., vol. 1 (Paris, 1862), p. 7, quoted in Theodore S. Hamerow, *The Birth of a New Europe: State and Society in the Nineteenth Century* (Chapel Hill: University of North Carolina Press, 1983), pp. 206–207.

SUGGESTED READING

Alter, George. *Family and the Female Life Course: The Women of Verviers, Belgium, 1849–80.* 1988. A reminder that women were usually not continuously in the industrial work force but entered and exited according to family needs.

Brimblecombe, Peter. *The Big Smoke: A History of Air Pollution in London Since Medieval Times.* 1987. An account of the causes of pollution and the attempts to control it.

Chinn, Carl. *Poverty Amidst Prosperity: The Urban Poor in England, 1834–1914.* 1995. Concentrates on the harsher aspects of industrialization.

Deane, Phyllis. *The First Industrial Revolution.* 1965. An excellent discussion of the importance of changes in production techniques.

Hilden, Patricia P. *Women, Work, and Politics: Belgium, 1830–1914.* 1993. Reveals the unique experience of women in the industrial work force in the first continental country to industrialize.

Himmelfarb, Gertrude. *The Idea of Poverty: England in the Early Industrial Age.* 1983. A work that describes the image of the poor among Victorian middle-class observers.

Hohenberg, Paul M., and Lynn Hollen Lees. *The Making of Urban Europe, 1000–1950.* 1985. A good general introduction to the impact of industry on urbanization, emphasizing less the pathology of cities and more their resilience.

Kelly, Alfred, ed. *The German Worker: Working-Class Autobiographies from the Age of Industrialization.* 1987. A collection of workers' accounts of their lives.

Landes, David S. *Prometheus Unbound.* 1969. A standard work emphasizing technological and cultural factors as explanations for industry.

Lynch, Katherine A. *Family, Class, and Ideology in Early Industrial France: Social Policy and the Working-Class Family, 1825–1848.* 1988. A study of social concerns in France over the corrosive impact of industry on working-class families.

Maynes, Mary Jo. *Taking the Hard Road.* 1995. An analysis of French and German workers' experiences during industrialization.

Mazlish, Bruce. *The Meaning of Karl Marx.* 1984. An easy-to-read introduction to the man and his thought, emphasizing the shaping of both by the era in which Marx lived.

Mokyr, Joel. *The Lever of Riches: Technological Creativity and Economic Progress.* 1990. A work that provides a comparative study of Western and Chinese technology, emphasizing cultural elements as explanations for the industrialization of the West.

Nardinelli, Clark. *Child Labor and the Industrial Revolution.* 1990. A work that represents child labor as less harsh than some contemporaries claimed and as a rational adjustment to existing economic conditions.

O'Brien, Patrick K., and Roland Quinault, eds. *The Industrial Revolution and British Society.* 1993. A broad set of essays on the origins and impact of industry on British society.

Pollard, Sidney. *Peaceful Conquest.* 1981. A reminder that although industrialization started in England, it occurred not throughout the whole country but only in specific regions; likewise when industry spread to the Continent, it spread only to specific regions.

Sylla, Richard, and Gianni Toniolo, eds. *Patterns of European Industrialization.* 1991. A volume describing the patterns of industrialization in a comparative perspective.

Thompson, E. P. *The Making of the English Working Class.* 1963. A work that emphasizes cultural factors that encouraged the development of working-class consciousness in England.

Tilly, Louise, and Joan Scott. *Women, Work and Family.* 1978. A description of the family wage economy in which all members contributed to the economy of the family, especially in the early stages of industrialization.

CHAPTER 20

New Powers and New Tensions, 1850–1880

I n 1866 when Prince Charles, a member of the Prussian royal family, was offered the throne of Romania, he reportedly had to look at a map to locate his future kingdom. His puzzlement was partly understandable, for a united Romania had existed for only five years. The prince and his contemporaries in the generation after 1848 witnessed the emergence of several new nation-states. And as the map of Europe changed, a much enlarged and more powerful United States also emerged.

The changing political scenery was accompanied by the development of new political institutions. To meet the demand for popular participation in government so dramatically expressed in 1848, every European state, except the Ottoman and Russian Empires, found it necessary to have a parliament. Rare before midcentury, such institutions became common thereafter. No longer was the demand for popular participation seen as a threat to the existing political and social order. In fact, popular participation, or the appearance of it, gave the existing order a legitimacy it had not enjoyed since the French Revolution. Nationalism flourished during this period, emerging as a decisive force in European affairs and in the United States, where it promoted territorial expansion and a determination to preserve the Union.

These political transformations occurred in an era of unprecedented economic growth and prosperity, touched off by the discovery of gold in California in 1848. The increased supply of gold allowed for the expansion of credit, which led to the founding of new banks and mass investments in growing industries. The iron output of Britain, France, and Germany tripled in the years between 1850 and 1878. During this same period the standard of living of every class rose significantly in industrializing nations. The middle class expanded dramatically, while the elites sought to re-establish their power in new ways.

In the first half of the century, international relations had been dominated by the congress system, in which representatives of the major European states met periodically to preserve the balance of power. This order disappeared in the second half of the century, as political leaders pursued the narrow interests of their state. Instead of negotiation, brute military force, or the threat of it, was employed to resolve international conflict. This was *Realpolitik*, a policy in which war became a regular instrument of statecraft, and its chief practitioner was the Prussian chancellor Otto von Bismarck.

～ *Questions and Ideas to Consider*

- What was the "congress system"? How did the Crimean War and the subsequent peace treaty change the system of international order? Were the decisions of the Congress of Paris honored?

- Why did Cavour want Napoleon III to help him win Italian unification? Why was Napoleon III willing to help? What does Napoleon III's decision to sign a treaty with Austria suggest about his attitude toward an Italian nation?

- Like Italian unification, German unification was won through military force, not liberal idealism. Yet the new Italian state was dominated by liberal Piedmont, while Germany was dominated by authoritarian Prussia. Discuss some of the other formative characteristics of the new German nation.

- In the United States, expansion—and tensions over the new territories—helped lead to the Civil War. Afterward, the democratic structure strained to adjust to new citizens and new calls for political participation. Discuss the political status of African Americans and women in this period.

- What was the Paris Commune? What kind of government was set up in France in its aftermath?

THE CHANGING SCOPE OF INTERNATIONAL RELATIONS

The Crimean War and its aftermath shaped European international relations for several decades. A new level of mutual suspicion arose, leading nations to act in their own self-interest and ignore the concerns of the other major players in the international system.

The Crimean War as a Turning Point, 1854–1856

The Crimean War had many causes. Principally, however, it was ignited by the decision of French and British statesmen to contain Russian power in the Balkans and keep it from encroaching on the weakening Ottoman Empire. Russian claims to have the right to intervene on behalf of Ottoman Christians had led to war between the two states in October 1853. The defeat of the Ottoman navy at Sinope in November left the Ottoman Empire defenseless.

British and French statesmen had considerable interest in the conflict. Britain had long feared that the collapse of the Ottoman Empire would lead Russia to seek territorial gains in the Mediterranean. Such a move would challenge Britain's supremacy. An explosion of public sentiment against Russia also obliged the British government to take an aggressive stance. Meanwhile, the French emperor, Napoleon III, viewed defeat of Russia as a way to eclipse one of the states most dedicated to preserving the existing European borders. He wanted to undermine existing power relations, hoping that a new order would lead to increased French power and influence. Napoleon also imagined that fighting side by side with Britain could lay the foundation for Anglo-French friendship. And so England and France rushed to defend the Ottoman Empire and declared war on Russia in March 1854.

The war was poorly fought on all sides. Leadership was woefully inadequate. The Russians had a standing army of a million men but never managed to use more than a fraction of

Crimean War This photograph shows the interior of the Sevastopol fortress after it had been battered into surrender. The Crimean War was the first conflict to be documented by photographers. *(Courtesy of the Board of Trustees of the Victoria & Albert Museum)*

CHAPTER CHRONOLOGY

1851	Louis Napoleon's coup d'état in France
1854–1855	Crimean War
1860	Italy united under Piedmontese rule
1861	The abolition of serfdom in Russia
1861–1865	Civil War in the United States
1862	Bismarck appointed prime minister of Prussia
January 1864	Austria and Prussia attack Denmark and occupy Schleswig and Holstein
June 1866	Austro-Prussian War
1867	The North German Confederation
	The "Second Reform Bill" in England
1870	Rome joined to Italy and becomes its capital
March–July 1870	Crisis over Hohenzollern candidacy for Spanish throne
July 19, 1870	France declares war on Prussia
1871	The Paris Commune and formation of the Third Republic
January 18, 1871	The German Empire declared in the Hall of Mirrors in Versailles
1878	Congress of Berlin

that number due largely to poor communications and supply systems. In Britain, failures in military supplies and leadership were denounced in the press and in Parliament. For the first time the press played an active role in reporting war, and photography brought to readers at home the gruesome realities of battle.

One of the few heroic figures to emerge from this conflict was Florence Nightingale (1820–1910), who organized a nursing service to care for the British sick and wounded. Before she arrived, there were five times more casualties from disease than from enemy fire. Her efforts produced a remarkable reduction of such casualties. Through the tremendous force of her intelligence and personality, she established new levels of cleanliness and order in hospitals. In the wake of her successes Nightingale was often described as an angelic maternal figure. However, her early writing demonstrates that she was not seeking to extend the female role of nurturer to the larger

Florence Nightingale in the Crimean War

Florence Nightingale used her influential family connections to win an appointment to the Crimean battlefield. Once there, she organized nursing for the wounded and was able to secure additional personnel and medical supplies for her hospital. In this letter, Nightingale describes the plight of the wounded in an army lacking sufficient supplies.

We have no room for corpses in the wards. The Surgeons pass on to the next, an excision of the shoulder-joint—beautifully performed and going on well—ball lodged just in the head of the joint, and fracture starred all round. The next poor fellow has two stumps for arms—and the next has lost an arm and leg. As for the balls, they go in where they like, and do as much harm as they can in passing. That is the only rule they have. The next case has one eye put out, and paralysis of the iris of the other. He can neither see nor understand. But all who can walk come into us for Tobacco, but I tell them that we have not a bit to put into our own mouths. Not a sponge, nor a rag of linen, not anything have I left. Everything is gone to make slings and stump pillows and shirts. These poor fellows have not had a clean shirt nor been washed for two months before they came here, and the state in which they arrive from the transport is literally *crawling*. I hope in a few days we shall establish a little cleanliness. But we have not a basin nor a towel nor a bit of soap nor a broom—I have ordered 300 scrubbing brushes. But one half the Barrack is so sadly out of repair that it is impossible to use a drop of water on the stone floors, which are all laid upon rotten wood, and would give our men fever in no time. . . .

I am getting a screen now for the Amputations, for when one poor fellow, who is to be amputated tomorrow, sees his comrade today die under the knife it makes impression—and diminishes his chance. But, anyway, among these exhausted frames the mortality of the operations is frightful.

Source: Letter to Dr. William Bowman, November 14, 1854, in Sue M. Goldie, ed., *"I Have Done My Duty": Florence Nightingale in the Crimean War, 1854–56* (Iowa City: University of Iowa Press, 1987), pp. 37–38.

society but searching for a way to avoid the cloistered, domestic role that women of the time were expected to fill. By almost single-handedly creating the idea and practice of nursing as a professional calling, Nightingale broadened the range of respectable middle-class female behavior and opened up another avenue of employment for working-class women. (See the box "Florence Nightingale in the Crimean War.")

The war ended in December 1855 when Russia surrendered the fortified port of Sevastopol after a long, bitter siege. Nightingale's efforts notwithstanding, the Crimean War killed three-quarters of a million people—more than any European war between the end of the Napoleonic Wars and World War I. The slowness with which each side mobilized, the lack of planning and foresight in staging battles, the large number of fatalities from causes other than enemy fire—all were reminiscent of hostilities from earlier eras. It was a futile, senseless war whose most important consequence was political, for it unleashed dramatic new changes in the international order.

The Congress of Paris and Its Aftermath

The former combatants met in Paris in February 1856 to work out a peace treaty. Their decisions—which pleased no one—shaped relations among European states for the next half-century. Russian statesmen were especially discontented. The Congress of Paris forbade Russia from having a fleet in the Black Sea and forced it to withdraw from the provinces of Moldavia and Wallachia, where it had enjoyed the right of intervention since the 1830s. Tsar Nicholas I had expected Austrian assistance in the war in return for his help in crushing the Hungarian rebellion in 1849. Instead, Austria's leaders had not only withheld aid but threatened to join the Western alliance. Nor did French leaders feel their nation had benefited. Although holding the congress in Paris flattered the emperor's pride, no other clear advantages emerged for France. The north Italian state of Piedmont, which had joined the allies, gained from the congress only a vague statement on the unsatisfactory nature of the existing situation in Italy. Prussia was invited to attend the congress only as an afterthought and hence also felt slighted.

Although the war seemed to have sustained the integrity of the Ottoman Empire, the peace settlement weakened it indirectly by dictating reforms in the treatment of its Christian populations. These reforms impaired the empire's ability to repress growing national movements. British political leaders, galled by the heavy sacrifices of the war, moved toward isolationism in foreign policy.

In the past the congress system had tried to ensure that no major power was dissatisfied enough to subvert the existing distribution of power, but the Crimean War and the peace treaty changed the situation. In the first half of the century the international order had been upheld in part by the cooperation of the conservative Eastern powers: Russia, Austria, and Prussia. Now these powers were rivals, and their competition contributed to growing instability in the international system. By and large, the decisions reached in Paris were either disregarded or unilaterally revised.

ITALIAN UNIFICATION

In the words of Prince von Metternich of Austria, Italy at midcentury was nothing but a "geographic expression." The revolution of 1848 had revealed an interest in national unification, but the attempt had failed. Yet within a dozen years what many believed to be impossible would come to pass. Idealists like Giuseppe Mazzini (1805–1872) had preached that Italy would be unified by its people, who would rise and establish a free republic. Instead, it was unified by royalty, by war, and with the help of a foreign state.

After the failed 1848 revolution, various Italian rulers resorted to repression. In Modena, the Habsburg duke Francis V jailed liberals, closed the universities, and personally caned passersby who did not tip their hat to him. In the Papal States, men were imprisoned for "appearing inclined to novelty." Pope Pius IX, who first had appeared sympathetic to Italian unification, opposed it as soon as he realized it was attainable only by war against Catholic Austria. In Parma, the duke was assassinated in 1854—to the relief of his people—and the uprising that accompanied this desperate act was suppressed by three thousand Austrian troops sent in by the duke's ally, the Habsburgs.

Compared to this dismal record, the kingdom of Piedmont in northern Italy appeared stable and successful. It was the only Italian state that kept the liberal constitution it had adopted in 1848, and it welcomed political refugees from other Italian states. Economically, it was a beacon to the rest of Italy, establishing modern banks and laying half the rail lines on the peninsula.

Since the late eighteenth century, some Italians had called for a *risorgimento*, a political and cultural renewal of Italy. By the mid-nineteenth century the idea was actively supported by a small, elite group of the educated middle class. For merchants, industrialists, and professionals, a unified state would provide a larger stage on which to pursue their ambitions. Members of these groups founded the National Society, a grassroots unification movement. This organization now looked to Piedmont to lead the peninsula to national unity.

Cavour Plots Unification

The statesman who was to catapult Piedmont to leadership in the dramatic events leading to

Italian unification was Count Camillo di Cavour (1810–1861). The son of a Piedmontese nobleman and high government official, he grew up speaking French, the language of the court in Piedmont, and mastered Italian only as an adult. Cavour was sympathetic to the aspirations of the middle class and saw in Britain and France models of what Italy ought to become, a liberal and economically advanced society.

Short, fat, and nearsighted, Cavour hardly cut a heroic figure. Yet he was ambitious, hardworking, and driven to succeed. In 1850 he joined the government of Piedmont. Two years later he was appointed prime minister. He shared the general enthusiasm of the middle classes for an Italian nation, but his vision probably did not include the entire Italian peninsula, only its north and center, which would dominate the rest of the peninsula in a loose federation. One fateful lesson he had learned from the failures of 1848 was that foreign help would be necessary to expel the Austrians from the peninsula.

When the Crimean War broke out in 1854, Cavour steered Piedmont to the allied side, hoping to advance his cause. He sent twenty thousand troops to the Crimea, one-tenth of whom died. This act gained him a seat at the Congress of Paris, where his presence boosted the kingdom's prestige—and where he and Napoleon III had an opportunity to meet and size each other up.

Napoleon III favored Italian liberation from Austrian rule and some form of unification of the peninsula. Austria had been France's traditional opponent; destroying its power in Italy might strengthen France. The French emperor and the Piedmontese prime minister met secretly in July 1858 at Plombières, a French spa, to discuss how Italian unity could be achieved. They agreed that Piedmont would stir up trouble in one of Austria's Italian territories in an effort to goad the Austrians into war. France would help the Piedmontese expel Austria from the peninsula, and the new Piedmont, doubled in size, would become part of a confederation under the papacy. In exchange, the French emperor demanded the cession of Nice and Savoy. Although Savoy was the heartland of the Piedmont kingdom, Cavour reluctantly agreed.

War between Austria and Piedmont broke out in April 1859. By June the combined Piedmontese and French forces had defeated the Austrians at Magenta and Solferino (Map 20.1). The bloodiness of these battles impressed contemporaries: The color magenta was named after the color of the blood flowing on the battlefield, and when a Swiss humanitarian, Henri Dunant (1828–1901), organized emergency services for both French and Austrians wounded at Solferino, he proposed the founding of voluntary relief societies in every nation, called the Red Cross.

Instead of following up these victories, Napoleon III decided to end the fighting. He was truly shocked by the bloodshed he had witnessed—and alarmed by Prussian mobilization on the Rhine on behalf of Austria. Also, there were popular uprisings in some other Italian states in June (Ravenna, Ferrara, Bologna), which Napoleon III feared might lead to requests for union. Such union would result in a much larger independent state than he had anticipated. Without consulting his ally, Napoleon signed an armistice with the Austrians, allowing Austria to keep part of Lombardy and all of Venetia and to participate in an Italian Confederation. Cavour was outraged by Napoleon's betrayal and resigned as prime minister; he returned to office, however, in January 1860.

Unification Achieved, 1860

The overthrow of the Austrian-backed rulers in Parma, Modena, and Tuscany led these areas in 1860 to vote in plebiscites to join Piedmont. Farther south, in central Italy, agitation against papal misrule also inclined the people of the Papal States toward Piedmont.

Cavour had envisioned no more than a united northern Italy. Unexpected events in the south, however, dramatically changed that vision. The centuries-old misgovernment of Naples led to an uprising, abetted by the revolu-

Map 20.1 The Unification of Italy, 1859–1870 Piedmontese leadership and nationalist fervor united Italy.

tionary firebrand Giuseppe Garibaldi (1807–1882), a rival of Cavour who favored unification and won a large popular following. In May 1860, with but a thousand poorly armed, red-shirted followers, he set sail for Sicily to help the island rise up against its Bourbon ruler. Winning that struggle, Garibaldi's forces crossed to the mainland. Victory followed victory, and enthusiasm for Garibaldi grew. His army swelled to 57,000 men, and he won the entire Kingdom of the Two Sicilies.

Threatened by the advance of Garibaldi's power, Cavour sent his army into the Papal States in September 1860. This action, a brutal attack on a weak state that had not harmed Piedmont, was viewed by many Catholics as aggression against the spiritual head of their church. However, as Cavour explained to his parliament, political necessity required it. The interests of Piedmont and the about-to-be-born Italy superseded traditional morality.

Although Garibaldi was a republican, he was convinced that Italy could best achieve unity under the king of Piedmont, and he willingly submitted the southern part of Italy, which he controlled, to the king, Victor Emmanuel II (r. 1849–1878). Thus by November 1860, Italy was united under Piedmontese rule (see Map 20.1). The territories that came under Piedmontese control all affirmed their desire to be part of the new Italy in plebiscites based on universal male suffrage. By huge majorities, the populations voted affirmatively. Undoubtedly there was pressure from the occupying army and the upper classes. Voting was not secret, and fraud was widespread. But the plebiscite gave legitimacy to the new state and won sympathy from liberally inclined states abroad.

Austria still held Venetia in the northeast; Rome and its environs were still held by the pope with the support of a French garrison. But within a decade, a propitious international situation enabled the fledgling country to acquire both key areas. After Austria was defeated in the Austro-Prussian War in 1866, Venetia was ceded to Italy. Then the Franco-Prussian War forced the French to evacuate Rome, which they had occupied since 1849. Rome was joined to Italy and became its capital in 1870. Unification was complete (see Map 20.1).

The Problems of Unified Italy

National unity had been achieved, but it was frail. The nation was divided between the modernizing north and the traditional south. From the beginning, the north behaved like a conquering state—sending its officials to the south, raising taxes, and imposing its laws. In 1861 an uprising of disbanded Neapolitan soldiers and brigands broke out. To crush the revolt, half the Italian army was sent south; the civil war lasted five years and produced more casualties than the entire effort of unification.

Other divisions remained. In 1861 only 2.5 percent of the population spoke the national language, Florentine Italian. The north was far more industrialized than the rural south. In the south, child mortality was higher, life expectancy was lower, and illiteracy approached 90 percent. The two regions seemed to belong to two different nations.

Piedmont imposed strong central control, resolutely refusing a federal system of government, which many Italians had hoped for. Piedmont was determined to project its power onto the rest of the peninsula and feared that any other form of government might lead to disintegration of the new state. The Civil War in the United States suggested the dangers of a federal system of government.

Piedmont imposed its constitution on unified Italy. This constitution limited suffrage to men of property and education, less than 2 percent of the population. Further, although parliamentarism was enshrined in the constitution, Cavour's maneuvering as prime minister had kept governments from being answerable to the parliament. Still, although Italian parliamentarism was far from complete, a liberal state recognizing legal equality and freedom of association had been established, providing more freedom for its citizens than the peninsula had seen for centuries.

The new Italian state was weakened by the hostility of the Catholic church. When Piedmont annexed Rome in 1870, the pope retained control of only a few square blocks around the papal palace, the Vatican. The popes considered themselves prisoners of the new Italian state and denounced it and all those who supported it, including those participating in elections. Thus the new state was contested by many Catholics, who refused to recognize it for decades.

In 1870, Italy, with its 27 million people, was the sixth most populous European nation. It was too small to be a great power and too large to accept being a small state. Italian statesmen found it difficult to define their country's role in international politics, and they lacked a firm consensus on Italy's future.

GERMAN UNIFICATION

Like Italy, Germany began as a collection of polities, first loosely united in the Holy Roman Empire and then, after 1815, equally loosely organized in the German Confederation. As Piedmont had done in Italy, Prussia, the most powerful German state, led the unification movement. And just as Italy had in Cavour a strong leader who imposed his will, German unification had a ruthless and cunning leader: Otto von Bismarck, prime minister of Prussia.

In 1848, German unification under Prussian leadership had appeared likely until the king of Prussia refused to accept a throne offered by an elected assembly. When national unity was ultimately achieved, it was due not to popular decision but to military force and the imposition of Prussian absolutism over the whole country.

The Rise of Bismarck

Austria under Metternich had always treated Prussia as a privileged junior partner. After Met-

ternich's fall in 1848, rivalry erupted between the two German states. Each tried to use for its own aggrandizement the desire for national unity that had appeared during the revolution of 1848.

In March 1850, Prussia invited various German rulers to a meeting in Erfurt to consider possible unification under its sponsorship. Austria, which had been excluded, insisted that the "Erfurt Union" be dissolved. Austrian leaders backed their demands with the threat of war; Prussia had to scuttle the Erfurt Union and accept Austrian leadership in Germany. At that time the Prussian military was not strong enough to challenge Austria. The new Prussian king, William I (r. 1861–1888), was committed to expanding the size and effectiveness of the army. When liberals in parliament opposed the increased costs that this would require, the king dissolved Parliament and appointed Otto von Bismarck as prime minister in 1862.

Bismarck was a Junker, a Prussian aristocrat known for his reactionary views, who had opposed the liberal movement in 1848. Bismarck sought to heighten Prussian power in Germany and throughout Europe. He faced down the newly elected parliament, telling the Budget Commission in 1862, "The position of Prussia in Germany will be decided not by its liberalism but by its power . . . not through speeches and majority decisions are the great questions of the day decided—that was the mistake of 1848–49—but by 'iron and blood.'"[1]

Bismarck tried to win over the liberals by suggesting that with military force at its disposal, Prussia could lead German unification. But the liberals resisted, and the Parliament voted against the military reforms. Bismarck decided to carry out the military measures anyway and to collect the taxes that would make them possible. The liberals who opposed Bismarck represented the business and professional classes who had received the vote as a result of the 1848 revolution. They had not implemented effective political or social programs, and they did not enjoy mass support. Bismarck met with no organized resistance.

German liberals were faced with a dilemma: Did they value nationhood or the principles of liberty more? In other countries statehood had preceded the development of liberalism, thus avoiding the conflict. Even in Italy, the liberals had faced a less harsh dilemma, for unification was led by the liberal state of Piedmont. That was not the case in Germany, where the natural leader, Prussia, had a long tradition of militarism and authoritarianism.

Bismarck's genius was to exploit the growing desire for German unification. Professional and cultural organizations now often extended beyond a single state, for instance, the German Commercial Association, the Congress of German Jurists, and the German Sharpshooters League. Many individual German states, each calculating possible political gains, launched proposals for unification in the 1860s. Although it had yet to find much resonance among the lower classes, the idea of a united Germany was gaining a wider audience.

Prussian Wars and German Unity

Neither the Prussian king nor Bismarck's fellow aristocrats were nationalists. Believing in a strong Prussia, they feared that a united Germany might dilute Prussian power and influence. German unification had been part of the liberals' program, not the conservatives'. Bismarck had to be clever. His first move was to enlarge Prussia's role in Germany at the expense of Austria. The provocation was a crisis over Schleswig-Holstein (Map 20.2). These two provinces, ethnically and linguistically German (except for northern Schleswig), were ruled by Denmark. When the Danish king, contrary to earlier treaty obligations, attempted to connect Schleswig more closely to the Crown in 1863, Holstein felt threatened. Although it was under Danish rule, Holstein was also a member of the German Confederation and called on the Confederation for protection. Acting on behalf of the Confederation, Prussia and Austria intervened, sending troops who won a quick, cheap victory

in 1864. Prussia occupied Schleswig, and Austria took Holstein.

Joint military action in no way united Prussia and Austria, who continued to be bitter rivals for domination of Germany. Bismarck believed that war was the only means to win this contest, and conflicts over the administration of Schleswig and Holstein served as a pretext to start one. With no declaration of war, Prussia attacked Austrian-administered Holstein in June 1866 and defeated the Austrian army at Sadowa (Königgrätz) on July 3. Austria sued for peace.

Prussia annexed its smaller neighbors who had supported Austria, thus creating a contiguous state linking Prussia with the Rhineland. This enlarged Prussia intended to dominate the newly formed North German Confederation, comprising all the states north of the Main River. Henceforth Austria was excluded from German affairs.

These events transformed Bismarck into a popular hero. Elections held on the day of the battle returned a conservative pro-Bismarck majority to the Prussian parliament. The legislature, including a large number of liberals mesmerized by the military victory, voted retroactively to legalize the illegal taxes that had been levied since 1862 to upgrade the military. The liberals rationalized that national unity ought to be gained first, with liberal constitutional institutions secured later. It did not turn out that way.

Bismarck hoped that the southern German states would eventually merge with the North German Confederation. Economically they continued to be dependent as a result of the Zollverein (the customs union). Many southern Germans favored unity, especially business people who saw in it the hope of an improved economy.

The Franco-Prussian War and Unification, 1870–1871

French leaders were determined to prevent German unity. They feared the loss of influence in the southern German states that had tradition-

Map 20.2 The Unification of Germany A series of military victories made it possible for Prussia to unite Germany under its domain.

ally been France's allies. More important, since the mid-seventeenth century, French security had been linked to a weak and divided Germany.

Both Berlin and Paris anticipated war. And war came soon enough, precipitated by a crisis over the Spanish succession. In 1868, a Catholic member of the Hohenzollerns, the reigning Prussian monarch's family, was offered the Spanish throne. The French viewed this candidacy as an unacceptable expansion of Prussian power. As passions heated, Bismarck was elated at the prospect of war. But the Prussian king was not. On July 12, 1870, he withdrew the young prince's candidacy, removing the cause for war. Bismarck was bitterly disappointed. Not satisfied, the French pushed their luck. On July 13 the French ambassador met the king of Prussia at Ems and demanded guarantees that no Hohenzollern would ever again be a candidate to the Spanish throne. The Prussian king refused.

William telegraphed an account of his meeting to Bismarck. The chancellor edited what became known as the Ems dispatch, making the exchange seem like a deliberate snub to the French ambassador. Faced by a flood of emotional demands for redress of the imagined slight to French national honor, Napoleon III declared war on July 19.

The Prussians led a well-planned campaign. An army of 384,000 Prussians was rushed by rail to confront 270,000 Frenchmen. Within a few weeks, Prussia won a decisive victory at Sedan, taking the French emperor prisoner on September 2. But the French continued the struggle, despite the odds. Infuriated, the Prussians resorted to extreme measures, taking hostages and burning down whole villages. They laid siege to Paris, starving and bombarding its beleaguered population.

Throughout Germany the outbreak of the war was met with general enthusiasm for the Prussian cause. Exploiting this popular feeling, Bismarck called on the other German states to accept the unification of Germany under the Prussian king. Reluctant princes, such as the king of Bavaria, were bought off with bribes. On January 18, 1871, the German princes met in the Hall of Mirrors of the Versailles palace, symbol of past French greatness, and acclaimed William I as *Kaiser*—German for emperor (see Map 20.2).

In May 1871 the Treaty of Frankfurt established the peace terms. France was forced to give up the provinces of Alsace and Lorraine and to pay a heavy indemnity of five billion francs. These harsh terms embittered the French, leading many to desire revenge and establishing a formidable barrier to future relations between France and Germany.

The Character of the New Germany

German unity had been forged by a series of wars—against Denmark in 1864, Austria in 1866, and France in 1870—and lacked the popular democratic base that had been present in Italy. Because the military had been instrumental in the formation of the new German *Reich* (German for empire), it remained dominant in the new state. Italian unity had been sanctioned by plebiscites. The founding act of the new Reich was the meeting of the German rulers on the soil of a defeated neighbor. Thus the rulers placed themselves above popular sanction.

The constitution of the new Germany was remarkably democratic on the surface. It provided for an appointed upper house, the *Bundesrat*, representing the individual German states, and a lower house, the *Reichstag*, which was elected by universal manhood suffrage. The latter seemed a surprising concession from Bismarck, the authoritarian aristocrat. But he knew the liberals lacked mass support and gambled that he would be able to create majorities that could be manipulated for his purposes.

The dominant state in the new Germany was, of course, Prussia, which also had two-thirds of its population. Within the Bundesrat, Prussia had 17 of the 43 seats and could block any legislation it opposed with the aid of only a few other states. The king of Prussia occupied the post of emperor, and the prime minister—now called the chancellor—was responsible not to parliament but to the emperor, as were the other cabinet members. The emperor alone could make foreign policy and war, command the army, and interpret the constitution. The authoritarianism of Prussia had been projected onto all of Germany.

The emergence of a strong, united Germany disrupted the European balance of power. In February 1871 the British political leader Benjamin Disraeli observed that the unification of Germany was "a greater political event than the French revolution of last century. . . . There is not a diplomatic tradition which has not been swept away. You have a new world. . . . The balance of power has been entirely destroyed."[2] Germany had become the dominant power on the Continent.

PRECARIOUS SUPRANATIONAL EMPIRES

In an age of nationalism that saw the creation of two new nation-states—Italy and Germany—the two multinational empires found themselves in a precarious position. The Habsburg and Ottoman Empires consisted of peoples speaking different languages, holding different religious beliefs, and having different historical traditions. In the past such multinational states had been quite normal in Europe, but in the nineteenth century they became increasingly anomalous. The peoples living under the authority of Vienna and Constantinople became more and more restive. Facing this severe challenge, the Austrian and Ottoman Empires attempted to strengthen themselves by restructuring their institutions.

The Dual Monarchy in Austria-Hungary

Austrian statesmen sensed the vulnerability of their empire. By 1860 they had lost much of their Italian possessions; in Hungary they met with resistance from the Magyars, a powerful group still resentful they had not won independence in 1848; and they faced the bitter struggle for German supremacy in Prussia. To give his government credibility, in February 1861, Emperor Francis Joseph (r. 1848–1916) issued what became known as the February Patents, which lib-

eralized the government, guaranteed civil liberties, and provided local self-government and an elected parliament.

The need to safeguard the remaining territories was clear. By 1866 the Austrian Habsburgs were no longer a German or Italian power (Venetia had been handed over to a united Italy). The strongest challenge to Habsburg rule came from Hungary, where the Magyars insisted on self-rule, a claim based on age-old historic rights and Vienna's initial acceptance of autonomy in 1848. Since Magyar cooperation was crucial, the government entered into lengthy negotiations with Magyar leaders in 1865. The outcome was the Compromise of 1867, which created a new structure for the empire that lasted until 1918. The agreement divided the Habsburg holdings into Austria in the west and Hungary in the east, linked by the person of the emperor of Austria, Francis Joseph, who was also king of Hungary. Hungary had full internal autonomy and participated jointly in imperial affairs—state finance, defense, and foreign relations. The new state created by the compromise was known as the dual monarchy of Austria-Hungary.

The emperor of the new state of Austria-Hungary had come to the throne as an 18-year-old in that year of crisis, 1848. Francis Joseph was a well-meaning monarch who took his duties seriously. He spoke several of his subjects' languages. In both halves of the empire, he was a much-loved, regal figure who provided a visible symbol of the state.

The compromise confirmed Magyar dominance in Hungary. Although numerically a minority, Magyars controlled the Hungarian parliament, the army, the bureaucracy, and other state institutions. They opposed self-rule by the Croats, Serbs, Slovaks, Romanians, and others in the kingdom and attempted a policy of Magyarization—teaching only Hungarian in the schools, conducting all government business in Hungarian, and giving access to government positions only to those fully assimilated in Magyar culture. This arrangement created frustrations and resistance among the various nationalities under their rule.

The terms of the compromise also gave the Hungarians a voice in imperial foreign policy. Magyars feared that the Slavic groups outside the empire who planned to form independent states or had already done so would inspire fellow Slavs in Austria-Hungary to revolt. To prevent that, the Hungarians favored an expansionist foreign policy in the Balkans, which the monarchy gladly embraced. Having lost its influence in Germany, Austria-Hungary found in the Balkans an area in which to assert itself. The policy was fraught with risks and, by bringing more discontented Slavs into the empire, led to hostility with other states.

The Ailing Ottoman Empire

At midcentury the Ottoman Empire was still one of the largest European powers, but it faced unrest within its borders and threats by the expansionist designs of its neighbors. The ailing empire was commonly referred to as "the sick man of Europe." Over the next twenty-five years, the empire shed some of its territory and modernized its government, but nothing could save it from decline in the face of nationalist uprisings in its Balkan possessions.

As early as the 1840s, the Ottoman Empire had begun various reform movements to bring more security to its subjects. Known as the *Tanzimat,* these changes were initiated by Sultan Abdul Mejid (r. 1839–1861), with the help of his able prime minister, Reshid Mustafa Pasha (1800–1858). Reshid had served as the Ottoman ambassador in London and Paris and was familiar with Western institutions, which he admired and wished to emulate. The reforms introduced security of property, equality of taxation, and equality before the law regardless of religion. Tax collection was regularized.

These reforms were strengthened by further edicts after the Crimean War. Contacts with the West encouraged Turks to think of transforming their empire into a more modern, Westernized state. Many young intellectuals were impatient with the rate of change, however, and, unable freely to express their opin-

ions at home, some went into exile in the late 1860s to Paris and London. Their hosts called them the "Young Turks," an expression that became synonymous with the desire for change and improvement.

Alarmed by challenges to its rule, the central government began to turn away from reform, and in 1871 the sultan decided to assert his personal rule. His inability successfully to wage war and hold onto the empire led to dissatisfaction, and in the spring of 1876 rioters demanded and won the establishment of constitutional government. Within less than a year, however, the new sultan, Abdul Hamid II (r. 1876–1909), dismissed the constitutional government and reverted to personal rule.

Opposition to the government increased, fueled by nationalist fervor. The empire tolerated religious diversity and did not persecute people because of their religion. But the central administration had lost control over its provincial officials, who were often corrupt and tyrannical. Much of the Balkan region was isolated from any benign control Constantinople might have wished to exercise. Christians, the majority population in the Balkans, blamed their suffering on Islamic rule, and many were inspired by the 1821 Greek war of independence and the revolutions of 1848 to seek their own independence.

The Romanians, who lived mainly in the adjoining provinces of Moldavia in the north and Wallachia in the south, began to express nationalist sentiments in the late eighteenth century. These sentiments were nurtured by Western-educated students, who claimed for their countrymen illustrious descent from Roman settlers of antiquity. News of revolution in Paris in 1848 helped trigger a revolt in both provinces demanding unification and independence. This uprising was quickly crushed by the Turks.

In 1856 the Congress of Paris had removed Russia's right of protection over Moldavia and Wallachia and provided for a referendum to determine their future. In 1859 the two provinces chose a local military officer, Alexander Cuza (r. 1859–1866), as ruler of each territory; and in

1862, the Ottoman Empire recognized the union of the two principalities in the single, autonomous state of Romania. At the Congress of Berlin in 1878, the full independence of Romania was recognized. Thus, in less than a quarter-century, two provinces of the Ottoman Empire merged and gained full sovereignty.

The path to independence was much more violent for the Bulgars. When a nationalist uprising in Bulgaria broke out in May 1876, the Christian rebels attacked not only symbols of Ottoman authority but also peaceable Turks living in their midst. The imperial army, aided by local Turk volunteers, quickly re-established Ottoman authority. Incensed by the massacre of fellow Muslims, the volunteers resorted to mass killing, looting, and burning of Christian villages. The "Bulgarian horrors" shocked Europe and made the continuation of Turkish rule unacceptable.

The Bulgar crisis was resolved by the Balkan wars of 1876–1878, which were provoked by the uprising of the westernmost Ottoman provinces of Bosnia and Herzegovina. Since many of the inhabitants of these two provinces were Serbs, they had the sympathy of Serbia, which believed it could unify the southern Slavs. Together with the neighboring mountain state of Montenegro, Serbia declared war on the Ottoman Empire. They were savagely defeated by the Turks.

Russia, which saw itself as the protector of the Slavic peoples, also declared war on the empire and forced the sultan to sue for peace. The resulting Treaty of San Stefano, signed in March 1878, excluded the Ottoman Empire from Europe and created a huge, independent Bulgaria as essentially a Russian satellite. The British, Austrians, and French were shocked at the extent to which the San Stefano treaty favored Russia. Under their pressure, the European powers met in Berlin in 1878 to reconsider the treaty. The Congress of Berlin reduced the size of the Bulgarian territory, allowing the rest to revert to Constantinople. Bosnia and Herzegovina were removed from Ottoman rule and put under that of Austria-Hungary (see Map 22.3 on page 595). Constantinople was forced to acknowledge the

Nationalistic Uprising in Bulgaria In this 1879 lithograph, Bulgaria is depicted in the form of a maiden—protected by the Russian eagle, breaking her chains, and winning liberty from the Ottoman Empire. *(St. Cyril and Methodius National Library, Sofia)*

independence of Serbia, Montenegro, and Romania and the autonomy of Bulgaria. The British insisted on being given the island of Cyprus to administer, an outpost from which they might prevent further challenges to the balance of power.

Thus Turkey was plundered, not only by its enemies but also by the powers that had intervened on its behalf. When France complained that it received no compensation, it was given the chance to grab Tunisia, another Ottoman province. The work of the congress reflected the power politics that now characterized international affairs. Neither morality nor international law restrained ambition.

THE EMERGENCE OF A POWERFUL UNITED STATES, 1840–1880

Across the seas a new power emerged in these years, the United States. It enlarged its territories, strengthened its national government, and broadened its democracy by including a large category of people previously excluded from the political process—African Americans. But these achievements came at the expense of the bloodiest conflict in American history, the Civil War. And through it all, this great democracy refused to enfranchise its female members, despite tremendous efforts by those lobbying for woman suffrage.

Territorial Expansion and Slavery

In the nineteenth century the United States gained huge territories through westward expansion. In 1803, President Thomas Jefferson, negotiating with the French, secured the Louisiana Purchase, which nearly doubled the size of the United States. In 1810, 1813, and 1819, Florida was acquired from Spain. Some Americans looked even farther, moving into Mexican-held territories in the Southwest and British-held territories in the Pacific Northwest. The United States, some began to insist, was destined to occupy the whole North American continent; expansion would fulfill what was often called America's Manifest Destiny. In 1845, Congress annexed Texas; in 1846 the United States gained the southern part of the Oregon territory after threatening war against Britain. Declaring war on Mexico in the same year, the United States won California and the Southwest in 1848. The United States now spanned the continent from the Atlantic to the Pacific.

The nature of the U.S. government was transformed in these years: From being a weak institution exercising authority only in a limited number of domains, the federal government became a powerful authority. This change represented the only practical resolution of regional disagreements that threatened to tear the country apart in the mid-nineteenth century.

Beginning in the 1820s the United States saw serious sectional clashes between east and west as well as north and south. The latter were more important. Many issues divided the two regions, notably a conflict between the industrial interests of the North and the agrarian interests of the South. What particularly sharpened this divide was the issue of slavery. As the United States annexed new territories, the question of whether they would be slave or free divided the North and South; the North opposed the spread of the "peculiar institution," while much of the South, fearing isolation, favored its spread.

The issue of slavery was passionately debated for decades. Some Americans wanted slavery abolished throughout the United States; if that could not be done, some of the most committed abolitionists advocated the secession of free states from the Union. On the other side, southerners threatened that if their way of life— meaning a society based on slavery—were not assured, then the South would secede. The threat of secession was lightly and frequently made by partisans of various causes for many decades. Commitment to national unity was weak.

The election of the Illinois Republican Abraham Lincoln (1809–1865) as president in November 1860 appeared to the South as a final blow. Lincoln opposed the spread of slavery beyond its existing borders and hence appeared to threaten its future. Within a few weeks, the South reacted to Lincoln's election.

Beginning in December 1860 a number of southern states voted to secede from the Union, forming in February 1861 the Confederate States of America. The South saw its cause as being one of states' rights, claiming that the people of each state had the right to determine their destiny. Southern states seized federal funds and property, and in April 1861 the Confederates bombarded federally held Fort Sumter, an island fort in the harbor of Charleston, South Carolina. Lincoln, inaugurated in March 1861, was determined to put down the insurrection and preserve the Union. A calamitous civil war (1861–1865) had begun.

Civil War and National Unity

The North had many advantages over the South. It was nearly three times as populous as the South, it had a strong industrial base that could supply an endless stream of manufactured weapons, and it had a more extensive rail system allowing for better transport of men and materiel to the front. Although there were a number of important military engagements between the two parties, the North essentially strangled the South, which toward the end of the war was short of men, money, and supplies.

During the war and its aftermath, the government took measures that centralized power in the United States, changing the nation from a loose federation of states to a more centrally governed entity. As one historian has noted, the United States changed from "they" to "it." The federal government intruded into areas of life from which it had before been absent. Slaves, previously considered property, were declared by Lincoln to be free with the Emancipation Proclamation in 1863. The Union imposed conscription, instituted a federal income tax, and replaced state banks with a uniform national banking system. The federal government provided massive subsidies for a national railroad system, and with the Morrill Land Grant College Act of 1862, it created a national system of state universities. As Senator John Sherman of Ohio declared during the war, "the policy of this country ought to be to make everything national as far as possible."

The principle of state sovereignty, which the Southern states had espoused and which the North had tried to accommodate before the war, now lay defeated. The North occupied the South in an attempt to "reconstruct" it. Reconstruction included efforts to root out the Confederate leadership and ensure full civil and political rights for the newly emancipated African Americans. The government also embarked on a short-lived campaign to provide freed slaves with enough land to assure them of a livelihood—another example of federal authority at work.

The Frontiers of Democracy

One of the major transformations in the United States that began in the 1820s was the inclusion of an ever greater number of people in the political process. By the late 1820s, under the impact of popular pressure, states abandoned restrictions on voting, and most adult white men received the vote. Symbolic of this new "age of the common man" was the election of Andrew Jackson as U.S. president in 1828. All his predecessors had been men of education and property—some were even described as "Virginia aristocrats"—but Jackson represented himself as a self-made man, a rugged frontiersman. State legislatures had in the past elected members to the presidential Electoral College, but in response to public calls for change, state legislatures altered the system so that Electoral College members were selected by direct popular vote.

National presidential campaigns became rough-and-tumble affairs, with emotional appeals to the public. Scurrilous attacks, many untrue, were mounted against opponents. Campaigns began to revolve around easily grasped symbols. When William Henry Harrison ran for president in 1840 he was depicted as a simple frontiersman; his supporters wore log-cabin badges, sang log-cabin songs, and carried log-cabin replicas on floats in parades. Such paraphernalia became a common sight in American elections. If some contemporary observers, such as the Frenchman Alexis de Tocqueville (1805–1859), were disappointed at the lack of a thoughtful and deliberate process in choosing political leaders, they thought democracy was nowhere in the world as fully developed as in the United States, where it foreshadowed the future of other societies.

When Abraham Lincoln was elected in 1860, nobody of his social standing occupied an equivalent position in Europe. At the news of his assassination in 1865, workmen and artisans, seeing in the dead president a kindred spirit, stood for hours in line outside the U.S. legation in London and the consul general's office in Lyon (France) to sign a book of condolence to express their sorrow. It was also a form of tribute to a nation that had elected a backwoodsman born in a log cabin to its highest office.

The frontiers of democracy appeared to have widened after the Civil War when amendments to the U.S. Constitution granted African American men full equality with white men. Slavery was forbidden throughout the United States, and citizenship was granted to all, regardless of "race, color, or previous condition of servitude." All American men were guaranteed the right to vote. During the first few years of Reconstruction, white men who had supported the Confederacy were deprived of the right to vote, and African American men represented a large voting bloc in the South. As a result, for the first time the United States saw the election of a black governor as well as several lieutenant-governors, senators, congressmen, postmasters, and innumerable county and town officials who were black. After the end of military occupation of the South, however, local white power reasserted itself and the rights of African Americans were sharply curtailed. Yet, compared to the situation before the Civil War, African Americans had advanced significantly.

Legislation allowing African American men to vote contrasted dramatically with the political situation of women in America. This was particularly true because women in the North had helped lead the movement to abolish slavery. In so doing, they had learned the processes of democratic action—writing petitions and gathering signatures, collecting funds, making speeches, and holding demonstrations. They had also learned, and personalized, the language of Enlightenment emancipatory ideals and liberal self-determinism. The first women's rights movement had been organized by Elizabeth Cady Stanton (1815–1902) and Lucretia Mott (1793–1880) in 1848. These women and others, most notably Susan B. Anthony (1820–1906) and Lucy Stone (1818–1893), were important abolitionists as well. For many women, struggling for the rights of slaves caused them to recognize the injustice of their own political situation. When emancipation of the slaves finally arrived, they expected that black men and all women would be given the

vote simultaneously. Instead, only black men got the vote.

Some of the white women were enraged to see those for whom they had labored suddenly transported to a political status that surpassed their own. They asked their white countrymen why an uneducated ex-slave should be able to influence public policy and a highly educated white woman should not. However, most black women felt that it was more important to secure black male suffrage than to hold out for universal suffrage. Some white women agreed and the women's movement split along these lines.

Still, by 1880 the United States had been transformed by unprecedented territorial expansion as well as the ordeal of the Civil War, which brought about the extension of federal authority and—however hesitatingly—the rights of citizenship to new groups. A large, powerful democracy had arisen on the North American continent.

STABILITY IN VICTORIAN BRITAIN

The mid-nineteenth century was a period of exceptional wealth and security for Britain as the population as a whole began to share in the benefits of industrialization. Britain enjoyed both social and political peace. The political system was not challenged, as it had been after the Napoleonic Wars. A self-assured, even smug, elite—merchants, industrialists, and landowners—developed a political system reflecting liberal values.

Parliamentary Government

Although suffrage was still very restricted, the parliamentary system became firmly established, with a government clearly responsible to the electorate. The importance of Parliament was symbolized by the splendor and size of the new building in which it met, finished in 1850. The form of government developed in its halls after midcentury represented a model that aroused the curiosity and envy of much of the world. (See the box, "Encounters with the West: A Japanese View of the British Parliament.") As we have

～ ENCOUNTERS WITH THE WEST ～

A Japanese View of the British Parliament

In 1862 the Japanese government sent its first diplomatic mission to Europe. Accompanying the delegation was its young translator, Fukuzawa Yukichi (1835–1901). Intrigued by what he saw and eager to interest his fellow Japanese in the West, Fukuzawa published several books. In fact, all books about the West in Japan came to be known as "Fukuzawa-bon." Toward the end of his life in his **Autobiography** *he described how, while in London, he had tried to understand the workings of the British Parliament.*

Of political situations at that time, I tried to learn as much as I could from various persons that I met in London . . . though it was often difficult to understand things clearly as I was as yet unfamiliar with the history of Europe. . . . A perplexing institution was representative government. When I asked a gentleman what the "election law" was and what kind of an institution the Parliament really was, he simply replied with a smile, meaning I suppose that no intelligent person was expected to ask such questions. But these were the things most difficult of all for me to understand. In this connection, I learned that there were different political parties—the Liberal and the Conservative— who were always "fighting" against each other in the government.

For some time it was beyond my comprehension to understand what they were "fighting" for, and what was meant, anyway, by "fighting" in peace time. "This man and that man are 'enemies' in the House," they would tell me. But these "enemies" were to be seen at the same table, eating and drinking with each other. I felt as if I could not make much out of this. It took me a long time, with some tedious thinking, before I could gather a general notion of these separate mysterious facts. In some of the more complicated matters, I might achieve an understanding five or ten days after they were explained to me. But all in all, I learned much from this initial tour of Europe.

Source: The Autobiography of Fukuzawa Yukichi, trans. Eiichi Kiyooka (Tokyo: Hokuseida Press, 1948), pp. 138, 143–144.

seen, Parliament consisted of an upper, hereditary House of Lords and a lower, elected House of Commons. Increasingly, the royal cabinet became answerable to Parliament.

In the twenty years after 1846, five different parties vied for power. Depending on the issue, parties and factions coalesced to support particular policies. After 1867, however, a clear two-party system emerged: Liberal and Conservative (Tory), both with strong leadership. This development gave the electorate a distinct choice. The Conservatives sought to preserve traditional institutions and practices, while the Liberals tended to be open to change.

Gladstone, Disraeli, and the Two-Party System

Heading these parties were two strong-minded individuals who dominated British political life for over a generation: William E. Gladstone (1809–1898), a Liberal, and Benjamin Disraeli (1804–1881), a Conservative. Gladstone came from an industrial family and married into the aristocracy; Disraeli was the son of a Jewish man of letters who had converted to Christianity. His father's conversion made his career possible —before the 1850s, Jews were barred from Parliament. Gladstone and Disraeli were master debaters;

Parliament and the press hung on their every word. Each was capable of making speeches lasting five hours or more and conducting debates that kept the house in session until 4 A.M. The rivalry between the two men thrilled the nation and made politics a popular pastime.

The competition between the Liberals and Conservatives led to a further extension of suffrage in 1867. The Second Reform Bill lowered property qualifications, extending the vote from 1.4 to 2.5 million electors out of a population of 22 million, and gave new urban areas better representation. Although some in Parliament feared that these changes would lead to the masses capturing political power—"a leap into the dark," one member called it—no radical change ensued. Extending the vote to clerks, artisans, and other skilled workers made them feel more a part of society and thus bolstered the existing system. John Stuart Mill, then a member of Parliament, championed the cause of women's suffrage (see page 585), but he had few allies and his effort failed.

As the extension of voting rights increased the size of the electorate, the parties became larger and stronger. Strong party systems meant a clear alternation of power between the Liberals and the Conservatives. With an obvious majority and minority party, the monarch could no longer play favorites in choosing a prime minister. The leader of the majority party had to be asked to form a government. Thus, even though Queen Victoria (r. 1837–1901) detested Gladstone, she had to ask him to form governments when the Liberals won parliamentary elections.

The creation of a broad-based electorate meant that politicians had to make clear appeals

Illustration of the Royal Family from *A Book of English Song* By carefully depicting herself as a devoted wife and mother, Queen Victoria appealed to her middle-class subjects and reflected their social ideals. In reality, she resented much about motherhood, privately complaining of the inconvenience and burden of childbirth and child rearing.

to the public and its interests. Public election campaigns became part of the political scene. The democratic "American" style of campaigning appealed to the common man. Also borrowed from across the seas was the "Australian ballot"—the secret ballot—adopted in 1872. This protected lower-class voters from intimidation by their employers, landowners, or other social superiors. In 1874 the first two working-class members of Parliament were elected, sitting as Liberals. Although their victory represented a very modest gain for workers' representation, it presaged the increasingly democratic turn Britain would take.

FRANCE: FROM EMPIRE TO REPUBLIC

Unlike Britain, which gradually transformed into a parliamentary democracy, France took a more tumultuous path. Revolutions and war overthrew existing political systems and inaugurated new ones. Each time the French seemed to have democracy within reach, the opportunity slipped away.

The People's Emperor, Napoleon III

The constitution of the Second French Republic provided for a single four-year presidential term. Frustrated by this limitation, Louis Napoleon by a coup d'état extended his presidency to a ten-year term in 1851. The following year, he called for a plebiscite to confirm him as Napoleon III (r. 1852–1870), emperor of the French. Although both of these moves were resisted in the countryside, the resistance was put down by massive repression.

In the rest of the country, huge majorities of voters endorsed first the prolonged presidency and then the imperial title. The new emperor seemed different from his predecessors. He believed in popular sovereignty (he maintained universal male suffrage, introduced in 1848), he did not pretend to reign by divine grace, and he repeatedly tested his right to rule by appealing to the popular vote. He seemed to combine order and authority with the promises of the Revolu-

tion—equality before the law, careers open to talent, and the abolition of hereditary rights.

The mid-nineteenth century was a period of prosperity for most Frenchmen, including urban workers and peasants. Louis Napoleon, in his youth the author of a book on pauperism, introduced policies congenial to labor, but repressive measures were also initiated. On the one hand, workers were required to keep a booklet in which their conduct was to be recorded by their employers; on the other hand, workers were granted limited rights to organize strikes, and labor unions were virtually legalized. The emperor expressed his desire to improve the workers' lot, and the government took a few concrete steps, such as providing some public housing. Slum clearance during the rebuilding of Paris drove many from their homes to the outskirts of the city, but it did provide healthier conditions for those who stayed behind, and the ambitious urban projects provided work for many (see page 553). Other public works projects, such as ports, roads, railroads, and monumental public buildings, also created jobs. For many, Louis Napoleon—the heir to the great Napoleon—was an incarnation of national glory.

Not all the French supported the emperor; many republicans could not forget that he had usurped the constitution of 1848. In protest, some went into exile, including the poet Victor Hugo. When Napoleon began to liberalize the government beginning in 1860 by easing censorship and making his government more accountable to the parliament, it facilitated the expression of opposition views. A coordinated republican opposition rebuked the economic policies of the empire.

Widespread hostility to the influence of the Catholic church—and the desire for more extensive freedoms of expression and assembly—helped forge a republican alliance of the middle classes and workers. This alliance was particularly powerful in the large cities and in some southern regions notorious for their opposition to central government control. Republicanism was better organized than in earlier years and had a more explicit program. Its proponents were prepared to take over the government, if the opportunity arose.

By 1869 the regime, which declared itself a "liberal empire," had fully evolved into a constitutional monarchy, responsible to the Legislative Corps, the lower house of the parliament. It might have endured, but in July 1870, Napoleon III rashly declared war against Prussia over the Ems dispatch and its fabricated slight to French national honor (see page 528). Defeat destroyed the empire. In September, at news of the emperor's capture, the republican opposition in the Legislative Corps declared a republic. It continued the war but had to sign an armistice in January 1871.

The leader of the new government was an old prime minister of Louis Philippe, Adolphe Thiers (1797–1877). To sign a definite peace, the provisional government held elections. The liberals, known as republicans since they favored a republic, were identified with continuing the war; the conservatives, mostly royalists, favored peace. Mainly because of their position on this issue, the royalists won a majority from a country discouraged by defeat.

The Paris Commune, 1871

The new regime had no time to establish itself before an extraordinary uprising shook France in the spring of 1871. The uprising was called the Paris Commune, a name that harked back to 1792–1794, when the Paris crowds had dictated to the government. The Commune insisted on its right to home rule. It was seen by both radicals and conservatives as a workers' revolt that was seeking to establish a workers' government. Karl Marx described it as the "bold champion of the emancipation of labor."

Although labor discontent played a role in the Paris Commune, other forces also contributed, most notably the Prussian siege of Paris during the Franco-Prussian War. Paris had become radicalized during the siege: The rich had evacuated the city. The remaining Parisians, largely working class, suffered much because of the siege. Angered at the lack of recognition for their economic needs and their courage in with-

standing the Prussians, they rose up against the new French government. Under their pressure, the Commune, composed largely of artisans, began governing the city.

In March 1871 the Commune declared itself free to carry out policies without hindrance from the central government in Versailles. During the two months that it lasted, Parisians developed a wide range of political clubs, public rituals, and cooperative workshops. They experimented with many socialist initiatives and, in general, the experience was described as exhilarating and celebratory. Political debates took place in every bar and meeting place; women formed separate clubs and also took an active part in many of the general clubs and events. Overall, the Commune's goals were quite moderate: It sought free universal education, a fairer taxation system, a minimum wage, and disestablishment of the official Catholic church. When the government sent forces to crush the Commune, soldiers set buildings on fire to force the Parisians out, and Parisians set official buildings on fire both to slow the soldiers and to burn the records of debt. Later, it was said that political women had set the fires. Such rumors and images of wild women proliferated as conservatives later tried to impose order by forcing women back into the domestic sphere. The end of the Commune was bloody: 25,000 people were massacred, 40,000 arrested, and several thousand deported.

The crushing of the Paris Commune signified the increasing power of the centralized state. The modern state had the strength to squelch popular revolts that in the past had seriously threatened regimes. Western Europe would not again witness a popular uprising of this magnitude.

Creation of the Third Republic, 1871–1875

Despite its brutality, the crushing of the Commune by Thiers's new government reassured many Frenchmen. "The Republic will be conservative, or it will not be," declared Thiers. The question now at hand was what form the new government would take. The monarchist majority offered the throne to the grandson of Charles X.

Manet: The Barricade In a detail from this 1871 painting, Edouard Manet catches a scene from the Paris Commune of 1871. With barricades, the communards are trying to protect themselves from the onslaught of government troops. Although fewer than a thousand government soldiers died, over 25,000 communards were killed. *(Reproduced by courtesy of the Board of Directors of the Budapest Museum of Fine Arts)*

However, he insisted he would become king only if the *tricouleur*—the flag of the Revolution, which long since had become a cherished national symbol—were replaced by the white flag of the House of Bourbon. The monarchists realized their project was unfeasible. France remained a republic. The republic, as Thiers put it, "is the regime which divides us the least."

By 1875 the parliament had approved a set of basic laws that became the constitution of the Third Republic. The parliament was to consist of two chambers: the Chamber of Deputies, elected by universal male suffrage, and the Senate, chosen indirectly by local officials. The two houses sitting jointly elected the president, who was to occupy essentially a ceremonial role as chief of state. The head of government—the premier—and his cabinet were responsible to the parliament. A century after the French Revolution, a lasting republican system of government in France was finally launched.

RUSSIA AND THE GREAT REFORMS

By the 1840s concern about the archaic nature and structure of Russian government was mounting. Many officials lamented the tendency of a timid bureaucracy to lie and mislead the public. Defeat in the Crimean War widened the critique of Russian institutions. Calls for *glasnost*—greater openness—became the leading motif in the great reforms of the 1860s.

The Abolition of Serfdom, 1861

The chief problem that needed resolution was serfdom. Educated opinion had long denounced serfdom as immoral, but this was not the principal reason for its abolition. Serfdom was abolished because it presented clear political disadvantages in both the domestic and international domains. The new tsar, Alexander II (r. 1855–1881), feared that if the abolition of serfdom did not come from above, it would occur from below—by a violent serf rebellion that would sweep away everything in its path, including the autocracy itself.

Serfdom was also linked to Russia's place in the world. Defeat in the Crimean War suggested that Russia could not depend on a soldiery of serfs for its defense. The Russian army would be more powerful if it consisted of free men with a stake in their society. In addition, the victorious Western states had won in part because their industrial might had furnished better weaponry and transportation networks. Industrial progress required a mobile labor force, not one tied to the soil. For many educated Russians, the defeat in the Crimea revealed general Russian backwardness; it was time to abolish serfdom.

In April 1861, the tsar issued a decree freeing the serfs. It was a radical measure to emancipate 22 million people from a system that allowed them to be bought and sold, separated from their families, and treated in the cruelest ways imaginable. Emancipation represented a compromise with the gentry, which had reluctantly agreed to liberate its serfs but insisted on compensation. As a result, the newly liberated peasants had to reimburse the government with mortgage payments for fifty years. The peasants received some land, but its value was vastly overrated and its quantity insufficient for peasant families. To make ends meet, the freed peasants continued working for their former masters.

The mortgage payments and taxes imposed on the peasants by the central government were handled by the local commune, the *mir*. The mir determined how the land was to be used, and it paid collectively for the mortgage and taxes on the land. As a consequence, the commune was reluctant for the peasants to leave the land, and they could do so only with its permission. Freed from serfdom, the peasants still suffered many constraints.

The tsar and his advisers feared the large mass of uneducated peasants as a potential source of anarchy and rebellion. Thus they depended on the mir to preserve control even though the commune system had some inherent economic disadvantages. Increased productivity benefited the commune as much as the individual peasant; hence there was little incentive for land improvement, and yields remained low.

Reforms in Russian Institutions

Alexander was called the "tsar emancipator" by his contemporaries, but he was wedded to the principles of autocracy. His aim in abolishing serfdom and introducing other reforms was to modernize and strengthen Russia and stabilize his divinely mandated rule. Like most Russians, Alexander believed that only the firm hand of autocracy could hold together a large, ethnically diverse country.

Clearly, however, the sudden freedom of 22 million illiterate peasants threatened to overwhelm existing institutions, and some changes had to be made. Although he surrendered no powers, Alexander did reform the government and the judicial and military systems so they could deal more effectively with all the changes in Russian society.

Government reform had paramount importance. Between about 1800 and 1850, the Russian population had increased from 36 to 59 million, and it had become more and more difficult to administer this vast country. Overcentralized, with a poorly trained civil service, the government was unable to cope with the problems of its people. Emancipation of the serfs greatly exacerbated this situation; an enormous number of people, freed from their owners' control, were abruptly in need of services. Thus in 1864 a law was passed providing for local governments, or *zemstvos*, at the village and regional level, giving Russians the authority and the opportunity to use initiative in local matters.

The zemstvos were largely controlled by the gentry and not particularly democratic. They were forbidden to debate political issues, and their decisions could be overridden or ignored by local officials appointed by the tsar. Some hoped that the zemstvos could become the basis for self-government at the national level and looked for the creation of an all-Russian zemstvo. But such hopes were firmly squelched by the tsar, who jealously insisted on undiminished power.

The tsar also created an independent judiciary that ensured equality before the law, public jury trials, and uniform sentences. Russian political leaders recognized that public confidence in the judiciary was a prerequisite for the development of commerce and industry. Businessmen would no longer fear arbitrary intervention by capricious officials and could develop enterprises in greater security.

In addition, censorship of the press was abolished. Under the previous tsar, Nicholas, all ideas that did not conform to government policy were censored. Censorship prevented the central government from being well informed about public opinion or the effects of its policies on the country. Under Alexander, openness in the press was viewed as a remedy for corruption and the misuse of power.

Reform also extended to the Russian army. Its structure and methods became more Western. Military service, previously limited to peasants, became the obligation of all Russians. Access to the officer corps was to be by merit rather than by social connection.

Although the tsarist regime remained autocratic and repressive, the reforms undertaken by Alexander II meant that a new page had been turned in Russian history.

SUMMARY

Novel configurations of power appeared in the period from about 1850 to 1880 as new or enlarged states were created through warfare or the threat of force. Liberal nationalists in the early nineteenth century had believed that Europe would be freer and more peaceful if each people had a separate nation, but they were now proved wrong. The Crimean War and its aftermath replaced the congress system, which had sought a balance of power among partners, with a system of rival states pursuing their own self-interest. The international order was severely shaken as Italy and Germany emerged from the center of Europe and Romania and Bulgaria were carved out of the Ottoman Empire in the east.

Both new and existing states faced a choice between federalism and centralized rule. In the process of unification, Italy and Germany could have opted for a loose federal union, but both Piedmont and Prussia chose central control. And the crushing of the Paris Commune spelled the doom of those who wanted a France of decentralized self-governing units. Strong, centralized governments increasingly became the norm. That was also the case across the ocean in the United States, where North and South fought a bloody civil war over the issues of slavery and state sovereignty, and the victorious federal government imposed its will on the rebellious states.

To achieve legitimacy, however, governments had to appear to have the consent of their peoples. Hence all European rulers except those of the Ottoman and Russian Empires found it necessary to have a parliament. France and Britain became increasingly democratic in these years, answerable to a growing electorate. In the United States white males already enjoyed freer and more open institutions than existed anywhere else, and the post–Civil War era marked a further enlargement of political participation when African American men were granted the rights of citizenship. Women did not have the right to vote in any of these states, but the women's suffrage movement had begun.

Two major changes for which liberals in 1848 had agitated had become reality: freer political institutions and the organization of nation-states. Although neither of these was fully implemented everywhere, both appeared to have been successfully established. Many Europeans could easily believe they were living in an age of optimism.

NOTES

1. Quoted in Otto Pflanze, *Bismarck and the Development of Germany*, vol. 1 (Princeton: Princeton University Press, 1990), p. 184.
2. Quoted in William Flavelle Monypenny and George Earle Buckle, *The Life of Benjamin Disraeli: Earl of Beaconsfield*, vol. 2 (London: John Murray, 1929), pp. 473–474.

SUGGESTED READING

Bensel, Richard Franklin. *Yankee Leviathan: The Origins of Central State Authority in America, 1859–1877.* 1990. Emphasizes the extent to which the Civil War led to centralization of government in the United States.

Blake, Robert. *Disraeli.* 1966. The authoritative biography of the Victorian statesman who helped shape the British parliamentary system.

Carr, William. *The Wars of German Unification.* 1991. A careful examination of the three wars that led to unification.

Coppa, Frank J. *The Wars of Italian Independence.* 1992. Views Italian unification within an international context.

Engle, Barbara Alpern. *Between the Fields and the City: Women, Work, and Family in Russia, 1861–1914.* 1994. An interesting and careful study of the complex experience of emancipation.

Evans, Eric J. *The Forging of the Modern State: Early Industrial Britain, 1783–1870.* 1983. Considers the development of political parties for the period covered in this chapter.

Goldfrank, David M. *The Origins of the Crimean War.* 1994. Blames the Russian Tsar Nicholas I for irresponsibly launching the war.

Grew, Raymond. *A Sterner Plan for Italian Unity.* 1963. Studies the role of the National Society in advancing the cause of unification.

Jelavich, Charles and Barbara. *The Establishment of the Balkan National States, 1804–1920.* 1977. Traces the emergence of independent states from the Ottoman Empire.

Kolchin, Peter. *Unfree Labor: American Slavery and Russian Serfdom.* 1987. The most recent study of Russian serfdom, of particular interest to American readers.

Lincoln, W. Bruce. "The Problem of Glasnost in Mid-Nineteenth Century Russian Politics." *European Historical Quarterly,* 11 (April 1981): 171–188. Considers the origins of the concept in the Russian bureaucracy.

Pearton, Maurice. *The Knowledgeable State: Diplomacy, War and Technology Since 1830.* 1982. Emphasizes the contribution of breakthroughs in science, technology, and social organization to military matters.

Pflanze, Otto. *Bismarck and the Development of Germany. I: The Period of Unification, 1815–1871.* 1990. Emphasizes Bismarck's flexibility and ability to improvise to accomplish long-range goals.

Rich, Norman. *Why the Crimean War? A Cautionary Tale.* 1985. Argues that the war was caused by the Western powers' decision to eliminate the Russian threat to the Ottoman Empire.

Shapiro, Ann-Louise. *Housing the Poor of Paris, 1850–1902.* 1985. A good discussion of the effect housing reform had on the working class.

Shaw, Stanford J. *History of the Ottoman Empire and Modern Turkey. II: Reform, Revolution and Republic: The Rise of Modern Turkey, 1808–1975.* 1977. Emphasizes the success of reform in the Ottoman Empire and sees its decline as essentially due to foreign aggression.

Sheehan, James. *German Liberalism in the Nineteenth Century.* 1978. Emphasizes the environment that conditioned the shaping of liberalism in a country that unified late and had to deal with a fast-emerging working class.

Sked, Alan. *The Decline and Fall of the Habsburg Empire, 1815–1918.* 1989. Provides a revisionist interpretation, concentrating on the strengths of the empire.

Smith, Dennis Mack. *Cavour and Garibaldi, 1860.* 1954. Contrasts the heroic, but sometimes naive, Garibaldi with the master manipulator, Cavour.

Smith, Page. *A People's History,* vols. 4 and 5. 1981 and 1982. Vol. 4 describes the development of the United States from 1828 to 1860. Vol. 5 covers the Civil War and Reconstruction. Both are marked by vivid prose and strong narrative.

Smith, William H. C. *Napoleon III.* 1972. Provides a sympathetic view of Napoleon III as a staunch believer in popular sovereignty who was devoted to the welfare of his people.

Williams, Roger L. *The French Revolution of 1870–1871.* 1969. Describes the Commune as the continuation of the French revolutionary tradition.

The Age of Optimism, 1850–1880

The first department store, "Bon Marché" (the good buy), opened its doors in Paris in the 1850s. The store sold a large range of products that previously had been available only in separate specialty shops, and it bought them in quantities that made it possible to lower prices considerably. Constructed of glass and iron, Bon Marché represented the new, modern age: technologically impressive, convenient, and opulent. The shoppers themselves exemplified the ideals of the age, for they were largely women: As men became increasingly associated with managing production in this age of "separate spheres," women became associated with managing consumption. The department store was where the "idle" middle-class woman negotiated the market for the benefit of her family, shopping for what her preindustrial counterpart would have made by hand.

In many ways, the department store serves as a summary of the various changes experienced by prosperous regions of the West after midcentury. Industrial innovation had lowered the price of glass and steel, so that these huge emporiums could be built at reasonable cost. Railroads brought customers from outside the city. The penny press provided advertising for the department store, while the expansion of the postal system facilitated catalog sales. And the higher incomes available to many people allowed them to purchase more than just the necessities. The consumer society had begun.

The new levels of European wealth also contributed to a change in attitudes. This was an era shaped to a large extent by a growing, optimistic middle class, convinced it was living in an age of progress. The application of science and technology to social problems created confidence that the world could be improved. The fertility of the soil was increased; the burgeoning cities were sanitized and regulated. Scientists used new methods to study and combat disease. Public authorities founded schools and trained teachers. Transportation and communication rapidly improved.

However, as many artists and intellectuals pointed out, not all of society benefited from the fruits of progress. Democracy and legal equality seemed on the rise, yet women were everywhere disenfranchised and often held the legal status of children. Eastern and southern Europe changed little, and even in the western part a large group of the population still lived in great misery. Some cities carried out ambitious programs of urban renewal, but others continued to neglect slums. Still, the tone of the age was set by the ascendant middle class in western Europe, which embraced change and believed that the era was heading toward even more remarkable improvements.

∾ Questions and Ideas to Consider

- Why is late-nineteenth-century culture associated with the middle class? Describe middle-class values. What was the ideology of "separate spheres"?

- How did the lives of the working class change during this period? Did a separate spheres ideology exist for this class? Why or why not?

- Why did this period experience so much urban renewal? What were the plans and goals of Baron Haussmann's rebuilding of Paris?

- Although the 1850s to 1880s saw a growing women's suffrage movement, women's rights activists worked for a variety of goals aside from the vote. What were they? What tactics were used to achieve them?

- The successes of science in this period promoted a general sense of optimism, but the new theories often gave rise to new fears. Discuss the impact of Darwin's evolutionary theory as well as the new ideas in physics and chemistry.

INDUSTRIAL GROWTH AND ACCELERATION

Beginning in the 1850s, western Europe experienced an unprecedented level of economic expansion. Manufacturers created new products and employed new sources of energy. An enlarged banking system provided more abundant credit to fund the expansion. Scientific research was systematically employed to improve methods of manufacture. A revolution in transportation speedily delivered goods and services to distant places. For many Europeans, daily life was profoundly changed.

The "Second Industrial Revolution," 1850–1914

The interrelated cluster of economic changes that began after 1850 is often called the "second industrial revolution." It was characterized by a significant speedup in production and the introduction of new materials such as mass-produced steel, synthetic dyes, and aluminum. Manufacturers replaced the traditional steam engine with stronger steam-powered turbines or with machines powered by new forms of energy—petroleum and electricity.

The invention of new products and methods of manufacture spurred industrial expansion. The second half of the nineteenth century has often been called the "age of steel." Up to then, steel production had been limited by the expense involved in its manufacture, but in 1856, Sir Henry Bessemer (1813–1898) discovered a much cheaper method, which produced in twenty minutes the same amount of steel previously produced in twenty-four hours. Over the next three decades, further advancements came from the French and English, halving the price of steel in Great Britain. Increased steel production made possible the expansion of the rail system, the creation of a steamship fleet, and an explosive growth in the building industry. No longer was steel a rare alloy used only for the finest swords and knives; it became the material that defined the age.

Significant changes in the supply of credit further stimulated economic expansion. Discovery of gold in California and Australia led to the inflow of huge amounts of the precious metal to Europe, expanding the supply of money and credit. This led to the establishment of the modern banking system.

CHAPTER CHRONOLOGY

1820s	The omnibus is introduced in France	1863	Building of underground railroad in London
1829	Robert Stephenson runs the *Rocket*		
1833	Invention of the telegraph	1864	Pope Pius IX issues the *Syllabus of Errors*
1840	Introduction of the penny stamp	1865	Transoceanic telegraph cable installed
1848	The Public Health Bill in England	1869	Opening of Suez Canal
	Seneca Falls Women's Rights Convention	1875	Alexander Graham Bell invents the telephone
1850s	Clipper ships		Electric lights in Paris
	Invention of the tramway	1885	Pasteur's rabies vaccine
1851	Crystal Palace Exhibition		
1859	Darwin publishes his doctrine of evolution		

Each advance made possible additional changes. Increased wealth and credit accelerated further expansion of industrial plants and the financing of an ambitious infrastructure of roads, railroads, and steamships, which in turn boosted trade. Between 1800 and 1840, the value of world trade had doubled. From 1850 to 1870 it increased 260 percent.

By the 1880s scientific discoveries increasingly fueled industrial improvements. Electricity began to be more widely used, replacing coal as a source of energy. Synthetic dyes revolutionized the textile industry, as did alkali in the manufacture of soap and glass. Dynamite, invented by the Swedish chemist Alfred Nobel (1833–1896) in the 1860s, made it possible to level hills and blast tunnels through mountains, facilitating construction. Five years after Nobel's death, his will established a prestigious prize named after its donor to honor significant contributions to science and peace.

Transportation and Communications

The rail system grew dramatically in the middle decades of the nineteenth century. When the English engineer Robert Stephenson (1803–1859) demonstrated his steam locomotive, the *Rocket*, in 1829, it ran on a track that was one-and-a-half miles long. By 1880 the total European railroad mileage was 102,000 (Map 21.1). In 1888 the Orient Express line opened, linking Constantinople to Vienna and thus to the rest of Europe. Meanwhile, the cost of rail transport steadily decreased, allowing for its greater use. Ocean transportation also changed dramatically. In 1869, the Suez Canal opened, reducing the distance between London and Bombay by 40 percent. More efficient ships were developed; by midcentury the clipper ship could cross the Atlantic in fourteen days. Steamships were also built, though they did not dominate ocean traffic until the 1890s. By 1880, European shipping carried nearly three times the cargo it had thirty years earlier.

The optimism born of conquering vast distance was reflected in a popular novel, *Around the World in Eighty Days* (1873), by the French writer Jules Verne (1828–1905). The hero, Phineas Fogg, traveled by balloon, llama, ostrich, steam locomotive, and steamship to accomplish in eighty days a feat that, only thirty years earlier, would have taken at least eleven months. Such was the impact of the new technology—and the Suez Canal.

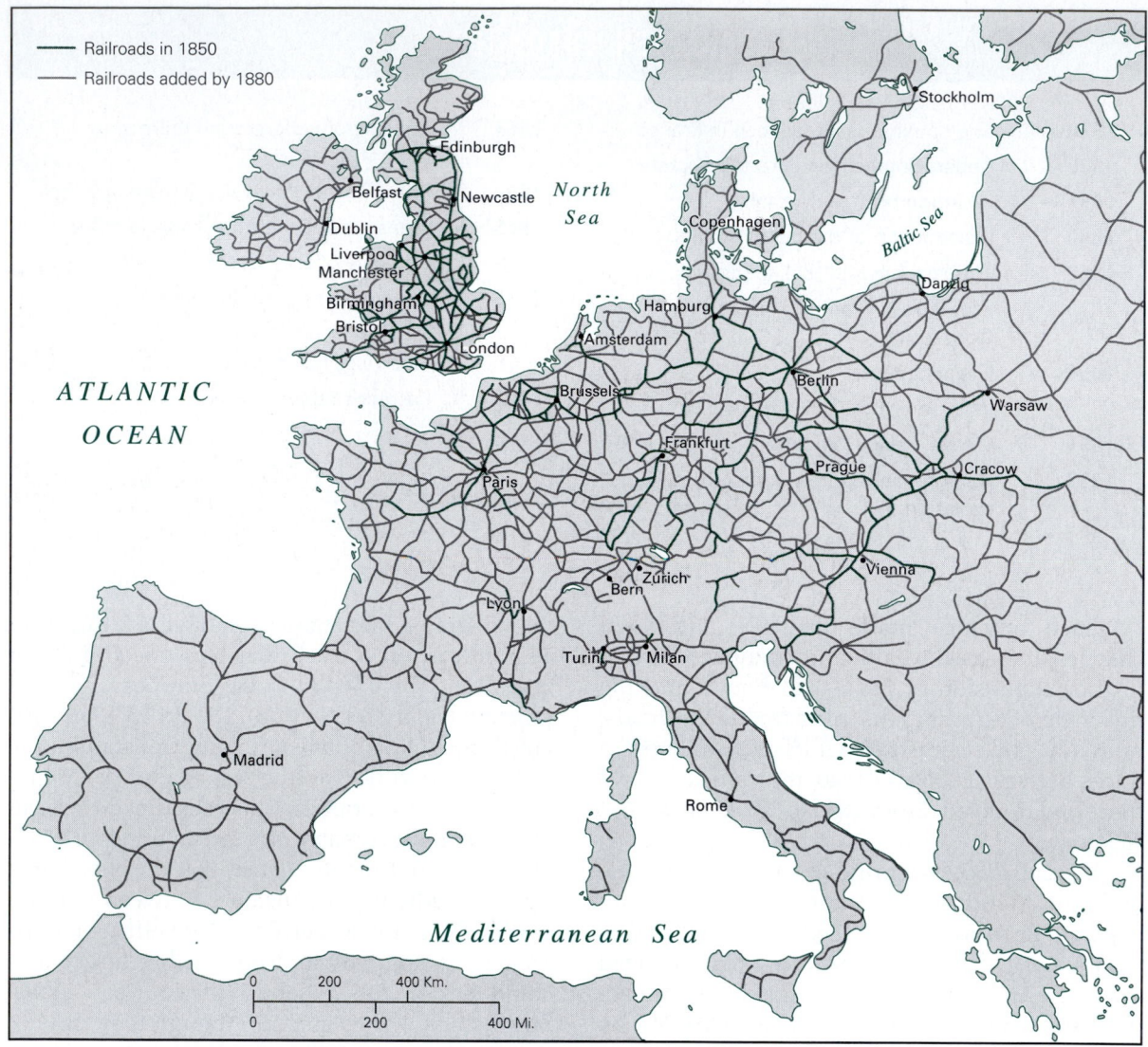

Map 21.1 Railroads of Western Europe, 1850 and 1880 During the mid-nineteenth century, European states built railroads at an increasing rate, creating a dense network by the 1880s. (*Adapted from Norman J. G. Pounds*, An Historical Geography of Europe, 1800–1914 *[New York: Cambridge University Press, 1985].*)

Along with the new speed, advances in refrigeration changed food transport. Formerly, refrigeration could be achieved only with ice cut out of frozen lakes, but this changed in the 1870s with the introduction of mechanical ice-making machines. By the 1880s dairy products and meat were being transported vast distances by rail and even across the seas by ship. Thanks to these advances, the surplus food of the Americas and Australia, rich in grass-lands, could offer Europe a cheaper and far more varied diet.

The Suez Canal Opened in 1869, the canal significantly shortened the voyage by ship from Europe to East Asia. The Suez Canal exemplified the speeding up of transportation and communication in the second half of the nineteenth century. *(AKG London)*

Regular postal service was another a child of the new era, because railroads and increased efficiency lowered the cost. In Great Britain the number of letters mailed in a year increased from 7 per person in 1840 to 32 by 1880. Combined with the transoceanic telegraphy system (1865) and the invention of the telephone (1875), regular postal service transformed the world of information. Now travelers could easily communicate with those at home, business could be transacted at a distance, and news from distant parts of the globe—of earthquakes, revolutions, or the outbreak of war—could reach Europe within minutes. In 1875 the American inventor Alexander Graham Bell (1847–1922) invented a machine

capable of transmitting the human voice by electrical impulses; in 1879 the first telephones were installed in Germany; two years later they appeared in France.

The speedy linking of distant places called attention to the need to standardize time. Until then, countries typically had innumerable time zones; each town established its time according to the location of the sun. Railroad traffic made these quaint differences a source of annoyance to travelers and railroad officials, and it became imperative to have a standard time for each European nation. The electric telegraph made it possible to set that time to the second.

CHANGING CONDITIONS AMONG SOCIAL GROUPS

Industrial advances transformed the traditional structure of European society. Fewer people worked the land; more worked in industry. The social and political influence of the landed aristocracy waned as wealth became far less dependent on the ownership of land. To varying degrees, this influence now had to be shared with the growing middle class. Although life for both industrial and farm workers generally improved in this period, there were great disparities, as many people continued to suffer from profound deprivation.

The Declining Aristocracy

Always a small, exclusive group, the European aristocracy represented less than 1 percent of the population in the nineteenth century. Many people of noble birth were quite poor and economically indistinguishable from their non-noble neighbors. Others owned vast estates and were fabulously wealthy.

Some ennoblements were of recent origin. In England, most titles were less than a hundred years old, having originally been conferred on individuals for service to the state, the arts, or the economy. In France both Napoleons had ennobled persons they wished to honor. In Germany, Bismarck arranged for the Kaiser to ennoble the Jewish banker Gerson Bleichröder (1822–1893) for helping finance the wars of the Prussian state.

As distinctions blurred between the aristocracy and the upper middle class, marriages were often arranged between the children of noble families in financial straits and children of wealthy merchants desiring status. Many nobles who previously had shunned manufacture became industrialists and bankers. Idle members of the nobility were now somewhat rare. Although many aristocrats still enjoyed a lavish lifestyle, others were far more restrained and might be mistaken for successful business people. Nobles played varied roles across Europe, generally dominating the ranks of officers, diplomats, and high-ranking civil servants. Many successful industrialists were also of noble birth. Their continued importance was obvious, but in most European states, nobles could no longer assert privileges based exclusively on birth.

The Expanding Middle Class

Up to the eighteenth century, society had been divided into legally separate orders based on birth. In the nineteenth century, it became more customary to classify people by their economic function. The large new group of industrialists, professionals, and merchants came to be known as the "middle class." These people were also frequently described as *bourgeois*, a term that had originated in the twelfth century to describe the new wealthy class based on urban occupations. The nineteenth century is often described as "the bourgeois century," especially in western Europe, where the middle class helped fashion much of society.

The middle class expanded dramatically in the wake of industrialization. More trade and manufacture meant more entrepreneurs and managers, while the increasingly complex society called for more engineers, lawyers, accountants, bankers, merchants, architects, and doctors. As industries matured, the increasing use of machinery and better industrial organization meant that fewer additional workers and more clerks and bureaucrats were needed. In the 1870s about 10 percent of urban working-class people reached lower-middle-class status by becoming storekeepers, lower civil servants, clerks, or salespeople.

Import-export businesses, insurance companies, and department stores provided opportunities of this kind, as did the expansion of government services. In the second half of the nineteenth century, France increased its teacher corps by 80,000 and the British postal service increased its staff sixfold. The significance for individuals was great. When the son or daughter of peasants became the village postmaster, a schoolteacher, or a clerk in a major firm, his or her whole family rose to the lower stratum of the middle class. Even more than income or material comfort, the promise of social respectability enticed the lower classes to strive for membership in the middle class. In midcentury Britain, the middle class represented 15 percent of the population; by 1881, 25 percent. Elsewhere, the proportion was lower, but it was growing in number and strength as the economy expanded.

A widening subgroup of the middle class consisted of members of the professions, those whose prestige rested on the claim of exclusive expertise in a particular field. In the early nineteenth century, requirements for exercising a profession varied, depending on the country. In France and Prussia, government regulation stipulated the qualifications necessary to practice medicine; in England anyone might practice it. As the professions attempted to create a monopoly for themselves and eliminate rivals, they established more standards. Medical doctors, for instance, began requiring specialized education to distinguish themselves from herbalists, midwives, and other rivals. By midcentury either professional associations or the state itself accredited members of the professions. Women had limited access to professions; typically their opportunities were confined to lower teaching positions and, as a result of Florence Nightingale's efforts (see page 519), nursing.

Middle-Class Lifestyles

The standard of living of the middle class varied considerably, from the wealthy entrepreneur who bought a château, or built one, to the bourgeois who dwelled in a modest apartment. But all members of the middle class lived in new standards of comfort. Their homes had running water, upholstered furniture, and enough space to provide separate sleeping and living quarters. They had several changes of clothing and consumed a varied diet. They read books and subscribed to newspapers and journals.

In some areas suburban living became fashionable. For further relief from the crowded cities, visits to resorts became popular. Throughout Europe, resort towns sprang up, devoted principally to the amusement of the well-off. It became fashionable to "take the waters"—bathing in hot springs and drinking the mineral waters thought to have special attributes. For the first time, tourism became big business. Thomas Cook (1808–1892), an Englishman, organized tours to the Crystal Palace exhibition of 1851 (see page 558). Discovering the large market for travel tours, he began running tours in England and on the Continent. Beginning in 1835, a German publisher, Karl Baedeker (1801–1859), issued a tourist guide to the Rhine, followed by guidebooks to various European countries and the Middle East. The Baedeker guides provided the pattern for the multitude of guidebooks that followed.

New wealth and leisure time also led to more hotels, restaurants, and cafés. In 1869 there was a hotel in Paris with seven hundred well-appointed rooms. Vienna's National Hotel, with three hundred rooms, had steam heat, spring water on every floor, and an icehouse providing cool drinks. At home or away, the bourgeois valued comfort.

Members of the middle class shared certain attitudes about the conduct of their lives. They believed their successes were due not to birth but to talent and effort. They wanted to be judged on their merits, and they were expected to abide by strict moral principles. Their lives were supposed to be disciplined, especially with regard to sex and drink. The age was called "Victorian" because the middle class in Britain saw in the queen who reigned for two-thirds of the century a reflection of its own values. "Victorian morality," preached but not always practiced, was often seen as hypocritical. Male sexuality was expected and condoned while female sexuality was repressed and negated. As a result, sexual behavior was veiled in social anxiety, and women were seen as either respectable virgins and mothers or disruptive mistresses and prostitutes. As the middle class increasingly dominated society, its values became the social norms. Public drunkenness was discouraged, and anti-alcohol movements

Ladies' Bicycling Fashion   This new mode of transportation suggested possibilities for female emancipation. *(From Karin Helm (ed.),* Rosinen aus der Gartenlaube *[Gutersloh: Signum Verlag, n.d.]. Reproduced with permission.)*

vigorously campaigned against drinking. Public festivals were regulated, making them more respectable and less rowdy. In several countries, societies for the protection of animals agitated against blood sports such as cockfights.

In spite of their differences in education, wealth, and social standing, most of the bourgeoisie resembled one another in dress, habits of speech, and deportment. Bourgeois men dressed somberly, in dark colors, and avoided decoration, reflecting their activity in the hard world of machines, money, and scientific attitudes. Such dress also reflected a conscious attempt to em-

phasize the achievement-oriented attitudes of the bourgeoisie in contrast to what was seen as the frivolous nobility.

The values that applied to bourgeois women were quite different. Confined to the running of the family home, bourgeois women expressed themselves through their clothes and their homes. They created extravagant, huge, beribboned dresses that literally took up space and defined their environments. Women's decorative ornamentation also defined the middle-class home. With the world of business and machines seen as ruthless and unforgiving, the home was reconceived from a place of production and reproduction to a haven of purity and love. Whereas the husband was limited to work for profit and was expected to be strong and rational, the wife was limited to work for affection and religious devotion and was expected to be gentle and emotional. Women did a great deal of work: They decorated and redecorated their homes with the seasons and the styles, supervised their servants, kept the accounts, watched over the children's homework and religious education, and involved themselves in charitable works. (See the box "Advice on Running the Middle-Class Household.") Yet all this activity was explicitly undervalued in a world concerned with material and intellectual progress. In the decades around midcentury, the idea of two separate spheres—one male and public, the other female and private—reached its height.

It is also true that many bourgeois women helped their husbands or fathers in the office, the business, or the writing of scientific treatises. Others achieved success on their own terms, running their own businesses, writing, painting, teaching. When Rosa Bonheur (1822–1899) was excluded from nude sketching sessions at her art school because she was a woman, she began painting animals and became the best-known painter of domestic animals in the nineteenth century.

The expectation that middle-class women would marry and be taken care of by their husbands led to the provision of inferior education for girls and young women. The husband's responsibility to support his wife—and any un-

Advice on Running the Middle-Class Household

In 1861 Isabella Mary Mayson Beeton, a London housewife, published **Mrs. Beeton's Book of Household Management,** *which in Britain was outsold only by the Bible. Her popular book provided British middle-class women with advice on running their households and reflected their values concerning discipline, frugality, and cleanliness.*

As with the commander of an army, or the leader of an enterprise, so is it with the mistress of a house. Her spirit will be seen through the whole establishment; and just in proportion as she performs her duties intelligently and thoroughly, so will her domestics follow in her path. Of all those acquirements, which more particularly belong to the feminine character, there are none which take a higher rank, in our estimation, than such as enter into a knowledge of household duties; for on these are perpetually dependent the happiness, comfort, and well-being of a family. . . .

Early rising is one of the most essential qualities which enter into good Household Management, as it is not only the parent of health, but of innumerable other advantages. Indeed, when a mistress is an early riser, it is almost certain that her house will be orderly and well-managed. . . .

Cleanliness is indispensable to health, and must be studied both in regard to the person and the house, and all that it contains. . . .

Frugality and economy are home virtues, without which no household can prosper. . . .

Charity and benevolence are duties which a mistress owes to herself as well as to her fellow-creatures; and there is scarcely any income so small, but something may be spared from it. . . . Great advantages may result from visits paid the poor, for there being, unfortunately, much ignorance, generally amongst them with respect to all household knowledge, there will be opportunities for advising and instructing them in a pleasant and unobtrusive manner, in cleanliness, industry, cookery, and good management. . . .

A housekeeping account-book should invariably be kept, and kept punctually and precisely. . . .

. . . The treatment of servants is of the highest possible moment as well to the mistress as to the domestics themselves. On the head of the house the latter will naturally fix their attention; and if they perceive that the mistress's conduct is regulated by high and correct principles, they will not fail to respect her. If, also a benevolent desire is shown to promote their comfort, at the same time that a steady performance of their duty is exacted, then their respect will not be unmingled with affection, and they will be more solicitous to continue to deserve her favour.

Source: Isabella Mary Mayson Beeton, *Mrs. Beeton's Book of Household Management* (London: S. O. Beeton, 1861), pp. 1–6.

married female members of their family—was often a source of great anxiety for men. For women, the problem was deeply frustrating. Even if they were brighter and more intellectually curious than their brothers, young girls did not receive an equal education. Proponents of women's rights argued strenuously for equal access to education and the professions. Slowly, secondary and university education was made available to young women, and very slowly they began to enter the professions.

Women more easily penetrated the lower levels of middle-class occupations. By the 1890s, two-thirds of primary schoolteachers in England

and half the post office staff in France were women; by 1914 nearly half a million women were working as shop assistants in England. Some new technologies created jobs that became heavily feminized, such as the positions of typist and telephone operator.

The Workers' Lot

Working-class women had always worked. They were generally paid much less than their male counterparts, but the jobs were there, families needed everyone to work, and there was no status to defend through enforced idleness. The increased prosperity and productivity of the period gradually improved the conditions of both male and female workers after 1850. Their wages and standard of living rose, and they enjoyed more job security. The workers' increased income enabled them to enjoy a better diet. In France the average number of calories consumed per adult male increased by one-third between 1840 and 1890. The quality of food also improved; people consumed more meat, fish, eggs, and dairy products.

In some ways, factory work became harder. There was an increased emphasis on efficiency, fewer informal breaks, and new machines that increased the tempo of work, frequently leading to accidents and exhaustion. Legislation gradually reduced the length of the workweek. The British workweek, typically 73 hours in the 1840s, was reduced to 56 hours in 1874. In France it was reduced to 10 hours a day, in Germany to 11.

As workers had more time and more money, their leisure patterns changed. Some leisure activities that had previously been limited to the upper classes became available to workers. Dance halls, popular theaters, and other enterprises sprang up to entertain them and make a profit. The railroad took them to resort towns for holidays.

Although most workers believed their lot had improved, they were aware that a vast gulf separated them from the middle and upper classes. In the 1880s in the northern French industrial city of Lille, the combined estates of 20,000 workers equaled that of one average industrialist. In Paris the gluttonous rich ate multicourse meals and the leftover scraps were collected by special vendors and sold to the poor.

Although a few members of the working class were able to enter the lower levels of the middle class, most remained mired in the same jobs as their parents and grandparents. Poverty was still pervasive, and urban diseases, such as tuberculosis, were common. Compared to the middle class, the workers continued to live in shabby and limited circumstances.

The Transformation of the Countryside

Before the nineteenth century, the countryside had hardly changed at all, but beginning at midcentury it was radically transformed. Agriculture became increasingly efficient, and the food supply grew significantly. More land was cultivated, and the yield per acre increased. In 1760 an agricultural worker in England could feed himself and one other person; by 1841 he could feed himself and 2.7 others. The population of Europe nearly doubled between 1800 and 1880, and yet it was nourished better than ever before.

The higher yields were due to an increased use of manure, augmented in the 1870s and 1880s by saltpeter imported from Chile and chemical fertilizers manufactured in Europe. In the 1850s steam-driven threshing machinery was introduced in some parts of western Europe. Organizational techniques borrowed from industry, including specialization and the insistence on regularity in the workplace, also contributed to greater productivity.

Life in the countryside became less isolated. Improved roads and dramatically expanded rail lines enabled farmers to extend their markets beyond the local area. In Brittany, in western France, a rail line to Paris led to a boom in dairy farming. Not only did rail lines connect farms to cities, but national school systems brought teachers into the villages. The local dialects and in some cases distinct languages that peasants had spoken for generations were replaced by a standardized national language. Local costumes became less common as styles adopted in the cities spread to the countryside via consumer catalogs. The farm girls who went to the cities to work as maids in middle-class homes returned to their villages with urban and middle-class ideals. Likewise, the military draft brought village youth into contact with urban folk and further spread city values to the countryside.

Even so, the rural world remained distinct from urban society. Many of the forces that contributed to modernity exacerbated rural problems. The expansion of manufacturing in cities contributed to the decline of cottage industry in rural areas, where agricultural workers had relied on the putting-out system to provide supplementary income. Thus, farmworkers were idle during slack seasons, and rural unemployment grew. In many cases railroads bringing goods made elsewhere wiped out some of the local markets on which cottage industry had depended. The steamship lowered the cost of transporting grain from distant Canada and Argentina, which often undersold wheat grown in Europe. The resultant crisis, worsened by a rural population explosion, led to the emigration of millions, who left the land for towns and cities or even migrated across the seas to the Americas and Australia. Although this process was painful for large segments of the rural population, the result was that for those who were able to remain on the land the situation eventually improved.

These developments had a striking effect on western Europe, but eastern Europe was hardly touched by them. In Russia, the average agricultural yield per acre in 1880 was one-quarter that of Great Britain. The land sheltered a large surplus population that was underemployed and contributed little to the economy. In the Balkans, most peasants were landless and heavily indebted.

URBAN PROBLEMS AND SOLUTIONS

By 1851 the majority of English people lived in cities; by 1891 the majority of Germans did as well. To cope with urban growth and its attendant problems—epidemics, crowding, traffic jams—cities developed public health measures and introduced planning and rebuilding programs. They adapted the new technologies to provide such urban amenities as streetlights, public transportation, water and sewer systems, and police forces. Cities became safer and more pleasant places to live, although city dwellers continued to suffer high mortality rates.

City Planning and Urban Renovation

Most of Europe's cities had begun as medieval walled cities and had grown haphazardly into major industrial centers. Their narrow, crooked streets could not accommodate the increased trade and daily movement of goods and people, and traffic snarls were common. City officials began to recognize that broad, straight avenues would resolve the traffic problem and bring sunlight and fresh air into the narrow and perpetually dank lanes and alleys. In the 1820s, London saw the first ambitious street-widening initiative. On Regency Street, old hovels were torn down and replaced with fancy new houses, and the poor were usually displaced. Later projects followed this pattern.

The most extensive program of urban rebuilding took place in midcentury Paris. Over a period of eighteen years, Napoleon III and his aide, Baron Georges Haussmann (1809–1891), transformed Paris from a dirty medieval city to a beautiful modern one. Broad, straight avenues were carved through what had been dingy slums. The avenues were lined with trees and graced with elegant houses. Enhancing the city were public monuments and buildings, such as the new opera house. The tremendous costs of this ambitious scheme kept the city of Paris in debt for decades. In addition, the slum-removal program drove tens of thousands of the poorest Parisians to the outskirts of the city, leading to greater social segregation than had previously existed.

Haussmann's extensive work in Paris served as a model for other cities, and although none was rebuilt as extensively, many underwent significant improvements. The cities of Europe

Pissarro: L' avenue de l' Opéra, Sunlight, Winter Morning Camille Pissarro, one of the leading impressionists, portrayed the broad new avenue designed by Baron Haussmann. The avenue leads to the new opera, in background, also planned during the Second Empire. (*Musée Saint-Denis, Reims/Giraudon/Art Resource, NY*)

began to display an expansive grace and sense of order, supporting the middle-class belief that theirs was an age of progress.

The Introduction of Public Services

Beginning at midcentury, government at the central and local levels helped make cities more livable by legislating sanitary reforms and provid-ing public transportation and lighting. In the 1820s medical practitioners had observed that dis-ease and higher mortality were related to dirt and the lack of clean air, clean water, and sunshine. Since diseases spreading from the poorer quarters of town threatened the rich and powerful, there was a general interest in improving public health by clearing slums, broadening streets, and sup-plying clean water.

Reform began in England, where the lawyer and civil servant Edwin Chadwick (1800–1895) drafted important plans for reform that became the basis for legislation. The Public Health Bill of 1848 established national standards for urban sanitation and required cities to regulate the installation of sewers and the disposal of refuse. The 1875 Health Act required cities to maintain certain basic health standards such as clean water and drainage.

As running water in the home became standard rather than a luxury, bathing became more common. The English upper classes had learned the habit of daily baths from their colonial experience in India; on the Continent it was not the custom until about the third quarter of the nineteenth century. French artist Edgar Degas (1834–1917) frequently painted bath scenes portraying the new European habit.

All these changes had a direct impact on the lives of city dwellers. Life became healthier, more comfortable, and more orderly. Between the 1840s and 1880, London's death rate fell from 26 per thousand to 20 per thousand. There was a decline in the incidence of diseases associated with filthy living conditions. Improved water supplies provided a cleaner environment and reduced the prevalence of water-borne diseases such as cholera and typhoid. In addition, a number of states became involved in the fight against disease: Norway and Sweden introduced mandatory vaccination for smallpox in 1810 and 1816, respectively. England followed in 1867 and Germany in the 1870s.

Other improvements also contributed to a better quality of life. With the introduction of urban transportation, city dwellers no longer had to live within walking distance of their work. Early public transportation was seen in the French omnibus service of the 1820s—a system of horse-drawn carriages following fixed routes. The bicycle also became an important means of transportation for some city dwellers. New gaslights made cities easier and safer to move around at night. The first electric lights appeared in Paris in 1875, although they were not common until the end of the century.

Cities significantly expanded their police forces to impose order, control criminal activity, and discourage behavior deemed undesirable, such as dumping garbage on the street, relieving oneself in public, or singing loud, raucous songs late at night. In 1850 London was the best-policed city in Europe with a five-thousand-man force, and Paris had around three thousand policemen. The numbers continued to increase.

SOCIAL AND POLITICAL INITIATIVES

New groups emerged to tackle the social and political inequalities of the period, as well as the critical urban problems that had followed in the wake of economic growth. The women's movement emerged. The state intervened in the economy in new ways. Private charitable groups sprang up. And socialist parties, exclusively dedicated to improving the lot of workers, gained in numbers and strength.

Feminism

A significant women's movement developed in the second half of the nineteenth century. In 1840, women working for the abolition of slavery found themselves barred from attending the World Anti-Slavery Convention in London. The outrage of the excluded U.S. delegates helped to inspire the organization of the first Women's Rights Convention, held in Seneca Falls, New York, in 1848. In Europe, similar conventions and associations appeared throughout the 1850s and 1860s.

In France, many of these associations formed during the political movements of 1848 and 1871. In both of these upheavals, women worked and fought alongside men and expected to reap some political and economic benefits. For instance, the Commune Commission for Education ruled to raise the salaries of women teachers to match those of men, "seeing that the necessities of life are as imperative for women as for men."[1] In general, these goals were not achieved. The government's re-establishment of order was, in both cases, partially structured around returning women to the private sphere. For instance, after the "June Days" of 1848, the government forbade women to form political clubs.

The strongest women's rights movement of the period developed in England. Largely made up of middle-class women from reform-minded families, the movement was led by Barbara Bodichon (1827–1891). Bodichon had written a pamphlet investigating the lack of legal rights for women, especially after they married. Incensed by what she found, she put together a petition asserting that married women ought to have control of their property and earnings. The petition was signed by a number of distinguished women of the day, including the poet Elizabeth Barrett Browning, the novelist Elizabeth Gaskell, and the political theorist Harriet Martineau. When Parliament rejected the proposal in 1856, the women around Bodichon redoubled their efforts.

These women and those who later joined them launched a number of important initiatives in the 1860s—a club where women could read and discuss issues, the feminist *Englishwoman's Journal*, and the Society for the Promotion of the Employment of Women to give women the skills they would need to be clerks and bookkeepers, instead of just governesses. They continued to lobby Parliament for married women's right to control their earnings and won this battle in 1878; in 1882 they secured married women's control of their own property.

Another major women's rights initiative, the repeal of the Contagious Disease Acts, was led by Josephine Grey Butler (1828–1906). In 1864, in response to the spread of venereal disease, the English government had given police in a number of ports and towns the right to arrest and examine any woman suspected of being a prostitute. Suspicion could be based on little more than a woman walking alone after dark. The acts clearly held women to blame for disease, put the burden of controlling prostitution on the prostitutes rather than their customers (or the wider economic system), and put all women, of whatever class, in danger of harassment by the state.

Butler, who came from a family of reformers, had fought to abolish slavery and had worked for the spread of education to impoverished women. The humiliating ideas behind the Contagious Disease Acts radicalized her—to the distress of some of her more conservative supporters. Through Butler's tireless efforts, and using political techniques she had learned in her abolitionist work, the acts were overturned in England in the 1880s. Butler also called attention to the plight of prostitutes on the Continent. Butler believed that women needed to obtain extensive political power, writing that "we have passed through an education—a noble education. God has prepared in us, in the women of the world, a force for all future causes which are great and just."[2]

The women's movement led by Barbara Bodichon put its numbers and prestige behind Butler's campaign and, in these same years, also campaigned for women's education. Although British universities admitted women, the University of London did not grant them degrees until after 1878, and the most prestigious British institutions, Oxford and Cambridge, did not grant degrees to women until after World War I. The situation was similar in the rest of Europe. In spite of discriminatory laws, harassment by male students, and initial obstruction by professional and accrediting groups, a few female doctors and lawyers practiced in England by the 1870s and on the Continent in the following decades.

The women's movement also continued to press for the right to vote, supporting John Stuart Mill in his run for Parliament and forming the Women's Suffrage Committee to organize further initiatives (see page 473). Nightingale, Martineau, and others, such as the mathematician Mary Somerville, joined 1499 prominent women in petitioning for the vote in 1866 but made little progress. In the coming century, women would use more aggressive tactics and achieve a great deal.

State Intervention in Welfare

The difficult conditions industry imposed on workers led to debates in several countries about the need for the state to protect the workers. The growing militancy of organized labor also forced the authorities to consider ways to meet the workers' needs. Although some rejected government intervention in the free market, others argued that the laws of supply and demand had caused wrongful exploitation—especially in the cases of very young children and pregnant women. Also, some advocates for worker protections were motivated by fear rather than compassion, as organized labor grew increasingly militant and socialist parties gained strength.

To correct some of the worst abuses, the Scottish philanthropist Robert Owen (1771–1858) agitated in Parliament for the first effective British factory act, which passed in 1819. The act forbade labor for children under the age of 9 and limited the workday of older children to twelve hours. Then, beginning in 1833, a series of factory acts further limited the work hours of children and women in factories and mines and funded inspections to enforce these laws. French laws protecting children were passed as early as 1841, but it was not until 1874 that funding was approved to enforce them. When France's defeat in the Franco-Prussian War was blamed on inadequate troops due to a falling birthrate—especially in comparison to its rival Germany—the government began to limit the work hours of children and women. French bourgeois liberals advocated "Solidarism," an ideology of mutual social responsibility intended to appease moderate socialists and defuse class war.

In Germany, the Kaiser's government wanted to show workers the benefits they could gain from the state so they would abandon the growing Socialist party. In the 1880s the government provided a comprehensive welfare plan that included health insurance and old-age pensions. By offering these benefits to the people on its own initiative, the German government enacted reform without seeming to have been forced. The German government was the first to express a national responsibility for the welfare of its citizens, and German social programs became models for the rest of Europe.

In much of Europe, however, the state did little on behalf of workers' welfare. In eastern Europe, where industry was still in its infancy, there was no protection of workers. More surprising was Belgium's inaction: It was the earliest country on the Continent to industrialize and one of the last to provide protection from the harsh industrial conditions.

The middle and upper classes supplemented government programs by developing private initiatives to better the workers' lot. Concern among these groups and individuals arose from a mixture of pity for workers' condition, religious teachings about their responsibilities for the less fortunate, and fear of the consequences of unrelieved misery. In Paris, three thousand private charitable organizations were founded between 1840 and 1900; their combined outlay in aid equaled the public charity available. In London the sum of £6 million—more than the total budget of many European states—was spent to aid the poor in 1890.

Middle- and upper-class women were largely responsible for volunteer charity work. Socially prohibited from working for profit and responsible for the spiritual well-being of the family, women embraced charity work as a focus for their talents and energies. By the end of the nineteenth century, as many as half a million Englishwomen were contributing their time to provide charity to the less fortunate. In Sweden women founded refuges for the destitute, old-age homes, a children's hospital, an asylum for the mentally handicapped, and various societies to promote female industry.

In Catholic and Protestant countries, the churches had traditionally identified with the rights of employers and seemed to ignore the lot of the workers. However, a number of Christians, lay and clerical, began to emphasize the need to address social issues. In Germany, Bishop Wilhelm von Ketteler (1811–1877) preached the need for the well-off to take responsibility for the less privileged. His message was taken up in France, Italy, and Spain among what became known as "social Catholics." In England, Protestants' concern for the poor was evidenced by the founding of the Salvation Army in 1878. Religious groups also hoped they could win converts among the poor by demonstrating concern for their plight.

Increasingly, states, municipalities, volunteer groups, and churches accepted responsibility for the well-being of others. This trend marked the beginning of an evolution that would eventually lead to the welfare state in much of twentieth-century Europe.

Educational and Cultural Opportunities

At the beginning of the nineteenth century, governments took little responsibility for providing education. The upper classes educated their children with private tutors, parents from more modest economic groups taught their children what they knew, and the poor attended the few small schools run by charitable and religious groups. With the rise of national democracies, however, leaders grew concerned that only an educated electorate could vote responsibly. Governments also wanted a chance to indoctrinate children in beliefs that would lend stability to the country: enthusiasm for the present form of government; nationalism, especially in opposition to any common enemy; and secular rationalism—especially for boys. England and France initiated mandatory primary school education in the 1880s. In Britain, one million children attended school in 1865; by 1880 more than three million attended.

Public education included not only reading, writing, and arithmetic but other skills as well. By insisting on punctuality and obliging students to carry out repetitive skills such as copying letters, words, or sentences, schools encouraged people to fit into the emerging industrial society. Obedience and respect for authority and the government were also taught, shaping the nation's future soldiers, factory workers, mothers, and voters. Secondary education was, on the whole, available only to the wealthy and the upper-middle class. University was available only to the sons of the elite, with the exception of a very small number from the lower-middle class.

In the spirit of public education, grand exhibitions were set up, and libraries, museums and art galleries gradually became accessible to the general public. The greatest public symbol of progress was the Great Exhibition of 1851, held

in London and housed in the Crystal Palace. This was the first World's Fair, and with 100,000 objects on display—half from Great Britain and its empire and the other half from foreign nations—it was intended to celebrate the accomplishments of the century, of industry, of each nation, and of an imagined bountiful future. The Crystal Palace itself was an immense glass and steel marvel of technology that became a model for the Bon Marché (see page 543) and many other architectural wonders of the nineteenth-century world. During peak attendance, 110,000 people were in the building at the same time, having come from all over the world and from all classes. Indeed, the entrance fee was lowered on certain days to ensure that the working class could view the stunning opulence and abundance and its promise for the future.

Despite the exuberant mood at the Great Exhibition, there were signs of the darker side of progress. A display of new cannons by the German arms manufacturer Alfred Krupp hinted of the coming mechanization of war. Colonial displays were enjoyed as collections of exotic delights, but they were also reminders that the European empires rested on the domination of other peoples. For some visitors, the most troubling aspect of the Great Exhibition was the crass materialism of it all. Charles Dickens complained, "There's too much," and many agreed. Nevertheless, world's fairs took place frequently for several decades as each nation sought to demonstrate its grandeur to the world.

Less ornate, but considerably more permanent, new libraries and museums also brought a wide range of cultural experiences to the general public. Between 1840 and 1880, the number of large libraries in Europe increased from forty to five hundred. The French national public library, the Bibliothèque Nationale, was established in Paris in the 1860s. Constructed of iron and glass, it was an impressive monument to the idea of an expanded reading public. Many provincial cities, as well as the glittering capitals of Europe, were endowed with new libraries.

Less grandiose, but probably more important for mostly rural populations, were the traveling libraries. Museums and art galleries, which in the previous century had been open to only a select few, gradually became accessible to the general public. The first museum to open to the public was the Louvre in Paris after the French Revolution. The rest of Europe lagged behind in making their cultural heritage available to the masses. The British Museum was open only to the wealthy, for there was widespread fear of the possible destruction that the "vulgar classes" might cause if they were allowed to visit. But the sedate behavior of the crowds during the Crystal Palace exposition reassured British authorities, and finally, in 1879, the museum was opened daily—without restrictions.

CULTURE IN AN AGE OF OPTIMISM

The improving economic and material conditions of the second half of the nineteenth century buoyed European thinkers. Many believed that women and men were becoming more enlightened, and they expressed faith in humankind's ability to transform the world with new scientific and technical breakthroughs. The world seemed knowable and perfectible. This faith advanced secularism while it undermined the certainties of traditional religion. The arts reflected these new values, emphasizing realism and science—as well as an underlying foreboding of the dark side of this "age of optimism."

Darwin and the Theory of Evolution

By midcentury most thinkers accepted the notion of change and transformation of society—and by analogy of the natural environment. The intellectual culture of the era was dominated by positivism, a philosophy of French thinker Auguste Comte (1798–1857). Viewing human progress as inevitable and ever increasing, positivists upheld the significance of empirical investigation and scientific thought, confident that their methods would assure the continued progress of humanity.

In the field of geology, the Englishman Charles Lyell (1797–1875) maintained that the earth was far older than the Bible suggested. He argued that its geological formations—the mountains, valleys, and seas—had been subjected to natural forces that, over hundreds of thousands, even millions, of years, had transformed them. Most educated people accepted his theory (there were, after all, seashells on mountaintops), which led many to wonder if the animal kingdom had also evolved.

Although evolution in the biological realm had been suggested as early as the end of the eighteenth century, Charles Darwin (1809–1882) was the first to offer a plausible explanation of the process. As the naturalist on an official British scientific expedition in the 1830s, he had visited the Galápagos Islands off the coast of South America. There he found species similar to but different from those on the mainland—and different from one another. Darwin hypothesized that they were not the result of separate creation but that they had adapted differently to their varying environments. Darwin had read Malthus's *Essay on the Principle of Population* (see page 472), and it influenced his reasoning. Darwin observed that there are almost always more creatures born than can be supported by the environment. This gives rise to what Darwin called a "struggle for existence," in which some creatures die off. Those that survive do so because they have some attribute that proved helpful in their specific environment. The survivors reproduce and pass on the helpful attributes to the next generation. Darwin called this imperceptible but continuous evolutionary mech-anism "natural selection." Though Darwin understood that the "fittest" creature for a given environment might not be the smartest, most complex, or most noble, many thought that his theory confirmed the era's faith in progress. Darwin did not suggest that human beings also evolved until *Descent of Man* (1871), where he clearly stated that humans had developed like other species of the animal kingdom. (See the box "Darwin's Basic Laws of Evolution.")

Many Christians were shocked by Darwin's assertions, and some denounced his findings.

Darwin's Basic Laws of Evolution

Darwin's **On the Origin of Species** *(1859) uses several kinds of arguments. In the passage below, Darwin suggests an objection to his theory and then refutes it. He also uses metaphors from geology and animal domestication to help his theory seem familiar. Lastly, he distances evolution from charges of atheism and vulgarity.*

Nothing at first can appear more difficult to believe than that the more complex organs and instincts have been perfected, not by means superior to, though analogous with, human reason, but by the accumulation of innumerable slight variations, each good for the individual possessor. Nevertheless, this difficulty, though appearing to our imagination insuperably great, cannot be considered real if we admit the following propositions, namely, that all parts of the organisation and instincts offer, at least, individual differences—that there is a struggle for existence leading to the preservation of profitable deviations of structure or instinct—and, lastly, that gradations in the state of perfection of each organ may have existed, each good of its kind. The truth of these propositions cannot, I think, be disputed. . . .

As geology plainly proclaims that each land has undergone great physical changes, we might have expected to find that organic beings have varied under nature, in the same way as they have varied under domestication. And if there has been any variability under nature, it would be an unaccountable fact if natural selection had not come into play. . . .

There is grandeur in this view of life, with its several powers, having been originally breathed by the Creator into a few forms or into one; and that, whilst this planet has gone cycling on according to the fixed law of gravity, from so simple a beginning endless forms most beautiful and most wonderful have been, and are being evolved.

Source: Charles Darwin, *On the Origin of Species by Means of Natural Selection*, 6th ed., vol. 2 (1872; reprint, New York: Appleton, 1923), pp. 267–268, 279, 305–306.

Some atheists and anticlerics celebrated evolutionary ideas as proofs against religion. Most moderate Christians, however, saw no reason why God could not have created the world through natural forces. Still, in the long run, Darwinism did much to undermine the authority of religion and literal interpretations of the Bible because, for the first time, there was a reasonable secular answer to the question of human existence.

Physics, Chemistry, and Medicine

Dramatic scientific breakthroughs in the nineteenth century reinforced the belief that human beings could understand and control nature. In physics, laws regarding electricity, magnetism, and thermodynamics were articulated by Michael Faraday (1791–1867), James Clerk Maxwell (1831–1879), and James Joule (1818–1889). In 1869, Russian chemist Dmitri Mendeleev (1834–1907) developed the periodic table, leaving blank spaces for several unknown elements whose discovery he predicted. When several were later discovered, it further added to the prestige of science.

Prolific research yielded discoveries in one field of knowledge that could be transferred to another. For example, chemists produced new dyes, enabling biologists to color slides of microorganisms and better study their evolution. Scientific breakthroughs also led to technical advancements that had industrial uses; for instance, inventions in chemistry led to the development of the first artificial fertilizers in 1842 and synthetic dyes in the 1850s.

Science became increasingly specialized. In the eighteenth century, the scientist had been a learned amateur practicing a hobby. In the nineteenth century, as the state and industry became increasingly involved in promoting scientific research, the scientist became a professional, employed by a university, a hospital, or other institution. New theories and discoveries were disseminated by scientific journals and at meetings of scientific associations.

Internationally, scientific cooperation became common, but there was also much nationalist rivalry. When cholera broke out in Egypt in 1883, a French and a German team of scientists rushed to the area to discover its cause. The German team, led by Robert Koch (1843–1910), uncovered the cholera bacillus as the source; on returning to his homeland Koch was feted as a national hero who had vindicated German superiority in science.

Around the midcentury mark, a number of important breakthroughs occurred in medicine. Before the development of anesthesia, surgery had been nearly impossible. With only alcohol to dull the patient's pain, even the swiftest surgeons could manage only modest surgical procedures. In the 1840s, the introduction of ether and then chloroform allowed for more extensive surgery. Painkillers were also increasingly used in childbirth, a procedure made popular when Queen Victoria herself used chloroform to ease her pain.

The greatest change in medicine was the shift from seeing disease as an imbalance in the patient's physical and moral system to understanding that it was caused by microscopic organisms. Among the many figures involved in making this conceptual leap, Louis Pasteur (1822–1895) was the most significant. Pasteur also pioneered certain methods of disease prevention. He demonstrated that the body could build up immunities to a disease when vaccinated by a weaker form of the bacilli that caused

it. His were not the first vaccines: People had long noticed that milkmaids' exposure to cowpox made them immune to smallpox, and in the eighteenth century, the English physician Edward Jenner (1749–1823) had developed a successful vaccine based on this principle. However, until Pasteur, no one knew why it worked or how to apply the procedure to other diseases.

The development of measures to prevent contamination also followed the pattern of observation preceding understanding. The Hungarian doctor Ignaz Semmelweiss (1818–1865) noticed that if he delivered a baby just after performing an autopsy, the new mother often contracted puerperal fever and died. He found that he could radically reduce infection rates by washing his hands with a chlorine solution before touching patients. Effective but inexplicable, Semmelweiss's method was lambasted and his career was ruined. Later, in England, the surgeon John Lister (1827–1912) developed an effective disinfectant, carbolic acid, to kill the germs that caused gangrene and other infections in surgical patients. Incidents of puerperal fever were reduced when midwives and especially doctors—who so often carried germs from sickbeds into healthy homes—began washing their hands and sterilizing equipment. Surgery was transformed as the diminished risk of infection allowed for more operations. The first surgical kidney removal took place in 1876; the first successful brain surgery in modern times occurred three years later.

The increasingly scientific base of medicine and its visible success in combating disease improved its reputation. The medical profession began to control access to its ranks by establishing powerful professional associations: The British Medical Association was founded in 1832, the American association in 1847, and the German association in 1872. Medical journals also emerged to spread scientific knowledge.

Science was fashionable. In 1869, Empress Eugénie in France had Louis Pasteur come to tea, draw blood from her finger, and examine it under a microscope, all to the astonishment of her guests. Some frogs, brought in for experimentation, escaped down palace corridors. The spectacle of science as the chic entertainment of an empress was a reminder of the increasing attention it commanded in the later nineteenth century.

Birth of the Social Sciences

The scientific method, so effective in uncovering the mysteries of nature, was now applied to history, society, and psychology. History flourished in the nineteenth century. In an era of vast transformations, many people were eager to employ scientific methods to explore their past. The father of modern historical writing is the German Leopold von Ranke (1795–1886). Departing from the tradition of earlier historians, who explained the past as the fulfillment of some overall purpose such as God's will or the liberation of humanity, Ranke insisted that the role of the historian was to "show how things actually were." Like a scientist, the historian must be objective and dispassionate. History became a discipline with common standards of evidence. Historians studied and interpreted original (or "primary") sources; they collected and published their findings; and they founded professional organizations and published major journals.

New social sciences emerged in this period. Anthropology had been the subject of speculative literature for hundreds of years, but it now combined interest in non-European societies with a search for biological sources of the intelligence and character of Europeans. The Anthropological Society, founded in Paris in 1859, searched for differences in the brains of factory workers and professionals, women and men, criminals and the law-abiding, and various nationalities and races. Led by the medical doctor Paul Broca (1824–1880), French anthropologists measured thousands of heads and reading their own prejudices into the measurements, they pronounced women, members of the working class, and nonwhite races to be naturally inferior. Even at the time some anthropologists, such as the Frenchman Léonce Manouvrier (1850–1927), argued against these methods and conclusions, and today they are considered quite meaningless. Anthropology is now understood as the comparative study of people in differing societies, but in its origins it gave apparent "scientific" backing to the era's racism, sexism, and classism.

In Britain, the main anthropological theorist was Edward Tylor (1832–1917). The son of a brass manufacturer, Tylor traveled because of ill health and came into contact with non-European peoples, who aroused his curiosity. He believed that societies were subject to discoverable scientific laws that followed evolutionary patterns. Theorizing that evolution had to do with geography as well as time, he believed that as one became distanced from Europe, humankind became increasingly primitive. The contemporary African was at a level of development similar to that of Europeans in an earlier era. Tylor believed that the conditions of non-Europeans were due not to biology but to a function of their institutions. Although they disagreed on the causes, both physical and social anthropologists generally believed in the superiority of the European race. Tylor was appointed to the first university chair in anthropology in 1884. Anthropology was slower to gain legitimacy as a profession in France because the science of human difference and inequality clashed with the stated ideals of the new democratic government. Sociology gained professional status considerably earlier.

The term *sociology*, originally coined by Comte, meant the study of society. This study began in earnest in the latter part of the century, for three reasons. First, the rise of statistics in the 1840s demonstrated that cases of human distress like suicide, disease, and infant mortality could be predicted. Even though these predictions related to the whole society and not to individuals, prediction implied the possibility of control. Second, Darwinism had sparked theorists like Herbert Spencer in England to investigate the natural evolution of human behaviors (see page 510). Third, the secular French government was concerned that society could not remain ethical in the absence of religion, and it seemed that sociology might help solve this problem. Emile Durkheim (1858–1917) led the new discipline of sociology by insisting that it was a verifiable science and that it could provide a nonreligious, factual morality. He occupied the first chair of sociology at a French university in 1887 and later founded a journal of sociology.

In the past, history, anthropology, and sociology had been the purview of amateurs; now professional historians, anthropologists, and sociologists were engaged full time in research and teaching. This led to significant advances in several disciplines, but it also led to the fragmentation and compartmentalization of knowledge. People of broad learning and expertise became far less common.

The Challenge to Religion

The scientific claims of the era seemed to clash with the traditions of religion. A number of scientists, including Darwin himself, found their Christian faith undermined by theories on evolution. Although most Europeans continued to be strongly influenced by traditional religious beliefs, they appeared less confident than in earlier eras.

After the revolutions of 1848, religion was regarded as a bulwark of order. In France, Napoleon III gave the Catholic church new powers in education, and the bourgeoisie flocked to worship. In Spain, moderates who had been anticlerical began to support the church, and in 1851 they signed a concordat declaring Roman Catholicism "the only religion of the Spanish nation." In Austria in 1855, the state surrendered to the bishops full control over the clergy, the seminaries, and the administration of marriage laws.

The papacy had been nearly overthrown in 1848, and in 1860 it lost most of its domains to Italy. Thus Pope Pius IX became a sworn enemy of liberalism, and in the *Syllabus of Errors* (1864) he condemned a long list of what he perceived to be modern errors, among them "progress," "liberalism," and "modern civilization." To establish full control over the clergy and believers, the Lateran Council in 1870 issued the controversial doctrine of papal infallibility, declaring that the pope, when speaking officially on faith and morals, was infallible. This doctrine became a target of anticlerical opinion.

The political alliance the Catholic church struck with reactionary forces meant that when new political groups came to power they moved against the church. Since the church had discouraged the unification of Italy, conflict raged between the church and the new state. When Protestant Prussia unified Germany, Chancellor Bismarck eyed Catholics with suspicion and launched a campaign against them, the *Kulturkampf* ("cultural struggle").

In France, the revolutionaries of 1789 had vilified the church along with the monarchy, for both were seen as authoritarian, hierarchical, and conservative. The antagonism between scientific republicans and religious monarchists had only grown since then. Democrats of the early Third Republic bitterly resented the church's support of the monarchist party. Anticlerics were also strongly influenced by Comte's ideas of positivism, believing that France would not be a free country until the power of the church was diminished and its antiscientific disposition was overcome. The Third Republic reduced the role of the church in education as well as some other clerical privileges.

Movements toward state secularism were sometimes accompanied by an acceptance of religious diversity. In 1854 and 1871, England opened university admission and teaching posts at all universities to non-Anglicans. Anti-Catholicism, at times a popular and virulent movement, declined in the 1870s. In France, the position of religious minorities improved. Some of the highest officials of the Second Empire were Protestants, as were some early leaders of the Third Republic.

Legal emancipation of Jews, started in France in 1791, eventually spread to the rest of the Continent. England removed restrictions on Jews when the House of Commons, in 1858, and the House of Lords, in the following decade, allowed Jews to serve in Parliament. Germany and Austria-Hungary granted Jews the rights of citizenship in the 1860s. Social discrimination continued, however, and Jews were not accepted as equals in most of European society. Although some Jews occupied high office in France and

Italy, in Germany and Austria-Hungary they had to convert before they were eligible.

In the expanding economy of western Europe, where the condition of most people was improving, the enhanced opportunities for Jews aroused relatively little attention. In other parts of Europe, they were not so fortunate. When they moved into commerce, industry, and the professions in eastern Europe, they were resented. Rashes of violence against them, called *pogroms,* broke out in Bucharest, capital of Romania, in 1866 and in the Russian seaport of Odessa in 1871. Although economic rivalries may have fueled this anti-Semitism, they do not completely explain it. In most cases anti-Jewish sentiment occurred in the areas of Europe least exposed to liberal ideas of human equality and human rights.

As the continued anti-Semitism showed, religion was still a passionate issue in the nineteenth century. In fact, despite the rise of secularism, religiosity grew in some ways. In France there were frequent reported sightings of the Virgin Mary. A shepherdess in 1858 claimed to have seen and spoken with her at Lourdes, which became an important shrine whose waters were reputed to heal the lame and the sick. In 1872 construction of a rail line allowed 100,000 people a year to visit the town.

Church attendance continued to be high, especially in rural areas. In England villagers usually attended church, many twice or more each Sunday, and children attended Sunday schools. Advances in printing made it possible to distribute large quantities of cheap religious tracts to a sizable and avid readership. The faithful eagerly engaged in proselytizing, sending missionaries to all corners of the globe.

Art in the Age of Material Change

The new era of technology, science, and faith in progress was reflected in the arts. Photography, for instance, had a direct impact on painting. Experiments in the late eighteenth century and the inventions of the Frenchman Louis Daguerre (1789–1851) made the camera relatively usable in the 1830s. By the 1860s, photographic services were in high demand; in Paris alone, thirty thousand people made a living from photography and allied fields. After the invention of the miniature camera in the 1870s and celluloid film in the 1890s, the camera came into wide use. Unlike paintings, photography was accessible to the public. Many Europeans became amateur photographers—Queen Victoria and Prince Albert had a darkroom at Windsor Castle.

The ability of photography to depict a scene with exactitude had a significant impact on art. On the one hand, it encouraged artists to reproduce on the canvas a visual image akin to that of a photograph. On the other hand, in England, the pre-Raphaelites reacted against materialism, copying the symbolic imagery and innocent style of painters prior to Raphael.

In a scientific spirit, many artists discarded myths and symbols, describing the world as it actually appeared to them—everyday life in all its grimness. The realist painter Gustave Courbet (1819–1877) proclaimed himself "without ideals and without religion." Similarly, his fellow Frenchman, Jean-François Millet (1814–1875), refused to romanticize peasants as earlier artists had, depicting the harsh conditions in which they labored. In painting historical scenes, artists undertook meticulous research of the landscape, architecture, fauna, and costumes of their subjects. To paint the Dead Sea in *The Scapegoat,* English artist Holman Hunt (1827–1910) traveled all the way to Palestine to guarantee an accurate portrayal of the site.

In the past, artists had been concerned about perfectly balanced composition. Under the influence of photography, they began to paint incomplete, off-center pictures. *Orchestra of the Paris Opera* by French artist Edgar Degas looks as if it has been cropped, with only half of a musician showing on each edge and the top half of the ballet dancers missing.

In 1874, Degas (1834–1917), Claude Monet (1840–1926), Camille Pissarro (1830–1903), Auguste Renoir (1840–1919), Alfred Sisley (1839–1899), and Berthe Morisot (1841–1895) opened an exhibition in Paris that a critic disparagingly called "impressionist." The impressionist artists

Courbet: The Stone Breakers This realistic 1849 painting depicts the rough existence of manual laborers. The bleakness of the subject matter and the style in which it was carried out characterized much of the realistic school of art. *(The Stone Breakers, 1849 [destroyed 1945], by Gustave Courbet [1819–1877], Gemaldegalerie, Dresden, Germany/Bridgeman Art Library, London/New York)*

increasingly painted outdoors, in the natural light. Monet was particularly interested in painting several views of the same scene, showing how the image of a street or cathedral varied with small changes in viewpoint, weather, and time of day.

The school of realism also influenced literature, especially the novel. In realist novels, life was not glorified or infused with mythical elements; the stark existence of daily life was seen as a suitable subject. Charles Dickens (1812–1870), who came from a poor background and had experienced the inhumanity of the London underworld, wrote novels depicting the lot of the poor with humor and sympathy. The appalling social conditions he described helped educate his large middle-class audience on the state of the poor. And yet, reflecting his own rise to the middle

class, he provided numerous examples of individuals who improved their circumstances through cleverness and hard work.

Another realist, the French novelist Gustave Flaubert (1821–1880), consciously debunked the romanticism of his elders. His famous novel, *Madame Bovary*, describes middle-class life as bleak, boring, and meaningless. The heroine seeks to escape the narrow confines of provincial life through adulterous and disastrous affairs.

Emile Zola (1840–1902), another Frenchman, belonged to the naturalist school of literature—distinguished from realism by its interest in precise, objective analysis offered without philosophical or moral commentary. The writer, Zola claimed, should be like a surgeon or chemist, providing a scientific cause and record of human behavior. In his Rougon-Macquart series,

~ ENCOUNTERS WITH THE WEST ~

A Chinese Official's Views of European Material Progress

Educated in European universities, Ku Hung-Ming rose to become a high official in the Chinese court. His essays were penned under the impact of the European military intervention in China during the Boxer Rebellion in 1900. Ku denounced European notions of superiority over Asia, arguing that material progress was an inappropriate measure of a civilization.

In order to estimate the value of a civilisation, it seems to me, the question we must finally ask is not what great cities, what magnificent houses, what fine roads it has built and is able to build; what beautiful and comfortable furniture, what clever and useful implements, tools and instruments it has made and is able to make; no, not even what institutions, what arts and sciences it has invested: the question we must ask, in order to estimate the value of a civilisation,—is, *what type of humanity, what kind of men and women it has been able to produce.* In fact, the man and woman,—the type of human beings—which a civilisation produces, it is this which shows the essence, the personality, so to speak, the soul of that civilisation. Now if the men and women of a civilisation show the essence, the personality and soul of that civilisation, the language which the men and women in that civilisation speak, shows the essence, the personality, the soul of the men and women of that civilisation. . . .

To Europeans, and especially to unthinking practical Englishmen, who are accustomed to take what modern political economists call "the standard of living" as the test of the moral culture of or civilisation of a people, the actual life of the Chinese and of the people of the East at the present day, will no doubt appear very sordid and undesirable. But the standard of living by itself is not a proper test of the civilisation of a people. The standard of living in America at the present day, is, I believe, much higher than it is in Germany. But although the son of an American millionaire, who regards the simple and comparatively low standard of living among the professors of a German University, may doubt the value of the education in such a University, yet no educated man, I believe, who has travelled in both countries, will admit that the Germans are a less civilised people than the Americans.

Source: Ku Hung-Ming, *The Spirit of the Chinese People*, 2d ed. (Beijing: Commercial Press, 1922), pp. 1, 144–145.

---

which describes the lives of several generations of a family, Zola incorporated the anthropological ideas of the era. His characters are deeply defined by their heredity, such that a moral or a criminal ancestor determines a character's biological destiny either to succeed or to fall into degradation.

The Russian novelist Leo Tolstoy (1828–1910) brought a new perspective to the historical novel in *War and Peace.* Instead of a heroic approach to battle, he showed individuals caught in forces beyond their control. Small and insignificant events, rather than major ones, seem to govern human destiny. Another Russian novelist often associated with the realist school, Feodor Dostoyevsky (1821–1881), aimed to portray realistically the psychological dimensions of his characters in *Crime and Punishment* (1866), *The Idiot* (1868), and *The Brothers Karamazov* (1879–1880). Though realism was often associated with science, Dostoyevsky used it to emphasize the spiritualism of his characters. When his books were translated into French and English, they had a striking effect on readers in western Europe.

Although material progress was generally celebrated in this era, a number of intellectuals reacted against it. Many feared the uniformity and valuelessness of a world based on mass production and consumption. They denounced the smug and the self-satisfied. In Britain, the historian Thomas Carlyle (1795–1881) wrote that his was not the age of progress but of selfishness and spiritual decline.

Another Englishman, John Ruskin (1819–1900), looked back to the Middle Ages as an ideal era in human history. People then did not produce with machines, but exercised craftsmanship; they had a stronger sense of community and labored for the common good. Ruskin was one of the founders of the Arts and Crafts movement, which emphasized the need to produce goods for daily use with an eye for beauty and originality. "Industry without art is brutality," Ruskin warned. As is clear in the works of Zola and Flaubert, French intellectuals also tended to reject the modern vision of progress. And some abroad were also unimpressed. (See the box "Encounters with the West: A Chinese Official's Views of European Material Progress.")

Thus, all was not optimistic in the age of optimism. If many people celebrated what they viewed as an age of progress, others claimed that under the outer trappings of material comfort lay a frightening ignorance of aesthetic, moral, and spiritual values.

half of the century. Perhaps the most striking of these middle-class values was the ideology of separate spheres based on gender. Men and women both struggled with the constraints of this ideal, but it was most confining for women, and women's movements arose all over Europe. The new wealth and technologies of this period led to improvements in both the countryside and the cities. Governments provided new services such as public education, cultural facilities, and expanded welfare.

The material changes in society were reflected in intellectual currents. Change and evolution were embraced as an explanation for the origin of species. A new confidence in scientific research led to many scientific and technical breakthroughs. Novelists and painters aimed to dissect the world around them, creating realism in the arts. Some intellectuals, however, criticized the worship of industry, science, and materialism.

Progress, as Europeans were to learn in a later era, was two-edged: The very forces that improved life for many also threatened it. The same breakthroughs in chemistry that led to the development of artificial fertilizers also provided more powerful military explosives. The expansion of education and reduction of illiteracy meant an end to ignorance but also the creation of a public that could more easily absorb messages of hate against a rival nation or against minorities at home. Material progress and well-being continued, but there were new forces in the shadows that would ultimately undermine the comforts, self-assurance, and peace of this age.

SUMMARY

During the second half of the nineteenth century, advances in industry created for many westerners an era of material plenty, providing more comforts to a larger population than ever before. It was a self-confident age that believed in progress and anticipated further improvements in its material and intellectual environment.

Economic changes transformed the class structure of many European countries, and middle-class values and tastes defined the second

NOTES

1. Quoted in Edith Thomas, *The Women Incendiaries* (London: Secker and Warburg, 1976), p. 100, as cited in Bonnie S. Anderson and Judith P. Zinsner, *A History of Their Own*, vol. 2 (New York: Harper and Row, 1988), p. 282.
2. Quoted in F. K. Prochaska, *Women and Philanthropy in Nineteenth-Century England* (Oxford: Clarendon Press, 1980), p. 220, as cited in Anderson and Zinsner, p. 184. The discussion of Butler is indebted to Anderson and Zinsner, pp. 181–184.

SUGGESTED READING

Adams, Carole Elizabeth. *Women Clerks in Wilhelmine Germany*. 1988. Provides a history of female store employees.

Bowler, Peter J. *Evolution—The History of an Idea*. Rev. ed. 1989. Written by a scientist who examines the history and development of the concept while evaluating the scientific merit of the debates.

Briggs, Asa. *Victorian Things*. 1989. Provides an amusing and instructive history of the various new objects that became part of consumer culture.

Chadwick, Owen. *The Secularization of the European Mind in the Nineteenth Century*. 1973. Considers the rise and spread of secular attitudes at the cost of religion.

Clark, T. J. *Image of the People: Gustave Courbet and the 1848 Revolution*. 1973. Explores the impact of the sociopolitical environment on Courbet's paintings and the audience's reactions to them.

Cocks, Geoffrey, and Konrad H. Jarausch, eds. *German Professions, 1800–1950*. 1990. Describes the relationship between the professions and the state.

Geison, Gerald L., ed. *Professions and the French State, 1700–1900*. 1984. Considers the development of the various professions in France.

Goldstein, Jan. *Console and Classify: The French Psychiatric Profession in the Nineteenth Century*. 1987. Excellent examination of the rise of psychiatry within the broader cultural, intellectual, religious, and political history of France.

Hobsbawm, Eric J. *The Age of Capital, 1848–1875*. 1979. Particularly strong on social and economic developments.

Lees, Andrew. *Cities Perceived: Urban Society in European and American Thought, 1820–1940*. 1985. Depicts how various writers in Europe and the United States perceived their cities.

Mayer, Arno. *The Persistence of the Old Regime—Europe to the Great War*. 1981. Argues for the persistence of the aristocracy throughout the nineteenth century.

Miller, Michael B. *The Bon Marché—Bourgeois Culture and the Department Store, 1869–1920*. 1981. Views the first and largest department store in Paris as both manifestation and promoter of bourgeois culture.

Peterson, M. Jeanne. *Family, Love, and Work in the Lives of Victorian Gentlewomen*. 1989. Offers a revisionist examination of the view that women were passive in the Victorian era.

Pilbeam, Pamela. *The Middle Classes in Europe, 1789–1914: France, Germany, Italy, and Russia*. 1990. Reviews the formation and values of the bourgeoisie in four continental European nations.

Pinkney, David. *Napoleon III and the Rebuilding of Paris*. 1958. The standard work on the urban renewal of Paris.

Pool, Phoebe. *Impressionism*. 1985. Studies the origins, accomplishments, and legacies of impressionism.

Prochaska, F. K. *Women and Philanthropy in Nineteenth Century England*. 1980. Reveals the important role women played in charity work throughout the century.

Robertson, Priscilla. *An Experience of Women and Change in Nineteenth Century Europe*. 1982. Describes the private lives of bourgeois women in the nineteenth century, emphasizing the differing national cultural traditions.

Smith, Bonnie G. *Ladies of the Leisure Class—The Bourgeoises of Northern France in the Nineteenth Century*. 1981. Emphasizes the separate world of domesticity bourgeois women created and maintained.

Thompson, F. M. L. *The Rise of Respectable Society—A Social History of Victorian Britain, 1830–1910*. 1988. Depicts considerable social mobility and well-being in Britain in the second half of the nineteenth century.

Walkowitz, Judith. *City of Dreadful Delight*. 1993. Fascinating study of the nineteenth-century urban world.

Weber, Eugen. *Peasants into Frenchmen: The Modernization of Rural France, 1870–1914*. 1976. A lively description of the process by which the French peasantry was modernized.

Weisberg, Gabriel P., ed. *The European Realist Tradition*. 1982. A multinational study revealing the pervasiveness of realism in European art.

Youngson, A. J. *The Scientific Revolution in Victorian Medicine*. 1979. A record of innovation in British medicine.

CHAPTER 22

Escalating Tensions, 1880–1914

I n the spring of 1914, U.S. President Woodrow Wilson, concerned over the growing international crisis, sent his aide, Colonel Edward House, to Europe. The colonel toured several capitals—Berlin, Paris, and London—and on May 29, 1914, he reported, "The situation is extraordinary. It is militarism run stark mad. Unless some one . . . can bring about a different understanding there is one day to be an awful cataclysm."[1] This prediction was far more accurate than House could have imagined; nine weeks later Europe was at war.

Yet the preceding years in Europe had on the whole been peaceful and prosperous. Contemporaries often characterized the generation before the war as "*la belle époque*"—the beautiful era. A growing economy provided expanding opportunities for many. The arts flourished and were celebrated. Parliamentary government continued to spread; in several nations, suffrage was extended. Yet hand in hand with these trends of apparent progress came troubling new tendencies. Several developments in the generation before 1914 undermined and threatened all the accomplishments of these years.

In many societies, governing became more complex as populations increased. The population of Europe jumped from 330 million in 1880 to 460 million in 1914. A larger population coupled with extended suffrage meant that more people participated in the political system, but it became harder to find consensus. The example of democracy in some countries led to frustration in the autocratic ones. In the same way, prosperity and economic growth aroused resentment in those who did not share in the benefits.

Intellectuals revolted against what they viewed as the smug self-assuredness of earlier years. They no longer felt certain that the world was knowable, stable, subject to comprehension and mastery by rational human beings. Some jettisoned rationality, glorifying emotion, irrationality, and, in some cases, violence.

The anxieties and tensions that beset many Europeans took a variety of forms. Ethnic minorities became the target of hatreds. Overseas, non-Europeans were forcibly put under white domination as European states embarked on a race for empire throughout the world. On the European continent, states increasingly felt insecure, worried that they would be subject to attack. They established standing armies, shifted alliances, drafted war plans, and, ultimately, went to war.

∼ *Questions and Ideas to Consider*

- Socialism had a variety of champions between 1880 and 1914. Describe some of the contrasting strategies and goals. Consider the Fabians, Ferdinand Lassalle, Karl Kautsky, and Clara Zetkin.

- Colonial conquest was not very lucrative and often quite costly. Why did the Europeans pursue new overseas empires in the late nineteenth century?

- By the end of the nineteenth century, Britain, France, and Italy were all having difficulty winning broad consensus for their policies. Why? Discuss the violent tactics associated with the Irish "home-rule" issue, the women's suffrage movement, the 1907 strikes in the Midi, and the Sicilian labor movement.

- Why were the states of Europe unafraid of war in 1914?

- How did World War I begin? How did France, Britain, and Germany get involved in a struggle over the Balkans?

FROM OPTIMISM TO ANXIETY: POLITICS AND CULTURE

Many of the beliefs and institutions that had seemed so secure in the "age of optimism" came under attack in the next generation. Forces hostile to liberalism became increasingly vocal. In the arts and philosophy, confidence was replaced by doubt, relativism, and a desire to flee the routines of everyday life.

The Erosion of the Liberal Consensus

In 1850 liberalism appeared to be the ascendant ideology, and liberals assumed that with the passage of time more and more people would be won over to their world-view. But by 1900, liberalism was facing serious challenges. Principles eroded within the liberal camp, while various ideas and movements—some new, some rooted in the past—eroded the liberal consensus. Prominent among these were socialism, anarchism, a new political right, racism, and anti-Semitism.

The undermining of the liberal consensus began among liberals themselves, who, in the face of changing circumstances, retreated from some of their basic tenets. One of the principal emphases of liberalism had always been free trade. But under the pressure of economic competition, liberals supported tariffs at home and created closed markets for the mother country overseas in the empire.

Historically, liberals had stood for the expansion of civil liberties, yet several groups were denied their rights. Power remained an exclusively male domain, and liberal men saw nothing wrong or inconsistent in denying women the vote and equal access to education and professional advancement. In the face of labor agitation, many liberals no longer unconditionally supported civil liberties and favored instead the violent crushing of strikes.

Similarly, liberals had always upheld the sanctity of private property, but under the pressure of events, they abandoned this principle as an absolute goal. To ensure workers' safety, they placed limits on employers by passing legislation on working conditions. In some countries, they supported progressive income taxes, which many perceived as a serious invasion of private property. When it became clear that a free market was unable to meet many human needs, liberals

CHAPTER CHRONOLOGY

1864	Founding of the International Workers' Association
1873	Three Emperors' League (Germany, Austria-Hungary, and Russia)
1879	Alliance between Germany and Austria
	Bismarck bans the Socialist party
1882	Triple Alliance (Germany, Austria, and Italy)
1884	Renewal of Three Emperors' League
	Fabian Society founded in Britain
1886	Gladstone proposes home rule for Ireland
1887	Reinsurance Treaty (Germany and Russia)
1889	Second International
1893	Independent Labour party established in Britain
1894	Franco-Russian Alliance
1897	Dreyfus affair rages in France
1898	Battle of Omdurman
1899	Kipling's poem "White Man's Burden"
1903	Pankhurst founds the Women's Social and Political Union
1904	Anglo-French Entente
1905	Einstein proposes the theory of relativity
	Law separating church and state in France
1907	Anglo-Russian Entente
1911	Italy occupies Libya
1914	Archduke Francis Ferdinand and his wife assassinated

supported the introduction of welfare programs in several countries. These reforms were intended to strengthen the state by winning support from the masses, but they constituted a breach of liberal principles. The meaning of liberalism was changing and amid such inconsistency and uncertainty, many began to feel that liberal ideology could not deal with the problems of the day.

The Growth of Socialism and Anarchism

Among the groups challenging the power and liberal ideology of the middle classes were the socialist parties, both Marxist and non-Marxist, whose goal was to alleviate the plight of the workers. Socialists varied in their notions of how their goals should be achieved. Some thought they could be achieved gradually and peacefully; others were dedicated to a violent overthrow of capitalist society. Some felt that "the woman question" could be solved after the triumph of

socialism; others asserted that oppression based on sex and oppression based on class were fundamentally linked, and both required immediate attention.

In Britain, where the Liberal party was more responsive to the needs of workers than in other European states, a separate socialist party, the Independent Labour party, was established relatively late, in 1893. More influential in the late nineteenth century was the Fabian Society, founded in 1884 and championed by such figures as the social investigators Beatrice Webb (1858–1943) and Sidney Webb (1859–1947) and the playwright George Bernard Shaw (1856–1950). The Fabians believed that by gradual, democratic means, factories and land could be transferred from the private sector to the state, which would employ them for the benefit of society as a whole. Socialism would come into being not through class war but through enlightened ideas. This gradualist approach became the hallmark of British socialism.

In Germany there were two competing socialist parties. The first, founded in 1863 by Ferdinand Lassalle (1825–1864), viewed universal suffrage as the means of assuring workers' well-being. A second socialist party, formed in 1868 and influenced by Marx, called for a workers' revolution. In 1875 the two parties united around a common program.

Unification did not prevent the German Social Democratic party from a bitter debate soon to be echoed in all European socialist parties. A German socialist leader, Eduard Bernstein (1850–1932), who had visited England and soaked up the influence of the Fabians, argued in his book, *Evolutionary Socialism* (1898), that Marx was wrong in his assumption that capitalism necessarily led to increasing wretchedness for the working class. Working conditions had actually improved. By piecemeal democratic action workers could gradually win power and legislate on behalf of their interests. Since he argued for a revision of Marxist theory, Bernstein was labeled a "revisionist."

Opposing Bernstein in this debate was the party theoretician Karl Kautsky (1854–1938). Although Kautsky agreed that in material terms the workers' lot had not worsened, he insisted that workers were worse off in political terms. In Germany, he argued, workers could come to power only if they first overthrew autocracy. A violent revolution would be necessary to institute socialism. Although the German Social Democratic party officially rejected revisionism and seemed to embrace the doctrine of a violent proletarian revolution, it in fact practiced the former. It had become a part of established society and was not ready to overthrow it.

Similarly ambiguous developments occurred in neighboring France. One of Marx's French disciples, Jules Guesde (1845–1922), founded a socialist party with a strong working-class membership devoted to carrying on a workers' revolution. Opposing his brand of socialism was Jean Jaurès (1859–1914), an idealistic schoolteacher who saw socialism as an ethical system. Jaurès believed that socialism could be achieved peacefully, in cooperation with the more enlightened members of the middle class.

In 1905 the socialist parties led by Guesde and Jaurès merged, and Jaurès became virtual party leader. Although Jaurès' brand of gradual democratic socialism influenced the daily functioning of the party, the French Socialist party formally continued to adhere to Guesde's doctrine of revolution. In 1914, on the eve of war, Jaurès called on his government to avoid war, and a furious nationalist assassinated him for it.

Another movement that sought to liberate the downtrodden was anarchism, which proclaimed that humans could be free only when the state had been abolished. According to anarchist theory, in a stateless society people would naturally join together in communes and share the fruits of their labor. Some anarchists believed their goal could be reached by attacking authority. The Russian nobleman Michael Bakunin (1814–1876), frustrated at the authoritarianism of his homeland, became a lifelong anarchist. He challenged tsarism at home and participated in the 1848 revolutions throughout Europe. He viewed all governments as repressive and declared war on them: "The passion for destruction is also a creative passion." His ideas were particularly influential in Italy, Spain, and parts of France, especially among the artisan classes.

Many anarchists of this period wanted to bring about the new society by "propaganda of the deed." An attack on the bastions of power, these anarchists believed, could bring about the dissolution of the state. They formed secret terrorist organizations that assassinated heads of state or those close to them. Between 1894 and 1901, the president of France, the prime minister of Spain, the empress of Austria, the king of Italy, and the president of the United States were killed by anarchists. These murders fixed the popular image of anarchism as a violence-prone ideology and produced no particular improvement in the lives of the working-class people.

Without accepting the anarchists' methods, some in the labor movement shared their hostility toward parliamentary institutions. A working-class program, labor activists argued, could be implemented only by a pure workers' movement, such as unionization. According to this line of thought, known as *syndicalism* (after the French word for unions), workers should amass their power in unions and, at the right moment, carry out a general strike, crippling capitalist society and bringing it down.

European socialism also attempted to have an international presence. In 1864, Marx had participated in the founding of the International Workers' Association, which fell prey to internal dissension and dissolved after a few years. It was followed by a more robust organization, the Second International, in 1889. The movement's staunchly patriarchal outlook was challenged by the socialist-feminist theoretician Clara Zetkin (1857–1933). In her important work of 1889, *The Question of Women Workers*, Zetkin argued that feminism and socialism were fundamentally linked: Men were oppressed by bosses, women were oppressed by bosses and men, and freedom for all could come only from economic emancipation. Later feminists would argue that cultural stereotypes of inferiority and social double standards needed to be addressed along with economics, but Zetkin was successful for her time. Impressed by her logic and pressured by her followers, the German Socialist party began supporting women's suffrage in 1895.

Male or female, socialists were concerned over the worsening relations among European states. As early as 1893 the International called on European states to resolve their conflicts by mandatory arbitration. In 1907, sensing impending war, the International called on the workers to strike and refuse military service. However, once war broke out most socialists were swept up in nationalist fervor and went willingly to war. Zetkin and others who hoped the workers of the world would refuse to fight each other were bitterly disappointed.

The New Right, Racism, and Anti-Semitism

The traditional opponents of liberalism on the political right were the conservatives, wedded to preserving the existing order. Beginning in the 1880s, however, a populist "new right" emerged.

Although conservatives had been wary of nationalism, the new right embraced it. Many in the new right rejected doctrines of human equality and embraced racist ideologies.

Racist thinking was common in the nineteenth century. Many Europeans believed that they were the epitome of humankind while members of other races belonged to lesser groups. In midcentury the Frenchman Arthur de Gobineau (1816–1882) published his *Essay on the Inequality of Human Races*, declaring that racial inequality "dominates all other problems and is the key to it." Biologists and early anthropologists made similar statements, giving racism a scientific aura. Some races were relegated to near subhuman levels.

These ideas helped fuel anti-Semitism. For centuries Jews had been the object of suspicion and bigotry. Originally, the basis of the prejudice was religious. As early as the Middle Ages, however, the argument emerged that "Jewish blood" was different. With the popularization of scientific racist thinking in the nineteenth century, Jews were commonly viewed as a separate race, unworthy of the same rights as Christians.

Historically, Christians had relegated the Jews in their midst to marginal positions. In the Middle Ages, when land was the basis of wealth and prestige, Jews had been confined to such urban trades as cattle trading and moneylending. They incurred high risks by lending money: They often were not paid back and faced unsympathetic courts when they tried to collect on debts. To counteract these risks, Jewish moneylenders charged high interest rates that gave them the reputation as usurers.

The emancipation of the Jews, which began in France with the Revolution and spread to Germany and Austria by the 1860s, provided them opportunities they had not had before, and some members of society found it hard to adjust to the prominence a few Jews gained. Because their increased prominence and success occurred concurrently with the wrenching social transformations of industrialization and urbanization, anti-Semites pointed to the Jews as the perpetrators of these unsettling changes. Many people perceived Jews as prototypical of the new capitalist class. Although most Jews were of modest means, resentment of the rich often was aimed at Jews.

Political movements based on anti-Semitism were founded in the 1880s. They depicted Jews as dangerous and wicked and called for their exclusion from the political arena and certain professions. In some cases they suggested that Jews be expelled from the state. The mayor of Vienna, Karl Lueger (1844–1928), was elected on an anti-Semitic platform. In Berlin, the emperor's chaplain, Adolf Stöcker (1835–1909), founded an anti-Semitic party. In France, Edouard Drumont (1844–1917) published one of the best-sellers of the second half of the nineteenth century, *Jewish France,* which attributed all the nation's misfortunes to the Jews.

In Russia organized *pogroms,* or mass attacks, on Jews killed two thousand people in the 1880s and one thousand in 1905, frightening 2 million Jews into exile, mostly to the United States. Russian Jews lived under social as well as legal disabilities, winning full emancipation only with the Bolshevik Revolution of 1917.

In the face of growing hostility, some Jews speculated that they would be safe only in their own nation. The Austrian Jewish journalist Theodore Herzl (1860–1904), outraged by the Dreyfus affair in France, in which a Jewish officer was imprisoned on trumped-up charges of treason (see page 587), founded the Zionist movement. He advocated establishing a Jewish state in the Jews' ancient homeland of Israel. In the beginning, the Zionist movement won a following only in eastern Europe, where the Jews were particularly ill-treated, but in 1948, it would lead to the founding of the state of Israel.

Various manifestations of anti-Semitism revealed the vulnerability of the principle of toleration, one of the basic tenets of liberalism. It became eminently clear that racism, with its penchant for irrationality and violence, could easily be aroused.

Irrationality and Uncertainty

In contrast to the confidence in reason and science that prevailed at midcentury, the era starting in the 1880s wrestled with the issues of irrationality and uncertainty—in philosophy, in science, in the arts, even in religion. The positivism of the earlier era had neglected the emotive and intuitive aspects of life. By the 1890s a neoromantic mood, emphasizing emotion and feeling, stirred major intellectual movements.

The intellectuals who matured in the 1890s, and thus are known as "the generation of 1890," stressed the extent to which irrational forces guide human beings and their relation to one another. Nonetheless, they remained strongly affected by the positivists, adopting their scientific methods to study irrationality and hoping to find ways to make human beings more rational. Following this group came those intellectuals who matured around 1905, known as the "generation of 1905." Like their seniors, they believed human beings were irrational and the world was unknowable, but they did not express any regret at this condition. Rather, they glorified it.

The intellectual trends of the 1890s were exemplified in the work of the Austrian Sigmund Freud (1856–1939), who founded *psychoanalysis,* a method of treating psychic disorders by exploring the unconscious. Freud believed that people were motivated not only by observed reality but also by their unconscious feelings and emotions. Whereas earlier physicians had described hysteria as a physical ailment, Freud saw its roots as psychological, the result of unresolved inner conflicts. Although Freud's work was influenced by rational methods, he stressed that irrational forces played a significant role in human behavior.

In philosophy, the tension between reason and emotion was expressed in the work of the German philosopher Friedrich Nietzsche (1844–1900), who proclaimed that rationality had led humankind into a meaningless abyss. Reason would not resolve human problems, but neither would religion now that modernity had broken it down. Nietzsche famously announced that "God is dead." He celebrated this because he saw Judeo-Christian ideas of good and evil as part of a "slave morality" that cherished obedience and docility over independence and heroism. With no God, humankind was free of outside constraints. Nietzsche admonished his readers to challenge existing institutions and accepted truths and to create new ones. Realizing that these ideas could be terribly dangerous if misunderstood, he warned his readers against such misconceptions, but to little avail. Across Europe, interpretations of Nietzsche's ideas were often used to support violent, racist doctrines.

In contrast to Nietzsche, the French philosopher Henri Bergson (1859–1940) reflected the values of the generation of 1905. He argued that science—and indeed life—must be interpreted not rationally but intuitively. "Science," Bergson declared, "can teach us nothing of the truth; it can only serve as a rule of action." Meaningful truths could best be understood emotively, such as the truth of religion, literature, and art.

The scientists of this period seemed to underscore the philosophers' conclusions. In 1905, the German physicist Albert Einstein (1879–1955) proposed the theory of relativity, which undermined the certainties of Newtonian physics. Einstein demonstrated that time and space are not absolute but exist relative to the observer. Much of the research in atomic theory also revealed variations and unexplained phenomena. The work of German physicist Max Planck (1858–1947) in quantum theory showed that energy was absorbed or emitted not continuously, as previously assumed, but rather discontinuously. Some scientists were finding it increasingly difficult to believe in ultimate certainties.

In the arts, the idea of being *avant-garde*—French for "at the forefront"—took hold among creative people. Artistic movements proclaimed idiosyncratic manifestos and constantly called for the rejection of existing forms of expression and the creation of new ones. The symbolists in France and Italy, the expressionists in Germany, the futurists in Italy, and the secessionists in Austria all reflected the sense that they were living through a fractured period.

Uncomfortable with the mass culture of their day, many artists no longer wanted to portray public ideals; rather, they tended to be interested in portraying their inner conflicts and emotions.

The public at large found it difficult to decipher the meaning of the new art, but a number of patrons confirmed the avant-garde artists' talent and insight.

Unlike the realists who preceded them, artists in the 1890s surrendered to neoromanticism, trying to investigate and express inner forces. As the French painter Paul Gauguin (1848–1903) noted, the purpose of painting was to communicate not how things looked but the emotions they conveyed. The Russian Wassily Kandinsky (1866–1944) asked viewers of his art to "look at the picture as a graphic representation of a mood and not as a representation of objects." Artists appeared to be examining the hidden anxieties of society. The Austrian artist Egon Schiele (1890–1918) and the Norwegian painter Edvard Munch (1863–1944) emphasized scenes of violence, fear, and sheer horror.

Religion, too, felt the effects of these intellectual trends. Although large numbers of people still held traditional religious beliefs and followed traditional practices, indifference to organized religion spread. In urban areas of western Europe, church attendance declined. But with the decline of traditional Christian practices, various forms of mysticism became more widespread. Some people were attracted to Eastern religions like Buddhism and Hinduism and other mystical beliefs. These attitudes may have reflected a loss of faith in Western culture itself. As the century came to an end, a number of intellectuals argued that their culture was destined for decline.

THE NEW IMPERIALISM

The age of empire building that started in Europe in the sixteenth century seemed to have ended by 1750. Then, in the 1880s, the European states launched a new era of expansionism and conquered an unprecedented amount of territory. In only twenty-five years, Europeans seized 10 million square miles and subjugated 500 million people—half of the world's non-European

Munch: The Scream Painted in 1893, this work reflects the fear and alienation of modern life. (*Edvard Munch,* The Scream, *1893. Tempera and oil pastel on cardboard. 91 × 73.5 cm. Photo: J. Lathion, Nasjonalgalleriet, Oslo*)

population. European expansion was also manifest in a massive movement of people; between 1870 and 1914, 55 million Europeans migrated overseas, mainly to Australia, the United States, Canada, and Argentina.

This era of ambitious conquest is often called the "new imperialism" to differentiate it from the earlier stage of empire building. Whereas the earlier imperialism focused on the Americas, nineteenth-century imperialism centered on Africa and Asia. And unlike that in the earlier period, the new imperialism occurred in an age of mass participation in politics and was accompanied by expressions of popular enthusiasm.

Economic and Social Motives

The hope of profit overseas was crucial in the dynamic of the new imperialism. When the British explorer Henry Stanley (1841–1904) returned from Africa in the late 1870s, he told the Manchester Chamber of Commerce, "There are forty million people beyond the gateway of Congo, and the cotton spinners of Manchester are waiting to clothe them." An economic downturn in 1873 had led to a decade-long European depression, and many hoped that colonization would help solve this economic crisis. Colonies, it was believed, would provide markets for European goods that would stimulate production at home. "Colonial policy is the daughter of industrial policy," declared French Prime Minister Jules Ferry (1832–1893). Rising tariff walls between European nations made colonial markets especially attractive.

However, there is considerable evidence that colonies did not represent large markets for the mother countries. In 1914, France's colonies represented only 12 percent of its foreign trade. Great Britain's trade with its colonies represented one-third of its foreign trade, but most of that was with the settlement colonies and not those acquired through direct conquest. As for Germany, colonial trade represented less than 1 percent of its exports. France, Germany, and Great Britain continued to be one another's main customers. Still, many Europeans contended that the colonies would turn out to be profitable in the long run.

Some proponents of empire, known as social imperialists, argued that possession of an empire could resolve social issues by giving employment to the working classes and thus keeping them satisfied with their lot. British colonial secretary Joseph Chamberlain (1836–1914) was a vigorous proponent of empire and claimed that if it were lost, "half at least of our population would be starved." His fellow imperialist Cecil Rhodes (1853–1902) claimed that Britain's empire was saving the country "from a murderous civil war." In Belgium, King Leopold II (r. 1865–1909) believed that the political strife between Catholics and liberals in his state could be overcome by territorial acquisition overseas.

An empire could be an outlet for a variety of domestic frustrations, especially for nations concerned about overpopulation. German and Italian imperialists often argued that their nations needed colonies to settle their multiplying poor. Once the overseas territories were acquired, however, few found them attractive for settlement.

Nationalistic Motives

To a large extent, empire building was triggered by the desire to assert national power. At the end of the nineteenth century, two major powers emerged: Russia and the United States. Compared to them, western European nations seemed small and insignificant, and many of their leaders believed they needed to acquire large territories to compete effectively on the world stage.

The British Empire, with India as its crown jewel, was the largest, most powerful, and apparently wealthiest of all the European domains. It was the envy of Europe. Although the real source of Britain's wealth and power was the country's industrial economy, many people believed possession of a vast empire explained Britain's success. And so the British example stimulated other nations to carve out empires.

Once the European states entered the fray, they excited mutual suspicion and fear. When the French appeared to be expanding in West Africa in the 1890s, the British, afraid they would be cut off from the trade of the Niger Valley, aggressively conquered huge tracts of land that previously had been ignored. The French had begun their conquests believing that they needed to reach the Niger before the British did (Map 22.1). Thus the scramble for Africa was triggered by European rivalries, by fear of missing an opportunity that would never return. Similarly in Asia, Britain annexed Burma in 1885 under the impression that France was about to do so, while France expanded in Indochina in the 1880s and 1890s for fear the British would beat them to the punch.

France, defeated by Prussia in 1870, found in its colonies proof that it was still a Great Power. Germany and Italy, which formed their national identities relatively late, cast a jealous eye on the British and French Empires and decided that if they were to be counted as Great Powers, they too would need overseas colonies. King Leopold II of Belgium spun out plans to acquire colonies to compensate for his nation's small size. And Britain, anxious at the emergence of rival economic and political powers in the late nineteenth century, viewed its colonies as a guarantee for the future.

Worldwide strategic concerns also stimulated expansion. Because the Suez Canal assured the route to India, the British established a protectorate

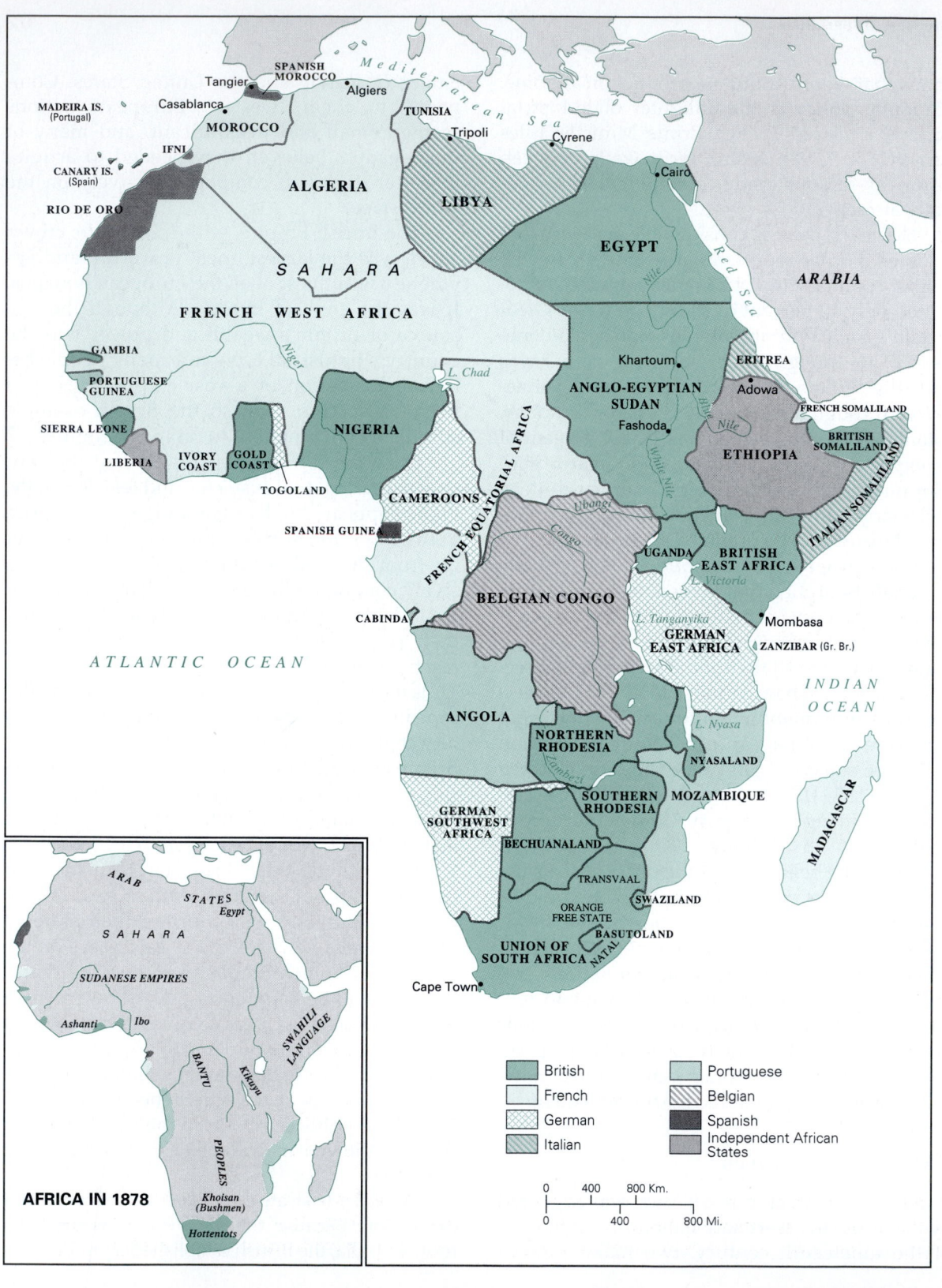

Mediterranean Sea

MADEIRA IS.
(Portugal)

SPANISH MOROCCO
Tangier
Casablanca
Algiers
TUNISIA
Tripoli
Cyrene

IFNI
CANARY IS.
(Spain)
MOROCCO

ALGERIA
LIBYA
EGYPT
Cairo

RIO DE ORO

ARABIA

S A H A R A

FRENCH   WEST   AFRICA

Red Sea

Niger

GAMBIA
PORTUGUESE
GUINEA

SIERRA LEONE

LIBERIA
IVORY
COAST
GOLD
COAST

TOGOLAND

L. Chad

NIGERIA

CAMEROONS

SPANISH GUINEA

Khartoum
ANGLO-EGYPTIAN
SUDAN
Fashoda

Blue Nile

White Nile

ERITREA
Adowa
FRENCH SOMALILAND
BRITISH
SOMALILAND

ETHIOPIA

ITALIAN SOMALILAND

FRENCH EQUATORIAL AFRICA

Ubangi

Congo

CABINDA

BELGIAN CONGO

UGANDA
BRITISH
EAST AFRICA

L. Victoria
L. Tanganyika

GERMAN
EAST AFRICA

Mombasa
ZANZIBAR (Gr. Br.)

ATLANTIC   OCEAN

INDIAN
OCEAN

ANGOLA

NORTHERN
RHODESIA

Zambezi

L. Nyasa

NYASALAND

MADAGASCAR

GERMAN
SOUTHWEST
AFRICA

SOUTHERN
RHODESIA

MOZAMBIQUE

BECHUANALAND

TRANSVAAL

SWAZILAND

ORANGE
FREE STATE
BASUTOLAND
NATAL

UNION OF
SOUTH AFRICA

Cape Town

ARAB
STATES
Egypt

SAHARA

SUDANESE EMPIRES

Ashanti
Ibo

BANTU

Kikuyu

SWAHILI
LANGUAGE

PEOPLES

Khoisan
(Bushmen)

AFRICA IN 1878

Hottentots

British
French
German
Italian

Portuguese
Belgian
Spanish
Independent African
States

0   400   800 Km.

0   400   800 Mi.

over Egypt in 1882. Then, in 1900, fearing that a rival power might threaten their position by encroaching on the Nile, they established control over the Nile Valley all the way south to Uganda. Russian expansion southward into central Asia toward Afghanistan was intended to avert a British takeover of this area, while the British movement northwestward to Afghanistan was designed to prevent Russia from encroaching on India. The "great game" played by Russia and Britain in central Asia lasted the entire nineteenth century, ending only in 1907.

Much of the expansion was due to the desire to control the often turbulent frontiers of newly acquired areas. Once these frontiers had been brought under control, there were, of course, new frontiers that had to be subdued. As the Russian foreign minister remarked, "The chief difficulty is to know where to stop." The imperial powers rarely did.

Much of the pace and direction of empire building was directed not by European governments but by "the man on the spot," the European official dispatched overseas. In 1883, British Prime Minister Gladstone sent General Charles Gordon (1833–1885) to the Sudan to supervise the withdrawal of British troops who had temporarily entered the country. Gordon disregarded his orders and tried to overthrow the local political and religious leader, the Mahdi, who counterattacked and killed Gordon. In the face of public outrage over the killing, the British annexed the Sudan.

Similarly, in 1883 France dispatched Commander Henri Rivière (1827–1883) to the southern part of Vietnam, already under French authority. Exceeding his orders, Rivière marched northward, and he and his troops were massacred. When news reached Paris, the National Assembly unanimously voted an expedition of twenty thousand men, who more than avenged the hapless commander. They brought northern Vietnam under French control.

Map 22.1 Africa in 1914 European powers conquered most of Africa in the late nineteenth century. Only Liberia and Ethiopia were left unoccupied by 1914.

Other Ideological Motives

In addition to the search for profit and nationalistic pride, a strong sense of mission was used to rationalize imperialism. Because Europeans were endowed with technical and scientific know-how, many imperialists believed it was Europe's duty to develop Africa and Asia. Railroads, telegraphs, hospitals, and schools would transform colonial peoples by opening them to what were seen as the beneficent influences of Europe. If necessary, these changes would be realized by force.

Influenced by Darwinian evolutionary theory, many argued that just as competition among species existed in nature, so did groups of humans struggle for survival. Dubbed "Social Darwinists," these thinkers envisioned a world of fierce competition. They believed that the most serious struggle was among the races.

At the same time that Europeans were making substantial material progress as a result of industrialization, their widescale expansion overseas brought them into contact with Africans and Asians who had not created an industrial economy. Europeans assumed that the dramatic disparity between their own material culture and that of colonial peoples was proof of their innate superiority.

Social Darwinists claimed that the laws of nature dictated the eclipse of weaker races and the victory of the stronger and presumably better race. Others believed that the "white man" had an obligation to dominate and lead the "lesser breeds" to a "higher stage." The British author Rudyard Kipling (1865–1936) celebrated this view in his poem "White Man's Burden" (1899):

Take up the White Man's burden—
Send forth the best ye breed—
Go bind your sons to exile
To serve your captives' need. . . .

Pointing to historic antecedents, imperialists colored their activities with a hue of heroism. Many Europeans took satisfaction in the idea that their countries were performing feats akin to those of ancient Rome or the Crusaders, spreading "civilization" to far-flung empires. Colonial writers, including Kipling, celebrated the heroism of white "men of action," while portraying "natives" as cowardly and weak.

Missionary groups were motivated by strong ideals favoring expansion. David Livingstone (1813–1873), a missionary doctor who had explored central and East Africa in the 1850s, had come across slave caravans and other practices that he found shocking. If the area were opened to commerce, he proclaimed, then Christianity and civilization would follow. His *Travels* and posthumous *Last Journals* were widely read by the British public, and they seemed to suggest that Africa would be vastly improved if it were "opened" to European contact. Missionaries were gripped by the notion of millions of "heathens" in Africa and Asia, and they welcomed European expansion to ensure the spread of Christianity.

Missionaries sometimes unwittingly started incidents that ended in conquest because they explicitly threatened indigenous social and political structures as well as religions. The execution of French missionaries in Vietnam in 1851 and 1852 led to reprisals by the French navy. The killing of missionaries in China also brought intervention by Europe. In Madagascar, competition between British Protestant and French Catholic missionaries for influence over the Malagasy queen precipitated French military intervention and conquest in 1896.

Much of the literature celebrating empire building described it in gendered terms. European men were seen as proving their virility by going overseas, conquering, and running empires. This image did not change when women heroically explored distant lands. For instance, Englishwoman Mary Kingsley (1862–1900) went on two exploration trips into Africa. Her popular books focused British interest on overseas territories, but they did not shake the established view that empire was a manly enterprise.

Conquest, Administration, and Westernization

Industrialization gave Europeans the means to conquer overseas territories. They manufactured rapid-fire weapons and had steam-driven gunboats and oceangoing vessels. Telegraphic communications allowed Europeans to gather information and coordinate military and political decision making. Such advantages made them virtually invincible in colonial conflicts. One remarkable exception was the defeat of the Italians in Adowa in 1896, when they faced an Ethiopian force that was superior in numbers and better armed.

Conquest was often brutal. In September 1898, British-led forces, armed with the recently developed machine gun, slaughtered twenty thousand Sudanese at the Battle of Omdurman. From 1904 to 1908, an uprising in southwest Africa against German rule led to the killing of an estimated sixty thousand of the Herero people; the German general, who had expressly given an order to exterminate the whole population, was awarded a medal by William II. In many colonies resistance continued long after conquest had officially been declared. Continuous skirmishes, in some cases full-scale wars, were fought. In Indochina, it took the French twenty years to defeat the "Scholars' Revolt," led by mandarins who resisted the protectorate.

Colonial governments could be brutally insensitive to the needs of the indigenous peoples. (See the box "Encounters with the West: Chief Montshiwa Petitions Queen Victoria.") To save money, France in the 1890s put large tracts of land in the French Congo under the administration of private rubber companies, which systematically and violently coerced the local people to collect rubber. When the scandal broke in Paris, the concessionary companies were abolished and the French state re-established its control.

The most notorious example of exploitation, terror, and mass killings was the Belgian Congo. Leopold II of Belgium had acquired it as a personal empire, and he mercilessly exploited it and its people. An international chorus of condemnation finally forced the king to surrender his empire and put it under the administration of the Belgian government, which abolished some of the worst features of Leopold's rule.

Though brutal and exploitive, imperialism's spread of Western technologies and values had

∽ ENCOUNTERS WITH THE WEST ∽

Chief Montshiwa Petitions Queen Victoria

In 1885 Bechuanaland in southern Africa became a British protectorate. The Bechuana leaders saw British protection as a means to prevent takeover by the Boers, Dutch-speaking white settlers who were aggressively expanding in South Africa. The British were cavalier about their responsibilities, however, and a few years later allowed the British South Africa Company, a particularly exploitive enterprise, to take control of Bechuanaland. In protest, Chief Montshiwa (1815–1896), a major chief of the Baralong people, petitioned Queen Victoria for redress. His petition was supported by missionary lobbying, and most of Bechuana was saved from the clutches of the company.

Mafeking, 16 August, 1895

To the Queen of England and Her Ministers:

We send greetings and pray that you are all living nicely. You will know us; we are not strangers. We have been your children since 1885.

Your Government has been good, and under it we have received much blessing, prosperity, and peace. . . .

We Baralong are very astonished because we hear that the Queen's Government wants to give away our country in the Protectorate to the Chartered Company; we mean the B[ritish] S[outh] A[frica] Company.

Our land there is a good land, our fathers lived in it and buried in it, and we keep all our cattle in it. What will we do if you give our land away? My people are increasing very fast and are filling the land.

We keep all the laws of the great Queen; we have fought for her; we have always been the friends of her people; we are not idle; we build houses; we plough many gardens; we sow. . . .

Why are you tired of ruling us? Why do you want to throw us away? We do not fight against your laws. We keep them and are living nicely.

Our words are No: No. The Queen's Government must not give my people's land in the Protectorate to the Chartered Company. . . .

Peace to you all, we greet you;
Please send a good word back.

I am etc,

Montshiwa

Source: S. M. Molema, *Montshiwa, 1815–1896* (Cape Town: G. Struik, 1966), pp. 181–182.

some positive results. By 1914, Great Britain had built 40,000 miles of rail in India—nearly twice as much as in Britain. In India and Egypt, the British erected hydraulic systems to irrigate previously arid lands. Colonials built cities often modeled on the European grid system, and some neighborhoods were equipped with running water and

modern sanitation. Schools, patterned after those in Europe, taught the imperial language and spread Western ideas and scientific knowledge—though to only a small percentage of the population.

Colonial rulers imposed laws and practices modeled after those of the home country. In India the colonial administration prided itself on

Victoria Terminus, Bombay Europeans' tendency to transfer values and institutions to their colonies included the export of architectural style. Various traditional European architectural styles, mainly the neo-Gothic that was so popular in nineteenth-century England, shaped this edifice, completed in 1888. *(The British Library, Oriental and India Office Collections)*

safeguarding the condition of Indian women by, for instance, abolishing in 1829 the tradition of "suttee," whereby widows were burned on their husband's funeral pyre. However, European models sometimes reduced the rights of indigenous women. In Hindu law a wife could leave her husband, but British law introduced into India the right of a husband to force his wife to return to him. In Kerala, in the southern part of the subcontinent, inheritance and descent were matrilineal (meaning they followed the mother's family line); the British tried to legislate this tradition out of existence since it disturbed their notion of the proper relationship between the sexes.

The European empire builders created political units that had never existed before. The British joined the whole Indian subcontinent under a single authority for the first time. Through a common administration, rail network, and trade, Britain gave Indians the sense of a common con-

dition, leading in 1885 to the founding of the India Congress party. Initially the party demanded reforms within the British colonial system; eventually it became the major nationalist group and called for constitutional government, representative assemblies, and the rule of law.

The ties of empire affected metropolitan cultures as well. The Hindi word for bandit became the English word *thug;* the Hindi number five, denoting the five ingredients necessary for a particular drink, became *punch.* Scenes from the colonial world often were the themes of European art, such as Paul Gauguin's paintings of Tahiti. After the turn of the century, Pablo Picasso's cubism reflected his familiarity with African art. In running the largest empire in the world, the British cultivated competitive sports and stern schooling, which, they believed, would develop "character." A growing number of people from the colonies also came to live in European cities. By 1900 some former colonists, despite various forms of discrimination, had become full participants in the life of their host country; two East Indians won election to the British parliament in the 1890s.

Overseas Migrations and the Spread of European Values

European migration overseas had begun with the expansion of European power abroad in the sixteenth century. Around 6 million people left Europe between the sixteenth and eighteenth centuries. These numbers pale in comparison to the 55 million Europeans who left the Continent for the New World, Australia, and New Zealand between 1870 and 1914 (Map 22.2).

Economic crises and overpopulation in rural Europe led many men and women to look overseas for new opportunities. They either settled permanently or labored as migrant workers to save enough money to bring back home to pay the mortgage or buy more land for their families. As many as three-quarters of all immigrants to the United States were young men. This shifted with changing economic situations: During some decades women who were domestic servants dominated Irish immigration to the United States.

The introduction of the steamship provided cheap and rapid communications with other continents. A transatlantic ticket did not cost much, and in many cases employers in the Americas advanced the price of a ticket in efforts to recruit labor. The trip was relatively short—a crossing from Liverpool to New York took no more than two weeks. In the past people had trekked for weeks from their village to the city in search of work; in the same amount of time they could now reach New York or Buenos Aires. Many envisioned the move as temporary. Of the 34 million migrants to the Americas, about a third returned to Europe. Many were truly seasonal workers, known as swallows in Italian, who went back and forth between Europe and the Americas every year.

Increased literacy, cheaper printing, and the ease of correspondence with the outside world spread what was called "America fever." Between 1900 and 1906, 3 million letters were sent to eastern Europe from the United States, and correspondence to relatives and friends boasted of the material advantages of life in the New World. A Swede who had settled in the United States wrote home, "And I can tell you that here we do not live frugally but here one has egg pancake and canned fish and fresh fish and fruits of all kinds, so it is different from you who have to sit and hold herring bones." Such letters, often reprinted in local newspapers or gathered in pamphlets, unleashed mass waves of migration.

Certain European groups migrated to specific areas. Scandinavians settled in the upper Midwest of the United States, Italians in Argentina, Germans in Paraguay, Britons in South Africa, Portuguese in Brazil, each group deeply influencing its adopted land. The upper Midwest was known as "the great desert," but Scandinavians used farm techniques from their homelands to cultivate these dry lands. German Mennonites who settled in Kansas brought with them a strain of wheat that became the basis of the state's prosperity. Durban in South Africa looks like an English city, and the Germans who came to Milwaukee, Wisconsin, made it a city of beer and strong socialist convictions.

Emigration scattered peoples and extended cultures overseas. By 1914 nearly half of all the Irish and Portuguese lived outside Europe. The settlers consumed many European goods and produced for the European market, increasing the centrality of Europe in the world market. The migrations across the globe were an added force to that of imperial conquest, further putting Europe's imprint on peoples and societies abroad.

THE DEMOCRATIC POWERS

By the end of the nineteenth century, most of Europe's political systems were in crisis. The major powers with democratic institutions—Great Britain, France, and Italy—confronted volatile public opinion and had difficulty winning broad consensus for their policies. They struggled with

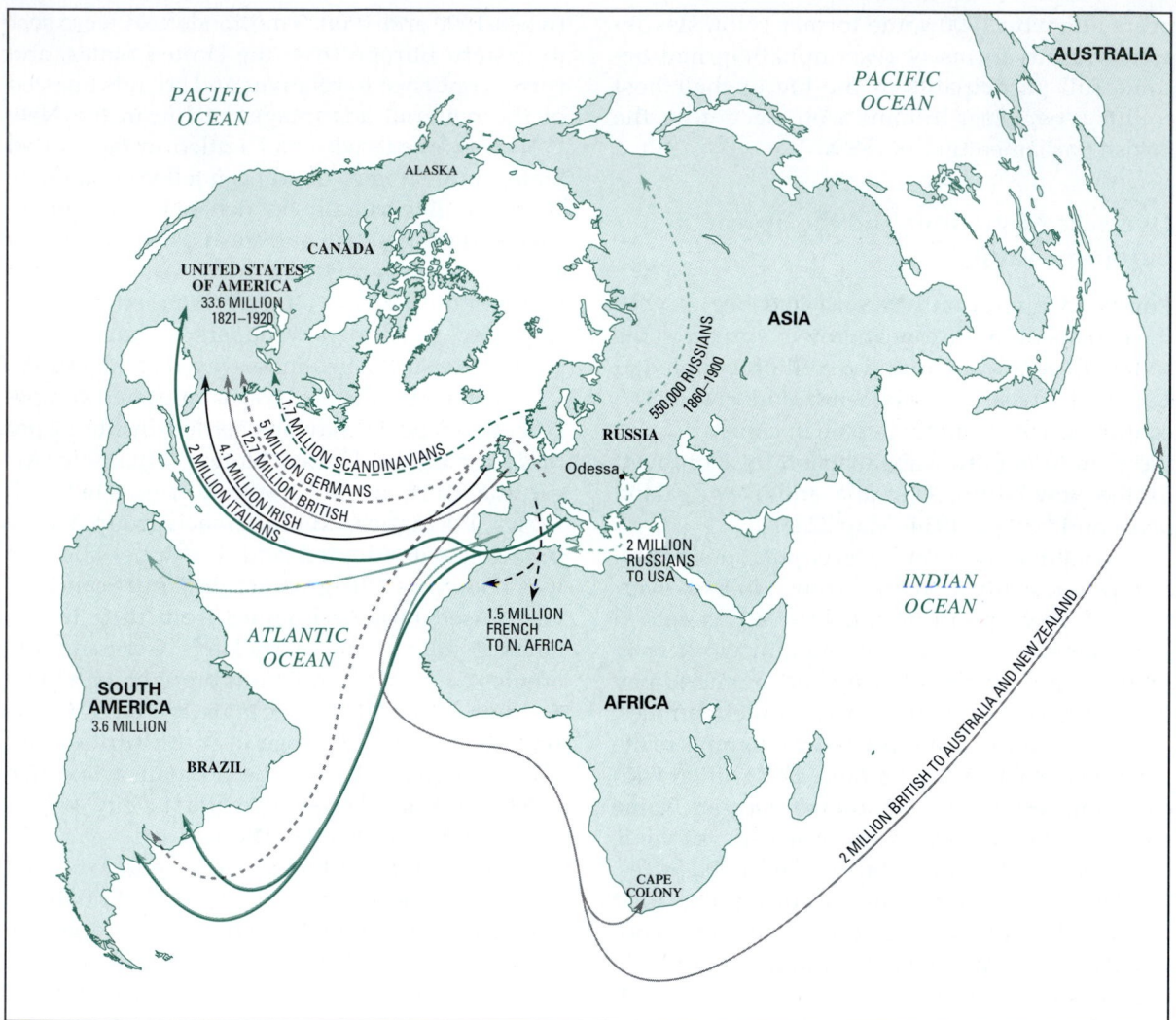

Map 22.2 European Migrations, 1820–1910 Throughout the nineteenth century, millions of Europeans left home for overseas; most headed for the United States. (*Source:* Reproduced from *The Times Atlas of World History,* 3d ed., by kind permission of Times Books. Some data from Eric Hobsbawm, *The Age of Empire, 1875–1914* [New York: Pantheon, 1987].)

new challenges emerging from an expanded electorate. Turning away from the democratic precept of resolving differences through the ballot and legislation, many people—both in government and out—were willing to resort to extraparliamentary means, including violence, to see their interests prevail.

Great Britain

In Great Britain the Reform Bill of 1884 had transformed the political landscape by doubling suffrage—giving the vote to two of every three adult men. To appeal to this enlarged electorate politicians were tempted to make promises that were often broken, to the frustration of their constituents. It was also more difficult to reach a compromise in a Parliament that no longer consisted of a fairly limited class of people with common interests and values. The British political system was faced with issues it was unable to resolve peacefully, and it was obliged—uncharacteristically—to resort to force or the threat of force.

As in earlier periods, Ireland proved to be a persistent problem. The political consciousness of the Irish had risen considerably, and they seethed under alien rule. In an attempt to quell Irish opposition in 1886, Prime Minister Gladstone proposed autonomy, or "home rule," for Ireland. The most serious objection to this plan was that if Ireland, a predominantly Catholic country, ruled itself, the Protestant majority in Ulster would be overwhelmed. "Home rule is Rome rule," chanted the supporters of Ulster Protestantism. Among Gladstone's own Liberals, many opposed changing the existing relationship between England and its possession. They seceded from the Liberals and formed the Unionist party, which, in coalition with the Conservatives, ruled the country from 1886 to 1905. When the Liberals returned to power in 1906, they proposed home rule again, but it was obstructed in the House of Lords and delayed until September 1914.

In the process of debating the Irish issue, many segments of British society resorted to extralegal tactics and even violence. Protestants in northern Ireland armed themselves, determined to resist home rule. Catholic groups, also armed, insisted on the unity of the island under home rule. The Conservative party in Britain, which opposed home rule, called on Ulster to revolt. British officers threatened to resign their commissions rather than fight Ulster. Only the outbreak of world war in 1914 delayed a showdown over Ireland, and then for only a few years.

Returned to power in 1906, the Liberals committed themselves to a vast array of social reforms but were frustrated by the difficulty of getting their program through the House of Lords. The feisty Liberal chancellor of the Exchequer, David Lloyd George (1863–1945), expressed his outrage that the will of the people was being thwarted by a handful of magnates in the House of Lords, sitting there not by election but by hereditary right.

The Liberals' social reform program included old-age pensions. To finance them, Lloyd George proposed raising income taxes and death duties and levying a tax on landed wealth. A bill with these measures easily passed the House of Commons in 1909 but was stymied in the upper chamber, where many members were prominent landowners. The House of Lords technically had the power to amend or reject a bill passed by the Commons, but for nearly 250 years it had been understood that it did not have the right to reject a money bill. Nonetheless, motivated by economic self-interest and personal spite against the Liberals, a majority in the House of Lords voted against the bill.

In reaction, in 1911, the Liberal government sponsored a bill to limit the House of Lords to a suspensive veto. This would mean that a bill defeated in the House of Lords could be prevented from going into effect for only a predetermined period—in this case, two years. The bill was quickly passed by the House of Commons, but the House of Lords had to be compelled to pass it: At the request of the government, the king threatened to appoint four hundred new lords. Under this threat, the House of Lords passed the bill.

During the debate over the bill, Conservatives, supposedly the upholders of decorum, resorted to brawling and refused to let the prime minister speak—for the first time in British parliamentary history. The British Parliament, considered the best model of free institutions, had shown itself unable to resolve issues in a reasoned manner.

Violence also appeared in another unexpected place: the women's suffrage movement. Most liberal men, when speaking of the need to extend human liberty, had excluded the female gender. Women had begun to organize groups devoted to winning the vote in the middle of the nineteenth century (see page 555). Their methods were peaceful—and they had little success. In the early twentieth century, both these factors changed.

A Suffragist Attempts to Chain Herself to the Gates of Buckingham Palace, 1914 In their effort to win the vote, women resorted to public protests, and the police often violently intervened. *(Popperfoto/Archive Photos)*

In 1903, Emmeline Pankhurst (1858–1928) and her two daughters founded the Women's Social and Political Union, whose goal was immediate suffrage. Angered by their lack of progress, the suffragists (referred to by contemporaries as "suffragettes") led by the Pankhursts began in 1906 a more militant program of protest—disturbing proceedings in Parliament, breaking windows at the prime minister's residence, burning down empty houses, dropping acid into mailboxes, and throwing bombs. There were even threats on the lives of the prime minister and king. Suffragists who were arrested often engaged in hunger strikes. In a painful and humiliating process, the authorities force-fed the women. Female protesters were also physically attacked by male thugs. (See the box "Pankhurst on Women's Rights.") At the dawn of World War I, protesters for women's

suffrage had drawn considerable attention to their cause. Women's contributions to the war effort would make it difficult for governments to continue to ignore their demands.

France

The Third Republic, founded in 1870 after France's humiliating defeat at the hands of the Prussians, also continued to face an ongoing series of crises. Challenged by enemies on the political left and right, the regime found itself buffeted from all sides.

The French government contributed to an unstable political situation by its lack of strong leadership. The need to build coalitions among the several parties in the parliament rewarded politicians who had moderate programs and

Pankhurst on Women's Rights

In 1908 the suffragists, led by Emmeline Pankhurst, issued a handbill calling on the people of London to "rush" Parliament and win the vote for women. The legal authorities interpreted their action as a violation of the peace, and several suffragists, including Pankhurst, were put on trial. They put up a spirited defense, in which Pankhurst movingly explained her motives for leading the suffragist cause.

I want you to realise how we women feel; because we are women, because we are not men, we need some legitimate influence to bear upon our law-makers.

Now, we have tried every way. We have presented larger petitions than were ever presented for any other reform, we have succeeded in holding greater public meetings than men have ever had for any reform, in spite of the difficulty which women have in throwing off their natural diffidence, that desire to escape publicity which we have inherited from generations of our foremothers; we have broken through that. We have faced hostile mobs at street corners, because we were told that we could not have that representation for our taxes which men have won unless we converted the whole of the country to our side. Because we have done this, we have been misrepresented, we have been ridiculed, we have had contempt poured upon us. The ignorant mob at the street corner has been incited to offer us violence, which we have faced unarmed and unprotected by the safeguards which Cabinet Ministers have. We know that we need the protection of the vote even more than men have needed it. . . .

We believe that if we get the vote it will mean better conditions for our unfortunate sisters. We know what the condition of the woman worker is . . . and we have been driven to the conclusion that only through legislation can any improvement be effected, and that that legislation can never be effected until we have the same power as men have to bring pressure to bear upon our representatives and upon Governments to give us the necessary legislation. . . .

I should never be here if I had the same kind of power that the very meanest and commonest of men have—the same power that the wife-beater has, the same power that the drunkard has. I should never be here if I had that power, and I speak for all the women who have come before you and other magistrates. . . .

If you had power to send us to prison, not for six months, but for six years, for sixteen years, or for the whole of our lives, the Government must not think that they can stop this agitation. It will go on. . . .

We are here not because we are lawbreakers; we are here in our efforts to become lawmakers.

Source: F. W. Pethick Lawrence, ed. *The Trial of the Suffragette Leaders* (London: The Women's Press, 1909), pp. 21–24.

were flexible. Thus there was little premium on firm ideas and commitments. Further, lackluster leadership appealed to republicans, who continued to fear that a popular leader might—as Louis Napoleon had in 1851—exploit his support to make himself dictator.

The regime lurched from scandal to scandal. The most notorious was the Dreyfus affair. In October 1894, Captain Alfred Dreyfus (1859–1935) of the French army was arrested and charged with passing military secrets to the German embassy. Dreyfus seems to have attracted suspicion because he was the only Jewish officer on the general staff. The evidence was flimsy—a letter written in a handwriting that some thought resembled that of Dreyfus.

Using this letter and materials that later turned out to be forged, the army court-martialed Dreyfus and sentenced him to life imprisonment on Devil's Island off the coast of South America. By March 1896, the general staff had evidence that it was another officer, Major Esterhazy, who was actually the spy. But to reopen the case would be to admit the army had made an error, and the general staff refused to do so.

By late 1897, when the apparent miscarriage of justice became widely known, French society split over "the affair." The political left, including many intellectuals, argued for reopening the case. For them it was crucial that justice be carried out. The army and its supporters, right-wing politicians, royalists, and Catholics, argued that the decision should not be changed. As the bulwark against internal and foreign threats, the army should be above challenge, and the fate of a single man—guilty or innocent—was immaterial.

The affair unleashed a swirl of controversy and rioting, which led the government to order a retrial in 1899. But the court again found Dreyfus guilty—this time with "extenuating circumstances" and the recommendation that he be pardoned. Finally, in 1906, Dreyfus was fully exonerated. He ended his days as a general in the army that had subjected him to so much suffering.

The strong encouragement Catholics had given to those who supported the original verdict confirmed the republicans' belief that the church was a menace to the regime. The Radical party, the staunchest backers of Dreyfus, won the elections in 1898. Despite its title, the Radical party favored moderate social reforms. It was uncompromising, however, in its anticlericalism. In 1905 the parliament passed a law separating church and state, ending the privileged position the Catholic church had enjoyed. Violent language and physical confrontations on both sides accompanied this separation. Catholics trying to prevent state officials from entering churches to take required inventories sometimes resorted to force,

using weapons or, in one case, a bear chained to the church. Armed soldiers broke down church doors and dragged monks away.

Labor problems also triggered confrontations with the government. Increased labor militancy produced long, drawn-out strikes, which in 1904 alone led to the loss of 4 million labor-days. There was agitation in the countryside, too, particularly in 1907 in the Midi, the south of France. This region had witnessed increased rural proletarianization as population grew and larger landholdings were concentrated under smaller numbers of owners. Rural militancy led to a revolt in 1907. Troops were sent in, killing dozens and winning for the Radical government the title "government of assassins."

Italy

Although unification had taken place in 1860, Italy found genuine unity elusive. The country was plagued by regionalism, social strife, and an unrepresentative political system. As in the past, the south especially challenged the central government. Assertive regionalism, brigandage, and poverty hardened the areas resistant to most government programs.

The parliamentary system established in 1860 was far from democratic. Property qualifications limited suffrage to less than 3 percent of the population. And government corrupted and co-opted the opposition so that electoral choice was short-circuited.

Between 1870 and 1890 the Italian government introduced some important reforms, but it was difficult to improve the standard of living for a people undergoing rapid population growth. In the fifty years after unification, the population increased from 25 to 35 million. In the south, a few wealthy landowners held large *latifundia*, or private estates, while the majority of the peasants were landless and forced to work for minimum wages. In the north, industrialization had started, but the region was not rich in coal or iron. To be competitive, industry paid very low wages, and the workers lived in abject misery.

Conditions on the land and in the factory led to widespread protests, followed by stern government repression. In 1893 a Sicilian labor movement won the adherence of 300,000 members, who seized land and attacked government offices. The government responded with massive force. In 1896, with unrest spreading throughout the peninsula, the government placed half the provinces under military rule. A cycle of violence and counterviolence gripped the nation. In this general atmosphere of violence, an anarchist killed King Umberto I on July 29, 1900.

After the turn of the century, a new prime minister, Giovanni Giolitti (1842–1928), tried to bring an end to the upheaval. He showed a spirit of cooperation toward the workers. Seeking to broaden his popularity by appealing to nationalist fervor, Giolitti launched an attack on Libya in 1911, wresting it from the ailing Ottoman Empire. The territory was arid and bereft of economic promise, but its conquest was championed as a proof of national virility and the foundation of national greatness.

Domestically, the nation also returned to force. A wave of workers' discontent seized the nation again, and in June 1914 a national strike led to rioting and the seizure of power in many municipalities, including Bologna. In the Romagna, an independent workers' republic was proclaimed. It took 100,000 government troops ten days to restore order. The workers' actions led some nationalist right-wing extremists to form "volunteers for the defense of order," anticipating the vigilante thugs who were to make up the early bands of Italian fascism.

THE AUTOCRACIES

Four major autocracies dominated central and eastern Europe: Germany, Austria-Hungary, the Ottoman Empire, and Russia. If the democracies were faced with difficulties in these years, the autocracies faced even more severe problems. Resistance to the autocracies included broad popular challenges to the German imperial system, the reduction of Austria-Hungary into a nearly ungovernable empire, and revolution in the Russian and Ottoman Empires.

Germany

Although Germany had a parliament, the government was answerable to the Kaiser, not the people's electoral representatives. And in the late nineteenth century, Prussia, the most reactionary part of the country, continued to dominate.

To rule effectively, Chancellor Otto von Bismarck maneuvered and intrigued to quell opposition. In the face of socialist growth, he used an attempt to assassinate the emperor as the excuse to ban the Socialist party in 1879. He succeeded in winning over both conservative agrarian and liberal industrial interests by supporting tariffs on imported foodstuffs and industrial goods. He also turned against the Catholics, who were lukewarm toward Protestant Prussia, persecuting them and their institutions. These measures, however, did not prevent the growth of the Socialist and Catholic Center parties.

Unfortunately for Bismarck, whose tenure in office depended on the goodwill of the emperor, William I died in 1888, to be succeeded first by his son, Frederick, who ruled only a few months, and then by his grandson, William II (r. 1888–1918). The young Kaiser William intended to rule as well as reign, but he was ill fit to govern. Convinced of his own infallibility, he bothered to learn very little. He hated any hints of limitation to his powers, announcing, "There is only one ruler in the Reich and I am he. I tolerate no other." He dismissed Bismarck. The schism between the two men was ideological as well as personal. William believed that Bismarck's suppression of the socialists had been ineffective and divisive. He ended the ban against the Social Democrats and sought to undermine their popularity through more subtle means, such as propaganda in the state schools.

The emperor was determined to make Germany a world power. He wanted it to have colonies, a navy, and major influence among the Great Powers. This policy, *Weltpolitik,* or "world politics," alarmed Germany's neighbors, but within Germany, it won support. Steel manufacturers and shipbuilders received lucrative contracts; workers seemed assured of employment.

Although the nationalist appeals impressed many Germans, the nation could not be easily managed. The emperor's autocratic style was challenged, and his behavior was increasingly viewed as irresponsible. In the elections of 1912, one-third of all Germans voted for the Socialist party. Thus the largest single party in the Reichstag was at least rhetorically committed to the downfall of the capitalist system and autocracy. Labor militancy reached new heights. In 1912, 1 million workers—a record number—went on strike. More and more Germans pressed for a parliamentary system with a government accountable to the people's elected representatives.

The emperor could not tolerate criticism. He frequently talked about using the military to crush socialists and the parliament. To some observers it seemed likely that the days of German autocracy were numbered—or that there would be a violent confrontation between the army and the people.

Austria-Hungary

The Austro-Hungarian Empire also faced a series of crises. In an age of intense nationalism, a multinational empire was an anomaly, as Emperor Francis Joseph (r. 1848–1916) himself acknowledged. Although the relationship between the two parts of the empire was regulated by the compromise of 1867 (see page 529), the agreement did not prevent conflict between Austria and Hungary, particularly over control of their joint army.

In the Hungarian half of the empire, the Magyars found it increasingly difficult to maintain control of the other nationalities. The Hungarian government resorted to censorship and jailings to silence nationalist leaders. In the Austrian half of the empire, the treatment of nationalities was less harsh, but the government was equally strife-ridden.

There were no easy solutions to the conflicts that the empire faced. Since much of the national

agitation was led by middle-class intellectuals, the Habsburg government introduced universal male suffrage in 1907 in an effort to undercut their influence. However, the result was an empire even more difficult to govern. It became nearly impossible to find a workable majority within a parliament that included thirty ethnically based political parties.

The virulence of debate based on nationality and class divisions grew to unprecedented extremes. Within the parliament, deputies threw inkwells at each other, rang sleigh bells, and sounded bugles. Parliament ceased to be relevant. By 1914 it had been dissolved and Austria was being ruled by decree. Emperor Francis Joseph feared the empire would not survive him.

The Ottoman Empire

In the years before 1914, no political system in Europe suffered from so advanced a case of dissolution as the Ottoman Empire, undermined by both secessionist movements within its borders and aggression from other European powers. Sultan Abdul Hamid II (r. 1876–1909) ruled the country as a despot and authorized mass carnage against those who contested his rule, earning him the title of the "Great Assassin."

Young, Western-educated Turks—the "Young Turks"—dismayed at one-man rule and the continuing loss of territory and influence, overthrew Abdul Hamid in a coup in July 1908. They set up a government responsible to an elected parliament. The Young Turks hoped to stem the loss of territory, but their efforts had the opposite effect. The various nationalities of the empire resented the attempts at "Turkification," the imposition of Turkish education and administration. Renewed agitation broke out in Macedonia, Albania, and among the Armenians. The government carried out severely repressive measures to end the unrest, killing thousands of Armenians.

For foreign powers, the moment seemed propitious to plunder the weakened empire. In 1911, Italy occupied Libya. Greece, Bulgaria, and Serbia formed an alliance, the Balkan League, which prosecuted a successful war against the empire in 1912. Albania became independent, and Macedonia was partitioned among members of the league. The empire thus lost its European possessions except for the capital, Constantinople, and a narrow strip of surrounding land.

Russia

Through the great reforms of the 1860s (see pages 539–541), the Russian autocracy had attempted to resolve many of the problems facing its empire and people. But the reforms and the major social changes of the period unleashed new forces, making it even more difficult for the tsars to rule.

The needs of a modernizing country led to an increase in the number of universities. The newly educated Russian youths began almost instantly an ardent, sustained critique of autocracy. In the absence of a large group upholding liberal, advanced ideas, university students and graduates, who came to be known as the intelligentsia, saw it as their mission to transform Russia. In the 1870s, university youths by the thousands organized a populist movement, hoping to bring change to the countryside. These youths included young women, known at the time as "Russian Amazons," who coupled their fight for peasants' rights with dedication to women's emancipation.

These youthful idealists intended to educate the peasants and make them more politically aware. But they met with suspicion from the peasantry and repression by the government. Large numbers of populists were arrested and put on trial. Frustrated, some disaffected young radicals formed the People's Will, which turned to murdering public officials to hasten the day of revolution.

Although the regime intensified repression, it also sought to broaden its public support. But in 1881, just as Tsar Alexander II was about to take a small step toward a parliamentary form of government, he was assassinated by members of the People's Will. The new ruler, Tsar Alexander III (r. 1881–1894), who had witnessed the assassination, blamed his father's leniency for his death

and sought to weaken his reforms. When Alexander's son, Nicholas II (r. 1894–1917), succeeded his father on the throne in 1894, he declared he would be as autocratic as his father. But he was a pleasant man who wanted to be liked. He lacked the forcefulness to establish a coherent policy for his troubled country.

Since the great reforms, serious problems had accumulated that threatened the stability of the regime. In the countryside the situation worsened steadily as the population exploded. The provisions that had accompanied the freeing of the serfs left considerable discontent. The peasants were not free to come and go as they pleased; they had to have the permission of the village council. Agriculture remained inefficient, far inferior to that of western Europe; hence the allotted land was insufficient to feed the peasants.

The modernization of Russia had changed it more dramatically and rapidly than any other central or eastern European state. In the 1890s an ambitious railroad-expansion program had triggered industrial development. Some factories and mining concerns were unusually large, with as many as six thousand employees. When workers grew incensed at their condition, they engaged in massive strikes that crippled industry.

Revolutionary socialist groups continued to flourish. The heirs to the populists were the Social Revolutionaries, who believed that the peasants would bring socialism to Russia. In 1898 the Russian Social Democratic party was founded. In 1903 this Marxist party split between the Mensheviks and the Bolsheviks. The Mensheviks insisted that Russia had to go through the stages of history Marx had predicted—to witness the full development of capitalism and its subsequent collapse—before socialism could come to power. The Bolsheviks, a minority group, were led by Vladimir Lenin (1870–1924), who insisted that a revolutionary cadre could seize power on behalf of the working class. Lenin favored a small, disciplined party, like the People's Will, while the Mensheviks favored a more open, democratic party.

At the turn of the century these groups were small and played a limited role in the mounting opposition to tsarism. But popular opposition

Workers' Demonstration in Moscow, 1905 In 1905 workers as well as peasants protested against the Russian autocracy. To bring the revolution under control, Nicholas II was obliged to grant several concessions. *(Novosti)*

soon grew in the face of Russian military ineptness in the war against Japan, which had broken out in February 1904 in a dispute over northern Korea. Antagonism to the tsarist regime escalated as a result of social tensions, heightened by an economic slowdown.

In January 1905, a series of demonstrations, strikes, and other acts of collective violence began. Together, they were dubbed "the revolution of 1905." One Sunday in January 1905, 400,000 workers seeking redress of their grievances gathered in front of the tsar's palace. Rather than hear their protests, officials ordered soldiers to fire on them, resulting in 150 deaths and hundreds more wounded. "Bloody Sunday" angered the populace. The tsar, instead of being viewed as an understanding, paternal authority, had become the murderer of his people. As reports reached Russia of more defeats in the war with Japan, the regime's prestige was further undermined. By September 1905, Russia had to sue for peace. Challenged in the capital, where independent workers' councils called *soviets* had sprung up, the government also lost control over the countryside, the site of widespread peasant uprisings.

Nicholas hoped to split the forces challenging him by meeting the demands for parliamentary government and granting major constitutional and civil liberties. At the end of October, the tsar established an elective assembly, the Duma, with restricted male suffrage and limited political power. When it quickly became the arena for criticism of autocracy, he suspended it and changed its electoral base and rules of operations.

The government tried to win support by reducing the peasants' financial obligations and extending local self-rule to the peasants, but it was not enough. Between emancipation and 1914 the peasant population had grown by 50 percent, but it acquired only 10 percent more land. In 1891 famine had broken out in 20 provinces, killing a quarter of a million people. Rural poverty and discontent were widespread.

Labor unrest also mounted among industrial workers. In 1912 there were 725,000 strikers, but by the first half of 1914 there were twice that number. When the French president visited St. Petersburg on the eve of the outbreak of the war, barricades were rising in workers' neighborhoods.

THE COMING WAR

Instability and upheaval characterized international relations in the years between 1880 and 1914. However, there was nothing inevitable about the outbreak of war. Good common sense dictated against it, and some intelligent people predicted that in the new modern era, war had become so destructive that it was unthinkable. Nevertheless, the Great Powers pursued diplomatic and military policies that brought them to its brink.

Power Alignments

Germany enjoyed an unchallenged position in the international order of the 1870s and 1880s. It was allied with Russia and Austria-Hungary in the Three Emperors' League, formed in 1873 and renewed by treaty in 1884. And it was part of the Triple Alliance with Austria and Italy. France was isolated, without allies. Britain, with little interest in continental affairs, appeared to be enjoying its "splendid isolation."

Germany's alliance system was not free from problems. Austria-Hungary and Russia were at loggerheads over control of the Balkans. How could Germany be the friend of both? To reassure the Russian government, Bismarck signed the Reinsurance Treaty in 1887, promising that Germany would not honor its alliance with Austria if the latter attacked Russia. After Bismarck's resignation in 1890, William II allowed the Reinsurance Treaty to lapse. Alarmed, the Russians signed the Franco-Russian Alliance in January 1894, by which each side pledged to help the other in case either was attacked by Germany.

The Great Powers on the Continent were now divided into two camps, the Triple Alliance (Germany, Austria-Hungary, and Italy) and the Franco-Russian Alliance. Britain formally belonged to neither. For a time it leaned toward the German-led alliance because France and Russia both rivaled Britain for influence in Asia, and France challenged Britain for control of Africa. However, distrust of Germany led Britain and France to resolve their difficulties overseas. In 1904, Britain and France signed an understanding, or *entente*, resolving their rivalries in Egypt, and in 1907, Great Britain and Russia regulated their competition for influence in Persia (present-day Iran) with the Anglo-Russian Entente. Now the Triple Alliance faced the Triple Entente of Great Britain, France, and Russia.

The Momentum for War

A series of crises solidified these alignments to the point where their members were willing to go to war to save them. France's attempts to take over Morocco twice led to conflict with Germany. In 1905, Germany insisted that an international conference discuss the issue and deny France this kingdom adjacent to its colony of Algeria. In 1911, when France grabbed Morocco anyway, Germany accepted the situation only after extorting compensation from the French, who deeply resented what they viewed as German bullying.

Britain also began to view Germany as a serious international menace. Over the years, Britain had developed a navy equal to none. An island nation, dependent on international trade for its economic survival, Britain saw its navy as a necessity. Germany began building its own navy in the 1890s, expressly for the purpose of challenging Britain's supremacy on the seas.

The heightened international rivalry forced the European states to increase their arms expenditures. In 1906 the British introduced a new class of ships with the launching of the *Dreadnought*. Powered by steam turbines and heavily armored, it was faster than any other ship and could not be easily sunk. Its ten 12-inch guns made it a menace on the seas. When Germany built equivalent ships, British naval supremacy was gone. Britain was feeling less secure than at any time since the Napoleonic Wars, and it continued an expensive and feverish naval race with Germany.

In Germany the changing military capacity of Russia created great anxieties. When Japan defeated the tsarist empire in 1905, the Russian military was revealed to be inferior. As a result Germany was not particularly afraid of its eastern neighbor. But stung by that humiliation, Russia had quickly rebuilt its army and planned to establish an extensive rail network in the west. To many Germans, their country appeared encircled by Russia and France. Beginning in 1912 many in the military and within the government started thinking about a preventive war. If war was inevitable, many Germans argued, it should occur before Russia became even stronger.

Many political leaders viewed the escalating arms race as a form of madness. Between 1904 and 1913 French and Russian arms expenditures increased by 80 percent; that of Germany by 120 percent; Austria-Hungary by 50 percent; and Italy by 100 percent. British Foreign Secretary Sir Edward Grey (1862–1933) warned that if the arms race continued, "it will submerge civilization."

On the whole warfare was not feared. Except for short, victorious colonial wars, the Western powers had not experienced a major conflict since the Crimean War. Russia's war against Japan in 1905 had been a calamity, but Russia could imagine that this was a nonreplicable disaster. Most policymakers believed that the next war would be short. The wars of the past half-century, notably the Austro-Prussian War of 1866 and the Franco-Prussian War of 1870, had been decided in a few weeks. Many of Europe's leaders did not dread war enough to make a major effort to prevent it.

It was the territorial rivalry between Austria and Russia that triggered international disaster. For decades the two empires had vied for control of the Balkans (Map 22.3). In 1903, following a bloody military coup that killed the king and queen of Serbia, a pro-Russian party took control of the Serbian government. It spread anti-Austrian propaganda and sought to unify under its banner the Slavs living in the Balkans, including those under Austrian rule. Many Austrian officials became convinced that the survival of the Austro-Hungarian Empire required that Serbia be destroyed.

On June 28, 1914, the heir to the Habsburg throne, Archduke Francis Ferdinand, visited Sarajevo in Austrian-ruled Bosnia. A young Bosnian Serb nationalist, hostile to Austrian rule, who had been trained and armed by a Serb terrorist group called the Black Hand, assassinated the archduke and his wife.

The assassination of the heir to the throne provided Austria with a pretext for military action. Kaiser William II, fearing that failure to support Vienna would lead to Austrian collapse and a Germany bereft of any allies, urged Austria to attack Serbia. On July 23, Austria issued an ultimatum to Serbia, deliberately worded in such a way as to be unacceptable. When Serbia refused the ultimatum, Austria declared war on July 28.

Perceived self-interest motivated each state's behavior in the ensuing crisis. Russia's status as a Great Power demanded that it not allow its client state to be humiliated, much less obliterated. In the past the French government had acted as a brake on Russian ambitions in the Balkans. France now counseled restraint, but it did not withhold its aid. France feared isolation in the face of what it perceived as growing German aggressiveness and believed that to remain a Great Power, it needed to help its ally.

German leaders may have seen the crisis as a propitious moment to begin a war that was going to occur sooner or later anyway. Germany declared war on Russia and, assuming that France would come to Russia's aid, invaded France through Belgium. The British, concerned by the threat to their ally France, and outraged by the violation of Belgian neutrality to which all the Great Powers had been signatories since 1839, declared war on Germany. Events had hurtled forward between the Austrian declaration of war on Serbia on July 28 and the British decision on August 4. Europe was at war.

SUMMARY

On the surface, the years from 1880 to 1914 seemed comfortable. More people than ever before enjoyed material advantages and an improved standard of living. Literacy spread. Death rates went down; life expectancy rose. But a revolution of rising expectations had been created, and people grew more demanding, insisting in sometimes violent ways on their political and economic rights. Although mass movements such as socialism and the women's suffrage movement generally made use of peaceful means in their campaigns to change society, some of their members advocated and employed force. Anarchism appeared to stalk Europe. And in turn, states did not hesitate to use force in efforts to quell various protest movements, even resorting to martial law.

Reflecting these trends, intellectuals like Freud and Bergson and artists like Schiele and Munch suggested that there was a hidden, irrational dimension of life beneath surface appearances. Behind the façade of security lay many disturbing impulses such as racism, anti-Semitism, and the desire to replace the emerging democracies with dictatorships.

In their relations with Africa and Asia, Europeans resorted to force to an unprecedented degree, conquering most of Africa and much of Asia. The new empires were intended to provide Europe with new sources of wealth, trade, and the trappings of power. Europeans found it nat-

Map 22.3 The Balkans in 1914 By 1914 the Ottoman Empire was much diminished, containing virtually none of Europe. Political boundaries did not follow nationality lines. Serbia was committed to unite all Serbs at the expense of the Austro-Hungarian Empire.

ural to regard themselves as belonging to a master race, destined to dominate the world.

Although most Europeans were optimistic about their future, some had serious doubts. Intellectuals spoke of decadence and decline. Statesmen, anxious to avoid the threat of national decline, resorted to extreme measures such as empire building overseas and armed competition in Europe. Among European thinkers and statesmen, force became widely accepted as the means to an end, and some leaders—notably those of Austria-Hungary and Germany—favored war over negotiation in July 1914.

The major powers—except Britain, confident in its naval dominance—built up large standing armies with millions of men and much modern equipment. Europe's network of alliances created more tension. If there were some leaders who feared war, more dreaded the consequences of not fighting, believing that war would save their regimes from the internal and external challenges they faced. Few could foresee the dire consequences of such a choice.

NOTES

1. Charles Seymour, ed. *The Intimate Papers of Colonel House,* vol. 1 (Boston: Houghton Mifflin, 1926), p. 249.

SUGGESTED READING

Baumgart, Winfried. *Imperialism—The Idea and Reality of British and French Colonial Expansion, 1880–1914.* 1989. A comparative study, emphasizing the political aspects of imperialism.

Brédin, Jean-Denis. *The Affair: The Case of Alfred Dreyfus.* 1986. The most authoritative account, written by a French lawyer; covers both the details of the affair and its context.

Bridge, F. R. *The Habsburg Monarchy Among the Great Powers, 1815–1918.* 1990. Contrary to most works on the Habsburg empire, praises Austrian leaders for preserving the empire as long as they did.

Clark, Linda L. *Schooling the Daughters of Marianne.* 1984. A study of the schooling and socialization of girls in France at the turn of the century.

Gay, Peter. *Freud—A Life for Our Time.* 1988. An admiring study by a prominent historian and trained psychoanalyst.

Hobsbawm, Eric. *The Age of Empire, 1875–1914.* 1987. A fine survey, emphasizing social change, by a leading British historian.

Hoerder, Dirk, and Leslie Page Moch, eds. *European Migrants—Global and Local Perspectives.* 1996. A collection of up-to-date articles on migrations of Europeans.

Hughes, H. Stuart. *Consciousness and Society: The Reorientation of European Social Thought, 1890–1930.* 1979. A classic on changes in European social thought.

Joll, James. *The Origins of the First World War.* 1984. A clear, concise, readable history emphasizing strategic interests and nationalist passions leading to the outbreak of the war.

Katz, Jacob. *From Prejudice to Destruction, 1700–1933.* 1980. A survey of two centuries of European anti-Semitism.

Kennedy, Paul. *The Rise and Fall of the Great Powers, 1500 to 2000.* 1987. Masterfully summarizes the factors that led to the shifting fates of the Great Powers.

Kohut, Thomas A. *Wilhelm II and the Germans—A Study in Leadership.* 1991. A psychohistorical study, analyzing the German emperor's youth and unsatisfactory relations with his parents.

Levine, Philippa. *Victorian Feminism.* 1987. Shows that Victorian women were involved in several campaigns for their rights, including the suffragist movement.

Mayeur, Jean-Marie, and Madeleine Réberioux. *The Third Republic—From Its Origins to the Great War, 1871–1914.* 1987. The most up-to-date survey of France in these years, emphasizing the emergence of republican government and the challenges it faced.

Silverman, Debora L. *Art Nouveau in Fin-de-Siècle France: Politics, Psychology, and Style.* 1989. An examination of the relationship among psychology, politics, and art.

Strobel, Margaret. *European Women and the Second British Empire.* 1991. Considers the role of women in the formation of the British Empire.

Teich, Mikulas, and Roy Porter, eds. *Fin de Siècle and Its Legacy.* 1990. A collection of critical essays summarizing the cultural trends at the end of the century.

Tickner, Lisa. *The Spectacle of Women: Imagery of the Suffrage Campaign, 1907–1914.* 1988. An extensively illustrated study of radical suffragism in Britain.

Townshend, Charles. *Political Violence in Ireland.* 1983. Studies the social and economic origins of violence in Ireland since 1848.

Wilson, Keith, ed. *Decisions for War, 1914.* 1995. A collection of articles, based on the most recent scholarship, highlighting the actions of the major and some minor powers in the crises of July 1914.

CHAPTER 23

War and Revolution, 1914–1919

**A**s the European powers prepared for a military showdown, an Egyptian-Sudanese intellectual, Mohammed Ali Duse (1867–1944), contemplated the long-term consequences the war might have: "We can only watch and pray. Unarmed, undisciplined, disunited, we cannot strike a blow; we can only await the event. But whatever that may be, all the combatants, the conquerors and the conquered alike, will be exhausted by the struggle, and will require years for their recovery, and during that time much may be done. Watch and wait! It may be that the non-European races will profit by the European disaster. God's ways are mysterious."[1] Duse was right. The fighting that began in August 1914 would become the first "world war"—a dramatic turning point in world history and the beginning of the end of European hegemony.

In Europe the overwhelming majority initially welcomed the war, but the eventual consequences for Europeans were often cataclysmic, most dramatically in the countries that met defeat. Long-standing empires and dynasties fell apart, so the map of Europe had to be redrawn after the war. World War I, known to contemporaries as "the Great War," shattered the old European order, with its assumptions of superiority, rationality, and progress.

The war proved such a turning point because the fighting, which had been expected to produce a quick result, instead bogged down in a stalemate during the fall of 1914. By the time it finally ended, in November 1918, the war had strained the whole fabric of life, affecting everything from economic organization to literary vocabulary, from journalistic techniques to the roles of women and men. The war also led to a communist revolution in Russia that had an incalculable impact on the subsequent history of the twentieth century.

∾ *Questions and Ideas to Consider*

- How did the new technologies in warfare favor those in the defensive position? What were the consequences of this?

- "Total war" required new social arrangements and innovative techniques to control public opinion. What changes occurred at the home front? What were their long-term results?

- Why did the Russian Revolution end Russia's participation in the war? Why was Lenin so concerned that the revolution spread to other European countries?

- In 1918, Germany was in a relatively favorable military situation. Many Germans wanted to work out a compromise peace while they had the chance, but military leaders persuaded Emperor William II to keep fighting. Why?

- What were the major concerns of each nation at the end of the war? In light of these concerns, was the Paris peace settlement a success?

THE UNFORESEEN STALEMATE, 1914–1917

When the war began in August 1914, enthusiasm and high morale, based on expectations of quick victory, marked both sides. But fighting on the crucial western front led to a stalemate by the end of 1914, and the particularly brutal encounters of 1916 made it clear that this was not the sort of war most had expected at its start. By early 1917 the difficulties of the war experience brought to the surface underlying questions about what it was all for—and whether it was worth the price.

August 1914: The Domestic and Military Setting

The outbreak of fighting early in August produced a wave of euphoria and a remarkable degree of domestic unity. To many, war came almost as a relief; at last, the issues that had produced

tension and intermittent crisis for the past decade would find definitive solution.

An unexpected display of patriotism by the socialist left fed the sense of domestic unity and high morale. Despite their long-standing call for international proletarian solidarity, members of the socialist parties of the Second International rallied to their respective national war efforts almost everywhere in Europe. To socialists and workers, national defense against a more backward aggressor seemed essential to the eventual creation of socialism. French socialists had to defend France's democratic republic against autocratic and militaristic Germany; German socialists had to defend German institutions, and the strong socialist organizations that had proven possible within them, against repressive tsarist Russia. The German Socialists' vote for war credits in the Reichstag on August 4 dramatically symbolized working-class support for the war.

In France the government had planned, as a precaution, to arrest roughly one thousand trade union and socialist leaders in the event of war, but no such arrests seemed necessary when the war began. Instead, the order of the day was "Sacred Union," which even entailed Socialist participation in the new government of national defense. Germany enjoyed a comparable "Fortress Truce," including an agreement to suspend labor conflict during the war, although no Socialist was invited to join the war cabinet.

The high spirits of August were possible because so few Europeans could foresee what they were getting into. It would be "business as usual," as the British government put it—no shortages, no rationing, no massive government intervention. Each side had reason for optimism: The forces of the Triple Entente outnumbered those of Germany and Austria-Hungary, but the Central Powers had potential advantages in equipment, coordination, and speed over their more dispersed adversaries.

After the fighting began, a second tier of belligerents intervened one by one, expanding the war's scope and complicating its strategy. In November 1914 the Ottoman Empire, fearful of Russia, joined the Central Powers, thereby extending

CHAPTER CHRONOLOGY

August 1914	Fighting begins	**November 1917**	Second Russian revolution: the Bolsheviks take power
September 1914	French forces hold off the German assault at the Marne		
		March 1918	Treaty of Brest-Litovsk between Germany and Russia
May 1915	Italy declares war on Austria-Hungary		
		March–July 1918	Germany's last western offensive
February–December 1916	Battle of Verdun		
		July 1918	Second Battle of the Marne
July–November 1916	Battle of the Somme		
January 1917	Germans resume unrestricted submarine warfare	**July–November 1918**	French-led counter-offensive
March 1917	First Russian revolution: fall of the tsar	**November 1918**	Armistice: fighting ends
		January 1919	Peace congress convenes at Paris
April 1917	U.S. declaration of war		
July 1917	German Reichstag war-aims resolution	**June 1919**	Victors impose Treaty of Versailles on Germany

the war along the Russo-Turkish border and on to Mesopotamia and the approaches to the Suez Canal in the Middle East. For Arabs disaffected with Ottoman rule, the war presented an opportunity to take up arms—with the active support of Britain and France. Italy, after dickering with both sides, committed itself to join the Entente with the Treaty of London of April 1915. This secret agreement specified the territories Italy was to receive in the event of Entente victory—primarily the Italian-speaking areas still within Austria-Hungary. In September 1915, Bulgaria entered the war on the side of the Central Powers, seeking territorial advantages at the expense of Serbia. Romania intervened on the side of the Entente in August 1916, hoping to seize Transylvania from Hungary.

Thus the war was fought on a variety of fronts (Map 23.1). This fact, combined with uncertainties about the role of sea power, led to ongoing debate among military decision makers about strategic priorities. Because of the antago-

nism that the prewar German naval buildup had caused, some expected that Britain and Germany would quickly be drawn into a decisive naval battle. Britain promptly instituted an effective naval blockade of Germany, but the great showdown on the seas never materialized. World War I proved fundamentally a land war.

Germany faced not only the long-anticipated two-front war against Russia in the east and France and Britain in the west; it also had to look to the southeast, given the precarious situation of Austria-Hungary. On the eastern front, Germany managed decisive victories during 1917 and 1918, forcing first Russia, then Romania, to seek a separate peace. But it was the western front that proved decisive.

Into the Nightmare, 1914

With the lessons of the wars of German unification in mind, both sides had planned for a short war based on rapid offensives. According to the

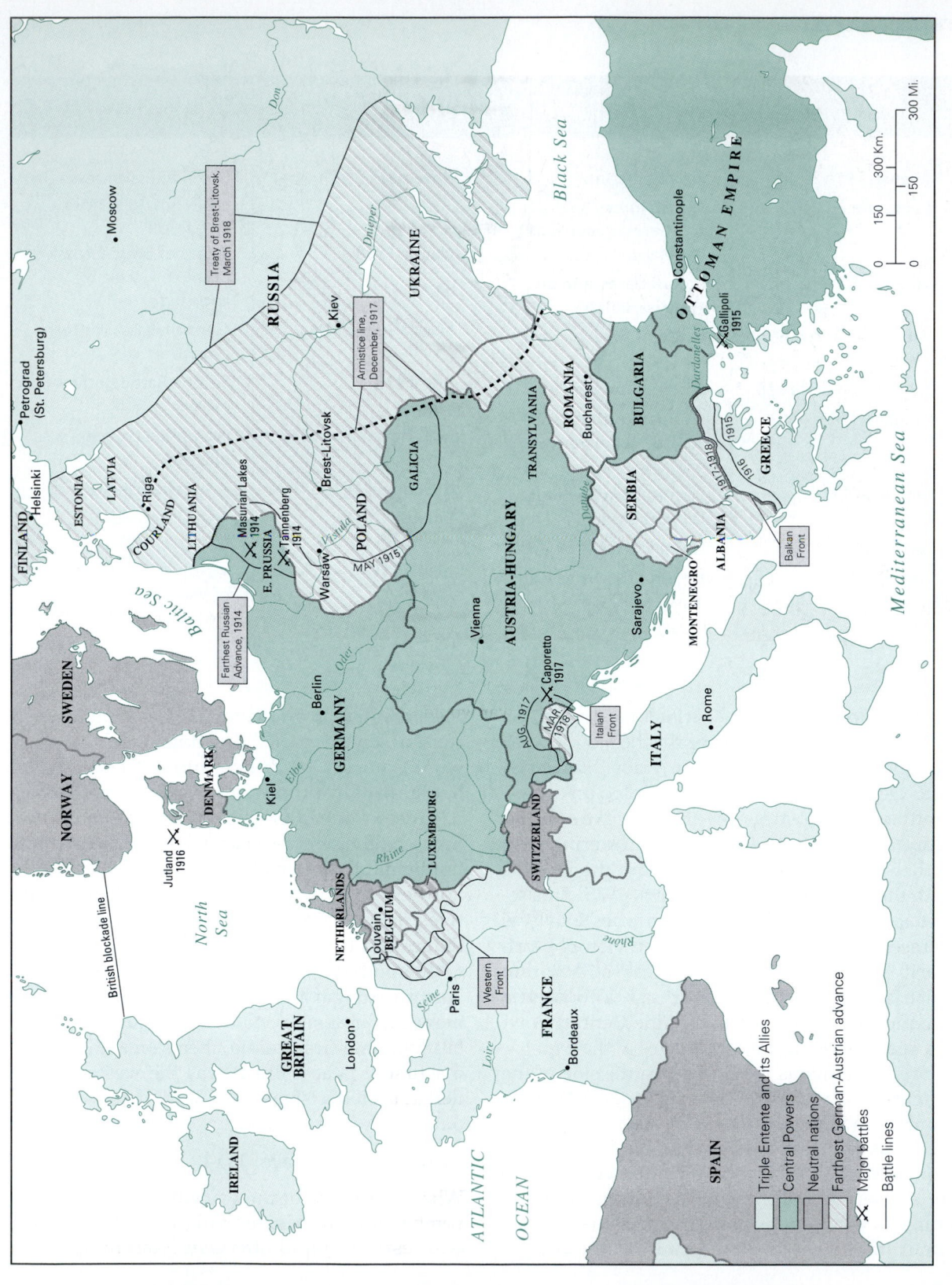

No Trenches in Sight Spirits were high early in August 1914, as soldiers like these in Paris marched off to war. None foresaw what fighting this war would be like. None grasped the long-term impact the war would have. (*Archives Larousse-Giraudon*)

Schlieffen Plan, drafted in 1905, Germany would concentrate first on France, devoting but one-eighth of its forces to containing the Russians, who were bound to need longer to mobilize. After taking just six weeks to knock France out of the war, Germany would then concentrate on Russia. French strategy, crafted by General Joseph Joffre (1852–1931), similarly relied on rapid offensives. The boys would be home by Christmas—or so it was thought.

Map 23.1 Major Fronts of World War I Although World War I included engagements in East Asia and the Middle East, it was essentially a European conflict, encompassing fighting on a number of fronts. A vast territory was contested in the east, but on the western front, which proved decisive, fighting was concentrated in a relatively small area.

Although German troops encountered more opposition than expected from the formerly neutral Belgians, they moved through Belgium into northern France during August. By the first week of September they had reached the Marne River, threatening Paris and forcing the French government to retreat south to Bordeaux. But French and British troops under Joffre counterattacked September 6–10, forcing the Germans to fall back. By holding off the German offensive at this first Battle of the Marne, the Entente had undercut the Schlieffen Plan—and with it, it turned out, any chance of a rapid victory by either side.

During the rest of the fall of 1914, each side tried—unsuccessfully—to outflank the other. When active fighting ceased for the winter in November, a military front of about 300 miles had been established all the way from Switzerland

Trench Warfare British soldier guards a trench at Ovillers, on the Somme, in July 1916. *(Trustees of the Imperial War Museum)*

to the North Sea. This line failed to shift more than 10 miles in either direction over the next three years. The result of the first six weeks of fighting on the western front was not gallant victory by either side but a grim and unforeseen stalemate.

The two sides settled into a war of attrition, constructing an elaborate network of defensive trenches. Enemy trenches were sometimes within shouting distance, so there was occasionally banter back and forth, even attempts to entertain the other side. But the trenches quickly became almost unimaginably grim—filthy, ridden with rats and lice, noisy and smoky from artillery fire, and foul-smelling, partly from the odor of decaying bodies.

As defensive instruments the trenches proved quite effective, especially because each side quickly learned to take advantage of barbed wire, mines, and machine guns to defend its positions. The machine gun had been developed before the war as an offensive weapon; few anticipated the

decided advantage it would give the defense. It proved possible to defend trenches even against massive assaults—and to impose heavy casualties on the attackers. In 1916 the tank was introduced to counter the machine gun, but, as skeptics had warned, tanks proved too unreliable to be widely effective. Although the French used them to advantage in the decisive Allied offensive in 1918, tanks were not crucial to the outcome of the war.

Though the defensive trenches had formidable advantages, neither side could give up the vision of a decisive offensive to break through on the western front. The troops were periodically called on to go "over the top" and then across "no man's land" to assault the enemy trenches. Again and again, such offensives proved futile, producing incredibly heavy casualties: "Whole regiments gambled away eternity for ten yards of wasteland."[2]

For the soldiers on the western front the war became a nightmarish experience in a hellish

Into the Trenches

As the initial offensives on the western front turned into stalemate, ordinary soldiers on both sides began to experience unprecedented forms of warfare in an eerie new landscape. Writing home to his family from France in November 1914, a young German soldier, Fritz Franke (1892–1915), sought to convey what this new war was like. He was killed six months later.

Yesterday we didn't feel sure that a single one of us would come through alive. You can't possibly picture to yourselves what such a battlefield looks like. It is impossible to describe it, and even now, when it is a day behind us, I myself can hardly believe that such bestial barbarity and unspeakable suffering are possible. Every foot of ground contested; every hundred yards another trench; and everywhere bodies—rows of them! All the trees shot to pieces; the whole ground churned up a yard deep by the heaviest shells; dead animals; houses and churches so utterly destroyed by shellfire that they can never be of the least use again. And every troop that advances in support must pass through a mile of this chaos, through this gigantic burial ground and the reek of corpses.

In this way we advanced on Tuesday, marching for three hours, a silent column, in the moonlight, toward the Front and into a trench as Reserve, two to three hundred yards from the English, close behind our own infantry.

There we lay the whole day, a yard and a half to two yards below the level of the ground, crouching in the narrow trench on a thin layer of straw, in an overpowering din which never ceased all day or the greater part of the night—the whole ground trembling and shaking! There is every variety of sound—whistling, whining, ringing, crashing, rolling . . . [ellipses in the original] the beastly things pitch right above one and burst and the fragments buzz in all directions, and the only question one asks is: "Why doesn't one get me?" Often the things land within a hand's breadth and one just looks on. One gets so hardened to it that at the most one ducks one's head a little if a great, big naval-gun shell comes a bit too near and its grey-green stink is a bit too thick. Otherwise one soon just lies there and thinks of other things. . . .

One just lives from one hour to the next. For instance, if one starts to prepare some food, one never knows if one may'nt have to leave it behind within an hour. . . .

. . . Above all one acquires a knowledge of human nature! We all live so naturally and unconventionally here, every one according to his own instincts. That brings much that is good and much that is ugly to the surface.

Source: A. F. Wedd, ed., *German Students' War Letters,* translated and arranged from the original edition of Dr. Philipp Witkop (London: Methuen, 1929), pp. 123–125.

landscape. Bombardment by new, heavier forms of artillery scarred the terrain with huge craters, which then became muddy, turning the landscape into a near swamp. (See the box "Into the Trenches.") Beginning early in 1915, tear gas, chlorine gas, and finally mustard gas were used by both sides. Although the development of gas masks significantly reduced its impact, the threat of poison gas added another horrible element to the experience of those who fought the war. The notions of patriotism, comradeship, duty, and glory began to seem absurd.

Although the Germans had been denied their quick victory in the west, by the end of 1914 they occupied much of Belgium and almost one-tenth of France, including major industrial areas and mines producing most of France's coal and iron. On the eastern front, the Germans had won some substantial advantages in 1914—but not a decisive victory.

The first season of fighting in the east suggested that the pattern there would not be trench warfare but rapid movement across a vast but thinly held front. When the fighting began in August, the Russians came more quickly than anticipated, confronting an outnumbered German force in a reckless invasion of East Prussia. By mid-September German forces under General Paul von Hindenburg (1847–1934) and his chief of staff, General Erich Ludendorff (1865–1937), repelled the Russian advance, taking a huge number of prisoners and seriously demoralizing the Russians.

As a result of their victory in East Prussia, Hindenburg and Ludendorff emerged as heroes, and they would play major roles in German public life thereafter. Hindenburg became chief of staff of the entire German army in August 1916, but the able and energetic Ludendorff remained at his side, and Ludendorff gradually assumed control of the whole German war effort, both military and domestic.

Seeking a Breakthrough, 1915–1917

In 1916, German leaders decided to launch a massive offensive against the great French fortress at Verdun, hoping to inflict a definitive defeat on France. The Germans gathered 1220 pieces of artillery for attack along an 8-mile front. Included were thirteen "Big Bertha" siege guns, weapons so large that nine tractors were required to position each of them; a crane was necessary to insert the shell, which weighed over a ton. The level of heavy artillery firepower that the Germans applied at Verdun was unprecedented in the history of warfare.

German forces attacked on February 21, taking the outer defenses of the fortress, and appeared poised for victory. The tide turned, however, when General Philippe Pétain (1856–1951)

assumed control of the French defense at Verdun. Pétain had the patience and skill necessary to organize supplies for a long and difficult siege. Moreover, he proved able to inspire affection and confidence among his men. By July the French had repelled the German offensive, although only in December did they retake the outer defenses of the fortress. The French had held in what would prove the war's longest, most trying battle—one that killed 600,000 men on both sides. For the French the Battle of Verdun would remain the epitome of the horrors of World War I.

Meanwhile, early in July 1916, the British had led a major attack at the Somme River that was similarly bloody—and that affected Britain much as Verdun affected France. On the first day the British suffered 60,000 casualties, including 21,000 killed. Fighting continued into the fall, though the offensive proved futile. One-third of those involved, or over 1 million soldiers, ended up dead, missing, or wounded.

Dominated by the devastating battles at Verdun and the Somme, the campaigns of 1916 marked the decisive end to the high spirits of the summer of 1914. Both sides suffered huge losses apparently for nothing. By the end of 1916, the front had shifted only a few miles from its location at the beginning of the year.

The French turned to new military leadership, replacing Joffre with Robert Nivelle (1856–1924), who sought to prove himself with a new offensive during the spring of 1917. Persisting even as it became clear that this effort had no chance of success, Nivelle provoked increasing resistance among French soldiers, some of whom were refusing to follow orders by the end of May.

With the French war effort in danger of collapse, the French government replaced Nivelle with General Pétain, the hero of the defense of Verdun. Pétain re-established discipline by adopting a conciliatory approach—improving food and rest, visiting the troops in the field, listening, even dealing relatively mercifully with most of the resisters. To be sure, many of the soldiers who had participated in this near-mutiny were court-martialed, and over 3400 were convicted. But of the 554 sentenced to death, only 49 were actually executed.

1917 as a Turning Point

Meanwhile, the Germans decided to concentrate on the eastern front in 1917 in an effort to knock Russia out of the war. The German offensive helped spark revolution in Russia, and in December 1917, Russia's new regime asked for a separate peace. This freed the Germans to concentrate on the west, but by this time France and Britain had a new ally.

On April 6, 1917, the United States entered the war on the side of the Entente in response to Germany's controversial use of submarines. Germany lacked sufficient strength in surface ships to break Britain's naval blockade, so the Germans deployed submarines to interfere with shipping to Britain. Submarines, however, were too vulnerable to be able to surface and confiscate goods, so the Germans had to settle for sinking suspect ships with torpedoes. In February 1915, Germany served notice that it would torpedo not only enemy ships but also neutral ships carrying goods to Britain. This German response was harsh, but so was the British blockade, which violated a number of earlier international agreements about the rights of neutral shipping and the scope of wartime blockades.

In May 1915 a German sub torpedoed the *Lusitania*, a British passenger liner, killing almost 1200 people. Partly because 128 of those killed were Americans, U.S. President Woodrow Wilson issued a severe warning, which contributed to the German decision in September 1915 to pull back from unrestricted submarine warfare. But as German suffering under the British blockade increased, pressure steadily mounted to put the subs back into action.

The issue provoked bitter debate among German leaders. Chancellor Theobald von Bethmann-Hollweg and the civilian authorities opposed resumption out of fear it would provoke the United States to enter the war. But Ludendorff and the military prevailed, arguing that even if the United States did intervene, U.S. troops could not get to Europe in time to have a major impact. Germany announced the resumption of unrestricted submarine warfare on January 31, 1917, and the United States responded with a declaration of war on April 6. Although it would take at least a year for the American troops to arrive in force, the entry of the United States gave the Entente at least the promise of more fighting power.

THE EXPERIENCE OF TOTAL WAR

As the war dragged on, the distinction between the military and civilian spheres blurred. Suffering increased on the home front, and unprecedented governmental mobilization of society proved necessary to wage war on the scale that had come to be required. Because it became "total" in this way, the war affected not simply international relations and the power balance but also culture, society, and the patterns of everyday life.

Hardship on the Home Front

The war meant food shortages, and thus malnutrition, for ordinary people in the belligerent countries, although Britain and France, with their more favorable geographical positions, suffered considerably less than others. Germany was especially vulnerable and promptly began suffering under the British naval blockade. With military needs taking priority, the Germans encountered shortages of the chemical fertilizers, farm machinery, and draft animals necessary for agricultural production. The government began rationing bread, meat, and fats in 1915. The scarcity of foodstuffs produced sharp increases in diseases like rickets and tuberculosis and in infant and childhood mortality rates in Germany.

The need to pay for the war produced economic dislocations as well. Government borrowing covered some of the cost, but to cover the rest governments all over Europe found it more palatable to inflate the currency, by printing more money, than to raise taxes. The idea was that the enemy would be made to pay once victory had been achieved. But financing the war this way meant rising prices and severe erosion of purchasing power for ordinary people all over Europe. In both France and Germany, the labor truce of 1914 gave way to increasing strike activity during 1916.

With an especially severe winter in 1916–1917 adding to the misery, there were serious instances of domestic disorder, including strikes and food riots, in many parts of Europe during 1917. In Italy, there were major strikes in Turin and other cities over wages and access to foodstuffs. The strains of war even fanned the flames in Ireland, where an uneasy truce over the home-rule controversy had accompanied the British decision for war in 1914. Unrest built up again in Ireland, culminating in the Easter Rebellion in Dublin in 1916. The brutality with which British forces crushed the uprising intensified demands for full independence.

Domestic Mobilization

Once it became clear that the war would not be over quickly, leaders realized that the outcome would not be determined on the battlefield alone. Victory required mobilizing all of the nation's resources and energies. So World War I became a total war, involving the whole society.

The British naval blockade on Germany, which made no distinction between military and nonmilitary goods, was a stratagem characteristic of total war. The goal was to damage Germany's long-term war-making capacity. And the blockade did prove significant, partly because Germany had not made effective preparations— including stockpiling—for a long war.

By the end of 1916, Germany had developed a militarized economy, with all aspects of economic life coordinated for the war effort. Under the supervision of the military, state agencies, big business, and the trade unions were brought into close collaboration. The new system included rationing, price controls, and compulsory labor ar-

bitration, as well as a national service law enabling the military to channel workers into jobs deemed vital to the war effort. Also, the Germans did not hesitate to exploit the economy of occupied Belgium, requisitioning foodstuffs even to the point of causing starvation among the Belgians themselves. They forced 62,000 Belgian workers to work in German factories under conditions of virtual slave labor. Although this practice was stopped in February 1917, by then nearly a thousand Belgian workers had died in German labor camps.

Although Germany presented the most dramatic example of domestic coordination, the same pattern was evident everywhere, even in France, with its economic individualism and distrust of an interventionist state. In Britain, the central figure was David Lloyd George (1863–1945), appointed to the newly created post of minister of munitions in 1915. During his year in that office, ninety-five new factories opened, soon overcoming the shortage of guns and ammunition that had impeded the British war effort until then. In fact, types of ammunition that had formerly taken a year to manufacture were now being produced in weeks, even days. His performance as munitions minister made Lloyd George seem the one person who could organize Britain for victory. He became prime minister in December 1916.

Shifting Gender Roles

The war effort quickened the long-term socioeconomic changes associated with industrialization. Government orders for war materiel fueled industrial expansion. The needs of war spawned new technologies—advances in food processing and medical treatment, for example—that would carry over into peacetime. And with so many men needed for military service, women were called on to assume new economic roles—running farms in France, for example, or working in the new munitions factories in Britain.

During the course of the war, the number of women employed in Britain rose from 3.25 million to 5 million. (See the box "Domestic Mobilization and the Role of Women.") In Italy, 200,000

Domestic Mobilization and the Role of Women

Early in 1917, the British writer Gilbert Stone published a remarkable collection of statements intended to illuminate the new experiences that British women were encountering in the workplace. The following passage by Naomi Loughnan, a well-to-do woman who worked in a munitions factory, makes it clear that the new work experience during the war opened the way to new questions about both gender and class.

Engineering mankind is possessed of the unshakable opinion that no woman can have the mechanical sense. If one of us asks humbly why such and such an alteration is not made to prevent this or that drawback to a machine, she is told, with a superior smile, that a man has worked her machine before her for years, and that therefore if there were any improvement possible it would have been made. As long as we do exactly as we are told and do not attempt to use our brains, we give entire satisfaction, and are treated as nice, good children. Any swerving from the easy path prepared for us by our males arouses the most scathing contempt in their manly bosoms. . . . Women have, however, proved that their entry into the munitions world has increased the output. Employers who forget things personal in their patriotic desire for large results are enthusiastic over the success of women in the shops. But their workmen have to be handled with the utmost tenderness and caution lest they should actually imagine it was being suggested that women could do their work equally well, given equal conditions of training—at least where muscle is not the driving force. This undercurrent of jealousy rises to the surface rather often, but as a general rule the men behave with much kindness, and are ready to help with muscle and advice whenever called upon. If eyes are very bright and hair inclined to curl, the muscle and advice do not even wait for a call.

The coming of the mixed classes of women into the factory is slowly but surely having an educative effect upon the men. "Language" is almost unconsciously becoming subdued. There are fiery exceptions who make our hair stand up on end under our close-fitting caps, but a sharp rebuke or a look of horror will often bring to book the most truculent. . . . It is grievous to hear the girls also swearing and using disgusting language. Shoulder to shoulder with the children of the slums, the upper classes are having their eyes pried open at last to the awful conditions among which their sisters have dwelt. Foul language, immorality, and many other evils are but the natural outcome of overcrowding and bitter poverty. If some of us, still blind and ignorant of our responsibilities, shrink horrified and repelled from the rougher set, the compliment is returned with open derision and ribald laughter. . . . On the other hand, attempts at friendliness from the more understanding are treated with the utmost suspicion, though once that suspicion is overcome and friendship is established, it is unshakable.

Source: Naomi Loughnan, "Munition Work," in Gilbert Stone, ed., *Women War Workers: Accounts Contributed by Representative Workers of the Work Done by Women in the More Important Branches of War Employment* (New York: Thomas Y. Crowell, [1917]), pp. 35–38.

women had war-related jobs by 1917. Women also played indispensable roles at the front, especially in nursing units. The expanded opportunities of wartime intensified the debate over the sociopolitical role of women that the movement for women's suffrage had stimulated. Some antiwar

ON HER THEIR LIVES DEPEND

WOMEN MUNITION WORKERS

Enrol at once

Mobilizing Women Responding to appeals like this, women quickly become prominent in the munitions industry in Britain as elsewhere. The chance to perform valued public roles during the wartime emergency proved a watershed for many women. (*Trustees of the Imperial War Museum*)

feminists argued that women would be better able than men to prevent wars. Women should have full access to public life, not because they could be expected to respond as men did but because they had a distinctive—and valuable—role to play. At the same time, by giving women jobs and the opportunity to do many of the same things men had done, the war undermined the stereotypes that had long justified restrictions on women's political roles and life choices.

For many women, serving their country in this emergency situation afforded a new sense of accomplishment, as well as a new taste of independence. Women were now much more likely to have their own residences and go out in public on their own, eating in restaurants, even smoking and drinking. Yet while many seized new opportunities and learned new skills, women frequently had to combine paid employment with housework and child rearing, and those who left home—to serve in nursing units, for example—often felt guilty about avoiding traditional family roles.

Propaganda and the "Mobilization of Enthusiasm"

Because the domestic front was crucial to sustaining a long war of attrition, it became ever more important to shore up civilian morale as the war dragged on. The result was the "mobilization of enthusiasm"—the manipulation of collective passions by national governments on an unprecedented scale. Everywhere there was extensive censorship, even of soldiers' letters from the front. Because of concerns about civilian morale, the French press carried no news of the Battle of Verdun and its horrifying casualties. In addition, systematic propaganda included attempts to discredit the enemy, even through outright falsification.

At the outset of the war, the brutal behavior of the German armies in Belgium made it easy for the French and the British to discredit the Germans. At Louvain late in August 1914 the Germans responded to alleged Belgian sniping by shooting a number of hostages and setting the town on fire, destroying the famous old library at the university. This notorious episode led the London *Times* to characterize the Germans as "Huns," a reference to the Mongol tribe that invaded Europe in the fourth century. Stories about German soldiers eating Belgian babies began to circulate.

The unprecedented propaganda combined with the unexpected destruction to give the war an increasingly catastrophic aura. Some came to believe that real peace with an adversary so evil, so different, was simply not possible. Thus, there must be no compromise, but rather total victory, no matter what the cost. At the same time, however, war-weariness produced a tendency to seek a "white peace," a peace without victory for either side. Both sets of impulses were at work in 1917, when dramatic events in Russia changed the meaning of the war for everyone involved.

TWO REVOLUTIONS IN RUSSIA: MARCH AND NOVEMBER 1917

Strained by war, the old European order finally cracked in Russia in 1917. Revolution against the tsarist autocracy seemed at first to lay the foundations for parliamentary democracy. But by the end of the year, the Bolsheviks, the smallest and most extreme of Russia's major socialist parties, had taken power, an outcome that was hardly conceivable when the revolution began.

The Wartime Crisis of the Russian Autocracy

The Russian army performed better than many had expected during the first year of the war, and as late as June 1916, it was strong enough for a successful offensive against Austria-Hungary. Russia had industrialized sufficiently by 1914 to sustain a modern war, at least for a while, and the country's war production increased significantly by 1916. But Russia suffered from problems of leadership and organization that made it less prepared for a long war than the other belligerents. Even early in 1915, perhaps a fourth of Russia's newly conscripted troops were sent to the front without weapons, instructed to pick up rifles and supplies from the dead.

Tsar Nicholas II (1868–1918) assumed personal command of the army in August 1915, but his absence from the capital only accelerated the deterioration in government. An illiterate but charismatic Siberian monk, Grigori Rasputin (ca. 1872–1916), had won favor at court for his al-

leged ability to control the hemophilia of the tsar's son, Alexis, the heir to the throne. With the tsar away, Rasputin emerged as the key political power and made a shambles of the state administration. Many educated Russians wondered if pro-German elements at court were responsible for the government chaos. Asked one Duma deputy of the government's performance, "Is this stupidity, or is it treason?" Finally, late in December 1916, Rasputin was assassinated by aristocrats seeking to save the autocracy, an act that indicated how desperate the situation was becoming.

By the end of 1916, the immediate difficulties of war had combined with the strains of rapid wartime industrialization to produce a revolutionary situation in Russia. The country's urban population had increased rapidly, and now the cities faced severe food shortages. Strikes and demonstrations spread from Petrograd (the former St. Petersburg) to other cities during the first two months of 1917. In March renewed demonstrations in Petrograd, spearheaded by women protesting the lack of bread and coal, led to revolution.

The March Revolution and the Provisional Government

At first, the agitation that began in Petrograd on March 8, 1917, appeared to be just another bread riot. Even when it turned into a wave of strikes, the revolutionary parties expected it to be crushed by the Petrograd garrison. But when called out to help the police break up the demonstrations, the soldiers generally avoided firing at the strikers. Within days, they were sharing weapons and ammunition with the workers; the garrison was going over to what was now becoming a revolution.

Late in the afternoon of March 12, leaders of the strike committees, delegates elected by factory workers, and representatives of the socialist parties formed a *soviet*, or council, following the example of the revolution of 1905, when such soviets had first appeared (see page 592). Regiments of the Petrograd garrison also began electing representatives, soon to be admitted to the Petrograd Soviet, which officially became the Council of Workers' and Soldiers' Deputies. This soviet was now the ruling power in the Russian capital. It had been elected and was genuinely representative—though of a limited constituency of workers and soldiers. Following the lead of Petrograd, Russians elsewhere began forming soviets, so that over 350 local units were represented when the first All-Russian Council of Soviets met in Petrograd in April. The overwhelming majority of representatives were Mensheviks and Socialist Revolutionaries; only about one-sixth were Bolsheviks.

On March 14 a committee of the Duma, recognizing that the tsar's authority had been lost for good, persuaded Nicholas to abdicate, then formed a new provisional government. Because it derived from the Duma elected in 1907, under extremely limited suffrage, this government was supposed to be temporary and pave the way for an elected constituent assembly, which would establish fully legitimate institutions.

Russia had apparently experienced the bourgeois revolution necessary to develop a Western-style parliamentary democracy. Even from an orthodox Marxist perspective, this was the revolution to expect, and Marxists could only help consolidate bourgeois democracy. The pursuit of socialism could take place within that new political framework. But the March revolution proved only the beginning.

The provisional government had to operate with the potentially more radical Petrograd Soviet, the keystone of the network of soviets across the country, looking over its shoulder. At first the Petrograd Soviet was perfectly willing to give the provisional government a chance to govern. In this bourgeois revolution, it was not up to socialists and workers to take responsibility by participating directly in government. Even among the Bolsheviks, there was widespread support for acceptance of the new government. Although the Bolshevik leader, Vladimir Lenin, disagreed, he was in exile in Switzerland.

The provisional government took important steps toward Western-style liberal democracy, es-

tablishing universal suffrage, civil liberties, autonomy for ethnic minorities, and labor legislation, including provision for an eight-hour workday. In response to pressure from feminists, women obtained the right to vote in all elections—along with a host of civil rights including the right to equal pay. But the government failed in two key areas, fostering discontents that the Bolsheviks soon exploited. First, it persisted in fighting the war. Second, it dragged its feet on agrarian reform.

The provisional government's determination to renew the war effort stemmed from genuine concern about Russia's obligations to its allies, about the country's national honor and position among the great powers. The educated, well-to-do Russians who led the new government expected that ordinary citizens, now free, would fight with renewed enthusiasm, like the armies that had grown from the French Revolution over a century before. These leaders failed to grasp how desperate the situation of ordinary people had become.

The March revolution had begun in the cities, but in the aftermath the peasantry had moved into action as well, seizing land and sometimes burning the houses of their landlords. By midsummer, a full-scale peasant war seemed to be in the offing in the countryside, and calls for radical agrarian reform became increasingly insistent. Partly from expediency, partly from genuine concern for social justice, the provisional government promised a major redistribution of land, but it insisted that the reform be carried out legally—not by the present provisional government, but by a duly elected constituent assembly.

Calling for elections would thus seem to have been the first priority, but the new political leaders kept putting it off. As unrest grew in the countryside, the authority of the provisional government diminished and the soviets gained in stature.

The Bolsheviks Come to Power

In the immediate aftermath of the March revolution, the Bolsheviks had not seemed to differ substantially from their rivals in the socialist movement. But the situation began to change in April, when Lenin returned from exile in Switzerland, thanks partly to the help with transportation that the German military provided. The Germans assumed—correctly, it turned out—that the Bolsheviks would undermine the Russian war effort. Largely through the force of Lenin's leadership, the Bolsheviks soon assumed the initiative.

Lenin (1870–1924), born Vladimir Ilich Ulianov, came from a comfortable upper-middle-class family. He was university-educated and trained as a lawyer. After an older brother was executed in 1887 for participating in a plot against the tsar's life, Lenin followed him into revolutionary activity. He was arrested for the first time in 1895, then exiled to Siberia. After his release in 1900, he made his way to western Europe, where he remained, except for a brief return to Russia during the revolution of 1905, until the renewal of revolution in 1917.

The Bolshevik party was identified with Lenin from its beginning in 1903, when it emerged from the schism in Russian Marxist socialism. Because of his emphases, Bolshevism came to mean discipline, organization, and a special leadership role for a revolutionary vanguard. Lenin proved effective because he was a stern and somewhat forbidding figure, disciplined, fiercely intelligent, sometimes ruthless. As a Bolshevik colleague put it, Lenin was "the one indisputable leader . . . a man of iron will, inexhaustible energy, combining a fanatical faith in the movement, in the cause, with an equal faith in himself."[3]

When Lenin began taking the initiative in 1917, his reading of the situation astonished even many Bolsheviks. He held that the revolution was about to pass from the bourgeois-democratic to a socialist phase involving dictatorship of the proletariat in the form of government by the soviets. It was time, then, for active opposition to

Lenin as Leader Although he was in exile during much of 1917, Lenin's leadership was crucial to the Bolshevik success in Russia. He is shown here addressing a May Day rally in Red Square, Moscow, on May 1, 1919. *(ITAR-TASS/Sovfoto)*

the provisional government, and this meant both criticism of the war, as fundamentally imperialist, and calls for the distribution of land from the large estates to the peasants. This latter measure had long been identified with the Socialist Revolutionaries; most Bolsheviks had envisioned collectivization and nationalization instead.

Lenin believed that a Bolshevik-led revolution in Russia would provide the spark to ignite the proletarian revolution elsewhere in Europe, especially in Germany. Although some remained skeptical, Lenin's strategic vision won acceptance among most of his fellow Bolsheviks.

In April 1917 moderate socialists still had majority support in the soviets, so the Bolsheviks sought to build gradually, postponing any decisive test of strength. Events escaped the control of the Bolshevik leadership in mid-July when impatient workers, largely Bolshevik in sympathy, took to the streets of Petrograd on their own. The provisional government had no difficulty getting military units to quell the uprising, killing two hundred in the process. Though this disturbance had developed spontaneously, Bolshevik leaders felt compelled to offer public support, and this gave the government an excuse to crack down on the Bolshevik leadership. Lenin managed to escape to Finland.

With the Bolsheviks on the defensive, counterrevolutionary elements in the Russian military attempted a coup. The provisional government, now led by the young Socialist Revolutionary Alexander Kerensky (1881–1970), had to rely on whomever could offer help—including the Bolsheviks. Bolshevik propaganda led the soldiers to refuse orders from their counterrevolutionary commanders. Within days, the Bolsheviks won their first clear-cut majority in the Petrograd Soviet, then shortly gained majorities in most of the other soviets as well.

During the fall of 1917, the situation became increasingly volatile, eluding control by anyone. People looted food from shops; peasants seized land, sometimes murdering their landlords. Desertions and the murder of officers increased within the Russian military.

With the Bolsheviks at last the dominant power in the soviets, Lenin, from his hideout in Finland, began urging the Bolsheviks to prepare for armed insurrection. The task of organizing the seizure of power fell to Leon Trotsky (1870–1940), who skillfully modified Lenin's aggressive strategy by playing up its defensive character. He argued that the provisional government would continue dragging its feet, inadvertently giving right-wing officer leagues time for another counterrevolutionary coup. This notion led people who wanted simply to defend the Petrograd Soviet to support the Bolsheviks' initiative.

During the night of November 9, armed Bolsheviks and regular army regiments occupied key points in Petrograd, including railroad stations, post offices, telephone exchanges, power stations, and the national bank. Able to muster only token resistance, the provisional government collapsed. In contrast to the March revolution, which had taken about a week, the Bolsheviks took over the capital and overthrew the government literally overnight, and almost without bloodshed. A wave of popular euphoria followed. But though the Bolsheviks had taken Petrograd, they would need three more years and a civil war to extend their control across the whole Russian Empire. No one yet knew if the Bolshevik Revolution in Russia would ignite revolution elsewhere in war-weary Europe, or if the Bolshevik regime could survive in Russia on its own.

The Russian Revolution and the War

Having stood for peace throughout the revolution, the Bolsheviks promptly moved to get Russia out of the war, agreeing to an armistice with Germany in December 1917. They hoped that Russia's withdrawal would speed the collapse of the war effort on all sides and that this, in turn, would intensify the movement toward revolution elsewhere in Europe. The Russian Revolution, they believed, was but a chapter in a larger story. As Lenin noted to Trotsky, "If it were necessary for us to go under to assure the success of the German revolution, we should have to do it.

The German revolution is vastly more important than ours."[4]

The Bolsheviks hoped to spark wider revolution by demonstrating the imperialist basis of the war. They published the tsarist government's secret documents concerning the war—the treaties and understandings specifying how the spoils were to be divided in the event of victory. In doing so, the Bolsheviks hoped to show ordinary people elsewhere that this had been, all along, a war on behalf of capitalist interests. The Bolshevik initiative added fuel to the controversy already developing in all the belligerent countries over the war's purpose and significance.

THE NEW WAR AND THE ENTENTE VICTORY, 1917–1918

Because the stakes of the war changed during 1917, the outcome, once the war finally ended in November 1918, included consequences that Europeans could not have foreseen in 1914. German defeat brought revolution against the monarchy and the beginning of a new democracy. Grand new visions competed to shape the postwar world.

The Debate over War Aims

The French and British governments publicly welcomed the March revolution in Russia, partly because they expected Russia's military performance to improve under new leadership, but also because the change of regime seemed to have highly favorable psychological implications. With Russia no longer an autocracy, the war could be portrayed—and experienced—as a crusade for democracy. At the same time, the March revolution could only sow confusion among the many Germans who had understood the war as a matter of self-defense against reactionary Russia. But the November revolution required a deeper reconsideration for all the belligerents.

Entente war aims agreements, like the Treaty of London that had brought Italy into the war in 1915, had remained secret until the Bolsheviks published the tsarist documents. Products of old-style diplomacy, those agreements had been made by a small foreign policy elite within the governing circles of each country; even the elected parliaments were generally not aware of them. The debate over war aims that developed in 1917 thus became a debate over decision making as well. In addition, there were exhortations for all the parties in the war to renounce annexations and settle for a white peace. It was time to call the whole thing off and bring the soldiers home.

To counter such sentiments, the idealistic U.S. president, Woodrow Wilson (1856–1924), insisted on the potential significance of an Allied victory. First in his State of the Union speech of January 1918, and in several declarations thereafter, Wilson developed "Fourteen Points" to guide the new international order. Notable among them were open diplomacy, free trade, reduced armaments, self-determination, a league of nations, and a recasting of the colonial system, recognizing the rights of the indigenous populations.

Lenin and Wilson, then, offered radically different interpretations of the war, with radically different implications. Yet they had something in common compared to the old diplomacy. They seemed to represent a whole new approach to international relations—and the possibility of a more peaceful world. Thus they found an eager audience among the war-weary peoples of Europe.

In Germany, antiwar sentiment grew within the Social Democratic party (SPD), finally leading the antiwar faction to split off and form the Independent Socialist party (USPD) in April 1917. A large-scale debate on war aims, linked to considerations of domestic political reform, developed in the Reichstag by the summer of 1917 and culminated in the Reichstag war-aims resolution of July 19. Affirming that Germany's purposes were solely defensive, the measure passed by a solid 60 percent majority. Germany, too, seemed open to a white peace.

But just as the dramatic events of 1917 interjected important new pressures for moderation and peace, pressures also mounted in the opposite direction. War aims grew more grandiose as it began to seem that the war offered an opportunity to secure advantages for the more contentious world that would follow. The shape of the present war convinced top German officials that Germany's geography and dependence on imports made it especially vulnerable in a long war. The purpose of the war for Germany increasingly seemed the conquest of the means to fight the next war on a more favorable footing.

When Germany established the terms of peace with Russia, it became clear how radically annexationist Germany's war aims had become. The outcome of negotiations at Brest-Litovsk early in 1918 was a dictated peace that Russia finally had no choice but to accept. Germany was to annex 27 percent of Russia's European territory, including the agriculturally valuable Ukraine, 40 percent of its population, and 75 percent of its iron and coal. All the German Reichstag parties except the Socialists accepted the terms of the treaty, which produced a new wave of enthusiasm for a victorious peace.

France, less vulnerable geographically than Germany, tended to be more modest. But news of the terms the Germans had imposed at Brest-Litovsk inflamed the French, supporting the notion that France must push on to definitive victory in order to secure substantial advantages against the German menace.

The Renewal of the French War Effort

The domestic division in France that followed the failure of Nivelle's offensive reached its peak in the fall of 1917. In November, with pressure for a white peace intensifying and France's ability to continue fighting in doubt, President Raymond Poincaré called on Georges Clemenceau (1841–1929) to lead a new government. The 76-year-old Clemenceau was known as a "hawk"; his appointment portended a stepped-up prosecution of the war.

Clemenceau moved decisively on both the domestic and military levels. By cracking down on the antiwar movement—imprisoning antiwar leaders, suppressing defeatist newspapers—he stiffened morale. Choosing a new commander of all Allied forces in the west, Clemenceau by-

passed Pétain and picked General Ferdinand Foch (1851–1929). From Clemenceau's perspective, Pétain was too passive, even defeatist. After some initial friction, Clemenceau let Foch have his way on the military level, and the two proved an effective leadership combination.

The German Gamble, 1918

As the campaign of 1918 began, Germany seemed in a relatively favorable military position: Russia had been knocked out at last, and American troops were yet to arrive. Moderates in Germany wanted to take advantage of the situation to work out a compromise peace. But the military leadership persuaded Emperor William II that Germany could still win a definitive victory on the western front if it struck quickly. Germany would be out of reserves by summer, so the alternative to decisive victory in the west would be total German defeat.

The German gamble almost succeeded. From March to June 1918, German forces seized the initiative in four months of sustained attacks. By May 30 they had again reached the Marne, where they had been held in 1914, and again Paris, only 37 miles away, had to be evacuated (see Map 23.1). As late as mid-July, Ludendorff remained confident of victory, but by mid-August it was becoming clear that Germany lacked the manpower to exploit its successes.

By mid-1918, American involvement was becoming a factor. On June 4, over a year after the U.S. declaration of war, American troops went into action for the first time, bolstering French forces along the Marne. It was a small operation, in which the Americans' performance was amateurish compared to that of their battle-seasoned allies. But as the Allied counterattack proceeded, 250,000 U.S. troops were arriving every month, boosting Allied morale and battlefield strength. By early August the whole western front began to roll back. With astonishing suddenness, the outcome was no longer in doubt, although most expected the war to drag on into 1919. Few realized how desperate Germany's situation had become.

Military Defeat and Political Change in Germany

In late September, Ludendorff realized that his armies could not stop the Allied advance, so he informed the government that to avoid invasion, Germany had to seek an immediate armistice. Hoping to secure favorable peace terms and to make politicians take responsibility for the defeat, Hindenburg and Ludendorff asked that a government based on greater popular support be formed. A leading moderate, Prince Max von Baden (1867–1929), became chancellor, and the Reichstag again became significant after its eclipse during the virtual dictatorship of the military. Prince Max replaced Ludendorff with General Wilhelm Groener (1867–1939), who seemed more democratic in orientation. It was clear that ending the war could not be separated from the push for political change in Germany.

After securing a written request for an armistice from Hindenburg, Prince Max sent a peace note to President Wilson early in October, asking for an armistice based on Wilson's Fourteen Points. During the month that followed, Prince Max undertook a series of measures, passed by the Reichstag and approved by the emperor, that reformed the constitution, expanding voting rights in Prussia and making the chancellor responsible to the Reichstag. At last Germany had a constitutional monarchy. President Wilson encouraged speculation that Germany could expect better peace terms if William II were to abdicate and Germany became a republic. But if it seemed likely that Germany was to become a parliamentary democracy, it was also possible to imagine a more radical change, perhaps inspired by the Russian example.

A radical outcome seemed a real possibility. As negotiations for an armistice proceeded in October 1918, the continuing war effort produced instances of mutiny in the navy and breaches of discipline in the army. By early November workers' and soldiers' councils were being formed all over the country, just as in Russia the year before. In Munich, on November 7, antiwar socialists led an uprising of workers and soldiers that expelled the king of Bavaria and proclaimed a new Bavarian republic, which sought its own peace negotiations with the Allies. In Berlin on November 9, thousands of workers took to the streets to demand an immediate peace, and the authorities could not muster enough reliable military force to move against them.

The senior army leadership grew concerned that the collapse of governmental authority would undermine the ability of army officers even to march their troops home. So Hindenburg and Groener persuaded the emperor to abdicate. Having lost the support of the army, William II accepted the inevitable and left for exile in the Netherlands.

With the German right, including the military, in disarray, and the centrist parties discredited by their support for what had become an annexationist war, the initiative passed to the socialists. But the socialists had divided in 1917, mostly over the question of response to the war. To many leftist socialists, the fact that the reformist mainstream of the SPD had supported the war for so long had discredited the party irrevocably. The most militant of these leftist socialists, led by Rosa Luxemburg (1870–1919) and Karl Liebknecht (1871–1919), envisioned using the workers' and soldiers' councils as the basis for a full-scale revolution.

Partly to head off the extreme left, SPD moderates proclaimed a parliamentary republic on November 9, just hours before the revolutionaries proclaimed a soviet-style republic. The next day the soldiers' and workers' councils in Berlin elected a provisional executive committee, to be led by the moderate socialist Friedrich Ebert (1871–1925). As the new republic sought to consolidate itself, the radical leftists continued to promote further revolution. So for Germany the end of the war meant a leap into an unfamiliar democratic republic, which had to establish itself in conditions not only of military defeat and economic hardship but also of incipient revolution on the extreme left.

Birth from military defeat was especially disabling for the new republic because the German people were so little prepared for the defeat when it came. Censorship had kept the public from any grasp of Germany's real situation, so the request for an armistice came as a shock. At no time during the war had Germany been invaded from the west, and in mid-1918 the German army had seemed on the brink of victory. It appeared inconceivable that Germany had lost on the battlefield. Thus the "stab in the back" myth, the notion that political intrigue had undermined the German military effort, developed to explain what seemed an inexplicable defeat.

THE OUTCOME AND THE IMPACT

After the armistice officially ended the fighting on November 11, 1918, those responsible for a formal peace settlement faced unprecedented challenges. The war's casualties included the Habsburg and Ottoman Empires, so the peacemakers had to deal not just with defeated adversaries but with a changed political and territorial order. And the volatile sociopolitical situation in the wake of war and revolution inevitably colored their deliberations. After all that had happened since August 1914, it was not clear what a restoration of peace and order would require.

The Costs of War

Raw casualty figures do not begin to convey the war's human toll, but they afford some sense of the magnitude of the catastrophe. Estimates differ, but it is generally agreed that from 10 to 13 million military men lost their lives, with another 20 million wounded. In addition, between 7 and 10 million civilians died as a result of the war and its hardships. In the defeated countries, food shortages and malnutrition continued well after the end of the fighting. Adding to the devastation in 1918 was a pandemic of influenza that killed 20 million people worldwide.

Germany suffered the highest number of military casualties, but France suffered the most in proportional terms. Two million Germans were killed, with another 4 million wounded. Military

deaths per capita for France were roughly 15 percent higher than for Germany—and twice as severe as for Britain. Of 8 million Frenchmen mobilized, over 5 million were killed or wounded. Roughly 1.5 million French soldiers, or 10 percent of the active male population, were killed—and this in a country already concerned about demographic decline. The other belligerents also suffered in great numbers. Among the military personnel killed were 2 million Russians, 500,000 Italians, and 114,000 Americans. Especially in light of the assumptions about European superiority and progress, this unprecedented bloodletting deeply affected the European self-image. It was the worst loss of life Europe had suffered since the Black Death of the fourteenth century.

Economic costs were heavy as well. Europeans found themselves reeling from inflation and saddled with debt, especially to the United States, once the war was over. Although the immediate transition to a peacetime economy did not prove as difficult as many had feared, the war and its aftermath produced an economic disequilibrium that lingered, helping to produce a worldwide depression in 1929.

The Search for Peace

The war had begun because of an unmanageable nationality problem in Austria-Hungary, and it led not simply to military defeat for Austria-Hungary but to the abdication of the emperor and the breakup of the Habsburg monarchy. The end of the war brought bright hopes for self-determination to the Czechs, Slovaks, Poles, Serbs, and Croats. Even before the peacemakers began deliberating in January 1919, some of these groups had begun creating a new order on their own. A popular movement of Czechs and Slovaks established a Czechoslovak republic on October 29, 1918, and a new Yugoslavia and an independent Hungary also emerged from indigenous movements. Some of these new amalgams of ethnic groups would unravel in the future, for many of these countries lacked traditions of self-government that might have helped them to survive.

The triumph of a revolutionary regime in Russia immeasurably complicated the situation, because in the unsettled conditions of the former Habsburg territories, as in Germany, the revolution seemed poised to spread in the wake of defeat—precisely according to the script the Russian revolutionaries were reading to the world. Still a precarious minority within Russia in 1918, the Bolsheviks continued to bank on revolution elsewhere in Europe until 1920. Shortly after taking power, they had rechristened themselves "Communists," partly to jettison the provincial Russian term *bolshevik*, but especially to underline their departure from the old reformist socialists of the Second International. Communism meant revolution along Russian lines. Before they were suppressed, enthusiastic Communist regimes governed for brief periods in parts of Hungary and Czechoslovakia and in the German state of Bavaria.

Fears that the Russian Revolution might spread fueled foreign intervention in Russia in June 1918, when 24,000 French and British troops entered the country. As long as the war with Germany lasted, military concerns helped justify this course, but after the armistice of November 1918, the intervention became overtly anticommunist. A series of thrusts, involving troops from fourteen countries at one time or another, struck at Russia from diverse points on its huge border. That effort aided the counterrevolutionary Whites, especially members of the old elites dispossessed by the Bolsheviks, who waged a civil war against the communists from 1918 to 1920. Although there was never a coordinated strategy between the Whites and the foreign troops, foreign intervention was intended to help topple the new regime.

The fourth prewar regime to disappear was the Ottoman Empire, which had controlled much of the Middle East in 1914. The Arab revolt against the Turks that developed in the Arabian peninsula in 1916 did not achieve its major military aims, though it endured, causing some disruption to the Turkish war effort. Its success was due partly to the collaboration of a young British officer, T. E. Lawrence (1888–1935), who proved an effective military leader and an impassioned advocate of the Arab cause. The support that Britain had offered the Arabs suggested that independence, perhaps even a single Arab kingdom, might follow from a defeat of the Ottoman Empire.

But British policy toward the Arabs was uncertain and contradictory. Concerned about the Suez Canal, the British government sought to tighten its control in Egypt by declaring it a protectorate in 1914. British and French diplomats agreed on a division of the Ottoman territories in the Middle East into colonial spheres of influence. France would control Syria and Lebanon, while Britain would rule Palestine and Mesopotamia, or present-day Iraq.

Potentially complicating the situation in the region was Zionism, the movement to establish a Jewish state in Palestine. Led by Chaim Weizmann (1874–1952), a remarkable Russian-born British chemist, Zionists reached an important milestone when British foreign secretary Arthur Balfour (1848–1930) cautiously announced, in the Balfour Declaration of November 1917, that the British government "looked with favor" on the prospect of a "Jewish home" in Palestine. At this point, British leaders sympathetic to Zionism saw no conflict in embracing the cause of the Arabs against the Ottoman Turks at the same time; indeed, Arabs and Jews, each seeking self-determination, could be expected to collaborate.

In the heat of war, the British established their policy for the former Ottoman territories of the Middle East without careful study. Thus, they made promises and agreements that were not entirely compatible.

The Peace Settlement

The peace conference opened in Paris in January 1919. Its labors led to five separate treaties, with each of the five defeated states, known collectively as the Paris peace settlement. The first and most significant was the Treaty of Versailles with Germany, signed in the Hall of Mirrors of the Versailles Palace on June 28, 1919. Treaties were also worked out, in turn, with Austria, Bulgaria, Hungary, and finally Turkey, in August 1920.

This was to be a dictated, not a negotiated, peace. Germany and its allies were excluded, as was renegade Russia. Having won the war, France, Britain, the United States, and Italy were to call the shots on their own, with the future of Europe and much of the world in the balance. However, spokesmen for many groups—from Slovaks and Croats to Arabs, Jews, and pan-Africanists—were in Paris as well, seeking a hearing for their causes. Both the Arab Prince Faisal (1885–1933), who would later become king of Iraq, and Colonel T. E. Lawrence were there to plead for an independent Arab kingdom. (See the box "Encounters with the West: Prince Faisal at the Peace Conference.") The African American leader W. E. B. Du Bois (1868–1963), who took his Ph.D. at Harvard in 1895, led a major pan-African congress in Paris concurrently with the peace conference.

The fundamental challenge for the peacemakers was to reconcile the conflicting visions of the postwar world that had emerged by the end of the war. U.S. President Wilson represented the promise of a new order of peace and cooperation. Clemenceau, now the French prime minister, stressed that only a permanent preponderance of French military power over Germany, and not some utopian league of nations, could guarantee a lasting peace. The negotiations at Paris centered on this fundamental difference between Wilson and Clemenceau. Although Britain's Lloyd George took a hard line on certain issues, he also sought to mediate, helping engineer the somewhat awkward compromise that resulted. When, after the peace conference, he encountered criticism for the outcome, Lloyd George replied, "I think I did as well as might be expected, seated as I was between Jesus Christ and Napoleon Bonaparte."[5]

In Article 231 of the final treaty, the peacemakers assigned responsibility for the war to Germany and its allies. The treaty forced Germany to pay reparations to reimburse the victors for the costs of the war; Article 231, the so-called "War Guilt Clause," seemed to establish a moral basis for these exactions. The determination to make Germany pay for what had become an enormously expensive war was one of the factors militating against a compromise peace in 1917. Thus the peacemakers decided to fix a reparations responsibility, although the amount to be paid was not established until 1921.

In addition, Germany was forced to dismantle much of its military apparatus. The treaty severely restricted the size of the German army and navy, and Germany was forbidden to manufacture or possess military aircraft, submarines, tanks, heavy artillery, or poison gas. France took back Alsace and Lorraine, the provinces it had lost to Germany in 1871 (Map 23.2). But for France, the crucial security provision was the treatment of the adjacent Rhineland section of Germany itself. For fifteen years Allied troops were to occupy the west bank of the Rhine River in Germany—the usual military occupation of a defeated adversary. But this would be only temporary. The long-term advantage for France was the permanent demilitarization of all German territory west of the Rhine and a strip of 50 kilometers along its east bank.

French interests also helped shape the settlement in east-central Europe. Wilsonian principles called for self-determination, but in this area of great ethnic complexity, ethnic differences were not readily sorted out geographically. So that Germany would again face potential enemies from both east and west, the French envisioned building a network of allies starting with the new Poland, created from Polish territories formerly in the German, Russian, and Austro-Hungarian Empires. That network might come to include Czechoslovakia, Yugoslavia, and Romania as well. These states would be weak enough to remain under French influence but, taken together, strong enough to replace Russia as a force against Germany.

The new Czechoslovakia not only was an amalgam of Czechs and Slovaks but also included Germans and Magyars. Indeed, Germans, mostly from the old Bohemia, made up 22 percent of the population of Czechoslovakia. Yugoslavia had an even more diverse population. French policymakers were so determined to foster a strong Czechoslovakia and Yugoslavia that they ordered the

∽ ENCOUNTERS WITH THE WEST ∽

Prince Faisal at the Peace Conference

With the war nearing its end in October 1918, British authorities permitted Faisal ibn-Husayn (1885–1933) to set up a provisional Arab state, with its capital at Damascus. In the memorandum of January 1919 that follows, Faisal outlined the Arab position, mixing pride and assertiveness with a recognition that the Arabs would continue to need the support and help of Western powers.

We believe that our ideal of Arab unity in Asia is justified beyond need of argument. If argument is required, we would point to the general principles accepted by the Allies when the United States joined them, to our splendid past, to the tenacity with which our race has for 600 years resisted Turkish attempts to absorb us, and, in a lesser degree, to what we tried our best to do in this war as one of the Allies. . . .

We believe that Syria, an agricultural and industrial area thickly peopled with sedentary classes, is sufficiently advanced politically to manage her own internal affairs. We feel also that foreign technical advice and help will be a most valuable factor in our national growth. We are willing to pay for this help in cash; we cannot sacrifice for it any part of the freedom we have just won for ourselves by force of arms.

. . . The world wishes to exploit Mesopotamia rapidly, and we therefore believe that the system of government there will have to be buttressed by the men and material resources of a great foreign Power. We ask, however, that the Government be Arab, in principle and spirit, the selective rather than the elective principle being necessarily followed in the neglected districts, until time makes the broader basis possible. . . .

In Palestine the enormous majority of the people are Arabs. The Jews are very close to the Arabs in blood, and there is no conflict of character between the two races. In principles we are absolutely at one. Nevertheless, the Arabs cannot risk assuming the responsibility of holding level the scales in the clash of races and religions that have, in this one province, so often involved the world in difficulties. They would wish for the effective super-position of a great trustee. . . .

In our opinion, if our independence be conceded and our local competence established, the natural influences of race, language, and interest will soon draw us together into one people; but for this the Great Powers will have to ensure us open internal frontiers, common railways and telegraphs, and uniform systems of education. To achieve this they must lay aside the thought of individual profits, and of their old jealousies. In a word, we ask you not to force your whole civilisation upon us, but to help us to pick out what serves us from your experience. In return we can offer you little but gratitude.

Source: J. C. Hurewitz, *Diplomacy in the Near and Middle East: A Documentary Record: 1914–1956* (Princeton, N.J.: D. Van Nostrand, 1956), vol. 2, pp. 38–39.

French police to force the spokesmen for Slovak and Croat separatism to leave Paris. Thus, Poland, Czechoslovakia, Yugoslavia, and Romania ended up as large as possible. Austria, Hungary, and Bulgaria, on the other hand, were diminished. What remained of Austria, the German part of the old Habsburg empire, was prohibited from choosing to join Germany.

Concern to contain and weaken Communist Russia was also at work in the settlement

Legend:

- ▬▬▬ Boundaries of German, Russian, and Austro-Hungarian empires in 1914
- Areas lost by Austro-Hungarian Empire
- Areas lost by Russian Empire
- Areas lost by German Empire
- Areas lost by Bulgaria
- Areas lost by Ottoman Empire
- Demilitarized Zones
- ▬▬▬ Boundaries of 1926
- ▬ ▬ ▬ Areas controlled under mandates from the League of Nations, 1920

NORWAY
Oslo
SWEDEN
Stockholm
North Sea
GREAT BRITAIN
FINLAND
Helsinki
Tallinn
Leningrad (St. Petersburg)
Baltic Sea
ESTONIA
Riga LATVIA
Memel
LITHUANIA
Vilnius
DENMARK
Copenhagen
NETHERLANDS
Amsterdam
Brussels
BELGIUM
RUHR
Cologne
GERMANY
Berlin
Danzig
POLISH CORRIDOR
EAST PRUSSIA
POLAND
Warsaw
Paris
LUX.
FRANCE
LORRAINE
ALSACE
Weimar
Frankfurt
Strasbourg
Prague
CZECHOSLOVAKIA
GALICIA
Kiev
Geneva
Bern
SWITZ.
Vienna
AUSTRIA
Budapest
HUNGARY
BESSARABIA
Locarno
Milan
S. TYROL
Venice
Trieste
Zagreb
CROATIA
ROMANIA
Bucharest
Genoa
Rapallo
ITALY
YUGOSLAVIA
Belgrade
Danube
Corsica
Rome
MONTENEGRO (To Yugoslavia 1921)
SERBIA
BULGARIA
Sofia
Black Sea
Sardinia
Naples
ALBANIA
Istanbul (Constantinople)
Ankara
Batum
Kars
Baku
Caspian Sea
GREECE
TURKEY
Tabriz
Mediterranean Sea
Izmir (Smyrna)
Athens
Crete
Cyprus (Gr. Br.)
Annexed by Turkey 1939
Aleppo
SYRIA (French Mandate)
Beirut
Damascus
Baghdad
IRAQ (MESOPOTAMIA) (British Mandate)
Kut el Amara
PERSIA (IRAN)
TUNISIA (French)
PALESTINE (British Mandate)
Jerusalem
Amman
TRANSJORDAN (British Mandate)
Basra
KUWAIT (Gr. Br.)
NEUTRAL ZONES
Cairo
Suez Canal
LIBYA (Italian)
EGYPT (Independent 1922)
NEJD (SAUDI ARABIA)
Red Sea
Sicily
Riyadh
Medina

RUSSIAN EMPIRE
(Became Union of Soviet Socialist Republics, 1922)
Volga
Ural
Don
Dnieper

0   200   400 Km.
0   200   400 Mi.

in east-central Europe. A band of states in east-central Europe, led by France, could serve not only as a check to Germany but also as a shield against the Russian threat. Romania's aggrandizement came partly at the expense of the Russian Empire, as did the creation of the new Poland. Finland, Latvia, Estonia, and Lithuania, all part of the Russian empire for over a century, now became independent states (see Map 23.2).

The overall settlement cost Germany almost 15 percent of its prewar territory, including major iron- and coal-producing regions, as well as about 10 percent of its prewar population. But the great bitterness that developed in Germany over the terms of the peace stemmed above all from a sense of betrayal. In requesting an armistice, German authorities had appealed to Wilson, who seemed to be saying that the whole prewar international system, not one side or the other, had been to blame for the current conflict. In 1919, however, the peacemakers treated Germany as the guilty party, greatly intensifying the sting of defeat.

Although Wilson had been forced to compromise with French interests in dealing with east-central Europe, he achieved a potentially significant success in exchange—the establishment of the League of Nations. According to the League covenant worked out by April, disputes among member states were to be settled no longer by war but by mechanisms established by the League. Other members were to participate in sanctions, from economic blockade to military action, against a member that violated League provisions.

Map 23.2 The Impact of the War: The Territorial Settlement in Europe and the Middle East The defeat of Russia, Austria-Hungary, Germany, and Ottoman Turkey opened the way to major changes in the map of east-central Europe and the Middle East. A number of new nations emerged in east-central Europe, while in the Arab world the end of Ottoman rule meant not independence but new roles for European powers.

Wider Consequences

How could Wilsonian hopes for a new international order be squared with the imperialist system, which seemed utterly at odds with the ideal of self-determination? As Mohammed Ali Duse had anticipated in 1914 (see page 597), the war had sown the seeds of dramatic change. Elites among the colonial peoples tended to support the war effort in the hopes of achieving greater autonomy. The Indian leader Mohandas Gandhi (1869–1948), for example, who had been educated in the West and admitted to the English bar in 1889, actively supported the British war effort, even helping recruit Indians to fight on the British side. But his aim was to speed Indian independence, and he led demonstrations that embarrassed the British during the war. After over a century of British rule, the war unleashed expectations and demands that led the British, in 1917, to promise home rule for India.

Colonial peoples participated directly in the war on both sides. In sub-Saharan Africa, for example, German-led Africans fought against Africans under British or French command. France brought colonial subjects from West and North Africa into front-line service during the war. The experience expanded political consciousness among the peoples subject to European imperialism.

Duse's *African Times and Orient Review* found reason for optimism in March 1917: "[A] Franco-British success will mean a greater freedom of the peoples we represent than they have previously experienced. The once despised black man is coming to the front in the battle for freedom, and the freedom which he helps to win for the white man, must also be meted out to him when the day of reckoning arrives."[6] The same line of thinking led China and Siam (now Thailand) to associate with the Allied side in 1917, in an effort to win international stature and thereby eventually to regain their lost sovereignty. China sent 200,000 people to work in France to help ease France's wartime labor shortage.

German colonies and Ottoman territories were not simply taken over by the victors, in the old-fashioned way, but came under the authority of the League, which assigned them as mandates to one of the victorious powers, which was to report back to the League annually. There were various classes of mandates, based on how prepared for sovereignty the area was taken to be. In devising this system, the Western powers formally recognized for the first time that non-Western peoples under Western influence had rights and that, in principle, they were progressing toward independence.

Still, the mandate approach to the colonial question was a halting departure at best. Although Britain granted considerable sovereignty to Iraq in 1932, the victorious powers generally operated as before, assimilating the new territories into their existing empires. Given the hopes raised in the Arab world during the war, this outcome produced a sense of betrayal among Arab leaders, who had expected complete independence.

The Chinese also felt betrayed. The victors acquiesced in special rights for Japan in China, causing a renewed sense of humiliation among Chinese elites and provoking a wave of popular demonstrations. In this instance, Western leaders were allowing a non-Western power, Japan, access to the imperial club, but they were hardly departing from imperialism. Those whose political consciousness had been raised by the war came to believe not only that colonialism should end, but that the colonial peoples would themselves have to take the lead in ending it.

In the United States, debate arose over the American role as President Wilson sought Senate ratification of the peace treaty. Wilson's opponents worried about U.S. commitments to France and Britain and that League membership would compromise U.S. sovereignty. An isolationist backlash had developed as Americans increasingly questioned whether the United States had been wise to become involved, for the first time, in a war in Europe. Late in 1919, at the height of the debate, Wilson suffered a disabling stroke. The Senate then refused to ratify the peace treaty, thereby keeping the United States out of the League of Nations. By 1920 the United States seemed to be pulling back from the leadership role it had been poised to play in 1918.

During the peace conference, a member of the British delegation, the economist John Maynard Keynes (1883–1946), resigned to write *The Economic Consequences of the Peace* (1920), which helped undermine confidence in the whole settlement. Keynes charged that the vindictive policy of the French, by crippling Germany with a punishing reparations burden, threatened the European economy and thus the peace of Europe over the long term. The lack of consensus about the legitimacy of the peace profoundly increased the postwar sense of disillusionment.

After the war was over, many of those who had fought it felt a sense of ironic betrayal; their prewar upbringing, the values and assumptions they had inherited, had not equipped them to make sense of what they had lived through. Beginning in the late 1920s a wave of writings about the war appeared. Many were memoirs, such as *Goodbye to All That* by the English writer Robert Graves (1895–1985) and *Testament of Youth* by Vera Brittain (1893–1970), who had served as a British army nurse at the front. The most famous exploration of the war was the antiwar novel *All Quiet on the Western Front* (1929) by German writer Erich Maria Remarque (1898–1970), which sold 2.5 million copies in twenty-five languages in its first eighteen months in print.

Although Remarque had seen front-line action, his novel said more about the cynical mood after the war than it did about the actual experience of those in the trenches. By the end of the 1920s an element of mythmaking was creeping into these efforts to make sense of the war experience. Still, there was something undeniably genuine in the laments of loss of innocence, in the sense of belonging to a "lost generation," that marked much of this writing. Not only were many friends dead or maimed for life, but all the sacrifices seemed to have been in vain.

What followed from the war, most fundamentally, was a sense that Western civilization was neither as secure nor as superior as it had seemed. The celebrated French poet Paul Valéry (1871–1945), speaking at Oxford shortly after the war, observed that "we modern civilizations have learned to recognize that we are mortal like the others. We had heard . . . of whole worlds vanished, of empires foundered. . . . Elam, Nineveh, Babylon were vague and splendid names; the total ruin of these worlds, for us, meant as little as did their existence. But France, England, Russia . . . these names, too, are splendid. . . . And now we see that the abyss of history is deep enough to bury all the world."[7] Valéry went on to warn that the transition to peace would be even more difficult and disorienting than the war itself. So traumatic might be the convulsion that Europe might be shown up for what it was in fact—a pathetically small corner of the world, a mere cape on the Asiatic landmass. Astounding words for a European, yet even Valéry, for all his foresight, could not anticipate what Europe would go through in the decades to follow.

SUMMARY

Europe was optimistic on the eve of war. After a century of relative peace and apparent progress, people everywhere believed that the war would be brief, purifying, and jubilantly successful. The nations of the Triple Entente and the Central Powers all believed that the war would confirm their own cultural, technological, and even racial superiority. Instead, in the west, trench warfare gave the defense the advantage, creating a tedious and traumatic stalemate that stretched over four years. In the east, the war produced an even more shocking outcome: the Russian Revolution.

For all the belligerent countries, this long war of attrition was made possible by industrial technology, but it was ultimately dependent on the will of the people. As such, controlling popular opinion became crucial to the war effort. Soldiers had to be kept obedient, dedicated, and optimistic. Women had to be recruited for munitions work and other previously masculinized labors. Colonial subjects of the European nations were also drawn into the war with promises of recognition and emancipation.

People wanted to believe that the world would be better after the war and that their nation would somehow be reimbursed for the emotional, physical, and financial tolls that the war had taken. When U.S. troops finally broke the stalemate, its allies could believe that such recompense was on the way. Before long, however, it became clear that most wartime wishes would not soon be fulfilled. The serious discrepancies between expectation or perception and reality would have profound consequences.

As the Treaty of Versailles demonstrated, after World War I the chief struggle in the West would be between those who would attempt to recreate the prewar world and the values that it now seemed to represent and those who wanted to create a new world with new values. In either case, the disintegration of the old order produced a sense of vulnerability hard to overcome. The vast casualties, the terrifying new weapons, the destruction of monuments—all gave the war an apocalyptic aura that heightened its psychological impact.

By destroying the Habsburg empire and the imperial regime in Germany, World War I seemed to have solved the immediate problems that caused it. Yet the war also produced a new set of tumultuous circumstances. The Russians had produced a communist revolution and were angling for other countries to join them. In many nations, women's demand for the vote could no longer be ignored after their great service and sacrifice. New nations were born out of the peace settlement, while others were pressing for recognition. And still, for most, the magnitude of violence itself created the greatest of the changes: A deep sense of disillusionment and doubt replaced Europe's optimism and expectation of eternal progress.

NOTES

1. From *African Times and Orient Review*, August 4, 1914; quoted in Imanuel Geiss, *The Pan-African Movement*, translated by Ann Keep (London: Methuen & Co., 1974), pp. 229–230.
2. Thus wrote the German poet Ivan Goll in 1917; quoted in Modris Eksteins, *Rites of Spring: The Great War and the Birth of the Modern Age* (Boston: Houghton Mifflin, 1989), p. 144.
3. By A. N. Potresov, as quoted in Richard Pipes, *The Russian Revolution* (New York: Random House, Vintage, 1991), p. 348.

4. Quoted in Koppel S. Pinson, *Modern Germany: Its History and Civilization*, 2d ed. (New York: Macmillan, 1966), p. 337.

5. Quoted in Walter Arnstein, *Britain Yesterday and Today: 1830 to the Present*, 6th ed. (Lexington, Mass.: D. C. Heath, 1992), p. 266.

6. Unsigned editorial, *African Times and Orient Review*, March 1917; quoted in Geiss, *The Pan-African Movement*, p. 479, n. 2.

7. Paul Valéry, *Variety*, 1st series (New York: Harcourt, Brace, 1938), pp. 3–4.

SUGGESTED READING

Becker, Jean-Jacques. *The Great War and the French People*. 1985. A landmark study of the relationship between battlefield fortunes and wider public responses as France bore the brunt of the fighting during World War I.

Brayborn, Gail, and Penny Summerfield. *Out of the Cage: Women's Experiences in Two World Wars*. 1987. A comparative study of the impact of the two world wars on women, relying especially on direct testimony.

Eksteins, Modris. *Rites of Spring: The Great War and the Birth of the Modern Age*. 1989. An original and provocative exploration of the relationship between culture and the war experience.

Ellis, John. *Eye-Deep in Hell: Trench Warfare in World War I*. 1989. A compelling account of life and death in the trenches, covering topics from trench construction to eating, drinking, and sex. Includes striking photographs.

Fitzpatrick, Sheila. *The Russian Revolution, 1917–1932*. 2d ed. 1994. An ideal introductory work that places the events of 1917 in the sweep of Russian history.

Fromkin, David. *A Peace to End All Peace: The Fall of the Ottoman Empire and the Creation of the Modern Middle East*. 1989. A detailed but gripping account of the role of the war and the peace process in transforming the lands of the Ottoman Empire.

Fussell, Paul. *The Great War and Modern Memory*. 1975. A widely admired study of the attempts to forge the new language, through literature, necessary to make sense of the British war experience.

Hanna, Martha. *The Mobilization of Intellect: French Scholars and Writers During the Great War*. 1996. Challenges the widespread notion that World War I galvanized a unified assault of French intellectuals against German culture.

Higonnet, Margaret Randolph, et al., eds. *Behind the Lines: Gender and the Two World Wars*. 1987. Sophis-

ticated essays on the role of women during the two world wars, concerned especially with the impact of war on gender definition.

Hough, Richard. *The Great War at Sea, 1914–1918*. 1983. A survey of naval operations, featuring the British navy. Includes photographs.

King, Jere Clemens, ed. *The First World War*. 1972. A superior documentary history, with selections on an array of topics, from military operations to diplomacy to the role of women in the war.

Kocka, Jürgen. *Facing Total War: German Society, 1914–1918*. 1984. Using concepts of class and monopoly capitalism in a flexible way, a leading German historian analyzes the impact of the war on German society.

Leed, Eric J. *No Man's Land: Combat and Identity in World War I*. 1979. A pioneering study of the experience of World War I, which explores its challenge to masculine identity.

Mayer, Arno J. *The Politics and Diplomacy of Peacemaking: Containment and Counterrevolution at Versailles, 1918–1919*. 1967. Emphasizes the impact of domestic political concerns and fears of spreading revolution.

Mosse, George L. *Fallen Soldiers: Reshaping the Memory of the World Wars*. 1990. Shows how the encounter with mass death in World War I led to new ways of sanctifying and justifying war.

Service, Robert. *Lenin: A Political Life*. 3 vols. 1985, 1991, 1995. A landmark, readable biography that does justice both to Lenin's ruthlessness and to the visionary purpose that made him one of the decisive actors of the twentieth century.

Sharp, Alan. *The Versailles Settlement: Peacemaking in Paris, 1919*. 1991. A brief, clear, and balanced overview that seeks to do justice to the magnitude of the task the peacemakers faced.

Von Laue, Theodore H. *Why Lenin? Why Stalin? Why Gorbachev? The Rise and Fall of the Soviet System*. 3d ed. 1993. A widely used survey. Accents the larger context of international preoccupations that helped shape the revolution and the system that developed from it.

Winter, J. M. *The Experience of World War I*. 1989. An ideal introductory work that proceeds via concentric circles from politicians to generals to soldiers to civilians, then to the war's long-term effects.

———. *Sites of Memory, Sites of Mourning*. 1995. Using an effective comparative approach, a leading authority argues that Europeans relied on relatively traditional means of making sense of the bloodletting of World War I.

CHAPTER 24

From Stability to Crisis, 1919–1939

I n 1925, Josephine Baker (1906–1975), a black entertainer from St. Louis, moved to Paris and quickly became a singing and dancing sensation. Also a favorite in Germany, she was the most famous of the African American entertainers who took the cultural capitals of Europe by storm during the 1920s. After the disillusioning experience of war, many Europeans found a valuable infusion of vitality in Baker's jazz music, exotic costumes, and "savage," uninhibited dancing.

The attraction to African Americans as primitive, vital, and sensual reflected a good deal of racial stereotyping, and black performers like Baker sometimes played to them. But there really was something fresh and uninhibited about American culture, especially its African American variant. Baker herself was a woman of great sophistication who became a French citizen in 1937, participated in progressive causes, and was decorated for her secret intelligence work in the anti-Nazi resistance during World War II.

The prominence of African Americans in European popular culture during the 1920s was part of a wider infatuation with all things American. As expatriates gathered in the Paris salon of the American writer Gertrude Stein (1874–1946), a new set of cultural values began to take shape. Old conventions had been shattered, and Stein represented the artistic innovation and social freedom that had appeared in the wake of the war.

But when the Great Depression began at the end of the decade, serious sociopolitical strains became evident throughout most of the Western world, and the open culture of the 1920s grew tense and constricted. The mechanisms used to realign the international economy after World War I seemed effective for most of the 1920s, but by 1929, they were beginning to backfire. The promise of democracy, so bright in the 1920s, was beginning to darken.

The Sensational Josephine Baker A native of St. Louis, the African American Josephine Baker moved to Paris in 1925 and quickly created a sensation in both France and Germany as a cabaret dancer and singer. Playing on the European association of Africa with the wild and uninhibited, she featured unusual poses and exotic costumes. *(Hulton-Getty/Liaison)*

New forms of government were emerging in Stalinist Russia and fascist Italy—both of which relied heavily on violence and intimidation. In Germany, the rise to power of the Nazi leader Adolf Hitler intensified the ideological polarization in Europe, and his policies produced a series of diplomatic crises that eventually led to a new European war.

～ *Questions and Ideas to Consider*

- To many, the rise of mass society meant cultural innovation and a democracy more re-

sponsive to the will of the people. Others saw only a debasement of cultural standards. Discuss some of the specific positions on both sides of this debate.

- Who was the "new woman," and what did she symbolize during the prosperous 1920s? How were women represented in the anxious years after 1929?

- Because its failure led to Nazism, the Weimar Republic has been much scrutinized. What might its leaders have done differently to produce a more viable democracy? Are the republic's immediate problems enough to explain its failure, or was Germany's history of authoritarianism crucial as well?

- What were the central positions of Nazism? Did Nazism succeed electorally because most people agreed with these positions?

- Compare the regimes of fascist Italy, Nazi Germany, and Stalinist Russia. Were they all totalitarian? In what ways can it be said that Nazi Germany had more in common with Stalinist Russia than it did with fascist Italy?

ECONOMY AND SOCIETY IN THE INTERWAR YEARS

Readjustment to peace caused wild economic swings just after the war, yet by the later 1920s, Europe was enjoying renewed prosperity. Culture also seemed vibrant and optimistic in the 1920s. By the close of the decade, however, Europe was in crisis. In the wake of the Wall Street crash of 1929, a cataclysmic depression struck the world economy. With the Great Depression came extraordinary suffering for many and great anxiety for many others. The creation of a "mass society"—through literacy, democracy, and technology—had seemed progressive and emancipatory in the 1920s. In the 1930s, many began to worry that the masses were too easily led and deceived, and too eager to lower cultural standards.

Economy and Society in the Interwar Years

627

New Trends in Labor and Lifestyle

The wartime spur to industrialization produced a large increase in the industrial labor force all over Europe, and a good deal of labor unrest accompanied the transition to peacetime. Some of that agitation challenged factory discipline and authority relationships. Business leaders and publicists fostered a new cult of efficiency and productivity, partly by adapting Taylorism and Fordism, influential American ideas about mass production. On the basis of his "time-and-motion" studies of factory labor, Frederick W. Taylor (1856–1915) argued that breaking down assembly line production into small, repetitive tasks was the key to maximizing efficiency. In contrast, Henry Ford (1863–1947) linked the gospel of mass production to mass consumption. In exchange for accepting the discipline of the assembly line, the workers should be paid well enough to be able to buy the products they produced—even automobiles. Not all Europeans welcomed the new ideas from America. In the new cult of efficiency some saw an unwelcome sameness and a debasement of cultural ideals.

In light of the major role women had played in the wartime labor force, the demand for women's suffrage proved irresistible in Britain, Germany, and much of Europe, though not yet in France or Italy. Although female employment remained higher than before the war, many women were pushed out of the work force to make jobs available to the returning soldiers. Working-class women continued to work, of necessity, but often lost their higher-paying war jobs. Still, many women felt freer as fashion and culture in the 1920s and 1930s deliberately broke away from the stultifying bourgeois respectability that had so constrained the actions of women. The "new woman," with short hair, a job, and her own apartment, was a central symbol of modernity. Dance crazes and jazz concerts defined a new culture of freedom in which women could function with considerable autonomy.

The desire to be "modern" also produced a more open, unsentimental, even scientific discussion of sexuality and reproduction. The new

CHAPTER CHRONOLOGY

March 1919	Founding of the Italian fascist movement
November 1920	End of fighting in the Russian civil war
October 1922	Mussolini becomes Italian prime minister
January 1924	First Labour government in Britain
	Death of Lenin
August 1924	Acceptance of the Dawes Plan on German reparations
October 1925	Locarno Agreement
May 1926	Beginning of general strike in Britain
August 1929	Acceptance of the Young Plan on German reparations
October 1929	U.S. stock market crash leads to Great Depression
January 1933	Hitler becomes German chancellor
March 1935	Hitler announces rearmament in defiance of the Versailles treaty
October 1935	Italy invades Ethiopia
July 1936	Beginning of the Spanish civil war

"rationalization of sexuality" fed demands that governments provide access to sex counseling, birth control, and even abortion as they assumed ever greater responsibilities for promoting public health. This direction was especially prominent in Germany, although German innovators learned from experiments in the new Soviet Union and from the birth control movement that Margaret Sanger (1883–1966) was spearheading in the United States. The more open and tolerant attitude toward sexuality fostered the development of a gay subculture, prominent in the vibrant cabaret scene that emerged in Berlin during the 1920s.

Arts and Leisure in the "Roaring Twenties"

As the new prosperity spread the fruits of industrialization more widely, ordinary people increasingly set the cultural tone, partly through new mass media like film and radio. To some, the advent of mass society portended a welcome revitalization of culture and a more authentic kind of democracy, while others saw only a decline in standards and a susceptibility to populist demagoguery.

With the eight-hour day increasingly the norm, growing attention was devoted to leisure. More and more people began to have the time and means to take vacations. European beach resorts grew crowded. An explosion of interest in soccer among Europeans paralleled the growth of baseball and college football in the United States. Huge stadiums were built across Europe.

During the early 1920s radio became a commercial venture, reaching a mass audience in Europe, as in the United States. Although movies had begun to emerge as vehicles of popular entertainment before the war, they came into their own during the 1920s, when the names of film stars became household words for the first time. The rapid development of film showed that new, more accessible media could nurture extraordinary innovation. Germany led the way with such films as *Metropolis* (1927) and *The Blue Angel* (1930), but the Russian Sergei Eisenstein (1898–1948) became perhaps the most admired filmmaker of the era with *Potemkin* (1925), his brilliant portrayal of the Russian revolution of 1905. And American film was on the rise: Marlene Dietrich (1901–1992) was among a number of German film celebrities who went to Hollywood.

Perhaps the quintessential positive symbol of the postwar period was air travel. The new technology symbolized freedom and possibility, and the American pilots Charles Lindbergh (1902–1974) and Amelia Earhart (1897–1937) captured the European imagination with their brav-

ery. Earhart's feminism won her many fans as well. It seemed that there still were heroes, despite the ironies of the war and the ambiguities of the peace.

Cultural Anxiety and Alienation

World War I had accelerated the long-term "modernization" process toward large industries, cities, and bureaucracies, and toward mass politics, society, and culture. That process was positive, even liberating, in certain respects, but it was also disruptive and disturbing. Thus a wide variety of concerns were expressed by intellectuals and artists in the years between the two world wars.

Many artists and writers attempted to capture the agonies of the war. The German artist Käthe Kollwitz (1867–1945) portrayed in sculpture and woodcuts the intense emotions of bereaved parents and orphaned children. Her own son had died in the war, and her images came to represent the grief and exhaustion of the era.

While Kollwitz depicted the ordeals of the masses, others began to worry over their character—and the fate of the culture they now controlled. In *Revolt of the Masses* (1930), the influential Spanish thinker José Ortega y Gasset (1883–1955) concluded that ordinary people were intolerant and illiberal, incapable of creating standards, and content with the least common denominator. Communism and fascism indicated the violence and intolerance of the new mass age. But Ortega found the same tendencies in American-style democracy.

Concern with cultural decline was widespread. To Sigmund Freud, the eruption of violence and hatred during the war and after indicated a deep, instinctual problem in the human makeup. In his gloomy essay *Civilization and Its Discontents* (1930), he suggested that the progress of civilization entails the bottling up of aggressive instincts, which are directed inward as guilt or left to erupt in violent outbursts.

The sense that there is something incomprehensible, even nightmarish, about modern civilization, with its ever more complex bureaucracies, technologies, and cities, found vivid expression in the works of the Czech Jewish writer Franz Kafka (1883–1924), most notably in the novels *The Trial* and *The Castle*, published posthumously in the mid-1920s. In a world that claimed to be increasingly rational, Kafka's individual is the lonely, fragile plaything of forces utterly beyond reason, comprehension, and control. In such a world, the quest for law, or meaning, or God is futile and ridiculous.

While some sought renewal from within the tradition, others insisted that a more radical break was needed—but also that the elements for a viable new cultural tradition were available. Reflecting on the situation of women writers in 1928, the British novelist Virginia Woolf (1882–1941) showed how women in the past had suffered from the absence of a tradition of writing by women. By the 1920s, women had made important strides, but Woolf suggested that they had to study their historical role in order to go further. Culture advances by drawing on the accomplishments of the past, but, explained Woolf, women's work and accomplishments were not written about and were thus lost to history. Most basically, women needed greater financial independence so that they could have the time for scholarship, the leisure of cultivated conversation, and the privacy of "a room of one's own." Woolf wrote about a hypothetical "Shakespeare's sister," suggesting that women geniuses had been born but had never been given the most rudimentary requirements of time, space, and respect. Woolf asserted that although the work of her own generation of women might not be noticed, it would eventually change the world for a future Shakespeare's sister, so that "when she is born again she shall find it possible to live and write her poetry."[1]

A very different effort to establish a new tradition developed in Paris in the early 1920s as the poet André Breton (1896–1966) spearheaded the surrealist movement. Surrealism grew directly from Dada, an artistic movement that had emerged during the war. Protesting the war, Dada artists developed shocking, sometimes nihilistic, forms to deal with a reality that seemed senseless and out of control. Some made collages

from trash; others indulged in nonsense or relied on chance. The results were sometimes amusing and often disturbing. By the early 1920s, the surrealists were adapting Dada's use of chance to gain access to the subconscious, which they believed contains a deeper truth.

Readjustment and the New Prosperity

In their effort to return to normal, governments were quick to dismantle wartime planning and control mechanisms. The needs of war had stimulated innovations that helped fuel the economic growth of the 1920s. New industries such as chemicals, electricity, and advanced machinery led the way to a new prosperity in the 1920s. The automobile, a plaything for the wealthy before the war, began to be mass-produced in western Europe. In France, which had pioneered automotive manufacture, the production of automobiles shot up dramatically, from 40,000 in 1920 to 254,000 in 1929.

But the heady pace masked problems that lay beneath the relative prosperity of the 1920s, even in victorious Britain and France. While new industries prospered, old ones declined in the face of new technologies and stronger foreign competition. In Britain, the industries responsible for the country's earlier industrial preeminence—textiles, coal, shipbuilding, and iron and steel—were now having trouble competing. Rather than investing in new technologies, companies in older industries sought government protection and imposed lower wages and longer hours on their workers. At the same time, British labor unions resisted the mechanization necessary to make older industries more competitive.

Rather than realistically assessing Britain's prospects in the more competitive international economy, British leaders sought to return to the prewar situation, based on the gold standard, and with London the world's financial center. For many Britons, the government's announcement in 1925 that the British pound was again freely convertible to gold at 1914 exchange rates was an indication that normality had returned at last. Yet the return to 1914 exchange rates overvalued the pound relative to the U.S. dollar, making British goods more expensive in export markets and making it still more difficult for aging British industries to compete. Further, Britain no longer had the capital to act as the world's banker. By trying to do so, Britain became all the more vulnerable when the international economy reached a crisis in 1929.

In Britain the Labour party supplanted the Liberals to become the dominant alternative to the Conservatives by the early 1920s. The Labour party got a brief taste of power when Ramsay MacDonald (1866–1937) formed Britain's first Labour government in January 1924. As a result, the governmental elite was significantly expanded to include those with working-class backgrounds.

Although the rise of Labour was significant, it was the Conservative leader Stanley Baldwin (1867–1947) who set the tone for British politics between the wars in three stints as prime minister between 1923 and 1937. Baldwin deliberately departed from the old aristocratic style of Conservative politics. He was the first British prime minister to use radio effectively, and he made an effort to foster good relations with workers. Yet Baldwin's era was one of growing social tension.

With exports declining, unemployment remained high in Britain throughout the interwar period, never falling below 10 percent. The coal industry, the country's largest employer, had become a particular trouble spot in the British economy. In 1926, a coal miners' strike turned into a general strike, involving almost all of organized labor—about 4 million workers—in the most notable display of trade-union solidarity Britain had ever seen. For nine days the British economy stood at a virtual standstill.

If the structural decline of older industries was clearest in Britain, inflation and its psychological impact was most prominent in Germany and France. In response to German foot-dragging in paying reparations, the French sent troops to occupy the Ruhr industrial area in January 1923. By the summer it was clear that the move had backfired, transforming an already serious inflationary problem, stemming from wartime deficit spending, into one of the great hyperinflations in

history. At its height, when it took 4.2 trillion marks to equal a dollar, Germans were forced to take wheelbarrows of paper money to buy groceries. Simply printing the necessary currency was a severe strain for the government. By the end of 1923, the government managed to stabilize prices through currency reform and drastically reduced government spending. But the rampant inflation had wiped out the life savings of ordinary people while profiting speculators and those in debt, including some large industrialists. This inequity left scars that remained even as Germany enjoyed a measure of prosperity in the years that followed. Inflation was less dramatic in France, but it was severe there, too—and particularly upsetting because before the war the value of the French franc had been stable for over a century.

Although some in prewar France had worried about falling behind rapidly industrializing Germany, the victory seemed to have vindicated France's more cautious, balanced economy, with its blend of industry and agriculture. Thus, the prewar mistrust of rapid industrial development continued, and the French pulled back even from the measure of state responsibility for the economy that had developed during the war. Government grants helped reconstruct almost eight thousand factories, but most were simply rebuilt as they were before the war. Moreover, the working class benefited little from the relative prosperity of the 1920s. Housing remained poor, wages failed to keep up with inflation, and France continued to lag behind other countries in social legislation.

The Great Depression

Although the stock market crash of October 1929 in the United States helped usher in the world economic crisis of the early 1930s, it had this effect only because the new international economic order after World War I was extremely fragile. By October 1929, in fact, production was already declining in all the major Western countries except France.

Certain economic sectors, especially coal mining and agriculture, were already suffering severe problems by the mid-1920s. British coal exports fell partly because oil and hydroelectricity were rapidly developing as alternatives. In agriculture high prices during the war had produced oversupply, leading to a sharp drop in prices once the war was over. The result of low agricultural prices was a diminished demand for industrial goods, which impeded growth in the world economy.

Throughout the 1920s, finance ministers and central bankers had difficulty juggling the economic imbalances created by the war, centering on war debts to the United States and German reparations obligations to France, Britain, and Belgium. The shaky postwar economic system depended on U.S. bank loans to Germany. By 1928, however, U.S. investors were rapidly withdrawing their capital from Germany in search of higher returns in the booming U.S. stock market. This tightened credit in Germany. Then the crash of the overpriced U.S. market in October 1929 suddenly forced strapped American investors to pull still more of their funds out of Germany. This process continued for two years, weakening the major banks in Germany and central Europe.

The Germans seemed to have no choice but to freeze foreign assets—that is, to cease allowing conversion of assets held in German marks to other currencies. In this atmosphere, investors seeking the safest place for their capital tried to cash in currency for gold—or for British pounds, which could then be converted to gold. The flight to gold soon put such pressure on the British currency that Britain was forced to devalue the pound and sever it from the gold standard in September 1931. This proved the definitive end of the worldwide system of economic exchange based on the gold standard that had gradually crystallized during the nineteenth century.

The absence of a single standard of exchange, combined with various currency restrictions, made foreign trade more difficult and uncertain. So did the scramble for tariff protection that proved a widespread response to the developing crisis. Crucial was the U.S. Smoot-Hawley Tariff Act of June 1930, which raised taxes on imports by 50 to 100 percent, forcing other nations to take comparable steps.

The decline of trade spread depression throughout the world economic system. By 1933 most major European countries were able to export no more than two-thirds, and in some cases as little as one-third, of the amount they had sold in 1929. By 1932 the European economies had shrunk to a little over half their 1929 size. With less being produced and sold, the demand for labor declined sharply. Unemployment produced widespread malnutrition, which led, in turn, to sharp increases in such diseases as tuberculosis, scarlet fever, and rickets.

During the first years of the Depression, economic policymakers based their responses on the "classical" economic model, which suggested that a downward turn in the business cycle was a normal and necessary adjustment and that government interference would only upset this self-adjusting mechanism. By 1932, however, it was clear that the conventional response was not working, and governments began seeking to stimulate the economy. Strategies varied widely. In the United States, Franklin D. Roosevelt (1882–1945) defeated the incumbent president, Herbert Hoover, in 1932 with the promise of a New Deal—a commitment to increase government spending to restore purchasing power. In fascist Italy (see pages 638–641), a state agency created to infuse capital into failing companies proved a reasonably effective basis for collaboration between government and business. In Nazi Germany (see pages 644–648), government measures sealed off the German mark from international fluctuations, stimulated public spending, partly on rearmament, and kept wages low.

High unemployment in Norway, Sweden, and Denmark helped social democrats win power in all three countries by the mid-1930s. The new left-leaning governments responded to the crisis by pioneering the "welfare state," providing such benefits as health care, unemployment insurance, and family allowances. To pay for the new welfare safety net, the Scandinavian countries adopted a high level of progressive taxation and pared military expenditures to a minimum. The Scandinavian model attracted much admiration as a "third way" between free-market capitalism and the various dictatorial extremes.

The Depression Worldwide

The Depression had a major impact on the non-Western world and its relations with the West. The radical restriction of international trade meant a sharp decline in demand for the commodities that colonial and other regions exported to the industrialized West. The value of Latin American exports declined by half. With foreign exchange scarce, Latin Americans had to curtail imports and intensify their efforts to industrialize on their own. This enterprise required a greater role for the state—and often entailed political change in an authoritarian direction.

In colonial nations, strains from the Depression further undermined the prestige of the liberal capitalist West and fed nationalist, anti-Western sentiments. In India, the increase in misery among rural villagers spread the movement for national independence from urban elites to the rural masses. In this context Mohandas Gandhi, who had become known by 1920 for advocating noncooperation with the British, became the first Indian leader to win a mass following throughout the Indian subcontinent. Encouraging villagers to boycott British goods, Gandhi accented simplicity, self-reliance, and an overall strategy of nonviolent civil disobedience based on Indian traditions. (See the box "Encounters with the West: Gandhi on Nonviolence.")

In Japan, the strains of the Great Depression helped produce precisely the turn to imperialist violence that Gandhi sought to counter. Lacking essential raw materials, Japan was dependent on international trade and thus reacted strongly as increasing tariffs elsewhere cut sharply into Japanese exports. Led by young army officers eager for their country to embrace a less subservient form of Westernization, Japan turned to aggressive imperialism. Attacking in 1931, Japanese forces quickly reduced Manchuria to a puppet state, but the Japanese met stubborn resistance when they began seeking to extend this conquest to the rest of China in 1937.

Japanese pressure indirectly furthered the rise of the Chinese communist movement, led by Mao Zedong (1893–1976). Securing a base in the Yanan district in 1936, Mao began seeking to apply Marxism-Leninism to China through land reform and other measures to link the communist elite to the Chinese peasantry. Mao was adapting Western ideas to build an indigenous movement that would overcome Western imperialism and create an alternative to Western capitalism.

The Depression, and the halting responses of the democracies in dealing with it, enhanced the prestige of the new regimes in the Soviet Union, Italy, and Germany, which appeared to be dealing with their economies more effectively. Capitalism seemed to be on trial—and so, increasingly, did parliamentary democracy. In east-central Europe, new democracies seemed to take root after the war, but except in Czechoslovakia and Finland the practice of parliamentary government did not match the promise of the immediate postwar period. Democracy seemed divisive and ineffective, so one country after another adopted a more authoritarian alternative during the 1920s and early 1930s.

Poland offers a dramatic example. Although its democratic constitution of 1921 established a cabinet responsible to parliament, the parliament fragmented into numerous parties. Poland had fourteen different ministries from November 1918 to May 1926, when a coup d'état led by Marshal Josef Pilsudski replaced parliamentary government with an authoritarian regime stressing national unity. The suppression of democracy came as a relief to many Poles—and was even welcomed by the trade unions. The regime held power until Poland was invaded by Nazi Germany in 1939.

THE STALINIST REVOLUTION IN THE SOVIET UNION

In making their revolution in 1917, the Bolsheviks had expected to spark a series of revolutions elsewhere. But a decade later, revolution elsewhere was nowhere in sight, and it seemed that,

~ ENCOUNTERS WITH THE WEST ~

Gandhi on Nonviolence

Mohandas Gandhi, a successful English-educated lawyer, emerged as a major force in the movement for Indian independence just after World War I. The following excerpts from articles published in 1935 and 1939—years notable for outbreaks of violence elsewhere—explain the significance of nonviolence to Gandhi's overall strategy.

Non-violence to be a creed has to be all-pervasive. I cannot be non-violent about one activity of mine and violent about others. That would be a policy, not a life-force. That being so, I cannot be indifferent about the war that Italy is now waging against Abyssinia. . . . India had an unbroken tradition of non-violence from times immemorial. But at no time in her ancient history, as far as I know it, has it had complete non-violence in action pervading the whole land. Nevertheless, it is my unshakeable belief that her destiny is to deliver the message of non-violence to mankind. . . .

. . . India as a nation is not non-violent in the full sense of the term. . . . Her non-violence is that of the weak. . . . She lacks the ability to offer physical resistance. She has no consciousness of strength. She is conscious only of her weakness. If she were otherwise, there would be no communal problems, nor political. . . . [I]f we, as Indians, could but for a moment visualize ourselves as a strong people disdaining to strike, we should cease to fear Englishmen whether as soldiers, traders or administrators, and they to distrust us. Therefore if we became truly non-violent . . . we being millions would be the greatest moral force in the world, and Italy would listen to our friendly word. . . .

. . . [W]hen society is deliberately constructed in accordance with the law of non-

violence, its structure will be different in material particulars from what it is today. But I cannot say in advance what the government based wholly on non-violence will be like.

What is happening today is disregard of the law of non-violence and enthronement of violence as if it were an eternal law. The democracies, therefore, that we see at work in England, America and France are only so called, because they are no less based on violence than Nazi Germany, Fascist Italy or even Soviet Russia. The only difference is that the violence of the last three is much better organized than that of the three democratic powers. Nevertheless we see today a mad race for outdoing one another in the matter of armaments. . . .

Holding the view that without the recognition of non-violence on a national scale there is no such thing as a constitutional or democratic government, I devote my energy to the propagation of non-violence as the law of our life—individual, social, political, national and international. I fancy that I have seen the light, though dimly. I write cautiously, for I do not profess to know the whole of the Law. If I know the successes of my experiments, I know also my failures. But the successes are enough to fill me with undying hope.

Source: Raghavan Iyer, ed., *The Essential Writings of Mahatma Gandhi* (Delhi: Oxford University Press, 1991), pp. 245–247, 262–263. Copyright 1991 by the Navajivan Trust. Reprinted by permission of the Navajivan Trust.

for the foreseeable future, the communist regime in Russia would have to go it alone as it sought to transform itself under new leadership.

Seeking to build "socialism in one country," Joseph Stalin led the Soviet Union during the 1930s through one of the most astounding transformations the world had ever seen. It mixed great achievement with brutality and terror in bizarre and often tragic ways. The resulting governmental system, which gave Stalin unprecedented power, proved crucial to the outcome of the great experiment that began with the Russian Revolution of 1917. But whether the fateful turn of the 1930s had been implicit in the Leninist revolutionary model or stemmed mostly from unforeseen circumstances and Stalin's idiosyncratic personality remains uncertain.

Consolidating Communist Power in Russia, 1917–1921

Even after leading the revolution that toppled the provisional government in November 1917, the Bolsheviks could not claim majority support in Russia. When the long-delayed elections to select a constituent assembly were finally held a few weeks after the revolution, the Bolsheviks ended up with fewer than one-quarter of the seats, while the Socialist Revolutionaries won a clear majority. But over the next three years the Communists, as the Bolsheviks renamed themselves, consolidated their power, establishing a centralized and nondemocratic communist regime. Power lay not with the soviets, and not with some coalition of socialist parties, but solely with the Communist party. The Communists also established centralized control of the economy, subjecting workers to more rigorous discipline.

During its first years, the new communist regime encountered a genuine emergency that seemed especially to require a monopoly of power. For over two years the communist Red Army had to fight a brutal civil war against counterrevolutionary "Whites," people who had been dispossessed by the revolution or who had grown disillusioned with the Communist party. The Whites drew support from foreign intervention and from separatist sentiment, as several of the non-Russian nationalities of the old Russian Empire sought to defect.

Although the counterrevolutionary assault seriously threatened the young communist regime, the Whites were unable to rally much popular support. Peasants feared that a White victory would mean the restoration of the old order, including the return of their newly won lands to their former landlords. By the end of active fighting in November 1920, the communist regime had regained most of the territory it had lost early in the civil war.

Many communist initiatives were tabled due to the demands of fighting counterrevolutionaries supported by foreign troops. Nevertheless, the commissar for public welfare, Alexandra Kollontai (1872–1952), established some child-care facilities to aid working parents and began structuring public medical care, though such programs were limited by lack of funds. A disciple of the German Socialist Clara Zetkin (Rosa Luxemburg had introduced them in 1906), Kollontai was the representative of women's concerns in Lenin's regime and as such she promulgated a decree transforming marriage from a religious arrangement legally dominated by the male partner into a civil arrangement between two equals. She also pushed through laws for equal schooling for girls, free hospital maternity care, easy divorce based on equal grounds for men and women, and ready access to birth control and abortion. Kollontai believed that communism could not survive without ensuring women the right to fulfilling work—which required the state to provide for familial domestic chores. She also argued for increased social equality and insisted on an end to double standards in sexual behavior, but these were radical new ideas with little immediate impact, especially under the strains of conterrevolution.

The counterrevolutionary and separatist movements also created a sense that the non-Russian nationalities required close control. Thus, when the Union of Soviet Socialist Republics (U.S.S.R.) was organized in December 1922, it was only nominally a federation of autonomous republics; strong centralization from the Communists' new capital in Moscow was the rule from the start.

Although they had to concentrate on the civil war from 1918 to late 1920, the Russian communists founded the Third, or Communist, International—commonly known as the Comintern—in March 1919. The Russian communists expected to lead the international socialist movement, but the Comintern's aggressive claim to leadership led to a lasting schism in the European socialist movement by early 1921. All over the world socialist parties split between "communists," who chose to affiliate with the Comintern, and "socialists," who rejected Comintern leadership.

At first, many European socialists opted for the Comintern, but as the implications of membership became clearer over the next few years, the balance shifted to favor the socialists. Late in 1923 the Comintern finally concluded that revolution elsewhere could not be expected soon. The immediate enemy was not capitalism or the bourgeoisie but the socialists, communism's rival for working-class support. The communists' incessant criticism of the socialists, whom they dubbed "social fascists," weakened the European left, especially in the face of the growing threat of fascism.

From Lenin to Stalin, 1921–1929

Although it managed to win the civil war, the communist regime was clearly in crisis by the beginning of 1921, partly because of "war communism," the rough-and-ready controlled economy that the war effort seemed to make necessary. With industrial production only about one-fifth the 1913 total, there were strikes in the factories, and peasants were resisting further requisitions of grain. In March 1921, sailors at the Kronstadt naval base mutinied, suffering considerable loss of life as governmental control was re-established.

With the very survival of the revolution in question, Lenin replaced war communism with the New Economic Policy, or NEP, in March 1921. Although transport, banking, heavy industry, and wholesale commerce remained under state control, the NEP restored considerable scope for private enterprise, especially in the retail sector and in agriculture. The economy quickly revived and by 1927 was producing at prewar levels. But what about the longer term? The Marxist understanding of historical progress required industrialization, and so debate focused on industrial development—the scope for it under Soviet conditions and its relationship to the creation of socialism.

This debate about priorities became bound up with questions about the leadership of the new regime. Lenin suffered the first of a series of strokes in May 1922 and died in January 1924, setting off a struggle among his possible successors. Leon Trotsky, a powerful thinker and architect of the Red Army, was by most measures Lenin's heir apparent. Although he favored tighter economic controls to speed industrial development, Trotsky planned for the Soviet Union to concentrate on spreading the revolution to other countries.

But it was Joseph Stalin (1879–1953) who gradually assumed power after Lenin's death. Born Josef Djugashvili into a lower-class family in Georgia, Stalin became party secretary in 1922, enabling him to establish his control of the Soviet system by 1929. Though he lacked Trotsky's charisma and knew little of economics, Stalin proved a master of backstage political maneuvering, playing his rivals against each other and accusing his critics of lack of faith in the Soviet working class. He outmaneuvered Trotsky and his allies, removing them from positions of power, and finally forced Trotsky into exile in 1929. Bitterly critical of Stalin to the end, Trotsky was murdered by Stalin's agents in Mexico in 1940.

Crash Industrialization and Forced Collectivization, 1929–1933

Stalin believed that the Soviet Union had to catch up with the West—and quickly. By 1929, he had instituted a policy of crash industrialization, favoring heavy industry and based on forced agricultural collectivization. This attempt to mobilize and control society was without precedent in Western history, and it affected the whole shape of the regime, including cultural policy. In 1929, Soviet officials began demanding "socialist realism," which portrayed the Soviet revolution in an inspiring, heroic light intended to encourage the intense new productive demands.

Promoting Industrial Growth With the turn to crash industrialization by 1929, the Soviet regime harnessed art to inspire enthusiastic participation in the common effort to build an industrial economy. The mix of images in this poster from about 1932 suggests that, working together, the state and the people were rapidly raising the country's socioeconomic level. *(David King Collection)*

Beginning in 1930, the peasants were forcibly herded into large, government-controlled collective farms. Communist leaders wanted to control agricultural pricing and distribution so that they could squeeze a surplus from agriculture to be sold abroad, earning money to build factories, dams, and power plants. So unpopular was this measure that many peasants killed their livestock or smashed their farm implements rather than let them be collectivized. During the first two months of 1930, as many as 14 million head of cattle were slaughtered, resulting in an orgy of meat eating and a shortage of draft animals. In 1928, there had been 60 million cattle in the Soviet Union; by 1934 there were only 33.5 million.

Collectivization served, as intended, to squeeze from the peasantry the resources needed to finance industrialization. But it was carried out with extreme brutality. What was being squeezed was not merely a surplus—the state's extractions cut into subsistence. So although Soviet agricultural exports went up after 1930, large numbers of peasants starved to death. The great famine of 1932–1933 resulted in between 5 and 6 million deaths, over half of them in Ukraine.

By 1937 almost all Soviet agriculture took place on collective farms, and significant increases in industrial output had established solid foundations in heavy industry, including the bases for military production. But, despite its successes, the forced development program created many inefficiencies and entailed tremendous human costs. The Soviet Union could probably have done at least as well, with much less suffering, through other strategies of industrial development. Moreover, Stalin's program departed from certain socialist principles—egalitarianism in wages, for example—that the regime had taken very seriously in the late 1920s. New labor laws established harsh punishments for absenteeism or tardiness and severely limited the freedom of workers to change jobs. There was no collective bargaining and no right to strike.

From Opposition to Terror, 1932–1939

Stalin's radical course, with its brutality and uncertain economic justification, quickly provoked opposition. During the summer of 1932, a group centered around M. N. Ryutin (1890–1937) circulated among party leaders a two-hundred-page tract calling for a retreat from Stalin's economic program and a return to democracy within the party. Stalin promptly had Ryutin and his associates expelled from the party, then arrested and imprisoned. But as the international situation grew menacing during the 1930s, Stalin became ever more preoccupied with the potential for further opposition.

In 1934 the assassination of Sergei Kirov (1888–1934), party leader of Leningrad (the former Petrograd), gave Stalin an excuse to intensify the crackdown against opponents. Though not conclusive, the evidence suggests that Stalin himself was responsible for killing Kirov. In any case, the event served Stalin's interests by creating a sense of emergency justifying extraordinary measures. The eventual result was a series of bizarre show trials, deadly purges, and, ultimately, a kind of terror, with no one safe from arrest by the secret police.

Between 1936 and 1938, famed Bolshevik veterans confessed to a series of sensational trumped-up charges: that they had been behind the assassination of Kirov, that they would have killed Stalin if given the chance, that they constituted an "anti-Soviet, Trotskyite center," spying for Germany and Japan. Many "confessed" because they thought it would help the regime. Almost all the accused were convicted and executed. Ryutin refused to "confess" and was shot in secret early in 1937.

A purge of the army in 1937 wiped out its top ranks, with 35,000 officers—half the entire officer corps—shot or imprisoned in response to unfounded charges of spying and treason. The Communist party underwent several purges, culminating in the great purge of 1937 and 1938. Of the roughly two thousand delegates to the 1934 congress of the Communist party, over half were shot during the next few years. The purge of the party got rid of the remaining "old Bolsheviks," those who had been involved in the revolution in 1917 and thus retained a certain independence. By 1939, Stalin loyalists constituted the entire party leadership.

The purge process touched virtually everyone as the net widened by 1938. Everybody knew someone who had been implicated, so everyone felt some measure of vulnerability to arrest, which would be followed by execution or exile to forced-labor camps. Moreover, there was a random, arbitrary quality to the purges. Ordinary people were tempted to denounce others, if only to demonstrate their own loyalty. Many believed that there was some treason in their midst: The unending talk of intrigues and plots had affected them deeply. The contrast between propaganda showing heroic achievement and the reality of shortages and hardships further suggested that a vast conspiracy was at work.

Somewhat ironically, Stalin's need to control his population centered on birth as well as death: In 1936 he ended the reproductive freedom that Alexandra Kollontai had put in place after the revolution. Abortion was outlawed, and birth control information became difficult to obtain. Stalin was clearly interested in replacing the depleted population, but these measures also served to regulate women's lives and choices and to make the family reflect the authoritarianism of the state.

The final toll of the purges was staggering. Of the approximately 160 million people in the Soviet Union, something like 8.5 million were arrested in 1937 and 1938, and of these perhaps 1 million were executed. Half the total membership of the Communist party—1.2 million people—was arrested; most were executed or died in forced-labor camps. Altogether, the purges resulted in approximately 8 million deaths. The death toll from Stalin's policies between 1929 and 1939, including forced collectivizations, was perhaps 20 million.

This fateful turn in the development of the communist regime in the Soviet Union proved to be one of the pivotal events of modern history. Some insist that Stalin was pursuing a deliberate policy, seeking to create an all-encompassing system of control. Others argue that though Stalin's ultimate responsibility is undeniable, he was simply responding on an improvised basis to a chaotic situation. Either way, Stalin's personal idiosyncrasies and growing paranoia were crucial to the peculiar development of the Soviet system.

Stalin had won his position based on his backroom political skill, not his popular appeal. Although a special aura came to surround him by the end of the 1930s, his style of leadership remained distinct from that of Mussolini and Hitler, who based their power on a direct relationship with the people.

FASCIST ITALY

Although Soviet communism was something new, it had developed from within the tradition of Marxist socialism. The pedigree of fascism was much less clear. Its leader, Benito Mussolini (1883–1945), had begun as a socialist, but by the end of the war he had left the socialist mainstream behind and was looking for a new constituency. The fascist movement that Mussolini forged in March 1919 proved violent and disturbing, yet it attracted considerable support among those disillusioned with parliamentary politics and hostile to the Marxist left.

The term *fascism* derived from the ancient Roman symbol of power and unity, *fasces,* a bundle of rods surrounding an ax. Stressing national solidarity, the fascists were hostile not only to liberal individualism and parliamentary democracy, but also to Marxist socialism with its emphasis on class struggle. Fascism was not traditionally con-

servative either. It claimed to be a new alternative to both liberal democracy and Marxist communism, based on values forged in the war.

The Crisis of Liberal Italy and the Creation of Fascism, 1919–1925

The Italian experience of World War I proved especially controversial because the Italians could have avoided it. No one attacked Italy in 1914, and the country could have received significant territorial benefits just by remaining neutral. Still, many Italians felt that participation in this war would be a revitalizing test of the young nation's strength. When Italy finally intervened on the side of the Triple Entente in May 1915, it was because France and Britain had promised specific territorial gains at the secret Treaty of London in April.

Despite the near collapse of the Italian armies in October 1917, Italy lasted out the war and contributed to the victory over Austria-Hungary. Supporters of the war felt that this success could lead to a thoroughgoing renewal of Italian public life, but to many—especially Socialists and Catholics—intervention had been a tragic mistake. Thus, despite Italy's participation in the victory, division over the war's significance immensely complicated the Italian political situation.

The situation became even more volatile when Italy did not reap all the gains expected at the Paris Peace Conference. Italy got most of what it had been promised in the Treaty of London, but appetites increased with the dissolution of the Austro-Hungarian Empire. To some Italians, the disappointing outcome confirmed that the war had been a mistake, its benefits not worth the costs. Others were outraged at what seemed a denigration of the Italian contribution by France, Britain, and the United States. Thus the outcome fanned resentment of Italy's allies, and also of the country's political leaders, who seemed too weak to deliver on their promises.

Amid this tension, Socialist leaders talked of imitating the Bolshevik Revolution. During 1919 and 1920, a wave of quasi-revolutionary labor unrest included several national strikes and a series of factory occupations. Although there was a revolutionary atmosphere in these years, Italian Socialist leaders did not carry out the planning and organization necessary for a Leninist-style takeover.

With the established political system of old liberal politics at an impasse, and the Socialist party too inflexible and too romantic to lead a radical transformation, fascism emerged, claiming to offer a third way. It was bound to oppose the Socialists because of conflict over the meaning of the war and the kind of transformation Italy needed. This antisocialist posture made fascism attractive to reactionary interests. By early 1921 landowners in northern and central Italy were footing the bill as bands of young fascists drove around the countryside beating up workers and burning down socialist meeting halls. But fascist spokesmen claimed to offer something other than mere reaction: a new politics that would prove better than Marxist socialism at pursuing the interests of the working class.

At the same time, important sectors of Italian industry, which had grown rapidly due to government orders during the war, looked with apprehension toward the more competitive postwar international economy. Nationalist thinkers and business spokesmen questioned the capacity of the parliamentary system to provide the vigorous leadership that Italy needed. Prone to bickering and partisanship, politicians lacked the vision to pursue Italy's long-term international economic interests and the will to impose the necessary discipline on the domestic level. Thus, the government had been relatively weak in responding to the labor unrest of 1919 and 1920.

In postwar Italy, then, there was widespread discontent with the established forms of politics, but those discontented were socially disparate, and their aims were not compatible. Some had been socialists before the war; others were nationalists hostile to socialism. While some envisioned a more intense kind of mass politics, others thought the masses already had too much power. Still, these discontented groups agreed on the need for change.

The person who seemed able to translate these discontents and aspirations into a new political force was the one-time socialist Benito Mussolini. From the Romagna region of central Italy, where his father was a blacksmith and a socialist and his mother a teacher, Mussolini became editor of the Socialist party's national newspaper, *Avanti!*, in 1912, when only 29 years old. Many saw him as the fresh face needed to revitalize Italian socialism.

His concern with renewal had made Mussolini an unorthodox socialist even before 1914, and after war broke out, he was prominent among those on the left who called for Italian intervention. The fact that socialists in France, Germany, and elsewhere had rallied to their respective national war efforts caused him to reconsider the old socialism, based on international proletarian solidarity. But the Socialist party refused to follow his call for intervention, remaining neutralist and aloof, so Mussolini found himself cut off from his earlier constituency.

Through his new newspaper, *Il popolo d'Italia* (*The People of Italy*), Mussolini promptly emerged as a leading advocate of Italian participation in the war. He saw military service once Italy intervened, and after the war he aspired to translate the war experience into a new form of politics. But after founding the fascist movement in March 1919, Mussolini became embroiled in periodic disputes with important sectors of his movement. Young fascist militants wanted to replace the existing parliamentary system with a wholly new political order, but Mussolini seemed more prone to use fascism as his personal route to power within the existing system. When his maneuvering finally won him the prime minister's post in October 1922, it was not at all clear that a change of regime was in the offing.

At first, Mussolini emphasized normalization and legality. Fascism had apparently been absorbed within the political system; with Mussolini as prime minister, there would be changes, but not revolutionary changes. Government would become more vigorous and efficient, the swollen Italian bureaucracy would be streamlined, and the trains would run on time. Those

Benito Mussolini The founder of fascism is shown with other fascist leaders in 1922, as he becomes prime minister of Italy. Standing at Mussolini's right (with beard) is Italo Balbo, later a pioneering aviator and fascist Italy's air force minister. *(Corbis-Bettmann)*

who had envisioned more sweeping change were increasingly frustrated.

In June 1924 the murder of Giacomo Matteotti (1885–1924), a moderate socialist parliamentary deputy, sparked a crisis that forced Mussolini's hand. Shortly after a speech denouncing fascist violence, Matteotti was killed by fascist thugs. A great public outcry followed, as Italians questioned whether the government—or Mussolini himself—was responsible for the crime. Many from the establishment who had tolerated Mussolini as the man who could keep order now deserted him. A growing chorus called for his resignation.

Mussolini sought at first to be conciliatory and reassuring, but more radical fascists saw the crisis as an opportunity for fascism to end the

compromise with the old order and to create a whole new political system. On December 31, 1924, thirty-three militants called on Mussolini to demand that he make up his mind. The way out of the crisis was not to delimit the scope of fascism but to expand it. Mussolini was the leader of fascism, *Il Duce,* and in that role he would have to implement the fascist revolution.

In a speech to the Chamber of Deputies a few days later, on January 3, 1925, Mussolini finally committed himself to a more radical course. Defiantly claiming the "full political, moral, and historical responsibility for all that has happened," including "all the acts of violence," he promised to accelerate the transformation that he claimed to have initiated with his agitation for intervention in 1914 and 1915.[2]

Innovation and Compromise in Fascist Italy, 1925–1930

Early in 1925, the fascist government imprisoned or exiled opposition leaders and outlawed the other parties and the nonfascist labor unions. But fascism was not seeking simply a conventional monopoly of political power; the new fascist state was to be totalitarian, all-encompassing, limitless in its reach. Under the old liberal regime, the fascists charged, the state had been too weak to promote the national interest, and the society had been too fragmented. So Mussolini's regime expanded the state's sovereignty and mobilized the society to create a deeper sense of national identity. For example, a new system of labor judges settled labor disputes, replacing the right to strike. And the Fascist party fostered new forms of participation in public organizations and clubs.

The centerpiece of the new fascist state was *corporativism*, which entailed mobilizing people as producers by organization of the workplace. Groupings based on occupation or economic function were to replace parliament as the basis for political participation and decision making. Beginning in 1926, corporativist institutions were established in stages until a Chamber of Fasces and Corporations at last replaced the old Chamber of Deputies in 1939.

It was through this corporative state that the fascists claimed to be providing the world with a third way beyond outmoded democracy and misguided communism. The practice of corporativism never lived up to its grandiose rhetoric, but the effort to devise new forms of political participation was central to fascism's self-understanding. The effort attracted much attention abroad, especially during the Great Depression.

The social component of fascism emphasized masculine virility, female subordination, and large families destined to pack the work force and the army. To forcibly change the status of women, the fascists doubled school fees for girls and ordered women to be fired from a range of occupations. In 1927, all women's salaries were reduced by 50 percent. Mussolini's endless praise for war widows and good mothers did strike a chord for many women, hard-pressed by the years of war and the demands of modernity, but overall the strategy was a failure. Fertility did not rise.

In this matter and others, it was difficult to determine whether the fascist regime was really new or actually represented a revival of tradition. In 1929, Mussolini worked out an accord with the Catholic church, formally ending the dispute between the church and the Italian state that had resulted from national unification. The compromise seemed to imply a kind of endorsement of Mussolini's government on the part of the church and the establishment in Italy. But the gesture displeased many fascists, leading to a partial crackdown on Catholic youth organizations in 1931, as Mussolini continued to juggle traditionalist compromise and revolutionary pretension.

GERMANY: FROM THE WEIMAR REPUBLIC TO NATIONAL SOCIALISM

Just as hopes for democratic renewal had met with frustration in Italy, many Germans found their desire for political participation eclipsed by their desire for government stability. With the Weimar Republic of 1918–1933, Germany experienced full-fledged parliamentary democracy for the first time, but this democracy had great difficulty establishing its legitimacy and was unable to address the ills of the Great Depression. As a result, the Nazi leader Adolf Hitler (1889–1945) got a chance to govern early in 1933. He immediately began creating a new regime, the Third Reich, intended as the antithesis of Weimar democracy.

Germany's Cautious Revolution, 1919–1933

The Weimar Republic had two strikes against it from the outset: It was born of national defeat, and it was forced to take responsibility for the harsh and dictated Treaty of Versailles in 1919. During its first years, moreover, the regime encountered severe economic dislocation, culminating in the hyperinflation of 1923, as well as ideological polarization that threatened to tear the country apart.

The initial threat to the new German republic, proclaimed in November 1918, came from the left, stimulated by the Russian example. Spearheaded by Rosa Luxemburg and Karl Liebknecht in Berlin (see page 615), revolutionary unrest reached a peak in December 1918 and January 1919. Even after Luxemburg and Liebknecht were captured and murdered in January, there remained a serious chance of revolution through May 1919, and communist revolutionary agitation continued until the end of 1923.

For this reason, the new government made repression of the extreme left a priority—even though it meant retaining some of the old imperial institutions. New forces of repression were born as well: When the regular army, weakened by war and defeat, proved unable to control radical agitation in Berlin, the government began to organize "Free Corps," irregular volunteer paramilitary groups to be used against the revolutionaries.

During the first five months of 1919, the government unleashed the Free Corps to crush leftist movements all over Germany, often with wanton brutality. In relying on right-wing paramilitary groups, the republic's leaders were playing with fire, but the immediate threat at this point came from the left. In 1920, however, the government faced a right-wing coup attempt, the Kapp Putsch. The army declined to defend the republic, but the government managed to survive thanks largely to a general strike by leftist workers. The republic's early leaders had to juggle both extremes because, as one of them put it, the Weimar Republic was "a candle burning at both ends."

Though sporadic street fighting by paramilitary groups continued, by 1924 the republic had achieved an uneasy stability. But Germany's postwar revolution remained confined to the political level. There was no effort to build a loyal republican army and no attempt to purge the bureaucracy and the judiciary of antidemocratic elements from the old order. When right-wing extremists assassinated prominent leaders, such as the Jewish industrialist Walther Rathenau in

1922, the courts often proved unwilling to prosecute those responsible. In general, those who ran the new government were skeptical of democracy, even hostile to the new regime.

Elections in January 1919 produced a constituent assembly that convened in Weimar, seat of what seemed the best traditions of German culture, to draft a democratic constitution. The elections had taken place before the peace conference produced the widely detested Treaty of Versailles. When the first regular parliamentary elections were finally held in June 1920, the three moderate parties that had led the new government and been forced to accept the treaty suffered a major defeat. Those were the parties most committed to democratic institutions, but they were never again to achieve a parliamentary majority. The 1920 elections, like many of those that followed, revealed an extreme lack of consensus in the German electorate.

The lack of consensus produced a multiparty system and a fragmented Reichstag. No single party ever won an absolute majority during the Weimar years, so governments were always unstable coalitions. Not only was the Weimar party system fragmented and complex, but it encompassed a wide ideological array, including extremes of both left and right bent on sabotaging the new democratic institutions. On the left, the Communists constantly criticized the more moderate Socialists. On the right, the situation was more complex. The extreme right National Socialists, or Nazis, were noisy and often violent, but they did not attract much electoral support until 1930. More damaging to parliamentary democracy for most of the Weimar period was the right-wing Nationalist party (DNVP), which played on nationalist resentments and fears of socialism.

Still, all was not necessarily lost for the republic when the three moderate parties were defeated in 1920. Germans who were unsupportive or hostile at first might be gradually won over. After the death of President Friedrich Ebert in 1925, Paul von Hindenburg, the emperor's field marshal, was elected president. Hindenburg's presidency suggested to skeptics that the new regime was legitimate and a worthy object for German patriotism.

The individual with the best chance of winning converts to the Weimar Republic in the early 1920s was Gustav Stresemann (1878–1929), the leader of the German People's party (DVP), a conservative but relatively flexible party that seemed capable of broadening the republic's base of support. As chancellor, and especially as foreign minister, Stresemann was the republic's leading statesman.

Stresemann became chancellor in August 1923, when inflation was raging out of control. Within months his government had Germany back on its feet, partly because the other powers were becoming more conciliatory. By November 1923 even the French agreed that an international commission should review the reparations question. In the summer of 1924, a commission led by the American financier Charles G. Dawes produced the Dawes Plan, which remained in force until 1929. The plan worked well by lowering payments, providing loans, and securing the stability of the German currency.

Stresemann understood that better relations with the victors had to be a priority if Germany was to overcome the present crisis and return to the councils of the great powers. French foreign minister Aristide Briand (1862–1932) shared Stresemann's desire for improved relations, and together they engineered the more conciliatory spirit in international relations evident by 1924. Its most substantial fruit was the Locarno Agreement of October 1925. France and Germany accepted the postwar border between them, which meant that Germany gave up any claim to Alsace-Lorraine. France, for its part, renounced the sort of direct military intervention in Germany that it had attempted with the Ruhr invasion of 1923 and agreed to begin withdrawing troops from the Rhineland ahead of schedule. Germany accepted France's key advantage, the demilitarization of the Rhineland, and Britain and Italy explicitly guaranteed the measure.

By accepting the status quo in the west, Stresemann freed Germany to concentrate on eastern Europe, where he envisioned gradual but substantial revision in the territorial settlement. Especially with the creation of Poland, that settlement had come partly at Germany's expense. Stresemann, then, was pursuing German interests, not subordinating them to some larger European vision. But he was willing to compromise and, for the most part, to play by the rules.

With the Locarno treaty, the victors accepted Germany as a diplomatic equal for the first time since the war. Germany's return to good graces culminated in its entry into the League of Nations in 1926. Stresemann and Briand were joint winners of the Nobel Peace Prize for 1926.

With the expiration of the Dawes Plan in 1929, the Young Plan, conceived by American businessman Owen D. Young, removed Allied controls over the German economy and specified that Germany pay reparations until 1988. Since the annual amount was less than Germany had been paying, it was expected that this plan would constitute a permanent, and reasonable, settlement. Nevertheless, the Young Plan produced resentment in Germany, leading, yet again, to political gains on the right.

When Stresemann died in October 1929, Weimar Germany was considerably better off than it had been in 1923, but the political consensus remained weak, the party system was still fragmented, and unstable coalition government remained the rule. The onset of the economic depression at the end of 1929 produced problems that Germany's fragile new democracy proved unable to handle. The pivotal issue was unemployment insurance. A Socialist chancellor, Hermann Müller (1876–1931), was leading the government when the Depression began, and as the crisis deepened, his party demanded increases in insurance coverage. When the Socialists failed to convince their coalition partners, the Müller government resigned in March 1930. That proved to be the end of normal parliamentary government in Weimar Germany.

President Hindenburg called on Heinrich Brüning (1885–1970), leader of the moderate Catholic Center party, to replace Müller as chancellor. Brüning promptly proposed an economic program that avoided unemployment insurance and public works projects in favor of directly deflationary measures. Brüning's program encountered opposition not only from socialists but also from conservatives, eager to undermine the republic altogether. As a result, Brüning could get no parliamentary majority. Rather than resigning or seeking a compromise, he invoked Article 48, the emergency provision of the Weimar constitution, which enabled him to govern under presidential decree.

When this expedient provoked strenuous protests, Brüning dissolved the Reichstag and scheduled new elections for September 1930. The outcome was disastrous—for Brüning and ultimately for Germany as well. Two of the democratic, pro-Weimar parties lost heavily, and the two political extremes were the big winners. The Communists gained 23 seats, for a total of 77 deputies in the Reichstag; the National Socialists did even better, climbing from the 12 seats they had garnered in 1928 to 107.

Brüning continued to govern, relying on President Hindenburg and Article 48 rather than majority support in the Reichstag. Meanwhile, the growth of the political extremes helped fuel an intensification of the political violence and street fighting that had bedeviled the Weimar Republic from the beginning. As scuffles between Nazis and Communists sometimes approached pitched battles, the inability of the government to keep order further damaged the prestige of the Republic.

In May 1932, Hindenburg's advisers finally persuaded him to dump Brüning in favor of an antidemocratic conservative. By this point the republic was a mere shell covering the backroom manipulation and dealing in Hindenburg's circle. The results of the July 1932 elections were the republic's death knell. The Nazis won 37.3 percent of the vote (230 seats) and the Communists 14.3 percent (89 seats). Together, the two extremes controlled a majority of the seats in the Reichstag, and each refused to work in coalition with any of the mainstream parties. Although he resisted for months, Hindenburg found it difficult not to give Adolf Hitler, as the leader of the largest party in the Reichstag, a chance to govern.

During the brief and tortured history of the Weimar Republic, there were twenty different cabinets, lasting an average of eight-and-a-half months each. The experience of instability, divisiveness, and finally paralysis reinforced the perception, long prominent in Germany, that parliamentary democracy was petty and ineffective. By 1932, the majority of Germans had lost confidence in the institutions of parliamentary democracy. Even those who voted for the Nazis were not clear what they might be getting, but, in light of economic depression and political impasse, it seemed time to try something else.

THE RISE OF NAZISM, 1919–1933

The National Socialist German Workers' party (NSDAP), or Nazism, emerged from the turbulent situation of Munich just after the war. A center of leftist agitation, the city also became a hotbed of the radical right, nurturing a number of new nationalist, militantly anticommunist political groups. One of them, a right-wing workers' party, attracted the attention of Hitler, who soon gave it his personal stamp.

Adolf Hitler was born in Austria in 1889, the son of a lower government official. By 1913 he had become a German nationalist hostile to the multinational Habsburg empire, and he immigrated to Germany. He volunteered for service in the German army in World War I, and it was during the war, he said later, that he "found himself."

He joined the infant German Workers' party late in 1919, and when his first political speech at a rally in February 1920 proved a resounding success, he began to believe he could play a special political role. But Hitler jumped the gun in November 1923 when, with Erich Ludendorff at his side, he led the Beer Hall Putsch in Munich, an attempt to launch a march on Berlin to overthrow the republic. On trial after this effort failed, Hitler gained greater national visibility as he denounced the Versailles treaty and the Weimar government. Still, *Mein Kampf (My*

Battle), the political tract that he wrote while in prison during 1924, sold poorly.

His failure in 1923 convinced Hitler that he should exploit the existing political system, but not challenge it directly, in his quest for power on the national level. Yet Hitler never intended to play by the rules: The Nazi party maintained a paramilitary arm, the Sturmabteilung (SA), which provoked a good deal of antileftist street violence.

In 1928 the Nazis attracted only 2.6 percent of the vote in the Reichstag elections. But, in the elections of September 1930, the first since the onset of the Depression, they increased their share dramatically, and in July 1932 their vote exploded to 37.3 percent, making them the largest party in the Reichstag.

As the crisis of the Weimar Republic deepened in 1932, conservative fears of a Marxist outcome played into Hitler's hands. President Hindenburg was relying heavily on a narrow circle of advisers who wanted to take advantage of the Nazis' mass support for conservative purposes. One of those advisers, Franz von Papen (1878–1969), lined up a new coalition that he proposed to Hindenburg: Hitler would be chancellor, Papen himself vice chancellor, and Alfred Hugenberg (1865–1951), the leader of the Nationalist party, finance minister. Still wary of Hitler, Hindenburg felt this combination might work to establish a parliamentary majority, box out the left, and contain Nazism. Hitler became chancellor on January 30, 1933.

The Consolidation of Hitler's Power, 1933–1934

When Hitler became chancellor, it was not obvious that a change of regime was beginning. Like his predecessors, he could govern only with the president's approval, and governmental institutions like the army, the judiciary, and the diplomatic corps were not in the hands of committed Nazis. But although an element of cultivated ambiguity remained, a revolution quickly began, creating the Third Reich.

On February 23, just weeks after Hitler became chancellor, a fire engulfed the Reichstag building in Berlin. It was set by a young Dutch communist acting on his own, but Hitler used it as an excuse to restrict civil liberties and imprison leftist leaders, including the entire Communist parliamentary delegation. Support from the Nationalists and the Center party enabled the Nazis to win Reichstag approval for an enabling act granting Hitler the power to make laws on his own for the next four years, bypassing both the Reichstag and the president.

Although the Weimar Republic was never formally abolished, the laws that followed fundamentally altered government, politics, and public life in Germany. The other parties were either outlawed or persuaded to dissolve so that in July 1933 the Nazi party was declared the only legal party. When President Hindenburg died in August 1934, the offices of chancellor and president were merged, and Germany had just one leader, Adolf Hitler.

During this period of power consolidation, Hitler generally accented normalization. To be sure, his methods occasionally gave conservatives pause. In an especially dramatic episode, the "blood purge" of June 30, 1934, he had several hundred people murdered. The purge was primarily directed against the SA, led by Ernst Röhm (1887–1934). Because Röhm had had pretensions of controlling the army, his removal seemed evidence that Hitler was taming the radicals in his movement. In fact, this purge led to the ascendancy of the Schutzstaffel, or SS, the Nazi elite, led by Heinrich Himmler (1900–1945), which became the institutional basis for the worst aspects of Nazism.

Nazi Aims and German Society

Hitler acted on the basis of a world-view that had coalesced by about 1924. (See the box "Hitler's World-View: Nature, Race, and Struggle.") The central components of his thinking—geopolitics, biological racism, anti-Semitism, and Social Darwinism—were by no means specifically German. They could be found all over the Western world by the early twentieth century.

Geopolitics claimed to offer a scientific understanding of world power based on geographical determinism. To remain sovereign in the

Hitler's World-View: Nature, Race, and Struggle

Hitler outlined his beliefs and aims in **Mein Kampf,** *which he wrote while in prison in 1924. The following passages reveal the racism, the anti-Semitism, and the emphasis on nature and struggle that formed the core of his world-view.*

No more than Nature desires the mating of weaker with stronger individuals, even less does she desire the blending of a higher with a lower race, since, if she did, her whole work of higher breeding, over perhaps hundreds of thousands of years, might be ruined with one blow.

Historical experience . . . shows with terrifying clarity that in every mingling of Aryan blood with that of lower peoples the result was the end of the cultured people. . . .

Here, of course, we encounter the objection of the modern pacifist, as truly Jewish in its effrontery as it is stupid! "Man's rôle is to overcome Nature!"

. . . [T]his planet once moved through the ether for millions of years without human beings and it can do so again some day if men forget that they owe their higher existence, not to the ideas of a few crazy ideologists, but to the knowledge and ruthless application of Nature's stern and rigid laws. . . .

In the Jewish people the will to self-sacrifice does not go beyond the individual's naked instinct of self-preservation. . . .

If the Jews were alone in the world, they would stifle in filth and offal; they would try to get ahead of one another in hate-filled struggle and exterminate one another. . . .

Source: Adolf Hitler, *Mein Kampf* (Boston: Houghton Mifflin, Sentry, 1943), trans. Ralph Manheim, pp. 286–289, 299, 301–302. Copyright 1943, renewed 1971 by Houghton Mifflin. Reprinted by permission of Houghton Mifflin Company and Random Century Group UK. All rights reserved.

new era of global superpowers like the United States, Hitler warned, Germany would have to expand its territory. By expanding into Poland and the western part of the Soviet Union, Germany could conquer the living space, or *Lebensraum,* necessary for agricultural-industrial balance—and ultimately for self-sufficiency.

The other strands of Hitler's world-view were much less plausible, though each had become prominent during the nineteenth century. Biological racism insisted that built-in racial characteristics determine what is most important about any individual. Anti-Semitism went beyond racism in claiming that Jews play a special and negative role. Social Darwinism accented the positive role of struggle among racial groups.

The dominant current of racist thinking labeled the "Aryans" as healthy, creative, superior.

In much racist thinking, Germanic peoples were somehow especially Aryan, though race mixing had produced impurity—and thus degeneration. For the sake of racial purity and historical progress, it was the duty of superior races to supplant backward races. To Hitler, the Jews were not simply another of the races involved in this endless struggle. Rather, as landless parasites, they had played a special historical role, embodying the principles—from humanitarianism to class struggle—that were antithetical to the healthy natural struggle among unified racial groups.

Although Hitler's world-view provided the underlying momentum for the Nazi regime, it did not specify a consistent program, and the regime often adopted short-term expedients that conflicted with its long-term aims. Thus it was possible for Germans living under Nazi rule in the 1930s to embrace aspects of Nazism without seeing where it was all leading.

Hitler's leadership was based on a charismatic relationship with the German people, a nonrational bond resting on common race. To create a genuine racial community, or *Volksgemeinschaft*, it was necessary to unify society and instill Nazi values, making the individual feel part of the whole—and ultimately an instrument to serve the whole. This entailed more or less forced participation in an array of Nazi organizations, from women's groups to the Hitler Youth, from the Labor Front to the Strength Through Joy leisure-time organization.

The Nazis devised unprecedented ways to stage-manage public life, using rituals like the Hitler salute, symbols like the swastika, new media like radio and film, and carefully orchestrated party rallies. The documentary film of a Nuremberg Nazi party rally, *Triumph of the Will* by Leni Riefenstahl (b. 1902), has long been recognized as one of the most compelling propaganda films ever made. Nazi insistence on a circumscribed role for women could shift markedly when women's labor—in this case the work of a promising young director—was deemed essential.

The constraint that Nazi policy put on the lives of women had several sources, but the government's desire to direct human breeding proved crucial. During the summer of 1933, Hitler's government began offering interest-free loans to help couples set up house if the woman agreed to leave the labor force, and Nazi women's organizations endlessly celebrated motherhood and large families. Yet family size continued to decrease in Germany as elsewhere in the industrialized world during the 1930s.

Efforts to control fertility took horrific form as the regime sought to stop the "unhealthy" from reproducing. Just months after coming to power, Hitler engineered a law mandating the compulsory sterilization of persons suffering from certain allegedly hereditary diseases. Medical personnel sterilized some 400,000, the vast majority of them "Aryan" Germans, during the Nazi years. (Forced sterilization was not limited to Nazi Germany in these years; the United

Hitler and Children Adolf Hitler was often portrayed as the friend of children. This photograph accompanied a story for an elementary school reader that described how Hitler, told it was this young girl's birthday, picked her from a crowd of well-wishers to treat her "to cake and strawberries with thick, sweet cream." *(From Heinrich Hoffman,* Jugend um Hitler. *© "Zeitgeschichte" Verlag und Vertriebs-Gesellschaft Berlin. Reproduced with permission. Photo courtesy Wiener Library, London)*

States and other democracies were experimenting with it as well, though not to this degree.)

Despite such extreme measures, Hitler's regime enjoyed considerable popular support, for even after Hitler was well entrenched in power, most Germans did not grasp the regime's deeper dynamic. Certainly some welcomed the feeling of belonging, and Hitler himself was immensely popular as a charismatic and decisive leader after the near paralysis of the Weimar years. Most important, before the coming of war in 1939, he seemed to go from success to success, surmounting the Depression and repudiating the major terms of the hated Versailles treaty.

The skillful work of Hitler's propaganda minister, Joseph Goebbels (1897–1945), played on these successes to create a "Hitler myth," which made Hitler seem at once heroic and a man of the people. This myth became central to the Nazi regime, but it merely provided a façade behind which the real Hitler could pursue deeper, long-term aims. These aims were not publicized directly, because the German people did not seem ready for them. In this sense, then, support for Hitler and his regime was broad but shallow during the 1930s.

Did Germans feel constantly under threat of the Gestapo, the secret police? In principle, the Gestapo could interpret the will of the *Führer*, or leader, and decide whether any individual citizen was "guilty" or not. But the Gestapo's victims were not picked at random. They were generally members of specific groups or people suspected of active opposition. So it cannot be said that the German people were coerced into participation through a general atmosphere of terror.

For Jewish Germans it was a different matter. Within weeks after Hitler became chancellor in 1933, new restrictions limited Jewish participation in the civil service, in the professions, and in German cultural life—and quickly drew censure from the League of Nations. The Nuremberg Laws, announced at a party rally in 1935, included prohibition of sexual relations and marriage between Jews and non-Jewish Germans.

About 11 percent of Germany's 550,000 Jews emigrated during 1933 and 1934, and perhaps 25 percent had gotten out by 1938. The fact that the regime stripped emigrating Jews of their assets made emigration more difficult, because countries were unwilling to take in substantial numbers of penniless Jews.

On November 9, 1938, using the assassination of a German diplomat in Paris as a pretext, the Nazis staged the Kristallnacht (Crystal Night) pogrom, during which almost all the synagogues in Germany and about seven thousand Jewish-owned stores were destroyed. Between 30,000 and 50,000 relatively prosperous Jews were arrested and forced to emigrate.

The systematic physical extermination of the Jews began only during the war, but the killing of others deemed superfluous or threatening to the racial community began earlier, with the euthanasia program initiated under volunteer medical teams in 1939. Its aim was to eliminate chronic mental patients, the incurably ill, and people with severe physical handicaps. Those subject to such treatment were primarily ethnic Germans, not Jews or foreigners. Because a public outcry developed, especially among relatives and church leaders, the program had to be discontinued in 1941, but by then it had claimed 100,000 lives.

The euthanasia program was based on the sense, fundamental to radical Nazism, that readiness for war was the real norm for society. Struggle necessitates selection, which requires overcoming humanitarian scruples—that "weakness" calls for special protection. Thus it was desirable to kill even ethnic Germans who were deemed unfit, as "life unworthy of life."

Preparation for war was the core of Nazism in practice. The conquest of living space in the east would provide not only the self-sufficiency necessary for sovereignty but also the land-rootedness necessary for racial health. Such a war of conquest would strike not only the Slavic peoples of the region but also Soviet communism. Beginning in 1936 the Nazis began to bend the economy to serve their long-term aims of war-making.

The Nazi drive toward war during the 1930s transformed international relations in Europe. The other European powers sought to understand Hitler's Germany in terms of the increasingly polarized political context of the period, betting that Hitler would stop short of engaging Europe in another war.

FASCIST CHALLENGE AND ANTIFASCIST RESPONSE

Communists and adherents of the various forms of fascism were bitterly hostile to each other, and beginning in 1934 communists sought to join with anyone who would work with them to fight the fascists. In France and Spain, this effort led to the formation of antifascist popular front coalition governments that struggled to defend democracy. In both cases, however, the Depression restricted maneuvering room, and these governments ended up furthering the polarization they were seeking to avoid.

The Reorientation of Fascist Italy, 1933–1939

By the mid-1930s, it was clear that Italian businessmen were managing to maintain their autonomy against the fascist effort to subordinate business to the political sphere. The corporative institutions never developed into genuine vehicles of mass participation through the workplace—if anything, in fact, they served to regiment the working class.

Mussolini was increasingly frustrated by the limitations he had encountered on the domestic level. On the international level, however, the new context after Hitler came to power offered him some space for maneuver. So as the fascist revolution in Italy faltered, Mussolini began concentrating on foreign policy.

Though Italy, like Germany, remained dissatisfied with the territorial status quo, it was not obvious that fascist Italy and Nazi Germany had to end up in the same camp. Italy was anxious to preserve an independent Austria as a buffer against Germany. There was considerable sentiment among Germans and Austrians for unification of the two countries, and such a greater Germany might threaten the lands Italy had won from Austria in 1919. When Germany seemed poised to absorb Austria in 1934, Mussolini helped stiffen the resistance of Austria's leaders and played a part in forcing Hitler to back down. Mussolini even warned that Nazism, with its racist orientation, posed a significant threat to the best of European civilization.

As it began to appear that France and Britain might have to work with the Soviet Union to check Germany, French and British conservatives pushed for good relations with Italy to provide ideological balance. So Italy was well positioned to play off both sides as Hitler began shaking things up on the international level after 1933. In 1935, just after Hitler announced significant rearmament measures, unilaterally repudiating provisions of the Versailles treaty for the first time, Mussolini hosted a meeting with the French and British prime ministers at Stresa, in northern Italy. To contain Germany, the three powers agreed to resist "any unilateral repudiation of treaties which may endanger the peace of Europe."

Mussolini was already preparing to extend Italy's possessions in East Africa to encompass Ethiopia (formerly called Abyssinia), assuming that the French and British, who needed his support against Hitler, would not offer significant opposition. Italian troops invaded in October 1935, prompting the League of Nations to announce sanctions against Italy.

The sanctions were applied haphazardly, largely because France and Britain wanted to avoid irreparable damage to their longer-term relations with Italy. In any case, the sanctions did not deter Mussolini, whose forces prevailed through the use of aircraft and poison gas by May 1936. But they did make Italy receptive to German overtures in the aftermath of its victory. And the victory made Mussolini more restless. Rather than continuing to play the role of European balancer, he began sending Italian troops and materiel to aid the antidemocratic Nationalists in the Spanish civil war (see the next section), further alienating democratic opinion elsewhere.

Conservatives in Britain and France continued to hope for a revival of the "Stresa Front" against Hitler. Some even defended Italian imperialism in East Africa. But Italy continued its drift toward Germany. Late in 1936, Mussolini spoke of a new Rome-Berlin axis for the first time. He and Hitler exchanged visits in 1937 and 1938. Finally, in May 1939, Italy joined Germany in an open-ended military alliance, the Pact of Steel, though Mussolini made it clear that Italy could not be ready for a major European war before 1943.

To cement this developing relationship, fascist Italy adopted anti-Semitic racial laws modeled on Germany's, even though Italian fascism had not originally been anti-Semitic and indeed had attracted Jewish Italians to its membership in about the same proportion as non-Jews. The increasing subservience to Nazi Germany displeased even many committed fascists. Such opposition helped keep Mussolini from entering the war until May 1940, eight months after it began.

From Democracy to Civil War in Spain, 1931–1939

By the mid-1930s the threat of fascism was so pressing that the Communists had to begin actively promoting electoral alliances and governing coalitions with Socialists and even liberal democrats to resist its further spread. From 1934 until 1939, Communists everywhere consistently pursued this "popular front" strategy. Nowhere was this strategy more apparent than in Spain.

The Spanish republic was born in April 1931 amid great optimism. In June, elections for a constituent assembly produced a solid victory for a coalition of liberal democrats and Socialists. But the leaders of the new republic dragged their feet on land reform, alienating landowners without satisfying the peasants. Socialists and agricultural workers became increasingly radical, producing upheaval in the countryside. A right-wing coalition (the CEDA) grew in response, becoming the largest party in parliament with elections in November 1933 and joining the government in October 1934. It seemed to the left that the growing role of the CEDA was a prelude to fascism.

The Spanish left may have been too quick to see the right-wing CEDA as fascist, but the German left had been criticized for its passive response to the advent of Hitler and the Spanish

left wanted to avoid the same mistake. Thus, during the fall of 1934 the left responded to the opening of the government to the CEDA with quasi-revolutionary uprisings in Catalonia and Asturias, which were crushed.

In February 1936 a popular front coalition of Republicans, Socialists, Syndicalists, and Communists won an absolute majority in parliament. The new government began to implement the land reform that had been promised earlier. But it was too late to undercut the growing radicalization of the masses: A wave of land seizures began in March, followed by a revolutionary strike movement. To many, the government's inability to keep order had become the immediate issue. By the early summer of 1936, the extremes of left and right were each preparing an extralegal solution.

A Nationalist military uprising led by General Francisco Franco (1892–1975) took control of substantial parts of Spain, but elsewhere the Nationalists failed to overcome the resistance of Republican Loyalists determined to defend the republic. Thus began a brutal civil war. Substantial Italian fascist and Nazi German intervention on the Nationalist side intensified the war's ideological ramifications. At the same time, the remarkable, heroic resistance of the Loyalists captured the imagination of the world. Indeed, forty thousand volunteers came from abroad to fight for the Spanish republic.

It proved a war of stunning brutality on both sides. Loyalist anticlericalism led to the murder of perhaps one-eighth of the parish clergy in Spain. On the other side, the German bombing of the Basque town of Guernica on a crowded market day in April 1937—represented unforgettably in Pablo Picasso's painting—came to symbolize the violence and suffering of the whole era.

Although Republican Loyalists assumed that Franco and the Nationalists represented another instance of fascism, Franco was really a traditional military conservative. Nevertheless, Franco's forces did find it expedient to take advantage of the appeal of the Falange, a fascist movement that had emerged under the leadership of the charismatic young José Antonio Primo de Rivera (1903–1936).

They Shall Not Pass! Women were prominent in the citizen militias defending Madrid and other cities during the Spanish civil war. This example of Loyalist poster art celebrates the sacrifices and courage of men and women. Compare this example of propaganda with those shown in the photos on pages 636 and 647. *(Biblioteca Nacional, Madrid)*

Meanwhile, the Republicans had to deal with an anarchist and syndicalist revolution in their own ranks. Ironically, the Communists insisted that this was no time for revolutionary experiments and put down the revolt of anarchist munitions workers in Catalonia. Under these extraordinary circumstances, the Communists gained the ascendancy on the Republican side, partly because they were disciplined and effective, partly because Soviet assistance enhanced their prestige. "They shall not pass," proclaimed the eloquent Spanish communist Dolores Ibar-

ruri (1895–1989), whose impassioned speeches and radio broadcasts captured the attention of the world. But in the end they did pass. Despite considerable heroism, the Loyalists were overwhelmed, and Madrid fell to the Nationalists in March 1939. General Franco's authoritarian regime governed Spain until his death in 1975.

France in the Era of the Popular Front

In France, concern to arrest the spread of fascism also led to a popular front coalition, here including

Socialists, Communists, and Radicals, which governed the country from 1936 to 1938. Although it did not lead to civil war, the popular front experience of the 1930s helped undermine confidence in the Third Republic.

In 1934, the French Communists took the initiative in creating a popular front coalition against fascism. Various nationalist, anticommunist, profascist, and anti-Semitic leagues had gathered momentum in France during the early 1930s, and in defense, the Communists were willing to reach out to the Socialists and even to the Radicals, making no demand for significant economic reforms. But as in Spain, the highly charged ideological climate favored extreme reactions.

In 1936, the popular front won a sizable majority in the Chamber of Deputies, putting Léon Blum (1872–1950) in line to become France's first socialist prime minister. This produced a wave of enthusiasm among workers that escaped the control of popular-front leaders and culminated in a spontaneous strike movement that spread to all major industries nationwide. The major trade union confederation, the Communists, and most Socialists, including Blum himself, saw the strikes as a danger to the popular front, with its more modest aims of defending the republic, and eagerly pursued a settlement, the Matignon Agreement. Workers got collective bargaining, elected shop stewards, and wage increases as a direct result of Matignon, then a forty-hour week and paid vacations in a later reform package.

In the enthusiasm of the summer of 1936, there were other reforms as well, but after that the popular front was forced on the defensive. The left grew disillusioned when a new government under the Radical Edouard Daladier (1884–1970) began dismantling some of the key gains in 1938. Meanwhile, businessmen and conservatives began blaming the workers' gains—like the five-day week—for slowing French rearmament.

As France began to face the possibility of a new war, the popular front was widely blamed for French weakness. When war came at last, resignation and division were prevalent, and when France fell to the Germans, the democratic Third Republic fell with it.

SUMMARY

The 1920s proved a contradictory period of vitality and despair. The era began with bright hopes for democracy, yet the outcome of the democratic experiment in east-central Europe was disappointing. In Germany as well, the new democratic republic remained on the defensive, then failed to weather the economic depression that began in 1929. Even Italy, heir by the 1920s to a respectable tradition of democracy, gave rise to the troubling new phenomenon of fascism. A hopeful new spirit of international conciliation drew France and Germany closer together by the end of 1925, and in early 1929 restabilization seemed to have taken hold in Europe. Germany, Italy, and the Soviet Union, the most volatile and potentially disruptive of the major countries, seemed to be settling down. But it would all come apart over the next decade.

The Depression and the challenges from new political regimes called both capitalism and democracy into question. The most important new political systems of the interwar period—Italian fascism, German Nazism, and Stalinist communism—were not merely authoritarian in the old-fashioned, predemocratic sense. In each of the three regimes, the sovereignty of the state was to become all-encompassing, breaking down the distinction between public and private. Thus Mussolini's boast that there was "nothing outside the state" in fascist Italy and the proclamation of Robert Ley, head of the Nazi Labor Front, that "the private citizen has ceased to exist."

The common totalitarian direction is important, but it glosses over differences, especially in origins and purposes, that are at least as important. Racism and anti-Semitism, fundamental to radical Nazism, were not central to Italian fascism, and Italy's experimentation with ideas of a "corporative state" was not shared by the Nazis.

Communism's philosophical origins distinguish it from fascism. Twisted though it became, the Marxist vision of human liberation, based on long-standing Western values, was still manifest in the ongoing Soviet revolution during the Stalinist 1930s. Committed communists believed that extreme measures were necessary if they were to carry out a transformation that would eventually benefit all humanity. Nazism never claimed a comparably universal aim. Hitler's world-view was the antithesis of the humanistic tradition.

But whatever the differences in values and intentions, the final reckoning must rest on the results. Stalin's way of implementing the Marxist revolution made individual human lives expendable, just as they were for Hitler. The outcome of both Stalinism and Nazism was mass murder on a horrifying scale.

NOTES

1. Virginia Woolf, *A Room of One's Own* (New York: Harcourt, Brace and World, 1975 [1929]), p. 118.
2. Benito Mussolini, speech to the Italian Chamber of Deputies, January 3, 1925, from Charles F. Delzell, ed., *Mediterranean Fascism, 1919–1945* (New York: Harper & Row, 1970), pp. 59–60.

SUGGESTED READING

Bessel, Richard, ed., *Life in the Third Reich.* 1987. Essays on the connections between the Nazi regime and German society. An ideal introductory work.

Bridenthal, Renate, Atina Grossmann, and Marion Kaplan, eds. *When Biology Became Destiny: Women in Weimar and Nazi Germany.* 1984. Excellent studies of Nazi gender ideology, examining issues of work, reproduction, and social organization.

Carr, Raymond. *The Spanish Tragedy: The Civil War in Perspective.* 1977. An accessible account, blending narrative with analysis and commentary. Particularly useful on the politics of the Nationalist zone.

Conquest, Robert. *The Great Terror: A Reassessment.* 1990. An updated edition of an influential work first published in 1968. Offers a gripping account of the Stalinist purges of the 1930s, emphasizing Stalin's personal responsibility.

Eichengreen, Barry. *Golden Fetters: The Gold Standard and the Great Depression, 1919–1939.* 1992. Accents the role of the gold standard both in intensifying the destabilizing process that led to the Depression and in limiting the responses of policymakers.

Fischer, Klaus P. *Nazi Germany: A New History.* 1995. Comprehensive, well researched, and carefully balanced, this is perhaps the best one-volume treatment of Nazism in English.

Fitzpatrick, Sheila. *Stalin's Peasants: Resistance and Survival in the Russian Village after Collectivization.* 1994. A probing study of the peasant response to the forced collectivization that inaugurated Stalin's rule in the Soviet Union.

Fitzpatrick, Sheila, Alexander Rabinowitch, and Richard Stites, eds. *Russia in the Era of NEP: Explorations in Soviet Society and Culture.* 1991. Illuminating scholarly essays accenting the ambiguities of the transitional 1920s, when class identity, economic activity, and gender roles had been radically disrupted but had not yet settled into the forms that came to characterize the Soviet experiment.

Gentile, Emilio. *The Sacralization of Politics in Fascist Italy.* 1996. A masterful account of the cult of political involvement that fed the first overtly totalitarian experiment.

Grossmann, Atina. *Reforming Sex: The German Movement for Birth Control and Abortion Reform, 1920–1950.* 1995. An innovative study tracing German debate and policy across three distinct political regimes.

Jackson, Julian. *The Popular Front in France: Defending Democracy, 1934–1938.* 1988. Combines narrative with thematic chapters on the most controversial issues surrounding the popular front experience.

Kent, Susan Kingsley. *Making Peace: The Reconstruction of Gender in Interwar Britain.* 1993. A concise and accessible work examining the use of traditionalist representations of gender roles in response to the anxieties unleashed in Britain by the war.

Kolb, Eberhard. *The Weimar Republic.* 1988. Provides a good overall survey, then pinpoints the recent trends in research.

Koonz, Claudia. *Mothers in the Fatherland: Women, the Family, and Nazi Politics.* 1987. An influential and accessible study of women in Nazism, accenting their active roles in implementing Nazism on the grassroots level, while ultimately stressing their subordination within the wider Nazi universe.

Noakes, J[eremy], and G[eoffrey] Pridham, eds. *Nazism: A History in Documents and Eyewitness Accounts, 1919–1945.* 2 vols. 1990. An invaluable collection of documents, with running commentary by the editors.

Nolan, Mary. *Visions of Modernity: American Business in the Modernization of Germany.* 1994. Examines the ambiguous impact of Americanism on Germany in the 1920s, when the United States seemed to stand both for economic success and for an impersonal, alienating mass culture.

CHAPTER 25

The Era of the Second World War, 1939–1949

"The effects could well be called unprecedented, magnificent, beautiful, stupendous and terrifying. No man-made phenomenon of such tremendous power had ever occurred before. . . . Thirty seconds after the explosion came first, the air blast pressing hard against the people and things, to be followed almost immediately by the strong, sustained, awesome roar which warned of doomsday and made us feel that we puny things were blasphemous to dare tamper with the forces heretofore reserved to The Almighty."[1]

So wrote Brigadier General Thomas F. Farrell, having just witnessed the birth of the atomic age. On July 16, 1945, watching from a control shelter 10,000 yards away, Farrell saw the first explosion of an atomic bomb at a remote, top-secret testing ground in New Mexico. Within weeks, the United States dropped two other atomic bombs—first on Hiroshima, then on Nagasaki—to force the surrender of Japan. In using the atomic bomb, the Americans not only ended the war but assured that a new set of anxieties would accompany the return to peace.

World War II proved more destructive than World War I and more truly global. Japan's far greater involvement in World War II brought the full brunt of the war to Asia and the Pacific and dramatically changed military strategy. Moreover, because the war expanded as it did, it affected the place of Western civilization in the world, speeding the dissolution of the Western colonial empires.

The ironic outcome of World War II was a cold war between the United States and the Soviet Union, allies in the victorious struggle against Germany, Italy, and Japan. By the end of the 1940s, the United States and the Soviet Union had divided Europe into competing spheres of influence.

Competition between these two superpowers almost immediately became global in scope and world-ending in possible consequence: The nuclear weapons that had ended the war were now being stockpiled, redefining the human condition.

The experience of World War II itself also changed the world forever. Before finally meeting defeat, the Nazis had begun implementing their "new order" in Europe. As part of this effort, in what has become known as the Holocaust, they began systematically murdering Jews in extermination camps, eventually killing as many as 6 million. The most destructive of the camps was at Auschwitz, in Poland. Auschwitz and Hiroshima came to stand for the war's new forms of death and destruction, both of which continued to haunt the world long after the war had ended.

∼ Questions and Ideas to Consider

- Why did the democratic nations of the West allow Hitler to revise Germany's status? Why did Britain and France finally declare war against Germany?

- What was the *Blitzkrieg*? Why was France so quick to surrender? What were the consequences for France and her former allies?

- Why does the Holocaust stand out as a new kind of human brutality? What purpose did it serve?

- Describe the Lend-Lease Act and the Atlantic Charter. Why was the United States reluctant to enter the war, and what made Roosevelt finally commit U.S. troops?

- What were the origins of the cold war? Could it have been avoided?

THE COMING OF WORLD WAR II, 1935–1939

Still under the long shadow of World War I, most Western leaders were determined to preserve the peace during the two ensuing decades. In Germany and eastern Europe, the peace settlement that had followed the war created new problems, and Hitler had consistently trumpeted his intention to overturn that settlement. What scope was there for peaceful revision?

The Germans Strike: Austria, Czechoslovakia, and Appeasement

During his first years in power, Hitler could be understood as merely restoring German sovereignty, revising a postwar settlement that had been misconceived in the first place. However uncouth and abrasive he might seem, it was hard to find a basis for opposing him. Yet in commencing German rearmament in 1935, and especially in remilitarizing the Rhineland in March 1936, Hitler fundamentally reversed the power balance established in France's favor at the peace conference.

France's special advantage had been the demilitarization of the entire German territory west of the Rhine River and a 50-kilometer strip on the east bank. The measure had been reaffirmed at Locarno in 1925, with Germany's free agreement, and it was guaranteed by Britain and Italy. Yet on a Saturday morning in March 1936, German troops moved into the forbidden area. The French and British acquiesced, uncertain what else to do.

But Hitler was not likely to stop there. Three new countries—Austria, Czechoslovakia, and Poland—bordered Germany, and in each the peace settlement had left trouble spots involving the status of ethnic Germans. In 1934, Hitler had moved to absorb his homeland, Austria, but strenuous opposition from Italy led him to back down. The developing understanding with Italy by 1936 enabled Hitler to focus again on Austria—initiating the second, more radical phase of his prewar foreign policy. On a pretext, German troops moved into Austria in March 1938, and it was promptly incorporated into Germany. This time Mussolini was willing to acquiesce, and Hitler was genuinely grateful. The Treaty of Versailles had explicitly prohibited this *Anschluss*, or unity with Germany, but that prohibition violated the principle of self-determination, and

CHAPTER CHRONOLOGY

September 1938	Munich conference ends Sudetenland crisis	**July 1943**	Allied landings in Sicily; fall of Mussolini
August 1939	Nazi-Soviet non-aggression pact	**November 1943**	Teheran conference
September 1, 1939	Germany invades Poland	**June 6, 1944**	D-Day: Allied landings in Normandy
May 10, 1940	Germany attacks the Netherlands, Belgium, and France	**February 1945**	Yalta conference
		May 7–8, 1945	German surrender
June 22, 1941	Germany attacks the Soviet Union	**June 1945**	Founding of the United Nations
August 1941	Churchill and Roosevelt agree to the Atlantic Charter	**July–August 1945**	Potsdam conference
		August 6, 1945	U.S. atomic bombing of Hiroshima
December 7, 1941	Japanese attack Pearl Harbor	**March 1947**	Truman Doctrine speech
January 1942	Wannsee conference; Nazi plan for the extermination of the Jews	**June 1948– May 1949**	Berlin Blockade and airlift
		August 1949	First Soviet atomic bomb
August 1942– February 1943	Battle of Stalingrad	**September 1949**	Founding of the Federal Republic in West Germany
April–May 1943	Warsaw ghetto revolt		

it was widely believed in the West that most Austrians favored unity with Germany. The Anschluss could be justified as revising a misconceived aspect of the peace settlement.

Czechoslovakia presented quite a different situation. It included restive minorities of Slovaks, Magyars, Ruthenians, Poles, and—concentrated especially in the Sudetenland—about 3.25 million Germans. After having been part of the dominant nationality in the old Habsburg empire, those Germans were frustrated with their minority status in the new Czechoslovakia. Hitler's agents actively stirred up their resentments.

Leading the West's response, when Hitler began making an issue of Czechoslovakia, was Neville Chamberlain (1869–1940), who had become Britain's prime minister and foreign minister in May 1937. An intelligent, vigorous, and public-spirited man from the progressive wing of the

Conservative party, Chamberlain sought to master the difficult international situation through creative bargaining. The excesses of Hitler's policy resulted from the mistakes of Versailles; redo the settlement on a more realistic basis, Chamberlain felt, and Germany would behave responsibly. Moreover, in Britain as elsewhere, there were some who saw Hitler's resurgent Germany as a bulwark against communism.

As the Sudeten Germans escalated their demands for autonomy, tensions between Czechoslovakia and Germany mounted. In September 1938 war appeared imminent—the French and the British began mobilizing. Since 1929, the French had been constructing a fortified line along their border with Germany, from Switzerland to the Ardennes Forest at the border with Belgium. In 1938, troops were sent in to man the "Maginot Line" for the first time.

A 1924 treaty bound France to come to the aid of Czechoslovakia in the event of aggression. The Soviet Union, according to a treaty of 1935, was bound to assist Czechoslovakia if the French did so. Throughout the crisis, the Soviets pushed for a strong stand in defense of Czechoslovakia. But for both ideological and military reasons, the British and French were not anxious for a war on the side of the Soviet Union. The value of the Soviet military was uncertain, at best, at a time when the Soviet officer corps had just been purged.

Hitler seemed eager to smash the Czechs by force, but when Mussolini proposed a four-power conference, he was persuaded to talk again. At Munich late in September, Britain, France, Italy, and Germany settled the matter, with Czechoslovakia—and the Soviet Union—excluded. Determined not to risk war over what seemed to be Czech intransigence, Chamberlain agreed to what Hitler had wanted all along—German annexation of the Sudetenland.

All Sudeten areas with German majorities were to be transferred to Germany; plebiscites would be held in areas with large German minorities, and Hitler pledged to respect the sovereignty of the newly diminished Czechoslovak state. Chamberlain and his French counterpart, Edouard Daladier, returned home to a hero's welcome, having transformed what had seemed certain war to, in Chamberlain's memorable phrase, "peace in our time."

But in March 1939, Germany sent troops into Prague. Slovakia was spun off as a separate nation, while the Czech areas became the Protectorate of Bohemia and Moravia. Less than six months after the Munich conference, most of what had been Czechoslovakia had landed firmly within the Nazi orbit. It was no longer possible to justify Hitler's actions as seeking to unite all Germans in one state.

The Invasion of Poland and the Nazi-Soviet Pact

With Poland, the German grievance was still more serious, for the new Polish state had been created partly at German expense. Especially galling to Germans was the Polish corridor, which cut off East Prussia from the bulk of Germany in order to give Poland access to the sea. The city of Danzig, historically Polish (Gdansk) but part of Germany before World War I, was left a "free city," supervised by the League of Nations.

Disillusioned by Hitler's dismemberment of Czechoslovakia, and angered by the Germans' menacing rhetoric regarding Poland, Chamberlain announced in the House of Commons on March 31, 1939, that Britain and France would intervene militarily in the event of a threat to Poland's independence. Chamberlain was abandoning the policy of appeasement, now possible because Britain was rapidly rearming.

Hitler continued to stress how limited and reasonable German aims were. Germany simply wanted Danzig and German transit across the corridor; it was the Polish stance that was rigid and unreasonable. As the crisis developed, doubts were increasingly expressed, on all sides, on whether the British and French were really prepared to aid Poland—that they were willing "to die for Danzig."

Although they had been lukewarm to Soviet proposals for a military alliance, Britain and France began to negotiate with the Soviet Union more seriously during the spring and summer of 1939. And then, even as negotiations between the Soviet Union and the democracies seemed to continue, the Soviet Union came to an agreement with Nazi Germany on August 22, 1939, in a pact that astonished the world. At this point a nonaggression pact with Germany seemed to serve Soviet interests best. To the Soviets, the democracies seemed no more trustworthy, and potentially no less hostile, than Nazi Germany. So the Soviets and the Germans agreed that each would remain neutral in the event that either became involved in war.

The Nazi-Soviet Pact seemed to have given Hitler the free hand he wanted in Poland. With the dramatic change in alignment, the democracies were surely less likely to intervene. But after Hitler ordered the German invasion of Poland on September 1, the British and French declared war on September 3.

With each step on the path to war, Hitler had alternated between apparent reasonableness and wanton aggressiveness. But he always intended a war of conquest—first against Poland, but ultimately against the Soviet Union. War was essential to the Nazi vision, and only when the assault on Poland became a full-scale war did the underlying purposes of Nazism become clear.

THE VICTORY OF NAZI GERMANY, 1939–1941

Instead of the enthusiasm evident in 1914, the German invasion of Poland on September 1, 1939, produced a grim sense of foreboding, even in Germany. Well-publicized incidents like the German bombing of civilians during the Spanish civil war and the Italian use of poison gas in Ethiopia suggested that the frightening new technologies introduced in World War I would now be used on a far greater scale, making the conflict a much uglier war, involving civilians more directly.

Still, as in 1914, there were hopes that this war could be localized and brief. Hitler did not expect a protracted war with Britain. In light of the Nazi-Soviet Pact, war between Germany and the Soviet Union seemed unlikely. And isolationist sentiment in the United States made U.S. intervention doubtful.

Hitler and the German high command envisioned a *Blitzkrieg,* or "lightning war." At first events seemed to confirm German expectations. When Poland fell after just over a month, Hitler publicly offered peace to Britain and France, seriously thinking that might be the end of it. The British and French refused to call off the war, but from 1939 through 1941 the Nazis won victory after victory, establishing the foundation for their new order in Europe.

Initial Conquests and "Phony War"

The Polish army was large enough to have given the Germans a serious battle. But in adapting the technological innovations of World War I, Germany had developed a new military strategy based on rapid mobility. This Blitzkrieg strategy employed swift, highly concentrated offensives based on mobile tanks covered with concentrated air support, including dive-bombers that struck just ahead of the tanks. The last Polish unit surrendered on October 2, barely a month after the fighting had begun. The speed of the German victory stunned the world.

Meanwhile, the Soviets began cashing in on the pact they had made with Nazi Germany a few weeks before. On September 17, with the German victory in Poland assured, Stalin sent Soviet forces into Poland. Poland was again divided between Germany and Russia. Stalin looked next to the Baltic States, which had been part of the Russian Empire before World War I. Although initially let off with treaties of mutual assistance, Estonia, Latvia, and Lithuania were incorporated as republics within the Soviet Union during the summer of 1940. The Nazi-Soviet agreement had assigned Lithuania to the German orbit, but the Germans agreed to let the Soviets have it in exchange for an additional slice of Poland.

The Soviets invaded Finland in November 1939. In the ensuing "Winter War," the Finns held out bravely and inflicted heavy casualties until the Soviets managed to prevail by March 1940. These difficulties seemed to confirm suspicions that Stalin's purge during the mid-1930s had substantially weakened the Soviet army. Still, by midsummer 1940 the Soviet Union had regained much of the territory it had lost during the upheavals surrounding the revolution of 1917.

In the West, little happened during the strained winter of 1939–1940, known as the "Phony War." Then, on April 9, 1940, the Germans attacked Norway and Denmark to preempt a British and French scheme to cut off the major route for the shipment of Swedish iron ore to Germany. Denmark fell almost at once, while staunch resistance in Norway took a few weeks to overcome. The stage was set for the German assault on France.

The Fall of France, 1940

The war in the West began in earnest on May 10, 1940, when the Germans attacked France and the Low Countries. They launched their assault on France through the Ardennes Forest, above the northern end of the Maginot Line—terrain so difficult the French had discounted the possibility of an enemy strike there. As in 1914, northern France became the focus of a major war pitting French forces and their British allies against invading Germans. But this time, in startling contrast to World War I, the Battle of France was over in less than six weeks, a humiliating defeat for the French. What had happened?

The problem for the French was not lack of men and materiel, but strategy. Germany had no more than a slight numerical advantage in tanks. But it used the tanks to mount rapid, highly concentrated offensives. French strategy, in contrast, was based on the lessons learned in World War I. Anticipating another long, defensive war, France dispersed its tanks among infantry units along a broad front. Once the German tank column broke through the French lines, it quickly cut through northern France toward the North Sea. France's poor showing convinced the British that they should get out and regroup for a longer global war. Finally, 200,000 British troops—as well as 130,000 French—escaped German encirclement and capture through a difficult evacuation at Dunkirk early in June.

As the French military collapsed, the French cabinet resigned, to be replaced by a new government under Marshal Philippe Pétain, the hero of the Battle of Verdun during World War I. Pétain's government asked for an armistice and then engineered a change of regime. The French parliament voted by an overwhelming majority to give Pétain exceptional powers, including the power to draw up a new constitution. So ended the parliamentary democracy of the Third Republic. The republic gave way to the more authoritarian Vichy regime, named after the southern resort city to which the government retreated as the Germans moved into Paris. The end of the fighting in France resulted in a kind of antidemocratic revolution.

According to the armistice agreement, the French government was required to collaborate with the victorious Germans. French resistance began immediately, however. In a radio broadcast from London on June 18, Charles de Gaulle (1890–1970), the youngest general in the French army, called on French forces to rally to him to continue the fight. The military forces stationed in the French colonies, as well as the French troops that had been evacuated at Dunkirk, could form the nucleus of a new French army. Given the circumstances, de Gaulle's appeal seemed quixotic at best, and most French colonies went along with what seemed the legitimate French government at Vichy. To the new Vichy government, de Gaulle was a traitor. Yet a new Free French force grew from de Gaulle's remarkable appeal, and its subsequent role in the war helped overcome the humiliation of France's quick defeat in 1940.

Winston Churchill and the Battle of Britain

With the defeat of France, Hitler seems to have expected that Britain, now apparently vulnerable to German invasion, would come to terms. But the British, having none of it, found a new spokesman and leader in Winston Churchill (1874–1965), who had replaced Neville Chamberlain as prime minister when the German invasion of western Europe began on May 10. Although Churchill had been prominent in British public life for years, his career had not been noteworthy for either judgment or success. He was obstinate, difficult, something of a curmudgeon. Yet he rose to the wartime challenge, becoming one of the notable leaders of the modern era. In speeches to the House of Commons during the remainder of 1940, he uttered perhaps the most memorable words of the war as he sought to inspire the nation. Some Britons, hoping for a negotiated settlement with Germany as the Battle of France ended, objected to Churchill's rhetoric, but his dogged promise of "blood, toil, tears, and sweat" helped rally the British people, so that later he could say, without exaggeration, that "this was their finest hour."

After the fall of France, Britain moved to full mobilization for a protracted war. Churchill consolidated economic policy under a small committee that gave Britain the most thoroughly coordinated war economy of all the belligerents. Between 1940 and 1942, Britain outstripped Germany in the production of tanks, aircraft, and machine guns. In 1941 the National Service Act subjected men aged 18 to 50 and women aged 20 to 30 to military or civilian war service. The upper age limits were subsequently raised to meet the demand for labor.

Hitler weighed his options and decided to attack. In light of British naval superiority, he hoped to rely on aerial bombardment to knock the British out of the war without an actual invasion. The ensuing Battle of Britain culminated in the nightly bombing of London from September 7 through November 2, 1940, killing 15,000 people and destroying thousands of buildings. But the British held. Ordinary people holed up in cellars and subway stations, while the fighter planes of the Royal Air Force fought back effectively, inflicting heavy losses against German aircraft.

Although the bombing continued into 1941, the British had withstood the worst the Germans could deliver, and Hitler began looking to the east, his ultimate objective all along. In December 1940 he ordered preparations for Operation Barbarossa, the assault on the Soviet Union. Rather than continuing the attack on Britain directly, Germany would use submarines to cut off shipping—and thus the supplies the British needed for a long war. Once Germany had defeated the Soviet Union, it would enjoy the geopolitical basis for world power, while Britain, an island nation relying on a dispersed empire, would be forced to come to terms.

Italian Intervention and the Spread of the War

Lacking sufficient domestic support and unready for a major war, Mussolini could only look on as the war began in 1939. But as the Battle of France neared its end, it seemed safe for Italy to inter-

vene and share in the spoils. Thus in June 1940, Italy entered the war, expecting to seize Corsica, Nice, and Tunisia from France. Italy hoped eventually to supplant Britain in the Mediterranean—and even to take the Suez Canal.

Although Hitler and Mussolini got along remarkably well, their relationship was sensitive. When Hitler seemed to be proceeding without Italy during the first year of the war, Mussolini grew determined to show his independence and finally, in October 1940, ordered Italian forces to attack Greece. The Greeks mounted a strong resistance, thanks partly to the help of British forces from North Africa.

Meanwhile, Germany had established its hegemony in much of east-central Europe without military force, often by exploiting grievances over the outcome of the peace conference in 1919. In November 1940, Romania and Hungary joined the Axis camp, and Bulgaria followed a few months later. But in March 1941, just after Yugoslavia had similarly committed to the Axis, a coup overthrew the pro-Axis government in Yugoslavia, and the new Yugoslav government prepared to aid the Allies.

By this point Hitler had decided to push into the Balkans with German troops, both to reinforce the Italians and to consolidate Axis control of the area. By the end of May 1941, Germany had taken Yugoslavia and Greece.

At the same time, the war was spreading to North Africa and the Middle East because of European colonial ties. The native peoples of the area sought to take advantage of the conflict among the Europeans to pursue their own independence. Operating from Syria, Germans aided anti-British Arab nationalists in Iraq. But most important proved to be North Africa, where Libya, an Italian colony since 1912, lay adjacent to Egypt, where the British presence remained strong. In September 1940 the Italian army drove 65 miles into Egypt, initiating almost three years of fighting across the North African desert. A British counteroffensive drove the Italians back into Libya, prompting Germany to send some of its forces from the Balkans into North Africa. Under General Erwin Rommel (1891–1944), the famous "Desert Fox," Axis forces won remarkable successes. But the German forays into the Balkans and North Africa had delayed the crucial attack on the Soviet Union.

THE ASSAULT ON THE SOVIET UNION AND THE NAZI NEW ORDER

The Germans penetrated well into the Soviet Union, reaching the apex of their power in 1942. German conquests by that point enabled Hitler to begin constructing his new European order. Although in western Europe the Nazis generally sought the collaboration of local leaders, in Poland and the Soviet Union the new order meant brutal subjugation of local populations. It was at this point that the Nazis began exterminating the Jews of Europe in specially constructed death camps.

Operation Barbarossa and Hitler's New Order

In ordering preparations for Operation Barbarossa in December 1940, Hitler was betting that the purges of the 1930s had severely weakened the Soviet Union. If Germany were to defeat the Soviet Union, it could gain control of oil and other resources required for a longer war against Britain and, if necessary, the United States.

Attacking the Soviet Union on June 22, 1941, German forces at first achieved notable successes, partly because Stalin was so unprepared for the German betrayal. By late November, German forces were within twenty miles of Moscow. But the Germans were ill equipped for Russian weather, and as an early and severe winter descended, the German offensive bogged down. The Soviets counterattacked near Moscow in December. Although their initial assault had stalled, the Germans still had the advantage, and they reached Stalingrad in November 1942. This proved the deepest penetration of German forces—and the zenith of Nazi power in Europe.

Hitler could now begin to put his new order into effect.

By the summer of 1942, Nazi Germany dominated the European continent as no power ever had before (Map 25.1). Satellite states in Slovakia and Croatia and client governments in Romania and Hungary owed their existence to Nazi Germany and readily adapted themselves to the Nazi system. Elsewhere in the Nazi orbit, some countries proved eager collaborators; others did their best to resist; still others were given no opportunity to collaborate but were ruthlessly subjugated instead.

The Nazis' immediate aim was to exploit the conquered territories to serve the continuing war effort. Precisely as envisioned, access to the resources of so much of Europe made Germany considerably less vulnerable to naval blockade than it had been during World War I. France proved a particularly valuable source of raw materials; by 1943, for example, 75 percent of French iron ore went to German factories.

But the deeper purposes of the war were clear in the different way the Nazis treated the territories under their control. In western Europe, there was plenty of brutality, but Nazi victory still led to something like conventional military occupation. However, in Poland and later in the conquered parts of the Soviet Union it at once became clear that the Nazi order would entail something very different.

After the conquest of Poland, Nazi leaders proclaimed a new era of German resettlement in eastern Europe. By mid-1941, 200,000 Germans, carefully selected for their racial characteristics, had been resettled—primarily on farms—in the part of Poland annexed to Germany. Many were ethnic Germans who had been living outside Germany. During the fall of 1942, the Schutzstaffel (SS), under the leadership of Heinrich Himmler, began to expel peasants from the rest of Poland to make way for further German resettlement. By 1943 perhaps 1 million Germans had been moved into what had been Poland.

After the assault on the Soviet Union, Himmler told SS leaders that Germany would have to exterminate 30 million Soviet Slavs to

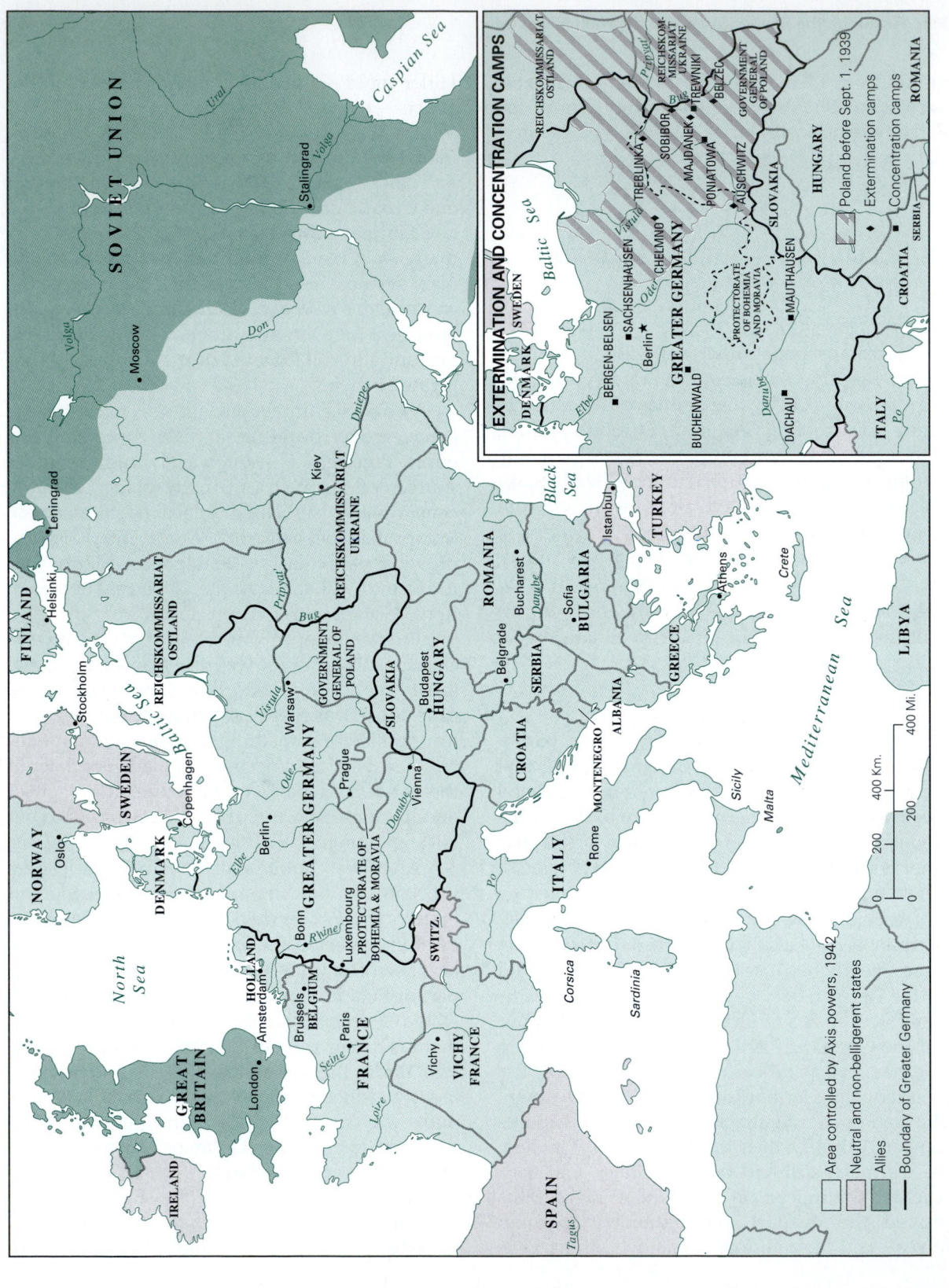

EXTERMINATION AND CONCENTRATION CAMPS

REICHSKOMMISSARIAT OSTLAND

REICHSKOMMISSARIAT UKRAINE

GOVERNMENT GENERAL OF POLAND

Pripyat'

Bug

SWEDEN

Baltic Sea

BELZEC

TREBLINKA

SOBIBOR

MAJDANEK

PONIATOWA

AUSCHWITZ

CHELMNO

Oder

Elbe

Vistula

DENMARK

BERGEN-BELSEN

SACHSENHAUSEN

Berlin

GREATER GERMANY

BUCHENWALD

PROTECTORATE OF BOHEMIA AND MORAVIA

MAUTHAUSEN

Danube

DACHAU

ITALY

Po

SLOVAKIA

HUNGARY

CROATIA

SERBIA

ROMANIA

- ■ Poland before Sept. 1, 1939
- ◆ Extermination camps
- ■ Concentration camps

SOVIET UNION

Ural

Volga

Stalingrad

Volga

Caspian Sea

Don

Moscow

FINLAND

Leningrad

Helsinki

REICHSKOMMISSARIAT OSTLAND

Kiev

Black Sea

TURKEY

NORWAY

Oslo

Stockholm

SWEDEN

Baltic Sea

Copenhagen

DENMARK

Elbe

Berlin

Bonn

GREATER GERMANY

Luxembourg

PROTECTORATE OF BOHEMIA & MORAVIA

Prague

Odra

Warsaw

Vistula

Pripyat'

Bug

REICHSKOMMISSARIAT UKRAINE

GOVERNMENT GENERAL OF POLAND

Dnieper

SLOVAKIA

Budapest

HUNGARY

Vienna

Danube

SWITZ.

Rhine

HOLLAND

Amsterdam

Brussels

BELGIUM

Paris

Seine

FRANCE

Loire

Vichy

VICHY FRANCE

GREAT BRITAIN

London

IRELAND

North Sea

Belgrade

CROATIA

SERBIA

MONTENEGRO

ALBANIA

ROMANIA

Bucharest

Danube

Sofia

BULGARIA

GREECE

Athens

Istanbul

Crete

Rome

ITALY

Po

Corsica

Sardinia

Sicily

Malta

Mediterranean Sea

LIBYA

SPAIN

Tagus

- □ Area controlled by Axis powers, 1942
- □ Neutral and non-belligerent states
- ■ Allies
- — Boundary of Greater Germany

400 Mi.

400 Km.

200

200

0

prepare for German colonization. But there, in contrast to Poland, the program barely got started during the war.

The Holocaust

Conquest of the east gave the Nazis the opportunity for a more radical solution to the "Jewish problem." Under the cover of war, they began the systematic extermination of the Jews that has come to be known as the Holocaust.

When and why this policy was chosen remains controversial. Although prewar Nazi rhetoric suggested the possibility of physical destruction, the "final solution to the Jewish problem" seemed to mean forced emigration. In 1940, the Nazis began confining Polish Jews to ghettos set up in Warsaw and five other cities. Himmler and the SS were making tentative plans to develop a kind of superghetto for perhaps 4 million Jews on the island of Madagascar. However, as the Polish ghettos grew more crowded and difficult to manage, Nazi officials in Poland began pressing for a more definitive policy.

In 1940, Hitler seemed to endorse the Madagascar plan, but he cultivated ambiguity on the operational level—and he left no paper trail—so the precise chain of events remains uncertain. The evidence suggests, however, that Hitler ordered the physical extermination of the Jews in the spring of 1941, before the German assault on the Soviet Union in June. By the fall, the Nazis were actively impeding Jewish emigration from the occupied territories and sending large numbers of German and Austrian Jews to the ghettos in Poland.

Map 25.1 The Nazi New Order in Europe, 1942
At the zenith of its power in 1942, Nazi Germany controlled much of Europe. Concerned most immediately with winning the war, the Nazis sought to coordinate the economies of their satellite states and conquered territories. But they also began establishing what was supposed to be an enduring new order in eastern Europe. The inset shows the location of the major Nazi concentration camps and the six extermination camps the Nazis constructed in what had been Poland.

With the invasion of the Soviet Union, special SS "intervention squads" were assigned to get rid of Jews and Communist party officials. By late November, the Nazis had killed 136,000 Jews, most by shooting, in the invaded Soviet territories. But as it became obvious that mass shooting was impractical, Nazi leaders sought a more systematic and impersonal method of extermination. In late July 1941, Reinhard Heydrich of the SS began developing a detailed plan, which he explained in January 1942 at a conference of high-ranking officials at Wannsee, a suburb of Berlin, though by then the plan was already under way.

The Nazis took advantage of the methods, and especially the deadly Zyklon-B gas, that had proven effective during the earlier euthanasia campaign in Germany. By March 1942 they had constructed several large extermination camps with gas chambers and crematoria, designed for efficient murder and disposal. The first targets of the full-scale mass killing were the Polish Jews already confined to ghettos. The ghettos became mere way stations on the journey to the death camps. The Nazis brutally suppressed attempts at resistance, like the Warsaw ghetto uprising of April and May 1943.

The Nazis constructed six full-scale death camps, although not all were operating at peak capacity at the same time. All six were located in what had been Poland (see inset, Map 25.1). The concentration camps in Germany, such as Dachau, Buchenwald, and Bergen-Belsen, were not extermination camps, although many Jews died in them late in the war.

The largest death camp was the Auschwitz-Birkenau complex, which became the principal extermination center in 1943. The Nazis shipped Jews from all over Europe to Auschwitz, which was killing about twelve thousand people a day in 1944. Auschwitz was one of two extermination camps that included affiliated slave-labor factories, in which Jews most able to work were literally worked to death. Among the companies profiting from the arrangement were two of Germany's best-known, Krupp and IG Farben.

The Jews typically arrived at the camps crammed into cattle cars on special trains. Camp personnel, generally SS medical doctors, subjected new arrivals to "selection," picking some for labor assignments and sending the others, including most women and children, to the gas chambers. Camp personnel made every effort to deceive the Jews who were about to be killed, to lead them to believe they were to be showered and deloused. Even in camps without forced-

Children at Auschwitz   Images from the Nazi camps haunted the decades that followed World War II. The Auschwitz-Birkenau complex proved the largest and most destructive of the camps that the Nazis created specifically for mass killing. The overwhelming majority of those sent to these camps were Jews, most of whom were killed by gassing shortly after their arrival. Those deemed fit for work might be spared, at least for a while, but children were typically killed at once. *(Hulton-Getty/Liaison)*

labor factories, Jews were compelled to do much of the dirty work of the extermination operation. But under the brutal conditions of the camps, those initially assigned to work inevitably weakened; most were then deemed unfit and put to death.

Himmler constantly sought to accelerate the process, even though it required labor and transport facilities desperately needed for the war effort. He and the other major SS officials, such as Adolf Eichmann, who organized the transport of Jews to the camps, portrayed the extermination of the Jews as a difficult "historical task" that they, the Nazi elite, must do for their racial community. For some camp guards, the extermination process became the occasion to act out sadistic fantasies. But though this dimension is surely horrifying, the bureaucratic, factory-like nature of the extermination process is in some ways more troubling.

Despite an overriding emphasis on secrecy, reports of the genocide reached the West almost immediately in 1942. At first, most tended to discount them as fabricated wartime propaganda. Many people believed that Jews were being interned for the duration of the war, much as Japanese-Americans were interned in camps in the western United States at the same time. But even as the evidence grew, Allied governments, citing military priorities, refused pleas from Jewish leaders in 1944 to bomb the rail line into Auschwitz.

The Nazis' policy of murdering "undesirables" also included communists, homosexuals, Gypsies, and Poles. But the Jews constituted by far the largest group of victims—5.7 to 6 million, almost two-thirds of the Jews in Europe.

Collaboration and Resistance

In rounding up Jews for extermination and in establishing their new order in Europe, the Nazis found willing collaborators in some of the countries within their orbit. Croatia, the most pro-Nazi of the satellite states, was eager to round up Jews and Gypsies as well as to attack Serbs on its own. Romania was happy to deliver foreign-born Jews to the Germans, though it dragged its feet when the Germans began demanding acculturated Romanian Jews. The degree of collaboration varied widely across Europe. Denmark did especially well at resisting the German effort to round up Jews, as did Italy and Bulgaria.

Vichy France was somewhere in the middle, and thus it has remained particularly controversial. When the Vichy regime was launched in the summer of 1940, there was widespread support for Marshal Pétain, its 84-year-old chief of state. Pétain promised to maximize French sovereignty and shield his people from the worst aspects of Nazi occupation. At the same time, the Vichy government claimed to be implementing its own "national revolution," returning France to authority, discipline, and tradition after the shambles of the Third Republic. Vichy's revolution was anti-Semitic and hostile to the left, so it seemed compatible with Nazism. And at first Germany seemed likely to win the war. Thus, Pétain's second-in-command, Pierre Laval (1883–1945), collaborated actively with the Nazis. The Vichy regime did much of the Nazis' dirty work for them—rounding up workers for forced shipment to German factories, hunting down members of the anti-German resistance, and picking up Jews to be sent to the Nazi extermination camps. After the war, Pétain, Laval, and others were found guilty of treason by the new French government. Because of his advanced age, Pétain was merely imprisoned, while Laval and others were executed. But the shame of Vichy collaboration continued to haunt the French.

The great majority of those living under German occupation came to despise the Nazis as their brutality became ever clearer. Nazi rule meant pillage; it meant rounding up workers for forced labor in Germany; it meant randomly killing hostages in reprisal for resistance activity. In one notorious case, the Germans killed everyone in the Czech village of Lidice in retaliation for the assassination of SS security chief Reinhard Heydrich.

Clandestine resistance movements gradually developed all over Europe. Resistance was prominent in France and, beginning in 1943,

northern Italy, which was occupied by Germany after the Allies defeated Mussolini's regime. But the strongest anti-German resistance was in Yugoslavia, Poland, and the occupied portions of the Soviet Union, where full-scale guerrilla war against the Germans and their collaborators produced the highest civilian casualties of World War II.

The role of the resistance proved most significant in Yugoslavia, where the Croatian Marxist Josip Broz, taking the pseudonym Tito (1892–1980), forged the opponents of the Axis powers into a broadly based guerrilla army. Its initial foe was the pro-Axis Croatian state that the Germans carved out of Yugoslavia. But Tito's forces soon came up against a rival resistance movement, led by Serb officers, that tended to be pro-Serb, monarchist, and anticommunist. By 1943, Tito led 250,000 men and women in what had become a brutal civil war that deepened ethnic divisions and left a legacy of bitterness. Tito's forces prevailed, enabling him to create a communist-led government in Yugoslavia late in the war.

In France and Italy, communists played a leading role in the resistance movements. As a result, the Communist party in each country overcame the disarray that followed from the Nazi-Soviet Pact of 1939 and after the war enjoyed a level of prestige that would have been unthinkable earlier. In the French case, there could have been conflict between the indigenous resistance, with its significant communist component, and the Free French under Charles de Gaulle, operating outside France until August 1944. But it is striking how well they were able to work together. Still, de Gaulle took pains to cement his own leadership. Among the measures to this end, he decreed women's suffrage for France, partly because women were playing a major role in the resistance.

Some depictions of the resistance, such as those by the French writer Marguerite Duras (b. 1914), detail the extreme difficulty of the movement and the isolation of its members. For the most part, however, western European resistance movements were greatly romanticized, their extent and import overstated. The resistance movements did make some military contribution, especially through sabotage, but in many cases their most significant impact was to create a measure of national self-esteem for countries humiliated by defeat.

Toward the Soviet Triumph

The failure of the Nazi assault on the Soviet Union was the decisive fact of World War II. Although supplies from its new allies—Britain and eventually the United States—helped the Soviet forces to prevail, the most important factor was the unexpected strength of the Soviet military effort.

Although the Germans reached Stalingrad by late 1942, they could not achieve a knockout. Fighting street by street, the Soviets managed to defend their city in what was arguably the pivotal military engagement of World War II. By the end of January 1943, the Soviets had captured what remained of the German force, about 100,000 men. The victory came at an immense price: A million Soviet soldiers and civilians died at Stalingrad.

The war had turned. By February 1944, Soviet troops had pushed the Germans back to the Polish border. The Soviet victory was incredible in light of the upheavals of the 1930s. Stalin was able to rally the Soviet peoples by appealing to patriotism, recalling the heroic defenses mounted against invaders in tsarist times. Moreover, when the Germans invaded in 1941, Soviet leaders dismantled the plants and equipment of 1500 industrial enterprises and shipped them by rail for reassembly farther east, out of reach of German attack. Finally, the earlier purges of the armed forces proved to have done less long-term damage than outside observers had expected. If anything, the removal of so many in the top ranks made it easier for talented young officers to move quickly into major leadership positions.

When the United States entered the war in December 1941, the Soviets were fighting for survival. They immediately began pressuring the United States and Britain to open another front in Europe. But the Allies did not invade northern France until June 1944. By then the Soviets had turned the tide in Europe on their own.

A GLOBAL WAR, 1941–1944

European colonial links spread the war almost at once, most dramatically to North Africa but also to East Asia and the Pacific. The Soviet Union also had interests in Asia and the Pacific, where it had long bumped up against the Japanese. During the 1930s, the United States, too, had become involved in friction with Japan. By 1941, President Franklin Roosevelt was openly favoring the anti-Axis cause, though it took a surprise attack by the Japanese in December 1941 to bring the United States into the war.

Japan and the Origins of the Pacific War

As a densely populated island nation lacking the raw materials essential for industry, Japan had been especially concerned about foreign trade and spheres of economic influence as it modernized after 1868. By the interwar period, the Japanese had become unusually dependent on exports of textiles and other products. During the Great Depression, when countries all over the world adopted protectionist policies, Japan suffered from increasing tariffs against its exports. This situation tilted the balance in Japanese ruling circles from free-trade proponents to those who favored a military-imperialist solution.

To gain economic hegemony by force, Japan could choose either of two directions. The northern strategy, concentrating on China, would risk Soviet opposition as well as strong local resistance. The southern strategy, focusing on southeast Asia and the East Indies, would encounter the imperial presence of Britain, France, the Netherlands, and the United States.

In 1931, Japan opted for the northern strategy, taking control of Manchuria in northeastern China. But the Japanese attempt to conquer the rest of China, beginning in 1937, led to an impasse by 1940. Japanese aggression drew the hostility of the United States, a strong supporter of the Chinese nationalist leader Jiang Jieshi (Chiang Kai-shek, 1887–1975), as well as the active opposition of the Soviet Union. Clashes with Soviet troops along the border between Mongolia and Manchuria led to significant defeats for the Japanese in 1938 and 1939. The combination of China and the Soviet Union seemed more than Japan could handle.

World War II, however, seemed to offer a precious opportunity for Japan to shift to a southern strategy. To keep the Soviets at bay, Japan agreed to a neutrality pact with the Soviet Union in April 1941. Rather than worry about China, the Japanese would seek control of southeast Asia, a region rich in oil, rubber, and tin—precisely what Japan lacked.

Japan had joined Nazi Germany and fascist Italy in an anticommunist agreement in 1936. In September 1940, the three agreed to a formal military alliance. For the Germans, alliance with Japan was useful to help discourage U.S. intervention in the European war. Japan, for its part, could expect the major share of the spoils of the European empires in Asia. However, when Japan assumed control of Indochina, nominally held by Vichy France, the United States imposed sanctions, and the British and Dutch followed, forcing Japan to begin rapidly drawing down its oil reserves. Conquest of the oil fields of the Dutch East Indies now seemed a matter of life and death to the Japanese.

These economic sanctions brought home how vulnerable Japan was and heightened its determination to press forward aggressively now, when its likely enemies were weakened or distracted. The Japanese did not expect to achieve a definitive victory over the United States in a long, drawn-out war. Rather, Japanese policymakers anticipated, first, that their initial successes would enable them to grab the resources to sustain a longer war if necessary, and, second, that Germany would defeat Britain, leading the United States to accept a compromise peace giving the Japanese what they wanted—a secure sphere of economic hegemony in southeast Asia.

The Japanese finally provoked a showdown on December 7, 1941, with a surprise attack on Pearl Harbor, a U.S. naval base in Hawaii. The next day, Japanese forces seized Hong Kong and Malaya, both British colonies, and Wake Island and the Philippines, both under U.S. control. The United States promptly declared war on Japan; in response, Hitler kept an earlier promise to Japan and declared war on the United States. World War II was now unprecedented in its geographical scope (see Map 25.2).

Much like their German counterparts, Japanese forces got off to a remarkably good start. By the summer of 1942, Japan had taken Thailand, the Dutch East Indies, the Philippines, and the Malay Peninsula. Having won much of what it had been seeking, it began devising the Greater East Asia Co-Prosperity Sphere, its own new order in the conquered territories. (See the box "Encounters with the West: Japan's 'Pan-Asian' Mission.")

The United States in Europe and the Pacific

During the first years of the war in Europe, the United States under President Franklin Roosevelt had not been a disinterested bystander. Although the United States did not have armed forces commensurate with its economic strength—in 1940 its army was smaller than Belgium's—it could be a supplier in the short term. And if it chose to intervene, it could become a major player over the longer term. With the Lend-Lease Act of March 1941, intended to provide war materiel without the economic dislocations of World War I, the United States lined up on the side of Britain against the Axis powers. In August 1941, a meeting between Churchill and Roosevelt aboard a cruiser off the coast of Newfoundland produced the Atlantic Charter, the first tentative agreement about the aims and ideals that were to guide the war effort. The Americans extended lend-lease to the Soviet Union the next month.

But though President Roosevelt was deeply committed to the anti-Axis cause, it took the Japanese attack on Pearl Harbor to overcome isolationist sentiment and bring the United States into the war as an active belligerent. By May 1942 the United States had joined with Britain and the Soviet Union in a formal military alliance against the Axis powers.

~ **ENCOUNTERS WITH THE WEST** ~

Japan's "Pan-Asian" Mission

This selection from an essay written just after the bombing of Pearl Harbor by the well-known author Nagayo Yoshio (1888–1961) accents Japan's claim to be freeing Asians from Western imperialism. Although it served Japan's own economic interests and was often applied brutally, Japanese "pan-Asianism" helped fuel the reaction against Western imperialism in Asia and the Pacific, with lasting results after the war.

While desperately fighting with a country which we made our enemy only reluctantly we were trying to find out a principle, an ethic based upon a new view of the world. . . .

. . . We would have nothing to say for ourselves if we were merely to follow the examples of the imperialistic and capitalistic exploitation of Greater East-Asia by Europe and the United States. . . .

. . . It is true that the science of war is one manifestation of a nation's culture. But from this time on we have to realize the increasing responsibility on our part if we are to deserve the respect of the people of East-Asian countries as their leaders, in the sphere of culture in general (not only the mere fusion and continuance of Western and Oriental cultures but something surpassing and elevating them while making the most out of them) such as the formation of national character, refinement, intellect, training to become a world citizen, etc. . . .

The sense of awe and respect with which the Orientals have held the white race, espe-cially the Anglo-Saxons, for three hundred years is deep-rooted almost beyond our imagination. It is our task to realize this fact and deal with this servility at its root, find out why the white people became the objects of such reverence. It goes without saying that we cannot conclude simplemindedly that their shrewdness is the cause. Also we have to be very careful not to impose the *hakko ichiu* [the gathering of the whole world under one roof] spirit arbitrarily upon the Asians. If we make this kind of mistake we might antagonize those who could have become our compatriots and thus might also blaspheme our Imperial rule. . . .

To sum up, we have finally witnessed the dawn of a new principle which we had been searching for over ten years. . . . [T]he phrase "Greater East-Asian Coprosperity Sphere" is no longer a mere abstract idea.

Source: Nagayo Yoshio, "Our Present War and Its Cultural Significance," in William H. McNeill and Mitsuko Iriye, eds., *Modern Asia and Africa* (New York: Oxford University Press, 1971), pp. 232–236. Reprinted by permission of William H. McNeill.

The two democracies had joined with Stalin's Soviet Union in a marriage of expediency, and mutual suspicions marked the relationship from the start. Initially, Britain and the United States feared that the Soviet Union might even seek a separate peace, as Russia had in World War I. The Soviets worried that their newfound allies, with their long-standing anticommunism, might hold back from full commitment or even seek to undermine the Soviet Union.

In response to pressure from Stalin, Britain and the United States agreed to open a second front in Europe as soon as possible. Since the Nazis dominated the Continent, opening such a

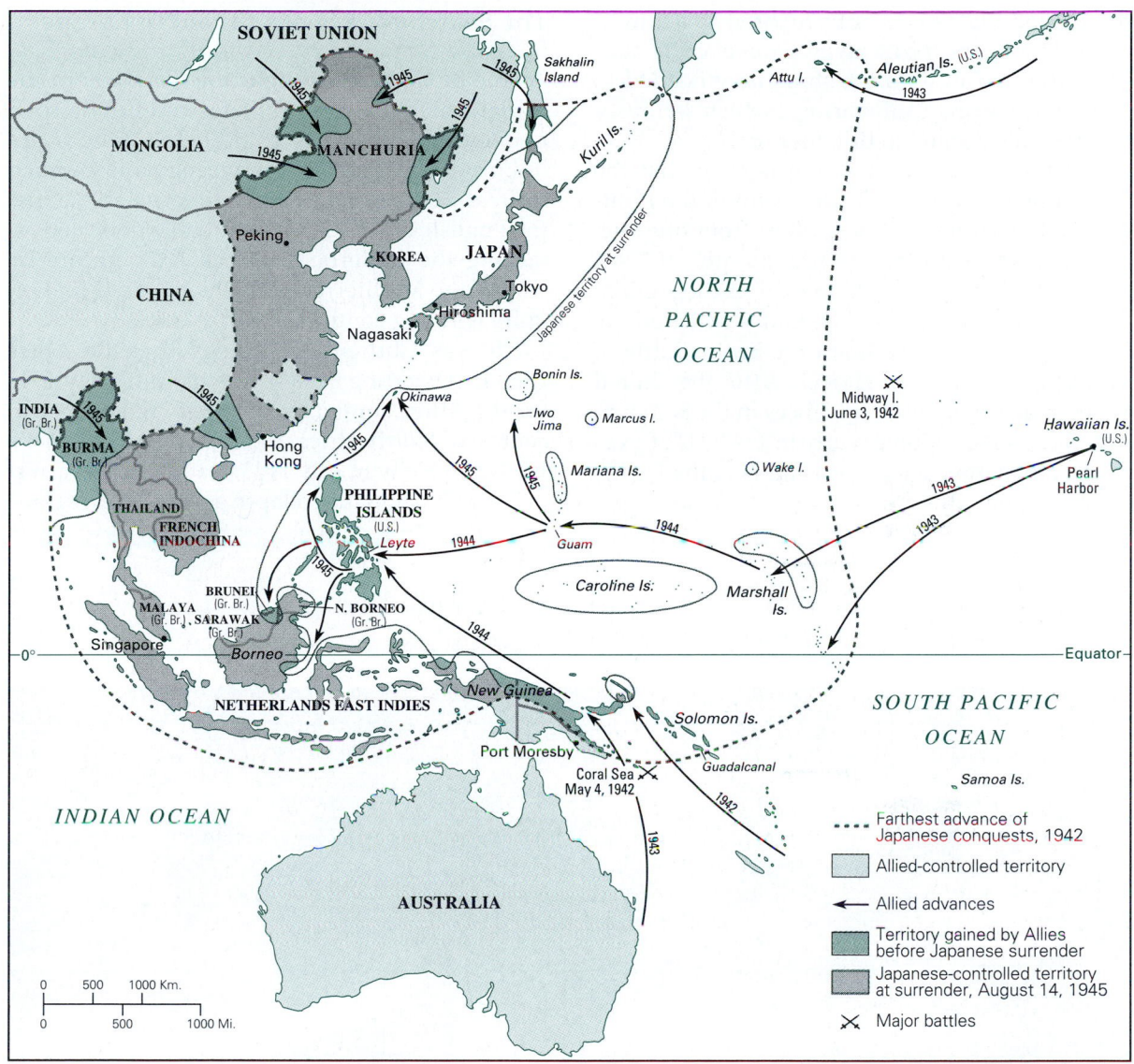

Map 25.2 The War in East Asia and the Pacific After a series of conquests in 1941 and 1942, the Japanese were forced gradually to fall back before U.S. forces. When the war abruptly ended in August 1945, the Japanese still controlled much of the territory they had conquered.

front required landing troops from the outside. It proved far more difficult to mount an assault on Europe than either Churchill or Roosevelt anticipated in 1942. The delays furthered Stalin's suspicions that his allies wanted the Soviet Union to do the bulk of the fighting against Nazi Germany—and weaken itself in the process.

The United States agreed to give priority to the war in Europe. But because it had to respond to the Japanese assault in the Pacific (Map 25.2), the United States was not prepared to act militarily in Europe right away. However, it supplied the British with the ships they needed to overcome German submarines, which seriously threatened shipping to Britain in 1942.

In the Pacific theater, it was clear that the United States would bear the brunt of the fighting. Although the Japanese went from one success to another during the first months of 1942, they lacked the resources to exploit their initial victories. In June, the United States defeated the Japanese navy for the first time in the Battle of Midway, northwest of Hawaii. After the United States stopped Japanese advances in the Solomon Islands and New Guinea early in 1943, U.S. forces began advancing across the islands of the Pacific toward Japan.

The Search for a Second Front in Europe

As the Soviet army fought the Germans in the Soviet Union, the United States and Britain tried to determine how they could help tip the scales in Europe, now an almost impregnable German fortress. Stalin kept urging a direct assault across the English Channel, but Churchill advocated attacking the underbelly of the Axis empire by way of the Mediterranean, which would first require winning control of North Africa.

It was Churchill's strategy that the Allies tried first, starting in 1942. It took until May 1943 for the Allies, joined by the Free French, to win control of North Africa. From there, Allied troops landed in Sicily in July 1943, leading to the arrest of Mussolini and the collapse of the fascist regime.

D-Day, 1944 Allied forces land at Normandy, early in the morning of June 6, 1944, at last opening a major second front in Europe. *(National Archives, Washington)*

Allied forces then moved on to the Italian mainland, but the Germans quickly occupied much of Italy in response. They even managed a rescue of Mussolini and re-established him as puppet leader of a new rump republic in northern Italy. It was a full nine months later before the Allies reached Rome, in June 1944. So Churchill's strategy of assaulting Europe from the south proved less than decisive.

Only when Churchill, Roosevelt, and Stalin met for the first time, at Teheran, Iran, in November 1943, did they agree that the next step would be to invade western Europe from Britain. Preparations had been under way since early 1942. Finally, Allied troops crossed the English Channel to make an amphibious landing on the beaches of Normandy, in northern France, on June 6, 1944, known to history as D-Day.

The D-Day invasion opened the second major front in Europe at last. Now American-led forces from the west and Soviet forces from the east advanced systematically on Germany. The one substantial German counterattack in the west, the Battle of the Bulge in December 1944, slowed the Allies' advance, but on March 7, 1945, Allied troops crossed the Rhine River.

Now, with the defeat of Germany simply a matter of time, Churchill wanted to strike east-central Europe to prevent Soviet domination of the region after the war. But the Americans thought these concerns were misguided. So the Allies concentrated instead on a secondary landing in southern France in August 1944. This assault, in which Free French forces were prominent, led quickly to the liberation of Paris. It was the Soviets alone who drove the Germans from east-central Europe and the Balkans, and this fundamentally affected the postwar order.

THE SHAPE OF THE ALLIED VICTORY, 1944–1945

The leaders of the Soviet Union, Britain, and the United States sought to mold the postwar order at two notable conferences in 1945. They brought different aspirations for the postwar world, but they also had to face the hard military realities that had resulted from the fighting: Each had armies in certain places but not in others. Those military realities led to the informal division of Europe into spheres of influence.

The most serious question the Allies faced concerned Germany. The country was widely held responsible for both world wars, as well as for Nazism with all its atrocities—including the concentration and extermination camps, discovered with shock and horror by the advancing Allied armies in 1945. How should Germany be treated?

In the Pacific theater, as in Europe, the way the war ended had major implications for the postwar world. The United States decided to use the atomic bomb, forcing Japan to surrender in a matter of days. The suddenness of the ending helped determine the fate of the European empires in Asia.

Victory in Europe

Although the tide had turned in 1943, Germany managed to continue the war by exploiting its conquered territories and by more effectively allocating its domestic resources for war production. Germany still had plenty of weapons even as the war was ending, but it was running out of military manpower, and it was running out of oil.

Despite making effective use of synthetics, the Nazi war machine depended heavily on oil from Romania. Late in August 1944, however, Soviet troops crossed into Romania, taking control of the oil fields. In addition, beginning in mid-1944, U.S. and British planes successfully bombed German oil installations.

From the start of the war, some, especially among British military leaders, insisted that bombing could destroy the economic and psychological basis of the enemy's ability to wage war. Beginning in 1942, British-led bombing attacks destroyed an average of half the built-up area of seventy German cities, sometimes producing huge firestorms. The bombing of the historic city of Dresden in February 1945 killed more than 135,000 civilians in the most destructive air

The Soviet Victory in Europe After forcing the Germans back for almost two years, Soviet troops reached Berlin in April 1945. Although it required a day of heavy fighting and bombardment, the Soviets took the Reichstag building, in the heart of the now devastated German capital, on April 30. Here two Soviet sergeants, Yegorov and Kantariya, plant the Soviet flag atop the Reichstag, symbolizing the Soviet victory in the decisive encounter of World War II in Europe. *(ITAR-TAS/Sovfoto)*

assault of the war in Europe. But the widespread destruction did not undermine morale or disrupt production and transport to the extent expected.

The more precise targeting favored by U.S. strategists proved more effective. In May 1944, the United States began bombing the oil fields in Romania and refineries and synthetic oil plants in Germany. Soon Germany lacked enough fuel even to train pilots, so that by 1945 German industry was producing more aircraft than the German air force could use.

Soviet troops moving westward finally met U.S. troops moving eastward at the Elbe River in Germany on April 26, 1945. With his regime thoroughly defeated and much of his country in ruins, Hitler committed suicide in his under-

ground military headquarters in Berlin on April 30, 1945. The war in Europe finally ended with the German surrender to General Dwight D. Eisenhower (1890–1969) at Reims, France, on May 7 and to Marshal Georgi Zhukov (1896–1974) at Berlin on May 8. While the world celebrated the end of the fighting in Europe, East-West differences were already upsetting the anti-German alliance.

The Atomic Bomb and the Capitulation of Japan

In the Pacific, Japan had been forced onto the defensive, but it mounted two major counterattacks in 1944 to challenge American naval supremacy.

The Japanese wanted to prevent American reconquest of the Philippines, which would cut Japan off from its vital raw materials farther south. But the naval battles of 1944 led only to further Japanese defeat.

As the situation grew more desperate, Japanese ground soldiers battled ever more fiercely, often fighting to the death, or taking their own lives, rather than surrendering. Beginning late in 1944, aircraft pilots practiced *kamikaze*, suicidally crashing planes filled with explosives into U.S. targets.

In the spring of 1945, American forces were close enough to be able to launch air raids on the Japanese home islands. But though the United States was now clearly in control, it seemed likely that an invasion of Japan would be necessary to force a Japanese surrender. Some estimated that an invasion might cost the United States as many as 1 million additional casualties, because the Japanese could be expected to fight more desperately to defend their own soil. It was especially for this reason that the Americans decided to try to end the war in an altogether different way, by using an atomic bomb.

In 1939 scientists in several countries, including Germany, had advised their governments that new, immensely destructive weapons based on thermonuclear fission were theoretically possible. The German economics ministry began seeking uranium in 1939, but Hitler favored jet- and rocket-propelled terror weaponry instead. Still, fear that the Nazis were developing atomic weapons lurked behind the Allied effort to produce an atomic bomb as quickly as possible.

Although the British were the first to initiate an atomic weapons program, by late 1941 the Americans were building on what they knew of British findings to develop their own crash program, known as the Manhattan Project. Constructing an atomic bomb was extremely difficult and costly—it was only with great effort that the United States had atomic weapons ready for military use by mid-1945.

The U.S. decision to use the atomic bomb, dropping two of them on Japanese civilians, has been one of the most controversial of modern history. The decision fell to the new president, Harry Truman (1884–1972), who had known nothing of the bomb project when Roosevelt died in April 1945. Over the next few months, Truman listened to spirited disagreement among American policymakers. Was it necessary actually to drop the bomb to force the Japanese to surrender, or would it be enough simply to demonstrate the new weapon to the Japanese in a test firing?

President Truman first warned Japan that if it did not surrender at once, it would be subjected to destruction immeasurably greater than Germany had suffered. The Japanese decided to ignore the American warning, although the United States had begun area-bombing Japanese cities a few months before. The bombing of Tokyo in March produced a firestorm that gutted one-fourth of the city and killed over 80,000 people. Since the Japanese refused to surrender, the use of the atomic bomb could seem the logical next step.

At 8:15 on the morning of August 6, 1945, from a height of 32,000 feet above the Japanese city of Hiroshima, an American pilot released the first atomic bomb to be used against an enemy target. The bomb exploded after 45 seconds, 2000 feet above the ground, killing 80,000 people outright and tens of thousands more in the aftermath. Three days later, on August 9, the Americans exploded a second atomic bomb over Nagasaki. Although sectors of the Japanese military held out for continued resistance, Emperor Hirohito (1901–1989) finally surrendered on August 14.

Death Counts and the Question of Guilt

Between 50 and 60 million people died in World War II—three times as many as in World War I. About that same number were left homeless for some length of time, many of them as refugees. The Soviet Union and Germany suffered by far the highest casualty figures. An appalling 23 million Soviet citizens died, of whom 12 to 13 million were civilians. Germany lost 5 to 6 million, including perhaps 2 million civilians.

In contrast, casualty rates for Italy, Britain, and France were lower than in World War I. Italy suffered 200,000 military and 200,000 civilian deaths. Total British losses, including civilians, numbered 450,000, to which must be added 120,000 Australians, Canadians, Indians, and others from the British Empire. Despite its quick defeat, France lost more lives than Britain because of the ravages of German occupation: The 350,000 deaths among French civilians considerably exceeded the British figure, closer to 100,000.

The United States lost 300,000 servicemen and 5000 civilians. Figures for Japan are problematic, partly because the Japanese claim that 300,000 of those who surrendered to the Soviets in 1945 remain unaccounted for. Apart from this number, 1,740,000 Japanese servicemen died from 1941 to 1945, more from hunger and disease than from combat, and 300,000 civilians died in Japan, most from U.S. bombing.

The great majority of Jews, Poles, and other "undesirables" shipped to Nazi death camps died during the war. Of those Jews who were still alive when the Nazi camps were liberated, almost half died within a few weeks. Even those who managed to return home sometimes faced pogroms when they arrived; forty Jews were killed in the worst of them, at Kielce, in Poland.

The redrawing of Germany's borders contributed to the huge wave of refugees after the war. To guarantee the permanence of the new territorial configurations, the Soviets and Poles began expelling ethnic Germans from historically German areas that were now part of Poland, and the Czechs expelled Germans from the Sudetenland area of Czechoslovakia. So a flood of German refugees was forced to move west after the war, into the shrunken territory of the new Germany. They were among the 16 million Europeans who were permanently uprooted and transplanted between 1939 and 1947.

As the war was ending, Europeans began attempting to assess guilt and punish those responsible for the disasters of the era. In the climate of violence, resistance forces in France, Italy, and elsewhere often subjected fascists and collaborators to summary justice, sometimes through quick trials in ad hoc courts. In Italy, this process led to 15,000 executions; in France, 10,000. After the war, governments sought to dispense justice in a more orderly way, but the results differed widely across Europe. In Belgium, 634,000 of a population of 8 million were prosecuted for collaborating with the Nazis, whereas in Austria, with a comparable population, only 9000 were brought to trial.

In Germany the occupying powers imposed a program of de-Nazification. In the areas occupied by the United States, Britain, and France, German citizens were required to attend lectures on the virtues of democracy and view the corpses of the victims of Nazism. In this context, the Allies determined to identify and bring to justice those responsible for the crimes of the Nazi regime. This effort led to the Nuremberg trials of 1945 to 1946, the most famous of a number of war crimes trials held in Germany and the occupied countries after the war.

Although Hitler, Himmler, and Goebbels had committed suicide, the occupying authorities tried twenty-four individuals who had played important roles in Hitler's Third Reich. All but three were convicted of war crimes and "crimes against humanity." Of the twelve sentenced to death, two committed suicide and the other ten were executed.

TOWARD THE POSTWAR WORLD, 1945–1949

Differences between the Soviets and the Western democracies soon undermined the wartime alliance, producing the division of Germany and a bipolar Europe. Thus the conclusion of World War II led directly to the danger of a nuclear war, threatening the extinction of life on earth. Outside Europe, the war brought to the forefront a new set of issues, from anticolonialism to the Arab-Israeli conflict to the spread of communism to the non-Western world.

The Yalta and Potsdam Conferences

Stalin, Roosevelt, and Churchill met at Yalta, a Soviet Black Sea resort, in February 1945, when

Allied victory was assured but not yet accomplished. The Yalta conference has long been surrounded by controversy. Western critics have charged that the concessions made there to Stalin consigned east-central Europe to communist domination and opened the way to the dangerous cold war of the next forty years. At the time, however, the division of Axis territory was already becoming evident, and, in light of the location of Allied troops, the alignment was probably inevitable. Also, the anticipation of victory produced a relatively cooperative spirit among the Allies. Thus, they firmed up plans for military occupation of Germany in separate zones, for joint occupation of Berlin, and for an Allied Control Council, which would make policy for all of Germany by unanimous agreement.

After Germany fell, the victorious Allies had to decide how to implement their plans. The leaders of the United States, Britain, and the Soviet Union confronted the question at their last wartime conference, at Potsdam, just outside Berlin, from July 17 to August 2, 1945. The circumstances were dramatically different from those at Yalta just months before. With Hitler dead and Germany defeated, there was no longer a common military aim in Europe to provide unity. Of the three Allied leaders who had been at Yalta, only Stalin remained. President Roosevelt had died in April, so his successor, Harry Truman, represented the United States. In Britain, Churchill's Conservatives lost the general election during the first days of the conference, so Clement Attlee (1883–1967), the new Labour prime minister, assumed the leadership of the British delegation.

Germany, devastated by bombing and left without a government, depended on the Allied occupying forces even for its day-to-day survival. The Allies had agreed that Germany was to be forced to surrender unconditionally, but it was not yet clear what would be done with the country over the longer term. U.S. policymakers had even considered destroying Germany's industrial capacity in perpetuity. However, cooler heads understood that the "pastoralization" of

Reconstruction Begins Shortly after the end of the war, women in Berlin pass pails of rubble along a line to a dump. Wartime bombing had severely damaged cities throughout much of Europe, although destruction was greatest in Germany. *(Hulton-Getty/Liaison)*

Germany would not be in anyone's economic interests. Moreover, as the democracies grew increasingly suspicious about Soviet intentions, an economically healthy Germany seemed necessary to help in the balance against the Soviet Union.

The Soviets had reason to take a much harder line against Germany. Having been invaded—and devastated—by German forces twice within living memory, the Soviet Union wanted to weaken Germany both territorially and economically. Of the three victors, the Soviets had suffered a greatly disproportionate share of the wartime destruction and economic loss, so they demanded heavy reparations. The United States and Britain accepted the Soviet proposal that Germany's eastern border with Poland be shifted substantially westward; as a result, the size of Germany was reduced by about 20 percent. Each of the four Allies had responsibility for administering a particular zone of Germany and of Berlin, but they were supposed to coordinate their activities in a common policy toward Germany.

Conflicting Visions and the Coming of the Cold War

To ensure the peace, the Allies agreed to create a new international body—the United Nations. At a conference in San Francisco from April to June 1945, delegates from almost fifty anti-Axis countries created a charter for the new United Nations. The major powers—the United States, Britain, France, the Soviet Union, and China—were given a privileged position in the organization as permanent members of the Security Council, each with veto power. To dramatize its departure from the Geneva-based League of Nations, which the United States had refused to join, the United Nations was headquartered in New York. In July 1945 the American Senate approved U.S. membership.

The cold war soon cast a heavy shadow over the new organization. Whereas the United States envisioned a world order based on the ongoing cooperation of the victors, the Soviet Union gave top priority to creating a buffer zone of friendly

states in east-central Europe, especially as a bulwark against Germany. While seeking this sphere of influence in east-central Europe, Stalin gave the British a free hand to settle the civil war in Greece, and he did not push for revolution in western Europe. The strong communist parties that had emerged from the resistance movements in Italy and France were directed to work within broad-based democratic fronts rather than try to take power. Stalin saw this moderate position in western and southern Europe as a tacit exchange with the West for a free hand in east-central Europe.

The United States refused to acquiesce as the Soviets established their sphere of influence in east-central Europe. The American reluctance to abandon the peoples of east-central Europe to Soviet hegemony is understandable. But U.S. policymakers failed to grasp the historical and strategic basis for Soviet priorities and assumed that the Soviets were primarily trying to spread communism. As a result, the cleft between the emerging superpowers widened.

The area of greatest potential stress between the Soviets and the democracies was inevitably Germany. At first, the Western Allies were concerned especially to root out the sources of Germany's antidemocratic, aggressive behavior, but that concern faded as communism, not Nazism, came to seem the immediate menace. At Potsdam, the West had accepted Soviet demands for German reparations, but rather than wait for payment, the Soviets began removing German factories and equipment for reassembly in the Soviet Union. The United States and Britain, in contrast, gave priority to economic reconstruction and quickly began integrating the economies of the western zones for that purpose.

Friction developed after 1945 as the West insisted on reduced reparations and a higher level of industrial production than the Soviets wanted. Finally, as part of their effort to spur economic recovery, the United States and Britain introduced a new currency without Soviet consent. Stalin's response, in June 1948, was to blockade the city of Berlin, cutting its western sectors off from the main Western occupation zones, almost 200 miles west. The Western Allies responded with a massive airlift that kept their sectors of Berlin supplied for almost a year, until May 1949, when the Soviets finally backed down.

The growing split with the Soviet Union reinforced the determination of the United States and Britain to ensure that western Germany would become a viable state—economically, politically, and even militarily. With Allied support, a "parliamentary council" of German leaders met in 1948 and 1949 and produced a document that, when ratified in September 1949, became the "basic law" of a new Federal Republic of Germany. It was intended to be a provisional new state, with a temporary capital in the small city of Bonn, but the Soviets responded by setting up a new state in their zone, in eastern Germany. The Communist-led German Democratic Republic, with its capital in East Berlin, was born in October 1949.

The "Iron Curtain" and the Emergence of a Bipolar World

In east-central Europe, only Yugoslavia and Albania had achieved liberation on their own, and the communist leaders of their resistance movements had a plausible claim to political power. Elsewhere, the Soviet army had provided liberation, and the Soviet military presence remained the decisive political fact as the war ended. To be sure, each country had local political groups that now claimed a governing role, but their standing in relation to the Soviet army was uncertain.

Under these circumstances, the Soviets were able to work with local communists to install new communist-led regimes friendly to the Soviet Union in most of east-central Europe. But though Churchill warned as early as 1946 that "an iron curtain" was descending from the Baltic to the Adriatic, the process of Soviet power consolidation was not easy, and it took place gradually over several years. The Communist-led government of Poland held elections in January 1947—but rigged them to guarantee a favorable outcome. In Czechoslovakia, the communists faced serious losses in upcoming elections and so finally took power outright in 1948. In 1949 there

were communist governments relying on Soviet support in Poland, Czechoslovakia, East Germany, Hungary, Romania, and Bulgaria. Yugoslavia and Albania were also communist but were capable of a more independent line.

Communism might have spread still farther in Europe, but the West drew the line at Greece. There, as in Yugoslavia, an indigenous, communist-led resistance movement had become strong enough to contend for political power by late 1944. But when it sought to oust the monarchical government that had returned from exile, the British intervened to help the monarchy. Although Stalin gave the Greek communists little help, communist guerrilla activity continued, thanks partly to support from Tito's Yugoslavia. In 1946 a renewed communist uprising escalated into civil war.

After the financially strapped Labour government in Britain reduced its involvement early in 1947, the United States stepped in. In March, President Truman announced the Truman Doctrine, which committed the United States to the "containment" of communism throughout the world. American advisers began re-equipping the anticommunist forces in Greece. Faced with this determined opposition from the West, Stalin pulled back, but the Greek communists, with their strong indigenous support, were not defeated until 1949.

Thus the wartime marriage of expediency between the Soviet Union and the Western democracies fell apart in the war's aftermath. The antagonism between the two superpowers became more menacing when the Soviets exploded their first atomic bomb in August 1949, intensifying the postwar arms race. By then the United States was on its way to the more destructive hydrogen bomb. The split between these two nations, unmistakable by 1949, established the framework for world affairs for the next forty years. (See the box "The Soviet View of the Cold War.")

The West and the New World Agenda

At the same time, other dramatic changes around the world suggested that, with or without the cold war, the postwar political scene

The Soviet View of the Cold War

The first cold war document the Soviet government made available to Western scholars was a telegram that Nikolai Novikov, the Soviet ambassador to the United States, sent from Washington to Soviet Foreign Minister Vyacheslav Molotov on September 27, 1946. Novikov sought to pinpoint the essential features of the new foreign policy the United States seemed to be pursuing after its victory in World War II. In releasing the document in 1990, Soviet authorities contended it had been of central importance in the Soviet effort to understand postwar American intentions and to formulate their own policy in response.

The foreign policy of the United States, which reflects the imperialist tendencies of American monopolistic capital, is characterized in the postwar period by a striving for world supremacy. This is the real meaning of the many statements by President Truman and other representatives of American ruling circles: that the United States has the right to lead the world. All the forces of American diplomacy—the army, the air force, the navy, industry, and science—are enlisted in the service of this foreign policy. For this purpose broad plans for expansion have been developed and are being implemented through diplomacy and the establishment of a system of naval and air bases stretching far beyond the boundaries of the United States. . . .

. . . [W]e have seen a failure of calculations on the part of U.S. circles which assumed that the Soviet Union would be destroyed in the war or would come out of it so weakened that it would be forced to go begging to the United States for economic assistance. Had that happened, they would have been able to dictate conditions permitting the United States to carry out its expansion in Europe and Asia without hindrance from the USSR. . . .

One of the most important elements in the general policy of the United States, which is directed toward limiting the international role of the USSR in the postwar world, is the policy with regard to Germany. In Germany, the United States is taking measures to strengthen reactionary forces for the purpose of opposing democratic reconstruction. . . .

Careful note should be taken of the fact that the preparation by the United States for a future war is being conducted with the prospect of war against the Soviet Union, which in the eyes of American imperialists is the main obstacle in the path of the United States to world domination. This is indicated by facts such as the tactical training of the American army for war with the Soviet Union as the future opponent, the siting of American strategic bases in regions from which it is possible to launch strikes on Soviet territory, intensified training and strengthening of Arctic regions as close approaches to the USSR, and attempts to prepare Germany and Japan to use those countries in a war against the USSR.

Source: "The Novikov Telegram," *Diplomatic History,* vol. 15, no. 4 (Fall 1991), pp. 527–528, 536–537. Reprinted by permission of Blackwell Publishers.

would be hard to manage. Events in India in 1947, in Israel in 1948, and in China in 1949 epitomized the new hopes and uncertainties that had emerged directly from World War II.

Although the British, under U.S. pressure, had reluctantly promised independence for India in order to elicit Indian support during the war, British authorities and Indian leaders had continued to skirmish. Mohandas Gandhi was twice jailed for resisting British demands and threatening a massive program of nonviolent resistance to British rule. But by 1946 the British lacked the will and the financial resources to maintain their control in India. Britain acquiesced in Indian independence, proclaimed on August 15, 1947.

Questions about the fate of the Jews, who had suffered so grievously during World War II, were inevitable. Almost two-thirds of the Jews of Europe had been killed, and many of the survivors either had no place to go or had concluded that they could never again live as a minority in Europe. Many insisted that they must have a homeland of their own. For decades such Zionist sentiment (see page 617) had centered on the biblical area of Israel, in what had become, after World War I, the British mandate of Palestine. In 1947, pressure from Zionists in Jerusalem and the United States led the British to withdraw from Palestine, leaving its future to the United Nations. The UN voted to partition Palestine, creating both a Jewish and an Arab Palestinian state. Skirmishing between Jews and Arabs became full-scale war in December, and in that context the Jews declared their independence as the new state of Israel on May 14, 1948.

In 1949 the communist insurgency in China under Mao Zedong (Mao Tse-tung) (see page 632) triumphed over the Chinese Nationalists under Jiang Jieshi (Chiang Kai-shek), who were forced to flee to the island of Taiwan. After their victory, the Chinese Communists enjoyed great prestige among other "national liberation" movements struggling against Western colonialists. To many in the West, however, the outcome in China by 1949 intensified fears that communism was poised to spread in the unsettled postwar world.

SUMMARY

World War II brought to a close an era of European history dominated by fascism. As a result of the war, the two major fascist powers collapsed and fascist forms of politics, with their hostility to democracy and their tendencies toward violence and war, stood at least temporarily discredited. But Nazism and fascism continued to haunt the Western mind, especially with the discovery of the Nazi camps.

Because the Soviets bore the brunt of the war in Europe, the Soviet Union—and its communist system—emerged with enhanced prestige. At the same time, an overseas war had again drawn the United States, which was now prepared to play an ongoing leadership role in world affairs.

With the Soviet Union and United States emerging from the war as superpowers, the center of gravity in the West changed dramatically. Weakened and chastened, the once-dominant European countries seemed destined to play a diminished role in world affairs. It quickly became apparent that the costs of the war had left even Britain, a full partner in the Allied victory, too weak to remain a great power. Almost at once, the Europeans began retreating from their long-standing imperial roles, though not without resentment, resistance, and more bloodshed. By 1949 the division of Europe, the advent of nuclear weapons, and the events in India, Israel, and China made it clear that the world's agenda had been radically transformed in the ten years since the beginning of World War II.

Whereas there had been, for a while, some illusion of a "return to normal" after World War I, it was obvious after World War II that the old Europe was gone forever and that the relationship between the West and the rest of the world would never be the same. Indeed, much of Europe's proud culture, on the basis of which it had claimed to lead the world, lay in the ruins of war, apparently exhausted. What role could Europe play in Western civilization, and in the wider world, after all that had happened?

NOTES

1. From Farrell's full account as related by General Leslie Groves in his "Memorandum to the Secretary of War," dated July 18, 1945, in Philip L. Cantelon, Richard G. Hewlett, and Robert C. Williams, eds., *The American Atom: A Documentary History of Nuclear*

Policies from the Discovery of Fission to the Present, 2d ed. (Philadelphia: University of Pennsylvania Press, 1991), pp. 56–57.

SUGGESTED READING

Campbell, John, ed. *The Experience of World War II.* 1989. Focusing on the experience of those touched by the war, this collaborative volume covers everything from prisoners of war to the uses of the arts for propaganda purposes.

Eisenberg, Carolyn Woods. *Drawing the Line: The American Decision to Divide Germany, 1944–1949.* 1996. A detailed, scholarly account that uses newly available sources to accent the American role in the process that culminated in the division of Germany by 1949.

Ellis, John. *On the Front Lines: The Experience of War Through the Eyes of the Allied Soldiers in World War II.* 1991. Based partly on oral testimony, a vivid account of the experiences of those who fought the war on the Allied side in Europe, Africa, and the Pacific.

Gaddis, John Lewis. *We Now Know: Rethinking Cold War History.* 1997. Taking advantage of newly available Russian and Chinese documents, a leading authority reassesses the cold war, from its origins to the Cuban missile crisis of 1962.

Glantz, David M., and Jonathan M. House. *When Titans Clashed: How the Red Army Stopped Hitler.* 1995. A detailed but compelling account of the decisive encounter in World War II, based partly on newly available materials from the former Soviet Union.

Harrison, Mark. *Soviet Planning in Peace and War, 1938–1945.* 1985. Shows how Soviet economic planners responded to invasion in 1941, enabling the Soviet Union to defeat Nazi Germany and emerge from the war as a great power.

Hilberg, Raul. *Perpetrators, Victims, Bystanders: The Jewish Catastrophe, 1933–1945.* 1992. The dean of Holocaust historians offers an accessible, compelling account by weaving capsule portraits delineating the many layers of involvement and responsibility at issue in the Holocaust.

Laqueur, Walter. *A History of Zionism.* 1989. Surveys the five decades of European Zionist activity that helped bring about the establishment of the state of Israel.

Marrus, Michael. *The Holocaust in History.* 1987. An ideal introduction to the major issues. Readable and balanced.

Paxton, Robert O. *Vichy France: Old Guard and New Order.* 1975. A widely admired study that assesses Vichy claims to have shielded the French from the worst features of Nazi occupation.

Pedersen, Susan. *Family, Dependence, and the Origins of the Welfare State: Britain and France, 1914–1945.* 1993. An effective comparative study showing how concerns about gender roles and family relations helped shape discussion and policy as government assumed greater responsibility for social welfare.

Pelling, Henry. *Winston Churchill.* 1974. Among the best single-volume biographies of Churchill. Balanced and readable.

Rhodes, Richard. *The Making of the Atomic Bomb.* 1988. An acclaimed study that combines science, politics, and personality in an especially dramatic way.

Summerfield, Penny. *Women Workers in the Second World War: Production and Patriarchy in Conflict.* 1989. Shows how the disruptions of war affected women's opportunities and self-understanding.

Wright, Gordon. *The Ordeal of Total War, 1939–1945.* 1968. A masterly synthesis of all aspects of the war experience, from the battlefield to the scientific laboratory, from the Nazi "new order" to the coming of the cold war.

Yahil, Leni. *The Holocaust: The Fate of European Jewry.* 1990. A clear and comprehensive account that accents the underlying continuity in Nazi policy and assesses the Jewish response.

CHAPTER 26

An Anxious Stability: The Age of the Cold War, 1949–1985

Sampling an American hotdog at a meatpacking plant in Iowa in 1959, the leader of the Soviet Union, Nikita Khrushchev, wryly observed that "we have beaten you to the moon, but you have beaten us in sausage-making." Khrushchev was in the midst of a two-week visit to the United States at the invitation of President Dwight Eisenhower. The Soviet leader found much to praise in American society, and he took every occasion to stress the possibility of "peaceful coexistence." Still, Khrushchev also took it for granted that vigorous competition would continue between the two countries. It was time to recognize, Khrushchev insisted, that each side fervently believed in its own system; hence, there was no point in trying to convince each other. The two sides would simply compete—and the competition could be peaceful.

But in 1960, less than a year after Khrushchev's visit, the Soviet military shot down a U.S. spy plane over the Soviet Union. The incident wrecked a previously planned summit meeting, and relations between the Soviet Union and the United States cooled. Although they would eventually warm again, this complex postwar era was characterized by ideological competition, mutual suspicion, and a costly and dangerous arms race. It seemed possible that, virtually overnight, the cold war could develop into a hot war that could lead to nuclear annihilation.

Both halves of Europe had to operate within the bipolar framework, but the Western and Soviet blocs each confronted different challenges. Dependent on U.S. leadership, unable to resist the tide of decolonization, the countries of Western Europe adjusted to a diminished international role. The change led many to advocate some form of European union, which might eventually enable the Western Europeans to deal with the superpowers on a more equal basis. On the domestic level, postwar reconstruction rested on a new consensus that government must play a more active role in promoting economic growth and social welfare. By the 1960s the promise of shared prosperity had been realized to a remarkable extent. But changing circumstances by the early 1970s threatened the consensus that postwar prosperity had made possible.

∼ *Questions and Ideas to Consider*

- Discuss some of the ways in which European intellectuals tried to make sense of human existence in the aftermath of World War II. What were the central questions posed, and what solutions were offered?

- Why did Western governments take on the responsibilities of the "welfare state"? Why did the question of welfare seem to demand a re-evaluation of gender roles in the West?

- Why did some colonies manage to gain their independence with relative ease, while others struggled bitterly for years? What factors other than relative military strength influenced these outcomes?

- Discuss the main tenets of Khrushchev's regime. Generally speaking, what was his foreign policy?

- In 1968 much of the West experienced popular protests, often by groups new to the political stage—or long absent from it. How did these new protests differ from earlier political initiatives?

THE SEARCH FOR CULTURAL BEARINGS

The events from World War I to the cold war added up to an unprecedented period of disaster for Europe. Europeans were bound to ask what had gone wrong, and what could be salvaged from the ruins of a culture that had made possible the most destructive wars in history, as well as fascism, totalitarianism, and the Holocaust. The cold war framework inevitably affected the answers. Some embraced the Soviet Union or sought a renewed Marxism. Others returned to religious or classical traditions or embraced new ideas associated with America's recent successes. In Western Europe this effort to take stock led to renewed determination and fresh ideas that helped produce the dramatically successful postwar reconstruction.

Absurdity and Commitment in Existentialism

The postwar mood of exhaustion and despair found classic expression in the work of the Irish-born writer Samuel Beckett (1906–1989), especially in his plays *Waiting for Godot* (1952) and *Endgame* (1957). Through Beckett's characters, we see ourselves going through the motions, with nothing worth saying or doing, ludicrously manipulating the husks of a worn-out culture. The only redeeming element is the comic pathos we feel as we watch ourselves.

The same sense of anxiety and despair led to existentialism, a movement that marked philosophy, the arts, and popular culture from the later 1940s until well into the 1950s. Existentialism developed from the ideas of the German thinker Martin Heidegger (1889–1976), especially from his *Being and Time* (1927), one of the most influential philosophical works of the century. Though it was a philosophy, existentialism was most significant as a broader cultural tendency, finding expression in novels and films. The existentialists explored what it means to be human in a world cast adrift from its cultural moorings.

The most influential postwar existentialists were the Frenchmen Albert Camus (1913–1960) and Jean Paul Sartre (1905–1980), each of whom had been involved in the French resistance. For both, an authentic human response to a world spinning out of control entailed engagement, commitment, responsibility. Camus sought to show how we might go on living in a positive, affirmative spirit, even in an absurd world. Peo-

CHAPTER CHRONOLOGY

1947	Marshall Plan announced	1957	Treaty of Rome establishes Common Market
1949	Formation of NATO		
1951	Formation of the European Coal and Steel Community	1958	Beginning of Fifth Republic under de Gaulle
1953	Death of Stalin	1961	Berlin Wall erected
	Workers' revolt in East Germany	1962	Algerian independence from France
1954	Defeat of France in Vietnam		Cuban missile crisis
1955	Bandung conference of non-Western countries in Indonesia	1964	Ouster of Nikita Khrushchev
	West Germany joins NATO	1968	Days of May uprising in France
	Warsaw Pact		Prague Spring reform movement crushed
1956	Khrushchev speech to the twentieth party congress	1969	Willy Brandt becomes West German chancellor
	Peace terms in Vietnam yield north-south partition	1973	First OPEC oil crisis begins
	Suez crisis; defeat for Britain and France in Egypt	1975	Independence of Mozambique and Angola from Portugal
	Hungarian reform movement crushed		Reunification of Vietnam

ple suffer and die, but as we come together to help as best we can, we might at least learn to stop killing one another.

Camus split from Sartre in a disagreement over the ongoing value of Marxism and the communist experiment in the Soviet Union. Though never an orthodox communist, Sartre found potential for human liberation in the working class, in communist parties, even in the Soviet Union itself, which he saw as the strongest alternative to U.S. imperialism. By the 1950s, he was portraying existentialism as fundamentally a way to revitalize Marxism.

By contrast, Camus, who had started as a communist in the 1930s, had grown disillusioned even before the war. Establishing new bases for human happiness and solidarity meant recognizing limits to what human beings could accomplish, limits even to our demands for freedom and justice. These were precisely the limits that the new political movements of the century had so disastrously overstepped. Communism, like fascism, was part of the problem, not the solution.

Marxists and Traditionalists

Sartre was among the many European intellectuals who believed that Marxism had won a new lease on life from the wartime resistance. As they saw it, Marxism could be revamped for the West without the Stalinist excesses of the Soviet Union. Marxism remained a significant strand in the political culture of the West during the cold war era, but it also attracted periodic waves of denunciation.

In Italy, as in France, the communists' major role in the resistance enhanced their prestige, preparing the way for the extraordinary posthumous influence of Antonio Gramsci (1891–1937), a founder of the Italian Communist party who had spent most of the fascist period in prison. His *Prison Notebooks*, published during the late 1940s,

Sartre and de Beauvoir Among the most influential intellectual couples of the century, Jean-Paul Sartre and Simone de Beauvoir emerged as leaders of French existentialism by the later 1940s. See the box on page 689. (*G. Pierre/Sygma*)

helped make Marxism a powerful force in post-war Italian culture. Gramsci pointed Marxists toward a flexible political strategy, attuned to the special historical circumstances of each country.

However, others, like Camus, held that Marxism was inherently flawed and denied that any recasting could overcome its deficiencies. Damaging revelations about the excesses of Stalinism during the 1930s seemed to confirm this view. Such writers as the Hungarian-born Arthur Koestler (1905–1983) and the Italian Ignazio Silone (1900–1978), who had believed in communism during the 1930s, now denounced it as "the God that failed." Whatever its initial promise, Marxism would inevitably lead to the kind of tyranny that had developed in the Soviet Union. In the mid-1970s, the disturbing portrait of the Stalinist *gulag*, or forced-labor-camp system, by the Soviet writer Alexander Solzhenitsyn (b. 1918) stimulated another wave of anticommunist thinking.

Those hostile to Marxism often insisted that the West had to reconnect with older traditions if it were to avoid further horrors like those it had just been through. Especially in the first years after the war, many, like the French Catholic thinker Jacques Maritain (1882–1973), held that only a return to religious traditions would suffice.

The Intellectual Migration and Americanism

The extraordinary migration of European artists and intellectuals to the United States to escape persecution during the 1930s and 1940s profoundly affected the cultural life of the postwar period. An array of luminaries arrived on American shores, from the composer Igor Stravinsky to the theoretical physicist Albert Einstein, from the architect Walter Gropius to the philosopher Hannah Arendt.

Before this cross-fertilization, American culture had remained slightly provincial, sometimes proudly and self-consciously so. All the direct contact with the Europeans by the 1940s helped propel the United States into the Western cultural mainstream. No longer could "Western" culture be identified primarily with Europe. In some spheres—painting, for example—Americans were now confident enough to claim leadership for the first time.

With the abstract expressionism of the later 1940s, American painters began creating visual images the like of which had never been seen in Europe. In comparison with the raw, energetic painting of Jackson Pollock (1912–1956), the work of the Europeans seemed merely "pretty"—and the newly brash Americans were not shy about telling them so. New York began to supplant Paris as the art capital of the Western world.

Some Europeans were eager to embrace what seemed distinctively American, because America had remained relatively free of totalitarian ideologies. By the 1950s there was much talk of "the end of ideology," with America pointing the way to a healthier alternative, combining technology, value-free social science, and scientific management.

Such Americanism fed the notion that Europe needed a clean break based on technological values. If such a break was necessary, however, what was to become of the European tradition? Did anything distinctively European remain, or was Europe doomed to lick its wounds in the shadow of America? These questions lurked in the background, but first Europeans faced the difficult task of economic and political restoration.

THE NEW SOCIAL COMPACT IN WESTERN EUROPE

Democracy quickly revived in Western Europe after World War II, taking root more easily than most had thought possible. The bipolar international framework helped. The United States actively encouraged democracy, and Europeans nervous about communism and the Soviet Union were happy to follow the American lead. Success at economic reconstruction was important as well. Not only was there greater prosperity, but governments could afford to deliver on promises of enhanced security, social welfare, and equality of opportunity.

From Economic Reconstruction to Economic Miracle

It is hard to imagine how desperate the situation in much of Western Europe had been in 1945. Major cities like Rotterdam, Hamburg, and Le Havre lay largely in ruins, and normal routines suffered radical disruption. Production had declined to perhaps 25 percent of the prewar level in Italy, to 20 percent in France, and to a mere 5 percent in southern Germany. Cigarettes, often gained through barter from American soldiers, served widely as a medium of exchange.

Although the U.S. commitment to help reconstruct Europe was not originally a cold war measure, the developing cold war context made it seem all the more necessary. The Marshall Plan, outlined by U.S. secretary of state General George Marshall in 1947, had channeled $13.5 billion in aid to Western Europe by 1951. The need to rebuild gave Europeans a chance to start over, using the most up-to-date methods and technologies. Though rebuilding strategies differed, the Western European countries made remarkable recoveries.

The new German government cut state aid to business and limited the long-standing power of *cartels* (groups of enterprises that worked together to minimize competition through price fixing and production quotas). The state was permitted to intervene in the economy only to assure free competition. In France, by contrast, many were determined to use government to modernize the country, and France adopted a flexible, pragmatic form of government-led economic planning.

In 1946, French economist Jean Monnet (1888–1979) launched the first of the French postwar economic plans, which brought government and business leaders together to agree on production targets. Economic planning enabled France to make especially effective use of the capital that the Marshall Plan provided, and French industrial production returned to its prewar peak by 1951. Strong and sustained rates of economic growth were achieved throughout much of Western Europe through the mid-1960s, with only Britain lagging behind.

During the first years of rapid economic growth, the labor movement remained fairly passive in Western Europe, even though wages stayed relatively low. After an era of depression and war, workers were grateful to have jobs, free trade unions, and at least the promise of greater prosperity in the future. By the 1960s, however, labor began demanding—generally with success—to share more fully in the new prosperity. Now, rather abruptly, much of Western Europe assumed the look of a consumer society, including widespread ownership of automobiles and televisions.

Social Welfare and the Issue of Gender

European governments had begun to adopt social welfare measures on a large scale late in the nineteenth century, and by the 1940s some degree of governmental responsibility for unemployment insurance, workplace safety, and even old-age pensions was widely accepted. Some Europeans found an attractive model in Sweden and Denmark, where the outlines of a welfare state had emerged by the 1930s. Sweden attracted attention as a "middle way" that avoided the extremes of Soviet Marxism, with its coercive statism, and American-style capitalism, with its commercialism and selfish individualism.

Sweden's economy remained fundamentally capitalist, based on private ownership, but the system of social insurance in Sweden was the most extensive in Europe. The government worked with business to promote full employment and steer the economy in directions deemed socially desirable. Moreover, the welfare state came to mean a major role for the Swedish trade unions, which won relatively high wages for workers and even enjoyed a quasi–veto power over legislation.

At the same time, the Swedish government began playing a more active role in spheres of life that had formerly been private, from sexuality to child rearing. Drugstores were required to carry contraceptives beginning in 1946, and Sweden was the first country to provide sex education in the public schools—on an optional basis in 1942, then on a compulsory basis in 1955. By 1979 the Swedes were limiting corporal punishment—the right to spank—and prohibiting the sale of war toys. This deprivatization of the family stemmed from a sense that society is collectively responsible for the well-being of its children.

Britain's decision to move toward the welfare state evidenced its widening appeal. Though Winston Churchill had led his country through the darkest days of the war, Churchill's Conservatives suffered a crushing loss in the 1945 elections. Early in the war most Britons had come to take it for granted that major socioeconomic changes would follow from victory, and the Labour party, led by Clement Attlee (1883–1967), seemed better equipped to deliver on that promise.

The success of government planning and control during the war suggested that government could assume responsibility for the basic needs of the British people in peacetime as well. The welfare state was an alternative to socialism, avoiding large-scale nationalization and concentrating on social welfare measures that significantly affected the lives of ordinary people. These included old-age pensions; insurance against unemployment, sickness, and disability; and allowances for pregnancy, child rearing, widowhood, and burial. The heart of the system was free medical care, provided by the new National Health Service, which was operating by 1948.

In Britain as elsewhere, gender roles were inevitably an issue as government welfare measures were debated. Were married women to have access to the welfare system as individuals or as members of a family unit, dependent on their husbands as breadwinners and responsible for child rearing? Should government seek to enable women to be both mothers and workers, or should it help make it possible for mothers not to have to work outside the home? The answers varied widely.

The percentage of women in the work force had increased significantly during World War II, but in the immediate postwar period traditional domestic patterns seemed to have returned. In

Social Welfare in Sweden With the state playing a major role, Sweden proved a pioneer in responding to the family and children's issues that became increasingly prominent after World War II. Here children play at a day-care center in Stockholm in 1953. *(Roland Janson/ Pressens Bild, Stockholm)*

many cases, women had little choice in the matter as they were fired from their higher-paying war jobs so that men could claim them. For middle-class women this generally meant returning to the solitary and often monotonous world of the home. Often this was welcomed as a return to normality, but many women soon missed the self-sufficiency, creative challenges, and camaraderie that their war jobs had provided. For working-class women, being fired "so a man could have the job" generally meant returning to tedious, low-paid, menial labor.

British feminists at first welcomed provisions of the British welfare state. The government was to ease burdens by providing family allowances, to be paid directly to mothers, for more than one child. This seemed a progressive step beyond the long-standing British trade union demand for a "family wage"—a wage high enough to enable the male breadwinner to support a family so that his wife would not have to work. The new provisions singled out mothers for benefits, enabling them to stay home with their children. But they also reinforced the traditional assumption that marriage meant economic dependence for women and assumed that child care was women's work.

It seemed to some theorists that the relationship between parents, children, and work was going through another monumental shift, comparable to the shift that accompanied the rise of wage labor and the rise of the state. Wage labor demanded that some member of the family work at a distance from the house, and as a result parenting and earning were no longer compatible. Men were able to enter the modern work force and participate in the state because they had a support staff: women. As ideologies of individual freedom progressed, women fought for the opportunity to become full participants in the work force and the state, which would be possible only with a new support system.

France did the best job of responding to these new conditions, and its innovative approach to gender and family issues eventually made France a model for others. After the experience of defeat, collaboration, and resistance, the French were determined to pursue both economic dynamism and individual justice. But they also remained concerned with population growth, so they combined incentives to encourage large families with measures to promote equal opportunity and economic independence for women. Thus, as they expanded the role of government after the war, the French tended to assume that paid employment for women was healthy and desirable. The French also recognized that pregnancy and infant care were demanding tasks and that fathers shared the responsibility for parenting. The challenge was to combine equal treatment and equal employment opportunities with support for child rearing.

New laws gave French women equal access to civil service jobs and guaranteed equal pay for equal work. In addition, the French welfare system treated women as individual citizens, regardless of marital or economic status. Thus they were equally entitled to pensions, health services, and job-related benefits. Yet the French system also provided benefits for women during and after pregnancy. There were also family allowances that treated both parents as equally essential.

Although female participation in the paid labor force in Western Europe declined after the war, it began rising steadily during the 1950s, then accelerated during the 1960s, reaching new highs in the 1970s and 1980s. Thanks partly to the expansion of government, the greatest job growth came in the service sector—in social work, health care, and education, for example—and many of these new jobs went to women. From about 1960 to 1988, the percentage of women aged 25 to 34 in the labor force rose from 38 to 67 in Britain, from 42 to 75 in France, and from 49 to 87 in Germany. But even as their choices expanded in some respects, women became more deeply aware of enduring limits to

their opportunities. Their awareness energized a new feminist movement in the 1960s (see page 706). That movement drew intellectual inspiration from *The Second Sex*, a pioneering work published in 1949 by the French existentialist Simone de Beauvoir (1908–1986). Starting with the existentialist emphasis on human freedom, de Beauvoir demonstrated how cultural conventions continued to restrict the range of choices for women. In a profoundly influential phrase, de Beauvoir asserted that "women are made, not born," meaning that so-called "feminine" character traits and abilities are in fact invented and reinforced by the culture and not biologically innate. Men, she argued, had made themselves the standard of humanity, defining women as the "Other" and making them the repository of male fantasies and fears. (See the box "Human Freedom and the Origins of a New Feminism.")

Restoration of Democracy in Germany, France, and Italy

With its turn to a welfare state, Britain was seeking to renew a long-standing democracy after an arduous victory. Much of continental Western Europe faced a deeper challenge—to rebuild democracy after defeat and humiliation. The outcome of the effort to restore democracy was by no means certain in the late 1940s. Communism was weak in the new Federal Republic of Germany, but in France and Italy strong Communist parties had emerged from the wartime resistance and claimed to point the way beyond conventional democracy.

The Federal Republic of Germany held its first election under the Basic Law in 1949, launching what proved a successful democracy. Partly to counter the Soviet Union but also to avoid what seemed the disastrous mistake of the harsh peace settlement after World War I, the victors sought to help get Germany back on its feet as quickly as possible. At the same time, German political leaders, determined to avoid the mistakes of the Weimar years, now better understood the need to compromise. To prevent instability, the Basic Law discouraged splinter parties and allowed the courts to outlaw extremist parties.

Human Freedom and the Origins of a New Feminism

The renewed feminism that became prominent during the later 1960s took inspiration from **The Second Sex,** *a pioneering work by the French existentialist Simone de Beauvoir that was first published in 1949. Even while valuing sexual difference, she showed the scope for opening the full range of human choices to women.*

[T]he nature of things is no more immutably given, once for all, than is historical reality. If woman seems to be the inessential which never becomes the essential, it is because she herself fails to bring about this change. . . .

To decline to be the Other, to refuse to be a party to the deal—this would be for women to renounce all the advantages conferred upon them by their alliance with the superior caste. Man-the-sovereign will provide woman-the-liege with material protection and will undertake the moral justification of her existence; thus she can evade at once both economic risk and the metaphysical risk of a liberty in which ends and aims must be contrived without assistance. Indeed, along with the ethical urge of each individual to affirm his subjective existence, there is also the temptation to forgo liberty and become a thing. . . .

If a caste is kept in a state of inferiority, no doubt it remains inferior; but liberty can break the circle. Let negroes vote, and they become worthy of having the vote; let woman be given responsibilities and she is able to assume them. . . .

. . . [T]here will be some to object that . . . when woman is "the same" as her male, life will lose its salt and spice. . . .

. . . There is no denying that feminine dependence, inferiority, woe, give women their special character; assuredly woman's autonomy, if it spares men many troubles, will also deny them many conveniences; assuredly there are certain forms of the sexual adventure which will be lost in the world of tomorrow. But this does not mean that love, happiness, poetry, dream, will be banished from it.

. . . New relations of flesh and sentiment of which we have no conception will arise between the sexes; already, indeed, there have appeared between men and women friendships, rivalries, complicities, comradeships—chaste or sensual—which past centuries could not have conceived. . . .

. . . [T]here will always be certain differences between man and woman; her eroticism, and therefore her sexual world, have a special form of their own and therefore cannot fail to engender a sensuality, a sensitivity, of a special nature. . . .

. . . [W]hen we abolish the slavery of half of humanity, together with the whole system of hypocrisy that it implies, then the "division" of humanity will reveal its genuine significance and the human couple will find its true form.

Source: Simone de Beauvoir, *The Second Sex*, trans. H. M. Parshley (New York: Random House, Vintage, 1989), pp. xxv, xxvii, 728–731. Copyright 1952 and renewed 1980 by Alfred A. Knopf, Inc. Reprinted by permission of Alfred A. Knopf, the Estate of Simone de Beauvoir, and Jonathan Cape.

The courts outlawed both the Communist party and a neo-Nazi party during the formative years of the new German democracy. Two mass parties, the Christian Democratic Union (CDU) and the Social Democratic party (SPD), were immediately predominant, although a third, the much smaller Free Democratic party (FDP), proved important in building governing coalitions.

Konrad Adenauer (1876–1967), head of the CDU, the largest party in 1949, emerged as

Germany's leading statesman. Mayor of Cologne during the Weimar Republic, Adenauer had withdrawn from politics during the Nazi period, re-emerging after the war to lead the council that drafted the Basic Law. As chancellor from 1949 until 1963, he oriented German democracy toward Western Europe and the Atlantic bloc led by the United States.

The new bipolar world confronted West Germany with a cruel choice. If it accepted the bipolar framework, the country could become a full partner within the Atlantic bloc. But if it tried to straddle the fence instead, it could keep open the possibility that Germany could be reunified as a neutral and disarmed state. When the outbreak of war in Korea intensified the cold war in the early 1950s, the United States pressured West Germany to rearm and join the Western bloc. Although some West Germans resisted, Adenauer led the Federal Republic into NATO in 1955.

In the late 1950s the West German economy was recovering nicely, and the country was a valued member of the Western alliance. Adenauer's CDU seemed so potent that the other major party, the SPD, appeared to be consigned to permanent opposition. Frustrated, the SPD began to shed its Marxist trappings in an effort to widen its appeal. Prominent among those pushing in this direction was Willy Brandt (1913–1992), who became mayor of West Berlin in 1957 and the party's leader in 1963.

Adenauer stepped down in 1963 at the age of 87, after fourteen years as chancellor. The contrast with Weimar, which had known twenty-one different cabinets in a comparable fourteen-year period, could not be more striking. The Adenauer years proved to Germans that liberal democracy could mean stable and effective government and economic prosperity.

From 1963 to 1969, the CDU proved it could govern without Adenauer, while the SPD came to seem ever more respectable, even joining as junior partner in a government coalition with the CDU in 1966. Finally, in October 1969, Brandt was elected chancellor, and the SPD became responsible for governing West Germany for the first time since the war. Brandt sought to provide

a genuine alternative to the CDU without undermining the consensus that had developed since 1949. He wanted to improve relations between West Germany and the Soviet bloc. Under Adenauer, the Federal Republic had refused to deal with East Germany at all. So Brandt's opening to the East, or *Ostpolitik*, was risky, but he pursued it with skill and success.

In treaties with the Soviet Union, Czechoslovakia, and Poland, West Germany accepted the main lines of the postwar settlement. Brandt also improved relations with East Germany. The two countries agreed to mutual diplomatic recognition and were admitted to the United Nations in 1973. Brandt's overtures made possible closer economic ties and broader opportunities for ordinary citizens to interact across the east-west border.

In France and Italy, unlike West Germany, communists emerged powerful from their major roles in wartime resistance movements. Indeed, in either nation they might have made a bid for power as the war was ending. But Moscow, concerned with the larger picture in Europe, called for the moderate route of participation in coalitions. The United States intervened persistently to minimize the communists' role in both countries. When the first parliamentary elections were held in the new Fourth Republic in France in 1946, the Communists won the largest number of seats, and their support continued to rise until 1949. Partly because of pressure from the United States, they were forced out of the coalition government in 1947, and after 1949 their strength began leveling off.

As the leader of the resistance effort, Charles de Gaulle assumed the dominant political role after the liberation of France in August 1944. But he withdrew, disillusioned, from active politics early in 1946, as political life under the new Fourth Republic seemed to return to the patterns of the old Third Republic: multiparty coalitions and constant instability. Governments rose and fell every six months, on the average, over the twelve-year life of the Fourth Republic. This finally ended in 1958, when de Gaulle returned to politics during the Algeria crisis (see page 695).

Although de Gaulle became prime minister within the Fourth Republic, it was clear that his return signified a change of regime. The French legislature gave his government full powers for six months, including a charge to draft a new constitution, which was approved by referendum in the fall of 1958. The result was the Fifth Republic, which featured a stronger executive—and soon a president elected directly by the people and not dependent on the Chamber of Deputies.

Italy's political challenge, after more than twenty years of fascism, was even more dramatic. Shortly after the war, the Italians adopted a new democratic constitution and voted to end the monarchy, making modern Italy a republic for the first time. But much depended on the balance of political forces, which quickly crystallized around the Christian Democratic party (DC) and the Communist and Socialist parties. As the cold war developed, the United States intervened periodically to support the Christian Democrats as a bulwark against the Communists. Many Italian moderates with little attachment to the Roman Catholic church supported the DC for the same reason.

Well into the 1970s, the DC was invariably the largest single party, yet not a majority, so it was forced to work in coalition with smaller parties. Beginning in the early 1960s, with the much-trumpeted "opening to the left," this even included the Socialist party (PSI), which typically won 10 to 15 percent of the vote in national elections. This total fell far behind that of the Communist party, which for decades remained the second largest at 25 to 35 percent. The relative strength of the political parties established the framework for the curious combination of surface instability and deeper stability—or immobility—that came to characterize the new Italian democracy. Domination by the Christian Democrats was the fundamental fact of Italian political life until the early 1990s.

Unlike their counterparts in France, the Italian Communists did not settle for a role of opposition and protest. They organized cooperatives, won regional elections, and garnered the support of intellectuals and journalists. At one time or another, they ran many of Italy's local governments and generally did well at it. Heavily communist Bologna, for example, was one of the best-governed cities in Europe.

As the years after World War II turned to decades, the Italian Communists' successes raised awkward questions. What were the Communists trying to accomplish on the national level, and how long was it supposed to take? Could a communist party function as a governing party within a democratic political system? Meanwhile, the Christian Democrats grew ever more entrenched, arrogant, and corrupt.

WESTERN EUROPE AND THE WORLD

By the early 1950s, the old Europe seemed dwarfed by the two global superpowers. The colonial networks that had symbolized European predominance were unraveling rapidly. One obvious response was some form of European unity. A unified Europe might eventually have the clout to stand as a global superpower in its own right. Although the first steps toward European unity did not go as far as visionaries had hoped, they established lasting foundations by the late 1950s—and they served European prosperity and security well.

NATO and the Atlantic Orientation

As the Soviets tightened their grip on east-central Europe, fears of Soviet expansion into Western Europe led to the creation of the North Atlantic Treaty Organization (NATO) under U.S. leadership in April 1949. In pooling the forces of its member countries under a unified command, NATO went beyond the usual peacetime military alliance. The Atlantic bloc assumed definitive shape in 1955, when it encompassed the newly rearmed West Germany (see Map 26.2 on page 698). Although the prospect of German rearmament made the French nervous at first, by 1954 they had come to agree that this was the best course for French security.

Ban the Bomb As nuclear tension escalated during the 1950s, some people built air-raid shelters, and others took to the streets in antinuclear protest. The protest movement was especially prominent in Britain. Here demonstrators march from Trafalgar Square in London to the Atomic Weapons Research Establishment in Reading to protest the H-bomb. (*Hulton-Getty/Liaison*)

The Soviets had considerable superiority in conventional forces and ready access to Western Europe. U.S. nuclear superiority balanced this and served as the cornerstone of the NATO alliance. As a consequence it seemed crucial for the United States to maintain its superiority in nuclear weapons, a fact that helped fuel the continuing arms race.

When the Soviet Union developed the capacity for a nuclear strike at the United States, Europeans began asking whether the Americans could be counted on to respond to a conventional Soviet attack on Western Europe. Such doubts became especially widespread in France, where President de Gaulle, citing concerns for French

sovereignty and security, accelerated the development of a French nuclear force in the 1960s.

The Varieties of Decolonization

World War II had proven a major catalyst for anticolonialist independence movements throughout the world. In southeast Asia and the Pacific, the quick Japanese conquests had revealed the vulnerability of France, the Netherlands, and Britain. Also, the United States took a dim view of European colonialism. Still, the process of decolonization was varied and uneven, partly because the local independence movements differed but also because the interests of Europeans varied. Where there were large numbers of European settlers or their descendants, the remaining colonial powers—Britain, France, Belgium, the Netherlands, and Portugal—were reluctant to yield. But everywhere they were more likely to yield if they could preserve property rights and the possibility of continued influence (Map 26.1).

The effort of the Netherlands to regain control of the Dutch East Indies led to four years of military struggle before Indonesia became independent in 1949. Britain generally sought to avoid such struggles, but policy was inconsistent. Although India, the crown jewel of the empire, had won independence in 1947, many Britons still envisioned extending Commonwealth status to former British colonies as a way of retaining economic ties and political influence. But the Commonwealth became little more than a voluntary cooperative association. Despite illusions and hesitations, however, Britain proved the most realistic of the European colonial powers, grasping the need to compromise and work with emerging national leaders.

Nevertheless, even Britain decided to resist in 1956, when it provoked an international crisis over the status of the Suez Canal in Egypt. Once a British protectorate, Egypt had remained under British influence even after nominally becoming sovereign in 1922. A revolution in 1952 produced a new government of Arab nationalists, led by the able and charismatic Colonel Gamel Abdul Nasser (1918–1970). In 1954, Britain agreed to leave the Suez Canal zone within twenty months, though the zone was to be international, not Egyptian, and Britain was to retain special rights there in the event of war. In 1956, however, Nasser announced the nationalization of the canal, partly so that Egypt could use its revenues to finance public works projects.

Led by the Conservative prime minister Anthony Eden (1897–1977), Britain decided on a showdown. Eden won the support of Israel and France, each of which had reason to fear Nasser's pan-Arab nationalism. Israel had remained at odds with its Arab neighbors since its founding in 1948, and Nasser was helping the Arabs, who were taking up arms against French rule in Algeria. Late in 1956, Britain, Israel, and France orchestrated a surprise attack on Egypt, but the troops met stubborn Egyptian resistance and were defeated. The United States and the Soviet Union both opposed the Anglo-French-Israeli move, as did world opinion. The outcome of the Suez crisis demonstrated the new strength of non-European nations within the new bipolar framework.

Still, the outcome in 1956 did not convince France to abandon its struggle to retain Algeria. And that struggle proved the most dramatic, wrenching experience that any European country was to have with decolonization. However, the process started not in North Africa but in Indochina, in southeast Asia, during World War II.

Led by the communist Ho Chi Minh (1890–1969), the Indochinese anticolonialist movement gained strength resisting the Japanese during the war and established a political base in northern Vietnam in 1945. Although the French re-established control in the south after the war, negotiations between the French and the Vietnamese nationalists seemed at first to be moving toward some form of self-government for Vietnam. There was considerable opposition to this in France, especially within the army, and in 1946 French authorities in Indochina deliberately provoked an incident to start hostilities. Eight years of difficult and expensive guerrilla war followed.

With its strongly anticolonialist posture, the United States was at first unsympathetic to the French cause. But the communist takeover in China in 1949 and the invasion of South Korea by the North in 1950 made the French struggle in Indochina seem a battle in a larger war against communism in Asia. By 1954 the United States was covering 75 percent of the cost of the French effort in Indochina. Nonetheless, when the fall of the fortified area at Dien Bien Phu in May 1954 signaled a decisive French defeat, U.S. President Eisenhower decided to accept a negotiated settlement. Eisenhower had concluded that the Soviet threat in Europe must remain his principal concern.

France worked out the terms of independence for Vietnam in 1955. The country was

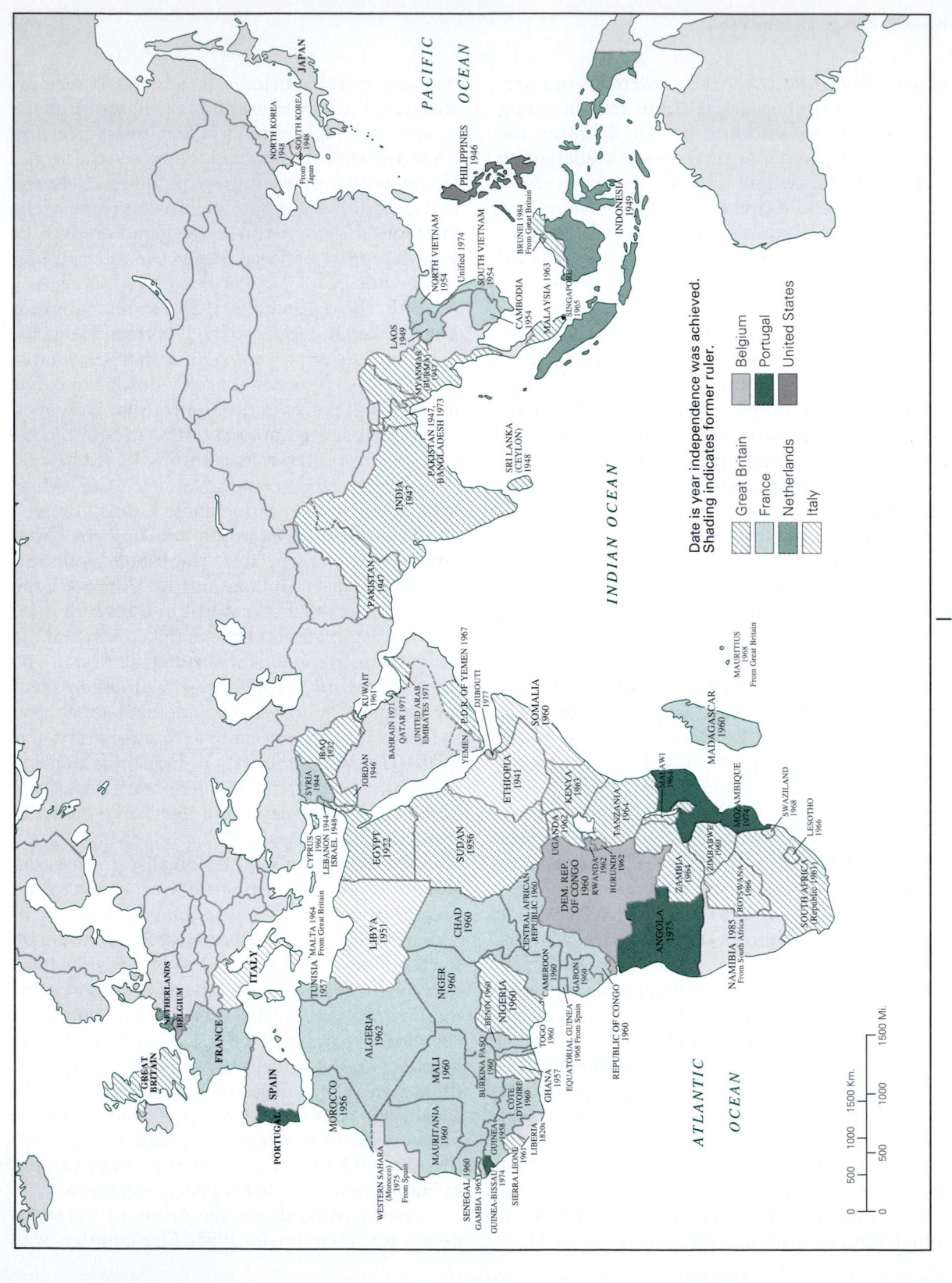

divided into northern and southern parts to separate the communist and anticommunist forces, pending elections to unify the country. The anticommunist regime the United States sponsored in the south resisted holding the elections, so the country remained divided (see Map 26.1). Only in 1975, after a brutal war with the United States, would the communist heirs of those who had led the fight against the French assume the leadership of a unified Vietnam.

In France, the defeat in Indochina left a legacy of bitterness, especially among army officers, many of whom felt that French forces could have won had they not been undercut by politicians at home. When the outcome in Indochina emboldened Arab nationalists in North Africa to take up arms against the French colonial power, the French army was eager for a second chance. The French government was willing to give it to them and agreed to independence for Tunisia and Morocco by 1956, in order to concentrate on Algeria. Algeria had been under French control since 1830, and it had over a million ethnic Europeans, 10 percent of the population.

France gradually committed 500,000 troops to Algeria, but the war bogged down into a stalemate, with increasing brutality on both sides. The war became a highly volatile political issue in France, finally coming to a head during the spring of 1958. The advent of a new ministry, rumored to favor a compromise settlement, led to violent demonstrations, engineered by the sectors of the French army in Algeria. Military intervention in France itself seemed likely to follow— and with it the danger of civil war.

It was at this moment that Charles de Gaulle returned to lead the change to the Fifth Republic. Those determined to hold Algeria welcomed de Gaulle as their savior. But de Gaulle fooled them, working out a compromise with the rebels that made Algeria independent in 1962. Only

Map 26.1 From Colonialism to Independence During a thirty-five-year period after World War II, the European empires in Africa, Asia, and the Pacific gradually came apart as the former colonies became independent nations.

de Gaulle could have engineered this outcome without provoking still deeper division in France. As for Algeria, the anticolonial movement there gave rise to a more radical political order than had been the case in Tunisia and Morocco. The new Algerian government's policy of expropriation and nationalization led most of the French settlers to relocate to France.

As the colonies of sub-Saharan Africa moved toward independence in the decades following World War II (see Map 26.1), the response of the European powers varied considerably. Of the major imperial powers, Britain had done the best at preparing local leaders and proved the most willing to work with indigenous elites. Belgium and Portugal—less certain they could maintain their influence—were the most reluctant to give up imperial status.

The transition was smoothest in British West Africa, where the Gold Coast achieved independence as Ghana, first as a dominion in the Commonwealth in 1957, then as a fully independent republic in 1960. There were few British settlers in that part of Africa, and the small, relatively cohesive African elite favored a moderate transition, not revolution. Where British settlers were relatively numerous, as in Kenya and Rhodesia, the transition to independence was much more difficult. The very presence of Europeans had impeded the development of cohesive local elites, so movements for independence in those areas tended to become more radical, advocating the expropriation of European-held property.

Nowhere was decolonization messier than in the two largest Portuguese colonies in Africa, Mozambique and Angola. Portugal had run the most repressive of the African colonial regimes, with elements of the earlier system of forced labor lingering into the 1960s. Portuguese intransigence radicalized the independence movement, which took advantage of help from the communist world to resist the colonizers militarily. Finally, in 1974, sectors of the Portuguese military, weary of a colonial war they lacked the resources to win, engineered a coup at home. The new government washed its hands of the debilitating struggle, granting independence to both Mozambique and Angola in 1975.

The process of decolonization led to a remarkable transformation in the thirty-five years after World War II. But decolonization hardly offered a neat and definitive solution. In formerly colonial territories, the boundaries often stemmed from the way Europeans had carved things up, rather than from indigenous ethnic or national patterns. Moreover, questions remained about the long-term economic relationships between Europeans and their former colonies.

The leader of Ghana, Kwame Nkrumah (1909–1972), used the term *neocolonialism* in arguing that more subtle forms of Western exploitation had replaced direct rule. But attempts by the former colonies to do without economic ties to the West often proved counterproductive, and in some areas reasonably good relations, compatible with Western economic interests, eventually developed. Generally, postcolonial leaders were highly ambivalent toward the West, where many of them had been educated.

At the same time, the context of superpower rivalry created new challenges and opportunities for the postcolonial world. In April 1955 the leaders of twenty-nine Asian and African nations met at Bandung, Indonesia, in a conference that proved a watershed in the self-understanding of what was coming to be called the "Third World." The most influential, like India's Jawaharlal Nehru, Egypt's Nasser, and Indonesia's Achmed Sukarno (1901–1970), were charismatic nation-builders, at once anti-Western and Westernizing. Along with Tito of Yugoslavia, Nehru was the leading proponent of *nonalignment*, navigating an independent course between the Western and Soviet blocs. Third World leaders often found ways of exploiting the superpower rivalry to their own advantage.

The reaction against Eurocentrism that accompanied the turn from colonialism was not confined to those who had been subjected to European imperialism. It contributed to the vogue of *structuralism*, as developed in anthropology by Claude Lévi-Strauss (b. 1908). While raising deep questions about any notion of Western superiority, Lévi-Strauss expressed a certain nostalgia for a world untouched by Western influence. There was also much interest in the West in the work of Frantz Fanon (1925–1961), a black intellectual from Martinique who became identified with the cause of the Algerian rebels. In *The Wretched of the Earth* (1961), Fanon found the West spiritually exhausted and called on the peoples of the non-Western world to go their own way, based on their own values and traditions. (See the box "Encounters with the West: The Legacy of European Colonialism.")

Economic Integration and the Coming of the European Union

As the old colonialism fell into disrepute, many found in European unity the best prospect for the future. Although hopes for political unity were soon frustrated, the movement for European integration achieved significant fruit in the economic sphere, especially through the European Economic Community (EEC), or Common Market, established in 1957.

The impetus for economic integration came especially from a new breed of "Eurocrats"—technocrats with a supranational, or Pan-European, outlook. Two remarkable French leaders, Jean Monnet and Robert Schuman (1886–1963), set the pattern. As French foreign minister after World War II, Schuman was responsible for a 1950 plan to coordinate French and German production of coal and steel. The Schuman Plan quickly encompassed both Italy and the Benelux countries to become the European Coal and Steel Community (ECSC) in 1951. Monnet served as the ECSC's first president and continued to push for more economic integration. In March 1957, leaders of France, Germany, Italy, Belgium, the Netherlands, and Luxembourg signed the Treaty of Rome, establishing the Common Market, or EEC. Over the next four decades the EEC's membership gradually expanded to include Denmark, Ireland, and Britain (1973), Greece (1981), Spain and Portugal (1986), and Austria, Finland, and Sweden (1995) (Map 26.2).

The immediate aim of the EEC was to facilitate trade by eliminating customs duties within

∾ ENCOUNTERS WITH THE WEST ∾

The Legacy of European Colonialism

In the following passage from **The Wretched of the Earth** *(1961), Frantz Fanon probes the negative consequences of colonialism—for both colonizers and colonized—and tries to show why a radical, even violent break from colonialism was necessary.*

The violence which has ruled over the ordering of the colonial world, which has ceaselessly drummed the rhythm for the destruction of native social forms and broken up without reserve the systems of reference of the economy, the customs of dress and external life, that same violence will be claimed and taken over by the native at the moment when, deciding to embody history in his own person, he surges into the forbidden quarters. . . .

. . . The colonialist bourgeoisie, in its narcissistic dialogue, expounded by the members of its universities, had in fact deeply implanted in the minds of the colonized intellectual that the essential qualities remain eternal in spite of all the blunders men may make: the essential qualities of the West, of course. . . . Now it so happens that during the struggle for liberation, at the moment that the native intellectual comes into touch again with his people, . . . [a]ll the Mediterranean values—the triumph of the human individual, of clarity, and of beauty— . . . are revealed as worthless, simply because they have nothing to do with the concrete conflict in which the people is engaged.

Individualism is the first to disappear. . . . The colonialist bourgeoisie had hammered into the native's mind the idea of a society of individuals where each person shuts himself up in his own subjectivity, and whose only wealth is individual thought. Now the native who has the opportunity to return to the people during the struggle for freedom will discover the falseness of this theory. The very forms of organization of the struggle will suggest to him a different vocabulary. Brother, sister, friend— these are words outlawed by the colonialist bourgeoisie, because for them my brother is my purse, my friend is part of my scheme for getting on. The native intellectual . . . will . . . discover the substance of village assemblies, the cohesion of people's committees, and the extraordinary fruitfulness of local meetings and groupments. Henceforward, the interests of one will be the interests of all, for in concrete fact *everyone* will be discovered by the troops, *everyone* will be massacred—or *everyone* will be saved.

Source: Frantz Fanon, *The Wretched of the Earth,* trans. Constance Farrington (New York: Grove, 1968), pp. 40–47. Copyright © 1963 by Presence Africaine. Reprinted by permission of Grove/Atlantic, Inc.

the Common Market and establishing a common tariff on imports from the rest of the world. Tariff reduction entailed the advantage of access to wider markets abroad, but also the risks of new competition in each member country's domestic market. It was hard to be sure who might gain and who might lose. However, the EEC proved advantageous to so many that tariff reduction proceeded well ahead of schedule. Trade among the member countries nearly doubled between 1958 and 1962, and by 1968 the last internal tariffs had been eliminated.

After the merger of the governing institutions of several European supranational organizations in 1967, the term "European Community" (EC) and later "European Union" (EU)

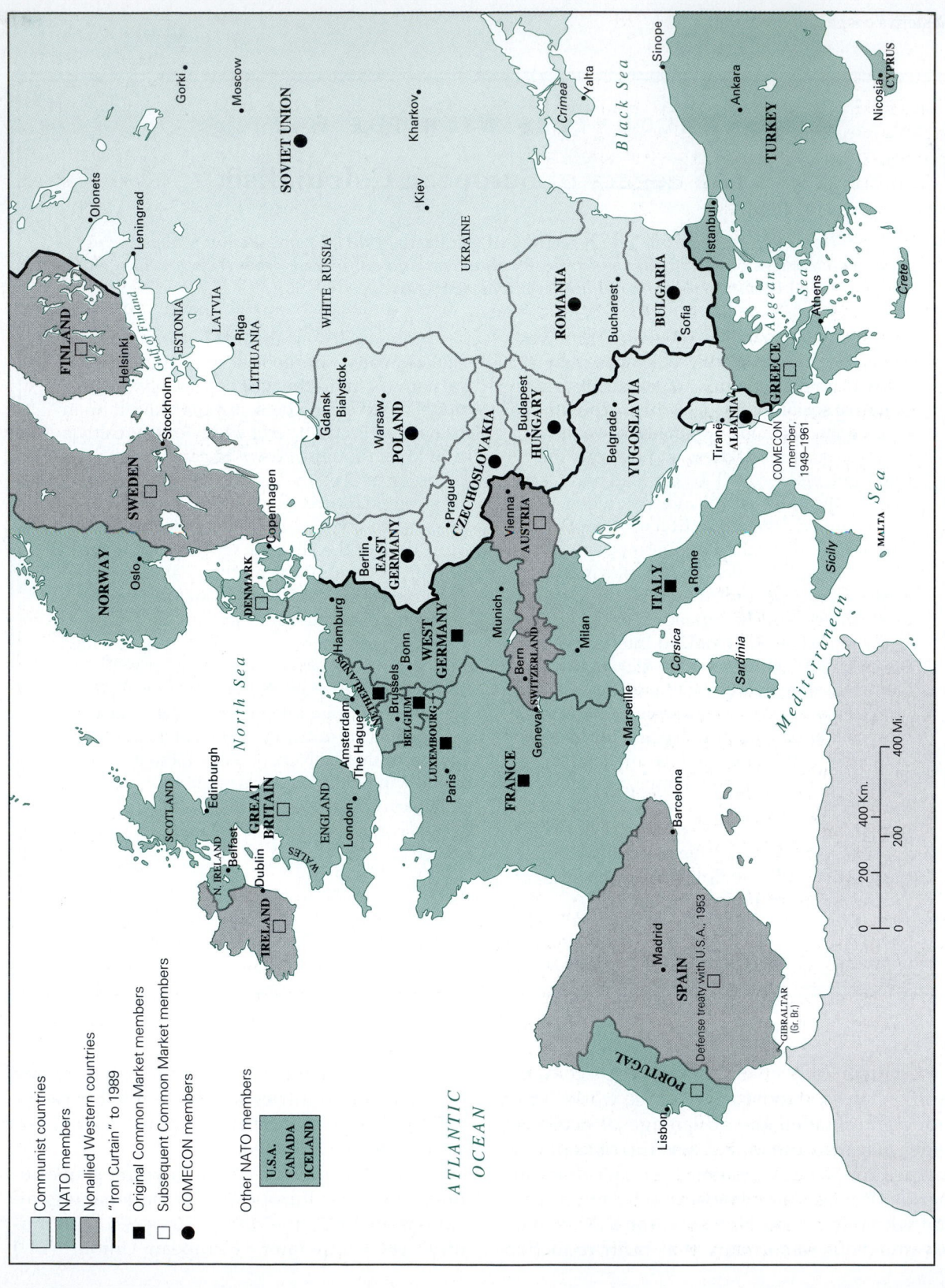

Communist countries
NATO members
Nonallied Western countries
"Iron Curtain" to 1989
Original Common Market members
Subsequent Common Market members
COMECON members
Other NATO members

U.S.A.
CANADA
ICELAND

FINLAND
Olonets
Leningrad
Helsinki

SOVIET UNION
Gorki
Moscow
Kharkov
Kiev

Black Sea
Sinope
Valta
Crimea

Ankara
Nicosia
CYPRUS
TURKEY

SWEDEN
Stockholm
Oslo
NORWAY

Gulf of Finland
ESTONIA
LATVIA
Riga
LITHUANIA

WHITE RUSSIA
UKRAINE

ROMANIA
Bucharest
BULGARIA
Sofia
Istanbul
Aegean Sea
GREECE
Athens
Crete

Copenhagen
DENMARK
Hamburg

Gdansk
Bialystok
Warsaw
POLAND

Prague
CZECHOSLOVAKIA
Vienna
AUSTRIA
Budapest
HUNGARY

Belgrade
YUGOSLAVIA
Tirane
ALBANIA

COMECON member, 1949–1961

Berlin
EAST GERMANY

NETHERLANDS
Amsterdam
The Hague
Brussels
BELGIUM
LUXEMBOURG
Bonn
WEST GERMANY
Munich
Bern
SWITZERLAND
Geneva
Milan

ITALY
Rome
Corsica
Sardinia
Sicily
MALTA
Mediterranean Sea

North Sea

Edinburgh
SCOTLAND
Belfast
N. IRELAND
Dublin
IRELAND
GREAT BRITAIN
ENGLAND
London
WALES

Marseille

Barcelona
Madrid
SPAIN
Defense treaty with U.S.A., 1953
GIBRALTAR (Gr. Br.)
PORTUGAL
Lisbon

ATLANTIC OCEAN

400 Mi.
400 Km.
200
200
0
0

replaced the terms "Common Market" and EEC. This broadening of the EEC did not occur without vigorous debate. The goal of the Common Market—to enable goods, capital, and labor to move freely among the member countries—required some coordination of the social and economic policies of the member states. Thus state sovereignty became an important issue.

In the mid-1960s, President de Gaulle of France forced some of the underlying uncertainties about the Common Market to the fore. De Gaulle was not prepared to compromise French sovereignty, and he was not persuaded that supranational integration offered the best course for postwar Europe. After the Algerian War ended in 1962, de Gaulle's France began playing an assertively independent role in international affairs, developing an independent French nuclear force, curtailing the French role in NATO, and recognizing the communist People's Republic of China.

De Gaulle's stance checked the increasing supranationalism of the Common Market. As the economic context became more difficult in the 1970s, it became harder to maintain the cohesion of the EEC. So though the Common Market proved an important departure, it did not give Western Europe a new world role during the first decades after World War II.

THE SOVIET UNION AND THE COMMUNIST BLOC

By the late 1950s, there was increasing concern in the West that the Soviet Union might have signif-

Map 26.2 Military Alliances and Multinational Economic Groupings in the Era of the Cold War The cold war split was reflected especially in the two military alliances: NATO, formed in 1949, and the Warsaw Pact, formed in 1955. Each side also had its own multinational economic organization, but the membership of the EEC, or Common Market, was not identical to that of NATO. Although communist, Yugoslavia remained outside Soviet-led organizations, as did Albania for part of the period.

icant advantages in the race with the capitalist democracies. Westerners worried about producing enough scientists and engineers to match the Soviets, and some economists held that central planning might prove as efficient as capitalism. Nonetheless, flaws in the political and economic system that had emerged under Stalin continued in the Soviet Union, and its system of satellites in east-central Europe presented new dilemmas. Efforts to make the Soviet system more flexible after Stalin's death in 1953 proved sporadic at best, and the Soviet suppression of the reform movement in Czechoslovakia during the "Prague Spring" of 1968 confirmed the rigidity of the Soviet system.

Dilemmas of the Soviet System in Postwar Europe

The Soviet Union had suffered enormously in leading the victory over Nazi Germany. Especially in the more developed western part of the country, thousands of factories and even whole towns lay destroyed, and there were severe shortages of everything from labor to housing. Yet the developing cold war seemed to require that military spending remain high.

At the same time, the Soviet Union faced the challenge of solidifying the system of satellite states it had put together in east-central Europe. Most of the region had no desirable interwar past to try to reclaim, and thus there was widespread sentiment for significant change, including nationalization of industry. The Soviet system seemed to have proven itself in standing up to the Nazis, and many believed that a socialist economic system could work. So a measure of idealism and enthusiasm surrounded postwar reconstruction even in the satellite states.

Partly in response to U.S. initiatives in Western Europe, the Soviets sought to mold the new communist states into a secure, coordinated bloc of allies. The Soviets founded a new organization, COMECON, as part of the effort to lead the economies of the satellite states away from their ties to the West and toward the Soviet Union (see Map 26.2). For example, before the war only

7 percent of Poland's foreign trade had been with the Soviet Union; by 1951 the figure was 58 percent. Through such mechanisms as artificial pricing of imports and exports, these new economic relationships often entailed outright exploitation of the satellite states for the benefit of the Soviet Union.

In the military-diplomatic sphere, the Soviets countered the admission of West Germany to NATO in 1955 by creating the Warsaw Pact, which provided for a joint military command and mutual military assistance in the Soviet bloc. The Warsaw Pact established a new basis for the continuing presence of Soviet troops in the satellite states, but the tensions within the Soviet-dominated system in east-central Europe soon raised questions about what the pact meant.

Yugoslavia had been a point of vulnerability for the Soviet system from the start. Communist-led partisans under Tito had liberated Yugoslavia from the Axis on their own, and they had not needed the Red Army to begin constructing a new communist regime. Tito was willing to work with the Soviets, but he could be considerably more independent than those elsewhere whose power rested on Soviet support. When Soviet demands, including control of the Yugoslav police and army, became intolerably meddlesome from the Yugoslav point of view, Tito broke with the Soviet Union in 1948. Yugoslavia began developing a more flexible socialist economic system, with greater scope for local initiatives.

Stalin's initial response to Tito's defection in 1948 was a crackdown on potential opponents throughout the Soviet bloc. As in the 1930s, Stalin relied on the secret police, who executed those suspected of deviation, inspiring fear even among those closest to him. As the arrest and execution of communist leaders continued in the satellite states, strikes and demonstrations developed as well, reaching a crisis point in East Germany in 1953.

The East German communist leader, Walter Ulbricht (1893–1973), feared that, as the United States pressed West Germany to rearm and join NATO, Soviet leaders would opt for a reunified but strictly neutral and disarmed Germany. German reunification, however, would entail free elections, which the East German Communists could not hope to win. Ulbricht thus intensified the industrial development of East Germany to make his country too valuable an ally for the Soviet Union to sacrifice. The resulting pressure on labor produced strong opposition.

In June 1953, a workers' protest in East Berlin led to political demands, including free elections and the withdrawal of Soviet troops. Disturbances spread quickly to other major East German cities. Though this spontaneous uprising was not well coordinated, Soviet troops had to intervene to save the Ulbricht government. The East German example helped stimulate antigovernment demonstrations elsewhere in the Soviet bloc, convincing Soviet leaders that something had to give. But at this point, shortly after Stalin's death, the leadership of the Soviet Union was still being sorted out.

De-Stalinization Under Khrushchev, 1955–1964

The nature of the struggle for succession after Stalin's death foreshadowed a turn from the extremes of Stalinism. The political infighting involved a reasonable degree of give and take, as opposed to terror and violence. Although one of the eventual losers was sent to Siberia to run a power station and the other was made ambassador to Outer Mongolia, it was a major departure that the winner, Nikita Khrushchev (1894–1971), had neither of them exiled or executed.

Khrushchev had not been Stalin's heir apparent, but he gradually established himself as the new leader by building up patronage networks and playing off factions. Slightly crude, even something of a buffoon, he won out by 1955 partly because his opponents repeatedly underestimated him. Although his period of leadership was brief, it was eventful—and in some ways the Soviet system's best chance for renewal.

At a closed session of the Soviet Communist party's twentieth national congress in February 1956, Khrushchev made a dramatic late-night speech denouncing the criminal excesses of the

Stalinist system and the "cult of personality" that had developed around Stalin. Khrushchev's immediate aim was to undercut his hard-line rivals, but he also insisted that Stalinism had amounted to an unnecessary deviation from Marxism-Leninism. It seemed that Khrushchev might bring liberalization and reform.

At the same time, however, popular discontent in the satellite states placed the whole system in crisis. In the face of the East German uprising of 1953, the Soviets began making room for more moderate communists. Khrushchev even sought to patch things up with Tito, publicly condemning Stalin's treatment of him, exchanging visits in 1955 and 1956, and suggesting that different countries might take different routes to communism.

In Poland beginning in June 1956, strikes against wage cuts took on a political character, fi-nally provoking the intervention of Soviet troops in October. Nonetheless, the Soviets tolerated reform within Poland because it pledged to continue to uphold the Warsaw Pact as a bulwark against Germany. Later that year, however, the Hungarians dismantled their collective farms and moved toward a democratic coalition government. They called for Soviet troops to withdraw, to enable Hungary to leave the Warsaw Pact and become neutral. These were not changes within the system, but changes that would undermine the system itself. So after a democratic government was set up in October, the Soviets used tanks to crush the Hungarian reform movement. Thousands were killed during the fighting or executed and 200,000 Hungarians fled to the West.

The Soviets understood that the system had to become more palatable, but they made it clear

Revolution and Restoration in Hungary Led by students and faculty from the Karl Marx University of Economics, Hungarians march across the Chain Bridge in Budapest on October 23, 1956, initiating the revolutionary phase of the movement for change in communist Hungary. Within two weeks, a Soviet-led crackdown, including shelling by Soviet tanks, had crushed the revolution, inflicting 27,000 casualties on the Hungarians. *(MTI/Eastfoto/Sovfoto)*

that liberalization had to be kept within certain limits. Reformers could not challenge the system itself, especially communist one-party rule and the Warsaw Pact. Hungary's new leader, János Kádár (b. 1912), collectivized agriculture more fully than before, but he also engineered a measure of economic decentralization. There was eventually an amnesty for political prisoners, as well as considerable liberalization in cultural life, so that Hungary came to enjoy freer contact with the West than the other satellites.

East Germany's communist leaders had every reason *not* to distance themselves from the Soviets. Walter Ulbricht, who remained in power until his retirement in 1971, concentrated on central planning and heavy industry in orthodox fashion, and he made the East German economy the most successful in the Soviet bloc.

Still, because that economic growth was built on low wages, East German workers were tempted to immigrate to West Germany as the West German economic miracle gleamed ever brighter during the 1950s. The special position of Berlin, in the heart of East Germany yet still divided among the occupying powers, made emigration relatively easy; 2.6 million East Germans left for the West between 1950 and 1962. With a population of only 17.1 million, East Germany could not afford to let this hemorrhaging continue. Thus, in August 1961 the Ulbricht regime erected the Berlin Wall, a grim reminder that despite periodic thaws in East-West relations, the iron curtain remained in place.

From Liberalization to Stagnation

The most intense phase of the cold war ended with Stalin's death in 1953. In his speech to the twentieth party congress in 1956, Khrushchev repudiated the Soviet tenet that the military showdown between Western capitalist imperialism and the communist world was inevitable. However, despite summit conferences and sporadic efforts at better relations, friction between the Soviet Union and the United States continued.

A new peak of tension was reached in October 1962 when the Soviets placed missiles in Cuba, which had developed close ties with the Soviet Union after the 1959 revolution led by Fidel Castro (b. 1926). Although the United States had its own offensive missiles in Turkey, adjacent to the Soviet Union, the Soviet attempt to base missiles in Cuba seemed an intolerable challenge. For several days, military confrontation appeared a distinct possibility, but President John F. Kennedy (1917–1963) managed an effective combination of resistance and restraint in responding to the Soviet move. The Soviets withdrew their missiles in exchange for a U.S. promise not to seek to overthrow the communist government in Cuba. The outcome was essentially a victory for the United States, which retained its offensive missile capacity adjacent to the Soviet Union. The Cuban missile crisis was the closest the superpowers came to armed confrontation during the cold war period.

Meanwhile, it was becoming clear that international communism was not the monolithic force it had once seemed. The most dramatic indication was the Sino-Soviet split, which developed during the 1950s as the communists under Mao Zedong solidified their regime in China. After taking power in 1949, the Chinese communists pursued their own path to development. The Soviets came to fear that the Chinese might challenge the Soviet leadership of international communism. By the early 1960s, the communist Chinese path had become especially appealing in the non-Western world. The antagonism between China and the Soviet Union added another layer of uncertainty to the cold war era.

As a domestic leader, Khrushchev proved mercurial and erratic, but he was an energetic innovator, willing to experiment. He jettisoned the worst features of the police state apparatus, including some of the infamous Siberian prison camps, and offered amnesties for prisoners. He also liberalized cultural life and gave workers greater freedom to move from one job to another. The government expanded medical and educational facilities and, between 1955 and 1964, doubled the nation's housing stock, alleviating a severe housing shortage.

As part of the domestic thaw in the Soviet Union after Stalin, divorce became easier and abortion was again legalized. Women received liberal provisions for maternity leave, and some measures were taken to assure equal access to higher education and the professions. Still, women were concentrated in lower-paying occupations and rarely rose to the top echelons. Although they were prominent in medicine in the Soviet Union, Soviet doctors did not have the status—or the incomes—that their counterparts enjoyed in the West.

Though living standards remained relatively low, Khrushchev's reforms helped improve the lives of ordinary people by the early 1960s. His claim in 1961 that the Soviet Union would surpass the Western standard of living within twenty years did not seem an idle boast. After all, the Soviets had launched *Sputnik I* in 1957 and put the first human into space in 1961. Such achievements suggested that even ordinary Soviet citizens had reason for optimism. More generally, the communist regimes throughout the Soviet bloc had achieved excellent rates of economic growth during the 1950s. Yet Khrushchev had made enemies with his erratic reform effort, and this led to his forced retirement in October 1964. But not until 1968 did it become clear that the liberalization of the Khrushchev era was over.

By early 1968 a significant reform movement had developed within the Communist party in Czechoslovakia. Determined to avoid the fate of the Hungarian effort in 1956, the reformers emphasized that Czechoslovakia would remain a communist state and a full member of the Warsaw Pact. But within that framework, they felt, it should be possible to invite freer cultural expression and democratize the Communist party's procedures. However, efforts to reassure the Soviets alienated some of the reformers' supporters, who stepped up their demands as a result. Soviet leaders grew concerned, and in August 1968 Soviet tanks moved into the Czech capital, Prague, to crush the reform movement.

The end of the "Prague Spring" closed the era of relative flexibility and cautious innovation in the Soviet bloc that had begun in 1953. A period of relative stagnation followed under Leonid Brezhnev (1906–1982), a careful, consensus-seeking bureaucrat. Now setting the tone was the "Brezhnev doctrine": The Soviet Union would help established communist regimes remain in power against any "counterrevolutionary" threat.

Poland, too, experienced a reform effort in 1968, but it was initiated by students and failed to attract the support of workers. The Polish communist government provided subsidized food, housing, and medical care, but to pay the bill the Polish government had to borrow from foreigners. So even in Poland, where the communist regime seemed to satisfy the workers, its way of doing so was increasingly artificial—and unsustainable.

After the successes of the 1950s and early 1960s, the Soviet Union was finding it ever harder to match the West in economic growth and technological innovation. And despite periodic efforts at economic reform, the satellite states did not do appreciably better. Ordinary people became increasingly frustrated as the communist economic system proved erratic in providing even the most basic consumer goods.

Frustration grew especially among women, who seemed to bear a disproportionate share of the burdens. Women were more likely to be employed outside the home in the Soviet bloc than in the West. Around 90 percent of adult women in the Soviet Union and East Germany had paid jobs outside the home by 1980. Yet not only were women concentrated in jobs with low pay and prestige, but they also still bore the major responsibility for child care, housework, and shopping. They had few of the labor-saving devices available in the West, and they often had to spend hours in line to buy ordinary consumer items. Dissatisfaction among women fed a new underground protest movement that began in the mid-1970s—a further indication of the growing strains in the overall system.

DEMOCRACY AND ITS DISCONTENTS, 1968 AND AFTER

The year 1968, which saw the end of the "Prague Spring," proved a turning point in Western

Europe as well. By this point, a generation after World War II, democracy seemed to have succeeded remarkably. But in the late 1960s it became clear that, despite prosperity and stability, political alienation had been building in Western Europe. The dissatisfactions that began erupting in 1968 fundamentally changed the tone of politics in Europe and the West. Economic difficulties that began in 1973 only added fuel to an already smoldering fire.

Democratic Consolidation and Political Alienation

Observing the success of democracy in the most developed parts of Western Europe, Spain, Portugal, and Greece established workable democracies after periods of dictatorial rule. After the death of Francisco Franco in 1975, democracy returned to Spain more smoothly than most had dared hope. Franco established that a restoration of the monarchy would follow his death, and King Juan Carlos (r. 1975–) served as an effective catalyst in the transition to democracy.

When the first democratic elections in Spain since the civil war were held in 1977, the big winners were a democratic centrist party and a moderate socialist party. The Socialists won a parliamentary majority in the next elections, in 1982, and a moderate Socialist replaced the centrist leader as prime minister. It appeared that Spain had quickly found its way to an effective two-party system. Meanwhile, the new constitution of 1978 dismantled what was left of the Franco system. A comparable transition from military rule to democracy took place in Portugal and Greece. For all three, EEC membership became a pillar of the solidifying democratic consensus.

At the same time, however, political disaffection threatened the consensus in the more established democracies of Europe. The most dramatic eruption of radical protest was the "Days of May" uprising that shook France in May 1968. The movement accused de Gaulle's Fifth Republic of having slighted domestic issues such as housing and education in its preoccupation with raising the international status of the country.

The uprising of 1968 started with university students, who sought to reach out to others, especially industrial workers, by offering a broad critique of the present system. But union activists and workers generally declined to join the movement, and the students ended up settling for relatively limited concessions. Still, the uprising made it clear that the university system needed a complete overhaul—and that students and faculty had to be involved in the changes. Over the next several years, the Education Ministry carried out reforms, breaking existing institutions into smaller units, with more local control over budgets and instructional methods. Student and faculty participation in institutional governance tended to politicize French universities, some of which became communist strongholds, others bastions of the right.

The effort to come to terms with the events of 1968 deepened divisions within the Communist party. Unable to transcend long-standing class categories and embrace the aspirations of those, like the students, who were newly disaffected, French communism increasingly seemed old and stale. In contrast, the French Socialist party gained dramatically during the 1970s. Claiming the mantle of the new left that had emerged in 1968, the Socialists proclaimed that the promise of that year could be translated into substantial change.

The Oil Crisis and the Changing Economic Framework

As the political situation in Western Europe became more volatile, events outside Europe made it clear how interdependent the world had become—and that the West did not hold all the trump cards. In the fall of 1973, Egypt and Syria attacked Israel, seeking to recover the lands they had lost in a brief war in 1967. The assault failed, but the Arab nations of the oil-rich Middle East came together to retaliate against the Western bloc for supporting Israel. By restricting the supply of oil, the Arab-led Organization of Petroleum Exporting Countries (OPEC) produced a sharp increase in oil prices and a severe economic disruption all over the industrialized world. In Western Europe, in January 1975, the price of oil was six times what it had been in 1973, and this increase remained a source of inflationary pressure throughout the West until the early 1980s.

The 1970s proved to be an unprecedented period of *stagflation*—sharply reduced rates of growth combined with inflation and rising unemployment. Increasing global competition, technological change, and high unemployment created new economic strains. The economic miracle was over.

Problems in the Welfare State

A tighter economy made it harder for governments to afford the welfare measures that had helped establish the political consensus since World War II. The Swedish case dramatized the problems of managing a welfare state in conditions of economic stringency.

In the early 1970s, 40 percent of Sweden's national income went for taxes to finance the system—the highest rate of taxation in the world. At the same time, Sweden found itself less competitive because its wages were high and it was not keeping abreast of technological developments. In Sweden, as elsewhere, there were growing doubts that the welfare state could nurture the initiative and productivity needed for success in the increasingly competitive global economy. By 1980 unemployment and efforts to cut government spending led to the most severe labor unrest the country had experienced since the war.

In Britain a dramatic assault on the welfare state developed at the same time. The British economy lagged behind those of the rest of the industrialized West, suffering especially during the 1970s. Between 1968 and 1976, the country lost 1 million manufacturing jobs, and there was no consensus on how to apportion the pain of the necessary austerity measures.

Both of Britain's major political parties made a serious effort to deal with the situation, but neither succeeded. The election of the militantly conservative Margaret Thatcher (b. 1925) as Con-

servative party leader in 1975 proved the turning point. When she became prime minister in 1979, it was clear that Britain was embarking on a radically different course.

In contrast, during the early 1980s a revitalized socialist party in France marginalized the communists and, for a time, seemed poised to reorient government. François Mitterrand (1916–1996) was elected president in 1981, promising to create the first genuinely democratic socialism. But he gradually abandoned his talk of socialism in the face of economic and political pressures. By the end of the decade, he was questioning the relevance of long-standing socialist tenets and playing up the virtues of entrepreneurship, the profit mechanism, and free-market competition.

The Democratic Consensus and Its Limitations

Discontent with the political consensus after 1968 led to a variety of new political alignments and expedients, some of them violent. In Italy the Communists responded to the economic crisis and political alienation by offering to share power—and responsibility—with the Christian Democrats on the national level for the first time. In 1976, the Communist party's share of the vote in national elections reached an all-time high of 34.4 percent. By the end of the 1970s, however, their efforts had led nowhere; their share of the vote steadily declined, as did their support among younger people and intellectuals. But the Christian Democrats were also losing electoral support. Their message seemed ever less relevant as Italy became more secular. And as the Italian Communists declined, many found it less important to support Christian democracy as a bulwark against communism.

In the 1970s, frustration with political immobility gave rise to a new wave of terrorism, especially in Italy and Germany. Terrorists in such groups as the Red Brigades in Italy and the Baader-Meinhof gang in Germany assassinated a number of prominent public officials and businessmen, including the long-time Italian Christian

Democratic leader Aldo Moro (1916–1978). Left- and right-wing extremism fed on each other, and it was right-wing extremists who were responsible for Italy's most deadly terrorist episode, a bombing in the railway station in Bologna that killed eighty-five people in August 1980.

Political frustration also found productive outlets, as new coalitions developed around newly politicized issues—from abortion to the environment—that had not been associated with the Marxist left. In Germany, the Green movement formed by peace and environmental activists during the late 1970s took pains to avoid acting like a conventional party. Concerned that Germany, with its central location, would end up the devastated battleground in any superpower confrontation, the Greens opposed deployment of additional U.S. missiles on German soil and called for an alternative to the arms race. Socialists and Conservatives held their own, leaving Germany with essentially a two-party system, as the strength of the Green party leveled off at 10 to 15 percent of the vote in the 1980s.

Prominent among the new political currents that emerged after 1968 was a new feminist movement. This new movement arose out of the politically charged atmosphere in Europe and the United States as women found themselves insisting on civil rights for others, only to realize that they, too, represented an oppressed class: Women were officially and unofficially barred from a wide range of educational and employment opportunities. They were denied equal pay for equal work. They were rarely considered for leadership roles in the political or business worlds.

Simone de Beauvoir's *The Second Sex* and Betty Friedan's *The Feminine Mystique* guided women's struggle to redefine themselves within society. These books argued that women were regarded not as human beings but as something inferior and auxiliary, and, as such, they were raised to put the needs and desires of men above their own. Some women struggled against this, explained both de Beauvoir and Friedan, but most were convinced from childhood that they were less capable and less important. They thus concentrated on endearing themselves to men, devoting their time to becoming beautiful, helpful, and noncompetitive.

Feminists forced new issues onto the political stage, working to liberalize divorce and abortion laws throughout the Western world, to obtain some equality in the division of housework and child care, and to address the ways that girls were encouraged to be beautiful and passive. At "consciousness-raising" groups, acting on the notion that "the personal is political," women brought extremely private matters to public attention. These ideas had a tremendous impact in the 1970s, and an even deeper sense of gender issues would become central to public debate and personal choice during the last two decades of the century.

SUMMARY

In the decades that followed World War II, a bipolar framework, dominated by the United States and the Soviet Union, shaped world affairs. The states of Western and central Europe continued to decline in influence and lost their remaining colonial possessions. The new bipolar framework opened certain possibilities but also limited political options in both halves of newly divided Europe. The Western European states had to follow the U.S. lead, especially in matters of national security, though France under de Gaulle grew especially restive. But Western Europe achieved remarkable prosperity and took significant steps toward multinational integration in the European Economic Community (EEC).

In the communist bloc, Stalin's death in 1953 ended the most repressive features of the Soviet regime. Under his successor, Nikita Khrushchev, the Soviet Union seemed able to compete with the United States in areas from education to economic growth to the exploration of outer space. But the experiment with central planning in the Soviet bloc proved ever less successful. At the same time, the fate of a series of opposition and reform efforts, from East Berlin in 1953 to Prague in 1968, made it clear that the Soviets intended to keep their east-central European satellite states on a relatively tight leash.

In Western Europe, the shared experience of wartime led to a new social compact based on greater government responsibility for economic well-being and social welfare. The implicit promise of growing prosperity for all made possible a measure of cooperation between business and labor that eroded earlier assumptions of irreconcilable class struggle. The new consensus provided a foundation for democracy, which became solidly established in Western Europe during the first two decades after the war.

In 1968 strains began to appear in the Western democracies, and slower economic growth during the 1970s jeopardized the postwar settlement. A diffuse discontent developed among many Western Europeans, who felt left out as the most important decisions were made by party leaders, technocratic planners, EEC Eurocrats, or the executives of multinational corporations. A quest for new forms of political participation began in 1968 and continued throughout the 1970s. The Green movement drew attention to the environment. The feminist movement forced Western civilization to extend its principles of human choice and freedom to women. Since women make up more than half of humanity—and the behaviors between the sexes affect all of humanity—this was a deeply significant change.

To a large degree, all these changes had more impact in the West than in the East. In Western Europe there was more room for change in the atmosphere of prosperity and the relative comfort of political legitimacy. Eastern Europe was not as fortunate. There, a persisting sense of social imbalance threatened to undermine the anxious stability that characterized the era from 1949 to 1985.

SUGGESTED READING

Brinkley, Douglas, and Clifford Hackett, eds. *Jean Monnet: The Path to European Unity*. 1991. A collection of essays on Monnet's central role in the movement toward European integration.

Dedman, Martin J. *The Origins and Development of the European Union, 1945–1995: A History of European Integration*. 1996. A concise and accessible introductory work.

Ellwood, David W. *Rebuilding Europe: Western Europe, America and Postwar Reconstruction*. 1992. A readable, well-balanced survey of the course of reconstruction in Western Europe in the decade after World War II.

Hosking, Geoffrey. *The First Socialist Society: A History of the Soviet Union from Within*. Enlarged ed. 1990. Looks at family, religion, nationality, and the experience of factory workers.

Hughes, H. Stuart. *Between Commitment and Disillusion: The Obstructed Path and the Sea Change, 1930–1965*. 1987. An updated edition of two previously published works by an influential intellectual historian. *The Sea Change* covers the intellectual migration from Europe to America.

Kuisel, Richard F. *Capitalism and the State in Modern France: Renovation and Economic Management in the Twentieth Century*. 1981. A thorough study tracing the emergence of economic planning and a technocratic ethos in France.

Laqueur, Walter. *Europe in Our Time: A History, 1945–1992*. 1992. A comprehensive, well-balanced survey by a leading authority on twentieth-century Europe.

Maier, Charles S., ed. *The Cold War in Europe: Era of a Divided Continent*. 3d ed. 1996. A series of essays especially helpful on the implications of the cold war framework for Western European development.

Marks, Elaine, and Isabelle de Courtivon, eds. *New French Feminisms*. 1980. A very strong collection of writings from the French women's movement.

Mommsen, Wolfgang J., and Jürgen Osterhammel, eds. *Imperialism and After: Continuities and Discontinuities*. 1986. A collection of essays by leading scholars. Analyzes the ways European influence continued after the end of formal imperial control.

Morgan, Kenneth O. *The People's Peace: British History, 1945–1990*. 1992. A thorough survey that seeks to avoid overemphasis on decline and pessimism.

Pulzer, Peter. *German Politics, 1945–1995*. 1995. A brief yet probing account of political developments in both East and West Germany.

Rothschild, Joseph. *Return to Diversity: A Political History of East Central Europe Since World War II*. 2d ed. 1993. A straightforward survey that makes sense of the differences as well as the similarities among the Soviet bloc countries during the cold war.

Ruggie, Mary. *The State and Working Women: A Comparative Study of Britain and Sweden*. 1984. A sophisticated comparative study that seeks to explain why women achieved greater economic equality in Sweden than in Britain.

CHAPTER 27

The West and the World in the Late Twentieth Century

During the fall of 1989, three teenaged Muslim girls were suspended from a public school near Paris because they insisted on wearing the headscarves traditional for Islamic women. School authorities cited the law barring religious displays in France's strictly secular school system. The leader of France's largest teachers' union also contended that "this flaunting of a clear symbol of women's subordination negates the teaching of human rights in schools." Thus, when the French minister of education defended the students' right to wear the scarves, he was widely criticized.

In fact, the education minister simply wanted to keep these girls—and the many others like them—in school, to expose them to secular influence and promote their assimilation into French culture. France's prestigious Council of State soon ruled that the scarves did not violate the constitutional separation of church and state, as long as they were not worn in an effort to flaunt religion or to proselytize. But the riddles of multiculturalism at issue in this "affair of the scarves" kept coming up in France and elsewhere by the late twentieth century.

As the population exploded in the less developed world, the prosperous countries of the North were increasingly a magnet for the disadvantaged from around the world. The resulting immigration created new social and political pressures that raised questions about citizenship and assimilation, pluralism and diversity, identity and community.

Such questions came to center stage partly because of the end of the cold war, which had overshadowed all else for decades after World War II. In 1989, dramatic change in the Soviet bloc came to a head, leading to the end of communism and the dissolution of the Soviet Union. The unraveling of the Soviet system brought an abrupt end to the postwar era, which had rested on a tense balance between the communist states and the capitalist democracies. Everywhere, the pace of political, economic, and technological change seemed almost too rapid. Moreover, key decisions seemed to be made increasingly by multinational corporations or supranational organizations beyond democratic control. By the early 1990s, a new set of anxieties and uncertainties had replaced those of the cold war era.

≈ *Questions and Ideas to Consider*

- Discuss the relationship between greater social equality and traditional social order. In what ways did the changing social role of the French state intersect with the growing feminist movement in France?

- Why did the communist bloc disintegrate when it did? List some of the contributing factors and discuss their relative importance.

- In the late twentieth century, supranational initiatives became increasingly important—and brought new problems and fears. Discuss some of the positive and negative attributes of supranational and global decision making.

- Has democratic capitalism triumphed? What evidence supports this notion, and what evidence suggests a more uncertain future?

- Given the increasing concern for a wider history—one that includes the experiences of women in the West and of all peoples elsewhere—should we continue the "Western Civ" course as it is? Why or why not?

CHALLENGES OF AFFLUENCE IN THE WEST

After the economic dislocations of the 1970s, most of Western Europe again enjoyed strong economic growth in the early 1980s. In Italy a "second economic miracle" enabled the country to surpass Britain and become the world's fifth largest economy. But in Italy and elsewhere in Western Europe, growth was uneven, confined to certain sectors and regions. By the 1990s prosperity mixed with ongoing worries about international competition, unemployment, and environmental constraints in a small and crowded continent.

By the 1980s democracy had become the unchallenged norm in Western Europe. The radical right was largely discredited and the Marxist left seemed to have been domesticated for good. In important respects, conservatives and social democrats sounded more and more alike. But at the same time there was a weakening of the postwar consensus about governmental responsibility for social and economic well-being, as new questions arose about the scope of the public sphere, the reach of the state.

Many of the trends important in Europe were visible in the United States as well. The widening gap between rich and poor, the weakening of organized labor, the increasing awareness of human responsibility for the environment, the growing prominence of women in the work force, the increasing concern about such family issues as child care—all were characteristic of Western civilization in general by the late twentieth century.

The Changing Economies: Prosperity, Imbalance, Limitation

In the early 1980s unemployment in Western Europe reached levels not seen since the Great Depression. Even after solid growth resumed by 1983, unemployment hovered stubbornly at around 10 percent throughout much of the region. This would have seemed unimaginable fifteen years before and was much higher than the rates of 5 to 7 percent in the United States during the same period.

This combination of prosperity and unemployment stemmed in part from the technological changes that produced a "third industrial

CHAPTER CHRONOLOGY

1979	Margaret Thatcher becomes prime minister of Britain
	First direct elections to European parliament
1980	Formation of Solidarity in Poland
1981	Mitterrand elected president of France
1982	Death of Leonid Brezhnev in the Soviet Union
1985	Gorbachev comes to power in the Soviet Union
1986	Explosion at Chernobyl nuclear power plant
1989	Collapse of communism in east-central Europe
1990	Reunification of Germany
	Persian Gulf War begins
1991	Collapse of communism in the Soviet Union; dissolution of the Soviet Union
	Beginning of fighting in Yugoslavia
	Maastricht agreement expands scope of the European Union
1996	Peace in Bosnia
	Yeltsin re-elected as Russian president

revolution" during the late twentieth century. Based most dramatically on the computer, it encompassed everything from robotics to fiber optics. The advent of new technologies in the context of increasing global competition produced new winners, but it also transformed the workplace and patterns of employment in worrisome ways.

Such technologies created opportunities for new firms able to start from scratch, without the problems of redundant workers or outmoded plants and equipment that older competitors faced. Benetton, an Italian clothing firm founded in 1964, quickly made effective use of computer technology in all aspects of its operation. Benet-

ton was successful partly because it needed fewer workers. Manufacturing jobs tended to be lost as competition forced the industrial sector to become more efficient through computers and automation. In the German steel industry over half the jobs disappeared during the 1970s and 1980s.

Changing labor patterns reinforced the decline of organized labor, while the increasing danger of unemployment undercut the leverage of the unions. And as the economy grew more complex, workers were ever less likely to understand themselves as members of a single, unified working class.

Affluence and Secularization

Postwar economic growth had created a secular, consumerist society throughout much of Western Europe by the mid-1960s. Growing prosperity meant not only paid annual vacations of three to four weeks but also the luxury of spending them away from home, often at crowded beach resorts. Television was virtually universal in households across Europe by the early 1980s. Spectator sports grew more popular, with soccer, the undisputed king, drawing rowdy and sometimes violent crowds.

In Western Europe, as in the United States, a remarkable baby boom had followed the end of the war and continued into the early 1960s. The birthrate declined rapidly thereafter, however. In Italy the number of births in 1987 was barely half the number in 1964, when the postwar baby boom reached its peak. By 1995 the population was not sustaining itself in Italy or Spain.

Increasing affluence led to rising expectations and demands for still wider opportunity. Such pressure focused especially on access to higher education, the chief vehicle for upward mobility. As university admissions increased in France, Italy, and West Germany, the development of a mass-based university system produced new dilemmas. In France, the market value of the state diploma declined substantially, as did the prestige of the faculty. In some cases, quality had actually fallen; in others, formerly elite groups simply mourned their past status.

Secularization diminished the once central role of the churches in popular culture, which had long revolved around religious festivals and holy days. Regular church attendance declined steadily. The Catholic church undertook a notable modernization effort under the popular Pope John XXIII (r. 1958–1963), but under his more conservative successors, the church became caught up in controversies such as birth control, abortion, and women's ordination that put it on the defensive.

In France, Italy, and Spain, many people considered themselves "cultural Catholics" and ignored church rulings they found inappropriate, especially those concerning sexuality, marriage, and gender roles. The easier availability of contraception—especially the birth control pill, widely obtainable by the late 1960s—fostered a sexual revolution that was central to the new secular lifestyle. In referenda in 1974 and 1981, two-thirds of Italians defied the Vatican by voting to legalize divorce and approve abortion rights. Even in heavily Catholic Ireland, the electorate narrowly approved the legalization of divorce in 1995.

The Significance of Gender

As the cases of class and religion indicate, long-standing bases of identity and the problems they sometimes gave rise to were becoming less important as an affluent, secular society emerged. At the same time, new questions about identity appeared. By the 1980s a growing consciousness of socially defined gender roles—and the limitations they created—had arisen out of the quest for equality of opportunity and individual self-realization.

As it matured, the feminist movement that had crystallized in the late 1960s found it necessary to expand its focus beyond the quest for equal opportunity. Examining subtle cultural obstacles to equality led feminists to the more general issue of gender—the way societies perceive sexual difference and define social roles. There was much interest in the innovative ideas of the French existentialist Simone de Beauvoir, who had raised in 1949 precisely the issues that came to the fore during the 1980s (see page 688). As the debate expanded from "women's issues" to gender roles, conceptions of masculinity were at issue as well.

Insofar as differentiated gender roles are purposefully "constructed" by particular societies, the notion of gender had been important throughout the long history of the West. Indeed, "gendering" had been central to the socialization process whereby young people learn how to function in their societies. But since most of the gender roles dictated by society were assumed to be natural, gender was only rarely as explicit and controversial an issue as it became in the late twentieth century. By the 1990s the gender issue was central not only to public policy but also to private relationships and to decisions about life choices in much of the Western world.

Male and female feminists fought for government-subsidized day care that would enable both parents to engage in fulfilling, paid employment while raising a family—without saddling women with a double burden. Seeking to enhance both equality of opportunity and long-term economic productivity, governments assumed responsibility for combining productive working parents with effective childhood development.

Setting the pace was France, where the government began making quality day care available to all in the 1980s. Government subsidy kept costs within reach for ordinary working families. In addition, 95 percent of French children aged 3 to 6 were enrolled in the free public nursery schools available by the early 1990s. Comparable figures for Italy (85 percent) and Germany (65 to 70 percent) were also high, although Britain lagged at 35 to 40 percent.

The increasing reliance on child care both reflected and reinforced a decline in the socializing role of the traditional family. This trend prompted concern about the long-term consequences for the socialization of children—and thus for the future of society. At issue was the interaction of family roles, individual self-realization, and the well-being of children.

In any case, the French model seemed to work well. Moreover, in France social services were delivered with less paperwork and intrusiveness

Demonstration for Reproductive Freedom In the late twentieth century, street rallies, marches, and demonstrations became a common and generally peaceful way for groups to make their views public. Here women in Rome, representing a number of organizations, unite in support of women's access to birth control and abortion. *(Gamma-Liaison)*

than elsewhere. In the 1990s, the question was simply whether France could still afford such benefits. And this question reflected a wider set of concerns, becoming central everywhere, about the political order and the role of government.

Re-evaluating the Role of Government

The most dramatic and single-minded assault on the welfare state came in Britain after Margaret Thatcher became prime minister in a new Conservative government in 1979. Thatcher insisted that Britain could reverse its economic decline only by fostering a new "enterprise culture," restoring the individual initiative that had been sapped, as she saw it, by decades of dependence on government. Thatcher took it for granted that the free market, undistorted by government intervention, pro-

duced optimum economic efficiency and thus, in the long term, the greatest social benefit.

Abandoning its aristocratic vestiges, the Conservative party now appealed to the upwardly mobile, entrepreneurial middle class. In light of the socioeconomic difficulties Britain had suffered in the 1970s, Thatcher's message had broad appeal across the social spectrum. With Labour increasingly isolated, identified with decaying inner cities and old industrial regions, Thatcher easily won re-election in 1983 and 1987.

Three immediate priorities followed directly from Thatcher's overall strategy. First, her government made substantial cuts in taxes and corresponding cuts in spending for education, national health, and public housing. Second, the government fostered privatization, selling off an array of state-owned firms from Rolls Royce to British Airways. The government even sold public housing to tenants, at as much as 50 percent below market value, a measure that helped Thatcher win considerable working-class support. Third, Thatcher curbed the power of Britain's labor unions.

Several new laws curtailed trade-union power, and Thatcher refused to consult with union leaders as her predecessors had done since the war. A showdown was reached with the yearlong coal miners' strike of 1984 and 1985, one of the most bitter and violent European strikes of the twentieth century. The strike's failure further enhanced Thatcher's prestige among her supporters. Yet the violent encounters between police and picketing strikers, carried nationwide on TV, indicated the cracks in the relative social harmony that Britain had long enjoyed. In addition, riots by unemployed youths broke out in several major industrial cities in 1981 and again in 1985.

In another important conservative move, Thatcher's government sponsored the Nationality Act of 1982, which restricted immigration from the former British colonies. The right-wing tendency to blame immigrants (largely from Britain's former colonies) for unemployment and urban crime gained Thatcher support from the otherwise hostile city dwellers. With her nationalist bent, Thatcher resisted the growing power of the multinational European Union. Her stance on this issue helped provoke opposition within her own party, which finally ousted her as party leader, and thus as prime minister, in 1990.

Controversy over the significance of the Thatcher years mounted after her departure. On the plus side, her efforts helped boost the competitiveness of British industry. Productivity grew at a rate 50 percent above the average of the other industrial democracies. This striking improvement stemmed partly from the attack on the trade unions, which had limited productivity by protecting redundant labor. Privatization found increasing approval, while the number of new businesses reflected a revival of entrepreneurship—apparently the basis for better economic performance over the longer term. Whatever the gains during the Thatcher years, however, the gap between rich and poor widened and the old industrial regions of the north were left ever further behind.

France and Italy prospered as never before but seemed unable to afford all the benefits their governments had gradually come to promise—mostly because of intensifying economic competition. But what the developed countries of the West could afford for education, welfare, or health care could not be established objectively; at issue, rather, were societal priorities, to be worked out through the political process. As the economy became more ruthlessly competitive and the gap in incomes widened, the winners seemed ever more reluctant to pay for those who were less successful. The growing preoccupation with cost reflected an erosion of the sense of community and fairness that had been essential to the postwar consensus—and that had led to the expanded government role in the first place.

ON THE RUINS OF THE COMMUNIST SYSTEM

In the early 1980s, the system hammered out by Stalin and his successors still seemed firmly entrenched in the Soviet Union and its satellites in east-central Europe, despite a lackluster period under the aging leadership of Leonid Brezhnev and his allies. Yet crises were building in both the Soviet Union and the satellite states, producing forces for change that finally engulfed the whole communist bloc. Although the process began in Poland, Hungary, and Czechoslovakia, the ultimate outcome depended on the Soviet response.

So the death of Leonid Brezhnev in 1982 and the beginning of a concerted reform effort in the Soviet Union in 1985 were the decisive moments. By the end of the 1980s the forces for change in the Soviet Union and its satellites had intersected, leading the whole communist system to unravel. The dangerous but stable bipolar world that had emerged from World War II had suddenly vanished, and the countries of the former Soviet bloc began seeking to rejoin the rest of Europe.

Crisis and Innovation in the Soviet Bloc

The impressive rates of economic growth achieved in the Soviet Union and several of its satellite states after World War II continued into the 1960s. However, much of that success came from adding labor—women and underemployed peasants—to the industrial work force. By the end of the 1960s that process was reaching its limits.

Even compared to those elsewhere in the communist bloc, the command economy in the Soviet Union was particularly centralized and inflexible. The persistent shortages of many consumer goods, understandable during the transformation to an industrial society, seemed less and less tolerable. And by the late 1970s the Soviet Union was falling behind in high technology, which required the freedom to experiment and exchange ideas that was notably lacking in the Soviet system. As that system bogged down, the expense of the arms race became increasingly untenable.

For all its terrible excesses, Stalin's regime had continued to inspire a measure of genuine idealism during his lifetime. But by the 1970s the Soviet system had settled into narrow routine or outright corruption. Its major functionaries were a class apart, enjoying access to special shops and other privileges. Brezhnev himself took enormous pleasure in his collection of expensive automobiles.

Brezhnev's death in 1982 made possible the rise of Mikhail Gorbachev (b. 1931), who became party secretary in 1985 and who represented a new generation, beyond those who had been groomed for party careers during the Stalinist 1930s. He quickly charted a reform course—and attracted the admiration of much of the world.

Gorbachev's effort encompassed four intersecting initiatives: arms reduction; liberalization in the satellite states; *glasnost,* or "openness" to discussion and criticism; and *perestroika,* or economic "restructuring." This was to be a reform within the Soviet system. There was no thought of giving up the Communist party's monopoly on power or embracing a free-market economy. The reformers still took it for granted that communism could point the way beyond Western capitalism, with its widespread crime, its illegal drugs, its shallow consumerism. So a measure of idealism guided the reformers' efforts. But they had to make communism work.

Gorbachev understood that "openness" was a prerequisite for "restructuring." The freedom to criticize was necessary to overcome the cynicism of the workers and improve productivity. Openness was also imperative to gain the full participation of the country's most creative people. The main thrust of restructuring was to depart from the rigid economic planning mechanism by giving local managers more autonomy. It did not have to entail privatization or free-market capitalism. It could mean, for example, letting workers elect factory managers.

The Crisis of Communism in the Satellite States

For many intellectuals in the Soviet bloc, the suppression of the Prague Spring in 1968 ended any hope that communism could be made to work. The initial outcome was a sense of hopelessness and resignation, but by the mid-1970s an opposition movement, centering on underground (or *samizdat*) publications, had begun to take shape in Hungary, Poland, and Czechoslovakia.

The first push toward real systemic breakdown came from an international conference in 1975. High-level representatives of thirty-five countries, including all of the Soviet bloc except Albania, came together in Helsinki, Finland. The parties recognized all borders, as the Soviets had wanted, but they also adopted a detailed agreement on human rights, which came to be known as the Helsinki Accords. Through various "Helsinki Watch" groups monitoring civil liberties, opposition intellectuals managed to assume moral leadership.

The most significant such group was Charter 77 in Czechoslovakia. In 1977, protesting against the arrest of an anti-establishment rock group called "The Plastic People of the Universe," 243 individuals signed "Charter 77." In the face of the powerful, heavy-handed communist government, dissidents proposed that change could be won if people simply lived according to their real beliefs. When people used their own names and addresses on the Charter 77 petition, they were carrying out this idea of "living the truth" by acting as if they were free to register such an opinion.

A leader in Charter 77 was the writer Václav Havel (b. 1936), who argued that hope for change depended on people organizing themselves, outside the structures of the party-state, in diverse, independent social groupings. (See the box "Power from Below: Living the Truth.") Havel and a number of his associates were in and out of jail as the government sought to stifle this protest. Despite the efforts of Havel and his colleagues, ordinary people in Czechoslovakia remained relatively passive until the late 1980s. For quite different reasons, Hungary and Poland offered greater scope for change.

Even after the failed reform effort of 1956, Hungary proved the most innovative of the European communist countries. Hungary was relatively prosperous by the late 1970s, though it faced difficulties paying off its foreign debt. The Hungarians responded, as nowhere else, by committing the economy to the discipline of the world market by joining the International Monetary Fund and the World Bank in 1982. This move required economic austerity, and Hungarian living standards declined during the early 1980s. But the country promoted its "second economy"— its autonomous private sector. By the mid-1980s alternative forms of ownership were responsible for one-third of Hungary's economic output.

This openness to experiment in the economy enabled reformers within the Hungarian Communist party to gain the upper hand. Finally, in 1988, the reformers ousted the aging János Kádár, who lacked the vision for continued reform. Increasingly open to a variety of viewpoints, the Hungarian communists gradually pulled back from their claim to a monopoly of power.

With growing concern for the Hungarian minority in Romania helping to galvanize political consciousness, new political clubs proliferated in Hungary. In June 1989, popular pressure led to the ceremonial reburial of Imre Nagy, who had led the reform effort in 1956. After having been convicted of treason, executed, and buried in obscurity, Nagy had been derided as a counterrevolutionary traitor in official government pronouncements. His reburial indicated the importance of historical memory—and who controls it.

The reform effort that built gradually in Hungary had stemmed especially from aspirations in the governing elite. More dramatic was the course of change in Poland, where there was already a tradition of labor militancy, especially among shipyard workers on the Baltic coast.

It was crucial that, whereas Polish workers had not supported dissident students and intellectuals in 1968, the two sides managed to come together during the 1970s. An extra ingredient from an unexpected quarter also affected the situation in Poland, perhaps in a decisive way. In 1978 the College of Cardinals of the Roman Catholic church departed from long tradition and, for the first time since 1522, elected a non-Italian pope. But even more startling was the fact that the new pope was from Poland, behind the iron curtain. He was Karol Cardinal Wojtyla (b. 1920), the archbishop of Kracow, who took the name John Paul II.

After World War II, the Polish Catholic church had been unique among the major churches of east-central Europe in maintaining and even enhancing its position. It worked just enough with the ruling communists to be allowed a measure of autonomy. For many Poles, the church remained an institutional alternative to communism and the focus of nationalist feelings. The new pope's visit to Poland in 1979 had an electrifying effect on ordinary Poles, who took to the streets by the millions to greet him—and found they were not alone. This boost in self-confidence provided the catalyst for the founding of a new trade union, Solidarity, in August 1980.

Led by the remarkable shipyard electrician Lech Walesa (b. 1944), Solidarity first emerged in response to labor discontent in the vast Lenin shipyard in Gdansk, on the Baltic Sea (see Map 27.1). Demanding the right to form an independent trade union, seventy thousand workers took over the shipyards, winning support both from

Power from Below: Living the Truth

Considering the scope for change in the communist world by the late 1970s, Václav Havel imagines a conformist grocer who routinely puts a sign in his window with the slogan "Workers of the world, unite!" simply because it is expected. That same grocer, says Havel, has the power to break the stifling sociopolitical system, which ultimately rests on those innumerable acts of everyday compliance.

[T]he real meaning of the greengrocer's slogan has nothing to do with what the text of the slogan actually says. Even so, this real meaning is quite clear and generally comprehensible because the code is so familiar: the greengrocer declares his loyalty . . . in the only way the regime is capable of hearing; that is, by accepting the prescribed *ritual*, by accepting appearances as reality, by accepting the given rules of the game. In doing so, however, he has himself become a player in the game, thus making it possible for the game to go on, for it to exist in the first place. . . .

Let us now imagine that one day something in our greengrocer snaps and he stops putting up the slogans merely to ingratiate himself. He stops voting in elections he knows are a farce. He begins to say what he really thinks at political meetings. . . . He rejects the ritual and breaks the rules of the game. He discovers once more his suppressed identity and dignity. . . .

. . . He has shown everyone that it *is* possible to live within the truth. Living within the lie can constitute the system only if it is universal.

The principle must embrace and permeate everything. There are no terms whatsoever on which it can coexist with living within the truth, and therefore everyone who steps out of line *denies it in principle and threatens it in its entirety*. . . .

And since all genuine problems and matters of critical importance are hidden beneath a thick crust of lies, it is never quite clear when the proverbial last straw will fall, or what that straw will be. This . . . is why the regime prosecutes, almost as a reflex action preventively, even the most modest attempts to live within the truth.

. . . [T]he crust presented by the life of lies is made of strange stuff. As long as it seals off hermetically the entire society, it appears to be made of stone. But the moment someone breaks through in one place, when one person cries out, "The emperor is naked!"—when a single person breaks the rules of the game, thus exposing it as a game—everything suddenly appears in another light and the whole crust seems then to be made of a tissue on the point of tearing and disintegrating uncontrollably.

Source: Václav Havel et al., *The Power of the Powerless: Citizens Against the State in Central-Eastern Europe* (Armonk, N.Y.: M. E. Sharpe, 1985), pp. 31, 37, 39–40, 42–43. Reprinted with permission from M. E. Sharpe, Inc., Armonk, NY 10504.

their intellectual allies and from the Catholic church. Support for Solidarity grew partly because, to pay its foreign debts, the government was cutting subsidies and raising food prices. But the new union developed such force because it placed moral demands first—independent labor organizations, the right to strike, and freedom of expression. The tense situation came to a head in December 1981, when the government under General Wojciech Jaruzelski (b. 1923) declared martial law and outlawed Solidarity, imprisoning its leaders.

So much for that, it seemed. Another lost cause, another reform effort colliding with inflexible communist power in east-central Europe, as in 1953, 1956, and 1968. But this time, it was different. The ideas of Solidarity continued to spread underground. Walesa remained a powerfully effective leader, able to keep the heterogeneous movement together. The advent of Gorbachev in 1985 changed the overall framework of the communist bloc, for he was convinced that the restructuring of the Soviet system required reform in the satellites as well. In the spring and summer of 1988, strikes demanding the relegalization of Solidarity alternated with government repression and military force, until eventually, with the economy nearing collapse, the government recognized that it had to negotiate.

When negotiations began early in 1989, Walesa and his advisers sought to secure the legalization of Solidarity within the communist-dominated system. But as the talks proceeded, the government gave ever more in exchange for Solidarity's cooperation, agreeing to make the forthcoming elections free enough for the opposition genuinely to participate.

The elections of June 1989 produced an overwhelming repudiation of Poland's communist government. Even government leaders running unopposed failed to win election as voters crossed out their names. In the aftermath of the elections, President Jaruzelski finally decided to give Solidarity a chance to lead. Tadeusz Mazowiecki (b. 1927), Walesa's choice and one of the movement's most distinguished intellectuals, agreed to form a government.

The chain of events in Poland culminated in one of the extraordinary developments of modern history—the negotiated end of communist rule. It happened partly because the Soviet Union under Gorbachev had become much less likely to intervene militarily. It also mattered that the Polish Catholic church acted as mediator, hosting meetings, reminding both sides of their shared responsibilities in the difficult situation facing their country. But most important was the courage, the persistence, and the vision of Solidarity itself.

The Anticommunist Revolution, 1989–1991

The Polish example suggested that the communist system was open to challenge. During 1989, demands for reform and, increasingly, for an end to communist rule spread through east-central Europe. By the end of that year, the Soviet satellite system was in ruins (Map 27.1).

Though strikes and demonstrations took place throughout the region, the end of the communist order in Hungary, Czechoslovakia, East Germany, Bulgaria, and Albania was more peaceful than anyone would have dreamed possible a few years before. Starting with Hungary, these countries followed the Polish model and negotiated the transfer of power from the communists to opposition leaders. In Czechoslovakia, the transition was so peaceful that it was dubbed the "Velvet Revolution." The signal exception was Romania, where the communist dictator Nicolae Ceausescu's bloody crackdown on the reform movement provoked an armed revolt. The opposition executed Ceausescu and his wife on Christmas Day 1989.

The possibility of violent repression was never far from the surface. In June 1989, the communist leadership in China had crushed a comparable movement for democracy in Tiananmen Square in Beijing. As the opposition movement grew in East Germany early in the fall, with weekly demonstrations in Leipzig attracting 300,000 people, the East German communist leader Erich Honecker (1912–1994) began preparing for a "Chinese solution" in his country. But a dramatic appeal for nonviolence by local opposition leaders in Leipzig helped persuade the police to hold off. Gorbachev, too, called for moderation. Honecker was soon forced to make way for communists favoring reform.

A marked increase in illegal emigration from East Germany to the west had been one manifestation that the whole satellite system was starting to unravel. If the communist reformers in East Germany were to have any chance of turning the situation around, they had to relax restrictions on travel and grant the right to emigrate. They began preparing legislation to both ends, amid a host of reforms intended to save the system. On November 9, 1989, the regime in East Germany did what had long seemed unthinkable: It opened the Berlin Wall, which was promptly dismantled altogether. Germans now

traveled freely back and forth between east and west. The liberalization effort proved too late, however. The communist system in the east quickly dissolved, and steps toward reunification followed almost immediately in 1990.

The opening of the Berlin Wall signaled the end of the cold war. The immediate result in the West was euphoria, but few failed to recognize that a still more difficult task lay ahead. To be sure, reformers in the former communist countries claimed to want individual freedom, political democracy, and free-market capitalism. But it would be necessary to build these on the ruins of the now-discredited communist system and its command economy, a task never confronted before.

Meanwhile, in the Soviet Union, Gorbachev sought to avoid alienating hard-line communists, so he compromised, watering down the economic reforms essential to perestroika. The resulting half-measures only made things worse. The structures of the command economy were weakened, but free-market forms of exchange among producers, distributors, and consumers did not emerge to replace them.

In 1986 an accidental explosion at the nuclear power plant at Chernobyl, in Ukraine, released two hundred times as much radiation as the atomic bombs dropped on Hiroshima and Nagasaki combined. The accident contaminated food supplies and forced the abandonment of villages and thousands of square miles of formerly productive land. According to later estimates, the radioactivity released would eventually hasten the death of at least 100,000 Soviet citizens. Despite his commitment to openness, Gorbachev reverted to old-fashioned Soviet secrecy for several weeks after the accident, in an effort to minimize what had happened. As a result, the eventual toll was far greater than it need have been. The accident and its aftermath seemed stark manifestation of all that was wrong

Tearing Down the Wall In 1989 the much-graffitied Berlin Wall was dismantled—in part by ordinary citizens such as this woman. The event marked the end of the cold war. Pieces of the wall itself are now in museums and kept by private individuals as symbols of the times. (*Gamma-Liaison*)

Map 27.1 Europe After the Cold War The reunification of Germany and the breakup of the Soviet Union, Yugoslavia, and Czechoslovakia fundamentally altered the map of Europe by the early 1990s.

with the Soviet system—its arrogance and secrecy, its premium on cutting corners to achieve targets imposed from above.

By the end of the 1980s, Soviet citizens felt betrayed by their earlier faith that Soviet communism was leading to a better future. A popular slogan spoke sarcastically of "seventy years on the road to nowhere." While the economic situation was deteriorating, people were free to discuss alternatives as never before. As the discussion came to include once unthinkable possibilities like privatization and a market economy, it became clear that the whole communist system was in jeopardy.

In 1990, the union of Soviet republics itself tottered on the verge of collapse. Lithuania led the way in calling for outright independence. The stakes were raised enormously when the Russian republic, the largest and most important in the U.S.S.R., followed Lithuania's lead.

In June 1990 the newly elected chairman of Russia's parliament, Boris Yeltsin (b. 1931), persuaded the Russian republic to declare its sovereignty. He hoped to force Gorbachev's reform effort beyond the present impasse. As a further challenge to Gorbachev, Yeltsin dramatically resigned from the Communist party during the televised twenty-eighth congress in July 1990. In the free elections of June 1991, the anticommunist Yeltsin was elected the Russian republic's president by a surprising margin.

Gorbachev sought a return to reform after Yeltsin's dramatic election as president of Russia in June 1991. Late in July, Gorbachev prepared a new union treaty that would have given substantial powers, including authority over taxation, to the constituent republics. He also engineered a new party charter that jettisoned much of the Marxist-Leninist doctrine that had guided communist practice since the revolution.

These measures promised the radical undoing of the Soviet system, and now the hard-liners finally struck back, initiating a coup in August 1991. They managed to force Gorbachev from power—but only for a few days. As the world held its breath, Yeltsin, supported by ordinary people in Moscow, stood up to the conspirators. Key units of the secret police, charged to arrest Yeltsin and other opposition leaders, refused to follow orders. The coup quickly fizzled, but the episode galvanized the anticommunist movement and radically accelerated the pace of change.

Although Gorbachev was restored as head of the Soviet Union, the real winner was Yeltsin, who quickly mounted an effort to dismantle the party apparatus before it could regroup. Spontaneous anticommunist demonstrations across much of the Soviet Union toppled statues of Lenin and dissolved local party networks. In a referendum in December 1991, Ukraine, the second most populous Soviet republic, voted overwhelmingly for independence. The Soviet Union was simply disintegrating.

The dissolution of the Soviet empire brought a new set of problems. What was to become of the 27,000 nuclear weapons stationed in four of the Soviet republics? What would be the economic relationship between the new countries? Some new form of coordination and unity seemed essential. Thus in December 1991, the leaders of Russia, Ukraine, and Belarus spearheaded the creation of a new Commonwealth of Independent States, which replaced the Soviet Union with a much looser confederation of eleven of the fifteen former Soviet republics. Late in December, Gorbachev finally resigned. The Soviet Union officially dissolved on January 1, 1992 (see Map 27.1).

Life After Communism

All over the formerly communist part of Europe, calls for Western-style democracy accompanied the end of the old order. But the area had little experience with democratic politics or a free-market economy. Political prospects would rest in large part on the success of the economic transition, but the economies in the former communist countries were close to chaos in the early 1990s. The attempt to construct a market economy brought unemployment, inflation, and widespread corruption. No longer could ordinary people count on the subsidized consumer goods or the welfare safety net that the communist regimes, for all their inadequacies, had provided. While many ordinary citizens suffered great hardship, some former communist functionaries got rich by taking over state-owned companies, provoking widespread resentment. Still, the transition to a market economy seemed to be working by the mid-1990s, though the course of change varied considerably from one country to the next.

Some of the postcommunist governments concentrated on privatizing existing state-owned concerns while others sought to foster entrepreneurship and innovation. Privatization lagged in Poland, but a buoyant new private sector emerged as the Poles proved adept at starting new businesses. Privatization was greatest in the

Czech Republic under the forceful leadership of Václav Klaus, a passionate partisan of market economics. By the end of 1995, the Czechs had achieved a solid annual economic growth rate of 4 percent with low unemployment and relatively low inflation.

Privatization was also rapid in Russia, where two-thirds of state-owned industry had been privatized by 1994. However, the fairness of the process was subject to much dispute. Optimists emphasized that 40 million Russians now owned shares in newly privatized companies. But even they could not deny that in certain sectors the process had included much insider dealing. In Russia, more than anywhere else in the former communist world, privatization benefited former Communist party functionaries, some of whom became instant multimillionaires.

The governmental weakness that accompanied the fall of communism in Russia yielded a chilling increase in lawlessness—from ordinary street crime like auto theft to sophisticated, organized crime with a significant role in the nation's economy. The nostalgia for the stability of communism led many Russians to vote communist in 1995 and 1996.

Communism had far deeper roots in Russia than elsewhere in the former Soviet bloc. Russian communists never dropped the communist label and never fully embraced democratic principles. During the 1996 presidential election, the communists, led by Gennady Zyuganov, exploited economic discontent, winning support especially from workers and older pensioners. The incumbent, Boris Yeltsin, in contrast, enjoyed the support of Russia's powerful new entrepreneurial class, which opposed any retreat from free-market principles; he capped a remarkable uphill struggle by defeating Zyuganov in a runoff election in July 1996. The campaign and election gave Russians their fullest experience of democracy to date.

The end of communism opened up divisive new questions across the former Soviet bloc. It quickly became clear that political freedom did not necessarily bring wider rights and liberties. For example, the eclipse of communism in Poland initially promised a major role for the Ro-man Catholic church, but angry debate followed when, in 1990, the government ordered that children be taught the Catholic religion in school and the head of the Polish church called for an end to the "communist-inspired" separation of church and state. An effort to pass a strong anti-abortion bill in time for a visit by Pope John Paul II in 1991 caused more heated debate; public opinion polls indicated that a majority of Poles favored abortion rights.

Abortion was similarly a major issue when the former East Germany was incorporated into the Federal Republic of Germany in 1990. Abortion law had been more liberal in the communist east than in the west. In the same way, East Germany was considerably more generous than the Federal Republic in providing maternity leave, day care, and other measures to enable mothers to work outside the home. Some East German feminists feared that the transition to capitalism could mean diminished employment opportunities for women. Though a compromise was worked out on the abortion issue, the differences in priorities that surfaced between West and East German feminists made it clear that the end of communism was no panacea.

In the former satellite states, as in several of the republics of the former Soviet Union, autonomy and democracy quickly opened the way to ethnic tensions that occasionally led to outright rebellion. Ethnic repression and conflict were not new to the region, but they had been kept largely submerged within the Soviet bloc.

In Czechoslovakia, the Slovak minority broke away to form an independent republic at the beginning of 1993. By 1995 the government was making Slovak the only official language, angering the large Hungarian minority in Slovakia and drawing protests from Hungary. The status of the Hungarian minority in Romania was an ongoing concern as well. But most dramatic—and tragic—was the situation in Yugoslavia, where ethnic and religious conflict produced not only the disintegration of the country but also a brutal, multisided war among Serbs, Croats, and Bosnian Muslims (see Map 27.2). One of the defining events of the 1990s, this war proved a major challenge for the new international order that had emerged from the cold war.

EUROPE AND THE WEST AFTER THE BIPOLAR PEACE

The dissolution of the Soviet system meant the swift, unexpected end of the cold war framework that had defined the era since World War II. Though it seemed only a balance of terror at the time, the cold war had provided a measure of order and security in the years from 1949 to 1989. What sort of international configuration was to follow? Though it could claim to have won the cold war, the United States had declined in relative strength from the unprecedented preeminence it had enjoyed after World War II.

The new framework seemed to invite Western Europe to become a superpower in its own right, so the movement toward European integration intensified, producing a more integrated union of fifteen members by the mid-1990s. But obstacles remained, stemming especially from traditional concerns about national sovereignty. And fighting in the former Yugoslavia raised questions about the ability of the European Union, or any international body, to assure stability.

The Changing International Framework

As the potential threat from the Soviet Union dissolved, the United States lost some of its leverage in Europe because American support no longer seemed essential for European security, and by the early 1990s, the Americans could no longer claim the same kind of leadership in any case. The role of superpower had taken its toll on the United States, just as it had on the U.S.S.R. The arms race had burdened the budgets of both of the big winners of World War II, while the war's major losers, Germany, Japan, and Italy, pulled back from any great power role and prospered as never before.

The ambiguities of the new international situation came to the fore during the first major international crisis of the post–cold war period, the Persian Gulf War, which the United States led against Iraq in 1990 and 1991. With superpower rivalry no longer an issue, the United States assembled a broad coalition that reversed an Iraqi takeover of oil-rich Kuwait. The United States had to pass the hat among its prosperous allies to pay for the Gulf War, and those called on to contribute seemed unlikely to settle for such arrangements again. This was especially true of Japan and Germany, each of which was engaged in reassessing its international role.

The collapse of communism in east-central Europe had paved the way for German reunification in 1990. Despite some nervousness, the four occupying powers—the United States, Britain, France, and the Soviet Union—gave their blessing as the Federal Republic simply incorporated the five states of the former East Germany. Although some in West Germany were hesitant about immediate reunification, especially because of the economic costs that seemed likely, West German Chancellor Helmut Kohl (b. 1930) sought to complete the process as quickly as possible. By early 1990 emigration of East Germans to the west had become a flood. West German law treated these Germans as citizens, entitled to social benefits, so their arrival in such numbers presented a considerable financial burden.

Reunification prompted anxiety about the role the new Germany, already a major economic power, might seek to play in Europe and the world. Germany, however, remained eager to prove its good intentions by leading the continuing movement toward European integration. Some worried that the European Union would become a vehicle for German domination, but the Germans took care to offer reasoned, cautious leadership, with no hint of bullying.

Reunified Germany also encountered new domestic problems that promoted caution. Because reunification proved far more costly than Kohl had expected, his government found it hard to keep some of the promises it had made to Germans in the east. When his government pulled back from its promise of wage equality between east and west in 1993, workers in the former East Germany mounted the most serious strikes the Federal Republic had experienced since World War II.

The French were particularly restive about the reunification of Germany, which threatened France's leading role in Western Europe. But France was still willing to act independently— and it could be influential in doing so. When the post–cold war international system fell into discredit with the multisided ethnic fighting in the former Yugoslavia, French pressure helped bring the situation to a head. President Jacques Chirac's threat to pull France out of the multinational peacekeeping force in the region influenced U.S. President Bill Clinton to step up the U.S. role. Though the French initiative in this case manifested the new complexity in relations among the Western allies, the outcome confirmed the centrality of U.S. leadership.

The brutality that characterized the fighting in Bosnia, and the halting efforts of the international community in response, brought to an abrupt end the optimism that at first surrounded the end of the cold war. The Serbs were widely accused of "ethnic cleansing"—brutal forced relocation or killing to rid much of Bosnia of its Muslim inhabitants (Map 27.2). Muslim enclaves in Bosnia suffered grievously under Serb fire. In the Bosnian capital, Sarajevo, a culturally diverse city long known for its tolerant, cosmopolitan atmosphere, more than 10,000 civilians, including 1500 children, were killed by shelling and sniper fire during a Serb siege from 1992 to early 1996. Finally, in August 1995, NATO forces responded with air strikes that led to peace accords and the end of four years of fighting by early 1996. The tide turned partly because a Western embargo had devastated the economy of what remained of Yugoslavia, forcing its Serb leader, Slobodan Milosevic, to cooperate with those seeking a peaceful solution.

Although the peace agreement envisioned a unified Bosnian state, the contending Serbs, Croats, and Bosnian Muslims quickly began carving out separate spheres, violating the rights of minorities as they did so. Traditions of statehood were weak in this part of the Balkans, so it remained unclear whether the forces of disintegration at work in the former Yugoslavia were simply an anomaly in the greater scheme of twentieth-century Western history or an indication of potential disintegrative forces at loose in Europe and the West. If every ethnic minority were to claim territorial autonomy, the future would be uncertain indeed.

Although it was a NATO force that imposed peace in the former Yugoslavia, NATO's future was uncertain. The alliance had been formed to check Soviet expansion in Europe and with the end of the Soviet threat, it made sense for members to rethink their military priorities. Some suggested that henceforth each nation ought to look after its own defense. Others envisioned expanding NATO to encompass certain of the former Soviet bloc countries, and this plan prevailed. In the fall of 1996, President Clinton announced that he wanted NATO to add a first round of new nations by 1999. For this to occur, Russia had to be convinced that such expansion would not threaten its security, and at the same time conservatives in the West had to be assured that an expanded NATO could still serve to contain Russia, if necessary. In March 1997, Clinton met with Russian president Boris Yeltsin in Helsinki, and the two established Russian tolerance of the proposed changes in NATO. Two months later, NATO and Russia signed a "Founding Act" of mutual cooperation and security between the alliance and its former adversary. A new Russia-NATO council offered Russia a voice in the alliance, but the North Atlantic Council remained the supreme decision-making body and did not include Russia. In June, NATO leaders invited Poland, the Czech Republic, and Hungary to join the Western alliance.

The European Union

The end of the cold war added urgency to the process of European integration. Although a full customs union had technically been achieved by the late 1960s, national governments continued to compromise the open market, especially by favoring certain companies to give them an advantage in international competition. For domestic political

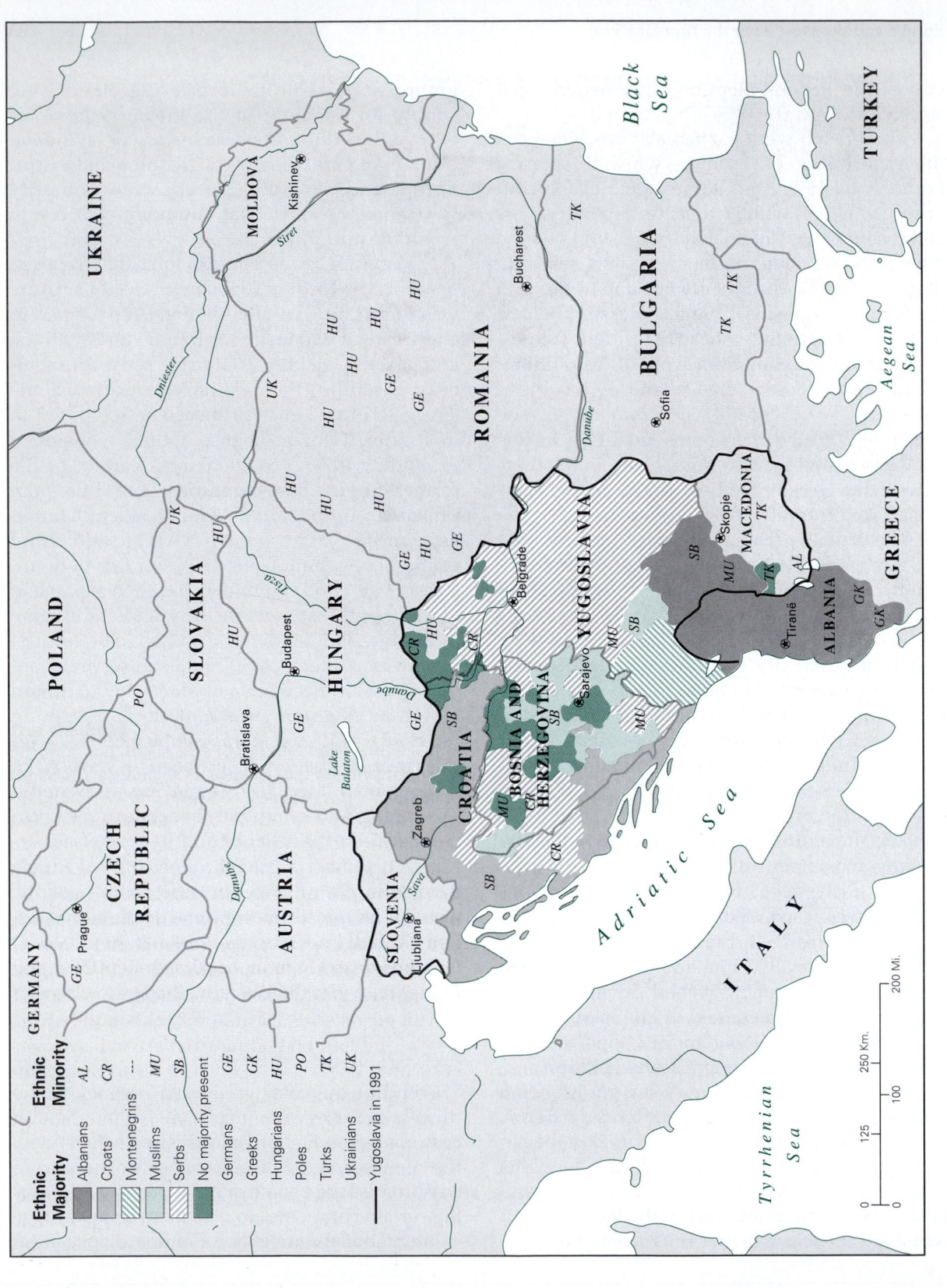

The Agony of Bosnia The wars that accompanied the breakup of Yugoslavia during the 1990s made it tragically clear that the end of the cold war was no guarantee of peace in Europe. The Serb shelling of the Bosnian capital, Sarajevo, from 1992 to 1996 caused widespread destruction and forced many to flee the city. Here Bosnian Muslims return to the Dobrinja area of Sarajevo in March 1996, just after the end of the Serb siege. (*Christopher Morris/Time/Black Star*)

reasons, governments sometimes confined their purchases to national firms or granted subsidies to domestic producers, enabling them to offer artificially low prices.

Still, movement toward the full-scale integration of the member economies continued by fits and starts. Amid increasing concern about "Eurosclerosis," or lack of innovation and competitiveness, the EEC's twelve members committed themselves in 1985 to the measures necessary to create a true single market by the end of 1992. Provisions included uniform product standards and equal competition for the government contracts of each country, as well as the free

Map 27.2 Ethnic Conflict in East-Central Europe The Balkans have long been an area of complex ethnic mixture. The end of communist rule opened the way to ethnic conflict, most tragically in what had been Yugoslavia. This map shows ethnic distribution in the region in the early 1990s.

circulation of goods, services, and money among the member countries. By the late 1980s, the thrust toward economic integration increasingly assumed a political dimension. A European Parliament had developed from the assembly of the European Coal and Steel Community by 1962, though it had little importance at first. By the mid-1990s the European Union included a network of interlocking institutions in Brussels, Strasbourg, and Luxembourg. Among them the European Parliament and the European Court of Justice played increasingly important roles.

At a meeting in Maastricht, The Netherlands, in 1991, the members of the European Union buttressed the powers of the European Parliament, agreed to move toward a common policy of workers' rights, and committed to a common currency and central banking structure by 1999. But this Maastricht agreement required the approval of the EU members, and in one country after another the ensuing debate over

European integration proved more divisive than expected. In addition to the concern over German domination, some feared entrusting vital decisions to faceless bureaucrats in foreign cities.

Although most of the Maastricht agreements were eventually ratified by the EU's members, implementation was not always smooth. Most controversial was the provision for an Economic and Monetary Union (EMU), based on a common currency, the euro. By eliminating the costs and uncertainties of currency exchange, this measure promised to boost trade among the member countries significantly. To become part of the mechanism, countries had to maintain budget deficits no higher than 3 percent of gross domestic product, requiring most of them to decrease their deficits substantially. Governmental efforts to comply with this provision produced conflict on the domestic level, as the thrust toward European union crashed against the social compact, already under pressure, that had produced high government spending for social welfare. Concerned with these pressures, Britain chose not to commit itself to the EMU, though future involvement was not ruled out.

In a televised speech in 1995, President Chirac emphasized his determination to cut the government's budget deficit to enable France to meet the Maastricht criteria for economic and monetary union. The required austerity would include reducing welfare and pension payments and restructuring the debt-plagued state railways. Chirac's initiative prompted intense popular reaction during the fall of 1995. Railroad workers led the most serious wave of strikes that France had experienced in a decade, including periodic interruptions of public services. Students joined in, insisting that the university system needed more money, not less. For many in France, embracing the EU seemed to jeopardize the egalitarianism that had helped sustain social cohesion among the French.

As of the spring of 1998, the euro was slated to go into circulation on January 1, 2002, with local currencies no longer accepted as of the following July.

Supranational Initiatives and Global Issues

Although less visible than the EU, other supranational entities also wielded increasing clout during the late twentieth century, making decisions that deeply affected the lives of ordinary people. Most obvious were multinational corporations, but the World Bank and the International Monetary Fund also played important roles, helping to keep the industrial economies synchronized and the less developed economies on a free-market path. These organizations could strongly influence domestic policies—by refusing, for example, to lend to countries spending heavily on defense.

At the same time, international cooperation took on greater urgency because of growing concern with the environment. Such problems as global warming, the destruction of rain forests, and the deterioration of the ozone layer were inherently supranational in scope. Yet environmental concerns complicated relations between the industrialized nations and the rest of the world. Countries seeking to industrialize encountered environmental constraints that had not been at issue when the West industrialized. The challenge for the West was to foster protection of the environment in poorer regions of the globe without imposing unfair limitations on economic growth.

Changing demographic and economic patterns suggested that "North-South" tensions between the prosperous countries, concentrated in the northern hemisphere, and the poorer ones, more likely to be found farther south, might replace the East-West tensions of the cold war. World population reached 5.5 billion in 1993, having doubled in forty years. This was the fastest rate of world population growth ever, and virtually all of the growth in the 1990s was in Africa, Asia, and Latin America. The population of Europe was growing at only 0.2 percent per year, and in several countries, including Italy, Germany, and Spain, the population would actually have declined without the boost provided by immigration.

Immigration and Citizenship

As the European Union and other supranational organizations became more prominent, forces in the opposite direction—subnational, religious, ethnic, tribal—simultaneously grew more powerful. Subgroup conflict was most tragic in east-central Europe (see Map 27.2), but it grew in Western Europe as well. In Northern Ireland violent polarization between Protestants and Catholics defied solution even after a 1998 peace compromise. In Spain the restoration of democracy gave the long-restive Basque and Catalan minorities the chance to press openly for autonomy. Even in Belgium, there was growing antagonism between Flemish-speaking Flemings and French-speaking Walloons during the 1990s.

With immigration growing sharply in Western Europe by the 1980s, questions about citizenship became politically central, giving a new twist to the interaction with the non-Western world that had helped define "the West" from the beginning. Demographic pressure in the less developed countries contributed to the rising immigration to Western Europe that made Africans selling jewelry, figurines, and sunglasses familiar in European cities by the early 1990s. In 1995 there were 11 million legal immigrants living in the European Union—including, as the largest contingent, 2.6 million Turks. There were also as many as 4 million illegals. As Europeans faced the problems of an increasingly competitive world economy, such immigration became a divisive political issue. In France the government's expulsion of illegal African immigrants sparked a major protest in 1996.

At issue were not only new immigrants, but long-settled immigrant families. Some of those raising questions were not seeking simply to preserve economic advantages by limiting access. Rather, they were concerned about community, diversity, and national identity—about what it meant to belong. Because of differences in tradition, individual countries tended to conceive the alternatives differently.

Germany had actively recruited foreign workers during the decades of economic boom and labor shortage after the war. In 1973 noncitizens constituted 2.6 million workers, or 11.9 percent of the work force. At first these "guest workers" were viewed as temporary, almost migrant, workers. But as they remained in Germany, their family patterns came to approximate those of the rest of the country, though their birthrates were considerably higher. By the 1980s, Germany had a large and increasingly settled population of non-Germans, many of them born and educated there.

In addition, the German Federal Republic had adopted a generous asylum law in an effort to atone for the crimes of the Nazi period. After the fall of communism, the newly reunified Germany found sixty thousand new arrivals seeking asylum every month by 1993. At that point Germany had a foreign population of 6.4 million.

The 1913 law governing citizenship for immigrants reflected a long-standing assumption that citizenship presupposed German ethnicity. Ethnic Germans—over a million of whom moved to Germany from the Soviet bloc between 1988 and 1991—were immediately accorded German citizenship. But many Turks who had been born in Germany could not become citizens.

As the new wave of immigration from the east swelled the "foreign" population, Germans subject to economic pressures felt that foreigners and asylum-seekers were getting a better deal than ordinary citizens such as themselves. In 1992 there were two thousand attacks on foreigners, some of them fatal. Those responsible were sometimes "skinheads," young people with uncertain economic prospects who claimed to admire Nazism. The violence provoked massive counter-demonstrations, but as reaction against refugees and foreign workers grew, the German parliament voted to restrict the right of asylum in 1993.

Although these issues provoked particular controversy in Germany, the claims of immigrants and refugees confronted all the Western democracies with difficult questions about the meaning of citizenship. In France the right-wing National Front, led by Jean-Marie LePen, forced the issue to center stage in the 1980s. The French accorded citizenship automatically to second-generation immigrants, assuming that the offspring of immigrants would be assimilated into the national community. But as France began to attract rising numbers of immigrants, especially from Algeria and other Islamic countries of North Africa, critics like LePen attacked the French citizenship law as too loose, charging that too many recent immigrants did not want to assimilate. Whereas the French left defended cultural diversity and its compatibility with citizenship, the right complained that citizenship was being devalued as a mere convenience, requiring no real commitment to the national community. This difference in perspective helps explain the controversy over the Muslim girls' headscarves that gripped France in 1989 (see page 708).

As these issues became ever more central in the West, representatives of twenty-seven Mediterranean countries—some European, some Middle Eastern, some African—met in Barcelona in 1995 to seek common ground. The Europeans pledged to help the other Mediterranean economies as a way to limit the flow of immigrants. The need to protect competing EU agriculture made it hard to deliver, however. The Barcelona conference dramatized the web of interlocking difficulties that surrounded Western Europe's relations with its neighbors by the late twentieth century.

IN THE SHADOW OF HISTORY: THE EXPERIMENT CONTINUES

The rapid change at the end of the twentieth century raised new questions for Europeans about the meaning of their history and traditions. Some worried that prosperity necessarily entailed "Americanization," the unwelcome sameness of mass consumer culture. For the formerly communist countries of east-central Europe, the challenge was to find a positive way of reconnecting with their national histories. In some cases, this return of history and memory contributed to the

renewed emphasis on ethnic identity, which itself produced conflict and repression.

The collapse of communism in the Soviet bloc seemed to mean the triumph of democratic capitalism. But rapid economic and technological change introduced problems that proved hard to handle within the democratic political sphere. And during the 1990s, divisive issues all over the Western world—from the role of the state to environmental protection to immigration and cultural diversity—threatened to disrupt the political consensus that had crystallized since World War II.

Europe and America, Old and New

Having weakened itself disastrously in the two world wars, Western Europe found itself dependent on the United States, first for its economic recovery, then for its defense. For decades after 1945, Europe seemed to have no choice but to follow the U.S. lead. Such subservience troubled some Europeans, and a kind of love-hate relationship with the United States developed in Western Europe during the later twentieth century.

Even after Europe's recovery, the United States continued to set the pace in high-technology industries, prompting concerns that Europe would become a mere economic satellite of the United States. Europe seemed to be caught in a dilemma: To retain its distinctiveness over the long term, it apparently had to become more like America in the short term. By the 1980s much of Western Europe had caught up with the United States in standard of living, and the Western Europeans set the pace in confronting some of the new problems that resulted from socioeconomic change. The French day-care system was one prominent example (see page 711). Nonetheless, concerns about Americanization deepened at the same time. By the late 1980s consumerism and the widening impact of American popular culture—from blue jeans and American TV to shopping malls—suggested a growing homogenization in the capitalist democracies. A Euro-Disneyland opened in France in 1992 and, after a slow start, proved increasingly popular. Tangible reminders of Europe's distinctive past remained, but the growing "heritage industry" in Britain and elsewhere suggested that they were merely commodities to be packaged like any other.

Postmodern Culture

The sense that history itself had been commodified seemed to put the whole notion of authenticity into question. Many contemporaries felt that truth and reality were no longer useful categories, that the world could be represented from an infinite number of viewpoints and through an endless array of interpretive ideas—and no single representation could encompass all these simultaneous truths. Embracing uncertainty as a fundamental fact was part of what came to be called postmodernism. Whereas the modern styles and theories of the first half of the century had been devoted to the explosion of traditional forms, artists in the postmodern period felt compelled to bear witness to the horrors of World War II and were moved to revive some formal elements from the past in order to communicate effectively. The result was a multitude of innovations that did not have a formal credo in common—the various artists did not comprise a cohesive movement—but rather were joined by their common use of historical references, scientific imagery, and an attempt to depict reality from several vantage points. There was also tremendous interest in selectively borrowing from the techniques of advertising and mass media in an attempt to satirize and undermine the manipulative effects of the dominant culture.

The sometimes playful, sometimes disturbing use of "found images" by Robert Rauschenberg

Sherman: Untitled #92 (1981) Photographs seem to record reality and yet, like paintings, are creative products of a human mind even if they are not staged or altered. Often featuring the artist herself disguised as a film starlet or a figure from a historical painting, Cindy Sherman's work comments on the way in which we look at different images and the way in which these images shape our ideas of gender and class. (*Courtesy of Cindy Sherman and Metro Pictures*)

Holzer: Truisms Installation (1989) Spiraling down the ramp of New York's Guggenheim Museum, Jenny Holzer's "truisms" progressed along LED signs. The odd and constantly changing messages created a heightened version of the postmodern ironic relationship to news, advertisement, historical wisdom, soundbites, and philosophical truth. At the center are more skewed aphorisms, carved into a circle of granite benches. *(Courtesy of Jenny Holzer Studio, New York. © Jenny Holzer. Photo: David Heald)*

(b. 1925) took seriously the visual information of everyday life while substantially transforming the images and conceptually redefining them. The American artist Cindy Sherman (b. 1954) combined performance and painting in her often huge photographic studies. Sherman's subject was the relationship between the human form, mass-produced commodities, and the fantasies that overlay the modern experience of these things—especially in relation to sex and conceptions of femininity. Another important American artist, Jenny Holzer (b. 1950), decorated various sites with sets of phrases, most of which sounded like familiar platitudes but carried strange, disjointed sentiments, especially in relation to one another. Each overall display seemed to close the

distance between wisdom and nonsense, and disrupt the notion that the culture could produce valid declarations of any kind. In a more traditional artistic medium, the neoexpressionist German painter Anselm Kiefer (b. 1945) reflected the continuing struggle to represent the unrepresentable: the cataclysms of the recent past.

Though there was considerable eclecticism in arts and letters in the second half of the century, they were guided by some broad theoretical innovations. Philosophy underwent a "linguistic turn" as new works asserted that the age-old attempt to understand existence did not make sense because humans primarily know existence through the imperfect medium of language. Following the lead of the Austrian

Ludwig Wittgenstein (1889–1951), philosophers began to concentrate on how language works, what its limitations are, and to what extent it creates a shared reality. The linguistic focus became a central part of postmodernism. Also essential to postmodernism was the thought of French writer Michel Foucault (1926–1984). In his many historical-philosophical works, Foucault studied the development of modern codes of normality, sickness, madness, criminality, and sexual perversion. Following Nietzsche, Foucault and other postmodern thinkers questioned the legacy of the Enlightenment, most notably the idea that increasing rationality and science would lead to freedom and justice. Events of the twentieth century suggested that new power structures had replaced the more obvious hierarchies of the premodern world and that the rationalist classifications of abnormality had become powerful controlling forces in the lives of ordinary people.

The Uncertain Triumph of Democratic Capitalism

The end of the cold war, the discrediting of communism, and the domestication of socialism all seemed to mean the triumph of political democracy and free-market capitalism. But though there was a good deal of self-congratulation in the West at first, what followed its victory was not a period of untroubled confidence but a deeper questioning of capitalist democracy.

In light of the Western political experience so far, few denied that what worked best, and afforded the only basis for political legitimacy, was representative democracy based on universal suffrage within an open, pluralistic society guaranteeing individual freedom. There must be freedom not only to inquire and criticize but also to pursue individual advantage within a market economy. At the same time, that free-market system had to be bounded by some measure of governmental responsibility—for education, for social welfare, for workplace and product safety, and for the environment. But difficult questions remained about the proper role for government in coordinating or balancing market forces.

As the former communist East struggled to catch up to the West, Western affluence increasingly seemed brittle and uncertain. High unemployment persisted in Western Europe, and although unemployment was considerably lower in the United States, new jobs were often poorly paid, with few health and insurance benefits. Moreover, Americans did not have the security that the European welfare states provided—in health care, most notably. Real wages advanced little between the mid-1970s and the mid-1990s, though by 1998 they were beginning to go up in the United States. Still, for most, the widening gap between the well-off and those barely getting by suggested the emergence of a "winner-take-all" society.[1]

Although the socialist left had won reforms that were now central to the consensus around democratic capitalism, it had abandoned much of what it had stood for—from class struggle and revolution to state ownership and a centrally planned economy. Socialism could apparently serve only as the mildly left-leaning party within the framework of capitalist democracy. Several corruption scandals served to further discredit the Socialist parties. In France such scandals brought the Socialists massive defeat at the polls in 1993 and 1995. In Italy, too, the Socialists were central to a corruption scandal that began in 1992 and quickly spread to discredit the Christian Democrats as well—and indeed the whole entrenched Italian political class.

With the decline of socialism as a political alternative, the new right, which had been associated especially with anti-immigrant sentiment at first, grew in prominence in the 1990s. Although differing considerably in priorities, respectability, and success, right-leaning political leaders from LePen in France and José Maria Aznar in Spain to Jörg Haider in Austria and Gianfranco Fini in Italy tapped into the growing political frustration and economic uncertainty.

What did it mean to be "right wing" or conservative in the late twentieth century? In Italy and Austria, new right politicians criticized the prevailing understanding of the recent past—the era of fascism and World War II—playing up the patriotic, anticommunist thrust of the interwar right. But as far as present priorities were concerned, conservatives sometimes differed sharply among themselves. In Britain the Thatcher government had tamed the labor unions and sold state-owned industries, but it had also expanded centralized control over local government, health care, and education. With its ideological agenda, the Thatcher government had been activist and interventionist, not cautious, gradualist, and pragmatic—not truly conservative. In addressing economic anxieties, the new right sometimes articulated problems that mainstream politicians ignored, but it seemed unable to propose viable solutions.

Extreme though it was, the Italian corruption scandal of the early 1990s dramatized troubling tendencies in the democratic political system of the later twentieth century. The need for money to finance electioneering and political patronage kept the whole system on the edge of corruption. Democracy seemed to place a premium on short-term advantage over vision and principle. By the early 1990s, declining voter turnout suggested growing political cynicism and disillusionment all over the Western world.

At the same time, participation in national politics came to seem less significant partly because key decisions were often made elsewhere, by multinational corporations or supranational organizations not directly subject to democratic control. As global competition intensified, the logic of capitalism seemed increasingly to overwhelm the capacities of democratic politics.

CONCLUSION: WESTERN CIVILIZATION IN A GLOBAL AGE

In the late twentieth century, the West was part of a world that was dramatically less Eurocentric than it had been a century before, when European imperialism was at its peak. Events in the West competed for attention with OPEC meetings, Japanese economic decisions, and the financial crisis in Asia. A planetary culture, a threatened environment, and an interdependent international economy required people to think and react in global terms as never before. All over the world, people were seeing the same films, listening to the same music, chatting over the Internet, and purchasing the same clothing from internationally powerful companies. Yet along with this increasing uniformity, the culture has shown vibrant interest in highlighting human differences based on nationality, ethnicity, religion, gender, and sexual orientation, and this too runs counter to the nineteenth-century notion that there was one correct version of respectable normality and one standard path toward national progress.

One of the defining characteristics of the modern period in the West had been a "master narrative"—a conception of all human development—that took the Europe as a model and assumed that everyone else was trying to catch up. Such developmentalist assumptions were linked to the arrogant sense of superiority that had been used to justify Western imperialism. Even though Westernization continued at the end of the twentieth century, it was increasingly recognized that the West was not necessarily the standard of development.

Since World War II, at least, there was a growing interest in the non-Western world and increasing respect for its diverse traditions. Scholars showed how Western images of the non-Western world had become stereotypes, reinforcing assumptions of Western superiority. Others investigated the long-standing assumptions of masculine superiority. And just as the prejudices of race and gender had reinforced one another, "multiculturalism" and feminism were mutually supportive as each worked to identify and dismantle deeply ingrained mechanisms of oppression. (See the box "Encounters with the West: The Case of 'Orientalism.'")

Such insights led some to deny that Western civilization merited privilege as an object of study. Given the injustices that had long been performed in the name of that civilization, this stance was understandable but not particularly practical. Over the course of several thousand

~ **ENCOUNTERS WITH THE WEST** ~

The Case of "Orientalism"

*In his influential book **Orientalism**, published in 1978, the Palestinian-American scholar Edward Said explored the process through which Westerners had constructed the "Middle East"—as different from the West. Though critical of the West, Said appealed to our common humanity in an effort to overcome the ongoing tendency, which was not confined to the West, to understand oneself as superior by stereotyping others. In the final analysis, he suggested, we all need to learn from one another.*

The Orient is not only adjacent to Europe; it is also the place of Europe's greatest and richest and oldest colonies, the source of its civilizations and languages, its cultural contestant, and one of its deepest and most recurring images of the Other. In addition, the Orient has helped to define Europe (or the West) as its contrasting image, idea, personality, experience. . . .

. . . The relationship between Occident and Orient is a relationship of power, of domination, of varying degrees of a complex hegemony. . . . There is very little consent to be found, for example, in the fact that Flaubert's encounter with an Egyptian courtesan produced a widely influential model of the Oriental woman; she never spoke of herself, she never represented her emotions, presence, or history. *He* spoke for and represented her. He was foreign, comparatively wealthy, male, and these were historical facts of domination that allowed him not only to possess Kuchuk Hanem physically but to speak for her and tell his readers in what way she was "typically Oriental." . . .

. . . [E]nough is being done today in the human sciences to provide the contemporary scholar with insights, methods, and ideas that could dispense with racial, ideological, and imperialist stereotypes of the sort provided during its historical ascendancy by Orientalism. I consider Orientalism's failure to have been a human as much as an intellectual one; for in having to take up a position of irreducible opposition to a region of the world it considered alien to its own, Orientalism failed to identify with human experience, failed also to see it as human experience. . . . I hope to have shown my reader that the answer to Orientalism is not Occidentalism. No former "Oriental" will be comforted by the thought that having been an Oriental himself he is likely—too likely—to study new "Orientals"—or "Occidentals"—of his own making. If the knowledge of Orientalism has any meaning, it is in being a reminder of the seductive degradation of knowledge, of any knowledge, anywhere, at any time. Now perhaps more than before.

years, a civilization had been developing—defining and redefining itself through the writing of history. Poets commented across time to other poets; philosophers interpreted each other's work in the context of a new historical moment. From social theorists to inventors, athletes to cosmologists, the project of human existence continued to refer back through its history. Increasingly the events of that history were seen not as inherently and grandly important, as if part of some preordained narrative, but rather as a series of guideposts, a source of ideas, a catalog of errors, and a reminder of heroic responses to a difficult world.

Though debate continues regarding the importance of Western civilization as a category of study, some consensus seems to be forming that knowledge of Western history is crucial—if only because that history continues to shape the West and, less directly, the world. Many people believe that the Western narrative is terribly flawed as a model for humanity: Its assumptions of ascending progress seem questionable at best. But understanding had to come first. The invitation to think freely about the Western tradition, to criticize it, and to build a better future on it rested on precisely that tradition—and remained perhaps its most fundamental legacy.

The effort to make a better civilization begins in knowledge of the civilization that has been inherited. Fortunately, that civilization—wretchedly unfair as it has often been to many of its members—is still one that offers extraordinary intellectual and cultural pleasures. Many voices have been silenced, but the conversation across centuries is still incalculably rich. The many voices that *can* be heard, whether part of the dominant culture or at its fringes, whether long canonized or even now half-hidden in its shadows—these voices can still provide insight, strength, and passion as the new millennium begins to unfold.

NOTES

1. Robert H. Frank and Philip J. Cook, *The Winner-Take-All Society* (New York: Free Press, 1995).

SUGGESTED READING

Barkan, Joanne. *Visions of Emancipation: The Italian Workers' Movement Since 1945.* 1984. A sympathetic account of the postwar Italian labor movement.

Best, Steven, and Douglas Kellner. *Postmodern Theory: Critical Interrogations.* 1991. A difficult but extremely interesting introduction to postmodern theory emphasizing its social and political ramifications.

Bridenthal, Renate, et al., eds. *Becoming Visible: Women in European History.* 1987. A major collection of essays on women's history, including seven that deal with twentieth-century topics.

Brubaker, Rogers. *Citizenship and Nationhood in France and Germany.* 1992. A lucid comparative study showing how very different conceptions of citizenship emerged in the two countries as a result of their contrasting historical experiences.

Cheles, Luciano, et al., eds. *The Far Right in Western and Eastern Europe.* 2d ed. 1995. A superior collection of essays on the revival of the extreme right in the 1980s and 1990s.

Funk, Nanette, and Magda Mueller, eds. *Gender Politics and Post-Communism: Reflections from Eastern Europe and the Former Soviet Union.* 1993. A country-by-country analysis and critique by feminist scholars from the region, with an effective mixture of outside perspectives.

Garton Ash, Timothy. *The Magic Lantern: The Revolution of '89 Witnessed in Warsaw, Budapest, Berlin, and Prague.* 1990. Firsthand testimony on the fall of communism by a British intellectual with close contacts among anticommunists in east-central Europe.

Glenny, Misha. *The Fall of Yugoslavia: The Third Balkan War.* 3d rev. ed. 1996. An influential account of the disintegration of Yugoslavia, combining historical analysis with dramatic treatment of the fighting.

Havel, Václav. *Disturbing the Peace: A Conversation with Karel Hvífizfidala.* 1991. Part autobiography, part history, part philosophy. Demonstrates the moral vision that made Havel so effective as a leader in the Czech opposition to communism.

Kuisel, Richard F. *Seducing the French: The Dilemmas of Americanization.* 1993. An illuminating study of the French response to all things American in the half-century that followed World War II.

Laba, Roman. *The Roots of Solidarity.* 1991. Seeks to show that workers, not the Polish intelligentsia, were the driving force behind Solidarity.

Mosse, George L. *The Image of Man: The Creation of Modern Masculinity.* 1996. Traces the idea and image of the masculine from the advent of nineteenth century bourgeois society to the late twentieth century.

Remnick, David. *Lenin's Tomb: The Last Days of the Soviet Empire.* 1994. An acclaimed and compelling account of the fall of the communist regime. Makes effective use of oral testimony.

Stokes, Gale. *The Walls Came Tumbling Down: The Collapse of Communism in Eastern Europe.* 1993. Dramatic and comprehensive, the first standard account of the dissolution of communism in east-central Europe.

Index